Perl
Developer's Guide

Perl

Developer's Guide

Ed Peschko
Michele DeWolfe

McGraw-Hill

New York ▪ San Francisco ▪ Washington, D.C. ▪ Auckland
Bogotá ▪ Caracas ▪ Lisbon ▪ London ▪ Madrid ▪ Mexico City
Milan ▪ Montreal ▪ New Delhi ▪ San Juan ▪ Singapore
Sydney ▪ Tokyo ▪ Toronto

McGraw-Hill

A Division of The McGraw·Hill Companies

The views expressed in this book are solely those of the author, and do not represent the views of any other party or parties.

1 2 3 4 5 6 7 8 9 0   AGM/AGM   0   5   4   3   2   1   0

P/N 0-07-212628-0
PART OF ISBN 0-07-212630-2

The sponsoring editor for this book was Rebekah Young and the production supervisor was Daina Penikas. It was set in Sabon by V&M Graphics, Inc.

Printed and bound by Quebecor/Martinsburg.

Product or brand names used in this book may be trade names or trademarks. Where we believe that there may be proprietary claims to such trade names or trademarks, the name has been used with an initial capital or it has been capitalized in the style used by the name claimant. Regardless of the capitalization used, all such names have been used in an editorial manner without any intent to convey endorsement of or other affiliation with the name claimant. Neither the author nor the publisher intends to express any judgment as to the validity or legal status of any such proprietary claims.

 This book is printed on recycled, acid-free paper containing a minimum of 50% recycled de-inked fiber.

Dedication

To Elizabeth, Yosef, and Leora, the coolest nieces and nephew on the planet.
I could not have written this book without you. I thought of you every page, every sentence.

I love you all, dearly.

To Debra Finegold for going through the first edition with a fine-tooth comb,
and for humbling me with exactly how many mistakes she found in the process.

To Margot Maley for being a really cool agent and keeping tempers cool when deadlines loomed.

Ed

To Buffy the Wonder Dog: I missed your company while doing this book.
Here's hoping the squirrels on the other side are slower than the ones here.

Michele

Contents

Contents

Contents

Contents

Contents

Contents

Foreword

> Hamlet   : Do you see yonder cloud that's almost in shape of a camel?
> Polonius : By the mass, and 'tis like a camel, indeed.
> Hamlet   : Methinks it is like a weasel.
> Polonius : It is backed like a weasel.
> Hamlet   : Or like a whale?
> Polonius : Very like a whale!

This book was a lot of work. No, let me rephrase that. It was an ordeal, a trial by fire. It took about twice as much time as expected, ended up twice as long, and took about one and a half years solid to write.

Also to be perfectly honest, I could have added a good 400 extra pages, excepting that (1) the book would break the spine of any good-quality book binding out there, and (2) I had to compromise somewhere for length. Some books come out cleanly onto the page, and others sort of grow and are fed—like the man-eating plant in Little Shop of Horrors. This book was of the latter type.

So after the dust had settled and the last word was was written, I started thinking of why it was such a mammoth effort. My intent was to fill a gap in the Perl literature that I feel was growing readily apparent: the lack of a decent respectable developer's guide for the perl language.

And as I thought about it further, the quote from *Hamlet* came to mind. Perl is known as the "camel" langauge. Larry Wall, its author, is fond of saying that "Perl may not look good, or smell good, but it gets the job done."

But the quote from *Hamlet* is doubly ironic when applied to Perl. Perl is not only the "camel" language, Perl is also the changeable language; changeable as the cloud-shaped camel in Hamlet's fantasy. And Perl is always changing shape—Perl has the stubborn habit of not being able to be pinned down to a particular problem. The more you look at Perl, the more things you can do with it.

Is perl a text processing language? Well, yes, it was designed as such. Is it a networking language? Well, yes... it has sockets/ simple client-server protocols built in.

Is it a system administration language? Well, yes, it manages world-wide networks. Does Perl let you get simple tasks done fast? Well, yes, "one-liner" scripts are common.

Is Perl a Web scripting language? Well, yes... the most popular on the Internet.
And so on. You can:

- Generate code with it
- Write quick GUIs with it (via Tk)
- Program Perl inside your C and C++ programs, and C/C++ inside your Perl programs
- Use it to filter mail
- Test GUI applications
- Use it for data warehousing
- Do source control
- Do spider searches on the web

The "reach" of Perl is astounding. You can write a one-million-line project in Perl, yet write a meaningful one line script. You can write interfaces into other packages, and several people have: including interfaces to Mathematica, Microsoft IIS server, Oracle, Sybase, Informix, Java, Win32, XML—anything in fact with a C "backend".

You can compile your Perl code, or link your Perl code into Java. Add to all this that Perl is a mature, well-tested language which is available on almost any platform—and of no cost, to boot—and you get one frustratingly hard technology to categorize, but one that will become absolutely essential in your day-to-day working life.

This book is an attempt to teach you some of that diversity, and more importantly to show perl through examples.

It does not require prior knowledge of perl—you need only be familiar with "programming in general", yet it is designed to go quite far into Perl's depths, giving a fairly complete tour of how to debug various types of Perl programs, and how to effectively program classes in Perl. In other words, you can do quite a bit with 1000 pages of text. And as an encore—we include a few appendixes on how to actually use the book—one appendix showing syntax examples, one index on using the CD, and one index on web resources for the perl developer's guide (the latter two can be found on the CD).

I hope you enjoy it; although it is long, it is thorough. I have tried to keep the examples relevant, and the code as technically correct as possible. The first manifestation of this book—*Perl 5 Complete*—had more errors than I care to mention; they have been eradicated for this edition due to lots of vigilant readers (special thanks goes to Deborah Finegold for her services—she went through this book line by line(!) looking for them). In addition, we have added a new index and appendixes added, per reader request.

Anyways, I hope you like it. If you are looking for a scholarly treatise on perl, you are probably better off going somewhere else. If you are just concerned about getting your job done—like the rest of us—this book may be for you.

Ed Peschko

1

Setting Up the Perl 5 Environment

The goal of this chapter is to introduce you to Perl and show you how to use Perl effectively. A large part of using Perl effectively is installing it on your system correctly. Installing Perl is only the first step. You also need, or should know how to find, information on:

- Customizing Perl for your situation
- Places where you can get answers for questions about Perl
- Talking with experts about Perl
- Professional Perl support and training

You must also be able to use the documentation for the day-to-day programming issues you will run into. Perl has some of the best on-line documentation available anywhere, whether in commercial or freeware packages. You should be able to easily consult it for problems you may encounter. This chapter will orient you to these resources, and be a quick pointer to where you can find more information.

Chapter Overview

In this chapter, we will go through each step most people go through in setting up Perl for use on their operating system. We start with the first Perl programming decision: Are you going to be using an already installed Perl, or installing a new version? Each has its benefits and drawbacks.

We will take each decision in turn. First, we will give you instructions on how to find an already installed Perl on Unix, NT/Win95/98, Macintosh, OS/2, and VMS, and tell you what to look for in these installations.

Second, we will look at installing Perl from scratch on the same five operating systems, and give instructions on how to test your new Perl and what to look for in the installation. Third, we will look at installing Perl modules and customizing the installation with modules that people have written on the Net. These canned solutions include CGI, making graphic user interfaces with Perl/TK, and so forth. Fourth, we will look at the Perl documentation, how to use it, and how to print it out in formats such as html, postscript, man, and just plain text.

Finally, we will look at the basic Perl support that exists on the Internet. If you need more detailed information than this, please refer to the Appendixes or the CD.

Perl is truly a language that is a living, breathing entity. No formal committee decides what is best for the language. People who *use* the language decide its content. Hence, there are always developments, changes, and new news in the Perl community. Getting into the "Perl flow" is part of learning the language effectively.

Installation of Perl 5

Perl has been ported to most every platform around, so there is no possible way we can cover all the platforms here. You can get Perl 5 working on almost every flavor of Unix, Windows NT, Windows 95/98, Win3.1, MS-DOS, VMS, Mac OS, plan9, AS/400, mainframes running MVS (or OS/390), and, VM/ESA. In fact, if you are a mainframe programmer and want to get an idea of how Unix will feel, learning Perl is the ideal way. Likewise, if you are a Unix programmer who wants to test the waters with NT, learning Perl is ideal.

Perl is so widespread, we must be picky in the operating systems we cover. We shall cover the installation of Perl on:

1. Unix
2. NT/Windows 95/98
3. OS/2
4. VMS
5. MacOS
6. MS-DOS

Note

We have not begun to mention all the systems Perl supports. Some others: AmigaOS, Atari, VOS, Next, Machten, lynxOS, and a bunch of systems that we haven't even heard of: mpe, acorn, aos, etc.

If you are using one of the operating systems that I do not cover, I strongly suggest you join the mailing list for your particular OS. Most of the examples in this book *should* work on these operating systems, but I cannot vouch for all of them. This book is guaranteed (as much as anything in the world of computers is guaranteed) only for Windows NT, Windows 95/98, and Unix variants. With a few exceptions (that are labeled), all the examples should work transparently between the Windows and Unix platforms.

Getting Started on the Perl 5 Installation

There are two basic choices on how to proceed. You can:

1. Find an already installed Perl
2. Build one out of the box, either by downloading a Perl executable prebuilt or building it yourself

We will be going over the things you need to type from scratch up until the point that you have installed Perl correctly. Why? Perl is an *Esperanto* language, meaning it looks and feels pretty much the same, everywhere. Hence, one of the great reasons to use Perl is to become familiar with an unknown environment, whether the environment is Unix, NT, VMS, or whatever.

If you compile Perl on any one of those systems, your woes about learning that operating system are about 90 percent over. This means that we will assume that you are a new user of the system on which you are going to install Perl. If you are not, you probably will not need to read the following text.

Finding an Already Installed Perl

Perl has been installed almost everywhere, and using preinstalled Perl has several advantages:

1. *Maintainability*—You don't need to maintain Perl yourself. If you have any difficulties, you can ask the system administrator.
2. *Centralized administration*—You can ask the person who installed Perl to extend or update it.
3. *Traceability*—If many people are using Perl, they can all use one copy rather than having individual copies lying around. If you are debugging other people's programs, you can guarantee it is not an error due to Perl's version.
4. *Low overhead*—You need not do anything as far as installation is concerned.

Likewise, there are some disadvantages:

1. *Loss of control*—If you want to update Perl yourself, you can't. Usually Perl is in a centralized place, such as **/usr/local/bin** on Unix, and can be modified only by a system administrator. This means you must ask the powers that be if you wish to modify it.
2. *Loss of flexibility*—You are at the mercy of the version of Perl and options installed by the system administrator.

If you are using an existing Perl, you are passing the responsibility of maintaining Perl to the system administrator. In doing so, you lose some of the freedoms you would have if you installed it yourself. Of course, how much freedom you lose depends on the operating systems you install it on; larger, more scalable systems (Plan9, Unix, VMS, NT) will benefit more from custom installation.

If you decide to use an already installed Perl, you must locate it and make sure it is the correct version. Your goal in finding Perl is twofold. One, you are going to want to find out *which* version of Perl is installed. Two, you should find out *where* Perl is installed. Finding Perl on a system is a somewhat system-dependent task. Let's go over each system.

Finding Perl on a Unix System

To find which version of Perl is installed on a Unix system, you can say something like:

```
prompt% perl -v
```

in which `prompt%` is your command prompt, and `perl` is the most common default name for the Perl executable. If this fails, other commands you can use are:

```
prompt% perl5.00X -v
```

or

```
prompt% perl5 -v
```

where `perl5` and `perl5.00X` (*X* being a number) are other, common alternative names for the Perl executable.

After this, you can use `whence`, or `which`, to tell you where the Perl executable is installed. This:

```
prompt% whence perl
```

would give you the complete path to your Perl executable. If this doesn't work, try:

```
prompt% which perl
```

because whether your system has whence, or which, is system dependent.

These commands will work only if Perl is in your path—if your system setup includes the directory where Perl is installed. If you cannot find it using the commands above, you can use some extremely common system commands on the Unix platform to find Perl. For example, **find** can locate Perl easily. The following command:

```
prompt% find / -name "perl*" -print -perm -550
```

will find all files on your system that begin with the string perl* and are executable by you (-perm 550). Hence, it finds Perl executable *candidates*. You can also look in some centralized places for Perl. Common central locations for Unix are **/usr/bin**, **/usr/local/bin**, and **/usr/sbin**.

If you find Perl this way, and it was located in the directory **/usr/local/bin**, say something like the following to get the version of Perl:

```
prompt% /usr/local/bin/perl -v
```

Then, add to your path variable something like:

```
PATH=$PATH:/usr/local/bin
```

This is the syntax for kern shell or Bourne shell; it lets you execute perl without having to type **/usr/local/bin** in front of it all the time. In any case, you are aiming for a window that looks something like Figure 1.1.

Figure 1.1
Output of a
Successful Version
Check on Unix

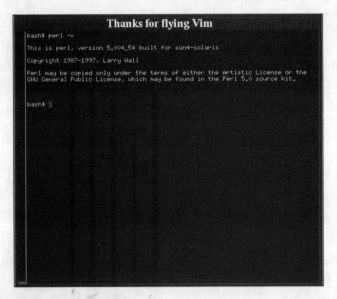

If you see this, then you are on the right track.

Finding Perl on NT/Windows 95/98

There are a couple of ways to find Perl on Windows NT. One is from the command line. Open up a DOS shell and type:

```
C:\> perl -v
```

This will check to determine whether Perl is installed in the centralized place, and whether or not the executable directory has been added to your path. You can also type the following in case Perl is installed in the regular place, but not yet set up in your path:

```
C:\> \perl\bin\perl -v
```

Note that you are going to want to save the information about which version of Perl you have, which is the output of this command.

You can also search for Perl on your whole disk drive by saying something like:

```
C:\> dir perl* /s
```

or going into Explorer and doing a **find** for files named **perl**. If it is a nonstandard place, write that place down and add it to your path by saying:

```
set PATH="%PATH%";C:\path\to\perl\binary
```

where \path\to\perl\binary is the name of the Perl binary. (This is so that you need not type the full path to Perl each time to run Perl scripts.) In any case, after setting the PATH variable, C:\> perl -v should give you something like what you see in Figure 1.2.

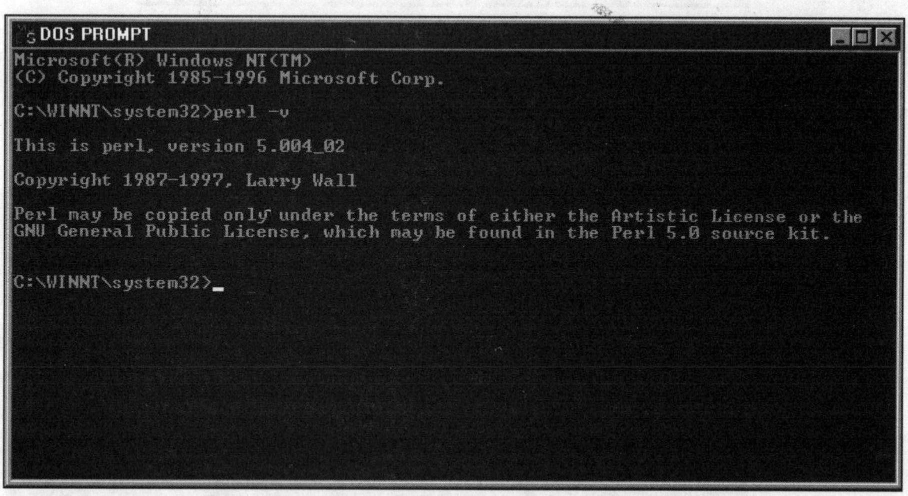

Figure 1.2
Successful NT
Check for Perl

```
DOS PROMPT                                                              _ □ ✕
Microsoft(R) Windows NT(TM)
(C) Copyright 1985-1996 Microsoft Corp.

C:\WINNT\system32>perl -v

This is perl, version 5.004_02

Copyright 1987-1997, Larry Wall

Perl may be copied only under the terms of either the Artistic License or the
GNU General Public License, which may be found in the Perl 5.0 source kit.

C:\WINNT\system32>_
```

The `C:\> perl -v` command indicates the type of Perl you have.

Finding Perl on the Macintosh

Unlike Windows and Unix, Macintosh has a GUI interface that is used to run Perl. It is called the "MacPerl application." (There is a command-line version of Perl that comes with MPW—a professional command-line Mac development tool—but the most popular way is through the GUI with MacPerl.)

Finding the MacPerl application (thanks to Matthias Neeracher) is like finding any other file on the Mac. Simply go to the **find** option in the system 7 tool, and look for the string MacPerl. If you find MacPerl, you are going to see a distribution that looks something like Figure 1.3.

Figure 1.3
MacPerl
Directory
Structure

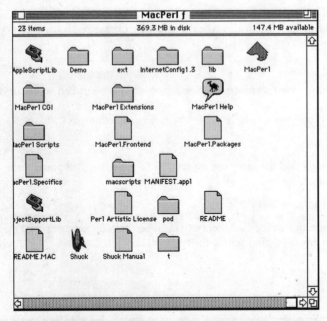

This software has gotten the award for the "coolest icons" in the Perl world.

To find the version of Perl you want to run, double-click the MacPerl icon (the one with the camel), and go to the Script submenu. Choose **one liner** and type as shown in the dialog box in Figure 1.4.

Figure 1.4
Command
to Get
Version
of Perl

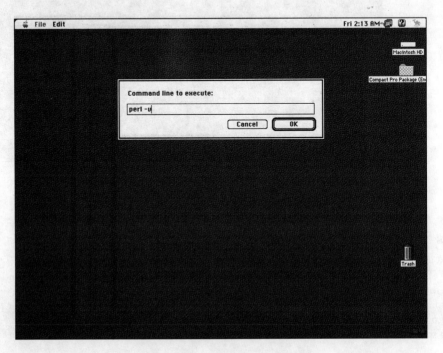

This will give you the display shown in Figure 1.5

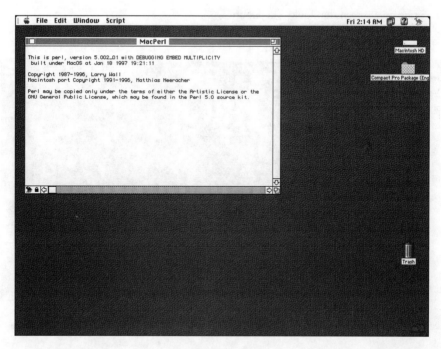

Figure 1.5
Successful
Macintosh Check

Note that the Macintosh version of Perl is unlike every other version discussed here, as it is only up to perl5.002.

Also note that you may find a different version here, the *Macintosh Programming Workshop* MPW version. This version is Perl in a command-line environment. If you want to use this version, you are going to have to get MPW. The easiest way to do so is to go to Metrowerks at *http://www.metrowerks.com* and order it from there through a package called CodeWarrior.

Metrowerks provides a very Unix-like command-line environment, along with a complete development kit to write C (and Perl) programs without the overhead of a GUI.

Finding Perl on OS/2

Finding Perl on OS/2 (thanks to Ilya Zakharevich) is pretty much like finding Perl on Unix and Win32. All you need to do is get a shell under the 'command prompts' folder, and type:

```
[H:] perl -v
```

If the Perl binary is in your PATH, you will get information on which version of Perl you have installed. As in Unix or NT, if you can't find Perl this way, you can do a **find**:

```
[H:] find "perl*"
```

which will show all of the files named Perl on your system. When you find the correct binary (**Perl.exe**), then you can say:

```
[H:] set PATH="%PATH%";\path\to\perl\executable;
```

which will then set it so your environment can find Perl automatically. Typing:

```
[H:] perl -v
```

should then bring up a screen that looks like Figure 1.6.

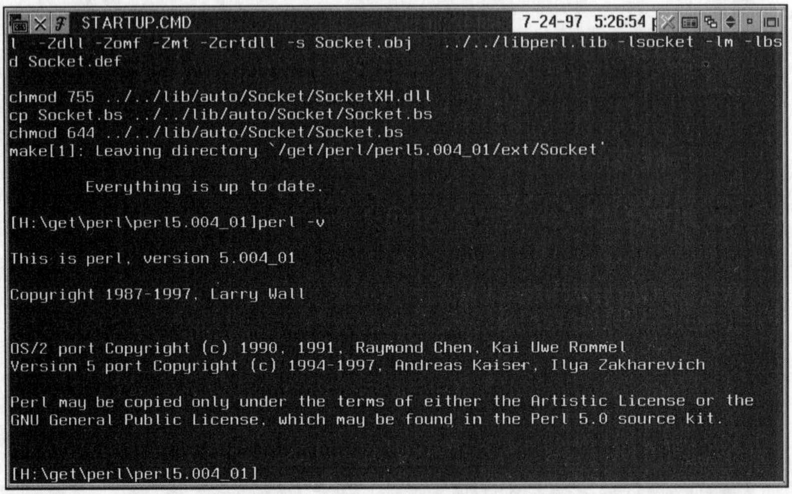

Figure 1.6
Perl Version
for OS/2

```
STARTUP.CMD                                    7-24-97  5:26:54
l  -Zdll -Zomf -Zmt -Zcrtdll -s Socket.obj   ../../libperl.lib -lsocket -lm -lbs
d Socket.def

chmod 755 ../../lib/auto/Socket/SocketXH.dll
cp Socket.bs ../../lib/auto/Socket/Socket.bs
chmod 644 ../../lib/auto/Socket/Socket.bs
make[1]: Leaving directory `/get/perl/perl5.004_01/ext/Socket'

          Everything is up to date.

[H:\get\perl\perl5.004_01]perl -v

This is perl, version 5.004_01

Copyright 1987-1997, Larry Wall

OS/2 port Copyright (c) 1990, 1991, Raymond Chen, Kai Uwe Rommel
Version 5 port Copyright (c) 1994-1997, Andreas Kaiser, Ilya Zakharevich

Perl may be copied only under the terms of either the Artistic License or the
GNU General Public License, which may be found in the Perl 5.0 source kit.

[H:\get\perl\perl5.004_01]
```

This indicates you are on the right track. Check to see that you have the correct version number of Perl, and go from there.

Finding Perl on VMS

Finally, we consider locating Perl on VMS versions 6.2 and above (thanks to many folks, especially Peter Prymmer, Charles Bailey, and Dan Sugalski). If you are sitting down at a DCL prompt (if you are a Unix user, the shell equivalent in the VMS world), type:

```
$ perl -v
```

just like any other OS to show you the Perl version. If you want to see where the Perl is located, on disk, you can say:

```
$ show symbol perl
     PERL == "$PERL_ROOT:[000000]PERL"
```

which shows—in VMS-ese—where PERL is installed. (If you are unfamiliar with VMS, `$PERL_ROOT` is a *logical*, which means it hides all the physical details about the computers, paths, etc., where Perl is installed. The $ indicates that 'PERL' is a binary executable.) (DKA600 is a *device* or disk drive; PERL5.004_01 is a directory.) The syntax:

```
$ show logical perl_root
     "PERL_ROOT" = "DKA600:[PERL5_004_01.]"  (LNM$PROCESS_TABLE)
```

gives you a more concrete look at where Perl actually is. (DkA600 is a *device* or disk drive; Perl5.004_01 is a directory.)

Finally, if nothing seems to be working, say:

```
$ DIR DISK:[*...]perl
```

where `DISK` is the disk drive(s) that finds where the Perl executable is located. This must be typed separately for each and every disk. A Perl script does this very nicely, so you can use older versions of Perl to "piggyback" the installations of newer ones.

Then set the variable `PERL_ROOT` to what you find:

```
$ define/translation=concealed perl_root disk$dka100:[perl5_004_01.]
```

with:

```
$ perl -v
```

you should see something that looks like Figure 1.7.

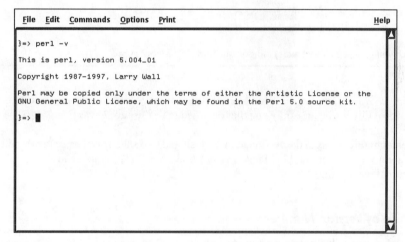

Figure 1.7
Perl Version
for VMS

```
}=> perl -v

This is perl, version 5.004_01

Copyright 1987-1997, Larry Wall

Perl may be copied only under the terms of either the Artistic License or the
GNU General Public License, which may be found in the Perl 5.0 source kit.

}=> █
```

What To Do After You Find Perl

When you have found Perl, you should have two pieces of information:

1. What version of Perl you have (in "gory" detail)
2. Where Perl is installed

The Significance of Perl's Version

When you say something like:

```
C:\>perl -v
```

The `-v` flag gets the version of Perl. The text that comes out of `perl -v` is pretty much independent of the operating system you are running on. The text you get will look something like this:

```
This is perl, version 5.6.0
        built under solaris at Apr 12, 2000 16:06:39
        + suidperl security patch

Copyright 1987-2000, Larry Wall

Perl may be copied only under the terms of either the Artistic License or the
GNU General Public License, which may be found in the Perl 5.0 source kit.*
```

The preceding text contains a lot of useful information. Some small points: The GNU General Public License lets you modify and distribute the source code at will, in code *or* executable form, provided you keep the notices of recognition in the code (see the file **Artistic** in the standard distribution).

Note

If you want even more gory details than this, you can say:

```
prompt% perl -V (on Unix, OS/2, MS-DOS, WinNT)
    $ perl "-V" (on VMS)
```

which will give you almost everything about how Perl is configured.

The line +suidperl security patch (and lines like it) bear witness to some pretty traumatic bugs that were found and fixed. As of this writing, the only bug that qualified to be this severe was the *suidperl* bug, which is gone in versions 5.003 and above.

It is important that this results in the version number. It should be 5.000 or higher, preferably 5.005. Certain operating systems are not at version 5.005 (MacPerl is at 5.003), but Perl's version should be 5.005 on any other operating system that we mention.

The Importance of Version Numbers

The version number is especially important because of the changes that are made between even small versions. Perl has a unique versioning system. In a Perl version tagged 5.001, the *1* in the thousandth place is almost as important as the *5*. Supposedly, this is to allow for versions 5.001 through 5.999, but it seldom gets this far. Version 4 lasted up to 4.036, taking more than 3 years, and then there was a collective decision that making Perl object-oriented warranted a 5.000.

Even small releases of Perl are done with care (and are really not that small). For example, Perl5.004 to Perl5.005 added:

1. *Compiler support*—Ability to compile to Perl-like bytecode (portable, machine-like code) or standard C.
2. *Thread support*—Ability to make processes "talk" together by sending messages back and forth.
3. *Unix to Windows 'code merge'*—Perl used to be split into two separate ports: the central distribution, and ActiveState's version. This used to be a pain for portability. There is now one central distribution, and it is working wonders.

On a more pragmatic note, you probably want to make sure that the version installed is version 5.004 or higher, preferably version 5.005. This book assumes 5.005, but works transparently with version 5.004 for most issues.

If you want a list of the changes for any given revision of Perl, you can see the **Changes** file found in the standard distribution. This brings us to the question: *How* do you get a standard distribution of Perl? The next sections describe the installation of Perl.

Installing Your Own Perl

Suppose you want the latest, greatest Perl, or to learn a lot about your operating system. Then you will want to install your own Perl. Here are some advantages of getting/using your own Perl:

1. *You learn more by doing the installation.* Perl has 10 years of experience in figuring out how to install itself on different systems. The Perl installation script squiggles through your operating system, finding out such esoteric things as "whether or not your integers are big-endian," which system calls your operating system supports, and so on. Perl understands how to use the information it retrieves.

2. *You can compile Perl with the options you choose.* We give some of the more helpful ways to compile Perl. The debugging switch, for example, lets you see the "guts" of how Perl is doing things.

3. *You can add modules very easily.* Perl has a special place called *CPAN* (stands for Comprehensive Perl Archive Network), which contains many user-contributed modules. These are pieces of code that people have built to do anything from date parsing to database connection.

4. *You can avoid network problems.* If you are using centrally installed Perl from **/usr/local/bin**, or **E:\perl>**, then you are using Perl over a network (LAN or Network File System). This makes you vulnerable to having that network go down. Hence, if you are to use Perl for mission-critical applications, you definitely want to get a secure copy.

5. *You can make a self-contained package.* Some people package the Perl executable they build with the source code they write. That way, if they need to sell this code, or move it to a different system, there is a self-contained package.

Here are some disadvantages of compiling your own Perl:

1. *You need a C compiler to make your own* Perl. For example, the Unix variant Solaris doesn't come bundled with a C compiler, so you need to get your own or buy it from Solaris. This drawback is somewhat offset by ActiveState, which has a packaged Windows 95/98, Windows NT binary.

2. *Compiling it yourself is more work.* Once compiled, you need to maintain Perl yourself. Since you are building it yourself, you are responsible for making sure that it works. This may be unacceptable.

3. *More knowledge is required for installation.* This is true if you are not using a precompiled version. You need to understand the compile steps and how to execute them.

4. *If you are not careful, everybody will be installing their own Perl.* At one extreme, you can have one centralized Perl. This may be too restrictive. At the other extreme, you have a Perl for each user (which may bring the storage capacity of the system to its knees). Therefore, if you install your own executable, you need to gauge the lack of flexibility versus the amount of maintenance you must do. Your system administrator may be able to help with this, too.

Given these advantages and disadvantages, I still say that it is a good thing for any Unix users to install their own Perl (even if they delete it after they are finished with the installation). Installation of Perl is a good learning experience on any OS.

Following are the steps to compile and install a new Perl binary. Just go to the correct OS, and follow the steps.

Installing Perl on Unix

The only option for installing Perl on a Unix box is to get the source code and install it yourself. If you are lucky, you can get a binary version for your Unix operating system, but you are probably better off building it yourself.

There are three steps to installing Perl on a Unix system:

1. *Get the source code.* Go to one of the Comprehensive Perl Archive Network (CPAN) sites and get it via **ftp**.
2. *Configure Perl to be installed on your particular machine.* Customize Perl for your particular configuation.
3. make, test, *and* install *Perl on your machine.* This step is usually the easiest step because Perl gets the installation correct almost 100% of the time.

If you are impatient and want to get going right away, here is a (pretty much) verbatim list of what you are going to type:

```
prompt% cd <temporary_directory>
prompt%ftp ftp.cs.colorado.com          (or ftp.cs.colorado.edu,
                                         or any of the sites mentioned
                                         here after you log in.)

(login as anonymous, password email address)
ftp> cd /pub/perl/CPAN/src
ftp> get latest.tar.gz
ftp> exit
prompt% gunzip latest.tar.gz
prompt% tar xvf latest.tar.gz
prompt% cd perl5.004                     (or whatever version is
                                         installed)
prompt% sh configure —prefix='/where/you/want/perl/installed'
prompt% make            ( makes perl into a local executable
prompt% make test       ( test Perl to see if it built correctly.)
prompt% make install    ( installs Perl into the correct place )
```

In fact, all of the steps, apart from the **ftp** step, are automatic. (The **ftp** step would be automatic if you had had Perl installed in the first place. This is a catch-22. You could script this if you had Perl, but you would not need to run the script if you had Perl in the first place!)

Usually, when I am consulting, I write a small shell script that does everything just listed for me given an argument (such as the release number). I then do the **ftp** manually. The CD gives a couple of examples of this 'support scripting.' You may want to look there for more information.

We go into each of the above steps in more detail next.

Getting the Perl Distribution

The first thing you must do to install Perl is get the source code and a C compiler, if you do not have one already. If you do not have a compiler, there are two choices:

1. Get **gcc**, the standard default compiler
2. Buy a C compiler

Of course, you need to compile the **gcc** compiler, so step 1 is not the easiest one. If your system does not have **gcc** installed, you must find a binary. Usually, the best place to get a binary is by talking to a newsgroup associated with the OS (**comp.unix.solaris**, for example).

Alternatively, you might ask for a Perl binary from **comp.lang.perl.misc**. As far as I know, there are very few standard Perl binaries for Unix, because there are as many types of Unix as there are pebbles on a beach.

Assuming you have a Perl compiler, you can get the latest source code from any one of the CPAN sites. (We shall see quite a bit of CPAN in this book.) Table 1.1 gives a list of some of the more important CPAN sites, along with their traffic levels.

Table 1.1 CPAN Sites		
	ftp.funet.fi/pub/languages/perl/CPAN	medium (Finland)
	uiarchive.uiuc.edu/pub/lang/perl/CPAN	moderately heavy (fast link)
	ftp.cs.colorado.edu/pub/perl/CPAN	relatively light
	ftp.cdrom.com/pub/perl/CPAN	medium (fast link)
	ftp.digital.com/pub/plan/perl/CPAN	moderately heavy (fast link)
	ftp.perl.com/pub/perl/CPAN	heavy and slow (Perl home page)
	ftp.demon.co.uk/pub/perl/CPAN	medium (UK)
	ftp.sai.msu.su/pub/lang/perl/CPAN	unknown (Moscow)
	ftp.cs.ruu.nl/pub/PERL/CPAN	unknown (Netherlands)
	ftp.uni-hamburg.de/pub/soft/lang/perl/CPAN	medium (Germany)

There are many more CPAN sites (95 in total), but this is a good sampling. To download them, you say:

```
prompt%ftp ftp.cs.colorado.edu          (or ftp.demon.co.uk
                                         or any of the sites mentioned
                                         here after you log in.)

(login as anonymous, password email address)
ftp> cd /pub/perl/CPAN/src
ftp> get latest.tar.gz
ftp> exit
prompt% gunzip latest.tar.gz
prompt% tar xvf latest.tar.gz
```

Or, if you prefer a browserfan, simply point it to *http://www.perl.com/perl/info/software.html* and look where it says:

```
Just click to download the latest Perl source (currently Perl version 5.004_01) from a
fast link. This version is a stable, production release (not beta) that compiles out
of the box for virtually all flavors of Unix (its native environment), plus VMS, OS/2,
and 32-bit Windows platforms as well. Check out its installation notes for details (or
see the INSTALL file in the src directory). Read the beta release notes and/or
documentation.
```

If you click **latest Perl source**, this will do exactly the same thing—probably better than the **ftp** because it is platform-independent.

After you get the Perl source, type:

```
prompt% gunzip latest.tar.gz;
prompt% tar xvf latest.tar
```

to unpack the software. If **gunzip** is not on your system, you are going to need to go to *ftp.gnu.ai.mit.edu*. Go into the directory that is created by **tar** and it looks something like Figure 1.8.

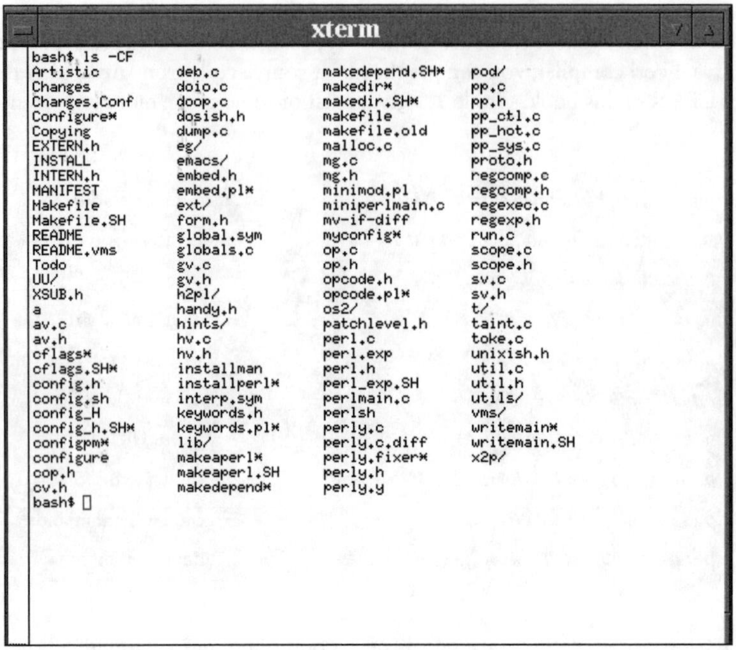

Figure 1.8

Perl Distribution
Directory

```
                                    xterm
bash$ ls -CF
Artistic         deb.c          makedepend.SH*    pod/
Changes          doio.c         makedir*          pp.c
Changes.Conf     doop.c         makedir.SH*       pp.h
Configure*       dosish.h       makefile          pp_ctl.c
Copying          dump.c         makefile.old      pp_hot.c
EXTERN.h         eg/            malloc.c          pp_sys.c
INSTALL          emacs/         mg.c              proto.h
INTERN.h         embed.h        mg.h              regcomp.c
MANIFEST         embed.pl*      minimod.pl        regcomp.h
Makefile         ext/           miniperlmain.c    regexec.c
Makefile.SH      form.h         mv-if-diff        regexp.h
README           global.sym     myconfig*         run.c
README.vms       globals.c      op.c              scope.c
Todo             gv.c           op.h              scope.h
UU/              gv.h           opcode.h          sv.c
XSUB.h           h2pl/          opcode.pl*        sv.h
a                handy.h        os2/              t/
av.c             hints/         patchlevel.h      taint.c
av.h             hv.c           perl.c            toke.c
cflags*          hv.h           perl.exp          unixish.h
cflags.SH*       installman     perl.h            util.c
config.h         installperl*   perl_exp.SH       util.h
config.sh        interp.sym     perlmain.c        utils/
config_H         keywords.h     perlsh            vms/
config_h.SH*     keywords.pl*   perly.c           writemain*
configpm*        lib/           perly.c.diff      writemain.SH
configure        makeaperl*     perly.fixer*      x2p/
cop.h            makeaperl.SH   perly.h
ov.h             makedepend*    perly.y
bash$ []
```

Some important files to read right away:

> **README:** The **readme** file for various Unix OS's.
> **INSTALL:** More information on installation for Unix.
> **Artistic:** Information on the "Free Software" concept. This should satisfy most lawyers that you *can* use Perl for free.

You can proceed to the next step after you have skimmed through each of these files.

Configuring Perl for Unix

The second thing to do when compiling Perl is to configure it so Perl knows on which system it is being installed. You have two choices:

1. Configure Perl 5 interactively, which is particularly helpful for beginners.
2. Configure Perl 5 noninteractively using system defaults.

Both of these use Perl's artificial intelligence program called **Configure** to figure out your system. (Yes, it is artificial intelligence—there is no other way to describe it.)

Configure is the script created by **metaconfig**, another program written by Larry Wall. It goes through your system to diagnose exactly how Perl will be created. As I said, there are as many different types of Unix as there are angels that can dance on the head of a pin; it is **Configure**'s job to fine-tune how Perl will build on your particular brand.

Configuring Perl Interactively

If you wish to configure Perl interactively, and give yourself the chance to see what is going on, type:

```
prompt% sh Configure
```

in the directory where you put the Perl distribution. Then answer questions such as what operating system you use, which version of **rm** you use, etc. Perl is almost 100% accurate in these cases, but it can be fooled by particularly strange variants of Unix.

By typing:

```
prompt% sh Configure
```

you give yourself a chance to override what Perl thinks it already knows. At each step where **Configure** needs a value, it will prompt you for one. Press **Return** to accept the default or type what you want to change.

A sample of the output given by the **Configure** script is given in Figure 1.9.

Figure 1.9
Configure
Script Output

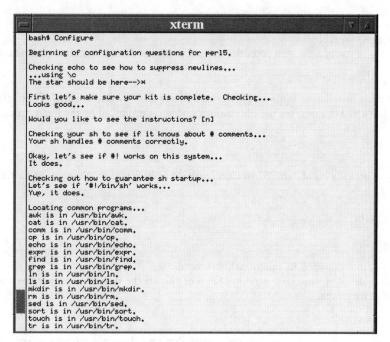

```
bash$ Configure

Beginning of configuration questions for perl5.

Checking echo to see how to suppress newlines...
...using \c
The star should be here-->*

First let's make sure your kit is complete.  Checking...
Looks good...

Would you like to see the instructions? [n]

Checking your sh to see if it knows about # comments...
Your sh handles # comments correctly.

Okay, let's see if #! works on this system...
It does.

Checking out how to guarantee sh startup...
Let's see if '#!/bin/sh' works...
Yup, it does.

Locating common programs...
awk is in /usr/bin/awk.
cat is in /usr/bin/cat.
comm is in /usr/bin/comm.
cp is in /usr/bin/cp.
echo is in /usr/bin/echo.
expr is in /usr/bin/expr.
find is in /usr/bin/find.
grep is in /usr/bin/grep.
ln is in /usr/bin/ln.
ls is in /usr/bin/ls.
mkdir is in /usr/bin/mkdir.
rm is in /usr/bin/rm.
sed is in /usr/bin/sed.
sort is in /usr/bin/sort.
touch is in /usr/bin/touch.
tr is in /usr/bin/tr.
```

As I said, do not worry about the questions that are there. Simply be aware of what is going on and see the defaults. After the questions are over, you are ready to make Perl.

Configuring Perl 5 Automatically

You have probably answered about 100 questions if you went through the Perl configuration process interactively. Most likely, you accepted the default for most every question, because Perl already knew the answer! If you did have to enter something different, it was the exception and not the rule.

You can use a different configure script to build things automatically. This configure script is called **configure** (lower case); it does basically the same thing as **Configure** (upper case) but does it automatically. Simply type:

```
prompt% sh configure     (plus command switches here)
```

Perl will now let you sit and watch it build without user input.

This second form of configuring Perl is especially helpful if you want to have several versions of Perl around. By putting extra command switches on after `sh configure`, you are giving Perl directives on how to build. You can do the same thing with the interactive **Configure**, but that is much more error-prone because you are answering hundreds of questions and may mistype an answer or miss a question altogether. Here is an example of using switches with **configure**. Let's say you want to install a personal copy of Perl in your home directory. Type:

```
prompt% sh configure --prefix=~/perl --html=~/perl/html
```

Now when you install Perl, it will install in your home directory, under **$HOME/perl**, and install the html-ified documentation in **$HOME/perl/html**.

Or, if you want to compile Perl with the debugging flag turned on (great for seeing how Perl works), type:

```
prompt% sh configure -D ccflags='-DDEBUGGING'
```

to turn on the debugging switch.

Another option is to use **gcc**, the gnu compiler instead of **cc**, the default-installed compiler, by using:

```
prompt% sh configure -D'cc=gcc'
```

There are many of these installation options. However, they are scantily documented. These are the three most used ones. For the full set of options, see the file **config.sh** which is produced by the build process.

'Making' Perl

You are now ready to actually build Perl. When **Configure** is finished, it says 'Now you must run a make'. Type:

```
prompt% make
```

and watch it go. After this is complete, type:

```
prompt% make test
```

to see Perl test itself to make sure all its functionality is there.

Finally, if you are installing your own version of Perl or you are the system administrator and want to install it in a centralized directory, type:

```
prompt% make install
```

This copies all the binaries, libraries, etc., that come with Perl into the place where you specified your 'prefix' (e.g., **sh configure --prefix=***/my/directory/please* will install into **/my/directory/please**).

After you are finished installing Perl, test your version in a more informal way. First, put Perl in your path by typing:

```
prompt% PATH=$PATH:/my/directory/please;
```

with **ksh**, or

```
prompt% setenv PATH "$PATH:/my/directory/path"
```

with **tcsh**. After this script is done, you should be able to say something like what is shown in Figure 1.10.

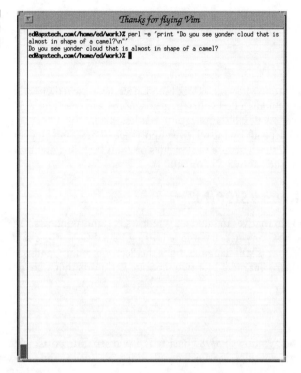

Figure 1.10
Unix Testing Shell

If Perl is installed correctly, it should bounce back the statement for you.

If Something Goes Wrong

Perl almost always installs correctly onto your Unix box, but not always. Troubleshooting is a complicated art, but there are three basic things you can do that will point out (or correct) about 80 percent of the errors encountered during an installation:

1. Remove **config.sh** and then install again.
   When Perl gets installed by the preceding **configure** script, it creates a **config.sh** file that contains all the information found regarding your system. However, and this is important, **config.sh** does *not* go away the next time you build Perl. You must remove this file if you want to install it on a different OS. Suppose you are working on an older platform of SunOS and the platform is upgraded. Chances are, your **config.sh** just became obsolete; when you try to install it again, BOOM. Therefore, make sure you remove it before installing again.
2. Try installing on a machine with the same OS.
   Perl depends on many components on your OS, and they may have bugs from time to time, or may be misinstalled. If Perl installs correctly on the "other" machine, you know it is a problem with one of the underlying components, which you can see by the Perl install steps.
3. Try replacing component by component.
   Replacing component by component will reveal perhaps 70 percent of the problems. This is a good, brute force method in case everything fails and you need to get Perl installed in a hurry.

There are also the resources listed at the end of the chapter, which may help tremendously. When everything else fails, contact other people to get help. After all, you may have even found a bug in Perl itself!

Summary of Building Perl on Unix

You can do two basic things if you want to use Perl on a Unix box: Check to see whether Perl is there, or build it yourself. Both have plusses and minuses: Building Perl yourself means more hassle yet a more flexible application, while using an installed version means a less flexible application, but less work.

Deciding which one you wish to do depends on the relative importance of flexibility in your use of Perl. If you want more flexibility, install it yourself. Otherwise, use the system's prebuilt Perl. Just don't forget to check if the preinstalled Perl is a "good" Perl or not (i.e., above version 5.003).

Building Perl 5 on Windows 95/98/NT

Unlike the build on Unix, you have two alternatives to build on Windows NT and Windows 95/98. You can install a binary that comes directly out of the box, or you can compile it using Visual C++ or Borland C++.

First, we must talk about an issue that is still hanging about the Perl community and is still the cause for a great deal of confusion. That issue is the recent merger of two separate Perl ports that were developed by different groups. This is discussed next.

The Great Perl Merge

Until recently, Perl on Windows NT and Windows 95/98 consisted of two separate ports, which, unfortunately, were incompatible. These two ports were developed to work on Windows platforms, and each was supported by a separate group. These ports were

1. The standard distribution version of Perl.
2. The ActiveState version of Perl.

The standard distribution was the Perl that we talked about earlier. It is available for almost any OS and was maintained by the central perl5 porters group. The ActiveState version of Perl sprung from the company ActiveState. This was a company funded by Microsoft to create a fully Win32-aware Perl.

The ActiveState version of Perl had much of the Windows-specific functionality, such items as interfaces into OLE (or ActiveX), ODBC, the Registry, etc. Table 1.2 lists them in no particular order.

Table 1.2 Windows Modules		
Win32::ChangeNotify	Allows you to monitor when a file or directory changes
Win32::EventLog	Allows you to monitor the NT event log (NT only)
Win32::File	Sets attributes in a file for windows NT
Win32::FileSecurity	Sets permissions for windows NT files
Win32::Mutex	Allows for Mutually shared objects, (so you can synchronize more than one process together)
Win32::Semaphore:	Makes a Semaphore object (lets you control flow between multiple processes. An extension of the Mutex

Table 1.2	Win32::NetAdmin:	Manages users and groups in WinNT (only works on NT)
Windows	Win32::NetResource:	Manages resources (printers, disks, etc.) over a network
Modules	Win32::Process:	Execute's a Windows process inside Windows 95/NT
(continued)	Win32::Registry:	Gives access to the Registry
	Win32::Service:	Allows you to start services on a given computer (ftp, etc.)
	Win32::WinError:	Allows you to handle Windows errors automatically
	OLE	Allows for you to use object linking and imbedding
	ODBC	Allows you to connect to an ODBC style database. NOT included in the internal distribution, but available, and on the accompanying diskette.

As any Windows programmer knows, having these types of modules is absolutely essential to Windows programming, especially OLE. However, ActiveState had some problems. It wasn't usable with the vast number of Unix modules available, it wasn't easily extendable (writing C or C++ extensions was a black art in ActiveState's Perl), and it had some syntactical differences with regular Perl.

On the other hand, the standard distribution of Perl was stable, extendable, widely used, developing at a rapid pace, and running rampant in popularity. But it did not have the essential Windows modules that allow for true Windows programming.

It was natural that the two versions of Perl should merge; the merge has already proved to be a great success. Having the same source code to implement the Perl language on both platforms (rather than simply a specification that companies can follow and break at will, as in the case of C++ and Java) has made for a very smooth experience in porting from NT to Unix and vice versa.

Note

There are some headaches due to the way that Unix and NT operating systems differ, which are summarized neatly inside the **README** files that come with the distribution.

This merge happened relatively recently, however, and the one practical thing you should take from this discussion is do *not* use any binary from ActiveState before version 5.005. If you have a binary prior to 5.005, you are going to want to re-install this binary over the one you have. This means that you will want to:

1. Check the version of your Perl executable.
2. Install the newest Perl (to be on the safe side).

There are two different ways of installing a new Perl executable: by getting an already built binary and by installing it yourself.

Installing a Self-Extracting Binary

To install a self-extracting binary on Windows 95/98 or NT, obtain the latest binary version of Perl 5 which is available on *http://www.ActiveState.com* or on the disk that comes with this book. (You can also pick up binary distributions as well, which give more than just the "bare bones" of Perl. They provide huge numbers of modules;

so go to that site for more information.) This is a self-extracting archive; all you must do is copy it to a folder. If you see the box in Figure 1.11, you know the installation is going well.

Figure 1.11
Starting window
for installing
ActiveState Perl

Click next to continue. This will bring up the following screen, where you choose which action you are going to do.

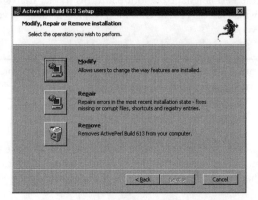

Figure 1.12
Options for
installing Perl

Note that, with perl5.6, the ActiveState version of perl gives you the option to upgrade if you have perl, or do a fresh clean install if you don't. Since we already have a previous version of perl (on the machine that generated this figure) we press 'repair' to continue. Windows will then go into the standard installer procedure which asks you where to install perl, what components you want, and so on. Very slick.

Building Perl from Source Code on NT or Win 95/98

For those of you who wish to fiddle with the guts of perl, you can install Perl via a compiler. Perl5.005 and above will compile out of the box with both Visual C++ and the Borland C++ compiler.

Getting NT/Win 95/98 Source Code

Getting the NT source code is, well, exactly the same as getting the Unix source code. After all the code *itself* is the same!

However, there are two main mirrors you may want to see to get the Perl source code. You can get it from ActiveState (*http://www.ActiveState.com*) or from the Perl home page (*http://www.perl.com/perl/info/software.html*). The ActiveState page provides some Windows-specific information, and the Perl home page is very comprehensive; you should check out both.

Installing NT/Win 95/98 Source Code

When you download the Perl source code from one of these two sites, you are going to need to install it a bit differently than on Unix. The source code comes with the **.tar.gz** extension, which (for those of you who aren't familiar with Unix tools) is a "tarred," "gzipped" file that you must uncompress and install. The easiest way to do this is to get the WinZip shareware package from *http://www.winzip.com*, which handles quite a few different formats for you as zipped files, compressed files, and tarred files.

I've heard of a couple of problems with this when installing the popular Unix editor emacs on NT, but never for Perl. If you *are* having problems with installation via winzip, look at getting the freeware **gunzip.exe** and **tar.exe** from *ftp://ftp.cs.washington.edu/pub/ntemacs/latest/i386/utilities/i386* which are used like their Unix counterparts (as shown earlier). (If you are an emacs fan on the Unix side, you may as well pick this up, too.)

Note that while you are uncompressing Perl, you will get a "nonexistent" or "false" error. There are two files in the Perl distribution—**Configure** and **configure**—that look the same to NT because of the case-insensitivity of NT. Ignore this error. It was calculated as the best way to keep backward compatibility with the Unix Perl, which probably has *millions* of scripts with "Configure" in it!

Installing Perl Using nmake or dmake

It is a little known fact, but both Borland and Visual C++ have a tool to build projects *outside* their graphical interface. Unix affiliates will recognize the tool: make.

Visual C++'s version of make is called **nmake**, and Borland's version is called **dmake**. Because Perl came from a Unix (command-line driven) background, it made sense that it used these familiar tools on NT and Windows 95/98. Below are the core steps for installing Perl using a Windows NT/95/98 compiler. (The process we have chosen to detail is **nmake** with Visual C++.)

Making a Perl executable with **gcc** is possible, but I have never tried it and cannot guarantee that the executable produced can use any of the Windows compilers. See the **README.cygwin32** file that comes with the standard distribution for more information.

Reading README.win32

Reading **README.win32** is a prerequisite to a good, successful install. It is contained in the standard distribution, and has all the steps described next, fleshed-out in greater detail. It also gives some helpful tips on troubleshooting. In particular, you need a 32-bit compiler (any compiler after version 2 for VC++ should be fine), and about 15 MB of disk space.

If you do not have a C++ compiler, and are not planning on doing GUI development with Visual C++, you can get the Learning Version for about $400 less. Since Perl doesn't have GUI calls inherent in it (although it can manipulate GUI's through OLE), it works just fine! The last time I checked, the learning edition cost $99, so it might be worth it even if you're not a "hard-core" programmer.

Step #1: Set Up the Compile Environment

First, get a **cmd** command tool. The **cmd** tool you want is found under the default drop-down list box under **Start,** under **Programs,** and labeled **Command Prompt.**

Get a shell, and look for the **vcvars32.bat** file that comes with Visual C++. Mine is under **Program Files\DevStudio\VC\bin,** so I would type:

```
c:\> C:\Program Files\DevStudio\VC\bin\vcvars32
```

which is the file that sets up a command-line programming environment, and comes with the Visual C++ distribution.

This bat file contains all the environmental variables that make **nmake** work (**nmake** is the tool you will use to build Perl on the command line). Go to Step #2.

Step #2: Edit the Makefile Inside the win32 Directory

The Makefile that creates Perl on Windows machines should work straight out of the box. It is located in the **win32** subdirectory under the standard distribution. Go into that directory:

```
C:\> cd <perl_install_directory>\win32
```

where `<perl_install_directory>` is the directory that contains the unpacked Perl distribution (**perl5.005,** for example). Take a look at the file **Makefile,** as this contains the instructions that VC++ will use to build Perl for you.

Even though the **Makefile** is fairly straightforward, there are a few things you can customize here. You should really look it over before you flip the switch and start compiling:

1. The variable INST_DRV controls on which drive Perl is to be installed. The default is C:.
2. The variable INST_TOP controls in which directory Perl is to be installed. Right now, the default is to have Perl installed in the directory **\perl.**
3. If you want to make a debug version of Perl, uncomment the line saying **CFG=debug.** We shall use the debug version of Perl later to debug regular expressions, and other such things.

You will probably want to make both types of Perl—regular and debugging—and store them as different names. For instance, you might want to make a regular version of Perl, and install it as **Perl,** and make a debug version of Perl and call it **perldebug.**

Step #3: Compile, Test, and Install

Now you are ready to actually go ahead and compile Perl. Simply make sure that you are in the win32 directory by saying:

```
C:\> cd <perl_install_version>\win32
```

where `<perl_install_version>` is, again, the place where you unpacked Perl. Now say:

```
C:\> nmake
```

which should display something like what you see in Figure 1.13

Figure 1.13
Making Perl
with NT

```
Command Prompt - nmake                                                  _ □ ✕
Could Not Find D:\perlinst\PERL5~1.004\PERL5~1.004\win32\miniperlmain.obj
Could Not Find D:\perlinst\PERL5~1.004\PERL5~1.004\win32\*.ilk
Could Not Find D:\perlinst\PERL5~1.004\PERL5~1.004\win32\*.pdb

D:\perlinst\PERL5~1.004\PERL5~1.004\win32>nmake

Microsoft (R) Program Maintenance Utility   Version 1.62.7022
Copyright (C) Microsoft Corp 1988-1997. All rights reserved.

        del /f config.h
Could Not Find D:\perlinst\PERL5~1.004\PERL5~1.004\win32\config.h
        copy config_H.vc config.h
        1 file(s) copied.
        cl.exe -c -nologo -W3 -I.\include -I. -I.. -DWIN32 -D_CONSOLE -DPERLDLL
 -Od -MD -DNDEBUG -Fo..\miniperlmain.obj ..\miniperlmain.c
miniperlmain.c
        cl.exe -c -nologo -W3 -I.\include -I. -I.. -DWIN32 -D_CONSOLE -DPERLDLL
 -Od -MD -DNDEBUG -Fo..\av.obj ..\av.c
av.c
        cl.exe -c -nologo -W3 -I.\include -I. -I.. -DWIN32 -D_CONSOLE -DPERLDLL
 -Od -MD -DNDEBUG -Fo..\deb.obj ..\deb.c
deb.c
        cl.exe -c -nologo -W3 -I.\include -I. -I.. -DWIN32 -D_CONSOLE -DPERLDLL
 -Od -MD -DNDEBUG -Fo..\doio.obj ..\doio.c
```

This actually creates a Perl executable. You now need to test it to make sure the Perl executable is OK:

```
C:\> nmake test
```

which should display what you see in Figure 1.14 when finished.

Figure 1.14
Testing Perl
on NT

```
Command Prompt - nmake test                                             _ □ ✕
        xcopy /f /r /i /d ..\perlglob.exe ..\t\
D:\perlinst\PERL5~1.004\PERL5~1.004\perlglob.exe -> D:\perlinst\PERL5~1.004\PERL
5~1.004\t\perlglob.exe
1 File(s) copied
        cd ..\t
        ..\perl.exe -I..\lib harness
base/cond...........ok
base/if.............ok
base/lex............ok
base/pat............ok
base/term...........ok
comp/cmdopt.........ok
comp/colon..........ok
comp/cpp............skipping test on this platform
comp/decl...........ok
comp/multiline......ok
comp/package........ok
comp/proto..........ok
comp/redef..........ok
comp/script.........ok
comp/term...........ok
comp/use............ok
cmd/elsif.......,...ok
cmd/for.............ok
cmd/mod.............
```

Note that several tests will be 'skipped on this platform.' This indicates that Perl cannot do the certain function on NT because it is not supported or is irrelevant for the operating system.

Note

This will not be much of a problem if you are writing scripts for both Unix and NT, because Perl warns you loud and clear if you try to call a function that isn't supported on NT. The main thing you are going to have to look for if you are a Unix programmer is the **fork()** system call. It doesn't work on NT, whereas it is pretty common on Unix.

Given that you see an 'All tests successful', you should now say:

```
C:\> nmake install
```

which will install Perl into wherever you set INST_TOP. Add to your path the place where the Perl binary was installed with a statement like:

```
C:\> set path = C:\perl\bin;"%PATH%";
```

and do a preliminary test, something like Figure 1.15.

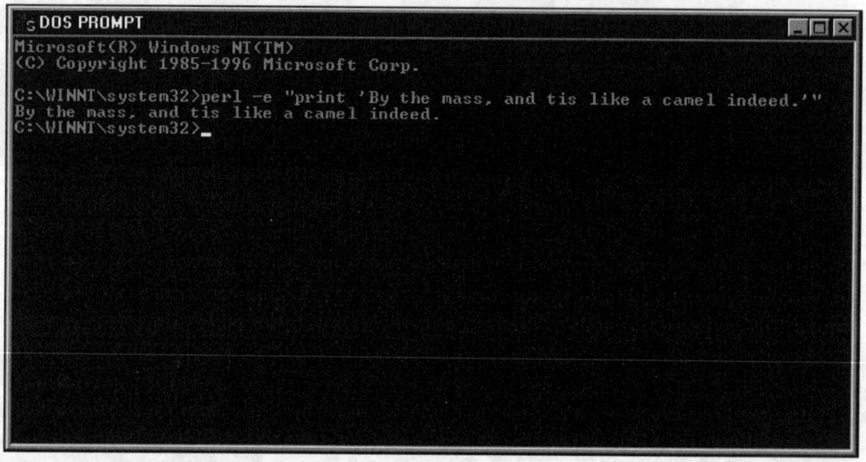

Figure 1.15

Testing the New
Executable

Now you are ready to use Perl.

If Something Goes Wrong

Perl is easier to install onto NT or Windows 95/98 than Unix in many ways. After all, there are only two operating systems that must be supported, and if Perl works on one, it will work on them all. At least that is the theory. Although problems with Perl are rare on NT, when they do arise, they are often very difficult to detect and eliminate. This is because of the central way that NT and Win95/98 do their administration.

NT and Win95/98 have a centralized "black box" (meaning you cannot look at it easily) called the *Registry*, where installed programs register themselves to make the installation as seamless as possible. Unfortunately, if a program decides to install a certain driver that makes another program break, that's the other program's problem. But by extension, it is also your problem.

Perl bypasses the Registry, avoiding many of these problems, but if you are dealing with modules that use other resources on your machine (ODBC, OLE, etc.), you may run into difficulty. There are quite a few things you can do to get out of these difficulties:

1. *Install a binary version and see if the problem goes away*. For whatever reason, you may have compiled Perl incorrectly, or your compiler was faulty. (I have heard of a couple of cases in which VC++ 4.2 thought it was version 5.0, which caused problems.) If the problem goes away after installing the binary, you at least know where to look the next time you install.
2. *Reinstall your C++ compiler*. If #1 is the case, you have probably installed your C++ compiler improperly. Reinstall your compiler and rebuild Perl and see if the problem goes away.

3. *Use a "Registry Doctor."* There are several products devoted to the problems that can occur with both Windows 95/98 and Windows NT versions of the registry. Check out *Norton Disk Doctor* as one of the best products to deal with problems.

4. *Mail to perlbug or apxtech.* Finally, if you think you have a bug in Perl, post the bug to *perlbug@perl.com*, by using the **perlbug** utility (detailed later). If you are not sure that it is a bug, but are still having problems with installation on Windows, mail to apxtech.com (*perlhelp@apxtech.com*, Perl's support line at the company I work for) and they will help you figure out what is going on and what to do to correct the situation.

This line is primarily for corporate technical support, but we don't mind helping out. Please don't abuse this!!

As I said, installation and usage bugs are fairly rare on NT. You should get by with no problem.

Summary of Building Perl on NT

You have two ways to build Perl on NT: by installing a prebuilt version and by compiling it yourself.

Using the prebuilt Perl can get you up and running right away, but you are pretty much confined to installing it in one place. If you want to use the extra modules rewritten for Perl, you are dependent on the people who write these modules, i.e., making a binary form and putting it out on CPAN.

Building Perl yourself can be fun and gives you a lot more functionality, but it does require a Windows-aware C++ compiler. The best option in this case would be to get the "learning" C++ compiler from Microsoft (provided you are not too concerned about writing Windows programs). It cost $99 the last time I checked, and contains a completely functional 32-bit compiler that will work for *everything* in installing Perl.

Building Perl on the Macintosh

Building Perl on the Macintosh is done exclusively through a self-installing archive. You are going to need to:

1. Get the correct, compacted distribution
2. Unpack that distribution

After you have done that, run and enjoy! Of all the operating systems listed here, Perl on the Macintosh is the easiest to install. Let's go through the two steps listed here. But before you do that you are going to need an unpacker utility (i.e., *Stuffit Expander*) to help with the files.

Getting Stuffit Expander

The distribution listed below is in Mac BinaryII format. Although you could get many different types of utilities to uncompress this format, *Stuffit Expander* is the best. It is available at *http://www.aladdinsys.com* as shareware, and if you don't have it now, you are probably going to want to get it. Simply follow the site from the home page, download it, and double-click on the **stuffit expander file**. Then go to the next step.

Downloading the Macintosh Distribution

You are going to need to go to CPAN to download the Macintosh distribution. Go to the central Perl site at *http://www.perl.com/perl/info/software.html*; from there use the CPAN multiplexer explained above in the install

Unix session, or go directly to one of the CPAN sites themselves (listed in Table 1.1). MacPerl is under the **ports/mac** directory in CPAN; hence, you could go to the site *ftp://ftp.cs.colorado.edu/pub/perl/CPAN/_ports/mac* and download it directly from there.

There is an important thing you need to know about MacPerl. As stated earlier, there are two separate distributions for the Mac. One is in a file that will have the following format: *ftp://ftp.cs.colorado.edu/pub/perl/CPAN/ports/mac/Mac_Perl_513r2_tool.bin*.

Here, "513r2" is a version, and the "tool" designation is what you are looking for. Another is a file with the format: *ftp://ftp.cs.colorado.edu/pub/perl/CPAN/ports/mac/Mac_Perl_513r2_appl.bin*.

Unless you have CodeWarrior (and thus the package MPW) from *http://www.metrowerks.com*, you are going to want to get the **appl.bin** version of the file. The **tool.bin** file will appear as garbage on your Mac with no icons at all. This version is for CodeWarrior; read the **MacPerlFAQ.txt** file that is in the same directory.

Expanding and Installing MacPerl

Warning: There will probably be a false error reported such as "Mac BinaryII will be used to inflate the file." Ignore it. Assuming Stuffit Expander is installed, double-click on the file you have downloaded (****appl.bin**). This expands it into a 'Stuffit Expander' archive.

After you have unstuffed the MacPerl file you downloaded and double-clicked on it, you should get the screen shown in Figure 1.16.

Figure 1.16
Mac Installation Prompt

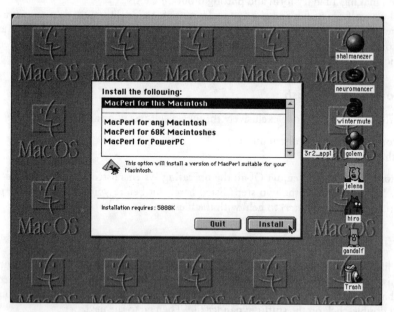

Tell Perl where you want to install it, and you can then use your new binary.

The binary is called **MacPerl** (it is the one with the camel and the pyramid, what else!), and double-clicking starts it. Figures 1.17 and 1.18 give a bit more information on how the MacPerl application works. Figure 1.19 shows where you will actually be running your scripts.

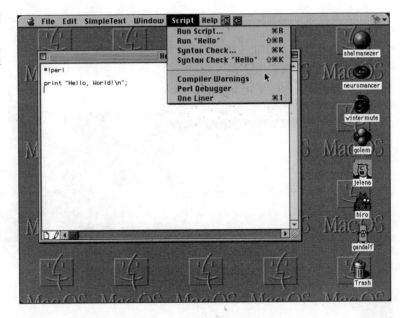

Figure 1.17
Running a
MacPerl Script

Under the Scripts menu item are two main ways you run Perl. At the bottom there is a "one liner" where you can type any Perl command you want. The other way is by loading a file. Both ways have their uses.

Figure 1.18 shows the other main thing that you need to know; how to customize your environment.

Figure 1.18
Customizing Your
Macintosh Perl
Environment

This menu is found under **Edit:Preferences**, and is where you will tell Perl where all your libraries are, how you want to edit your scripts, and so forth.

To test your new install, simply say something like what you see in Figure 1.19, in the "one liner" section under scripts.

Figure 1.19
Testing MacPerl

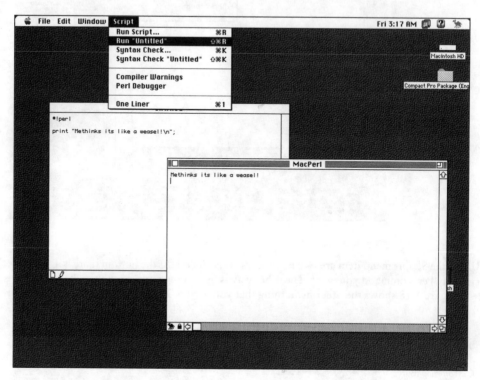

There are other ways of running the Macintosh Perl application. If you are interested, take a look at the **mac.pod** file that comes with the Macintosh distribution.

Building Perl on OS/2

Building Perl on OS/2 is a bit more complicated than building on other platforms, because you need to get other software (besides such simple things as decompression software) and install that before touching the OS/2 distribution. Next is a quick summary of what you need, along with a common install path.

For more information on this read the **README.os2** file that comes with the documentation. There are many options for installing onto OS/2 and you should look at them closely.

You can also build Perl on MS-DOS, Win3.1, Win95/98, and NT if you want to this way, and we will briefly talk about this. If you are on Win95/98 and WinNT, you are probably better off using the "native" way of building Perl as described earlier.

I suggest installing Perl on Win95/98 or Windows NT by going with the standard distribution. The way that I suggest installing Perl on MS-DOS systems is with a very decent DOS Perl port called DJGPP, which is available on CPAN.

Note

Prerequisites to Build Perl on OS/2

You will need a couple of things before you install your OS/2 executable. First, you are going to need a package called EMX or RSX. EMX is available in *ftp://ftp.cdrom.com/pub/os2/emx09c/emxrt.zip* and RSX is available in *ftp://ftp.leo.org/pub/comp/os/os2/leo/devtools/emx+gcc/contrib/rsx*.zip*. EMX and RSX act as a DOS extender, which means that you can compile Perl this way on other platforms as well as OS/2. (You can get a working version of Perl on Win-NT, Win-95/98, Win-31, and even MS-DOS without Windows!)

What's the difference?

RSX needs a server called DPMI running on your system; this provides subroutines on MS-DOS, Win-31, etc., that approach the multitasking that other operating systems pretty much take for granted. (DPMI—for those of you uninitiated in MS-DOSish—stands for DOS Protected Mode Interface, and is available on the Win platforms.)

EMX works on an older version of DPMI called VCPI (for Virtual Control Program Interface). Unfortunately, VCPI and DPMI are not compatible, so EMX won't work on DPMI, and RSX will not work on VCPI!

Table 1.3 provides the operating system cross-reference that you will need to get up and running.

Table 1.3 RSX and EMX	File	Operating System
	ftp://ftp.cdrom.com/pub/os2/emx09c/emxrt.zip	OS/2 MS-DOS
	ftp://ftp.leo.org/pub/comp/os/os2/leo/devtools/emx+gcc/contrib/rsx510.zip	Win3.1 Win95
	ftp://ftp.leo.org/pub/comp/os/os2/leo/devtools/emx+gcc/contrib/rsxnt131.zip	NT 3.51 or above

If you are on DOS, get EMX. If you are anywhere else, get RSX. (And if you are paranoid, get both.) The two packages are smart enough to figure out which one is supposed to run. While you are there, you might as well pick up the gnu development tools. Yes, you can build **gcc**, Perl, and even **emacs** on a DOS box; if you are so inclined, you can get a Unix-like environment, too, with **bash**. Follow the instructions in the distributions on how to do this.

Once you have either EMX or RSX, you will have to configure **Config.SYS** to run automatically when you start your computer. Then reboot and go to the next step.

Getting the Perl Distribution

You can get the regular distribution and also get the **gcc** tools to compile Perl, but there is also an automatic install process you might want to check out. In any case, you need **unzip.exe**. It is available in several places. The best place to get it is *http://www.cdrom.com/pub/infozip* which is an exhaustive source for zip on more than 30 platforms.

Then, you can either download the source or you can get the zipped executables themselves. These are available on any CPAN site (see Table 1.3). This is one such fully qualified path: *ftp://ftp.cs.colorado.edu/mirrors/CPAN/authors/id/ILYAZ/os2/latest*.

There will be many zip files in this directory: you need them all. They are listed below.

```
plinst10.zip   plINSTAL.zip   plREADME.zip   perl_utl.zip   perl_ste.zip
perl_sh.zip    perl_pod.zip   perl_mlb.zip   perl_man.zip   perl_mam.zip
perl_inf.zip   perl_exc.zip   perl_blb.zip   perl_aou.zip
```

Put these all into one directory, and make sure that **unzip.exe** is in your path.

We talk about the installation of OS/2 Perl next. If you are going to build Perl on any of the Microsoft platforms, you will need to follow the directions in the **README.os2** file; they get quite complicated! You might want to check out the DJGPP port instead (instructions given later).

Using the Self-Installer for OS/2

Unzip **plinst10.zip**. This is the master control switch for installing Perl on OS/2. To flip this master control switch, type:

```
[H:] install.exe
```

The first thing you should see is something like Figure 1.20.

Figure 1.20
Install Screen

This is the Perl camel, the trademark of pretty much all Perl-dom.

It also happens to be on the cover of *Programming Perl* by Larry Wall and Associates, and is trademarked by O'Reilly and Associates.

Note

If you see this, you are on the right track. Read the instructions that come up next, and continue.
The next milestone looks something like Figure 1.21.

Figure 1.21

Install Components

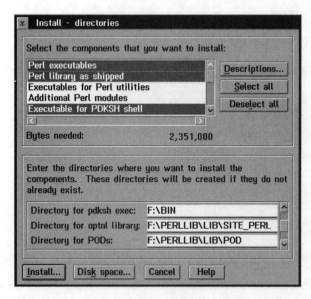

Each directory corresponds to a separate component of Perl that you may or may not choose to install. Go ahead and install them all, after clicking the **descriptions** button to familiarize yourself with what is available. Finally, a progress screen will come up, telling how close you are to being done. When you are done, you should be able to do the test shown in Figure 1.22. If Perl echoes back the statement, you know that you are done.

Figure 1.22

Testing OS/2

Building Perl on VMS

The next operating system we will deal with is VMS. VMS's installation is very much like that of Unix and NT, but the syntax differs quite a bit.

Prerequisites for Installing Perl on VMS

You are going to need these prerequisite programs to install Perl on VMS:

1. **gunzip**
2. **tar**
3. a C compiler
4. **MMS** (DEC's **make** analog), or the freeware equivalent **MMK**

There are no surprises here. Uncompress the Perl source code, un-archive it, and then compile it into an executable using a **make**-like product. Chances are you already have these programs. If you type:

```
$ gunzip --help
$ tar
$ gcc -version OR $ cc/version nl  OR $ cc/list=file.lis nl:
$ mmk/ident     OR mms/ident
```

and any of these items come up blank, you will need to get them, install them, and put them in your path before going forward.

Every one of the programs outlined above (except MMK) has source code at *ftp://ftp.gnu.ai.mit.edu/pub/gnu*, and, being a gnu archive site, this is mirrored at quite a few places. Note that you cannot use **gmake** here because VMS uses *conditional compilation*. It lets you define certain steps inside the **make** process as dependent on flags that you give to it on the command line.

If you are interested in getting prebuilt binaries (you pretty much have no choice for MMK), you can go to the VMS binary site at *ftp://ftp.digital.com/pub/VMS* or *ftp://ftp.wku.edu/vms/fileserv*, which has a good deal of compiled images you can look at. MMK is found at *ftp://ftp.wku.edu/madgoat/*. GCC (the stand-alone compiler) can be found at *ftp://ftp.cco.caltech.edu/pub/rankin/*. In each case, when you get these programs, you can make an alias by saying:

```
$ tar == "$mydev:[mydir]vmstar-vax.exe"
```

where $mydev indicates to the shell (CLI) that the file is a binary, rather than a script (which is indicated by "@"). mydir is the physical directory where you have stored the compiled binaries.

Obtaining Perl for VMS

You are now ready to compile Perl. VMS has been integrated into Perl's core source code, so you can compile right out of the box. Get the standard Perl distribution by going to *http://www.perl.com/perl/info.html* and clicking on **grab the latest source**. This will automatically transfer you to a random fast link to get Perl.

Note that VMS has a limitation here; you can have only one dot (.) in any given filename. Hence, you may have to do a little name juggling to convert **latest.tar.gz** to **latest.tar-gz**; most ftp clients make this easy.

Installing Perl on VMS

The installation of VMS is all command-line driven. The first two steps are simple:

```
$ gunzip latest.tar-gz
$ tar -xvf latest.tar
```

You will probably want to do this where you can have many deep directories (as DISK$DEVICE:[000000]). When you untar the **latest.tar** file in step #2, all the files will go to a default directory; namely **[.perl<version>]** (where **version** is the version of Perl, such as **[.perl5_004]**).

Then change into that directory:

```
$ set default [.perl<version> ]
```

and look at the two major files that hold all the information you need in order to build Perl:

```
$ type/page README.vms
$ type/page [.vms]descrip.mms
```

The first file has copious amounts of information about how to build Perl on VMS. There are quite a few ways of doing it. The simplest way is to use MMS (DEC's formal project builder) or MMK (the **make** clone listed earlier). As of now, there is no **Configure** product available (as there is for Unix) and as there are many different types of VMS, you need to look at the file (**config.vms**) and provide the right defaults when you actually compile Perl.

Note

Once it comes into being, the command: `$ @[.vms]Configure "-des"` will automatically recognize what configuration you are on. By the time this book is published, it should be in existence.

Then, find out which C compiler you are using by probing the version again:

```
$ cc/version nl:
    DEC C V5.3-006 on OpenVMS Alpha V7.1
```

or if that does not work:

```
$ cc/list=file.lis nl:
```

or:

```
$ gcc --version
```

Cross-referencing the response you get from these commands with the **[.vms]descrip.mms** file, you can then choose the correct qualifiers for the mms executable (or mmk) to tell which Perl you are building:

```
$ mms/descrip=[.vms] /macro=("decc=1","__AXP__=1")
$ mms/descrip=[.vms] /macro=("decc=1","__AXP__=1") test
$ define/translation=concealed perl_root disk$dka200:[perl5_004_01.]
$ mms/descrip=[.vms] /macro=("decc=1","__AXP__=1") install
```

Steps #1, #2, and #4 correspond to the **make, make test,** and **make install** commands on other OSs; this particular command builds Perl on an AXP machine with DEC's C compiler as the default.

Note

The **define/... perl_root** command tells mms where to install Perl; this should be another directory that has many deep directories.

This is the simplest one-line script you can do. (**perl -e 1;** is shorter, but not as interesting.)

Building Perl on MS-DOS

The last OS we will consider installing Perl on is MS-DOS. MS-DOS may not be the most glorious of systems, but it sure is the most widespread; the ability to turn a 386 PC into a workstation without having to switch OSs is a powerful incentive for many businesses to use Perl. Instead of switching OSs, they can use Perl to do the difficult jobs that MS-DOS can't do.

Believe it or not, the OS running on 85% of all IBM PCs is (you guessed it) MS-DOS with Win3.1. Sometimes it's just MS-DOS. As such, they make great, cheap machines for Web servers or thin clients, which can get information from other sources, collate mail, and so on. MS-DOS machines tend to run the menial tasks that all the other machines in the office are too expensive to do. However, to do this magic of turning a 386 into a Perl machine, you will need a couple of things.

Prerequisites for Installing Perl on MS-DOS

The MS-DOS Perl port is built off an initiative by Delorie Software (and blessed by the Free Software Foundation) called DJGPP.

Note

DJGPP stands for DJ's Gnu Programming Platform or somesuch (I don't think they have come up with a name for it yet), and is quite popular. The 3D game *Quake* was programmed with DJGPP tools.

DJGPP's goal is to make a 32-bit programming platform available for DOS machines that in reality could be either 32-bit or 16-bit, and greater than a 386. It works because the 386 and above are 32-bit machines, even though DOS is not. Check out *http://www.delorie.com/djgpp* for more detail.

The DJGPP port is totally stand-alone, so you need no extra files besides **pkzip** (*http://www.pkzip.com*). However, if you are a Unix user, you might want to pick up the DJGPP version of **bash**, a Unix shell at the DJGPP site: *ftp.simtel.net/pub/simtelnet/gnu/djgpp/bshXXXXb.zip*.

Note

You might want to pick up all your favorite Unix tools at the same time: compiler, **awk sed, gawk, grep, sh-utils, textutils, fileutils, diffutils, make**, and **findutils**. But you do not need any of them for a perl install. They just make DOS workable if you are a Unix user.

Installing Perl via Binary

You can install Perl either via its binary distribution, or by downloading the DJGPP development platform, plus associated tools, and compiling it. We discuss installing only the binary here. Go to the central distribution under the directory **DJGPP** for more information on installing via compilation.

First, you need to get the Perl binary by going to the CPAN site nearest you: *ftp://ftp.cs.colorado.edu/ pub/_perl/CPAN/ports/msdos/djgpp/perlxxx.zip*. Then, you need to unzip the binary package **perl54b.zip**, preserving the directory structure. Make sure you have created a directory before you do this! Say:

```
c:\djgpp> pkunzip -d perlxxx.zip
```

Be careful that you have the –d modifier; otherwise, Perl will come out in one, flat directory, and it won't work.

If you want to have Perl in a different directory other than the default **C:\djgpp**, you need to edit the file **lib\perl5\Config.pm**, and replace every **c:/djgpp** with your path. Suppose you wanted to install Perl inside **C:\perl**. You would say:

```
c:\perl> pkunzip -d perlxxx.zip
c:\perl> bin/perl -i~ -pe "s'c:/djgpp'C:/perl'i;" lib\perl\Config.pm
```

The second line is simply Perl-ese to actually do the substitution correctly. It goes through the file **Config.pm** and replaces all the text strings **C:/djgpp** with **C:/perl** and backs up a copy of the original in **lib\perl\Config.pm~**.

Make your environment know where to find the Perl variable by editing **autoexec.bat** or typing at the DOS prompt:

```
c:\> set PATH = "%PATH%;C:\perl\bin\perl"
```

or wherever you wanted to install it, and do a quick test of your new Perl application (see Figure 1.23).

Figure 1.23
Testing the
MS-DOS
Application

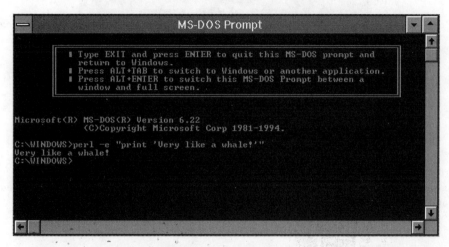

You should be in business. The MS-DOS port is a very robust one. It is built-in virtual memory, works with Win95/98 or DOS, and works with most standard Unix modules. Generally, MS-DOS is a much more pleasant place with Perl installed than without it. Trust me!

Installing Perl Add-On Packages

Let's shift gears. When you get Perl installed, you also get a whole bunch of predefined functionality in what are called *modules*. The additional functionality in ActiveState's port (that handled NT) is all in modules. Likewise, the standard distribution of Perl has many useful modules.

Modules are files that contain functions that are helpful to use, but don't need to be included with the Perl executable itself. They are extensions of the language—a special form of library. For example, the standard distribution contains a module called **Benchmark** which is helpful in timing Perl code, or to see how fast it is on average.

While the standard distribution has a lot of functionality in the form of modules, one of the key principles that Perl 5 was founded on was that it must be *easily extendable*. People need to be able to program functions that others would want to use, and then make them accessible for all.

This is the purpose of CPAN. The index for CPAN is located on *http://mox.Perl.com/CPAN*. Look there for more information. This is actually several sites in one. Pick the one most convenient for you. These sites list all the publicly available modules for Perl. As the saying goes, "Don't reinvent the wheel." There are modules here that I have found very useful and touch on in this book. A screen shot, complete with URL, is shown in Figure 1.24.

Figure 1.24
CPAN and Some
of the Modules
It Contains

As you can see, there are many things here, including database interfaces, World Wide Web interfaces (through CGI), and text manipulation, to name a few.

Package Installation Steps

There are two ways you can install modules: the easy way and the difficult way. More descriptively, you can either directly install them, or use a module called **CPAN**, which is the way I prefer to do things. We go over each next.

Manual Installation of Packages

The default, old way to install a package on Unix or NT was as follows. You first needed to download it, using **ftp**. Then you typed something like:

```
prompt% gunzip Module.tar.gz
prompt% tar xvf Module.tar
prompt% cd Module
prompt% perl5 Makefile.PL  (this uses the Perl5 configuration information stored when
                            you said 'sh configure')
prompt% make
prompt% make test
prompt% make install
```

This would automatically make the instructions on how to build the module ('perl Makefile.PL' makes this instruction set in a 'Makefile'), and would put the module in a place that you could use it.

To test if the install copied the files correctly, you should be able to say:

```
use Module;
```

at the top of a script to include that module, without needing to know where that module is installed. This way doesn't really have any advantages, though Perl itself is the best tool I know of for automating things, and Andreas Koenig with his **CPAN** module made things much easier. Of course, you can also get modules from the CD that accompanies this book; this has certain benefits too. We shall cover both of these methods below.

Installation via CPAN

For UNIX users, the best way to install new modules is via CPAN; from various people I've heard it described as 'the best thing since indoor plumbing" and as "making large-scale Perl distributed development possible". It does, however, require two things:

1. A TCP/IP connection to the internet.
2. A C/C++ compiler if you are going to do any installing of modules that have C or C++ components.

Note

If you do not have a C/C++ compiler and are on a Solaris/Linux/Windows box, then PPM might be for you. See section on PPM below.

So what is CPAN? CPAN is a catalog of available modules, a road map if you will, of what Perl functionality there is out on the Web. Not only that, CPAN allows you to look at what is out there and:

1. Update modules that you already have
2. Install new modules
3. Install "bundles" of related, new modules.

To use CPAN, you simply type:

```
prompt% perl -MCPAN -eshell
```

This is to be read as 'invoke Perl, using the module CPAN, and then evaluate the function shell() inside the module CPAN." After you type this, you should get a prompt:

```
Cpan shell - CPAN exploration and moudles installation (v1.54)
Readline support available (try "install Bundle::CPAN")
Cpan>
```

Take its advice. Type:

```
Cpan> install Bundle::CPAN
```

And watch it go! The things it installs are:

- MD5 - a security module
- Data::Dumper - a debugging module
- Net::Telnet - a module for handling telnet

- libnet - a module for handling command-line manipulation
- Term::ReadKey - a module for handling command-line manipulation
- CPAN::WAIT - enhanced CPAN functionality
- CPAN - latest version

You have just gotten and installed many of the things you need to do Web development. This is an example of the bundle concept; these are modules that work very well together. Next, you can say:

```
cpan> I /Bundle/
```

To see exactly what bundles are available. The most important bundles are:

- Bundle::Apache - bundle for the Apache Web server
- Bundle::CPAN - bundle for CPAN (see above)
- Bundle::LWP - bundle for Web protocols
- Bundle::Tk - bundle for Tk programming
- Bundle::libnet - bundle for net protocols

There are other tricks you can do. You can see which modules of yours are out of date by typing:

```
cpan> r
```

This gives you reinstall suggestions. You can also say:

```
cpan> I /Debug/
```

To get information about all modules pertaining to debugging.

Installation via PPM

Note that above, we said that you needed to have a C/C++ compiler in order to use CPAN. However, for certain platform/module combinations, you can use PPM - which allows for binary installs instead, and available only on ActiveState's version of perl. This is a life saver for those of you running on Windows' platforms, where compilers aren't readily available on the platform.

To use ppm, you say:

```
C:\> ppm
```

which should respond with:

```
PPM interactive shell (1.1.3) - type 'help' for available commands.
PPM>
```

This is the PPM prompt. Type the command help, and you get:

```
Commands:
    exit                    - leave the program
    help [command]          - prints this screen, or help on 'command'.
    install PACKAGES        - installs the specified PACKAGES.
    quit                    - leave the program.
    query [options]         - query information about installed packages.
    remove PACKAGES         - removes the specified PACKAGES from the system.
    search [options]        - search information about available packages.
```

```
        set [ options ]         - set/display current options.
        verify [ options ]      - verifies current install is up to date.

PPM>
```

The most important commands here are 'install' and search. 'search' gives you a list of possible modules, and install installs them. Hence:

```
PPM> search ldap
```

Gives you the following:

```
Packages available from
    soap://www.activestate.com/cgibin/SOAP/ppmserver.plex?class=PPM::SOAPserver:
  perl-ldap [ 0.11] perl-ldap is a library of modules implementing an LDAP client.
    The aim of the perl-ldap project is to implement a very portable LDAP client in
    perl by relying on as little compiled code as possible
To then install the ldap module, you would say:

PPM> install perl-ldap
Retrieving package 'perl-ldap'….
Installing C:\Perl\site\lib\URI\ldap.pm
Writing C:\Perl\site\lib\auto\perl\ldap\.packlist
PPM>
```

Note that the 'search' command can take a substring, and will list out all available modules for that substring. Install on the other hand takes only a complete module name. And also note that both ppm and CPAN keep track of what you have installed - if you have installed ldap in the past, and a new version of ldap comes out, CPAN and PPM will keep your installation up to date.

Installation via the CD

The CD that accompanies this book also has several of the most commonly used modules, including all of the modules for accessing the internet, doing CGI, Webcrawler programs, for database access, etc. In fact, the CD is really a wrapper around both CPAN and PPM; allowing for CPAN to be used in cases where a compiler is present (most unix variants) and allowing for PPM to be used in cases where a compiler is not present (ie: the windows box). To use, slip the CD into the CD drive,and follow the instructions below:

On unix, type

```
prompt% sh install.sh
```

This will lead to a series of questions in installation, starting with:

```
Mounting point for the CD [ default /home/horos/ver2 ]?
```

Follow the series of questions, after you are done, you will have an install of perl, common perl modules, and the more common supporting tools (like make) inside of one directory.

For Windows variants, the install has a few more bells and whistles. In addition to the install of perl, and the common perl modules, you get the documentation in html format, and a windows desktop icon to run your install. If done correctly, the result of the install looks like figure 1.25:

Figure 1.25
Install menu
for Perl

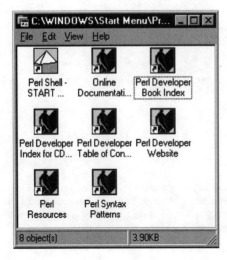

Other Support

By now you should have gotten Perl up and running on your machine. Suppose you want to get support for your Perl code. There are four major ways: Web sites, newsgroups, mailing lists, and professional Perl support. We cover the basics next. There are quite a few more of these resources, including books, in the Appendix included later on in this book.

Web Sites

There are hundreds of small Web sites out there dealing with Perl. Ninety-nine percent of your requests can be handled by remembering *http://www.perl.com*, the Perl home site.

The Perl home page has pretty much any information that you would want about Perl: pointers to code, **CPAN**, the latest Perl news, answers to frequently asked questions, CGI help, and so forth. You will want to start here, and maneuver around inside this massive amount of documentation before doing anything else.

Newsgroups

There are several Usenet newsgroups that can help you with Perl. You should be aware of the three most useful.

- **comp.lang.perl.announce** tells about new developments in the Perl community. It is mostly a read-only group. This is one way to find out if a new extension or release of Perl is available.
- There is also **comp.lang.perl.tk** which talks about how to write GUI programs in Perl using the **perl/tk** extension. It is heavily Unix based, since **tk** is currently only a Unix extension.
- Finally, there is **comp.www.authoring.cgi**, which is not strictly Perl, but nonetheless has quite a few Perl programmers and comments, since Perl is the most popular CGI programming language.

Mailing Lists

Mailing lists tend to be focused, concentrating on specific issues, rather than the gamut of Perl. There are quite a few, some even concentrating on a single Perl module.

However, there is one mailing list that is basic enough to mention right now. This is *perl-win32 users@ActiveState.com*. If you are a Windows Perl programmer, this is the place to go for information. Make a message with the message body:

```
SUBSCRIBE perl-win32-users
```

or, if you want the digest form:

```
DIGEST perl-win32-users
```

and send it to *ListManager@ActiveState.com*.

In addition, *perlbug@perl.com* is a place for reporting Perl bugs. Perl has a nice interface called **perlbug**, which is included in the distribution. Type:

```
prompt% perlbug
```

to report a given bug. This script does everything for you: reports the version, particulars, etc. The only thing you have to do is write the bug! The script will even mail it for you.

Professional Support

Perl has pretty much integrated itself into the enterprise and there are a number of companies out there where you can get contracts for Perl support.

The company I work for—ApexTech—has technical support contracts available for Perl, specializing in C++ and Perl support for the enterprise. We also maintain a Perl help desk, at *perlhelp@apxtech.com*, which can help answer any simple Perl question that you might have, or point you to the right place for a solution. Mail to *perlhelp@apxtech.com* for more details, or point your browser at *http://www.apxtech.com/perl*.

For information on professional training classes, simply point your browser to *http://www.perl.com/perl* (again, the Perl home page). Tom Christiansen has been doing Perl training courses for years, and he maintains the most popular Web site for Perl. E-mail *perl-classes@perl.com* for more information.

Another good site for professional Perl support is *http://www.perl.co.uk*, "The Perl Clinic." It is headed by Tim Bunce who has done a lot of work tying relational databases and Perl together, as well as core work in making Perl as useful as it is today. E-mail *perl-support-info@perl.co.uk* for more information.

I haven't done much research on this subject, but given that the company I work for does it and (as far as I know) my company is not unique, there are probably quite a few other sources. Cygnus software (*www.cygnus.com*) and ActiveState (*www.activestate.com*) might have more information.

Summary

We covered quite a bit in this chapter, and here is a checklist of things that you should have completed at this point in order to get the most out of this book and your learning efforts:

1. You should have made and installed Perl.
2. You should have ready access to the Perl documentation.
3. You should have perused a couple of on-line sites, especially *http://www.perl.com/perl*. (If you are using Win32, *http://ActiveState.com*.)

Now that you have Perl installed, the documentation in an accessible place, and subscribed to a mailing list or news-group, what happens next? Chapter 2 gets you started on programming in Perl by giving a very high-level overview of the Perl 5 development environment. After that, we get into brass tacks, going through many examples of how Perl works, and actual scripts that will work on both NT and Unix. (This is the job of Chapters 3 to 11.)

So take it nice and easy (and relax!). We've got a lot of ground to cover, but fortunately we've got a lot of space to do it in. Next, a high-level overview of what this Perl thing is all about.

Perl at 30,000 Feet: An Overview of Perl

This chapter demonstrates how to run Perl 5, and introduces Perl syntax. The following chapters build on this one (so much so that you might consider this chapter a map for the chapters to come). Before proceeding, I strongly suggest that you have Perl installed, and the man pages printed out, so that you may test the code examples given here.

If you are familiar with Perl, you might want to go to the next chapter. For a Perl veteran, the examples in this chapter will be fairly simple. However, if you want to get back into Perl programming after being a bit rusty, this chapter is for you.

Chapter Overview

One of the best ways to learn a language is to look at it as a whole, without concerning yourself with the parts. This chapter is designed around that principle: to give you a smattering of everything, before we take out our microscope and focus on a bit at a time. Hence, there will be four major parts in this chapter.

First, we will go over some simple uses of Perl, which have been around as long as Perl has been around, solving problems that "fall in the gap" between what an operating system provides, and what products companies provide.

Second, we will go over how to actually run Perl on Unix and Windows 95/ Windows NT platforms. In particular, we will show several ways to make Perl work with the windowing platform, and some of the flags we can use with the Perl executable.

Third, we will give an overview of Perl-ish syntax. This is where we enter the "30,000 feet" territory that gives the chapter its name. We consider Perl variables, functions, comments, statements (simple and compound), control structures, and common Perl errors. In short, we will discuss in 20 pages what we later expand to 200.

Finally, we will give some examples of Perl in action, going over examples of how you can become instantly productive in Perl. We will consider six such examples, ranging from logging onto an Internet service provider, to interacting with Excel via OLE.

As the chapter says, this is the 30,000-foot view. For those of you who like to be closer to the ground, the rest of the book will be a bit more methodical.

introduction

Perl was designed as a "just do it" language; many of our Perl programs today are simple time-savers. The standard saying is that "Perl was designed as a combination of the best features of sh, C, awk, and sed," the standard Unix toolkits. Perl, in other words, was and still is a language for tool building.

Although we will see that Perl is much, much more—it is capable of managing million dollar projects, mission-critical data, and large Web sites—never forget that one of its primary functions is as a tool builder. If you find yourself confronted with a repetitive task, chances are that you can code a simple, 10-line script that will save you much time.

Some Simple Uses of Perl

As we have seen, the original use of Perl evolved from the shortcomings of other shell tools. One of the primary uses of Perl is to do simple administrative tasks, and do them quickly.

Consider the following tasks:

1. E-mailing members of your team when a process is done.
2. Cleaning a disk with many junk files on it.
3. Performing version control (checking to make sure that a database, or files, applications, etc., are up to date).
4. Summarizing a large amount of text into a report (what Perl was actually designed for in the first place).

Consider an environment that has many of these little, critical path problems. These tasks can't be ignored, because if they are, then *other* people can't do their job. But if you pay attention to them, and do them by hand, then you can't do your job! In other words, they become housekeeping tasks that take over a project.

If you have many junk files, you will potentially run out of disk space. If an important process finishes, and you don't automatically inform people, you are setting yourself up for failure. If you forget, they will be twiddling their thumbs waiting for an already finished process. Effective reports can save you and your co-workers lots of time.

This is where Perl is a lifesaver, and why I was attracted to it. Perl has a very short "ramping up" time: people can learn it quickly. Perl has also become a serious programming language, object-oriented with debuggers, embedded documentation, and links to C/C++, making it the perfect language for learning programming techniques.

Perl allows you to become almost instantly productive, yet it won't close any doors on you. You can learn object-oriented programming, modular programming, database interfaces, and even effective data management, and at the same time be productive in your job. You won't have to take off six months to learn to be productive. The magic of Perl is that it allows you to learn while doing.

Running Perl

There are a few ways of running Perl; each operating system tends to develop its own. Unix users favor using the #! syntax at the beginning of their commands, Macintosh users favor running their commands through a GUI, and Windows NT users haven't actually figured out what they like the best quite yet.

Therefore, we will go through a number of these uses. We will start with the generic way of running a Perl command (that will work everywhere, except perhaps for Macintosh), and then turn to specialized ways of running Perl for Unix and Windows.

But first, we will talk about what is actually going on when you run a script through Perl in the "generic" portion next.

Running Perl Generically

The general syntax for a Perl command that will work on pretty much any platform is:

```
prompt%  perl ScriptName;
```

where 'prompt%' is the prompt you would get in a Unix-like environment, and:

```
C:\> perl ScriptName;
```

is the equivalent syntax on an NT or Windows 95 through MS-DOS. In other words, Perl takes whatever input is in the file ScriptName, and checks its syntax, verifying that what you have given it is a correct Perl file, and executes it if it is.

Note that the above usage assumes that you have a file called *ScriptName*. Alternatively, if you don't want to have a file created, you can type a simple one-line Perl script by saying:

```
prompt%  perl -e "ScriptText";
```

which is simply Perl's way to interpret the text between the single quotes on the command line as a small Perl program and run with it. The following command:

```
prompt%  perl -e "print 'Hello, World\n';"
```

prints out "Hello, World\n" on the screen and then exits.

Running Perl Tenets

As you can see, this philosophy differs quite a bit from other computer languages. Almost all other languages—apart from such languages like tk and shell—require a certain amount of effort to run a given program.

Suppose I was using C/C++. To write this and use it on my Unix box, I'd have to:

1. Open the editor
2. Type in the following file and save it with a specific suffix, namely .c:

```
#include <stdio.h>
void main()
{
    printf ("Hello World!\n");
}
```

3. Close my editor
4. Type **cc hello.c** (assuming we named it as such) to compile the program into machine language in a file called **a.out.** This is also different on different platforms.
5. Type **a.out**

This cycle is edit/formally define/compile/execute. Perl avoids it almost completely.

> **Note** More accurately, Perl lets you decide how much of the cycle you want to participate in. If you want to formally define things, you can. If you want to make a subroutine `main`, you can. You just don't have to—it is not needed to program Perl. Adding as much or as little as you want in rigor is a common topic throughout this book.

Look at the sample Perl code again:

```
prompt% perl -e 'print "Hello, World\n";'
```

If you are a C programmer, you will note the lack of a `main()` subroutine, the lack of declarations, and the lack of everything except to print out `Hello World` and then a carriage return.

Therefore, running Perl is a simple matter of typing what you want Perl to do, and then hitting return.

There is another very helpful thing that Perl does for you, although you need not be aware of it. Perl checks the syntax fully before it actually starts running. Unlike other "simple to use" tools, like older versions of Tcl or shell, Perl isn't so slack as to execute only a part of your program before finding a syntax error and dying. There are no half measures in Perl. Perl checks the full syntax of the command before executing it.

These other languages execute the language a statement at a time, which means they can go halfway through a script and then die, with very unpleasant effects. If Perl does not like the script, it will complain loudly. Following is an example of a simple compilation mistake:

```
prompt% perl -e "print 'hello, world' print 'hello, world2'"

syntax error at -e line 1, near "'hello, world' print"
Execution of -e aborted due to compilation errors.
```

This dies because there is no semicolon between the two print statements. For more information on common syntax, and common syntax problems, see the section "General Perl Syntax" later in the chapter.

Now, this is not the only generic way to run Perl through the command line. Perl also offers a number of "Perl switches" that ease the task of doing certain common actions with Perl. The switch **-e** that we used earlier was one example. We now turn to look at some others.

Perl Switches

There are quite a few specialized switches that Perl recognizes when executing a Perl program. You will hear about one of them, **-w,** quite a bit in the course of this book. It allows Perl to give warnings if the variables in programs are *probably* not being used correctly, if there is a problem with a function infinitely deep in recursion, and numerous other potential problems.

Common switches we will be concerned with in this book include:

-w   A warning switch that you will want to make standard. This is because it does much of the debugging for you by warning you when variables are: not declared; used only once; and many other things. In fact, future versions of Perl may turn on this as a default.

-d   used to run the Perl debugger.

-D   used to use the "debugging" flags that give indications of how Perl is parsing the program. This switch is not available by default; you need to compile Perl with the "debugging flag." (See the section "installing Perl" for more details on how to do this.) -D will be the focus of chapter 22 when we talk about the debugger.

-c   used to use the syntax checker. With -c, Perl checks the syntax of the program without actually running it.

-S   used to execute a script via searching in the user's path. This flag is used to make Perl search through your path to find the script after -S and to execute it if it has the correct permissions. The -S switch is used most often with a method for running Perl we shall describe later.

These are just a few of the switches available for use in Perl. If you are interested in further command line switches, we strongly suggest that you consult the **Perlrun** `manpage` that comes with this documentation for more details.

Running Perl on Different Operating Systems

Unless you are using the Perl switches, you rarely need to type **perl scriptname** to get a Perl script to run. It is somewhat redundant—you want people to be focusing on the *script,* and not on the Perl executable.

In this section, we will be concentrating on the different ways to run Perl on Unix and Windows NT/95.

Running Perl on Unix

Unix is the parent operating system that Perl was developed on, and as such, has a couple of well-entrenched ways of executing a Perl script. They are listed next.

The #! Method

The #! method is available to any shell that supports the #! syntax for programs, which means pretty much any shell out there. The trick is to simply put the full path to the Perl interpreter at the top of the script and change the permissions of that script so it becomes executable. If your Perl binary was located in **/usr/local/bin**, you would say something like:

```
#!/usr/local/bin/perl
```

at the beginning of your script to run it, and then you would say a statement like:

```
prompt% chmod 755 script.p
```

to change the permissions of the script so that it was runnable for everybody. If we do this, our simple **Hello world** example becomes:

```
#!/usr/local/bin/perl
print "Hello World\n";
```

After changing the modifications to the script, the program **script.p** can be executed without explicitly saying that it is a Perl script:

```
prompt%  script.p
```

This line is then internally translated by your shell into:

```
prompt%  /usr/local/bin/perl script.p
```

and makes for a convenient way to run your scripts. You can also run your scripts with flags in them. Hence:

```
#!/usr/local/bin/perl -w
```

turns into

```
prompt% /usr/local/bin/perl -w
```

when put onto the command-line.

Running Scripts via eval and env

This shortcut does not always work correctly, and is definitely not bombproof. If you move your script to a place where Perl is not installed in **/usr/local/bin**, your command will not work.

The result is something like "command not found." Some operating systems, like HP/UX, also throw away long names like:

```
"#!/this/is/an/extremely/long/path/to/perl/so/it/will/not/work"
```

by simply truncating the line to the first 32 characters.

However, on Unix, there are a couple of methods that can let you get around this limitation and make your scripts much more portable. First, there is the **/bin/env** method. You can say something like:

```
#!/bin/env perl
.. script here
```

which uses the program **env** on a Unix box to find the correct version of Perl to execute. This isn't totally bulletproof, since **/bin/env** may not exist on your system or **env** may be located in a different place (although I haven't seen any Unix system like this yet), but it's pretty close, and a pretty simple construct to use. For an almost completely bulletproof method you can say something like:

```
#!/bin/sh # -- perl
eval 'exec perl $0 -S ${1+"$@"}'
      if $running_under_some_shell;
```

This takes advantage of the fact that we know that **sh** (the bourne shell) has a command named eval (which evaluates a given string as a shell script) that can execute a command named **perl**, which happens to be in the user's path.

This otherwise horrid construct will make your scripts much more portable—at least to other Unix machines. For example, if Perl is installed in **/usr/local/bin** on one machine, and **/usr/bin** in another, you can run the same script on both machines, because the eval 'exec allows you to dynamically determine where Perl is.

Otherwise, when you move your scripts to the new machine, it will no longer find the Perl executable, and your Perl scripts will not work.

Running Perl on Windows 95 and Windows NT

Because Perl has become popular on Windows 95 and NT rather recently, the number of ways of running Perl on NT has become large. Time will tell which is the best, but for now I will give them all (apart from the generic use we discussed earlier).

As it stands, you cannot use the #! syntax by default. The MS-DOS shell **cmd.exe** is just not sophisticated enough to understand #!, and scripts on NT are made executable by certain *extensions* to the files (such as **.bat** or **.exe**). Hence, having a **.p** or **.pl** extension will not work. However, there are three basic ways you can run Perl scripts on the Win32 platform, as discussed next.

Using an NT-to-Unix Converter

If you want to use the #! syntax, you should install **gnu-win32** and **bash** for Win95/NT (*http://www.cygnus.com*) or djgpp (*http://www.delorie.com*).

Both provide packages for basically turning your NT box into a Unix box. If I had to choose between the two, I'd choose **djgpp** because it works on a larger group of platforms (Win31, Win95, and WinNT), but that's a pretty slim margin. They both give you Richard Stallman's excellent GNU utilities (*http://www.fsf.org*), which make the NT world a little bit easier for Unix users.

Both products come with the CD that accompanies this book. If you have them installed and set up, you can type:

```
C:\> bash
```

to get a working Unix shell, and assuming that **script.p** has **#!/path/to/perl** as the first line, you can say:

```
bash$ script.p
```

to execute the Perl program. This method is especially helpful for those of you who need to run Perl scripts transparently between platforms. It is a bit of a hack, but all you have to do is either:

1. Install Perl inside a path equivalent to the path where you have Perl on your Unix box (something like **C:/usr/local**).
2. Install **bash** inside **C:/bin** and make a copy of **bash.exe** to **sh.exe**.

Then, consult the earlier section on running Perl on Unix. Either of these ways can work wonders if you are dealing with a Perl project that has to work on both machines. If you don't have this "cross-platform runnability," you will find it an extreme annoyance when you have to change each and every script just so Perl can run on one platform or another.

Making Stand-Alone Scripts via Batch Files

If you don't want to have the overhead of getting a Unix-to-NT converter, and *still* want to simply say 'ScriptName' to invoke a script, Perl provides two different scripts in the standard distribution to help you. The first is the **pl2bat.bat** script. If you say something like:

```
C:\> pl2bat a.pl
```

then **pl2bat** will take **a.pl**, strip off the **.pl** and create a batch file called **a.bat**. Then you can run the Perl executable as:

```
C\> a
```

which will then run your script named **a**. When using this method, you can only have scripts with no extension, or an extension with a **.pl** on the end. This is because if you have a script named **a.p**, and you call the program **pl2bat** with:

```
C:\> pl2bat a.p
```

it will create a script, **a.p.bat**. This script does not know how to execute correctly due to the DOS command line not knowing what to do with the '.p.bat' extension.

The second script provided in the standard distribution is the **runperl.bat** script. **runperl.bat** takes the opposite tack from **pl2bat.bat**. Instead of copying the code that you have into another file and appending a header, you copy **runperl.bat** into something like **a.bat** and then this batch file runs your original script. **runperl.bat** is available inside the **bin** directory associated with your Perl installation. If you say something like:

```
C:\perl\bin> copy runperl.bat a.bat
```

and then type:

```
C:\perl\bin> a
```

DOS will run the associated script a for you.

runperl.bat has benefits over **pl2bat**. First, because you are *copying* the wrapper **runperl.bat** around instead of the underlying code (as you are doing with **pl2bat**), you need not maintain two separate versions of the code.

Second, running your Perl scripts is a one-step process. Once you have made the original copy from **runperl.bat** to **a.bat**, each time you make a change to your original script **a**, you can run the script with the associated changes straight off.

However, it shares the same limitations with **runperl.bat** in that you are forced to have Perl scripts without a suffix. It also creates some overhead because a function named **exec** must be run each time you start a script that has been "**runperl**-ized."

Making Perl Scripts Associated with Perl into Icons

On Windows95/NT, you can also make it so you can double-click on an icon to launch a Perl application. To do this, go into Windows Explorer and select a Perl file (such as **ScriptName.p**). Select **Open With** and scroll down the list this option provides (see Figure 2.1) until you find the executable **Perl**. You have now associated *all* of the files that end with **.p** with Perl. Hence, if you name all of your scripts with a consistent suffix (**script1.p**, **script2.p**, **script3.p**, and so on), you only need do this step once.

There are advantages and disadvantages to associating a Perl script with an icon. One advantage is that you can double-click an icon to get the behavior you want. The disadvantage, however, when you use Perl this way is that you lose out on much of the power Perl provides in the form of command-line arguments. In other words, you could say:

```
perl script.p
```

and

```
perl script.p -input_file my_input
```

instead of making two different scripts (one that handles an input file, and one that doesn't).

Another disadvantage of associating an icon with a Perl script is that only a couple of switches will work, and you will have to hard code them into the script with the associated Perl variable. For example:

```
$^D = 512;
$a =~ m"pattern";
```

turns on the debugging flag for regular expressions. See **perlrun** for more detail.

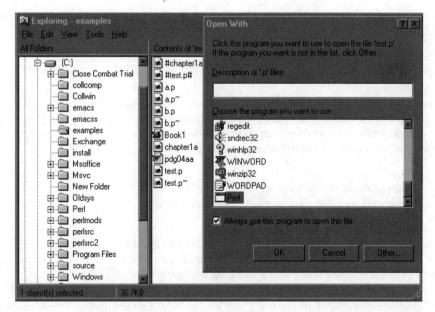

Figure 2.1

Associating a
Perl Script
with an Icon

Yet another disadvantage of this method is that your scripts will execute, and then disappear after they are done executing. Perl is a DOS application and as such opens a DOS window to do its processing. Therefore, when you click on the icon you have formed via associating a script with the Perl executable, your script may run really fast showing output, and then—boom—close down the MS-DOS prompt, taking your output with it.

Note

To get the flexibility of the command line in a GUI form, you might also consider making a perl/tk GUI out of your scripts. We consider this in Chapters 12, 22, and 23. Or, you might consider using one of the tk examples we develop in Chapter 12 (**runscript.p,** which captures the text from a Perl script run into a GUI window).

Summary of Running Perl

You can run Perl pretty much anywhere with the following statement:

```
C:\> perl script_name.p
```

where `script_name.p` is a legal series of Perl statements. If you want more convenient usage for Unix, you can use a shell trick:

```
#!/usr/local/bin/perl
<text_of_script_here>
```

This will only work out of the box for Unix. For NT, your best bet is something like:

```
C:\perl\bin> copy runperl.bat a.bat
```

where `C:\perl\bin` is the place where Perl is installed on your machine, and `a.bat` is the Perl script name that you have, plus the **.bat** extension. However, this solution will allow you to make scripts only without extensions such as **.p** or **.pl**. To run your scripts in a Unix-like way, you are best off getting the **djgpp** or **gnu-win32** packages described above.

General Perl Syntax

Up to this point, you should have Perl installed and running on your system. You should also have a general idea of some tasks that Perl can do for you. Finally, you know how to create and invoke a Perl program. Now let's take a 30,000-foot view, so to speak, of the general syntax of Perl.

In this section we will take an introductory look at the following:

1. Special characters
2. Functions, variables, and subroutines
3. Gluing functions, variables, and subroutines into statements
4. The most common errors that are made in Perl

I may be accused of syntactic terrorism by throwing you directly into the thick of Perl, but let's take the chance. Perl is notorious for all of its special characters. To the untrained eye, a code noise Perl script can look as familiar as the clicks and hums of the !kung sound to an English speaker.

But this disorientation is only temporary. After you take the time to learn a few Perl principles and look at a few Perl scripts, Perl seems very natural. It "flows well." In fact, of all the programming languages I have used, Perl seems the most like English.

All this said, if you are new to Perl, just accept the strangeness for now; I have found that one of the best ways to learn a language is to simply jump in.

Perl Variables

Unlike most languages, Perl represents its different types of variables by *special characters*, not by declaring them as char name[80] as done in C. Also, you can have variables that are the same name, but that point to different variables. @variable, $variable, and %variable point to three separate types of variables. @variable is an array, $variable is a scalar, and %variable is a hash. These are the three major types of variables and we take each in turn.

Scalars

$ denotes a *scalar*, which is a variable that contains anything—numbers, letters, or special characters—of any size.

One can remember the denotation of scalar by thinking of $ as an *s* as in *scalar*, or *single*. Its purpose is to point to a single value, which could be anything (a string, a number, a bunch of binary data, etc.). I will have much to say about this in chapters to come, but here are a couple of examples of scalar assignment:

```
$string = "This is a string!\n";
$number = 33.4;
```

In other words, when making a scalar that is a string, you use either " " or ' ' to indicate when a string begins or ends. (You do not need these quotes if you are assigning a number.)

Unlike other languages, you need not worry about how these variables are stored on the computer. They grow and shrink on demand. A common mistake for C programmers is to say something like:

```
print $string[0];
```

and expect to see *T* be printed. They expect $string to be an array of characters, as it would be in C. This just doesn't work. Instead, this statement looks for the first element in the list called @string. You have to do something like:

```
print substr($string,0,1);
```

which takes a substring of the text in $string.

Arrays

@ denotes an *array*, which is a variable that contains a list of items (scalars) that can be referred to by number. An example is $ARGV[0], which is the first element in the array @ARGV, or the command stack.

If a scalar is a single value, then an array is a bunch of scalars. You can remember it by thinking *@=at*, *at=array*. Since arrays are bunches of scalars, you can get at an individual element in an array by *subscripting* that array with an [<element_number>].

Again, we have pretty much devoted Chapter 3 to these variable types, but here are some examples:

```
@arrayName = (1,2,3,4,'hello','goodbye');    # sets the array '@arrayName'
print $arrayName[0];        # prints '1'
print $arrayName[5];        # prints 'goodbye'
```

Note a couple of things about these examples. First, you can intermix any type of text in an array (strings, numbers, anything). Second, you need not tell Perl how many elements are in the array, Perl does it for you automatically.

Hashes

% denotes a *hash*, which is a variable that contains a series of items that can be referred to by a string, instead of an element number by place, as in arrays. An example is $ENV{'PATH'}, which refers to the environmental variable PATH in the operating system.

Hashes are Perl's way of creating a dictionary. If you think about it, when you open up a dictionary, and look for a definition, you are looking for a string, and trying to get the value for that string. For example:

dog   (n.) mammal of the canine family, domesticated by humans.

Perl's way of encoding this relationship would be to say something like:

```
$dictionary{'dog'} = '(n.) mammal of the canine family, domesticated by humans.'.
```

This statement says "the definition of 'dog' in the 'dictionary' is '(n.) mammal, etc., etc.' "

Here are a few more examples:

```
%hashName = ('key' => 'value', 'key2' => 'value2' );
print $hashName{'key'};
print $hashName{'key2'};
```

The first example sets a hash. Just like a dictionary, a hash contains a series of 'key value' pairs, indicated by the syntax 'key' => 'value'. To get a value out of them, say $hashName{'key'}, which corresponds to the definition of 'key' in %hashName. So, $hashName{'key'} prints 'value', and $hashName{'key2'} prints 'value2'.

Hashes are infinitely valuable. They are also the hardest structure to become accustomed to for programmers of other languages. You simply have to get used to them through examples (of which we shall have several).

Unfortunately, I can't think of a good mnemonic for them! Unless you think of the percent sign as sort of a scratch mark—which is sort of a 'hash' mark—but that really is stretching it.... Ah, well.

Filehandles

The `FH` in `open(FH, "file")` and `close(FH);` denotes a filehandle. A *filehandle* is a variable that allows Perl to get data from and write to files, as in `$line = <FH>`, denotes a read on a filehandle. The read process actually reads a line from an input source and stuffs it into variable `$line`. The next call to `$line = <FH>` will read the next line, and so on.

Filehandles are a bit of an oddity in Perl. They don't have a special character denoting them (like hashes, arrays, and scalars do). They are pretty much a leftover from the early days of Perl when it was strictly a shell-like language.

You may prefer to use:

```
my $FH = new FileHandle("file");
```

which does the same thing as:

```
open(FH, "file");
```

but does it in an object-oriented way. It makes a filehandle look like a scalar, which is nice because you only have three types of variables to remember. Filehandles are Perl's main way of interfacing with the outside world. For example you could say:

```
<code>
$ line = <FH>
<code> or
$ line = $FH getline ()
```

to get a line of data out of the file named 'file'.

These are just the basics of variables. How to manipulate them, their operators, and so forth will be covered in Chapter 3.

Other Oddments

Here are some of the other items you shall see in following examples.

Functions

`function_name()` denotes a *function call* in Perl, to either a built-in or programmer-predefined function. To make a function call in Perl, you simply say something like:

```
function_name('argument1','argument2','argument3'):
```

and the corresponding function definition is:

```
sub function_name    #denotes a function definition in Perl.
{
    my ($argument1, $argument2, $argument3) = @_;
}
```

Again, this is a simple overview of what functions look like.

Regular Expressions

One of the most useful features of Perl—one that sets it apart from almost every other language out there—is its ability to match patterns in a string. Suppose you had a variable (a scalar) that looked something like:

```
$scalarName = 'this is a scalar with a pattern in it';
```

Perl gives you the ability to look for a pattern inside that variable. This is called *pattern matching* and it is done by what are called *regular expressions*. If you say something like:

```
$scalarName =~ m"pattern";    # denotes a 'matching' regular expression in Perl.
```

then Perl looks into the string `$scalarName`, doing something like what you see in Figure 2.2.

Figure 2.2
How Perl
Matches a
Regular
Expression

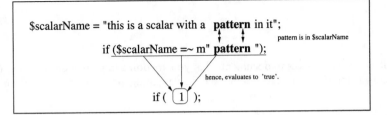

If you then say something like:

```
if ($dogName =~ m"bowser")
{
    print "HERE!\n";
}
```

it will only print `Here` if the variable `$scalarName` contains the pattern `bowser`.

Now, say you want to search for, and replace, a pattern. If you say something like:

```
$line =~ s"pattern"other_pattern";
```

then this looks for the string `pattern`, and replaces it with the string `other_pattern`, as in Figure 2.3.

Figure 2.3
Substitution in
Regular
Expressions

Before: $pattern = "this has a **pattern** in it";

$pattern =~ s" **pattern** " **other pattern** ";

regexp operator   other pattern substituted for pattern

After: $pattern = "this has a **other pattern** in it";

This comes in extremely handy for creating reports, sifting through log files looking for pertinent data, giving a Web page the ability to do keyword searches (if you have ever seen Yahoo or Lycos, you know what I mean). You can do thousands of things with regular expressions. They are really a language unto themselves. We have devoted Chapter 9 to their usage.

Simple Perl Syntax Rules to Remember

Up to this point, we have seen some important concepts in Perl including the variables—scalars, arrays, and hashes—filehandles, functions, and regular expressions. Now, how do you glue these structures together in a meaningful way?

Perl syntax is a difficult thing to grasp, and is even a more difficult thing to define. When you are speaking, you are aware if someone isn't "getting" the language. The statement "He cleaned the brush with the dog" is just plain wrong, but does it help anyone who is learning the language to say "Oh, you mixed up the object of the sentence with the noun in the prepositional phrase"? Probably not. The explanation is more complicated than the problem it solves. In this case, one is better off pointing out what the error looks like, and how to correct it.

Hence, we shall take the same approach. If you want a complete guide to the syntax of Perl, see the Perl man page named **Perlsyn**. In fact, one could consider this small section to be a primer to that document.

Now, in the rough, a given Perl program consists of a series of comments, statements (simple and complex), and declarations.

Comments

Comments are, well, comments: places to document what you are doing in your code. They are indicated by a #. The rule for comments is simple. If you place a # marker, then anything that follows it up to the newline is ignored by Perl. Hence:

```
exit();    # exits the program, because of foo
```

exits the program and the following comment tells other programmers why you are doing it.

Simple and Compound Statements

Simple statements are like sentences in Perl; they tell the computer to do something, and then finish the intention with a semicolon. In other words, they are of the following form:

```
do_something;
```

There are no restrictions on whether or not your statements are on one line. Perl is a free-form language; whitespace doesn't count. Hence, you could say:

```
do
    something;
```

and Perl wouldn't mind.

Listing 2.1 shows some simple statements.

Listing 2.1

```
chop($answer = <STDIN>);
```

This says to take a line of input from the keyboard, assign it to the variable $answer, and then chop off the end character (i.e., get rid of the newline).

```
open (FILE, "fileName")
                || die "Couldn't open fileName";
```

This says to open the file named fileName. If it can't be opened, stop the program with the statement Couldn't open fileName.

```
print "answer equals 'y'" if ($answer eq 'Y');
```

This statement says to print answer equals 'y' only if the variable $answer equals the value 'Y'.

```
function_call('value','value2','value3');
```

This is an example of a user function call. It calls the function function_call with the arguments value, value2, and value3.

All of these are valid simple statements.

Compound statements are basically like compound sentences are to English: They contain multiple simple statements in them, and group a set of statements to be executed based on a "modifier" or "clause." They look like:

```
if (something) { simple_statement1; simple_statement2; }
while (something) { simple_statement1; simple_statement2; }
```

In other words, compound statements are groups of simple statements controlled by a conditional (if) or a looping mechanism (while). The main thing to remember here is that they are opened and closed by matching squiggly brackets ({ and }). Perl is rich in these control structures.

Sample compound statements are shown in Listings 2.2, 2.3, and 2.4.

Listing 2.2
if_block.p

```
if ($answer eq 'Y')
{
    print "You answered yes....";
    print "Deleting file now\n";
    unlink($filename);
}
```

Listing 2.3
reading_file.p

```
my $FD = new FileHandle("log_file");
while ($line = <$FD>)
{
    if ($line =~ m"ERROR")
    {
        push (@error_list, $line);
    }
}
```

Listing 2.4
countdown.p

```
$variable = 10;
print "Counting Down from 10 to 1!\n";
while ($variable)
{
    print "$variable ";
    $variable--;
}
```

The first example prints You answered yes...Deleting file now and then unlinks the file pointed to by the variable $filename, but does so only if the variable answer equals the character 'Y'.

The second example goes through each line of the file log_file and checks to see if the line has the string ERROR in it (as per regular expressions). If it does have the string ERROR in it, it is added to the variable @error_list.

The third example prints Counting Down from 10 to 1 <newline> 10 9 8 7 6 5 4 3 2 1'. The variable $variable is being decremented, one at a time. When the count reaches zero, then while ($variable) ceases to be true, and the compound statement ends.

Simple and complex statements are the heart of Perl. Although you need to declare subroutines, (and by option declare packages), most of Perl is just telling the computer to do stuff.

Declarations

Finally, *declarations* simply associate a piece of code with a name. The only thing you need to declare in Perl are subroutines. We have seen their form already and they look like:

```
sub subroutineName
{
    do_something;
    do_something_else;
}
```

Notice again that this is a simple extension of the compound statement. There are open and closed brackets at the beginning and ending of the subroutine definition.

Common Errors

All the rules of syntax, variables, and functions translate into some common errors for beginning Perl programmers. If you want a full list of errors, please turn to the **perldiag** man page (that comes with the distribution).

Perl errors can be classified into two types: variable and syntax.

Variable Errors

One simple variable error that pretty much everyone makes is forgetting $, @, or % in front of variables. Since all variables in Perl are prefixed by a special character, a common error is forgetting that special character. Hence:

```
variable = 'value';
array = (1,2,3,4);
```

is not going to work. It's going to say:

```
Unquoted string "variable" may clash with future reserved word at script.p line 4.
Can't modify constant item in scalar assignment at a.p line 4, near "'value';"
script.p had compilation errors.
```

Perl is not clairvoyant: You must tell it somehow that you are dealing with either an array, a hash, or a scalar. Using an array when you mean a scalar, a scalar when you mean an array, and so forth is another common variable error.

Perl's syntax is flexible here, but it can do unexpected things. If you say:

```
$scalarName = @arrayName;
```

this is not an error, *per se*. It just may have unexpected consequences. This simply translates `@arrayName` (a list of elements) into a form that `$scalarName` can understand. In this case, it sets `$scalarName` equal to the number of elements in `@arrayName`.

This is called *context* and we shall have much more to say about this later on.

Syntax Errors

A common syntax error that people make is assuming that Perl has multiline comments.

There are no multiline comments in Perl, but beginning Perl programmers often forget this, and try to "bounce" (match) between the #. For example:

```
# this is the beginning of a comment.
  which is multiline but won't work #
```

This simply will not work, and Perl will "complain" about the 'which' statement on line 2 not existing.

Forgetting to put a semicolon after each statement is another common syntax error. Listing 2.5 shows a piece of code that has this syntax error.

Listing 2.5
mistake1.p

```
print "Hello, World"      # mistake.
print "The above line has a mistake in it!";
```

Now, when you type:

```
prompt% perl mistake1.p
```

the result is:

```
syntax error at mistake1.p line 3, near "print"
Execution of mistake1p aborted due to compilation errors.
```

because Perl is interpreting this as:

```
'print "Hello World"   print "The above line has a mistake in it!\n"'.
```

and ignoring all of the whitespace in between, concatenating the two statements together into one. Perl thinks that the second `print` is an argument to the first `print` and becomes confused.

A common error is to omit either an opening quote or a closing quote, because Perl uses single quotes (' ') or double quotes (" ") to mark strings.

Hence:

```
print 'aha;      print 'here'
```

will not work because the first quotation marks after `aha;` aren't closed. Likewise:

```
print "asdfasdf; print "here";
```

does not work because the quotation marks aren't balanced.

Not balancing of parentheses and forgetting commas in arguments are also common mistakes. Perl uses ( ) a lot. In particular, it is used in functions, lists, and conditionals. Because Perl-ish functions look like:

```
function_name($argument1, $argument2, $argument3);
```

and lists look like:

```
( 1, 2, 'string3' );
```

and conditionals look like:

```
if ($variable1 > $variable2) { do this(); }
```

a common error is to not balance or forget the parentheses. To say:

```
function_name($argument1;
    ($variable1, $variable2, $variable3;
    if $variable1 > $variable2
```

are all mistakes, as is:

```
function_name ($argument1 $argument2);
```

because Perl uses a comma to separate two elements.

Complex statements use { } to determine their end, and a common error is to omit them. Hence, the following are syntax errors (Listing 2.6):

Listing 2.6

```
Error #1: using a 'then' in an if clause
if ($condition) then do_something($variable1, $variable2);
Error #2: Forgetting a bracket at the end of a function name
sub function_name
{
    do_something();
Error #3: Forgetting a bracket at the end of a while condition:
while ($condition)
{
    do_something();
```

Summary of 30,000-Foot View of Perl

If you are a C or shell programmer, Pascal, Fortran, Ada, or BASIC programmer, then at least some of the syntax above should look familiar to you. That's because Perl is the ultimate pidgin language, developed out of combinations of already existing languages.

If you stick to the given rules, and keep your Perl programming simple, you should be able to learn it fairly quickly. The syntax just given should satisfy you 90 percent of the time. Many people get in trouble with Perl because they get overly complicated, overly fast. Perl has extreme expressive power, as we shall see. Sometimes you can, for convenience sake, ignore these rules.

You do yourself a favor by sticking to the basics. The important thing is to master the main concepts of Perl: $ stands for a single, scalar variable; @ stands for an array; and % stands for a hash, which is sort of like a dictionary. And be as plain as you can when programming, at first. Then, and only then, should you try more difficult syntax.

Perl Examples

Each of the following examples represents a concrete instance I have encountered in the workplace. In each case, the problem was solved by a simple Perl script.

Do not be alarmed if your first reaction to these programs is "What is that mess on the page?" This is especially true if you have never seen a Perl script before—it is a natural reaction. If you are unsure what to make of the syntax, refer to the capsule definitions we have given earlier.

Each of these parts of Perl is discussed in much detail in the following chapters. We are just providing enough here to get you started.

Figure 2.4 shows a list of the special symbols we covered earlier, and what they mean.

Figure 2.4
Special
Characters
in Perl

Symbol	Concept	Definition	Mnemonic	Usage
$	Scalar	A scalar is a 'single' variable either number or string	$ for 'single' or 'scalar'	$number = 42 $string = 'aha'
@	Array	An array is a group of scalars indexed by a subscript ([1])	@ for 'at' which alliterates w/ array	@arrayName = (1,2,3); print $arrayName[0];
%	Hash	A hash is a dictionary - it has a bunch of key value pairs	% looks like it is hashed up	%age = ('Ed' => '27', 'Lana 24','Joe 32'); print $age{'Ed'}; # prints 27
;	Terminator	terminators end a computer statement	; is traditional way to end statements in C or pascal	chop($line); open(FD, "$file") || die;
#	Comment	a place for programmers to store information about the program	# is a scratch mark, put your scratchings afterwards	exit(); # comment -- exits for 'foo'

()	List	a group of elements	parens are traditional in C or pascal in passing argument lists into functions	@arrayName = (1,2,3);
				function(@arrayName);
				if ($value > $value2)

{}	brackets	brackets are ways to group simple statements into a compound one; also used to get values out of a hash	brackets are traditional in C for grouping of statements and in conditionals.	if ($condition) { exit(); }
				sub true { return(1); }
				while ($true) { do_this(); }
				print $hash{'key'};

=~	Regular Expression	a 'regular expression' is a way to tell if one string has another string in it.	=~ can be looked at as 'semi equal', and substrings inside strings are 'semi-equal'	$string =~ m"substring"; 'this string' =~ m"this"; $string =~ s"1"2"g;

This is a small taste of Perl. Take a look at the following real-life problems and Perl solutions for a more wideeyed view.

Example #1: Accessing Data, and Printing Data from a Bunch of Flat Files, ASCII Format

Let's start with a subject that is near and dear to the hearts of many a business: the processing and flow of data. Consider that you have a bunch of reports (hundreds), all in flat files with extensions **.rpt,** and all of the format in Table 2.1.

Table 2.1

```
Person:      Expense Amount    Rationale for Expense
-------------------------------------------------------
Joe N.       45.00             Office supplies
Sally S.     415.00            Travel to conference
....
```

In other words, these are flat files. The first 11 characters represent the person, the next 18 represent the amount, and the final 20 represent the rationale.

Suppose you want to nail down the travel budget for a given person. The following Perl script will do the job (Listing 2.7):

Listing 2.7
simple_report.p

```perl
 1  #!/usr/local/bin/perl
 2
 3  use FileHandle;
 4  my @files = @ARGV;
 5  my ($file, $line, %expenses);
 6  foreach $file (@files)
 7  {
 8      my $FH = new FileHandle("$file");
 9      while ($line = <$FH>)
10      {
11          my ($person, $expense, $reason) =
12                          (substr($line,0,11),
13                           substr($line,11,18),
14                           substr($line,29,20));
15          if ($reason =~ m"travel"i)
16          {
17                  $expenses{$person} += $expense;
18          }
19      }
20  }
21  foreach $person ( keys %expenses)
22  {
23      print "$person => $expenses{$person}\n";
24  }
```

Now for an explanation of what is going on here. First, the usage of this script is going to be:

```perl
simple_report.p <file_list>
```

In which `file_list` is a list of all the files given as an argument. We see this by the line `@files = @ARGV;`. `@ARGV` is simply a list of all the arguments given at the command line. This statement simply copies the argument list to another variable which makes more sense to the programmer.

Second, the line `my ($file, $line, %expenses)` simply states which variables we are going to be using. We didn't have to do this (only subroutines must be declared), but the keyword `my` lets Perl do some pretty cool, extra debugging checks.

Third, the code goes through a `foreach` loop. This is a construct like `while`, but it goes through each element in an array, setting the value of what is termed the index variable (`foreach $file (@files)`) to that element.

```perl
foreach $file (1,2,3)
{
}
```

sets $file to 1 first (run the loop), 2 second (run the loop), and 3 third (and then run the loop). This construct goes through each of the files on the command line. For each file, the code:

1. Opens it (my $fh = new FileHandle("script");).
2. Goes through each line in the file (while ($line = <$FH>)).
3. Splits each line into its three component parts, based on its position in the file ($person, $expense...) = (substr($line,0,11), ...). This cuts up the file based on characters.
4. Checks to see if the reason for the expense had something to do with travel (if ($reason =~ m"travel"i)). I means to match without regard to case (case Insensitive). If so, adds the amount to the expenses for that person ($expenses{$person} = $expense;).

What we have done is gone through all the lines in all the files we have, and basically collapsed the report into the one hash called %expenses. After we are done, expenses will contain (again, in a dictionary) information on how much each person spent. If you don't believe this, consider that the first time we see a name, say 'Joe', the value $expenses{'Joe'} is empty. Next, when we say:

```
$expenses{'Joe'} += 200.00;
```

it will increment the value to 200.00.

The second time we run through, and say:

```
$expenses{'Joe'} += 50.00
```

the hash has remembered that Joe's expenses were 200.00, and thus increments them by 50 (to 250.00).

After all is said and done, we have the data we need to collapse all the files into a summary of who spent what. The statement:

```
foreach $person (keys %expenses)
{
    print "$person => $expenses{$person}\n";
}
```

is a simple way of spilling all of this information out. keys %expenses is basically a way of getting out what words are in our dictionary. If we only had two people who spent money on travel ('Joe' and 'Sally'), then keys %expenses would output who had what.

Example #2: Accessing Data, and Printing Data from a Bunch of Flat Files, Excel Format

Let's take the same example and use Perl to tie Excel spreadsheets instead. We may be getting ahead of ourselves a little, but often PC reports don't come in the form of ASCII files (although, with Excel's help you can easily make them ASCII). You will need the ActiveState of Perl with NT extensions (see the section "Installing Perl on NT with ActiveState" in the last chapter). You will also need Excel.

Consider whether you have the same problem, but in this case, you have hundreds of Excel files, all of which look like what is shown in Figure 2.5.

Figure 2.5
Excel
Spreadsheets
Interacting with
Perl

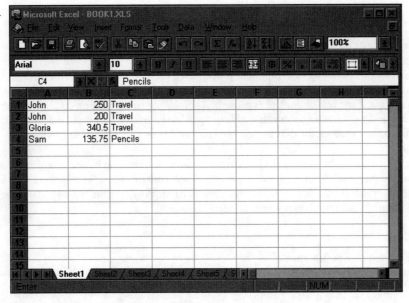

These Excel spreadsheets have exactly the same data as the text report listed earlier. It is just the format that is different. One example goes through flat files and the other through Excel. Hence, the logic will be the same, but we will be using OLE to do the various functions (because Excel can't be accessed directly). Listing 2.8 shows this way of using Perl.

Listing 2.8
Excel1.p

```
1   #!/perl/bin/perl
2   use OLE;
3   @files = @ARGV;
4   my $app = CreateObject OLE "Excel.Application" || die "Couldn't open Excel\n";
5   my ($file, $counter, %expenses);
6   foreach $file (@files)
7   {
8       $app->Workbooks->Open($file);
9       $done = 0; $counter = 1;
10      while (!$done)
11      {
12          my ($person, $expense, $reason) =
13                      ($app->Range("A$counter")->{'Value'},
14                       $app->Range("B$counter")->{'Value'},
15                       $app->Range("C$counter")->{'Value'}
16                      );
17          if ($reason =~ m"travel"i)
18          {
19                  $expenses{$person} += $expense;
20          }
21          if (!$person && !$expense, && !$reason)
22          {
```

```
23                 $done = 1;
24          }
25          $counter++;
26      }
27      $app->Workbooks->Close($file);
28 }
29 $app->Quit();
30
31 foreach $person ( keys %expenses)
32 {
33      print "$person => $expenses{$person}\n";
34 }
```

Note that this is almost a direct translation of the logic from the flat file example, but because we cannot directly access the Excel spreadsheets (to do the manipulation ourselves), we need to go through OLE. Note the 'i' on the end of the regular expression m"travel"i on line 17—this indicates that the preceding expression is case insensitive.

OLE lets you control Windows applications such as Excel through Perl. You create a new OLE object through the call:

```
my $app = CreateObject OLE "Excel.Application" || die "Couldn't open Excel\n";
```

and then proceed to open up files via:

```
$app->Workbooks->Open($file);
```

and close them with:

```
$app->Workbooks->Close($file);
```

The $app->Range("A$counter")->{'Value'} call then gets a value out of the opened Excel spreadsheet, which we then manipulate via Perl's syntax. The scalar $counter call is incremented to access each and every value. We access:

```
$app->Range("A1")->{'Value'};
```

first, access:

```
$app->Range("A2")->{'Value'};
```

second, and so on. We iterate through each column in the Excel spreadsheet, taking data out, and putting it into a hash.

Run this by saying either:

```
C:\> perl Excel1.p *.xls
```

or (if you have **bash**):

```
prompt$ Excel1.p *.xls
```

from the directory where the Excel files reside.

Going through thousands of Excel spreadsheets and summing their contents can save quite a bit of time. However, note that the syntax for OLE is a bit more complicated than the regular Perl syntax. In fact, it is a good example of Perl's object-oriented capabilities, which we go into in great detail when we get to the second part of the book. If you install ActiveState's port, there is also the **oleauto** man page, which shows more about how to automate OLE.

For now, if you are comfortable with this syntax, go for it. A good way to get comfortable with this syntax is to look at Visual Basic programs which do OLE. The syntax is almost exactly the same. We shall also (occasionally) make some OLE examples.

If you are not comfortable, a good way to get around in Windows is to save Excel spreadsheets as flat files, and then use the 'flat file' metaphor in Example 1. This makes life easy, because you can then manipulate the reports in straight text format.

Example #3: E-mailing Members of Your Project When a Process Is Complete

Suppose there is a process that is extremely important, and needs attention when it is finished. Everyone on your group must be notified when it is done. One solution is to e-mail a notification message to everyone. With the Perl system command, you can perform any command the local operating system allows (Listing 2.9).

Listing 2.9
MailAfterDone.p

```
 1   #!/usr/local/bin/perl5
 2
 3   system("important_process");
 4
 5   open (FILE, "> /tmp/process_complete");
 6   print FILE "hey all -- the process is complete!\n";
 7   close(FILE);
 8
 9   foreach $user ('abel', 'baker', 'charlie')
10   {
11       system("elm -s 'process is complete' $user < tmp/process_complete");
12   }
```

OK, now for a pseudo-code explanation of what happened:

1. Do the process `system: ("important_process");`.
2. Open a temporary file, write the message that we are to send in that file, and close the file. This actually creates a file on the system that you can look at through any editor.
3. Go through the list of users `'abel'`, `'baker'`, and `'charlie'`, and mail the message. This occurs in the line `system ("elm ...")`. You may, of course, substitute the command-line mailer of your choice. There is also a module called **Mail::Send** (included on the CD) that does this sort of thing for you (but requires the command **Sendmail**, which is primarily a Unix command). Or you could make your own simple wrapper module, which we will also do in the section on objects.

This example shows that at its most simple, Perl has a great role as "traffic cop." However, keep portability in mind; this example will not work on an NT system unless you substitute **elm** with the proper NT command. In particular, for Microsoft Exchange, you would access this functionality via OLE. (Microsoft Exchange is fully OLE-automatable.)

Example #4: Connecting to an Internet Service Provider

Example #3 is an example of a convenience script—one that saves you strain on the typing muscles. The idea is to connect to an internet service provider (ISP) from a Linux system. Before this script, it was necessary to:

- Make a temporary copy of a file
- Edit that copy, and change one thing
- Save the file
- Invoke a shell script on the copied file

Why do all that if Perl can turn it into a one-step affair?

To connect to an outside network, Linux provides **pppd** and **chat**, which basically automate the login process. A **chat** file looks like the following (not Perl syntax, but still pretty ugly) in Listing 2.10.

Listing 2.10
chat.p

```
exec /usr/local/bin/chat -v \
  TIMEOUT  10   \
  ABORT '\nBUSY\r'    \
  ABORT '\nNO ANSWER\r'   \
  ABORT  '\nRINGING\r\n\r\nRINGING\r' \
  ''   AT   \
  'OK-+++\c-OK' ATH0     \
  TIMEOUT  45   \
  OK  ATDT 555-1212   \
  CONNECT  ''    \
BIS ''      \
  Username:--Username: YOUR_ACCOUNT_HERE    \
  Password: PASSWORD  \
  '>' ppp
```

After creating the script, run something like:

```
pppd modem /dev/tty01 19200 'chat'
```

to connect to the ISP. (**pppd** is the process which actually creates the link.)

chat is an appropriate name for this process. When run, **chat** starts a dialog with a server on the other side of the phone line. The process is as follows:

1. Picks up the phone (with the OK-+++ line).
2. Dials the number (with the OK ATDT 555-1212 line).
3. Waits till it sees the string Username:, and sends the string YOUR_ACCOUNT_HERE.
4. When it sees the string Password:, sends the string PASSWORD.
5. Sends the string ppp after logged in.

This is all fine and dandy, but what happens if you aren't assigned a stable password? This is true with systems which use a SecurId card. With a SecurId or a similar card, the password fluctuates each minute. This means the password changes, which makes things very secure, but also very inconvenient for scripting. In fact, this security feature makes such a script as the previous one impossible.

Consider what you put in the PASSWORD entry in the script. If there were a stable password, *foobar*, you could say something such as:

```
Password:  foobar
```

and it would connect fine. But the SecurId card makes this impossible, since the password is constantly changing. A way to vary the **chat** script every single time you log in (depending on the reading on the SecurId card) is needed. Here is where Perl comes in (Listing 2.11).

Listing 2.11
login_helper.p

```
1  #!/usr/local/bin/perl
2
3  open(TEMPLATE,"chat_template");              # opens the chat file above for reading
4  open(CHATFILE, "> /tmp/chat");               # opens a 'temporary' chat file for writing
5
6  print "What does your SecurId card say:\n";  # prints out to STDIN, asking a question
7  chop($answer = <STDIN>);                     # gets an answer from STDIN.
8
9  while ($line = <TEMPLATE>)                    # goes through the file, a line at a time.
10 {
11    if ($line =~ m"YOUR_ACCOUNT_HERE"g)        # looks for the string
12    {
13        $line =~ s"YOUR_ACCOUNT_HERE"$answer";
14    }
15    print CHATFILE $line;
16 }
17 close(TEMPLATE);
18 close(CHATFILE);
19
20 system("pppd modem /dev/tty01 19200 '/tmp/chat'");
21 unlink("/tmp/chat");
```

And that's it. This script:

1. Opens the chat_template file (line 3).
2. Opens a temporary chatfile called /tmp/chat (line 4).
3. Prompts the user for a string (lines 5 and 6). This is where you would enter your SecurId number.
4. Loops through the file, a line at a time (line 8).
5. Looks for the pattern YOUR_ACCOUNT_HERE, and substitutes it with what the user typed (lines 10 through 13). This is an example of regular expressions, the process of matching text in Perl.
6. Prints the line, substitutions included, to a temporary chatfile (line 14).
7. Closes the filehandles, flushing the output to disk (lines 16 and 17).
8. Launches the command ("pppd modem /dev/tty01 19200 /tmp/chat") via a 'system' call (line 19).
9. Deletes the temporary file that you created (unlink("/tmp/chat");) (line 21).

When run, the script output is:

```
What does your SecurId card say:
```

Perl is now waiting for your input. Suppose you type:

```
What does your SecurId card say:
passwd1
```

Perl will then execute pppd modem /dev/tty01 /tmp/chat. *Voila!* If you have given the correct temporary password, you will be connected. To see why, simply look at /tmp/chat. It will look exactly like chat_template with one difference:

```
....
....
Password: passwd1  \
```

See how this works? Perl copied the file with *one* difference: it filled in the password you have supplied. The **chat** function now works seamlessly with dynamic passwords. Just type:

```
prompt% login_helper.p
```

and Perl connects to the Internet. And, because the password is dynamic, you need not worry about security.

This little trick works well to automate any program that uses a **config** file. If a program reads from a flat ASCII file, you can simply make a copy of that file, "flip a couple bits" to modify its execution, and then run it from the command-line.

Example #5: Unsupplied Functions on Differing Systems: *cat*

Now, we (hopefully) aren't going to get in a religious war here, but one of the good things that Perl does is give the power of the command-line interface to Windows applications. Unfortunately, this particular issue is the cause of much active debate (and flame wars) on the Internet. Hence, a bit of diplomacy is in order.

One might say that the command-line interface is "obsolete." Some folks are perfectly satisfied with GUI applications. On the opposite end, one might say that GUI interfaces are overhyped. Some folks are only satisfied with command-line interfaces.

Whatever. Like it or not, the truth is that GUI applications have their benefits and drawbacks, and command-line tools have their benefits and drawbacks. Neither is predominant, or we would be living in a "one or the other" world.

This section concentrates on giving you the power of both on the Windows platform (although the commands listed here will work on Unix as well).

There are three well-known Unix functions that have no direct equivalent functions in the "command.com" world: **cat, grep,** and **find**.

Note This is not quite true. There are several packages out there that perform the functions **cat, grep,** and **find**. These packages give Unix functionality to NT. Three of these packages are: *NuTCracker* (which costs a considerable amount of money), *MKS toolkit* (which costs money), and the *gnu-win32 project* (which is free, but takes some time and knowledge to install). There are also public domain tools that do these functions via GUI. But the point still stands: If you are doing things in bulk, and you need ultimate flexibility, you are probably better off programming it yourself.

---

cat displays file listings to the screen. Take the following file:

```
List me out to the screen..
I dare you..
```

The command **cat file** will echo out the contents of that file, kind of like the Window shell's **type**:

```
%prompt    cat file
List me out to the screen..
I dare you..
```

Here is **cat** as programmed in Perl (Listing 2.12).

Listing 2.12
cat.p

```
 1 #!/usr/local/bin/perl
 2
 3 foreach $file (@ARGV)        # we iterate through the command list
 4 {
 5     open(FILE, $file);       # we open each file from command line
 6     while ($line = <FILE>)   # we iterate through each line in the file.
 7     {
 8         print "$line\n";     # we print out the current line we are looking at
 9     }
10     close(FILE);             # we close the file.
11 }
```

In pseudocode, the process is:

1. Loop through the argument list via `foreach $file (@ARGV)`.
2. Open a filehandle to that file: `open(FILE,$file);`.
3. Loop through the lines in the file: `while ($line = <FILE>);`.
4. Print that line to the screen: `print "$line\n";`.
5. Close the file: `close(FILE)`.

Here is the minimalist form of **cat** (Listing 2.13):

Listing 2.13
cat_minimal.p

```
 1 #!/usr/local/bin/perl
 2
 3 while (<>) {   print; } # we iterate through every line in the file,
 4                         # and print it out, transparently
 5                         # opening and closing files.
```

Surprisingly, this code does exactly the same thing as the earlier, more verbose version. It uses many special variables that Perl uses as defaults. `while (<>)`, for example, goes through each line in every file specified on the command line. And `print;`, by itself, prints the same line set by the `while(<>)` loop, the one set in the `$_` variable.

We stay away from minimalist Perl in this book. It hinders, rather than helps, and understanding the code and can be downright difficult to debug for anything but the most simple scripts. However, it is helpful if you need to write a simple, throwaway script. Those of you interested in minimalist Perl can go to the **Perlvar** man page for more examples.

Example #6: Unsupplied Functions on Differing Systems: *grep*

grep looks for a pattern in a group of files, and prints matching lines. For those of you unfamiliar with **grep**, it is extremely useful for debugging, tracking down dependencies in code, looking for examples of code usage, and about a million other things. Here is the simplest version of **grep** in Perl (Listing 2.14).

Listing 2.14
minimal_grep.p

```
1 #!/usr/local/bin/perl
2
3 $pattern = shift @ARGV;     # make first argument the pattern we are looking
4                             # for, and shift it off the @ARGV array.
5 while (<>)                  # go through each line in each file
6 {          # @ARGV array.
7   if (m"$pattern")  { print; }  # match the pattern against this line
8 }
```

Let's take this code and expand it to see what is really going on. For fun, we will even add a command switch, -1, to **grep** that only shows which files match a given pattern, not the patterns themselves (Listing 2.15).

Listing 2.15
fuller_grep.p

```
1  #!/usr/local/bin/perl
2
3  use Getopt::Std;        # gives you access to 'simple' command line processing.
4
5  getopts('l');           # adds the command switch 'l'  Both take no arg.
6                          # sets the variable $opt_l.
7
8  my $pattern = shift @ARGV;        # The pattern '$pattern' is first argument
9
10 foreach $file (@ARGV)              # we now loop through files on command line.
11 {
12    open (FILE, $file);            # we open each file.
13    while ($line = <FILE>)         # we go through each line of the file.
14    {
15       if ($line =~ m"$pattern")   # is the pattern in the line?
16       {
17            print "$file" if ($opt_l);    # if so, and -1 given, print filename
18            last if ($opt_l);             # we've found the pattern.. we don't
19                                          # need to go through the file again.
20
21            print "$file: $line" if (!$opt_l);  # if no(ie:!) -1 given, print
22                                                # the file, and line.
23       }
24    }
25    close(FILE);
26 }
```

As in the **chat** example, the processing for **grep** is straightforward:

1. Include the module **Getopt::Std**. This gives us the function **getopts**, which lets us do command-line processing.
2. Process the arguments on the command line getopts('l'). If we say something such as grep.p -1, this will set $opt_l as a variable, which reminds Perl that the user has typed −1.

3. Perl provides a special array variable, `@ARGV`, which corresponds to the arguments on the command-line. We shift (that is, take the first element off the array), and set it to the variable `$pattern` (`$pattern = shift @ARRAY`).
4. Loop through each file in the argument list, using `foreach $file (@ARGV)`.
5. Open each file for reading to search for patterns: (`open(FD, $file);`).
6. Go through each line of the file using the `while ($line = <FILE>)` construct.
7. Look for the pattern `if ($line =~ m"$pattern")` in each line of the file.
8. If the line matches the pattern, check to see if the user has typed −l on the command line. If so, simply print the name of the file and go to the next file: `print "$file" if ($opt_l); last if ($opt_l);`.

If the user did NOT type −l, print each occurrence to the screen `print "$file: $line\n" if (!$opt_l)`. That pretty much sums up the processing. Using the file **grepfile** listed below:

```
PATTERN1
PATTERN2
PATTERN3
```

we can say:

```
%prompt  grep.p PATTERN1 grepfile
grepfile:  PATTERN1
```

This simply matches `PATTERN1` in the file **grepfile**. The output looks like:

```
%prompt  grep.p PATTERN grepfile
grepfile: PATTERN1
grepfile: PATTERN2
grepfile: PATTERN3
```

This matches every line, because "PATTERN" is in all lines in **grepfile**. The command:

```
%prompt  grep.p -l PATTERN grepfile
```

gives the output:

```
grepfile
```

This simply shows that "PATTERN" is somewhere inside the file **grepfile**.

There are thousands of versions of **grep**, and most of them are written in Perl. Among the more common:

cgrep.p—*context grep*. If a pattern match happens, give the surrounding five or so lines that contain that pattern.

rgrep.p—*recursive grep*. Look for a pattern recursively, through a directory.

greplist.p—Look for a list of patterns in a file, rather than just one.

All three of these commands are very useful, and we shall see how to implement them in Chapter 12. Now let's look at one more example in the realm of the simple commands: **find**. Unix buffs are very familiar with **find**. If you are in system administration, it is what makes your job possible.

Example #7: Unsupplied Functions on Differing Systems: *find*

find lists files in a directory given a certain criteria. Suppose you forgot where a file named **cow_report** was located in an environment with thousands of files. **find** is a handy way to, well, find the file. If you are from the Windows world, it's like the Explorer GUI, but much more powerful. For example, suppose there was the following directory structure:

```
directory1/
  file3
  subdirectory/
    file2
    cow_report
```

In Unix, to locate file **cow_report** the command is:

```
find directory1 -name 'cow_report' -print;
```

and given the criteria "the name of the file is **cow_report**," this will print out:

```
directory1/subdirectory1/cow_report.
```

This syntax is quite cryptic, and no good in terms of portability. Even inside the world of Unix, you cannot count on **find** to be equal syntactically. AIX's **find** and Solaris's **find** may return subtly different values given an expression. And, of course, Windows NT does not have a bundled command line version of **find**. This is where Perl comes in. Let's make a **find** that says something like:

```
prompt% find.p cow_report directory1 directory2
```

which will look for **cow_report** in **directory1** and **directory2** and print exactly the same output as the **find** above. Here it is (Listing 2.16).

Listing 2.16
find.p

```
1   #!/usr/local/bin/perl5
2
3   use File::Find;            # 'File::Find' is a pre-packaged library that we use.
4                              # Supplies the function 'find' given below.
5
6   my $pattern = shift @ARGV; # gets an argument off of the command stack @ARGV.
7   my @directories = @ARGV;   # we take the directories from rest of command line.
8
9   find (\&matchPattern, @directories);  # function call in Perl, with callback.
10
11  sub matchPattern                # A subroutine in Perl.
12  {
13      if ($File::Find::name =~ m"$pattern")  # if the file name ($File::Find::name)
14                                             # matches the pattern given:
15      {
16          print "$File::Find::name\n";          # print it out.
17      }
18  }
```

Note that this is a bit of a paradigm shift from what we did with **grep**. The details of looping through directories, as well as the inconsistencies between Windows NT and Unix and how they handle directories, are hidden behind the function **find**. This is a good example of programming abstraction.

First **include** the module **use File::Find;**. This gives the function **find**, which we will use later. Then, take the first argument off the command-line:

```
find.p cow_report directory1 directory2
```

and stick it into the variable $pattern.

```
find.p cow_report directory1 directory2
```

The rest of the command stack we assume is directories, and we stick them into the array @directories.

The line find (\&matchPattern, @directories); is a little tricky: What does it mean? First, **find** is a function, and @directories is a list of directories, a simple array which is passed into the function as an argument. But what about \&matchPattern? \&matchPattern is a *callback*. Callbacks are not functions. They are references to functions, which are often passed to a function to tell it how to perform.

In this particular case, the function **find** does all the looping and iterating through the directories, and calls the function **matchPattern** each time it loops through. Each time it loops through, it sets the variable $File::find::name to the name of the file or directory it is dealing with. And in each case, it calls the function **\&matchPattern**.

In the **cow_report** case, the command:

```
prompt%  find.p cow_report directory1 directory2
```

on the directory tree:

```
directory1/
   file1
   subdirectory/
      file2
      cow_report'.
```

results in:

```
directory1/subdirectory/cow_report
```

The detailed flow of processing is described below.

```
Loop #1:
   $File::find::name set to 'directory1';
   Calls \&matchPattern: does 'directory1' contain the string 'cow_report'? No..
   (i.e.: $File::find:name =~ m"$pattern")
Loop #2:
   $File::find::name set to 'directory1/file1';
   Calls \&matchPattern -- does 'directory/file1' contain 'cow_report'? No...
Loop #3:
   $File::find::name set to 'subdirectory/file2';
   Calls \&matchPattern -- does 'subdirectory/file2' contain 'cow_report'? No...
Loop #4:
   $File::find::name set to 'subdirectory/cow_report'
   Calls \&matchPattern -- does 'subdirectory/cow_report' contain 'cow_report? Yes...
   print it out!
```

find, like **grep**, is infinitely useful, and is the wellspring of thousands of commands. In particular, you could combine this example with the one that did reporting. Then, when you ran the program, it would automatically look through all the Excel spreadsheets in a certain directory. Or perhaps you could use **find** to delete garbage files. (I would be *very* careful about doing this, since this involves doing something that could have serious repercussions on your system if done incorrectly.)

Summary

This chapter has been a bit of a whirlwind. It touched on many subjects and touched quickly. If you are new to Perl and don't understand all the syntax, don't worry. All these aspects are covered in chapters to come, along with many more examples. The point of this chapter is to get you acclimated to Perl syntax, and start thinking in the "Perl-ish" way.

We hope to make Perl syntax almost second nature to you and enable you to pound out these scripts in absolutely no time. This is essential when we get to the heart of this book, which is object-oriented programming in Perl.

If you must have a list of things to keep in mind, here it is:

1. Perl requires no declarations, except in the case of subroutines. Hence, you can just do what you need and exit.
2. Perl can be run in quite a few ways. The most common is saying:

   ```
   prompt% perl <script>
   ```

   at the command-line, and placing:

   ```
   #!/usr/local/bin/perl
   ```

   at the beginning of a Perl file.
3. The important thing in becoming productive in Perl is to start constantly thinking in terms of automating tasks: "What in my job am I doing day after day? How can I change this?" If you think this way, you will get hundreds of programming examples for practice, and at the same time improve productivity on the job.
4. Be careful when you program Perl scripts, especially if you are going to do such nasties as delete backup files (see earlier). Always use caution, wrapping sensitive commands such as **unlink** with prompting that will tell you what a given problem is going to do. And learn some rigor in your programming; that is, take the time to learn the next few chapters fairly well.

If you are going to remember any syntax, remember the table in Figure 2.4 with all the special characters and their definitions. The next few chapters are going to be in-depth analyses on these symbols and how they work.

3

Variables in Perl

This chapter concerns a basic strength of Perl, and why it has grown so popular as a data-manipulation language: its policy toward *variables*. This chapter is not meant to be considered a complete reference. For that, consult the **Perlvar** manpage.

Perl looks at variables a little bit differently than other languages do. Languages such as LISP give one or two basic types of variables, and a few functions for their manipulation. This is the minimalist approach, in which the programmer is expected to have the knowledge to create from only a few building blocks.

Other languages, such as C, take an opposite tack. The number of types of variables in these languages is huge (`int`, `float`, `double`, `long`, `short`, `char`, etc.). Hence the process for manipulating these variables can get quite complex.

Perl tries to strike a balance between minimalist and complex. Perl's overall philosophy is pragmatic: It hides the complexity of having a thousand datatypes, but realizes that giving one datatype to the user may be restrictive. Therefore, Perl has settled on four basic datatypes, each of which is admittedly a compromise between elegance and functionality. These datatypes have been hammered out over 10 years of hard experience. The amount of functionality that these four datatypes cover is quite impressive. The types are:

Scalars—A single chunk of data
Arrays—A bunch of scalars, indexed by number
Hashes—A bunch of scalars, indexed by a scalar called a *key*
Handles—A pointer that enables programmers to open resources from the operating system (files, directories, sockets, etc.)

This chapter is designed to teach you "successful wrangling" of these datatypes. Once you get used to thinking in scalars, arrays, hashes, and handles, and start using them correctly, you can do some pretty cool things.

Chapter Overview

As there are four different types of variables in Perl, it may come to no surprise that there are four major parts to this chapter. However, there are some issues that arise from the fact that there are only four datatypes available, so each section on variables is divided into subsections.

First, we will talk about the scalar, and its role as "universal Perl datatype." We will see how it differs from variables like the ones provided by languages such as C, and talk about a technique called *interpolation*, which allows the scalar to become the universal Perl datatype. We then consider some of the more common operations to manipulate scalars.

Second, we talk about the array, which is Perl's way of representing a group of scalars, ordered by key. We go over its philosophy, and how you can manipulate the array via built-in functions.

Third, we go over the hash, which lets you keep data in Perl as a dictionary does, in a set of key-value pairs. We go over functions to manipulate individual key-value pairs, or manipulate the entire hash.

Finally, we go over handles, which let Perl interact with data external to the Perl program, such as files and directories.

That and a section of examples make up the bulk of this chapter. But first, let's take a look at the "big picture" in a little more detail.

Basic Perl Datatypes

What makes Perl so special? What sets its variables so far apart from other languages? And why do data-manipulation tasks such as generating html pages come so naturally to Perl? A large part of this is due to the inherent ease behind Perl's variables. You need not declare variables as you would in C or FORTRAN. The following is a no-no:

```
Scalar $scalarName;
Array @arrayName;
Hash %hashName;
Handle HandleName
```

This is usually a C programmer's beginning mistake in Perl. Perl variables *carry* their datatype alongside them (so to speak). Scalars are always prefixed with $, arrays with @, and hashes with %. If you have something that you know is a variable, and it doesn't have a special character in front of it, you know it is a filehandle. Table 3.1 lists the special characters.

Table 3.1 Perl's Special Characters	Special Character	What it Denotes	Example
	$	Scalar	$number = 123.44;
			$string = 'aaaa';
	@	Array	@numberArray =(1,2,3);
			@stringArray = ('elmt1', 'elmt2',3);
	$<var>[ ]	Array Element	print $stringArray[2]; # prints 3
			$stringArray[4] = 'newstring'; # sets 5th element
	%	Hash	%hashName = ('key' => 'value', 'key2'=>'value2');
	$<var>{ }	Hash Lookup	print $hashName{'key'}; # prints 'value'
			$hashName{'key3'} = 'value3'; # sets 'key3'

There are other things you need not worry about with Perl variables. You don't need to worry about memory management with Perl; Perl takes care of that for you. Variables grow on demand. Perl variables also hold *any* type of data, so you need not worry about data being truncated or mutilated in any way.

Finally, Perl provides a robust set of internal functions to help you manipulate your data. Programming in Perl sometimes feels like you are cooking (yes, in a kitchen). You "chop" variables, "split" them, and "splice" them. You "shift" them and "map" them. You "join" them and "chomp" them.

At my workplace, we have sort of blurred this line; once you have the analogy in your head, you inevitably go too far and start calling your data directories "medium_to_well".

Note

Let's look at each of these datatypes in close examination, and go over them in detail.

Scalars (Denoted by $)

Although there are four built-in datatypes in Perl, there is only one basic datatype in Perl: the scalar. *Scalars* are simply blocks of information. These blocks of information may represent integers, strings, floats, binary information, or whatever else the programmer dreams up. Scalars are denoted by a $ (dollar sign).

Scalars are one of the reasons why Perl is as powerful as it is. As stated earlier, you need not worry about how big to make your scalar. Perl will make your variables as big as necessary, even if your scalar is a file several megabits in size. Pictorially, you can think of scalars as a whole entity, hiding the details on how they are stored. Figuratively, scalars look like they do in Figure 3.1.

Figure 3.1
A Scalar

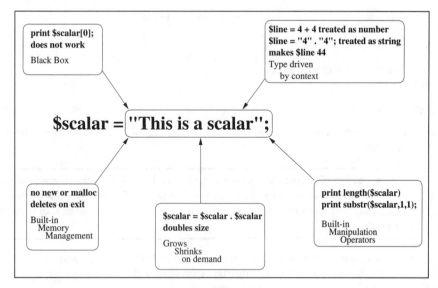

Scalars, Figuratively Speaking

The traditional variable (something like C's `char` variable and how it is used to make strings) might look something like what is shown in Figure 3.2. When programming in C, the programmer needs to worry about such low-level details, whereas in Perl, the details are hidden so you need not worry. To assign a scalar to another scalar, you simply say:

```
$string1 = "This is a scalar";
```

or

```
$string1 = $string2;
```

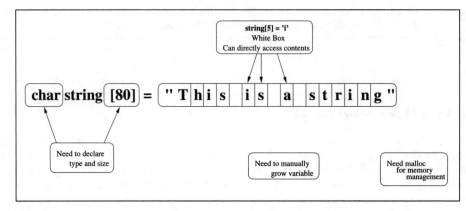

Figure 3.2
A String in C

Scalars allow programs to be much shorter and less complex for several reasons. One reason is that there are fewer issues with boundary conditions. To do the same thing, a C program might look something like:

```
char *string1 = (char *) malloc(sizeof(string2)+1);
int xx = 0;
while (string2[xx] != NULL)
{
    string2[xx] = string1[xx];
    xx++;
}
string2[xx] = '\0';
```

because of the explicit need in C to worry about each character. This also fails if one of the characters in the string is a null (\0) character.

Note

C and its brethren (C++, etc.) are really easy to pick on because they are so low-level. This isn't totally fair. The two languages evolved to handle different concerns, and C is concerned with making things as fast as possible. The above piece of code is fast. So if you are a C/C++ programmer, take such comparisons with a grain of salt.

This points to another thing that you need not worry about in Perl: type inconsistency. C has floats, doubles, unsigned chars, chars, longs, shorts, etc. The difference between a float and a double is in how the variable is stored on the computer (i.e., the precision of the variable).

Perl deems this sort of information too low-level for a programmer to worry about. Therefore, scalars are floats, doubles, chars, longs, and shorts, all at the same time. In C, when you say something like:

```
int yy = 32767;
yy++;
```

what do you get? Well, depending on the compiler you are working on, you get:

1. −32767: The integer wrapped around because it was only 16 bits wide.
2. 32768: The integer is 32 or 64 bits, so you have plenty of space left.
3. Program crash: Your program segmentation faults, and aborts with some sort of cryptic message.

If you hit number 3, what is probably going on is the same as in number 1, but the C/C++ compiler is nice enough to *die* for you instead of silently corrupting your data. Of course, it doesn't tell you why it died.

You need not worry about this sort of thing in Perl. `$xx = 32767; $xx++;` will always return `32768`. If your integers go too high, adding more numbers to them will return floats.

There are other universal benefits to this scalar. There are no keywords to memorize, and no need for you to worry about conflicting keywords. Scalars allow unlimited length of both variable name and the variable's data. There is no need to do anything specific to denote binary or special characters as there is in many other languages.

There is also nothing special to be done with embedded null characters. In other words, scalars allow almost total freedom to program effectively and efficiently. Of course, with this freedom must come some responsibility. If you aren't careful, you could load that 100MB file into one gigantic scalar, and give your machine a seriously bad day. Also, there are a few caveats you should be aware of, because Perl has made the ubiquitous scalar what it is by a compromise of elegance and pragmatism.

Overall, the loose typing of variables enables much design leeway. For example, if you think something is going to be an integer, and it turns out to be a float, there are usually no changes to be made to the code. There are a few exceptions to this rule, which we will discuss in the chapter on Perl syntax.

Creating a Scalar

The syntax for creating a scalar is:

```
$variableName = <value>
```

in which *value* may be numeric (integer or float):

```
string
reference (scalar, array, hash, code, or package)
or boolean (True or False)
```

The variable name can be any legal word string (a–z, A–Z, 0–9 or _) that starts with a lowercase or capital letter. Perl is case-sensitive, so be sure to create a standard for the programming project.

Perl is similar to shell scripting when assigning values to a variable. The single quote (') indicates that the text is to be used verbatim and the double quote (") indicates that the text is going to be interpreted.

Following are some simple examples of scalars (note the pound sign # used for comments):

```
$scalar1 = 'this is a scalar';    # simple scalar assigned 'this is string'
$print = 10.0;                    # simple scalar assigned 10 (rounding is done)
$print = '10.0';                  # number that is also a string, assigned 10.0.
$scalar2 = "this is $print";      # interpolation, assigned 'this is 10.0'
$scalar3 = 'this is $print';      # non-interpolation, assigned 'this is $print'
$emptyString = '';                # empty string.
```

We may be getting ahead of ourselves here, but this example shows a couple of things about Perl. One is that quotes are important. If you say something like:

```
$line = '$';
```

you are using single quotes, and `$line` gets the value $. If on the other hand, you use a double quote, something like:

```
$print = 10;
$line = "this is $print";
```

then `$print` is evaluated as a variable, and `$line` gets the value "this is 10." This is called *interpolation*, and we shall have a lot more to say about it in Chapter 6 on contexts. Interpolation allows for a very natural way to make scalars out of other scalars, blocking them together. Here are some more complicated examples of assigning values to variables in Perl:

```
$octalData = "\07\04\00\01";                # octal data. (\01 equals '1' octal)
$binaryData = "\x0B\0F\xAC\xBC"             # hexadecimal data. 'hello' in ascii
$LooksLikeBinaryDataButIsnt = '\x0b\x0f';  # value is \x0b\x0f (single quotes)
$ReadFromFile = <FD>;                       # Filehandle read ( line from file)
$AssignSingleQuote = '\'';                  # backticking (\') which provides
                                            # ability to assign a single quote
$assignDoubleQuote = "\"";                  # assigning a double quote by \"
$assignTabsNewlinesBackslashes ="\t\n\\";   # \t = tab, \n = newline, \\ = backslash
$MultiLineString = ' Example: this shows
                  how Perl can be assigned a multiline string
';                                          # Example.. multiline string
$4illegalVariableName1;                      # Illegal variable starts with number
$Illegal%VariableName2;                      # Illegal -- has a % in it
$return = "return value";                    # 'return' is keyword nonetheless
                                            # $return is a legal variable.
```

These examples show some of the ways that Perl handles such dilemmas as making a variable equal a quote, and how to handle binary data, octal data, make "return characters," and so on. Perl has one general rule for making special characters:

If you affix a backslash to the beginning of something, you can make it a special character.

Hence, \n becomes a newline; \t becomes a tab, and \r becomes a linefeed. If you want to print a single quote inside single quotes, you say \'.

These examples also show another useful thing, that Perl inherited from the shell: The ability to have completely unambiguous references to variables, without the fear of conflicting with keywords. Because Perl attaches the type of variable to the variable itself, `$return` is a variable, different from **return** the keyword. Hence, if you really want to, you could say something like:

```
if ($if)
{
print $print;
} elsif ($elsif)
{
chop($chop);
}
```

and Perl will understand what you are doing, even if you don't. After all, `$elsif`, `$chop`, and `$print` are just variables.

This ability to make variables that have the same name as keywords can confuse programmers who are used to programming in low-level languages such as C. There are other caveats to remember about scalars that we will look at next.

Scalars as the "Generic Datatype"

A question going through your mind may be: "Exactly how does Perl make scalars work overtime, that is, make them work as floats, ints, doubles, and strings?" Well, Perl simply decides on the right interpretation based on the context that the variable is in. If a variable is in a place where it looks as though it should be interpreted as a string, it *is* interpreted as a string. If a variable is in a place where it looks like a number, it *is* interpreted as a number, and so forth.

This idea of context runs all the way through the language. We will discuss it in detail in Chapter 6 on contexts.

The following three rules approximate the behavior Perl follows when assigning values to a variable, but these rules are by no means exclusive. In other words, you can have a string that is also a number that is also a boolean. (See the **Perldata** man page if you want the complete reference.)

String Interpolation

A scalar is interpreted as a string if it is part of a string comparison operator, or is a built-in function requiring a string, or part of the `" "`, or `' '` construction syntax. A list of places where scalars are interpreted as strings is given in Table 3.2.

Table 3.2	quotes	`'', ""`	$string = 'a', $string = 'b'
Scalars Interpreted as Strings	comparison operators	gt, lt, eq, cmp,ne	'9' gt '10', '1.1' ne '1'
	dot operator	.	$a = 1; $b =2; print $a . $b # prints 12
	hash keys	{ }	$hash{10.0} = 1; print $hash{10.0}; # prints 1

Let's take a look at a few of these elements more closely; they tell a lot about how Perl can get away with only having one datatype.

Quotes (`' '` and `" "`)

Quotes go a long way to tell how a variable is being interpreted. When you see quotes, think of strings. One thing that newcomers to Perl get confused about is that:

```
if ('9.0' eq '9');
```

is *not* the same as:

```
if (9.0 == 9);
```

This is because the quotes are a dead giveaway that 9.0 is to be interpreted as the string 9.0, rather than the number 9. Hence the string 9.0 does *not* equal the string 9. (They aren't the same characters, but the number *9.0* does numerically equal *9*.)

The String Comparison Operators (gt, lt, eq, cmp, ne)

The operators gt, lt, eq, cmp, and ne do certain string comparisons. gt means "greater than," lt is "less than," eq is "equal," and ne is "not equal," (cmp is a special operator for sorting; don't worry about it right now). These string comparison operators compare variables in alphabetical order. Any scalars attached to them are interpreted as strings. If you see some code like:

```
print "yep.. aaa is greater than bbb\n" if ('aaa' gt 'bbb');
```

then Perl is interpreting both aaa and bbb as strings, and then checking to see whether aaa is greater than bbb (gt); it isn't and is therefore false. If you say:

```
print "9.0 does not equal 9" if ('9.0' ne '9');
```

you might not get what you expect because the string 9.0 doesn't equal the string 9, and this message will always get printed. Likewise:

```
print "10 isn't always bigger than 9" if ('10' gt '9');
```

evaluates to true because *10* is smaller than *9* when evaluated as a string.

There is a caveat here, however. If you don't have parentheses around a numeric string, it will be interpreted first as a number, and second a string. For example:

```
if (9.0 eq 9) { print "HERE!\n"; }
```

is true because 9.0 gets trimmed to 9 (rounded) before the string compare. Again, I refer you to the **Perldata** manpage for more detail.

The . Operator

The '.' symbol denotes the concatenation operator in Perl. The operator takes two scalars, and combines them in one scalar. As such, to the scalars to the left and right are interpreted as strings in this scenario. Hence:

```
$line = $line . 'end of the';
```

appends the string end of the to the end of $line.

```
$nineHundredTen = '9' . '10';
```

is the string '910', and not *9.10* as the unwary might expect, because the *9* and *10* are being concatenated. However, note that this is not the same as:

```
$ninepointTen = 9 . 10;
```

where the dot *isn't* a concatenation operator.

Number Interpolation

A scalar is interpreted as a number if it is part of an array subscript, is in a numeric comparison operator, or is in a built-in function requiring a number.

In other words, if a scalar *looks* like it should be interpreted as a number, it generally is interpreted as a number. Table 3.3 has a list of places in which a scalar is interpreted as a number.

Table 3.3 Scalars Interpreted as Numbers	numeric operators:	+, -, /, *, **, %(mod)	"45"+23; 5%4, "error"/"error"
	numeric comparisons	>, <, <=, >=, ==	'1e+23' > '5e+22', 2344.32 == "2344.32"
	array subscripts	[ ]	$array[15], $array["aa"]
	built-in functions	int(), localtime().	int("1111.5") localtime(34234234)

The main thing to recognize here is that in statements such as $array["aa"] and "error"/"error", Perl converts these to the number 0 (zero) for you. However, if it is something like 2344.32, it is a numerical format, and Perl will leave it as it is.

Perl recognizes quite a few numerical formats. The only rule you need to remember here is not to use quotes, or you will end up with strings rather than numbers, (and they may or may not be converted into numbers when necessary for you). Table 3.4 shows the formats.

Table 3.4 Numerical Formats	Number	Type	Number-to-String Autoconvert
	114123	integer	converts: "114123" == 114123
	1123141.111	float	converts: "1123141.111" == 1123141.111
	1_344_454	integer (with underscores for thousands)	does not convert: "1_344_454" != 1344454;
	0x3FFFFF	hexadecimal	does not convert: "0x3FFFFF" != 0x3FFFFF;
	0x3ffff	hexadecimal	does not convert: "0x3ffff" != 0x3ffff;
	03777	octal	does not convert: "03777" != 03777;
	5.432e+300	exponential	does not convert: "5.432e+300"!= 5.432e+300;
	5.224E300	exponential	does not convert: "5.224E300"!= 5.224E300

Remember, '1_000_000' is *not* the same as 1_000_000. The quotes make all the difference in the world. (The underscores make the number easier to read. Don't use commas, as they have special significance in Perl as the list separator.) Note the quotes again: 1_000_000 denotes the number 1 million, and '1_000_000' denotes the string 1, followed by an underscore, three zeros, another underscore, and three more zeros. Hence:

```
(1000000 == 1_000_000);
```

is always true, since the underscores simply make the number easier to read. Whereas:

```
(1000000 == "1_000_000")
```

is always false, since "1_000_000" is not a number because of the quotes.

Following are more examples of variables interpreted as numeric values:

```
$scalar = $scalar +5;   # Easy, add 5 to the variable
if ($biggerScalar > $lesserScalar) { print "$biggerScalar is bigger than
$lesserScalar\n"; }
$onehundred = 10**2;              # ten to the second power is 100.
$five = $two + $two;              # math in the book '1984'
$subscript = "1"
print $array[$subscript];
```

The last code example is a bit tricky. The quotes should tip you off that what you are looking at is a string, but because $subscript is used in a context which takes a number, $subscript is forced to become a number. This evaluates as:

```
print $array[1];
```

The same thing happens with expressions such as:

```
$sum = "111.00" + 12;
```

The + turns the string 111.00 into a number so $sum becomes 123. Likewise with:

```
$value = "non_number" + 1231;
```

you are forcing a string that is normally not a number to become a number. Once a string is so forced, it becomes zero.

This is a caveat you can locate by using the **-w** (warning) flag. If you run the script as follows:

```
prompt% perl5 -w -e "$value = 'non_number' + 1231; "
```

you will get the message:

```
Argument 'non_number' isn't numeric at line 1.
```

Refer to the section "Debugging Perl" for more information.

Confusing? Well, yes. The best way to get over any awkwardness and avoid mistakes is to always use the -w flag in your scripts. -w will notify you about many potential problems with your scripts.

After you get used to this automatic conversion, it becomes quite natural. The best practice for people new to the language is to get used to using -w and looking at the output it creates.

Boolean Interpolation

Consider in detail what happens when you say something such as if ($a gt $b). A scalar is interpreted as a Boolean if it is part of a conditional clause. *Conditional clauses* in Perl are such constructs as if, then, while, and do while. If the scalar is empty, exactly zero ("0"), or the special value "undefined" (discussed later in this chapter), this corresponds to the FALSE value. If the scalar is non-empty, or is a reference, this corresponds to TRUE.

This is a gross simplification, but one that will do until we give it more treatment later in the section "Operators." For an example of what can lie in wait for Perl programmers, consider the value "0.000". Is this false? It certainly looks false, because "0.000" looks as if it is numerically 0.

However, remember that strings are denoted by the quotes ("). Hence, "0.000" is simply a string that *looks* like zero, but isn't a zero as far as Perl is concerned. By our definition therefore, "0.000" is true, and if you say something such as:

```
print "This is true" if ("0.0000");
```

then this will always print This is true. It's something to think about.

Following are examples of variables being interpreted as Boolean values:

```
my $nameOfScalar = "something";

if ($nameOfScalar)
{
    print "True";
}
```

This example always evaluates to true, because $nameOfScalar has a length greater than 0.

```
$scalar = "";
if ($scalar)
{
    print "This never gets here";
}
```

This will never perform the code inside the loop, because $scalar is null and therefore false.

Variable Interpolation Summary

Scalars can be interpreted as either strings, numbers, or Boolean (true or false). Generally, if something looks like a number, it is a number; if it has quotes around it, it is interpreted as a string; and if it is in a comparison (>, =, <, eq, ne, cmp), the value that results from it is a Boolean.

The main thing to watch out for with loosely typed variables is strings being mistaken for numbers. If you say something such as:

```
$varb = "hello" + "goodbye";
```

then you don't get "hello goodbye", you get 0, because + forces "hello" and "goodbye" to be numbers, and this expression evaluates as 0 + 0 which equals 0. The best way to catch such beasts is by the use of the warning flag (**-w**).

Again, all this complication, rules, and confusing mass of steps that Perl goes through can be mostly avoided if you use **-w** in your scripts. This way, you learn by easy experience rather than by hard knocks.

Functions and Operators to Manipulate Scalars

Perl invests much of its functionality in scalars. Perl provides quite a few functions and operators to manipulate scalars. Following are some of the most widely used functions for manipulating scalars. This is by no means an exhaustive set of functions, but surprisingly, they should suffice for 90 percent of the operations you would ever want to perform on scalars:

Calculating Length: length Function

length is a built-in function that gives the length of a scalar:

```
$scalar = "Sample scalar";
$length = length($scalar);   # $length becomes 13.
```

In this example, the function length counts the letters in the scalar $scalar.

Truncating Last Character in Scalars: chop Function

The following is the built-in function chop, which chops a character off the end of a scalar:

```
$scalar = "HO\n";
chop($scalar);             # makes $scalar 'HO'.
chop($scalar);             # makes scalar 'H'
$scalar = 12323;
chop($scalar);             # returns 1232 (chop works on numbers, too!)
```

In each case, you end up with a scalar that is one character less than what went in. Note that you do not say something like:

```
$scalarName = chop($scalarName);
```

This simply doesn't work, because it returns the character that was chopped rather than the abbreviated string.

Truncating Last Character in Scalars: chomp Function

chomp is another built-in function that chops characters off of scalars. It is an intelligent chop, which is usually used for getting rid of newlines on the ends of Perl input. Let's say you define a special character to be \n (a newline). Then a statement such as:

```
$scalar = "This has a newline\n";
chomp($scalar);
```

would return This has a newline. In other words, the newline is gone, and chomp gets rid of the newline. However, if you say:

```
$scalar = "This doesn't have a newline";
chomp($scalar);
```

The original contents of $scalar remain the same because there is no special character chomp-ed from the end.

See the difference? chomp is safer because chop would end up with This doesn't have a newline. It is all controlled by a special variable (called $/) which contains the characters that you don't want to be chopped. This can be set to any value you want, as in the following:

```
$/ = "AAAAA";
$scalar = "ChoppingAAAAA";
chomp($scalar);
print ($scalar);               # prints 'Chopping'
```

The variable $/ does quite a bit more than this. It is called the Input record separator, and we will have more to say on it in the section "Special Variables and Operators", Chapter 10.

Getting Substrings: substr

A scalar is considered to be a "whole," or a unit. You can't simply reach in and grab parts of a scalar. For example, the following will not work:

```
$scalarName = "dog";
print $scalarName[0]; # will NOT print 'd'.
```

because $scalar[0] represents an array element, not the first character of the scalar $scalarName.

Perl provides the substr function (substring) to extract parts of a scalar. If you wanted to get the first character of a scalar, you would say something like:

```
$scalarName = "dog";
$letterD = substr($scalarName,0,1);
```

which is read as "starting at the zeroth (first) letter in $scalarName, take one character, and stuff it into scalar $letterD.

If you want, you can also use the short form of substr and take, say, the fifth and following characters:

```
$vowels = "AEIOUANDSOMETIMESY";
```

```
$andsometimesy = substr($vowels, 5);
print $andsometimesy;
```

This prints ANDSOMETIMESY.

Substr is infinitely useful. Do this if you want to chop off two characters from the scalar $chop:

```
substr($chop, -2) = '';
```

which says that negative subscripts are OK, and they count backward from the end of the string.

Manipulating Case: *uc()* and *lc(); ucfirst();* and *lcfirst()*

uc() returns an uppercase version of the string that you give it. For example, if you say something like:

```
$name = uc("Huey");
print $name;
```

this prints "Huey".

ucfirst() returns a capitalized version:

```
$name = ucfirst("huey");
print $name;
```

and prints "HUEY".

Likewise, lc() and lcfirst() return lowercased versions of strings. lc returns all lowercase. lcfirst() makes the first character uncapitalized (although why anybody would want to do that is beyond me).

defined and *undef*

Scalars can come into being any time necessary without a formal definition statement. You can say:

```
print $scalarName;
```

without first initializing $scalarName. All variables are said to have a special value before they are explicitly created. This value is called *undefined*, and it plays quite a large role in Perl.

If you need to test whether or not a scalar has a defined value, simply say something like:

```
if (defined $scalarName)
{
    print "The scalar has been defined\n";
}
```

Likewise, if you want to set a value to be undefined, or simply want to pass the undefined value around, you can simply say:

```
return(undef);          # returns the undefined value from a
                        # function.
$string = undef;        # sets string to the undefined value.
undef($string);         # undefines the string (same as above). Equal to $string = undef;
```

This doesn't do undef and defined nearly enough justice. There are several cases where defined/undef is used in Perl to a programmer's great advantage:

1. When a filehandle or directory handle reaches its end, the last value returned is undef. See the section on handles for more information on this.

2. Some special functions return `undef` as the last value. See below, and the Perlfunc page for more details.
3. Arrays and hashes can also be `undef`'d; this is described in more detail later.

Summary of Scalars

Scalars are Perl's heavily overloaded, jack-of-all-trades datatype. They take some patience to get used to, but if you take the time to learn them well, they will do you yeoman's service.

Scalars are so ubiquitous, and so close to how people naturally think about how variables should operate, that you will find yourself using them in ever-more-complicated ways. Remember:

1. Scalars operate as numbers, strings, and Boolean.
2. They are abstractions in that you can't simply reach in and manipulate them internally. You need functions to do so.
3. You need not know how these variables are stored. They manage themselves.

Arrays (Denoted by @) and Lists

Are you wondering why we spent so much time on scalars? If you know scalars inside and out, you know arrays (and hashes) inside and out as well. Arrays are simply groups of scalars that are indexed by a number. Arrays in Perl grow and shrink automatically, unlike some programming languages that require the size of an array to be preset. Arrays are represented by @ (at sign). Arrays in Perl are like arrays in C in that they start at the zeroth element and progress upward.

The values of the individual elements in simple, one-dimensional arrays are assigned in the same way as scalars by the following construct:

```
@arrayName = (value1, value2, value3);    #this assigns values starting at index 0
```

When dealing with strings that are in order, or with numbers, you can also simply say:

```
@arrayName = (1..10);
```

where .. is a special symbol that says the same thing as:

```
@arrayName = (1,2,3,4,5,6,7,8,9,10);
```

Or you can say:

```
@arrayName = ('a'..'e');
```

which creates an array with the following contents:

```
@arrayName = ('a','b','c','d','e');
```

in which the .. expands into a series of elements.

Each array element is a scalar. Therefore, the element may be assigned a value individually by index number with the following construct:

```
$arrayName[index] = value;
```

Again, C programmers can get especially confused by this. This is not getting the `<index>`th character of the scalar `$arrayName`. Instead, it is the `<index>`th element of `@arrayName`, something like what is shown in Figure 3.3.

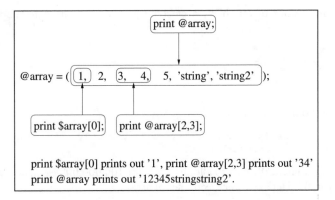

Figure 3.3
Reading Array
Syntax in Perl

Here are some simple examples of arrays and array elements:

```
@array1 = ('This', 'is', 'an', 'array');     # four-element array
@numberArray = (1, 2, 3, 4, 5);              #  array of numbers
@emptyArray = ();                            #  empty array
$array2[0] = 'elem0';                        # element 0 of array2 equals 'elem0'
```

The following example prints all the elements in the array in order:

```
print "@array1\n";         # Example: printing out
                           # an array -- by default
                           # prints "This is an array".
                           # See $/ to change this behavior
```

and the following copies @array2 into @array1:

```
@array1 = @array2;         # Example of copy
                           # constructor for arrays
                           # copies each element so
                           # array1 equals array2
```

The next two examples demonstrate manipulating arrays directly (i.e., copying two arrays into one). However, you should realize that Perl provides a function to do this (push), which you should probably use instead.

```
@array1 = (@array2, @array3);     # Makes @array1 equal
                                  # to @array2 concatenated with @array3.
@array1 = (@array1, 'element1');  # appends onto array1 element 1.
```

The following code shows some more interesting things you can do with arrays:

```
@array = ($scalar1, $scalar2, $scalar3);             # Example of scalar assignment to arrays
@ArraySlice[3,4,5] = ('elem3','elem4','elem5');      # Example of slicing an array
                                                     # which assigns string "elem3" to
                                                     # $arraySlice[3], and so on
```

The following demonstrates moving the value of elements to other elements in the same array. This example moves the value of element three to element one, the original value of element one to element two, and the original value of element two to element three:

```
@swap[1,2,3] = @swap[3,1,2];      # Example of swapping elements.
```

This is called *slicing*; it makes transposition of variables extremely easy because you need no temporary variables or loops. It is equivalent to:

```
@swap2 = @swap;
$swap[1] = $swap[3];
$swap[2] = $swap[1];
$swap[3] = $swap[2];
```

Here's another example that you should be aware of:

```
$tooBig[100000000] = '1';    # Too big an array, will probably make your system thrash
                             # and perhaps die.
```

Since arrays grow by default, this automatically tries to allocate space for 100,000,000 elements, which will probably exhaust your memory. Be careful. Here are other examples of arrays:

```
@array = <FD>;                    # Will assign @array the entire file via a filehandle
@array1 = qw(This is an array);   # Example of qw (quoted word) syntax
                                  # Results in ('This', 'is', 'an','array')
@array1 = (This, is, an, array);  # Example of quoteless  assignment
$array[0] = "@array1";            # Example of scalar interpolation context
                                  # see section contexts for more info.
                                  # makes the first element of the array
                                  # 'This is an array'
```

The first example shows what you can do with arrays and how they can be assigned to a filehandle (which we shall talk about shortly). The last example shows another ubiquitous thing about arrays. If you use double quotes (" ") around an array, you are using what is called *array interpolation*. The double quotes join all the elements into one big scalar.

Manipulative Functions on Arrays

This section discusses the functions that manipulate arrays. This is not by any means a full list, but it contains the more important ones.

Getting the Length of an Array (`scalar` and `$#`)

There is a function that returns the number of elements in an array; it just isn't the function that you would expect. The function is called `scalar`, and it forces the array into a scalar context, much as you force strings into a number context.

This example:

```
@array = (1,2,3,4);
$number_of_elements = scalar(@array);
```

returns the number 4.

In practice, the `scalar` function is seldom used. Once you understand how contexts work (see the section on "Contexts" in Chapter 6), you can safely drop the `scalar` word and say:

```
$number_of_elements = @array;
```

instead, because it does the same thing.

The old way of doing this was to say:

```
$number_of_elements = $#array; +1
```

but be careful to put the '+1' on the end if you use it, because it returns one less than the statement above (i.e.; if @array = ('1','2'), then $#array equals 1 not 2).

scalar(@arrayName) shows a simple way for you to iterate through all the elements of an array. You simply say:

```
for ($xx = 0; $xx < scalar(@arrayName); $xx++)
{
    print $arrayName[$xx];
}
```

and the scalar function supplies you with the size of the array through which to iterate. In practice, the scalar is dropped, so this becomes:

```
for ($xx = 0; $xx < @arrayName; $xx++)
{
    print $arrayName[$xx];
}
```

Appending to an Array: The push Function

The push function pushes an element or elements to the end of an array. Remember, the size of arrays is not pre-defined, so it is OK to keep adding elements to the end of the array.

```
@array = ('another', 'array', 'of', 'scalars');
push(@array, 'pushed element');              # pushes an element onto the array
                                             # Afterwards, the array contains (another,
                                             # array, of, scalars, pushed element)
@array = ('one');
push(@array, @array);                        # doubles the array
                                             # Afterwards, the array equals
('one','one')
push(@array, ('list','of','elements'));      # appends ('list','of','elements') onto
                                             # array which now contains
                                             # "one, one, list, of, elements"
```

push is a very handy function to put in your toolbox for manipulating the contents of arrays. It is not necessary to read through the whole array to add elements to the end, nor is it necessary to know the number of elements in the array to create the next one. Finally, it is a safe way to combine the contents of arrays.

Taking Elements Off Arrays: pop Function

pop is the opposite of push. pop takes an element off the end of an array. pop then returns the element's value as a scalar. Again, you need not know the number of elements in an array in order to operate on the last element.
The following is an example of using pop:

```
@array = ('another', 'array', 'of', 'scalars');
$scalar = pop(@array);        # @array now contains ( 'another', 'array', 'of' )
                              # $scalar becomes string 'scalars'
push(@array, 'aha'):          # does a push
$scalar = pop(@array);        # undoes that push
                              # $scalar becomes string 'aha'
                              # array now contains ('another', 'array', 'of'), and
                              # 'scalars' is off the stack
```

Note that pop only undoes one scalar at a time. Hence the following are not exact equivalents:

```
push(@array, @array);
$scalar = pop(@array);
```

unshift and shift Functions

unshift does the exact thing as push, but it adds to the beginning of an array rather than the end. Following is an example of unshift:

```
unshift (@array, 'element');   # adds element to beginning of array
unshift (@array, @array);      # 'doubles' the size of the array
```

Likewise, shift does exactly the same thing as pop, but removes the element to the beginning of an array, not the end.

```
unshift( @array,'element');    # adds element to beginning of an array. ('add')
                               # becomes ('element','add').  See above example
$scalar =  shift (@array);     # $scalar becomes 'element' which undoes the 'unshift'
```

Complicated Array Management: splice Function

Because there are functions for manipulating elements at the beginning and end of arrays, you might expect there is a function that manipulates the middle elements. There is, and it is called splice. splice is quite powerful. In fact, every function above can be rewritten in terms of splice.

splice does just what it sounds like it does: It takes a list and then removes or adds elements to that list in any order specified. General usage is: @array is the array to be affected; $position is the starting position to be affected; $length is the length to be affected; and @list is value to be added.

splice usage is:

Usage 1: splice(@array, $position, $length, @list);

This can be probably better explained in pictorial form, as shown in Figure 3.4.

Figure 3.4
splice Arguments

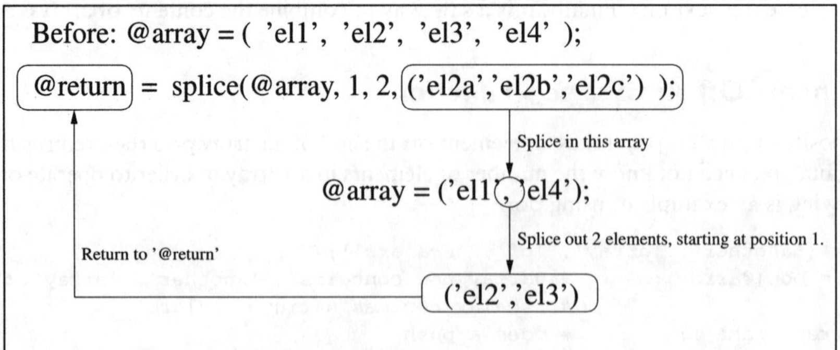

Before: @array = ('el1', 'el2', 'el3', 'el4');

@return = splice(@array, 1, 2, ('el2a','el2b','el2c'));

Splice in this array

@array = ('el1', 'el4');

Splice out 2 elements, starting at position 1.

Return to '@return'

('el2','el3')

After: @array = ('el1', 'el2a','el2b','el2c', 'el4');

Usage 1 takes elements out of `@array` starting at `$position`, and continuing for `$length` (i.e.: elements between `$position` and `$position+$length`) and adds elements of `list` in its place.

> **Usage 2:** `splice(@array, $position, $length);`

Usage 2 removes elements between `$position` and `$position+$length`, and does no adding of elements.

> **Usage 3:** `splice(@array, $position);`

Usage 3 removes elements starting at `$position` and continuing to the end of the array. All usages return a `list` to the left-hand side. Following are examples of usage of `splice`:

```
@array = ('el1','el2','el3','el4');
$scalar = splice(@array, $#array);     # Equivalent to 'pop(@array);'
                                       # @array becomes ('el1', 'el2', 'el3')
                                       # $scalar becomes 'el4'
@returnArray = splice(@array, 1,2);    # @returnArray becomes ('el2','el3');
                                       # @array becomes ('el1','el4');
                                       # Read as: 'take out 2 elements from
                                       # @array, starting at position 1

@addArray = ('el2a','el2b');
splice(@array, 2, 0, @AddArray);       # @array becomes (el1,el2, el2a,el2b, el3, el4)
                                       # Read as 'take out zero elements, starting
                                       # at position 2, and add @AddArray

splice(@array, 2, 0, ('el2a','el2b'));
                                       # exactly the same as
                                       # the example above, except that list is explicit now
```

reverse

`reverse` takes an array, and turns it "inside out." Hence, if you say something like:

```
@array = (1..10);
```

and then say:

```
print "Counting down...\n";
foreach $element (reverse(@array))
{
    print "$element ";
}
```

it prints:

```
"10 9 8 7 6 5 4 3 2 1"
```

The array has been reversed.

Making Arrays Out of Scalars: `split` Function

`split` provides a method to take a scalar and split it into an array. `split`'s most common forms are with two or three arguments. The default form takes a given regular expression or pattern, and then splits it into as many pieces as specified by $limit. If the string could be split into more pieces than specified by $limit, then the rest of the string is stuffed into the last element. And if $limit is omitted, Perl splits up the variable into as many pieces as it possibly can.

The syntax of split is as follows:

```
@array = split(REGEXP, $scalar, $limit)
```

where $limit is an optional, numeric string, and REGEXP is a regular expression (see the section "Using Regular Expressions" in Chapter 9 for more detail).

Following are examples of split:

```
@arrayOfChars = split( '', $scalar);    # splits up scalar into its
                                        # associated chars. eg, 'here' turns into
                                        # ('h','e','r','e')
@arrayOfWords = split(' ', $scalar);    # splits up scalar into its
                                        # associated words based on spaces
@arrayOfWords = split(m#\s+#, $scalar);
                                        # splits up scalar into its associated
                                        # words by matching spaces
```

These are relatively simple—they split on spaces. With the optional limit argument, you can ensure that an array will be made with a fixed number of elements.

```
$scalar = "Last word will be 'many words after split'";
@arrayOfWords = split(m"\s+", $scalar, 5);
                                        # split jams ''many words after split''
                                        # into $arrayOfWords[4]
```

To get the most use out of split, you really should know how regular expressions work. The above example splits on spaces (m"\s+" is to be read as "match any space").

For a more in-depth way on regular expressions and regular expression functions like split, and how to use them, see the section "Using Regular Expressions" in Chapter 9.

Making Scalars Out of Arrays: *join() Function*

join does the very opposite of split. It takes an array, and then turns it into a scalar. It has the following syntax:

```
$scalarName = join("chars_to_join", @arrayName);
```

For example, with:

```
@arrayName = (1,2,3,4,5,6,7,8,9,10);
```

you can say:

```
$scalarName = join(' ',@arrayName);
```

to get the scalar:

```
"1 2 3 4 5 6 7 8 9 10";
```

Or, to join a list directly by colons, you could say:

```
$scalarName = join(':', ('my','list'));
```

to produce the following scalar:

```
"my:list";
```

Array Truncation: `undef()`, `chop()`, and `chomp()` Functions

Arrays have their own version of these three functions. That is, you can simply do something like:

```
undef(@arrayName);
```

and the array will become blank (i.e., it will contain no elements).

Likewise `\chop(@arrayName)` and `chomp(@arrayName)` take every element in `@arrayName` and get rid of the end characters in the same manner as `chop` and `chomp` did earlier. They simply save you some typing.

Hashes

Hashes are groups of scalars that are indexed by another scalar, rather than a number. Like arrays, hashes grow and shrink automatically when you add or subtract elements. They do not need to be presized.

Hash structure is similar to the traditional structure of arrays, but the indexes themselves are scalars. Again, they are like dictionaries. The following:

```
$dictionary{'dog'} = 'Domesticated mammal';
```

defines `dog` as `Domesticated mammal`. As in dictionaries, you can look up 'dog' and get 'Domesticated mammal' as a definition:

```
print $dictionary{'dog'};  # prints 'Domesticated mammal'.
```

Pictorially, you read hashes as shown in Figure 3.5.

Figure 3.5
Interpreting the
Hash Syntax

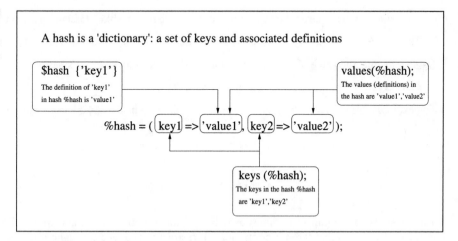

Hashes can be much more flexible than arrays because you can use most any scalar as a key element. However—this is very important—hashes lose all concept of order when they are put together. In other words, you would not want to locate an element by the key and then march through X number of records; the results would be unpredictable.

Hashes are represented by a % (percent sign) when values are assigned. The construct for creating a hash is:

```
%hashName = (key1, value1, key2, value2);
```

or

```
%hashName = (key1 => value1, key2 => value2);
```

Note

> The second syntax example uses the symbol ' => ' which is known as *syntactic sugar*. This makes the code much more appealing to look at. The => is really just a ' , ' in disguise.

There is no separate syntax for the initial creation of a hash as there is in Java and other programming languages. The hash is created in memory the first time it is referenced. The syntax for assigning a hash element is:

```
$hashName{key1}=value1;
```

Following are simple examples of hashes:

```
%hash1 = ('key1' , 'value1');      # simple hash construct
%hash1 = ('key1' => 'value1');     # does the same thing as above, but is more readable
```

The following example shows the assignment of multiple values in one statement:

```
%hash2 =
    (                              # Example: hash with two values
      'key1' => 'value1',
      'key2' => 'value2'
    );
```

Finally, the next example shows the explicit assignment of a value to a hashkey (assigning a word a definition):

```
$hash2{'key1'} = 'value1';     # Example of setting a hashkey explicitly.
```

This code fragment prints the value of a hash element using the preceding example's hash:

```
print "$hash2{'key2'}\n";      # prints 'value2'
```

The following example shows incorrect usage of assigning values to a hash. key2 has no value assigned to it.

```
%hash1 = (                     # Example of INCORRECT
   'key1' => 'value1',         # USAGE. Need hashkey pair
   'key2'
   );
%hashNname = ()                # Empty hash. If deleting a hash, use 'delete' instead
                               # (see the section on "Hash Operators") .
```

As you can see, hash value assignment is almost exactly equivalent to array value assignment. Both use the ( ) syntax. The main difference is that the subscripts and values are interchanged throughout the assignment. Aside from the fact that the array has a concept of order, the two following examples are equivalent in value:

```
@arrayName = ('val0','val1','val2','val3','val4');
%hashName =
    (
        0 => 'val0', 1 => 'val1',
```

```
            2 => 'val2', 3 => 'val3',
            4=>  'val4'
    );
```

In other words, $hashName{0} and $arrayName[0] both equal 'val0'. However, printing all the values of %hashName and @arrayName leads to something different:

```
    print @arrayName;
```

prints:

```
    val0val1val2val3val4
```

On the other hand,

```
    print values(%hashName);
```

does not print a fixed sequence at all, because, again, hashes have no concept of order.

The following are more complicated examples:

```
    @arrayName = ('key', 'value', 'key2', 'value2');
    %hashName = @array;          # An example
                                 # of array context (see Chapter 6)
    $hashName{key} = 'value';
    $hashName{key2} = 'value2';
    %hashName =                  # Example of hash assignment via scalars
        (
            $key1 => $value1,
            $key2 => $value2
        );
    %hash1 = %hash;              # Example of copying hashes by value
    %hash1 =                     # Example of copying hashes by value,
        (
            hash0,               # and adding an additional key
            'additional_key' => 'additional_value'
        );
```

Many of these examples use a bit of semantic trickery. You probably want to use the functions listed next instead, but then again, it's your choice.

Manipulative Functions on Hashes

Hashes are basically "black boxes" in that you put something into them, and it is difficult to predict where it goes in the hash structure. This results in no easy way to print an entire hash structure with a statement similar to print "%hashName"; , because, again, of the order thing. Hashes need special retrieval functions.

With 'tie'ing, (see the section, Tie-ing Variables in Chapter 16) there is also the problem of hashes becoming extremely large. I worked with one hash that was hundreds of megabytes in size. Hence, there is a need for a function that will manipulate hashes one element at a time. These functions are described below.

keys Function

The keys function returns a list of keys that is in a given hash, in array format. The syntax for keys is:

```
    @arrayName = keys (%hashName);
```

which assigns to @arrayName the keys of %hashName in an indeterminate order. Following are examples of assigning values to hash elements and then retrieving those values:

```
%hashName =
    (
        key1 => value1,
        key2 => value2,
        key3 => $scalar
    );
@arrayName = keys(%hashName);      # @arrayName equals ('key1','key2','key3')..or is it
                                   # ('key2','key3','key1') ?;
```

The keys function is also used to move interactively through a hash. For example, the following code fragment prints all the key value pairs in the hash %hashName:

```
foreach $keyName (keys %hashName)
{
    print "$keyName => $hashName{$keyName}\n";
}
```

The foreach control structure is described in Chapter 4.

values Function

The values function returns a list of values that is in a given hash and returns that list in array format. The syntax is:

```
@arrayName = values(%hashName);
```

The following example assigns a value to a scalar, $scalarName, and then assigns values to keys in hash %hashName. Finally, the values in the hash are returned in array format in @arrayName.

```
$scalarName = 'value3';
    %hashName =
        (
            key1=>value1,
            key2=> value2,
            key3=>$scalarName
        );
@arrayName = values(%hashName);    # @arrayName now equals (value1,value2,value3);
                                   # or is it ('value2','value1','value3');
```

values and keys are the primary windows into the hash data structure. Through them you can iterate through each element in the hash, or see what you have stored in the hash. However, realize the overhead that occurs when you say:

```
@keys = keys(%hashName);
```

This creates an array element for every key value, and if the hash is large, you will end up with a huge array. If this is the case, you will probably want to use each, described next.

each Function

The each function is the way to handle very large hashes without overflowing your memory space. It returns a ($key, $value) list pair for each element in the hash. After it is done, each returns an empty list. Following is an example of the usage of each:

```
%hashName = ('very_large_hash');              # pseudocode!

while (($key, $value) = each %hashName)
{
  print "$key, $value\n";
}
while (($key, $value) = each %hashName)  # you can nest them.
{
  while (($key2, $value2) = each %hashName2)
  {
  }
}
```

By using each here, you ensure that you don't overwhelm the local internal memory. You can nest each functions because every individual hash has its own each attached to it; they will not conflict.

Note

Do not add to the hash while iterating through the list. When you first perform an each on a hash, an iterator is created for that hash, which is then tied to values of that hash. This iterator is shared by values, keys, and each; it persists until the FALSE value returns. This iterator becomes "confused" if you start adding hash values in the middle of it, and this problem can be very hard to track down. In other words, results are unpredictable.

```
while (($key, $value) = each (%hash))
{
  $hash{'newkey'} = 1;   # EXTREMELY BAD IDEA.
  delete $hash{$key};    # ANOTHER BAD BAD IDEA.
}                        # INDETERMINITE BEHAVIOR
```

delete Function

The delete function is the way to remove one element from a hash, since, after all, each element in a hash is a scalar. It is safe to use on any hash, unlike the undef function described next. It can be used on tied hashes as well as nontied hashes. (See the section Tie-ing for more information on tied functions.)

Following are examples with delete:

```
delete $ENV{PATH};                # deletes PATH environment variable
foreach $key (keys %hashName)     # accesses hash elements iteratively. Note use of Keys function.
{
    delete $hashName{$key};       # deletes every hash element
}                                 # in hash %hashName.
```

undef Function

Hashes also have their own version of the undef function. This example:

```
undef(%hashName);
```

has the effect of deleting the entire hash. This may or may not be what you intended to do. It is equivalent to %hashName=();

exists Function

The above functions show how you get values out of a hash, but how do you test to see if a value is in a hash? This is the job of the `exists` function. If you say something such as:

```
if (exists($dictionary{'dog'}))
{
    print $dictionary{'dog'};
}
```

`exists` goes into the hash `%dictionary` and determines whether `%dictionary` has the key 'dog'. If it does, it returns `true`. If not, it returns `false`.

Summary of Hashes

Hashes, also called associated arrays, are usually not inherent in other languages (such as C). They take a bit of getting used to. You basically put values into the hash by defining it as in the following:

```
%hash = ('this'=>'is', 'a'=>'hash');
```

which is found in `key/value` pairs. Then, if you wish to access a value, you can say:

```
print $hash{'this'};
```

to print 'is', or:

```
print $hash{'a'};
```

to print 'hash'. You can also say:

```
$hash{'newkey'} = 'new definition';
```

to directly set the definition of newkey in the hash `%hash`.

Handles

Hashes, scalars, and arrays make up the total of all of the strict datatypes of Perl. They hold data, and you will use hashes, arrays, and scalars to manipulate any data you might conceive.

However, there is, of course, the question of where that data will come from. To do this, Perl provides something called a *handle*. If scalars, hashes, and arrays are Perl's data, then handles are Perl's method of getting that data. Perl provides two types of handles:

- File handles
- Directory handles

which provide Perl the ability to interface with files, processes, sockets, and, in the case of directory handles, directories. We shall be concerned here with filehandles. Directory handles will get treatment in section "Perl Odds and Ends."

Rather than being distinguished by a special character, handles have the convention of being distinguished by being in all uppercase. Hence,

```
print FD "file name\n";
```

should be read as "print to the filehandle FD, the value `file name\n`."

Filehandles

Filehandle is a bit of a misnomer. You can use filehandles to have Perl read/write to files, but you can also use them to read/write to pipes, and read/write to sockets. They are Perl's primary window to the outside world.

Using a filehandle consists of three steps. First you open that filehandle, then you read or write to that filehandle, and then you close that filehandle.

To open you say:

```
open(FD, "fileName");
```

which ties the filehandle FD to the file "fileName." This is to be read as "open file fileName (read-only) and tie it to the file descriptor FD." This open statement forms a connection to the file fileName. If you then say something like:

```
$line = <FD>;
```

then $line will contain the next line in the file descriptor FD. This is the read. Alternatively, you can say:

```
print FD $line;
```

to write to the filehandle. (To do this you would have to open it like: open(FD, "> fileName") or open(FD, ">> fileName".)

Finally, you close the filehandle when done. You say:

```
close(FD);
```

to indicate that the operating system can close the connection for you and output information to the OS. This is extremely useful in getting data from the operating system, and only touches the surface of what filehandles can do.

Operations on Filehandles

Below are some common functions for dealing with filehandles:

open—opens a filehandle, and prepares that data handle for reading
< >—reads from a filehandle
print—prints to a filehandle
close—closes a filehandle

We also introduce below the package FileHandle, which comes with the Perl standard distribution and can be used for filehandles, but is cleaner than the filehandles Perl provides.

open Function

open is the primary way that you create a filehandle. If you say something like:

```
open(FD, "> output_file") || die "Couldn't open output file!\n";
```

you are making the file descriptor FD synonymous with the file output_file (and you so happen to delete any existing output_file at the same time). You are opening the file for writing and the die says that if you don't correctly open the connection, you "die."

Other things you can do with filehandles are listed next.

```
open(FD, ">> output_file") || die;     # append to file or die
```

This will append to a file (or die if it cannot write to it).

```
open(FD, "input_file") || die;        # get data from a file or die
```

This will open a file for reading (or die if it can't).

```
open(FD, "process | ") || die;        # get data from a process or die
```

This will open a process for reading (or die if it can't).

```
open(FD, " | to process") || die;     # pipe data to a process or die
```

This will pipe data to a process (or die if it can't). Typically in the Windows world you don't pipe output to processes. This tends to happen in Unix and NT. If you prefer, you can also say something like:

```
my $fh = new FileHandle(">> output_file") || die;
```

which does the same thing, but ties the filehandle to the scalar $fh instead of FD. For the bulk of this book we shall use the FileHandle syntax rather than open. It is cleaner and, if you use it consistently, will help you avoid many problems.

Note

Specifically, file handles via open are pretty odd items in the Perl world. They are bare words that stick out from the more elegant hashes, scalars, and arrays, which can be localized fairly effectively. If the statement:

```
open(FD,"file") || die "Couldn't open file!\n";
```

occurred in the heart of a program, and then:

```
sub filedesc
{    open(FD, "file2") || die "Couldn't open file2!\n";
}
```

was in a subroutine, the subroutine's file descriptor overrides the one in main (i.e., just like a global variable). It is highly recommended that you use the FileHandle package instead, and use the second of the constructs above. For example:

```
use FileHandle;
sub filedesc
{
    my $fileHandleName = new FileHandle("fileName") || die "Couldn't open filename!\n";
    $line = <$filehandle>.
}
```

As we shall see, the my makes it so the variable $fileHandleName is 'inside' the function, so that if you have another $fileHandleName variable in the code, there is no conflict.

---

open is useless by itself. (After all, you want to do reading and writing as well!) Hence, open goes in tandem with the other functions listed next.

Reading from a Filehandle (< >)

Suppose you have opened a file or process for reading via:

```
open(FD, "input_file") || die;
```

or

```
open(FD, "dir |") || die;
```

Both statements create a tie between the file descriptor FD and the file `file`, and you can do something such as:

```
$line = <FD>;        # or $line = <$FD>; to use the FileHandle object.
```

The `<>` syntax means that we are reading the file descriptor FD, and putting the results into the variable `$line`. This descriptor knows which type of variable it is reading into. Hence, you can say something like:

```
@lines = <FD>;
```

to slurp the entire file into the variable `@lines`. Now, to read through a file sequentially, we can simply use some form of the construct:

```
while (defined $line = <FD>) {  }  # or while (defined $line = <$FD>) with FileHandle
```

Take this construct and use the data file:

```
----- DATA FILE -----
line1
line2
line3
```

On the first iteration through, `while (defined $line = <FD>)` will set:

```
$line = "line1\n";
```

the second iteration will set:

```
$line = "line2\n",
```

and the third call will set:

```
$line = "line3\n".
```

Voila! Your file is read. Note that the `<FD>` operator reads the line with the ending character ("a newline") intact. If you want this character to be removed, simply do a `chop()` or a `chomp()` on the resulting scalar.

The technique for reading from a process is quite similar, as follows:

```
open(FD, "dir |") || die "Couldn't open pipe!\n"; # $FD = new FileHandle("ls |") ||
                                                   #  die "Couldn't open pipe!\n";
```

This opens a file descriptor for the process `dir`. In English, this is read as "take the output from the Win32 command **dir** and stick it into the file descriptor FD."

This technique is called *piping*. Piping occurs when the output of `ls` is routed to the file descriptor FD.

This Perl functionality is very powerful. However, this is a place where you must be extremely careful about portability; `ls` may not exist when you try to port over to another operating system and, in particular, **dir** does not exist on Unix. The following construct will print all the files in a directory on a Unix system:

```
open(FD, "ls |") || die "Couldn't open pipe!\n";  # $FD = new FileHandle("ls |") ||
                                                   # die "Couldn't open pipe!\n";
while ($line = <FD>)                               # while ($line = <$FD>)
{
    print $line;
}
```

Just as before, the FD argument keeps track of the last line you read in your filehandle; hence, you can iterate through them.

print *Function*

The usage of print is:

```
print (@arrayName)
```

or

```
print FILEHANDLENAME (@arrayName)
```

print is a commonly used function. We have seen several examples of print already, as shown in the following code:

```
print "@ARGV\n";
                        # prints the array using interpolation, see both the section
                        # 'special variables' and $" ($LIST_SEPARATOR) and
                        # $\ ($OUTPUT_RECORD_SEPARATOR)
                        # and the section on interpolation in previous chapters.
print "\n\tHello\n";    # prints a newline, tab, Hello then a newline
print functionName();   # prints the output from the function functionName.
```

All of these examples show forms of the usage (print (arrayName)). Although invisible, Perl prints to a special filehandle called STDOUT if you fail to give print a filehandle of its own.

If instead, you want to print to STDERR, the error stream (and another standard variable Perl provides), use:

```
print STDERR "@ARGV\n";
```

or to a defined (writeable) filehandle, use:

```
my $fileHandleName = new FileHandle("> output_file");
print $fileHandleName "@ARGV\n";
```

This again, will destroy the file that you open. If you want to append to this file instead, say:

```
my $fileHandleName = new FileHandle(">> output_file");
print $fileHandleName "@ARGV\n";
```

Remember that chomp had a special variable associated with it? There is a Perl special variable that you should be aware of ($|), which is intimately tied to print. It is the flushing mechanism in Perl. If you want your output to go *immediately* to a file, rather than be buffered, just set $| as equal to one (1). Then you won't be waiting for the system to write a block of output at a time. Immediately after a print, that text will go to the specified file.

For example, you may do something such as:

```
my $fh = new FileHandle("> file");
$| = 1;
foreach $line (@lots_of_lines)
{
    print $fh "$line\n";
}
```

Note the second line ($| = 1;). $| is the 'piping' variable in Perl. It controls whether or not output goes to a filehandle right away. With $| set, you are guaranteed that your output goes to the filehandle immediately. Without it, it can accumulate in the buffer, which may be lost if the process goes down. (The price of this security is speed—with $| set output goes a tad slower, but it is well worth it in my humble opinion . . .)

Shutting Filehandles: `close`

The usage of `close` is:

```
close (FILEHANDLENAME)
```

`close` is the logical opposite of open, or the opposite of "new Filehandle." When you:

```
close ($FileHandle);
```

or:

```
$fileHandle->close();      # this IS object oriented, after all!
```

it breaks the pipe between the filehandle and the file associated with it, which causes several things, such as follows:

1. If the corresponding open was writing to the file, i.e.,

```
$filehandle = new FileHandle("> file");
```

then any buffered output from `print $filehandle` is put into the file right before the `close`.

2. The `$filehandle` iterator gets reset to read from the beginning of the file again.
3. If the corresponding open was a pipe, then the command doing the pipe is terminated.

Both open and the phrase `"new FileHandle"` do an implicit `close` when the filehandle goes out of scope. For example:

```
sub openFile
{
    my $fh = new FileHandle("> log") || die "Couldn't open log!\n";
    print $fh "LOG ENTRY";
}
```

will both close the filehandle `$fh`, and save the buffered output LOG ENTRY into a file when the function openFile is finished. Likewise:

```
open(FD, "> log");
print FD "LOG ENTRY\n";
```

will implicitly close the filehandle FD right before the Perl script exits.

Summary of Filehandles

Filehandles are used in Perl to connect to the outside world. First, tie a handle to its corresponding file via:

```
use FileHandle;                      # Uses the filehandle object.
my $filehandle = new FileHandle("file");
```

Next, either read or write from that filehandle:

```
my $line = <$fh>;                    # reads a line from the file
print $fh $line;                     # prints to the file
```

Then, close the filehandle:

```
close($fh);
```

This is the simplest form of filehandle usage. You can also read from processes, write to processes, and slurp entire files into either arrays or scalars.

Examples

Perl's variables have a great deal of synergy. If you look at the datatypes Perl provides, you see that there are certain hooks to translate different types of variables into each other. For example, if you say something like:

```
@words = split(' ', $paragraph);
```

you are taking a scalar (`$paragraph`) and turning it into an array (`@words`). If you then decide that you want to reverse the words, you can say:

```
$paragraph = join(' ', reverse(@words));
```

This reverses the words and sticks them together into a backward paragraph.

Here are some admittedly arbitrary things you can do to manipulate text. Don't worry about doing anything productive for now; simply look at how Perl's special variables can make the manipulation of text so easy.

One task made very easy by Perl is loading an entire file into an array. To do this, simply say:

```
use FileHandle;
my $fh = new FileHandle("file_name");
my @arrayName = <$fh>;
```

After this, `@arrayName` will contain a list of lines in a given file. If we wanted to load the entire file into a scalar, we could simply say:

```
use FileHandle
local($/) = undef;
my $fh = new FileHandle("file_name");
my $scalarName = <$fh>;
```

and then `$scalarName` contains the whole file.

Suppose you wanted to go through a file, line by line, backward, take out the first field of that file, and print it. The following table illustrates this example:

```
a:b
c:d
d:e
```

The code to perform this task looks like:

```
1 use FileHandle;
2 my $fh = new FileHandle("my_file");
3 my @lines = <$fh>;
4 my $line;
5 foreach $line (reverse(@lines))
6 {
7     @words_in_line = split(m":", $line);
8     print "$words_in_line[0]\n";
9 }
```

The filehandle $fh is combined with the array @lines to slurp the entire file into memory. We then traverse through @lines one line at a time, and in reverse order (5), split the line by colons (7), and then print the first word onto the line (8).

This then results in the following text (if fed the above file):

```
d
c
a
```

Another task well suited for Perl is to manipulate text within a file. As an example, let's "auto-abbreviate" a file, splitting the paragraph into words, truncate each word in that file to five characters, join the paragraph together again, and then finally write out the file to another file:

```
1 use FileHandle;
2 my $fh = new FileHandle("in_file");
3 my $fh2 = new FileHandle("> out_file");
4
5 while ($line = <$fh>) { $paragraph .= $line; }
6
7 @words = split(' ', $paragraph);
8
9 foreach $word (@words) { $word = substr($word, 0,5); }
10
11 $paragraph = join(' ', @words);
12
13 print $fh2 $paragraph;
14 close($fh2);
15 close($fh);
```

We open the files (2,3), go through the files and slurp the file into one big line ($paragraph), snip off the first five characters in the word (9), print the paragraph (13), and then close the file (14,15).

Hence, a paragraph like:

```
"Courtesy itself must convert to disdain if you come in her presence"
```

becomes:

```
"Court itsel must conve to disda if you come in her prese"
```

Let's do the opposite by taking a file and making an array of words that are over nine characters long. To do this, simply say:

```
1 use FileHandle;
2 my $fh = new FileHandle("in_file");
3
5 while ($line = <$fh>) { $paragraph .= $line; }
6
7 @words = split(' ', $paragraph);
8
9 my ($word, @longWords);
9 foreach $word (@words) { if (length($word) > 9) { push(@longWords, $word); } }
10 print "@longWords\n";
```

To continue this line of thought, another form of file manipulation is to make a concordance out of any given file. Hence, we shall have the following interface. If we say:

```
print $number{'the'}
```

it prints the number of occurrences of the word *the* in an input file, as shown in the following code:

```
1 use FileHandle;
2 my $fh = new FileHandle("in_file");
3 my $fh2 = new FileHandle("> out_file");
4 my ($line, %number, @words);

5 while ($line = <$fh>) { $paragraph .= $line; }
6
7 @words = split(' ', $paragraph);
8 foreach $word (@words) { $number{$word}++; }
9 print $number{'the'};
```

This works as follows. The logic for taking a paragraph and turning it into words is the same (1–7). But now, we go through each word (8), and then note that we have found an occurrence of the word by adding on to the end of a hash ($number{$word}). Hence, with the input:

"In the beginning, there was the word, and the word was God,"

the resulting hash from line 8 becomes:

```
%number =
    (
        'In' => 1,        'the' => 3,
        'beginning => 1,  'there' => 1,
        'was' => 2,       'word' => 2,
        'and'=> 1,        'God' => 1
    );
```

This works because the hash remembers the number of times it has seen each word and therefore line 9 will print 3.

Let's get a bit more practical. Suppose you want to get a listing of files, such that we can say something such as:

```
print $size{'my_file'}
```

This prints out the size of my_file on a Win32 platform:

```
1 use FileHandle;
2 my $fh = new FileHandle("dir |");
3 while ($line = <$fh>)
4 {
5     my @stats = split(' ',$line);
6     $size{$stats[-1]} = $stats[-4];
7 }
```

Here, we simply open a filehandle to the process "dir |", and then go through each line of the output, splitting it by spaces. Hence, (2) opens the output to the process **dir**, and reads it into Perl via (3).

We then take the line from the output. Note that the ending word (subscript −1) holds the name of the file, and the fourth word from the end (subscript −4) holds the size of the file. Hence, the hash assignment:

```
$size{$stats[-1]} = $stats[-4];
```

expands to something like:

```
$size{'file'} = '20,000';
```

so we can look up the size from the name of the file.

Summary of Perl Variables

Perl's variables are tailor-made for the fast manipulation of data. Instead of getting low-level access to data directly stored in the computer (as you would in such languages as Basic or C), you get access to a rich variety of functions that let you manipulate them to your heart's desire.

Scalars, denoted by $, are Perl's "jack-of-all-trades" variable. You can store any type of information in them, and then split them to form arrays, chop or chomp them to take a character off the end, take a look at their length, and manipulate them either as strings or numbers. (Another thing you can do, which we have not discussed here, is to look for patterns in them. This is the domain of *regular expressions*, to which we have dedicated an entire chapter, Chapter 9.

Arrays, denoted by @, are groups of scalars indexed by a number. They grow and shrink for you, and can be manipulated as easily as scalars. To access an element of them, say $variable[$index], where "variable" is a valid array variable, and "$index" is the position on which the array holds. You push (onto the end of the array) and unshift (onto the beginning of the array) them to make them longer, and pop and shift them to make them shorter. You splice to remove certain elements, and join them to make scalars. You can also chop and chomp characters off the end.

Hashes, denoted by %, are groups of scalars indexed by a scalar. They also grow and shrink for you. To access them, you say $variable{$key}, where "variable" is a valid hash variable, and "$key" is a valid hash key. To delete an element from a hash, you delete; to add an element you say $variable{$key} = $value. To get a listing of keys in a given hash, you say keys(%hashName). To get a list of values in that hash, you say values(%hashName). To go through the keys and values one at a time, you say ($key, $value) = each (%hashName).

Finally, handles are Perl's way of reaching out to the operating system. To get a filehandle, you open it with an associated process or file. When you are done with the filehandle, you close it. If you want to print to the file, you print and if you want to extract from the file, you say $varb = <FH> or @varb = <FH> where FH is the name of the filehandle. People may want to consider saying my $fh = new FileHandle(OPEN_EXPR); instead, because it is generally a cleaner way to approach handles.

That's about all it takes to introduce the basic data structures of Perl. Perl's variables let you do a lot of data wrangling. If you learn how to use these data structures properly, you will be able to solve problems with ease that would be very difficult in other languages.

Perl Control Structures and Operators

There is a richness of control structures in Perl. *Control structures* are the traffic police of Perl. In other words, they tell the process which way to proceed in the code, and are your main line of attack when creating algorithms and subroutines in Perl.

Unless you want to use a different control structure for each line, it is probably not worthwhile to memorize them all. The purpose of this chapter is to explain the more common control structures.

Likewise, the purpose of this chapter is not to give a comprehensive list and usage summary of operators, but instead to relate some of the more common patterns of operators, as well as the common "gotchas."

Check out the **perlop** or **perlsyn** reference pages that come with Perl if you want a comprehensive list of operators and control structures.

Chapter Overview

Perl's control structures and operators are some of the most flexible—and complicated—in computer language today. Hence, you should probably just review the chapter to see if you are missing any pieces of knowledge regarding control structures and operators. We have divided this chapter into four sections.

First, we talk about a thorny topic in Perl: how Perl determines if a statement is true or false. This is a topic that many people don't completely understand, because the underlying logic Perl uses is quite complicated.

Second, we talk about the many control structures in Perl: `if`, `while`, `foreach`, `for`, `until`, and `unless`. Each has its uses, although you need not know them all to be effective. We also talk about how to modify how these control structures execute to our liking. There are three major control-structure modifiers that exist: `redo`, `next`, and `last`. (There is a `goto`, but it will remain undiscussed.) In addition, you can tag any piece of code with a label, which we also discuss.

Third, we go into Perl's operators. Perl has quite a few operators, and quite a few orders of precedence. We give a few simple rules on how to maneuver when determining operator precedence.

Finally, we will discuss common Perl patterns. Common Perl patterns are snippets of code syntax used over and over again when dealing with Perl; we go over 17 of these patterns and how they are used. If you are familiar with Perl syntax, in a hurry, or anxious to get to the later chapters, just take a look at the common patterns toward the end of the chapter. Otherwise, knowing the way Perl operators work is a cornerstone of learning the language.

The Nature of Perl-ish Truth

Before we get into the specific conditionals in Perl, let's go over how Perl decides whether an expression is true or false.

Since Perl only has three datatypes (hashes, arrays, and scalars), it needs to be a little tricky in how it evaluates expressions as true or false. In particular, there are four different cases in which a condition evaluates to false, which we'll cover now.

1. False if the Condition Evaluates as Zero

The following statement will execute 10 times, and stop when `$counter` hits zero:

```
$counter = 10;
while ($counter) { print "$counter\n"; $counter--}
```

This prints "10 9 8 7 6 5 4 3 2 1" and stop at zero, since the expression `while ($counter)` has evaluated to false when `$counter` reaches zero.

Note that Perl has a very special meaning of what zero is in this context. Remember the discussion in Chapter 3 of string, number, and Boolean contexts? Well:

```
if (0)
{
}
```

evaluates to false, but

```
if ("0.0000")
{
}
```

evaluates to true. Why? Because the second case has `0.0000`, a *string*. And because strings always numerically evaluate to zero, if Perl translated `0.0000` to `0` in this case, it would also translate "a" to zero, which would mean:

```
if ("a")
{
}
```

would also be false. Hence, the only case in which something is zero is where it is 1) the string "0", or 2) a number (not in quotes) that translates to zero. Hence:

```
if (0.000)
{
}
```

evaluates to false.

2. False if the Condition Evaluates to ' '

If you are dealing with strings, then the false condition cannot be 0 (although if you end up with a string like this, it will also evaluate to false). The following will print h e l l o and stop:

```
@arrayofLetters = ('h','e','l','l','o','', 'a','l','l');
$counter = 0;
while ($letter = $arrayofLetters[$counter++])
{
        print "$letter ";
}
```

It does not print the all because after the o in hello, $letter becomes ' ', and the loop terminates.

3. False if the Condition Evaluates to the Empty List

More subtly, if you are dealing with an array or a hash, and you get zero elements in an array (i.e., something evaluates to the empty list ()), the loop processing terminates. Hence, the following:

```
%hashName = ('This','is','a','hash');
while (($key, $value) = each (%hashName))
{
print "$key $value ";
}
```

prints this is a hash (or a hash this is) and then stops.

What happens here is that %hashName gets one key-value pair ($key $value), out of the hash, which is put into the list. The loop stops when the last hash element has been put into this list.

This form of terminating is very helpful when using function calls. Often when a function call like each is performed, it will return a () when it is done.

4. False if a Function Ever Returns the Value from the Function undef

The following also terminates after printing 123:

```
@arrayName = (1,2,3,undef,4,5,6)
$counter = 0;
while ($arrayName[$counter])
{
        print $arrayName[$counter];
        $counter++;
}
```

Again, this terminates since the fourth element of arrayName is undef.

Remember these rules as we discuss the Perl control structures next. Of course, it helps to know exactly how you can make a control structure in Perl in order to apply this knowledge! To that end, we now turn to the syntax of Perl's control structures.

Perl Control Structures

The four Perl control structures most useful to know are while, for, foreach, and if ...elsif...else (elsif and else are optional here). There are also a couple of very convenient keywords for jumping around within control structures, next and last.

In addition, there are the esoteric control structures unless and until, and one more respectable statement used to jump around in control structures: redo. (Perl supports a goto but isn't very proud of it.)

These are the most common forms of the control loop, the ones you will use 90% of the time. Now let's look at each form in detail.

while

while is almost exactly like its equivalent in C. There is a condition for the while loop to satisfy, and the loop will be executed as long as that condition holds, i.e., until it is evaluated to false. Also, as in C, the text of the while loop is *only* evaluated if the while condition is true. In other words, there are no initial executions of the while loop.

while Loop Syntax

Figure 4.1 shows the three forms the while loop can take, along with the logic which drives them.

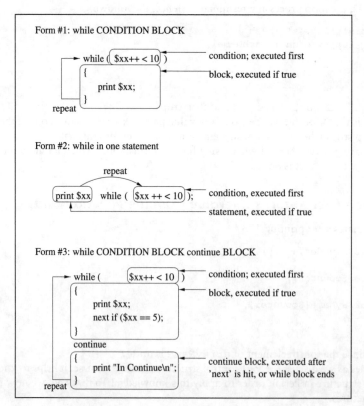

Figure 4.1
The Different
Forms of while

1. The condition is first evaluated, then checked to see whether the condition is true or false.
2. If—and only if—it is true, the internal loop commands are performed.

Then the condition is checked again, and so on. If the condition is false, then the next command in the program is executed.

`while` Form 1

The first form is the "regular" `while`, or "vanilla" `while`. Here, the statements look like:

```perl
my $xx = 0;
while ($xx++ < 10)
{
    print "$xx\n";
}
```

where $xx is printed if it is less than 10, printing 0 1 2 3 4 5 6 7 8 9, and terminating when the condition becomes false.

`while` Form 2

The second form of `while` is the one-line form. This is a convenient, shorthand form, looking like:

```perl
print "$xx\n" while ($xx++ < 10);
```

which prints the same thing as the longhand form of `while` given earlier (0 1 2 3 4 5 6 7 8 9). If you want, you can perform multiple statements in this form of the `while` loop by separating the statements with commas, and putting the whole thing in parentheses although you need to be pretty careful about orders of precedence here:

```perl
(print ("$xx\n"), print (FD "$xx\n")) while ($xx++<10);
```

`while` Form 3

The third form of `while` has a *continue* block on it. A continue block is done after the loop is finished and before the next condition's evaluation. It is most often used with the `next` keyword to break out of the current loop (see notes on `next` later in the chapter). Therefore:

```perl
my $xx = 0;
while ($xx++ < 10)
{
    ($form = 1, next) if ($xx == 5);
    print "$xx ";
}
continue
{
    (print (":IN CONTINUE $xx:"), $form = 0) if ($form == 1);
}
```

will print:

```
0 1 2 3 4 :IN CONTINUE 5: 6 7 8 9 10"
```

Each time the loop ends, Perl drops down to the continue block. However, only if $form is set to 1, does it print out the :IN CONTINUE string.

Continue blocks are good when you want to break out of a loop prematurely, and then do something before going to the next iteration of the loop. For example:

```
$FALSE = 0; $TRUE = 1; $WANTED = $TRUE;
while (defined ($line = <FD>))
{
    ($wanted = $FALSE, next()) if ( tooLong($line));
    ($wanted = $FALSE, next()) if ( tooShort($line));
    ($wanted = $FALSE, next()) if ( tooFat($line));
    ($wanted = $FALSE, next()) if ( tooThin($line));
}
continue
{
    process() if ($wanted == $TRUE);
    $wanted = $TRUE;
}
```

Here, it makes sense to use `continue`, because as soon as you find out that the `$line` is `tooLong()`, you don't need to check whether it is `tooShort()`, `tooFat()` or `tooThin()`. You can safely skip to the end of the loop and go to the next line.

for Control Structure

`for` is also like its C equivalent. The structure has a starting variable, a test condition, and an incremental variable to act upon each time the loop is executed.

for Loop Syntax

A sample `for` loop is shown in Figure 4.2, along with its logic:

Figure 4.2
The Different
Forms of `for`

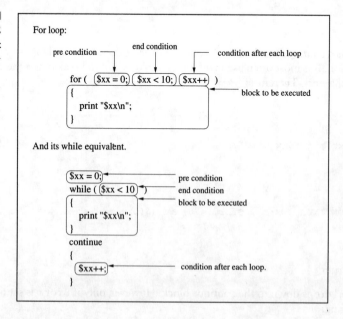

This works exactly as it does in C. Perl first sets the initial condition and then proceeds to loop through the body of the `for` loop as long as the end condition evaluates to true. After each `for` loop, the last statement in the `for` (in this case, `$xx++`) is performed, and the loop starts again. Two things to note here:

1. The last statement in the `for` (xx; yy; zz) is only performed *after* the loop has executed and *before* the next evaluation of the end condition. The following, for example, will never execute any of the `for` loop:

    ```
    for ($counter = 0; $counter == 1; $counter++)
    {
    }
    ```

    since the test `$counter == 1` is performed before `$counter++`.
2. All the statements in the `for` loop can be any legal Perl statement.

The following is the usual way that one uses the `for` loop to loop through the elements of an array:

```
for ($counter = 0; $counter < @arrayName; $counter++)
{
    do_something($arrayName[$counter]);
}
```

In other words, `$counter` is set to zero, the loop is performed, `$counter++` increments to one, and *then* `$counter` is tested to see if it is less than `@>arrayName`, which is the number of elements in the array.

However, this is not the limit of usability of the `for` loop. Any `while` loop can be translated into a `for` loop, although it is not always wise to do so. For example, one of the `while` loops in the previous section becomes:

```
for ($line = <FD>; defined $line; $line = <FD>)
{
    do_function($line);        # loop continues until '$line' is blank
    do_function2($line);       # $line is incremented
}
```

Here we read a line at a time and if it is not defined, it is terminated; if it is defined, we go on to read the next line.

`foreach` Control Structure

`foreach` is very similar to the "for..in" structure in Bourne Shell. It combines much of the logic of `for` and `while`. `foreach` has a built-in array manipulator, which iterates through each of the elements of an array or hash, and, in the process, makes each element writable. `foreach` is very convenient when modifying several elements of a writable array, or when iterating over an array or hash without having to resort to a counter.

`foreach` Loop Syntax

There are three types of `foreach` loops, as shown in Figure 4.3. Perl begins with the first element in `@>arrayName` and loops through to the end of the array `@>arrayName`.

The tasks requested in the loop are performed in turn on every element from the starting element to the end of the array or hash.

Figure 4.3
foreach **Forms**

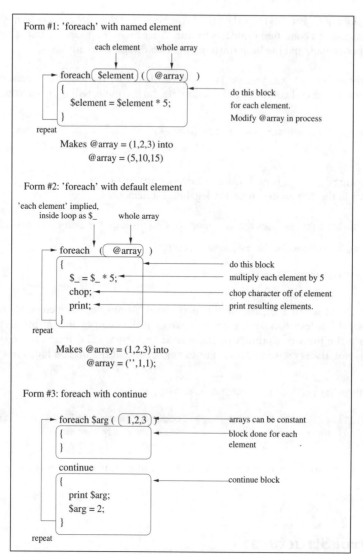

Form #1: 'foreach' with named element

each element   whole array

foreach($element) ((@array))
{
    $element = $element * 5;
}

— do this block
for each element.
Modify @array in process

repeat

Makes @array = (1,2,3) into
@array = (5,10,15)

Form #2: 'foreach' with default element

'each element' implied,
inside loop as $_   whole array

foreach ((@array))
{
    $_ = $_ * 5;   — do this block
    chop;   — multiply each element by 5
    print;   — chop character off of element
}   — print resulting elements.

repeat

Makes @array = (1,2,3) into
@array = ('',1,1);

Form #3: foreach with continue

foreach $arg ((1,2,3)   — arrays can be constant
{   — block done for each
}   element

continue
{   — continue block
    print $arg;
    $arg = 2;
}

repeat

One of the primary uses of foreach is to modify each element in an array. To do this, all you have to do is modify the element after the foreach, i.e., the bold variable in the following; foreach **$element** (@array). Hence:

```
@array = (1,2,3,4);              # set the array
foreach $el (@array)
{
    $el++;                       # increment each of the elements in the array
}

print "@array\n";                # prints 2,3,4,5
```

increments the value of each element in @array, by making $el each of the elements of the array in turn, and then incrementing it. This turns 1,2,3,4 into 2,3,4,5.

You can also use foreach as a type of while loop. The following code:

```
foreach $key (keys %hash)    # for each of the keys in a hash
{
    print $hash{$key};       # print the value associated with that key
}
```

goes through each element in the hash, and then prints which element is associated with that key.

There are a couple of other things to understand about foreach. Although the most common usage is to go through elements as we did above, you can also use any array or list. The following prints all the letters from A to Z:

```
foreach $letter ('A'..'Z')
{
    print "$letter\n";
}
```

where .. is, again, the list construction operator that we encountered in Chapter 3, and the following prints the return values from a function:

```
foreach $element (functionReturningArray())
{
    print "$element\n";
}
```

If you try to set any of the above values, you will get an error. The following code gives a syntax error:

```
foreach $element (1..10) { $element++; }
```

Because each of the values in (1..10) is read-only, they cannot be altered in the same way that foreach $element (@array) can modify @array. You will get an error such as:

```
Modification of read-only value attempted at script.p line 1
```

which refers to the fact that the digits 1..10 cannot be modified because they are constants.

Note that if you want to do something such as go through only a select number of elements in a foreach statement, you can use the following:

```
foreach $element (@array[1,2,3])
{
}
```

which uses *slicing* to access array elements 1, 2, and 3 of @array.

Two extra tidbits: First, foreach, like while, has a continue form, although I've never used it. Second, and more useful, as of perl5.005_03, Perl has a final form of foreach in which the foreach loop has an implicit my. In other words, you can say something like:

```
foreach my $element (@array)
{
        print $element;
}
```

which then makes $element a lexical variable inside the foreach loop. Again, we will cover this in more detail in the next chapter, but this basically makes:

```
1    my $element = 2;
2    foreach my $element (1,2,3)
3    {
4            # no operation;
5    }
6    print $element;
```

print out '2' instead of printing '3'. The two variables $element in lines 1 and 2 are different altogether. Perl used to force you to do this in two statements; you save some screen real estate by rolling it into one.

if..elsif..else Control Structure

The if..elsif..else control structure is similar to C's except that C has else if instead of Perl's elsif (only Larry Wall knows the reason why). Anyway, the if..elsif..else statement is Perl's way of deciding between different courses of action, and can be used much like Pascal's and C's switch statement. Below are some forms.

if..elsif..else Syntax

Formally, the if..elsif..else syntax looks like Figure 4.4.

Figure 4.4
if..elsif..
else

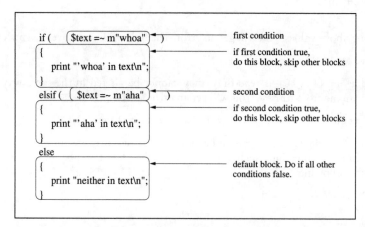

Here, $text=~m"whoa" and $text=~m"aha"could be any Perl statement. The if interprets them as a "true/false" condition, and then evaluates the corresponding block for the first statement it finds that is true. (For the way Perl evaluates whether a statement is true or false, see either the description earlier in this chapter, or the one in the chapter on Perl variables.) Hence, in the following:

```
if ($string1 gt $string2 && $number > $number2)
{
    doSomething();
}
elsif ($string lt $string2)
{
    doSomethingElse();
```

```
}
else
{
    doADefaultSomething();
}
```

the first case (`$string gt $string2 && $number > $number2`) is evaluated to be either true or false—the code associated with it being executed if true. The second case is evaluated if the first evaluates to false (`$string1 lt $string2`), and the default case is executed if both the first two cases evaluate to false.

This means that only the first condition to evaluate to true is tested, and that control then skips to the first code block *after* the `if`. This means that:

```
if (5 > 4)
{
    print "FIVE IS GREATER THAN FOUR";
}
elsif (3 > 2)
{
    print "THREE IS GREATER THAN TWO";
}
```

will print FIVE IS GREATER THAN FOUR. Since order matters in an `if..else..elsif` block, think carefully about the order in which you write the conditions in the `if` block. For example, the following code to compare dates will not work if we switch the `'year'` and `'month'` conditions, because a month field is less important than the year in determining which date is earlier:

```
if ($a{'year'} > $b{'year'})
{
    print "date a happened later than date b";
}
elsif ($a{'year'} < $b{'year'})
{
    print "date b happened later than date a";
}
elsif ($a{'month'} > $b{'month'})
{
    print "date a happened later than date b";
}
elsif ($a{'month'} < $b{'month'})
{
    print "date b happened later than date a";
}
elsif ($a{'day'} > $b{'day'})
{
    print "date a happened later than date b";
}
elsif ($a{'day'} < $b{'day'})
{
    print "date b happened later than date a";
}
else
{
    print 'date a happened either on the same day as date b';
}
```

As stated, order is important here. After performing the first block of code within the control structure (that happens to be true), the processing resumes at the next line after the structure.

Perl also has a short form of if. As an alternative to the example just given, you could say:

```
(print("date a happened later than date b\n"), $found = 1)
                               if ($a{'year'} > $b{'year'});
(print("date b happened later than date a\n"), $found = 1)
                               if ($a{'year'} < $b{'year'});
(print("date a happened later than date b\n"), $found = 1)
                               if ($a{'month'} > $b{'month'} && $found != 1)
(print("date b happened later than date a\n"), $found = 1)
                               if ($a{'month'} < $b{'month'} && $found != 1)
(print("date a happened later than date b\n"), $found = 1)
                               if ($a{'day'} > $b{'day'} && $found != 1);
(print("date a happened later than date b\n"), $found = 1)
                               if ($a{'day'} < $b{'day'} && $found != 1);
 print("date a happened either on the same day or earlier than date b")  if (!$found);
```

where you use $gt as a tag that tells you whether or not you have found that date a is greater than date b.

Control of Control Structures

There are often cases where you want to nest control structures and then break out of them, as opposed to completing a certain set of iterations. Suppose we want to break out of a loop if a condition holds true, as in the following:

```
foreach $line (@lines)
{
    # how do we get out, without iterating through all the lines?
}
```

In this case, Perl provides three ways to move around in control structures: next, last, and redo. next provides the functionality to stop the current version of the loop, and evaluate the next one. last, on the other hand, breaks out of the current loop and returns to the loop in which it was nested. Finally, redo is a specifically Perlish keyword, which says for the control loop to "re-evaluate the expression."

We shall cover each of these in turn.

next

Formally, the syntax of next is simple. Put it in control structures at any point where you want to skip to the next evaluation of the loop, as shown in Figure 4.5. We have already seen an example of next when dealing with the while loop and continue. Here's an example of how next works in nested loops:

```
for ($xx = 1; $xx < 4; $xx++)
{
    foreach $value ( 1,2,3,4,5,1,2,3) # point A
    {
        if ($value > 3)
        {
            next;                # goes to point A. 'Short Circuits' the loop, to
                                 # go to the next evaluation of the loop.
        }                        # if there was a continue loop here would go there
```

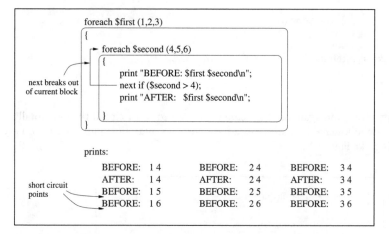

Figure 4.5
next Used in
Flow Control

```
foreach $first (1,2,3)
{
    foreach $second (4,5,6)
    {
        print "BEFORE: $first $second\n";
        next if ($second > 4);
        print "AFTER:  $first $second\n";
    }
}
```

next breaks out
of current block

prints:

BEFORE: 1 4	BEFORE: 2 4	BEFORE: 3 4
AFTER: 1 4	AFTER: 2 4	AFTER: 3 4
BEFORE: 1 5	BEFORE: 2 5	BEFORE: 3 5
BEFORE: 1 6	BEFORE: 2 6	BEFORE: 3 6

short circuit
points

```
        print "$value ";
    }
    print "\n";
}
print "DONE";
```

This prints out:

```
1 2 3 1 2 3
1 2 3 1 2 3
1 2 3 1 2 3
DONE
```

In each loop, the values *4* and *5* are skipped because the next routes back to *A*, and hence skips the print. next then passes control to foreach, which evaluates the next loop, in this case, picking the next number.

The following prints next finishes the loop:

```
foreach $word ('next','finishes','skip','skip','the','loop')
{
    next if ($word eq 'skip');
    print "$word ";
}
```

Note that it doesn't print the word skip but still continues to the end of the loop.

next is very handy for ignoring items inside a given control structure. For example, the following ignores any line with comments in them:

```
foreach $line (@lines)
{
    next if ($line =~ m"#");    # ignores lines with # in them.
    doSomethingWithNonCommentedLines();
}
```

and the following ignores the first 100 lines of a file:

```
my $lineNo = 0;
while ($line = <FD>)
```

```
    {
        next if ($lineNo++ < 100);
    }
```

As we shall see, next is often used in conjunction with last.

last

last is just as easy to use, and again has the default behavior to short-circuit the loop totally, turning control to the next block of code following the last. last has a formal syntax (just put it where you need to "break out" of a loop) something like Figure 4.6.

Figure 4.6
last Used in
Flow Control

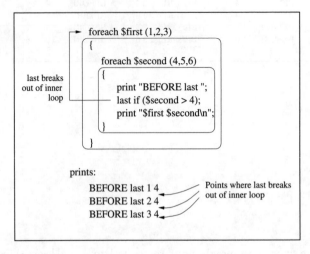

Note that last does not totally break out of every loop. It simply cuts to the next controlling block, which may or may not be inside another loop. Hence, the following:

```
1  foreach $value (1,2,3,4,5,1,2,3)
2  {
3      if ($value > 3)
4      {
5          last;  # jumps to point A
6      }
7      print "$value ";
8  }
9  # point A
10 print " DONE";
```

prints 1 2 3 DONE. However:

```
1  for ($xx = 1; $xx < 4; $xx++)
2  {
3      foreach $value (1,2,3,4,5,2,3)
4      {
5          last if ($value > 3);  # goes to point B
6          print "$value ";
7      }
```

```
8        # point B
9        print "\n";
10 }
```

This prints out:

```
1 2 3
1 2 3
1 2 3
```

The last statement short-circuits the inner loop, going to line 8 every time $value becomes greater than 3.

last is good for exiting on an error, or after a particular piece of data has been found. The following example returns only the first 1,000 lines of a file:

```
my $lineCount = 0;
while ($line = <FD>)
{
    last if ($lineCount++ > 1000);
}
```

The following pseudocode returns an error status if an error occurs while evaluating through the elements (the error is flagged by the subroutine errorInLine($line) returning true, and the subroutine doSomething is called if an error has occurred):

```
1    foreach $line (@lines)
2    {
3        if (errorInLine($line))
4        {
5            $error = 1;
6            last;                    # breaks out of loop to point A
7        }
8    }
9    # point A
10 if ($error == 1)
11 {
12     doSomething();
13 }
```

Suppose you wanted to determine whether a given array had an element greater than 10. last would be helpful here, too:

```
1 @bigArray = (1,2,11,...... (ie: thousands of elements))
2 foreach $element (@bigArray)
3 {
4     if ($element > 10)
5     {
6         $largeElementFound = 1;
7         last;
8     }
9 }
```

After the first element greater than 10 is found, we need not go through the rest of the array. All that matters is that we found one.

Finally, last is very helpful when you want to force a user to enter data in the correct format before continuing with a "retry" if the user doesn't enter the correct data:

```
1 my ($input1, $input2);
```

```
2 while (1)
3 {
4     print "Please enter two values.\n";
5     chop($input1 = <STDIN>, $input2 = <STDIN>);
6     last if (($input1 !~ m"^(\d+)$") || ($input2 !~ m"^(\d+)$"));
7     print
8     "Please enter numbers for input1 and input2! you said $input1 and $input2\n";
9 }
```

This will force the user to keep entering text until both $input1 and $input2 are integers.

redo

Now we will touch briefly on the redo keyword, which is a bit of an oddity. It "stalls" a loop, going back to the loop like next does, but reevaluates it. The best way to understand redo is in action. For example:

```
1 my $xx = 1;
2 foreach $element (1,2,3,4,5)
3 {
4         print "$element ";
5         $xx++;
6     redo if ($xx % 2 == 1);
7 }
```

prints 1 1 2 2 3 3 4 4 5 5, in effect doubling the array. In short, the redo statement looks at a counter, $xx, and based on whether or not the remainder of that counter divided by 2 equals 1 (1/2 = 0 mod 1, for example), redoes the expression, going through each element twice. Hence, the following is an infinite loop:

```
foreach $element (0) { redo }
```

redo is fairly uncommon, but there are a few places you will find it useful. For example, the following insures that each element in a foreach loop will get input that has a *y* in it:

```
foreach $question (@questions)
{
    $question;
    redo if (($answer = <STDIN>) !~ m"y");
    push(@answers, $answer);
}
```

Labeling Your Control Structures

For those of you who don't think that next, last, and redo are powerful enough in their native form, there are labels you can put on them. This works much like a label for a goto, but is better because you are limited to going only to loops above the one that next or last is in. This is helpful for doing algorithms in which you have deeply nested constructs. Figure 4.7 shows an example of labels breaking out of a loop. As you can see, the label makes the next, last, or redo affect the labeled loop rather than the loop that contains the next, last, or redo.

For example, the following:

```
1  LABEL: foreach $valueouter (1,2,3)   # LABEL this is where the next goes.
2  {
3         foreach $valueinner (1,2,3,4,5,1,2,3)
```

Figure 4.7
Labels Breaking
Out of a Loop

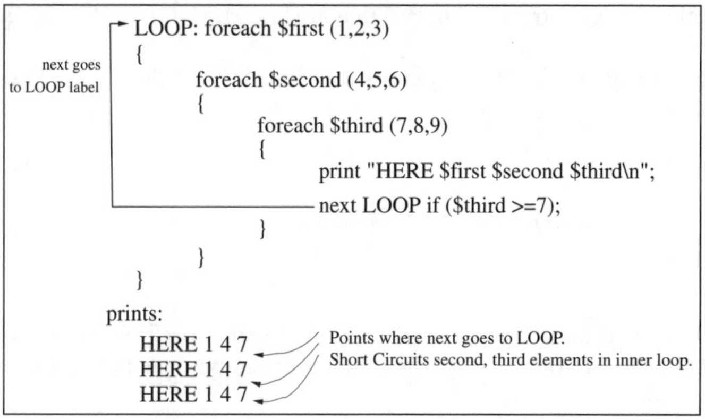

```
       next goes       LOOP: foreach $first (1,2,3)
     to LOOP label     {
                               foreach $second (4,5,6)
                               {
                                       foreach $third (7,8,9)
                                       {
                                               print "HERE $first $second $third\n";
                                               next LOOP if ($third >=7);
                                       }
                               }
                       }
                       prints:
                           HERE 1 4 7          Points where next goes to LOOP.
                           HERE 1 4 7          Short Circuits second, third elements in inner loop.
                           HERE 1 4 7
```

```
4       {
5               if ($valueinner > 2)
6               {
7                   next  LABEL ;                # Goes to LABEL (valueout loop)
8                                                # *instead* of going to foreach  $valueinner.
9               }
10              print "VALUEOUT: $valueouter VALUEIN $valueinner\n";
11      }
12      print " DONE\n";
13 }
```

prints:

```
VALUEOUT: 1 VALUEIN: 1
VALUEOUT: 1 VALUEIN: 2
VALUEOUT: 2 VALUEIN: 1
VALUEOUT: 2 VALUEIN: 2
VALUEOUT: 3 VALUEIN: 1
VALUEOUT: 3 VALUEIN: 2
DONE
```

What happens here is that the behavior of the next is being applied not to the default label (the $valuein loop), but to the LABEL. Hence, the next short-circuits the current loop it is in ($valuein) completely, and then causes the $valueout label (where it goes) to jump to the next value.

If last was here instead of next, the printout would be:

```
VALUEOUT: 1 VALUEIN: 1
VALUEOUT: 1 VALUEIN: 2
DONE
```

because last is now short-circuiting both loops. The process flow hits a value greater than 2 in valuein, goes to the label LABEL, immediately kills both iterators, and then jumps to print DONE.

Last Word on Perl Control Structures

This is really all you need to know about Perl control structures. You could even forget about LABEL if you really wanted to. In some instances it helps make code really clean, as when looping through multiple arrays and deep nested structures. There are other looping structures in Perl that are like while, for, foreach, and if, but with a twist.

until is like while, but it negates the expression instead. In other words, while (!$expr) and until ($expr) both mean the same thing.

```
until ($a == $b)   # OR while ($a != $b)
{
   doSomething();     # does stuff until $b equals $a;
   $a++;
}
```

do..while is a control structure like while, but it automatically does the first loop before the evaluation. Since the while comes at the end of the loop, the block is executed once before the condition is tested. Hence:

```
do { print "HERE!\n"; } while ( 1 == 0);
```

always prints HERE, whereas:

```
while(1 == 0) { print "HERE\n"; }
```

never prints HERE.

The unless control structure is like if, except for the negation. if (!$expr) and unless ($expr) mean the same thing. Finally, do..until does exactly the same thing as do..while but does it "oppositely;" i.e., it evaluates an expression until a condition is true (not false, as in do..while).

Again, these structures can be useful in certain situations, but they can also clutter your code. Use them sparingly, but well.

Introduction to Perl Operators

Perl has many operators, and the precedence of the operators is quite complicated. Fortunately (at least for people who know C/C++), all the operators that Perl shares with C/C++ have the same precedence as they do in those languages.

These operators can also make for very unclear code, and are responsible for many of the Just Another Perl Hacker (JAPH) scripts out there, such as the one provided by Jan-Pieter Cornet (*johnpc@xs4all.net*):

```
# perl
++$_;$!=$_+++$_;($:,$,,$/,$*)=$!=~/.(.)...(.)(.).(.)/;$!=$_+$_;
($@,$\,$~)=$!=~/(.)(.).(.)/; $_="$,$/$:"; $@++; $~="$~$_"; ($_)=
\$$=~/\((.)/;$|=++$_;$_++;$|++;$~="$~ $@$:";`$~-$/$\$*$, $|>&$_`
```

Wouldn't it be easier to read this as:

```
print 'Johnpc';
```

Of course, this takes all the fun out of it, but it makes a point. It is very easy to get very cryptic with Perl-ish syntax. Remember this while reading further.

Note

There is a specific type of obfuscated Perl scripts out there called JAPH. (Just Another Perl Hacker). These are scripts dedicated to printing out Just Another Perl Hacker, in a way that again highlights the "interesting" syntactics made possible by Perl's rubberband syntax.

Randal Schwartz pioneered the technique; here is an example given by Abigail (*abigail@fnx.com*):

```
perl5.004 -wMMath::BigInt -e'$^V=new
Math::BigInt+qq;$^F$^W783$[$%9889$^F47$|88768$^W596577669$%$^
W5$^F3364$[$^W$^F$|838747$[8889739$%$|$^F673$%$^W98$^F76777$=56;;$^U=substr($],$
|,5)*(q.25..($^W=@^V))=>do{print+chr$^V%$^U;$^V/=$^U}while$^V!=$^W'
```

And yes, this prints out `Just Another Perl Hacker`. Note that this is not only obscure, but it also is version dependent in that it only works with perl5.004.

To make it work with perl5.005 you have to cheat, and realize that $] is the variable which handles the version of perl, and modify it so that perl5.005 doesn't affect the output. I'll leave this as an exercise to the reader.

Obfuscated perl actually has grown (a bit more than it probably should). Check out `http://orwant.www.media.mit.edu/tpj/obfusc-1-writeup` for more ridiculously obfuscated code.

Perl Operator Precedence

Table 4.1 is a list of all the Perl operators and their order of precedence. This list is taken straight from the **perlop** man page. The operators are listed in order of precedence, highest to lowest. Following this list are sections that describe the most important sets of operators and give examples on their usage. As you can see, there are quite a few levels! We turn next to how to deal with this complexity, which is both a blessing and a curse.

Table 4.1
Operator
Precedence

'Order	Operator	Name and Definition
left	list operators	Includes functions, variables, items in parentheses.
left	->	Dereferencing operator. See chapter on references.
NonA	++, --	Increment and decrement. ++$aa adds one to $aa.
right	**	Exponentiation. $a**$b raises $a to the $b power.
right	!, ~,+,-\	Not, bit negation, reference op, unary +/-(i.e., -4).
left	=~,!~	Matching operators with regular expressions.
left	*,/,%.x	Times, divided, modulus, string, and list multiplier.
left	+,-,'.' (one dot)	Plus, minus, string operator.
left	<<, >>	Binary shift left operator, binary shift right operator.
NonA	named unary ops	Functions that take one argument, filetest operators (-f -X split examples, see **perlref** for more info).

continued next page

Table 4.1
Operator
Precedence
(continued)

Order	Operator	Name and Definition
NonA	<,>,<=,>=	Numeric less than, greater than, less than or equal to, or greater than or equal to.
	lt,gt,le,ge	String less than, greater than, less than or equal to, greater than or equal to.
NonA	==, !=, <=>	Numeric equal to, not equal to, comparison operator.
	,eq,ne, cmp	String equal to, not equal to, comparison operators.
left	&	Binary and... does a bit match on each bit in strings.
left	|,^	Binary or: does an or bit match on each bit in strings. Binary xor: does an xor bit match on each strings.
left	&&	and operator, evaluates to true if both are true.
left	||	or operator, evaluates to true if both are true.
NonA	..	List operator, as in (1..50) == (1,2,3..50).
right	? :	Conditional operator as in ($a = ($b == 1)? '0' : '1'.
right	=,+=,-=,*=, **=, &=, <<= &&=	Equals, plus equals, etc.
left	',',=>	List separator, another list separator as well.
left	not	Synonym for ! except lower precedence.
left	and	Synonym for && except lower precedence.
left	or	Synonym for || except lower precedence.

As you can see, there are quite a few levels! We turn next to how to deal with this complexity, which is both a blessing and a curse.

Techniques to Clarify Perl Expressions

The complexity of Table 4.1 can create real difficulties. One of the more frustrating aspects of Perl is that the code can be full of ambiguities if you are not careful. In other words, what task will Perl do first? In situations where the code seems ambiguous, you have three possible options to make it clear:

1. Split the offending statement into multiple substatements.
2. Put parentheses around a given ambiguity.
3. Use the operator precedence table to determine precedence.

These tactics are given in the order in which you *should* prefer them. In other words, splitting a complicated statement into substatements should be preferred over parenthesizing, and so on. We discuss each next.

Splitting Perl Statements

This is the simplest technique, and the one that should be preferred. One bad thing about Perl is the power it gives programmers to "ramble at the mouth" too long. You can make horrifically complicated sentences in Perl. You can often get a burst of clarity by splitting Perl sentences. The statement:

```
$num = $sub**power + log($sub2);
```

can become the following two statements:

```
$num = $sub**$power;
$num+= log($sub2);
```

This not only helps you with your coding, but helps others to read your code. You get fewer bugs, and when other people maintain your code, they will thank you. Likewise:

```
print log $sqrt, " "x length ($sqrt);
```

becomes:

```
$log = log($sqrt);
$length = " " x length($sqrt);
print $log . $length;
```

Of course, it is up to you to decide how long is too long. People just starting with Perl might find the above comforting, whereas experienced Perl programmers may wonder why there are three lines, and not one.

Parenthesize It

Perl also provides the parentheses, (), as an easy mechanism to clarify Perl operators. In general, if you have a question about an operator's precedence, simply add parentheses around the concerned expression, and your precedence question is solved.

Note

Using parentheses to clarify operators does not always work in some pathological cases. For example:

```
&function('a', exit());
```

will call exit (and perform an exit) before the subroutine is called. Hence, you should say something like:

```
function('a'), exit();
```

instead (i.e., you need to cut the offending statement into several lines).

However, it is also very easy to take parentheses to extremes. Consider the following Perl statement:

```
print (($a)+($b));        # Exhibit A: parenthesesitis.
```

This is "parentheses-itis," the practice of *always* putting parentheses around things. There's a fine line between the above and:

```
print $a+$b;              # Exhibit B: minimalismitis
```

or:

```
print ($a+$b);            # Exhibit C:
```

Which of these is easiest to read? We vote for Exhibit C. print ($a + $b); emphasizes the functional part of the statement. After all, you are printing the sum $a+$b, so they should be grouped together.

Exhibit A is too paranoid, and Exhibit B, although if you get used to it can be rather freeing, begs the question of whether or not print munges all its arguments before or after being evaluated. In other words, does Exhibit B evaluate to:

```
(print ($a))+$b;
```

or:

```
print ($a+$b);
```

In this case, the code evaluates to the second statement, print ($a + $b), but the lack of parentheses will bite you someday if you aren't careful. If you say something like:

```
print 'done','printing','arguments',exit();
```

it will exit without printing anything. Perl evaluates this to:

```
print ('done','printing','arguments',exit());
```

which then evaluates the exit before passing it to print. Therefore, the program exits. In this case:

```
print ('done','printing','arguments'), exit();
```

isn't just more clean, but is also syntactically correct.

The point of all this is to make the code as clear as possible without being verbose. Remember, the person who maintains that code may be you!

Using the Precedence Table

This should be a last resort, because most of your code should be clean enough that you shouldn't have to deal with precedence rules. The classic example is:

```
$yy = ++$xx%2;
```

In other words, does the % (modular) operator go before the ++? Is the following code equal to 5%2 or 4%2?

```
$xx = 4;
$yy = ++$xx%2;
```

We can use the rule table above to figure out that this is actually equal to:

```
$yy = (++$xx)%2
```

and the ++ goes before the %. But why not say so in the first place?

If you opt for using the precedence table, there are two rules to remember. The first rule is that items at the top of the table are of higher precedence than items at the lower level. Consider the following statement:

```
if  (1 > 0 or 2 > 1 and 3 < 4)  # if 1 is greater than 0 OR 2
{                               # is greater than 1 AND
}                               # three is less than 4.
```

This statement could be ambiguous. To see how it would be executed, we can look at the operator precedence table. Since > and < are of higher precedence than or and and, we can put parentheses around each <>. The statement becomes:

```
if ((1 > 0) or (2 > 1) and (3 < 4))
{
}
```

and since and is of higher precedence than or, we can similarly put parentheses around the and expressions:

```
if ((1 > 0) or ((2 > 1) and (3 < 4)))
{
}
```

This is how Perl interprets this statement. For human eyes, this is coming pretty close to "parentheses-itis," so we just might consider taking the parentheses off the > signs to have the expression read:

```
if (1 > 0 or ( 2 > 1 and 3 < 4))
{
}
```

This seems like the right balance between ambiguity and verbosity. Again, parentheses are around the point where it makes a logical difference in how the statement is executed. After all, the construct:

```
if((1 > 0 or 2 > 1) and 3 < 4)
{
}
```

does exactly the opposite.

The second rule to remember when looking at the operator precedence table is that when you are confronted with an expression that contains more than one of the same precedence rules, those rules are executed in the order given by the Order column in the operator precedence table.

This almost never happens. Most of the time, as in the case of + and *, the order in which the statement is evaluated does not matter. In the cases where it does matter, it's better to put parentheses around the offending expression for clarity, or split it. However, we can interpret:

```
$a = 2**3**$exponent;
```

to be equal to $a = 2**(3**$exponent);, because ** is right-associated, and the rightmost part of the expression is evaluated first. And:

```
$a +=$b *=5;
```

is equal to $a += ($b *=5); because it too is evaluated right to left. Likewise, since subtraction is sensitive:

```
$a = 10 - 1 + 1;
```

becomes:

```
$a = (10 -1) + 1;
```

Such exercises will help you become accustomed to Perl's precedence levels. However, I would stay away from the precedence table, instead splitting long statements and parenthesizing statements first.

Common Operators in Perl

As you can see from the precedence table, not only are there many *levels* to consider when dealing with Perl, there are many *operators*.

Two points will keep you sane here. First, there is much overlapping in this area between C and Perl. Second, although the number of operators in Perl is large, only a fraction of them are frequently used. However,

C and Perl aren't exactly the same as far as operators go, and you sometimes do want to use the infrequently used operators.

Following is an introduction to Perl operators; the idea is to give you enough to satisfy you for a long time to come. Those who want to get the complete reference, see the **Perlop** man page.

Arithmetic and Increment Operators in Perl

Perl has all the arithmetic operators that C has. In fact, they work exactly the same as their equivalents in C. Just be sure that you are using numeric strings when dealing with them. After all, 'a' + 'b' is interpreted as 0 + 0 in Perl.

Note

If you are doing complicated math processing, you are better off making a C module and linking it with Perl. Perl is simply too slow for calculations.

Your best source of information for this is the **perlxs** man page, and the package **swig** on the accompanying CD.

You may also want to check out the **Math::ematica** interface to Stephen Wolfram's *Mathematica,* and everything on CPAN under the category **Math::**.

```
$a = $b + $c;
$a = 'MISTAKE' + 20;              # ERROR ('MISTAKE' will be treated as '0', and
                                  # $a becomes 20. (debugger -w will catch this)
$a = (@arguments + @array2) * 20; # sets $a equal to number of elements in
                                  # @arguments plus number of elements in
                                  # @array, times 20.
$speed = (1/2) * $acceleration * ($time **2);
$a = 10; $a++;                    # incrementor. $a becomes 11;
$a = 10; $a—;                     # decrementor. $a becomes 9;
```

There is actually an exception to the string interpolation rule when dealing with incrementing—++. There is some special "magic" associated with this operator that allows you to do the following:

```
$aa = 'AA'; $aa++;     # $aa becomes 'AB';
$aa = 'zz'; $aa++;     # $aa becomes 'aaa';
$aa = '01'; $aa++;     # $aa becomes '02';
$aa = '09'; $aa++;     # $aa becomes '10';
```

This happens for all characters that are alphanumeric (a–z, A–Z, 0–9). It does *not* happen for non-numeric characters. Hence:

```
$a = '+'; $a++;
```

does not work.

Perl Conditional Operators

There are two sets of conditional operators in Perl:

- The set dealing with numerics (==, >=, <=, >, and so on).
- The set dealing with strings (lt, gt, le, ge, eq).

Likewise, there are two new operators:

- $a <=> $b is a comparison function for *numbers*. <=> returns –1, 0, 1 depending on whether $a is numerically less than, equal to, or greater than $b.
- $a cmp $b is a comparison function for strings. cmp returns –1, 0, 1, depending on whether $a is alphanumerically less than, equal to, or greater than $b.

These comparison operators will be most helpful when we cover sorting (see Chapter 10).

Perl interpolates a variable into either string or numeric context based on comparison operators, which are in the same vein as the arithmetic operators. You should not be doing gymnastics such as:

```
if (9 gt 10)      # evaluates to true but does not do what you would want.
{                 # The statement does so since 9 is greater than 10 lexically
}
if ('string' == 'strung')    # also evaluates to true but does not do what you would
{                            # want. Two strings are *always* equal
}                            # numerically since they both
                             # evaluate to zero in numeric context.
```

when what you probably want is:

```
if ('aaa' gt 'b')           # works, evaluates to false.
{
}
if (10 > 5)                 # works too, evaluates to true.
{
}
```

Perl Logical Operators

Perl provides logical operators for use in statements. They are:

- && logical and (1 && 1 == 1).
- and synonym for && (1 and 1 == 1).
- || logical or (1 || 0 == 1).
- or synonym for || (1 or 0 == 1).
- xor exclusive or (1 xor 1 == 0) or (1 xor 0 == 1).

These logical operators behave like their C equivalents in many cases. They always evaluate to either true ('1') or false (''').

```
if (10 > 9 && 20>10)        # evaluates to 1 (true).
{                           # since both subcases are true.
}
if (10 == 10 || 14 < 10)    # evaluates to 1 (true) since
{                           # one of the two subcases are true.
}
```

Short-Circuiting

|| and &&, and or and and have some extra functionality that is very handy, and makes for very readable code:

```
functionReturningScalar() || warn "Expression was false!\n";
```

```
                              # Example of short-circuiting.  Tries to do
                              # 'functionReturningScalar()'.  If this returns
                              # '' or 0 (false) , prints 'expression was false'.
@array = functionReturningArray() || @otherArray || ();
                              # sets @array equal to the array returned
                              # by the functionReturningArray(), or
                              # if this is empty, @otherArray.
printItWorkedIfTrue() && print "IT WORKED!\n";
                              # opposite of '||'. If 'printItWorkedIfTrue()'
                              # returns a non-zero (true) value,
                              # then (and only then) print 'IT WORKED!'
```

These examples show a technique called *short-circuiting*, which is a handy way to make your code more readable and less verbose at the same time.

In the case of ||, to evaluate an expression to true (nonzero or ' '), all Perl really need do is *find* the first expression that is true. Hence, what Perl does is *stop* evaluating an expression as soon as a true value is found. In other words:

```
0 || 0 || 0 || 1 || 1;        # evaluates first four expressions
                              # stops at first '1'.
                              # Does not evaluate last expression.
```

Likewise, in the case of &&, to evaluate an expression to true, Perl needs to have *every* subexpression true. In other words, as soon as a false expression is reached, Perl stops:

```
1 && 1 && 1 && 0 && 0;        # evaluates first four expressions
                              # stops at first '0'. Does not evaluate last expression.
```

In addition, the synonyms for these operators, namely or and and, do exactly the same thing as their || and && counterparts. They short-circuit as well, but in a very handy way. Because they are so low on the precedence scale (in fact, the lowest), you can say:

```
open FD, "filename" or die;
```

which will open a file descriptor or die if it cannot. The thing to note here is the lack of parentheses. I prefer to put parentheses around this simply because I like having function calls always denoted by (), but in some ways this is clearer (even the fact that it is in English, rather than ||, makes it clearer). Do what feels appropriate for you.

The Conditional Operator

Perl borrows from C the very handy conditional operator, the expression? trueCase: falseCase form. It works like Cs in that if you say the following:

```
$length = (@array > 2)? 'more than two elements' : 'two or less';
```

this acts exactly like:

```
if (@array > 2)
{
    $length = 'more than two elements';
}
else
{
    $length = 'two or less';
}
```

In other words, one line ((condition) ? trueCase : falseCase;) can take the place of six lines of code. This is extremely handy for shortening code with many separate if.. then.. else clauses. Here's a switch statement:

```
$value = ( $value eq 'Mon')? 'Monday'      :
         ( $value eq 'Tue')? 'Tuesday'     :
         ( $value eq 'Wed')? 'Wednesday'   :
         ( $value eq 'Thu')? 'Thursday'    :
         ( $value eq 'Fri')? 'Friday'      :
         ( $value eq 'Sat')? 'Saturday'    :
         ( $value eq 'Sun')? 'Sunday'      :
         "Not a day of the week!";
```

which basically expands the days of the week into their longer forms. This works because the "false" case itself is a conditional, which in turn has a 'false' case of its own, and so on. Although you may want to write this as:

```
%days = ( 'Mon' => 'Monday', 'Tue' => 'Tuesday', 'Wed' => 'Wednesday',
          'Thu' => 'Thursday', 'Fri' => 'Friday', 'Sat' =>'Saturday',
          'Sun' => 'Sunday' );
$value = ($days{$value})? $days{$value} :
                "Not a day of the week!\n";
```

where the hash takes place of the bulk of the switch statement, and the only case for ? : is where $value is *not* a day of the week.

Perl File and Command Operators

The usage of file operators and command operators is dealt with in some detail in both Chapter 3, "Variables, C" and Chapter 10, "Special Perl Functions". However, here we introduce the concept of file and command operators, as well as their syntax.

Perl has a built-in interface into each operating system to which it has been ported. This interface allows Perl to interact with files on disk and to execute a shell command directly. This is an important concept for Perl, and one of the reasons Perl is so portable and powerful. We will take a look at file handling and shell command execution next.

The <FILEHANDLE> File Operator

<FD> reads from the filehandle FD into a scalar you specify on the left-hand side. If you want to read one line from the file called fileName, do this:

```
open(FD, "fileName");    # open syntax to process a file.
$line = <FD>;            # reads a line out of the file.
close(FD);               # closes the file.
```

After all, you won't have the luxury of having terabytes of RAM! Many times the important data is on disk (or tape or CD-ROM, etc.), and Perl's job is to make reading that data as easy as possible.

The Backticks Operator (` `)

The *backticks operator* (` `) takes a string, interpolates it, and then executes the command as a shell command. The following puts the output from a find command into the variables @>lines and $line, respectively:

```
my @lines = `find . -print`;   # executes a find operation, puts the results into @lines.
$line = `find . -print`;       # executes a find operation, puts the results into $line.
```

Beware of nonportability here. The command **find** is not available on all systems, and backticks (` ` ` `) should be avoided whenever portability is important. Use Perl builtins instead. (We will discuss these builtins in Chapter 11.)

Summary of Perl Control Structures and Operators

The control structures and operators make Perl an extremely "freeing" language in which to program. Compared to languages like C++ or C, Perl becomes much more like a "natural" language. In fact, you can say a statement like:

```
sleep until $sun eq 'up';
```

which parses in Perl. However, too much freedom can be a "bad" thing. (Although they are cool, JAPH scripts are probably *not* your best examples of readable code.)

Hence, the purpose of the next part of the chapter is to show some common templates of expressions in Perl and when they are used. They should be able to handle most of your programming needs.

Examples: Common Expression Patterns in Perl

As we have said before, a good thing about Perl code is that it is infinitely flexible. And a bad thing about Perl code is that it is infinitely flexible. Hence, the idea of this section is to show some of the more clean, and common, expression patterns for Perl.

Out of the *huge* number of possible Perl expressions, there are really only a few that you should actually be using. In fact, I would say that the smaller the number of expression patterns you have, the better. The less types you have, the easier it will be for others to understand your code, and the easier it will be to maintain your code.

Likewise, a limited number of expression patterns also creates the possibility for you to build tools to help manage your complexity. There is nothing cooler than writing your own tools that actually debug your programs for you, or give you a "road map" to what is going on. If you keep your syntax minimal, you'll find it a much easier when it comes time to build C/C++ extensions.

In other words, let your object-oriented or modular syntax do the work, not the tricks of the interpreter. We discuss object-oriented Perl techniques in the second part of this book.

Here, we examine the more commonly found expressions and our preferred method for parsing them. We call these structures *patterns* because they are extremely common, and you can almost use them as "cookie-cutters" to create your own, specific solutions.

Pattern 1: Arithmetic Expressions

With arithmetic expressions, use as many parentheses as you can to make the meaning clear. In practice, there are fewer arithmetic expressions in Perl than one might think since it is not the speediest in this area!

Use the precedence table as your guideline. The following statements avoid "parentheses-itis" by functionally clustering items that go with parentheses:

```
$val = $variable**$exponent + log($sum - $var);
$val = ($var + $val) ** 2;
```

These two statements seem pretty clear, because ** is much more binding than +, and the function call log is much more binding than –; hence the need for parentheses. However, if you feel uncomfortable with this, you could say:

```
$val = ($variable**$exponent) + (log($sum-$var));
```

although this seems like overkill. But, again, it is better to have more parentheses and get the answer right than a minimal amount and get the answer wrong.

Pattern 2: *if Patterns with Multiple and/or Clauses*

These patterns occur where one has an `if` condition with multiple `and/or` clauses. Here, `&&` and `||` (or their cousins `and/or`) are the focus points for the expression.

Here, you probably want to limit yourself to putting parentheses around the statements that are logically tied together. For example:

```
if (($scalar > $scalar2 && $scalar2 > $scalar3) || $scalar3 > $scalar4)
{
}
```

ties the `$scalar > $scalar2` and `$scalar2 > $scalar3` groups together, because without the parentheses the statement would be logically wrong. But:

```
if ((($scalar > $scalar2) && ($scalar2 > $scalar3)) || $scalar3 > $scalar4)
{
}
```

doesn't use "economy of parentheses" and therefore becomes cluttered.

Pattern 3: Expressions in a Condition

Expressions in a condition are Perl statements inside a compare clause: `>`, `<`, `==`, etc. In these cases, parentheses force precedence and add to readability, as in the following example:

```
if (($scalar1+$scalar2) > 5)
{
}
```

In this, the parentheses around `$scalar1` and `$scalar2` aren't strictly necessary. Since `+` is higher in precedence than `>`, the expression means the same without them, but still "looks" like it might be wrong. Hence, the parentheses are added for clarity. If the expression becomes too complicated, you can always split it to enforce readability, as in:

```
my $var = $scalar1 + $scalar2;
  if ($var > 5) { }
{
}
```

Pattern 4: Functions Without Any Arguments

This expression pattern is an easy one. Perl has several forms for functions, and even more for functions without arguments. All of these:

```
function;
function();
&function;
&function();
```

are legal, but you should not use them all. The following is the correct way to go here:
Parentheses make for clarity here, too, and the '&' seems redundant. Hence, function();

Pattern 5: Functions With Regular Arguments

Functions with arguments should be focal points in your code. As such, even though you don't need to put parentheses around the function in the following function call:

```
function $a, $b, $c;
```

it doesn't "shout" that this is a function call, either (it could be a syntax error). And if you say:

```
print function $a, $b, $c;
```

does it say "print to the screen the evaluation of function with the arguments $a, $b, and $c", or "print to the filehandle function $a, $b, and $c"?

Again, the parentheses on the end of the function calls add to readability, as well as work to clarify. It is worthwhile to train your mind to expect that when you see the pattern word (), you are seeing a function call.

```
function($a, $b, $c);
internalFunction($a, $b, $c);
```

Functions such as print are so common that it is sometimes OK to drop the parentheses.

```
print STDERR "HERE!\n";      # printing to a screen
```

However, each one of these cases (like print) should be thought out carefully. And if you decide to drop the parentheses, force yourself to *always* do so (except on rare occasions when not adding parentheses makes the expression wrong, like print("HERE"), exit()). Force of habit will make your code easier to read.

Pattern 6: Functions Inside a Function Call

What about functions that are called inside of other functions, such as:

```
function($arg1, internalFunction $arg2, internalFunction $arg3)
```

In this case, it could be ambiguous. Is the function internalFunction2 inside internalFunction (an argument to it), or is it a separate argument to &function? Is it:

```
&function($arg1, internalFunction($arg2, internalFunction($arg3));
```

or:

```
&function($arg1, internalFunction($arg2), $internalFunction($arg3));
```

This ambiguity can cause you much grief. Therefore, you are better off putting parentheses around every function call, as in:

```
internalFunction($arg1, $arg2, internalFunction($arg4));
push(@args, extract_array_values());
```

This will prevent many precedence mistakes.

Pattern 7: Expressions Inside a Function Call

In the case of an expression within a function call, you can drop the parentheses between the expressions. This is because we can use commas in a list operator as well as parentheses, since they are extremely low in precedence. Hence:

```
print ($scalar+length($a), $scalar * $length);
```

is equal to:

```
print (($scalar+length($a)), ($scalar * $length));
```

but the first form seems a bit cleaner.

Pattern 8: Expressions That Are Evaluated Inside a Function Call

There are times when an expression is evaluated from inside the function call. In other words, the internal expression is evaluated first, and the result is sent as an argument to the function. This is the case with Perl built-in functions. Something like:

```
chop($line = <FD>);          # retrieves a line from a file descriptor FD, then
                             # chops the last character off of it.
```

could be cut up into two lines $line = <FD>; chop($line); because chop modifies $line. It is common practice to use this form, as it saves typing and is fairly maintainable.

Doing two steps in one or more lines of code is a fairly common pattern in Perl; in fact, there is a term for it in Perl called *chaining* (which we will get to in Chapter 6 on contexts.) The important thing here is to always know what you are doing when you chain, and to always use parentheses around the logically joinable parts.

Pattern 9: Temporary Copies of a Variable, With the Temporary Variable Being Manipulated

This pattern is really a spiced-up example of Pattern 8. This pattern happens so frequently that it isn't worth it to split the code into two lines:

```
($tmp = $line) =~ tr[A-Z][a-z];
                        # copies $line into $tmp, and then (in $tmp)
                        # 'translates' all A-Z chars to a-z chars
                        # (lowercase) without touching $line.
($tmp = $number)++;     # copies $number into $tmp, and then increments $tmp.
($tmp = $line)=~s{\bWORD\b}{word};
                        # copies $line into $tmp and then (in $tmp)
                        # substitutes instances of WORD with word.
```

Here, again, we use parentheses around the patterns that we are going to evaluate first: $tmp = $line happens, and *then* the operation (++, tr, s"""") happens.

Pattern 10: Getting the Results of a Pattern Match, Function, or Translate, and Sticking Them in a Variable

This pattern is the flipside of the last pattern. In this case, the variable gets assigned *after* a manipulation is made. For example:

```
$count = ($line =~ tr{A-Z}{a-z});  # gets a count of the uppercase characters in $line,
                                   # and sticks it into $count
```

This is an example of the translate operator in action. It substitutes capitals for lowercase letters in $line, first, and, as a side effect, counts the number of uppercase characters in $line and sticks them into $count. Likewise,

```
($user, $password, $uid) = ($line =~ m{(.*?):(.*?):(.*?)}s);
                            # gets the results of a pattern match (see section
                            # 'regular expressions') and puts that result into
                            # the array ($user, $password, $uid).
```

is an example of the match operator, which basically matches a pattern inside $line. Because of the parentheses around $line, the match is done first, and only after the match is done are the results of that match put into the variables $user, $password, and $uid. Note that in each case we have taken the concept we were dealing with, and compressed it into one statement. We could have said:

```
$line =~ m{(.*?):(.*?):(.*?)}s;
$user = $1;
$password = $2;
$uid = $3;
```

but it is longer and as we shall see later, less precise and more prone to error: Sometimes long expressions make sense in Perl; sometimes they don't.

Pattern 11: Short-Circuiting in Executing a Command

As we saw, the following statement:

```
open(FD, 'filename') || die();
```

means "open the file filename, and tie it to the filehandle FD. If unsuccessful, die." This is an example of short-circuiting.

In this case, parentheses are necessary around open(FD, ..) because the || operator is of higher preference than the , operator. If you said:

```
open FD, 'filename' || die();
```

it is equivalent to:

```
open FD, (filename || die());
```

which is not what you want. However, this is what the or and and operators are for. They have extremely low precedence, so:

```
open FD, "filename" or die;
```

is a perfectly valid Perl sentence.

Nevertheless, it's a good idea to put parentheses around functions anyway, since they logically bind the arguments of the function to that function. The following:

```
open(FD, "filename") or die "Unable to open filename!\n";
                        # opens a file descriptor. If it cannot, it dies
```

is not strictly needed, because the main focus of the statement is the function open, not the short-circuiting.

Pattern 12: Use of Conditional Operator in Assignment

The expression:

```
if ($condition1)
{
    $value = $value1;
```

```
}
elsif ($condition2)
{
        $value = $value2;
}
else
{
        $value = $value3;
}
```

is unnecessarily verbose, and you can use the conditional operator instead:

```
$value = ($condition1)? $value1 :
    ($condition2)? $value2 :
    $value3;
```

Here, the parentheses are not strictly necessary around the condition since the ? is of low priority. However, as in the following cases:

```
$value = ($string gt $otherString) ? $string : $otherString;
                                        # sets $value to the highest
                                        # lexical valued string.
@value = (@array1 > @array2) ? @array1 : @array2;  # sets @value to the array with
                                        # the greatest number of elements.
```

having the parentheses makes sense because they group what is logically associated together.

Pattern 13: Assignment With Short-Circuiting

This pattern is used as a good way of setting a variable to several possible versions on the same line:

```
$variable = $ENV{'LOGDIR'} || getlog() || 'DEFAULT';  # tries $ENV{'LOGDIR'} first
                                        # function getlog() second,
                                        # and if both blank, sets
                                        # to default.
```

It has the same effect as Pattern 12, taking the place of needless if.. then clauses.

Pattern 14: Assignment in *if.. then, while, or foreach* Constructs

Pattern 14 takes advantage of the fact that any statement inside a conditional is evaluated before the conditional actually evaluates as true or false.

Hence, there are two steps to this pattern: 1) evaluating the statement inside the conditional, and 2) using the results of this evaluation to decide whether the condition is true or false.

This pattern is very common:

```
if (@files = getFileNames())          # get files from a function.
{                                      # evaluates to false if get_file_names
  print "@files\n";                    # returns (), or undef
}
elsif (outOfFilenames())
{
}
```

Here, if `getFileNames()` returns one or more strings in the array to `@>files`, the `if` will be evaluated as true. If `getFileNames` returns `undef`, or `()`, the `if` will be evaluated as false. Either way, `@>files` will be set.

Likewise:

```
while(($key, $value) = each (%hash))     # assigns a $key, $value pair
{                                        # each time thru the expression.
}                                        # evaluates to false if each returns
                                         # ().
```

iterates through a hash, calling each before evaluating whether or not each returned a `()`. And:

```
foreach $file (@files = <FD>)     # get files from a file descriptor
{                                 # -<FD>, and iterate through them, while setting '@files'.
}
```

both makes a list of files (in `<@>files`) and iterates through them afterwards, setting `$file` to each element in `@>files`. The `split` in:

```
foreach $word (split(/,/, $list))     # split up the list by commas,
{                                     # use each $line of this as an element
}                                     # in the array.
```

evaluates first, making an array of words out of a comma-separated list (something like `$list` being equal to `1,2,3,4,5`. Finally:

```
while ($line = getLine())     # get a line from the function 'getLine'
{                             # iterate through this function
}                             # until getline() returns nothing.
```

repeatedly calls the function `getline()`, setting the value in `$line` until `$line` runs out of values.

Pattern 15: Using Functions and Operators to Assign Values to Internal Perl Variables

Internal Perl variables, such as `$_` and `$@`, are variables Perl uses by default.

As such, Pattern 15 is usually just shorthand for Pattern 14: Use of conditional operators in assignment. We tend to think it makes things unclear, but it is also very common.

```
while (defined <FD>)     # sets $_ to a line from the filehandle <FD>
{                        # goes through each line in filehandle <FD>.
    chop();              # chops that variable (ie: takes off
}                        # the last character.)
```

is equivalent to:

```
while (defined ($_ = <FD>))
{
    chop($_);
}
```

Likewise, the following will iterate through each `@>ARGV`:

```
for (@ARGV)     # again, sets $_, iterates through
{               # each argument.
}
```

As it iterates, each argument is set to $_, which you can then access via special functions or by name.

Pattern 16: Iterating Through a Regular Expression

We devote a whole chapter to regular expressions. Think of this as a preview of what is to come.

In this pattern we use a regular expression as an iterator. In the following example, $line is not actually changed. Instead, each number in the scalar $line is picked out and assigned to $1, one by one:

```
while ($line =~ m/([0-9]+)/g)      # simple regular expression that picks out
{                                   # all of the integer numbers in a
    print "$1\n";                   # regular expression. (see section
                                    # 'regular expressions')
}
```

Right now, simply note the g at the end. This stands for *global,* which means in this case "match as many times as you can." If you had:

```
$line = '1 x 2 y 343 z';
```

as a string, this snippet of code would print out:

```
1
2
343
```

Pattern 17: Filehandle Joins as an Argument to a Subroutine, or Function List

The following assignment operator makes @>lines all the lines in files FD, FD2, and FD3:

```
@lines = (<FD>, <FD2>, <FD3>);
```

which works by evaluating each of the filehandles in the (), and joining them into one huge list.

Summary of Perl Expression Patterns

There is no "magic" about these expression patterns. We present them here in order to help you create the most unambiguous, maintainable code possible. Mixing and matching these patterns should give you a framework for the majority of your programming needs.

Summary

Of all the things in Perl, the precedence table (which defines the order in which symbols are evaluated) is by far the most complicated. It has to be in order to be "natural." If you think about it, English is full of complicated (and contradictory) rules, special cases, and so forth, to which we seem to have adapted.

Perl's idiom set is extremely rich, but on the downside, it takes time to get used to. Almost every other language has about half the precedence rules of Perl. (At least Perl doesn't have contradictory rules like natural languages!) So how do you learn and work with Perl's idiom set? Well, there are two things you can do:

1. Have the precedence table in front of you the whole time you are programming. Likewise, look at the **perlop** man page for more examples. This will get you used to the syntax in a hurry.

2. One of the best ways to learn is by imitation. You may also want to have the common Perl patterns in front of you, just to get the hang of Perl syntax.

Once you get the hang of it, Perl's complexity becomes a real blessing. You find solutions to problems that would take 10 times longer to write in other languages. You will have fun finding little nooks and crannies of the language, little inventive patterns that are both functional and somewhat surprising. (I've been programming in the language for nine years, and I still find these things!)

Anyway, you'll start to have fun. The next chapters deal with the heart of the language and use these common expressive patterns quite frequently.

5

Functions and Scope

Perl is very much like other computer languages in that it has larger units of measurement than the expression. In other words, you can build larger computer structures that can be used interchangeably in other programs. Perl supports *functions*, and collections of functions into *packages* or *libraries*. Perl also supports two types of *scope*, which is the segmentation of variables so that they are only visible to certain parts of the program.

Those of you who are already familiar with these concepts should keep in mind that, as with everything else in the language, Perl looks at functions and scope in a nontraditional way.

The purpose of this chapter is to provide the basic syntax, pitfalls, and principles behind effective use of functions and scope, as well as give several examples of their use inside actual code. Take a look at the **perlsub** and **perlmod** man pages for further information.

Chapter Overview

This chapter covers the first of two major ways Perl allows you to scale up your code: the combination of the function and the scope. The other way, dealing with packages, libraries, and classes, will be discussed in the next part of the book. This chapter is divided into three main sections.

First, we talk about functions and how they operate: the syntax of functions, how you pass and manipulate arguments to them, how you get values out of them, common subroutine errors (and tips to avoid them), recursion, `wantarray`, and more.

Next we talk about the other half of the puzzle: scope. *Scope* is the method used by computer languages so that variables don't "collide." Proper use of scoping methods means you need not worry about having 10 different variables named get in the same program. Perl has two different policies for scope, *lexical* and *dynamic*, and we will cover these in detail below. We consider their definitions in detail, and the places in your programs where each is used.

Finally, we will go over some examples: programming recursion in Perl, using references in subroutines (covered in more detail in Chapters 7 and 8), and finally using Perl itself to settle issues of scope.

Functions

Every computer language has functions, even the simplest of the simple. Perl is no exception.

A *function* returns a set of outputs given a certain set of inputs. Because functions are by nature repeatable and reusable, they are very handy in cutting down programming efforts. The code to perform certain tasks may be used in many different places in a program, but may have to be written only once.

Functions are often called *subroutines* because they do their work outside of the main line of program logic. Because they are out of the way, functions allow you to clarify the main logic flow of a program.

Perl has some special ways of working with functions. For example, Perl has no strict typing that forces you to write a function a certain way. There is no structure in Perl like the following C function:

```
int functionName(int argument1, string *argument2);
```

Perl does not require "types" or "named parameters" for the function. Instead, a Perl function often looks like:

```
sub functionName
{
    my ($argument1, $argument2) = @_;
    # ... do stuff.
    return($function).
}
```

In other words, the function is said to be *freely defined* or *free flowing*. As such, the return value for a function can be interpreted in many different ways depending on the context in which that function was written.

Perl also has *built-in* functions, which are functions that are compiled with the language. These are described in Chapter 12, "Built-in Functions and Variables in Perl."

Syntax

The general form of a Perl function is as follows:

```
sub subroutineName
{
  my (@argsToSubroutine) = @_;      # Not essential, shows
                                    # the way that arguments are passed to subroutines.

  doStuff();                         # Here, do subroutine. Can be a list of commands.

  return(@returnValues);            # Again, the return isn't
                                    # necessary.  You simply can, by default, return
                                    # the value of the last expression evaluated.

}
```

There are six ways to call a function:

```
$return = &subroutineName(@args_to_subroutine);    # Usage 1;
$return = subroutineName(@args_to_subroutine);     # Usage 2;
@return = subroutineName();                        # Usage 3;
@return = &subroutineName();                       # Usage 4;
@return = subroutineName;                           # Usage 5;
@return = subroutineName @args_to_subroutine;      # Usage 6;
```

Usages 2 and 3 should be preferred since they are the most explicit, yet the least cluttered.

The & or () here signifies a subroutine. Also, whatever can be put in a list can be put in a subroutine. Passing () is equivalent to passing a NULL set to the list. $return and @return are return values from the subroutine—you can return hashes via %return but it is not common practice. Figure 5.1 shows how the two items are related.

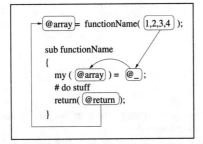

Figure 5.1
Relationship between Calling a Subroutine and Its Return Value

The arguments to the subroutine are passed into the subroutine by the incoming array @args_to_subroutine. These values are passed back to the left-hand side of the equation by the value in return(@returnVals);.

Let's take a closer look at these two elements: the argument stack and the return stack.

The Argument Stack

The *argument stack* is denoted by a special variable, @_, and is local to the subroutine being called. Arguments are put into @_ each time you call a subroutine. @_ works much like the stack in C and C++.

Since the argument stack is an array, there is no limit to the number of arguments that can be passed to a function, each argument being a scalar. Let's take a moment and play with this concept. If you start with a function that looks like:

```
sub subroutineName
{
    my (@args) = @_;
}
```

you could just as easily call this function with:

```
subroutineName(1);
```

or:

```
subroutineName(1,2,3,'alpha','bravo','charlie');
```

or:

```
subroutineName(@argumentsToArray);
```

or even:

```
subroutineName(%hashValue);
```

This last example is, technically, allowable although it may not be advisable (hashes go into subroutines with no idea of order). It may be useful if you want to use the hash in the subroutine, however. But even here, you may want to use a reference to a hash instead (see "References," Chapter 7, and the section "Passing Arguments by References," later in this chapter).

Hence, the length of the argument stack does not matter when calling a subroutine. Perl will dutifully make @_ whatever is passed to your subroutine, and it is up to the subroutine to decide whether or not an argument will be paid attention.

Now, the length of argument stack does matter within the subroutine. Let's start with the following function call:

```
$value = add(1,2,3);
```

add is defined as:

```
sub add
{
    my ($value1, $value2) = @_;
    return($value1 + $value2);
}
```

You are setting yourself up for a bug search here. add ignores the third element in the list. To add insult to injury, the function does *not* tell you that the third element is being ignored.

Remember, it is up to you to check the validity of the passed-in arguments—Perl will not do it for you.

The variable nature of Perl's argument stack can be used to your advantage. If you want a more robust subroutine, try the following:

```
1  sub add
2  {
3      my (@values) = @_;
4      my $return;
5      foreach $value (@values)
6      {
7          $return += $value;
8      }
9      return($return);
10 }
```

Here, you have not gotten rid of your bug, but have actually made the subroutine more powerful. By going through each argument and then adding it to $return (in lines 5–8), you have made a general-purpose addition function, one that can take several arguments, not just two.

There are a couple of points that you need to know about the argument stack, which are discussed next.

Manipulating the Argument Stack

There are several ways to manipulate the argument stack. First, since the @_ array is like any other array, you can access each element by subscript. Therefore, $_[1] gives the second element of the function (remember, the array subscript in Perl starts at zero).

Second, you can also access the @_ through the shift and pop functions, which have some magic attached to them when being converted to a subroutine (see the following code):

```
mySubroutine(1,2,3,4);

sub mySubroutine
{
    $firstArgument = shift;  # accesses the first element on the stack.
                            # $firstArgument becomes '1', @_ becomes (2,3,4).
    $secondArgument = shift;# accesses the second element on the stack.
                            # $secondArgument becomes '2', @_ becomes (3,4);
    $lastArgument = pop;    # accesses the last element on the stack. $lastArgument
                            # becomes '4', @_ becomes (3).
}
```

In all these examples, shift and pop are used with shorthand, and are equivalent to shift(@_) and pop(@_), respectively. Each time you call them, they take either the first argument (shift) or the last argument (pop) off the stack. Then they store the argument in the variable on the left-hand side, shortening @_ as you go. Following are some more examples of manipulating @_:

```
sub subroutine
{
    my (@array) = @_;       # Simple. @array becomes the argument list.
}

sub sub                     # No conflict here! Even though subroutine name is sub
{
    my $firstarg = shift;   # shift and pop automatically,
    my $secondarg = shift;  # access the @_array.
    my $lastarg = pop;      # $firstarg becomes the first argument,
                            # and @_ is shortened
    my (@restofargs) = @_;  # $lastarg becomes the last, and @_ is shortened

    my $return;
    $return = 'returnValue';# returns scalar returnValue to main return
}
```

Local @_ Stacks

Another important thing to remember about @_ is that it is *localized*. This means that if you call a function inside a function, you needn't worry about the first function impacting the second.

Therefore, you can do things like this:

```
a(1,2,3);
sub a
{
    b(1,2,3,4);
    print "@_\n";
}
```

Here, a's @_ becomes 1,2,3, and b's @_ becomes 1,2,3,4. Hence, you can use @_ without worry here. The example prints "1 2 3", as well as running b().

This flexibility allows you to perform *recursion* in Perl, in which a subroutine is defined in terms of itself. Recursion is very handy for parsing through text and listing permutations of strings. For example, the following subroutine will call itself 10 times, and then exit:

```
simple_recursion(0);
sub simple_recursion
{
    my ($number) = @_;
    return() if ($number > 10);
    simple_recursion($number + 1);
}
```

Perl keeps track of the 10 separate argument stacks that are necessary in order to complete this task, evaluating the above as:

```
simple_recursion(0)
     calls simple_recursion(1);
          calls simple_recursion(2);
             . . .
                 calls simple_recursion(11);
                      returns '' to simple_recursion(10);
                 returns '' to simple_recursion(9);
             . . .
     returns '' to subroutine;
```

which, as we shall see, lets you tackle complicated problems much more simply than otherwise possible.

Summary of the Argument Stack (@_)

In short, having only one mechanism (@_) for passing arguments to subroutines is incredibly powerful. This concept lets you:

- Make incredibly broad subroutines, which perform a general task, no matter how few or many arguments there are. The add function, for example, simply adds numbers—not two numbers, or three, or four, but as many numbers as are passed in.
- Make quick changes to subroutines, without having to formally declare those changes.
- Provide this functionality while still giving you the flexibility to use such advanced techniques as recursion.

The Return Stack

The argument stack is the main way of having Perl pass arguments to subroutines. (Aside from the sort built-in function sort, it is the only way.) Its opposite is the *return stack*, which is Perl's method of returning values to the calling subroutine.

As you may recall, the usual method of calling a subroutine is:

```
@values = subroutine($arguments);
```

In this situation, the return stack of the function subroutine is copied into the variable @values. And, like the argument stack, the return stack is also in array form.

There are two major ways for a subroutine to return values to the main (calling) routine:

1. By use of the special function return.

2. By default (i.e., looking at the last expression in the subroutine).

Let's look at both of these points in detail.

Return Keyword

The `return` keyword allows you to immediately cut short a subroutine, returning the values inside its argument stack to the subroutine. Hence, if you say something like:

```
sub dbroutine
{
    my (@argument) = @_;
    return(1);
    return(2);
}
```

the `return(2)` will never be called, since the `return(1)` has already returned the value 1 to the subroutine.

Suppose we write a simple routine to compare two dates. The dates are in the form "MM-DD-YYYY" or "MM/DD/YYYY." The function returns negative if the first date is earlier than the second, 0 if the first date is equal, and positive if the first date is greater than the second:

```
sub datecompare
{
    my ($date1, $date2) = @_;
    my ($month1, $day1, $year1) = split(m"[-/]", $date1);      # splits by - or / into
three elements
    my ($month2, $day2, $year2) = split(m"[-/]", $date2);      # does same for date2 -
see split
    return(-1) if ($year1 < $year2);
    return(-1) if (($month1 < $month2) && ($year1 == $year2));
    return(-1) if (($day1 < $day2) && ($month1 == $month2) && ($year1 == $year2));
    return(0) if (($year1 == $year2) && ($month1 == $month2) && ($day1 == $day2));
    return(1);
}
```

This translates into "first compare the year, then compare the month, then compare the day." If the first year is less than the second, we need go no further, and so on.

In short, each `return` immediately goes back to the place where the function was called, so that we need not evaluate any further. This simplifies the logic, and makes it possible for us to write a rather convoluted bunch of `if` conditions on several short lines, rather than "jamming" it together into a complicated `if`.

Now we could use our `datecompare` function as in:

```
if (datecompare("1996/11/30", "1995/12/11") < 0)
{
    print "1996/11/30 is less than 1995/12/11!\n";
}
```

to get a freeform comparison of dates. Let's extend this function to return the number of years, months, and days difference between two arbitrary dates (let's assume for simplicity's sake that there are 30 days to the month):

```
sub datediff
{
    my ($date1, $date2) = @_;
    my ($month1, $day1, $year1) = split(m"[-/]", $date1);
    my ($month2, $day2, $year2) = split(m"[-/]", $date2);
```

```
    my $days1 = 365 * $year1 + 30 * $month1 + $day1;
    my $days2 = 365 * $year2 + 30 * $month2 + $day2;
    my $daysdiff = $days2 - $days1;
    return(int($daysdiff/365), (int($daysdiff/30))%12, $daysdiff%30);
}
```

Here we calculate the number of days each date has, subtract them from each other, and then return the following:

- Number of years in element 0(int($daysdiff/365))
- Months in element 1 (between 0 and 11)
- Days in element 2 (between 0 and 29)

It is up to the place where datediff is called to assure that these three elements are used correctly.

Default Return

You might get tired of typing "return" all the time to indicate you are returning a value to the main program. Enough Perl programmers were tired enough for it to be decided that return was not a necessary thing, and could be ignored, or made implicit. Therefore, as a shorthand, you will see a lot of code doing the following:

```
sub subName
{
    my (@arguments) = @_;
    my $return;
    $return;
}
```

Here, the last statement in the subroutine is a scalar. You might also see:

```
sub subName
{
    my (@arguments) = @_;
    my @argsToReturn;
    @argsToReturn;
}
```

in which the last statement in the subroutine is an array. You might even see:

```
sub subName
{
    my (@arguments) = @_;
    my @argsToReturn;
    @argsToReturn = (1..10);
}
```

in which the last statement in the subroutine is actually an assignment. It assigns an array to the statement @argsToReturn, and then @argsToReturn is returned to the stack.

In each case, it is immaterial whether the last statement is a hash, array, or scalar. In the absence of a return, the last statement evaluated in an array is the return stack, or the value that is returned to the subroutine.

Using this logic, the following example is a simple way to return all the lines in a file, sorted alphabetically:

```
sub sortedLinesInFile
{
    my ($file) = @_;
    my $fh = new FileHandle("$file") || die "Couldn't open $file!\n";
    @lines = sort (<$fh>);
}
```

@lines contains the sorted lines from the file $file, which is passed in as an argument. Being the last statement in the subroutine, @lines automatically becomes the return stack. This subroutine could be called like so:

```
my @fileLines = sortedLinesInFile("my_file");
```

to get, after execution, all the sorted lines in the variable @fileLines.

Note that it does not matter whether or not the return stack is the last statement in the subroutine *positionally*. The return stack is the last statement *evaluated*. For example, if you have a subroutine that is one giant if clause, as in the following:

```
sub betweenLowerGreater
{
    my ($firstValue, $secondValue, $compare) = @_;
    if (($firstValue > $compare) && ($secondValue > $compare))
    {
        "less than";
    }
    elsif (($firstValue > $compare) && ($secondValue < $compare))
    {
        "in between";
    }
    elsif (($firstValue == $compare) || ($secondValue == $compare))
    {
        "equal";
    }
    else
    {
        "greater than";
    }
}
```

then this will do what you expect: namely, return whether or not the $compare element is between, greater than, less than, or equal to the two other elements, because the last statement evaluated is either the less than, in between, equal, or greater than.

wantarray

Let's suppose that we want to improve on the datecompare function we were working with earlier. Remember that there were two separate incarnations of it. The first returned a scalar that indicated whether or not the first date was earlier or later than the second:

```
$earlier_or_later = datecompare('1996/11/11', '1996/12/11');
```

The second incarnation of the routine returned the number of years, months, and days the two dates were separated by:

```
($years, $months, $days) = datediff ('1996/11/11','1996/12/11');
```

These are basically the same function. If we wanted to use datediff to implement datecompare, we could say:

```
my ($years, $months, $days) = datediff('1996/11/11','1996/12/11');
$earlier_or_later = ($years < 0 || $months < 0 ||  $days < 0)? -1 :
                    ($years ==0 && $months == 0 && $days == 0)? 0 :
                                                                1;
```

because we know that one date is earlier than another date if the years, months, or days are more negative than the other years, months, or days, and so on. However, we cannot do something like:

```
if (datediff('1996/11/11','1996/12/11') < 0)
{
    # do something
}
```

because `datediff` returns an array with years, months, and days difference, and not a scalar. It would be great to have a function do "double duty," able to return a scalar *and* an array.

The function `wantarray` is Perl's way to perform double duty. `wantarray` senses whether or not a function is being used in a context that requires an array, or one that requires a scalar. From that information, the function can decide what to return. For example, in the following code:

```
sub subName
{
    my (@arguments) = @_;
    wantarray() ? doSomething() : doSomethingElse();
}
```

if `wantarray` evaluates to true, a function has called it, such as:

```
@array = subroutine();
```

in which the subroutine is expecting an array. On the other hand, if `wantarray` evaluates to false, this means a function has called it, such as:

```
$scalar = subroutine();
```

This is represented in Figure 5.2.

Figure 5.2
wantarray
Contexts and
Usage

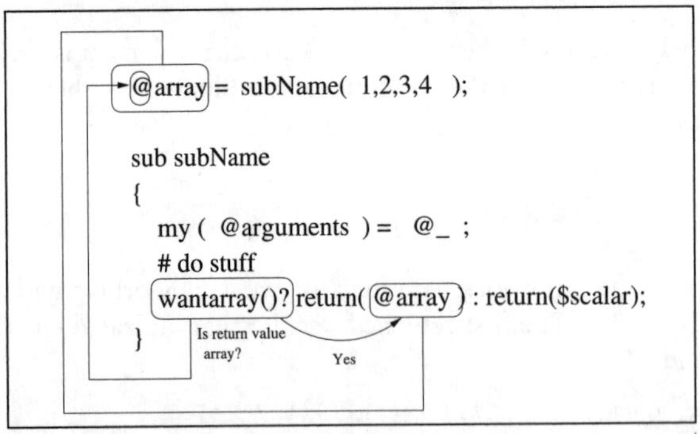

With our knowledge of `wantarray`, let's rewrite the `datediff` routine to handle returning a scalar or an array.

If called in scalar context, the return value will indicate whether the first date is less than the second. If the function is in array context, it will return an array containing the difference in years, months, and days.

```
sub datediff
{
    my ($date1, $date2) = @_;
    my ($month1, $day1, $year1) = split(m"[-/]", $date1);
    my ($month2, $day2, $year2) = split(m"[-/]", $date2);
    my $days1 = 365 * $year1 + 30 * $month1 + $day1;
```

```
        my $days2 = 365 * $year2 + 30 * $month2 + $day2;
        my $daysdiff = $days1 - $days2;
        wantarray()?
            return(int($daysdiff/365), (int($daysdiff/30))%12, $daysdiff%30) :
            return( $daysdiff cmp 0);
    }
```

Now, if we say something like:

```
    my ($years, $months, $days) = datediff("12/13/1966", "1/11/1985");
```

wantarray "senses" that we are calling `datediff` from a context that needs an array, and therefore evaluates as true and returns a three-element array. If, instead, we say:

```
    my $comparison = datediff("12/13/1966","1/11/1985");
```

this returns either -1, 0, or 1 depending on whether the first date is less than, equal to, or greater than the second.

Passing Multiple Arrays or Hashes to Functions

So far we have discussed passing scalars and arrays to a subroutine. You can also pass any other data structures that you choose to a subroutine. However, these arguments are passed in *list* context, so you must remember the cardinal rule of lists here: Lists are mangled into one giant list, losing any concept of location within the list. In other words, separate elements are joined into one long stream of data.

Here are some *bad* ideas for function calls. In these function calls, @argument1, @argument2, %argument1, and %argument2 all lose their identities inside the function itself. In other words:

```
    wrongFunction(@argument1, @argument2);      # bad idea!
    wrongFunction(%argument1, %argument2);      # bad idea again!
    wrongFunction(@argument1, $scalararg2);     # still bad!
```

If you do this type of thing, it will hurt you. There is only *one* array that is important here (from the point of view of the function), @_. This array contains both @argument1 and @argument2. This means that when you actually run the following function:

```
    sub wrongFunction
    {
      my (@argument1, @emptyargument) = @_;   # does not work @argument1 gets all the values,
    @emptyargument gets none.
    }
```

@argument1 is "greedy," and takes all the arguments passed into the function into itself, something like what is shown in Figure 5.3. There is no pointer that tells @_ "The @argument1 array ends here" or "The @argument2 array starts here." Therefore, @emptyargument gets nothing passed into it from the calling routine.

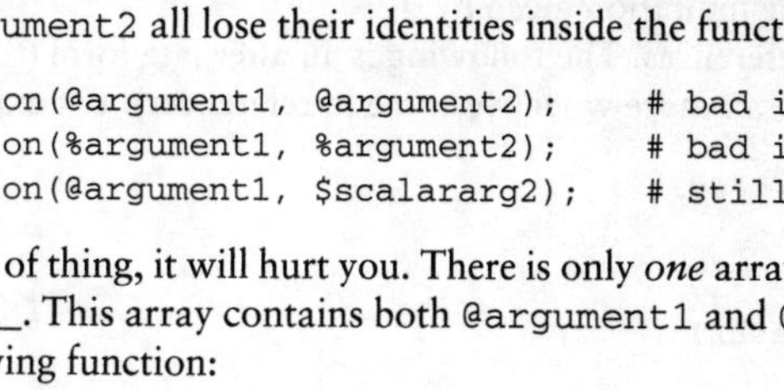

Figure 5.3
List Cramming

Likewise, hashes lose their concept of hash value-pair when passed by value, and they need to be "hashified" when they are copied out of the stack:

```
hashArgumentFunction (%hash)

sub hashArgumentFunction
{
   my (%argument1) = @_;     # '%hash' gets transmuted to @_  which
                             # becomes an array.  Array @_ gets copied back
                             # to hash %argument1!
}
```

This bottleneck made by having only one array (@_) for the argument stack causes three shortcomings in passing hashes or arrays when constructing subroutines:

1. There can only be one array or hash in a subroutine at given time.
2. If you want to name your arguments, you are forced to copy the data structure into the form you want (such as my (@arrayName) = @_;).
3. If you want to write back the incoming arguments to the function, you need to directly access the @_ variable itself.

All of these are a bit of a nuisance and a pain, especially point 1.

There are several cases in which you might want to pass more complicated structures around, such as when you wish to pass an object, or a reference to a "glob" of data that you get from a database. In these cases, you cannot pass multiple arrays or hashes because of the limitation given by @_.

To get around this, you will have to pass references. The following is an alternate form (that works) to pass two arrays to a function. (We will get to the syntax more when we come to references). For example:

```
referenceArrayFunction(\@array1, \@array2);
```

or two hashes:

```
referenceHashFunction(\%hash1, \%hash2);
```

or objects:

```
my $objectName = new Object();
reference($objectName);
```

You could, for example, access the arrays in referenceArrayFunction as follows:

```
sub referenceArrayFunction
{
    my ($array1, $array2) = @_;    # array functions.
    print "printing out array1 @$array1\n";
    print "printing out array2 @$array2\n";
}
```

where @$array1 *dereferences* the reference passed into the subroutine, to get back the actual values in the array. But this is just a taste of things to come. We will talk a lot about these concepts in Chapters 7 and 8.

Perl Function Caveats

As we have seen repeatedly, Perl has a looser interpretation of how functions are composed (and of functions in general) than do most other languages. There are no rules "set in stone" about the amount of arguments passed in, nor the amount returned, nor even the type of arguments or return values that a function should return. With this expressive freedom comes a cost that you should bear in mind. Proper contemplation of the following caveats could save you hours of debugging.

Caveat #1: Error Checking

Perl has the philosophy that the programmer should worry about matching up the arguments in the function call to the subroutine. This was hinted at earlier. If you have a function call that looks like:

```
sub mySub
{
    my ($argument1, $argument2) = @_;
}
```

and you then call this function in this manner:

```
mySub($argument1, $argument2, $argument3);
```

you may be surprised when argument3 drops off the edge of your subroutine into nothingness.

There are three ways to cope with this feature/bug:

1. Generalize the subroutine (make it broader).
2. Put error checking into the subroutine itself.
3. Use the -w flag to capture errors.

We shall take each of these in turn.

Generalizing Subroutines

Suppose that you have the following subroutine, which returns the size of a file you pass in, or returns zero if the file is a directory:

```
sub filesize
{
    my ($file) = @_;
    (-f $file) ? -s $file: 0;
}
```

This is a situation in which you are probably better off making this subroutine generalized, so that it takes an unlimited number of arguments and returns the combined size of all the files passed to it:

```
sub filesize
{
    my (@files) = @_;
    my ($file, $size);
    foreach $file (@files)
    {
        $size += (-f $file) ? -s $file : 0;
    }
    $size;
}
```

By making the function more generalized, there is no need to have an exact count of the arguments being passed in. The function can handle any number of arguments; you don't have to think about the interface and how many arguments it takes.

Putting Error Checking in Subroutines

Whether or not it makes sense to generalize the function, it does not hurt to put error checking in the subroutine, or perhaps even build in a usage for your subroutines, where the subroutine figures out how many values were passed into it. For example, you might want to put a check in the add subroutine, to make sure each of the arguments is a number:

```
1   sub add
2   {
3       my (@numbers) = @_;
4       my @nonNumbers;
5       if (@numbers) { print "Usage: add( @numbers )\n"; }
6       if (@nonNumbers = grep($_ == 0 && $_ ne '0', @numbers))
7       {
8           print "Warning! You passed the following non numbers to add! @nonNumbers\n";
9       }
10      foreach $number (@numbers) { $return += $number; }
11      $return;
12  }
```

Here, the usage statement is in line 5 where we tell the user of our function exactly how to call the subroutine. The meat of the error checking is in the statement (lines 6–10). Note that the grep statement in line 6 is simply a fancy way to determine whether or not a scalar is a number.

Note

More to the point, usage checks each element in @numbers to see if the element evaluates to zero. If it does, chances are good that it is a string (because strings evaluate to zero in an ==). Just to make sure, the function compares that scalar with the string zero. This works 99.9 percent of the time, but you can fool it by passing in, for example, the string 0.00.

You may want to consider always using -w, which will always warn you if something is a non-number. However, it is hard to force people to use the -w switch if they use your code. See -w below.

Another situation that calls for the use of error checking within a function is making sure that only two arguments are passed to a function. It doesn't make sense, after all, to pass three arguments to a datediff function.

```
sub datediff
{
    my ($date1, $date2) = @_;
    warn "You need to pass two arguments to datediff!\n" if (@_ != 2);
#   ...
}
```

This code manually checks the amount of arguments the user passes into the function. You can get pretty sophisticated with this warning technique. For example, you could make it so that a user, passing in a special flag, could get the usage of the subroutine:

```
sub datediff
{
    my ($date1, $date2) = @_;
    warn "Usage: datediff('MM/DD/YYYY','MM/DD/YYYY')\n"; if ($_[0] eq 'usage');
# rest of subroutine...
}
```

where if the user said datediff('usage'), it would print a special message on how the subroutine is used.

Using the -w flag

Let's take another look at the add function shown earlier, line by line:

```
1 sub add
2 {
3     my (@numbers) = @_;
4     my (@nonNumbers, $return, $number);
5     if (@nonNumbers = grep($_ == 0 && $_ ne '0', @numbers))
6     {
7         print "Warning! You passed the following non-numbers to add! @nonNumbers\n";
8     }
9     foreach $number (@numbers) { $return += $number; }
10    $return;
   }
```

Perl provides you with a bundled package of warnings (which we shall talk about extensively in this book) that are triggered if you run the script with -w. If you use -w in your program, you can take out lines 4–9, and instead let Perl do the warning for you:

```
1 #!/usr/local/bin/perl5 -w                    # -w flag for warning
2 add('apples', 'bananas');
3 sub add
4 {
5     my (@numbers) = @_;
6     foreach $number (@numbers) { $return += $number; }
7     $return;
8 }
prompt% perl -w add.p
Argument 'apples' isn't numeric at line2.
Argument 'bananas' isn't numeric at line2.
```

Here, if you put -w on the command-line with which you run Perl, or put it in the interpreter line #!/usr/local/bin/perl5 -w, or even set the variable $^W, Perl itself provide detailed warnings. This is quite important; in fact, we devote a whole chapter to items like this in Chapter 22, "Perl Debugging Tips."

The more checks you put in your code like this, the happier people who use your code will be. This user-friendliness makes all the difference in how much your code is utilized. Perl lends itself to adding this feedback.

More to the point, it is up to you to decide how much user-friendliness, warnings, and so forth to put in your code. The language doesn't enforce this; you do. This is a tenet we will see time and time again; it is a philosophy worth getting used to with Perl.

Caveat #2: Passing by Reference and Passing by Value

Another behavior you should be aware of is that Perl never actually makes a copy of the arguments it passes to a function. It never really uses "pass by value" in its functions. Instead, @_ is a synonym for the list that is passed into the function. This code:

```
$scalar1 = 5;
function($scalar1, $scalar2);
print "Scalar equals $scalar1\n";

sub function
  {
    $_[0] = 1;
  }
```

actually overrides $scalar1, and prints "Scalar equals 1."

Likewise, if you try to pass in a read-only element into a function:

```
&functionWithReadOnlyElements(3.1415925);

sub functionWithReadOnlyElements
{
  $_[0] = 0;                    # trying to modify what was passed in.
                                # Since it is a read-only value
                                # (3.1415925 is a number) this gives an error.

}
```

it gives the error:

```
'Modification of read-only value attempted at line <lineNo>'.
```

because you are trying to directly assign a constant to a number. This is akin to the statement:

```
3.1415925 = 0;
```

which, obviously, is absurd.

Summary of Caveats

Knowing these caveats can help save you hours of debugging effort:

1. You are responsible for doing error checking for subroutine calls; Perl will not help you. This gives you the freedom to do as much or as little verification as you want (sort of like going along with the Unix philosophy of giving yourself enough rope to hang yourself). However, if you make your subroutines fairly user-friendly, you will do yourself a great favor.

2. You would be wise to use -w in your subroutines. Such an error as the number of return values not equaling the number of values on the left-hand side of the equals statement will be caught:

   ```
   ($value1, $value2, $value3) = subroutine();
   ```

   where the subroutine is defined as:

   ```
   sub subroutine
   {
       return($value1, $value2);
   }
   ```

   This error is extremely difficult to find by yourself. $value3 simply becomes nothingness. Use -w to protect yourself from such bugs.

3. Perl never really passes by value. It passes by reference instead. Hence, if you change the @_ array, you change the values that you pass in.

4. In addition, be wary of the fact that you can pass only one array or one hash into a subroutine and hope to keep that array or hash's identity. If you pass more than one, Perl will flatten the two variables into one long list. Use references for more than one value.

Summary of Functions

All in all, you should remember the following three things about Perl's functions:

1. They are called with the following structure:

```
    <RETURN_STACK> = subroutine(<ARGUMENT_STACK>);
```

in which RETURN_STACK is either a scalar, array, or hash and represents the values coming out of the subroutine, and ARGUMENT_STACK is the list of values being passed into the subroutine.

2. The general form of a function:

```
    sub subroutine
    {
        my(<ARGUMENT_STACK>) = @_;
        # do stuff
        return(<RETURN_STACK>);
    }
```

where @_ is a special variable indicating the function's arguments, where ARGUMENT_STACK is an optional copy of the values coming into the subroutine, and where RETURN_STACK represents the values going back to the call.

3. You are responsible for providing all error checking (as much or as little as you like). Error checking takes many forms, but two of the most common error checking statements are accomplished by using use strict; and -w at the top of your program.

Perl's Scoping Methods

Scope is the policy of variable management. It is absolutely crucial to understand Perl scoping methodology if you want to make programs larger than 100 or so lines. This stems from another fact we mentioned earlier; global variables spring into existence in Perl (if they are not currently there). This is—as many things are in Perl—both a blessing and a curse. For example, consider the following simple subroutine:

```
    sub isZeroByte
    {
        ($file) =  @_;
        (-z $file) ? 1: 0;
    }
```

Is there anything wrong with this example? Yes, there is, and it will bite you quite strongly some day if you don't learn scoping rules. Remember, by just saying $file = @_;, you are creating the global variable $file, which is visible everywhere. If you say something like:

```
    $file = "otherFile";
    if (isZeroByte("thisFile"))
    {
        print "thisFile is zero bytes long!\n";
    }

    open(FD, "$file");
```

$file is silently overwritten in the subroutine isZeroByte. It is important to see here that the last open statement is not going to open otherFile. Instead, it is going to open thisFile, because it was silently changed by the call to isZeroByte.

There is a good chance you could spend hours tracking down why this is the case, because it has changed *silently*.

The purpose of this section is to prevent you from this agony (which I have gone through quite a few times). Imagine if you said to delete $file instead of opening it and deleted the wrong file!

There are three major methods you need to know to effectively deal with your programs and avoid "variable suicide" (in which you kill your variables by bad variable policy):

1. `my`
2. `local`
3. `"use strict"`

`local` and `my` are Perl's actual methods for scoping. `'use strict'` is a technique, a package you can use to have Perl actually police the proper use of variables by always declaring them.

Using `my` and `'use strict'` in your programs can make them nearly bulletproof to the variable suicide example shown earlier. `local`, on the other hand, is a holdover from Perl 4 later which is used in specific instances that we shall discuss. Ultimately, `local` should go away, leaving the more stable `my` in its place.

We will take a look at these three items in some detail. But first, let's deal with a simple issue in Perl: What exactly comprises a scope?

Scope Syntax

A *scope* is simply an area within which a variable is usable and visible. Fortunately, Perl's rules for scoping are fairly simple. It works on areas in the code called *blocks*. There are two types of blocks:

1. A special block called a *global block*, which is the entire Perl file.
2. Each { } in an `if (condition) { }`, `while { }`, `do { }`, and any other conditional loop defines a block. In fact, *any* use of brackets where you can insert code (i.e., any place beside brackets that make hashes) defines a block, and not just subroutine calls.

Blocks can be nested, or internal to other blocks, and generally are completely wrangle-able. (Within reason! If you try to define a subroutine in an `if` block, you aren't going to get what you want unless you really know what you are doing.) Figure 5.4 shows some common Perl-ish blocks. So what do blocks have to do with scoping? The special keywords, `my` and `local`, figure out where variables are to be visible. Let's look at each in turn.

Figure 5.4
Pictorial
Representation of
Perl-ish Blocks

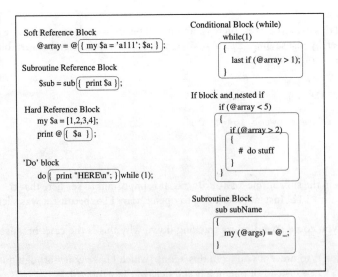

my and Lexical Scoping

The most common way to avoid globals is by the use of my. If you look back at the subroutines we created, you will notice that we made heavy use of it. We did this for a good reason: Every single time you say something like:

```
my ($variable);
```

Perl actually creates space for another, private variable called $variable, which is good until the block that it is in goes away. For example:

```
for ($xx = 0; $xx < 10; $xx++)
{
    my $data = 2;
}
print "$data\n";
```

prints nothing, because the block is the bracketed for loop, and here my $data = 2; indicates that a new copy of $data is created and destroyed every single time the for loop runs its course. You can see this in the following Perl script:

```
my $xx;
for ($xx = 0; $xx < 10; $xx++)
{
    my $data = 2 if ($xx == 0);
    print $data;
}
```

Here, the only time that 2 is printed is on the first loop (where the my is executed). All other times, it simply prints blank. This is because the my variable has been destroyed after the first for loop exits, and is now undefined.

my variables have *lexical scope*, which means they have the following two properties:

1. They are defined for the duration of the block that they are in.
2. They are not visible to subroutines (except, as we shall see, in the case where they are defined at a global level).

For example, if you say something like:

```
my ($xx, $yy) = (1,1);
if ($xx > 0)
{                                    # OUTER BLOCK
    my $variable = 'this is xx\'s';
    if ($yy > 0)                     # INNER BLOCK
    {
        print "$variable\n";         # print "this is xx's"
    }                                # INNER BLOCK
}                                    # OUTER BLOCK
print "This prints nothing! $variable\n";
```

Perl then prints this is xx's, since $variable is visible inside the inner block (marked as INNER BLOCK). Then, after the outer block, the routine prints This prints nothing:: since after the outer block, $variable has been destroyed.

In the following code:

```
if ($xx > 0)
{
    my $variable = 'this won\'t work!';
```

```
    function();
}
sub function()
{
    print "$variable\n";
}
```

$variable won't be printed because function(), even though the function is in block where $variable was defined, is inside a function call, and is therefore invisible to the subroutine.

So, given these rules, guess what happens when you say the following:

```
my ($xx, $yy) = (1,1);
if ($xx > 0)
{
    my $variable = 'this is xx\'s';
    if ($yy > 0)
    {
        my $variable = 'this is yy\'s';
        print "$variable\n";
    }
    print "$variable\n";
}
```

It actually prints :

```
this is xx's
this is yy's
```

Surprised? Even though you have defined $variable in the meantime as this is yy's, the two $variables are actually altogether *different*. They happen to have the same name, but they are in different blocks. This code snippet:

```
{
    my (@array) = (1,2);
    {
        my (@array) = (2,3);
        {
            my (@array) = (3,4);
        }
    }
}
```

defines three separate arrays, and then destroys them at the end of their respective blocks, even though the syntax is quite silly.

my Pseudo-Globals and Static Variables

There is a cool behavior you should be aware of with my. When a my variable is created at the global level (one that is at the same level as subroutine declarations), it is visible to all subroutine declarations at the same level.

These are sometimes called static variables, because the variables "stay around" for the duration of the program. In other words, if you say something like:

```
use FileHandle;
my $fh = new FileHandle("readFile");
myRead();
```

```
sub myRead
{
    print <$fh>;
}
```

then the variable `$fh`, due to being defined at 'file scope,' will be visible to the function myread, and the print statement will work as intended.

Although we have said before that my variables are not visible to subroutine calls, this works, because `$fh` is defined at the same level as the subroutine definition. This means that it prints out the entire file via `print <$fh>`, even though `$fh` was never passed into the function via a parameter. This behavior is a little alarming at first, but can be quite useful when creating static variables.

Static variables are variables that persist from function call to function call, but are not global. For example, the following function will keep a memory of what was added to it, returning a larger array every time it is called:

```
BEGIN
{
    my @staticVarb;
    sub addArray
    {
        my (@values) = @_;
        push(@staticVarb, @values);
    }

    sub getArray
    {
        @staticVarb;
    }
}
```

Now, if you call this like:

```
addArray(1,2,3,4);
addArray(5,6,7);
addArray(8,9,10);
print "@{[ getArray() ]}\n";
```

it prints out 1 2 3 4 5 6 7 8 9 10, because even though @staticVarb is a my variable, it is defined at the same level as the subroutine declarations addArray and getArray. This routine also shows a use of BEGIN, which basically tells Perl to "execute this code first, before anything else." (BEGIN is described in more detail in Chapter 11.)

my and foreach

Finally, there is a new form in Perl for my variables and looping, as of perl5.005. You can say something like:

```
foreach my $varb (@varbs)
{
    print $varb;
}
```

which implicitly makes $varb lexical and bound to the scope inside the foreach. It is equivalent to:

```
my $varb;
```

```
foreach $varb (@varbs)
{
    print $varb;
}
```

I usually don't use this form, since my scripts are not always running on perl5.005. Your mileage may vary.

my Caveats

As with all things in Perl, my has a couple of caveats you should be aware of. First of all, the following two statements are *not* equivalent:

```
my ($varb, $varb2);
my $varb, $varb2;
```

The first statement does what you would expect (i.e., defines two my variables). The second statement (my $varb, $varb2') translates into something like:

```
my $varb;
$varb2;
```

In other words, it makes the first variable $varb a my variable, and the second one $varb2 a global variable. This is quite a common "gotcha," and we shall see how to overcome it by use strict.

Second, notice that:

```
if ($condition1)
{
    my $variable = 'value1';
}
elsif ($condition2)
{
    my $variable = 'value2';
}
```

also doesn't work. You are creating the variable $variable, but it is also being destroyed right afterward! You probably want to say something like this instead:

```
my $variable;
if ($condition1)
{
    $variable = 'value1';
}
elsif ($condition2)
{
    $variable = 'value2';
}
```

in which you declare the my variable beforehand. One of the biggest caveats is that you cannot use my to localize special Perl variables. If you say:

```
sub localArgv
{
    my ($_) = "\n";
}
```

it will result in:

```
Can't use global $_ in 'my'
```

which should be fixed soon (it's on the "to do" list for the Perl folks).

Summary of *my*

my is Perl's special keyword for declaring a variable to be *lexically scoped,* which is really just a fancy term to say that it belongs to the block in which it was created. my variables exist for as long as the duration of the block in which they were created.

The main thing to remember about my variables is that they are not only visible to blocks "underneath" where they are declared, they are also visible to subroutines declared at the same level. Hence:

```
if ($condition) { my $a = 1; a(); }

sub a
{
    print $a;
}
```

does not work, whereas:

```
my $a = 1;
a();
sub a
{
    print $a;
}
```

works, primarily because it is defined at the same level as the subroutine. my is the main way to perform scoping.

`local` and Dynamic Scoping

local was the primary way Perl performed scoping before the addition of my in Perl 5. I only mention it here because there is one place where you still need to use local: with special variables such as $_, which we have seen briefly and shall talk about more later.

The following example does not acually create a new variable:

```
sub subRoutine
{
    local($") = "|";
}
```

Instead, it changes the value of the already existing global variable for the duration of the block that this subroutine is in. This is called *dynamic scoping,* which refers to the fact that the values of the global variable are dynamic (change) based on where local is called.

Based on this concept, the following code:

```
$hmm = "permanent variable!";
for ($xx = 0; $xx < 5; $xx++)
{
    local($hmm) = "temporary change";
    print "$hmm\n";
}
```

```
    print "$hmm\n";
```

prints:

```
temporary change
temporary change
temporary change
temporary change
temporary change
permanent variable!
```

Even though the global has been changed five times to temporary change in the for loop, it is actually a global variable in disguise. So far, this is the same as my variables. But the main effect of this is to have the local variable visible to underlying subroutines. The following code:

```
if ($a > $b)
{
    local($varb) = 1000;
    printvarb();
}
sub printvarb
{
    print "$varb\n";
}
```

prints 1000, because varb is still a global variable and is visible everywhere. It just temporarily changed the value for the purposes of the subroutine.

Again, you are going to want to use local only in cases when you need to use a Perl special variable in a subroutine. Hence:

```
sub getWholeFile
{
    my ($file) = @_;
    local($/) = undef;
    my $fh = new FileHandle("$file");
    $return = <$fh>;
    return($return);
}
```

slurps the entire file my_file into string $return, and then returns its value to the main subroutine. (See the section "Special Variables in Perl", Chapter 10 for more information on $/. It is the variable in Perl that controls how much is read from a filehandle by the <> operator. Setting it to undef makes it so <> reads in the entire file, \n makes it so <> reads in to the newline, etc.)

If we don't localize this variable, as sure as night follows day a situation will arise in which you are doing a bunch of file slurping. The following then happens:

```
$line = getWholeFile("my_file");              # doesn't localize $/... $/ is now
"undef"
my $fd = new FileHandle("my_other_file");
while (defined ($otherline = <fd>))
{
    # process each line by itself? No! you are processing the entire file in one chunk!
}
```

Without local($/) being set inside 'getWholeFile', there is a very subtle bug here. getWholeFile does get the entire file into the string $line, but as a side effect sets $/ to undef for the rest of the program. This means that when you are expecting one behavior from `<>` (to read to the next newline), you get another behavior instead (reading to the end of the file).

Hence, as of now, the primary use of local in Perl is to prevent this action at a distance. We really don't want to have this behavior 1,000 lines before we set '$/' to undef, and then find out later that one of our subroutines uses this changed value. Here are some other common examples of localizing special variables:

```
sub printoutPipeDelimitedLines
{
    my (@fields) = @_;
    local($") = "|";
    print "@fields\n";
}
```

$" controls what comes between elements when they are interpolated in "" (printoutPipeDelimited-Lines(1,2,3) prints "1|2|3").

These are the two most common cases for localizing special variables. For more information on special variables, go to section "Perl Special Variables" in Chapter 12, and the **perlvar** man page.

'use strict'

At this point you know pretty much all you need to know about effective scope management in Perl. You know how to avoid globals by the use of my and local. Now the question is how do you effectively follow these rules?

As said before, Perl has some caveats with my. Especially unbidden is the fact that when you say:

```
my $varb1, $varb2;
```

the my keyword takes only $varb1 to be a my variable, and ignores $varb2. Likewise, when you say:

```
if ($condition1)
{
    my $varb1 = "probably a mistake";
}
print $varb1;
```

it doesn't exactly work as planned, as $varb1 has been destroyed after the edge of the if. Hence, instead of printing probably a mistake, it prints nothing.

There is a way to avoid the use of globals—and effectively use my and local—without tracing through the preceding code for these mistakes (even when Perl is being obstinate), and that is to use the phrase 'use strict'. If you say:

```
use strict;
my $varb1, $varb2;
```

it prints:

```
'Global symbol "varb2" requires explicit package name at test.p line 2. Execution of
test.p aborted due to compilation errors.
```

indicating that you haven't actually used my and local effectively, and that there is a global variable lurking somewhere. In this case, it is the global $varb2, which you can correct by saying:

```
use strict;
my ($varb1, $varb2);
```

'use strict' is absolutely essential for any program larger than 100 lines. You will see it in abundance in this book.

Summary of Scoping Rules in Perl

There are four major things you need to know about scoping:

1. Scoping happens in terms of blocks, or is a logical piece of code.
2. Variables are defined with the my keyword. This makes a variable bound to a given block ('if ($condition) { my $a = 1; } binds $a to the if block). Variables inside the block get created by the my, and are then destroyed when the block ends.
3. 'use strict' and –w will save you hours of time when it comes to actually debugging programs. They enforce that all variables that you create are my variables.
4. local is used to localize special variables, such as $/ and $_, where you want to get a special behavior out of Perl operators (like having <> slurp in an entire file). See the section "Special Variables" in Chapter 10 for more information.

Examples of Subroutines

In this section we take what we have learned about scoping, and concentrate on form in the creation of subroutines. Let's take a look at examples of three types of subroutines:

1. Subroutines that use recursion
2. Subroutines that use references
3. Subroutines that use wantarray

With that in mind, here are five examples of subroutines.

Examples of Subroutines That Use Recursion

Recursion can be used to turn subroutines that would usually take 50 or more lines of code into an elegant 10 lines. Here are two examples of subroutines that use recursion to good effect.

The following example prints a directory tree. The routine, named find, is called:

```
simple_find("directory_name");
```

The subroutine looks like what is shown in Listing 5.1.

Listing 5.1
simple_find.p

```
 1 use strict;
 2
 3  sub simple_find
 4  {
 5      my ($input) = @_;
 6      my $file;
 7      print "$input\n" if (-f $input);
 8      if (-d $input && $input ne '.' && $input ne '..')    # ignore . and ..
 9      {                                                     # directories or infinite
10          opendir(FD, $input);                              # loop.
11          my @files = readdir(FD);
```

```
12              closedir(FD);
13              foreach $file (@files)
14              {
15                      simple_find("$input/$file");     # recursive call
16              }
17      }
18  }
```

This example works by looking at the input, printing the input if it is a file (and thereby stopping the recursion [line 5]), or opening the directory and recursively applying itself to each of its contents (lines 14–16).

Notice the heavy use of my here. We enforce its use via 'use strict' (line 1) and then proceed to make all the variables internal to the subroutine my variables. This isn't just good practice; it is necessary. If we didn't do this, the call to simple_find (line 15) would overwrite the @files variable and create a big mess.

Likewise, the following will give all the combinations of a string, returning an array of them. It works by "picking apart" the string, and then calling itself on the substrings. Following is the usage:

```
@combos = combinations("string")
```

The subroutine is shown in Listing 5.2.

Listing 5.2
combinations.p

```
1  sub combinations
2  {
3      my ($string) = @_;
4
5      my %return;
6      return($string) if (length($string) == 1);
7      my (@letters) = split(//, $string);
8
9      my ($xx);
10     for ($xx = 0; $xx < length($string); $xx++)
11     {
12         @letters[0,$xx] = @letters[$xx, 0];
13         my ($first_letter, $sub_string) =
14                     ($letters[0], join('', @letters[1..(length($string)-1)]));
15
16         my @permute_array = combinations($sub_string);
17         grep($return{$first_letter . $_} = 1, @permute_array);
18     }
19     return(keys %return);
20 }
```

This is a bit difficult to envision. *Note*: In line 12, we swap each of the characters for the first one; in line 16, we do the actual recursive call; and in line 17, we "mark" the fact that we have seen certain combinations of strings (using a hash). Pictorially, it kind of looks like Figure 5.5. This figure doesn't do the combination function true justice. In particular, line 6 (return ($string) if (length($string) eq '1';) prevents us from recursing indefinitely; if we had forgotten *one* my variable, this function would not have worked. The my again makes it so each of the variables @permute_array, %return, $xx is associated with only one combination function. If we had not done this, then as the combination function was called recursively, the variables would have collided values.

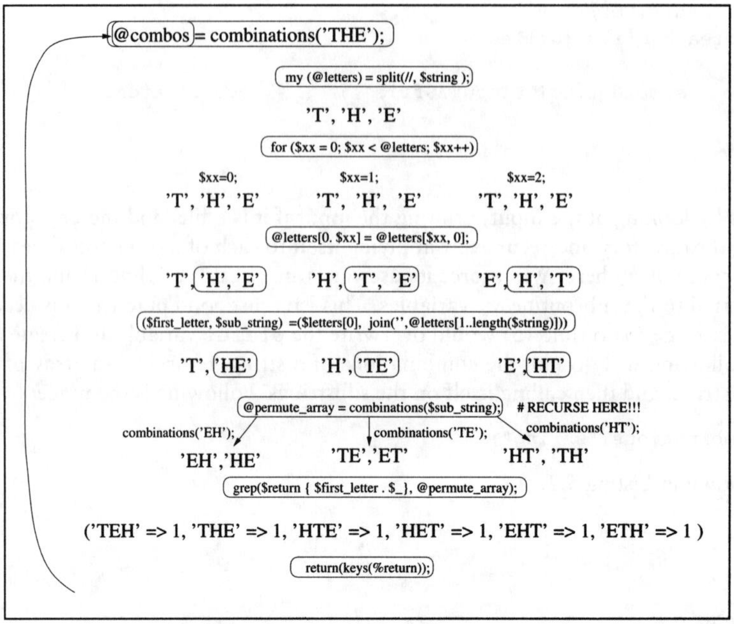

Figure 5.5
The
combination
Function, and
How It Works

The combinations of the larger string are defined in terms of combinations of each of the smaller strings. These two functions are simple examples of the expressive power you get by using recursion. Once you get in the habit of looking at certain operations as recursive, you can form very elegant solutions, especially in Perl.

Examples of Subroutines That Use References

Although we haven't talked about them yet in detail, *references* will be your primary way to deal with complicated data structures. Hence, the following example shows a couple of things you can do with references when you pass them into functions. The following merges two hashes into one return hash:

```
my %hash = hashMerge(\%hash1, \%hash2);
```

The subroutine itself looks like Listing 5.3.

Listing 5.3
hashMerge.p

```
1   use strict;
2
3   sub hashMerge
4   {
5       my ($hashref1, $hashref2) = @_;
6       my ($key, %return) = ('', ());          # () is an empty hash.
7       foreach $key (keys %$hashref1)
8       {
9           $return{$key} = $hashref1->{$key};  # $hashref->{$key} gets $key for
10      }                                       # a hash reference.
11      foreach $key (keys %$hashref2)
```

```
12      {
13          $return{$key} = $hashref2->{$key};
14      }
15      return(%return);
16  }
```

This works by first stuffing %return with the hash pointed to by %$hashref1, and then stuffing %return with %$hashref2. Because no error checking is made here, the second call may overwrite the values of the first call. For example, if called with arguments like:

```
%hash1 = (1 => 2);
%hash2 = (1 => 4);
my %return = hashMerge(\%hash1, \%hash2);
```

then return will become (1 => 4) because the second hash is overwriting the first.

The following switches the values of two arrays. It is called like this:

```
switchArrays(\@argument1, \@argument2);
```

It corresponds to the subroutine shown in Listing 5.4.

Listing 5.4
switchArrays.p

```
1  use strict;
2  sub switchArrays
3  {
4      my ($argument1, $argument2) = @_;      # Array References.
5      my @tmp;
6      @tmp = @$argument1;
7      @$argument1 = @$argument2;
8      @$argument2 = @tmp;
9  }
```

This works because lines 7 and 8 "reach in" to the reference and set the value that the reference points to, sort of like what is shown in Figure 5.6.

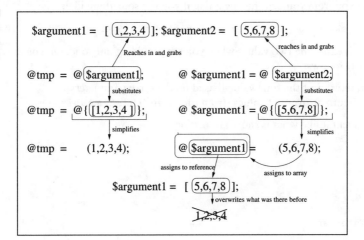

Figure 5.6
Simple Reference
Manipulation

We will have much more to say about references later. You can get a lot more complicated than this, having references to references, references to references to references, and so on. See Chapter 9 for more detail, or be patient; we will get there soon.

Subroutine `wantarray` Examples

Let's see more examples where `wantarray` may be useful. Consider a subroutine in which it makes no sense to call a subroutine in array context. Say you are computing compound interest, based on an amount, a percentage, and a number of time units, as in Listing 5.5.

Listing 5.5
compoundInterest.p

```
 1  use Carp;
 2 use strict;
 3
 4  my $origAmount = 100.00;
 5  my $percent = .05;
 6  my $timeUnits = 60;
 7  my $amount = compoundInterest($origAmount, $percent, $timeUnits);
 8
 9  sub compoundInterest
10 {
11      my ($origAmount, $percent, $timeUnits) = @_;
12
13      carp "You need to use this function in scalar context!\n" if (wantarray());
14      my $xx;
15      for ($xx = 0; $xx < $timeUnits; $xx++)
16      {
17          $origAmount += $origAmount*$percent;
18          $origAmount = sprintf("%.2f", $origAmount);   # rounds to
19      }                                                  # two decimal places
20      $origAmount;
21  }
```

Here, line 13 will protect you from yourself, raising a flag if you say something like:

```
my ($value1, $value2) = compoundInterest($origAmount, $percent, $timeUnits);
```

because the left-hand side is expecting two values when you are providing only one. Or, you may decide that you want to have two usages as follows:

1. In scalar context, return just the final value (based on the three parameters).
2. In array context, return an array of values (from time units 0 to `$timeUnits`).

You might want to implement it like what is shown in Listing 5.6.

Listing 5.6
compoundInterest2.p

```
 1  use strict;
 2
 3  sub compoundInterest
 4  {
```

```
5       my ($origAmount, $percent, $timeUnits) = @_;
6
7       my ($xx, @arrayOfAmounts, $newAmount);
8       for ($xx = 0; $xx < $timeUnits; $xx++)
9       {
10          $origAmount += $newAmount if (defined($newAmount));
10          push(@arrayOfAmounts, $origAmount);
11          $newAmount += $newAmount*$percent;
12          $newAmount = sprintf("%.2f", $newAmount);
13      }
14      wantarray()? @arrayOfAmounts: $origAmount;
15  }
```

If you use this function like:

```
foreach $value (compoundInterest(100,.05, 10))
{
    print "\$$value ";
}
```

it prints out a list of 10 values, something like:

```
$100 $105 $110.25 $115.76 $121.55 $127.63 $134.01 $140.71 $147.75 $155.14
```

whereas if you call it like:

```
$value = compoundInterest(100, .05, 10); print "\$$value\n";
```

you get only the last value ($155.14).

Scope Examples

Finally, let's consider a couple of extended scope examples. Simply look at it as several examples crammed together.

In the first example, we denote the value of each variable at any given time, next to the variable itself, along with the type of variable it is. Hence:

```
print $my_variable1;    # undef;
```

indicates that $my_variable1 is not visible at the scope specified. Let's look first at the effect of scope on visibility in subroutines as in Listing 5.7.

Listing 5.7
scopeExample.p

```
1   $global = 'global';
2   my $my_at_global_block = 'my at global block';
3   if (1 > 0)
4   {
5       my $my_in_if_block = 'my in if block';
6       local $local_in_if_block = 'local in if block';
7       beginSub()
8   }
9
10  BEGIN
11  {
```

```
12    my $my_in_begin_block = 'my in begin block';
13    local($local_in_begin_block) = 'local in begin block';
14    sub beginSub
15    {
16        print $global;              # 'global';
17        print $my_at_global_block   # 'my at global block'
18        print $my_in_begin_block;   # 'my in begin block'
19        print $local_in_begin_block; # undef
20        print $my_in_if_block;      # undef
21        print $local_in_if_block    # ;local in if block'
22    }
23  }
```

Here the subroutine `beginSub` shows how each of the different variables prints out:

1. `$global` (line 16) prints 'global' because it is a global.
2. `$my_at_global_block` (line 17) prints 'my at global block' because the `sub beginSub { }` declaration is defined in a sub-block of the global file.
3. `$my_in_begin_block` (line 18) prints 'my in begin block' because the declaration of `sub beginSub` is defined inside the `BEGIN` block where the variable is declared, and because `beginSub` holds a reference to it.
4. `$local_in_begin_block` (line 19) does *not* print anything because the `BEGIN` block has gone away by the time `beginSub()` was called, and there is no such thing as references to a local variable.
5. `$my_in_if_block` (line 20) does *not* print anything because the subroutine `beginSub()` is not defined in the `if` block itself, like `'if () { my $a; sub beginSub { print $a }}`.
6. `$local_in_if_block` (line 21) does print 'local init block' because it is actually a global in disguise (a copy of a global) and globals are seen everywhere.

Now let's look at what happens when we start making variables with the same names as in Listing 5.8.

Listing 5.8
scopeExample2.p

```
24 while ($xx++ < 1)
25 {
26    my $my_in_while_block = 'while1';
27    local($local_in_while_block) = 'while1';
28    local($global) = 'while1';
29    while ($yy++ < 1)
30    {
31        my $my_in_while_block = 'while2';
32        print $my_in_while_block;   # 'while2'
33        print $global;              # 'while1' not 'global'
34        print $local_in_while_block # 'while1'
35    }
36    print $my_in_while_block;       # 'while1'
37 }
38 print $global;                     # 'global';
```

Here, in turn:

1. In line 32, the `$my_in_while_block` prints `while2`, because it was defined in line 31, and this "covers" the previous definition in line 26.

2. In line 33, the `$global` prints while1, not global, because the local definition in line 28 covers the previous global definition.
3. In line 34, the `$local_in_while_block` prints while1, because it was defined in line 27, and locals are seen everywhere.
4. In line 36, the `$my_in_while_block` prints while1 because the previous definition in line 32 goes out of scope.

Summary

The most important things to remember from this chapter are:

1. Subroutines have the following form:

```
sub subName
{
        my (@arguments) = @_;
        return($return_value);    # or @return_value
}
```

2. Subroutines are called by:

```
my $value = subName(@arguments);
```

3. Perl defines a bunch of related code as blocks which are delineated by a { }.
4. The keyword my makes variables nonglobal (in what is termed lexical scope). my variables cannot be seen in subroutine calls, but can be seen in blocks that are "below" (inside) the block where the my variable was defined.
5. `'use strict'` and -w are crucial in warding off typical bugs and typical errors. If you don't use them, code at your own peril.

In the next chapter, we will go into more detail about an important issue that was raised here with wantarray. We shall talk about contexts and what they mean to Perl. Contexts basically account for 80 percent of Perl's functionality (and headaches, of course), so if you are just starting with Perl, you will definitely want to pay close attention.

6

Contexts in Perl 5

This chapter covers an important concept that sets Perl apart from most computer languages: contexts.

Contexts are Perl's way of making the language seem more natural and less computer-like. With contexts, variables can mean different things, depending on where they are put in an expression. This helps the language "flow" because you capture your thoughts in Perl-ish "sentences." In other words, sometimes I get the feeling that I am "speaking" Perl and not programming in it, because it feels like a natural language to me. (But then again, I probably need to get out more.)

As usual, the on-line documentation is extremely helpful and detailed. Once you have mastered the basic concepts in this chapter, the relevant man page is **perldata**, which deals with contexts.

To use the power of Perl, it is essential that you understand contexts.

Chapter Overview

The richness of Perl's contexts are a feature pretty much unique to Perl. Most other computer languages don't make the emphasis on contexts that Perl does, so we will go into them in great detail. This chapter is divided into three sections that try to make the process of learning contexts as painless as possible.

First, we will go over the definition and simple examples of scalar contexts. *Scalar contexts* are places in which scalars, arrays, or hashes are converted to a scalar; they account for about 80 percent of your code. We talk about the basic process of this conversion, as well as the "gotchas" when dealing with scalar contexts.

Next, we will cover list contexts, and how list contexts are affected if the list is an array as opposed to a literal list (i.e., in a '()'). *List contexts* are places where your datatypes (scalars, arrays, or hashes) are converted internally into a list; we talk about slicing, and the possibility of your arrays getting truncated in a nasty side effect of list contexts called *void contexts*.

Third, we will look at what might be called *context patterns*, which are ways that you can recognize if a Perl statement is in scalar or list context.

Finally, we will look at putting together all the building blocks to make Perl do some pretty cool things; we will talk about using the power in Perl's contexts to put into one line the functionality of what other statements require you to do in twenty.

Introduction to Data Context

Much of the confusion of programming in Perl comes from people using contexts incorrectly, although this is not overt: They simply don't realize that this is the mistake they are making. The point of this section is to get familiar with the concept of *context*, see why it is important, and then drive home how to make sure you are using contexts correctly. In other words, the most important rule you learn from this section should be:

Make sure you are using the variable in the context you meant it to be used in.

So, what is a context? A place to start to understand context is to think about natural languages. Certain words in natural languages are used in totally different ways, depending on the *context* in which the word appears. The word *set*, for example, has the most definitions by far of any word in the English language. (Well, at least according to the *Guinness Book of World Records*. If you take that for the gospel of truth, then you'll agree. At any rate, it has many definitions.)

Set means four different things in the following sentences:

1.   He *set* the book down on the table.
2.   After the point, it was game, *set*, and match.
3.   The agenda was *set* when the VP came by.
4.   She became *set* in her ways.

In computer terms, data contexts are simply clues to the interpreter on how to interpret a given dataset (rather than a word) in a given place. In other words, Perl parses each expression, and decides then and there what the meaning of each variable is going to be, or how it is going to be interpreted. This means you can say:

*   @arrayName = $scalarName;
*   @arrayName = @arrayName2;
*   @arrayName = %hashName

and have all of the above be syntactically legal. However, these statements mean quite different things. Note the different symbols again: @ for arrays, % for hashes, and $ for scalars. These symbols are important; if you are off by a symbol, you are saying something completely different to the interpreter than what you may have intended.

What these Perl sentences mean is based on the relationships between the variables on the right- and left-hand sides of the expressions. Again, this is much like a natural language, only with a lot less gray area.

Unlike natural languages, there are definite rules to determine what means what in each context. We cover the rules later in the chapter.

The two basic contexts in Perl 5 are:

*   Scalar
*   List

In addition, there is a special case where the 'list' in 'list context' is a variable, either an array or a hash. (For functionality's sake, Perl behaves a little differently when variables are involved.)

Anyway, it will pay to look closely at the following sections. A thorough understanding of contexts will greatly strengthen your Perl 5 programs.

Scalar Contexts

Scalar contexts are expressions in which Perl datatypes are interpreted as a *scalar*. Following are some simple examples:

```
$scalarName = "This is a scalar"
$scalarName = "@arrayName";
$scalarName = @arrayName;
```

This can be seen in Figure 6.1. Here, the equal sign is being used to figure out the context of the right-hand side by looking at the left-hand side of the equal sign. In other words, the equal sign "gauges" what the right-hand side is supposed to be; in the preceding examples, both sides of the equation are interpreted as scalars. Note in the third example that an array (or a hash—not shown here) can also be interpreted as a scalar in the correct context.

Figure 6.1
Captioned Scalar
Contexts in Perl

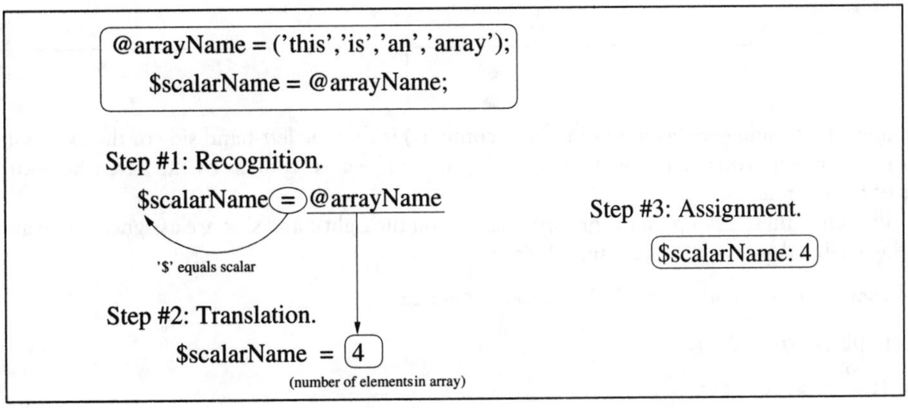

Therefore, a variable on the right-hand side (in this case `@arrayName`) does not determine the context. The left-hand side is the determining factor. `$scalarName =` says to Perl, "I am assigning to a scalar." Therefore, whatever is on the right-hand side (i.e., `@arrayName`) should be interpreted as a scalar. In this case, `$scalarName` is assigned the number of elements in `@arrayName`.

List Contexts

List contexts are places in which a Perl dataset is interpreted as a list. Again, lists are groups of scalars with a distinct order, so you can look them up by their position in the list. Here are some simple examples of list contexts:

```
($scalar1, $scalar2) = (@array1);
($scalar1, $scalar2) = ($scalar2, $scalar1);
($scalar1, @array1) = (@array1, $scalar1);
```

We have already seen some list contexts in the form of subroutine calls:

```
@returnStack = subroutine();
```

in which the subroutine returns an array to the @returnStack on the left-hand side of the expression. All these are represented in Figure 6.2.

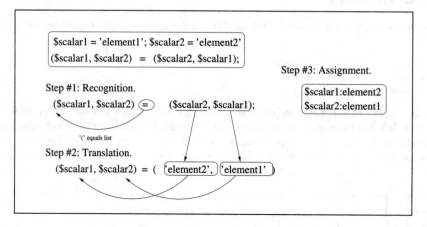

Figure 6.2
List Contexts
in Perl

The important thing here (as it was in scalar contexts) is that the left-hand side of the expression determines that it is a list context. You can tell an expression is going to be a list context by the parentheses around the left-hand side of the expression.

In each of these examples, the group of scalars on the right-hand side are assigned—one at a time—the scalars on the left-hand side of the equal sign. Hence:

```
($scalar1, $scalar2) = ($scalar2, $scalar1);
```

is a simple shorthand for:

```
$tmp = $scalar1;
$scalar1 = $scalar2;
$scalar2 = $tmp;
```

The differences between them are that you don't need a temporary variable, and it takes one line to write instead of three.

List contexts are special in the sense that they munge, or collapse, all their elements into a big, long list before doing assignments. Therefore, if you say something like:

```
(@array1, @array2) = (@array2, @array1);
```

it looks something like what is shown in Figure 6.3. We have already seen this when discussing functions: @array1 here gets all of the elements in @array2 concatenated with the elements in @array1. @array2 gets nothing! @array1 has been "greedy," and eaten up all the arguments on the left-hand side of the equation.

You can usually tell if something is in list context by the parentheses around it. Another thing you should be aware of with list contexts is that balance of the number of elements is important. If you say something such as:

```
($scalar1, $scalar2) = ($scalar2, $scalar1, $scalar3);
```

Figure 6.3
List Assignment in
List Context.
A Caveat

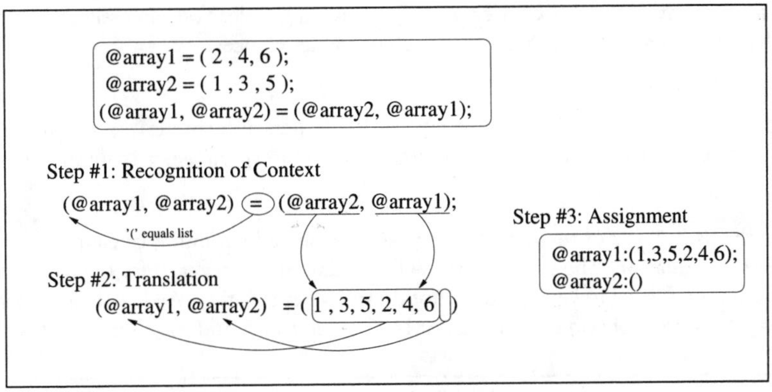

```
@array1 = ( 2 , 4, 6 );
@array2 = ( 1 , 3 , 5 );
(@array1, @array2) = (@array2, @array1);
```

Step #1: Recognition of Context

(@array1, @array2) = (@array2, @array1);

'(' equals list

Step #3: Assignment

```
@array1:(1,3,5,2,4,6);
@array2:()
```

Step #2: Translation

(@array1, @array2) = (1 , 3, 5, 2, 4, 6)

then `$scalar3` is dangling off the end and, therefore, gets assigned to nothing. This logic can be very difficult to track down and may not be what you intended. The `-w` flag, discussed earlier, can help, but it will not always catch these types of errors.

List Contexts with Arrays

As stated, Perl handles list contexts a little differently when arrays are involved. Internally, Perl turns all arrays into lists, and then does assignments. However, when you say something like ($a,$b) = ($a,$b,$c), $c "falls off the edge" because the left-hand side has a *fixed number of elements*. This makes no sense, however, with arrays because Perl *grows* its arrays on demand. Therefore, all of the following work as intended:

```
@arrayName1 = @arrayName2;
%hashName1 = %hashname2;
@arrayName = (1,2,3);
```

This looks like what you see in Figure 6.4. In the first example, we copy `@arrayName2` into `@arrayName1`. In the second, we copy `%hashName2` into `%hashName1`. In the third example, we assign the array `@arrayName` to a list (1,2,3). These examples show that you can have an array on one side of the equal sign, and a list on the other, and the assignment works fine.

Figure 6.4
Contexts with
Arrays Action

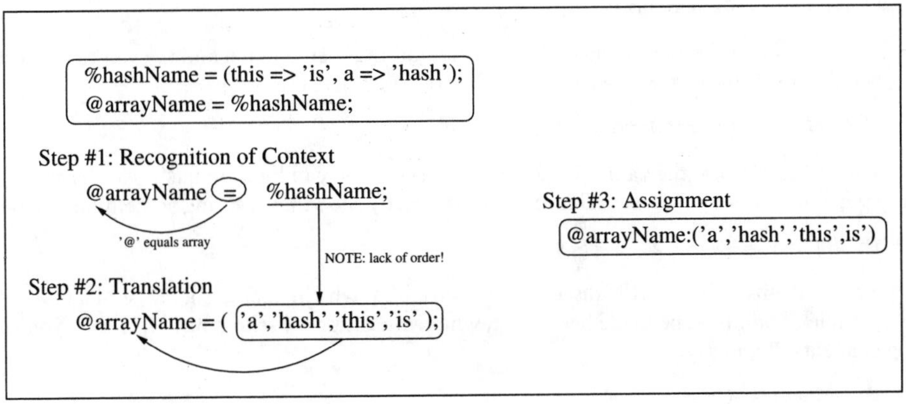

```
%hashName = (this => 'is', a => 'hash');
@arrayName = %hashName;
```

Step #1: Recognition of Context

@arrayName = %hashName;

'@' equals array

NOTE: lack of order!

Step #3: Assignment

@arrayName:('a','hash','this',is')

Step #2: Translation

@arrayName = ('a','hash','this','is');

In other words, array and list contexts are basically interchangeable. You can assign an array to a list, and vice versa. However, list and scalar contexts are *not* interchangeable. Hence:

```
$scalarName = @arrayName;
```

has meaning, because @arrayName is an array, and this gets interpreted as the number of elements in @arrayName. $scalarName = forces @arrayName to be interpreted as a scalar. However:

```
$scalarName = ('list', '2');
```

is not OK. Again, this is because of the need for the list to balance its number of elements with the elements on the left-hand side of the equation. The second form will lose data if you try it, since the list ('list', '2') needs to be forced into scalar context. However, it does not do so by being interpreted as the number of elements in the list (i.e., as @arrayName did). Because it is a list, it is trimmed to fit, and the element list is dropped.

Note

This is not quite true, but it is a helpful distinction. If you say something like:

```
($a, $b) = (1,2,exit());
```

what do you think will happen? The exit won't drop off, but will instead be evaluated, and your program will end. In other words, you can use commas as a way to separate arguments, in much the same way as a ; separates statements. Hence:

```
($arg1, $arg2, $arg3) = (shift(@array), shift(@array), shift(@array));
```

shifts off arguments one, two, and three from the array @array, and assigns them to $arg1, $arg2, $arg3, much like the following code does:

```
($arg1,$arg2,$arg3) = splice(@array,0,3);
```

What About Hashes?

It is important to note that hashes are handled slightly different from arrays, in list context. When there is a hash on the assignment side of the equal sign, it denotes a list context in disguise. The interpreter converts them from hashes into arrays. If you say something like:

```
%hashName = @arrayName;
```

you are actually making a hash where the keys are odd-numbered pairs, and the values to those keys are the even-numbered pairs. If @arrayName equals the list (1,2,3,4), then:

```
%hashName = @arrayName;
```

will make %hashName the value (1=>2, 3=>4). Hence, you can look on hashes as denoting a special type of an array when it comes to contexts. This example is exactly the same as doing something like the following:

```
%hashName = (1 => 2, 3 => 4);
```

You may recognize this from the discussion on variables, which, again, is a usage of a context in disguise. There are a couple of points to be made here. First, when you assign a list to a hash like this, you run the risk of dropping elements. If you say:

```
%hashName = (1=>2, 3=>4, 5);
```

the 5 will be dropped, along with giving the mandatory "severe warning":

```
Odd number of elements in hash list
```

Hashes need key-value pairs to work.

Second, the key-value nature of hashes is why we have been using the =>. => is really a spruced-up comma.

```
%hashName = ( 1,2,3,4 );
```

and:

```
%hashName = ( 1 => 2, 3 => 4)
```

are identical. It is just that the second one makes it easier to read. In fact, there is a pair of elements here, and the => has some special properties (if you use it, you don't have to put quotes around strings on the left side of the =>). The following code:

```
%hashName = ( this => 'is', a => 'hash');
```

is legal syntax.

Third, if you assign a hash to an array, going the opposite way, you will lose order in the hash. If you say something like:

```
@array = %hash;
```

the key-value pairs of the hash will be put into the array. And again, since you don't know which elements in a hash are first, the array will come out in semi-random order. Hence:

```
@array = %hash;
($key, $value) = (pop(@array), pop(@array));
%hash = @array;
```

is an inefficient way of removing a random hash element, and returning it to $key, $value.

Finally, if you put a hash in a scalar context, the hash returns an idea of how many key-value pairs are inside the hash. Hence, if you say:

```
$usage = %hash;
```

where:

```
%hash = (hash => 'name');
```

this returns:

```
1/8
```

This gives you an idea of how big the hash is. (It indicates that there are eight "buckets"—places to put keys—in the hash, and only one of the buckets is filled.) This gives you an idea of how fast the hash access is because the closer the number on the left is to the number on the right, the more efficient the hash is.

Slicing

There is another thing you should be aware of with list contexts: slicing. *Slicing* is a way for assignments to be given into part of an array or hash, without affecting the whole thing. If you say something like:

```
@array[1,2,3] = @array[3,1,2];
```

you are in effect saying:

```
@tmparray = @array;
$array[1] = $tmparray[3];
$array[2] = $tmparray[1];
$array[3] = $tmparray[2];
```

but you are doing it all at once. This means that you need not make any temporary variables. (The preceding code, as stated, would simply make @array's elements 1, 2, and 3 all $array[3].)

This syntax works for hashes, too. Hence,

```
@keys = (1,2,4);
@hash{@keys} = @hash{reverse(@keys)};
```

will do the same as the following:

```
%tmphash = %hash;
$hash{1} = $tmphash{4};
$hash{2} = $tmphash{2};
$hash{4} = $tmphash{1};
```

only, again, you don't need any temporary variables. The one thing to remember about slicing is that the following is not desirable:

```
$hash{@keys} = $hash{reverse(@keys)};
```

which, because of the $ in $hash, Perl interprets in scalar context and, therefore, evaluates as:

```
$hash{3} = $hash{3};
```

because the number of elements in @keys is 3.

Ways to Determine Context

One of the easiest ways to determine context is if there is an assignment involved. The rule is simple: If the variable on the left-hand side has a $, then the Perl sentence is in scalar context. If the left-hand side is a list, then the Perl sentence is in list context. If the variable on the left-hand side is an @ or %, then the Perl sentence is in list context.

We have seen several examples of conversions between assignments. But what happens if you don't have an assignment?

Fortunately, there is a clear set of simple rules to determine which context a given variable is in. These determinations are:

- By built-in function
- By operator
- By location

The following sections demonstrate the rules for determining context.

Using Built-in Functions to Determine Datatype

Perl has many handy, built-in functions, like print and time, which provide common functionality. We cover these in the chapter "Perl Built-in Functions."

   Certain built-in functions always require lists. Therefore, a variable given to that function will always be
in list context. Likewise, certain built-in functions always require scalars. Therefore, a variable given to them
will always be in scalar context. A simple example of a built-in function that forces a certain context is the
scalar function.

   As you might expect, the scalar function forces any variable you give it into scalar context. The following:

```
scalar(@value)
```

will interpret value as a scalar. So if you say something like:

```
@arrayName = scalar(@arrayName);
```

@arrayName becomes a one-element array, something like what is occurring in Figure 6.5.

Figure 6.5
Built-in Functions
and Context

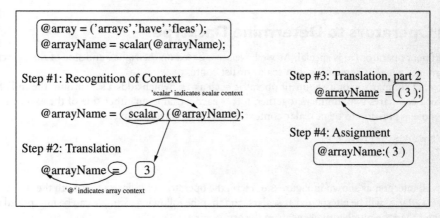

Listing 6.1 contains examples of built-in functions determining contexts.

Listing 6.1
internalFunc.p

```
@array = ('arrays', 'have', 'fleas');
print int(@array);       # int always takes a scalar, hence, in SCALAR
                         # context and prints '3' (number of elements in array).
print sort(@array)       # sort takes a LIST/ARRAY, and sorts it alphanumerically
                         # (by default) hence, prints out 'arrays fleas have'

print int(1,2,3,5);      # Legal, but A MISTAKE.
                         # int takes a scalar and (1,2,3,5) is a read-only list.
                         # Hence 1,2 and 3 are thrown out,prints '5'. use -w!
grep($_ > 10, @array);   # 'grep' is a function that takes an expression in first
                         # element, array second. hence'@array' is in list context
                         # @chars = grep($_ gt 'a', (split(//,function()));  );
                         # Here, the 'split(//, $function)' is in list context.
                         # This says, make an array of characters that come out of
                         # function()  and are greater than the letter 'a'
```

Unfortunately, the context of built-in functions is dependent on the function itself. So how do you determine the
context of a given function? For a starter, you can go to Chapter 10, "Perl Built-in Functions and Variables". This

will give you a pointer to the most important Perl functions and the types of arguments they take. Alternatively, you can go to the **perlfunc** man page, which lists all the internal functions and the arguments they take.

The **perlfunc** man page lists:

```
chr SCALAR
```

This means that the chr function takes a scalar, and only a scalar. chr is a built-in function to print out the ASCII value of a number (print chr(72); prints H, for example). If you then say:

```
chr(@arrayName);
```

this is probably not going to give you what you want. @arrayName becomes a scalar, and this scalar is interpreted as a number, and the ASCII value of the number of elements in the array is what is actually printed. If you so happen to have 72 elements in @arrayName, it will print H.

Using Operators to Determine Datatype

The assignment operator (=) is special. As we have seen, based on the right-hand side of the expression, the equal sign determines whether something is in scalar or list context.

Any other comparison or assignment operator, such as .=, which adds a scalar onto the end of another scalar, or ==, which compares two numbers together, forces each variable on either side of the expression to be scalars, and the whole expression to be in scalar context. If you say something like:

```
if ($size > @arrayName)
{
}
```

then Perl will interpret as shown in Figure 6.6. Here, the operator > indicates that both the scalar $size and the array @arrayName will be interpreted as scalars, and that the following example can be interpreted as: "if the scalar size is greater than the number of elements in the array array."

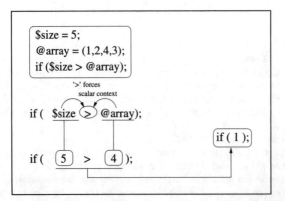

Figure 6.6

A Nonassignment
Operator Forcing
Scalar Context

This rule for scalar interpretation includes all the comparison operators (==, ne, >) and increment/decrement operators (++, --). Perl 5 gives extremely strange errors if you try to do weird things such as decrement an array (@arrayName--) or increment a hash (%hashName++). Do not attempt these actions. They won't do anything useful, and you may even crash Perl and get a core file.

The statement `@arrayName--` does not mean take the last element off of `arrayName`. Because `@arrayName` is in scalar context, this statement is interpreted as "try to decrement the number of elements in `@arrayName`," something akin to saying:

```
(3)--;
```

and since the number of elements in an array is a read-only value, this is a syntax error. Use `pop` instead, as in the following:

```
$element = pop(@arrayName);
```

Listing 6.2 contains a few examples of contexts for variables with operators other than assignment, and a couple of common conceptual mistakes that people make when they forget about context. Note that they are all in scalar context.

Listing 6.2
Scalar Samples.p

```
$a++;            # incrementor of $a.  Since SCALAR context.
@a--;            # decrementor of @a?  SCALAR context natively on an array. SYNTAX ERROR!
$a[1]++;         # better. $a[1] represents a scalar, hence is viable in SCALAR context.
if  (%a == %b)   # legal syntax -- but A MISTAKE
{                # %a resolves to  SCALAR context, as well as %b.
    print "matched!\n";
}
```

Are you trying to compare two hashes? This does not work, because you are interpreting `%a` and `%b` in scalar context. You must go through each element of the hash one at a time:

```
die if ($a{'a'} eq $b{'a'});
        #legal and better.  $a{'a'} represents SCALAR and is viable in scalar context.
do
{
    subroutine('a');
} if (@a > @b);
        # legal -- but REALIZE WHAT YOU ARE
        # COMPARING. NOT the elements of @a and
        # @b, but the number of elements in each
        # set. @a is an array in SCALAR context, and
        # resolves to a scalar (no. of elements).
```

Are you trying to compare two arrays, element by element? This does not work, either. You must go through each element one at a time:

```
@a .= @b;
        # Are you concatenating two arrays?
        # NO. This is a syntax error, since @a
        # resolves to a SCALAR as well as @b. Use push instead.
```

This does not work because `@a` and `@b`, attached by a nonassignment operator =, are scalar values. Hence, `@a` is read-only in this context (and unwritable). Use `push` instead, something like:

```
push(@a, @b);
```

Finally, consider this comparison example:

```
if ((3,4,5) < (4,5,6))   # legal -- but A MISTAKE.
{                        # < forces construct into SCALAR context.
    print "HERE!!!\n";   # Since (3,4,5) and (4,5,6) are lists,
}                        # (3,4) and (4,5) are thrown away, and only
                         # 5 and 6 are compared together.
```

Again, because both `(3,4,5)` and `(4,5,6)` are in scalar context, this expression simply compares 5 and 6, and throws away the other two elements. Consider what you are trying to do: Are you trying to compare each individual element with each other, and only print HERE if one is always less than the other? Or are you trying to compare the number of elements in the array? In each case, there would be a different solution, so be clear about what you want to do.

Advanced Contexts

Let's go over a couple more examples, just to hammer the points in. So far, we have been a bit simple in that we have not done any subscripting on variables, and we haven't tried tricks. The three Perl symbols ($, @, and %) can be extremely powerful tools of expression. But they can also be very misleading if you type them incorrectly. The following shows another wrinkle of how Perl determines contexts, and the order in which they evaluate:

```
@arrayIndexes = (1,2,3);
@arrayIndexes2 = (2,1,3); $arrayName[@arrayIndexes] = $arrayName[@arrayIndexes2];
            # Tricky. AND A MISTAKE.
            # @array turns into a SCALAR context as
            # well as @array2, because the left-hand
            # side variable ('$scalar[@array]' is a
            # scalar. Probably meant
            # @scalar[@array] = @scalar[@array2], if you want to copy an array
            # slice.
```

Again, even a mess like the preceding example can be evaluated if you know the rules about contexts, and remember how to determine what is a scalar and what is an array. The first thing to notice about the example is that the left-hand side of the equation ($arrayName[<\@>arrayIndexes]) denotes a scalar, and *not* an array, since it starts with a $. Therefore, this assignment is in scalar context, and both @arrayIndexes and @arrayIndexes2 get evaluated as scalars. This is a fancy way of saying:

```
$scalar[3] = $scalar[3];
```

You probably meant something like:

```
@array[@subscripts] = @array2[@subscripts];
            # Somewhat tricky as well.  OK if you are copying an array slice .
            # @array in List context, hence
            # @subscripts and @subscripts are in list
            # contexts. Hence, if @subscripts are
            # numeric, will copy the array slices.
```

Now `@array[@subscripts]` denotes an array (because it begins with an @), and the expression is evaluated in list context.

See the next example to see how tricky context can become. Try to follow along; if this makes sense to you, then you are well on your way to understanding how contexts work.

```
@array1 = (1,2,5,4,3);
@array2 = ('this','is','a','mistake');
```

```
$scalar = (@array1, @array2);  # another tricky one. And a
            # MISTAKE. @array1 and @array2 are
            # in SCALAR context because of $scalar
            # on the left-hand side.  Hence,
            # this is evaluated as
            # $scalar =
            # (number of elems in @array1,
            # number of elems in @array2); but
            # since lists and scalars don't mix,
            # the first element in the list gets
            # dropped off in translation to a scalar.
            # Hence, in this case
            # $scalar gets assigned the value 4, which is the number
            # of elements in @array2!
```

As you can see, context can become complicated in a hurry, just as the English language can become complicated in a hurry. Remember, one person's idea of complex may be well within the comfort area of another person. One way to deal with Perl's complexity is to avoid it. If you are not comfortable with doing something like:

```
@arrayName[3,1,2] = @arrayName[1,2,3];
```

as shorthand for:

```
@temp = @arrayName;
$arrayName[3] = $temp[1];
$arrayName[1] = $temp[2];
$arrayName[2] = $temp[3];
```

then don't do it! It's better to be explicit and understand what you are doing than to confuse yourself by complicated syntax. However, being explicit can clutter your code. The best thing is to learn how Perl deals with variables via the previous constructs, and then apply these principles to your own code.

Using Location to Determine Datatype

Location rules also dictate how Perl handles variables. There are four major rules to remember here. (We preface the rules with the punctuation marks you need to look for.)

1. " "—Scalars and arrays are interpreted in scalar context inside quotation marks, by a process known as interpolation. The relevant syntax for interpolation looks like this:

   ```
   print "@arrayName\n";
   ```

2. ( )—User functions: scalars, arrays, and hashes are interpreted in list context when they fall within user functions. The relevant syntax for function calls looks like this:

   ```
   myfunction($scalar1,$scalar2);
   ```

3. [ ]—Array references: scalars, arrays, and hashes are interpreted in list context when they fall within [ ], the symbols for array references. The relevant syntax for array references looks like this:

   ```
   $arrayRef = [$scalar1, $scalar2, @scalar3 ];
   ```

4. { }—Hash references: scalars, arrays, and hashes are interpreted in list context when they fall within { }, the symbols for hash references. The relevant syntax for hash references looks like this:

   ```
   $hashref = {'key1' => 'value1', 'key2' => 'value2'};
   ```

Let's go through each rule in detail.

Context Rules with Interpolation

Scalars and arrays inside the double quotes (" . . ") are interpreted in scalar context, as far as the variable to the left-hand side of any equal sign is concerned. There is another twist here. Through the trick of interpolation, arrays are expanded into their corresponding elements, rather than denoting the number of elements in the array. Therefore, if you say something like:

```
@arrayName = (1,2,3,4);
$scalarName = "@arrayName";
```

this prints out 1 2 3 4. Note the difference here. If you had just said:

```
$scalarName = @arrayName;
```

then $scalarName would have gotten the value 4. Perl is doing the following in Figure 6.7.

Figure 6.7
Interpolation in
Perl

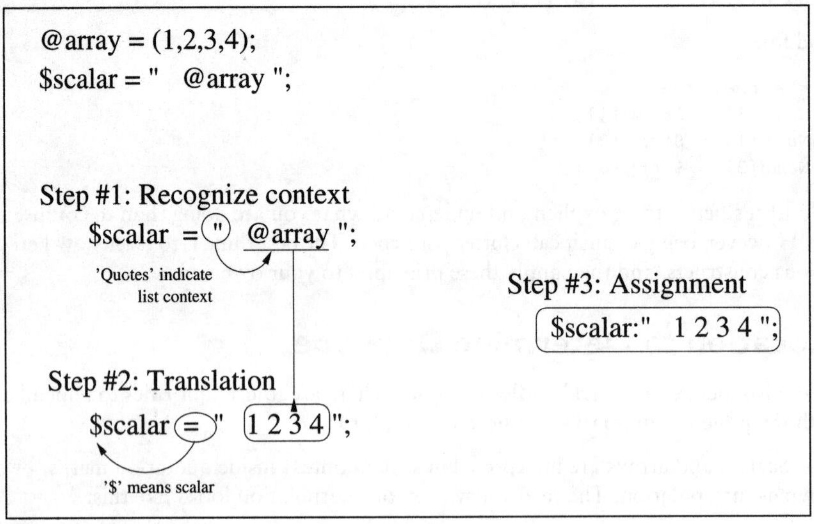

```
@array = (1,2,3,4);
$scalar = "   @array ";
```

Step #1: Recognize context
$scalar = " @array ";
'Quotes' indicate list context

Step #2: Translation
$scalar = " 1 2 3 4 ";
'$' means scalar

Step #3: Assignment
$scalar:" 1 2 3 4 ";

Hashes are *not* expanded inside double quotes—neither are lists. The following does *not* do what you might expect, and print this is a hash and 1 2 3 4, respectively:

```
%hash = ("this" => "is", "a" => "hash");
print "%hash";
print "(1,2,3,4)";
```

Instead, it prints %hash and (1,2,3,4). It treats the % and (as characters, not special symbols.

Special Symbols in Interpolation

Suppose you decide that you actually want to print an @, or a $. You have two options:

1. Backslash that character in double quotes. The following statement:

    ```
    print "\@array\n";
    ```

    prints @array. Note that you don't need to worry about printing spurious backslashes. If you backslash something that doesn't need backslashing, the backslash disappears. In other words, \@ is always a @, \\ is always a \, and \# is always a #, even though # does not need backslashing.

2. Use single quotes instead. Interpolation works only with double quotes. If you say:

    ```
    print '$scalarName';
    ```

    it will do exactly as you told it to do, which is print the string $scalarName. Single quotes are your way to tell Perl to be literal. The '$', '@', '%', etc., actually mean a dollar sign, an at sign, and a percent sign, rather than signifying a variable. If you want a literal ' (single quote), this is the only case in which you need to backslash inside single quotes.

This:

```
print 'This is an \ @ (at) sign';
```

prints This is an @ (at) sign. And:

```
print 'This is a \' (single quote)';
```

prints This is a ' (single quote). And:

```
print 'This is a \\ (backslash)';
```

prints 'This is a \ backslash'.

Contexts and Function Calls

As we saw in Chapter 5, when you are passing variables into a function, they are interpreted strictly as a list. We didn't say it at the time, but here is a perfect example of the importance of context in Perl. This is a case in which the assignment's role in determining context takes a back seat to the function call's role in determining context. When you say something like:

```
$return_value = functionName($array1, $array2);
```

you might think that $array1, $array2 would somehow be munged into a scalar because of the equal sign. But no, the arguments are insulated from being translated into a scalar simply because they are in a function call.

This logic allows you to pass in arguments as you please. On the other side of the tracks, so to speak, the function call looks like:

```
sub functionName
{
    my (@arguments) = @_;
    # ... function call here.
    return($return_value);
}
```

Arguments are passed by arrays, and the special variable @_ is assigned to all the values passed into the function (Figure 6.8).

Figure 6.8
Function Names
and Contexts

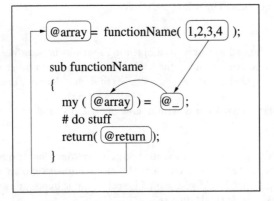

The boxes indicate what is being copied to and where. Attentive readers will recognize Figure 6.8 included in Chapter 5. For more details and pitfalls on writing user functions, please refer to Chapter 5.

Array References and Contexts

As we shall see, *references* are Perl's way of making "pointers" to data (so you make complicated data structures, a two-dimensional array being an array of pointers to their arrays). A reference constructor, denoted by { } (for hash references) and [ ] (for array references) is always a special type of scalar that is *insulated* from its surroundings. In other words, it—and its elements—cannot be coerced into scalars. This means that if you do something such as:

```
@array1 = (1,2,3); @array2 = (4,5,6,7);
$arrayRef = [@array1, @array2];
```

@array1 and @array2 are *not interpreted* as "the number of elements in @array1 and @array2." This is therefore *not* equivalent to:

```
$arrayRef = (@array1, @array2);
```

In the first case, inside [ ] $arrayRef becomes [1,2,3,4,5,6,7]. In the second, $arrayRef becomes '4'. Think of the internals of [ ] and { } as a miniature list context, insulated from the outside world, just like subroutine calls. Therefore, $arrayRef becomes [1,2,3,4,5,6,7], which is read as "$arrayRef points to the array that has the values [1,2,3,4,5,6,7]."

Likewise, as in the case with lists, if you put two arrays into one of these constructs, they will be interpreted internally as one big list and lose their identity. Here is an example of this insulation:

```
@array = ([1,2,3,4,5],[6,7,8,9,10]);
```

Here, each of the array references is treated as a scalar, and @array becomes 2 elements long, each being an array reference. By the way, this is Perl's way to construct a two-dimensional array (we will see in Chapter 7 how to get the data out). This example:

```
sort([1,2,3,4,5]);
```

is just plain nonsense, because the built-in function sort is expecting an array, and you are passing it a reference (which, being a scalar, becomes a one-element array).

The following code snippet:

```
if ({'a' > 'hash' } > {'another' > 'hash'})
{
}
```

is also nonsense, because it does not somehow get the number of elements in the hashes, and compare them (as if (@a > @b) would do with arrays). Instead, it returns a nonsense value.

Again, the importance of special characters rears its ugly head in Perl; if you haven't gotten them straight, they will cause you no end of pain. Remember:

```
1 $scalar = (@array);
```

and:

```
2 $scalar = [@array];
```

are very different! 1 makes $scalar the number of elements in @array, 2 makes $scalar a reference to @array itself.

Control Structures and Contexts

Control loops have their own special rules for contexts. However, most of these rules are fairly natural and pretty elegant (if you think about it). Table 6.1 shows the basic rules.

Table 6.1

Construct	Context
if,unless (...)	scalar
while (...)	scalar
foreach (...)	list
for (;;)	scalar
for ()	list

The first for construct is the standard for ($xx = 0; $xx < 10; $xx++). The second for is the less standard for (@array) construct, which is really a synonym for foreach.

The main thing to remember here is that each context rule works fairly well with its associated construct. Consider while. while's job is to evaluate the expression that exists inside the parentheses after it, and, if true, evaluate the code associated with its block. This example of a while loop:

```
while (defined ($line = <FD>))
{
}
```

evaluates the expression defined $line = <FD> one at a time, using the knowledge that <FD> will return the first row, then the second row, and so forth. Therefore, while evaluates this in *scalar* context. Hence,

```
while (@array)
{
}
```

is either an infinite loop or a no-operation, since @array evaluates to the number of elements in the array, either a number greater than zero (in which case while evaluates as true and it is an infinite loop), or a number equal to zero (in which case it evaluates to false, and the `while` loop ends). Therefore, it makes sense for `while` to evaluate expressions in a scalar context.

Likewise, it makes sense for `foreach` to evaluate expressions in a *list* context. The job of `foreach` is to iterate over a list of elements. This means that when you say:

```
foreach $line (<FD>)
{
    print "$line";
}
```

you are basically getting the same result as the equivalent `while` loop (printing the lines in the file denoted by the file handle `<FD>`). Realize that with the `<FD>` being evaluated in list context, you are slurping the entire file into an array that `foreach` subsequently processes. (Of course, this may not be the wisest idea; the 'while' is much more efficient, and the foreach slurps the file all into a big array.)

On the other hand, with this code:

```
while (defined ($line = <FD>))
{
    print "$line";
}
```

the scalar context makes it so that only one line is being processed at a time.

Finally, consider `if`. Because `if` does things in a scalar context, you can say things like:

```
if (@array)
{
}
```

to test if array has any elements or not. Or you can say something like:

```
if ($returnValue = myFunction())
{
}
```

which will test if the function `myFunction()` returns a true or false value, and only do the associated `if` clause if `$returnValue` is true.

Summary

Although there are only five basic rules for understanding 99 percent of contexts, they can get interesting fast. You can twist and bend Perl syntax into whatever shape you want, although that is sometimes not the best policy.

Instead, the point of this is that if you understand the examples above, you will know contexts pretty well, at least enough to come up with clever solutions of your own. Hopefully, your code will not be as "flashy" as some of the following examples. The following code exchanges terseness for understandability. You should weigh how much this is worth compared to the ability to understand your own code down the pike, let alone have somebody else understand it.

Here again are the five rules:

1. If the variables are tied together by an operator that is *not* the (=) sign, then the variables to both the right- and left-hand sides are scalars.
2. If the variable is inside a special function, that function determines the context.

3. If the variables are tied together by an assignment operator (=), then the left-hand side of the statement determines the right-hand side's context.

4. If you have variables in certain contexts (user-defined functions, array references, and hash references), those variables are in list context, and "insulated" from assignment (i.e., in `$a = myFunction(@b);`, `@b` does not get coerced to be a scalar, but is a list).

5. Items in a `while` loop are natively evaluated in scalar context, as are items in an `if` clause. Items in a `for` loop are in list context.

Now, let's look at how Perl's syntax can bend using these five rules. One of the main complexities we will see in Perl syntax is that you can design it such that the output of one expression is used as the input of the other. This process is known as chaining. With *chaining*, the possibilities for manipulating data are endless, as we shall see next.

Examples

We said earlier that Perl's policy toward contexts set Perl apart from other languages. This section is designed to show off that flexibility.

One of the big things Perl does is allow you to fit functions together as if they were Tinker Toys. Suppose a function happens to return an array. The output of that function could be passed to another function, which in turn alters the output in some way. Look at this example:

```
my @uppercase = split(//, uc($variable));
```

where $variable = 'this must be so' returns

```
('T','H','I','S',' ','M','U','S','T',' ','B','E',' ','S', 'O');
```

Taking the result of this, and then reversing it, say:

```
my @uppercase = reverse(split(//, uc($variable)));
```

returns:

```
('O','S',' ','E','B',' ','T','S','U','M',' ','S','I','H','T');
```

Now go ahead and join the resulting string:

```
my $uppercase = join('',reverse(split(//,uc($variable))));
```

returns:

```
'OS EB TSUM SIHT'
```

In short, we have done something that looks like what is shown in Figure 6.9. With a few lines of code, we have done a relatively complicated task: Reversing a string and making it uppercase. We did this by taking relatively simple functions (`join`, `reverse`, `split`, `uc`) and realizing the *contexts* those functions require. The only thing remotely difficult here is the `split(//` part. This is because `split` takes a regular expression in the first part, resulting in splitting the string into component characters, which we will talk about at length in Chapter 9 and Chapter 11.

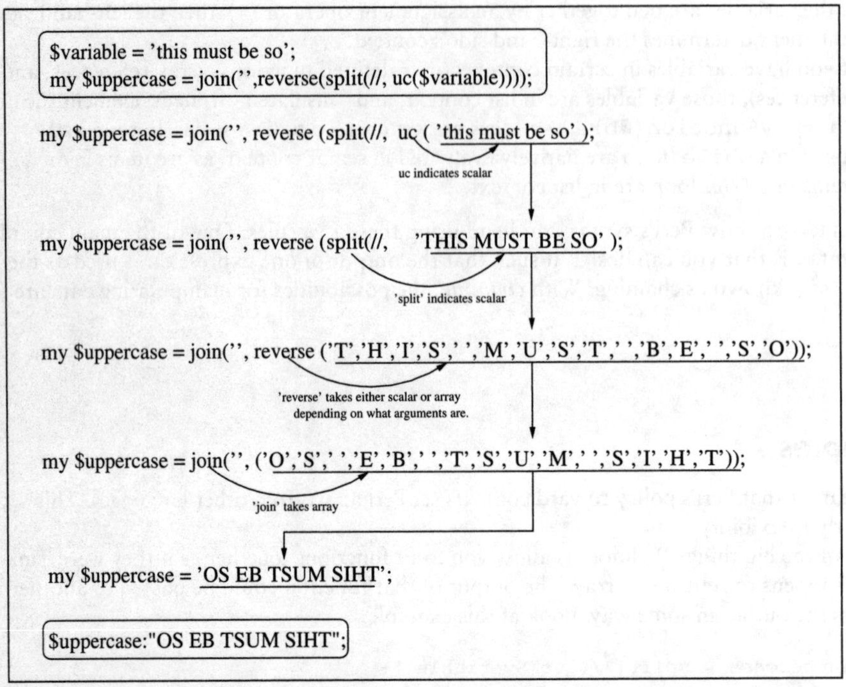

Figure 6.9
*Stringing
Functions
Together*

```
$variable = 'this must be so';
my $uppercase = join('',reverse(split(//, uc($variable))));
```

```
my $uppercase = join('', reverse (split(//,  uc ( 'this must be so' );
```
          uc indicates scalar

```
my $uppercase = join('', reverse (split(//,    'THIS MUST BE SO' );
```
          'split' indicates scalar

```
my $uppercase = join('', reverse ('T','H','I','S',' ','M','U','S','T',' ','B','E',' ','S','O'));
```
          *'reverse' takes either scalar or array
          depending on what arguments are.*

```
my $uppercase = join('', ('O','S',' ','E','B',' ','T','S','U','M',' ','S','I','H','T'));
```
          'join' takes array

```
my $uppercase = 'OS EB TSUM SIHT';
```

```
$uppercase:"OS EB TSUM SIHT";
```

We have also happened to reinvent the wheel. The following does exactly the same thing, without dealing with `split`:

```
my $reverseUC = uc(reverse('this must be so'));
```

because `reverse` can take a scalar argument, as well as an array.

There are two points to be made here. First, since it is relatively easy to tell, even by trial and error, what context functions take, it is easy to do this stacking. After all, there are only two choices at any given point: *scalar* or *list*. Second, it pays huge dividends to know what Perl's internal functions do, inside and out. You'll save yourself a lot of time by not doing this elaborate stacking.

With this in mind, here are some other examples of putting contexts together to do pragmatic things.

Example 1: Reversing a Hash

The statement:

```
%hash = reverse(%hash);
```

takes a hash that looks like:

```
%hash = ('key1' => 'value1', 'key2' => 'value2','key3' => 'value3');
```

and turns it into a hash that looks like:

```
%hash = ('value1' => 'key1','value2' => 'key2','value3' => 'key3');
```

It works, again, because of contexts. Because `reverse` takes an array as its only argument, %hash turns into an array, something like:

```
('key1','value1','key2','value2','key3','value3');
```

reverse then reverses it, to become:

```
('value3','key3','value2','key2','value1','key1');
```

Then this gets "stuffed" back into the hash with the values becoming the keys (the odd elements) and the keys becoming the values (the even elements). Note that this "reversal" is nondeterminant (i.e., if you have two or more keys with the same values, you will end up with a hash containing the first value encountered), as the following:

```
('key1' => 'value1','key2' => 'value1','key3' => 'value1');
```

becomes:

```
('value1' => 'key1') or ('value1'=> 'key2') or ('value1' => 'key3')
```

Example 2: Reading From Standard Input Until a Certain Type of Character Is Pressed

This is used all the time. If you say:

```
while (($line = <STDIN>)!~m"end")
{
    print (join('', reverse(split(//, $line))));  # sample code
}
```

then $line = <STDIN>, in scalar context, will catch a line of input that someone types at a keyboard. The regular expression !~ m"end" checks to see whether that line has the string end in it. (Again, see the section "Regular Expressions" for more detail. They are absolutely essential for understanding Perl!)

If it doesn't have the string end in it (' !~ means doesn't match), then go ahead and do the `while` loop, which in this case means print the reverse of what was just typed (a "palindrome").

Example 3: Splitting a String into Chunks 10 Characters Long

This example is a "teaser." It shows you what you can do with regular expressions, and is meant to entice you to read Chapter 9 on them (regular expressions really are quite useful). Here is the code:

```
$line = 'aaaaaaaaaabbbbbbbbbbcccccccccc';
@split = ($line =~ m"(.{1,10})"sg);
```

A bit of explanation is in order: the m".{1,10}" means match one to ten characters in the string line; . means any character; {1,10} means one to ten characters matched, the more the better; and the sg is a special signal to Perl to make it so the text that matches goes into an array (in list context), something like Figure 6.10.

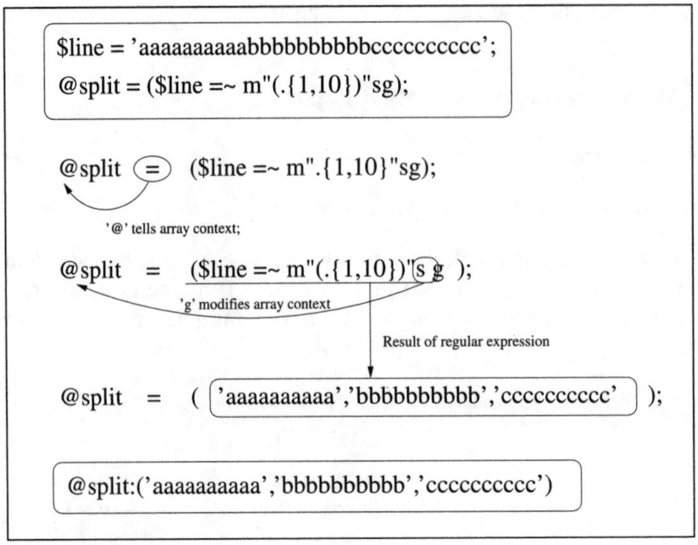

Figure 6.10
Regular
Expression
List Context

This does quite a bit of work, something equivalent to the code:

```
while ($counter < length($line))
{
    push(@split, substr($line, $counter, 10));
    $counter+=10;
}
```

which itself is a good example of contexts in general (and which you might want to do until you have got regular expressions down).

Example 4: Checking to See Whether a File Has the Same Number of Lines as Another File

```
my $FD1 = new FileHandle("file1");
my $FD2 = new FileHandle("file2");
if (@{[ <$FD1> ]} == @{[ <$FD2> ]})
{
    print "Same Number of lines!\n";
}
```

This example uses our old trick to make function calls into arrays (i.e., @{[functionCall()]}). You should have an idea of how to decode this (when we get to references, you'll have even more of an idea). When you say:

```
[<$FD1>]
```

it reads the file descriptor $FD1 in list context, getting all of the lines out and putting it into a reference. The construct:

```
@{[ <$FD1> ]}
```

dereferences the reference, turning it into a real array. And finally:

```
if ( @{[ <$FD1> ]} == @{[ <$FD2> ]} )
{
}
```

takes the two arrays, turns them into scalars (meaning the number of elements in the array), and then compares that value, to see if they are equal. If you don't want that much "magic" going on, you can say:

```
@lines1 = <$FD1>;
@lines2 = <$FD2>;
if (@lines1 == @lines2)
{
}
```

which is probably a saner way of doing it anyway.

Example 5: Finding Out Whether One File Has More Occurrences of the Word "the" Than Another File

Just to show you how sickening contexts can get, in one line (OK, technically six) this last example counts the number of occurrences of the word *the*, and compares it to another file's occurrences. Here's the code (brace yourself):

```
undef $/;    # makes it so Perl gets the whole file in one <> read (see special variables)
my $FD1 = new FileHandle("file1");
my $FD2 = new FileHandle("file2");
if (@{[    <$FD1> =~ m"\bthe\b"sg    ] } > @{[    <$FD2> =~ m"\bthe\b"sg ]})
{
    print "file1 has more occurrences of the word than file2!\n";
}
```

Confused yet? Again, it is simply a matter of unraveling contexts ($/ makes it so the whole file goes into file descriptors on one read of <>, full read mode). Again:

```
[ <$FD1> =~ m"\bthe\b"sg    ]
```

is in list context so this means "open up $FD1, and get all the data" (because of $/—if this wasn't there, it would get one line). Then, use regular expressions to match occurrences of *the* with bordered words around it (i.e., \b means match at a word boundary). A string like:

```
the sin of the flesh
```

would match at the places where *the* is bold, but

```
theocracy
```

would not because there is no word boundary on the right in theocracy. Anyway, in the string the sin of the flesh:

```
[ <$FD1> =~ m"\bthe\b"sg    ]
```

becomes:

```
[ 'the','the']
```

because of the two occurrences of the word *the* that matched. Hence:

```
@{[ 'the','the']}
```

becomes the array:

```
@array = ('the','the')
```

which in the scalar context:

```
if (<@{[ .... ]} > @{[ ... ]}
```

becomes the number:

```
2
```

which indicates the number of occurrences of the word *the* in the string the sin of the flesh. Whew! You probably would be better off doing this:

```
undef $/;
my @words1 = split(' ', <$FD1>);
my @words2 = split(' ', <$FD2>);
my @the1 = grep(m"\bthe\b", @words1);
my @the2 = grep(m"\bthe\b", @words2);
if (@the1 > @the2)
{
}
```

which does the same thing as the above example, but makes it a little more explicit. grep, if you aren't familiar with it, is Perl's way of making a filter on an array. The grep in the previous example only lets pass into the array @the1, the words that match the pattern \bthe\b. Or you may want to unroll this syntax even further. Start simple, and then get fancy.

Summary

For only having two major types of contexts (list and scalar), Perl gets quite a bit done. Athough there is no perfect method for determining whether a given variable or piece of data is in scalar or list context, there are some quick rules to do so:

1. Scalars on the left-hand side of an '=' force the right-hand side into scalar context.
2. Arrays or hashes on the left-hand side of an '=' force the right-hand side into scalar context.
3. References ([@array]) force list context for the variable @array.
4. Function calls (function(@array)) force @array into list context.
5. If a variable begins with $, the value inside a subscript ([ ], { }) is in scalar context.
6. Comparison operators (==, !=, gt, etc.) force scalar context.

That's about it. Learn these rules once and you will understand most contexts. Combine the knowledge of references and you will know the core of Perl fairly well.

7

References

References are Perl 5's way of representing pointers to data in the language, rather than the data itself. References are a big improvement over anything that existed in Perl 4. They allow you to make complicated data structures such as trees, multidimensional arrays, priority queues—pretty much any sort of data structure you desire—easily. Old guard Perl programmers should pay special attention to this section, because once you learn how easy it is to program with references, you'll never want to go back.

The purpose of this chapter is to get you accustomed to the elasticity of references (i.e., to make you understand how the syntax works behind them, and then, by extension, use them efficiently). If you are fond of documentation (as I am), the appropriate Perl reference page is **perlref** which goes into much detail-and with many examples—on the following material.

It was a pain to program data structures more complicated than the traditional arrays and hashes in Perl 4. To give you an example of how bad it was, look at the following, horrid construct:

```
@array = ("1$;2$;3$;4", "5$;6$;7$;8");
```

was used to implement a two-dimensional array. Each element was accessed by:

```
print ((split(m"$;", $array[1]))[2]);
```

which would print 7. Contextually speaking, this says "take the element `$array[1]` as a scalar, split it into an array of elements using the special variable `$;`, then dereference this array using the subscript `[2]`, and print it out."

Yuck. Just *try* to extend this to do three-dimensional arrays. Now, in Perl 5, the same construct looks like:

```
@array = ([1,2,3,4],[5,6,7,8]);
```

and element 7 is accessed by:

```
print $array[1][2];
```

Once again, if you are not familiar with references, you are going to want to read this chapter. Unless, of course, you want to go back to the Perl 4 syntax just listed, or something similar.

Chapter Overview

Perl's references are just like its contexts; there is a strict set of language rules. When combined, these language rules make for very powerful techniques in programming. This chapter deals with these language rules in detail.

First, we cover the definitions of the two types of references that Perl has—hard and soft—and go over the reasons why hard references should be preferred over their soft counterparts.

We then go over the syntax used to construct complex data structures—the various operators (backslash, ref, and anonymous arrays and hashes).

Once we have put the data into the references that we have built, we will go over the process of extracting that data. We will also go over the rules that are necessary to look inside the array, hash, and scalar references we constructed. In addition, we will look at the process of drawing/listing what a given data structure will look like in "raw form" (how it looks if we constructed it manually via Perl's syntax).

Finally, we again have examples: storing an HTTP access log into a data structure, recursive references to a directory/file hierarchy and turning it into a data structure, and quite a few others.

Introduction

For eight years, all Perl ever had in the way of data structures were these three datatypes: hashes, arrays, and scalars. Some pretty incredible things were done with them in spite of their limitations. As we saw earlier, people overcame these limitations by using specific Perl techniques that are totally unnecessary today.

Other difficult techniques were things such as: using `eval` to create variable names; manipulating the symbol table; using `typeglobs`, by making one-dimensional hashes/arrays "look" like two or more; and various other techniques that made the code obscure, hard to debug, and inflexible.

Note

If this sounds ugly, it is. `eval` and `typeglobs` have their uses, but not for data structure creation. We will briefly touch on these concepts in Chapter 11, so don't worry about their definitions for now.

With object-oriented Perl comes a new concept: references. *References* are simply pointers to items, whether they be hashes, arrays, or scalars. There are even pointers to functions, called *code references*, which we will cover later. References are used to create trees, recursive data structures, lists of lists, double-arrayed hashes, and any other data structures that you can think of quickly and painlessly.

For example, here is a double (or two-dimensional) array that uses references:

```
$doubleArray = [[1,2,3],[4,5,6],[7,8,9]];
```

Each individual element is accessed by:

```
$doubleArray->[1][1];
```

The first statement is read as "`$doubleArray` is a reference to an array that has three references to arrays in it: [1,2,3], [4,5,6], and [7,8,9]." The second statement is read as "access the second element (subscripted by zero) of the first element of the second array in `$doubleArray`."

References greatly expand the usability and maintainability of Perl. As you can see, references also make Perl a much more readable language. Much of the line noise in Perl 4 scripts was because of the lack of references. ("Line noise" is where there are more special characters than normal characters.) The job of this section is to teach you how to make references work, and how to decode them.

As with the rest of Perl, there are a few simple rules that determine 95% of what you need to know about references and their use. These rules are also discussed in this section.

Perl 5 References: Hard and Soft

References are tags that point to other variables, or to pieces of data on the system. Think of them like a postal address. A postal address *refers* to the place you live, but is not actually *the* place you live.

Perl has two types of references: hard and soft. *Hard references* are those that point, physically, to a piece of data on a system. They are not a separate datatype in Perl, but are instead stored in scalars, just like every other bit of data in Perl.

If you are a C programmer, you can think of hard references much like pointers in the sense that they "point" to an object. Likewise, they access the object pointed to by a process called *dereferencing*. Hard references are not the same in that you cannot perform pointer arithmetic with them. For example:

```
'$a = [1,2,3]; $a++'
```

does not make $a point to [2,3].

Perl references are also "smart." They keep track of how many different variables point to them, and only go away (their memory being automatically freed) when the last reference to them goes away. This is done by a process called garbage collection. If you say:

```
{
    my $a = [1,2,3];
    $b = $a;
}
print "@$b\n";
```

it prints out 1 2 3, because even though the variable $a would have gone away at the end of the loop, $b stays on in its place since a copy was made of the reference before $a went out of scope. This means that the variable stays around.

One way of making a hard reference to a piece of data is simply by affixing a \ to the front of a variable, and then assigning that variable to a scalar. For example:

```
@array = (1,2,3,4,5);
$hardRef = \@array;
```

@array is actually an array, (1,2,3,4,5), which takes up a chunk of memory. By virtue of the \, $hardRef now points to the same chunk of data in memory that @arrayRef does. Now you can manipulate @arrayRef by virtue of changing $hardRef. In other words, you have internally made a picture very much like what is shown in Figure 7.1.

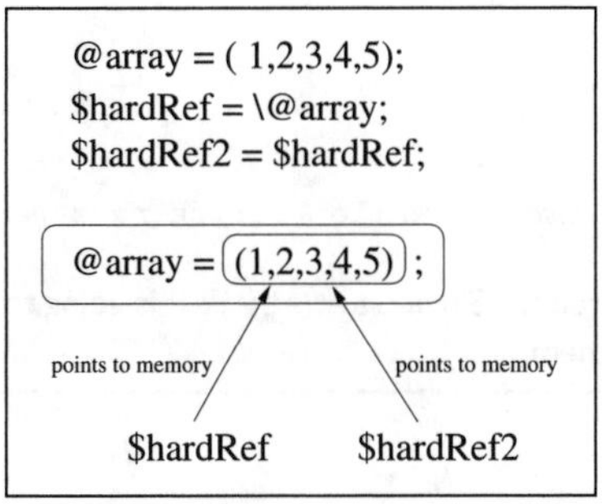

Figure 7.1
References and
Internal Memory
Management

```
@array = ( 1,2,3,4,5);
$hardRef = \@array;
$hardRef2 = $hardRef;
```

@array = (1,2,3,4,5) ;

points to memory   points to memory

$hardRef $hardRef2

You can now treat $hardRef exactly as if it were a copy of @array, by putting an @ in front of it to indicate that you are reaching into the reference to get the value stored within it. Then if you say:

```
@$hardRef = ('0');
print "@array\n";
```

it prints 0, because with @$hardRef = 0 you have changed the value of @array by changing the underlying array.

Soft references or "symbolic references," are references that work simply because one variable contains the name of another. Look closely at the following example:

```
$variable = 'scalar1'; $scalar1 = 'PRINT ME';
print $$variable;
```

Perl evaluates $variable to be scalar1. This is equivalent to:

```
print $scalar1;
```

Hence:

```
print $$variable1;
```

results in printing the string 'PRINT ME'.

Note

It's just my preference, but I strongly suggest *not* using soft references at all. You can't use them with my or lexically scoped variables. Hence:

```
my $varb = '1';
$name = 'varb';
print $$name;
```

will *not* print '1'. Instead, it will print nothing at all, or if you so happened to define a local or global version of $varb, it will print whatever happens to be inside this variable.

Soft references promote the use of global and local variables, which you should actively avoid.

In fact, with the directive use strict in your scripts (see section on Debugging, Chapter 21), you cannot use soft references at all. If you program something like the following:

```
use strict;
$var = 'scalar1';
$$var = 1;
print $scalar1;
```

you will get errors generated like:

Can't use string ("scalar1") as a scalar ref while "strict refs" in use at line 6.

This itself is reason enough not to use soft references. Since use strict is going to be your first line of defense against typos, you really want to avoid them.

Because of the inherent problems in using soft references, this book will be primarily concerned with hard references. Soft references existed in Perl 4, but have rapidly become only of specialized use because of hard references and their power. Hard references are by far the most scalable way to make complicated data structures in Perl.

Hard references are *hard* in the sense that if you link two variables by a reference and change one, you also change the other. They are also *hard* in the sense that references can exist alone, without any name to support them. The statement function([1,2,3]) is perfectly legal, and it passes in an array reference without a name.

Finally, if one of the variables gets eliminated, or goes out of scope, the other will stay around in its stead.

Recognizing References When You See Them—the ref Function

The first thing you should know about references is how to spot them. Perl provides a function, ref, that tells you whether or not a certain variable is a reference.

If you say something like:

```
print ref(\@arrayReference);
```

this dutifully prints ARRAY because the \@ indicates that you have an array reference. Likewise:

```
print ref(\%hashReference);
```

prints HASH since the \% indicates a hash reference. (ref prints nothing at all if its argument isn't a reference.)

Keep this in mind when you are going through the following material. Perl always has the answers at hand, and if you have a question about what type of data you are handling, you can always use ref to determine the type.

Manually Constructing Data Structures

There are two ways of constructing the data structures:

1. Using a \ to signify the reference.
2. Creating anonymous references.

For now let's be concerned with constructing these data structures. Later, we shall learn how to get our data out of them.

Using the Backslash Operator

We have already mentioned the backslash operator in the definition for hard references. The \ operator is a great way of creating hard references. Simply put a \ in front of any variable (array, scalar, or hash) and you've got a reference to it. You could, for example, create a two-dimensional array in the following way:

```
@array = (1,2,3,4);
@array2 = (5,6,7,8);
@array3 = (9,10,11,12);
@twodimaïrray = (\@array, \@array2, \@array3);
```

Each array is manually created and then stuffed into its appropriate "box" inside the "master" array. You've now made a picture like what is shown in Figure 7.2.

Figure 7.2
Two-Dimensional
Array

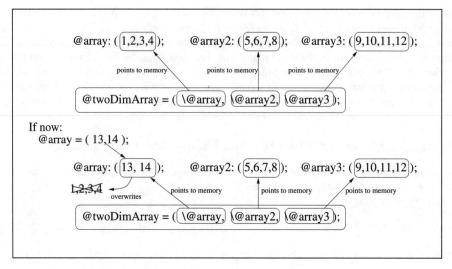

If you wanted to make a hash instead in which the members of the hash were themselves hashes, you could do the following:

```
%hash1 = (1 => 2,3 => 4);
%hash2 = (5 => 6,7 => 8);
%hash3 = (9 => 10,11 => 12);
%hash =
                (
                'key1' => \%hash1,
                'key2' => \%hash2,
                'key3' => \%hash3
                );
```

Here is how to make a reference to a scalar:

```
$scalarRef = \$scalar;
```

Note that $scalar itself is a reference. Hence, here is how to make a reference to a reference to a reference to a scalar:

```
$scalarRef = \\\'Text Here';
```

Note that in the last example, an important thing about the backslash is that you can stack your references, or make a reference to a reference. In this case, it's pretty silly. To actually print the text inside $scalarRef, you would have to do something like:

```
print $$$$scalarRef;
```

which is a real waste of $ signs.

However, there are some cases where you don't want to take the trouble of creating the temporary arrays (@array, @array2, @array3), and simply want to build them from scratch. This is a good case for anonymous arrays and hashes (created by, what else, anonymous array and hash constructors), which we touch on next.

Anonymous Arrays and Hashes and Their Constructors

When you say something like:

```
$arrayRef = \@array;
```

you are creating an array reference that points to the same value as what is in @array. However, @array is still the actual array here. What if you want to make something that looks like the following code, where *everything* is a reference to a piece of data that is sort of floating by itself in computer space? In Perl, the way to do this is by creating what are called *anonymous references*. If you say something such as:

```
$arrayRef = [1,2,3,4];
```

the [] is an *anonymous array constructor* which denotes that you are creating an array reference, rather than an actual array. What is created is something that looks like Figure 7.3.

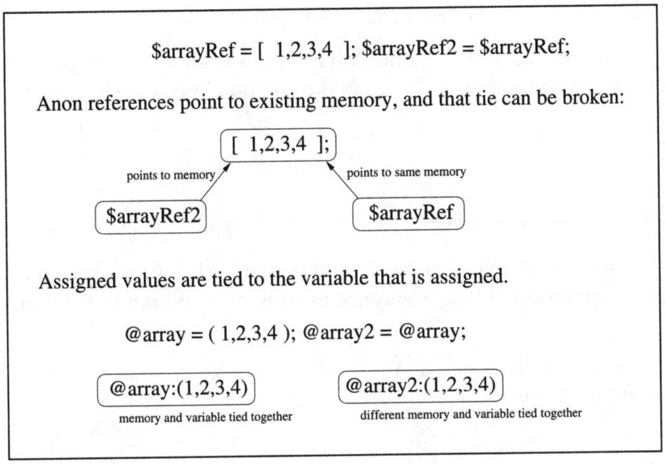

Figure 7.3
Anonymous
References

$arrayRef = [1,2,3,4]; $arrayRef2 = $arrayRef;

Anon references point to existing memory, and that tie can be broken:

[1,2,3,4];

points to memory   points to same memory

$arrayRef2 $arrayRef

Assigned values are tied to the variable that is assigned.

@array = (1,2,3,4); @array2 = @array;

@array:(1,2,3,4)   @array2:(1,2,3,4)

memory and variable tied together   different memory and variable tied together

The difference here is that if you say:

```
@array = (1,2,3,4);
```

@array is actually the array pointed to. $arrayRef simply points to an anonymous piece of data that Perl manages, or keeps track of, and you don't have to worry about. For example, if you say something like the following:

```
sub array
{
    my $arrayRef = [1,2,3,4];
}
```

where $arrayRef is a temporary bit of data, then after the reference goes out of scope, Perl cleans up after you. This cleanup happens by deleting the reference and reclaiming the memory automatically. This is *automatic garbage collection*, which we will discuss at the end of the chapter.

You can then add other pointers to the same piece of data, as in the following:

```
$arrayRef2 = $arrayRef1;
```

There are two types of anonymous references you can create: anonymous array references and anonymous hash references. Let's see how we can use these datatypes to create multidimensional, complex data structures.

Anonymous array references are denoted by a [ ]. Instead of saying something like:

```
@array1 = (1,2,3,4);
@array2 = (5,6,7,8);
@array3 = (9,10,11,12);
@twodimarray = (\@array1,\@array2,\@array3);
```

to create a two-dimensional array, you can instead say:

```
@twodimarray = ([1,2,3,4],[5,6,7,8],[9,10,11,12]);
```

See how this is working? These two statements are not only similar, they are computationally equal. The only difference is that instead of having @array1 as the pointer for the first element, @array2 as the second, and so forth, Perl keeps track of the elements for you.

In fact, if you wanted to, you could drop the need for having @twodimarray point to the actual two-dimensional array. You could say something like:

```
$twodimarrayRef = [[1,2,3,4],[5,6,7,8],[9,10,11,12]];
```

so that $twodimarrayRef is a reference itself; you don't have any variable actually pointing to the data.

Anonymous hash references are denoted by { }. To make an anonymous hash, you say:

```
$hashRef = { 'this' => 'is', 'a' => 'hashref'};
```

as opposed to:

```
%hash = ('this' => 'is', 'a' => 'hash' );
```

which has parentheses and a % to indicate that you are assigning to a hash, rather than to a hash reference. You could then go on to make a two-dimensional hash reference by saying something like the following:

```
$hashRef = {
             'key1' => {1 => 2, 3 => 4 },
             'key2' => {5 => 6, 7 => 8 }
           };
```

key1 has a value that is a hash reference and points to the hash 1=>2, 3=>4. Likewise, key2 has a value that points to 5=>6, 7=>8.

Like the \ operator, you can stack the anonymous array and hash constructors ([] and {}). To make a reference to a reference to a reference to an array, you could do the following:

```
$nestedArrayRef = [[[[1,2,3,4]]]];
```

which is a waste of brackets and something you shouldn't need to do too often. (It can be done, however. That's what Perl is about!)

Getting More Complicated

Using the backslash operator and the {} and [] constructs you can make structures as complicated as you want. Need a three-dimensional array? You could write:

```
$twoDarrayref1 = [[1,2],[3,4],[5,6]];
$twoDarrayref2 = [[7,8,9],['bob','cat']];
$threeDarrayref = [$twoDarrayref1, $twoDarrayref2];
```

in which the references are placed inside a variable, which is itself a reference. You've generated something that looks like Figure 7.4.

Figure 7.4

Three-Dimensional
Array Reference

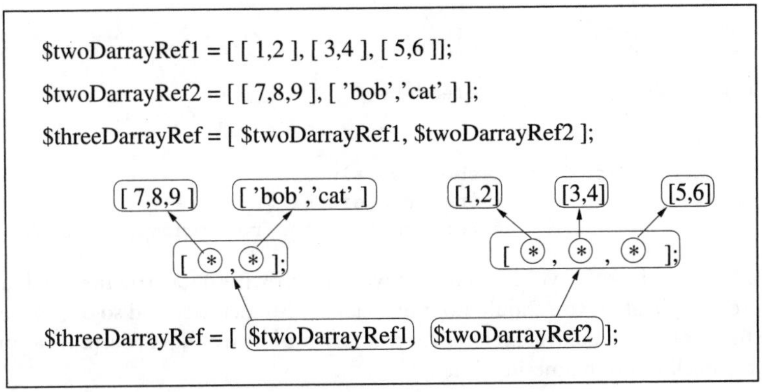

```
$twoDarrayRef1 = [ [ 1,2 ], [ 3,4 ], [ 5,6 ]];

$twoDarrayRef2 = [ [ 7,8,9 ], [ 'bob','cat' ] ];

$threeDarrayRef = [ $twoDarrayRef1, $twoDarrayRef2 ];
```

```
$threeDarrayRef = [ $twoDarrayRef1, $twoDarrayRef2 ];
```

Need an array that contains hashes? Try the following:

```
%hash = {'key5' => 'value5', 'key6' => 'value6'};
$arrayOfHashes = [
                   { 'key' => 'value' , 'key2' => 'value2'},
                   { 'key3' => 'value3', 'key4' => 'value4'},
                   \%hash
                 ];
```

As you can see, you can mix and match these constructs (intermixing { }, [ ], and \) to your heart's content although, for consistency's sake, you are probably better off sticking to either anonymous references, or explicit references through a backslash.

Here are some more examples of using references (just to get comfortable with the syntax):

```
$arrayref = [1 ,2 ,3, 4, [1,2,3,4]];
                # $arrayref is an array reference
                # which points to 5 elements one of which itself is an array
                # ref which contains 4 data points.
```

This shows a hybrid data structure. The first four elements in the array reference are scalars. The fifth one, however, is an array reference.

Following is an example of taking two arrays and putting them into their very own array reference:

```
my $arrayref = [@array1, @array2];
                # Example of array that is a reference
                # to @array1 and @array2 concatenated.
```

Here, @array1 and @array2 are concatenated and stuck in the reference $arrayref.

Finally, try to figure out what is going on in the following examples yourself. Remember, each time you use a \@ or a [, you are dealing with an array reference, and when you use a { or a \%, you are dealing with a hash reference.

```
$hashref =
{
  key1 => \@array1,
  key2 => \@array2,
  key3 => [ 'anonymous', 'array', 'reference']
};
# hash has keys that themselves are arrays
$hashref =
```

```
{
   key1 =>
   {
      subkey1 => ['array', 'of', 'elements']
   }
};
# hash that has keys which have hashes as values.
$hashref_of_ref = \$hashref;    # $hashref_of_ref is now a
                                # reference to the reference of the hash listed above!
```

This code shows the limits of how far you would ever want to go with data structures. Chances are if you are doing something more complicated, you should do it in a class, with methods and so on, for retrieving data. You have probably gone too far once you have a reference structure four or five levels deep. (I'm sure that you can see that this would not be much fun to maintain, either.)

Using Complicated Data Structures

Complicated data structures are used in Perl when you need more power than a simple hash or array can provide. If you wanted to, you could make an object out of the data you wish to model. However, making an object takes time and design knowledge, and you may not want to go to the trouble when a data structure will suffice. There are trade-offs to either one. These trade-offs between complex data structures and objects are discussed at length in the next major section in the book on objects.

Complex data structures are also very handy for translating data from a database into a structure through which you can iterate. Here's an example of parsing information from the command line. The statement:

```
script.p -option1 'value1' -option2 'array1 array2'.
```

translates very cleanly into:

```
$commandOptions =
   {
      'option1' => 'value1',
      'option2' => ['array1', 'array2']
   };
```

See how this works? option1 takes one argument, and becomes a hashkey in commandOptions. It has one value, which is a scalar, value1. Since option2 takes an array of values, we translate this into a hashkey in commandOptions with an anonymous array ['array1', 'array2'] as values.

Alternatively, you could do something like the following to denote a database table, with its name, type, and size of database fields:

```
$database_table =
   [
      {'name' => 'table_id', 'type' => 'int', 'size'=> 4 },
      {'name' => 'first_column', 'type' => 'char', 'size'=> 10 },
      {'name' => 'second_column', 'type' => 'char', 'size'=> 15 }
   ];
```

These are only some simple examples. There are many other times that you will want the power of more complicated data structures without taking the time and trouble to make a class. We will see many of these examples in chapters to come. We devote Chapter 8 to the more common complex data structures.

Summary of Manually Referencing and Constructing Data Structures

References point to a place in memory that contains data. The data may be a scalar, an array, or a hash. The simple way to remember the type of data structure you are referencing and constructing is:

- \$—scalars
- \@—[ ] arrays
- \%—{ } hashes

References may be stacked, moved, copied, or swapped. They are a handy way to access data. An anonymous reference is one in which a reference is created by the [ ] or { } syntax, and allocates a chunk of memory, without associating that memory directly with any particular variable.

Dereferencing Complex Data Structures

The previous section showed you how to create and populate data structures. Of course, it is always nice to be able to get that data back out of the data structure. *Dereference* means to turn a reference back into its component values.

So how do you go about getting the data out of the data structure? For one thing, you cannot simply print the references to get the data that is in them. This would be *implicit* dereferencing (i.e., done "behind the scenes"). This is an OK policy provided Perl always did it. (Python for example, always dereferences. It is a "pointer semantic language.")

As it stands, Perl can either access actual items, or references to actual items, so it must have a different syntax for doing each one. (After all, Perl is good but not a mindreader.) If a reference is directly printed, Perl shows text indicating the place in memory where it is, which is seldom what you want. This is shown in the following statements:

```
$scalarRef = \'the reference to a scalar';   # $scalarRef is a scalar reference
print $scalarRef;                            # reference. prints out
                                             # "SCALARREF(0x....)".
```

Printing the memory location instead of the data at that memory location also happens with arrays and hashes, as in:

```
$arrayRef = [ 1, 2, 3, 4 ];    # $arrayRef is a reference to an array.
print $arrayRef;               # prints out ARRAYREF(0x....).


$hashref = { key => value};    # $hashref is a reference to a hash.
print $hashref;                # prints out HASHREF(0x.....).
```

These print ARRAYREF(0x12323) and HASHREF(0x12123), respectively. Note that these are just strings and *not* usable as references. They are useful for debugging only, and for indicating what type of reference each item is. Because hashes only hash on strings, you can't use references as keys to hashes. This means you can't say:

```
$hash{$arrayRef} = {$arrayRef2};
```

or:

```
$hash{"$arrayRef"} = {$arrayRef2};
```

because each reference is interpreted as a string when going into the hash.

We need to get a little more complicated in coding to get our data back out of these data structures. Following are rules that govern the *dereferencing* of a data structure. These rules go from *most* readable and maintainable to *least*.

Rule 1: In simple cases, you can take whatever the variable is and dereference it by the appropriate symbol for the reference (i.e., $, @, or %). A simple example of this is:

```
$line = \'this is a scalar ref';
print $$line;                    # prints 'this is a scalar ref'
```

Notice the two dollar signs. In effect, this says "take the scalar variable reference and dereference that data." An equivalent can be done for arrays and hashes:

```
$arrayRef = [1,2,3,4];
print "@$arrayRef\n";
```

which prints 1 2 3 4.

The following prints key1 key2:

```
$hashRef = {'key' => 'value', 'key2' => 'value2' };
@keys = keys (%$hashRef);
print "@keys\n";
```

The following code gives an error:

```
$hashRef = ('key' => 'value', 'key2' => 'value2' };
print @$hashRef;
```

because you are trying to dereference an array reference, when $hashRef is actually a hash reference.

Rule 2: For array and hash references, elements can be accessed by the symbol->. This is called *direct access*. If you say:

```
$hashRef = {'key' => 'value'};
```

then:

```
print $hashRef->{'key'};
```

prints the string 'value', because the -> has gone inside the hash reference, and retrieved the definition for the key key, much the same way that $hash{'key'} grabs data inside a real hash.

Rule 3: For array and hash references, you can alternatively access each element by performing $$varb[] for arrays or $$varb{} for hashes. This is called *indirect access*. $varb is the name of the variable that you are using.

Rule 2 is by far the more readable. Rule 2 can also be *stacked*, which means you can use it on deeply nested constructs. This is a simple example of rule 2 and rule 3:

```
$line = [0,1,2,3];
print $line->[0];    # prints 0 (rule2);
print $$line[0];     # prints 0 (rule3);
```

This is a more complicated example of rule 2 (showing stacking):

```
$line = [[0,1]];
print $line->[0]->[0]; # prints '0' (rule2)
```

Note the second example. You could have just as easily said print $line->[0][0] because the second -> is not necessary. Both examples show how you would reach inside the data structure using the -> syntax.

In ambiguous cases brackets can be used to clarify. If you are using this rule often, your code is probably not very readable.

The following is a simple example:

```
$arrayRef = [0,1,2,3];
print ${$line}[0];    # prints 0;
```

As we said, you are probably not using references correctly if you often resort to rule 3. By judicious use of assignment, you can take rule 3 and break it into many instances of rules 1 and 2. If you have something such as this:

```
$complicatedRef = [1,2,3,[4,5,6]];
```

you could say something such as:

```
print "@{$complicatedRef->[3]}";
```

to print out 4 5 6. This directly reaches into the complicated data structure, returns an anonymous array associated to $complicatedRef, and then dereferences it. See Figure 7.5.

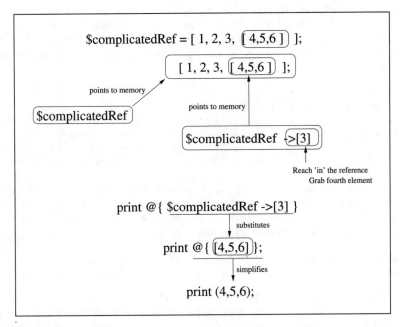

Figure 7.5
How
Complicated
Referencing
Works

But why bother with this complicated syntax? You are better off using a temporary placeholder:

```
my $ref = $complicatedRef->[3];
print @$ref;
```

This can make your code far more readable and maintainable. It shows your thinking process in all its steps instead of a *fait accompli*.

Again, let's take some examples of some complicated data structures and how you would want to dereference them.

```
$arrayref = [ 1, 2, 3, 4 ];    # a simple array ref.
print $arrayref->[1];          # use rule2, -> syntax   ( prints 2 )
print $$arrayref[1];           # use rule3, $$ syntax    ( prints 2 )
print ${$arrayref}[1];         # use rule3, {} to disambiguate ( prints 2 )
print @$arrayref;              # use rule1  ( prints 1 2 3 4 )
```

The following example shows several different, simple ways to access an array reference. It is as much a matter of taste, but rule 2 (for me) is clearest.

```
$arrayref = [' ', ' ',' ', ' ', [1,2]];
print $arrayref->[4]->[1];    # use rule2  ( prints 2);
print $arrayref->[4][1];      # use rule2. Note
                              # lack of '->' in second bracket. This is
                              # equivalent to the above statement because
                              # you don't need to write a second '->'
$complicatedRef = [{hmm => {hmm2 => ['key']}}];
print $complicatedRef->[0]{'hmm'}{'hmm2'}[0];   # uses rule 2. Note that we
                                                # can mix and match array and
                                                # hash constructors as we please!
```

Here we show the use of syntactic sugar. *Syntactic sugar* denotes a syntax construct equivalent to some more "verbose" syntax, but easier to write and, therefore, understand.

In this case, the -> can be omitted when you go more than one level deep in a reference. This is because once you get past the first level of an array call, you are dealing strictly with references. The -> is used only to distinguish between a data structure that is a reference, and a data structure that is the real thing. Here are some more examples:

```
$arrayref = [0,1,2,3,[a1,a2,a3,a4]];
print $$arrayref[4][2];      # use rule2b.
print ${$arrayref}[4][2];    # use rule4.
print "@{$arrayref->[4]};";  # use a combination of rule 2 and rule 4.
                             # getting kind of ugly.yet this prints out 'a1 a2 a3 a4';
print "@$arrayref->[4]\n";   # Note: NOT the same.. Prints out ARRAYREF(0x....)
```

The last line in the example does not print out a1 a2 a3 a4. @$arrayref->[4] turns into @{$arrayref} ->[4] which is interpreted as "show me the array slice associated with the fourth element of $arrayref," @a[4]. This prints ARRAYREF(0x....);. Again, this is getting way too complicated. We are better off creating a placeholder for all of this data, as in the following:

```
my $placeholder = $arrayref->[4]  # better way to handle ambiguity.
print @$placeholder;              # now $placeholder holds [a1,a2,a3,a4].
```

@$placeholder dereferences and prints a1 a2 a3 a4.

This shows the confusion you can create when you do not split the dereferencing into separate parts. It is an easy place for people to get confused. @$array->[4] seems a very natural way to dereference a data chunk. Unfortunately, it is ambiguous, and if you are doing stuff like this, make sure to do it in two separate steps; this will force you to be clear in your thoughts.

Here's a subtle issue you should be aware of when using the -> operator:

```
@ArrayOfArrayRef = (1,2,3,4,[a1,a2,a3,a4]);
print $ArrayOfArrayRef[4][2];
```

Note the difference here between this and $ArrayRefOfArrayRef. Since we are directly assigning to @ArrayOfArrayref, it is an array first (note the @ here). We need to assign to @ArrayOfArrayRef in list context, which forces a (). Note how we access it. There is no -> between the Ref and the [4] because ArrayOfArrayRef is an actual array, not an array reference. Hence, the -> is only good in the case of array references, not arrays. A good maxim to remember is to only use the -> syntax when you are dealing with references, not actual pieces of data. Only use a -> at the top level of a data structure. You don't need to do it at lower levels.

You can use these three rules in combination with the methods for access we gave last chapter to access and print some pretty complicated data structures. As a final example, suppose we want to print the following data structure:

```
$hashref =
{
    key1 =>
        {
            key1a => value1a,
            key1b => value1b
        },
    key2 =>
        {
            key2a => value2a,
            key2b => value2b
        }
};
}
```

This is a hash made of hashes. The idea is traverse down the data structure, and, at each level, print all the data structures below. Hence, we can use the following code to dereference the data structure:

```
1  foreach $key (sort keys (%$hashref))
2  {
3                                            # accessing the first level of the
4                                            # data structure by rule 1 (% in front of $)
5                                            # gets keys (key1, key2). We do a 'sort'
6                                            # to retain order;
7      my $ref = $hashref->{$key};           # sets the reference equal to the values
8                                            # for key1, key2.
9      foreach $key2 (sort keys(%$ref))      # going through the second data structure.
10     {
11         my $value = $ref->{$key2};            # get the value out of the hash.
12         print "$key -- $key2 -- $value\n"; # print out data.
13     }
14 }
```

The foreach line `foreach $key (sort keys (%$hashref))` loops around the keys inside the top level of the hash. The `my $ref = $hashref->{$key}` line gets the data structure pointed to by the key $key, namely something like:

```
'key1' => { 'key1a'=>'value1a','key2a' => 'value2a' }
```

The `foreach $key2 (sort keys(%$ref))` loop then gives us access to keys inside this hash, namely key1a and key2a. Then `my $value = $ref->{$key2}` gets the values associated with these keys, namely value1a and value2a, and finally the `print` line prints everything out.

So, the upshot of this is when this loop is done, it prints:

```
key1 -- key1a -- value1a
key1 -- key1b -- value1b
key2 -- key2a -- value2a
key2 -- key2b -- value2b
```

Make sure you understand how this is working as it is a common metaphor in Perl. We have seen it once, and we will see it again.

As with everything else in Perl, you have a choice. This functionality could be written by using the shorthand of rule 3 (using brackets to clarify):

```
foreach $key (sort keys (%$hashref))
{
    foreach $key2 (sort keys %{$hashref->{$key}})
    {
        ....
```

I personally prefer the first structure over the second, because I'm forced to think about what I am doing. The second example blithely goes through the levels of the data structure without being explicit on how the levels interact with each other, although the code is much shorter. It lacks clarity of thought; unless you know exactly what the syntax means, and how this is working, I would stick to using the placeholder technique.

Summary of Dereferencing Data References

This section discussed the various methods of retrieving data from memory once it had been put there in scalar, array, or hash form. *Dereferencing* means interpreting a reference to see where it points, going there, and retrieving the data. This occurs all in one step.

The most important rule with dereferencing and deconstructing is, as with all of Perl, keep it simple. It is better to use multiple lines of code to show your intentions than to try to show off your brilliance through complexity (which usually has the opposite effect!). In particular there are four rules you should remember:

1. Use @, $, or % to dereference references of the appropriate type: If you say $hashRef = {'my', 'hash'}, then $hashref->{'my'} equals 'hash'.
2. Use ->, as in $hashRef->{'key'} or $arrayRef->[1], to access elements of a hash reference or an array reference.
3. Use $$arrayRef[0] or $$hashRef{'key'} as alternate methods to access elements. Use in moderation, as rule 2 is much cleaner.
4. Use brackets to clarify the two ways of referring to these structures. Hence, ${$arrayRef}[0] is the same as $$arrayRef[0], only more clear.

Remember that you can use these things in conjunction with each other: ${$arrayRef->[0]}[0] might refer to an element in a two-dimensional array (although the cleaner $arrayRef->[0][0] might be preferable).

The next section shows another way to create data and data structures.

Creating Data Structures by Assignment

Perl provides the programmer with a powerful way to create data structures implicitly. This is through *assignment* of a value. In other words, there is no need to take two steps to create a structure and then assign values to it.

If you want a three-dimensional array, you can write:

```
$array3D[4][2][1] = 1;
```

and the array is created for you. As always, Perl is nice enough to handle memory management transparently for you. Perl sizes up the 3D array and makes a chunk of memory at least five elements by three elements by two elements in size (remember 0 subscripts).

Before you go into this section, you should thoroughly understand the above two sections on constructing and deconstructing references. The reason is that Perl delivers a loaded weapon into the developer's hand: the ability to make complicated data structures without thinking of the consequences of the complication. In other words, it is easy to write:

```
$a->{'sam\'s'}{'account'}[1]{'January'} = ['list', 'of', 'purchases'];
```

without thinking of how to access the structures underlying what you are doing. There is a general rule for creating complex data structures by assignment, and this is more a programmer's style rule than anything else.

If you are going to create a complex data structure by simple assignment, know what the anonymous reference of what you just created looks like, from the point of view of where you created it. The above example (with list of purchases) looks like:

```
$a = {'sam\'s' => {'account' => ['',{'January' => ['list', 'of', 'purchases']}]}}};
```

Ugly, right? And when code looks that ugly, you should consider breaking the data structure creation into several separate steps, and think about capturing the substeps into functions. In other words, think about what the process will be for recovering your data, and if that data is better served in a class.

 As a personal rule, I try never to directly access data structures more than two levels deep. This forces clarity and, hopefully, makes life easier for my fellow programmers.

Note

The Process for Creating Data Structures by Assignment

The process for creating a data structure by assignment is extremely easy. Simply write down the data structure you want, being careful of contexts, and Perl will do all the variable management for you.

For example, the following creates a three-dimensional array with at least one element in each column. It also sets the 0, 0, 0 element to 1:

```
$threeDarray[0][0][0] = 1;  # Creates a three-dimensional array, i.e.,
                            # [[[1]]]
```

The next example creates a three-dimensional array with an initial size of 2 elements in the first column, 3 elements in the second column, and 1001 elements in the third column. Since the 0..999 elements are not there, Perl creates them and stuffs them with blanks.

```
$threeDarray[1][2][1000] = 1;
```

It is possible to create hashes with arrays for the hash keys. The next example is a two-dimensional hash with an anonymous array as the entry for hashkey1 and hashkey2:

```
$twoDhash{hashkey1}{hashkey2} = [@array];
```

The following statements create the reference equivalents of the previous three examples. Note that there is an extra -> between the Ref and the first [ ]. This indicates that we are dealing with a reference here, *not* a real variable. It also makes the variable much easier to pass to functions:

```
$threeDarrayRef->[0][0][0] = 1;
$threeDarrayRef->[1][2][1000] = 1;
$twoDhashRef->{hashkey1}{hashkey2} = [@array];
complicatedFunction($threeDarrayRef, $twoDhashRef);
```

See how clean and easy this is? This will be a major point in chapters to come. Passing a real variable to a function looks like:

```
complicatedFunction(\@threeDarray, \%twoDhash);
```

which is a bit cluttered.

We have now seen the creation of a Perl data structure by way of an assignment to a variable. Just remember, this is not an explicit way to create variables and data structures. Code maintainers will think mean thoughts about you if you scatter newly created variables throughout your code without the appropriate comments. We are not calling for a return to the days of declaring all variables at the top of a program, but show some kindness to those who follow you.

Translating Direct Assignments into Equivalent Perl 5 Statements

When you 'translate direct assignments into equivalent Perl' statements you are basically attempting to 'mimic' what the Perl interpreter is doing with memory management, and do it in your head. For example, the assignment:

```
$array1[4] = 1;
```

turns into the Perl statement:

```
@array1 = (undef,undef,undef,undef,1);
```

See how this works? If you set the fifth element of `array1` to 1, then this creates, by default, four *undefined* elements in the array, before the 1 in the fourth element (because Perl is indexed by 0). This is what actually happens when you assign to an array element larger than the largest one: the array *extends*, filling the extra "spaces" with undefined elements.

Again, concentrate on the one statement. Forget about the rest of the data structure when doing these exercises.

There are many reasons why you want to be able to translate complicated data structures into references, such as:

1. For clarity, so you know exactly what you are doing
2. For regression testing
3. For debugging

Reason 1 is probably the most important. If you will be making complicated data structures, you must know exactly what you are doing. Turning an assignment into an anonymous reference (so you could build the data structure by hand if you wanted to) is an easy exercise to determine how clearly you are thinking.

Fortunately, there is an easy process for translating a data structure into an anonymous reference: Simply use the four rules used to dereference the variables to deconstruct the arrays, and put them into reference form. In this way, { } becomes a context { ... }, [ ] becomes an array context [...], and so on.

This subject is best explained by example. If you have the following assignment:

```
$array[4] = 1;
```

it becomes the following data structure/Perl statement:

```
@array = (undef,undef,undef,undef,1); # shows the data structure
                                       # @array after assignment.
                                       # note... only affects the place with the 1
                                       # doesn't affect the entire data structure.
```

Likewise, the assignment:

```
$array2D[4][0] = 1;
```

turns into:

```
@array2D = (undef,undef,undef,undef,[1]);
                        # shows the data structure @array2D after assignment.
                        # (undef,undef,undef,undef, [1])
                        # ArrayRef in fourth (indexed by 0) element
```

If we add the assignment:

```
$array2D[4][1] = 2;
```

to the data structure $array2D, we get:

```
@array2D == (undef,undef,undef,undef, [1,2] );
                      # arrayRef in fifth (indexed by 0) element
                      # added to.(in bold)
```

What happened here is that Perl has automatically grown the array for you. The 2 is added after the 1 to get the structure.

Now, if we do an assignment with a ->, a reference to an array or a hash is created instead:

```
#   $arrayRef->[4] = 1;
```

In the corresponding anonymous form, there are square brackets instead of the parentheses:

```
#   $arrayRef == [undef,undef,undef,1];  # Note... brackets here instead of ()
```

Here are a couple of three-dimensional examples. Notice that each bracket causes an extra level of nesting.

```
$arrayRef3D->[4][1][1] = 'ADDED ELEMENT1';
# Equivalent to:
#$arrayRef3D ==
#      [undef,undef,undef,undef
#         [undef,                      #arrayRef in fifth (indexed by 0) element.
#            [undef,'ADDED ELEMENT1']  #array Ref in second element of
#         ]                            #fifth element
#      ];
```

If we add something again:

```
$arrayRef3D->[4][0][2] = 'ADDED ELEMENT2';
# equivalent to
# $arrayRef3D == [undef,undef,undef,
                    [ [undef,undef,'ADDED ELEMENT2'],[undef,'ADDED ELEMENT1']]];
```

the added element gets put in the place where Perl grows the array.

Finally, in the following hash example:

```
$twoDhashRef->{hashkey1}{hashkey2} = [@array];
# Equivalent to
#   $twoDhashRef == {hashkey1 => {hashkey2 =>[@array]}};
```

each level of nesting in the hash causes an extra {. Since [@array] points to an array, the value of hashkey2 becomes a pointer to the elements of @array.

These examples show why it is so important to know exactly what you are doing before you do that long assignment. Think of what happens if you do something like:

```
$arrayRef3D->[4][0][1] = [@array];
```

and then:

```
$arrayRef3D->[4][0] = { %hash };
```

Let's turn this into the anonymous constructs as before. The first assignment $arrayRef3D->[4][0][1] = [@array]; becomes:

```
$arrayRef3D = [undef,undef,undef,undef,[[undef,[@array]]]];
```

with each indentation in $arrayRef3D becoming an extra dimension.

Now, when we add the hash, we get:

```
$arrayRef3D = [undef,undef,undef,undef,[{%hash}]];
```

See what happened? We replaced the [4][0] element with a hash. [@array] occupies the [4][0][1], element position. Since [@array] was part of that [4][0] element, it was clobbered, along with any other subscripts hanging off [4][0].

Because Perl does all of its own memory management implicitly, the array reference you are expecting disappears and is replaced by a hash. This is probably not what was intended. Be careful with this construct and use translation to debug.

Fortunately, there is a lot of help available for the programmer who is dealing with structures and debugging them. The built-in debugger has facilities for printing data structures as complicated as you would like. Also there is a gem of a module (imported from CPAN) that can take any reference Perl uses and turn it into the structure format listed. We will take a look at **Data::Dumper** later.

Simple example of **Dumper**:

```
use Data::Dumper;

$arrayref = [1,2,3,[1,2,3,4,{key1 => value1, key2 => value2}]];

print Dumper($arrayref);

  $VAR1 = [1, 2, 3,
      [1, 2, 3, 4,
        {
          key1 => value1,
          key2 => value2
        }
      ]
    ];
```

We discuss **Dumper** further in Chapter 21 "Programming for Debugging." It helps quite a bit.

Why learn how to turn a Perl assignment into a data structure equal to that assignment if Perl can do it for you? Because you can intuitively debug any Perl program if you know this method. If you are an experimenter, then read the above twice or thrice, look at the more complicated examples to follow, and then go ahead and turn to the section called "Dumper" and experiment with it.

The better you know the actual Perl translation of code, and the better you can understand how these data structures work, the cleaner your code will be. And those who maintain your code after you will sing your praises.

References and Scoping: Garbage Collection

There is one special property you should be aware of when dealing with references, and that is Perl's policy towards recollecting the memory of references that go "out of scope." This policy is called garbage collection by reference count and it works like the following. Remember when we said that the following statement:

```
if ($true)
{
    my $varb = [1,2,3,4];
}
```

actually created a new variable called $varb, assigned it the value [1,2,3,4], and then instantly destroyed $varb after the bracket? Well, there was a bit of complex machination going behind the scenes here.

Every time you say my ($varb) = [1,2,3,4] or somesuch, Perl marks down that the particular piece of memory [1,2,3,4] is being *referred* to by one variable, namely $varb. When the closing bracket is reached, the reference count for the piece of memory goes down by one ($varb is destroyed). And now, when the reference count is zero for [1,2,3,4], that piece of memory is reclaimed (and $varb is destroyed).

The important thing to remember here is that Perl does not claim memory back when a particular instance of a variable is destroyed, but only when the reference count for a piece of memory goes down to zero. It is very important to understand how Perl behaves in this situation; this is one of the primary ways that Perl differs from C, C++, or any other lower-level language. If you now say:

```
1 my ($saveVarb);
2 if ($varb)
3 {
4     my ($varb) = [1,2,3,4];
5     $saveVarb = $varb;
6 }
7 print "@$saveVarb\n";
```

the reference count for the piece of memory in [1,2,3,4] goes up by one (for my ($varb) = [1,2,3,4]), and then goes up to two (from $saveVarb = $varb). When the closing bracket is reached, the reference count goes down to one. $varb is destroyed as per scoping rules, but the piece of memory referred to by $varb does not get destroyed because the reference count is still one. Therefore, line 7 prints 1 2 3 4.

Here's another example:

```
1 sub subroutine
2 {
3     my (@array) = (@_, @_);
4     return(\@array);
5 }
```

This returns the argument stack – doubled – back to the caller in the form of an array reference. At line 3, the reference count to the data contained by @array is now one, and when you get to line 4, the reference count to @array is temporarily increased to two (since a variable on the right-hand side of the subroutine call is being assigned \@array, as in my $arrayRef = subroutine(@array)).

The reference count then goes back down to one after the main subroutine is entered. But the *memory* in @array persists.

This policy keeps memory management worry-free—99% of the time. If you say something like:

```
1 if ($true)
2 {
3     my $a = 'HERE';
4     $a = \$a;
5 }
```

Perl will never reclaim this memory. Instead, it persists. In line 3, the reference count for the piece of memory pointed to by 'HERE' becomes one. In line 4, it's bumped up to two (since $a is now pointing to 'HERE' as well). At line 5, the reference count goes down from two to one as $a is "destroyed."

Hence, the memory count here never reaches zero. You are going to have to explicitly do something like:

```
if ($true)
{
    my $a = 'HERE';
    $a = \$a;
    undef $$a;
}
```

to break this cycle (this may be common in cases where you make tree structures).

The point of this section is to trust Perl to do the right memory management most of the time, but be quick to jump on the "unable to free memory" error if it occurs.

Examples

Let's look closer at some examples of references to understand the syntax behind them. Let's start with an example of the flexibility behind Perl's access.

Example 1: Direct Anonymous Access

This example deals with something near and dear to the Perl coder's heart: Saving typing space. Consider the situation in which you want to temporarily treat an array as a hash and dereference it. For example:

```
@array = ('key1' => 'value1', 'key2' => 'value2', 'key3' => 'value3');
```

Suppose you want to treat this as a hash, such that key1's value is value1, and so on. The traditional approach (and not a bad one, I might add) is:

```
%hash = @array;        # sets the hash %hash equal to the array @array;
print $hash{'key1'};   # prints out 'value1'.
```

Can we get shorter than this? Of course! It's Perl! Hence, we could say something like:

```
print ( {@array}->{'key1'} );
```

See how this is working? @array, by virtue of being enclosed by { }, is being interpreted as a hash reference. -> dereferences that hash reference, and {'key1'} tells us that we are looking for the value that corresponds to 'key1'. This prints:

```
value1
```

This might seem a bit on the tacky side (it is), but you can actually use it to make complicated switch statements:

```
my $response = { 'option1' => 'value1', 'option2' => 'value2', 'option3' => 'value3'}->{$input};
```

which is equivalent to the more conventional (and probably better):

```
$response = ($input eq 'option1')? 'value1' :
            ($input eq 'option2')? 'value2' :
            ($input eq 'option3')? 'value3';
                                   'unknown';
```

which, of course, goes through each numbered option and compares $input to it. However, it is your choice to decide which is best. If you have a function that returns a hash, such as:

```
$days = { _getDays() }->{'Mon'};
```

where _getDays() returns a hash:

```
sub _getDays
{
    my %return = ('Mon' => 0, 'Tue' => 1, 'Wed' => 2, 'Thu'=>3, 'Fri' => 4, 'Sat' => 5, 'Sun' => 6);
    %return;
}
```

(This would make $days equal to 0, given the above call.)

Example 2: Reading a Flat File and Bundling It into a Data Structure

Let's take a bit more conventional example. Suppose you have a list of data that corresponds to time connected to a network. It looks something like this, which corresponds to an HTTP access log:

```
alpha.umn.edu - - [24/Feb/1997:09:03:50 -0700] "POST /cgi-bin/script1.cgi HTTP/
alpha.umn.edu - - [24/Feb/1997:09:04:15 -0700] "POST /cgi-bin/script1.cgi HTTP/
mcgraw.com - -    [24/Feb/1997:09:04:22 -0700] "POST /cgi-bin/script2.cgi HTTP/
rohcs.ats.com - - [24/Feb/1997:09:04:34 -0700] "POST /cgi-bin/script2.cgi HTTP/
rohcs.ats.com - - [24/Feb/1997:09:04:34 -0700] "POST /cgi-bin/script1.cgi HTTP/
```

Now, your job is to see which sites are accessing each particular file. In short, you might want to see the output be a data structure like:

```
$hash = {'/cgi-bin/script1.cgi' => {'alpha.umn.edu' => 2, 'rohcs.ats.com' => 1 }
```

which tells me, at first glance, that the script **script1.cgi** has been accessed twice from *alpha.umn.edu*, and once from *rohcs.ats.com*. To do this, you might want to do something like what is shown in Listing 7.1.

Listing 7.1
logParse.p

```
1 use FileHandle;

2  my $FH = new FileHandle("access_log");
3  my ($line, $accessHash) = ('',{});
4
5  while (defined $line = <$FH>)
6  {
7      $line =~ m"(.*?) .*POST (.*?) HTTP";
8      my $address = $1;
9      my $script = $2;
10     $accessHash->{$script}{$address}++;
11 }
```

The main thing here is line 7 and line 10. Note line 7: Here are regular expressions, *again*! This particular regular expression goes through the line, matches the address and script name, and saves them to the variables $1 and $2, respectively, as shown in Figure 7.6.

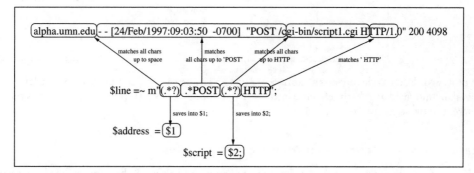

Figure 7.6
Regular
Expression to
Match Line from
Access Log

Anyway, the line here in question is 10. When you say:

```
$accessHash->{'/cgi-bin/script1.cgi'}{'alpha.umn.edu'}++;
```

it creates an entry in the hash `accessHash`, according to the rules we described earlier (substituting -> and {}{}, each for an anonymous hash). This is like:

```
$accessHash = {'/cgi-bin/script1.cgi' => {'alpha.umn.edu' => 1 }}
```

After the `while` loop is done, the data structure looks like:

```
$accessHash =
        {
            '/cgi-bin/script1.cgi' => {
                                        'alpha.umn.edu' => 2,
                                        'rohcs.ats.com' => 1
                                      },
            '/cgi-bin/script2.cgi' => {
                                        'rohcs.ats.com' => 1,
                                        'mcgraw.com' => 1
                                      }
        };
```

Using the rules of dereferencing, we can untangle this (it is a "hash of hashes," as we shall see in Chapter 8). For example, if we want to get the particular sites that access **/cgi-bin/script1.cgi**, we can say:

```
my $script1Hash = $accessHash->{'/cgi-bin/script1.cgi'};
my @accessSites = keys(%$script1Hash);
print "Access sites for script1: @accessSites\n";
```

which works to dereference this, and print out "Access sites for **script1: alpha.umn.edu mcgraw.com**," as in Figure 7.7.

Figure 7.7
Dereferencing a
Hash of Hashes

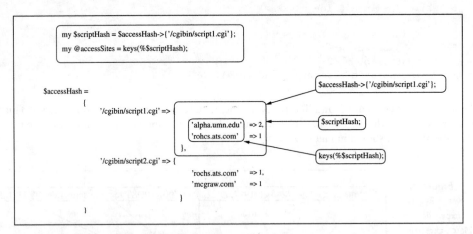

In other words, the code `$accessHash->{'/cgi-bin/script1.cgi` goes down one level into the hash, and saves an "intermediate" hash reference into `$script1Hash`. `keys(%$script1Hash)` gets the keys for the hash referenced by `$script1Hash`.

Example 3: A Recursive Data Structure for Files

OK, let's take one more example, one complicated enough to tie in all the concepts we have seen in this chapter. If you say something like:

```
C:\> dir
```

and get:

```
Volume in drive C has no label
Volume Serial Number is 4631-1803
Directory of C:\WINDOWS

.               <DIR>        11-16-96  5:10p .
..              <DIR>        11-16-96  5:10p ..
COMMAND         <DIR>        11-16-96  5:14p COMMAND
SYSTEM          <DIR>        11-16-96  5:14p SYSTEM
HELP            <DIR>        11-16-96  5:14p HELP
NETDET   INI         7,885   07-11-95  9:50a NETDET.INI
FORMS           <DIR>        11-16-96  5:38p FORMS
SMARTDRV EXE        45,145   11-16-96  5:01p SMARTDRV.EXE
REGEDIT  EXE       120,320   07-11-95  9:50a REGEDIT.EXE
...SKIP LOTS HERE.
         242 file(s)      12,379,223 bytes
          21 dir(s)      438,534,144 bytes free
```

it can be looked on as a recursive data structure, or a tree. Each directory corresponds to a branch that can be expanded, and each file corresponds to an edge, or leaf. Now, doing a directory command on the entire structure on disk can cost time. Instead, we'd like to do it only once (if possible), and then *cache*, or *save*, the fact that we have done it in memory. So, we could do something like:

```
my $tree = findTree("/");
```

where findTree takes a directory ("/") as an argument, and returns a data structure representing a file tree, and

```
my @files = getFiles($tree, "export/home/epeschko");
```

retrieves information about files underneath the directory export/home/epeschko, relative to the data structure itself, without actually having to read the disk again. This turns into a data structure like:

```
$tree =
        { "COMMAND"       => { 'file list_in_command' }.
          "SYSTEM"        => { 'file_list in system' }.
          "NETDET.INI"    => "FILE",
          "FORMS"         => { 'file_list_in_forms' }.
          "SMARTDRV.EXE"  => "FILE",
          "REGEDIT.EXE"   => "FILE",
          "HELP"          => { "ACCESS.TXT" => "FILE",
                               "HELP.TXT"   => "FILE",
                               "WHATVR" =>   { "TEST1" => "FILE",
                                               "TEST2" => "FILE"
                                             }
                             }
        };
```

Here, each hash represents a directory encountered, and each subhash represents either files or directories under that directory. Here, HELP is expanded for you (to see the files underneath it).

Now this is a job for recursion, and we have already seen a recursive solution from Chapter 5 that did something very similar.

Listing 7.2
simpleFind.p

```
1   sub simple_find
2   {
3       my ($input) = @_;
4       my $file;
5       print "$input\n" if (-f $input);
6       if (-d $input)
7       {
8           opendir(FD, $input);
9           my @files = readdir(FD);
10          closedir(FD);
11          foreach $file (@files)
12          {
13              next if ($file eq '.' || $file eq '..');
14                          # don't want to self-recurse
15              simple_find("$input/$file");
16          }
17      }
18  }
```

What must we do to modify this to get what we want? First, we need to realize that we are simply printing the input here, rather than putting it into a data structure.

Second, simple_find("$input/$file") will print the whole path to the file itself, printed out by print $input. This is not what we want. Again, we are shooting for:

```
$tree = { 'dir' => {'dir1' => { 'file1' => 'FILE' },
                              { 'file2' => 'FILE' }
                  }
        }
```

not:

```
$tree = { 'dir' => 'dir/dir1' => {'dir/dir1/file1' => 'FILE' } } }
```

Hence, we have two problems. One, the code as stated does not put its results into a data structure. Two, it prints out too much information. (We want to have only one level of the directory structure per branch.) These two problems translate into a modified subroutine like what is shown in Listing 7.3.

Listing 7.3
findTree.p

```
1   sub findTree
2   {
3       my ($input) = @_;
4       my ($file, $dirhash) = ('', {});
5       return ("FILE") if (-f $input);
6       if (-d $input)
7       {
8           opendir(FD, $input);
9           my @files = readdir(FD);
10          closedir(FD);
11
12          chdir ("$input");
```

```
13          foreach $file (@files)
14          {
15            next if ($file eq "." || $file eq '..');
16            $dirhash->{$file} = findTree("$file");
17          }
18          chdir("..");
19     }
20     return($dirhash);
21  }
```

The first thing we notice is that the print is gone. Instead we have in line 5 return("FILE") if (-f $input). This checks to see whether $input is a file. If so, it returns a leaf to the findTree that called it, saying that the argument passed to it was a file.

Second, the call returns a hash called $dirhash if—and only if—$input is a directory. Whether or not $input is a file or directory, notice that the heart of the subroutine is in line 16:

```
$dirhash->{$file} = findTree("$file");
```

This innocent-looking statement is what builds our data structure for us. At the top level, $dirhash is the entire structure that is returned to the main subroutine. In recursive calls to findTree, $dirhash->{$file} is the portion of the tree that is below the file (or directory $file). Say we call this routine on the file structure:

```
$tree = findTree('.');
'dir'
'dir\dir1'
'dir\dir1\dir2'
'dir\dir1\file1'
'dir\file1'
```

This corresponds to the data structure:

```
$tree =
    {
        dir => {
                dir1 => {
                            dir2 => {   },
                            file1 => 'FILE',
                        },
                        file1 => 'FILE'
        };
```

Now, if you say:

```
$dirRef = $tree->{'dir'}->{'dir1'};
```

you get the data structure:

```
        {
         'dir2' => {  },
         'file1' => 'FILE'
        }
```

which is all the files and directories under **dir/dir1**. Furthermore, this points to a solution to our second problem, namely, a way of retrieving information from this structure. Let's look at how we wanted to call it:

```
my @files = getFiles($tree, "export/home/epeschko");
```

A sample way of doing this is shown in Listing 7.4.

Listing 7.4
getFiles.p

```
1   sub getFiles
2   {
3       my ($tree, @path) = @_;
4       my $pathPart = shift(@path);
5       my $subtree = $tree->{$pathPart};
6
7       if (@path)
8       {
9           return getFiles($subtree, @path);
10      }
11      else
12      {
13          listFiles($subtree);
14      }
15  }
```

This is our "stub" routine, which lets us have the usage we want. Passing in export/home/epeschko with the data structure is user-friendly, but it is *not* "computer-friendly." It requires the computer to parse out the structure, so the job of lines 6-9 is to take the path apart, turning it into (export, home, epeschko), and then in line 8, to go down to the appropriate level in the hash ($subtree = $subtree->{$pathPart}). At that point and only that point do we call listFiles(), our recursive subroutine that does most of the work. This is shown in Listing 7.5.

Listing 7.5
getFiles.p II

```
15  sub listFiles
16  {
17      my ($hash, $pretty) = @_;
18      $pretty = "" if (not defined $pretty);
19      foreach my $key (keys (%$hash))
20      {
21          if ($hash->{$key} eq "FILE")
22          {
23              print "$pretty$key\n";
24          }
25          else
26          {
27              print $pretty . uc($key) . " =>\n";
28              listFiles($hash->{$key}, "$pretty\t");
29          }
30      }
31  }
```

Here, we use ref, and traverse the data structure going down. foreach $key (%$subtree) in line 7 gets all the keys in the data structure at our current level, and line 10 checks to see if the key $key points to a hash or a regular element.

If $subtree->{$key} is a hash reference, then listFiles is called recursively (lines 10–13). If $subtree->{$key} is a scalar (i.e., not a reference), we know that it is a file and push it onto the return list (line 16) (see Figure 7.8).

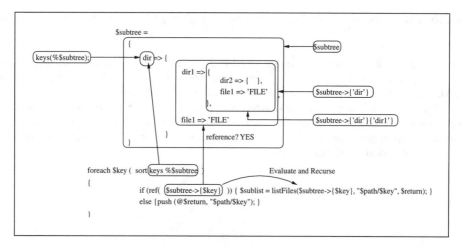

Figure 7.8
Getting the Data
Out of the
Findtree
Structure

This example shows even more. Look at how we are calling our subroutine. To save time, when we do our recursive call, we are putting the values into an array reference. Hence:

```
push(@$return, "$path/$key");
```

is the only place where we do any copying of any sort. Hence, in the subroutine call:

```
listFiles($tree, "export/home/epeschko", $return);
```

$return is actually getting changed by the subroutine. The push statement in the earlier example actually references what is inside of $return, and actually changes it. The $return variable is, therefore, "along for the ride."

This has been a long and rather arduous example, but it shows much about how Perl's subroutine structure works. It is available on the accompanying CD and if you have questions about it, one of the best ways to figure it out is by taking it apart. In fact, you will learn more about Perl by taking this one group of subroutines apart than most people learn about Perl in months.

Summary of References

References are Perl's way of creating extremely complicated data structures. If you are going to remember anything from this chapter, remember how to:

1. Create an arbitrary data structure via references; that is, know what $anonHash ={key =>{ key => {key => [@array]}}} means.
2. Get values out of a data structure; that is, know that $anonHash->{key}{key}{key}[1] gets the value $array[1].
3. Turn an assignment into a Perl construction; that is, know that $array->[0][2][1] = 'ADDED' taken by itself turns into the data structure $array = [['','',['','ADDED']]].

In other words, if you can manipulate hard references and go backward and forward with them in your mind, then you are ready to use **Data::Dumper**. This will help you immensely to understand references. In fact, it will also help you to debug your programs quite well. We will see much more use of Dumper throughout this book.

Remember also, the policy on how Perl reclaims memory that is allocated in a process called garbage collection. In short, Perl does what you want 95 percent of the time, and only when you start making statements like:

```
my $a = 1;
$a = \$a;
```

are you going to get memory leaks. Even then, you can explicitly tell Perl not to leak by saying something like:

```
undef $$a; .
```

Also, please look over the three examples in this chapter. Chapter 8 will also give many examples (in fact, it is devoted to pragmatic examples about references), but these three really help with the concepts involved behind them. Master them, and the next chapter's examples will be almost too easy.

Finally, don't get too complicated with references. If you need a complicated data structure, you might as well use a class instead. Classes have other inherent plusses to them. (One value of classes is that they are not generic.) You can also simplify your interface. Therefore, we will show some of the more common data structures next, and then move on to package and class syntax.

More on Perl 5 References and Common Data Structures

To this point in the book we have been talking about the very lowest level of Perl 5 data structures: scalars, hashes, and arrays. We have also discussed references, which are ways to point to and access data from within a given structure. Now we are going to put these pieces together into a more complex format.

There are data structures that come up again and again in Perl; most of the time, these are all you need to get along even without modules or objects. Indeed, these structures are often used in conjunction with modules and classes: They handily return data to the programmer that is too complex for a simple array or hash reference to provide.

Chapter Overview

In this chapter, we will go over four of these commonly used data structures. These data structures are:

- Array of Arrays
- Array of Hashes
- Hash of Hashes
- Hash of Arrays

In each case, there are three basic things you need to know about each of these structures, in addition to examples, to actually use them:

1. How to recognize them
2. How to construct them
3. How to get values out of them

This chapter is split into four parts, each dedicated to a different data structure, looking at the three issues, and seeing actual examples of their usage. We will also consider hybrid data structures, ones that combine elements of the four data structures into structures that are either more complicated (like Array of Hash of Hashes) or more irregular.

Finally, we shall talk a bit about passing complicated data structures inside programs and functions.

Note

There is a slight simplification in talking about these data structures that you should know about. When we talk about Array of Arrays or Array of Hashes, etc., we are really talking about what you might call a reference to an Array of Arrays or an Array of Hashes.

I mention them without the "reference" part because I have found it wise to always use references when dealing with data structures that are more complicated than your standard hash or array. If you always use references, it will simplify your life.

This is an "applied" chapter. The previous chapter talked quite a bit about the theory behind Perl references, and gave some examples, but didn't go into the nuts and bolts behind the most common Perl data structures. (Perl 4 programmers also need a bit of orientation to actually get used to them.)

If you are not quite sure of how references work, or want more examples of their usage, this chapter is recommended. People who are looking for even more examples on the way Perl references work are advised to turn to the reference page (**perlLoL**). As always, this page goes up and down and inside out, giving many examples on the subject.

First, let's take a look at the data structure most people get to know when they first learn Perl references: an Array of Array.

Array of Arrays (AoA)

An *Array of Arrays* is a simple, two-dimensional array sort of like a checkerboard with the elements being the reference points to the squares on a board.

The Array of Arrays data structure isn't used as often as one might think; as we shall see, getting individual values out of these structures requires that one knows the numeric subscript for that value, which can make them difficult to debug. (You often find yourself asking questions such as: "Is the element I want in $value->[7][6]<, or $value->[7][5]?")

However, they are the first reference data structures that people learn, as they resemble two-dimensional arrays in other languages. They are also important in cases where you have data in a table-like form, where you are assured that the data is in a regular structure. Or, in cases where you need to keep the order of the data, and that data is too complicated to keep in an array.

How to Recognize an Array of Arrays

If you were to construct an Array of Arrays, or create it out of a direct assignment, it would look something like this:

```
$AoA =
[
    ['element1a', 'element2a', 'element3a','element4a'],
    ['element1b', 'element2b','element3b','element4b']
];
```

Here, the outermost set of brackets (the [] encompassing *everything*) indicates that $AoA is a reference to an array. Each inner set of brackets equals a subarray, or the second dimension of the array.

Note

This is also the output you would get if you used the **Data::Dumper** module, and did something like:

```
use Data::Dumper;
print Dumper($AoA);
```

given, of course, that $AoA is an Array of Arrays, and contains the values given in the previous example.

Array of Arrays Direct Access

As we said, Array of Arrays work well in cases where the data layout is well-known. Such a dataset might be seen in a database table (say, customer), where each row in that database consists of four columns: ID, name, address, and type. Suppose the data looked like the following:

```
1111|George Hammond|12 Elk Pkwy | GOOD
1112|Susie Wayland|15 Sachs Road | CANCELED
1113|Michael Thurmond|1115 Cherry St |GOOD
```

This could, fairly easily, be turned into a Perl-ish data structure that looked like the following:

```
$ArrayOfCustomers =
[
    [ 1111, 'George Hammond','12 Elk Pkwy','GOOD'],
    [ 1112, 'Susie Wayland','15 Sachs Road','CANCELED'],
    [ 1113, 'Michael Thurmond','1115 Cherry St','GOOD']
];
```

This is an Array of Arrays. Each row of the database table corresponds to an array *inside* the Array of Arrays. Let's look at five ways you may want to access this internal element.

First, let's say you want to get the first customer's name. Each element in an Array of Arrays can be directly accessed by using the following syntax:

```
$AoA->[$dim1][$dim2];
```

$dim1 and $dim2 are the subscripts of each dimension in the array you want to access. Hence, something like:

```
print $ArrayOfCustomers->[0][1];
```

prints the first character's name, printing out the boldface element:

```
$ArrayOfCustomers =
[
    [ 1111, 'George Hammond','12 Elk Pkwy','GOOD'],
    [ 1112, 'Susie Wayland','15 Sachs Road','CANCELED'],
```

```
    [ 1113, 'Michael Thurmond','1115 Cherry St','GOOD']
];
```

Second, suppose you want to print the data of a customer directly. In other words, you want to print an entire row consisting of ID, name, address, and status. Well, the syntax for printing a subarray is just as simple:

```
my $arrayRef = $AoA->[$dim1]; print "@$arrayRef";
```

$dim1 is the first dimension of the array (the row you wish to access). Given this data, the statement:

```
(@{$AoA->[0]});
```

points to the boldface customer in the following code:

```
$ArrayOfCustomers =
[
    [ 1111, 'George Hammond','12 Elk Pkwy','GOOD'],
    [ 1112, 'Susie Wayland','15 Sachs Road','CANCELED'],
    [ 1113, 'Michael Thurmond','1115 Cherry St','GOOD']
];
```

and the statement:

```
print "@{$AoA->[1]}\n";
```

prints "1112 Susie Wayland 15 Sachs Road CANCELED".

Third, suppose you want to extract only the names from your data structure. This is a job for map (as we shall see in Chapter 10 on built-in functions and special variables):

```
@names = map($_->[1], @$ArrayOfCustomers);
```

map goes through each array in the array @$ArrayOfCustomers and pulls out the second element in each, and then passes this back to @names:

```
@names = ('George Hammond', 'Susie Wayland', 'Michael Thurmond');
```

It could be rewritten as:

```
foreach $name (@$ArrayOfCustomers)
{
    push(@names, $ArrayOfCustomers->[1]);
}
```

Fourth, suppose you want to get the name and address for the third customer in the list. The following code:

```
($name, $address) = @{$ArrayOfCustomers->[2]}[1,2];
```

works by going into the second array element of $ArrayOfCustomers and grabbing its second and third members, accessing the following boldfaced elements:

```
$ArrayOfCustomers =
[
    [ 1111, 'George Hammond','12 Elk Pkwy','GOOD'],
    [ 1112, 'Susie Wayland','15 Sachs Road','CANCELED'],
    [ 1113, 'Michael Thurmond','1115 Cherry St','GOOD']
];
```

The fifth and final way to access an internal element is as follows: Suppose that you want to get the customers that only have IDs greater than 1111. This is a job for grep:

```
    my $greatIDS = [];
    @$greatIDS = grep($_->[0] > 1111, @$ArrayOfCustomers);
```

Here, grep simply weeds out all customers with a first element less than, or equal to 1111 and keeps all elements that satisfy the condition. Hence, $greatIDS will contain the following elements in boldface:

```
$ArrayOfCustomers =
[
    [ 1111,  'George Hammond','12 Elk Pkwy','GOOD'],
    [ 1112,  'Susie Wayland','15 Sachs Road','CANCELED'],
    [ 1113,  'Michael Thurmond','1115 Cherry St','GOOD']
];
```

Notice that we make $greatIDS a reference, and then assign to that reference rather than to the array itself. This allows the data structure to mirror the one that it was derived from. This makes it look like:

```
$greatIDS =
[
    [1112,'Susie Wayland','15 Sachs Road','CANCELED'],
    [1113,'Michael Thurmond','1115 Cherry St','GOOD' ]
];
```

Again, grep will be discussed in Chapter 10 on built-in variables. It is basically equivalent to the following:

```
foreach $array (@$ArrayOfCustomers)
{
    if ($array->[0] > 1111) { push(@$greatIDS, $array); }
}
```

This code goes through each array in the Array of Arrays and compares it to 1111.

A Common Misconception in Array of Arrays

Many Perl programmers make the following mistake when accessing elements inside an Array of Arrays reference. If we said:

```
@greatIDS = grep($_->[0] > 1111, @$ArrayOfCustomers );
```

then @greatIDS is no longer a reference, and the data structure would look like:

```
@greatIDS =
(
    [1112,'Susie Wayland','15 Sachs Road','CANCELED']
    [1113,'Michael Thurmond','1115 Cherry St','GOOD' ]
);
```

Note the parentheses here. You would then access the first name ('Susie Wayland') with:

```
print $greatIDS[0][1];
```

instead of:

```
print $greatIDS->[0][1];
```

although with this usage you would again have to be careful about passing @greatIDS to functions. If you said:

```
function(@greatIDS, @greatIDS2);
```

then it would be wrong if you want to pass these variables distinctly to a function call, something like:

```
function(\@greatIDS, \@greatIDS2);
```

because again, Perl will take anything that looks like (@greatIDS, @greatIDS2) and munge it into one, gigantic list.

Figure 8.1 summarizes all of the basic methods to access an Array of Arrays, albeit in a simpler example.

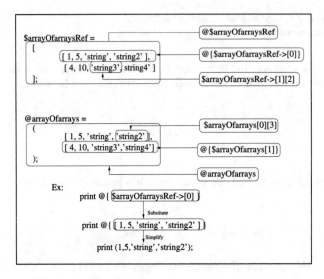

Figure 8.1
Access Methods
on Array of Arrays

You must be careful not to mismatch references and actual variables. If you say something like:

```
@array = @{$AoA->[1]};
```

then @array is an actual array, a nonreference. Whereas if you say:

```
@$array = @{$AoA->[1]}
```

then $array is now a reference to an array, and therefore more convenient to be passed to functions.

If you truly understand how each of these access methods is working, then you will have a good idea of how everything in Perl is working.

Creating an Array of Arrays

One thing we have kind of ignored was how to actually turn the following:

```
1111|George Hammond|12 Elk Pkwy | GOOD
1112|Susie Wayland|15 Sachs Road | CANCELED
1113|Michael Thurmond|1115 Cherry St |GOOD
```

into:

```
$ArrayOfCustomers =
[
    [ 1111, 'George Hammond','12 Elk Pkwy','GOOD'],
    [ 1112, 'Susie Wayland','15 Sachs Road','CANCELED'],
```

```
        [ 1113, 'Michael Thurmond','1115 Cherry St','GOOD']
];
```

We need to make a *constructor*. This problem extends to situations in which there is not a simple flat file from which we are accessing records from a database or parsing data from commands or other sources of information. For the simple purposes of this flat file example, the constructor will look like the following:

```
my $AoA = makeArrayOfArrays('filename');
```

where makeArrayOfArrays takes a filename, opens it, parses the data in the format just given, creates an Array of Arrays, and passes the reference back to $AoA on the right-hand side. Let's consider two possible attacks, one bad and one good.

Direct Constructor of Array of Arrays

First, let's look at a suboptimal (probably bad) way of creating an Array of Arrays from a flat file.

This is the direct method: Take each individual element, one at a time, and put that element into its appropriate slot, something like this:

```
1111|George Hammond|12 Elk Pkwy |GOOD
1112|Susie Wayland|15 Sachs Road |CANCELED
1113|Michael Thurmond|1115 Cherry St |GOOD
```

Set 1111 first so the data structure looks like:

```
[['1111']]
```

and set George Hammond second (the data structure looks like [['1111', 'George Hammond']]). Codewise this becomes what is shown in Listing 8.1.

Listing 8.1
makeArrayOfArrays.p

```
0   use FileHandle;          # we need filehandle module for 'new FileHandle'
1   sub makeArrayOfArrays
2   {
3       my ($file) = @_;     # Assume that we are passed in a filename
4       my $return = [];     # return value;
5       my (@lines);         # lines for file.
6
7       my $fd = new FileHandle("$file") || die "Couldn't open $file\n";
8       chomp(@lines = <$fd>); # get all lines, chop the return off of each line
9
10      my ($line, $xx, $yy);
11      for ($xx = 0; $xx < @lines; $xx++)
12      {
13          my (@elements) = split(m"\|", $line);
14          for ($yy = 0; $yy < @elements; $yy++)
15          {
16              $return->[$xx][$yy] = $elements[$yy];
17          }
18      }
19      return($return);
20  }
```

This is a common metaphor for C programmers just beginning in Perl. The heart of the Array of Arrays construction is in lines 11 through 17, which is basically two nested for loops; it is suboptimal for three reasons:

1. It requires two variables, $xx, $yy, to manually iterate through each element in the two-dimensional array.
2. It is way too verbose. As we shall see, we can compress this function down to three lines.
3. It has no sense of abstraction. In creating this data structure, we must worry about each and every element in it.

Point 3 is perhaps the most important point, one on which we will spend a great deal of time in the latter part of this book. What happens if we decide to enhance the function so it can ignore certain elements in the file, as in the following:

```
$AoA = makeArrayOfArrays('filename', {IGNORE => [1,2]});
```

where the '{IGNORE => [1,2]}' parameter simply tells makeArrayOfArrays to ignore fields 1 and 2 in this particular filename? If we wanted to do this, we would have to add code to the function itself (see Listing 8.2).

Listing 8.2
makeArrayOfArrays2.p

```
0    use FileHandle;              # we need filehandle module for 'new FileHandle'
1    sub makeArrayOfArrays
2    {
3        my ($file, $config) = @_;           # Assume that we are given filename
4        my ($return, @lines) = ([],());     # return value, lines for file;
5        my $ignoreElements =
6               $config->{IGNORE} || [];     # we get the items we want to ignore
7
8        my $fd = new FileHandle("$file") || die "Couldn't open $file\n";
9        chomp(@lines = <$fd>);              # get all lines,chop return off lines
10
11       my ($line, $xx, $yy);
12       for ($xx = 0; $xx < @lines; $xx++)
13       {
14           my (@elements) = split(m"\|", $line);
15           for ($yy = 0; $yy < @elements; $yy++)
16           {
17               if (!grep ($_ == $yy, @$ignoreElements))  #
18               {
19                   $return->[$xx][$yy] = $elements[$yy];
20               }
21           }
22       }
23       return($return);
24   }
```

Here, the added code is in boldface. The grep statement basically looks through the @$ignoreElements array, checking to see whether any of the elements happen to be $yy. English-wise, it translates as "Ignore if $yy happens to be in the list @$ignoreElements." (grep is infinitely useful. See Chapter 10 on built-in functions for more examples.) Note two things here:

- The subroutine is getting rather long (24 lines).
- The subroutine is subtly incorrect. Notice that line 19 will give you a structure that looks like:

```
$AoA =
[
    ['1111','',''.'GOOD'],
    ['1112','',''.'CANCELED'],
    ['1113','',''.'GOOD']
];
```

where each of the ignored elements will leave behind a "ghost" element (a ' ') in its place. This may be desired, but most likely is not. This is a consequence of Perl's policy of variables.

In any case, the upshot is that by doing this direct assignment, you limit your coding flexibility. If you need to add functionality, then more likely than not, you will have to go through a lot of discomfort to make your functions work.

Let's take a look at a better constructor for this particular data structure.

Indirect Constructor of Array of Arrays

As said, the code noted above is bad because it does not allow coding flexibility. By relying on directly creating the array, you are painting yourself into a corner by not allowing your code to expand.

So, how do you overcome these limitations? The solution is to abstract your data structure creation. In this case, think of your lowest unit of measurement as a "line" in a file, rather than each individual element.

Listing 8.3 is a constructor that does basically the same thing, but does it in a way that will allow more room to grow.

Listing 8.3
makeArrayOfArrays3.p

```
0   use FileHandle;              # use FileHandle package to get below functionality.
1   sub makeArrayOfArrays
2   {
3       my ($file) = @_;         # Assume that we are passed the
4                                # file name.
5       my $return = [];         # return value;
6       my (@lines);             # lines in file
7
8       my $fd = new FileHandle("$file") || die "Couldn't open $file\n";
9       chomp(@lines = <$fd>);
10      foreach $line (@lines)
11      {
12          push(@$return, [ split(m"\|", $line) ]);
13      }
14      return($return);
15  }
```

As you can see, this is much cleaner. Notice also that the code is shorter. In particular, one line (line 12) takes the place of four in the direct constructor! There are also no iterator variables ($xx, $yy). Overall, the subroutine is shorter by about 10 lines. We could compress it further, too, if pressed. In particular, lines 9–12 could become:

```
@$return = map {[split(m"\|", $ )]} @lines;
```

which basically is a synonym for lines 10–13, pushing onto a return array a changed version of an input variable (@lines).

However, the main benefit of this approach is flexibility. Suppose we want to add the same functionality that we tried (and failed) to add before, namely:

```
$AoA = makeArrayOfArrays('filename', {IGNORE => [1,2]});
```

where `IGNORE` signals the `makeArrayOfArrays` function to ignore the second and third elements. Well, the key to adding this is to recognize that line 11 is a perfect line to replace with a function call (Listing 8.4).

Listing 8.4
makeArrayOfArrays4.p

```
0   use FileHandle;                # use FileHandle package to get below functionality.
1   sub makeArrayOfArrays
2   {
3       my ($file,$config) = @_;   # Assume that we are passed the
4                                  # file name.
5       my $return = [];           # return value;
6       my (@lines);               # lines in file
7
8       my $fd = new FileHandle("$file") || die "Couldn't open $file\n";
9       chomp(@lines = <$fd>);
10      foreach $line (@lines)
11      {
12          push(@$return, getArrayRef($line, $config));
13      }
14      return($return);
15  }
```

Here, `getArrayRef` returns an array reference, given the passed-in line, and the configuration hash. In this case, `getArrayRef` might look like this:

```
1   sub getArrayRef
2   {
3       my ($line, $config) = @_;
4       my @return;
5       my $ignoreElements = $config->{IGNORE} || [];
6       my $yy;
7       my @elements = split(m"\|", $line);
7       for ($yy = 0; $yy < @elements; $yy++)
8           { push(@return, $elements[$yy]_) if (!grep($_ == $yy,@$ignoreElements));}
9       return([ @return ] );
10  }
```

Hence, we delegate the task of deciding which elements we want to a subfunction. Line 7 is responsible for weeding out the elements in our "ignore list," and we return an array reference to the ones that are left over (line 8). We end up, therefore, with a data structure that looks like:

```
$AoA =
[
    ['1111', 'GOOD'],
    ['1112', 'CANCELED'],
    ['1113', 'GOOD']
];
```

Because we have abstracted out what we do with lines, we can split our function into several manageable chunks, rather than a monolithic whole.

Anyway, now that we have created our function to make this data structure, let's take a look at a generic function to access the data structure.

Array of Arrays Access Function

We are now in a position to create a function that will print out any Array of Arrays. Let's go further with the access methods we talked about. Remember that:

```
$AoA->[2][1]
```

directly accessed the element in a two-dimensional array, and:

```
$arrayRef = $AoA->[2];
print @$arrayRef;
```

prints the array slice associated with that array.

Suppose we want to print the entire data structure. Given that:

```
$account =
[
    ['name','type','address','amount'],
    ['name2','type2','address2','amount2']
];
```

we want to print name type address amount\name2 type2 address2 amount2.

We need a *generic function* that does this for us, which traverses down our data structure and prints what we need in the way we need it.

Listing 8.5 is such a function. We assume that we are passed an Array of Arrays reference.

Listing 8.5
printAoA.p

```
 1  sub printAoA
 2  {
 3    my ($AoA) = @_;                  # we are passed the AoA reference.
 4    my ($return);
 5
 6    foreach $arrayref (@$AoA)        # gives an array ref.
 7    {
 8      my $scalar = "@$arrayref\n"; # simply print the reference out, as a scalar.
 9      $return .= $scalar;
10    }
11    $scalar;
12  }
```

Here, lines 6–10 do most of the work. We go through each reference in the Array of Arrays reference passed in, and simply make a scalar out of it (line 8). By the rules of interpolation, this comes out to be a space-separated scalar. We might want to add a parameter for a configuration hash, as we did with the constructor, so you could say something like:

```
printAoA($AoA, {DELIM => '|'});
```

to print a pipe-delimited field. This would look like what is shown in Listing 8.6.

Listing 8.6
printAoA2.p

```
1  sub printAoA
2  {
3    my ($AoA, $config) = @_;              # we are passed the AoA reference.
4    my ($return);
5    local($") = $config->{DELIM} if ($config->{DELIM});
6    foreach $arrayref (@$AoA)             # gives an array ref.
7    {
8    my $scalar = "@$arrayref\n";          # simply print the reference out, as a scalar.
9        $return .= $scalar;
10   }
11   $return;
12 }
```

Here, the special variable $" = "|" makes the expression "@$arrayref\n" equal to something like "1|2|3|4", rather than "1 2 3 4". In other words, this would give you the "magic" required to print an array with any delimiter you wanted (you could do a similar trick with $\ to print any ending character you wanted).

The upshot of all this is that this function can be made very generic. Since we are not concerned anywhere in this function about the size of the arrays involved (as Perl is nice enough to keep track of this for us), this can be used on any Array of Arrays. Therefore, foreach $arrayRef (@$AoA) traverses the first dimension of AoA and:

```
print "@$arrayRef";
```

by default, traverses the second dimension.

Array of Arrays Example: Filtering Columns from Excel

Now let's take a look at an example of the use of Arrays of Arrays, to try to show where they are helpful. Keep in mind that we are talking about flat files, although with extensions like SybPerl, OraPerl, or OLE, you could do the same thing with a database or Microsoft programs (you could do the following inside Excel, for example). We provide these packages on the accompanying CD. Suppose that you have a table (in a file) that looks something like this:

```
"Raymond Burton",31,"Architect","Sampson Architecture"
"Sam Ireland",34,"Administrative Assistant","USV"
"Jim Hampton",35,"Senior VP","Tyco LTD"
```

This is your standard, vanilla "comma-separated values" file, which any Excel program can spit out. Now, suppose you want to get a summary that simply lists the name and title of each person in the file, and print it to a file, in alphabetical order. Use the following section, "Plan of Attack," as a guide.

Plan of Attack

There are four steps:

1. Parse the file and put it into a data structure.
2. Sift through the data structure and take out the elements that you want.

3. Sort these elements into an alphabetically ordered reference.
4. Print out these elements to a file.

Now steps 1, 2, and 4 look very similar to what we were doing with `makeArrayOfArrays` and `printAoA`. Hence, we will modify the functions to do these steps of the task that we require in two statements:

```
my $modifiedAoA = makeArrayOfArrays("CSVfile", {IGNORE => [1,3], DELIMITER => "," });
printAoA($modifiedAoA, {OUTPUT_FILE => "newfile", DELIMITER => ","});
```

The first statement (`makeArrayOfArrays`) actually:

1. Creates the array of arrays, separating words by a comma (`,`).
2. Ignores the second and fourth elements.

The second statement (`printAoA`):

1. Prints the modified elements to an output file.
2. Uses the delimiter `,` to do so.

The sorting then would be done by a different routine which we have yet to write.

Now this is probably the best way to do it, as you are reusing code and making a powerful subroutine in the process. However, it probably isn't the best way to learn about Array of Arrays syntax, so I leave it as an exercise for you.

Let's make a complete program that does this. This program takes as its first argument an input file, CSV, and as its second argument an output file, and cuts out the second and fourth elements. Here is a first crack:

```
1 my $ifh = new FileHandle("$ARGV[0]");
2 my $ofh = new FileHandle("> $ARGV[1]");
3 my $line;
4 my $AoA = [];
5 while (defined ($line = <$ifh>))
6 {
7     @elements = split(m",", $line);
8     push(@$AoA, [@elements[0,2]]);
9 }
```

Note

This is subtly wrong, and if you look at comma-separated value files, you can see why. Suppose you have something like the following in `$line`:

```
"Struthers, Aaron", 54, "Bouncer","Sam's Grill"
```

Then when you split (m`","`, `$line`);, you get *five* elements:

```
('"Struthers','Aaron"',54,'"Bouncer"','"Sam\'s Grill"');
```

rather than four, because there is a comma in `"Struthers, Aaron"`. Fortunately, Perl provides a package called **Text::Parsewords**, which let's you do something like:

```
use Text::ParseWords;
@elements = quotewords(",", 1, $line);
```

and parse it correctly, because the comma is in the middle of double quotes.

This routine does your data structure creation. Line 7 (with caveats) does the splitting of your input lines (into elements), and line 8 actually populates the Array of Arrays with the two elements we want (name and occupation). Our structure now looks like this:

```
$AoA =
[
    ['"Raymond Burton"','"Architect"'],
    ['"Sam Ireland"','"Administrative Assistant"'],
    ['"Jim Hampton"','"Senior VP"']
];
```

Now, we need to sort them:

```
1 @$AoA = sort {$a->[0] cmp $b->[0]} @$AoA;
```

`sort` is a built-in function in Perl that lets you sort elements in any way, shape, or form you desire. Here, we happen to be sorting the names in the file in alphabetical order, because we know that name is element 0. Because each element in @$AoA is itself an array, this function reaches in, gets the first element out of two of the elements in @$AoA, and then compares them. After this, we have a structure like:

```
$AoA =
[
    ['"Raymond Burton"','"Architect"'],
    ['"Jim Hampton"','"Senior VP"'],
    ['"Sam Ireland"','"Administrative Assistant"']
];
```

Now that we have sorted it, print it out:

```
1 my $element;
2 local($") = ",";
3 foreach $element (@$AoA)
4 {
5     print $ofh "@$element\n";
6 }
```

Again, we use the $" variable to make interpolation work a certain way, and then print using that interpolation. This trick works quite a bit; you should get used to it.

Summary of Array of Arrays

The data structure Array of Arrays is good for cases in which you have tabular data in which you care about its order. Such cases include data printouts, formatted reports, matrices, and other structures. To access a certain slice of data (say the second row), you say something like:

```
my @array = @{$AoA[1]};
```

which would access the boldface elements in the following data structure:

```
$AoA = [ [1,2,3,4], [5,6,8,9,10] }
```

To access an individual element, you instead say:

```
my $element = $AoA->[1][2];
```

Array of Hashes (AoH)

An Array of Hashes is an array of elements, each of which is a hash. This is much more useful in making data structures "name-friendly." After all, we tend to associate data with names, rather than numbers. Suppose we want to print all the names in a data structure that looks like the following:

```
$accounts =
[
        ['name1','type1','address1','amount1'],
        ['name2','type2','address2','amount2']
];
```

In other words, an Array of Arrays. You could say something like:

```
foreach $arrayRef (@$accounts)
{
        print $arrayRef->[0];
}
```

However, this relies on you knowing that "row zero" equals "name." Of course, you could always define a hash to translate:

```
%account = ('name' => 0, 'type' => 1, 'address' => 2, 'amount' => 3 );
```

and then say something such as:

```
foreach $arrayRef (@$accounts)
{
    print $arrayRef->[$account{'name'}];
}
```

where $account{'name'} translates into "0," which is then the index that points to named data. This is ugly, slow, and unnecessary. It also does not insulate your code against change (we'll talk about this later). It's much better to build the translation into the data structure itself. This is the Array of Hashes.

Anonymous Reference Structure

In the following code:

```
$AoH =
[
    {'key1a' => 'value1a', 'key2a' => 'value2a', 'key3a'=>'value3a'},
    {'key1b' => 'value1b','key2b' => 'value2b', 'key3b'=>'value3b'}
];
```

note the [indicates the first level of the data structure, and the comma-separated { indicates the second. These indicate that the primary structure is going to be an array, and that the secondary structure is going to be a hash.

In the example with these accounts the data structure will look like:

```
$accounts =
[
    {'name' => 'fred', 'type' => 'book binding',
          'account'=> 'stable', 'amount' => 'owes $250'},
    {'name' => 'john doe', 'type' => 'insurance',
```

```
                 'account' => 'risky', 'amount' => 'owes $60K' }
];
```

To use data structures, we would need to know just two things, as we did in the Array of Arrays: how to access the function, and how to build it.

Array of Hashes Direct Access

There are four common ways to access an Array of Hashes, detailed in the following sections.

1. Access a Given Element

Given this structure, then, each element in the Array of Hashes can be accessed by the following syntax:

```
$AoH->[$dim1]{$key1};
```

where $dim1 is the dimension that the Array of Hashes $AoH is based on, and $key1 is the key to the hash.

Then, in this example, $account->[0]{'name'} accesses the following element in the hash, equaling 'fred'. Here it is in the hash (in boldface):

```
$accounts =
[
    {'name' => 'fred', 'type' => 'book binding',
          'account'=> 'stable', 'amount' => 'owes $250'},
    {'name' => 'john doe', 'type' => 'insurance',
          'account' => 'risky', 'amount' => 'owes $60K' }
];
```

2. Access the Entire Row

Suppose we want to access the entire row for fred. Well, hashes inside the array can be accessed by this syntax:

```
my $hashref = $AoH->[$dim1]; %hash = %$hashref;
```

where $dim1 is the first dimension of the array.

The following syntax can be used to print the Array of Hashes from the example:

```
my $hashref = $account->[0]; my @values = values %$hashref; print "@values\n";
```

Here is the relevant data in the structure itself:

```
$accounts =
[
    {'name' => 'fred', 'type' => 'book binding',
          'account'=> 'stable', 'amount' => 'owes $250'},
    {'name' => 'john doe', 'type' => 'insurance',
          'account' => 'risky', 'amount' => 'owes $60K' }
];
```

Again, only the values are referenced because we used the function values. If you said something like 'print "@{[%$hashref]}\n" (using the trick to interpolate any array), you would reference the whole row.

Now the output of values %$hashref could be "fred book binding stable owes $250." Or it could be "book binding stable fred owes $250," or something like it.

Remember, hash elements do not come out of the hash in a predetermined order. This is one of the things that Array of Arrays has in advantage over Array of Hashes, since arrays have a concept of order.

3. Get All the Names of a Certain Element

Let's get all the names out of our Array of Hashes:

```
my @names = map ( $_->{name}, @$accounts);
```

This makes @names (fred, john doe), or the boldface elements in:

```
$accounts =
[
    {'name' => 'fred', 'type' => 'book binding',
        'account'=> 'stable', 'amount' => 'owes $250'},
    {'name' => 'john doe', 'type' => 'insurance',
        'account' => 'risky', 'amount' => 'owes $60K' }
];
```

Here, you are guaranteed to get things out in the order "fred," "john doe." It is an Array of Hashes, and you are accessing each element, sequentially, with map in an array.

4. Getting a Slice of Elements Out of the Hash

Let's get the name and amount of the second account in the array:

```
my ($name, $account) = @{$accounts->[1]}{('name','account')};
```

This uses slicing to directly access the name and account. However, this is becoming convoluted, so let's split it up:

```
my $hashRef = $accounts->[1];
my ($name, $account) = ($hashRef->{name}, $hashRef->{account});
```

In this example, we make a placeholder ($hashRef) and then access directly into this to get the name and account elements inside it. Here are the relevant structures:

```
$accounts =
[
    {'name' => 'fred', 'type' => 'book binding',
        'account'=> 'stable', 'amount' => 'owes $250'},
    {'name' => 'john doe', 'type' => 'insurance',
        'account' => 'risky', 'amount' => 'owes $60K' }
];
```

As you can see, this is exactly the same as referencing an Array of Arrays. The only difference is the {} instead of the [], and the fact that slicing (getting a portion of a hash or array) is a little more complicated.

Summary of Array of Hashes Access

Accessing an Array of Hashes is quite similar to accessing an Array of Arrays. Figure 8.2 gives the most common access forms, and what they refer to. Get these forms right, and understand the principles behind them, and you will understand Arrays of Hashes quite well.

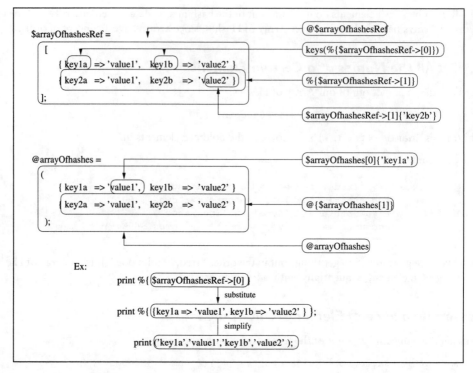

Figure 8.2
Accessing an
Array of Hashes

Array of Hashes Sample Constructor

So let's see how we can construct an Array of Hashes from a flat file that consists of a list of delimited rows. In order to do so, you need to have a way to construct the hash part of the Array of Hashes. Something like this is appropriate:

```
name        |type           |account        |amount
fred        |book binding   |stable         |owes $250
john doe    |insurance      |risky          |owes $60K
```

in which the first row indicates what you are going to be hashing on, and the second and later rows indicate the data to be put in the hash.

Hence, the code will be quite similar to the Array of Arrays constructor. The central function is shown in Listing 8.7a.

Listing 8.7a
makeArrayOfHashes.p

```
1   use FileHandle;                        # we need FileHandle for 'new FileHandle' call
2   sub makeArrayOfHashes
3   {
4       my ($filename) = @_;                                   # we are given filename
```

```
5        my $fh = new FileHandle("$filename") || die;     # we open up the file.
6        my ($line, $return, $hash) = ('',[],'',());
7                                                # $line = '',$return =[], etc
8     chomp($line = <$fh>);                      # we chomp newlines off $line
9     my @lines;                                 # we'll hash against line
10    my $hashRef = getHashKeys($line);          # we make keys out of $line
11    chomp(@lines = <$fh>);                      # we get rest of the lines
12    foreach $line (@lines)
13    {
14          push (@$return, getRef($line, $hashRef));
15    }
16    return($return);
17 }
```

We might say that this is the "outline" of our Array of Hashes constructor. As is appropriate with functions, we stuff the "hard bits" [getting the keys we need to hash on (line 10), and the actual "turning a line into a hash" (line 14)] into functions. We could then reuse them. The function getHashKeys then becomes what is shown in Listing 8.7b.

Listing 8.7b
makeArrayOfHashes.p (continued)

```
1  sub getHashKeys
2  {
3     my ($line) = @_;                           # we pass in a line
4     my (@hashElements) = split(m"\|", $line);  # we split it by '|'
5     my ($element, $return, $xx) = ('', {},0 ); # another multiple set
6     foreach $element (@hashElements)           # we go through each element.
7     {
8           $element =~ s"^\s+""g;                # get rid of leading spaces
9           $element =~ s"\s+$""g;                # and trailing spaces.
10          $return->{$xx++} = $element;          # we make 'translation' hash.
11    }
12    $return;
13 }
```

This function does something very useful for us. It makes a translation table so we know that the first element of the table happens to be the name, the second an account, etc. The heart of the algorithm is in line 10, which returns something like:

```
$return == { 0 => 'name', 1=> 'type', 2 => 'account', 3 => 'amount' };
```

It works like what you see in Figure 8.3. What do we use this for? Well, here is the plan of attack. Since we want to make a structure like:

```
$accounts =
[
    {'name' => 'fred', 'type' => 'book binding',
         'account'=> 'stable', 'amount' => 'owes $250'},
    {'name' => 'john doe', 'type' => 'insurance',
         'account' => 'risky', 'amount' => 'owes $60K' }
];
```

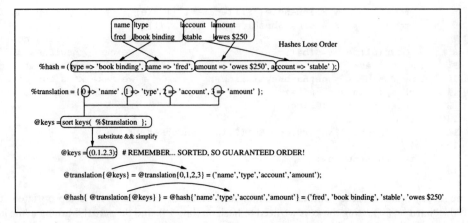

Figure 8.3
Creating a
Translation Table
in Perl

we need a way to turn the array we get from splitting up a line into a hash reference. With a translation table, we can say:

```
my (@elements) = split(m"\|", $line);
$hash{$return->{0}} = $elements[0];
```

to actually say:

```
$hash{'name'} = 'fred';
```

because `$return->{0}` resolves to name, and `$elements[0]` resolves to fred. More formally, we put it in a function called getRef, as shown in Listing 8.7c.

Listing 8.7c
makeArrayOfHashes.p (continued)

```
 1  sub getRef
 2  {
 3      my ($line, $hashKeys) = @_;
 4      my ($element, @elements);
 5      my ($return) = {};
 6      my ($xx);
 7      @elements = split(m"\|",$line);              # split $line on "\|".
 8      for ($xx = 0; $xx < @elements; $xx++)
 9      {
10          $element = $elements[$xx];
11          $element =~ s"^\s+""g;                    # strip leading spaces.
12          $element =~ s"\s+$""g;                    # strip trailing spaces
13          $return->{$hashKeys->{$xx}} = $element;   # magic turning array
14      }                                             # into a hash.
15      $return;
16  }
```

Line 13 is where we take the lookup table we have built (row 0 equals the name field, for example), and turn it into the hash that we return in line 15 to the main routine, to be stuffed into the data structure by:

```
push (@$return, getRef($line, $hashRef));
```

We then iterate through the file (for each line), adding a hash onto the array as we go.

Array of Hashes Access Function

By creating the data structure in this way (Array of Hashes), we are granted more freedom in how we access it. Now, instead of doing:

```
foreach $arrayRef (@$accounts)
{
    print $arrayRef->[0];    # prints out the names of the accounts.
}
```

we can do:

```
foreach $hashRef (@$accounts)
{
    print $hashRef->{'name'};
}
```

which is infinitely more useful for accessing data elements, and also quite a bit more useful if something in your code changes.

Suppose that the field 'name' is moved to the third column of account (if you are dealing with databases), so you have:

```
type, account, name, amount. # $arrayRef->[0] now points  to type
```

Any code that says $arrayRef->[0] is going to break, because it now points to type. Or if a field is prepended:

```
id, name, type, account, amount # $arrayRef->[0] now points to id
```

any code that says $arrayRef->[0] is going to point to the id. If you use an Array of Hashes to access these elements, your code will be insulated against this change. If you were dealing with an Array of Arrays, then suddenly your code is using type where it should be using name.

Note that in this example, there still are some changes you must be wary of. If someone changes the field from name to Name, you will still break. This is another good reason for **-w:** It will warn you when you are using a hash value that is undefined. Hence:

```
#!/usr/local/bin/perl -w

my $AoH = getAoH('filename');
my $hashRef = $AoH->[0];
print $hashRef->{'name'};
```

will issue a warning about undefined columns if name happens to be undefined.

Let's now print an Array of Hashes in exactly the same way that we printed an Array of Arrays. It may not be as useful as the Array of Arrays example given earlier. Again, this is because of the orderless nature of hashes. You won't be guaranteed of the order that text prints out.

Let's call the function printAoH. It will look something like what you see in Listing 8.8.

Listing 8.8
makeArrayOfHashes.p (continued)

```
1   sub printAoH
2   {
3       my ($AoH) = @_;
```

```
 4      my ($hashRef);
 5      foreach $hashRef (@$AoH)                # go through each hash in array.
 6      {
 7          my $key;
 8          foreach $key (keys (%$hashRef)) # go through each key in the hash.
 9          {
10              print "$key => $hashRef->{$key} ";
11          }
12          print "\n";
13      }
14 }
```

The above function is generic, and prints the entire Array of Hashes structure, just as the Array of Arrays function did. It does it explicitly by going through each key in the hash and printing that. We could make it shorter, via some trickery, as shown in Listing 8.9.

Listing 8.9
makeArrayOfHashes.p (continued)

```
1 sub printAoH
2 {
3     my ($AoH) = @_;
4     my ($hashRef);
5     foreach $hashRef (@$AoH)                # go through each hash in the array.
6     {
7         print "@{[ %$hashRef ]} \n";    # print out using interpolation trick
8     }
9 }
```

Line 7 takes on the job of lines 7–12 in the other example. Again, it takes $hashRef, dereferences it, turns it into an array, and then interpolates that array so it prints elements with space delimited (a lot of work for one line).

But, of course, this isn't very useful because of that "order thing" (unless you want to just see the Array of Hashes). Most of the time, you will be doing reporting using specialized functions. Here's an example of a reporting function:

```
1 sub reportAoH
2 {
3     my ($AoH) = @_;     # passed in from above.
4     foreach $hashRef (@$AoH)
5     {
6         print "$hashRef->{'name'}\t$hashRef->{'account'}\n";
7     }
8 }
```

Again, if you substitute reportAoH, for the function printAoH, it will print the name and account fields in the table account, rather than the whole thing.

Array of Hashes Example: Dealing with Incomplete Data

Arrays of Hashes are used interchangeably with Arrays of Arrays; hence, the examples that work for AoAs also work for AoHs. (You could easily rewrite the Excel example to work for AoHs.)

However, there are a couple of situations in which you can do things with Array of Hashes that you *cannot* do with an Array of Arrays. Suppose the file you were accessing had data that looked like:

```
Record #1:
    name:  'George Simpson'
    age: 25
    occupation: 'Plumber'
    salary:       $45000
Record #2:
    name: 'Sam Plinkton'
    age:  56
    occupation: 'Accountant'
Record #3:
    name: 'Heather Sanford'
    occupation: 'botanist'
```

In other words, your data is incomplete. You have a lot of data with associated tags, but they contain only certain information about a given item. Let's take a file like this and prepare a report of occupations and their associated salaries (in alphabetical order), and print it to an output file. The "plan of attack" is detailed next.

Plan of Attack

There are four steps here:

1. Turn the file into a data structure.
2. Get the data that we need out of that data structure.
3. Sort those elements into a sorted reference.
4. Print out those elements into a file.

However, because the format of the file that we want is different, and because we are asking for a different task (reporting occupations and their assorted salaries), the code itself will be quite different. Here's a possible solution, having the user say `script.p <input_file> <output_file>` (Listing 8.10a).

Listing 8.10a
incompleteRead.p

```
1   use FileHandle;
2   use strict;
3   my $ifh = new FileHandle("$ARGV[0]");
4   my $ofh = new FileHandle("> $ARGV[1]");
5
6   my ($hashRef, $AoH) = ({}, []);
7   while ($hashRef = getHashRecord($ifh))
8   {
9       $hashRef->{'occupation'} = 'UNKNOWN' if (!defined $hashRef->{'occupation'});
10      $hashRef->{'salary'} = 'UNKNOWN' if (!defined $hashRef->{'salary'});
11      push(@$AoH, $hashRef);
12  }
13  @$AoH = sort { $a->{'occupation'} cmp $b->{'occupation'} } @$AoH;
14  foreach $hashRef (@$AoH)
15  {
16      print $ofh "$hashRef->{'occupation'}: $hashRef->{'salary'}\n";
17  }
```

The only thing out of the ordinary here is that we are parsing the file differently in line 7. Instead of the usual:

```
while (defined ($line = <$ifh>))
```

we have:

```
while ($hashRef = getHashRecord($fd))
```

Why? Because our input file is of the format:

```
Record #1:
    name:  'George Simpson'
    age: 25
    occupation: 'Plumber'
    salary:       $45000
Record #2:
    name: 'Sam Plinkton'
    age:  56
    occupation: 'Accountant'
Record #3:
    name: 'Heather Sanford'
    occupation: 'botanist'
```

with multiple lines per record. Furthermore, each line corresponds to a hash. Hence, we need a function to make a hash reference out of this, returning:

```
$hashRef = {'name' => 'George Simpson', 'age' => 25,
                  occupation => 'Plumber', 'salary => '$45000' }
```

the first time, and returning:

```
$hashRef = { 'name' => 'Sam Plinkton', 'age' => 56,
                  'occupation' => 'Accountant' }
```

the second, and so on. Below is such a function. Let's use the module **Text::Parsewords** to handle splitting up each of the lines, as shown in Listing 8.10b.

Listing 8.10b
incompleteRead.p (continued)

```
1   use Text::ParseWords;
2   use strict;
3   sub getHashRecord
4   {
5       my ($fh) = @_;
6       my ($return, $line)  = (undef, undef);
7       while (defined ($line = <$fh>))
8       {
9           return($return) if (($line =~ m"Record #")&&(keys (%$return) != 0));
10          next if ($line =~ m"Record #");      # ignores "Record #"returns if
11                                               # created hash,and'Record #' found
12                                               # (this indicates next record)
13          my ($key, $value) = quotewords(":", 0, $line);  # splits to name,value
14          $key =~ s"^\s+""g;    $key =~ s"\s+$""g;
15          $value =~ s"^\s+""g; $value =~ s"\s+$""g;
16          $return->{$key} = $value;
17      }
18      return($return);
19  }
```

Here, we use a small trick to handle the format of the incoming record. The heart of the subroutine is in lines 7–17, where each line is read in turn, and then put into the data structure, until either the file ends (and we return on line 18) or the line contains the text `Record #` and we have already created an element in our hash (keys (`%$return`) != 0). In that case, the hash is returned on line 18. The running of it looks something like Figure 8.4. After each line of input, an extra record is made, which then is stuffed into a hash. When the string `Record #` is detected, the loop ends and keeps the filehandle pointing at the right place to pick up the *next* record. Hence:

```
while ($hash = getHashRecord($ifh))
```

Figure 8.4
Population of a
Hash Record
Based on an
Input File

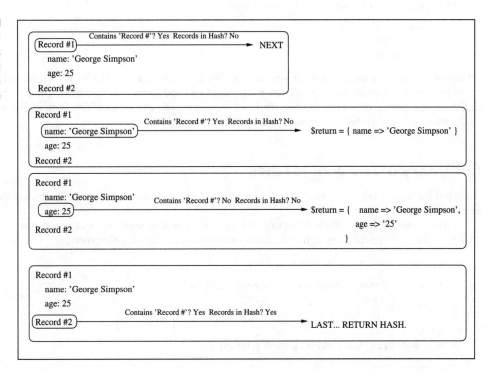

does what we want and picks up record 1, then record 2 returns a hash reference, much the same way that `while $line = <$fd>` returns a line of text. Let's go back to our original function (Listing 8.10a).

```
1   use FileHandle;
2   use strict;
3   my $ifh = new FileHandle("$ARGV[0]");
4   my $ofh = new FileHandle("> $ARGV[1]");
5
6   my ($hashRef, $AoH) = ({}, []);
7   while ($hashRef = getHashRecord($ifh))
8   {
9       $hashRef->{'occupation'} = 'UNKNOWN' if (!defined $hashRef->{'occupation'});
10      $hashRef->{'salary'} = 'UNKNOWN' if (!defined $hashRef->{'salary'});
11      push(@$AoH, $hashRef);
12  }
13  @$AoH = sort { $a->{'occupation'} cmp $b->{'occupation'} } @$AoH;
```

```
14 foreach $hashRef (@$AoH)
15 {
16     print $ofh "$hashRef->{'occupation'}: $hashRef->{'salary'}\n";
17 }
```

Now we can see where this fits in. Line 7 provides the bridge between our input source (a flat file) and a Perl data structure. The rest of the function is rather ordinary. We massage the data in lines 9–10, adding a couple of elements (an occupation or salary of UNKNOWN if it wasn't found in the data), and then in line 11 build our data structure. In line 13, we sort it (by occupation) and in lines 14–17, print it to the output file.

The upshot is that we get a file that looks like:

```
Accountant: UNKNOWN
botanist: UNKNOWN
Plumber: $45000
```

Of course, this is just a sample of what we could do. We could average the salaries, get a subset of the data (sorted by name), print it in a different format, lowercase the data, and so on. The important thing to remember here is that once you get the data into a format Perl can recognize, you can do anything with it. We will see this even closer when we look at the next data structure: Hash of Hashes.

Summary of Array of Hashes

Arrays of Hashes are what they sound like: an array (in our case, an array reference) in which each element of that array references itself as a hash.

They are more flexible than Arrays of Arrays, since you can make your data structure more resistant to change. Take a database example. If you have a table with the following elements:

```
id, name, account, address
```

and turn it into an Array of Arrays, your code will refer to:

```
$column->[0]
```

to get an ID.

Similar code in an Array of Hashes will refer to:

```
$column->{id};
```

instead, and won't break if someone switches around elements as follows:

```
name,id,account,address
```

Now, `$column->[0]` will break (because it refers to the name) but if you program it right, `$column->{id}` will *not* (because you have *named* the element as such).

Hash of Hashes

A Hash of Hashes is a simple two-dimensional hash. As you might expect, each hash key has a hash as a value. The anonymous form for a Hash of Hashes looks like this:

```
$HoH =
{
```

```
        level1key1 => { level2key1 => 'value1', level2key2 => 'value2' }
        level1key2 => { level2key1 => 'value1', level2key2 => 'value2' }
    };
```

Hashes of Hashes are great for an extremely common problem in the world of business, and a common database problem: unique keys.

Suppose that we have state information that is indexed by a unique identifier, an ID. Then, we could use the two-dimensional hash to "tag" all the unique accounts on the system, producing a data structure that looks like:

```
$stateKeys =
{
    ID421 => { state => 'Minnesota', capital => 'St Paul', state_weed => , 'dandelion' }
    ID221 => { state => 'South Dakota', capital => 'Pierre', state_weed => , 'crabgrass }
};
```

Notice what we are doing here. For each row of the state info table, we pick out and tag a given key as part of a two-dimensional hash. Let's look at how we can access it.

Hash of Hashes Access Methods

In a way, stuffing the data of a database into a Hash of Hashes makes that data less easy to access. Because a hash is a black box in that you need a method to see what is inside it, the syntax for accessing anything you don't know is there becomes more difficult.

Hence, given a data structure like:

```
$stateKeys =
{
    ID421 => { state => 'Minnesota', capital => 'St Paul', state_weed => , 'dandelion' }
    ID221 => { state => 'South Dakota', capital => 'Pierre', state_weed => , 'crabgrass }
};
```

let's access different parts of these data elements in the same way that we did with Arrays of Hashes and Arrays of Arrays.

You can access the state associated with the ID 'ID421' by saying:

```
print $stateKeys->{'ID421'}{'state'};
```

to print Minnesota.

To get a hash slice of the same data structure, you could say:

```
my $hashRef = $stateKeys->{'ID421'};
```

to get the hash referenced by 'ID421', i.e.,

```
$stateKeys =
{
    ID421 => { state => 'Minnesota', capital => 'St Paul', state_weed => , 'dandelion' }
    ID221 => { state => 'South Dakota', capital => 'Pierre', state_weed => , 'crabgrass }
};
```

but only if you know ID421 is there inside the hash. You can get this information by saying:

```
my (@keys) = keys(%$stateKeys);
```

which references the following keys (again, in boldface) in the Hash of Hashes:

```
$stateKeys =
{
    ID421 => { state => 'Minnesota', capital => 'St Paul', state_weed => , 'dandelion' }
    ID221 => { state => 'South Dakota', capital => 'Pierre', state_weed => , 'crabgrass' }
};
```

However, the syntax for getting, say, all of the states out of the hash becomes rather convoluted:

```
1 foreach $key (keys(%$stateKeys))
2 {
3     my $hash = $stateKeys->{$key};
4     push(@states, $hash->{state});
5 }
```

which references:

```
$stateKeys =
{
    ID421 => { state => 'Minnesota', capital => 'St Paul', state_weed => , 'dandelion' }
    ID221 => { state => 'South Dakota', capital => 'Pierre', state_weed => , 'crabgrass' }
};
```

It works by taking the keys of $stateKeys (ID421, ID221) in line 1, accessing the hash associated with that key (line 3), and putting it into a temporary hash ($hash). Then, we access the second level of the hash, and push it onto an array called @states (line 4). But this is not syntax that you'd write home about. The same goes for getting the records for all states that begin with letters greater than *N*:

```
foreach $key (keys(%$stateKeys))
{
    my $hash= $stateKeys->{$key};
    if ($hash->{'state'} gt 'N')
    {
        $states_gt_N->{$key} = $hash;
    }
}
```

This code does the trick, but again, it isn't simple and it isn't clean. You would end up with a Hash of Hashes in $states_gt_N, that weeded out Minnesota and ended up with just the bold elements in:

```
$stateKeys =
{
    ID421 => { state => 'Minnesota', capital => 'St Paul', state_weed => , 'dandelion' }
    ID221 => { state => 'South Dakota', capital => 'Pierre', state_weed => , 'crabgrass' }
};
```

Again, this isn't the easiest syntax. If you wanted to skip getting the key, and just get an Array of Hashes that started with letters greater than *N*, you could say:

```
my $hashList = [];
@$hashList = grep ($_->{state} gt 'N', values (%$stateKeys));
```

which would simply return an Array of Hashes, each element of which is a hash with states greater than *N*, something like:

```
$hashList =
[
```

```
        { state => 'South Dakota', capital => 'Pierre',
                    state_weed => , 'crabgrass }
];
```

But we are not guaranteed that the states we are getting are in any given order, because of the values statement.

Summary of Hash of Hashes Access Methods

Hash of Hashes access methods are a bit convoluted. If you don't know what is in your data structure, you need to use the keys() or values() keyword a lot. A summary is given in Figure 8.5. What we lose in accessibility, we gain in speed. The best thing about Hash of Hashes is that if you know the elements you are looking for, they are only a couple of hash accesses away.

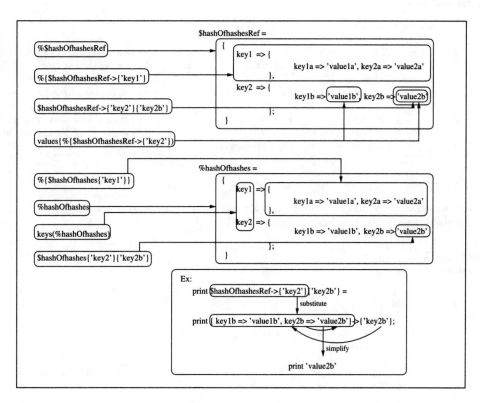

Figure 8.5
Hash of Hash Access Methods, Summarized

Hash of Hashes Sample Constructor

We are now in a position to make a generalized constructor for a Hash of Hashes. Again, we will assume that we have a file that looks something like:

```
id          |state          |capital        |state_weed
ID421       |Minnesota      |St. Paul       |dandelion
ID221       |South Dakota   |Pierre         |crabgrass
```

The benefit of reusing the format we had before is that we can reuse the code for getting the translation table we talked about before, which says something like:

```
$column = { 0 => id, 1 => state, 2 => capital, 3 => state_weed };
```

This lets us turn an array into a hash, by saying something like:

```
$return->{$column->{0}} = $element[0];
```

where $column->{0} becomes ID, and $return->{$column->{0}} becomes $return->{'id'} becomes 'ID421'. Here is the code from the section on Array of Hashes again (Listing 8.11).

Listing 8.11
getHashKeys.p

```
1   sub getHashKeys
2   {
3       my ($line) = @_;                             # we pass in a line
4       my (@hashElements) = split(m"\|", $line);   # we split it by '|'
5       my ($element, $return, $xx) = ('', {},0 );  # multiple assignment
6       foreach $element (@hashElements)            # iterate through elements
7       {
8           $element =~ s"^\s+""g;                   # strip off leading spaces
9           $element =~ s"\s+$""g;                   # strip off trailing spaces
10          $return->{$xx++} = $element;             # we make 'translation' hash.
11      }
12      $return;
13  }
```

While we are at it, we might use the code to actually translate an array into a hash as well, from our last example in the section on Array of Hashes (Listing 8.12).

Listing 8.12
getRef.p

```
1   sub getRef
2   {
3       my ($line, $hashKeys) = @_;
4       my ($element, @elements);
5       my ($return) = {};
6       my ($xx);
7       @elements = split(m"\|",$line);              # split $line on "\|".
8       for ($xx = 0; $xx < @elements; $xx++)
9       {
10          $element = $elements[$xx];
11          $element =~ s"^\s+""g;                    # strip off leading spaces.
12          $element =~ s"\s+$""g;                    # strip off trailing spaces
13          $return->{$hashKeys->{$xx}} = $element;#  array to hash magic
14      }
15      $return;
16  }
```

Line 13 does all the work for us. If we use this code again, our job becomes exceedingly simple in making a constructor, given a filename, as shown in Listing 8.13.

Listing 8.13
makeHoH.p

```
1   use FileHandle;
2   sub makeHoH
3   {
4       my ($fileName) = @_;
5       my $fh = new FileHandle($fileName) || die "Couldn't open $fileName";
6       my ($line, $return) = ('',{});
7       my $defLine = <$fh>; chomp($defLine);
8       my $transHash = getHashKeys($defLine);
9       my @lines = <$fh>; chomp(@lines);
10      foreach $line (@lines)
11      {
12          my $hash = getRef($line, $transHash);
13          $return->{$hash->{id}} = $hash;
14      }
15      $return;
16  }
```

Here, the key lines are 10–14. The $return->{$hash->{id}} takes the ID out of the hash that we created in line 12, and creates the following entry in $return:

```
'IDXXX' => { state => 'XXXXX', capital => 'XXXXX', state_weed => 'XXXX' };
```

iterating, then, through every line in the file makes our data structure, which is returned on line 15.

What happens if you have more than one field you wish to hash on? Simple: Replace line 13 with whatever field you wish to hash on. Say you wanted to hash on the capital and the ID. Then you would say:

```
$return->{$hash->{id}}{$hash->{state}} = $hash;
```

But this is a triple hash, or a HoHoH. We won't go into it in more detail here.

Hash of Hashes Access Function

Likewise, here is the general access function for extracting information from a Hash of Hashes. It is almost exactly the same as Arrays of Hashes and Hashes of Hashes, except that it uses the keys function in both dimensions (Listing 8.14).

Listing 8.14
printHoH.p

```
1  sub printHoH
2  {
3      my ($HoH) = @_;
4      my ($key);
5      foreach $key (keys %$HoH)
6      {
7          my $secondKey;
8          print "$key: ";
9          foreach $secondKey (keys (%$hash))
10         {
11             next if ($secondKey eq 'id');
12             print "$secondKey, $hash->{$secondKey} — ";
```

```
13              }
14          print "\n";
15      }
16 }
```

This will print all the keys and values of the second-level hash on the same line as its associated first-level key. Line 7 gets the first-level key; lines 9–12 print the keys and values associated with it. In our example, we would get an output with something like:

```
ID421: state, Minnesota —  state_weed, dandelion — capital, St.Paul
ID221: state, South Dakota — state_weed, crabgrass — Capital, Pierre
```

Again, the use of this is somewhat problematic because of the order with hashes.

Example of Hash of Hashes: Poor Person's Database

Let's use a Hash of Hashes to implement what we might call a "poor man's database," which uses flat files. It will be quite simple, with the ability to:

1. Add an entry.
2. Get an entry based on a key.
3. Check for duplicates (and disallow them).
4. Write out a file on closing.

Let's say there are four commands to this database. We will assume that each entry has a certain order (say ID, name, address, phone, and comment, delimited by colons). The commands are:

a—add.
g—get (based on key).
e—exit and store.
l—load from file.

Hence:

```
'a 16:Ed:1 trampoline blvd:444-3234:No telemarketing calls, please!'
```

adds a record, and `'g 16:name'` prints out `'Ed'`. `e file` stores the session to `'file'`, and `'l file'` would load the session from `'file'`.

Let's write the interface first. It will look something like what is shown in Listing 8.15a.

Listing 8.15a
poorMansDB.p

```
1  use FileHandle;
2  my ($HoH, $line) = ({}, '');  # Note predefinition of $HoH as reference.
3                                 # If you don't do this, can't pass into function.
4  my $config = { 0 => 'id', 1 => 'name',
5                      2 => 'address',3 => 'phone number', 4 => 'comment' };
6  while (defined(chop($line = <STDIN>)))
7  {
8      processAdd($HoH, $line) if ($line =~ m"^a");
9      processGet($HoH, $line) if ($line =~ m"^g");
10     processStore($HoH, $line) if ($line =~ m"^e")
11     processLoad($HoH) if ($line =~ m"^l");
```

```
12      print "Unknown Command\n" if ($line !~ m"^[agel]");    # if $line doesn't begin with a,g,e,l
13 }
```

This is about it. Line 2 shows the structure of our table (this is the translation hash that comes up again and again, translating an array to a hash). Each time the user enters a key, lines 4–8 check to see if the user has entered various commands. Now, all we need to do is write each one of these functions. We take them in turn, as shown in Listing 8.15b.

Listing 8.15b
poorMansDB.p (continued)

```
14 sub processAdd
15 {
16      my ($HoH, $line) = @_;
17      my ($hash, $xx) = ({},0);
18      $line =~ s"a\s+""g;
19      my @elements = split(m":", $line);
20
21      ( print ("Error in input! wrong no. of fields!\n"), return())
22                                      if (@elements != keys(%$config));
23      foreach my $element (@elements) { $hash->{$config->{$xx++}} = $element; }
24
25      ( print ("Duplicate key!\n"), return()) if (defined $HoH->{$hash->{id}});
26      $HoH->{$hash->{id}} = $hash;
27 }
```

Here, we make a quick check to see that the number of elements the user entered matches the number of rows in the database (line 20), make the hash out of the array (line 22), and then check for duplicate keys (line 24). If there is an error in input, or it is a duplicate key, we return. Otherwise we make the assignment into the data structure (line 25). Now that it is added, we can get various fields (Listing 8.15c).

Listing 8.15c
poorMansDB.p (continued)

```
27 sub processGet
28 {
29      my ($HoH, $line) = @_;
30      $line =~ s"^g\s*""g;
31      my ($id, @fieldsToPrint) = split(m":", $line);
32
33      if (!defined $HoH->{$id})
34      {
35          print "ID $id not defined!\n";
36          return();
37      }
38      my $hash = $HoH->{$id};
39      my $field;
40      if (!@fieldsToPrint)
41      {
42          my (@fields) = sort keys(%$config);
43          foreach $field (@fields) { print "$hash->{$config->{$field}} "; }
44          print "\n";
45      }
```

```
46      else
47      {
48              foreach $field (@fieldsToPrint) { print "$hash->{$field} "; }
49              print "\n";
50      }
51 }
```

There are a couple of things to note about this (rather long) subroutine. The bulk of its length is because of "user-friendliness." In lines 32–36, we check to see whether the ID is defined. And lines 40–44 show a small trick we can use to *pretend* a hash has order.

If a user enters a command like **g 16**, we assume that he or she wants to have all the information about ID 16. Hence, if we simply printed:

```
print "@{[%$hash]}\n";
```

we would get the information in no particular order. In line 16, we say:

```
@fields = sort keys(%$config);
```

where `keys(%$config)` is equal to the following elements in boldface:

```
my $config = { 0 => 'id', 1 => 'name', 2 => 'address',
                     3 => 'phone number', 4 => 'comment' };
```

Hence `@fields` refers to $(0,1,2,3,4)$, because `sort keys (%$config)` sorts them in numeric order (see Chapter 10 on special functions for more detail). When we say:

```
foreach $field (@fields) { print "$hash->{$config->{$field}} "; }
```

then `$config->{$field}` refers first to `$config->{0}`, (id) second to `$config->{1}`, (name), third to `$config->{2}` (address), etc. The upshot of this is that it is equivalent to:

```
foreach $field ('id','name','address','phone_number','comment')
{
    print "$hash->{$field}\n";
}
```

and therefore prints the fields in order, as if they were an array.

We don't have room for the other two functions, `processLoad` and `processStore`, right here. See if you can come up with a good solution and then compare your solution with the one on the accompanying CD. Because you are both loading and storing the file, you are free to pick any format you like.

Summary of Hash of Hashes

Hash of Hashes is probably the most difficult of the data structures to get used to.

Hashes of Hashes are best used when you have to model a "unique key," where that unique key is either a key from a database or a key from a flat file. They are more difficult to model, but if you know the information you want to get out of them, they are worth it.

They are also useful when you need to access data *fast*. Anything in a Hash of Hashes can be accessed in a hash lookup. In an Array of Hashes, the equivalent lookup would need to search through the entire array to find an element.

Hash of Arrays

A Hash of Arrays is a hash in which each of the values in the hash is an array. Below is the anonymous structure for a Hash of Arrays:

```
$HoA = {
    key1 =>   [ $scalar1a, $scalar1b, $scalar1c ],
    key2 =>   [ $scalar2a, $scalar2b, $scalar2c ]
    };
```

Making a hash of arrays is good for cases where you want to have direct access to a given dataset (based on a key), but don't care about the order in which the elements of that key are stored.

For example, suppose you want to model a simple directory structure. You could say something like:

```
my $files =
{
    directory1 => ['file1','file2','file3','file4'],
    directory2 => ['file1','file2','file3','file4']
};
```

and access the files in directory1 by saying:

```
my $directory1 = $files->{'directory1'};
print @$files;
```

This would print the libraries used by the program, etc. Following is the general form for a Hash of Arrays.

Hash of Arrays Direct Access Method

How do you access parts of a Hash of Arrays? It should be easy by now.

A particular element in a Hash of Arrays can be accessed by:

```
$HoA->{$key1}[$dim1];
```

where $dim1 is the dimension which the Hash of Arrays is based on, and $key1 is the key to the hash. Hence:

```
print $HoA->{'dierectory1'}[0];
```

accesses:

```
my $files =
{
    directory1 => ['file1','file2','file3','file4'],
    directory2 => ['file1','file2','file3','file4']
};
```

Arrays inside the hash can be accessed by my $arrayref = $files->{directory2}; print "@$arrayref\n"; .

This accesses the following, boldfaced elements:

```
{
    directory1 => ['file1','file2','file3','file4'],
    directory2 => ['file1','file2','file3','file4']
};
```

and prints 'file1 file2 file3 file4'. Slices can be done with the following syntax:

```
my @firstfiles = map($_->[0], values(%$files));
```

which accesses:

```
my $files =
{
    directory1 => ['file1','file2','file3','file4'],
    directory2 => ['file1','file2','file3','file4']
};
```

or, alternatively:

```
foreach $value (keys (%$files))
{
    push(@firstfiles, $files->{$value}[0]);
}
```

The rest of the forms of access are left as an exercise; they are directly determinable from the Hash of Hashes and Array of Arrays examples given earlier.

Hash of Arrays Sample Constructor

Let's look at how we would construct a data structure that looked like the previous example. Again, the output was that of a directory and its contents. Suppose the directory looks like:

```
file1
directory1/
    file1
    file2
    file3
    file4
directory2/
    file1
    file2
    file3
    file4
```

Let's read this in Perl, assuming that we do it directly using `readdir`. Let's add the twist that we are reading it in alphabetical order, and ignore recursion, as shown in Listing 8.16.

Listing 8.16
readDir.p

```
1  use DirHandle; # module implementing directory handles, like FileHandle does files
2  use strict;
3  sub readDirectory    # makes a hash of arrays.
4  {
5      my ($directory) = @_;
6      my $DH = new DirHandle ("$directory");
7      my ($entry, $return) = ('',{});
8      my @entries = readdir($DH);
9      foreach $entry (@entries)
10     {
11       next if ($entry eq '.' || $entry eq '..'); # get rid of '.', '..'
12         my $file = "$directory/$entry";
13         if (-d $file)
14         {
```

```
15              my $arrayDH = new DirHandle ("$entry");
16              my @files = grep($_ ne '.' && $_ ne '..', readdir($arrayDH));
17              $return->{$entry} = [ sort @files ];
18          }
19      else
20      {
21              $return->{$entry} = '';
22          }
23  }
24  }
```

Here, we get the directories and files from the operating system in line 7 (and sort them on the fly), and check to see whether each of those entries is a directory. If it is, we open it up (line 14), get its files, and stick them into a hash associated with that entry (line 15). If it is a file instead (lines 17–21), we simply make a "dummy" hash entry to show the file is there and stick that into the return value (line 19).

As a result, the directory structure:

```
file1
directory1/
     file1
     file2
     file3
     file4
directory2/
     file1
     file2
     file3
     file4
```

becomes:

```
$return =
{
    'file' => ['file'],
    'directory1' => ['file1','file2','file3','file4'],
    'directory2' => ['file1','file2','file3','file4']
};
```

which we then can manipulate to our heart's content.

Hash of Arrays Access Function

And, going with the flow, below is the access function to get the values out of an HoA. In the sample above (with the directories), this would print out:

```
directory1: file1 file2 file3 file4
directory2: file1 file2 file3 file4
file:
```

The relevant code is shown in Listing 8.17.

Listing 8.17
printHoA.p

```
1   sub printHoA
2   {
```

```
3        my ($HoA) = @_;        # we are passed the HoA reference
4        my ($key);
5        foreach $key (sort keys(%$HoA))
6        {
7            my $arrayRef = $HoA->{$key};
8            print "$key: @$arrayRef\n";
9        }
10 }
```

An easy one this time—we simply take each key, access the array associated with that key (lines 5–7) and then print out the key along with its associated value (line 8).

Example of Hash of Arrays: Processing Lists of Data/Key

Now let's take a look at another short example of a Hash of Arrays. (This chapter is too long already!) Let's suppose that you have a grocery list (where you always keep them, in flat files) that has the following items:

```
Cereal:    1.49, 1.59, 1.69, 1.49
Pizza:     1.99, 1.89, 2.05
Pop Tarts:2.55, 2.75, 2.67
Tofu:      2.39, 2.39
Cereal:    1.59
```

(You can tell I'm a bachelor, can't you!) You want a summary of the cost for each type of food that you purchase. Well, this is the natural place for a Hash of Arrays. We:

1. Read in the file to a data structure.
2. Manipulate the data structure.
3. Print out the summary.

The code is shown in Listing 8.18a

Listing 8.18a
readGroceries.p

```
1   use FileHandle;
2   use strict;
3
4   my $groceryHash = readGroceries("$ARGV[0]");        # take from first argument
5   sumAndPrint($groceryHash);
```

Now, we just fill in the blocks:

```
6 sub readGroceries
7 {
8        my ($filename) = @_;
9        my ($line, $hash) = ('', {});                    # need to make reference
10       my $fh = new FileHandle("$filename");
11       my @lines = <$fh>; chop(@lines);
12       foreach $line (@lines)
13       {
14           my ($hashElement, $list) = split(m"\s*:\s*", $line);
15           push(@{$hash->{$hashElement}}, split(m"\s*,\s*", $list));
16       }
```

```
17      return($hash);
18 }
```

Here, the heart of the algorithm is in lines 14 and 15, which take the line from the file, and first split it on the colon (:) to get the name of the element, and then split it on the comma (,) to get the associated prices. Line 15 then builds the data structure directly out of the list (in a sort of sneaky way, as we'll see next). We then proceed to sum up, and print the grocery list with what is shown in Listing 8.18b.

Listing 8.18b
readGroceries.p (continued)

```
19 sub sumAndPrint
20 {
21     my ($groceryHash) = @_;
22     my $item;
23     foreach $item (keys %$groceryHash)
24     {
25         my ($sum, $price);
26         my $arrayOfPrices = $groceryHash->{$item};
27         foreach $price (@$arrayOfPrices)
28         {
29             $sum += $price;
30         }
31         print "$item: $total\n";
32     }
33 }
```

This prints something like:

```
Cereal: 7.85
Pop Tarts: 7.97
Pizza: 5.93
Tofu: 4.78
```

Now, in the whole program, the only unusual thing about this syntax is in line 15:

```
push(@{$hash->{$hashElement}}, split(m"\s*,\s*", $list));
```

which so happens to be the center of our algorithm. $hash->{$hashElement} refers to "cereal" or "Pop Tarts", i.e., it is what we are hashing on. Hence:

```
push(@{$hash->{$hashElement}},
```

refers to the array in the Hash of Arrays, i.e.:

```
$HoA =
{
    'Cereal' => [ 1.59,1.69,1.49,1.59 ],
    'Pop Tarts' => [2.55, 2.75,2.67 ],
    'Pizza' => [ 1.99,1.89,2.05 ],
    'Soup' =>   [2.39,2.39]
};
```

This means that split(m"\s*,\s*", $list) must fill in the values here. It does this by splitting elements in the list by many characters zero or more spaces, followed by a comma (,), followed by zero or more spaces.

Hence:

```
1001,    1002,     10003
```

becomes `'1001','1002','1003'`, as the spaces are munged by the split. But we are getting ahead of ourselves.

Note

`split (m"\s*,\s*", $list)` doesn't work on the leading spaces of the first chunk to be split, or the trailing spaces of the last chunk to be split. The most bulletproof way of doing this is saying:

```
@elements = split(m",", $list);
foreach (@elements) { s"^\s+""g; s"\s+$""g; }
```

Summary of Common Data Structures

From the previous sections on Arrays of Arrays, Arrays of Hashes, Hashes of Hashes, and Hashes of Arrays, you can see that there are common elements that tend to flow from an application of two rules, which we discussed in the previous chapter. These rules are:

1. If you want to traverse through an array reference, dereference with the construct:

   ```
   foreach $elmt (@$aref)
   {
   }
   ```

   where `$aref` is an array reference. This will go through each element of the array.

2. If you want to traverse through a hash reference, dereference with the construct:

   ```
   foreach $key (keys %$href) {
        my $value = $href->{$key}
   }
   ```

   The `keys %$href` will give a list of keys, where `$href` is the hash reference. This will go through each element in the hash, one by one.

The data structure Array of Arrays was good at printing out nice, orderly tables of data. Array of Hashes was good at accessing tables via the name of their elements. Hash of Hashes was good at quick access to individual pieces of data, also known as a database, and Hash of Arrays was good at processing lists that so happen to be associated with a string (such as grocery lists).

Finally, as you can see from all the code of this chapter, making a Perl data structure is quite closely tied into reading a source of data. If you read from a certain type of file, then knowing Perl's functions for reading it in is *extremely* important. For if you get the data into Perl in the first place, half your battle is won.

Final Note

Where can you go from here?

Well, there are two ways to extend the above data structures.

The first is by *creating hybrid structures*. Sometimes, you will need a structure that doesn't exactly fit the mold of always having an array of elements that have arrays of their own, and so on. Something like this:

```
my $configHash =
{
            config1 => 'file1',
            config2 => ['-w','-s','-h']
            config3 => {key1 => 'value1',key2 => 'value2'}
};
```

is extremely common, but is not really a Hash of Arrays or a Hash of Hashes. Learning how to use these structures is a simple matter of understanding the rules from Chapter 7, and applying them.

The second way to extend data structures is by *making structures with more dimensions*. If you have a variable called HoHoA, then it's a good bet that it is a Hash of a Hash of an Array. Each letter where you encounter a 'H', you can say 'foreach $key (keys(%$. . .)) to get the keys out. And each time you encounter an 'A', you can get values out by saying something like foreach $element (@$. . .). So to get an HoHoA, you say:

```
foreach $key (keys %$HoHoA)
{
    my $HoA = $HoHoA->{$key}
    foreach $key2 (keys %$HoA)
    {
        my $arrayRef = $HoA->{$key};
        foreach $element (@$arrayRef)
        {
            print "$element";
        }
    }
}
```

And to get a $AoHoAoHoHoAoA, you can say:

```
foreach $HoAoHoHoAoA (@$AoHoAoHoHoAoA)
{   # A
    foreach $key (keys %$HoAoHoHoAoA)
    {    # H
        my $AoHoHoAoA = $HoAoHoHoAoA->{$key};
        foreach $HoHoAoA (@$AoHoHoAoA))
        {  # A
            foreach $key (keys %$HoHoAoA)
            {    # H
                my $HoAoA = $HoHoAoA->{$key};
                foreach $key (keys %$HoAoA)
                {  # H
                    my $AoA=$HoAoA->{$key};
                    foreach $arrayRef ($@$AoA)
                    {  # A
                        foreach $scalar (@$arrayRef)
                        {  # A
                            push (@scalars, $scalar);
                        }
                    }
                }
```

```
            }
        }
      }
   }
```

A piece of advice: if you are forced to do this in a real program, please rethink your design.

That's about it. If you skipped Chapter 7, or think that this chapter showed some chinks in your Perl armor, then I would strongly suggest going back to the last chapter for review. It contains more information on the guts of making Perl data structures, so it will open up the ways to creating tailor-made data structures.

# CHAPTER 9

Regular Expressions

If one were to come up with a list of things that were uniquely Perl, things that would come to mind would be the way that Perl handles its *data structures* and its *regular expressions*.

Even if you are not familiar with Perl, you might already be familiar with regular expressions. If you work with complicated editors (vi, emacs), or have programmed with a C regular expression package, programmed in icon, Python, tcl/tk, scripting languages, or Visual C++, or even taken finite automata in college (you know who you are), then you are probably familiar with them. Unequivocally, Perl has more powerful regular expressions than any of these languages or packages. This chapter covers this power in detail.

Chapter Overview

With this aforementioned power comes a complicated syntax. Perl's regular expression set is so powerful because it is so well integrated into the language. This is a result of it evolving through the years and gradually solving problems that were thrown at it, rather than starting from a preconceived notion of what should be in a regular expression package. In fact, you could probably say that about the language itself! Therefore, there will be several parts to this chapter, and eight principles we will talk about in conjunction with regular expressions, just to ease you into learning them.

The first thing we will talk about are the three basic regular expression operators that Perl has: m (for *matching*), s (for *substitution*) and tr (for *translating*). Of these three, 95 percent of your code will be either matching or substitution of regular expressions. It is a rare case when you use the tr operator, but it can be invaluable when you need it.

Then we will start in on the basic regular expressions' principles: a Perl expression only matches on a scalar; backtracking is used to deal with partial regular expression matches; how regular expressions translate Perl variables inside of them; and the use of "metacharacters" to match whether a character is in a certain set of characters.

We continue in this vein talking about Perl regular expressions' support for multiple "groupings" of characters (called multiple match operators), and about the forms of matching available to Perl—greedy and lazy. Then we get back to what are termed "backreferences."

Next, we talk about the various subscripts, (i, s, g, x, m, c, e and o), that we can add to regular expressions that really let the user customize the functionality inside his/her module to a great degree.

Finally, as always, we get to examples. Regular expressions are known for being difficult to learn, so we give approximately 15 pages of examples of them in action. We start from the very simple (going from "getting words in a text file") to actually building a complicated regular expression from scratch (when we build a double-quoted string).

Introduction

If you don't believe Perl's regular expressions are expressive and/or complicated, just look at the following list of actions Perl's regular expressions can perform. They can:

- Match any type of ASCII or binary data.
- Deal with any length of data.
- Contain expressions up to 65,535 (64K) bytes long.
- Iterate over patterns of data, "remembering" where the pattern matched last.
- Deal with alternate patterns of data (i.e., matching either an *a* or a *b*).
- Match classes of characters (i.e., uppercase, lowercase, numerics, binary chars, etc.).
- Deal with negative lookups, in which a pattern matches only if it is not followed by another pattern.
- Deal with both "greedy" matches (ones in which a character set matches the greatest amount of characters that it can match) and "nongreedy" matches (ones in which a character set matches the least amount of characters it can match).
- Easily be used to create a lexer and, along with **byacc**, make a parser.

In addition, Perl expression has an extra readability form which facilitates both your sanity and clearer thinking when dealing with regular expressions. This is a new feature in Perl. If you get nothing else out of this chapter, be sure to understand how to make "readable expressions."

Anyway, as Larry Wall would say, that's definitely enough hype. The flipside of regular expressions is that they can notoriously misbehave if you don't know how to use them. It's very important to understand the usage of regular expressions and, by extension, the general principles involved in their construction.

Perl's regular expression set is so unlike anything else available that even if you have training in other regular expression packages, you will find features in Perl that simply don't exist in others. Also, Perl sets itself apart by integrating regular expressions intimately, and cleanly, with the rest of the language.

In fact, this chapter doesn't do Perl's regular expressions justice. There is simply too much information to fit into one chapter. If you want more information, I suggest referring to the **perlref** page in the FAQ.

There is also a very well-done book, *Mastering Regular Expressions*, by Jeffrey Friedl (listed in the acknowledgements of this book). It has many well-designed, thoughtful examples, and goes into more depth about the material listed next (a couple of examples in this chapter were included by permission of the author, following and commented below.)

Basics of Perl Regular Expressions

A constant source of questions/comments on the newsgroup *comp.lang.perl.misc* is bugs in the string-matching operators of Perl—its regular expression engine.

This is a common mistake that both beginners and advanced programmers make. The Perl regular expression engine is *not buggy* (well, not *that* buggy). It is, in the best tradition of computer science, frustratingly logical.

Perl is frustratingly illogical, which can make it intimidating to the beginner. The Perl regular expression engine obeys your commands to the symbol, but often those commands don't do exactly what you want them to do. It's an example of people telling the computer to "do what I think, not what I said."

The surest way to learn and use regular expressions is to take simple examples and then progress to more complicated examples, while first taking to heart the principles underlying their construction. If you are new to them, the thorough understanding of regular expressions makes you instantly more productive in tasks ranging as far and wide as:

1. Code analysis
2. Correcting misspellings
3. Sorting through tons of data
4. Code generation

For example, genetic engineers are extremely happy using Perl for looking for patterns in gene sequences. And, on a more personal note, some of the formatting of this book was done with regular expressions.

For those of you who are unfamiliar with regular expressions, here's a concise definition:

- *Regular expression*: a pattern that uses a logical notation to represent a set of possible strings.

That's really all there is to it (and that's what 10 weeks and $500 told me in college). A group of strings, such as "cat," "cats," "catty," "tomcat," "alleycat," etc., can be matched by one regular expression:

```
$catstring =~ m/cat/;    # matches any of the above strings. Returns a '1'.
```

This is, in fact, the way Perl looks for "cat" in every one of these strings (i.e., tomcat, alleycat).

As with many of the items that make Perl so strong, regular expressions can be distilled to a few principles; learn them and you can do wondrous things. Although we call them "basic" regular expressions, they start at the *very* basic, and move into some fairly advanced material.

Principle 1: *There are three forms of regular expressions: matching, substituting, and translating.*

There are three regular expression operators listed in Table 9.1. Each expression is explained in more detail next.

	Operator	Meaning
Table 9.1 Regular Expression Operators	`m //`	"match"
	`s///`	"substitute"
	`tr///`	"translate"

- *Matching*: The form m/<regexp>/ indicates that the regular expression inside the // is going to be matched against the scalar on the left-hand side of the =~ or !~. As syntactic sugar, you can say /<regexp>/, leaving out the m.
- *Substituting*: The form s/<regexp>/<substituteText>/ indicates that the regular expression <regexp> is going to be substituted by the text <substititeText>. As syntactic sugar, you can say /<regexp>/<substituteText>/, leaving out the s.
- *Translating*: The form tr/<charClass>/<substituteClass>/ takes a range of characters— <charClass>—and substitutes them for <substituteClass>.

Note that translating (tr) isn't really a regular expression, but is often used to manipulate data in ways that are difficult to do with regular expressions. Hence tr/[0-9]/9876543210/ makes the strings 123456789, 987654321, etc.

You *bind* these expressions to a scalar by using =~ (in English: *does*, as in "does match") and by !~ (in English: *doesn't*, as in "doesn't match"). As an example of this, we give six sample regular expressions below, along with their corresponding definitions:

```
$scalarName =~ s/a/b/;          # substitute the character a for b, and return true
                                # if this can happen
$scalarName =~ m/a/;            # does the scalar $scalarName have an a in it?
$scalarName =~ tr/A-Z/a-z/;     # translate all capital letters with lower case ones,
                                # and return true if this happens
$scalarName !~ s/a/b/;          # substitute the character a for b, and return false
                                # if this indeed happens.
$scalarName !~ m/a/;            # does the scalar $scalarName match the character a?
                                # Return false if it does.
$scalarName !~ tr/0-9/a-j/;     # translate the digits for the letters a thru j, and
                                # return false if this happens.
```

If we say something like horned toad =~ m/toad/, this turns into Figure 9.1.

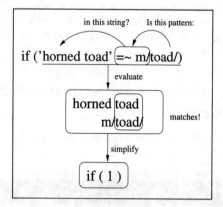

Figure 9.1
Simple
Pattern Match

In addition, if you are matching against the special variable $_ (as you might do in while loops, map, or grep), you can do without the !~ and =~. Hence, all of the following work:

```
my @elements = ('a1','a2','a3','a4','a5');
foreach (@elements) { s/a/b/;}
```

makes @elements equal to b1, b2, b3, b4, b5. And:

```
while (<$FD>) { print if (m/ERROR/); }
```

prints all the lines with the string 'ERROR' in them. And:

```
if (grep(/pattern/, @lines)) { print "the variable \@lines has pattern in it!\n"; }
```

prints something only if lines have the pattern pattern in them. This bears directly on the next principle.

Principle 2: *Regular expressions match only on scalars.*

Note the importance of scalars here. If you try something such as:

```
@arrayName = ('variable1', 'variable2');
@arrayName =~ m/variable/;    # looks for 'variable' in the array? No! use grep instead
```

then @arrayName matching will not work! It is interpreted as 2 by Perl, and this means you are saying:

```
'2' =~ m/variable/;
```

This is not going to give expected results, to say the least. If you want to do this, say:

```
grep(m/variable/, @arrayName);
```

which loops through each of the elements in @arrayName, returning (in scalar context) the number of times it matched, and, in array context, the actual list of elements that matched.

Principle 3: *A regular expression matches the earliest possible match of a given pattern. By default, it only matches or replaces a given regular expression once.*

This principle uses a process called *backtracking* to figure out how to match a given string. If it finds a partial match and then finds something that invalidates that match, it "backtracks" to the least possible amount in the string that it can without missing any matches.

This is probably the most helpful principle to understand what the regular expression is doing, and you don't need Perl-ish forms to understand what it is doing. Suppose you had the following pattern:

```
'silly people do silly things if in silly moods'
```

and you wanted to match the pattern:

```
'silly moods'
```

The regular expression engine matches silly, then hits the p in people. At that point, the regular expression engine understands that the first silly won't match, so it moves up to the p and keeps trying to match. It then hits the second silly, and tries to match moods. It gets a t (in things) instead, and moves up to the t in things, and keeps trying to match. The engine then hits the third silly, and tries to match moods. It does so, and the engine finally matches. Pictorially, this becomes something like what is shown in Figure 9.2.

Figure 9.2
Simple
Backtracking

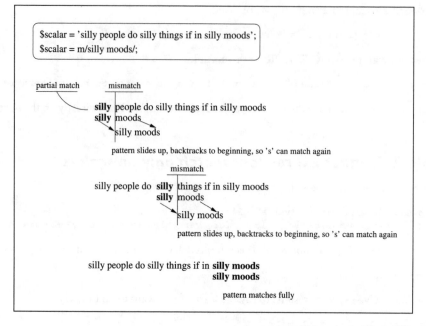

```
$scalar = 'silly people do silly things if in silly moods';
$scalar = m/silly moods/;
```

partial match   mismatch

silly people do silly things if in silly moods
silly moods

silly moods

pattern slides up, backtracks to beginning, so 's' can match again

mismatch

silly people do **silly** things if in silly moods
silly moods

silly moods

pattern slides up, backtracks to beginning, so 's' can match again

silly people do silly things if in **silly moods**
silly moods

pattern matches fully

Backtracking will become very important when we get to wildcards. If there are several wildcards in the same regular expression, all intertwined, then there are pathological cases where backtracking becomes very expensive. If you see an expression such as:

```
$line =~ m/expression.*matching.*could.*be.*very.*expensive.*/
```

the .* indicates a wildcard, which means "match any character (besides newline) zero or many times." It is possible that this could take a *long* time; if there are possible matches at the end of the string that don't work, the engine will backtrack like crazy. See Principle 6 on wildcards for more information on this.

If you see something like this, you can usually split up your regular expression into parts. In other words, *simplify* your regular expression.

Principle 4: *Regular expressions can take ANY and ALL characters that double-quoted strings can.*

In the first "compartment" of the s/// operator (s/*//), or the m// operator (m/*/), the items inside here are treated *exactly* like double-quoted strings (with some extra added functionality, namely special regular expression characters, described later). You can interpolate with them:

```
$variable = 'TEST';
$a =~ m/${variable}aha/;
```

and:

```
$a = "${variable}aha";
```

Both point to the same string; the first matches the string TESTaha in $a, the second sets $a to the string TESTaha.

Because regular expressions can take every single character that a double-quoted string can take, you can do things such as:

```
$expression = 'hello';
@arrayName = ('elem1','elem2');

$variable =~ m/$expression/;        # this equals m/hello/;
```

Here, we simply expand $expression into hello to get m/hello/. This trick works for arrays as well:

```
$variable =~ m/arrayName/;        # this equals m/elem1 elem2/;
```

Here, this is equal to m/elem1 elem2/. If the special variable $" was set to |, this would be equal to m/elem|elem2/, which, as we shall see, matches either elem1 or elem2 in a string. This works for special characters too:

```
$variable =~ m/\x01\27/;            # match binary character x01, and
                                    # octal character 27.

$variable =~ s/\t\t\t/   /;         # substitute three tabs for three spaces.
```

In fact, with a few exceptions that we will talk about now, Perl handles string processing in m// exactly as if it were in double quotes. But there *are* exceptions. There are certain characters that have significance to the regular expression engine itself. What happens, then, if you want to match something such as a forward slash (/) or parentheses (( ))? These characters have special significance to the regular expression engine. You can't say something such as:

```
$variable =~ m//usr/local/bin/;        # matches /usr/local/bin? NO! SYNTAX ERROR
```

because Perl will interpret the / as being the end of the regular expression. There are three possible ways to match something like the above.

The first way is to use a backslash to "escape" whatever special character you want to match—this includes backslashes. Hence, the example just given becomes:

```
$path =~ m/\/usr\/local\/bin/;
```

This tries to match /usr/local/bin in $path.

The second way is to use a different regular expression character. Using backslashes gets ugly fast if you have many special characters to match (path characters are especially bad).

Fortunately, Perl has a form of syntactic sugar that helps quite a bit here. Because you need to backslash every / when you say m// or s///, Perl can allow you to change the regular expression delimiter (/) into any character you like. For example, we can use a double quotation mark (") to avoid lots of backslashing:

```
$variable =~ m"/usr/local/bin";       # Note the quotation marks.
$variable =~ m"\"help\"";             # If you are going to match quotation
                                      # marks, you need to backslash them here. (as per \")
$variable =~ s"$variable"$variable2"; # works in s/// too.
```

We used this convention earlier in the book, and for good reason. If you start using " as your regular expression character, it serves as a good mnemonic to remember that what you are dealing with here is actually string interpolation in disguise. Likewise, quotation marks are a lot less frequent than slashes.

Perl also allows you to use { }, ( ), or [ ] to write regular expressions:

```
$variable =~ m{ this works well with vi or emacs because the parens bounce };
$variable =~ m( this also works well );
$variable =~ s{ substitute pattern } { for this pattern }sg;
```

This principle will come in very handy when we start dealing with multiple-line regular expressions. And because you can bounce parens here, you can start treating them as "miniature functions" (if you have a reasonably intelligent editor like emacs or vi). In other words, you can bounce between the beginning and ending of the expressions.

The third way is to use the `quotemeta( )` function to automatically backslash things for you. If you say something like:

```
$variable =~ m"$scalar";
```

then `$scalar` will be interpolated and turned into the value for scalar. There is a caveat here: Any special characters will be acted on by the regular expression engine, and may cause syntax errors. Hence, if scalar is:

```
$scalar = "({";
```

then saying something like:

```
$variable =~ m"$scalar";
```

is equivalent to saying: `$variable =~ m"({";`, which is a *runtime syntax error*. If you say:

```
$scalar = quotemeta('({');
```

it will make `$scalar` become `\(\{` and substitute `$scalar` for:

```
$variable =~ m"\{\{";
```

Then, you will match the string `({` as you like.

Principle 5: *A regular expression creates two things in the process of being evaluated: result status and backreferences.*

Every time you evaluate a regular expression, you get:

- An indication of how many times the regular expression matched your string (*result status*)
- A series of variables called *backreferences* if you wish to save parts of the match.

Let's go over each in turn.

Result Status

A *result status* is an indication of how many times a given regular expression matched your string. The way you get a result status is to evaluate the regular expression in scalar context. All the following examples use this result variable.

```
$pattern = 'simple always simple';
$result = ($pattern =~ m"simple");
```

Here, `result` becomes one, because the pattern `simple` is in `simple always simple`. Likewise, given `simple always simple`:

```
$result = ($pattern =~ m"complex");
```

makes `result` null because `complex` isn't a substring inside `simple always simple`, and:

```
$result = ($pattern =~ s"simple"complex");
```

makes `result` equal to one, because of the substitution from simple to complex works. Going further:

```
$pattern = 'simple simple';
$result = ($pattern =~ s"simple"complex"g);
```

becomes more complicated. Here, `$result` becomes two, because there are two occurrences of simple in simple simple, and the g modifier to regular expressions is used, which means "match as many times as you can." (See modifiers later in the chapter for more detail.) Likewise:

```
$pattern = 'simpler still';
if ($pattern =~ m"simple")
{
    print "MATCHED!\n";
}
```

uses `$pattern =~ m"simple"` in an if clause, which basically tells Perl to print `Matched!` if the pattern `$pattern` contains the substring `simple`.

Backreferences

Backreferences are a bit more complicated. Suppose you want to save some of your matches for later use. To facilitate this, Perl has an operator (the parentheses `()`) that you can put around a given set of symbols you wish to match.

Putting parentheses around a pattern inside a regular expression simply tells the interpreter "Hey, I wish to save that data."

The Perl interpreter obliges, and then saves the match that it finds in a special set of variables ($1, $2, $3 . . . . $65535), which can be used to refer to the first, second, third, etc., parentheses matches. These variables can then be accessed by looking at the relevant variable or by evaluating the regular expression in array context. For example:

```
$text = "this matches 'THIS' not 'THAT'";
$text =~ m"('TH..')";
print "$1\n";
```

Here, the characters THIS are printed out—Perl has saved them for you in $1, which is printed later.
However, there are more things this example shows, such as the following:

1. *Wildcards* (the character dot (.) matches any character). If THIS wasn't in the string, the pattern (TH..) would have happily matched THAT.
2. *Regular expressions* match the first occurrence on a line. THIS was matched because it came first. And, with the default regexp behavior, THIS will *always* be the first string to be matched. (You can change this default by modifiers, detailed later in this chapter.)

Figure 9.3 shows more about how this is working. In Figure 9.3, each parenthesis goes along with its own, numeric variable.

Here are some more examples:

```
$text = 'This is an example of backreferences';
($example, $backreferences) = ($text =~ m"(example).*(backreferences)");
```

Again, we use a wildcard to separate two text strings: example and backreferences. These are saved in $1 and $2, which are then immediately assigned to $example and $backreferences. This is illustrated in Figure 9.4.

```
$text = "this matches 'THIS' and 'THAT'";
$text =~ m"('TH..').*('TH..')";
print $1;
```

```
$text = "This is an example of lots of backreferences";
($example,$filler, $backreferences) = ($text =~ m"(example)(.*)(backreferences)");
```

Notice, however, that this only occurs when the text string *matches*. When the text string does not match, $example and $backreferences are empty. Here is pretty much the same example wrapped in an if statement, which prints $1 and $2 only if they match:

```
if ($text =~ m"(example).*(back)")
{
     print $1;      # prints 'example' -- since the first parens
                    # match the text example.
     print $2;      # prints 'back' -- since the second parens match the text back
}
```

So, what happens if your regular expression does not match at all? If you take the following pattern:

```
$text = 'This is an example of backreferences';
$text =~ s"(exemplar).*(back)"doesn't work";
print $1;
```

$1 will *not* get assigned because the regular expression didn't work. More importantly, Perl won't tell you that it hasn't assigned $1 to anything. This last example shows two important points about regular expressions:

1. A regular expression is an "all or nothing" deal. Just because the string back matches inside the pattern

   ```
   'This is an example of backreferences'
   ```

   does *not* mean that the entire expression set matches. exemplar is not in this string, so the substitution fails.

2. Backreferences do not get set if a regular expression fails. You cannot be sure what this is going to print. This is cause for much consternation and is a frequent Perl *gotcha* when tracking down a logic problem. $1 is simply a regular variable, and (contrary to some Perl myths out there) does not get set to "blank" if the regular expression fails. Some people think this is a bug, while others think it is a feature.

Nonetheless, the second point becomes painfully obvious when you consider the following code.

```
1 $a = 'bedbugs bite';
2 $a =~ m"(bedbug)";      # sets $1 to be bedbug.
3
4 $b = 'this is nasty';
5 $b =~ m"(nasti)";       # does NOT set $1 (nasti is not in 'this is nasty').
6                         # BUT $1 is still set to bedbug!
7 print $1;               # prints 'bedbug'.
```

In this case, $1 is the string bedbug, because the match in line 5 failed! If you were expecting nasti, well, that is your problem. This Perl-ish behavior can cause hours of bloodshot eyes and lost sleep. Consider yourself warned.

Common Constructions for Using Backreferences

If you want to avoid this very common bug (in which you expect a match, but do not get one and end up using a previous match instead), simply use one of the following three constructions in assigning backreferences to variables.

1. The short-circuiting method. Check for the match, and if it occurs, then—and only then—assign using '&&'. Example:

   ```
   ($scalarName =~ m"(regular expression)") && ($match = $1);
   ```

2. if clause. Put your match in an if clause, and if that if clause in matching is true, then—and only then—will the pattern be assigned.

   ```
   if ($scalarName =~ m"(nasti)") { $matched = $1; }
       else { print "$scalarName didn't match"; }
   ```

3. Direct assignment. Because you can assign a regular expression directly to an array, take advantage of this all the time:

   ```
   ($match1, $match2) = ($scalarName =~ m"(regexp1).*(regexp2)");
   ```

All of your pattern matching code should look like one of the previous three examples. Without these forms, you are definitely coding without a seat belt. And this will save you tons of time, as you will never have this type of bug.

Using Backreferences in the Regular Expression Itself

When you wish to use the s" " " operator, or in the case of some complicated patterns that are otherwise difficult to match with the 'm" "' operator, Perl provides a very helpful functionality of which you should be aware.

This functionality is that backreferences are available to the regular expression itself. In other words, if you put parentheses around a group of characters, you need not wait until the regular expression is over to use them. If you want to use backreferences in the second part of s" " ", you use the syntax $1, $2, etc. If you want to use the backreferences in m" " or the first part of s" " ", you use the syntax \1, \2, etc. Here are some examples:

```
$string = 'far out';
$string =~ s"(far) (out)"$2 $1";    # This makes string 'out far'.
```

We simply switch the words here, from far out to out far.

```
$string = 'sample examples';
if ($string =~ m"(amp..) ex\1") { print "MATCHES!\n"; }
```

This example is a bit more complicated. The first pattern (amp..) matches the string ample. This means that the whole pattern becomes the string ample example, where the underlined text corresponds to the \1. Hence, this matches sample examples.

Here is a more complicated example of the same vein.

```
$string = 'bballball';
$string =~ s"(b)\1(a..)\1\2"$1$2";
```

Let's look at this example in detail. This does match, but it isn't obvious why. There are 5 steps to the match of this string:

1. The first b in parentheses matches the beginning of the string, and is saved into \1 and $1.
2. \1 then matches the second b in the string, because it is equal to b, and the second character so happens to be b.
3. (a..) matches the string all and is stored into \2 and $2.
4. \1 matches the next b.
5. \2, because it is equal to all, matches the next and last three characters (all).

Put it together and you get the regular expression matching bballball, or the whole string. Since $1 equals 'b' and $2 equals all, the whole expression:

```
$string = 'bballball';
$string =~ s"(b)\1(a..)\1\2"$1$2";
```

translates (in this case) into:

```
$string =~ s"(b)b(all)ball"ball";
```

or, in the vernacular, substitute the string bballball for ball.

The regular expression looks pretty much as it does in Figure 9.5. There are some complicated backreferences in s" " ". If you understand the last example, you are pretty far along in understanding how Perl's regular expressions work. They can and do get worse.

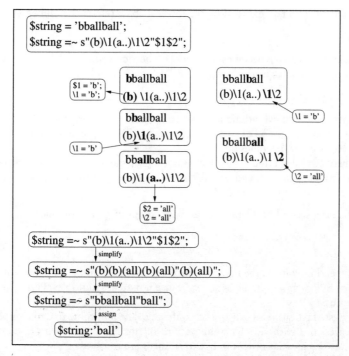

Figure 9.5
Inner Matching
in Action

Nested Backreferences

Nested backreferences serve well to match strings that are too complicated to be matched in a single order (one string following after the other). For example, the following expression:

```
m"((aaa)*)";
```

uses the * to match multiple occurrences of aaa: It matches ' ', aaa, aaaaaa, or aaaaaaaaa. In other words, Perl matches patterns with multiples of three *a*'s in a row. But it will not match aa. Suppose you want to do something like match the following string:

```
$string = 'softly slowly surely subtly';
```

Then the following regular expression will match, and we can use nested parens to capture some info about what matched:

```
$string =~ m"((s...ly\s*)*)";   # note nested parens.
```

Here, the outermost parentheses (( )) capture the whole thing: softly slowly surely subtly. The innermost parentheses (()) capture a combination of strings beginning with an s having three characters in the middle, and ending with an ly followed by spaces. Hence, it first captures softly, throws it away, then captures slowly, throws it away, then captures surely, and then captures subtly.

There is a problem here: In what order do the backreferences come? You can get caught quite easily in this problem. Do the outer parentheses come first or the inner parentheses? The simple answer is to remember the following three rules:

1. The earlier a backreference is in an expression, the lower its backreference number, as in:

    ```
    $var =~ m"(a)(b)";
    ```

    In this case, the backreference (a) becomes $1, and (b) becomes $2.

2. The more general a backreference is, the lower its backreference number, as in:

    ```
    $var =~ m"(c(a(b)*)*)";
    ```

    In this case, the expression with everything in it (m"(c(a(b)*)*)") becomes $1. The expression with the a nested inside it, m"(c(a(b)*)*)", becomes $2. The expression with the b nested inside it, (m"(c(a(b)*)*)"), becomes $3.

3. In case of conflicts between rules 1 and 2, rule 1 wins out. In the statement $var =~ m"(a)(b(c))", (a) becomes $1, b(c) becomes $2, and (c) becomes $3. Hence, in this case, (s...ly\s*)* becomes $1, and (s...ly\s*)* becomes $2.

Be sure to note that there is a second problem. Let's go back to our original, complicated, regular expression:

```
$string = 'softly slowly surely subtly'
$string =~ m"((s...ly\s*)*)";  # note nested parens.
```

What does (s...ly\s*)* end up with in the backreference $1? Well, as said, it matches multiple things: First softly, then slowly, then surely, and finally subtly. Since it matches multiples, Perl throws away the first matches and $2 becomes subtly.

Even with these rules, nested parentheses can *still* be confusing. The best thing to do is simply practice. Once again, do many regular expressions with various combinations of this logic, and then present these to the Perl interpreter. This allows you to see in what order the backreferences are resolved.

Principle 6: *The heart of the power of regular expressions lies in the wildcard and multiple-match operator.*

The *wildcard* operator lets you match more than one character in a string. If you are dealing with binary data, the wildcard matches a range of characters. The *multiple-match operator* lets you match zero, one, or many characters.

The examples we have looked at so far were instructive as far as teaching the basics of Perl are concerned, but they weren't very powerful. In fact, you could probably write a C subroutine to do any of them. The Perl regular expression set derives its power from its ability to match multiple patterns of text (that is, the ability to represent many distinct patterns of data by the logical "shorthand" mentioned previously). Perl just happens to have the best shorthand available.

Wildcards

Wildcards represent classes of characters. Suppose you had the following strings, but didn't know whether they were capitalized:

*   kumquat
*   Kristina
*   Kentucky
*   key
*   keeping

In this case, the following Perl expression would match the first letter of each word:

```
[Kk]
```

This is the example of character class. All wildcards in Perl can be represented by taking brackets [and putting the class of characters you wish to match between them, and then closing the brackets]. The previous wildcard tells the regular expression engine "OK, I'm looking for either a "K" or a "k" here. I'll match if I find either one." Here are some more examples of wildcards in action:

```
$scalarName = 'this has a digit (1) in it';
$scalarName =~ m"[0-9]";    # This matches any character between 0 and 9, that is, matches any digit.
$scalarName =~ 'this has a capital letter (A) in it';
$scalarName =~ m"[A-Z]";    # This matches any capital letter (A-Z).
$scalarName =~ "this does not match, since the letter after the string 'AN ' is an A";
$scalarName =~ m"an [^A]";
```

The first two examples are fairly straightforward. [0-9] matches the digit 1 in this has a digit (1) in it. [A-Z] matches the capital A in this has a capital letter (A) in it. The last example is a bit trickier. Because there is only one an in the pattern, the only characters that can possibly match are the last four an A.

However, by asking for the pattern an [^A] we have distinctly told the regular expression to match a, then n, then a space, and finally a character that is *not* an A. Hence, this does not match. If the pattern was match an A not an e, this *would* match, because the first an would be skipped, and the second matched! Like:

```
$scalarName = "This has a tab(    )or a newline in it so it matches";
$scalarName =~ m"[\t\n]"    # Matches either a tab or a newline.
                           # matches since the tab is present.
```

This example illustrates some of the fun things that can be done with matching and wildcarding. First, the same characters that you can have interpolated in a " " string also get interpolated in both a regular expression and inside a character class denoted by brackets ([\t\n]). Here, "\t" becomes the matching of a tab, and "\n" becomes the matching of a newline.

Second, if you put a ^ inside and at the front of your [ ], the wildcard matches the negation of the characters in the grouping. Likewise, if you put a - inside the [ ], the wildcard matches the range you give (in this case, all digits ([0-9]), all capitals ([A-Z])). These operators can be combined to get wildcards that are fairly specific:

```
$a =~ m"[a-fh-z]";       # matches any lowercase letter *except* g.
$a =~ m"[^0-9a-zA-Z]";   # matches any nonword character. (i.e., NOT
                         # a character in 0-9, a-z or A-Z)
$a =~ m"[0-9^A-Za-z]";    # a mistake. Does not
                          # equal the above. Instead matches 0-9,
                          #  A-Z,  a-z, OR A CARET (^).
$a =~ m"[\t\n ]";         # matches a space character: tab, newline or blank).
```

The important thing to note here is the third example. The caret in [0-9^A-Za-z] is a literal caret, not a negative, because it appears in the middle of a character class. Hence, if you want a negative character class, always put it at the beginning of the []. Don't forget the [], either: If you do, you've got a literal string of text, not a character class.

Common Wildcards

It so happens that certain wildcards are extremely common; you probably don't want to have to say something such as [0-9] every time you want to match a digit. In that case, Perl has several convenient shorthand wildcards that make things easy on the programmer. Here they are, along with an English expression describing what they represent, and the character grouping to which they are equivalent:

- \d—Matches a digit (character grouping [0-9])
- \D—Matches a nondigit (character grouping [^0-9])

- \w—Matches a word character (character grouping [a-zA-Z0-9_]) (underscore is counted as a word character here)
- \W—Matches a nonword character (character grouping [^a-zA-Z0-9_])
- \s—Matches a space character (character grouping [\t\n] (tab, newline, space)
- \S—Matches a nonspace character (character grouping [^\t\n]).
- . —Matches any character, except (in some cases) newline (character grouping [^\n]), matches any character, when you say m"(.*)"s. See modifiers later in this chapter.
- $ —Although not really a wildcard (it doesn't match any specific character), it is a widely used special character; it matches the "end of line," if placed at the end of a regular expression. *Zero Width Assertion.*
- ^ —Although not really a wildcard, it is a special character that matches "beginning of line" if placed at the beginning of a regular expression. *Zero Width Assertion.*
- \b, \B—Same as $ and ^; doesn't match a character, but matches a word boundary (\b) or a lack of word boundary (\B). *Zero Width Assertion.*

The first point we can see from this table is the "dot" wildcard (.). This gets used fairly often as filler between items, along with the multiple match operators. Take a look at the following match:

```
$a = 'Now is the time for all good men to come to the aid of their party';
$a =~ m"(Now).*(party)";        # matches, since '.' matches any
                                # character except newline
                                # and '*' means match zero or more characters.
```

The .* gobbles up all the characters between Now and party, and the match is successful. (*All* in this context means "zero or more, as many as possible." This is called *greediness*; we will talk about this when we talk about multiple match operators later.)

Here are some other examples of wildcards. Note that we use single quoted strings on the left side of the =~ (this is a simple way to test expressions):

```
1 '1956.23' =~ m"(\d+)\.(\d+)";              # $1 = 1956, $2 = 23
2 '333e+12' =~ m"(\D+)";                     # $1 = 'e+';
3 '$hash{$value}' =~ m"\$(\w+){\$(\w+)}";    # $1 = 'hash', $2 = 'value'
4 '$hash{$value}' =~ m"(\W)(\w+){(\W)*(\w+)(\W*)}";  # $1 = '$', $2 = 'hash',
                                             # $3 = '$', $4 = 'value'.
5 'VARIABLE =VALUE' =~ m"(\w+)(\s*)=(\s*)(\w+)";  # $1 = 'VARIABLE', $2 = ' ',
                                             # $3 = '', $4 = 'VALUE'
6 'catch as catch can' =~ m"^(.*)can$";      # $1 = 'catch as catch'
7 'can as catch catch' =~ m"^can(.*)$";      # $1 = 'as catch catch'
8 'word_with_underlines word2' =~ m"\b(\w+)\b";  # $1 = word_with_underlines
```

In each case, we show a different wildcard, in this case using * to mean "match zero or more wildcards in a row," and + to mean "match one or more wild cards in a row." Some of these examples are useful in themselves: Example 5 shows a good way to fortify expressions against errant spaces by using \s*; example 8 shows a generalized way to match a word; and example 4 shows a relatively general way to match a hash with key.

However, in particular, example 1 isn't a generalized way to match a Perl number. This is an exceedingly difficult problem, given all the formats Perl supports; we will consider it as a problem later.

There is another thing to notice from this table: Some of the wildcards are labeled "*Zero Width Assertion.*" We cover this next.

Zero Width Assertions and Positive Width Assertions

The characters in Table 9.2 are what you might call positive width assertions.

Table 9.2	\D	nondigit
Positive	\d	digit
Assertions	\w	word
	\W	nonword
	\s	space
	\S	nonspace
	'.'	anything but newline

These actually match a character in the string. Positive width means they match a character, and the regular expression engine "eats" them in the matching process. The characters in Table 9.3 are negative width assertions.

Table 9.3	^	beginning of the string
Negative	$	ending of string
Assertions	\b	word boundary
	\B	nonword boundary

These don't match a *character*, they match a *condition*. In other words, ^cat will match a string with cat at the beginning, but the ^ doesn't match any given character. Look at the following expressions:

```
$zigguratString = 'this matches the word ziggurat';
$zigguratString =~ m"\bziggurat\b";
$zigguratString =~ m"\Wziggurat\W";
```

The first one matches because it looks for ziggurat between two nonword characters (word boundaries). The string holds this condition.

The second one does not match. Why? The \W on the end is a positive width assertion and, therefore, *has* to match a character, and the string ends with ziggurat so there are no characters left to match. The "end of a line" is not a *character*, it is a *condition*. This condition is met by '\b' (a zero width assertion) but not '\W' (a positive width assertion). This is an important distinction.

Furthermore, even if it matched, the second one would eat the character involved. Hence, if you said something like:

```
$zigguratString = "This matches the word ziggurat now";
$zigguratString =~ s"\Wziggurat\W""g;
```

You would end up with This matches the wordnow, because you have substituted both the word and the intervening spaces. Hence:

- Zero width assertions such as \b and \B can match places where there are no characters. They never eat any characters in the process of a match.

Here are some other wildcard matching examples:

```
$example = '111119';
$example =~ m"\d\d\d";          # match the first three digits it can find in the string. Matches '111'.
$example = 'This is a set of words and not of numbers';
$example =~ m"of (\w\w\w\w\w)";  # Matches 'of words'.. Creates a backreference
```

Note the last example. Because there is an of at the beginning of the string (before words), the pattern matcher matches this particular of, and not the later of (the one before numbers). The last example also shows where we are going. It is a real chore to have to print \w five times in order to match five word characters. Hence, Perl provides multiple match operators to facilitate matching long patterns. We turn to this next.

Multiple Match Operators

There are six multiple match operators in Perl. They are used to avoid coding stuff such as saying \w five times in a row, as in the preceding section. Think of them as a shorthand shortcut.

The six Perl multiple match operators are:

- *—Match zero, one or many times.
- +—Match one or many times.
- ?—Match zero, or one time.
- { X }—Match 'X' many times exactly.
- { X, }—Match 'X' or more times.
- { X, Y }—Match 'X' to 'Y' times.

These two examples are equivalent, but which do you find easier to read?

```
$example = 'This is a set of words and not of numbers';
$example =~ m"of (\w\w\w\w\w)";   # Matches 'of words'.
$example =~ m"of (\w{5})";        # Usage of { X } form.  Matches 5 characters,
                                  # and backreference $1 becomes the string 'words'.
```

Hopefully, you find the second example easier to read. It uses multiple match operators to avoid boring, repetitive code.

You can also use special symbols to match an indeterminate number of characters. The regular expression a* matches '', a, aa, or aaa, or any number of as. It matches *zero* or *many* as. This example:

```
$example = 'this matches a set of words and not of numbers';
$example =~ m"of (\w+)";
```

matches the string words (of (\w+) = 'of words'). And

```
$example =~ m"of (\w{2,3})";   # Usage of {X, Y}. Matches the string 'wor'
                               # (the first three letters of the first match it finds.
                               # matches the string 'wor'
                               # ('of \w{2,3}' equals 'of wor' here)
```

And contrary to intuition, the m" " clause in:

```
$example = 'this matches a set of words and not of numbers';
$example =~ m"of (\d*)";
```

matches this string, even though we are looking for digits with \d*. Why? Because \d* means *zero to many*, and hence, matches zero digits! However:

```
$example =~ m"of (\d+)";
```

will not match the same string, because you have used a \d+ instead of \d*. Therefore, it is looking for one or more digits after the word of, which the string does not have.

Greediness

Now, all of these above examples show a major point about how the regular expression engine matches a given string with a given expression; that is, by default, multiple-match operators are *greedy*.

What does "greedy" mean in this sense? *Greedy* means that Perl multiple-match operators will, by default, gobble up the maximal amount of characters in a string and still have the ability to make a pattern match. You should learn this well. Understanding the nature of greedy Perl expressions will save you hours of tracking down weird regular expression behavior.

Here are a few simple examples of this greedy behavior that can drive a programmer mad. Let's start with the statement:

```
$example = 'This is the best example of the greedy pattern match in Perl5';
```

Suppose you want to match the is in this example. Accordingly, you do something such as:

```
$example =~ m"This(.*)the";
print $1;          # This does NOT print out the string 'is'!
```

You expect to see is when you print the $1. What you get is the following string:

```
'is the best example of'
```

This works as shown in Figure 9.6. This is because of the greediness of the multiple-match operator *. The * takes all the characters up to the last occurrence of the string the (the one before greedy). And, if you are not careful, you will get unexpected results from using regular expressions.

Figure 9.6
Greedy . *
with Caveats

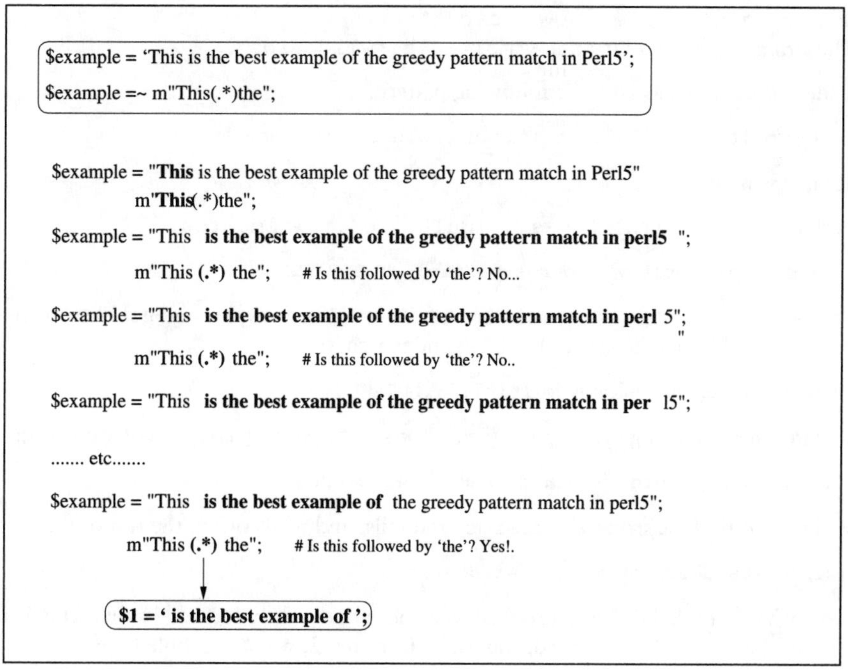

$example = 'This is the best example of the greedy pattern match in Perl5';
$example =~ m"This(.*)the";

$example = "**This** is the best example of the greedy pattern match in Perl5"
        m"**This**(.*)the";

$example = "This **is the best example of the greedy pattern match in perl5** ";
        m"This (.*) the";   # Is this followed by 'the'? No...

$example = "This **is the best example of the greedy pattern match in perl** 5";
        m"This (.*) the";   # Is this followed by 'the'? No..

$example = "This **is the best example of the greedy pattern match in per** l5";

.... etc.......

$example = "This **is the best example of** the greedy pattern match in perl5";

      m"This (.*) the";   # Is this followed by 'the'? Yes!.

$1 = ' is the best example of ';

Here are some more examples:

```
$example = 'sam I am';
$example =~ m"(.*)am";                          # stores 'sam I' in $1
$example = 'RECORD: 1   VALUE: A  VALUE2:  B';
$example =~ m"RECORD:(.*)VALUE";                # stores '  1  VALUE: A  ' in $1;
$example = 'RECORD';
$example =~ m"(\w{2,3})";                        # matches REC
```

The last example shows that even numeric multiple-match operators are greedy. Even though there are two word characters in RECORD, Perl prefers to match three, because it can. If you said 'RE'=~ m"\w{2,3}", it would match only two characters as that is the maximum amount possible.

Backtracking and Multiple Wildcards

OK, you've hung in so far; now it is time to tackle a thorny subject. As said earlier, the combination of wildcards and backtracking can cause some extremely slow performance for regular expressions. If you understand why, this is a good indicator that you are "getting" regular expressions.

Take the following example:

```
$string =~ m"has(.*)multiple(.*)wildcards";
```

This means that the regular expression is going to look for (in numerical order):

1. The pattern has (m"has.*multiple.*wildcards")
2. The maximum text it can find until it gets to the last multiple
   (m"has(.*)multiple(.*)wildcards)
3. The string multiple (m"has(.*)multiple(.*)wildcards")
4. The maximum text it can find until it gets to the last wildcards
   (m"has(.*)multiple(.*)wildcards")
5. The string wildcards (m"has.*multiple.*wildcards")

Consider then, what happens with the following pattern:

```
has many multiple wildcards multiple WILDCARDS
```

Well, what happens is:

1. Perl matches has (i.e., m" has(.*)multiple(.*)wildcards)

   has many multiple wildcards multiple WILDCARDS

2. Perl performs the m"has(.*)multiple(.*)wildcards part and gobbles up all the characters it can find until it hits the last multiple and matches:

   has **many multiple wildcards** multiple WILDCARDS

3. Perl matches the string multiple (i.e., m"has(.*)multiple(.*)wildcards):

   has many multiple wildcards **multiple** WILDCARDS

4. Perl tries to find the string wildcards and fails, and reads out to the rest of the string:

   WILDCARDS does not match 'wildcards'!

5. Now what does Perl do? Because there was more than one wildcard (*) character, Perl *backtracks*. The last place it could have made a mistake is in step 2, when it gobbled up:

has **many multiple wildcards** `multiple WILDCARDS`

Hence, it goes back to right after `has`:

```
has many multiple wildcards multiple WILDCARDS
  ^goes back here
```

6. Now it tries to rectify its mistake, and only gobbles up characters up to the next to last incidence of `multiple`. Hence, the pattern `m"has(.*)multiple(.*)wildcards"` matches:

    has **many** multiple wildcards multiple WILDCARDS

7. `multiple` in `m"has(.*)multiple(.*)wildcards"` then matches:

    has many **multiple** wildcards multiple WILDCARDS

8. Then the wildcard matches the space—(`m"has(.*)multiple(.*)wildcards"`) matches:

    has many multiple( )wildcards multiple WILDCARDS

9. Finally, `wildcards` (`m"has(.*)multiple(.*)wildcards`) matches:

    has many multiple **wildcards** multiple WILDCARDS

Therefore, the whole regular expression matches has `many multiple wildcards`. It gave the result that might be expected, but it sure took a torturous route to get there!

To be sure, the Perl algorithm that implements regular expressions has some shortcuts to improve performance, but the logic just given is basically correct.

I don't hesitate to add that this example may be the most important one in this chapter-even Perl veterans incorrectly parse regular expressions now and again (much to their chagrin). Go over it again and again, until the answer is second nature to you. After that, try to trace the way Perl matches the following:

```
$pattern = "afbgchdjafbgche";
$pattern =~ m"a(.*)b(.*)c(.*)d";
```

We'll give you this one for free:

```
afbgchdjafbgche (m"a(.*)b(.*)c(.*)d";)
afbgchdjafbgche (m"a(.*)b(.*)c(.*)d";) -- greedy, goes to last 'b'
afbgchdjafbgche (m"a(.*)b(.*)c(.*)d";)
afbgchdjafbgche (m"a(.*)b(.*)c(.*)d";) -- matches g.
afbgchdjafbgche (m"a(.*)b(.*)c(.*)d";)
afbgchdjafbgche (m"a(.*)b(.*)c(.*)d";) -- backtrack because no 'd'
afbgchdjafbgche (m"a(.*)b(.*)c(.*)d";) -- now we take up everything to the next to last b
afbgchdjafbgche (m"a(.*)b(.*)c(.*)d";)
afbgchdjafbgche (m"a(.*)b(.*)c(.*)d";) -- now the second .* becomes greedy.
afbgchdjafbgche (m"a(.*)b(.*)c(.*)d";)
afbgchdjafbgche (m"a(.*)b(.*)c(.*)d";) -- still no d. darn. backtracks
afbgchdjafbgche (m"a(.*)b(.*)c(.*)d";) -- wildcard becomes less greedy, gobbles to next to last c
afbgchdjafbgche (m"a(.*)b(.*)c(.*)d";)
afbgchdjafbgche (m"a(.*)b(.*)c(.*)d";) -- there is only one d in the expression and this matches up to it
afbgchdjafbgche (m"a(.*)b(.*)c(.*)d";) -- a match! matches 'afbgchd'.
```

Not very pretty. As you can see, if you have more than one greedy, multiple-match operator, things can get ugly—and inefficient—fast.

Possibly the simplest maxim that can be taken out of this example is that the multiple-match operators to the left get "first say" over their counterparts to the right. A pattern such as:

```
m"(.*)(.*)";
```

will *always*, in a string with no newlines in it, make the first backreference contain the whole string, and the second contain nothing. Errors like this are best dealt with by the **-Dr** command line option, as in, **Perl -Dr script.p.** We will talk about this in Chapter 20.

Anyway, what happens if you don't want to have this greediness? Well, as we will see in the next section, Perl (unique to any package out there) has the ability to have *nongreedy* versions of these characters.

Nongreedy Multiple-Match Operators

Greediness can be a blessing, but it can just as often be a hassle! Take a common example of C comments (so common it is an FAQ and in the documentation). Say you want to match the bold text in the following:

```
/* this is a comment */    /*another comment */
```

Try to think of a greedy solution here. We want to match a /* followed by all the text up to and including the next */. If we try:

```
m"/\*.*\*/";
```

then this will match:

```
/* this is a comment */    /*another comment */
```

The whole thing! Again, because the * is greedy.

This is the best greedy solution I could come up with:

```
$commentmatcher =~ m"/\*([^*]*|\**[^/*])*\*/";*
```

which is not the most readable of solutions. (Although, again, we could make it much more readable using the m""x, covered later.) We will go over this later because understanding this particular expression will help immensely in learning regular expressions in general! For now, just welcome the nongreedy versions. There is a simple rule to remember them by: Simply add a ? onto the end of any greedy multiple-match operator to make it nongreedy.

Hence, the previous commentmatcher becomes:

```
$commentmatcher =~ m"/\*(.*?)\*/";
```

which still isn't the most readable form, but it sure is much better! We can even describe this in simple English: "Take a /*, then take the minimum possible amount of characters, and then take the closing */," something like what is shown in Figure 9.7.

"Laziness" is another term used to describe ?. The regular expression engine can be thought of as lazily marching along, until it hits the first possible expression it can match. In this case, it is a */ that it hits to move it onto the next step. If you say:

```
$line =~ m"(.*?)(.*?)(.*?)";
```

each (.*?) will match *nothing*.

Why? Again, the minimum amount of characters that will match here is zero (because you have said * (zero to many)). Hence, by matching zero characters, each (.*?), has done its job, and, being lazy, passes control onto the next (.*?) which in turn takes zero characters.

Figure 9.7
Minimal Matching

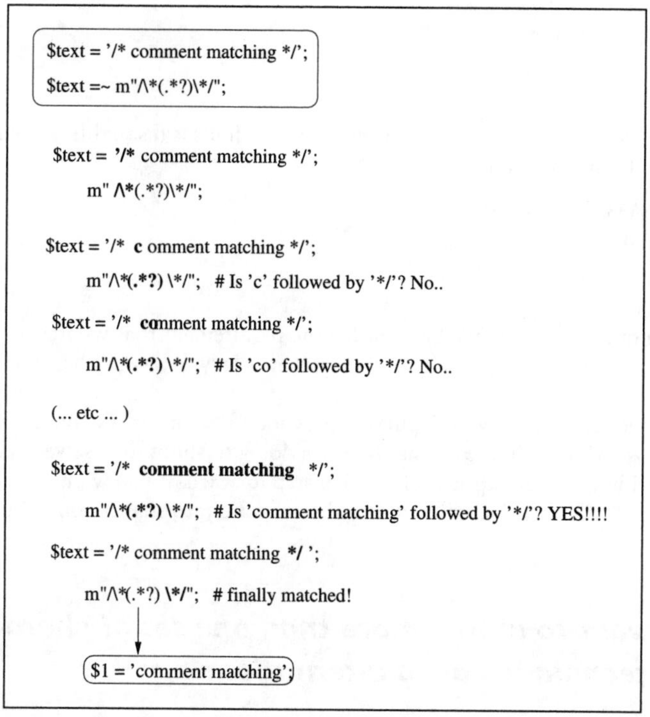

$text = '/* comment matching */';
$text =~ m"/*(.*?)*/";

$text = '**/*** comment matching */';
m" /*(.*?)*/";

$text = '/* **c** omment matching */';
m"/*(.*?) */";   # Is 'c' followed by '*/'? No..

$text = '/* **co**mment matching */';
m"/*(.*?) */";   # Is 'co' followed by '*/'? No..

(... etc ...)

$text = '/* **comment matching** */';
m"/*(.*?) */";   # Is 'comment matching' followed by '*/'? YES!!!!

$text = '/* comment matching ***/** ';
m"/*(.*?) */";   # finally matched!

$1 = 'comment matching';

Here are the generalized rules for lazy matchers. Simply append a character class (like `.`, `\d`, or `[123]`) onto them to get this lazy behavior.

- `*?`—Match zero, one or many times, but match the fewest possible number of times.
- `+?`—Match one or many times, but match the fewest possible number of times.
- `??`—Match zero, or one time, but match the fewest possible number of times.
- `{ X }?`—Match "X" many times exactly.
- `{ X, }?`—Match "X" or more times, but match the fewest possible number of times.
- `{ X, Y }?`—Match "X" to "Y" times, but match the fewest possible number of times.

Here are some more examples of minimal matchers in action, along with what would be matched with non-greedy ones:

```
$example = 'This is the time for all good men to come to the aid of their party';
$example =~ m"This(.*?)the";
```

This matches ' is '. If it was greedy it would match ' is the time for all good men to come to the aid of'. (Note the trickiness here—'their' contains the word 'the'!) And the following regular expression matches what is in bold:

```
$example = '1999211333333333333331';
if ($example =~ m"1(\d{3,}?)")
{
}
```

This expression says 'match a 1 followed by three digits (or more)'. However, since there is nothing after the '?', it basically says 'match a 1 followed by three digits'. So this matches '1999'.

```
$example = '1f9991333333333333333331';
if ($example =~ m"1(\d{3,}?)")
{
}
```

Here, we have the same expression, but the first 1 the pattern matcher finds is disqualified, since it is followed by an 'f'. It then goes to the next 1, and matches 1333.

```
$example = '1f9991333333333333333331';
if ($example =~ m"1(\d{3,}?)1")
{
}
```

Here, this matches something quite different. We have added the requirement that whatever digits we find with \d{3,}, a 1 must follow. Hence, even though the pattern matcher is lazy, it has to go to the end of the expression to find a match.

As you can see, one must be very careful with regular expression logic. Surprises abound for the uninitiated. There are endless ways for those who don't know what they are doing to shoot themselves in the foot!

Learning the principles behind regular expressions is a big step forward. If you want more information, turn to the section "Perl Debugging," Chapter 21, where we will give more information on debugging Perl regular expressions.

Principle 7: *If you want to match more than one set of characters, Perl uses a technique called alternation.*

Alternation

Alternation is the way to tell Perl that you wish to match one of two or more patterns. In other words, the expression:

```
(able|baker|charlie)
```

tells Perl "look for either the string able *or* the string baker *or* the string charlie" in a regular expression. As an example, start with the following statement:

```
$declaration = 'char string[80];' or $declaration = 'unsigned char string[80];'
```

Say you want to match strings char or unsigned char. It would be very convenient to match more than one string at a time. The following regular expression matches both:

```
foreach $declaration ( 'char string[80]',  'unsigned char string[80]' )
{
    if ( $declaration =~ m"(unsigned char |char )" )
    {
        print ":$1:";    # prints ':char:' first time around.
                         # prints ':unsigned char:' second time around.
    }
}
```

The | syntax means match either unsigned char or char and saves the string matched into a backreference. Alternation can be quite subtle, for there is an important thing to remember about its behavior:

- Alternation always tries to match the first item in the parentheses. If it doesn't match, the second pattern is then tried, and so on.

This is called *leftmost matching*, and it accounts for many of the bugs people have when they get to regular expressions. Take the earlier example. Let's say that we switch the order of the items in the parentheses, so the example becomes:

```
$declaration = 'unsigned char string[80]';
$declaration =~ m"(char |unsigned char )";
```

Does this match the string `unsigned char` (as in `unsigned char string[80]`)? No, it matches `char` (i.e., `unsigned char string[80]`). Because the `char string` is first in the list, it gets priority over the string `unsigned char`. The regular expression matches it, and thereby saves the wrong alternation in the backreference.

This mistake is so common that a point must be made here:

- Always put the highest-priority strings to match, the most specific strings, first.

If you don't do this, agony awaits. For example:

```
$line =~ m"(.*|word)";
```

never matches `word`. This is because `word` is an instance of `.*` (that is, four arbitrary characters). And because regular expressions match leftmost, it picks up the `.*` first. Hence:

```
$line = "wordstar";
$line =~ m"(.*|word)";
```

will match `wordstar` (i.e., the whole thing), and not `word`star. The `.*` matches any character, and because it is first in the alternation, it always takes precedence over the "word" part. This, however, does match `word` in `word`star:

```
$line =~ m"(word|.*)";   # since 'word' is first.
```

This is also helpful for situations such as when you don't know whether or not a word will be followed by a delimiter or an end-of-line character, or whether or not a word is plural, as in the following:

```
$line = 'this is a list of words in a string';
$line = 'the last word in this string is word';
$line =~ m"word(s|$)";   # matches both above; 'word' if last word in string.
                         # word may be followed by the character '!' or '$'.
```

Both of these match. This syntax will match the string `word` if it is either followed by the end of the string or followed by an `s`. Replace the `$` by:

```
$line =~ m"word(s|\b)";
```

and you get a good way for dealing with plurals.

Principle 8: *Perl provides extensions to regular expressions, in the (?..) syntax.*

One day in Perl history (around the transition from Perl 4 to Perl 5), it was decided that in order for the regular expression set to grow, Perl had to "get past the metacharacter standard." Some people seemed to argue that there were too many metacharacters, and some people disagreed, until there weren't too many metacharacters *left* on the keyboard!

It was then decided that it would be a good idea to make one distinctive construct that could be used to provide for several more expansions to come. The keyboard was looked at, and it was found that one rather common character (?) was hardly used anywhere. Hence, it was decided. The syntax looks like this:

```
(?<special character(s)><text>)
```

Here, `<special character(s)>` represents the extensions, and `<text>` is the text on which that expression acts. The four most common extensions are shown in Table 9.5.

Table 9.5	Extension	Meaning
Regular Expression Extensions	?=<regexp>	Matches the next group of text, but doesn't 'eat' it for further matches.
	?!<regexp>	Only match if not followed by <regexp>.
	?:<regexp>	Grouping, but non-backreference creating, parens.
	?xims	Built-in modifier to the regular expression.

In addition, there is an operator (`?#comment`) that would let you embed comments into regular expressions. This is now pretty much obsolete because of the x modifier.

Otherwise, these extensions work like any other regular expression construct. You slip them into the regular expression itself. If you say:

```
$line =~ m"I love (?!oranges)";
```

this matches `love figs`, but not `I love oranges`, since the (`?!`) prohibits oranges from following the string `I love`. However, this would match `I love orange`, or `I love ripe oranges`, because it only prohibits things that *start* with the string `oranges`. You could say:

```
$line =~ m"I love(?!.*orange)"
```

to prohibit these strings.

In fact, the (`?!`) modifier is probably the most understood construct in the language. People expect it to do stuff like:

```
$line =~ m"(?!oranges) I love";
```

and have this not match `oranges I love`. This simply doesn't work. The (`?!`) construct matches only if the next substring is *not* oranges. Hence, in this case, the only place this negates the match is at the beginning of the string—it doesn't do anything at any other place. The regular expression just goes along, and then finds that the next six characters aren't "oranges." Hence, the requirement is satisfied, and it proceeds to the next requirement.

The other two expressions used the most are (`?:...`) and (`?=...`). For example, (`?:...`) makes your regular expressions more efficient by getting rid of unwanted backreferences. If you say:

```
$line =~ m"(?:int|unsigned int|char)\s*(\w+)";
```

to get variable names, you may not wish to save the type of the variable; hence, the (`?:`). It matches the type, followed by any spaces, followed by the variable name (`\w+`). But it saves the variable name in `$1`, not `$2`. The (`?:`) is ignored for the purposes of backreferences. This saves on time and memory, especially in large pattern matches.

The other expression, (`?=`), is useful only when you use it with the g modifier, which we shall see below. The g modifier lets you start back at the point in an expression where you left off, without having to traverse from the beginning. For example, if you had data that looked like:

```
BLOCK1 <data> BLOCK2 <data2> BLOCK3 <data3>
```

and you wanted to match <data> first, <data2> second, and <data3> third (and last), and you said:

```
$line =~ m"BLOCK\d(.*?)(BLOCK\d|$)"g;
```

it would match <data> on the first run, but then place the "match pointer" in the wrong place, after the second BLOCK. If you say something like:

```
$line =~ m"BLOCK\d(.*?)(?=BLOCK\d)"g;
```

it matches the same amount of text, because it says "match the minimal amount of text between BLOCK1 and BLOCK2." It ignores BLOCK2 for the purpose of the next match, so that the next call to the regular expression can match <data2>. Figure 9.8 summarizes up the difference between the two.

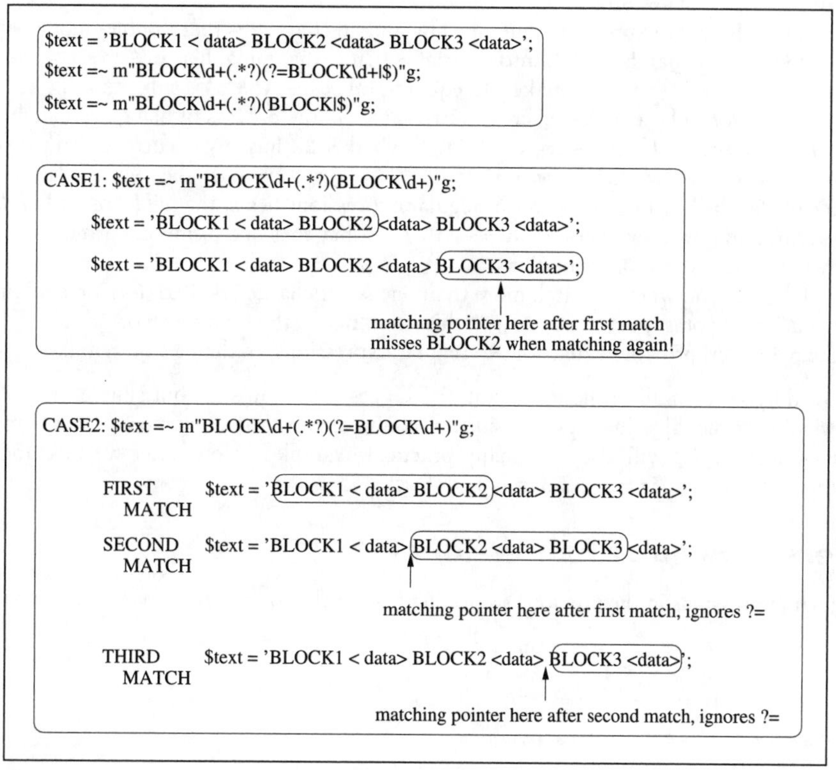

Figure 9.8 Difference between m"BLOCK(.*?)(?=BLOCK)"g and m"BLOCK(.*?)BLOCK"g

```
$text = 'BLOCK1 < data> BLOCK2 <data> BLOCK3 <data>';
$text =~ m"BLOCK\d+(.*?)(?=BLOCK\d+|$)"g;
$text =~ m"BLOCK\d+(.*?)(BLOCK|$)"g;
```

CASE1: `$text =~ m"BLOCK\d+(.*?)(BLOCK\d+)"g;`

`$text = 'BLOCK1 < data> BLOCK2 <data> BLOCK3 <data>';`

`$text = 'BLOCK1 < data> BLOCK2 <data> BLOCK3 <data>';`

matching pointer here after first match
misses BLOCK2 when matching again!

CASE2: `$text =~ m"BLOCK\d+(.*?)(?=BLOCK\d+)"g;`

FIRST MATCH   `$text = 'BLOCK1 < data> BLOCK2 <data> BLOCK3 <data>';`

SECOND MATCH   `$text = 'BLOCK1 < data> BLOCK2 <data> BLOCK3 <data>';`

matching pointer here after first match, ignores ?=

THIRD MATCH   `$text = 'BLOCK1 < data> BLOCK2 <data> BLOCK3 <data>';`

matching pointer here after second match, ignores ?=

With the (?=) version we can now say the following:

```
$line = 'BLOCK1 <data> BLOCK2 <data2> BLOCK3 <data3>'
while ($line =~ m"BLOCK\d(.*?)(?=BLOCK\d|$)"g)
{
    print "$1\n";
}
```

and have this print out <data>, then <data2>, and then <data3>. This works because of the g-modifier, which makes the regular expression 'iterate' over the text as shown above. We will see more use of the g modifier in the following section.

Summary of Regular Expression Principles

The previous section should be more than enough to get you working with regular expressions. Although we called them "basic" regular expressions, we will see that in various combinations, they make a formidable ally in the fight against data—it is a fight sometimes. The eight principles—again—are:

- Principle 1: There are three different forms of regular expressions (matching (m//), substituting (s///), and translating (tr///)).
- Principle 2: Regular expressions match only on scalars ($scalar =~ m"a"; works; array =~ m"a" has array treated as a scalar, and hence probably does not work).
- Principle 3: A regular expression matches the earliest possible match of a given pattern. By default, it only matches or replaces a given regular expression once ($a = 'string1 string2'; $a =~ s"string""; makes $a == '1 string2').
- Principle 4: Regular expressions can take any and all characters that double-quoted strings can ($a =~ m"$varb" expands $varb into a variable before matching; hence, $varb = 'a', $a = 'as', $a =~ s"$varb"" makes $a equal to s because the 'a' is substituted).
- Principle 5: A regular expression creates two things in the process of being evaluated: *result status* and *backreferences*. If $a =~ m"varb" tells whether $a has any occurrences of the substring varb, $a =~ s"(word1) (word2)"$2 $1" "turns around" the two words.
- Principle 6: The heart of the power of regular expressions lies in the *wildcard* and *multiple-match operator*, and how they operate. $a =~ m"\w+" matches one or more word characters; $a =~ m"\d*" matches zero or more digits.
- Principle 7: If you want to match more than one set of characters, Perl uses a technique called *alternation*. If you say m"(cat|dog)" this says "match the string cat or dog."
- Principle 8: Perl provides extensions to regular expressions, in the (?..) syntax.

Whew! How do you learn all of these principles? I suggest that you start out simple. If you learn that $a =~ m"ERROR" looks for the substring ERROR inside $a, you've already got much more power than you do in a lower-level language like C. We will also give many practical examples below, after we talk about two important concepts: modifiers to regular expressions and contexts.

Modifiers to Regular Expressions

All the regular expressions in the previous section had either the form:

```
$a =~ m//;    # m" " is synonym, as is m{ }
```

or:

```
$a =~ s///;    # s" " " is synonym, as is s { } { }
```

Both of these represent the default form of regular expressions. These match or substitute once, starting from the beginning of the expression.

Suppose we do not want to "match or substitute once." Suppose we want to substitute *all* occurrences of a for b in an expression, or we want to match case-insensitively. In other words, suppose we do not want the default behavior. Fortunately, there are some helpful modifiers we can put on regular expressions to overload their behavior to do something other than the default. In this modified form, the regular expressions look like the following:

```
$a =~ m//cgismxo; $a =~ s///geismxo;
```

with one or more modifiers "tacked on" to the end to alter the behavior of Perl's expressions. Let's deal with those that have features in common between the two (s, m, i, x, o) and then deal with the ones that have different meanings between operators (c, g, e). We deal with these next.

Modifiers in both Substitution and Matching

The constructs m" " and s" " " " have many operators in common. They are listed in Table 9.6. All five modifiers are described in detail next.

	Modifier	Meaning
Table 9.6 Regular Expression Modified	x	Readable regular expression form.
	i	Case-insensitive regular expression form.
	s	Treat expression as a single string.
	m	Treat expression as multiple strings.
	o	Compile a regular expression once.

x: Extended Readability Regular Expressions

Regular expressions can sometimes become a mess. You have seen it earlier, but that doesn't go half as far as some of the expressions in real life. Consider the following code that—roughly—matches a subroutine in Perl:

```
$line =~ m"sub\s+(\w+)\s+{(.*?)}\s*(?=sub)"s;
```

What does this mean? Even if you are an old hand at Perl, this expression still forces you to think quite a bit, even if it is commented. The lack of white space in particular is irksome, and the number of special characters can give you nausea.

The x operator was not available in Perl 4. It becomes a particular blessing because it makes it possible to put white space in regular expressions to make them readable, and allows room to put comments in. The expression:

```
$line =~ m"sub\s+(\w+)\s+{(.*?)}\s*(?=sub)"s;
```

becomes:

```
$line =~ m{
    sub\s+ (  \w+  ) \s+    # matches the 'sub' keyword, subroutine name
                            # and matches the white space afterwards.
    {                       # opening brace
      (  .*?  )             # matches the text of the sub. and saves it for
                            # further use.
    }                       # closing brace
    \s*(?=sub)              # the next sub keyword
}sx;                        # match as a multiline string and be readable.
```

While still pretty ugly, as anything with that many special characters is bound to be, you can see the logic behind it much more clearly. It more closely resembles the actual thought process of logic. The braces are in their correct places. And since you can put in comments, they help immensely to give a play-by-play of what is happening.

Note, however, a couple of caveats. Since white space is allowed in the regular expression, and filtered out, the following will not match:

```
$line = "multi line string\nhere";
$line =~ m"multi line string"x;    # this does not match the above because
                                   # the space above GETS MUNGED OUT.
```

Note that the x readability function works only in the *first* bracket of the `substitute` operator (i.e., in `s{ }{ }`). This is because *only* the first bracket has its values interpolated as a double string. Everything in the second bracket is literal. For example, the following is probably *not* going to do what you want:

```
$line = 'aaaaaa';        # we want 'bbbbbb' after the substitute below.
$line =~ s {
                a
           }
           {
                b
           } gx;         # we want to do a 'general' match, i.e., match
                         # ALL a's for b's. DOESN'T WORK!
    print $line;         # prints '                        b            b... etc'
                         # six times over.
```

What happened here is that the item in the second bracket does not have white space munged here. Instead, each instance of a (where white space does get munged) is substituted for three tabs, a b, and then a newline, resulting in a mess.

Readable regular expressions have a large role in helping you keep your sanity when dealing with more complicated things.

i: Case-Insensitive Matching

Regular expressions are case-sensitive by default. Using the i indicates that the matching will be done *case-insensitively* instead.

```
$pattern = 'Exercise';
$pattern =~ s"exer"EXER"i;  # matches first four characters of Exercise. (Exer)
$pattern = 'Edward Peschko';
$pattern =~s"[a-f]dward"Edmund"gi;  # matches 'Edward'. replaces with Edmund.
```

In both cases, these match: the first turning `Exercise` into `EXERcise`, and the second turning `Edward Peschko` into `Edmund Peschko`.

The i modifier is pretty much a shorthand for writing several tedious regular expressions, such as `$pattern =~ m"[Ee][Xx][Ee][Rr]";`.

s: Treat the Pattern as a Single Line

Without modifiers, a dot (.) matches anything but a newline and '\s' matches a space or tab. Sometimes the default behavior is helpful; sometimes it is very frustrating, especially if you have data that spans multiple lines. Consider the following case:

```
$line =
   'BLOCK1:
      <text here1>
    END BLOCK
    BLOCK2:
      <text here2>
    END BLOCK'
```

Now suppose you want to match the text between blocks `<text here[0-9]>`:

```
$line =~ m{
            BLOCK(\d+)
```

```
                    (.*?)
        END\ BLOCK      # Note backslash. Space will be ignored otherwise
   };
```

This does not work. Because the wildcard (.) matches every character *except* a newline, the regular expression hits a dead end when it gets to the first newline and it *stops matching right there*.

Sometimes, as in this case, it is helpful to have the wildcard (.) match *everything*, not just the newline. By extension, it is helpful to have the wildcard (\s) match [\n\t], not just tabs and spaces. This is what the s operator does.

It tells Perl not to assume that the string you are working on is one line long. The above then does work with an s on the end of the regular expression.

```
$line =~ m{
        BLOCK(\d+)
        (.*?)
        END\ BLOCK      # Note backslash. Space will be ignored otherwise
   }s;
```

With the s on the end, this now works.

m: Make '$' and '^' Match newlines($) and Characters after newlines(^).

The m modifier makes it so ^ and $ now match not only the beginning and ending of the string (respectively), but also make ^ match any character after a newline, and make $ match a newline. In the following example:

```
$line = 'a
b
c';
$line =~ m"^(.*)$"m;
```

the m modifier will make the backreference $1 become a instead of a\nb\nc.

o: Compile Regular Expression Only Once

The o modifier is helpful when you have a long expression. When you say something like:

```
$line =~ m"<very long expression>";
```

where <very long expression> is a paragraph, or even pages, long, as it stands, each time Perl hits this regular expression, it compiles it. This takes time, and if the pattern you need to match is exceedingly complicated, your regular expression will be exceedingly long.

In Jeffrey Friedl's book, there is an expression that matches e-mail addresses, which comes out to 6,598 bytes long! Without the o modifier it would be sunk, but if you compile it only once, it is usable.

However, there is one caveat you should be aware of. If you say:

```
$line =~ m"$regex"o;
```

you make a promise to Perl that $regex *will not change*. If it does, Perl will *not* notice your change. Hence,

```
$regex = 'b';
while ('bbbbb' =~ m"$regex"o) { $regex = 'c'; }
```

is actually an infinite loop in Perl. $regex changes, but it is not reflected in the regular expression. (This does not however, bind you to one only one regexp per program. Each instance of expressions with o is compiled before usage.)

Modifiers Specific to Substitution

The s, m, x, I, and o modifiers work exactly the same way with both substitution and matching (s///, m//), but there are a couple of modifiers that are made specifically for substitution. They are g and e. The modifier e is specific to substitution and is not found in the matching version. There is also a g modifier for matching, but the two g modifiers for substitution and matching are so different as to be distinct. They are listed next.

g: Substitute All the Patterns for Their Equivalents

By default, the s/// operator substitutes only the first time it sees something. If you want to substitute every single instance something into something else, use the g operator. The next three examples are equivalent:

```
$pattern = 'NUM1 NUM2 NUM3';

$pattern =~ s"NUM"LETTER"g;    # substitutes NUM for LETTER.
$pattern =~ s"num"LETTER"gi;   # Note -- you can stack these modifiers.
                               # does exactly the same thing as the above.
while ($pattern =~ s"NUM"LETTER") {}
```

All of these make $pattern LETTER1 LETTER2 LETTER3. The first does so with regard to case, the second does so with regard to case (gi modifiers), and the third does so slowly (each time s"NUM"LETTER" substitutes once, becoming LETTER1 NUM2 NUM3 first, LETTER1 LETTER2 NUM3 second, and finally LETTER1 LETTER2 LETTER3).

e: Evaluate the Second Part of the s/// as a Complete "Mini-Perl Program" Rather Than as a String

The e modifier for s/// is pretty cool, but also very involved. You can do pretty heavy wizardry with it. We'll just mention it briefly here, with an example. Let's say you wanted to substitute all the letters in the following string with their corresponding ASCII number:

```
$string = 'hello';
$string =~ s{ ( \w ) }            # we save the $1.
           {ord($1). " ";}egx;
```

This example prints out 104 101 108 108 111. Each character was taken in turn here and run through the ord function that turned it into a digit. Needless to say, this can do pretty powerful stuff in a short amount of time. It also runs the risk of being extremely obscure.

We suggest you use this logic as a last resort, when all other "tricks" have failed. Its use can sometimes hide a cleaner way of doing things. Is the above really clear? Or is the following better?

```
$string = turnToAscii($string);

sub turnToAscii
{
    my ($string) = @_;
    my ($return, @letters);

    @letters = split(//, $string);
    foreach $letter (@letters)
    {
        $letter = ord($letter) . " " if ($letter =~ m"\w");
    }
```

```
        $return = join('', letters);
        $return;
    }
```

The latter example is explicit and easily maintainable. However, it is also over 10 times as long and a few times slower; a judgment call must be made on when to use e.

Matching, and the g Operator

The modifiers x, i, s, and e work just the same with the matching operator m//. There is, however, one significant change in how the g operator works, and you will use it quite frequently.

As was seen before, the g operator in substitution meant that every single instance of a regular expression was replaced. However, this is meaningless in the context of matching. Backreferences indicate one and only one match. Hence, Perl uses the g operator in a different way with m// than it does with s///.

Perl attaches an iterator to the g operator. When you match once with $string =~ m" "g, Perl remembers where that match occurred. This means you can use this to match where you left off. When Perl hits the end of the string, the iterator is reset:

```
$line = "hello stranger  hello friend  hello sam";
while ($line =~ m"hello (\w+)"sg)
{
    print "$1\n";
}
```

This outputs:

```
stranger
friend
sam
```

and then quits, because the inherent iterator comes to the end of the expression. There is a caveat here. If you are using the g modifier, then any modification to the variable being matched via assignment causes this iterator to be reset.

```
$line = "hello";
  while ($line =~ m"hello"sg)
  {
    $line = "$line";
  }
```

This is an infinite loop! So restrain yourself and avoid modifying your string while you are matching it. (Make a copy instead!)

Matching, the c Operator, and the \G Zero Width Assertion

Note that there is a caveat with the above example. If the pattern does not match, then the position operator is reset! This does not work very well if you are building something like a parser. Suppose you want to match something like C code:

```
struct elt
{
    char *val;
    int pos;
}
```

```
for (xx = 0; xx < 10; xx++)
{
    fprintf(stderr, "%d", xx");
}
```

Then you are going to want something that works as a parser, something that is able to split the language into pieces, like this:

```
while (!$eof)
{
    if ($line =~ m"for"sg) { my $struct = _matchstruct(\$line, \$eof);        }
    elsif ($line =~ m"struct"sg) { my $forloop = _matchfor(\$line, \$eof);    }
    else { $eof = 1; }
}
```

where the subroutines _matchstruct and _matchfor match the struct and for loop, independently.

Unfortunately, there are two problems here:

1. When the parser hits the first matcher (m"for"sg) it will skip over the struct altogether, and proceed to the for loop.
2. If the for loop does not match, the position will reset so the beginning of the string is matched again.

Problem #1 prevents us from making a true parser—one that matches all of a given set of text. Problem #2 makes it so that we could match the same thing at the beginning many times—if the match fails, the position would reset and be subject to a false match without seeing the end of file record ($eof).

Perl gets around these two problems in the form of a zero width assertion (\G) and a modifier to the regexp engine (c). Lets take these in order. \G is a zero width assertion used in conjunction with the matching modifier g. It means "match, and only match right after where the last search with g left off". For example, the following will match 1, then 2, then 3, then 4, and then 5:

```
my $line = '12345abcde67890';
while ($line =~ m"\G(\d)"sg)
{
    print "$1\n";
}
```

When the regular expression engine sees 'a' in the string, this fails the \G zero width assertion. This short-circuits the while loop and it never gets to see 6,7,8,9, and 0.

OK, all fine and proper, but this still leaves the problem of the position being reset if a match fails (and hence screwing up any parsers we might write). For this, we have the modifier c. Looking at our original example:

```
while (!$eof)
{
    if ($line =~ m"\Gfor"sgc) { my $struct = _matchstruct(\$line, \$eof);       }
    elsif ($line =~ m"\Gstruct"sgc) { my $forloop = _matchfor(\$line, \$eof);   }
    else { $eof = 1; }
}
```

Note that we have added the \G and c modifiers to each regular expression. The \G makes it so that we are guaranteed not to miss any text in the string that we are parsing—only matches where we left off from the last match are allowed. The c maintains the position if we have a failure in matching 'for' or 'struct'; this allows us to have multiple regular expressions, each one matching a token in our parser. Filling the example out:

```
sub _matchstruct
{
```

```
        my ($line, $eof) = _;
        $$line =~ m"\G(\w+)\s*{(.*?)}"sgc || print "SYNTAX ERROR";
        my $return = { name => $1, text => $2 };
        $$eof = 1 if ( !pos($$line) );
        return($return);
    }

sub _matchfor

    {
        my ($line, $eof) = _;
        $$line =~ m"\G\((.*?)\)\s*{(.*?)}"sgc || print "SYNTAX ERROR";
        my $return = { condition => $1, text => $2 };
        $$eof = 1 if ( !pos($$line) );
    }
```

We take advantage of the fact that a reference to a scalar keeps the position of the scalar that it references, and therefore "split up" our parsing work into subroutines which then each handle part of the parsing job.

Modifiers and Contexts

If you were not familiar with Perl regular expressions before you started this chapter, your head is probably swimming with different modifiers, methods, special characters, and so forth. Let's take a moment to look at different forms of how regular expressions are used, and then finish this chapter with some common examples of regular expressions in use.

This has everything to do with context. Remember, in Perl, context is king, and if you pay attention to it, you can do many powerful things just by recognizing the context that different expressions are in. Let's simply "crystallize" the forms we've seen so far, and add a couple of new ones.

Substitution (No Modifier) in Scalar Context

This looks like:

```
if ($string =~ s"a"b") { print "Substituted Correctly"; }
```

This prints Substituted Correctly, returning a 1 to the if when the string in fact did match. It also substitutes the first instance of a for b at the same time.

Substitution (g Modifier) in Scalar Context

This returns the number of successful matches made. For example, using this method, if you say something like:

```
($string =~ s"a"b"g) == ($string2 =~ s"a"b"g) && print "Same number of a's\n";
```

Perl will tell you if $string has the same number of as in it as $string2, as well as perform the substitution. If you wanted, you could do this on whole files:

```
undef $/;                          # munge mode, do whole file.
my $fh = new FileHandle("File1");
my $fh2 = new FileHandle("File2");
(($line = <$fh>) =~ s"a"b") == (($line2 = <$fh2>) =~ s"a"b");
```

This counts the number of as in both files, comparing them while again doing the substitution.

Substitution (No Modifier) in Array Context and Substitution (g Modifier) in Array Context

These two are boring. They do exactly the same thing as substitutions in scalar context.

Matching in Scalar Context (No Modifier)

This is the same as substitution in a scalar context with no modifiers. If you say:

```
if ($line =~ m"a") { print "Matched an a!\n"; }
```

it simply checks to see whether $line has an a in it. If you say:

```
if ($line =~ m"\b(\w+)\b" ) { print "$1\n"; }
```

this checks to see if $line has any word in it, and then saves that in $1, printing it. And:

```
($line =~ m"\b(\w+)\b") && (print "$1\n");
```

is the same thing, only using short-circuiting to print it.

Matching in Array Context (No Modifier)

This matches the first position the regular expression can match, and simply puts the backreferences in a form that is quickly accessible. For example:

```
($variable, $equals, $value) = ($line =~ m"(\w+)\s*(=)\s*(\w+)");
```

takes the first reference, (\w+), and makes it $variable; it takes the second reference, (=), and makes it $equals; and it takes the third reference, (\w+), and makes it $value.

Matching in Array Context (g Modifier)

This takes the regular expression, applies it as many times as it can be applied, and then stuffs the results into an array that consists of all possible matches. For example:

```
$line = '1.2 3.4 beta 5.66';
matches = ($line =~ m"(\d*\.\d+)"g);
```

will make @matches equal to 1.2, 3.4, 5.66. The g modifier does the iteration, matching 1.2 first, 3.4 second, and 5.66 third. Likewise:

```
undef $/;
my $FD = new FileHandle("file");
comments = (<$FD> =~ m"/\*(.*?)\*/");
```

will make an array of all the comments in the file $fd.

Matching in Scalar Context (g Modifier)

Finally, if you use the matching operator in scalar context, you get a behavior entirely different from anything else in the regular expression world, and even the Perl world. This is that "iterator" behavior we talked about. If you say:

```
$line = "BEGIN <data> BEGIN <data2> BEGIN <data3>";
```

```
while ($line =~ m"BEGIN(.*?)(?=BEGIN|$)"sg)
{
    push(blocks, $1);
}
```

this matches the following text (in boldface), and stuffs it into @blocks on successive iterations of while:

```
BEGIN <data>(%)BEGIN <data2> BEGIN <data3>
BEGIN <data> BEGIN <data2>(%)BEGIN <data3>
BEGIN <data> BEGIN <data2> BEGIN <data3>
```

We have indicated via a (%) where each iteration starts matching. Note the use of (?=) in this example. It is essential to matching the correct way; if you don't use it, the "matcher" will be set in the wrong place.

Examples of Regular Expressions

Enough theory already! Keep the preceding information in mind (especially the "Modifiers and Contexts" section), go get a cup of hot chocolate, and relax.

Remember, there are only 177 different characters you can type with a keyboard. Regular expressions happen to use most of them. I feel that learning regular expressions happens to be worth the effort, because of the exceedingly powerful things you can do with them.

Below are several examples of real-life pattern matchings, from the simple to the complicated. They show the power of regular expressions. Understand how to parse them, and you are well on your way to writing Perl.

Example 1: Words in a Text File

```
undef $/;
use FileHandle;
my $fh = new FileHandle("$ARGV[0]");
my words = (<$fh> =~ m"\b(\w+)\b"g);
```

This is a simple example. Here, we simply open the file given to us by the first argument to the script, i.e., by typing **perl5 script.p filename**. In the fourth line, the pattern m"\b(\w+)\b"g iterates over the file, getting all of the words out of it and sticking it into the array words. Note the use of undef $/; this affects the filehandle so the entire file is slurped into one scalar.

Example 2: Words Fitting a Given Criteria in a File

Let's expand on this a little. Suppose we want to get all the words that start with the letter *t* in a file.

```
my words = grep(m"^t", (<$fh> =~ m"\b(\w+)\b"g));
```

or equivalently:

```
foreach my $word (<$fh> =~ m"\b(\w+)\b"g)
{
    push (words, $word) if ($word =~ m"^t");
}
```

In each case, the regular expression is in array context, with a g modifier; therefore, it passes back a list of words to the context in which it was called. In the first case, this was the function grep; in the second case, it was a foreach loop.

After this array is passed back, the m"^t" clause pushes onto the array stack any and all words that start with *t*. For example, this could be used to match words in a list:

```
my @%words = ('gofer' => 1,'Julie' =>1,'Doc' => 1,'bartender' => 1,'captain' => 1);
my @characters = grep ($words{$_}, (<$fh> =~ m"\b(\w+)\b"g));
```

or perhaps, make your own spelling checker:

```
1 use FileHandle;
2 my (%words, words);
3 my $fd = new FileHandle("/usr/dict/words");   # or any dictionary
4 grep { chop($_); $words{$_} = 1 } (words = <$fd>);
5 undef $/;
6 my $fh = new FileHandle("$ARGV[0]");
7 my @misspelled_words = grep(!$words{$_}, (<$fh> =~ m"\b(\w+)\b"g));
```

Here, we simply load all the words from /usr/dict/words into a hash in line 4. (We need to say @words = <$fd> because grep modifies the list by chopping off a newline, and we can't directly chop input from a filehandle.)

Then, we put Perl into "get whole file" mode (line 5), and proceed to slurp the whole file into one long string, cut it into words, and compare it against the hash to see if any word is not present (line 7). A lot of work for one line!

Example 3: Times (10:00AM)

Suppose you have a file of the form:

```
Picked up nuts and bolts 10:00AM
Sawed wood 11:00AM
Sanded 12:30PM
```

in which the description is followed by the time at which the deed occurred and you want to turn this into a hash that tells you what you did at what time. There are three steps:

1. Read in the file.
2. Extract out the times and events.
3. Create a hash.

With the use of regular expressions, step 2 becomes fairly straightforward. Our regular expression will look something like this:

```
m"^(.*?)(<regexp for time>)\s*$"mg
```

Here, matching the comment is easy. Given that every line is a comment/time pair, and consists of a comment first, and a time second, matching the comment becomes a simple matter of putting a .*? right after the beginning.

Furthermore, we use the m modifier, so that ^ means "match any character after either the beginning or a newline," and $ means "match any character that is a newline, or the end of the string."

Now we need only find what the regular expression for time is. We could roughly think of it as this:

```
m"(\d{1,2}:\d{2}\s*[AP]M)";
```

The first \d{1,2}: matches 10:, the second \d{2} matches 00-59, and [AP]M matches AM or PM. This expression also happens to match 99:99PM, but the chances of such a string occurring are slight, so we deem the risk acceptable. (In more "bulletproof" cases, we would have to consider this. See "Mastering Regular Expressions" for more detail on how to only match 0-11, or 0-23, or 0-59, i.e., "time" numbers.)

Anyway, we can now iterate through our file with this expression and make the hash. The code is below:

```
1   use FileHandle;
2   use strict;
3   undef $/;
4   my $fd = new FileHandle("$ARGV[0]");
5   my $line = <$fd>; my %commenthash;
6   while ($line =~ m"^(.*?)(\d{1,2}:\d{2}\s*[AP]M)\s*$"mg)
7   {
8       my $comment = $1; my $time = $2;
9       $commenthash{$time} = $comment;
10  }
```

The loop in lines 6 through 10 does most of the work, making the hash by taking the results of the regular expression (line 8) and hashifying it (line 9). You could then do whatever you like with the data.

Example 4: HTML Tags—Substituting Bold Text for Italic

You are probably aware of these. They are things like:

```
<H3 FOLDED_ADD_DATE="....">culture</H3>
```

or:

```
<TITLE>my bookmarks</TITLE>.
```

In general, we cannot match all these with one regular expression, because they can be recursive, as in the following:

```
<DL><p>
    <A ...>      </A>
</DL><p>
```

although we could write a recursive subroutine to do so.

But in a simple subroutine, the best we can do is pick a list of tags to match, and then use that information to match (assuming the tags are *not* recursive). This is usually a safe assumption.

Now, the general form of a tag is something like this:

```
<I> .... </I>
```

or

```
<A HREF = ...>      </A>
```

In other words, the first tag consists of a <, then a string, followed by either nothing or a space and other text describing the tag, plus a >. The tag is closed by a </STRING> where STRING equals the same string as before. To match:

```
<B> text </B>
```

we could say:

```
m"<B>(.*?)</B>"
```

assuming, of course, that this tag isn't recursive. How do we generalize this so it matches any tag? Well, let's say we wanted to match bold or italic (B or I). And furthermore, we don't know whether these strings have text after them (assume we don't know if <B description> is possible). We could use the following pattern:

```
m"<(B|I)(\s.*?)?>"
```

which says to match either `B` or `I` first, and then match (zero or 1 times) the combination of a space plus the minimum amount of characters. Why this complexity? Consider, if we say: m `"<(B|I).*?>"`, then:

```
<BODY>
```

will match. Hence, it is essential that we put in the facts that:

1. There could not be any more text after the <.
2. If there is any more text, it will be a *space* followed by any number of characters (up to, but not including, the next >).

In pictures, our expression m`"<(B|I)(\s.*?)?` works like Figure 9.9.

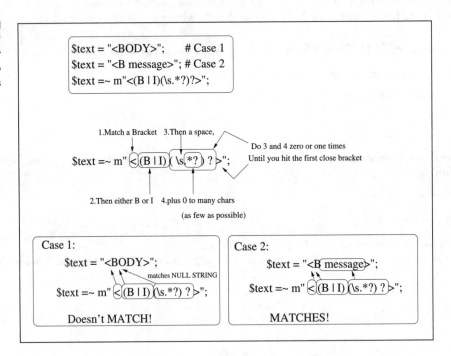

Figure 9.9
A Regular
Expression to
Match HTML Tags

If we now take (B|I) and substitute it with $pattern, where $pattern = `'B|I'`, we get:

```
m"<($pattern)(\s.*?)?>"
```

To match the first tag <B> and to match the "whole enchilada":

```
m"<($patterns)(\s.*?){0,1}>.*?</\1>"sg;
```

Here, `\1` is whatever pattern we had found in $patterns. Hence, this matches the whole tag (in this case, the B tag).

```
<B>hold</B>
```

For our code example, let's simplify, and only consider two possible strings to match: <B> and <I>. Furthermore, in this case, let's substitute bold text for italic, and vice versa.

However, let's write our code in such a way that it can be generalized. The code follows now:

```
1 undef $/;
2 my $fd = new FileHandle("$ARGV[0]");
3 my $line = <$fd>;
4 my (%substituteHash) = ('B' => 'I', 'I' => 'B');
5 my $patterns = join('|', keys(%substituteHash));      # makes B|I
6 $line =~ s|(<) ($patterns)((\s.*?)?>)    # opening tag (<B> or <I>)
7                (.*?)                      # text in between
8          (</) \2 (>)                      # closing tag (</B or </I>)
9          }{$1$substituteHash{$2}$3$5$6$substituteHash{$2}$7}sgx;# subsitute
```

Lines 5 through 9 are the killers. Let's look at them closely. The first thing we notice is that we have parenthesized everything: `(<)`, `($patterns)`, etc. This way, we ensure everything we save will be accounted for when we substitute back in.

Second, notice the sgx modifiers on the end. We must use the s modifier in case we have something like:

```
<B>
text here
</B>
```

We must use the x or the expression will become unreadable. We must use the g so that this matches more than one time.

Finally, notice the $1....$7 substitute variable. This is us, plunking in the data we have matched. In particular, the $substituteHash{$2} takes whatever tag we find, and converts from, say, B to I.

This example shows much about the crafting of regular expressions. The next example goes even further.

Example 5: http, ftp Tags

You know the ones I'm talking about:

```
http://members.aol.com/tlyco/KITH/index.html
ftp://ftp.x.org
```

Suppose you've got a file of text containing them (for simplicity sake, suppose they aren't split between lines), and you want to abstract them out. Well, the first thing we must do is come up with a regular expression to match these. Lets look at what we need to match:

1. `ftp:` or a `http:` followed by `//`.
2. An Internet address (`members.aol.com`, `128.101.22.1`).
3. Several, optional paths */tlyco/KITH/index.html*.

This translates into something that looks like this:

```
m"((?:ftp|http)://(?:\w+\.){2,5}\w*(/\S*)?)"g
```

This is outlined in Figure 9.10. This took a little trial and error. We use `(?:)` so we don't get any backreferences; the `(?:ftp|http)` is self-explanatory, but the `(?:\w+\.){2,5}\w*` needs some explaining, as does the `(/\S*){0,1}`.

In `(?:\w+\.){2,5}\w*` each `\w+\.` is meant to match `members.`, or `aol.`. However, this isn't enough to match the whole Internet address, because the Internet address has a trailing group of letters. `(?:\w+\.){2,5}` does not match `members.aol.com`; it matches `members.aol.`. We need to add a `\w*` to match the last bit (`com`).

Figure 9.10
Matching an
http, ftp Tag

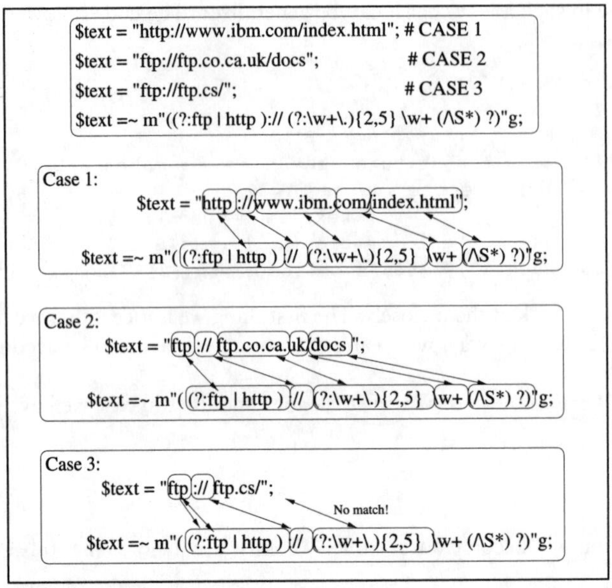

(/\S*)?—is saying "match a slash followed by as many nonspaces as you can find, and do it zero or one times." It refers to the fact that you can have a trailing path on an http or ftp address, but it is not a necessity. This results in the optional question mark.

This pattern is not perfect. If you have backslashed spaces in the http tag in particular, this won't work. Or, if you have an http daemon running on a different port (*http://site:8080*, for example), it won't work. However, it is, as we say, "close enough"; if you want to improve it to handle such cases, go right ahead.

Now let's make a loop that extracts all http and ftp tags from a given file. For example, a bookmarks file, as in the following:

```
1   undef $/;
2   my $fd = new FileHandle("$ARGV[0]");
3   $line = <$fd>;
4   my tags;
5   while ($line =~ m"((?:ftp|http)://(?:\w+\.){2,5}\w*(/\S*){0,1})"g)
6   {
7       my $tag = $1;
8       chop($tag);
9       push(tags, $tag);
10  }
```

Here, we chop off the last character, since in a bookmarks file these tags are in double-quoted strings. We will approach this problem more directly next, when we consider matching a double-quoted string.

Example 6: C Comments and Double-quoted Strings

There are two parts to this example: an easy one and a difficult one. If you understand the difficult one, then you're on your way to regular expression nirvana. Those who want to get more information can go to *Mastering Regular Expressions*, where these examples are fleshed out with much more detail.

We have already given the expression for finding C comments via lazy regular expressions. It looks like this:

```
$line =~ m"/\*.*?\*/"g;
```

in which we match a /* and then the minimum amount of characters until */, and then finally a */. To get all the comments in a given C file, you could say:

```
undef $/;
use FileHandle;
my $fh = new FileHandle("$ARGV[0]");
@comments = (<$fh> =~ m"/\*.*?\*"g);
```

which uses the common g form to get the comments out of the text, along with undef $/ which makes <$fh> get all the text out of the first file argument.

So much for the easy part. However, I also said there was another greedy version that does the same thing:

```
$expression = m"/\*([^\*/]|\*[^/])*\*+/";
```

Let's "readify" this a bit with /x:

```
$expression = m{
                (/\*)                          # matches beginning
                    ([^\*/]|\*[^/])*           # matches junk in middle, comment
                (\*+/)                         # matches ending
            }x;
```

This does exactly the same thing as the /*.*?*/. And why would anyone want to write something like this, instead of writing the relatively simple /*.*?.*/?

In this case, the only answer has to do with efficiency. When you have a lot of data, you can craft a greedy expression that can go much quicker than the corresponding lazy version. However, in most cases, you would probably want to write the simpler version, if anything, for readability and maintainability. In other cases, however, you cannot be so simple. The one we shall consider is the double-quoted string. In the first case, we might consider that we could match a double-quoted string by:

```
m/".*?"/;
```

But, alas, this is not to be. This works fine for "True Lies", but it does not work fine for "The Man who cried \"Uncle\"";. In this second case, we used the trick that Perl uses; we have escaped the special character " so it can be included in a " " string! Hence, the pattern ".*?" will match "The Man who cried \" instead of the whole statement.

So how do we get around this? Well, by trickery, that is, by suiting our regular expression to the pattern at hand and thinking, "We can overcome the problem."

Hence, let's consider some possible strings we need to match.

1. ""—empty string
2. "\""—one quote
3. "a"—one letter
4. "a\""—one letter, then a quote
5. "a\"a"—one letter, then a quote, then a letter.
6. "a\t\""—one letter, then a backslashed special character, then a backslashed quote.

These might be what we would consider *boundary* conditions. If we are going to screw up anywhere, it will be here. So, let's start building our regular expression from the ground up, so to speak. We first match the obvious:

```
m/".*?"/;
```

Which strings does this match? It matches 1 and 3.

Then, let's add the ability so that 2 can match by handling the case where a backslash is followed by a quote:

```
m/"(\\"|.*?)*"/g;
```

But this doesn't quite work in matching 4. If our string is `"a\""`, then `.*?` will match the `"a\""`. We would also have a trailing character, because the next time through the `*`, this will not let `\\"` match (the backslash is eaten). Hence, lets reconsider `.*?` here:

```
m/"(\\"|[^\\"]*)*"/g;
```

This eats up all the characters, but it doesn't quite work on example 6. The `\t` doesn't match alternation 1, and backslash isn't allowed by alternation number 2 at all. Hence, the regular expression stops at the a (in bold) in`'"a\t"'`. Therefore, we need to allow for a backslash followed by a character:

```
m/"(\\.|[^\\"]*)*"/g;
```

This now works on all six cases, and, therefore, works to match. However, we have run into a trap. What is this trap? Remember backtracking, in which the regular expression tries every single possibility, and gives up when all possibilities are tried? Well, this expression goes through an inordinate amount of work in figuring stuff out. Even a small string such as:

```
"bbb
```

goes through this much before it fails to match, even if we ignore the first alternation:

```
"bbb   (m/"([^\\"]*)*"/);      # matches ".
"bbb   (m/"([^\\"]*)*"/);      # inner bracket matches all 3 characters.
"bbb   (m/"([^\\"]*)*"/);      # outer bracket matches on one copy of inner
                               # three characters, fails on "
"bbb   (m/"([^\\"]*)*"/);      # Inner matches 2 chars
"bbb   (m/"([^\\"]*)*"/);      # Outer matches once on the two chars fails "
"bbb   (m/"([^\\"]*)*"/);      # Inner matches once on last char
"bbb   (m/"([^\\"]*)*"/);      # Outer matches once on last char, fails on "
"bbb   (m/"([^\\"]*)*"/);      # Inner matches once on first char
"bbb   (m/"([^\\"]*)*"/);      # Outer matches 3 times/first char,fails on "
```

Even in this case, with four characters in the string, we have a total of nine tried matches, 12 if you count the end parentheses, and 24 if you count the alternation we ignored! In other words, the two stars battle it out, where the inner one tries to match as many characters as it can, and the outer one then drives the inner one to try more and more combinations before finally quitting.

When the string being matched is a long one, this can take literally lifetimes. How do you recognize this error? First, realize that the backtracking principle is much more than just a mathematical curiosity. It can produce very palpable bugs, like this one.

Second, if you think you have a bug like this, try your script versus the -Dr switch on the command line, something like:

```
prompt% perl5 -Dr script.p
```

This will run your script, but show your compiled regular expressions on the screen. Notice that you need to compile Perl with the -DDEBUGGING script, or get a Perl binary built with that as internals. We will talk about this more in "Debugging Perl."

Finally, realize you will run into a couple of these. You can usually get around them by finding a way to do the same expression without the star. In this case:

```
m/"((?:[^"\\]|\\.)*)"/g;
```

will do the trick, because we don't *need* the internal star here. We also make it more efficient by putting the most common alternation first (`[^"\\]`) and by using `?:` so no backreferences are saved except the whole thing. This little regular expression we end up with is a gem, and can be used, for example, to rewrite the recognizing HTTP, and FTP addresses example: `HREF="ftp://ftp.perl.com"`. FTP and HTTP addresses are double-quoted strings inside html files, so this code becomes:

```
use FileHandle;
my $line = new FileHandle("$ARGV[0]");
while ($line =~ m/HREF="((?:[^"\\]|\\.)*)"/g)
{
    push(addresses, $1);
}
```

which will then go through each file and pick out the addresses for that file.

Summary

This chapter has been a long one primarily because 1) regular expressions are powerful, 2) regular expressions are heavily integrated into the rest of the language, and 3) people get confused about regular expressions and seldom use them correctly. If you learn their secrets, they make your life much easier, especially if you deal with large amounts of data.

Regular expressions almost form a "language within a language" in Perl. As you have seen, they can be fairly involved, and (let's face it) if you are not familiar with them now, you are not going to learn them without practice. Therefore, we suggest the following path for learning regular expressions.

Learn the principles in this chapter well. To use regular expressions effectively, you will need to know these principles, or you will be spinning your wheels often. Then try several regular expressions in actual use, working from simple to complicated.

Also, look at other examples in the book. I haven't included nearly as many as I would have liked in this chapter, so I stuffed a few in Chapter 12, just for good measure! Look at the sections about regular expression debugging, in the chapter on "Debugging Perl."

Be sure to check out the documentation in **perlref**. Also, check out Jeffrey Friedl's book, *Mastering Regular Expressions*. Whereas this chapter will get you started and give you some skill in regular expression manipulation, it cannot possibly give the same treatment that his book goes into. As far as I know, it's the only book of its kind out there—fully devoted to practical use of regular expressions.

Finally, let your knowledge about regular expressions evolve. Start with simple regular expressions, and as your knowledge grows, let your regular expressions grow.

10

Perl Built-in Functions and Variables

Perl is not a minimalist language when it comes to built-in functions. It is difficult to get far into Perl without using built-in functions and special variables.

We have already covered several of these variables and functions in detail. There are many, many more—so many, in fact, that people get lost deciding which ones to concentrate on.

This chapter is designed as a solution to that problem: It points out the most important variables and functions, and demonstrates their most common usage. For a complete reference, see the **perlrun**, **perlfunc**, and **perlvar** reference pages.

Chapter Overview

We don't want to duplicate the effort of the on-line manual, so we will confine ourselves to going over the common Perl functions and variables that we did not touch on in Chapter 3.

We will parse out the functions available in the "Perl core" into groups, and try to stay away (if at all possible) from the functions that are operating system (Unix)–specific; these will form the basic structure of this chapter.

The basic functional groups we will discuss are:

- Specialized quoting and formatting
- Functions for I/O on formatted data
- Functions for variable manipulation

- Time manipulation functions
- Debugging functions
- Functions to get information about files
- Process forking and management
- Functions emulating operating system commands

In each section, the emphasis will be on giving examples, and filling in the holes that I believe the on-line documentation has.

After going through these functions, we will turn to the internal variables Perl provides. These internal variables create many shortcuts in your actual programs; we discuss the most common:

- Internal tokens for use inside Perl code
- Internal filehandles inside Perl
- Named, internal variables
- One-character variables that affect the way an internal Perl function is executed
- One-character variables that are set as a side effect from other internal Perl functions

Even though this looks fairly extensive, please don't use this chapter as a reference! You will want to know the functions and variables described in this chapter pretty well, but you are doing yourself a disservice if you don't print the relevant documentation.

Introduction

If I were to chose a phrase to describe Perl, I would say it is "simple in the design and complicated in the details."

You have seen this is true from previous chapters, especially with regular expressions. Eight simple principles form the core of regular expressions. But Perl evolved to handle real-world problems (rather than being designed from scratch), so the engine evolved to be very intricate, with a lot of functionality behind each symbol.

The same is true with how Perl's built-in functions and special variables have evolved. The built-in functions each fill a pragmatic gap. To be on the safe side, some gaps have been filled more than once. We have already seen this before, in the form of `shift` and `splice`. The following two statements are equal:

```
my $return = shift(@arrayName);
my $return = splice(@arrayName,0,1);
```

Both take the first element off the beginning of @arrayName and stuff it into the variable $return. Or, if you want to count the number of characters in a string, try the following:

```
my $nochars = length($string);
my $nochars = @{[(split(//, $string))]};
my $nochars = $string =~ tr[\000-\377][\000-\377];
```

(I dare say that the first usage is a bit less noisome and much easier to read than the others.) The official Perl motto may be "There's more than one way to do it," but I am tempted to modify this: "There's more than one way to do it, but some are better than others."

This chapter is designed to exhibit some of the more powerful built-in functions and special variables that are built into Perl (some are Unix-specific, and then we give their NT counterparts). These functions are so much a part of the Perl programming experience that you should learn them and know them well.

There are a few simple rules you need to know about the default behavior of internal functions and operators. Then, if you run up against a real-life problem that does not exactly match this default behavior, chances are there is either a function or special variable that will help you resolve it.

For example:

```
@arrayName = ("This", "is", "an", "array");
$stringName = "@arrayName\n";    # $stringName becomes
print $stringName;               # 'This is an array'
```

prints "`This is an array`" by default. But what happens if you want "`This|is|an|array`" instead, perhaps to use in a regular expression, or to load into a database? Perl provides the variable $" (or $LIST_SEPA-RATOR), which determines what to put between the elements of the array (in string context). Here, setting:

```
$" = "|";                       # also use English; $LIST_SEPARATOR = "|";
                                # see below
print "@arrayName\n";           # prints 'This|is|an|array'.
```

does what you want, which is return a character string with "`|`" delimiters. There are thousands of these little tricks in Perl. Likewise, there are *classes* of tricks, such as the following:

- Tricks with functions
- Tricks with special variables
- Tricks with the order of execution

These tricks flow from the fact that Perl is such an expressive language. It is full of computer metaphors, similes, and other constructions. Learning these tricks is one of the biggest steps you will take in becoming a strong Perl programmer. In fact, it is *the* biggest step (aside from object-oriented Perl).

It is pretty much out of the scope of this book to explain all these small time savers, but the best way to learn them is to:

- Learn the principles we discussed in these last few chapters (contexts, variables, and references).
- Discover them on your own by combining these principles with what we will cover in this chapter.
- Look at the Perl source code for ideas. Thousands of lines are there at your beck and call.
- Talk to other Perl programmers (*comp.lang.Perl.misc* comes to mind).
- Just experiment.

Built-in Perl Functions

Built-in Perl functions are routines that are already recognized by the Perl interpreter. You get them for free; that is, you need no libraries to access them. They are "built in" to the language.

Principles Behind Built-in Functions

As you may expect, the main principle behind built-in functions is pragmatism. Who wants to have to remember two or more functions that basically do the same thing? Because ease of usage was the supreme goal behind Perl's design, its functions have evolved to be as painless as possible. Perl functions are smart. They know what type of variable has been passed to them, and how to treat it.

For example:

```
$line = "Please chop the letter T";
chop($line);                    # $line becomes "Please chop the letter "
```

works to chop the last character off of $line, whereas:

```
@listOfValues = ("Chop", "Every", "Letter", "Off");
chop(@listOfValues);     # @listOfValues becomes ("Cho", "Ever", "Lette","Of")
```

works to chop each character off of @listOfValues.

In other words, chop works the way you would expect it to: chopping one character off each scalar, and one character off each element in an array. chop performs a simple function, but does it "blind" to datatype.

What happens if you say:

```
%hash = ('key' => 'value', 'key2' => 'value2');
chop(%hash);
```

Well, pretty much the same thing. After this is done, the hash becomes:

```
%hash = ('key' => 'valu', 'key2' => 'value');
```

by chopping off each letter in the values, but leaving the keys alone. This is a somewhat startling, but entirely logical, way to program. If you chop a character off the key as well, you may end up with a hash that has empty keys, or a key with more than one value. The hash would no longer be viable. For example, suppose you had the following hash:

```
%hash = ('a' => 'bb', 'c' => 'dd');
```

and when you called:

```
chop(%hash);
```

it went ahead and chopped off both the value *and* the key. Then you would end up with something that looked like:

```
%hash == ('' => 'b', '' => 'd');
```

This is not viable. What happens if you tried to look up the following hash entry:

```
$hash{''};
```

Would Perl return 'b' or 'd'? Therefore, it is crucial that chopping only affect values where you cannot possibly destroy the integrity of the hash, and therefore leave the keys alone.

This evolution of usefulness is a result of much thought (and trial and error). Sweat and tears went into programming these built-in functions. You would be smart to learn them not only for their power, but for their ability to teach good programming style. Let's now turn to look at some of the more important ones (you can also go to the **perlfunc** man page for more detail).

The Main Functions

Unless you are doing specialty programming (sockets, Unix system administration, etc.), the following functions (combined with those you have already learned) are the ones you will be using 95 percent of the time.

Perl's built-in functions can be grouped by different functional groups. I supply a Windows 32 function if no internal Perl function works correctly on Windows 32 (this is especially the case in process management).

- Functions for specialized quoting and formatting: quotemeta(), qq(), qw(), q(), qx(), and **HERE** documents.
- Functions for IO to or on formatted data: read, printf(), and sprintf(). (For information on open, close, and print, turn to Chapter 3, where we go over filehandles in "Perl Variables.")
- Functions for variable manipulation: sort(), split(), grep(), and map(). For many others, turn to the "Perl Variables" section in Chapter 3.

- Time manipulation functions: `localtime()`, `timelocal()`, `time()`, `times()`, and `sleep()`.
- Debugging functions: `caller()`, `warn()`, and `die()`.
- Functions to get information about files: file tests, and `glob()`.
- Process forking and management: `system()`, `` `` ``, `fork()`, `exec()`, `wait()`, and `Win32::Process()`.
- Functions for emulating operating system commands: `rmdir()`, `mkdir()`, and `chdir()`.

Operations for Formatting Data

As a quick note, Perl has a couple of cool "pseudo" functions that will help you to keep your sanity, especially if you are writing code to generate more code, and dealing with regular expressions.

These functions are: `quotemeta()` and the specialized quote operators `qw()`, `qx()`, `qq()`, and `q{ }`. We look at them briefly next.

quotemeta()

Suppose you had the following text that you wanted to search for inside many files:

```
( aleph + beta ) ** 2;
```

and suppose you knew that this text could be matched *verbatim*. If you did the straightforward thing:

```
1 $text = '( aleph + beta ) ** 2';
2 foreach $file (@filelist)
3 {
4     open (FD, $file);
5     $line = <FD>;
6     print "Match" if ($line =~ m"$text");
7 }
```

you would come to grief. Why? Because when you put the text `( aleph + beta ) ** 2` into the regular expression (line 6), the regular expression treats the `(`, `+`, `)`, `*` characters as special characters. Hence, the text `$text` will *not* match the string `$line` in line 6.

`quotemeta()` changes all that. When you say:

```
$text = quotemeta( '( aleph + beta ) ** 2' );
```

it makes the resulting variable `$text` regular expression "friendly," backslashing all the right characters for you:

```
\( aleph \+ beta \) \*\* 2
```

which is a much easier way to write this type of regular expression.

qw(), qx(), qq(), and q{ }

These four "functions" are actually more readable forms of quotes, which are especially handy when writing Perl code to generate Perl code.

Suppose you wanted to generate the following code:

```
$line = "$text2$text"
```

in which you wanted to keep `$line` and `$text2` as variables, and interpolate `$text` into whatever it is on the command-line.

Well, if you did the following:

```
$code = "\$line = \"\$text2$text\"";
```

you will, before long, get a bad case of "backslash-itis." With qq(), you can say:

```
$code = qq(\$line = "\$text2$text");
```

which does exactly the same thing. qq() here is just a synonym for " ". Table 10.1 gives all of their meanings, plus examples.

Table 10.1
Specialized
Quotes

Symbol	Meaning	Example
qq()	double quotes	$text = 1; $text2 = qq($text) => $text2 = 1
q{}	single quotes	$text = 1; $text2 = q{$text} => $text2 = '$text'
qw()	word list	@array = qw(this is) => @array = ('this', 'is');
qx()	execute (`)	$text = qx(dir) => $text = `dir`;

Each has the benefit of not requiring you to backslash the respective quotes.

HERE Documents

Perl goes further than this in helping you print things such as code or data. Suppose you have several lines (tens to hundreds) that you want to print pretty much verbatim, but with one change: You want to interpolate any variables you find. Let's suppose there are many double quotes (you are generating C code). If you said:

```
$line =
"
char $variable\[$length\] = \"$value\";
...
";
```

then you've got two strikes against you for readability. First, you have extra newlines, because the returns are interpreted as returns. Second, you need to backslash any double quotes you see.

Enter the **HERE** document. **HERE** documents are ways for you to make literal text in Perl, and assign it to a variable or function. The previous example becomes:

```
$line =<<"EOL";
char $variable\[$length\] = "$value";
EOL
```

EOL is an arbitrary tag that tells Perl what to look for to stop interpreting the text as *text*, and look at the rest as Perl code. This is basically saying "Take all the text between EOL and the exact characters EOL and turn it into a Perl string." Because you are saying EOL, interpolation happens. Perl also ignores the beginning and ending returns so you get one line of text. (Note that we did not say EOL, at the end; this is a syntax error.)

Perl allows three types of **HERE** documents: EOL (single quotes/no interpolation), EOL (double quotes plus interpolation), and EOL (backticks for shell calls plus interpolation). The third type is quite intriguing. It basically lets you embed a shell script inside Perl, returning the text to a Perl variable:

```
$line =<<`ENDOFSCRIPT`
cd $dir1
dir /s
type filename
ENDOFSCRIPT
```

or, more helpfully:

```
my $fd = new FileHandle("scriptname"); my @script = <$fd>; close($fd);
$line =<<`ENDOFSCRIPT`;
@script
ENDOFSCRIPT
```

which will execute any script (Unix or Windows NT) and then pipe the results to the variable $line.

Reading and Writing Operations to Files and Variables

You have actually seen the three functions that are the most important for filehandle manipulation: open, print, and close. You can get a long way knowing these three functions. The functions that follow are really the icing on the cake. These functions, read, printf, and sprintf, aren't nearly as important as open, print, and close, but can be extremely helpful when dealing with special cases.

read, printf, and sprintf are good to know, especially when you hit data that can't be parsed easily by slurping it into a variable with a $line = <FD> (read). Another use is if you hit a case in which you want to have selective writing to a variable or filehandle (printf, sprintf). Following is more information on these built-in functions.

read

read is Perl's major way to read-in information, in bulk, from a filehandle. Its usage is as follows:

```
$bytes = read(FILEHANDLE, $scalar, $length, $offset);
```

where $scalar is the variable you want to populate with the data from FILEHANDLE, $length is the amount of data you want to read-in, and $offset (optional) is the point at which you want to write the data into the scalar. $bytes is the number of characters read. If there are no bytes to be read (i.e., the file is at an EOF), this returns 0. This makes it nice to use in a while loop (as in while (read(...))). For example:

```
open(FILEHANDLE, "file");
$bytes = read(FILEHANDLE, $input, 40, 20);
```

would read up to 40 characters from the open filehandle FILEHANDLE into the scalar $input, starting at the position 20. Something like:

```
$input = "<twenty nulls><read from filehandle>";
```

in which the string $input is padded with 20 nulls, and then (and only then) are the 40 characters inserted. Here, for example, is a simple program to make block text (text with no newlines) a little more user-friendly. It chops data into 80 character segments, putting a newline after each (use \r\n if you are using DOS or NT):

```
while (read(FILEHANDLE, $input, 80))
{
    print "$input\n";
}
```

I wouldn't suggest using this script on text that is more conversational in nature (i.e., many words with newlines on the end). In that case, the `read` statement has no way of knowing whether or not one of the characters it has read is a newline. Hence, you could get lines with only *one* word on them!

`read` should be used only when you know exactly what size blocks you need to slurp in from a filehandle, and when there is no real delimiter to the file. If there is a delimiter, such as a newline, or you want to read the entire file at once, use `$line = <FILEHANDLE>` instead. This will save you tons of trouble. Too many times I have thought that I knew something was of "fixed length" and used `read` only to find that the file in question was not always of fixed length, but off by a character or two. This caused strange errors when reading it.

printf

`printf` is sort of the opposite of `read`. Instead of reading in fixed amounts of data, `printf` gives you the option to output fixed amounts of data. Its usage is:

```
printf [FILEHANDLE] $format_string, @arrayOfValues;
```

For example:

```
use FileHandle;
my $FH = new FileHandle("> my_file");
$longvarb = "This has 23 chars in it";
printf $FH "%10.10s\n", $longvarb;
```

prints `This has 2` to the filehandle `$FH`. `printf` has chopped the scalar to fit into 10 characters. The `printf` statement should be read as "print 10 and only 10 characters of the variable `$longvarb` to the filehandle `$FH`." C programmers should be fairly familiar with this. `printf` does something similar to what we see in Figure 10.1.

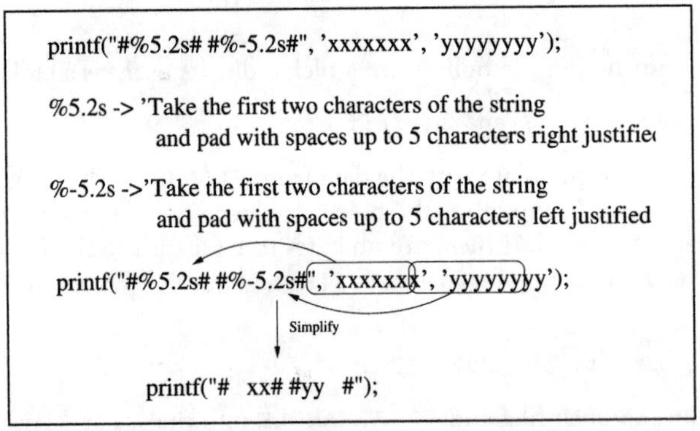

Figure 10.1
Reading `printf`

```
printf("#%5.2s# #%-5.2s#", 'xxxxxxx', 'yyyyyyyy');

%5.2s -> 'Take the first two characters of the string
            and pad with spaces up to 5 characters right justified

%-5.2s ->'Take the first two characters of the string
            and pad with spaces up to 5 characters left justified

printf("#%5.2s# #%-5.2s#", 'xxxxxxx', 'yyyyyyyy');

                    Simplify

printf("#  xx# #yy  #");
```

`printf` uses the percent sign (`%`) followed by a combination of numbers or letters that give it instructions on how to print out whatever follows in the argument list. To use `printf` correctly, you must have a "secret decoder ring" that tells you what each one of the `%` signs mean. Fortunately for C programmers, this is the same as the one in C. The more important elements are given in Table 10.2, which shows some popular combos to `printf`. Each of these formats takes two optional numbers (like `%10.10s`). If you said:

```
printf "%s\n", "This is a string";
```

it is equivalent to the statement:

```
print "This is a string\n";
```

Table 10.2	c	one character	%7c will pad out one character with six spaces.
printf combinations	d	number (integer) in decimal	%7d will pad out the decimal to seven places (right justified).
	f	float	%7.2f will be of precision 2, pad out to seven places (right justified).
	g	double	%-7.2g will be of precision 2, pad out to seven places (left justified).
	ld	long decimal	%7ld will do the same as %7d, except work with larger decimals.
	o	octal	%3o will right pad octals less than three places with spaces.
	s	string	%16.11s will take first 11 chars of string, pad to 16 with spaces.
	u	unsigned number	%-7u will pad out, left justified, any unsigned number.
	x	a hex number	%6x will pad out, right justified, hexadecimal numbers.

However, if you say:

```
printf ":%4.3s:", "This is a string";
```

this will print:

```
': Thi:'
```

because the %4.3s says to Perl "print out space for four characters, yet only print three characters in the string itself." It therefore truncates your string to the first three characters, and at the same time prints four characters (space padded):

```
printf("%5.2f", "1.333333333");
```

This would print to standard output by default, "1.33," because the 2 in 5.2 indicates how much precision will be printed in that number. You can use anything to match up with the percents, even user functions. Hence:

```
printf("hey %s\n", userFunction());
```

will stuff the results from userFunction() into the argument to printf, %s.

Perhaps the best way of showing the use of printf is to give examples.

```
printf(":%-15.10s:%7d:", "String incarnate", 222);
:String inc    :    222:
```

Again, the - means left-justified, and 15.10 means "take at most 10 characters, and stuff them into a space for 15."

```
printf(":%15s:%7d:\n", "String incarnate", -222);
:String incarnate:    222:
```

Since a second number wasn't specified here, the string is not chopped off, and the full string's length is given, even though it is more than 15 characters long:

```
printf(":%15s:%-7u:\n", "String", -222);
:         String:4294967074:
```

Here, you must be careful of conversions. Because `%u` indicates an unsigned number, a negative number behaves unexpectedly:

```
printf(":%8x:%8o:\n", 123123,123123);
:   1e0f3:  360363:
```

This converts `123123` into hexadecimal (`%x`) and octal (`%o`):

```
printf(":%d:\n", 13131313111);
:-1:
```

Here is another case in which you must be careful of conversions. `13131313111` is too large an integer for `%d` (or `%ld`) to handle (use `%s` instead).

```
$this = 13131313111;
printf("$this :%ld:\n", 13131313111);
13131313111 :2147483647:
```

Interpolation works, too. The argument to `%ld` shows that it, too, can overflow (and the largest integer possible for `%ld` is 2147483647).

`printf` is the most flexible way to print in Perl. We will see another cool way to do reports in Chapter 11, by using formats. But remember that you can do anything with `printf` that you can do with formats, plus more.

sprintf

`sprintf` is simply the analogue to `printf` which prints to *variables* rather than to *filehandles*. The usage of `sprintf` is:

```
$variable = sprintf($string, @arrayOfValues);
```

Hence, `$variable` gets whatever format to which string `$string` and `@arrayOfValues` evaluate. For example, the following:

```
my $hex = sprintf("%x", $decimal);
```

converts a decimal value to hex. To see more examples on this usage, see the previous discussion on `printf`.

Summary of Reading and Writing Operations to Filehandles

The main three functions for Filehandle reads are `open`, `print`, and `close`. Covered in this section are some more specialized read and write functions:

1. `read` reads chunks of data into memory.
2. `printf` prints out to a filehandle chunks of data using a special formatting string.
3. `sprintf` acts as printf on a string, rather than a filehandle.

Operations on Variables

Perl provides a myriad of ways of operating with variables. We have already seen some of these functions in detail, as in `delete`, `keys`, `each`, `push`, `pop`, `shift`, `unshift`, and `splice`. Others that will greatly empower you when programming with Perl are sort, split, grep, and map. These functions can take common, 20-line subroutines, and turn them into one-liners. Therefore, we will cover them in great detail.

As with any Perl component, these functions can be used or abused. For example, you probably don't want to do something such as:

```
grep(s"pattern1"pattern2", @list);
```

because it is slower than:

```
foreach (@list) { s"pattern1"pattern2"; }
```

Both examples will replace pattern1 with pattern2 inside the array @list, but the first construct creates a return list, which takes time and memory. Hence, they are functionally equivalent, but not equivalent in efficiency.

sort

The sort function allows you to sort an array using any sort function you feel is appropriate. sort's syntax can get quite involved; here are some of the more common usages:

```
sort (@arrayName);
sort { CODEBLOCK } @arrayName;
sort sort_function @arrayName;
```

The default usage of sort is to sort in alphanumeric order. Start with an array (@arrayName) as follows:

```
@arrayName = ('Apples','Bananas','Carrots');
```

To sort alphanumerically:

```
@arrayName = sort (@arrayName);
```

This syntax sorts the values in @arrayName in alphanumeric order. Hence, something such as:

```
@arrayName = (1,10,9);
@arrayName = sort(@arrayName);
```

is probably not going to work in the way you want, unless you want the order 1,10,9. Note that this is not an "inplace" sort. The sorted values are put in their own array, to be returned to the main program as necessary.

Another usage of sort is in passing a function to the sort. Since the previous example does not work (as in returning 1, 9, 10), and since people have a myriad of ways in which they can sort their data, Perl provides the ability to give a subroutine to the sort. If you define a subroutine that goes to a sort, do not use the regular method:

```
my ($variable) = @_;
```

Instead, sort uses the special values $a and $b (to denote element1 and element2) to pass to the sorting subroutine. Whatever the result of the compare between these two values determines the result.

Consider the following blocks of code:

```
@arrayName = (1,10,9);
@arrayName = sort numerically @arrayName;
print @arrayName;

sub numerically
{
    $a <=> $b;     # '$a' here means the first element
}                  # '$b' here means the second element
                   # does a numeric comparison, will come out
                   # in numeric order.
```

In this example, Perl takes all the elements in the array, and plugs them into the comparison function *numerically* in turn (as opposed to *alphanumerically*). Internally, the comparisons might look like:

```
($a => 1) <=> ($b => 10)    # a becomes 1, b becomes 10.  Do not switch
($a => 1) <=> ($b => 9)     # a becomes 1, b becomes 9... Do not switch.
($a => 10) <=> ($b => 9)    # a becomes 10, b becomes 9.  DO switch.
```

and so on.

This isn't real Perl syntax, but you get the idea. First, $a is 1 and $b is 10. These correspond to Perl comparing elements 0 and elements 1 together and Perl switches the appropiate elements in place, internally. (If you want to watch this order yourself, you can put a print statement in the sort routine.)

A shorthand method is to give a subroutine right before the sort, as in:

```
@arrayName = sort { $a <=> $b } @arrayName;
```

which does the same thing, but avoids writing a subroutine call.

You can also get really fancy with sorts. See the **perlfunc** man page for more details. In essence, you can do something such as:

```
@arrayName =
    @arrayName
    [
      sort
        {
          $arrayName[$b] <=> $arrayName[$a];
        }
        (0..$#arrayName)
    ];
```

This is a little wacky. It does the same thing as:

```
@arrayName = sort {$a <=> $b } @arrayName;
```

but it is more efficient because it sorts the *index* of the array, rather than the array itself. So, if the comparison function is pretty nasty, or the elements of array name are huge, you can avoid extra comparison or copying time. Again, see `sort` under **perlfunc** for more details.

split

`split` is the function that takes scalars and breaks them into arrays. `split` works by looking for either a delimiter or a regular expression, and then divides them on that boundary.

Usages of `split`:

```
@arrayName = split($text, $scalarName);
@arrayName = split(m"regexp", , $scalarName);
@arrayName = split(m"regexp", ,$scalarName, $NUM_ELEMENTS);
```

The following example splits $scalarName into the array (`'Comma'`, `'Separated'`, `'elements'`). In other words, `split` separates $scalarName by commas:

```
$scalarName = "Comma,separated,elements";
@splitArray = split(",", $scalarName);    # @splitArray becomes
                                          # ('Comma', 'Separated', 'elements')
```

If you had:

```
$scalarName = ',has,,,Extra Commas Here';
@splitArray = split(",", $scalarName);    # @splitArray =
                                          # @splitArray becomes ('','has','','','Extra
                                          # Commas Here');
```

you get an element for the initial space between the beginning of the line, and the first `,`. You also get extra elements for the null fields between two adjoining commas (`,,`). To avoid the second behavior, you can use a regular expression in the first argument of `split`:

```
@splitArray = split(m",+", $scalarName);
```

Since the regular expression is now matching on several commas in a row, they are combined into one comma as far as `split` is concerned. This produces:

```
('','has','Extra Commas Here')
```

If you want to get rid of the extra first space, you are going to have to do it with a `shift` function:

```
shift(@splitArray) if (!$splitArray[0]);
```

Likewise, you will have a trailing blank if the last element in `$scalarName` is a `,`. To get rid of that, do a pop:

```
pop(@splitArray) if (!$splitArray[-1]);
```

There are three behaviors of `split` you should be aware of. First, if you use any parentheses inside the regular expression (for back matches), those parentheses will turn up as fields in your split, as in:

```
$line = 'PIPE|DELIMITED|FIELD';
@arrayName = split(m"(   \|    )"x, $line);    # Note... modifiers to regular
                                               # expressions (x) work here.
                                               # We use the readable regexps to
                                               # clarify the statement by adding
                                               # white space.
```

In this example, `@arrayName` becomes:

```
( 'PIPE','|','DELIMITED','|', 'FIELD' )
```

Second, the following construction:

```
"$line = "       This   is   a     special    case    ";
@arrayName = split(' ', $line);
```

makes `@arrayName` (`'This'`, `'is'`, `'a'`, `'special'`, `'case'`). In other words, `split` gets rid of all the trailing and leading spaces for you and just gives the text in separated array elements.

Third, if you put a number in the third argument of `split`, it makes `split` create an array only as big as that number. In the following:

```
$line = "MULTI:LINE:COLON:DELIMITED:FIELD";
@line = split(m":", $line, 3);
```

`@line` becomes (`'MULTI'`, `'LINE'`, `'COLON:DELIMITED:FIELD'`);. This behavior makes your code more efficient, since Perl does not have to split as many fields for you.

`split` is especially useful for dealing with tabular data, in which there are nice, stately rows of data all delimited by a certain character. This is a very common metaphor:

```
($accountId, $firstName, $lastName) = split(m"\|", $accountField);
```

in which the names of the fields you are splitting are listed out while being split. Here is an example that (along with the block text example above) takes conversational text that so often happens to have the very bad habit of going over 80 characters per line (hence wrapping to the next line), and turns it into neat lines that fit on an editor screen. This example shows the power of regular expressions at its finest:

```
undef $/;
$line = <FD>;
chop($line);
$line =~ s"\n" "g;          # substitute, temporarily, newlines for spaces.
@eighty_char_lines = split(m"(.{1,79}\b)", $line);
$" = "\n";
print "@eighty_char_lines\n";
```

This works by using one of the properties of regular expressions. Remember that regular expressions are greedy by nature. In the line split(m"(.{1,79}\b)", $line); you are telling the regular expression engine to look for from one to 79 characters, the more the better, and to terminate these 79 characters by a word break (\b).

Note

OK, not exactly. There is a subtle bug here; if you spotted it, you are catching on quite well. By saying m"(.{1,79}\b)", we are telling split to take this regular expression as our *delimiter,* and not as the element itself. Without the parenthesis around (.{1,79}\b), the delimiter would match everything. Therefore:

```
('', 'eighty character string', '', another eighty character string','','etc');
```

in which the spaces are the actual elements that split matched. To get rid of these, you can say:

```
@eighty_char_lines = grep { length() > 0 } split(m"(.{1,79})\b)", $line);
```

where the grep weeds out strings of length 0. (grep is detailed below.)

The result of all this is that the split greedily chops up all of the lines into chunks as big as possible, but not exceeding 79 characters. It looks something like:

```
undef $/;
$line = <FD>;                    # read in the entire file
@words = split(' ', $line);      # split the line into words
do
{
    while ((length ($line . $words[$xx]) < 80) && (defined $words[$xx]))
    {
        $line .= " " . $words[$xx];
        $xx++;
    }
    print $line;
} while (defined $words[$xx]);
```

except much faster, and much more succinctly stated.

grep

grep is the all-purpose array manipulator in Perl. It is very similar to the Unix utility of the same name, but this grep works on Perl arrays and Perl functions. However, Perl's grep comes with traps for the unwary. Its usage is:

```
@arrayName = grep(EXPRESSION, @arrayToMatch);
```

```
ArrayName = grep { FUNCTION } @arrayToMatch;
```

This is how Perl's `grep` works. The array given in the second argument has all its values taken, one by one, and set to the special variable `$_` something like Figure 10.2.

This variable can then be used in the function or condition specified in the first argument. If that condition or function evaluates to nonblank or nonzero, then that element matched the condition of the `grep`, and is put on the return value of the `grep`.

grep is legendary for being obscure. The best way to explain it is to demonstrate its usage. A simple example may make `grep` clear:

```
my @integers = (0,1,2,3,4,5,6,7,8,9,10);
my @matches = grep($_ > 5, @integers);    # '@matches' now equals ( 6,7,8,9,10 )
```

grep took each value in `@integers`, stuck it in `$_`, and compared it to 5. If the comparison was true, (i.e., `$_ > 5` evaluated to one) grep pushed the matching element onto `@matches`. If not, grep went on to the next element. The one-line grep statement is pretty much equivalent to:

```
foreach $integer (@integers)
{
    if ($integer > 5)
    {
      push(@matches, $integer);
    }
}
```

It is also possible to use a function or a regular expression with `grep`:

```
@matches  = grep{  $_ > 5; } @integers;  # same as above, only has anonymous
                                         # subroutine aka sort.
@strings = (1, 'integers', 2, 'and', 3, 'strings');
```

```
@integers  = grep(m"^\d+$", @strings);    # matches (1,2,3). Doesn't match non
                                           # 'integers', 'and', 'strings'
```

And if the value of $_ changes while you are grep-ing through the function, it actually changes the array itself, as in:

```
@integers = (1,2,3);
grep ($_ = $_*2, @integers);        # makes @integers the array (2,4,6).
                                    # you may want to use map or foreach instead.
```

although this usage is slightly less efficient than:

```
foreach (@integers) { $_ *= 2 }
```

because it builds a list for returning to a variable, and you aren't using that return value!

There are several practical uses for grep. For example, you can use grep to turn an array into a hash whose keys are the elements in the array, and whose values are the number of times that element occurs in the array:

```
@words = ('be','very','very','very','afraid');
grep($concordance{$_}++, @words);
```

Now %concordance will look like:

```
%concordance = ('be' => 1, 'very' => 3, 'afraid' => 1);
```

Therefore, this is a true concordance. By saying $concordance{'very'} we find that this occurred three times in our input array.

In scalar context, grep returns the number of times a given pattern matched. If you use good coding style and always put your subroutines at the beginning of a line, as in:

```
sub mySub
{
}
```

then you can find out, say, if you have more than five subroutines in mySub by saying:

```
my $FH = new FileHandle("Module.pm");
my @code = <$FH>;
if (grep(m"^sub ", @code) > 5)
{
    (print " more than five subroutines in Module.pm\n"; )
}
```

This evaluates to true if there are more than five occurrences of ^sub in the code (sub at the beginning of a line). And:

```
if ((@sub_lines = grep (m"^sub\s+(\w+)", @code)) > 5)    # saves subroutine names.
{ print "found more than five subroutines in Module.pm"; }
```

evaluates to true on the same condition, and saves the matches in @sub_lines (which will happen to be your subroutine names).

Another interesting thing you can do with grep is weed out duplicates in arrays:

```
@duplicates = grep {  $marked{$_}++; $marked{$_} == 1; } @original;
```

This takes an array like (3,1,2,4,3,2,1,5) and turns it into (3,1,2,4,5) by marking each array element, and only returning true if that element was seen for the first time ($marked{$_} == 1).

Perhaps you need an array that consists only of values that are in ascending order, and throw out the middle values. The following:

```
@array = (1,4,6,2,8,1,11,32,16);
my $max;
my @ascending = grep { $max = $_ if ($_ > $max); } @array;
```

returns (1,4,6,8,11,32). This works by having a placeholder called $max, and only returns true if the value (again, passed through the special variable $_) is greater than $max.

Another idea is to get all the error lines out of a log file:

```
use FileHandle;
my $LOG_FILE = new FileHandle("log");
@error_lines = grep(m"ERROR", <$LOG_FILE>);
```

Here, the filehandle $LOG_FILE is slurped into a big list, and only the lines that have ERROR in them are passed back to the array @error_lines. We could also use this trick to get a concordance of words on an entire file:

```
grep($concordance{$_}++, (map { split(' ',$_) }  <FILEHANDLE>));
```

Attentive readers will notice that this is the same as an example given in Chapter 5. Twenty lines in the script are shrunken down to one, somewhat obscure, line. There must be a happy medium.

This borders a little too heavy on the code-hack side of things. If you can read this one line program and understand it, you are learning Perl pretty well. The map split takes all the lines in FileHandle, splits them into words, and then passes the result of that split through the grep engine, which dutifully marks each time it has seen a given pattern in the hash %concordance. This is illustrated in Figure 10.3.

Figure 10.3
Nasty grep
Example

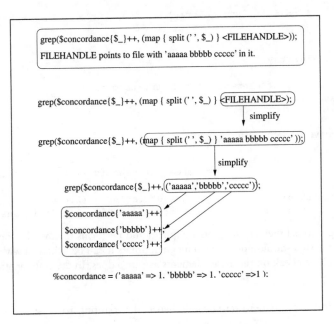

The major concept to remember about grep is not to accidentally trash your array while doing the compare. So, if you say something like:

```
@backup_files = grep (s"\.bak"", @files);
```

you will not only get a list of backup files, but will also make all the backup files in @files disappear, so the array @files ('file1','file2.bak','file3.bak') becomes ('file1', 'file2','file3') while @backup_files becomes ('file2','file3'). This is probably not the original intention of your code!

map

map begins with an input array, and transforms it into an output array given a function that you specify. It sort of is like a "map" in the sense that there is a relationship between the input values and the output values, and that you "map" one value to another given a transform function.

The usage of map is:

```
$arrayName = map( &function,  @source_array);
```

map is like grep in that it iterates through every element in an array, but different because map has no implicit filter that gets rid of undefined values. This is very important: map has no default filtering of values applied to elements that pass through the function function. Therefore:

```
@array = grep( 1 == 2, @newArray);
```

will always return an undef array(), whereas:

```
@array = map (1 == 2, @newArray);
```

will return, instead, a list of elements in @array that equals the size of the number of elements in @newArray. This array will be blank, since the condition 1==2 always evaluates to false.

In other words, the following statement using map:

```
@targetArray = map(function($_), @sourceArray);
```

is the logical equivalent to:

```
foreach $element (@sourceArray)
{
    $targetElement = function($element);  # do the target
    push(@targetArray, $targetElement);
}
```

The following two examples have the same result:

```
@integers = (1,2,3);
@twiceAsBig = @integers;                 # makes @twiceAsBig (1,2,3) temporarily.

grep($_ = $_*2, @twiceAsBig);            # makes @twiceAsBig (2,4,6).
@twiceAsBig = map($_*2, @integers);      # makes @twiceAsBig (2,4,6) in one step.
```

except that the example using map is much cleaner, more explicit, and performs the task in one step. (As stated many times, functionality in one step should not be the only goal, unless it can be achieved with clarity.)

Notice that map does not do a check on the array elements as grep does. In the statement:

```
@files = map (-f $_, @fileList);
```

map does not eliminate records that evaluate to zero or null; hence, the resulting array is:

```
(1,'',1,'','','','',1)
```

meaning that the first record matched was a file, the second wasn't, and so on. Whereas if you said:

```
@files =  grep(-f $_, @fileList);
```

you get a *list* of files instead of an array of ones and blanks.

Another important note about map is that it takes whatever is returned by the mapping function, and stuffs it into the return array. This means that you need not have the same number of elements in both. If you say something like:

```
@multiples = map { $_, $_*2 } @multiples;
```

then you have doubled your array size, turning (1,2,3,4,5) into (1,2,2,4,3,6,4,8,5,10). Likewise:

```
@greater_than_five = map { $_ > 5 ? ($_) : () } @multiples;
```

returns an array with less elements than you started with. You are probably better off doing this particular function as a grep.

Like grep, map is immensely useful. Suppose you have a data structure you want to flatten. Say, for example, you have an array of hashes that looks something like:

```
$AoH = [
        {
            'name' => 'Carmen',
        ....
        },
        {
            'name' => 'Peter'
        ...
        }
    ];
```

and you wish to extract all the names out of it into an array. With map, it is fairly straightforward. This is how to do it:

```
@names = map { $_->{'name'}} @$AoH;
```

Likewise, suppose you want to make some skeleton code given a list of subroutine names, to conform to coding standards, give a common interface to packages, etc. A good start would be something like:

```
@subNames = ('subroutine1','subroutine2','subroutine3');
@codeSubs = map { "sub $_\n{\n}" }  @subNames;
```

This would make @codeSubs look like:

```
@codeSubs = (
'sub subroutine1
{
}'.
'sub subroutine2
{
}',
'sub subroutine3
{
}'
);
```

which does the subroutine bit, but ignores any issues about package names, package variables, etc. Now all you have to do is figure out how to actually fill these subroutines with code!

Summary of Operations on Variables

As a Perl programmer, you really want to know `sort`, `grep`, `map`, and `split`. These functions are truly work-horses in Perl, being used for thousands of different applications.

1. `sort`, in its simplest application, sorts an array in alphabetical order, or by a user-defined function.
2. `split` takes a scalar and separates it based on the criteria that the user provides.
3. `grep`, in its simplest application, finds which elements in an array satisfy a condition.
4. `map`, in its simplest application, makes a new array based on a transform from the old array.

Time Functions

Perl has quite a few functions that help you to deal with either timing code, getting time of day, affecting the timing of running code, and just plain dealing with time. These applications are shown below.

localtime

`localtime` is Perl's major interface for getting information about what time the system thinks it is. It has two usages, depending on its context. The usage of `localtime` is:

```
($seconds, $minutes, $hours, $monthdays, $months, $years, $weekdays, $yeardays,
$daylightSavings) = localtime($secs); $timestring = localtime($secs);
```

The first usage, in array context, gives an array of time elements ($seconds, $minutes, $hours, etc.) based on the one argument to `localtime`, the number of seconds since 1970. In this example:

```
($secs, $min, $hr, $mday, $mnth, $yr, $wd, $yd, $ds)  = localtime();
```

Perl assumes that you mean the current time, something like:

```
$secs = 22;
$min = 24;
$hr = 22;
$mday = 7;
$mnth = 2;
$yr = 97;
$wd = 5;
$yd = 65;
$ds = 0;
```

You should know that *year* is number of years since 1900 and *month* starts with January being equal to month 0. Likewise, *weekday* starts with 0 being Sunday, 6 being Saturday. The following scalar form:

```
$timeString = localtime();
```

gives the current time in the format:

```
Fri Mar  7 22:22:50 1997
```

whereas something like:

```
    $timeString = localtime(0);
```

results in:

```
    Wed Dec 31 17:00:00 1969
```

because localtime is geared to the number of seconds since Jan 1, 1970, *Greenwich mean time.*

timelocal

timelocal is not strictly a built-in function. Instead, it is a function provided by the Perl package called Time::Local, a module that you need to include in your programs if you wish to use timelocal. It is the opposite of localtime in that it calculates the number of seconds since January 1, 1970. timelocal uses an array given by localtime to do this calculation.

The usage of timelocal is:

```
    use Time::Local;
    my $secs = timelocal(@arrayFromLocalTime);
```

The following example will always print the number of seconds from 1/1/1970:

```
    my $seconds = timelocal(localtime());
```

time

time simply gives the number of seconds since 1/1/1970. Since localtime takes the number of seconds since 1970, here is a way to find the time an hour ago:

```
    my $time = localtime(time()-3600);
```

Expanding on this, here is a small subroutine to find out times one second, minute, hour, etc., from the present:

```
    my %secs =
        (
        'second' => 1,
        'minute' => 60,
        'hour' => 3600,
        'day' => 86400,
        'year' => '31557600'
        );
    foreach $key (keys %secs)
    {
        my $time = localtime(time()-$secs{$key});
        print "Time one $key ago: $time\n";
    }
```

times

times is Perl's main way to benchmark code, to see how CPU-intensive it is.

The usage of times is:

```
    ($user, $system, $child_user, $child_system) = times();
```

The $user and $child_user times are the amount of time your process (and its children) utilize the CPU. The $system and $child_system times are the amount of time the operating system is engaged by the process.

Now—and this is important—remember that `times` does not give you any idea of elapsed time. You can get the "wallclock" time by the `time` function given earlier. Instead, `times` is good for figuring out how much of a CPU hog the process is. If you say:

```
($user1, $sys1, $child1, $childsys1) = times();
sleep(20);    # sleeps for 20 seconds (see below)
($user2, $sys2, $child2, $childsys2) = times();
```

it will not print out 20 seconds if you say `$user2-$user1`. Instead, it will print an extremely small number (like `.01`) because that is the amount of time you are engaging the CPU. If you want wallclock time, see `time` instead.

sleep

`sleep` pauses a process for *X* number of seconds. The usage of `sleep` is:

```
my $secondsSlept = sleep($seconds);
```

This lets you do things such as wait for another process to complete, or make an infinite loop with a check that is extremely CPU-intensive. If you said:

```
while (!-f "$filename")
{
}
```

to wait for a file to appear (perhaps from another process), this chews up the CPU, because the file test ('-f': see below) is particularly CPU-intensive, and the chances of the file being there .001 seconds after you first checked are slim. Instead, say:

```
while (!-f "$filename")
{
    sleep(20);
}
```

This is significantly better, because you are only checking for the file every 20 seconds.

Summary of Time Functions

Manipulating time is one of the biggest inconveniences ever faced by programmers. Another big inconvenience is optimizing code for speed, and being able to tell if wallclock elapsed time has been improved. This is why Perl provides low-level, built-in time functions:

1. `localtime` returns a time (either string or elements) based on the argument being the number of seconds since 1970.
2. `timelocal` does the opposite of `localtime`. It returns the number of seconds since 1/1/70. (Don't forget to specify "use **Time::Local**" in the code.)
3. `sleep` puts a process to sleep for a given amount of time.
4. `time` gives the number of seconds since 1/1/1970.
5. `times` gives CPU and system time for processes.

There is much more to it than this, but this is enough to get you started.

Debugging Functions

The following debugging functions are extremely helpful in locating problems in Perl programs. We shall go over these in detail in Chapter 22 "Perl Debugging Tips," but you should at least be aware of them for now.

caller()

The built-in function `caller` lets you take a quick peek into how a program is running. `caller` is invaluable, especially in its incarnations (`confess` and `carp`, in the package `Carp`) in tracing down why a certain error occurred. If you do something like:

```
a();
sub a { b(); }
sub b { c(); }
sub c { d(); }
sub d { print "HERE!!!\n";}
```

then you are making a calling stack, `a()` calls `b()`, which calls `c()`, and so on. This can be very difficult to debug, since finding the bug becomes a problem of navigation, or unwinding this stack. `caller` unwinds the stack for you at any given point. The usage of `caller` is:

```
($package, $filename, $line) = caller();
```

or:

```
($package, $filename, $line, $subroutineName, $arguments, $context) = caller($frame);
```

Let's take another look at the example, and use `caller` instead:

```
a();
sub a { b(); }
sub b { c(); }
sub c { d(); }
sub d { print "@{[ caller() ]}\n"; }
```

This prints:

```
main script.p 4
```

because d was called from subroutine c, which was in the `main` package, in the file **script.p,** on the fourth line. If we said:

```
a();
sub a { b(); }
sub b { c(); }
sub c { d(); }
sub d { print "@{[ caller(1) ]}\n"; }
```

instead (note the 1 here as the argument to `caller`), we've unwound the stack one frame; it now shows the function that called the function that called `caller`. This prints:

```
main script.p 3 main::c 1 0
```

because `main::c` was the function that called `main::d` that called `caller`.

    `caller` is usually not used directly, although we will see places where it is. Instead, a package called `Carp` is usually used, which contains the functions `carp` (lowercase *c*) and `confess`. If you use the function `confess`, as in the following:

```
use Carp;
a();
sub a { b(); }
sub b { c(); }
sub c { d(); }
sub d { confess "Dying here!\n"; }
```

then Perl will print out the entire stack:

```
Dying here!
main::d called at line 6
main::c called at line 5
main::b called at line 4
main::a called at line 3
```

and terminate the process. You can now debug at will. The function `carp` does the exact same thing, but doesn't terminate. It just shows you where you are at a given time.

die( )

`die` basically kills a process at a given point, printing the arguments it is given. Its usage is:

```
die @arguments;
```

If, for example, you say something like:

```
die "This program is not very correct, is it!";
```

you are telling Perl to exit the program, giving an indication of where it is in the program, and to put that message on the standard error stream, or STDERR. The preceding statement will say something like:

```
This program is not very correct, is it! at line 32.
```

`die` is used mainly with short-circuiting, so that if a condition is not met that is necessary for a program to continue, as in the following:

```
use FileHandle;
my $fh = new FileHandle("> file") || die "Couldn't open file!";
```

this will exit the program on the case in which a file cannot be opened.

warn( )

`warn` is like `die` except it only gives a warning on STDERR, and does not stop the execution of the program. If you say something like:

```
use FileHandle;
my $fh = new FileHandle("> file") || warn "Couldn't open file!";
```

it prints the same message as `die`, i.e.,

```
Couldn't open file! at line 32
```

but not `die`, or terminate the program. `warn` simply states the message instead.

Summary of Debugging Functions

Debugging functions make it possible to make Perl code scalable, and are the key to debugging and understanding object-oriented calls. You should also know these built-in functions quite well:

1. `caller` prints parts of an execution trace given a certain point.
2. `die` exits the code in a given spot, printing a message where it does die.
3. `warn` prints the same thing as `die` (a message to STDERR) but does not exit.

Perl Interfaces to Operating Systems: System Calls, Operating System Emulations, and File Operators

Perl started its useful life as a scripting language for Unix. As such, it was sort of a cross between a language meant for controlling system-level activities and for extracting other useful data in the form of reports. In its latest incarnation, it is—obviously—so much more.

One powerful advantage to the programmer is that Perl has retained its system-level roots and allows the programmer to easily perform system-level activities and do system-level checking from within a Perl program.

These functions come in two flavors: those which manage the running of other processes and those which allow Perl to perform common system calls cross-platform. Function calls [system, exec, fork, and `` (the backtick operator)] allow Perl to manage running other processes. The function calls chdir, mkdir, and others allow Perl to make common system calls totally portable between platforms.

Or so we wish! Perl, like almost everything else in the computing world, has been caught in the crossfire over the battle between differing operating systems. The current battle attracting the most attention is, of course, the one between Unix and NT; the dust has not yet settled. Yes, you can have portable Perl software. You should use these Perl internal calls (such as chdir) whenever possible, but this is not 100 percent bulletproof. You just have to be careful going about doing it.

You can also hedge your bets with this book, especially if you work for a large company and want to make sure that the software you developed on Unix will work on NT.

system and Win32::Spawn

`system` takes the supplied argument and executes it as if it were a command in an operating system shell, either Unix, NT, DOS, or anything else. `Win32::Spawn` does the same thing, but is NT-specific, and lets you make processes stand alone on an NT box.

Because `system` can execute platform-specific commands, by its very nature, `system` creates platform-dependent code. Since `Win32::Spawn` is only on NT, calls to it make code even more platform-dependent.

In general, Unix users are much more inclined to use system calls than are NT users (because NT is more "interactive" by nature). Much of the following example could be emulated in NT (by the specific calls to OLE, for example).

The usage is:

```
system($command);
```

and:

```
Win32::Spawn($executable, $arguments, $pid);
```

If your code executes something such as:

```
system("ls");
```

then you cannot hope to run your script on any system that does not have the executable `ls`. This is the same for `dir`:

```
system("dir");
```

will make an NT script totally bound to the NT world. One way to get around this is by using Perl's internal functions to EMULATE `ls` or `dir`. For example:

```
opendir(DIRHANDLE, ".");
while ($file = readdir(DIRHANDLE))
{
    print "$file\n";
}
```

approximates an `ls` or `dir`, in an extremely portable way. On Unix, the `system` command:

```
system("elm -s 'done with work' recipient < filename");
```

mails to the user recipient the filename `filename`. The following executes a source-control statement, and does so in the background:

```
system("rcs -u filename &");    # Unlocks the file filename, and does so in the background.
```

and the following directs output to a file:

```
system ("ls > file 2>&1");
```

Again, these functions are highly Unix-specific. In fact they depend on a Unix shell being available in order to work correctly. In particular, the `&` (the background character) is very OS-specific. This is where `Win32::Spawn` comes in:

```
use Win32;
Win32::Spawn("notepad.exe", "myNote.txt", $processid);
```

which runs `notepad.exe` in the background. This, too, is highly specific, and doesn't work on Windows 95, where there is no good workaround. This example runs an interactive program for the user and, when finished, returns:

```
system("vi filename")    # starts up vi on the file filename
```

Of course, these commands do not work if the particular system does not have `vi`, `elm`, `rcs`, `ls`, etc. Therefore, it is a good idea to minimize your use of this command, and in highly marked spots.

If you don't minimize your use of `system`, when the time comes to port your scripts to a new system, you will have to completely rewrite your system calls to deal with that system's inconsistencies. Also, consider using the Perl-ish versions of common system calls instead. In fact, in some places you simply can't get around using the Perl-ish equivalents. If you say something like:

```
chdir($dirname) || die "couldn't change directory to $dirname!";
```

this changes the directory for the duration of your Perl script, whereas:

```
system("cd $dirname") && die "Couldn't change directory to $dirname!";
```

simply will not work, because the system call doesn't "keep its side effects." This is a very important point to remember about `system`. If you use `system` to change environmental variables (some other aspect of your environment) and then try to use these side effects later on, you will simply be defeating your own purpose. If you say something like:

```
system("VARIABLE=value");
print $ENV{'VARIABLE'};
```

you are on the wrong track. `system` opens its very own small process, which has its own "mini" environment which it inherits from the Perl script (something like what is shown in Figure 10.4).

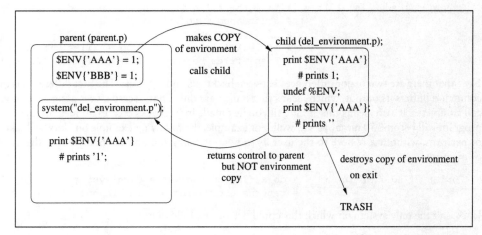

Figure 10.4
The Impermanence of System Calls

However, there is one thing the system call leaves behind for the Perl executable, and you should be aware of it. The system call sets `$?` which is nonzero if it fails. Hence, if you say:

```
system("bad_command");
if ($? ne 0)
{
    print "Error in command!\n";
}
```

will warn you that bad.command has failed.

Note

Notice, again this is not portable between Unix and other OSs! `$?` is a shell variable, and is, as of this writing, not emulated in the other versions of Perl.

`` (Backticks Command)

The backticks function or operator takes the string specified by COMMAND, interpolates it, runs it, and then returns the text of that command to either a scalar or an array. If it is in scalar context, the results of the command are slurped entirely into the scalar. If the backticks are in array context, Perl uses the variable `$/` (`$INPUT_FIELD_SEPARATOR`) to determine how to split the text.

Using backticks shares the same negative property as system: If you use it, you are almost guaranteed to anchor your program to a particular operating system.

Here is its usage:

```
$scalarName = `COMMAND`;
@arrayName = `COMMAND`;
```

This example uses the backticks operator to perform a system-level command, to get a listing of directories in Unix:

```
chop(@files = `ls -1`);    # take the files from the ls command, and
                           # stuff them into @files.
                           # if 'ls -1 returns:
                           # "file1\nfile2\nfile3" (three files with returns)
                           # then @files becomes ('file1','file2','file3').
```

Note that there are two major differences between backticks and system. The first difference is that the backticks command buffers its output, which means that it displays only on the screen, or is assigned to a variable, *after* the call completes. It also means that if the call you just made in backticks creates 50 megabytes of output, then your program will become 50 megabytes as well. For example, the following example on Unix will take a very long time to perform, without any note to the user as to what is going on, and probably cause the machine to run out of memory:

```
print `find / -print`;    # do a find on the whole darn system.
                          # returns every single file, in one long string.
```

Unix isn't the only system on which this could occur. The following:

```
print `cd \\ & dir /s`;
```

basically does the same thing, and dumps the entire contents of your DOS system into memory.

The second difference between system and backticks is that the backticks operator will not work on items that require human input, as in:

```
$badIdea = `interactive_program`;
```

since any text prompting the user for input is going to get buffered in the computer, and hence not displayed to the screen. Therefore, the user will not see what is expected from him or her, and the program will seem to hang.

The program has not hung. Instead, the computer has probably printed the message requiring human input, but it is invisible since the backticks are preventing it from being displayed until the command is done!

So, unless you can sense what the computer wants and act accordingly, this is a bad idea. In many cases, though, it makes a great deal of sense to retrieve the output from a command in the form of a string. Here are more examples, which again, will only be good on a Unix system:

```
$wordcount = `wc $file`;                 # gets the word count of 'file'
@matching_lines = `grep pattern @files`; # gets all the occurrences of pattern in @files.
@sorted_lines = `sort $file`;            # sorts file_name
```

However, one of your goals should be to limit your use of backticks, for the already-mentioned portability issue. In fact, all of the backtick commands could be rewritten in Perl. The word count becomes:

```
use FileHandle;
undef $/;                                # make it so <FD> slurps the whole file into a scalar.
my $FD = new FileHandle($file);          # see special variables for more info.
```

```
$stuff = <$FD>;
$chars = length($stuff);
$words = @{[ (split(' ', $stuff)) ] };      # splits 'stuff' into words and then
                                            # stuffst the count in $words.
$lines = @{[ (split(m"\n", $stuff)) ] };    # splits 'stuff' into lines and
                                            # then counts them.
$wordcount = "$chars $words $lines";        # prints everything out.
```

This shows the power of split (yet again) and the power of the @{[ ]} syntax we mentioned earlier to prevent temporary variables and put everything into one line. If you aren't comfortable with this syntax, split the above into two lines instead, and say:

```
@word_array = split(' ', $stuff);
$words = @word_array;
```

The grep command becomes:

```
use FileHandle;
foreach $file (@files)
{
    my $fh = new FileHandle("$file");
    push(@matching_lines, grep(m"pattern", <$fh>));
}
```

where the Perl-ish grep returns only those lines that match a given pattern, and then stuffs them into @matching_lines. The sort command becomes:

```
my $fh = new FileHandle("file_name");
@lines = <$fh>;
@sorted_lines = sort(@lines);
```

where we simply use the Perl-ish sort instead of the sort command. These not only work exactly the same as their backtick counterparts, they will also work cross-platform (i.e., on NT as well as Unix, as well as other OSs). Hence, if you are doing cross-platform development, you want to stay as far away as you can from using `` and system.

fork, wait, exec, and the Win32::Process Module

We should mention one last command here, or rather, command set. fork is its name, along with exec and wait. fork is an extremely powerful command. It is similar to system, but with better process control, for controlling whatever processes your programs spawn or generate. Unfortunately, NT does not natively support fork. To get fork-like functionality on, you use the process and module. (There *are* software packages that can make NT support fork. If, for example you use Perl with the package **gnu-win32** on Windows NT, you will get fork as well, since **gnu-win32** emulates Unix on NT.)

So without further ado, here they are: exec, wait, and fork. Their usage is as follows:

```
$processId = fork();
exec($commandString);
wait();
```

The function fork makes a copy of your process, and then proceeds to run both processes until they hit exit statements. It returns the processId of the child process that it generates, the unique identifier for that process on Unix systems.

The standard metaphor is:

```
if (!($pid = fork()))
{                           # if child -- the child will
                            # return a non-zero value for the $pid
    exec("script_name");
}
else
{
    wait();
}
```

This essentially splits the one process into two processes, each with its own namespace, etc. These two processes are called `parent` and `child`. The parent then goes into the `wait` loop, which waits for the child processes to finish. The `child` continues to execute in the `if` loop, in this case `exec(script_name)`, before exiting.

This is very helpful because it bypasses the overhead of a system call, and because it provides process control in the form of a pid. Unfortunately, NT does not have `fork`, and several Perl scripts have `fork()` calls in them. This is where **Win32::Process** comes in, NT's version of `fork`. Hence, it is a big issue for porting Perl to NT.

Note

In fact, you may want to have a "wrapper" around `fork`, which checks to see if your OS is Unix or NT, and acts accordingly. In the ActiveWare version of Perl, there is a group of functions that come with Perl itself, in a module called **Win32::Process** that do the same sort of stuff as `fork`. They work something like:

```
use Win32::Process;
$object = Create Win32::Process
        (
            "C:/windows/excel"    #executable
            "Excel spread.xls",   #command-line
            0,                    #whether the process inherits from the parent
            DETACHED_PROCESS,     # whether the process is detached or not.
            "."                   # Current Directory
        ) || die "Couldn't open Excel!";
    $object->Wait(INFINITE); # waits for call to finish

    $object->GetExitCode($ExitCode); # exits out, returns error code.
```

Notice that you need to be familiar with Perl's object-oriented syntax to do this, and notice that its syntax is quite nasty. You might wrap the forking off of a Perl script as in:

```
eval("use Win32::Process");      # effective way of including a module not knowing
                                 # if it is there or not (see eval, next chapter)

use Config;                      # gets configuration of Perl.
if ($Config{'osname'} =~ m"nix")
{
    if (!($pid = fork())) { exec($perlscript); }
    else { wait(); }
}
```

```
      else
      {

          $object = Create Win32::Process (
                  $perlscript,          #executable
                  $perlscript,          #command-line
                  0,                    #whether the process inherits from the parent
                  DETACHED_PROCESS,     #
                  ".") || die "Couldn't open Excel!";  #current dir
              $ProcessObj->Wait(INFINITE); # waits for call to finish

              $ProcessObj->GetExitCode($ExitCode); # exits out, returns error code.
      }
```

Internal Perl Functions to Emulate System Calls

Perl provides several functions to help you avoid the nonportability issue. We give some of the most important ones next.

chdir, unlink, link, mkdir, readdir, and opendir

The functions chdir, unlink, link, mkdir, readdir, and opendir provide a Perl-ish alternative to their Unix and DOS cousins. Table 10.3 shows the Perl command and the similar Unix/DOS command:

Table 10.3
Perl, Unix and
DOS commands

Perl command:	UNIX Command	Dos Command
chdir	cd	cd
unlink	rm	rm
readdir, opendir, closedir	ls	dir
mkdir	mkdir	mkdir
rmdir	rmdir	rmdir

There is also a hostname package (**Sys::Host**) and a find package (**File::Find**) that do things very much like hostname and find. Again, the main reason behind these scripts is portability. If you get used to using them, you won't be bitten when you move to new systems. Anyway, enough of a rant. Here are some examples. If you find yourself using system("cd dirname"), you haven't been paying attention. Use these instead:

```
chdir("C:/windows");                # changes to the windows directory. Sets
                                    # cwd inside Perl to be "C:/windows". Note - no need
                                    # for dos's slash.
opendir(DIR, "C:/windows") || die;# opens up the directory "C:/windows" for reading.
```

```
@list = readdir(DIR) || die;        # reads a list of files from the directory $dir.
                                    # equivalent to 'dir DIR'.
foreach $file (@list)
{
    if (-f $file)                   # if a file.
    {
        $status = unlink($file);    # delete it. and return the status.
    }
}
$status = unlink(@list);            # deletes all the files in the directory. better off
                                    # doing it one at a time, so you can get the
                                    # status. This 'status' is the number of files
                                    # the unlink actually does. The unlink
                                    # does not touch the directories!
rmdir("/tmp") || die;               # tries to remove the directory. Succeeds
                                    # if empty.
mkdir("/tmp", 0755) || die;         # tries to make the directory "/tmp" with the
                                    # permissions 0755.
unlink <file.*>;                    # tries to delete all the files in the cwd that
                                    # match file.
```

All these operators have a status, which you ignore at your own peril. For example, let's suppose that mkdir("/tmp", 0755) returned a status of 2. This means something went wrong during the making of that directory. If you do these commands without checking the status of the command, and part of your program depends on having, say, a directory created, and the directory isn't there, well, then "the gloves are off" as to the effects on your system.

It takes a while to get used to doing all these operations in Perl, but once you manage to do it, you lessen your dependence on the operating system a great deal. This, of course, makes your code more portable.

These functions are just a sampling of all the operating system functions available. You will see more of these throughout this book. In fact, it is this book's policy to use Perl if it can, rather than system calls or pipes. Once you decide to uphold this policy in your own code, you will find that the next time you need to port your scripts, it will be much easier.

File Operators

Perl has quite a few file operators it uses to check certain files. They all have a similar usage, inherited from the Unix shell.

Here is their usage:

```
(-OP SCALAR)
(-OP FILEHANDLE)
```

-OP is any one of a number of one-character switches that operate on a filehandle.

Table 10.4 shows some of the more important operators that Perl knows about.

Table 10.4

Perl file operators

-f filehandle or $filename (test whether or not the filehandle is a file)
-d filehandle or $filename (test if the filehandle points to a directory)
*-l filehandle or $filename (test if the filehandle points to a link)
*-r filehandle or $filename (test if the filehandle is readable by owner of script)
*-w filehandle or $filename (test if the file is writable by owner of script)
*-x filehandle or $filename (test if the file is executable by owner of script)
-z filehandle or $filename (test if the file has zero size)
-s filehandle or $filename (gives size of file)
-e filehandle or $filename (test if file exists)
-T filehandle or $filename (test if the file is a text file)
-B filehandle or $filename (test if the file is a binary file)

This is not a complete list. For more information, go to the **perlvar** man page. Also, note that not all these operators work on a Windows platform. The ones that do not are prefixed by an *, and do not work because there is no such functionality. Each operator returns a 1 if true, and a ' ' if false (except for the '-s' operator, which returns the size in number of bytes). Following are examples of their usage:

```
$fh = new FileHandle("FILE") || die;
print "symbolic link\n" if (-l $fh);  # if the filehandle points to a symbolic link, print
print "fileName is a file" if (-f "fileName");# if fileName is a file, print.
print "fileName is readable" if (-r _);  # if fileName is readable, print.
```

The last example shows the use of the _ variable, which is quite good at preventing more than one system call on the same file. This is because the file operators are all manifestations of the low-level call stat. stat is Perl's way to get information about files in the operating system. If, for example, you did the following:

```
if (-r "file" &&-e "file" && -s "file")  # looking for a readable, existing, non-zero
{                # size file. Unfortunately, this means three
}                # stat calls, which provide you all this info anyway!
```

it would be wasteful. Rather, you should use:

```
if (-r "file" && -e _ && -s _)     # much better -- ONE stat call only.
```

This saves big on processing resources, because stat calls are expensive. Some common, cross-platform uses of file operators follow:

```
if (!(-e $directory))
{
    mkdir("$directory") || die "Couldn't make directory!\n";
}
```

and:

```
if (!(-e $file))
{
    $fd = new FileHandle("> $dir");
}
```

which both make a directory, or touch a file if it does not yet exist.

glob( )

glob is Perl's function to get file names and directory names from the operating system, in a manner similar to how the OS itself does it. The usage is:

```
my @arrayName = glob($glob_pattern);
```

For example, if you want to get all the **.c** files in a given directory, this:

```
my @files = glob("*.c");
```

expands the * in the same manner the shell would, substituting * with all files that have **.c** on the end.

glob is portable between the Windows 32 and Unix worlds, because it isn't really using the underlying platform to expand the `"*.c"`, but is using an internal function to do it.

Summary of Internal Perl Functions to Emulate System Calls

These functions are a bit more portable between operating systems, and they perform some fairly low-level operations. The main ones to know are:

1. File operators, which get information on what is in a given file.
2. glob, which expands a pattern into its corresponding files in a system-independent way (like `"rm *"`).
3. rmdir, opendir, closedir, etc., are functions that do basic system calls for you.

Summary of Internal Perl Functions

Perl built-in functions provide a wide variety of functionality to the Perl shell. This is one of the reasons Perl is so useful in solving everyday problems; you know that however you wish to manipulate your data, or whatever system calls you wish to make, there is a Perl function built into the core that does it for you!

We outlined the most common Perl internal functions, and covered the everyday problems that people encounter, but you will want to check out **perlfunc** for a far more complete listing. I haven't counted them recently, but at last count there were over 300 internal Perl functions built in (if you count different uses as different functions).

Perl functions also have the property of being multiplexed, or as we shall call them in Chapter 20, "Layering and Perl." We gave the count of 300 as the number of internal functions, but the number of distinct names for internal functions is more like 80.

They simply work differently depending on the parameters you pass them. This is what makes Perl seem so simple to use even though the number of actual separate commands is gigantic.

Onward and upward. The next section deals with another aspect that makes Perl so useful; the Internal Perl Variables which gives a location for common data you will use in your Perl applications.

Internal Perl Variables

Perl has special variables provided, by default, with the Perl executable. It is important to note that these special variables are read-only.

Note

Throughout this chapter, you will see two forms of special variables: a "short" form and a "long" form (i.e., $" and $LIST_SEPARATOR). The short form is all we had in Perl 4. Those of us who are familiar with these short forms would not want to give them up as they save a lot of typing.

With Perl 5, however, there is a long-hand provided for these variables. For example:

```
use English;
```

used at the beginning of a program will make synonyms of the long form for all short variables. For example, Perl changes $` to $PREMATCH, $| to $OUTPUT_AUTOFLUSH, etc. Sometimes there are two such synonyms:

```
$, = $OFS = $OUTPUT_FIELD_SEPARATOR;     # These are the same thing
```

Don't worry about setting $, and forget about setting $OFS or $OUTPUT_FIELD_SEPARATOR. These are true synonyms: Once one of the values changes, the others change as well. (We will see in Chapter 11 how this is accomplished.)

Whether or not you want to use these long forms is another matter. If you like being explicit or remember easier in longhand, they are fine, but it is just as easy to look up the short form in a reference like **perlvar** as it is to look up the long value.

The practice of this book is to use the short form and then show a translation of the short form into the long form in a comment or two.

We have already seen examples of special variables: The $" ($LIST_SEPARATOR), as seen earlier, and the $` ($PREMATCH), $' ($POSTMATCH), and $& ($MATCH) as seen in regular expressions.

Why use special variables? Perl uses them in several ways:

- To hold very common data, frequently used in Perl programs.
- To modify the way that a Perl function or operator works, as in $" ($LIST_SEPARATOR) above, which modifies interpolation.
- To keep scratch data to help a function or operator, as in $MATCH, which holds the information about the last match, for the regular expression engine.

In general, they are used to make a complicated interface simple. Consider, for example, what would have to happen if you didn't have a $" operator. Then, you would have to have an interpolation function and pass the $" as an argument as in:

```
@arrayName = (1,2,3);
$line = interpolate( ' ', @arrayName);     # ' ' equals $" ($LIST_SEPARATOR)
                                           # unintuitive
```

This "pseudosyntax" is extremely cumbersome, and somewhat ugly. Compare it to the Perl-ish way:

```
@arrayName = (1,2,3);
$line = "@arrayName";                      # does what you expect.
```

This form is shorter and more concise, avoids a function call, and (if you get used to the idea that $ " is set to the default of " ") does what you would expect.

Internal variables are part of the reason that Perl is easy to write and one of the reasons why things can be done so fast in Perl. For example, the following example prints out the arguments supplied to a Perl program:

```
print "@ARGV\n";
```

The following prints the directories for which Perl searches for libraries:

```
print "@INC\n";
```

The following sections demonstrate some of the more important variables that Perl supports, with examples of their usage, sorted by category. Also, keep in mind that all the variables are global.

Internal Filehandles: STDIN, STDOUT, STDERR, ARGV and DATA

Perl provides quite a few special filehandles you can use to send output to various locations, which we cover next.

STDIN

STDIN provides a simple method for you to get data from the keyboard, the shell in which the user is typing. If you say:

```
chop( $value = <STDIN> );
```

then $value will contain what the user has typed (on the command-line). You also can use this on the left-hand side of an equation, like:

```
if (<STDIN> =~ m"Y") { print "user input contained a 'Y' in it! \n"}
```

or perhaps:

```
if (($value = <STDIN>) =~ m"Y") { print "User input contained a Y - in $value!\n" }
```

Both examples use STDIN to capture input, the second to save that input into a variable before matching it to a regular expression. This can be handy to have points at which you want the user to type a certain value, and die if the input doesn't contain yes.

STDOUT and STDERR

These are the two main ways to send text to the screen where the user typed the Perl command. STDOUT, in particular, is also the "filehandle" Perl uses by default in the print command. It stands for "Standard Output." When you say:

```
print "THIS GOES TO THE SCREEN!\n";
```

then Perl is silently translating this to:

```
print STDOUT "THIS GOES TO THE SCREEN!\n";
```

for you. STDERR also directs the text to the screen, although in a slightly different way. When you say something like:

```
print STDERR "filename!\n";
```

then this will go to the screen. But if you say something like:

```
prompt% perl -e "print STDERR 'filename!'" > file
```

this will *not* redirect the output to the file `file`, even though you have put in the >. (This works exactly the same way on NT, but not on Windows 95/98.) This allows you to split the two input streams on the command-line. And at least on Unix, the following command for a korn shell works to split the two filestreams into two separate files:

```
prompt% perl -e "print STDERR 'filename!'" > stdout 2>& stderr
```

One last note: Sometimes it is really annoying to have both STDOUT and STDERR streams going at the same time. Suppose you were capturing the output of a program that did this. The output text in this case tends to get garbled—STDERR and STDOUT are two different streams and they are both going to the same place.

In these cases it is helpful to redirect STDERR to STDOUT, either by doing so explicitly in the shell or by using a pipe to open up the relevant command. For example:

```
open (STDERR, "> STDOUT");    #
print STDERR 'HERE';
```

will send all the STDOUT text to STDERR. And:

```
open ( FD, "dir 2>&1 |");
```

will redirect STDOUT to STDERR inside the shell (again NT/Unix), so that you can actually see the **dir** command being executed by saying:

```
while ($line = <FD>) { print FD $line; }
```

Again, as of this writing, this does not work in Windows 95. (It may, however, by the time this book is published.)

ARGV

The ARGV filehandle is used in special cases where you want to actually treat all of the arguments on the command-line as files. ARGV will then act as a default filehandle for each and every entry in @ARGV. Hence, when you say:

```
while ($line = <ARGV>) { print "$line!\n"; }
```

you are actually saying this in disguise:

```
foreach $arg (@ARGV)
{
    open (FD, "$arg");
    while ($line = <FD>)
    {
        print "$line!\n";
    }
}
```

Hence, ARGV is just a cleaner way of stating things in a small subset of important scripts.

DATA

The DATA filehandle is another, simple mechanism to help write simple and quick scripts to parse data. It allows you to attach code to a piece of data, and thus process that piece of data "in place." If you say, for example, something like:

```
    while ($line = <DATA>)
    {
        print $line;
        @tokens = split ('|', $line);
        print $token[0];
    }
    __DATA__
    NUMBER 1|IS| A | PIPE | DELIMITED | LINE
    NUMBER 2| IS | ANOTHER | PIPE | DELIMITED | LINE
```

this prints:

```
    NUMBER 1
    NUMBER 2
```

Perl is reaching in and grabbing the data after the special symbol __DATA__. Hence, on the first iteration of the while loop, $line becomes NUMBER 1, and on the second, $line becomes NUMBER 2.

Internal Tokens: __FILE__, __LINE__, __DATA__, __END__

The special tokens, while not being strictly variables, are often used in conjunction with special filehandles (like DATA). They are listed next.

__FILE__ and __LINE__

__FILE__ and __LINE__ are used as quick ways of getting the file and line in which the current statement is executing.

As such, they give information similar to caller(). However, caller only reports the lines in the stack *above* the place where the statement is executing, not the actual place itself. Here is a statement that supplements caller by showing the file and line of the actual calling statement:

```
    print __FILE__, "    ", __LINE__, "@{[caller()]}\n";
```

Note that because they are not variables *per se*, you cannot put them in double quotes.

__DATA__ and __END__

__DATA__ and __END__ are used with the DATA special filehandle as shown earlier. The only difference between the two is that __DATA__ can be used more than once so that each package can have its own "DATA" handler. For example:

```
    A.pm:
    package A;
    while ($line = <DATA>)
    {
        print "$line in package A\n";
    }
    1;
    __DATA__
    package A line 1
    package A line 2
    package A line 3

    B.pm:
```

```perl
package B;
while ($line = <DATA>)
{
    print "$line in package B\n";
}
1;
__DATA__
package B line 1
package B line 2
package B line 3
```

This works via setting the filehandle A::DATA to point at the lines after package A, and the filehandle B::DATA to point at the lines after package B.

Internal Named Variables: @ARGV, @INC, %INC, %ENV, %SIG

Like named filehandles, Perl provides quite a few special named variables that help you interface with certain aspects of the shell. These will probably be some of the most widely used variables you will have in your programs.

@ARGV

@ARGV (no synonym) holds the arguments as passed into Perl via the command-line. The following:

```perl
print "@ARGV\n"
```

prints the arguments passed to the command. The following is a simplistic option processor that creates a hash out of all items that come after a –:

```perl
my (%options, @newARGV, $xx);
for ($xx = 0; $xx < @ARGV; $xx++)
{
    my $arg = $ARGV[$xx];
    my $val = $ARGV[$xx+1];
    if ($arg =~ m"^-")              # matches a '-' at the beginning of the argument
    {
        $options{$arg} = $val;
        $xx++;                      # we skip the 'value' part, since it has
                                    # already matched.
    }
    else
    {
        push(@newARGV, $arg);       # we save the argument that
                                    # is *not* a directive on a stack.
    }
}
@ARGV = @newARGV;                   # we then take @newARGV (the stuff we
                                    # just matched) and then copy it over
                                    # the old @ARGV stack. (we are done with it!)
```

If someone types:

```perl
command.p -option1 option_value -option2 value2 table1 table2 table3
```

you can then access whatever the user typed on the command-line by:

```
$options{'-option1'}  ;    # holds value 'option_value'.
```

For more robust option processing, see the module **Getopts**. Perl provides a module to do the above transparently, and we will see quite a few examples of this in the next section.

Perl also provides an ARGV filehandle in which each argument on the command-line is treated as a file, and opened. This example:

```
while ($line = <ARGV>) { $count++;}
print $count;
```

counts all the lines given from files on the command-line.

@INC

@INC shows the directory order in which Perl searches for libraries (either required or used), much like the **-I** flag for Unix C compilers. Perl looks for libraries in first-to-last order, which means if the @INC looks like:

```
('/usr/local/lib/Perl', 'mylib/Perl')
```

and there are the libraries:

```
/usr/local/lib/Perl/standardPerlLib.pm, mylib/Perl/standardPerlLib.pm
```

your library will be ignored when you do your use or require.

We will talk a lot more about @INC in Chapter 14, "The Syntax of Libraries and Modules."

%INC

%INC is the hash equivalent of @INC. Instead of giving information about where the libraries are coming from, %INC provides information about which libraries are actually in your workspace. For example, suppose you say something like:

```
use Data::Dumper;
use strict;
```

at the beginning of your code. If you then say:

```
print Dumper(\%INC);
```

it will contain the following two messages:

```
'Data/Dumper.pm' => '/usr/local/lib/perl5/site_perl/Data/Dumper.pm'.
'strict.pm' => /usr/local/lib/perl5/strict.pm'
```

which indicate which library is being used at the time.

%ENV

%ENV is an array that shows all the environmental variables of which Perl is aware. These come directly from the shell. For example, if you say something in korn shell such as:

```
export ENVIRONMENTAL_VARIABLE=/home/install/bin
```

then the Perl statement will print:

```
print $ENV{'ENVIRONMENTAL_VARIABLE'};   # This prints out '/home/install/bin'.

print keys %ENV;                        # This prints out your
                                        # entire environment
```

Notice that by the nature of the shell, if you modify an environment variable in Perl, you do not modify it in the original shell. All the changes that were made in the environment will be wiped clean as soon as the Perl script exits. This is sometimes an annoying behavior, but is unavoidable because of the way the shells are put together.

However, if you modify the environment, you do modify it for any processes the Perl script spawns, as in:

```
$ENV{PERL5LIB} = "/home/edward/Perlwork";
system("Perlcall.p");       # this is a simple 'system' command
                            # fires off 'Perlcall.p' as a subprocess,
                            # and waits for it to return.
```

In this case, `"Perlcall.p"` will see the changes you made to the environment and execute them.

Perl also provides a module, `Env`, that lets you see your environment as a bunch of scalars: `$ENV{'SHELL'}` becomes `$SHELL`, and so on. In other words:

```
use Env;              # uses the Environmental module.
print $PERL5LIB;      # prints out the environmental
                      # variable PERL5LIB.
```

prints the environmental variable `PERL5LIB`, and:

```
$PERL5LIB = "/full/path/for/perl5lib";
```

sets the environmental `PERL5LIB` variable.

This sometimes makes code much cleaner, especially in modules that manipulate the environment a lot. These are true synonyms that `Env` sets up. If you undefine `$ENV{PATH}`, you also undefine `$PATH`, and so on. You can do things such as:

```
use Env "HOME", "PATH";
```

which will only make a `$HOME` and a `$PATH` variable.

%SIG

The `%SIG` variable handles all the signal handlers that the Perl script knows about. It is, by default, set to an empty hash. If you want to get a list of signals your system supports, you can simply use the **Config** module.

This is done in the following way:

```
use Config;

print $Config{sig_name};     # prints out a list of signals that your system supports.
```

If you set any of the signals in that config list via:

```
$SIG{SIGNAL_NAME} = \&signal_function;   # code reference.
```

then, when the function SIGNAL_NAME gets "caught" by the process, the function `signal_function` is called instead of doing the default action that the signal does. The usual way signal handlers are used is to prevent the process from dying when a command is typed.

For example, if your machine supports an INT signal (both Windows and Unix do this):

```
$SIG{INT} = 'IGNORE';     # special keyword, IGNORE, which means 'just skip it'.
```

If someone types a **Ctrl-C** (or whatever equals "send an interrupt to the underlying process") now, the process will ignore it. Likewise, if you set the handler to:

```
$SIG{INT} = \&hit_control_c;
sub hit_control_c
{
    print "Ouch! Somebody hit a signal $_[0]\n";   # Note the $_[0] here.
}                                                   # if you print out this varb
                                                    # it shows which signal
                                                    # was actually pressed.
```

when someone types the interrupt sequence (**Ctrl-C**), it will print Ouch! Somebody hit a signal INT and continue.

Note

Perl also provides a special handle, __DIE__, for running a subroutine before the program exits abnormally, and __WARN__ for when a warning message is printed. It is extremely helpful in debugging, as in:

```
use Carp;

$SIG{__DIE__} = sub { confess(@_) };     # passes the text of the 'die' message
                # to the signal handler thru @_.

$SIG{__WARN__} = sub { warn(@_) };     # passes the text of the 'warn'
                # thru the signal handler.
```

This will give a stack trace when your program exits with an error condition. For more on Carp, confess, and warn, see the section "Debugging Perl."

Note

Signal handlers do not work right off with underlying processes. For example, if you say something such as:

```
$SIG{INT} = 'IGNORE';
system("command");     # forks off a command
```

and then press the interrupt char (**Ctrl-C**), if Perl is in the middle of command it will interrupt it, even though you told it not to.

Internal One-Character Variables

Now, we get to the somewhat hairy part of the chapter; we talk about those one-line variables that make Perl so lovable to people who like to write terse code, and are a turn-off to so many others.

If you belong to the second category, or are new to Perl and think longer names would help you learn the language better, the module **English** will come in very handy to give you an alternative. Just say:

```
use English;
```

and you will get the long filenames (instead of the terse ones).

Internal Variables That Modify the Behavior of Functions: $_, $\, $", and $/

We have seen only one of these already: $" ($LIST_SEPARATOR). This section discusses some of the similar variables like this, variables which change the internal state of some special Perl function or application.

$_ (Long Name $ARG)

I hesitated to include the variable $_ ($ARG), because it is often abused and it has so many meanings. However, its use is so prevalent that we must say something about it.

$_ acts as a default variable. It is a variable, used by several functions and in several contexts, that you never see. When a function has no arguments and you know it should take one, as in the following statements:

```
print;
die if (-f);
```

or, when you see what looks like a regular expression, and it doesn't have an =~ in it, as in:

```
if (m"whatever") { &do_something; }
```

this checks $_ to see if it has whatever in it; if it does, it does the routine do_something. $_ works with a foreach loop such as:

```
foreach (@args) {  }    # instead of foreach $arg (@args) { }
```

which goes through each element in @args, and sets $_ to it temporarily for the duration of the loop. Or in:

```
while (<ARGV>) {  print;   }
```

where this is actually a small program, the equivalent of:

```
while (defined $line = <ARGV>)
{
    print $line;
}
```

In the use with grep and map:

```
@dirs = grep(-d , @fileList);      # goes thru a @fileList, tests each instance to
                                   # see if it is a
                                   # directory  and returns a list of directories
                                   # into @dirs.
@value = map(ord, @charlist);      # turns characters in @charlist
                                   # into their ASCII values in @value.
```

where $_ is being used by grep and map as a temporary value to search through.

From this section you can see why $_ is attractive. With its use there is no need to set an extra variable. Syntax becomes shorter and quicker to write. But it is also extremely easy with $_ to become too cryptic. By explicitly setting $line, you are forcing yourself to remember that $line means something, that is, a line in a file described by the filehandle ARGV.

If you get into the constant habit of using $_, you are going to trip up somewhere, as in the following:

```
use FileHandle;
foreach (@ARGV)
{
    my $file = match_pattern();
    print;                                  # print out argument list (arg to @ARGV);
}
```

```
sub match_pattern
{
    my $FH = new FileHandle ("$_");
    while (defined <$FH>)
    {
        return(1) if (m"pattern");
    }
}
```

This trips up since the while line (while (defined <$FH>)) also uses $" for you, and this collides with the foreach loop. The big question is where do you draw the line? We say that you should use $_ in three cases: 1) when you have a quick and dirty script to do, and need to do it pronto; 2) in functions that require it, like grep and map; and 3) inside a small to medium-sized subroutine, where you *always* localize it, as in:

```
sub read_file
{
    my ($fileName) = @_;
    local($_);
    my $return = [ ];
    open(FD, "$fileName");
    while (<FD>)
    {
      push(@$return, $_);
    }
    $return;
}
```

Even here you aren't gaining much, just one less variable. You also have to be aware that the operator push() doesn't take $_ as an argument.

$" ($LIST_SEPARATOR), $, ($OUTPUT_FIELD_SEPARATOR or $OFS), and $\ ($OUTPUT_RECORD_SEPARATOR or $ORS)

We have already seen the internal variable $" ($LIST_SEPARATOR). It provides some magic for arrays printed inside quoted context. If an array is interpolated in a double-quoted string context:

```
@arrayName = ("Example", "Again");
$line = "@arrayName";     # prints "Example Again" if $" is
print $line;              # a space (default)
```

then $" is used to determine what to put between the elements of the list, the default of which is a space. By setting $" equal to "\n\t", you can say something such as:

```
local($") = "\n\t";                    # or $LIST_SEPARATOR = "\n\t"
@line = ("Example", "Again");          # with 'use English';
print "@arrayName\n";                  # prints "Example\n\tAgain";
```

Notice we have both put the words on separate lines and indented them. This comes in handy in two cases: 1) if you have multiple patterns that you want matched in a regular expression:

```
local($") = "|";        # $LIST_SEPARATOR = "|";
@patternlist = ('pattern1','pattern2','pattern3','pattern4');
$string = "we want to match pattern4";
if ($args = m"(@patternlist)")     # this equals
```

```
{                # (pattern1|pattern2|pattern3|pattern4)
}                # remember. regular expressions
                 # interpolate like double quotes!
```

and 2) in code generation. Suppose you had a list of fields that corresponded to a table definition, as in:

```
my (@fieldList) = ('char a(50)', 'int b', 'text c');
```

By setting the $" equal to say, a ",\n\t", you can say something such as:

```
my $tableName = "example";
local($") = "\n\t";
my $table = "create table $tableName (\n\t@fieldList )";
                                    # This prints out
                                    #   create table example (
                                    #       char a(50),
                                    #       int b,
                                    #       text c )
```

Note that this is totally, completely, syntactically correct SQL, and it is even prettified!

The same trick can be done for C and Perl:

```
$" = ";";
@declarationList = ('char a[50]', 'int intName');
```

The other two variables, $, ($OUTPUT_FIELD_SEPARATOR or $OFS) and $\ ($OUTPUT_RECORD_SEPARATOR or $ORS), aren't nearly as useful. We list them here only to understand print a little better. print is a pretty odd duck. Because it is so commonly used, Perl provides several modifiers to how its arguments are actually being printed. These three print statements will print different things, even though they are printing different aspects of @arrayName:

```
print "@arrayName";
print @arrayName;
print scalar(@arrayName);
```

The first and the third example print the number of elements in an array since scalar forces the arg to be a scalar; print sees a list with one element.

The second (because print is a function on arrays) does something different. Since it is printing @arrayName in an array context, and not in interpolated double quotes, it uses the $, variable instead. So if you want to use this construct, you have to remember to switch between $, and $".

$\ is a little more helpful. It indicates what character print is going to print after it finishes printing everything else. $\ is originally set to null, but if you set it, you'll get something like:

```
local($") = "|";
local($\) = "$";

@arrayName = ('regexp1', 'regexp2');
print "@arrayName";                  # prints regexp1|regexp2$
                                     # Note the '$' at the end here...
```

But still, you can always print the $ explicitly at the end, so this is useful only in heavy-duty code generation.

$/ ($INPUT_RECORD_SEPARATOR)

This variable, $/, is much more useful than its cousin, ($\ or $OUTPUT_RECORD_SEPARATOR). It indicates how the file descriptor reads its information. $/ is set to "\n" by default. For example:

```
local($/) = "\n";        # actually, the default.
open(FD, "$file");       # opens the file descriptor FD for information
$line = <FD>;            # Now -- line contains the 'line' from FD
                         # UPTO and INCLUDING
                         # the $INPUT_RECORD_SEPARATOR
                         # "\n";
```

If you have a file with the format:

```
THIS|IS|A|LINE|OF|DATA
THIS|IS|A|LINE|OF|DATA2
```

in which both lines of data are terminated by a "\n", and then after the preceding statement, you read in:

```
'THIS|IS|A|LINE|OF|DATA
'
```

with the return or $/ intact, and you want to get rid of the return, then you can do:

```
chomp($line);
```

```
chomp($line =<FD>);      # reads stuff in, and automatically chomps
              # off the '$/'.
```

chomp works on the '$/'; hence, it is safe. If, for some reason, you read in a line without a '$/' on it, as in:

```
'NO INPUT_RECORD_SEPARATOR'   # lacking a '\n';
```

then chomp does nothing. It only works on the '$/'. Its unsafe cousin, chop, on the other hand, chops off the R, giving:

```
'NO INPUT_RECORD_SEPARATO'.
```

Suppose you have a "record" file, in which there is a different row delimiter present:

```
'THIS|LINE
OF DATA|
HAS CONTROL NS IN IT| AND IS DELIMITED BY A CARET-RETURN ^
'
```

Then, you can set $/ to be:

```
local($/) = "^\n";
```

and the construct:

```
while (defined ($line = <FD>))
{
    chomp($line);     # gets rid of "^\n";
}
```

reads each logical line—everything up to and including the ^\n—and for each line, it gets rid of the row separator "^\n".

A final use of $/ is to suck in all the data from a file into one long string. We have already seen this in a couple of places. This is very powerful when combined with the regular expressions from the last chapter and there isn't a delimiter that is special (like the above). If you want to do this, you undef it and set it to blank.

Say, for example, we had a file of the format:

```
BLOCK1
    this is a block of text
    containing multiple lines.
BLOCK2
    this is another block.
```

Then, we might be able to iterate through this using something such as:

```
undef $/;

open(FD, "$file");
$line = <FD>;                         # now '$line' equals ALL of file $file!
while ($line =~ m"(.*?)(BLOCK\d+|$)"sg) # now we loop through the
{                                     # with the delimiter 'BLOCK'
    do_something_with_line($1);       # plus several digits.
}
```

This sets $1 to:

```
this is a block of text
containing multiple lines
```

first, and:

```
'this is another block'
```

second, using the power of regular expressions.

The $/ construct can be an arbitrarily complicated string. It can be used to parse code, manipulate documents, manipulate database definitions, etc. As long as the text is semireadable, you can do whatever you want with it.

Variables Set by Function Calls, and/or Support Various Functions and Operators: $`, $', $&, $$, $0, and $?

The role of these variables is to support underlying Perl functions so that the amount of syntax necessary in those functions is minimal.

Whereas the one-line variables in the previous section actually changed the way certain functions executed, the variables here go the other way around. They are set by various functions and basically make the operations of those functions smoother. In the chapter on regular expressions (Chapter 9) we already encountered a few ($` ($PREMATCH), $' ($POSTMATCH), and $& ($MATCH)). Here is a review of each, along with a few new ones. As always, the names of the English variables are given as well.

$` ($PREMATCH), $' ($POSTMATCH), and $& ($MATCH)

$` $PREMATCH, $& ($MATCH), and $' ($POSTMATCH) are set as "side effects" by the regular expression to equal respectively, the text preceding the match, the text that actually was matched, and the text after the match.

If you have the regular expression:

```
$line = "fee fie foe";
$line =~ m"fie";
```

then $` becomes the string fee, $& becomes the string fie and $' becomes the string foe.

$$ ($PROCESS_ID, or $PID)

$$ ($PROCESS_ID, or $PID) is the current process ID of the process running on your machine. This is incredibly useful for making temporary file names:

```
open(FD, "> $$");    # open a temporary file based on the PID.
                     # open for writing.
```

The reason this is incredibly useful is that if you are running processes on the same machine, there is no chance for collision when you run other processes that use $$ in this way. In other words, if **script.p** is the name of the program above that is opening a file, you can run:

```
prompt% perl_script.p    (PID 1123) (temporary file name /tmp/1123)
prompt% perl_script.p    (PID 1124) (temporary file name /tmp/1124)
prompt% perl script.p    (PID 1125) (temporary file name /tmp/1125)
prompt% perl_script.p    (PID 1126) (temporary file name /tmp/1126)
```

and the operating system keeps track of the file names for you. This again, is only good on Windows NT and Unix machines. Windows 95/98 does not have a concept of process IDs, and hence will not work here.

$0 ($PROGRAM_NAME) (Read as $ <zero>)

$0 (read as $<zero>) holds the name of the script, as you ran it. For example, if you name your script:

```
script_name.p
```

in the directory:

```
/home/utils
```

then the variable $0 becomes /home/utils/script_name.p.

This is extremely useful for modules that need to know from where they were called. We will use this logic when we go into our automatic documentation handler later. Suppose you want to make a module that kept track of what was run and when. You could simply do something such as:

```
package ModuleTrak;
sub log
{
    my $fh = new FileHandle(">> process_log");
    my $date = localtime;
    print $fh "$0 $date\n";
}
```

Then, on any call to:

```
ModuleTrak::log;
```

Perl will automatically keep track of the program that was run, without the package having to be "passed" that information.

$? ($CHILD_ERROR)

$? gives the last error status for any system call or command given in backticks. It is usually used to check for any errors returned from a given process:

```
system("cd $ROOT");
if ($?)
{
    print "Error in changing to $ROOT!\n";
}
@files = `ls -1 $DIR`;
if ($?)
{
    print "Error in getting files from $DIR!\n";
}
```

This shows the actual error that occured as it happened, as well as flagging that an error indeed happened.

Summary of Internal Variables

Again, as was the case with the internal functions we mentioned earlier, we have given only the most common of internal variables. There are many others, some with exotic names simply because Perl ran out of common keys on the keyboard ($^X holds the Perl executable name, for instance).

A quick scan of the **perlvar** man page shows that there are about 60 in all. So we again ask you not to take this chapter as gospel, and instead go to the on-line documentation.

Summary

The main purpose of this chapter is to supplement the documentation and focus on the more important special variables and built-in functions in one place. This chapter explained them in more detail, especially in regard to portability. After one has gotten used to the amount of detail here, one can then go on to the **perlvar**, and **perlfunc** man pages for more information, as well as the **Perl for Win32** documentation.

If I were to summarize what I thought were the most important functions to know (in a chapter of important functions), I would say that a good plan of attack for learning Perl functionality would be to:

1. Learn about variables and contexts first.
2. Learn `split`, `map`, `grep`, and `sort`.
3. Learn `caller` and `Carp`.
4. Learn the Perl interfaces to the OS (`mkdir`, `rmdir`, etc.) for portability.
5. Use the rest of the variables and functions as you see fit.

This approach emphasizes learning Perl in a Perl-ish way. `split`, `map`, `grep`, and `sort` are the most unique functions to Perl. If you learn them, then you will be easily able to pick up the other functions in their wake.

11

Perl 5 Odds and Ends

Perl has a lot of success behind it. Perl has become the most popular language on the Web to use for system administration, database administration, and for a myriad of other tasks. Perl has managed to become incredibly useful without the one thing that other languages have had: A formal design committee. To the contrary, Perl's design is about as anarchical as you could possibly imagine. In all likelihood, a given feature started with a "why don't we try this" post on the mailing list Perl5-porters. Likewise, much of the look and feel of Perl has occurred because of historical accident (Larry Wall's own personal historical accidents, so to speak), and the desire for "one more feature."

Chapter Overview

The upshot of this "one more feature" ideal is that there are a few concepts in Perl that don't fit very well with any of the other Perl features, yet are too powerful to overlook. This chapter is devoted to these features. The features we will cover are:

1. Formats
2. Coderefs
3. Globbing
4. `BEGIN/END`
5. `eval`

Formats are Perl's "what you see is what you get" way to generate ASCII reports. Formats are extremely helpful in generating quick-and-dirty analysis output for others to read (so you can get back to programming more edifying items in Perl). This chapter could be considered a primer on formats. You can get much fancier with formats than what will be shown here. You might want to check the **perlform** man page for more details.

Coderefs, or callbacks, let you pass functions into other functions, as you would data. In doing so, coderefs permit the construction of much more powerful modules and objects, and allow you to think about things in a much more object-oriented way. If you want more information, check the **perlref** man page for more details.

Globbing is Perl's ability to refer to more than one thing by the use of a wildcard. This chapter covers one form of globbing: type globbing.

BEGIN/END functions are Perl's method of performing certain tasks before the logical execution of a program, and after the end of the program. In other words, these functions allow you to do such things as global cleanup or global setup. They also are important for understanding how packages work. *Execution control* is my term for controlling the sequence of events followed by Perl when an executable runs. This includes when variables are assigned and when functions are defined. Understanding execution control can explain several strange errors you might get while running Perl.

Perl's function for executing strings as if they were small Perl programs is eval. It was necessary in Perl 4 to use eval much more than it is in Perl 5. In fact, it is best to forget about most of the uses of eval in Perl 4. For example, if you used eval to create complex data structures, you will now use references instead.

Each of these subjects is covered briefly in this chapter. If you need to get more in-depth information on these topics you can consult **perlform** for formats, and **perlfunc** for eval and BEGIN/END. Type globbing is covered in the Perl documentation, but you will need to dig for it in several places.

Those of you just starting in the language might want to read and understand formats, because they can make you productive immediately. Be sure to read about eval if you need to port your Perl scripts to many platforms. If you need to make your scripts run such that they are being fired off automatically (whether by cron or by a Web server), read about BEGIN/END. If you are going to be doing more than just a little object-oriented programming, be sure to read about callbacks.

The odds and ends covered in this chapter fill in the remaining gaps of the basics of Perl. They are rather "messy" because they don't fit into neat, tidy categories of what has come before. However, they are great at solving the particular problems that they were designed to solve—pragmatism is the key here. When you become familiar with Perl, you will want to add these to your repertoire.

Formats

Have you ever had need for a quick analysis of reams and reams of data? Do you feel that you are "drowning in data and starving for information?" Whether the report is on the performance of a certain piece of code, the bugs in a piece of software, or cost/benefit analysis, all reports share the three following steps:

1. Data collection
2. Data manipulation
3. Data output

Formats are Perl's way of handling the data output step in this chain. Formats allow you to change data into meaningful information. They do this in a very quick, "pretty enough but not too pretty" way. Formats are not very scalable, because complicated reports are difficult to make. When formats were devised, Perl was a very young language and there was no such thing as my variables. Hence, you need to use globals to write out reports.

In other words, formats are useful for simple reports because they let you easily extract data into an output file much faster than is possible with C or C++.

Format Syntax

Using formats involves a two-step process:

1. Define a *top* (header) and a body to the report.
2. Write data to the report.

Let's look at both steps in turn, in an actual example. Let's consider a program to summarize a Web log.

Example: Summarizing a Web Log

Perl is used for CGI creation and Web access. One of the main tasks one will encounter with CGI is summarizing tons of information. Here, we will use formats to define and execute this summary.

Defining the Format

The first thing we need to do in order to get a useful summary of what happens with our Web server is to define a report format that makes a good summary. Below is the format we will want to use:

```
Web Hits Report
Server Hits     Domain      Avg Connect Time    Total Xfer    Comments
-----------------------------------------------------------------------
1323            umn.edu     04 h 15 m 11 sec    55331 KB      Way too much
                                                              net lag
44              str.com     00 h 16 m 04 sec    432 KB        from T1 --
                                                              Fast transfer
```

You could define this in Perl with the following formats:

```
Listing 11.1 Webreport.p (format header)

1   format REPORT_TOP =
2   Web Hits Report
3   Server Hits      Domain       Avg Connect Time      Kbytes      Comments
4   -----------------------------------------------------------------------
5   .
6   format REPORT =
7   @<<<<<<          @<<<<<<<      @# hr @# min @# sec    @<<<<<<<    ^<<<<<<<<
8   $hits,           $domain,      $hr,  $min,  $sec,     $kbytes,    $comment.
9   .
```

In these two formats, REPORT_TOP corresponds to what the report prints at the beginning of each page. REPORT corresponds to the body of the report. The idea here is that you can define the report to look like the desired output without actually going to the trouble of making a GUI picture of the report, using a specialty application like Excel, or any of a hundred hurdles.

You do need to know some special characters to accomplish this, though. The special characters involved with formats are given in Table 11.1. Any other character in a format will be treated as a regular character in true Perl style.

Table 11.1	@	Indicates the beginning of a fixed variable.
Special	<	Indicates that the variable is to be left-justified.
Characters	>	Indicates that the variable is to be right-justified.
in Formats	|	Indicates that the variable is to be center justified.
	^	Indicates the beginning of a multiline variable.
	#	Indicates that the variable is to be a number.
	~~	Indicates that a multiline variable is to be indefinitely continued on the next line.
	.	Indicates that the end of the format is reached. This character must be by itself at the beginning of a line.

Let's look at some more examples. When you see something like:

```
format STDOUT =
Read:   @<<<<<<<
$variable
.
```

this is indicating that the scalar $variable is to be left-justified, and that any more than seven input characters are to be chopped off. This also means that you are to print your report to the screen, rather than a given file. Whereas if you see something like:

```
format STDOUT =
Center the following variable
@|||||||||||||||||||||||||||||||||||||||||||||||||||||||||
$variable
.
```

this indicates that the scalar $variable is to be centered, and that any extra characters that don't fit will fall off either edge of the line.

Now, something like:

```
format REPORT =
Comment: ^<<<<<<<<<<<<
         $variable
         ^<<<<<<<<<<<<
         $variable
.
```

indicates that the variable is to span more than one line. It also indicates that the first 13 characters will be spread on the first line, and the next 13 characters will be spread on the second.

Let's take another look at Listing 11.1:

Listing 11.1
Webreport.p (format header)

```
1   format REPORT_TOP =
2   Web Hits Report
3   Server Hits     Domain         Avg Connect Time     Kbytes      Comments
4   -------------------------------------------------------------------------
```

```
5   .
6   format REPORT =
7   @<<<<<<         @<<<<<<<    @# hr @# min @# sec    @<<<<<<<    ^<<<<<<<<
8   $hits,          $domain,    $hr,  $min,  $sec,     $kbytes,    $comment.
9   .
```

Now, how do we actually use this format to create something useful?

The write Function

First, we defined the report structure. Now we will go to the second step of the formatting process: using the format by calling the `write` function. To demonstrate this, we need to create some data to write out. Let's create a stub to do this. (In other words, some test data to test your application. The actual data would be located in your logs in your http server.)

Listing 11.2
Webreport.p (continued)

```
10  my $data = [
11              [ 12331, 'umn.edu', 4, 05, 36, 44232, 'too much lag time' ],
12              [ 44, 'str.com', 00,4, 6, 432, 'from t1 -- fast transfer']
13          ];
```

This is the data to print out. To create the report, we then say:

Listing 11.3
Webreport.p (continued)

```
14   open (REPORT, "> report_file");   # this 'binds' the
15                                      # REPORT file handle to the place we want to
16                                      # print out the report.
17   foreach $element (@$data)
18   {
19        ($hits, $domain, $hr, $min, $sec, $kbytes, $comment) = @{$element};
20        write REPORT;
21   }
22   close(REPORT);
```

See how easy this is? We simply populate the variables that are to be used in the format, and they are automatically put in the right place on the report. Because we have defined the handle REPORT_TOP, we have ensured that we have the same header on each page of the formatted report.

When we actually take the data from an http server instead of a stub, we shall simply replace the code @{$element} with a call that returns a data structure that mirrors the function shown.

The first thing to do when learning formats is concentrate on knowing the special characters that make them work. Realize that @ indicates a single line variable, whereas ^ indicates that the variable may go on for several lines. The special characters are quite straightforward. The special characters shown in our example should suffice for about 90 percent of the reports that you write.

How Formats Work (Advanced Formats)

There is some heavy "magic" going on here. First, there is a simple `write FILEHANDLE` statement, which removes the worry about explicitly passing in the variables that are being used in the format. It also appears that

Perl "auto-magically" right-justifies, centers, and left-justifies for you, as well as splits variables into many lines! Finally, Perl handles the length of the page for you.

How does Perl do all of this so easily?

There are quite a few variables associated with the format. As with much of Perl, these variables are of the "one special character" variety. (See Table 11.2.)

Table 11.2 Special Variables and Formats		
	$%	the page number that the corresponding format is on.
	$=	the number of lines per page (default 60).
	$-	the number of lines left on the page.
	$~	the name of the format (default STDOUT).
	$^	the name of the "header" (default STDOUT_TOP).

It is easy to tweak all of these variables to get certain effects. For example, suppose you are doing inventory reporting, and want to output only one inventory request per page. You define the report's look via the code shown in Listing 11.4.

Listing 11.4
inventory.p (format header)

```
1   format STDOUT_TOP =
2   Inventory Request for Date: @<<<<<<<<<<
3                               $date
4   Request Number: @<<<<<<<<<
5                   $%
6   ----------------------------------------
7   .
8   format STDOUT =
9   Part Number: @############        Name of parts: @<<<<<<<<<<<<<<
10               $part_number,                        $part_name
11  Cost: @######.##
12        $cost_of_part
13  Comments on request: ^<<<<<<<<<<<<<<<<<<<<<<<<<<<< ~~
14                       $comment
15  .
```

Notice the $% used here. It prints the page number on the report. Now look at what happens when we do the write again with test data:

Listing 11.5
inventory.p (continued)

```
16  $reportStuff = [
17                  [ 'Jun 15, 1996', 66423412, 'tongue depressors', 199.99,
18                      'These things are expensive!' ],
19                  [ 'May 1, 1995', 123122, 'squeegies', 1.19,
20                      'need replacements.. do not squeege effectively.'
21                  ]
22              ];
```

```
23 foreach $report (@$reportStuff)
24 {
25     ($date, $part_number, $part_name, $cost_of_part, $comment) = @{$report};
26     write STDOUT;
27     $- = 0;
28 }
```

Note the use of the `$-` here. By setting it to zero, you are telling the internal Perl formatter to restart the page. This produces the following output:

```
Inventory Request for Date: Jun 15, 1996
Request Number: 1
----------------------------------------
Part Number: 66423412          Name of parts: tongue depressors
Cost:      199.99
Comments on request: These things are expensive!
^L (page break)
Inventory Request for Date: May 1, 1995
Request Number: 2
----------------------------------------
Part Number: 123122            Name of parts: squeegies
Cost:        1.19
Comments on request: need replacements.. do not squeege effectively.
```

Since this reset happens every time we loop through the report, we get the effect of only having one report per page. The same effect would occur if we set `$=` to 10, since there would be only 10 lines per page.

What if you wanted to add an optional comment to the end of a given record, something that only applies to certain items in the list? In other words, you want to intermix print statements with `write`. This is possible, but you will have to manage `$-` (newpage) yourself.

Format Caveats

The idea in Perl that all it takes to output to the report is the simple statement `write FILEHANDLE;` is a direct result of the fact that Perl is using global variables with the `write` function.

This means that if you do something like:

```
format LOOSE =
This won't work: @>>>>>>>>>>>>>
                 $left_justify_me
.
my $left_justify_me = "variable_text";
write LOOSE;
```

it won't work because `$left_justify_me` is a my variable, because `write` is a function call, and because (as we have said) my variables simply don't work in function calls.

Also, you should realize that formats are one of the older, squeakier features of the language. As such, they tend to show the stress (via bugs) when used in too complicated a manner, and are not being maintained (my variables came along as a new feature and made formats much more confusing). One of the "to do" items is to make a format "package" that takes the functionality of formats out of the language, and places them into a module.

Therefore, formats should probably not be used in huge projects, and instead used only in small, throwaway scripts.

Coderefs

Coderefs are a bit troublesome from the perspective of this book. *Coderef* stands for *code reference*, and you could argue that they belong in the section on references. However, coderefs aren't really pointers to *data*, they are pointers to *functionality*. Hence, you could argue that they belong in the chapter on functions.

Anyway, I decided to put them in this odds and ends chapter, which is really sort of a pity because they are so powerful. In fact, they are necessary when doing anything more than simple object-oriented programming. We will see many code references in the chapters on object-oriented programming, Chapters 17 through 24.

Format of Coderefs

When you say something like:

```
my $functionReference = \&subr;
```

you are defining a code reference. $functionReference is a scalar that gets set to "point to the function &subr." If you now print $functionReference, it will look like:

```
CODE(0xa47ec)
```

indicating that it is a code reference that resides at the address 0xa47ec in memory.

Now you can use the & character to dereference $functionReference, much in the same way you used @ to dereference array references and % to dereference hash references. If subr looks like:

```
sub subr { my ($arg1, $arg2) = @_;    print "$arg1    $arg2\n"; }
```

then the following code:

```
my $functionReference = \&subr;
&$functionReference(1,2);
```

prints out 1   2.

Internally, Perl is going through gyrations that look something like what is shown in Figure 11.1. Hence, &$functionReference(1,2) becomes &{CODE(0xa47ec)}(1,2), which becomes &subr(1,2). The important thing is to remember what is pointing to what! If you try to dereference something that is not a code reference with an &, you will end up with a fatal error.

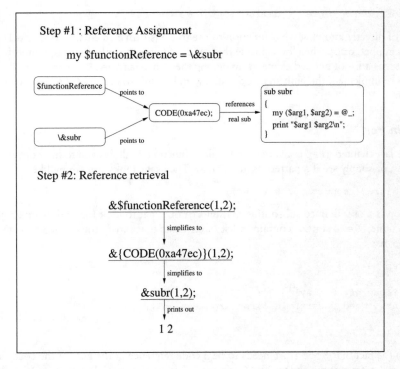

Figure 11.1
How Code
References Work

Anonymous Subroutines

Just as you can have anonymous data structures, you can have *anonymous subroutines*, which do not have a name associated with them, only pointers. If you say:

```perl
my $coderef = sub { print "@_\n"; };
```

then you are defining a code reference (note the semicolon at the end of the line). This is a statement, not a block. (If you understand the difference between these two concepts, you will learn Perl quickly.)

This statement is equivalent to:

```perl
my $coderef = \&subr;
sub subr { print "@_\n"; }
```

only cleaner and much more concise. To call the code reference, you say:

```perl
&$coderef('args', 'here','now');
```

which prints args here now.

Callbacks

The primary use of code references is to program callbacks. *Callbacks* are functions that fill in a bit of functionality that a function or object lacks. We have already seen some forms of callbacks, although we didn't point them out: grep and map are implemented in terms of callbacks. When you say:

```
my @definedElements = grep { defined($_) } @elements;
```

grep has no way of directly knowing what function to use to transform elements. { defined($_) } is a call-back in this code snippet. grep then looks inside this code, and uses this information to modify its behavior. As a result, grep returns a list of defined elements, assigning them to @definedElements.

For fun, let's re-implement the built-in grep function in Perl just to get an idea of how you might do this in your own projects.

grep Redone in Perl

As was said in the last chapter, grep is a very useful built-in function. It allows you to filter out elements that don't belong in an array, or simply see if a pattern is in an array. The usage looks something like:

```
@elements = grep( condition, @array );
```

where condition is a user-defined subroutine that tells grep what to look for, and @array is a user-defined array. After all is done, @elements contains a list of elements that satisfy the condition. Let's define the bare bones of mygrep as:

```
1 sub mygrep
2 {
3     my ($coderef, @array) = @_;
4     (print ("Need coderef in first argument!\n"), return())
5                                         if (ref($coderef) ne "CODE");
6 }
```

Here, we build in the fact that $coderef needs to be a code reference in the guts of the code. If we did not, as soon as we tried to dereference the code with &$coderef, Perl would croak in a most unfriendly fashion.

To fill this in, remember what grep() does. grep() goes through each element in an array and sorts through them, returning a list of the elements that match the condition specified. mygrep will look like what you see in Listing 11.6.

Listing 11.6
mygrep.p

```
1  sub mygrep
2  {
3      my ($coderef, @array) = @_;
4      my ($return, $element) = ([], '');
5      (print ("Need coderef in first argument!\n"), return())
6                                          if (ref($coderef) ne "CODE");
7      foreach $element (@array)
8      {
9          if ( &$coderef($element) )
10         {
11             push(@$return, $element);
12         }
13     }
14     return(@$return);
15 }
```

The heart of the algorithm is in lines 7 through 13. Processing goes through each element, and then calls the code reference $coderef in line 9. We don't care what it is as we hope that the user of the function knows what he or she is doing, whereas mygrep does not.

All we care about is that $element gets pushed on the stack $return, if indeed it does evaluate to true. If we called this now with the following:

```
@array = (1,12,11,10);
my @return = mygrep( sub { $_[0] > 10 }, @array);
```

then Perl essentially goes through the following logic:

Step 1: substitute

```
if (&{ $_[0] > 10 }(1))  { push (@$return, 1);  }
if (&{ $_[0] > 10}(12))  { push (@$return,12);  }
if (&{ $_[0] > 10}(11))  { push (@$return, 11); }
if (&{ $_[0] > 10}(10))  { push (@$return, 10); }
```

Step 2: evaluate

```
if (1 > 10)   { push (@$return, 1);  }
if (12 > 10)  { push (@$return, 12); }
if (11 > 10)  { push (@$return, 11); }
if (10 > 10)  { push (@$return, 10); }
```

Step 3: assign

```
push (@$return, 12);
push (@$return, 11);
```

Step 4: return

```
return(12, 11)
```

And then,

```
@array = (1,12,11,10);
my @return = mygrep( sub { $_[0] > 10 }, @array);
evaluates to @return = (12,11);.
```

If you understand this logic and the steps Perl is going through to make the magic happen, you will be able to debug Perl code with lightning speed. It is a simple matter of thinking the way the Perl interpreter thinks in order to get coding done fast.

Closures

Finally, we will give a nod to closures, which can actually be used to create your own object-oriented syntax. We won't, however; this is an exercise best left to the reader.

The process of making closures is simply the use of callbacks to generate a family of functions, based on another function. That may not sound simple, but when you get into the practice of *doing* it, making closures is fairly easy.

Suppose that you had the following function, which added two values together:

```
$val1 = 4; $val2 = 4;
sub add
{
    "Adding $val1 and $val2 to get ", $val1 + $val2;
}
my $addref = \&add;
print &$addref(), "\n";
```

This is not a good idea, because $val1 and $val2 are global. However, we can get rid of the global part by saying:

```
my ($val1, $val2) = (4, 4);
sub add
{
    print "Adding $val1 and $val2 to get ", $val1 + $val2;
}
my $addref = \&add;
print &$addref(), "\n";
```

We just added a my variable to get rid of a global value—Perl keeps track of what $val1 and $val2 are inside the code. The trick behind closures is to take this idea of encapsulating values one step further, to say something like the following:

```
sub addgen
{
    my ($val1, $val2) = @_;
    return sub
        {
            "Adding $val1 and $val2 to get ", $val1 + $val2;
        }
}
```

What have we done here? We now have made the variables $val1 and $val2 so that they are no longer static. They are dynamic, changing each time on a call to addgen. Furthermore, we have made addgen return a sub-reference each time it has been called. The following code:

```
my $ref1 = addgen(5, 5);
my $ref2 = addgen (6,6);
print &$ref1(), "\n";
print &$ref2(), "\n";
```

will print "Adding 5 and 5 to get 10" when you say print &$ref1(), and will print "Adding 6 to 6 to get 12" when you say print &$ref2().

In other words, addgen is a *subroutine generator*. Each time you call it, it binds the anonymous sub it returns with the values that are passed to it. This is useful, if not slightly dangerous.

The main thing to see about closures is that they are just as powerful as objects in their own right. You can use them when you want to store massive data structures inside a given sub, and then return that sub to the "world" with data it "remembers," just like objects.

Note

Those of you new to object-oriented programming will probably want to skip to Chapter 13 for more detail on objects and the benefits of OO programming.

However, I am not fond of closures. I mention them here in an effort to be complete; the functionality they provide can be given by the more standard object. There is more than one way to do it, though, and you can experiment with them if you like.

Summary of Code References

Code references are simply Perl's way of pointing to functions. Code references, and especially callbacks, are concepts you should learn fairly well. The whole of PerlTk—a method of making GUI Perl scripts—is built on their concept, as well as a few techniques we will discuss later in the book.

To make a code reference, you simply "point" a scalar variable at either an anonymous sub:

```
my $a = sub { print "HERE @_\n"; };
```

or at an already existing sub:

```
my $a = sub new { print "HERE @_\n"; };
```

and then $a will contain a code reference. To actually call the function in that code reference, you say:

```
&$a(1,2,3);
```

where the & dereferences the code reference to get the actual function. Doing so, you will print HERE 1 2 3.

From code references we build callbacks (where a code reference is used to fill in the gaps behind another function) and closures (functions that are code reference generators).

Globbing (Typeglobs)

Globbing is the process of referring to more than one thing by a special symbol. We have already seen globbing in some detail as it applies to filenames. For example, this statement:

```
my @files = glob("*.c");
```

tells Perl to reach into the operating system and grab all the files that end with a .c. *Filename globbing* is a quick workaround for interfacing with the operating system. (You might want to use opendir, readdir, and closedir instead, as suggested in Chapter 10.)

However, this statement:

```
*line = *variable;
```

demonstrates *typeglobbing*. This tells Perl to expand the * into each type of variable symbol that there is. Hence, this statement could be translated to mean:

```
$line = $variable;
@line = @variable;
%line = %variable;
&line = &variable;
```

all of which is being done at the same time, only the examples above will actually *copy* the different variables, whereas in globbing, no copying is being done. Everything is being done with references; the symbols line and variable are now truly aliased, which means that they point to the same reference. This is more like:

```
\$line = \$variable;
\@line = \@variable;
\%line = \%variable;
\&line = \&variable;
```

where each reference is tied together. Globbing is used because this syntax is illegal in Perl. After you say *line = *variable, if you change $line, you also change $variable, and so on.

Globbing Tricks

You can do some interesting things with globbing. Here are three:

- Alias individual variables
- Create read-only values
- Create subroutine aliases

Alias Individual Variables

Globbing not only works in aliasing all symbols together; you can also alias individual symbols. This code:

```
*alias = \@line;
```

would make it so @alias was exactly the same variable as line (until @alias was typeglobbed to something else).

Create Read-only Values

For a read-only value (array, scalar, or hash) you can say something like:

```
*PI = \'3.14';
*E = \'2.718';
```

and get a true, read-only value. With this value, the statement $E=3; prompts you with the following error:

```
'Modification of Read-only value attempted at line xxxx'
```

Create Subroutine Aliases

Because aliases work on any type of reference, including subroutines, you can make aliases to other subroutines. If you say:

```
*other = \&this;
```

you are aliasing the subroutine other to the subroutine this. Hence, anybody that called the function other, as in:

```
other('my','arguments');
```

would instead be calling the subroutine this.

Globbing and Exporter

Aside from globbing allowing these relatively useful tricks, a good reason to know about it is because it explains so much about how Perl works.

Warning: The following discussion gets rather intricate. If you have not done so already, review the section on namespaces and brush up on how Perl handles segmenting functions into different compartments called "packages" or "namespaces."

One of the key modules we will see in Chapter 13 when we come to modular and object-oriented programming is the module Exporter, which has at its heart the use of globbing and globbing tricks. We shall cover Exporter when we get to OO programming. As we will see, when you say something like:

```
1 package MyPackage;
2 use Exporter;
3 @EXPORT = (my_sub, my_sub2);
```

and then use this package inside another package/script, as in:

```
use MyPackage;
```

somehow the functions "magically" appear inside the `MyPackage` namespace, so you don't need to say `MyPackage::my_sub2()` to reference the function `my_sub2`. You simply need to say:

```
my_sub2();
```

and away you go. Globbing is the reason for this magic. The essence of Exporter can be summarized by the following line:

```
use Carp;
*{"${callpkg}::$sym"} =
        $type eq ''  ?  \&{"${pkg}::$sym"} :
        $type eq '&' ?  \&{"${pkg}::$sym"} :
        $type eq '$' ?  \${"${pkg}::$sym"} :
        $type eq '@' ?  \@{"${pkg}::$sym"} :
        $type eq '%' ?  \%{"${pkg}::$sym"} :
        $type eq '*' ?  *{"${pkg}::$sym"} :
        Carp::croak("Can't export symbol: $type$sym");
```

which appears in Exporter.pm module lines 158 to 164, which comes in the distribution. This rather elegant statement does a lot of magic; if you understand it, you understand Perl quite well. `${callpkg}` is the calling package, and `$sym` is the symbol to be evaluated. `${pkg}` is the package where Exporter is used. Let's go over this statement in a little more detail.

First, we define a package to export names:

```
1 package MyPackage;
2 use Exporter;
3 @EXPORT = (my_sub, my_sub2);
```

and then use:

```
use MyPackage;
```

in a script. Now your calling package (`$callpkg`) is main, the package where Exporter is used (`$pkg`) is `MyPackage`, and the type of symbol (`$sym`) is `''`. The upshot is that this expression evaluates as:

```
*{main::my_sub} = \&{MyPackage::my_sub};
```

Now, if you want to call `MyPackage`'s version of `my_sub`, you simply say:

```
my_sub();
```

Because the glob statement inside the exporter has aliased it for you, Perl knows which statement you mean. If you understand how this works, you understand much about the malleability (and usefulness) of Perl. If it isn't quite clear, go through it a couple of times, or even look at the Exporter.pm module. Your Perl skills will improve immeasurably if you understand what this module is doing.

How Perl Runs Your Program, and a Discussion of BEGIN/END

This section is devoted to folks who need to have a more complete picture of the sequence of events that occurs when Perl actually runs your programs, in other words, the steps that occur between when you type **script.p** and when Perl executes your program. This information can be extremely helpful in finding solutions to otherwise inexplicable problems, especially for people doing CGI programming. (CGI programs usually do not run by people typing them, but instead have a server run them, which can cause much confusion.)

Perl Compilation Steps

Exactly what happens when a Perl script is executed? Perl has two distinct steps in parsing a given script: compile time and run time.

Compile time is when Perl turns scripts or programs into what is called a parse tree. A *parse tree* is the internal representation of code that can be understood by the operating system, and is optimized by compilation. *Run time* takes the internal representation and actually executes whatever parse tree the interpreter came up with.

This simple picture is complicated quite a bit by the fact that Perl provides two special routines: BEGIN { } and END { }.

These routines allow you to have the usual order of events subverted such that some blocks of code are executed before anything else (BEGIN) and some blocks are executed last (END). In other words, if you put a BEGIN block anywhere in your code, Perl will parse and execute that piece of code before any of your other code is compiled. For example:

```
1 print "This will print second!\n";
2 BEGIN
3 {
4     print "This will print first!\n";
5 }
```

prints:

```
This will print first!
This will print second!
```

even though the `This will print first!` line comes after the `This will print second!` line.

Likewise, if you say:

```
1 END
2 {
3     print "This will print second!\n";
4 }
5 print "This will print first!\n";
```

you will get the same results (print second after print first) even though the END block comes before the print.

What is happening here is not simply semantics (i.e., Perl is not rearranging the code so that all BEGIN blocks happen first, and all the END blocks happen last). Instead, Perl is actually treating all BEGIN and END blocks as separate programs, much like eval does later. In other words, if you say:

```
1 BEGIN
2 {
```

```
3      print "Program #1\n";
4 }
5 print "Program #2\n";
6 END
7 {
8      print "Program #3\n";
9 }
```

these are actually three separately compiled programs, such that the BEGIN block is checked for syntax and executed first; the main body of the code (Program #2) is checked for syntax and executed; and finally the END block is checked for syntax and executed. The difference between this and simply writing three separate Perl scripts is that the BEGIN blocks and END blocks can communicate with the main process through variables or subroutines.

If you say:

```
1 BEGIN
2 {
3      $ENV{'PERL5LIB'} = "/my/path/to/perl";
4 }
5 print $ENV{'PERL5LIB'};
```

then this will first set the PERL5LIB key in the environment, and the print statement will output:

```
/my/path/to/perl
```

because the variables and such are shared.

The following list gives the exact order of what is going on in these situations. You will find it helpful for tracking down problems.

- For each given BEGIN block:
  - Step 1: Compile the given BEGIN block (this includes use as well).
  - Step 2: Run the given BEGIN block.
- For each END block defined (in the opposite order defined 'backwards'):
  - Step 1: Compile the given END block.
- For code outside of a BEGIN or END block:
  - Step 1: Compile the main code.
  - Step 2: Run the main code.
- For each END block defined (in the opposite order):
  - Step 1: Run the given END block. Also do this on the case that the program terminates abnormally (due to a die).
- Do global cleanup.
- Exit.

Hence, if your program is:

```
1 BEGIN
2 {
3      print "Hmmm.. this works";
4 }
5 print "This does too....\n";
6 END
7 {
8      print "Syntax ERROR!!!!\n
9 }
```

it outputs:

```
Hmm...this works
```

when run and then dies with a syntax error because END blocks are compiled before the main program is run.

More on Perl Parsing

Let's look at two common places of which you should be aware detailing how Perl parses programs.

1. When using modules.
2. When running noninteractive Perl. This is a common practice among CGI programmers (in which the computer is executing the scripts, not you).

Modules

In Chapter 14, we discuss how modules work, but for now, let's look at how modules relate to BEGIN {} and END {}. It is important to understand the Perl parsing order when programming with modules. For example, if you say something like:

```
use MyModule;
```

then, you are actually saying:

```
1 BEGIN
2 {
3      require MyModule;
4      eval("MyModule->import()");
5 }
```

where `import` is a user-defined function that may or may not exist in a package. That is why it is wrapped in an eval.

Therefore, modules are actually BEGIN blocks in disguise. This code:

```
1 use Config;
2 if ($Config{'osname'} =~ m"Win")
3 {
4      use WindowsModule;
5 }
6 else
7 {
8      use UnixModule;
9 }
```

is not going to work because use statements are inherently inside BEGIN blocks, the if ($Config' test is ignored, and there is an attempt to import *both* modules. This code turns into something like:

```
1 use WindowsModule;
2 use UnixModule;
3 if ($Config{'osname'} =~ m"Win")
4 {
5 }
6 else
7 {
8 }
```

This means that the program dies on the module that does not exist on the other platform.
Instead, you are going to have to say:

```
1  BEGIN
2  {
3      use Config;     # uses the module config which tells you if a certain
4                      # system is being used. This tells you what is or is
5                      # not on your system.
6      if (($Config{'osname'} =~ m"Win")   # look at OS type.
7      {
8          require 'NTModule.pm'; NTModule::import();
9      }
10     else
11     {
12         require 'UNIXModule.pm'; UNIXModule::import();
13     }
14 }
```

In other words, avoid the use statement and put everything in a BEGIN block. This is kind of messy, because you
have to put this block of code inside every script you want to use. An even better approach is:

```
package GenericModule;
use Config;

sub import
{
    # code up above... (lines 3-13)
}
1;
```

Now, when people use the package GenericModule in their code, all they have to say is:

```
use GenericModule;
```

and the details of what is Unix and what is NT will be hidden from them.

Other Uses of BEGIN/END

You will find quite a few uses for BEGIN and END once you get used to them. Suppose that you have a Perl script
that creates temporary files while checking on the status of various systems (pseudocode—you need to define
system_status() and network_down()):

```
1  my @systems = ('sampson', 'zulu', 'bravo','charlie');
2
3  my $system;
4
5  foreach $system (@systems)
6  {
7      my $fh = new FileHandle("> /tmp/system.$ext");
8      print $fh "Status of System: ".system_status($system);# prints status.
9      die "Fatal Error!!!\n" if (network_down());    # dies if network down.
10 }
11
12 &email_status_and_cleanup();
```

As it stands, this program has a flaw. What happens if the network goes down in line 9? Then `email_status_and_cleanup()` will *never* get called. `die` causes the script to terminate immediately.

There are two potential solutions to this problem. One is to pair the call to `email_status_and_cleanup` with the error, as in:

```
1 if (network_down())
2 {
3     email_status_and_cleanup();
4     die "Fatal Error!\n";
5 }
```

But this is no good if you have several separate calls to `exit()`, because you will need to copy the call to the function `email_status_and_cleanup()` to many places, which, of course, raises the chance for programmer error. What happens if you forget to call this function someplace?

It may also be feasible to say:

```
1 die_and_cleanup("Fatal Error!\n");
2
3 sub die_and_cleanup
4 {
5   my (@messages) = @_;
6   email_status_and_cleanup();
7   die "@messages\n";
8 }
```

But this is also a little unclean. Wrappers such as this are helpful, but suppose we want to catch several different types of errors? Then we would have to have several wrapper functions.

Note

We will see when we get to Chapter 23, "Perl Debugging Tips" that Perl has a variety of ways of dying. We even saw one of these above: **carpout** makes the script die in the form of an HTML page, for example.

END is the perfect solution here. END provides a convenient way of doing something right before the program exits, whether that program dies, exits, or whatever. It is important to note that END blocks will *not* be executed if a signal kills the program. Short of a kill signal or a syntax error in your main program, Perl guarantees that the following code:

```
1 END
2 {
3     &email_status_and_cleanup();
4 }
```

will *always* call `email_status_and_cleanup()`, because it is not part of the main execution cycle. In fact, this function occurs between the end of the main program and the exit of the program.

Likewise, suppose you wish to make sure that two programs do not run at the same time. You could do something like this:

```
1  BEGIN
2  {
3      exit if (-e "marker");
4      my $fh = new FileHandle("> marker"); close("marker");
```

```
 5  }
 6
 7  # ..... do your stuff
 8
 9  END
10  {
11      my $status = unlink("marker") ||
12      die "Couldn't delete marker!\n";
13  }
```

At the very beginning of the program, a marker file is created, and the `exit if (-e 'marker');` statement assures us that no second process will be able to start. Then, after the program exits, the marker is deleted so the program is runnable again.

> This scheme is fairly good for small processes. However, this could fail if multiple processes run at exactly the same time, since both processes would create the file **marker** at the same time. See the **perlfunc** man page under `flock` for a more bulletproof, if less portable, way of doing this (Unix only). We also consider this when making a mutex (mutually exclusive resource) object.

BEGIN and END are also good for timing programs, notifying people upon start and completion of a process, and diagnosing the output of a process, among other things.

Noninteractive Perl

The previous section demonstrated that knowing the order of execution within Perl can be helpful. Once you learn it, you can use it to your advantage with BEGIN/END. Another place where this knowledge comes in handy is when the machine executes the code, rather than a human (this includes CGI). The following, typed at the keyboard:

```
prompt% perl script.p
```

executes Perl with a hidden dependency. The executing program is dependent on the environment in which it is running. For example if **script.p** consists of:

```
#!/usr/local/bin/perl5

system("run_program");
```

then you are dependent on your PATH variable to find `run_program` (in both windows NT and Unix). If you don't have your PATH variable set correctly, this program will not run correctly: It will say `run_program not found`.

This all seems self-explanatory. However, things become more complicated when these same scripts do not run from the command line.

Trust me, you will find out exactly how dependent your scripts are on the environment in which they are running when you run this from a Web-server or a cron job! And it can be quite a struggle to remove these dependencies.

Let's look at a place where the environmental variables usually come into play. Listing 11.7 is a small, convenient CGI script that prints out the environment in which http servers run their scripts.

Listing 11.7

env_printer.p

```perl
1   #!/usr/local/bin/perl5
2
3   use CGI;                      # Uses CGI module
4
5   my $page = new CGI;          # makes an instance of the CGI module
6   print $page->header;         # prints out header for the page
7
8   print $page->start_HTML(     # what will show up on the top of the browser
9            -title=>'Environment Printer',
10           -BGCOLOR=>'white');
11
12
13  foreach $key (keys %ENV)      # print out the environment
14  {
15      print "$key= $ENV{$key}\n<br>\n";
16  }
17  print $page->end_HTML;        # end the page.
```

All Listing 11.7 does is create a Web page that shows the environment in which the script was run. Let's look at the differences when this is run from the command line, as shown in the following code and in Figure 11.2.

```
prompt% env_printer.p
```

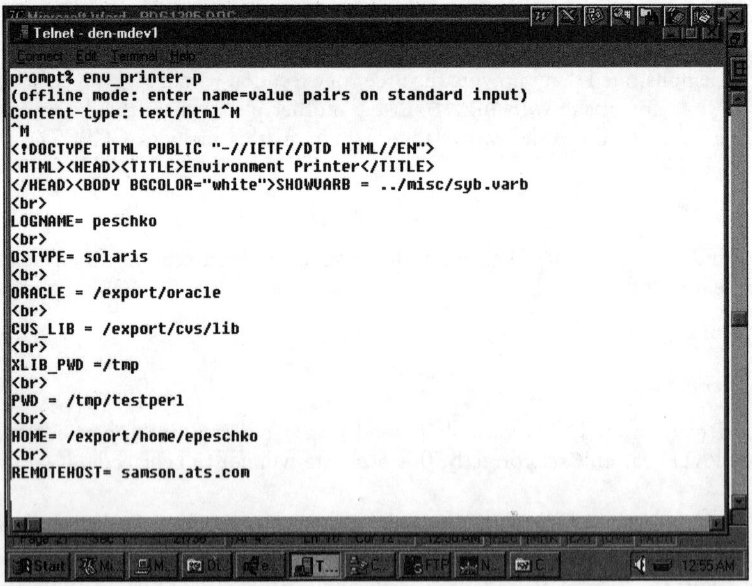

Figure 11.2

Output of

env_printer.p

at Command Line

```
prompt% env_printer.p
(offline mode: enter name=value pairs on standard input)
Content-type: text/html^M
^M
<!DOCTYPE HTML PUBLIC "-//IETF//DTD HTML//EN">
<HTML><HEAD><TITLE>Environment Printer</TITLE>
</HEAD><BODY BGCOLOR="white">SHOWVARB = ../misc/syb.varb
<br>
LOGNAME= peschko
<br>
OSTYPE= solaris
<br>
ORACLE = /export/oracle
<br>
CVS_LIB = /export/cvs/lib
<br>
XLIB_PWD =/tmp
<br>
PWD = /tmp/testperl
<br>
HOME= /export/home/epeschko
<br>
REMOTEHOST= samson.ats.com
```

And now look what happens when it is run from the CGI prompt (Figure 11.3).

Figure 11.3
Output of
env_printer
via Scripts

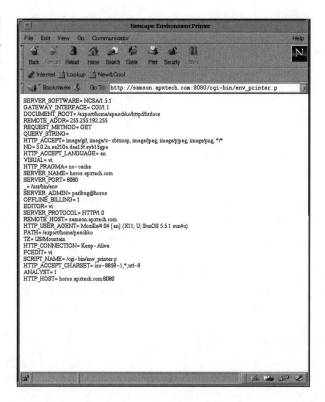

As you can see, the environments are totally different. In particular, the paths, when **env_printer.p** is run under the server, reflect the environment at the time the server was compiled. Therefore, any Perl script with dependencies on environmental variables that aren't in this list will not work.

This behavior brings up the following two problems for CGI developers.

Problem #1: Extensions for Third-Party Software

Consider the situation in which it is desired to add an extension for a database, or some other third-party software onto a site, as in Listing 11.8:

Listing 11.8
nifty_dbase.pl

```
1 use CGI;
2 use Sybase::DBlib;
3
4 my $page = new CGI;
5 my $sybLogon = new Sybase::DBlib($user, $password, $server);
```

Listing 11.8 will not work because in order to get a database connection, the Sybase::DBlib object needs to have access to environmental variable SYBASE that tells it where the database is located on the machine. Also, depending on how Sybase was installed, Sybase::DBlib may need the variable LD_LIBRARY_PATH to correctly link with Perl.

Thus, the problem is how to add `LD_LIBRARY_PATH` and `SYBASE` so the script knows about them.

Problem #2: Adding Include Paths for Libraries

Suppose you want to put together your own libraries in a certain location, and use them in a CGI script:

```
1 use CGI;
2 use lib "$ENV{MY_LIBRARIES}";
3
4 use MyObject;
5 $myobject = new MyObject();
6
7 $page = new CGI;
```

This will not work either. The environmental variable `MY_LIBRARIES` will not be found by the CGI script (since it was not compiled with the server), and `MyObject` will not be loaded. Both examples will blow up when you try to access them, giving the following result:

```
Internal Server Error:
The server encountered an internal error or misconfiguration.
```

which is the server's way of dealing with all the error messages a Perl script is generating (instead of sending HTML data). What is really happening is something like:

```
Can't locate MyObject.pm in @INC at myscript line 3.
BEGIN failed--compilation aborted at myscript.pl  line 3.
```

where the Perl script prints this out to `STDERR` and the browser isn't smart enough to recognize this as an error. How do you add the environmental variable `MY_LIBRARIES` to your HTML script?

Note

Of course, the reason for this behavior is security. If you let the cron job inherit the environment of the user, or let the http server inherit the environment of the user who runs the httpd, then, theoretically, a malevolent user could slip in a command of his or her own choosing, and run it against your computer with the authority of the http server. By restricting the environment of the server, you reduce the loopholes, and the threat of the attack is minimized.

Paranoid? Yes. Justifiable? Probably. Regardless, it is a fact of life, and we must deal with it while programming. Also it may (or may not) be as simple a solution as tacking on the correct environmental variables to a script that is not working.

The preceding two examples are part of a class of problems that a Perl script faces, namely, questions of *timing*. When, exactly, do things happen in a Perl script? In these two examples, we needed to add three different environmental variables to make the scripts work. The obvious solution (adding the environmental variable in the body of the script itself) may or may not work.

Solutions Using BEGIN/END

Surprisingly, adding these three environmental variables to a Perl script creates three separate problems, which require different solutions. They can be classed as:

1. Environmental variables that can be set inside the Perl script itself. For example, the environmental variable SYBASE, which is necessary for Sybase::DBlib to find the location of the databases.
2. Environmental variables that need to be set before the compilation step. For example, the environmental variable MY_LIBRARIES, which is necessary to find the package MyObject before running the program.
3. Environmental variables that need to be set before the Perl script runs. For example, the environmental variable LD_LIBRARY_PATH, which is necessary for Perl to find the C library associated with Sybase::DBlib. Another example is: PERL5LIB, which is looked at only once by Perl, when the Perl program starts.

Let's look at solving each of these in turn.

Solution 1: Environmental Variables Needed at Run Time

$ENV{SYBASE} was needed by the program to tell the Sybase module where to point to its database. Here, the solution is easy. Since the problem is a run-time problem, and Perl executes its statements sequentially, all we have to do is set the variables. These variables could be set at any time. The following code:

```
1 $ENV{'SYBASE'} = '/usr/lib/sybase';
2 $dbconnection = new Sybase::DBlib('user','password', 'SERVER');
3
4 $ENV{'SYBASE'} = '/usr/other/lib/sybase';
5 $dbconnection = new Sybase::DBlib('user','password', 'SERVER2');
```

could set up two simultaneous connections to databases, if so desired.

Solution 2: Environmental Variables Needed at Compile Time

To solve this problem, we again take advantage of the BEGIN block. Since we know that use blocks occur before the rest of the main program, and that they run sequentially, all we do is insert:

```
1 BEGIN
2 {
3   $ENV{'MY_LIBRARIES'} = '/use/my/libraries/now';
4 }
5 use Sybase::DBlib;
```

before the:

```
1 use lib "$ENV{'MY_LIBRARIES'}";
```

This forces the use to use the updated environment.

Solution 3: Environmental Variables Needed Before the Perl Script Is Run

Solving the problem of adding environmental variables needed before the script is run (such as LD_LIBRARY_PATH and PERL5LIB) is the most counter-intuitive of the bunch, and takes a bit of understanding of what is happening in the underlying environment.

After all, how do you add a definition to a Perl script that needs this definition before it executes? Seems like a catch 22, and it sort of is. The tricky part here is that you cannot use the following code to get around this problem:

```
1 BEGIN
2 {
```

```
3    $ENV{LD_LIBRARY_PATH} = '/correct/path/to/lib';
4 }
use Sybase::DBlib;
```

To understand why, consider the environment Perl runs in. It is a very basic fact of shell architecture that any script, program, binary, or whatever cannot change the parent environment in which it runs. This is a basic principle, but one that many people do not know, or vaguely comprehend. If your environment looks like:

```
prompt% env;
VARB1=1
VARB2=1
VARB3=1
```

and you write a script that looks like the following code and wipes out the environment:

```
undef %ENV;        # not necessarily the best thing to do!
```

if you run it, it will *not* affect your current workspace! When you say:

```
prompt% env_killer.p       # wipes out current environment
prompt% env;
VARB1=1
VARB2=1
VARB3=1
```

you get the same environment as before.

In other words, programs run in their own protected, safe environment. This is true cross-platform, Unix, DOS, or Windows NT. Pictorially, it looks like what is shown in Figure 11.4. The child is fenced in; it inherits all the environmental variables from its parent, but it is not allowed to change those variables.

Figure 11.4
Conceptual
Drawing of the
Shell Environment

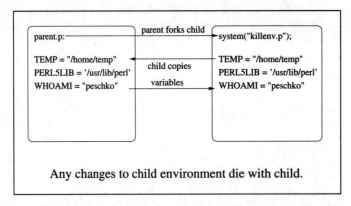

Any changes to child environment die with child.

In our case with LD_LIBRARY_PATH:

```
1 BEGIN
2 {
3 $ENV{LD_LIBRARY_PATH} = '1'
4 }
```

text looks like what is shown in Figure 11.5.

This will not work, because by the time the program starts, the thing that glues Perl together with outside libraries (the linker) has already found and used LD_LIBRARY_PATH. Hence, setting it in our process doesn't do a thing.

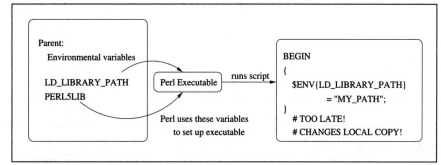

Figure 11.5
Caveats of
Running in the
Shell

What's a programmer to do? In this case we have two choices. The first is to compile the libraries statically rather than dynamically. This involves taking all the necessary libraries, and remaking Perl so that they are internal to Perl.

This solves our problem, because you have eliminated the dependency on finding the shared libraries, but it also makes a large executable, and is sometimes tough technically. Often, this is not an option, especially if the variable does not have to do with LD_LIBRARY_PATH (or libraries) at all, or you are using a precompiled Perl-like ActiveWare.

Another choice is to set the necessary variables, and then somehow trick the program into thinking that these variables are its own. To see how we can do this, let's take a look at our model of the environment Perl runs in.

This model has some limitations, but it does not say that we can't muck around in the child variable name-space. In particular, if we said something such as what is shown in Listings 11.9 and 11.10, it would print nothing.

Listing 11.9
parent.p

```
1 #!/usr/local/bin/perl
2
3 undef %ENV;
4 system("printenv.p");
```

Listing 11.10
printenv.p

```
1 #!/usr/local/bin/perl
2
3 foreach $key (keys %ENV)
4 {
5   print "$key => $ENV{$key}\n";
6 }
```

The **printenv.p** script is inheriting from its parent process (the script shown), and not from the shell proper. Therefore, we can use a pretty cool trick to force our original program to use the correct linker, as shown in Listing 11.11.

Listing 11.11
getlink.p

```
1 BEGIN
2 {
3     if ($ENV{'LD_LIBRARY_PATH'} eq '')
4     {
5         $ENV{LD_LIBRARY_PATH} = 'my_path';
6         exec($0);
7     }
8 }
```

This looks something like what is shown in Figure 11.6.

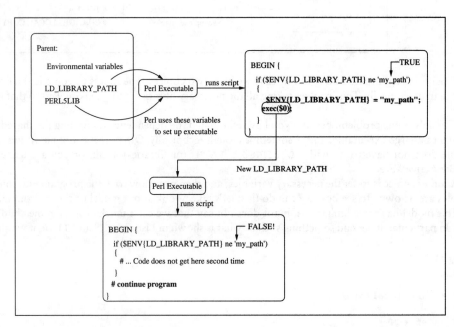

Figure 11.6
The Re-Execute Trick

See what this is doing? The first time around, it checks for an LD_LIBRARY_PATH variable. Because this variable is undefined, Perl goes ahead and defines it for us ($ENV{LD_LIBRARY_PATH} = 'my_path';), and then re-executes our program for us, keeping the modified environment intact. It forks off itself, so it inherits $ENV{'LD_LIBRARY_PATH'} from itself.

The exec re-executes the script, starting it over with the new environment. And since $ENV{'LD_LIBRARY_PATH'} is set the first time through, we don't go into an infinite loop. The child will re-execute, and since it finds LD_LIBRARY_PATH set—the child inherited it from its parent—Perl will ignore this BEGIN block and execute the rest of the code.

This is extremely useful because it makes Perl totally self-contained. We can internalize the environment we use inside the Perl scripts themselves, without resorting to wrappers, batch files, or other such inconveniences. Once you move your source code from one place to another seamlessly and silently, you will thank Perl for this power.

Using BEGIN for Debugging CGI

Finally, let's get rid of that very annoying "Internal Server Error" by using BEGIN:

```
An internal error occured, please check server configuration and try again.
```

The reason this occurs is because when you get an error such as:

```
Can't locate MyModule.pm in @INC at program_name.p
```

It is not a viable HTML page; hence, the complaint from the browser. By taking advantage of the fact that the BEGIN blocks come before the rest of the programs, we can make our errors turn into HTML pages!

We could do this by hand, but fortunately the CGI module provides us with a couple of really wonderful functions: carpout() and fatalsToBrowser(). Both functions will save you hours of tracking down bugs. Again, we can do this by using a BEGIN block. Insert the code shown in Listing 11.12 into any HTML program.

Listing 11.12
cgiDebug.p

```
1 BEGIN
2 {
3          use CGI::Carp qw (carpout fatalsToBrowser);
4          use FileHandle;
5          my $LOG = new FileHandle ( ">> /usr/local/lib/cgi/log/logname");
6          carpout($LOG);
7 }
```

and *voila*! Any time an error comes into your program, from any source, internal or external, it will be logged into the file pointed to by the filehandle object $LOG. Importing the function fatalsToBrowser redefines all the functions (die, confess, carp, and so on). With these two statements, you will trap both fatal errors (programming errors), or debugging output, getting displays like what is shown in Figure 11.7 for fatals.

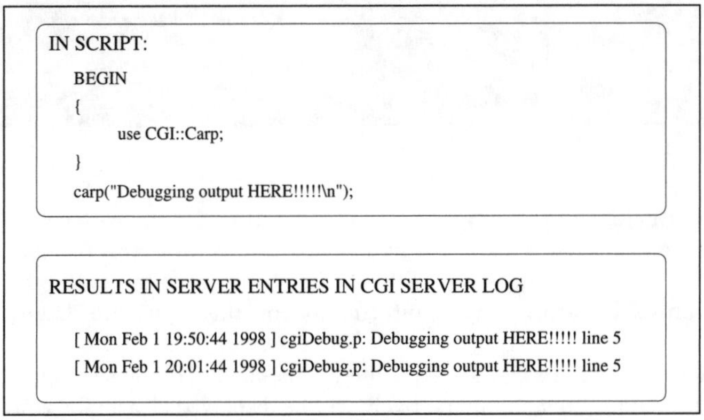

Figure 11.7
Fatals Output via
fatalsTo
Browser

```
IN SCRIPT:

  BEGIN
  {
       use CGI::Carp;
  }
  carp("Debugging output HERE!!!!!\n");
```

```
RESULTS IN SERVER ENTRIES IN CGI SERVER LOG

  [ Mon Feb 1 19:50:44 1998 ] cgiDebug.p: Debugging output HERE!!!!! line 5
  [ Mon Feb 1 20:01:44 1998 ] cgiDebug.p: Debugging output HERE!!!!! line 5
```

And, if you so desire, your own debugging output for debugging output will occur (see Figure 11.8).

Figure 11.8
Debugging
Output via
`carpout`

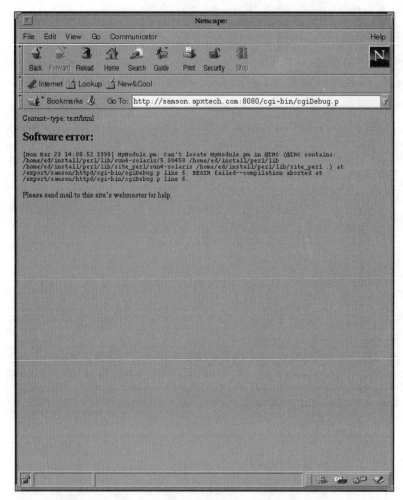

This is an extremely powerful function, and can save much time when dealing with environmental problems. You can test in the same environment that you are going to release your programs to (i.e., the cgi-bin server), which, as any systems engineer can tell you, is about 90 percent of the battle in developing systems. Read the documentation thoroughly on **CGI::Carp** for more information on this. This site details quite a few more useful tricks.

If you use `carpout` and `fatalsToBrowser`, your life will be made 10 times easier, because the environmental errors you get when running scripts noninteractively will be displayed clearly for you.

Summary of BEGIN/END and Flow Control

BEGIN and END are functions Perl provides in order to give the programmer more flexibility in deciding when things are to be done. BEGIN blocks are always compiled and run first, whereas END blocks wait until everything else in your main program is done running before they kick in.

Flow control, the process of understanding each individual step that Perl is doing to avoid coding mistakes, is an important thing to understand for Web programmers and folks that write cron jobs. (It doesn't hurt to learn it even if you do neither of these things.) Basically, Perl program execution has two steps: run time and compile time. Each step does several different things, but the main thing to remember is that the compile time step will not catch errors where subroutines are undefined.

eval

eval is a function in Perl with much significance, because it is used in Perl in a myriad of ways. eval takes a string, turns it into a Perl program, and executes it.

Hence, if you say:

```
$line = 'print "Eval par-excellence!\n";';
eval ($line);
```

this will go ahead and execute the line $line, printing Eval par-excellence!. eval is one of the really cool things Perl inherited from the shell. Try doing that in any compiled language!

Principles of Using eval

There are three things to remember when using eval:

1. eval goes through exactly the same routine as Perl itself when started up. eval checks the syntax of the program, assigns variables, and does everything short of starting a new process. Hence, there might be a considerable bit of overhead in using eval.

2. Although eval checks for syntax errors and fatal errors (such as die), it does *not* terminate the main program when this occurs. Instead, it *traps* the errors in a special variable, called $@. Likewise, eval will return ' ' if it did not execute correctly, or 1 if it did. If you say:

```
my $status = eval('print "This Works because it is correct syntax\n";');
print $@;
```

then $status returns a 1 because the eval worked, and $@ will become ' '. This policy allows you to determine whether eval worked cleanly.

3. eval can (and does) use all the variables it inherits from the main program. Furthermore, if you make any variables inside the eval, they will transfer to the "outside" unless they are my variables. For example, if you say:

```
my $a = 1;
eval('$b = $a;');
print "$b\n";
```

this will print 1. However, if you say:

```
my $a = 1;
eval ('my $b = $a;');
print "$b\n";
```

it will print ' ', because the variable $b is a my variable and has gone outside of the scope of the eval.

Usage of eval

You can do several things with eval. Let's go over some of them now.

Checking for Features on a System

One of the really cool things eval provides is the ability to check what system you are in, or what resources that system has.

Because eval can check to see whether code will pass or fail, and then return a status to the main script, you can wrap calls in an eval, and then make decisions based on what it returns. For example:

```
eval ("require 'OLE'") || ($system = 'Unix');
```

is a pretty safe way to determine whether or not you are on an ActiveState variant of Perl. After all, Unix doesn't have a built-in version of OLE, and so this statement will evaluate to false, short-circuit, and set the system to Unix. Likewise:

```
eval("getpriority(0,0);1;") || ($system = 'Unix');
```

will give you a pretty good idea of whether or not you are in a Unix system.

Using eval this way, knowing that certain Perl functions are not universals, and providing an alternative to those functions, is an extremely good way to bulletproof your programs.

Using Perl Syntax to Enhance User Interfaces

One of the smallest, yet most powerful Perl scripts out there is the **rename** Perl script (written by Larry Wall). It looks something like Listing 11.13 (I've made it a little more verbose):

Listing 11.13
rename.p

```
1 my $operation = shift (@ARGV);
2 foreach $argument (@ARGV)
3 {
4     $_ = $argument;
5     eval ("$operation");
      die "You must give a legal regular expression ($@)" if ($@);
6     $new_argument = $_;
7     if ($argument ne $new_argument)
8     {
9         rename($argument, $new_argument) || print "Couldn't rename $argument to $new_argument!\n";
10    }
11 }
```

This script is basically giving you the power to manipulate filenames as if they were strings in Perl. If you say:

```
prompt% rename 's"\.bak$"";' *.bak;
```

this script will take all the **.bak** files and get rid of the extension. Likewise:

```
prompt% rename 'tr"[A-Z]"[a-z]";' *
```

will rename all of your uppercase files to lowercase ones.

How is this working? The key to this script's power is in line 5:

```
eval ("$operation");    # was $ARGV[0]
```

The `foreach` loop (line 4) goes through each filename, and filters that filename through what was passed as the first argument. Hence `rename 's"\.bak"";' *.bak` makes the `eval` statement:

```
eval('s"\.bak"";');
```

which has the effect of chopping off the **.bak** from the end of the input. The results of that filter (**home.bak** becomes **home**) are then tested for equivalency. If they aren't equivalent, a rename is required, and the `rename` function is called (line 9).

Kind of cool, right? You can use similar tricks to give database access programs the power of Perl syntax. You could enhance `grep` to take a similar sort of syntax, such that:

```
grep 'm"[a-z]"' filelist
```

would find all files with lowercase letters in them.

You could make Perl-ish calculators or Perl-ish shells in which Perl input becomes the interface to the world, and people type in Perl expressions as if they were commands. You could make intelligent **config** files, which have Perl in them to drive other Perl scripts.

More information on what you can do with `eval` is in the **perlfunc** man page.

Increasing Program Performance

Since `eval` code can be generated before it is executed, you can use Perl to generate tons of code. This process is done for speed rather than readability.

Suppose you have files of the following form:

```
123123|Ron Cassidy|2552 Sycamore Street
144123|Thea Thompson|15 Orchard
155152|Helen Gaskell|544 Kentucky Court
```

This is a fairly common file format when dealing with databases. The file above is a flat file; it consists of data that will be loaded into a database, and loaded by a "bulk copy" command.

For various reasons, sometimes doing a bulk copy is not the most advantageous method. Instead, you may want to interact directly with the SQL engine and say something like:

```
insert into table message_text (123123, 'Ron Cassidy', '2552 Sycamore Street');
insert into table message_text (144123, 'Thea Thompson','15 Orchard');
insert into table message_text (155152, 'Helen Gaskell','544 Kentucky Court')
```

This also inserts data into the database, but does it in a safer way. Those of you who are database administrators will see that this fires off triggers (preserving data integrity), whereas the using bulkcopy doesn't.

This example shows a pretty good use of eval. In it we want to treat characters and integers differently (and floats, and dates, and so on). We want to put single quotes (`'`) around characters, and no quotes around integers. Assume that `$line` holds a line of input from the **input** file, and `@types` holds the type of each field (integer or character). Whereas previously:

- `$type[0]` equals integer
- `$type[1]` equals character
- `$type[2]` equals character

now, to generate these insert statements, we could say something like what is shown in Listing 11.14.

Listing 11.14
genInsertInefficient.p

```
1    my @types = ('integer', 'character','character');
2    my $line;
3    while ($line = <FD>)
4    {
5        my @rows = split(/\|/, $line);
6        my ($xx, @types);
7        for ($xx = 0; $xx < @rows; $xx++)
8        {
9                if ($types[$xx] eq 'character')
10               {
11                   $rows[$xx] = "'$rows[$xx]'";
12               }
13       }
14       local($") = ",";
15       my $insertStatement = "insert into table $table values (@rows)\n";
16       print "$insertStatement\n";
17   }
```

This is a little complicated, but the heart of the code is in lines 8–13, where we decide whether or not something is a character field. We check the type of the field, and if it is a character, we put quotes around it. However, the main thing to notice about this code is that it is so inefficient. For each row in the file that we are transmuting, we perform:

1. A complete loop through each element in that file.
2. A potential data copy
3. An `if then` statement.

This could translate into much lost time. Going through each element, one at a time, to find out what type it is is redundant and unnecessary. We would be better off knowing ahead of time what types the different fields are by saying something such as the following:

```
1    my $line;
2    local($") = ",";
3    while ($line = <FD>)
4    {
5        my @rows = split(/\|/, $line);
6        $rows[1] = "'$rows[1]'";
7        $rows[2] = "'$rows[2]'";
8        print "insert into table message_text values (@rows)\n";
9    }
```

where we know ahead of time that fields 1 and 2 are character fields. This way, we need not loop through the fields to find out what we already know. The code as it stands, though, is low-level, simple, and repetitive. If we had a hundred different tables, we would have to write a hundred different subroutines—not a fun thing. Hence, we generate it on the fly.

This is a job for eval. Listing 11.15 shows an implementation using eval.

Listing 11.15
genInsert.p

```
1 #!/usr/local/bin/perl5
```

```
2  my $code =
3  'local($") = ",";
4  while ($line = <FD>)
5  {
6      my (@rows) = split(/\|/, $line);
7  ';
```

This generates the header—no matter what the table or circumstances, this will always be the same. Note that this is a big variable assignment: The single quotes around lines 3–7 assign everything there to the variable $code. The code in Listing 11.16 adds on the code (line 13) each time a character field has been found.

Listing 11.16
genInsert.p (continued)

```
8      my $xx;
9      for ($xx = 0; $xx < @rows; $xx++)
10     {
11         if ($type[$xx] eq 'character')
12         {
13             $code .= '$rows[$xx] = \'$rows[$xx]\'' . "\n";
14         }
15     }
16     $code .= 'print "insert into table message_text values (@rows)\n";' . "\n";
17     $code .= '};';
18
19 eval $code;
```

When we get to the eval part of the processing, Perl has created the program for us. Instead of directly reading the variables, we create the program via making the Perl program itself the programmer.

Optimally, this avoids an entire order of magnitude in running times, and also some extra if then statements that consume running time. This can make the difference between a process taking a day or an hour when the file sizes that you traverse are megabytes upon megabytes in size.

This "unrolling of the loop" type of programming is pretty common in Perl, especially when you are dealing with splitting and manipulating files. If you think of places where Perl can write your code for you, you are in good shape and your productivity in certain tasks will skyrocket.

Summary of eval

eval is Perl's way of making strings into executable programs. Object-oriented types could think of it as the "method which makes a string an executable and runs that executable." Simply say:

```
eval($code);
```

and *voila*! whatever is in the string $code will be treated like a Perl program.

eval has quite a few uses and we took a look at three major categories:

1. Trapping errors in Perl code and doing cross-platform development.
2. Sprucing up a user interface with the power of Perl's syntax.
3. Generating code optimized for speed, not readability.

"Any problem can be solved by a layer of indirection," or so goes the saying, and eval shows this quite nicely. You can get quite complicated with eval, and usually that complication is a small negative compared with the benefits in code power you obtain. But you can overdo it. The worst I have gotten with eval is to have programs that generated programs, that, in turn, generated programs of their own. I don't suggest doing that (for your own sanity's sake), but the power for you to do so is there.

Summary

This chapter contained Perl concepts not easily tucked away in a box. However, these concepts are not trivial. In fact, knowledge and usage of these "odds and ends" will enable you to be a powerful, graceful Perl programmer.

# CHAPTER 12

Examples

In the introduction, I talked a little about the diverse way Perl has spread itself into the enterprise. Perl is a language with a couple of simple philosophy tenets:

- Expressability: being able to say what you mean without the language getting in the way.
- Humility: realizing that almost all good ideas have been implemented before, and searching for and finding ideas from these sources and incorporating them into Perl itself.
- Interoperability: being able to work easily with other tools.

These three tenets have paid off quite well, and now that you have seen 11 chapters of syntax, it is the time to see Perl in action. Here are quite a few Perl scripts for your perusal; modify them without compunction. That is the fourth tenet—public scrutiny of someone else's programming will do 90 percent of your work for you! (Please don't apply the tenet to college exams.)

Chapter Overview

This chapter concerns Perl scripts in action. We start with what are called "functional diagrams" that we'll use to clarify some of the logic in the longer scripts, and then we'll proceed to code. We have divided these scripts into nine different categories:

1. grep Programs
2. Text/File manipulation
3. Code generators

4. OLE (object linking and embedding)
5. Interacting with GUIs via Guido
6. Interacting with the Web via libwww
7. CGI scripting
8. Database programming with DBI
9. Creating GUI applications with Tk

In other words, start with what has been called the "traditional" role of Perl (text manipulation), and then proceed to items that are not normally assumed to be in Perl's native environment (Perl handles them quite well, though).

Realize, however, that these categories are relatively artificial. For example, we talk about a mail parser that can be programmed to get rid of junk mail. We code it as a simple Tk application with two buttons, and make it programmable so that you can enter into a file that does the parsing for you. What do you call this application? A code generator? A text/file manipulator? A GUI? It is all three of these things, but we choose the GUI because we have already talked about the other two aspects.

Anyway, enjoy. This chapter covers a rather large amount of territory, but I feel I owe it to the world in general to show that Perl is not just for one-liners anymore, and that there are quite a few real-world applications that fit hand-in-glove with Perl. Just realize that each of these categories probably could generate its own book. In some cases, it probably has.

I owe quite a few people for help and support on these examples. I have done a little bit of tweaking of their original applications, so blame me if it doesn't work, and I'll try to get it fixed.

Functional Diagrams

First, let's briefly mention a tool that we will use in some instances: The functional diagram.

Functional diagrams are diagrams that show what functions are calling other functions inside your programs. They are used to ensure that you know what you are doing, and that you have a fairly clean design for your code.

We will see many more of them as we get into the heftier pieces of code that we discuss in the OO section of this book.

If you have code that looks like the following:

```
a()
sub a {    b(); c();    }
sub b {    d();    }
sub c { print "END";  }
sub d { print "END";  }
```

then you have generated a functional diagram that looks something like Figure 12.1.

Figure 12.1

Sample Functional
Diagram

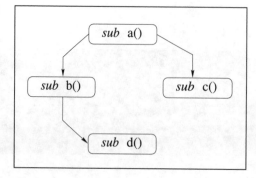

Hence, a() calls b() and c(), and b() calls d(): a nice clean hierarchy. This is what you want your functional diagrams to look like. If you see code like this:

```
a()
sub a {  b(); c();  }
sub b {  d();        }
sub c {  print "END"; }
sub d {  a(); c();    }
```

then you have generated a hierarchy that looks like Figure 12.2.

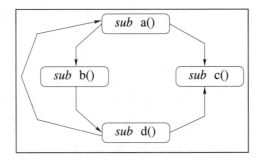

Figure 12.2
Functional
Diagram with
a Circular
Dependency

You want to avoid circular dependencies and cross-dependencies like this, at almost all costs. Circular dependencies make your code less changeable: If you change a component in d(), then you also have to potentially change a() and c(). Nice hierarchies limit your susceptibility to change.

Anyway, keep functional diagrams in mind. When we get to some of the more complicated scripts below, we will use them as an explaining tool.

grep Programs

One of the original tasks Perl was designed for was, of course, text manipulation. If you had gigabytes of text, then it was—and is—a short step to use Perl to actually find anything in that vast amount of information. The first type of program we will consider here is the grep.

Note If you are interested about word history, grep stands for globally search for a regular expression; print it out. It comes from ed the command-line editor.

When actually writing code, grep is infinitely useful for finding one's way through the detail inside the code, and getting a good picture of what the code is doing. For example, you can say:

```
prompt% grep custID <filelist>
```

where custId is a pattern, and filelist is the list of files that you are looking for custId in. The following command:

```
prompt% vi `grep -l custID <filelist>`
```

will actually let you look at all the files that contain the string custID. If you were editing code, this would help quite a bit.

Perl was, and is, used to build on that idea. With Perl, you can build a thousand specialized greps, each with its own personalized touch, and greps for different types of patterns. We implement two different types of grep next.

There's More Than One Way to Do It: Context grep

The first type of grep we will implement is the context grep. Notice that the preceding grep (that shows only one line) has limited use if you want to have an idea of a context for a given pattern.

Context grep is meant to change that. If you say something like:

```
C:<\> cgrep.p regular compdefinition
```

you will get output that looks like:

```
- - - - - - - - - - - - - - - - - - - - -

grep: tool a Unix command for searching files for lines matching a given regular
expression Named after the qed/ed editor subcommand "g/re/p" where re stands for
regular expression, to Globally search for Regular expression and Print the lines
containing matches to it. There are two other major variants, fgrep which searches
only for fixed strings and egrep which accepts extended RE's but is usually the

- - - - - - - - - - - - - - - - - - - - -
```

In other words, you get an idea of how the word is being used, so you can make a better judgment about whether that portion is important to you.

Since this is such a basic tool, it is also a good candidate for showing exactly how many different, yet equivalent, solutions you can derive in Perl. We will implement three separate and not necessarily equal solutions for the grep problem next.

One key point here will drive all of our solutions: Note that if we are not careful, we could get output like:

```
- - - - - - - - - - - - - - - - - - - - -

named after a theorem in calculus.
grep: tool a Unix command for searching files for lines matching a given regular
expression Named after the qed/ed editor subcommand "g/re/p" where re stands for
regular expression, to Globally search for Regular expression and Print the lines

- - - - - - - - - - - - - - - - - - - - -

grep: tool a Unix command for searching files for lines matching a given regular
expression Named after the qed/ed editor subcommand "g/re/p" where re stands for
regular expression, to Globally search for Regular expression and Print the lines
containing matches to it. There are two other major variants, fgrep which searches
only for fixed strings and egrep which accepts extended RE's but is usually the

- - - - - - - - - - - - - - - - - - - - -
```

Notice that the text is the same here. It looks as if we have double vision. This is quite annoying, and it happens if we do the simple thing, and just print two lines before and two lines after each time we see **regular**. Something like this:

```
for ($xx = 0; $xx < @lines; $xx++)
{
    if ($lines[$xx] =~ m"$pattern")
    {
        my ($low) = ($xx - 2 > 0)? 0 : $xx-2;
        my ($high) = ($xx + 2 > $#lines)? $#lines : $xx + 2;
        print "@lines[$low..$high];
    }
}
```

will lead to this doubling effect. To get the more useful squashing effect:

```
- - - - - - - - - - - - - - - - - - - - - -
grep: tool a Unix command for searching files for lines matching a given regular
expression Named after the qed/ed editor subcommand "g/re/p" where re stands for
regular expression, to Globally search for Regular expression and Print the lines
containing matches to it. There are two other major variants, fgrep which searches
only for fixed strings and egrep which accepts extended RE's but is usually the

- - - - - - - - - - - - - - - - - - - - - -
```

where the output is readable, we will need to be a bit more clever.

Context grep #1: via Regular Expressions

The first approach we can take to the context problem is to actually think of the entire context as one big regular expression. If our pattern was scout, the problem of matching the bold in:

```
boat cruise
relax breathe easy
campfire boundary waters
superior grandmarais
boy scout cooking
teepee camp fire
girl scout flintlock
woodsmoke tentpeg
merit badge mosquitos
samsonite tv
briefcase civilization
```

is a regular expression problem: matching the first three lines before the first occurrence of scout, and then continuing to match until we find two interrupted lines where scout does not occur as a pattern. Hence, we can load the entire file into a scalar, and simply treat the solution as a regular expression, as in Listing 12.1.

Listing 12.1
cgrepRegexp.p

```
 1  #!/usr/local/bin/perl5
 2
 3  use strict;
 4
 5  my $pattern = shift(@ARGV);
 6
 7  open(FD, "$ARGV[0]");
 8  undef $/;
 9  my $line = <FD>;
10  my ($beginning, $matched);
11
12  print "\n";
13  while (
14      $line =~ m{
15              (.*?)
16                  ($pattern)
17              (([^\n]*\n){0,3}[^\n]*?(?=$pattern)|([^\n]*\n){0,3})
18          }sgxo
19      )
```

```
20 {
21     my ($allBeforeText, $pattern2, $afterText) = ($1,$2,$3);
22
23   my ($beforeText) =($allBeforeText =~ m"((?:[^\n]*?\n){0,3}[^\n]*?)$"s);
24
25     print "----------------------------------\n"
26                 if ((!$beginning) || ($beforeText ne ''));
27
28
29   print "$beforeText$pattern2$afterText";
30
31     $beginning = 1;
32     $matched = 1;
33 }
```

We'll take this slow because the regular expressions in this are a handful. In all the following cases, what the regular expression matches is in boldface. First, lines 13–19 match:

```
boat cruise
relax breathe easy
campfire boundary waters
superior grandmarais
boy scout cooking
teepee camp fire
girl scout flintlock
woodsmoke tentpeg
merit badge mosquitos
```

(i.e., all the text from the beginning up to and including scout, plus the three lines after the pattern). Line 23 prunes the text before scout to:

```
relax breathe easy
boundary waters
campfire cooking
boy
```

and then line 29 prints the text we have found. On the second pass, the regular expression matches:

```
...
boy scout grandmarais
teepee superior
girl scout flintlock
woodsmoke tentpeg
```

and then prints this. Finally, on the third pass, it matches:

```
teepee superior
girl scout flintlock
woodsmoke tentpeg
merit badge mosquitos
samsonite tv
briefcase civilization
```

Line 29 prints the final text, plus a ------------ indicating that we are done.

Context grep #2: via References

The problem with the previous solution is that it is a bit slow (and just a bit unreadable). Regular expressions on the whole are pretty speedy, but in situations like this (where the regular expression gets quite complicated), the regular expression might end up doing a lot of backtracking. Hence, we might want to do this by references. Suppose we were trying to match the same text. We could turn something like:

```
boat cruise
relax breathe easy
campfire boundary waters
superior grandmarais
boy scout cooking
teepee camp fire
girl scout flintlock
woodsmoke tentpeg
merit badge mosquitos
samsonite tv
briefcase civilization
```

into two distinct matches, each with its own range. The first match would grab lines 2–6:

```
0   boat cruise
1   relax breathe easy
2   campfire boundary waters
3   superior grandmarais
4   boy scout cooking
5   teepee camp fire
6   girl scout flintlock
7   woodsmoke tentpeg
8   merit badge mosquitos
```

and the second match would grab lines 4–8:

```
2   campfire boundary waters
3   superior grandmarais
4   boy scout cooking
5   teepee camp fire
6   girl scout flintlock
7   woodsmoke tentpeg
8   merit badge mosquitos
9   samsonite tv
10  briefcase civilization
```

Now, if we keep track of all these matches, we could merge the two references together, thus removing all of the duplicate material:

```
2   campfire boundary waters
3   superior grandmarais
4   boy scout cooking
5   teepee camp fire
6   girl scout flintlock
7   woodsmoke tentpeg
8   merit badge mosquitos
```

Then we simply print out the distinct text.

The following script does this via references. It keeps track in an array, @matchedRange, of all such ranges that we will merge later. And then, at the end of each file we consider, the script merges these ranges, printing out blocks of code.

Listing 12.2
grepRef.p

```
1   #!/usr/local/bin/perl5
2
3   use Getopt::Long;
4   use FileHandle;
5
6   GetOptions
7   (
8       \%opt, "savelines=i", "filelist:s"
9   );
10
11  my $pattern = shift(@ARGV);
12
13  if (defined ($opt{filelist})) # files to open search.
14  {
15      my $fd = new FileHandle("$opt{filelist}") if ($opt{filelist});
16      chop(@files = <$fd>);
17  }
18  else
19  {
20      @files = @ARGV;
21  }
22
23  my $file;
24  my $sl = $opt{savelines} || 2;
25
26  foreach $file (@files)
27  {
28      my $fd = new FileHandle("$file") ||(print "Couldn't open $file!!!\n",next);
29      my @lines = <$fd>;
30
31      my ($xx, @matchRange);
32      for ($xx = 0; $xx < @lines; $xx++)
33      {
34
35          if ($lines[$xx] =~ m"$pattern"o)        # We've found a pattern
36          {                                       # Now we need to save surrounding
37      push                                        # line changes.
38      (
39          @matchRange, [
40              (($xx-$sl) > 0) ? $xx - $sl: 0,
41              (($xx+$sl) > $#lines) ? $#lines : $xx+$sl
42              ]
43      );
44          }
45      }
46      my $mr;
```

```
47      if (@matchRange)
48      {
49          print "$file<\\>n";
50
51          foreach $mr (@matchRange)
52          {
53              my $low  = $mr->[0];
54              my $high = $mr->[1];
55
56      foreach $xx ($low..$high)
57      {
58        if (!$printed{$xx})
59        {
60            print $lines[$xx];
61            $printed{$xx} = 1;
62        }
63      }
64          }
65          print "-------------------------------------------\n";
66          undef %printed;
67      }
68 }
```

Again, lines 37–43 grab the line range of what we want to eventually print, based on a match of our input pattern. And lines 56–62 keep track of the merge process. In particular, line 61 keeps track of a hash, which "tags" if a line has not been printed, so we print a line only once.

Context grep #3: via a Stack

Note

Idea and original code by Jan-Pieter Cornet (johnpc@xs4all.net).

What can we say about the second proposed solution? Well, it is more time-efficient (takes less time than the regular expression solution), but it sure isn't space-efficient. To get space efficiency, we need to move to the concept of a "shifting window."

Again, let's look at the sample text and what we want to match:

```
boat cruise
relax breathe easy
campfire boundary waters
superior grandmarais
boy scout cooking
teepee camp fire
girl scout flintlock
woodsmoke tentpeg
merit badge mosquitos
samsonite tv
briefcase civilization
```

What would it mean to have a stack here? Well, using a stack would involve keeping a limited history of what lines we matched before. Suppose you wanted to match three lines surrounding the pattern scout; you would first match the first three lines:

```
boat cruise
relax breathe easy
campfire boundary waters
superior grandmarais
boy scout cooking
```

and then shift through them, until you see a line that has scout in it, as in the following steps:

Step #1:

```
boat cruise
relax breathe easy
campfire boundary waters
superior grandmarais
boy scout cooking
```

Step #2:

```
boat cruise
relax breathe easy
campfire boundary waters
superior grandmarais
boy scout cooking
```

Now that you see scout, you then save the three lines in your stack (in boldface), and then get rid of the stack. You keep going:

Step #3:

```
boy scout cooking
teepee camp fire
girl scout flintlock
woodsmoke tentpeg
```

Step #4:

```
boy scout cooking
teepee camp fire
girl scout flintlock
woodsmoke tentpeg
```

and now, you save the two lines, because you have found the text scout again. In the process, you keep track of whether or not you have found three lines in a row without scout in them, at which point you print the lines you have saved.

Here is the code to do this, called **cgrepStack.p** (Listing 12.3).

Listing 12.3
cgrepStack.p

```perl
1   #!/usr/local/bin/perl5
2
```

```
 3  use strict;
 4
 5  my $line;
 6  my @stack;
 7  my @printed;
 8  my $countdown = 0;
 9
10  my $no;
11  if ($ARGV[0] =~ m"^\d+$")
12          { $no = shift(@ARGV) }
13      else
14          { $no = 3; }
15
16  my $pattern = shift(@ARGV);
17  $" = "";
18  my ($file, $fileprint);
19  foreach $file (@ARGV)
20  {
21      open(FD, $file);
22      while ($line = <FD>)
23      {
24          push(@stack, $line);
25          shift(@stack) if (@stack > $no);                # we get rid of a line
26                                                          # if stack too big
27
28          my $pushed;
29          if (($line =~ m"$pattern") && (@printed == 0))  # if pattern is found
30          {                                               # and we don't have
31                                                          # anything to print
32              $countdown = $no;
33              $pushed = 1;
34              push (@printed, @stack);                         # we push fact to printed stack
35          }
36          elsif ($line =~ m"$pattern")                    # if we find a new
37                                                          # occurrence before
38                                                          # print out
39          {
40              $countdown = $no;                           # we postpone
41          }                                               # printing out
42
43          if ($countdown > 0)                             # if we have not gone
44          {                                               # more than '$no'
45          if ($pushed == 0) { push(@printed, $line); }    # lines without seeing
46              else { $pushed = 0; }                       # pattern we push a
47              $countdown--;                               # line onto the stack
48          }                                               # to be printed.
49
50          if (($countdown == 0) && (@printed > 0))        # we are ready to
51          {                                               # print
52              if (!$fileprint) { print "$file:\n"; $fileprint=1; }
53                  print "--------------------\n";
54              print "@printed";
```

```
55              @printed = ();
56          }
57      }
58      if (@printed > 0)                          # print out
59          # remaining text
60      {
61          print "-------------------\n";
62          print "@printed";
63          @printed = ();
64      }
65      @stack = ();
66      $countdown = 0;
67      $fileprint = 0;
68      close(FD);                                  # end of file.
69 }
70
71 if (@printed > 0)
72 {
73      print "----------------\n";
74      print "@printed";
75 }
```

Lines 19–20 keep track of the stack, shifting as necessary. The rest of the lines keep track of what is to be printed and what is not to be printed. What can we say about this algorithm? Well, it definitely saves space. First, you might recognize that we are using:

```
while ($line = <>)
```

instead of:

```
for ($xx = 0; $xx < <\@>lines; $xx++)
```

which means we can save quite a bit of space. The only lines we need to store are the ones to be printed. Second, it is pretty fast. We are going through each line only once, and matching on that line twice. With a little optimization, we could probably bring this down to matching once as well. Therefore, this is probably the best of the three algorithms that we will see. We will use it next.

Using cgrepStack.p

Since this is the fastest algorithm that we came up with, let's give an idea of how it might be used. Coincidentally (and a very good example of using this script), I talked to someone about 6 months ago, and I had forgotten who had contributed the idea for this code.

Luckily, I have saved all mail I ever received, and to find out who had contributed the prototype code, I said:

```
prompt(/mail)% cgrepStack.p 10 'shift\(' Mail
```

The 10 means that I was looking for 10 lines of surrounding context, and the `'shift\('` means that I was looking for the pattern shift(. (Remember: These are Perl regular expressions, so you need to back-shift special characters like \ (.)

This can save you plenty of time for this type of problem (we could probably improve this version of cgrep a bit as well). I found that it was Jan-Pieter who in fact had contributed the code.

filegrep: Matching Multiple Files with Multiple Patterns

The second version of grep we will consider is called *filegrep*, which is useful in going in the opposite direction of cgrep: grabbing information on multiple patterns and summarizing it all into a report.

For example, suppose you had some code with a list of tables inside:

```
author
publisher
editor
binder
graphical_artist
```

and you want to find out:

1. A list of filenames where all the terms were used (each and every one).
2. Lines where one or more of the terms were used.
3. Files where none of the terms are used.

These issues are the staple of many computer science problems—migrating code to a new OS or tracking down changes in a data model—and, in general, they make you much more powerful in managing your data.

With the following script, you can do all these things. It is called **filegrep.p** because it supports the concept of having more than one pattern in a "pattern list" file, and more than one file in a "file list" file. Whereas in Unix you could say:

```
prompt% egrep 'a|b|c|d|e|f|g|h|i|j' *
```

with **filegrep.p** you could say:

```
prompt% filegrep.p -patlist patterns -filelist files
```

where `patterns` is a file that contains a list of patterns, and `files` is a file that contains a list of files. This script is quite useful on Unix, and is a lifesaver for doing development on NT, which has no real equivalent of 29
`filegrep.p`. Because it has been so useful in the past, it has sprouted quite a few options (Listing 12.4).

Listing 12.4
filegrep.p

```
1    #!/home/epeschko/perl50043/install/bin/perl
2
3    use FileHandle;
4    use Getopt::Long;
5    use strict;
6
7    my %varb;
8    my %already;
9    my ($opt, $usage) =
10       GetOptions
11          (
12              \%varb, 'filelist:s', 'patlist:s',
13              'show!','noshow!', 'and!', 'found!', 'notfound!' ,
14              'debug'
15          );
16
```

```
17
18  my ($file, $line);
19  my @files;
20  my @patterns;
21  my $pattern;
22  my $code;
23
24  if ($varb{'patlist'})                          # look for pattern list option
25  {
26      my $fd = new FileHandle("$varb{'patlist'}");
27      chop(@patterns = <$fd>);
28      close($fd);
29  }
30  else
31  {
32      @patterns = shift(@ARGV);
33  }
34
35  if ($varb{'filelist'})                         # look for file list option
36  {
37      my $fd = new FileHandle("$varb{'filelist'}");
38      chop (@files = <$fd>);
39      close($fd);
40  }
41  else                                           # files from command-line
42  {
43      @files = @ARGV;
44  }
45
46  @files = grep (!-d, @files);                   # strip one line directories
47
48  grep (s{   ([^\\])"   }{   $1\\"   }xg, @patterns); # we need to bacslash patterns
49                                                 # on command-line
50
51  $code = <<"END_OF_CODE";                       # generating code
52  my \$yy = 0;
53  foreach \$file (\@files)                        # @files comes from command
54                                                 # line, $file as well
55  {
56      my (\$matched, \$have) = (1,1);
57      my \$fd = new FileHandle("\$file");
58      my (\$marker, \@skip) = (0,());
59  #       print ("FILES: ", \$zz-1, "\\n") if ((\$zz++)%1000 == 0);
60      while (defined (\$line = <\$fd>))           # open each file
61      {
62          study(\$line);
63  #           print ("\tLINES: ", \$yy-1, "\\n") if ((\$yy++)%1000 == 0);
64  END_OF_CODE
65
66      my $xx = 0;
```

```
67   foreach $pattern (@patterns)                          # @patterns from command-line
68   {
69      if ($varb{'show'})
70      {
71         $code .="\t\t(print (\"\$file:\$line\"), next)
72            if (\$line =~ m\"$pattern\"o);\n";           # pattern $pattern is compiled
73                                                         # to a regexp
74      }
75      elsif ($varb{'noshow'})
76      {
77         $code .="\t\t(\$matched = 1, last ) if (\$line =~ m\"$pattern\"o);\n";
78      }
79      elsif ($varb{'nothave'})                           # various options generate
80                                                         # different code.
81      {
82         $code .= "\t\t(\$have = 1, last) if (\$line =~ m\"$pattern\"o);\n";
83      }
84      elsif ($varb{'and'})
85      {
86         $code .=
87   "\t\t(\$marker++, \$skip[$xx] = 1, \$marker == ${\($#patterns+1)} && last )
88                          if ((!\$skip[$xx]) && (\$line =~ m\"$pattern\"o));\n";
89         $xx++;
90      }
91      elsif ($varb{'found'})
92      {
93         $code .= "\t\t(print (\"$pattern\\n\"), \$already{$pattern} = 1)
94           if (\$line =~ m\"$pattern\"o && (!\$already{$pattern}));\n";
95      }
96
97      elsif ($varb{'notfound'})
98      {
99         $code .= "\t\t\$already{$pattern} = 1
100           if (\$line =~ m\"$pattern\"o && !\$already{$pattern});\n";
101      }
102      else
103      {
104         $code .="\t\t(print (\"\$file\\n\"), last)
105                if (\$line =~ m\"$pattern\"o);\n";
106      }
107   }
108   $code .=
109   "     }\n";                                           # end of pattern loop
110
111      if ($varb{'nothave'})                             # some code options have extra
112                                                         # functionality
113      {
114         $code .= "\n\t\tprint (\"\$file\\n\") if (!\$have);";
```

```
115      }
116      if ($varb{'noshow'})
117      {
118          $code .= "\n\t\tprint (\"\$file\\n\") if (!\$matched);";
119      }
120      if ($varb{'and'})
121      {
122          $code .= "\n\tprint (\"\$file\\n\") if (\$marker == ${\($#patterns+1)});";
123      }
124 $code .=
125 "
126      close(\$fd);
127 }                                          # end of file loop
128 ";                                         # end of code generation
129
130 if ($varb{'notfound'})
131 {
132      foreach $pattern (@patterns)
133      {
134 #        $code .= "\nprint \"$pattern :\$already{$pattern}:\n\";";
135          $code .="\nif (\$already{$pattern} != 1){ print \"$pattern\\n\"; }";
136      }
137 }
138
139 print $code if ($varb{'debug'});
140 eval $code if (!$varb{'debug'});
141 die $@ if $@;
142
```

filegrep.p's basic mechanism for working is code generation. If you say something like:

```
C:\> perl filegrep.p -patlist patterns -filelist files
```

where patterns contains:

```
pattern1
pattern2
pattern3
pattern4
pattern5
```

this generates the following code:

```
my $yy = 0;
foreach $file (@files)
{
    my ($matched, $have) = (1,1);
    my $fd = new FileHandle("$file");
    my ($marker, @skip) = (0,());
    while (defined ($line = <$fd>))
    {
        study($line);
        (print ("$file\n"), last) if ($line =~ m"$pattern1"o);
        (print ("$file\n"), last) if ($line =~ m"$pattern1"o);
```

```
            (print ("$file\n"), last) if ($line =~ m"$pattern1"o);
            (print ("$file\n"), last) if ($line =~ m"$pattern1"o);
            (print ("$file\n"), last) if ($line =~ m"$pattern1"o);
        }
        close($fd);
    }
```

The code it generates is pretty silly: a wrapper around a bunch of `if` statements. Lines 50–129 are the heart of this algorithm, starting at the "here document" of lines 50–62:

```
51  $code = <<"END_OF_CODE";
52  my \$yy = 0;
53  foreach \$file (\@files)
...
64  END_OF_CODE
```

and ending at the last `if` statement is where code is being generated. The heart of the flexibility is that different code is generated by different statements at the command-line. You can see this code generation in action by using the `-debug` flag, by saying:

```
prompt% filegrep.p -patlist pattern -filelist files -debug
```

which shows you the code generated, rather than executing the code.

Some uses of `filegrep.p` are listed next:

1. `filegrep.p pattern *` default that works like a regular grep, except it only prints filenames that have the pattern, rather than the line.
2. `filegrep.p -patlist patterns -show *` looks through all the files given by the expansion of `*` and actually shows the lines where a pattern inside the file **patlist** is given.
3. `filegrep.p -patlist patterns -filelist list -noshow` looks through all the files named inside **list,** and prints the ones that have one or more patterns inside them.
4. `filegrep.p -patlist patterns -filelist list -and` only lists filenames that have all the patterns contained inside the file **patterns.**

filegrep.p is my industrial strength tool to look for patterns. For me, it works wonders. If you are used to Unix and are working on NT, you can use **filegrep.p** along with **find2perl** to emulate much of the functionality you find on Unix.

Text/File Manipulation

Text/file manipulation is really a broader version of grep. The goal here is to transform data that you already know the structure of into something else that is useful.

This covers a slew of problems, and as Perl is the master of manipulating text in the first place, the number of applications Perl can support in this area is astounding. We cover the following five applications:

1. Indexing a file (so you can find occurrences of given words)
2. Comparing and contrasting directory structures
3. Deleting garbage files
4. Solving a simple cipher
5. Using a regular expression to match numbers

All of these are useful, some in their own right (I used a version of the indexing script on this book, for example). Others, like the regular expression to match numbers, you can use in your own code.

Indexing a File

Indexing a file is a major pain. It's hard to believe that, before the advent of computers, people actually made concordances of Shakespeare—where they listed every single word, and where it occurred in every play—by hand.

Of course, with Perl, the same concordances take about five minutes or less. (You can do a concordance in C as well, but writing the program might take as long as doing the concordance by hand!)

Here is a small program that does an index of where words are in documents, given the input files. If you say:

```
prompt% index.p -filelist file -wordlist words
```

where `file` contains a list of files you want to index, and `words` contains a list of words you care about, then Perl will produce a structure that looks like:

```
$VAR1 = {
          'shift' => [
                      './cgrepRef.p: 11',
                      './cgrepStack.p: 12',
                      './cgrepStack.p: 16',
                      './cgrepStack.p: 25',
                      './cgrepRegexp.p: 5'
                     ]
        };
```

I use **Data::Dumper** to dump out the data in a way that is sort of legible. You may wish to do more.

Listing 12.5
index.p

```
1    #!/usr/local/bin/perl5
2
3    use Getopt::Long;
4    use strict;
5    use Data::Dumper;
6    use FileHandle;
7
8    my (%opt);
9
10   GetOptions(\%opt, "--filelist:s", "--wordlist:s" ,     # more option handling
11                     "--page", "--line", "--delimiter");
12
13
14   my ($word, $words);                                    # going to be place to
15                                                          # store words
16   my (%inwords, %position);
17
18   if ($opt{'wordlist'})                                  # given word list flag?
19                                                          # Handles which words
20   {                                                      # to keep.
21       my $FH = new FileHandle($opt{'wordlist'});
22       foreach $words (<$FH>)
23       {
```

```
24                chop($word = $words);
25                $inwords{$word} = 1;
26          }
27    }
28
29    local($/) = ($opt{'page'})?    "        Page "          # we need some way to
30                                                            # 'count' pages
31            ($opt{'delimiter'})? $opt{'delimiter'}          # let's us define 'units'
32            ($opt{'line'})?        "\n"          :          # on which to index.
33                                   \n";
34
35
36    my ($file, $unit, @files);
37    if ($opt{'filelist'})                                   # which files are we
38                                                            # looking in
39    {                                                       # o'--filelist' argument
40        my $fh = new FileHandle($opt{'filelist'});
41        @files = <$fh>;
42    }
43    else
44    {
45        @files = @ARGV;
46    }
47
48    foreach $file (@files)                                  # for each file
49    {
50    my $fieldno = 0;
51        chomp($file);
52        my $fh = new FileHandle("$file") || next;
53
54        while (defined ($unit = <$fh>))                     # remember.. $ up above.
55        {
56            $fieldno++;
57            chop($line);
58            my @words = ($unit =~ m"((?:[\@\%\$]|\b)\w+)\b"sg);  # find all occurrences
59                                                                 # of all words
60            my $word;
61
62            foreach (@words) { tr"A-Z"a-z"; }              # make lower case
63            foreach $word (@words)
64            {
65                if (!$opt{'wordlist'} || $inwords{$word})
66                {
67                    push(@{$position{$word}}, "$file: $fieldno");  # mark where we
68                                                                   # saw word
69                }
70            }
71        }
72    }
73
74    print Dumper(\%position);                               # print out whole index
```

The key to this algorithm is in line 58, which splits what we are calling a *unit* into a series of words. They may be (not necessarily) preceded by an @, %, or $. This also allows for Perl variables to be indexed. In lines 62–71, we actually look to see if we want to process the word (line 65), and then push the information to about where the word is located onto a stack called $position (line 67). We go through each file, doing this for everything, and we finally print the whole data structure as found (line 74).

Other interesting things about this algorithm: Lines 29–33 actually let us index by other things, in addition to the line number. We can index by a different delimiter (if we say: -delimiter whatever on the command-line). Or, we can index by the special keyword Page, which happens to be something that the prints of this book were separated by. Combining this fact with the ability to automate the saving of this file into text (via OLE), with the context grepping we saw above, and, well, even a monster of a book like this wasn't too difficult to index.

Comparing and Contrasting Directory Structures

This script comes in quite handy when you are given a new installation of a package from another vendor. Suppose you have a piece of software, *Snappy Keys*, which happens to run your whole business software department. And one day, you get a new version of *Snappy Keys*, and it simply stops working.

There are two major ways to deal with this: One is to install the old software, tell *Snappy Keys* about it, and delay installing the new software until it is fixed. But this is a passive way and, unfortunately, sometimes it never gets fixed since the vendor of *Snappy Keys* can't tell what is wrong.

The second way is to troubleshoot the problem with *Snappy Keys*, and that is what the script in Listing 12.6 does. To use it, you have two parallel installations of products on disk; you specify, through an item called @G::WantedElements, exactly which elements you wish to compare. The script then goes through each sub-directory, comparing file by file, and noting the following:

1. Which files differ in the aspects that you mentioned via @G::WantedElements (default is size).
2. Which files exist in one distribution, but not in another.

With this information in hand, you can give the vendor an idea of where to look. (Surprisingly, I've found that vendors won't, or can't, do this type of analysis themselves. I wish vendors could do this; it would make them much more user-friendly.)

Anyway, this script works like a 'diff-r' in Unix, except 'that' by making GG::WantedElements anything you'd like, you can get a more detailed description of the differences between the two directions. Here's the longhand version, without thinking of reuse and 'File::Find'.

Listing 12.6
_dircompare.p

```
1    #!/usr/local/bin/perl5
2    #
3    use strict;
4    use DirHandle;
5    #
6    #%G::StatElements =
7    #            (
8    #                    'dev' => 0, 'ino' => 1, 'mode' => 2, 'nlink' => 3,
9    #                    'uid' => 4, 'gid' => 5, 'rdev' => 6, 'size' => 7,
10   #                    'atime' => 8, 'mtime' => 9, 'ctime' => 10, 'blksize' => 11,
11   #                    'blocks' => 12
12   #            );
13   # @G::WantedElements = ('mode','nlink','uid','gid','size','atime','mtime');
14   # @G::WantedElements = ('size');
```

```
15
16   my $firstRoot = $ARGV[0];
17   my $secondRoot = $ARGV[1];
18
19   die "Need Two Arguments!\n" if (@ARGV != 2);   # take two arguments at
20   filesystemDiff($firstRoot, $secondRoot);       # compare their command-line
21
22   sub filesystemDiff
23   {
24       my ($root1, $root2) = @_;
25
26       print "Comparing $root1 to $root2:\n";
27       print "-------------------------------\n";
28
29       my $diffs = diff($root1,$root2, 1);        # do the first comparison A to B
30       print @$diffs;
31
32       print "Comparing $root2 to $root1:\n";
33       print "-------------------------------\n";
34
35       $diffs = diff($root2,$root1, 1);           # then the second, compare B to A
36       print @$diffs;
37   }
38
39   sub diff
40   {
41       my ($dir1, $dir2, $reclevel) = @_;
42
43       my $diffs = [];
44       my $type1 = _type($dir1);                  # is this a file, direction, or doesn't it exist?
45       my $type2 = _type($dir2);
46
47   if ($type2 eq 'notexist')
48   { push(@$diffs, "\t" x $reclevel . "$dir2 does not exist\n");
49                              # put text on return stack
50
51   }
52   elsif ($type1 ne $type2)                       # different type of file:
53                                                  # one is directory, other file
54   {
55     push(@$diffs,
56     "\t" x $reclevel . "$dir1 is '$type1' => $dir2 is '$type2'\n");
57   }
58   elsif ($type1 eq 'file')
59   {
60     my $diff = statDiff($dir1, $dir2, $reclevel);  # check if files are same
61     push (@$diffs, $diff) if ($diff);
62   }
63   elsif ($type1 eq 'directory')
64   {
65     my $diff = statDiff($dir1,$dir2, $reclevel); # check if directories
66                                                  # are same
67
```

```
68    my $dh = new DirHandle($dir1);
69    my @filesAndDirs = $dh->read();
70    @filesAndDirs = sort by_type @filesAndDirs;
71    my $file;
72
73    foreach $file (@filesAndDirs)
74    {                                              # need to skip '.' and '..'
75        next if ($file eq '.');
76        next if ($file eq '..');
77        my $diff = diff("$dir1/$file","$dir2/$file", $reclevel+1);
78                                                    # go down a level
79        push(@$diffs, @$diff) if (@$diff);
80    }
81    }
82
83    return($diffs);
84    }
85
86  sub statDiff
87  {
88    my ($element1, $element2, $reclevel) = @_;
89    my $xx;
90    my $diffs1;
91
92    my (@stat1) = stat($element1);              # find out info about
93                                                 # each file seeing
94    my (@stat2) = stat($element2);              # globals for what is different
95
96    foreach $xx (@G::StatElements{@G::WantedElements})
97    {
98        if ($stat1[$xx] ne $stat2[$xx])
99        {
100            return( "\t" x $reclevel . "$element1 => $element2\n" );
101        }
102        }
103        return(0);
104 }
105
106 sub by_type
107 {
109    my $atype = _type($a);                      # get the types of files
110    my $btype = _type($b);
111
112    return(1) if (($atype eq 'file') && ($btype ne 'file'));
113    return(0) if (($atype ne 'file') && ($btype eq 'file'));
114    return($a cmp $b);
115 }
116
117 sub _type
118 {
119    my ($entry) = @_;
120
121    return
122    (
```

```
123                    (-d $entry )? 'directory' :
124                    (-f $entry )? 'file' :
125                    (!-e $entry)? 'notexist' :
126                    'unknown'
127           );
128 }
```

`dircompare` uses recursion to do this magic; line 77 shows the recursion. Basically, we open each directory, and from there proceed to compare the files inside the directories together and note any differences. Lines 47–84 show the comparisons: If we hit a directory, line 77 opens that directory to find out what files *underneath* that directory we need to compare.

We could have done this using source code from the standard distribution package called `File::Find`, but this is an awfully good example of recursion. With `File::Find`, you can say something like:

```
use File::Find;
find(\&wanted, "$directory");
sub wanted
{
        push (@files, $File::Find::name);
}
```

and get a list of files in one directory (recursively). Then you could take these files, and go through them one by one, substituting the `$directory` in `File::Find`, with the other directory you want to compare to. Your compare loop would then look like this:

```
foreach $file (@files)
{
    my $newfile = $file;
    $newfile =~ s"^$directory"$other_directory";
    stat_diff($file, $newfile);
}
```

This is a rough sketch, but we will fill in a bit more with the next example. Chalk this up to the "there's more than one way to do it" principle. Using `dircompare`, you can say:

```
c:\> perl dircompare.p dir1 dir2
```

and get output that looks something like this:

```
Comparing dir1 to dir2:
------------------------
        dir1/tmp/filename => dir2/tmp/filename
        dir1/hello does not exist
Comparing dir2 to dir1
------------------------
        dir1/tmp/filename => dir2/tmp/filename
        dir1/goodbye does not exist
```

This output is a bare-bones sketch, but it probably could be enhanced by showing exactly how the two files differ.

Deleting Garbage Files

Here's another annoyance that Perl can solve when working on large projects. Suppose you are working with editors and other tools that leave a backup file behind. MS Word, for example, leaves several copies of itself behind. The question is: How do you clean up the junk?

Well, the script in Listing 12.7 can help. It is called **delpat.p** (for delete pattern) and it looks through all the files you give on the command-line, and selectively deletes the ones that you label as *trash*. For example:

```
prompt% delpat.p '.bak$' *
```

will delete all files that have an extension of **.bak** on them, that live in the current directory or below. The script uses the `File::Find` library we talked about earlier and, therefore, does the recursion for you.

Listing 12.7
delpat.p

```
1    #!/usr/local/bin/perl5
2
3    use File::Find;
4    use Getopt::Long;
5    use strict;
6
7    my %varb;
8    GetOptions(\%varb, '-force!');              # give them the opportunity to
9
10   my $pattern = shift(@ARGV);
11   $pattern =~ s"\."\\\."g;                    # we make a 'dot' a wildcard 'force' a delete
12
13   my @files = grep (-f $_, @ARGV);            # deletes files and directories different ways
14   my @dirs =  grep (-d $_, @ARGV);            # deletes directories
15
16   find(\&del, @dirs);
17
18   my $file;
19   foreach $file (@files)
20   {
21       $File::Find::name = $file;
22       del();
23   }
24
25   sub del
26   {
27   if ($File::Find::name =~ m"($pattern)$"     # back for the pattern
28       {
29           if (!$varb{'force'})
30           {
31               print "Going to delete: $File::Find::name\n";
32               print "Do you wish to delete this file?!";
33               next if (<STDIN> !~ m"^[yY]");
34           }
35       print "Deleting file $File::Find::name\n";
36       unlink($File::Find::name) ||
37           print "Couldn't delete $File::Find::name\n";
38       }
39   }
```

Note how this is working. First, we shift off the first argument in line 10. (This will be the pattern we are going to delete.) Second, we split what is left on the command-line into files and directories (lines 13 and 14). In line 16, we call the function del (callback) on each of the files in each of the directories.

Then, we go through the files, and call del on each (lines 19–23). Finally, notice that the function del prompts the user on whether or not the file is to be deleted, unless -force is given on the command-line.

When you are doing something dangerous like deleting garbage files, one day you may delete something important. In fact, we already solved one of these hurdles in line 11. We always make a dot a literal dot and never its Perl equivalent.

Why? Well, because if we say:

```
C:\> perl delpat.p .bak *
```

we don't usually want the Perl regular expression version of dot, which means "any character." Instead, we want a literal, so we force it to be so with s"\."\.". Also, we have given the user a way out. You can say:

```
C:\> perl delpat.p .bak -force
```

and it will do the deleting by force. We could put an option called "yes to all" in, as well.

Solving a Simple Cipher

OK, here's an example to show off the power of Perl's syntax in manipulating text. The idea is to solve a simple cipher, where you rotate the letters a certain amount, something like:

```
The source for internet discussion groups
becoming:
Hvs gcifqs tcf wbhsfbsh rwgqiggwcb ufcidg.
```

Of course, the idea behind ciphers is that you don't have the information on how much the cipher has shifted letters. Notice how we deal with this problem in the code in Listing 12.8.

Listing 12.8
cipher.p

```
1    #!/usr/local/bin/perl5
2
3    use FileHandle;
4    use strict;
5
6    my $FH = new FileHandle("$ARGV[0]") || die "Couldn't open $ARGV[0]!\n";
7
8    undef $/;                                       # sets $/ globally, maybe
9                                                    # not the best idea!
10   local($") = "";
11   my $cipher = <$FH>;
12   $cipher =~ tr[A-Z][a-z];
13   my $dictionary = "/usr/dict/words";            # get our dictionary
14                                                   # (list of words)
15   my $dict = _setDictionary($dictionary);
16
17       my @letters = ('a'..'z');
18       my @newLetters = @letters;
19
```

```perl
20  my $xx;
21  my ($newCipher, $saveCipher);
22  my ($newMatch, $bestMatch);
23  for ($xx = 0; $xx <\<> 26; $xx++)
24  {
25    @newLetters=($newLetters[25],@newLetters[0..24]);        # shift last
26                                                             # letter to front
27    $newCipher = $cipher;
28    eval("\$newCipher =~ tr[@letters][@newLetters]");        # try a new cipher
29
30    if (($newMatch = _match($newCipher, $dict )) > $bestMatch) # we see if the
31    {
32      $bestMatch = $newMatch;                                # new cipher works.
33      $saveCipher = $newCipher;                              # better. If so, save it
34      }
35  }
36
37  print "HERE IS YOUR CIPHER: $saveCipher<\\>n";
38
39  sub _setDictionary                                         # we bascically
40  {                                                          # load the dictionary
41      my ($dictionary) = @_;                                 # into memory
42
43      my (@words, $word);
44      my ($line);
45      my $return = {};
46
47      my $FH = new FileHandle($dictionary) ||die "Couldn't open $dictionary!\n";
48      $line = <$FH>;
49      @words = _makeWords($line);
50
51      foreach $word ( @words) { $return->{$word} = 1; }      # we make a hash
52      $return;
53  }
54
55
56  sub _match
57  {
58      my ($cipher, $dict) = @_;                              # we get the cipher
59      my $matches = 0;
60
61      print $cipher;
62      my (@words) = _makeWords($cipher);                     # split it into words
63      my $word;
64
65      foreach $word (@words)
66      {
67          if ($dict->{$word})                                # test the word against
68          }
69              $matches
70      }
71      return($matches);
72  }
```

```
73
74    sub _makeWords
75    {
76        my ($cipher) = @_;
77        $cipher =~ s"\n" "g;
78        $cipher =~ tr"A-Z"a-z";
79        my <\@>words = split(' ', $cipher);
80        @words;
81    }
```

Lines 23–35 are the key here. We simply use the tr function to rotate the letters around, and then try to match each word against a dictionary. Suppose our cipher is:

```
rfcpc gq
```

Then we translate this into:

```
sgdqd hr
```

and check it against the $dict hash (the one in use here is /usr/dict/words; I know no equivalent on NT). We load that file into a hash, so that when we compare against it, we see that there is no such word as *sgdqd* or *hr*, so our score is zero. Then we continue to get:

```
pdana eo
qeb ob fp
rcfcpcgq
sgdgd hr
there is
```

and we have a match. If this were actually running, we would continue and do the other 19 permutations, to see if any of them actually worked better. Of course, the idea of a cipher is to "code up" pithy sayings. (*Games* magazine does this all the time, although theirs are real ciphers that can't be solved by such a simple scheme.) Here, I guess, is mine:

```
file cipher:
'W bsjsf ush am qoh rfiby - whg kfcbu hc uwjs zweicf hc obwaozg - pih kvohsjsf vs rcsg
cb vwg ckb hwas wg vwg pigwbsgg.'

print% cipher.p cipher

HERE IS YOUR CIPHER: i never get my cat drunk - its wrong to give liquor to animals -
but whatever he does on his own time is his business.
```

A Regular Expression to Match Perlish Numbers

Now, we will give a script that matches a list of numbers in a string. This one is especially useful if you put it into a library or a module. The idea is that you could use this regular expression to match arbitrary numbers inside a text field. It isn't completely (usably) accurate; for example, it would miss the numbers in:

```
1+4
```

because it assumes a space before and after the number. However, we could probably accommodate this by getting rid of the restriction.

Anyway, we construct the regular expression in a "top down" manner, dealing with each type of number, and stringing them together in a big chain of alternates, as shown in Listing 12.9.

Listing 12.9
numbers.p

```perl
1    #!/usr/local/bin/perl5
2
3    my $hexadecimal = q{
4                            0x                # leading trailer
5                            [0-9a-fA-F]+      # 0 through 9, a-f A-F
6                    };
7
8    my $float       = q{
9                            (?:\+|\-){0,1}    # beginning plus/minus
10                            [0-9]*\.          # stuff before the '.'
11                            [0-9]+            # stuff after the '.'
12                    };
13
14   my $integer     = q{
15                            (?:\+|\-){0,1}    # beginning plus/minus
16                            [0-9]+            # digits.
17                    };
18
19   my $scientific = qq{$float} ."      ".    # float plus E or e
20                   q{[E|e]} . qq{$integer};# plus integer makes scientific
21
22
23   my $underscore  = q{
24                            (?:\+|\-){0,1}    # leading plus/minus
25                            [0-9]{1,3}        # first three digits, up to _
26                            (?:_[0-9]{3})+    # underscores, plus groups of 3 digits
27                    };
28
29   my $number      = qq{
30                            (\\s+|^)        # leading spaces. since qq, need \\
31                            (
32                            ?:$hexadecimal|
33                               $underscore|
34                               $scientific|
35                               $float     |
36                               $integer
37                            )
38                            (?=\\s+|\$)     # again, trailing spaces, ?=
39                                            # because we don't want to throw
40                    };                      # away spaces
41   ########## END OF REGULAR EXPRESSION ####################
42
43   print $number;                           # prints full regular expression just for fun... ;-)
44
45   my $line = " This is 0 a test -1.233 of the 0. emergency 1.03e-24-
46   broadcast 543 system 4_223_233";
47
48   while ($line =~ m"($number)"sgxo)         # need to have x and o -- x will
49   {                                         # use comment mode, o compiles once.
50
51       print "$1 ";
52   }
```

Lines 3–27 concern themselves with building up the individual, different types of numbers. Line 29 actually sticks all this stuff together into one regular expression which we call in line 48. It is, as you might assume, huge.

Note that when we are putting together the alternates we put them together in a *specific* order. Floats must come first—before integers—because a float such as:

```
233.33
```

has an integer inside it, and we would always match the integer first. Also, notice that we use (?=) because the trailing spaces aren't part of the number itself. (In retrospect, it looks like \b would be just as good.)

Code Generators

Next, we come to code generators. Code generators are the top of the food chain for manipulating text (so to speak). If you can write code to make code, you can do things that (for some reason) seem to be magic to nontechnical people.

Note

When I submitted my first 50,000-line, automatically generated Perl script to perform database integrity checking to my manager of some years ago, he just shook his head in either shock or dismay; I couldn't really tell which.

Of course, to generate code, you need a language to automatically generate. There are several good ones out there that benefit from automatic generation:

1. C
2. C++
3. SQL
4. Perl (of course!)
5. Expect

For the purposes of this book, we chose Expect. Expect is probably the least known, but it fills in a gap that, for some reason, people in the Perl world have chosen to ignore until recently (there is an Expect module on CPAN — it is not very mature, however).

Suppose for example, you are running an ftp session. If you type:

```
prompt% ftp ftp.cs.colorado.edu
```

you get a string back:

```
Connected to freestuff.cs.colorado.edu.
220 freestuff.cs.colorado.edu FTP server (Version wu-2.4.2-academ[BETA-12](1) Fri Jan
24 13:06:52 MST 1997) ready.
Name (ftp.cs.colorado.edu:ed):
```

ftp is now expecting you to log in. The job of Expect, however, is to handle that request without you being present. An Expect script, built on top of tcl, looks something like this:

```
spawn ftp ftp.cs.colorado.edu
set timeout 60
expect {

    "Name*):*" { send "anonymous\r" }
    "failed" { send "quit\r"; exit 1 }
    timeout { puts "TIME_OUT\n"; exit 1 }
```

```
    }
    expect {
        "Password:" { send "myemail@myhost.com\r" }
        "Failed" { send "quit\r" }
        timeout { puts "TIMEOUT\n"; }
    }

    expect {
        "ftp>*"  { send "get file1\r" }
        timeout { puts "TIME_OUT\n"; }
    }
```

spawn spawns off a process and expect indicates what we expect to see as returned text from the program that we spawned off.

The key here is that if Expect sees the text on the left come back from the process it spawns, then it sends the text on the right. If it sees Name, it sends anonymous<carriage return>; if it sees Password, it sends myemail@myhost.com<carriage return>.

There are many intricacies to this process, and I don't want to have to learn another scripting language. Hence, I use Perl to generate the scripts that I use. I can copy sample text of Expect from a book; that's easy. I can have Perl generate the scripts that I use; that's semi-easy.

However, there is a large overhead in learning a scripting language when you use it for any one thing.

Although I say Perl has no Expect-like functions that are truly up-to-date, the **libnet** distribution has a couple of modules, **Net::Ftp** and **Net::Telnet**, that basically do the same thing as we do in the following examples, just not in an Expect-like way.

Hence, you can think of the following two programs as examples only. You'll probably want to install **libnet** via CPAN or the accompanying CD.

However, they *can* be used as templates for your own code when you need to automate programs that are not as standard as telnet. (I have done this several times in the past.)

Automating Telnet

Telnet is the standard (agreed upon by committee) way of two machines talking to one another. There are many request for comments (RFC) files that deal with the telnet standard and, hence, it is a fairly reliable way to handle processes that require more than one machine to complete.

See `http://wombat.doc.ic.ac.uk/foldoc/foldoc.cgi?query=telnet` for more details. This is another one of those on-line computer dictionaries that is invaluable sometimes.

On the command-line (or in the case of NT, through a GUI) you say something like:

```
prompt% telnet <site_name>
```

which then sends a request for connection to the site <site_name>. A telnet server that runs on the computer pointed to by <site_name> then recognizes that a computer is trying to talk to it, and sends back some text. The result is you get something like:

```
Trying 165.125.122.110…
Connected to mysite.apxtech.com.
Escape character is '^]'

UNIX(r) System V Release 4.0 (mysite)

Welcome to mysite.apxtech.com!
This system is a dual P-200 running Solaris 2.5.1, with 64 MB of RAM and plenty of
attitude. All communications to and fro are monitored for security purposes. By
proceeding, you consent to this monitoring.

login:
```

Again, the computer is waiting for your login. You enter it, and get:

```
Password:
```

You enter the password, for verification, and get a prompt:

```
ed@mysite.apxtech.com(%):
```

at which point you can do anything your user can do. However, all of this, as it stands, is interactive. Some computers have an **rsh** command (for remote shell) that implements this in an automated fashion, but even this command is limited.

The following script automates telnet from the command-line, so that you can send multiple commands to the remote machine. You store all the commands you want to run in a command file, something like **telnet_commands:**

```
      ---- telnet_commands ----
"ogin:" ,  "ed"
"Password:", "yeehaw!"
"(%):",  "ls"
"(%):",  "runscript.p"
    "(%):", "exit"
```

and then run the command with the following line:

```
prompt% telnet.p -site mysite.apxtech.com -execfile telnet_commands
```

This generates some Expect code, and you see your commands being executed on your screen.

If you are running NT, you must use the command provided on the CD.

Note

Listing 12.10 is the code for **telnet.p.**

Listing 12.10
telnet.p

```perl
1   #!/usr/local/bin/perl5
2
3   my $opt = {};
4
5   use strict;
6   use Data::Dumper;
7   use FileHandle;
8   use Term::ReadKey;
9   use Getopt::Long;
10  use Text::ParseWords;
11  use String::Edit;
12
13  main();
14
15
16  sub main
17  {
18  GetOptions
19    (
20        $opt,"--site:s","--execfile:s","--expect:s","--pass:s",
21        "--telnet:s", "--debug"                        # give options to user
22    );                                                 # site = where to go to
23                                                       # execfile = file to execute
24        modifyDefaults($opt);
25        my $code = _genTelnetCode($opt);
26        _execTelnetCode($opt, $code);
27  }
28
29  sub _modifyDefaults      # We get the options from the command-line, and then
30  {                        # proceed to modify them according to some
31      my ($opt) = @_;      # predetermined defaults.
32
33      my ($fileopt, @errors);
34      $fileopt = (defined ($opt->{'execfile'}))? _parseFile($opt) : {};
35      %$opt = (%$fileopt, %$opt);
36
37
38      $opt->{'site'}   = (defined($opt->{'site'}))? $opt->{'site'} :    # which place
39                                              $ENV{'EXPECT_TELNET_SITE'}; # to connect to
40
41  $opt->{'expect'} = $opt->{'expect'} || $ENV{'EXPECT_EXEC'} || "expect -i"; # which executable
42
43  $opt->{'user'} = $opt->{'user'}    || $ENV{'TELNET_USER'} ||
44                                      $ENV{'USERNAME'} || getpwuid($<);  # which user
45
46      if (!defined ($opt->{'pass'}))
47      {
48      print "Enter password for $opt->{'user'}\n";              # prompt for password
```

```
49            ReadMode 2; $opt->{'pass'} = <STDIN>; ReadMode 0;
50       }
51
52       $opt->{'telnet'}   = $opt->{'telnet'} || $ENV{'TELNET'}  || "telnet";
53
54       push (@errors, "You need to provide a telnet site!\n")
55                                          if (!defined ($opt->{'site'}));
56       push (@errors, "You need to provide a user!\n")
57                                          if (!defined ($opt->{'user'}));
58       push (@errors, "You need to provide a password!\n")
59                                          if (!defined ($opt->{'pass'}));
60       die @errors if (@errors);
61  }
62
63  sub _parseFile          # We look through the file for commands that we are to
64  {                       # pass to Expect.
65      my ($opt) = @_;
66      my $return = {};
67
68      my $fh = new FileHandle("$opt->{'execfile'}") ||
69                                          die "Couldn't open 'execfile'\n";
70
71      my @lines = <$fh>;
72
73      my ($line, $xx, $keep) = ('', 0, '');        # open up for reading commands
74                                                   # and configuration
75      foreach $line (@lines)
76      {
77          chop($line);
78          next if (!$line);   # ignore blanks
79
80          my @array;                               # flags have a '.' in them.
81          if (@array = _isaFlag($line))
82          {
83              $return->{$array[0]} = $array[1];
84          }
85          else
86          {
87              if ($xx == 0)              # first line of commands is always user
88              {
89                  my ($userprompt, $user) = _parseCommand($line);
90                  $opt->{userprompt} = $userprompt;
91                  if ($user ne 'USER') { $opt->{user} = $user; }
92              }
93              elsif ($xx == 1)           # second line of commands is password
94              {
95                  my ($passwordprompt, $password ) = _parseCommand($line);
96                  $opt->{'passwordprompt'} = $passwordprompt;
97                  if ($password ne 'PASSWORD') { $opt->{'pass'} = $password; }
98              }
99              else
100               {
```

```
101                      push (@{$return->{commands}}, [ _parseCommand($line) ] );
102              }
103          $xx++;
104      }
105  }
106      die "You need to have at least one command!\n"
107                                          if (!$return->{'commands'});
108      return($return);
109  }
110
111  sub _parseCommand        # command to take something like the line: "a", "b" and
112  {                        # turn it into a form that expect can use.
113      my ($line) = @_;
114      my $keep = 0;
115
116      my ($prompt, $action) = quotewords("\s*,\s*", $keep, $line);  # use quoteword module to split up
117      $prompt = trim($prompt);
118      $action = trim($action);
119      return($prompt, $action);
120  }
121
122  sub _isaFlag             # command to take flags from the exec file, and turn
123  {                        # them into options to pass to Expect.
124      my ($line) = @_;
125      my $keep = 0;
126      my (@array) = quotewords("\s*:\s*", $keep, $line);
127      @array = trim(@array);
128      if (@array == 2) { return (@array); }
129          else { return (()); }
130  }
131
132  sub _genTelnetCode       # command to make legal Expect code, based on
133  {                        # flags passed to program, plus command file.
134      my ($opt) = @_;
135
136      my ($commands, $line, $command, $key) = ($opt->{'commands'}, '', '', '');
137
138      foreach $key ('user','pass', 'userprompt', 'passwordprompt' )
139      {
140          $opt->{$key} =~ s"([\@\$\\])"\\$1"g;       # we need to substitute
141      }                                              # dollar signs and at signs
142                                                     # with their backslashed
143      foreach $command (@$commands)                  # equivalents - Expect does
144      {                                              # interpolation like Perl!
145          $command->[0] =~ s"([\@\$\\])"\\$1"g;
146          $command->[1] =~ s"([\@\$\\])"\\$1"g;
147      }
148                                                     # start of code generation
149                                                     # generation of user prompt.
150  $line .=<<"EOL"
151  set timeout -1
152
153  spawn $opt->{'telnet'} $opt->{'site'}
```

```
154 expect {
155     "$opt->{'userprompt'}" { send "$opt->{'user'}\\r" }
156     "failed" { send "quit\\r"; exit 1; }
157     "error*" { send "quit\\r"; exit 1; }
158     timeout  { puts "Timed Out\\n"; exit 1; }
159     "Service not available" { puts "Connection Dropped\\n"; exit 1; }
160     "ftp>*" { send "quit\\r"; exit 1 }
161 }
162 EOL
163 ;
164
165 if ($opt->{'passwordprompt'})                    # generation of password
166 {                                                 # part.
167 $line.=<<"EOL"
168 expect {
169     "$opt->{'passwordprompt'}" { send "$opt->{'pass'}\\r" }
170     "failed" { send "quit\\r"; exit 1; }
171     "error*" { send "quit\\r"; exit 1; }
172     "Service not available" { puts "Connection Dropped\\n"; exit 1; }
173     timeout  { puts "Timed Out\\n"; exit 1; }
174 }
175
176 EOL
177 }
178
179
180
181 foreach $command (@$commands)                     # generation of commands
182 {                                                 # to be executed.
183
184     $line.=<<"EOL"
185     expect {
186         "$command->[0]" { send "$command->[1]\\r" }
187         timeout { puts "Timed Out\\n"; exit 1; }
188     }
189 EOL
190 }
191     $line .=<<"EOL"
192     expect {
193         eof { exit 0 }
194         timeout { exit 1 }
195     }
196 EOL
197 ;
198     $line;
199 }
200
201 sub _execTelnetCode           # command to actually execute
202 {                                    # the telnet code that we have generated
203     my ($opt, $code) = @_;
204
205     my $exec = ($opt->{'expect'});
206     if ($opt->{'debug'})
207     {
```

```
208        print "Generated code:\n$code\n";
209    }
210    else
211    {
212    open (EXPECT, "| $exec");        # note; we 'pipe' commands to an excutable via filehandle
213        print EXPECT $code;
214        close(EXPECT);
215    }
216 }
```

This code is becoming a bit long, and when it gets long like this, we turn to the functional diagrams. Figure 12.3 shows a functional diagram that also outlines the logic of the program quite well. As you can see, we have designed **telnet.p** to be "top down." There are two major parts to the program: the interface and the code generation. Let's look at both, because they work so closely together.

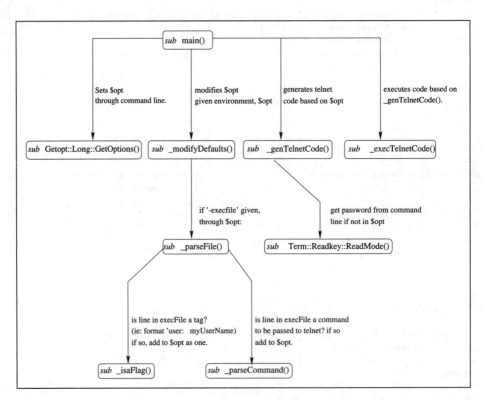

Figure 12.3
Functional Diagram of **telnet.p**

telnet.p Interface

There are three ways to give options to **telnet.p**; hence, there are three ways to give such things as passwords, user names, and so on:

1. The default options coming from the environment. For example, lines 38–39 in Listing 12.10 define $ENV{'EXPECT_TELNET_SITE'}; the users can set this inside their environment to avoid having to put it in the command file.

2. Options coming from the file -**execfile**. If you say something in your file about where you will execute commands, such as:

```
1 site:    my_site.here.com
2 "login:", "ed"
3 "Password:", "yummy2veg"
```

line 1 will tell **telnet.p** that you want to go to my_site.here.com.

3. Options from the command-line. You can say: telnet.p -site 'my_site.here.com, and **telnet.p** realizes that you want to go to my_site.here.com.

However, this flexibility can create conflicts: Someone could have specified they wanted to go to the site *A* in the environment, to site *B* in the command file, and to site *C* on the command-line!

In such a case, we prioritize. We assume that the command-line is the most urgent; if people are typing commands, it means they definitely want to go there.

The second most urgent place is the command file. If the command file has an entry like:

```
site: my_site.apxtech.com
```

we know that the user probably wants to go there.

Finally, the least urgent place is the defaults, the environmental variables that we set. These just "pick up the pieces" in case the first two methods come up blank.

This scheme allows many uses that are not otherwise apparent. For example, suppose that you have 50 sites you need to connect to, and do the same actions on—all at once. With this flexibility, you can say something like:

```
prompt% telnet.p -site 1 -execfile commandlist
prompt% telnet.p -site 2 -execfile commandlist
. . .
```

and so on, down the line, to run the commands on each and every site.

Code Generation

The code generation part takes all the flexibility that we have developed in the interface, and translates it into code. This is the job of gentelnetCode. You can see the code that it generates by adding -debug onto the end. For example, if you had a file, **command_list**, that looked like:

```
site:       happyface.org
"ogin:",    "ed"
"Password:","nya2ghh"
"]$",       "cd my_dir",
"]$",       "ls",
"]$",       "exit"
```

and you actually ran **telnet.p** with the following command:

```
prompt% telnet.p -site 2 -execfile commandlist -debug
```

you would generate the following code:

```
1   Generated code:
2   set timeout -1
3
4   spawn telnet happyface.org
5   expect {
6       "ogin:" { send "ed\r" }
```

```
 7          "failed" { send "quit\r"; exit 1; }
 8          "error*" { send "quit\r"; exit 1; }
 9          timeout { puts "Timed Out\n"; exit 1; }
10          "Service not available" { puts "Connection Dropped\n"; exit 1; }
11
12     }
13     expect {
14          "Password:" { send "nya2ghh\r" }
15          "failed" { send "quit\r"; exit 1; }
16          "error*" { send "quit\r"; exit 1; }
17          "Service not available" { puts "Connection Dropped\n"; exit 1; }
18          timeout { puts "Timed Out\n"; exit 1; }
19     }
20
21          expect {
22              "]\$" { send "cd my_dir\r" }
23              timeout { puts "Timed Out\n"; exit 1; }
24          }
25          expect {
26              "]\$" { send "ls\r" }
27              timeout { puts "Timed Out\n"; exit 1; }
28          }
29          expect {
30              "]\$" { send "exit\r" }
31              timeout { puts "Timed Out\n"; exit 1; }
32          }
33          expect {
34              eof { exit 0 }
35              timeout { exit 1 }
36          }
37
```

Notice the commands in boldface; these directly come out of the **execfile** we made. All we do in **getTelnetCode** is pad them into text which so happens to be a legal Expect program. The `timeout` directive tells Expect to do the action specified if the command times out (i.e., there is no response from the telnet server or your text doesn't match correctly). The other directives (`failed:`, `error*`) indicate commonly found strings in telnet servers.

There are a couple of things we must do to the input to do this: Add `\r` to the end of commands, and turn all the $ into \$ (since Expect does interpolation just like Perl).

Execution of Code

Finally, we need to take the code that we have just generated, and send it to Expect to actually be executed. This is done by _execTelnetCode in lines 201–216 of Listing 12.10, and we actually send the code that we just created to a pipe, as in:

```
212          open (EXPECT, "| expect -i");
213          print EXPECT $code;
214          close(EXPECT);
```

We could just as easily have done this with a system call (if you are using Windows 95, you may have to because the **dos** command prompt is pretty bad at this sort of thing), but doing it via a pipe has two advantages:

1.   No extra files are lying around.
2.   The passwords are much more secure (no place to trap them).

Number 2 is the critical point. By putting the code that we've just generated into a pipe, we make our system much more secure. Lines 212–214 can be used to talk to the pipe; when you print to the EXPECT handle, you actually make the EXPECT handle execute the code you mention.

Automating ftp

Once we get **telnet.p** down, we can use the base code to make other programs, which automates different things. One such commonly used program is *file transfer protocol*, or ftp, which is what makes the Internet go round.

However, when dealing with a browser, or on the command-line, you can only download one file at a time. With the **ftp.p** we are going to write (see Listing 12.11), you can say:

```
prompt% ftp.p -site prep.ai.mit.edu -filelist 'files'
```

where `'files'` contains a list of files to be found at the site, such as the following:

```
/pub/gnu/bash.tar.gz
/pub/gnu/fileutils.tar.gz
/pub/gnu/sharutils.tar.gz
```

Then ftp.p will connect to the site `prep.ai.mit.edu` and get all the files in that file list. This script is particularly good for people who have slow modem connections. You simply tell the program to transfer at night, and during the early daylight hours, ftp does its thing, downloading all the files, automatically.

Unlike telnet, Windows NT comes with a command-line version of ftp, so you need not do anything special to make it work. You do, however, need to install Expect from the CD in order for this to work.

Listing 12.11
ftp.p

```
1    #!/usr/local/bin/perl5 -w
2
3    my $opt = {};
4
5    use FileHandle;
6    use Getopt::Long;
7
8    main();
9
10   sub main
11   {
12       GetOptions
13           (
14               $opt, "site:s", "filelist:s", "expect:s", "ftp:s",
15                                                       # same arguments
16                   "user:s", "pass:s", "type:s", "ftpfile:s",
17                   "debug"
18           );
19
20       _modifyDefaults($opt);
21       my $code = _genFtpCode($opt);
22       _execFtpCode($opt, $code);
23   }
24
25
26   sub _modifyDefaults
```

```
27  {
28      my ($opt) = @_;
29
30      my $fileopt = _parseFtpFile($opt) if ($opt->{'ftpfile'});
31                                              # get defaults from ftp file
32      %$opt = (%$fileopt, %$opt);             # override command-line
33
34      $opt->{'expect'} = $opt->{'expect'} || $ENV{'EXPECT_EXEC'} ||
35                                   "/usr/local/bin/expect -i";
36
37      $opt->{'user'}      = $opt->{'user'} || $ENV{'EXPECT_USER'} || "anonymous";
38                                              # default for anonymous ftp
39      $opt->{'pass'}      = $opt->{'pass'} || $ENV{'EXPECT_PASS'} || "me@";
40      $opt->{'ftp'}       = $opt->{'ftp'}  || $ENV{'FTP'}         || "ftp";
41      $opt->{'type'}      = $opt->{'type'} || $ENV{'EXPECT_TYPE'} || "bin";
42
43      if ($opt->{'filelist'})
44      {
45          @{$opt->{'files'}} = split(' ', $opt->{'filelist'});
46      }
47
48      push( @{$opt->{'files'}}, @{$fileopt->{'files'}});
49  }
50
51  sub _parseFtpFile                               # we get the ftp file
52  {                                               # and open up for options
53      my ($opt) = @_;
54      my $return = {};
55
56      my $fh = new FileHandle("$opt->{'ftpfile'}")
57                          || die "Couldn't open $opt->{'ftpfile'}\n";
58
59      my $line;
60      while (defined ($line = <$fh>))
61      {
62          next if ($line !~ m"\w");
63          if ($line =~ m":") { _addopt($return, $line);  }  # colon indicates option
64          else               { _addfile($return, $line); }  # no colon
65                                                             # indicates file
66      }
67      $return;
68  }
69
70  sub _addopt
71  {
72      my ($return, $line) = @_;                         # options have special format
73      my ($key, $val) = ($line =~ m"^\s*(.*?)\s*:\s*(.*?)\s*$");
74      $return->{$key} = $val;
75  }
76  sub _addfile                                 # files are words on are line
77  {
78      my ($return, $line) = @_;
79
80      my ($val) = ($line =~ m"^\s*(.*)\s*");
81      push (@{$return->{'files'}}, $val);
```

```
 82  }
 83
 84  sub _genFtpCode                                    # actual generation of code
 85  {
 86      my ($opt) = @_;
 87
 88      my $line = '';
 89
 90      foreach $key ('user', 'pass') { $opt->{$key} =~ s"[\$\\]"\\$1"g; }
 91
 92  $line .=<<"EOL"
 93  set timeout -1
 94
 95  spawn $opt->{'ftp'} $opt->{'site'}
 96  expect {
 97      "Name*):*" { send "$opt->{'user'}\\r" }           \\# add user
 98      "failed" { send "quit\\r"; exit 1; }
 99      "error*" { send "quit\\r"; exit 1; }
100      timeout  { puts "Timed Out\\n"; exit 1; }
101      "Service not available" { puts "Connection Dropped\\n"; exit 1; }
102      "ftp>*" { send "quit\\r"; exit 1 }
103  }
104
105  expect {
106      "assword:" { send "$opt->{'pass'}\\r" }          \\# add password
107      "failed" { send "quit\\r"; exit 1; }
108      "error*" { send "quit\\r"; exit 1; }
109      "Service not available" { puts "Connection Dropped\\n"; exit 1; }
110      timeout  { puts "Timed Out\\n"; exit 1; }
111  }
112
113  expect {                                           # check if connected
114      "logged in" { send "\\r" }
115      "onnected to*" { send "\\r" }
116      "ftp>*" { send "\\r" }
117      "failed" { send "quit\\r"; exit 1; }
118      "error*" { send "quit\\r"; exit 1; }
119      "Service not available" { puts "Connection Dropped\\n"; exit 1; }
120      timeout { puts "Timed Out\\n"; exit 1; }
121  }
122
123  expect {                                           # send type: or binary ascii
124      "successful" { send "$opt->{'type'}\\r" }
125      "onnected to*" { send "$opt->{'type'}\\r" }
126      "ftp>" { send "$opt->{'type'}\\r" }
127      "failed" { send "quit\\r"; exit 1; }
128      "error*" { send "quit\\r"; exit 1; }
129      "Service not available" { puts "Connection Dropped\\n"; exit 1; }
130      timeout { puts "Timed Out\\n"; exit 1; }
131  }
132  EOL
133  ;
134                                                     #
135  foreach $file (@{$opt->{'files'}})                 # for each file
136  {
```

```
137     $file =~ s"[\$\\]"\\$1"g;                              # we need to protect '$' signs
138     my ($dir, $filename) = ($file =~ m"(.*)[/\\](.*)");# split directory from file
139     $dir = $dir || "/";
140     $filename = $filename || $file;
141
142     $line .=<<"EOL"
143     expect {                                              # go into directory
144         "failed" { send "quit\\r"; exit 1; }
145         "error*" { send "quit\\r"; exit 1; }
146         "ftp>"  { send "cd $dir\\r" }
147         Service not available" { puts "Connection Dropped\\n"; exit 1; }
148         timeout { puts "Timed Out\\n"; exit 1; }
149     }
150     expect {                                              # get file name
151         "failed" { send "quit\\r"; exit 1; }
152         "error*" { send "quit\\r"; exit 1; }
153         "ftp>"  { send "get $filename\\r" }
154         Service not available" { puts "Connection Dropped\\n"; exit 1; }
155         timeout { puts "Timed Out\\n"; exit 1; }
156     }
157 EOL
158 ;
159 }                                                         # end of code generation
160
161 $line .=<<"EOL"
162 expect {
163         "failed" { send "quit\\r"; exit 1; }
164         "error*" { send "quit\\r"; exit 1; }
165         "ftp>"  { send "quit\\r"; exit 0; }
166     Service not available" { puts "Connection Dropped\\n"; exit 1; }
167         timeout { puts "Timed Out\\n"; exit 1; }
168 }
169 EOL
170 ;                                                         # end of script generation
171     $line;
172 }
173
174 sub _execFtpCode
175 {
176     my ($opt, $code) = @_;
177
178     my $exec = $opt->{'expect'};
179     if ($opt->{'debug'})
180     {
181         print "Generated code:\n$code\n";
182     }
183     else
184     {
185         open (EXPECT, "| $exec");                         # we pipe command 2 filehandle
186         print EXPECT $code;
187         close(EXPECT);
188     }
189 }
```

Again, this code is almost exactly the same as **telnet.p.** In fact, I have simply cut and pasted many of the sections of code from the previous example, and modified them from there!

As one might expect, this isn't exactly the best practice, but many people do it at one time or another (including me). And if you don't know the techniques of modular or object-oriented programming, this is probably the only way to do code reuse.

OLE Automation: Object Linking and Embedding (NT/Win95)

Now, let's look at a couple of places where Perl is used on a specific platform: the Win32 platform. I hate to do this, because one of Perl's best features is portability, but two more of Perl's basic tenets are "let people do what they want to do" and "it is better to have a solution, than to have no solution at all."

In this case, we want to make it so that Perl can "talk" to MS-Office applications. The reasons for this are:

1. They are popular.
2. They can be used to make (mostly) formatted versions of raw data.
3. Perl can be used to streamline the process of dealing with large amounts of their data.

In other words, Perl can be used to translate between the free formats (ASCII, LEX, HTML) into the proprietary ones (Word documents, Excel spreadsheets). Thus, you gain power in controlling the data; OLE is Microsoft's primary way of making this control happen.

Note

If you have Microsoft Office 97, then you can install information on the methods, flags, and so forth that you can use.

However, I searched the Net for quite a while to try to find good information on pragmatic, free sources of OLE code. There is a knowledge base at `http://www.microsoft.com/kb` that could be extremely helpful. But if someone out there from Microsoft is reading this, please tell whomever is in charge of the knowledge base to:

1. get rid of dead links;
2. increase server bandwidth; and
3. do a serious cleaning job on the data they have, and put pragmatic information on the server. I have read a hundred times about what OLE is, and only half a dozen times on how to apply OLE (all from 1995 and 1996).

The one article I did find in the knowledge base was called http://support.microsoft. `com/support/kb/articles/Q167/2/23.asp`.

I didn't find it through the search engine, but through the newsgroup `microsoft.public.vb.ole.automation` (thanks to Rob Bovey). This didn't contain useful information, but it pointed to a Windows Help file that does. If the http server gives you trouble, you can get this file directly via ftp at `\ftp://ftp.microsoft.com/Softlib/MSLFILES/AUTO97.EXE`.

Note that this only deals with Office 97 automation. If anybody finds anything on automation for previous versions of the Office tools, let me know.

The packaged documentation for Office 97 is quite a bit better, but does not come in the "standard" install. You have to install it via a special option at install time.

Next we give a brief introduction on how to actually make OLE automated Perl scripts.

A Brief Overview of OLE

So here is the quick, 15-second tour of OLE.

OLE is a way to harness applications and run them automatically. As we saw with Expect, we could harness either the ftp server or the telnet server by running it and sending it keys.

However, GUIs are perceived to be more difficult to run in this manner (however, see Guido later for a rebuttal) so Microsoft came up with OLE. With OLE, you could say something like:

```
my $excelObject = new Win32::OLE('Excel.Application');
```

that would open the Excel application for you (don't worry about the syntax for now). If you then say:

```
$wordObject->Workbooks->Open('C:<\\>excel.xls');
```

this will open a workbook for you inside Excel, and you can sit back and automatically control it to your heart's desire.

If you are unaware of how to program OLE, the best way to program OLE scripts is to actually take a look at Visual Basic scripts, and "gut" the code for syntax. For example, the **AUTO97.EXE** file I mentioned earlier contains quite a few OLE automation examples in Visual Basic; the examples look somewhat like Listing 12.12.

Listing 12.12
word.bas

```
1       Dim WordDocument As Word.Document
2       Dim WordParagraph As Word.Paragraph
3       Dim WordApplication As Word.Application
4       Dim WordRange As Word.Range
5
6       Set WordApplication = CreateObject("Word.Application")
7
8       With WordApplication
9           .WindowState = wdWindowStateMaximize
10           .Documents.Add
11
12          Set WordDocument = WordApplication.ActiveDocument
13
14          Set WordRange = WordDocument.Range
15          With WordRange
16              .Font.Bold = True
17              .Italic = False
18              .Font.Size = 16
19              .InsertAfter "Running Word 97!"
20              .InsertParagraphAfter
21          End With
22          .ActiveDocument.SaveAs "c:\Temp\Aha.doc"
23          .Quit
24      End With
```

This harnesses Word for Windows 97 (version 8.0) to actually create a document and then save it as **C:\Temp\Aha.Doc**. You can convert this into the Perl script shown in Listing 12.13 (thanks to Jan Dubois for testing—I don't have Word for Windows 97).

Listing 12.13
wordcopy.p

```
1    use Win32::OLE;
2
3    use Data::Dumper;
4    use strict;
5
6    my $word = new Win32::OLE('Word.Application') || die "No Word App $!\n";
7
8    my $wdWindowStateMaximize = 1;
9    $word->{WindowState} =  $wdWindowStateMaximize;
10   $word->Documents->Add();
11
12   my $worddoc = $word->ActiveDocument();
13   my $wordrng = $worddoc->Range();
14
15   $wordrng->Font->{'Bold'} = 'True';
16   $wordrng->Font->{'Italic'} = 'False';
17   $wordrng->Font->{'Size'} = '16';
18   $wordrng->InsertAfter("Running Word 97!\n");
19   $wordrng->InsertParagraphAfter();
20
21   $word->WordBasic->SaveAs("C:\temp\aha.doc");
22   $word->Quit();
```

Notice three things here. First is the lack of declarations. Visual Basic's version is four lines longer because it needs to declare each variable and Perl has no such need. Second, line 6 institutes some error control: If you can't open a file, you can have your process die, and tell the user why your process is dying. Third—and most important—is that the syntax is similar. We substitute:

```
WordRange.Font.Bold = True
```

with:

```
$wordrng->Font->{'Bold'} = 'True'
```

and we substitute:

```
WordRange.InsertAfter "Running Word 97!\n"
```

with:

```
$wordrng->InsertAfter("Running Word 97!\n);
```

Hence, given a Visual Basic OLE automation script, the transfer between the two languages is fairly easy. The one thing that gets in the way sometimes is Visual Basic's use of odd little constants, like $wdWindowStateMaximize in line 8.

To get these constants, you are better off going to the source: to the MSOffice OLE documentation that comes with MSOffice, and is not installed by default. (Note: Newer versions of Win32::OLE have these constants built in.) So let's see some more OLE automation scripts, but this time, let's make them more general purpose (in the sense that they actually do something useful).

More Controlling Word with OLE

Here are two more scripts dealing with Word and OLE, that I've found somewhat useful. Both were translated from Visual Basic into Perl, and then warped into doing something generically useful. I am indebted to Eric Zimmerman for the original Visual Basic source code for both of the following examples, and to Jan Dubois for testing on Office 97 the two scripts that require that software package.

Printing Out Documents via OLE—An NT Version of lpr

If you use Word frequently, as some of us do (especially those who write books), one of the most annoying things about it is that everything is GUI-based. There is no way in Word of simply stacking and queuing 100 documents to print. In Unix, you could say:

```
prompt% lpr -P$PRINTER_NAME *
```

where $PRINTER_NAME pointed to a publicly available printer. Then, all 100 of your documents in your current directory print out. However, in the NT world, you have to

1. Open the 100 documents in turn.
2. Select **Print** from the file menu.
3. Hit **OK**.

To be fair, DOS has a 'print' command, but it has fallen into disrepair, and usually does not work. And anybody who has actually had to print 100 documents knows that it is a major pain. To compound things, sometimes you must wait for the print queue to empty before you can do the cycle again, so you could be sitting around with absolutely nothing to do for hours!

The following script fixes all that. To use it, simply say:

```
C:\ wordprint.p -delay 100 *
```

and Word will print documents, one by one with 100 seconds between each printing (the delay is optional). **wordprint** is shown in Listing 12.14.

Listing 12.14
wordprint.p

```
1    use FileHandle;
2    use strict;
3    use Win32::OLE;
4    use Getopt::Long;
5
6    my %opt;
7    GetOptions( \%opt, 'delay:i');
8
9    my @files;
10
11   if ($ARGV[0] =~ m"\.")       # if the first argument doesn't have a .
12   {                            # we assume that we are given a list of files
13       @files =  @ARGV;
14   }
15   else
16   {
17       my $fh = new FileHandle($ARGV[0]) || die "Couldn't open $ARGV[0]\n";
18       chop(@files = <$fh>);
19   }
```

```
20
21   my $wordObj=new Win32::OLE('Word.Basic')|| die "Couldn't open Word !\n";
22   print $wordObj;
23   $wordObj->{Visible} = 1;
24
25   my $file;
26   die "Need to input some files!\n" if (!@files);
27
28   foreach $file (@files)
29   {
30       $wordObj->FileOpen ($file, 'True');
31       $wordObj->FilePrint();
32       if ($opt{'delay'}) { sleep ($opt{'delay'}); }
33   }
34   $wordObj->Close();
```

This script came in very handy when I was writing this book; it is in pre-Windows 97 OLE because I don't have Word 97, but one of the big things I needed to do was print sections of text for cross referencing, or to give to other people for preview.

However, if you are going to use this effectively, you must make sure that your copy of Word is set up correctly. Perl follows to the letter exactly how your Word printer is set up; hence, if you aren't careful, you could send tons of output to the wrong printer.

Saving Documents in a Different Format

Another big way automation helped was to save documents into a different format. Since the Word format is proprietary, it is a big pain to index. You must rely on the Visual Basic methods for text processing, and Visual Basic simply wasn't made to handle text the way Perl was.

Again, OLE automation came in handy. Although I didn't have Word 97, I knew someone who did, and they used the following script to save everything as regular text documents (which can be manipulated quite easily by Perl). To use it, you say:

```
C:\> wordsave.p *
```

or:

```
C:\> wordsave.p test.doc
```

where the arguments to the script are legal Word documents. The code then saves everything with a txt extension for you, so you can look through the results with Perl (see Listing 12.15).

Listing 12.15
wordsave.p

```
1    #!/usr/local/bin/perl5
2
3    use FileHandle;
4    use strict;
5    use Win32::OLE;
6
7    my @files;
8
9    if ($ARGV[0] =~ m"\.")
10   {
11       @files =  @ARGV;
```

```
12  }
13  else
14  {
15      my $fh = new FileHandle($ARGV[0]) || die "Couldn't open $ARGV[0]\n";
16      chop(@files = <$fh>);
17  }
18
19  my $wordObj = new Win32::OLE('Word.Application')
20                                 || die "Couldn't open Word $! !\n";
21
22  die "Need to input some files!\n" if (!@files);
23
24  foreach $file (@files)
25  {
26          next if  ($file !~ m"\.doc$");
27          $wordObj->Documents->Open($file);
28          my $txtfile;
28          ($txtfile = $file) =~ s"\.doc"\.txt"ig;
29
30          $worddoc->ActiveDocument->SaveAs
31                                 (
32                                         {
33                                          FileName=> $txtfile,
34                                          FileFormat => 'wdFormatText'
35                                         }
36                                 );
37
38  }
39  $wordObj->Close();
```

Note lines 31–35: They show you another piece of the puzzle when translating Word code into Perl. If you wanted to do the equivalent in Visual Basic, you would say:

```
WordDoc.ActiveDocument.SaveAs FileName:= "C:\whatever\file"
                          FileFormat := wdFormatText
```

Unfortunately, this works only with Office 97. In version 7.0 and earlier of Word, you had to go through the `Word.Basic` OLE object (as in the example preceding this one).

Excel Example: Merging Two Spreadsheets

We gave an example of Excel in Chapter 2. Now, we are in a position to know exactly what is going on, and to better use references.

Excel works exceedingly well with references. If you think about it, a spreadsheet is a two-dimensional array (row A, column 10, for instance). If you have more than one spreadsheet open at the same time, this becomes a three-dimensional array.

Hence, you can manipulate Excel spreadsheets in Perl quite easily. Here's a small program that merges two or more spreadsheets together, and then saves them in the last workbook on the command-line. So if you say:

```
C:\ perl merge_excel.p 1.xls 2.xls 3.xls 4.xls
```

it will merge `1`, `2`, and `3.xls` into `4.xls`, stacking the spreadsheets on top of each other. The code is shown in Listing 12.16.

Listing 12.16
merge_excel.p

```
1    use Win32::OLE;
2
3    use Data::Dumper;
4    use strict;
5
6    my $excel = new Win32::OLE('Excel.Application') || die "ARRGH! $!\n";
7
8    $excel->{'Visible'} = 1;
9
10   print $excel;
11
12
13   my $workbook;
14   my $AoAoA = [];
15
16   foreach  $workbook (@ARGV)                       # each workbook on command-line
17   {
18                                                    # open it
19       $excel->Workbooks->Open($workbook);         # produces Array of Array
20       push(@$AoAoA, _processData($excel));
21       $excel->Workbooks(1)->Close();
22   }
23
24       _integrate($excel, $AoAoA);                  # put workbooks into one spread sheet
25       $excel->Save($ARGV[$#ARGV]);                 # save and quit,
26       $excel->Quit();
27
28   sub _processData
29   {
30       my($excel) = @_;
31
32       my $AoA = [];
33       my $value;
34       my ($row, $col) = ('A','1');
35
36       while (1)
37       {
38
39           while
40               (
41                    defined ($value =
42                    $excel->Workbooks(1)->Worksheets('Sheet1')->
43                            Range("$row$col")->{Value})
44               )
45           {
46
47               print "$row$col: $value\n";
48       $AoA->[ord($row) - ord('A')][$col-1] = $value; # stuff info into
49               $col++;                                      # Array of Array
50           }
51           last if ($value eq '' && $col == 1);
```

```
52              $row++; $col = 1;
53          }
54      print Dumper($AoA);
55      return($AoA);
56  }
57
58  sub _integrate
59  {
60      my ($excel, $AoAoA) = @_;
61
62      my $wb;
63      $excel->Workbooks->Add() || die "Couldn't open Workbook!\n";   # New workbook
64      print Dumper($AoAoA);                                          # testing
65
66      my %lastcol;
67      my ($rows, $cols, $rowcount, $colcount);
68
69      my $coltotal = 1;
70      foreach $wb (@$AoAoA)                                          # for each
71      {                                                             # Excel file
72          my $rows = $wb;
73          for ($rowcount = 0; $rowcount <  @>$rows; $rowcount++)     # for each row
74          {
75              $cols = $rows->[$rowcount];
76
77              for ($colcount = 0; $colcount <  @$cols; $colcount++)  # for each
78              {                           # column
79                  my $row = sprintf("%c", $rowcount+ord('A'));       # we need to
80                  my $col = $cols->[$colcount];                      # get an
81                  $lastcol{$row}++;                                  # equivalent
82                  my $range = "$row$lastcol{$row}";                  # column
83                  print "Adding $col to :$range:\n";
84              $excel->Range("$range")->{Value}=$col; # we add the value to the range
85              }
86          }
87      }
88  }
```

The only thing quirky about this is in the translation between the Excel spreadsheet and the double array. We have the line:

```
48              $AoA->[ord($row) - ord('A')][$col-1] = $value;
```

which does the translation. Excel rows go from A through Z, AA-ZZ, AAA-ZZZ, etc. And hence, as a quick translation, we can take the ASCII_value for *A (ord('A'))*, and subtract it from the name of the row to get a zero-based array element. If we had cell G12, this would translate into:

```
$AoA->[ord('G') - ord ('A') ][12-1]  = $value;
```

or:

```
$AoA->[71-65][11] = $AoA->[6][11] = $value;
```

So the translation of Excel to Perl is fairly straightforward. When we have our elements inside Perl two-dimensional arrays, the rest is easy. We accumulate the three arrays together, print them to the last element in the subroutine `integrate` in line 58, and then show what we are doing in line 82. By the time we get to saving the file (line 25) we have an Excel file consisting of our original Excel documents on the command-line.

Sending Mail via MAPI

Now we will consider sending mail via *MAPI*. MAPI stands for *Messaging Application Program Interface*, and is Windows' main method for automating mail. (Hopefully, by the time you read this, MAPI might be incorporated into the **Mail::Send** module of Graham Barr's, so you can get true, platform-independent mail, but we'll see.)

There are seven steps to sending a mail message with MAPI:

1. Making the OLE object
2. Logging into the OLE server
3. Configuring a message to be in the "Outbox"
4. Adding text to the message, and then saving it via **Update**
5. Figuring out where it is going by adding Recipients
6. Resolving those recipients via **Resolve**
7. Sending the mail

No wonder I yearn for a simple Perl interface to do all this! Here's some sample MAPI code. It acts as the command 'mail' does in Unix; if you say:

```
c:\> perl send_message.p help@internet.com pleasehelp@internet.com
```

Perl will tell you to enter a subject, and then the text to the message you are about to send. It saves this text in a message, which you then send to the MAPI server. The code is shown in Listing 12.17.

Listing 12.17
send_message.p

```
1    use Win32::OLE;
2    use strict;
3
4    my $ORIGINAL_MAIL   = 0;
5    my $FIRST_RECIPIENT = 1;
6    my $COPY_RECIPIENT  = 2;
7    my $BLINDCOPY_RECIPIENT  = 3;
8
9    my $SAVEMAIL = 1;
10   my $DONTSAVEMAIL = 0;
11
12   my $login = "Ed Peschko";
13   my $passwd = shift (@ARGV);
14
15
16          16  my @destination = @ARGV;
17   die "You need to have a message recipient!\n" if (!@destination);
18   my $mailobj = new Win32::OLE('MAPI.Session')
19              || die "Couldn't open a MAPI session! $!";  # special keyword for
20                                                          # mail session
21
22   my $logon = $mailobj->Logon($login, $passwd);              # logon for mail
23
24   print "Enter message please!\nSubject:";
```

```
25
26  my $subject = <STDIN>;
27  chop($subject);
28
29  print "Message Text: (.) to end\n";
30  my ($mail, $line);
31
32  while ($line ne '.')
33  {
34      chop($line = <STDIN>);
35      $mail .= "$line\n";
36
37  }
38
39  my $message = $mailobj->Outbox->Messages->Add();        # Add a message to queue
40
41  $message->{'Subject'} = $subject;
42  $message->{'text'} = $mail;
43  $message->Update();
44
45  my $type;     # first or second recipient?
46
47  foreach $mail (@destination)                        # go through each destination
48  {
49      if ($mail eq $destination[0]) { $type = $FIRST_RECIPIENT; }
50      else { $type = $COPY_RECIPIENT  = 2; }
51
52      my $sendto = $message->Recipients->Add();        # Add a recipient
53      $sendto->{'Name'} = $mail;
54      $sendto->{'Type'} = $type;    # the first person we list is the primary,
55      $sendto->Resolve();           # the second and further are copies.
56  }
57      $message->Send($SAVEMAIL,$AUTO,0);
58
59  $mailobj->Logoff();
```

Lines 39–59 are the actual MAPI part; lines 4–10 show some of the more common constants in MAPI. We use these constants in lines 49, 50, and 57; if we have more than one destination, we need to make the first person a "first recipient" and all the others "copy" recipients (lines 49 and 50). We therefore stack the people we are going to send to in line 52 (adding recipients as we go) and configure what types of recipients they are (line 54).

Finally, we send the mail (line 57) and quit the server (line 59). As I said, this seems to be an awful lot of work to send a message; hopefully you can look at **Mail::Send** on CPAN, and it will send mail on NT in one clean step.

LibWWW Examples

By now, about anybody who has to do with computers chokes on the incredibly ugly term *Information SuperHighway*. For one thing, the term is misleading; *Web* is a better term (also overused), and *mesh* might be more accurate.

In any case, not only do the newspeople have exceedingly bad taste for metaphors, but they are also missing out on about 80 percent of the Web as they know it.

The popular media concentrate on what they see on the Web: Home pages, people glued in front of computers, surfing, and so forth. However, nobody considers how the information that people are looking at actually got there in the first place.

This is the second side of the Web puzzle: If you can't collect information, you can't make an effective Web page. And if you can't make an effective Web page, then there is no Web.

In Perl, LibWWW is the primary way you would collect that information. LibWWW deals with the automation of collection of data off of the Web, and all that entails.

With LibWWW you can easily make a Webcrawler. You can easily download files from ftp sites on the Web. You can easily extract http tags from any Web page you come across, and you can easily make your applications interact with the Web for good effect. Most of this is more simple than people think; following are some small examples on how to do it.

Getting an html Page from the Web

If you go to any reasonable browser, like Netscape, you can see the source of a document by saying: View' => 'Document Source. This gives you an overview of what html is actually causing the page that you are witnessing. Listing 12.18 is a small Perl script that does exactly the same thing.

Listing 12.18
gethtmlpage.p

```
1    #!/usr/local/bin/perl5
2
3    use LWP::UserAgent;
4    $ua = new LWP::UserAgent;
5
6
7    $ua->agent('Mozilla/3.0');
8    my $req = new HTTP::Request( "GET" => "$ARGV[0]");
9    $req->header("Accept" => "text/html");
10   my $res = $ua->request($req);
11
12   if ($res->is_success) { $res->content(); }
13   else { print "Error: ". $res->code() . " " . $res->message(); }
```

Here, we do exactly the same thing. In line 4, we make a new UserAgent, which is an object like a portable mini-browser, only it is totally automated. In line 7, we lie to the user agent, telling it that it is in fact a Netscape browser (some Web pages look to see what browser is hitting them).

Then, we tell what type of request we are sending (a form, lines 7 and 8). We then pass that information to the user agent (line 10), which returns a string, which we then print.

Easy enough! If you say something like:

```
C:\> perl gethtmlpage.p "http://www.dejanews.com"
```

this will print:

```
<html>
<head>
<title> Deja News</title>
<meta name="keywords" content="dejanews usenet newsgroup articles search query">
</head>
<body background="/gifs/bgbar_gw.gif" bgcolor="#ffffff" text="#000000" link="#0000ff"
vlink="#52188c" alink="#ff0000">
# much deleted.
```

In other words, the *http://www.dejanews.com* home page. The question is: How do we manipulate this data? Well, we perform one type of manipulation next when we parse this information to get http tags.

Getting http Tags from a Web Form

To get the http tags from a form, we exploit one of Perl's greatest strengths: Its compilcated regular expressions. After all, when you think about it, a tag in a form looks something like:

```
<a href="http://www.dejanews.com">
```

where the tag is the item inside the double quotes. All we must do to extract this is make a regular expression that matches double quotes, precede that by an HREF, and then print the code. The code looks something like Listing 12.19.

Listing 12.19
simplehtmlparse.p

```
1    #!/usr/local/bin/perl5
2
3    use LWP::Simple;
4
5    my $doubleparen = q{"(([^\\\\"]|\\\\")*)"};               # reg exp for double quotes
6
7    print $doubleparen;
8    die "Need to supply an argument!\n" if (!defined $ARGV[0]);
9    $doc = get($ARGV[0]);                                      # simple way of getting a file
10
11   while ($doc =~ m/HREF=$doubleparen/sgi)
12   {
13       print ":$1:\n";
14   }
```

The regular expression is in line 5, and it should look familiar for we already covered it in the chapter on regular expressions.

Line 9 is an even simpler way of getting an html page than we covered earlier; all you do is say get(<url>) and you've got the text of that URL inside $doc.

Lines 11–13 cycle through the document and print the http tags they find.

These are fairly simple examples, but I hope you can see how valuable they are at extracting information off of the Web. In fact, a Webcrawler is really only a fancified version of a program that has three steps:

1. Extract the text and html tags off of one URL.
2. Save the text of that URL into a database.
3. Repeat steps 1 and 2 for all html tags we find.

We have already done steps 1 and 2; all we would have to do is take the stuff we programmed before, put it into a loop, and we have a Webcrawler.

Be careful if you are going to try making a Webcrawler. You can easily overload a system by sending out too many requests, and you might end up being banned if you don't introduce delays in your program (via sleep statements, and so forth).

    In addition, it seldom is very useful to start a general Webcrawler like this; sites like Lycos and Yahoo have already done it for you in a way that is far more extensive than a program of yours could ever do. The trick is selective searching: Webmasters are not happy if someone makes a Webcrawler that is CPU-intensive, and you could get into a lot of trouble. You have been forewarned.

A formbuilder Parsing Through an On-line form for User Information

We are now in a position to make a more complicated program. The one that we choose to make is called **formbuilder.p** and we will use it to actually make it so we can use the two simple scripts we described earlier (**simplehtmlparse.p** and **gethtmlpage.p**).

    The trick to how this script is going to be so useful is in the format which CGI scripts use to pass arguments. If you are working on Unix or NT, you can say:

```
C:\> perl script.p 1 2 3
```

and have your argument stack (@ARGV) look like:

```
@ARGV = (1, 2, 3);
```

Well, the arguments CGI receives are in hash value pairs, separated by a ?. Next time you go to Lycos or Yahoo, take a look at what happens when you enter something into the search window:

```
Search: perl script
```

The resulting `Location:` header will look something like this:

```
Location: http://search.yahoo.com/bin/search?p=perl+script
```

This is the server translating your search into an html tag. The application search is free to use the `p=perl+script` information any way it chooses. Yahoo so chooses to make it search its database for anything that has the keywords `perl` and `script` in it.

    Now the question is how do you find the correct arguments to any given script on the Web? After all, if we wanted to, we could bypass the Search Web page on Yahoo, if we find the location 'http://search.yahoo.com/bin/search?p=perl+script ourselves.

    The script has no way of knowing that the request came from the search page, or from you or your script. Hence, if we could find the correct arguments to pass to search, or any other script, we could bypass many forms on the Web, and automate the process quite a bit.

    The trick is to look at the Yahoo page itself for clues. If we look at the url http://www.yahoo.com, we see the following lines:

```
<form action="http://search.yahoo.com/bin/search">
<input size=30 name=p>
```

The first `action` tag is the script that is executed if we complete the form, and press **Submit**. The second is a named parameter, the one we are searching for. Both are used to combine into something like:

```
http://search.yahoo.com/bin/search?p=perl+script
```

for a valid tag that can be passed to a browser, or be automatically called by a script. Listing 12.20 is a script that handles much of the drudgery of looking at forms and figuring out the arguments to pass to them.

Listing 12.20
formbuilder.p

```
1    #!/usr/local/bin/perl5
2
3    use strict;
4
5    my $doubleparen = q#(?:[^\\"]|\\\\")*#;
6    my $noparen =    q#[^>=\s]+#;
7    my $selecttag = q#<SELECT.*?</SELECT>#;
8    my $inputtag = q#<INPUT .*?>#;
9    my $form =      q#<FORM .*?>#;
10
11   use LWP::UserAgent;
12   my $ua = new LWP::UserAgent();
13
14   $ua->agent("Mozilla/3.0");# we need to do this to get the 'right' web page
15                           # (the default gives you a sparse web page sometimes)
16
17   print "Web Site: $ARGV[0]\n";
18   print "-----------------\n";
19   my $req = new HTTP::Request("GET" => "$ARGV[0]");
20   $req->header("Accept" => "text/html");
21
22   my $res = $ua->request($req);
23
24   if ($res->is_success)
25   {
26   _buildForm( $ARGV[0], $res->content());                    # main function
27   }
28   else
29   {
30       print "Error: " . $res->code() . " " . $res->message();
31   }
32
33   sub _buildForm
34   {
35     my ($formname, $wholeform) = @_;
36
37     my ($formline) =
38         ($wholeform =~ m{
39                   ($form)    # form name    we get all embedded forms
40               }six
41         );
42
43     my @selects  =
44         ($wholeform =~ m{
45                   ($selecttag)  # -getting all selects
46               }sgix
47         );
```

```
48
49    my @inputs     =
50       ($wholeform =~ m{
51                  ($inputtag)                              # we get all inputs
52             }sgix
53        );
54
55    my $action      = _parseForm ( $formname, $formline ); # we see how script is to be executed
56    my $selectKeyValues =_parseSelect( $formname, \@selects ); # we get all selection Keys
57    my $inputKeyValues =_parseInput ( $formname, \@inputs ); # we get all input Keys
58
59       print <<"EOL"
60   Script Name:
61       $action
62
63   Actions:
64   @$selectKeyValues
65   @$inputKeyValues
66   EOL
67   }
68
69   sub _parseForm
70   {
71       my ($formname, $formline) = @_;
72
73       if ($formline =~ m#.*?ACTION.*?=.*?("$doubleparen"|$noparen)#si)    # actions can have form
74       {                                                     # 'ACTION = x' pr
75          my $scriptname = $1;                               # 'Action = "x."
76          return($scriptname);                              # Note case insensitive
77       }
78       else
79       {
80          print "WEIRDNESS!\n";
81          return('NO_SCRIPT');
82       }
83   }
84
85   sub _parseSelect                                          # form
86   {
87       my ($formname, $selects) = @_;
88
89       my ($select, $name, $values, $return) = ('','',[],[]);
90       local ($") = ",";
91       foreach $select (@$selects)
92       {
93          ($name) =
94             ($select =~ m{
95                         SELECT\s*NAME.*?          # gets junk before name
96                         ("$doubleparen"|$noparen) # gets the actual name
97                    }six
98             );
99
100         @$values =
101            ($select =~ m{
```

```
102                         <.*?VALUE.*?                # gets junk before value
103                         ("$doubleparen"|$noparen)   # gets actual value
104                         .*?>                        # gets junk after value
105                    }sgix
106          );
107      push (
108              @$return, sprintf("\tName: %-.20s\tValues: %-20s\n",
109                                              $name,"@$values")
110          );
111      }
112      return($return);
113  }
114
115  sub _parseInput
116  {
117      my ($formname, $inputs) = @_;
118
119      my ($input, $name, $default_value,$return) = ('','','',[]);
120      foreach $input (@$inputs)                # we go through all things user needs to enter
121      {
122          next if ($input =~ m#TYPE\s*=\s*("submit"|submit\s*)#i);# skip submit tags
123
124          ($name)  =
125              ($input =~ m{
126                          .*?NAME\s*=\s*                  # form...
127                      ( "$doubleparen"|$noparen)
128                  }six
129              );
130
131          ($default_value) =
132              ($input =~ m{
133                          .*?VALUE\s*=\s*
134                          ("$doubleparen"|$noparen)
135                  }six
136              );
137
138          push
139          (
140              @$return,                               # return text
141              sprintf (
142                      "\tName: %-.20s\tValues: %-20s\n",
143                                      $name, $default_value
144                  )
145          );
146      }
147      return($return);
148  }
```

This is getting kind of complicated, so let's draw another functional diagram (Figure 12.5).

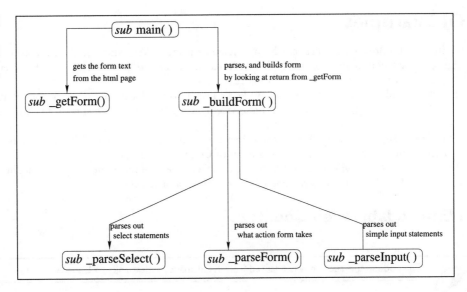

Figure 12.5
Functional
Diagram for
the Formbuilder

Here again, the key is regular expressions. The function _buildForm( ) parses out the whole html document into several pieces of text:

1. The action the form will take when executed (the regular expression m"<FORM .*?>")
2. The input tags we mentioned earlier (the regular expression m"<INPUT .*?>")
3. The radio buttons that occur in forms (the regular expression m"<SELECT.*?</SELECT>")

Each of these regular expressions keys for places that we can find the arguments that can be passed to CGI scripts. This is the first step. The rough text we get from matching for these three regular expressions we now send to _parseForm(), _parseSelect(), and _parseInput() for processing.

And finally, in lines 59–66, we print the output. This shows the arguments we can pass, at a best guess, to a given script. When we run this script for *http://www.lycos.com*, we get something like:

```
Web Site: http://www.lycos.com
-------------------------------
Script Name:
    /cgi-bin/pursuit

Actions:
    Name: cat        Values: lycos,sounds,graphics,point,geo,ups,bn,stockfind
    Name: matchmode  Values: and
    Name: query      Values: ""
```

We can use this information to build a reasonable URL_to do searches with. If we say something like:

```
http://www.lycos.com/cgi-bin/pursuit?cat=lycos&matchode=and&query=perl
```

this is then a legal URL for getting all the information on Perl from Lycos.

This is not the last time we will see this script. We will see it later when we use it to build a Meta-Web browser.

CGI Examples

Fortunately, and unfortunately, Perl has been saddled as being a Web language. Yes, it is true, Perl is the most popular scripting language for Web use, and yes, Perl can interface with Java, and yes, Perl has been integrated into Web servers like IIS and Apache (for performance reasons...).

But this popularity tends to overshadow Perl's uses in other locations, which I hope that this chapter is showing! Companies do themselves a great disservice by using Perl in only one area (the CGI area) and ignoring the rest.

One can't deny it though. One of the primary uses of Perl is on the Web, and any book calling itself *Perl Complete* must to give at least a few examples of CGI GUIs in action.

So here they are. We will start with a small example (a Web counter), move up to a medium-sized example (a metabrowser), and finish with a relatively large example (a bugtracker).

An Embeddable Web Counter

The code in this section was adapted from F. Cusmano, with thanks to Liang Gu.

Our first example shows up in many different contexts: A counter to count the accesses of a certain Web page. Although, in many ways, it has been done to death (the example, that is), it shows many important things about how CGI and html can work together.

The first thing we need to look at is the html in which we actually embed the counter. Listing 12.21 shows the sample Web page we are going to use.

Listing 12.21
counterinfo.html

```
1    <HTML>
2        <HEAD>
3            <TITLE>Interesting places to find counters</TITLE>
4        </HEAD>
5        <body bgcolor=#DDDDDD text =#000000">
6        <left>
7        <h2> List of sites to get more sophisticated counters from: </h2>
8            <ul>
9            <li><h3><a href = "http://www.worldwidemart.com/scripts"> Matt's Script Archive</a>
10            <li> <a href = "http://www.counter.com"> counter.com </a>
11            <li> <a href = "http://www.countestatsr.com"> counterstats.com </a>
12            <li> <a href = "http://www.countmania.com"> countmaina.com </a>
13            <li> <a href = "http://www.freecount.com"> freecount.com </a>
14            <li> <a href = "http://www.jinko.com/counters"> Jinko mania </a>
15            <li> <a href = "http://www.freecount.com"> countmaina.com </a>
16            <li> <a href = "http://www.digits.com"> Web counter</a>
17            </ul>
```

```
18    <img src="/cgi-bin/fcount.cgi">
19       </body>
20    </html>
```

This page is simply a list of links that show, well, more sophisticated examples of Web counters than we do here. The key to our example though, is in line 18, where we will get our Web counter; the script **/cgi-bin/fcount.cgi** will get the Web counter picture for us.

But how does html recognize that we aren't trying to access **/cgi-bin/fcount.cgi** itself as a picture? How does it interpret it as a script instead?

The key here is by *context*. **cgi-bin** is by definition for the Web server, a place where you keep binaries. Therefore, you can use the binary to generate or return pictures—whatever you like.

fcount.cgi, then, must return a bitmap that a user's browser can decode as a picture. Listing 12.22 is **fcount.cgi**. Notice that the picture it produces isn't exactly the greatest.

Listing 12.22
fcount.cgi

```perl
1    #!/usr/local/bin/perl
2
3
4
5    use CGI;
6
7    # create an array of digit bits for the XBM
8    #use the hex code (2chars) to define each line of the digits (working on graph paper helps)
Remember bits displayed lsb 1st
9
10   #                 00 11 22 33 44 55 66 77 88 99
11   my $digs =                                                  # the 'xbm' or bitmap
12      [
13         [qw (    00 00 00 00 00 00 00 00 00 00    )],
14         [qw (    00 00 00 00 00 00 00 00 00 00    )],
15         [qw (    3c 30 3c 3c 30 7e 38 7e 3c 3c    )],
16         [qw (    66 38 66 66 30 06 0c 66 66 66    )],
17         [qw (    66 30 60 60 38 06 06 60 66 66    )],
18         [qw (    66 30 60 60 38 06 06 60 66 66    )],
19         [qw (    66 30 30 60 34 06 06 60 66 66    )],
20         [qw (    66 30 30 38 34 3e 3e 30 3e 66    )],
21         [qw (    66 30 18 38 32 60 66 30 3e 7c    )],
22         [qw (    66 30 0c 60 32 60 66 30 66 60    )],
23         [qw (    66 30 0c 60 7e 60 66 18 66 60    )],
24         [qw (    66 30 06 60 30 60 66 18 66 60    )],
25         [qw (    66 30 06 60 30 66 66 18 66 60    )],
26         [qw (    3c 7c 7e 3c 30 3c 3c 18 3c 3c    )],
27         [qw (    00 00 00 00 00 00 00 00 00 00    )],
28         [qw (    00 00 00 00 00 00 00 00 00 00    )]
29      ];
30
31   if (!($fname = $ENV{'QUERY_STRING'})) { $fname = "fcount"; }
32
```

```
33   my ($fcnt, $flog, $cnt) = ( "$fname.cnt", "$fname.log", 0 );
34
35   if (open(FCNT, "<$fcnt"))      { $cnt = <FCNT>; close(FCNT); }   # open 10g fcount
36   if (++$cnt > 9999)             { $cnt = 1;  }                    # increment count
37   if (open(FCNT, ">$fcnt"))      { print FCNT $cnt; close(FCNT); } # print out new count
38
39   my @out = split('', sprintf("%04d", $cnt));
40
41
42   print "Content-type: image/x-xbitmap\n\n";                      # generate a bitmap
43   print "#define count_width  32\n";
44   print "#define count_height 16\n";
45   print "static char count_bits[] = {\n";
46
47   for ($ii = 0; $ii < 16; $ii++)
48   {
49       my $digit;
50       foreach $digit (@out) { print"0x$digs->[$ii][$digit]," }
51   }
52   print "};\n";
53
54   #now do the log file
55   if (open(FLOG, ">>$flog"))                                       # log of who accessed
56   {
57       $dd = localtime(time);
58       $ra = $ENV{'REMOTE_ADDR'};
59       $rh = $ENV{'REMOTE_HOST'};
60       $hu = $ENV{'HTTP_USER_AGENT'};
61       printf FLOG "$dd | $ra | $rh | $hu\n";
62       close(FLOG);
63   }
64
```

Lines 11–29 define the bitmap we will use. Word quoting (qw) comes in quite handy here. Otherwise there would be tons of extra quote marks (['00', '00', '00', '00']—yuck). Lines 35–37 get the number of users that have accessed the Web site. We increment that, and in lines 42–51 we proceed to generate the XBM that will be printed by the image = directive.

Then we do one more thing: Using the REMOTE_ADDR, REMOTE_HOST, and HTTP_USER_AGENT variables, we save a record into a log of each site that accessed the page, and what browser they were using. In lines 65 and 66, we end the form.

When it is all done, the combination of Web counter and script makes a page that looks something like Figure 12.6.

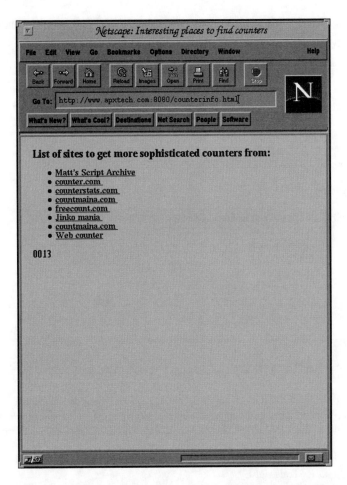

Figure 12.6
Counter Plus
Links to
More Elaborate
Counters

Well, not much, but by following the links on that page, you could probably find a counter to suit your needs.

A Meta-Browser

In this section, we will be using formbuilder to build a script (thanks to Alan Switzer). Let's go up a level (two levels?) in difficulty, and look at building a fairly complicated Web page. Remember our formbuilder script? Well, with a little elbow grease, we can use the output of our formbuilder to build what is called a *meta-browser*. Meta-browsers don't do much in themselves, except query other browsers to see what they know, and display their information in an easy-to-see way.

Well, if you remember from our earlier discussion, the way to make an engine search was to send the script that did the searching a certain string of arguments. For Yahoo, the script/search string combo looked like:

```
http://search.yahoo.com/bin/search?p=perl+script
```

First, what we need to do is collect a list of these script/search string combos. We do this by running **formbuilder**:

```
prompt% formbuilder.p http://www.lycos.com

Web Site: http://www.lycos.com
-----------------
Script Name:
    /cgi-bin/pursuit

Actions:
        Name: cat          Values: lycos,sounds,graphics,point,geo,ups,bn,stockfind
        Name: matchmode Values: and
        Name: query       Values: ""
        Name:    Values:


prompt% formbuilder http://www.altavista.com

Web Site: http://www.altavista.com
-----------------
Script Name:
    "http://www.altavista.digital.com/cgi-bin/query"

Actions:
        Name: what       Values: web,news
        Name: fmt        Values: ".",c,d

        Name: pg         Values: q
        Name: q Values: ""
```

From here, we can construct http tags that will work on pretty much any search engine. We choose *www.yahoo.com*, *www.altavista.com*, *www.excite.com*, *www.lycos.com*, *www.infoseek.com*, and *www.metacrawler.com*. So in a sense, we are making a "meta-meta-crawler" script, because *www.metacrawler.com* does exactly the same thing we are trying to do!

Anyway, that forms the heart of our script. The rest of it is shown in Listing 12.23. It becomes a bit of a mouthful to do this so that the usage feels right.

Listing 12.23
meta.cgi

```
1    #!/usr/local/bin/perl5
2
3    # meta.cgi - this perl script demonstrates how to create a cgi program that
4    #            can access multiple search engines on the web.
5
6    use CGI qw(:all);
7    use CGI::Carp qw (fatalsToBrowser confess);
8    use strict;
9
10   # Define JavaScript function for hit number validation
11   my $jscript=<<END;
12                    <!-- Hide script
13
14                    function validateHits(form)
15                    {
16                     var hitnum = parseInt(form.hits.value);
```

```
17                      if (isNaN(hitnum))
18                          {
19                            alert("Please choose an integer number of hits!");
20                              form.hits.focus();
21                              form.hits.select();
22                              return false;
23                          }
24                        return true;
25                      }
26                      // End script hiding -->
27   END
28
29   # Create the query CGI object
30   my $query = new CGI;
31
32   # Create an html document
33   print $query->header;
34   print $query->start_html
35                  (
36                  -title       => 'THE META SEARCH ENGINE',
37                  -author      => 'switzer.alan@decatech.com',
38                  -script      => $jscript,
39                  -BACKGROUND  => 'images/background.jpg'
40                  );
41
42   # Determine if script called with argument or not...
43   if (param())
44   {
45   my $subject = $query->param('subject');
46   my $hits = $query->param('hits');
47   my $engines = $query->param('engines');
48
49          print $query->h1('META SEARCH RESULTS:');
50
51          if ($subject)
52          {
53              # Display requested query string and number of hits for the search
54              print
55              "Your subject is: <B>", em($query->param('subject')), "</B>", hr(),
56          "You wanted to find <B>", em($query->param('hits')), "</B> hits", hr();
57
58              # Save array of information for each search engine's characteristics
59              my @search_engines =
60                  (
61                      {
62                          name => "Yahoo",
63                          url  => "http://search.yahoo.com",
64                  tag  => "/bin/search?p=$subject",
65                          img  => "images/yahoo.gif",
66                          txt  => "Yahoo hits for \"<B>$subject</B>\""
67                      },
68                      {
69                          name => "Lycos",
70                          url  => "http://www.lycos.com",
71                          tag  =>
```

```
72              "/cgi-bin/pursuit?cat=lycos&query=$subject&matchmode=and",
73                          img  => "images/lycos.gif",
74                          txt  => "Lycos hits for \"<B>$subject</B>\""
75                      },
76                      {
77                          name => "Alta-Vista",
78                          url  => "http://www.altavista.digital.com",
79          tag  =>
80           "/cgi-bin/query?what=web&fmt=.&pg=q&q=$subject",
81                          img  => "images/alta_vista.gif",
82                          txt  => "Alta-Vista hits for \"<B>$subject</B>\""
83                      },
84                      {
85                          name => "Infoseek",
86                          url  => "http://www.infoseek.com",
87          tag  =>
88        "/Titles?col=WW&qt=$subject&sv=IS&lk=noframes&nh=$hits",
89                              img  => "images/infoseek.gif",
90                              txt  => "Infoseek hits for <\\>"<B>$subject</B><\\>""
91                      },
92                      {
93                          name => "Excite",
94                          url  => "http://www.excite.com",
95          tag  => "/search.gw?trace=a&search=$subject",
96                              img  => "images/excite.gif",
97                              txt  => "Excite hits for \"<B>$subject</B>\""
98                      },
99                      {
100                             \name => "Metacrawler",
101                              url  => "http://www.metacrawler.com",
102 tag  => "/crawler?general=$subject&method=0&region=&rpp=20&timeout=10&hpe=$hits",
103                             img  => "images/metacrawler.gif",
104                             txt  => "Metacrawler hits for \"<B>$subject</B>\""
105                         }
106                 );
107
108         print "<table align=center>\n";
109
110         my $search;
111         foreach $search (@search_engines)
112         {
113             my ($yc, $xc) = (100,40);
114             my ($img, $url, $tag, $txt) =
115                 (
116                  $search->{'img'}, $search->{'url'},
117                  $search->{'tag'}, $search->{'txt'}
118                 );
119
120         if ($engines eq "All")
121         {
122             # Create links to all search engine results
123 print <<"EOF_PRINT";
124 <tr>
125     <td align=center>
126         <a href= "$url$tag">
```

```
127                 <img src="$img" align=center border=2 height=$xc width=$yc></a>
128         </td>
129         <td>
130             <a href= "$url$tag">
131             $search->{'txt'}</a>
132         </td>
133 EOF_PRINT
134                 }
135                 elsif ($engines eq $search->{'name'})
136                 {
137                     # Create a link to the specific search engine the user
138                     # asked for
139 print <<"EOF_PRINT";
140 <tr>
141     <td align=center>
142     <a href= "$url$tag">
143     <img src="$img" align=center border=2 height=$xc width=$yc></a>
144     </td>
145     <td>
146         <a href= "$url$tag"></a>
147         $txt
148     </td>
149 </tr>
150 EOF_PRINT
151                     last;
152                 }
153             }
154             # End the table
155             print "</table>\n";
156
157             # Provide a link back to the main page
158             print p(),
159             $query->a({href=>"meta.cgi"}, "Return to META SEARCH home");
160     }
161     else
162     {
163             # User didn't input a query string, create page to tell them
164             print "You submitted an empty query.", p(),
165             "Hit ", $query->b("back"), " on your",
166             " browser, or click below and ", $query->i("try again"), "!", p(),
167             $query->a({href=>"meta.cgi"}, "Return to META SEARCH home");
168     }
169 }
170 else
171 {
172     # Main/Start page creation
173     # Create a form to ask user for query, number of hits, and search
174     # engines to use
175     print $query->h1('META SEARCH ENGINE'),
176     start_form(-name=>'form1', -onSubmit=>"return validateHits(this)"),
177 "<table>",
178 Tr(), td(), "What subject do you want to look for?",
179 td(), $query->textfield('subject'),
180 p(), Tr(), td(), "How many hits do you want to find?   ",
181 td(), $query->textfield(-name=>'hits',-default=>'20'),
```

```
182   p(), Tr(), td(), "Your choice of search engines?",
183   td(),
184      $query->radio_group(-name=>'engines',
185                              -values=>['All', 'Yahoo', 'Lycos', 'Alta-Vista',
186                                        'Infoseek', 'Excite', 'Metacrawler'],
187                              -default=>'All', -linebreak=>'true'),
188                       "</table>", "<center>", $query->submit(), "</center>",
189      p(), end_form();
190  }
191
192  # End the html document
193  print end_html();
```

Although this looks quite complicated, the logic of it is fairly simple. There are two main pages that we create. The first one is created in lines 171–190 if the user gives no arguments to the script. This is shown in Figure 12.7. We give the user a series of questions in lines 178–183; in particular, we are constructing a table so the meta-search engine looks fairly respectable. The tr() and td() functions define table rows and table pieces of data, respectively. The radio_group function provides the group of buttons that actually determine on which sites the Perl script is going to seek out and find information.

Figure 12.7
Meta-Search
Engine
Home Page

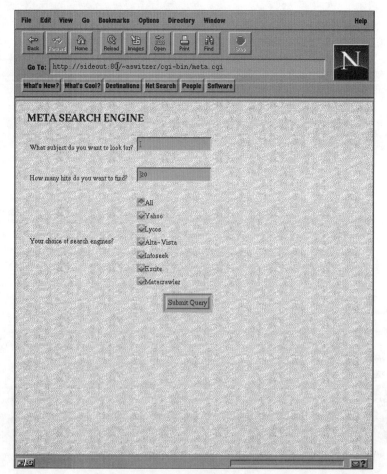

We also choose a picture background in line 39, as we kind of get sick of the gray that comes as a default with browsers, and we set up a callback that determines whether or not the person has entered a valid number of hits in line 176.

When a person hits the **submit query** button, the html page then uses the Javascript up top (lines 11–27) to look at the value for the hits parameter. If it is null (line 17), we call the alert function in Javascript (line 19) which puts up the warning shown in Figure 12.8.

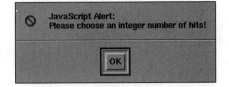

Figure 12.8
Alert Shown on
the Screen
Signifying
Null String

Now, if the user has entered legal values, they are used to generate the html page that shows links to browsers which you can then use to process your query.

The values you enter into the meta-search engine home page become parameters to the **meta.cgi** command-line. These parameters are then stored, and **meta.cgi** forks off a copy of itself.

When line 43 is hit (the check for `param()` or `parameters`), this statement then is true—there are parameters. (When you first started this example, this statement was false.) Then, Perl goes to work taking the parameters out of the command-line (lines 45–48), and creating a Web page out of the results. In a critical loop (lines 111–153) we create the links to the actual search engines we are interested in. This Web page looks like Figure 12.9.

There you have it. If you now hit on any one of these links, the meta-browser will pass these links on to the respective Webcrawler, which will then find the subject 'Perl' for you, and print out as many hits as you requested.

Figure 12.9
Results of the
Search

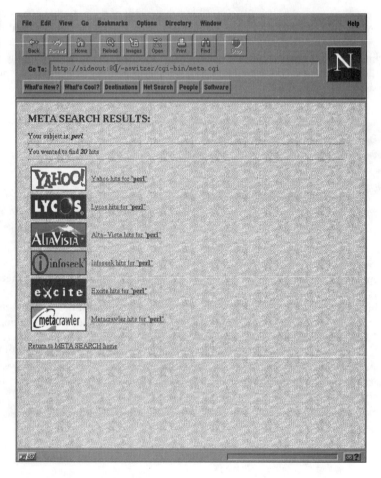

File   Edit   View   Go   Bookmarks   Options   Directory   Window   Help

Back   Forward   Home   Reload   Images   Open   Print   Find   Stop

Go To: http://sideout:80/~aswitzer/cgi-bin/meta.cgi

What's New?   What's Cool?   Destinations   Net Search   People   Software

META SEARCH RESULTS:

Your subject is: *perl*

You wanted to find *20* hits

Yahoo hits for "**perl**"

Lycos hits for "**perl**"

Alta-Vista hits for "**perl**"

Infoseek hits for "**perl**"

Excite hits for "**perl**"

Metacrawler hits for "**perl**"

Return to META SEARCH home

A bugtracker

In this section, we create a maintainable application for communicating bugs to team members (thanks to Sally Thompson), also known as a"bugtracker."

The last example showed something that is very peculiar to programming in CGI: It is essentially a "stateless" environment. We talk about this in great detail when we get to our "main" CGI programming project in Chapter 24 (porting scripts from a shell to making them GUIs on the Web). But for now, simply realize what this means.

The only information that any CGI script can get is from the command-line. Hence, if you take the time to make a huge structure in one window, and then forget to "unpack" this structure and put it on the command line, Perl will remember nothing about the structure.

Each time you hit that submit button, whatever you have built up in memory is gone, because Perl is firing off a new instance of itself and *wiping the slate clean*, so to speak.

There are several ways to deal with this limitation:

1. Ignore it, and pass long command-lines.

2. Use a permanent data structure to hold the information you have accumulated, and then load it back into memory each time a person hits **Submit**.

3. Use a permanent instance of Perl. Find a method to make it so the Perl interpreter "stays around" after the person hits **Submit**.

The first way can get silly, especially if you have lots of data you want to share between pages. The second way is done fairly frequently and will be done in the following script. It's a fair (workable) solution.

But if you can do it, the third way is the best way of approaching the problem. You have no overhead for starting Perl, and you can keep a much larger Web site than otherwise possible. Two major servers support an embedded Perl, Apache and IIS, and you may want to check out their home pages: *www.apache.com* and *www.microsoft.com*, respectively.

The interpreter embedded into Apache is called **mod_perl** and it is really cool. It lets you embed Perl syntax exactly as if it were JavaScript. There is also an equivalent script, by activestate, that lets you do the same with Windows NT servers.

Note

Here's a script that shows how one might create a *bugtracker*, where people enter bugs, and are assigned bugs from a centralized source. CGI is really adept at this because it can be extremely centralized, more so than any GUI. For example, a script like that shown in Listing 12.24 could be used to make a distributed development team that only communicated through e-mail, and bugs would be passed into a centralized database via browser.

Listing 12.24
bugtrack.p

```
1    #!/home/epeschko/perl5.004_50/install/bin/perl
2
3    use CGI;
4    use CGI::Carp qw (fatalsToBrowser confess);
5    use Data::Dumper;
6    use FileHandle;
7    use Date::Format qw(time2str);
8    use Date::Parse qw(str2time);
9
10    use strict;
11
12   my $JSCRIPT=<<EOF;
13   function do_submit()
14       {
15       document.forms[0].submit();
16       }
17   EOF
18   ;
19   select(STDOUT); $|=1;
20   my $query = new CGI;
21
22
23   print $query->header;                          # title of screen
24   print $query->start_html
```

```
25                      (
26                          -title=>     'Defect Track',
27                      -script=>    $JSCRIPT,
28                      -author=>    'sthompso\@elmer.tcinc.com'
29                  );
30
31  print $query->startform                     # form on screen
32                  (
33                      -name=>      'form2',
34                      -action=>    'bugtrack.p',
35                      -method=>    'get'
36                  );
37  my @severity=
38          (
39              'Catastrophic',
40              'No Workaround Avail',
41              'Workaround Exists',
42              'Cosmetic',
43              'Enhancement'
44          );
45
46  my @defectStat =
47          ('New', 'In Progress','Complete');     # status of bugs
48
49  my @phase=                                  # phase of bugs
50          ('System','Integration','Production');
51
52  my @area=
53          (                                   # where bugs are
54              'Software Tools',
55              'User Software',
56              'Scripts',
57              'Data',
58              'Documentation',
59              'Installation'
60          );
61
62  my @_fields =
63          qw (date defect_id status area short_desc long_desc severity phase);
64
65  my $defect_data = setup_defect_data();
66
67  main();                                      # three different screens
68
69  sub main
70  {
71    if ($query->param("submit_defect") )
72    {
73        save_defect_data($query);
74        $defect_data = setup_defect_data();     # set up screen
75    }
76
77    if ($query->param("submit") )  # query from last cgi cell script calls itself
78    {
```

```
79              &display_defects($defect_data);              # dislpay defect screen
80         }
81         else
82         {
83              &search_defects($defect_data);               # search defect screen
84         }
85         print $query->endform;
86    }
87
88
89    sub display_defects
90    {
91         my ($defect_data) = @_;
92         my ( $defect_id, $data, $date, $status, $area,
93                  $short_desc, $long_desc, $severity, $phase,
94                  $timeval);
95
96         my ($i) = -1;
97         my ($radio_button);
98
99         while ($date= $query->param('date.' . ++$i))        # information gathered
100        {                                                   #  from user to be displayed
101          my $radio_button = $query->param('select.' . $i);
102                                                            # on defect screen.
103          if ($radio_button eq 'on')
104          {
105               $defect_id = $query->param("defect_id.$i");
106               $data = $defect_data->{$defect_id};
107               $date=$data->{date};
108               $status=$data->{status};
109               $area=$data->{area};
110               $short_desc=$data->{short_desc};
111               $long_desc=$data->{long_desc};
112               $severity=$data->{severity};
113               $phase=$data->{phase};
114               last;
115          }
116        }
117
118        if (!defined $data)                                 # if no data, make new bug
119        {
120             $defect_id =_pick_defect_id($defect_data);
121             $timeval= time();
122             $date = localtime($timeval);
123             $date = substr($date, 4, 6) . ", " .  substr($date, 20, 4);
124             $status='NEW';
125             $area='';
126             $short_desc = '';
127             $long_desc='';
128             $severity='';
129             $phase='';
130        }
131
132        print "<HTML><H1><center>Defect Track</center></H1>";
```

```
133     print "<HTML><H2><center>Entry Screen</center></H2>";
134
135     print "<P><b>Date</b>",                    # make an input text field
136          $query->textfield
137               (
138                    -name=>'date',
139                    -value=>$date,
140                    -size=>20
141               );
142
143     print "<b>Defect Id</b>",                   # make an Id text field
144          $query->textfield                      # to look up old bugs
145               (
146                    -name=> 'defect_id',
147                    -value=> $defect_id,
148                    -size=>  20
149               );
150
151     print "<b>Ticket Status</b>",               # what status is ticket in?
152          $query->scrolling_list                 # give user only a few
153               (                                  # legal choices
154                    -name=>     'status',
155                    -values=> [@defectStat],
156                    -default=> $status,
157                    -size=>    1
158               );
159
160     print "<P><b>Short Description</b>",         # description?
161          $query->textfield
162               (
163                    -name=>    'short_desc',
164                    -value=>   $short_desc,
165                    -size=>    80
166               );
167
168     print "<P><b>Phase Found in</b>",
169          $query->scrolling_list
170               (
171                    -name=>'phase',
172                    -values=>[@phase],
173                    -default=>$phase,
174                    -size=>1
175               );
176
177     print "<P><b>Defect Severity</b>",
178          $query->scrolling_list
179               (
180                    -name=>'severity',
181                    -values=>[@severity],
182                    -default=>$severity,
183                    -size=>1
184               );
185
186     print "<b>Area Affected</b>",
```

```
187                  $query->scrolling_list
188                      (
189                          -name=>'area',
190                          -values=>[@area],
191                          -default=>$area,
192                          -size=>1
193                      );
194
195      print "<P><b>Long Description</b>",          # text box
196              $query->textarea
197                  (
198                      -name=>'long_desc',
199                       -default=>$long_desc,
200                      -rows=>10,
201                      -columns=>80
202                  );
203
204      $query->delete('submit');
205                                                   # submit button: note'submit'
206      print "<center>",                            # function
207              $query->submit
208                  (
209                      -name=>'submit_defect',
210                      -value=>'Submit'
211                  ),
212              "</center>";
213  }
214
215  sub search_defects
216  {
217      my ($defect_data) = @_;
218      my ($srchText);
219
220      print "<HTML><H1><center>Defect Track</center></H1>";
221      print "<HTML><H2><center>Search Screen</center></H2>";
222
223      print "<P><b>Enter Search Text</b>",
224              $query->textfield
225                      (
226                          -name     => 'srchText',
227                          -size     => 20,
228                          -onChange => "do_submit()",
229                          -value    => $srchText
230                      );
231
232      print "<center><table border>";              # make a table.
233      print "<caption><H4><b>Existing Defects</b></H4></caption>\n";
234      print "<th>Select</th>\n";
235      print "<th>Date</th>\n";
236      print "<th>Defect Id</th>\n";
237      print "<th>Area</th>\n";
238      print "<th>Defect Description</th>\n";
239      print "<P>\n";
240
```

```
241     my $i = 0;
242     my ($defect_id, $data, $date, $area, $short_desc);
243                                                 # $defect data is where
244     foreach $defect_id (keys %$defect_data)
245     {
246         $data = $defect_data->{$defect_id};    # all user input is
247         $date=$data->{date};                    # gotten from file
248         $area=$data->{area};
249         $short_desc=$data->{short_desc};
250         my $search = $query->param('srchText');
251 if ($query->param('srchText') && $short_desc !~ /$search/ig) {next};
252
253         print "<tr>>";
254         print "<td>",
255             $query->checkbox(-name=>"select.$i",        # we want to give
256                 label=>>>'',                            # them a place for
257                 -size=>1),                              # checking whether or
258                 "</td>";                                # not they want to see
259                                                         # the textfield
260         print "<td>",
261             $query->textfield(-name=>"date.$i",
262                 -value=>$date,
263                 -size=>9),
264                 "</td>";
265         print "<td>",
266             $query->textfield(-name=>"defect_id.$i",
267                 -value=>$defect_id,
268                 -size=>6),
269                 "</td>";
270         print "<td>",
271                 $query->textfield
272                 (
273                     -name=>"area.$i",
274                     -value=>$area,
275                     -size=>14
276                 ),
277                 "</td>";
278         print "<td>",
279
280         $query->textfield
281                 (
282                     -name=>"short_desc.$i",
283                     -value=>$short_desc,
284                     -size=>50
285                 ),
286                 "</td>";
287         $i++;
288         print "</tr>";
289     }
290
291     print "</table></center>\n";
292     print "<center>",
293             $query->submit
294                 (
```

```
295                              -name  =>  'submit',
296                              -value =>  'Submit'
297                      ),
298          "</center>";
299 }
300
301 sub save_defect_data                          # Ad back data base... bad
302 {                                             # performance, Use DBI
303     my ($query) = @_;
304     my @text;
305
306     local($") = "|";
307
308     my $defects = setup_defect_data();        # setup_defect_data gives old
309                                               # defects
310     my $field;
311     foreach $field (@_fields)
312     {
313         push(@text, $query->param($field));
314     }
315     my $new_defects = setup_defect_data("@text", $defects);
316
317     my $fh = new FileHandle("> $ENV{'DOCUMENT_ROOT'}/defect_data") ||
318             croak ("couldn't open $ENV{'DOCUMENT_ROOT'}/defect_data");
319
320     write_defects($fh, $new_defects);
321 }
322
323 sub write_defects                             # code to write defects
324 {      # writes entire file, each step.
325     my ($fh, $new_defects) = @_;
326
327     my ($key, $field, @text);
328     foreach $key  (keys (%$new_defects))      # each key, in all defects
329     {
330         my $defect = $new_defects->{$key};
331         foreach $field (@_fields)
332         {
333             my $text =     $defect->{$field};
334             if ($field eq 'date')
335             {
336                 my $secs = str2time($text);
337                 $text = time2str("%x", $secs);
338             }
339             push(@text, $text);
340         }
341         print $fh "@text\n";                   # we use pipe delimited files
342         undef (@text);                         # write it out
343     }
344     close($fh);
345 }
346
347 sub setup_defect_data               # we 'setup' defect data by loading it from files
348 {                                              # overloaded functions
```

```
349      my ($type, $defects) = @_;
350
351      my (@data);
352      my $return = {};                              # no args loads all defects
353      if (@_ == 0)
354      {
355          my $fh= new FileHandle("$ENV{'DOCUMENT_ROOT'}/defect_data");
356          chop(@data = <$fh>);
357      }
358      else                                          # with arguments , makes new defect
359      {
360          my $text = $type; @data = ($text); $return = $defects;
361      }
362
363
364      my ($row);
365
366      foreach $row (@data)                          # split defect rows;
367      {
368      my $defect = {};
369      my @stuff = split(/\|/,$row);
370
371      my $i = 0;
372      map ($defect->{$_fields[$i++]} = $_, @stuff);
373      $return->{$defect->{defect_id}}= $defect;  # populate data structure
374 }
375 $return;
376 }
377
378 sub _pick_defect_id                               # picks a new defect id
379 {
380      my ($defect_data) = @_;
381
382      my $xx = -1;
383      while (defined ($defect_data->{++$xx})) { }
384      return($xx);
385 }
```

Again, this is getting pretty hairy, so let's make a functional diagram. Figure 12.10 shows the bugtracker's skeleton.

Figure 12.10
Bugtracker
Functional
Diagram

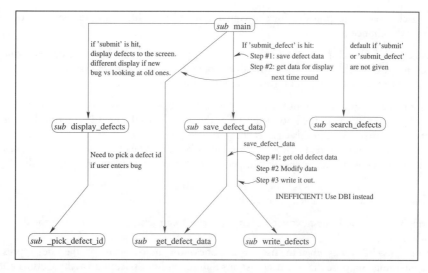

Here, we are again juggling two Web pages through a loop: the loop in lines 69-86. The first of the two Web pages we set is the "defect search" page, which the user sees when he or she enters the application. It looks something like Figure 12.11.

Figure 12.11
Defect Search
Screen

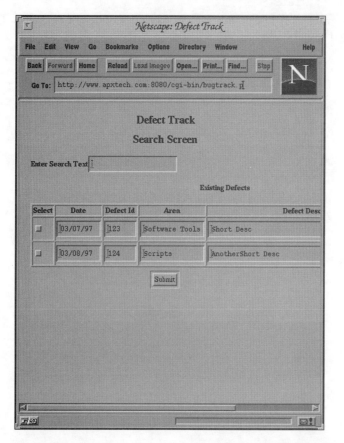

The defect search screen is responsible for showing at a high level what bugs are available to work on, and also to give the user the chance to:

1.   Select a specific bug for perusal by checking the appropriate radio box in the Select column.
2.   Enter in a search text string, and show all the bugs associated with that string.
3.   Do neither of these things, and instead submit a new bug.

When the user hits **Submit,** the current version of the script stops running, and like a runner handing a baton to the next runner, the script passes the knowledge what the user did to the next Perl script that fires up in the form of arguments in the http string. In this case, there were two possibilities.

The first was the user types text in the Search window. Suppose the user searches for the bugs given the search text typed in the Search window. Say he or she typed **perl. Bugtrack.p** creates an http tag that looks like:

```
'http://www.apxtech.com:8080/cgi-bin/tmp/bugtrack.p?srchText=perl&
(all the bugs matching that description)
```

With the string **srchTxt=perl,** the next version of the script **bugtrack.pl** knows to limit the display of bugs inside the text in line 251.

The second possibility was when the user presses one of the radio buttons on the side, or presses **Submit** without selecting anything. Suppose that the user just hits **Submit** without selecting anything else on the screen. In that case, **bugtrack.p** creates an http tag that looks like:

```
'http://www.apxtech.com:8080/cgi-bin/tmp/bugtrack.p?srchText=&submit=Submit (all the
bugs matching that radio button command)
```

This signifies to the bugtracker that it should prompt for a new bug description to be entered. Thus, the following, second screen comes up (Figure 12.12).

Figure 12.12
New Entry Screen
for **bugtracker.p**

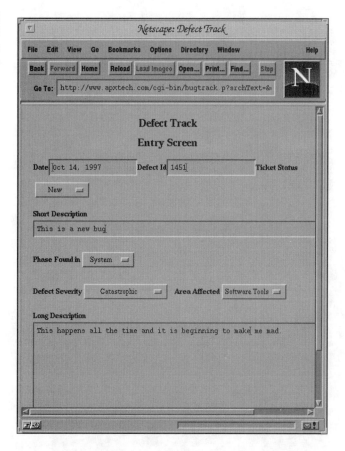

We are then free to enter in the information that we want, and when we are done, we hit **Submit**. This causes the http tag to be passed back to look like:

```
http://www.apxtech.com:8080/cgibin/tmp/bugtrack.p?srchText=&submit_defect=Submit (etc.)
```

Then we call the function string `save_defect_data()`, then `setup_defect_data()`, and then `search_defects()`. In other words, we save the data for the bug, get the new saved data from the place we saved it to (a file), and then redisplay the screen. When done, we get a screen that looks like Figure 12.13. If you are new to Web programming, this "passing by parameters" may seem a bit odd. It seems like you are passing the world around, and going through a massive amount of overhead in constructing these "batons" for communication between CGI scripts.

Figure 12.13
A New Bug
Added by
bugtrack.p

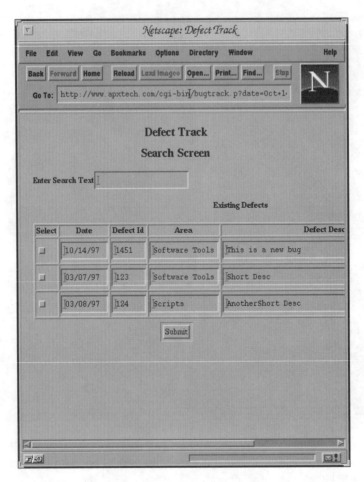

And if you feel that, you are right. You pretty much owe it to yourself to check out **mod_perl** with the Apache Web server, or PerlScript with the IIS Web server. Here the Perl-interpreter is built into the Web server so you don't have the overhead of starting or passing around parameters each time.

In any case you can pretty much see everything we talked about again in that one loop:

```
69   sub main
70   {
71      if ($query->param("submit_defect") )
72      {
73          save_defect_data($query);
74          $defect_data = setup_defect_data();
75      }
76
77      if ($query->param("submit") )
78      {
79          display_defects($defect_data);
80      }
81      else
82      {
```

```
83        search_defects($defect_data);
84     }
85    print $query->endform;
86  }
```

See how well this shows the Web design we talked about? Some people in fact think of this as a state machine, where depending on the state (`$query->param()`) you go to different functions (`display_defects`, `search_defects`).

One more note: What if you don't have **mod-perl** and Apache, or IIS and PerlScript, and therefore need to start a Perl interpreter each time? Well, by compiling your script you can reduce this overhead of running the Perl executable each time to *nothing*.

And, by saving your text in a database (via either DBI as we will talk about later, or DBM, which we will talk about in Chapter 16), you can reduce the overhead to where you are passing a single key around:

```
http://www.apxtech.com:8080/bugtracker.p?id=24234223123
```

In this case, the `id` would stand for a text string in a database, which **bugtrack** would then read to get more information on what to do next.

Summary of CGI

So there it is, a quick one-hour tutorial on the basic concepts of CGI by example. Of course, there is much more to it, but there are several good CGI books out there (*How to Set Up and Maintain a World Wide WebSite*, by Dr. Lincoln Stein, author of *CGI.pm*, comes to mind).

In short, there are four basic principles you need to remember:

1. Perl's interface for CGI is through the module **CGI.pm**. Methods in CGI are used to dynamically construct html pages.
2. html documents can communicate with Perl scripts via certain directives (`<img src = "/cgi-bin/counter.pl"`).
3. Where you are in a CGI server's hierarchy determines the behavior that you get via loading a document into a Web browser.
4. If you want to make programs that have more than one Web page, you need to pass around that information via the command-line.

Notice that we spent very little time talking about the interface of all of this. And for good reason—there are plenty of Web sites out there that do the CGI thing. Here are a couple of corollary principles you might want to remember:

1. To learn html, you can always see how something was done in html by going to **Document Source** on your favorite browser.
2. To get the pictures and/or structure from html pages, you can always go to **Document Info** inside your favorite browser.
3. The page *http://www-genome.wi.mit.edu/ftp/pub/software/WWW/examples/* is the only page on **CGI.pm** you will ever need.

Databases

I hate to say it, but databases are going to get a bit of a short shrift here—not because they are unimportant, but because of the *ease* in which you can manipulate them in Perl. Perl has about the easiest interface into databases I have ever seen. Of course, to use databases, you need to know SQL, and this section assumes that you do.

Like any other language, Perl talks to a database via the means of a driver. Perl sends data to that driver, which then goes to the database, retrieves the relevant information back, and hands it off to Perl (Figure 12.14).

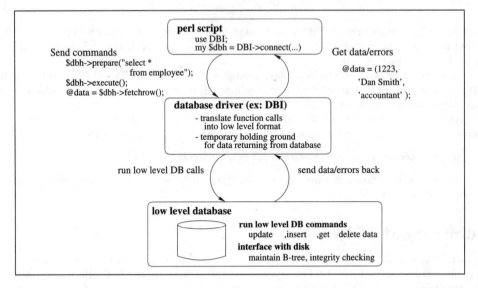

Figure 12.14
High-Level
Diagram of Driver
Communicating
to a Database

Now in this case, the "driver" can be one of many things. There are **oraperl**, **sybperl**, and **Win32::ODBC**; these are the old ways of doing database manipulation in Perl, and they still have merit.

However, the interface of Perl's future is called **DBI**, standing for *Database Interface*. DBI's idea is to make the most common commands for databases work for any given database vendor.

To do this, DBI acts as "traffic cop." Underneath the "hood" (so to speak) of DBI are modules called **DBD:** DBD::Sybase, DBD::Oracle, DBD::Informix, DBD::ODBC, etc., which you need to have installed in order for DBI to work with your particular system.

If you have Sybase, you need **DBD::Sybase**; for Oracle, you need **DBD::Oracle**. These are the database *drivers* that do the actual job of talking to the database.

So when you say "use DBI" (or load the DBI module), you are in effect saying "Load up the databases that I know about—I don't care what they are." And then DBI, through DBD, handles all the complexity of talking to the database for you.

From then on, it is simply a matter of sending the database commands. Here is a simple example that displays database information.

A Database Monitor: Viewing Database Information

One of the most frustrating things about databases is actually maneuvering inside them—especially for beginners.

There are several commands, tables, and objects in databases that make maneuvering in databases tough for beginners; it is usually a matter of groping around for a while, getting used to the command language in order to get anything done.

Of course, once you get the command language down you can work miracles; but that takes time. Listing 12.25 is a small script (thanks to Michael Peppler for this example) that displays any database objects in a Sybase database, and can help beginners learn the Sybase lingo. It comes from the **DBD::Sybase** distribution, and we show what the equivalent commands in the Sybase module are.

Listing 12.25
sqlDisplayDBI.p

```
1
2
3    use lib '.';
4
5    BEGIN
6    {
7        $ENV{'SYBASE'} = "/path/to/sybase";          # need to locate sybase
8    }
9
10    use strict;
11   use DBI;    #          use Sybase::DBlib;
12
13   use CGI;
14
15   my $query = new CGI;
16
17   print $query->header;
18   print $query->start_html(-title => "Show a Sybase Object"); # open new page
19                                                        # get
20   my $server   = $query->param('server');               #
21   my $database = $query->param('database');
22
23   my $state = $query->param('__state__') || 0;
24
25   if(!$database)
26   {
27       error("Please supply the <b>database</b> parameter.<p>");
28   }
29
30
31
32
33   #  WAS my $dbh = new Sybase::DBlib( "sa", undef, $server);
34
35   my $dbh = DBI->connect('dbi:Sybase:', 'sa','',
36                   {syb_dbd_server => $server });
37
38   ($dbh->do("use $database") != -2
39           || error("The database <b>$database</b> doesn't exist");
40   #   ($dbh->dbuse($database) == SUCCEED) ||
41   #            error("The database <b>$database</b> doesn't exist");
42
43
44   SWITCH_STATE:                                # infinite loop
45   while (1)                                    # if the user is on screen zero
```

```
46   {                                                    # get objects from server
47       ($state == 0) && do
48       {
49           my($values, $labels) = getObjects();
50           print "<h1>Show a Sybase objects definition:</h1>\n";
51           print "<p><p>Please select an object:<p>\n";
52           print $query->start_form;
53
54           print $query->scrolling_list
55                               (
56                                   -name     => 'object',
57                                   -values   => $values,
58                                   -labels   => $labels              # lost of different objects
59                                   -size     => 10
60                               );
61
62           $query->param(-name=>'__state__', '-values'=>1);        # set the state
63           print $query->hidden(-name=>'__state__');
64           print $query->hidden(-name=>'database');
65           print $query->hidden(-name=>'server');
66
67           print $query->submit;                          # submit button
68           print $query->end_form;                        # user goes to next screen.
69
70           last SWITCH_STATE;
71       };
72
73       ($state == 1) && do
74       {
75           print "<h1>Show a Sybase object's definition:</h1>\n";
76
77           my $objId = $query->param('object');           # we use the 'object' given
78           my $html = getText($objId);                    # from the last screen
79           print $html;                                   # and get an html object
80                                                          # for the page
81           last SWITCH_STATE;
82       };
83   }
84
85   print $query->end_html;
86   exit(0);
87
88
89   sub getObjects
90   {
91
92   #    WAS $dbh->dbcmd(
93
94   my $sth = $dbh->prepare              # makes the database ready for a command
95       (
96   "select distinct 'obj' = o.name, 'user' = u.name, o.id, o.type
97            from     dbo.sysobjects o,
```

```
98                     dbo.sysusers u,
99                     dbo.sysprocedures p
100              where  u.uid = o.uid
101                 and o.id = p.id
102                 and p.status & 4096 != 4096
103              order by o.name"
104          );
105
106
107
108 # WAS $dbh->dbsqlexec; $dbh->dbresults;
109
110  $sth->execute();                            # executes that command
111
112    my %dat;
113    my @values;
114    my %labels;
115    my $value;
116
117 #  WAS     while(%dat = $dbh->dbnextrow(TRUE))
118 #         {
119
120  while($dat = $sth->fetchrow_hashref)         # we get data from the
121  {                                            # a row at a time database
122 #  WAS      $value = "$dat{id} - $dat{type}";
123     $value = "$dat->{id} - $dat->{type}";     # we print out the column values
124
125     push(@values, $value);
126
127 #  WAS     $value = "$dat{id} - $dat{type}";
128     $labels{$value} = "$dat->{user}.$dat->{obj}";
129  }
130
131    return (\@values, \%labels);
132 }
133
134 sub getText
135 {
136    my $objId = shift;
137
138    $objId =~ s/[\D<\-\s]+$//;
139
140 #  WAS     $dbh->dbcmd ("select text from dbo.syscomments where id = $objId");
141
142   my $sth =                                        # gets info about
143  $dbh->prepare("select text from dbo.syscomments where id = $objId");    # objects
144
145 #   $dbh->dbsqlexec; $dbh->dbresults;
146
147  $sth->execute();                                  # executes query
148    my $html = '';
```

```
149     my $text;
150
151 #     WAS while(($text) = $dbh->dbnextrow)
152 while(($text) = $sth->fetchrow)              # fetches data, as scalar
153 {
154    $html .= $text;
155 }
156 TsqlToHtml($html);
157 }
158
159 sub TsqlToHtml                                # we use perl's regex to bold
160 {                                             # and italicize input
161     my $html = shift;
162     $html =~ s/\n/<br>\n/g;
163
164     local($") = '|';
165
166     # bolding the keywords
167     my @keywords = qw    ( as begin between declare delete drop else end exec
168                           exists go if insert procedure return set update values
169                           from select where and or create
170                              );
171
172     push(@keywords , 'order by');
173
174 $html =~ s"\b(@keywords)\b"<b>$1</b>"ig;       # the actual keywords being bolded
175
176     my @types =    qw  ( tinyint smallint int char varchar datetime
177                          smalldatetime money numeric decimal text binary
178                          varbinary image
179                       );
180
181     # italicising the types
182 $html =~ s"\b(@types)\b"<i>$1</i>"gi;
183
184 $html =~ s"\t"\ \ \ \ "g;
185 $html =~ s" "\ "sg;
186
187 $html;
188 }
189
190 sub error
191 {
192     print "<h1>Error!</h1>\n";
193     print @_;
194     print $query->end_html;
195     exit(0);
196 }
```

Again, here is a Web page that is implemented as a state machine. We won't say much about this aspect of it, except that lines 174 and 182 are really cool ways of italicizing (or boldfacing) words.

More to the point, we have boldfaced every single occurrence of a DBI call, and set it next to the corresponding **Sybase::Dblib** call.

When you are actually getting data out of the database with DBI, you go through four major steps:

1. **Logging in.** Lines 35 and 36 show the most common way of logging into a server:

```
35  my $dbh = DBI->connect('dbi:Sybase:', 'user','password',
36                            {syb_dbd_server => $server });
```

The first parameter is the type of database you are connecting to; the second and third parameters are user and password, respectively; and the syb_dbd_server is a hash reference parameter that tells which server to connect to.

2. **Preparing the SQL for processing.** Lines 142 and 143 show the preparation for an SQL command to be processed via DBI (and therefore by **DBD::Sybase**):

```
142     my $sth =
143  $dbh->prepare("select text from dbo.syscomments where id = $objId");
```

3. **Executing the SQL.** Line 147 shows the execution of an SQL command:

```
147 $sth->execute()
```

This actually tells the database to run the request, and to wait for any arguments to "fetch" the data.

4. **Getting the data out of the server.** Once you have executed the command, you can move the data into Perl via the form of an array:

```
152     while(($text) = $sth->fetchrow)
153     {
154         $html .= $text;
155     }
```

or a hash reference:

```
120     while($dat = $sth->fetchrow_hashref)
121     {
123         $value = "$dat->{id} - $dat->{type}";
```

where the id and type fields are actually the names of fields inside a table.

That's about it for simple database access. And, if you are familiar with doing this type of operation in C, you should realize exactly what a pain it is to do it in C when compared to Perl! In fact, it needn't be as complicated as the example; if you want to simply execute a piece of SQL you can say:

```
38  ($dbh->do("use $database") != -2
39                      || error("The database <b>$database</b> doesn't exist");
```

instead of going through all of the bother of actually preparing, executing, and so forth.

Now, let's turn to the application side of **sqldisplayDBI.p**. When you run **sqldisplayDBI.p**, you give it a command string; supplying it the database and the server like so:

```
http://www.apxtech.com/sqldisplay.p?server=MYSERV&database=mydatabase
```

When you do so, it gives you a window in which you can select an object for viewing (see Figure 12.15). If you then hit **Submit query**, **sqldisplayDBI.p** will open up that particular object's definition, and give you a display like Figure 12.16. Hence you get a "pretty printed" view of what the object actually is doing, which is a good technique for actually learning the database system itself!

Figure 12.15
sql displayDBI.p
Results in
Browser

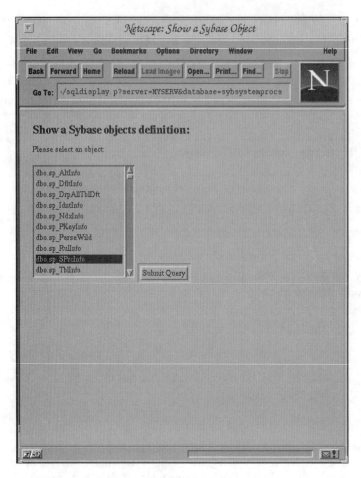

Figure 12.15
sql displayDB1.p
Results in
Browser

Figure 12.16
sqldisplayDBI.p
Showing the
Object Definition

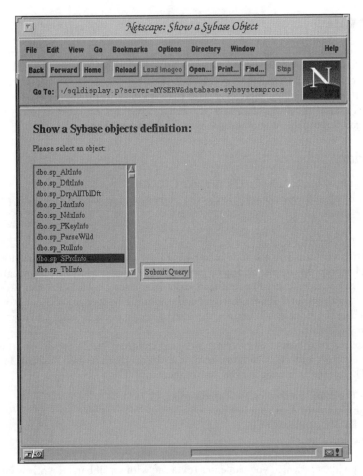

Database Summary

This is, of course, just a small example of what you can do with DBI. DBI and DBD are fully functional database programmer interfaces, which means that you can manipulate just about any aspect of a database with them.

However, as just a warning note, DBI is fairly solid code for certain database engines, but other database engines have a certain amount of "catchup" to play. For example, DBI with **DBD::Oracle** is stable, as is **DBD::Informix**, but **DBD::Sybase** is in an alpha stage.

Hence, for Sybase, you might want to use Sybperl instead, and indeed, notice that I put in comments at each and every equivalent **Sybase::Dblib** command.

Sybase::Dblib is stable, well-tested, and object-oriented, so you should probably be using it in the short term. Between **DBD::ODBC** and **Win32::ODBC**, it is a toss-up decision—I prefer DBI. For Oracle and Informix, however, there really is no choice; you *should* be using DBI, instead of oraperl and ingperl, the older Perl interfaces.

PerlTk Examples

The last subject we will cover is PerlTk, which is a way of making cross-platform GUIs that are fast, flexible, and easily configurable. It is based on the tcl/tk package of John Ousterhout, has much the same interface, and is available via CPAN or the accompanying CD.

However, PerlTk (I believe) is much more powerful than tcl/tk. (No offense to tcl, but it really needs to get object-oriented.) PerlTk has Perl's power of an interface, and the code that you create is totally OO. Before we get into the examples though, it's probably a good idea to give some background on Tk.

Small Tk Tutorial

Here is a small tutorial of how you can use PerlTk to make OO GUIs.

First, Tk uses what is called an *event loop*. Here is the simplest tk application you could possibly make:

```
use Tk;
MainLoop();
```

The `MainLoop()` function says that you are done configuring how your Tk application will look, and are ready to display your GUI application. All the `MainLoop()` function does is hand control of the program to a very simple-minded process, which basically (every few milliseconds) asks the screen: "Has the user pressed any buttons, or interacted with the Tk windows yet?" It does this over and over until the user actually does something, in which case the `MainLoop` handles the requests. Of course, this `MainLoop` process is simply an infinite loop, since we haven't actually made any GUIs yet.

Second, Tk is composed of widgets that have parents, and children. PerlTk works off of the principle of a geometry manager that controls *widgets*, which are graphical objects that are used to control a form. There are several widgets in PerlTk, but the following are the most important:

- `MainWindow`—The main window of your application.
- `Toplevel`—Subwindows inside your application.
- `Menu`—A menu for your applications.
- `Entry`—A single line of text.
- `Frame`—A place to put other widgets.
- `Text`—A type of widget in which you can enter text (one with scroll bars, the other without).
- `Canvas`—A canvas for displaying widgets in a free-form way.

Now, if you want to make a Tk screen, you make a `MainWindow` and then populate it with several other objects (such as `Menu`, `Canvas`, or what have you).

Some sample code might look like:

```
use Tk;
my $window = new MainWindow();     # add a main window
$window->title('this is a window');

my $text = $window->Text           # add a text object
                (
                        '-wrap' => 'word',
                        '-relief' => 'sunken',
                        '-borderwidth' => 2,
                        '-setgrid' => '1'
                );
my $button = $window->Button('-text' => 'Configure', '-command' => \&configure );
```

This would:

1. Make a MainWindow.
2. Entitle it this is a window.
3. Create (but not put) a text window inside this mainwindow.
4. Create (but not put) a button inside the window as well.

Hence, the MainWindow owns the subwindow, and it also owns the button inside the subwindow.

The third point in your Tk tutorial is that you configure widgets with hashes. Each one of these widgets is configured by passing it a hash when creating it (or in configuring it afterward). We already saw this in:

```
my $text = $window->Text
               (
                       '-wrap' => 'word',
                       '-relief' => 'sunken',
                       '-borderwidth' => 2,
                       '-setgrid' => '1'
               );
```

Here, we are making the Text widget (inside the window $window) have the following qualities:

1. It wraps around such that words are not split onto two lines.
2. The relief is sunken, such that it looks darker than the rest of the window.
3. The -borderwidth or empty space surrounding the text object is 2.

Note

setgrid is a bit more complicated. It is used to communicate with the top-level window for sizing reasons. See the 'Text' page included in the perlTk documentation for more details.

The fourth point is you pack, place, or grid objects to place them on the screen. When you have made a relationship between two objects, as we did with my $text = $window->Text(...), you have not yet put that object into the window it is associated with.

To do this, you need to call either the pack, place, or grid method. Leaving off where we were before, we could pack the $text and $button widgets onto the $window widget by saying:

```
$text->pack('-side' => 'top');
    $button->pack('-side' => 'top');
```

When you say this, PerlTk goes through a bit of magic. The pack algorithm is one of the coolest GUI things I've seen, and it makes building GUI applications extremely easy. The best way is to see it in an example. Listing 12.26 is a complete Tk application, which shows pack in action.

Listing 12.26
packexample.p

```
1   use Tk;
2   my $window = new MainWindow();
3   $window->title('this is a window');
4
5   my $text = $window->Text
6                   (
```

```
 7                          '-wrap' => 'word',
 8                          '-relief' => 'sunken',
 9                          '-borderwidth' => 2,
10                          '-setgrid' => '1'
11                        );
12 my $button = $window->Button('-text' => 'Configure');
13 $text->pack('-side' => 'top');
14 $button->pack('-side' => 'top');
15 MainLoop();
```

This creates something like what is shown in Figure 12.17. So what happened here? Well, we "packed" the text first, up at the top. And then, we "packed" the button. But because the text was packed first, it got priority and was put in the primary, top position. The button came next, as it was packed second.

Figure 12.17
Example of Pack in Action

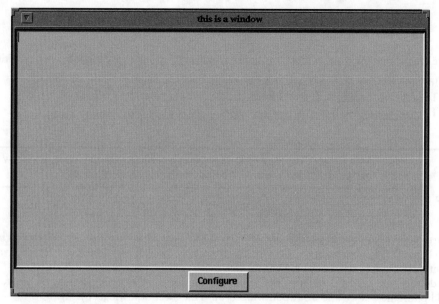

Pack has many cool options that we can only cover here in the basics. You can:

1. pack things to the left or to the right, or to the top or to the bottom.
2. -fill your objects so they take up all the available space in the x, y, or both dimensions.
3. -anchor your widgets to the n (north), ne (northeast), nw (northwest), w (west), s (south), se (southeast), sw (southwest), or the *center* (center is the default).

Read the documentation on pack (**pack.html**) for more details.

It is surprising, but this simple algorithm will actually solve about 95 percent of your simple GUI needs. If you need to go further, see the grid and place functions in the documentation; they provide you with a little more control.

The fifth and final point to make in your PerlTk tutorial is that you control what the application does via callbacks. All of the previous four tenets are good for is drawing "pretty pictures." It is the job of callbacks to actually take those pictures and have them do anything.

Callbacks, as you may remember from the last chapter, are Perl's way of calling functions without actually knowing their name. For example:

```
$a = \&b;
```

makes $a a reference to the function b, and:

```
&$a;
```

then actually calls the function &b.

In Tk, callbacks are used to make the application work. You define a callback and tie it to a button, menu event, or what have you. When that button is pushed, the callback behind that button is executed. Taking the small example that we had earlier, we can make it so the button puts text into the text box for us as shown in Listing 12.27.

Listing 12.27
packexample.p

```
1   use Tk;
2   my $window = new MainWindow();
3   $window->title('this is a window');
4
5   my $text = $window->Text                          # add text window
6                   (
7                        '-wrap' => 'word',
8                        '-relief' => 'sunken',
9                        '-borderwidth' => 2,
10                       '-setgrid' => '1'
11                  );
12  my $button = $window->Button('-text' => 'Configure', # add button
13              '-command' => [\&insert, $text,
14                       'My text to insert' ] );
15  $text->pack   ('-side' => 'top');
16  $button->pack ('-side' => 'top');
17  MainLoop();
18
19  sub insert
20  {
21      my ($textwidget, $text) = @_;
22      $textwidget->insert('0.0', $text);
23  }
```

The code outlined in bold defines the callback. The command \&insert is associated with the button $button. Hence, when you hit the **Configure** button in this example, Perl inserts the text My text to insert into the text box (line 22), as in Figure 12.18.

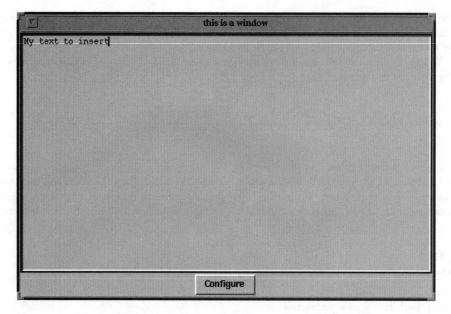

Callbacks like this glue your application together. They are used to take the disparate buttons, dials, knobs, menus, and the other widgets of your application and make them talk to each other. In the preceding example, we had the callback &insert, which took as a parameter $textwidget, and then inserted text into that $textwidget. We could have just as easily saved a file, loaded a file, or whatever.

Summary of PerlTk Introduction

PerlTk is a melding of Perl-the text manipulation language and Tk—the package for creating quick GUIs. Each of the tools complements the others, filling in weak spots.

There are five basic points that you need to know to become fluent in Tk:

1. Tk's main function (the one you will call all the time) is an event loop.
2. Tk works on the idea that widgets control other widgets through a parent/child relationship.
3. You configure each of the widgets with hashes.
4. You pack the widgets onto each other with the pack, place, and grid commands.
5. You use Perl callbacks to tie all the underlying widgets together.

We shall see exactly how powerful PerlTk is in the following two examples. First, we will consider the problem of junk mail and how to solve it; second, we will consider the problem of running applications inside a Windows environment in a clean fashion.

Mail Filter

The growth of computer networks around the world has had one bad result: Junk mail.

A day doesn't go by when I get mail about get-rich-quick schemes, pornography announcements, pyramid marketing, water filters, whatever; this is probably all based on the "sucker born every minute" principle. Unfortunately, the Internet makes this type of conning all the more easy. With automated tools, zero cost of distribution, and people selling 50-million-block chunks of e-mail addresses, the problem will grow and grow and grow.

Examples

Listing 12.28 is a small script that let's you filter out this type of junk. It is based the `eval` function in Perl, and the fact that there on is a cool module on CPAN called **Mail::Filter** that let's you construct filters like this pretty easily.

Listing 12.28
mailparse.p

```
1   #!/home/epeschko/perl50043/install/bin/perl
2
3   use Tk;
4   use FileHandle;
5
6   use strict;
7
8   my $window = new MainWindow();
9   $window->title('Mail Filter');
10
11  my $configure = $window->Button                  # define configure button
12                            (
13                                  'text' => 'Configure',
14                                  'command' => \&configure,
15                            )
16                            -> pack('side' => 'right');
17
18  my $filter     = $window->Button                 # define filter button
19                            (
20                                  'text' => 'Filter',
21                                  'command' => \&filter
22                            )
23                            -> pack('side' => 'left');
24  MainLoop();
25
26  sub filter
27  {
28      print "Filtering!!!!\n";
29      my (@delete_flags) = ('-delete', '1')  if ($ENV{'MAILFILTER_ON'});
30      my $file =   $ENV{'FILTER_FILE'}|| "$ENV{'HOME'}/.mailfilt";
31      my $mailbox = $ENV{'MAILBOX'}  || die "Need to have a mailbox to filter!\n";
32
33      my $folder = new Mail::Folder('AUTODETECT', $mailbox) ||
34                      error_window("You need to have the 'MAILBOX environmental
35      the Folder program couldn't detect
36      your type of mailbox! ");
37
38      require $file;
39      my $ft= new Mail::Filter( \&mailbox_filter );
40      $ft->filter($folder, @delete_flags);
41  }
42  sub configure                                   # configure screen to define filters
43  {
44      my $file =   $ENV{'FILTER_FILE'} || "$ENV{'HOME'}/.mailfilt";
45      my $editor = $ENV{'FILTER_EDITOR'} || '';
46      if (!$editor)                               # if no editor is defined, we make a simple one
```

```
47      {
48          my $textwindow = $window->Toplevel(-title => 'email filter');
49          my $text = gettext($file);
50          my $field = $textwindow->Scrolled        # add text window to hold input
51                                  (   'Text',
52                                      '-scrollbars' => 'e',
53                                      '-wrap' => 'word',
54                                      'relief' => 'sunken',
55                                      'borderwidth' => 2,
56                                      'setgrid' => '1'
57                                  );
58
59          $field ->pack  ( 'expand' => 'yes', 'fill' => 'both' );
60          $field->insert('0.0', $text);
61
62          my $save = $textwindow->Button          # add button for save
63                                  (
64                                      'text' => 'Save',
65                                      'command' =>
66                                          [ \&savetext, $field, $file  ]
67                                  )
68                                  -> pack( 'side' => 'left' );
69
70          my $dismiss = $textwindow->Button       # add button to dismiss window
71                                  (
72                                      'text' => 'Dismiss',
73                                      'command' =>
74                                          [ $textwindow => 'withdraw']
75                                  )
76                                  -> pack( 'side' => 'right' );
77      }
78      else
79      {
80          system("$editor $file");                # else fork off an editor
81          _checkText($file, 'file');
82      }
83  }
84
85  sub gettext                                     # sucks in text from a file
86  {
87      my ($file) = @_;
88      local($/) = undef;
89      my $fd = new FileHandle("$file") || return ('');
90      return(<$fd>);
91  }
92
93  sub savetext                                    # saves text to a file simple editor
94  {
95      my ($window, $file) = @_;
96      my $text = $window->get('0.0', 'end');
97
98      return(0) if (!_checkText($text, 'text'));
99
100     my $fd = new FileHandle("> $file");
```

```
101      print $fd $text;
102 }
103
104 sub error_window                        # defines an error screen
105 {
106      my ($window, $text, $file) = @_;
107
108      my ($height, $width, $type) = _dimensions($text); # figure out whether
109                                          # screen should be bolded or not.
110      my $errorwindow = $window->Toplevel();
111      my $error;
112
113      if ($type eq 'Scrolled')
114      {
115          $error = $errorwindow->Scrolled
116                          (
117                                  'Text',
118                                  'height' => $height,
119                                  'width' => $width,
120                                  'borderwidth' => 2,
121                                  'setgrid' => 'true'
122                          );
123          $errorwindow->title("Errors in mail filter file");
124      }
125      else
126      {
127          $error = $errorwindow->Text
128                          (
129                                  'height' => $height,
130                                  'width' => $width,
131                                  'borderwidth' => 2,
132                                  'setgrid' => 'true'
133                          );
134          $errorwindow->title("Errors in mail filter file");
135      }
136
137      $error->pack  ('expand' => 'no', 'fill' => 'both' );
138
139      $error->insert('0.0',
140 "Your mail filter program does not
141 have the correct syntax! Error:
142
143  $text"
144 );
145
146      my $button = $errorwindow->Button
147                          (
148                                  'text' => 'Dismiss',
149                                  'command' =>
150                                      [ $errorwindow => 'withdraw']
151                          )
152                          -> pack( 'side' => 'right' );
153 }
154
```

```
155 sub _checkText                                # check the text for errors.
156 {
157     my ($text,$type) = @_;
158     local($/) = undef;
159
160     if ($type eq 'file') { my $fd = new FileHandle($text); $text = <$fd>; }
161
162     eval ( "sub { $text } ");
163     if ($@) { error_window($window,$@); return(0) }
164     return(1);
165 }
166                                                # check the size of the text
167 sub _dimensions
168 {
169     my ($text) = @_;
170     my ($height, $width, $type);
171
172     my @lines = split(m"\n", $text);
173     grep
174         { my $tlength = length($_);
175
176           $width =   ($tlength + 2 > 80)? 80 :
177                      ($tlength > $width)? $tlength + 2
178                     : $width
179         }
180         @lines;
181
182     $height = (@lines < 2)? 5 : @lines + 3;
183
184     if ($height > 20) { $height = 20; $type = 'Scrolled'; }
185         else { $type = 'Text';     }
186
187     return($height, $width, $type);
188 }
```

What to say about this application? From the outside it looks pretty simple. If you run it, you get two buttons, looking like Figure 12.19.

Figure 12.19
Filter Top Two
Buttons

Now the idea is twofold. If you press **Configure**, you get a screen like Figure 12.20.

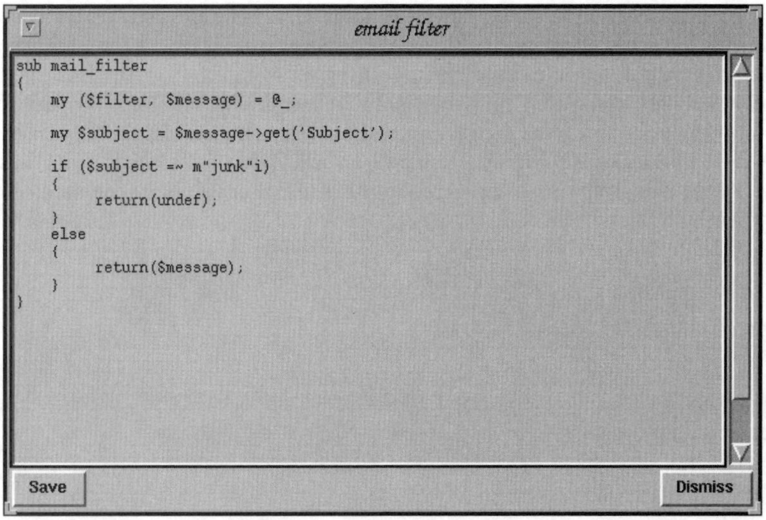

Figure 12.20
Configure Screen

```
email filter

sub mail_filter
{
    my ($filter, $message) = @_;

    my $subject = $message->get('Subject');

    if ($subject =~ m"junk"i)
    {
        return(undef);
    }
    else
    {
        return($message);
    }
}


         Save                                          Dismiss
```

The idea of this screen is for you to type a legal mail filter. As I said earlier, CPAN has a module called **Mail::Filter** by Graham Barr, which lets you take an arbitrary mailbox, and then filter it to any given criteria you want. Here, the mail filter will be applied to all messages in your mailbox, as supplied by the environmental variable $ENV{'MAILBOX'}.

In this sample, the mail filter will look for messages with the subject "junk" and get rid of them (this is what return(undef) does). Otherwise, it will keep them in your incoming mailbox. For more filters, see the **Mail Tools** available on CPAN or the accompanying CD.

Note that there are a couple of issues here: 1) Filtering your mailbox is a pretty dangerous thing to do, and 2) there needs to be a trigger to actually delete the junk mail for you.

The first problem we solve by introducing another environmental variable: MAILFILTER_ON. This prevents you from inadvertantly deleting any messages. When we do the filtering in line 40:

```
40      $ft->filter($folder, @delete_flags);
```

we need to pass it (-delete', 1) in order for the actual altering of the mailbox to occur. This allows you to test your mail filters before using them.

The second problem is solved by the **Filter** button. When you press **Filter**—and only when you press **Filter**—our mailbox is affected. This lets you have selective control over when you want to actually delete your junk mail.

The only question left is if this application only has two buttons, why is it 188 lines long? The answer is because we need to make auxilliary checks in order to insure stability. We must check the syntax of the filter people enter; if it is wrong, we need to print the errors. We need to save the filter to a file, or we would have to type it over again each time we entered the application.

Applications like this, although simple in purpose, can get pretty long in order to deal with all the different items that take place.

Running Scripts from Inside a Tk Application

As we saw in Chapter 2, Perl is a bit awkward to run on NT. As it stands, you need to either make your Perl script a batch file, run it from the command prompt, or associate icons with a Perl executable.

All three ways have drawbacks. Making a batch file is a pain, as is running it from the command prompt. And associating Perl script icons with a Perl executable only works halfway: It works for applications like Tk that are basically infinite loops until told when to quit but not others.

For command-line scripts, associating the icon is not that useful. Windows runs through your script, and then closes the dos prompt that was running the application, thus making it almost impossible to monitor what occurred.

Listing 12.29 presents a possible solution. It emulates a shell, giving you a place to run the command-line, and a directory to run it in. It also gives you an option to save the text that you just generated by the Perl script.

Listing 12.29
runscript.p

```
1   #!/home/epeschko/perl50043/install/bin/perl
2
3   use Tk;
4   use Tk::FileDialog;
5   use FileHandle;
6   use Cwd;
7
8   my $nolines = 0;
9
10    use strict;
11
12   my $window = new MainWindow();
13   $window->title('Run Script');
14   my ($text, %entries);
15
16   die "Need zero or one argument!\n" if (@ARGV > 1);
17   my ($directory, $command) = (@ARGV == 1)? _getFile($ARGV[0]) : (cwd(), '');
18   my (@labels) = ("run directory\t", "Command Line\t");
19
20  foreach $text (@labels)                                  # we make a loop to pack
21  {                                                         # different frames
22    my $frame = $window->Frame('borderwidth' => 2);
23
24    my $entry = $frame->Entry( 'relief' => 'sunken', 'width' => 60);
25    $entry->insert('end', $directory)if ($text eq "run directory\t");
26    $entry->insert('end', $command) if ($text eq "Command Line\t"); # together
27    $entry->bind("<Control-f>", [\&getdir, $entry ])         # calls getdir when control F pressed
28                    if ($text eq "run directory\t");
29    $entry->bind("<Control-f>", [\&getfile, $entry ])        # calls getfile when pressed
30                    if ($text eq "Command Line\t");
31
32    my $label = $frame->Label( 'text' => "$text" );
33
34    $frame->pack('side' => 'top', 'fill' => 'x');
35    $label->pack('side' => 'left');
36    $entry->pack('side' => 'left');
37    $entry->focus() if ($text eq 'directory');
38
39    $entries{$text} = $entry;
40    }
```

```
41
42   my $frame = $window->Frame( 'borderwidth' => 2 )->pack('side' => 'top');
43
44
45   $text = $window->Scrolled('Text', 'setgrid' => 'true', '-scrollbars' => '');
46
47   my $runbutton = $frame->Button              # buttons added from left to right
48                    (
49                       'text' => 'Run',
50      'command' => [\&run, \%entries, $text]    # calls 'run' routine when pressed
51                    )
52            -> pack('side' => 'left');
53
54
55   my $savetextbutton = $frame->Button         # save text added to left
56              (
57                    'text' => 'Save Text',
58      'command'=>[\&saveas, \%entries, $text]   # calls 'saveas' when pressed
59              )
60              -> pack('side' => 'left');
61                                               # save command added to RA
62   my $savecommandbutton = $frame->Button
63              (
64                   'text' => 'Save Command',
65      'command'=>[\&savecommand, \%entries, $text] # calls savecommand when pressed
66              )
67              -> pack('side' => 'left');
68
69
70   my $loadcommandbutton = $frame->Button       # next load
71              (
72                   'text' => 'Load Command',
73      'command'=>[\&loadcommand, \%entries, $text] # calls 'load command' when pressed
74              )
75              -> pack('side' => 'left');
76
77
78   my $clearbutton = $frame->Button             # next... clear
79              (
80                   'text' => 'Clear',
81      'command' => [\&clear => $text ]          # calls 'clear' sub when pressed
82              )
83              -> pack('side' => 'left');
84
85   my $quitbutton = $frame->Button
86              (
87                   'text' => 'Quit',
88      'command' => [$window => 'destroy']       # destroys window when pressed
89              )
90              -> pack('side' => 'left');
91
92
93   $text->pack('side' => 'bottom');
94
```

```
95   MainLoop();
96
97   sub run                                # subroutine attached to run button
98   {
99       my ($entries,$text) = @_;
100
101      my $dir = $entries->{"run directory\t"}->get();
102      my $script = $entries->{"Command Line\t"}->get();
103      $text->insert
104          (
105              'end',
106  "Running\n\t$script\nin\n\t$dir\n-----------------------------------------\n"
107          );
108      $nolines += 3;
109
110      my $line;
111      chdir($dir);
112
113      if ($script =~ m"\.p|\.pl|\.pm") { open (FD, "$^X -S $script 2>&1 |"); }
114          else { open(FD, "$script 2>&1 |"); }   # won't work on windows 95 *sigh*
115
116      while ($line = <FD>)
117      {
118          $text->insert( 'end', $line );
119          $nolines++;
120          $text->configure('-scrollbars' => 'e') if ($nolines > 22);
121      }
122      $text->yview('moveto', 1);
123  }
124
125  sub getdir                             # subroutine bound to directory field
126  {
127      my ($e) = @_;
128      my $filed = $e->FileDialog             # we make a new 'dialog box
129                      (
130                          '-Title' => 'Directories',
131                          '-SelDir' => 1,
132                          '-Path' => $e->get()
133                      );
134
135      my $dir   = $filed->Show('-Horiz' => 1);
136      $e->delete(0, 'end');
137      $e->insert('end', $dir);
138  }
139
140  sub getfile                            # subroutine attached to 'file' button
141  {
142      my ($e) = @_;
143
144      my $filed = $e->FileDialog             # make file dialog box
145                      (
146                          '-Title' => 'Files',
147                          '-Path' => $e->get()
148                      );
```

```
149
150     my $file = $filed->Show('-Horiz' => 1);
151     $e->delete(0, 'end');
152     $e->insert('end', $file);
153 }
154
155 sub clear                               # clear the text in the main box
156 {
157     my ($text) = @_;
158     $text->configure('-scrollbars' => '');
159     $text->delete('0.0','end');
160     $nolines = 0;
161 }
162
163 sub saveas                              # save command file
164 {
165     my ($entries, $textwidget) = @_;
166
167     my $startpath = $ENV{'TEXT_DIR'} || $entries->{"run directory\t"}->get();
168     my $command = $entries->{"Command Line\t"}->get();
169
170
171     my $filed = $textwidget->FileDialog
172                         (
173                             '-Title' => 'File To Save',
174                             '-Path' => $startpath
175                         );
176     my $file = $filed->Show('-Horiz' => 1);
177     return() if (!$file);
178     my $fh = new FileHandle( "> $file") || (error($file, $textwidget),return());
179     print $fh $text;
180 }
181
182 sub loadcommand                         # load a command, previously run
183 {
184     my ($entries, $textwidget) = @_;
185     my $path = $ENV{'COMMAND_DIR'} || $entries->{"run directory\t"}->get();
186
187     print "HERE $path\n";
188     my $filed = $textwidget->FileDialog
189                     (
190                         '-Title' => 'File To Save',
191                         '-Path' => $path
192                     );
193     my $file = $filed->Show('-Horiz' => 1);
194     return() if (!$file);
195     my $fh = new FileHandle( "$file") || (error($file, $textwidget), return());
196     my @lines = <$fh>;
197     chop(@lines);
198
199     $entries->{"run directory\t"}->delete(0,'end');
200     $entries->{"run directory\t"}->insert('0', $lines[$#lines-1]);
201     $entries->{"Command Line\t"}->delete(0,'end');
202     $entries->{"Command Line\t"}->insert('0', $lines[$#lines]);
```

```
203 }
204
205
206 sub savecommand                              # save command text to a file
207 {
208     my ($entries, $textwidget) = @_;
209
210     my $path = $ENV{'COMMAND_DIR'} || $entries->{"run directory\t"}->get();
211     my $command = $entries->{"Command Line\t"}->get();
212
213     my $filed = $textwidget->FileDialog
214                         (
215                             '-Title' => 'File To Save',
216                             '-Path' => $path
217                         );
218     my $file = $filed->Show('-Horiz' => 1);
219     return() if (!$file);
220     my $fh = new FileHandle( "> $file") ||(error($file, $textwidget), return());
221     print $fh <<"EOL";
222 #!$                                          # we make a shortcut
223                                              # generating perl code
224 my \$tmpfile = ".runfile.\$\$";
225
226 open(FD, "> .runfile.\$\$");
227 print FD <DATA>;
228 close(FD);
229
230 system("$  $0 \$tmpfile");
231 unlink(".runfile.\$\$");
232
233 __END__
234 $path
235 $command
236 EOL
237 }
238
239 sub _getFile
240 {
241     my ($file) = @_;
242     my $fd = new FileHandle("$file") || die "Couldn't open $file!\n";
243     my @lines = <$fd>;
244     chop(@lines);
245     return(@lines);
246 }
247
248 sub error                                    # error screen
249 {
250     my ($file, $tw) = @_;
251     my $errwindow = $tw->Toplevel();
252     my $text = $errwindow->Text
253                         (
254                             'setgrid' => 'true',
255                             'height' => 10, 'width' => 40
256                         );
```

```
257      $text->insert ('0.0', "Error in opening $file");
258      $text->pack('side' => 'top', 'fill' => 'x');
259      $errwindow->Button
260              (
261                      'text' => 'OK',
262                      'command' => [ $errwindow, 'withdraw' ]
263              ) -> pack ('side' => 'bottom');
264 }
```

This time, let's give a functional diagram to show the structure of this application (Figure 12.22). For now, we shall treat each button as having a separate function, and label them. We shall see that this is not far from the truth when we get to object-oriented programming.

Figure 12.21
The Structure of
runscript

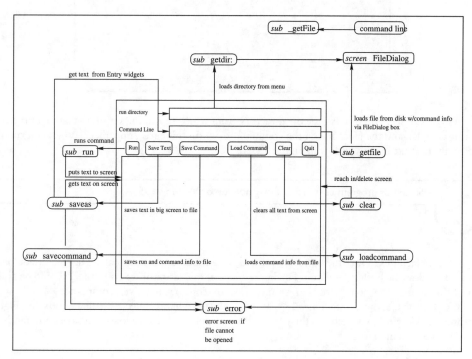

As you see, the addition of buttons, text objects, and toolbars makes the code a lot longer. It doesn't help that we are showing off—lines 27 and 28 actually bind keys to the text objects, so we can type **Control-F** instead of clicking the buttons!

The key lines are 21–94, which define the look of the application, and the run subroutine which actually runs the Perl application for us. Figure 12.22 shows **runscript** in action.

Figure 12.22
The **runscript**
Windows
Application

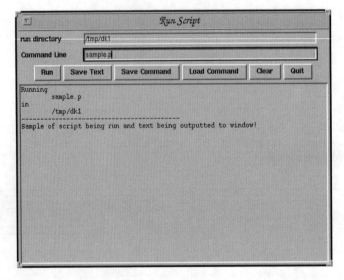

As you can see, you simply type the directory from which to run the script, the name of the command to run (in this case, **ls**), and the place to run the command from (in this case, **/tmp/dk1**). When you run the application, it displays the text in the window in Figure 12.22.

Since this program uses pipes, it may not run on Windows 95.

Note

We give facilities to save the buffer we created, save the command set that we have created, load the command from a file, clear the buffers, and quit. Further releases of this script (if we go farther) should be able to make icons out of this application, so that you can simply click an icon to run a given command.

Oh yes, and one more note. Lines 188–190 actually get what is called a file dialog box (see Figure 12.23). This is a prebuilt Tk window which lets the user pick a file, and we use it to load and save commands to files. You've probably seen them before.

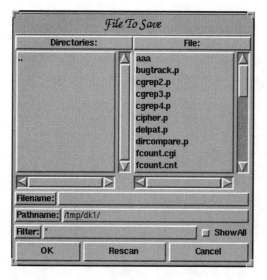

Figure 12.23
File Dialog Box

PerlTk has quite a few of these prebuilt windows lying around; I heartily recommend that you check out the on-line documentation and the on-line code that comes with PerlTk.

Summary of Tk Examples

PerlTk is one of the best ways in Perl to build GUI applications (the other way is CGI). We have given a small tutorial to help you get started with PerlTk. However, this is no substitute for the extensive on-line documentation that comes when you install PerlTk.

In addition, there is one good way to learn Tk that we didn't mention, and that is with the command:

```
C:\> widget
```

When you get PerlTk installed into your Perl 5 distribution, widget comes, too. It is a beautiful way to learn Tk because there are about 30 different applications that show you all of the tricks of the PerlTk trade installed interactively in the documentation.

Summary

One of the mottos of the Perl community (the writer of Perl, Larry Wall, said it first) is, "There's more than one way to do it." This statement talks about diversity of solutions, and how a problem can be tackled in more than one way.

However, just because Perl syntax is so flexible doesn't mean anything if you can only apply Perl to a small set of problems! And, as you have seen, the number of problems Perl can tackle will continue to grow, because Perl was designed extraordinarily well at quite a few levels.

Perl pretty much spans the gamut of applications, from utilities to find text, to database assistants, to scanning the Web, to actually publishing on the Web, to filtering e-mail, to making your tasks at printing or merging lots of documents easier.

And as we shall see in the next half of this book, you needn't stop here. Perl is just as flexible as an object-oriented language, and ideal for either learning OO programming, converting non-object-oriented scripts into objects, or building large, very flexible applications.

CHAPTER 13

Introduction to Object-Oriented Programming for the Uninitiated and the Unaware

This chapter is an introduction to learning and using object-oriented programming in Perl. A lot of ground is covered (in a short amount of space) on our 30,000 foot view of object-oriented programming. The chapters in this section flesh out the skeleton that we begin here.

Chapter Overview

There has been much attention, bordering on hype, paid to objects and object-oriented programming (OO). Programming languages are either praised or condemned for their "object-oriented–ness," or lack thereof.

This has gone a bit far: applications that work well are being converted, often with much anguish, to object-oriented languages, methodologies, and databases. The quickest resume stuffer is to say that you have done the "OO thing" and then list the OO projects you have done, and OO languages you know.

Why all the excitement? Just what does it mean to be object-oriented? How is it possible to use an OO-capable language and still not be doing object-oriented programming? This chapter is designed as a quick primer on why object-oriented programming is so hyped, and why you might consider learning OO if you don't already know it.

Let's look at the advantages and disadvantages of using object-oriented methodologies in application development.

The Advantages and Disadvantages of OO

The reason why there is so much hype is because the hype is based on reality. There are many good reasons for businesses to want to use OO, but if they want to use OO, they have to do it right. Appropriately applied, object-oriented programming is all of the following:

1. *Less expensive.* Projects developed using OO tend to cost companies less money over the long run than if another technique were used.
2. *Easier to change.* Projects developed using OO tend to last longer than projects without OO. This means OO applications are more likely to grow with an organization and adapt to changing needs.
3. *More manageable.* Projects developed using OO tend to lend themselves to being divided into well-defined chunks which can be given to developers.
4. *More scalable.* OO projects can be made larger and more complex than other projects. This is inherent in the technology of OO programming methodology and in combination with OO-capable databases.

In the rush to make projects OO, the "dark side" of object-oriented programming is often overlooked. The fact is that not every application should be made object-oriented. Object-oriented languages are not inherently superior, more foolproof, or more efficient in every case. The disadvantages of object-oriented programming are as follows:

1. OO is more difficult to learn than its rival procedural languages. Make no mistake about it, if you are used to procedural programming, you need to do some mental gymnastics to make the switch to OO.
2. OO requires more patience to implement. You must think before you act.
3. OO requires more of an up-front time commitment. It is very easy to negate the flexibility of the modularity of OO programming with poor design. OO languages can be used procedurally. Some projects out there have a million lines of code, using OO languages, and don't have a single object!
4. OO is harder to implement correctly. It is necessary to have the proper infrastructure in place for development, testing, and the rollout to production. Once again, this is often overlooked in the rush to program.
5. It can be difficult to find experienced, successful OO programmers, designers, and project leaders. On the flip side, because object-oriented programming is so effective and yet has such a steep learning curve, people who know OO can do extremely well in the business world.

Where does Perl fit in all of this? The great thing about Perl is that it lessens the learning curve for OO and lets you be productive at the same time.

Once you understand the concepts and a little syntax, you can start experimenting with object-oriented programming in Perl and, by extension, other OO languages. With Perl you can do some very effective object-oriented things such as database administration, system administration, and Web programming, among others, without worrying about getting caught in a dead end technically.

In other words, Perl lets you do OO while you learn its concepts.

Understanding Object-Oriented Programming

Let's first concentrate not on Perl's version of OO, but instead on what OO is itself. Object-oriented programming is a method of programming that concentrates on making effective, reusable building blocks of code.

Just as it is easier to make a building out of bricks, girders, and wires (and a good building plan) than it is to make a building out of lime, rock, and iron ore, so—OO claims—is it easier to build computer projects out of reusable components called classes, which implement objects, and to hook these classes together via a design notation.

OO has its associated terms, just as in any other discipline. The significant object-oriented terms are as follows:

- *Object.* A self-contained unit of data that has subroutines to access and manipulate that data.
- *Class.* A piece of code that implements objects. In Perl, classes are implemented via the keyword **package**.

- *Modules.* Object-oriented programming is often called "modular" because it has parts that can be moved and reused. In Perl, unfortunately, the term module is used in two different ways, which causes much confusion. One definition, which is also the OO one, is the file which contains a class. The second definition is a type of programming that concentrates on separating functions into reusable code, without worrying about the corresponding data. The second type of modular programming is what we will cover in Chapter 14.

Here are more important terms that deal with how OO programming is done:

- *Abstraction* is the process of taking units of code and separating them.
- *Encapsulation* is the process of making an object "self-sufficient" so users of that class do not need to directly access the inner pieces of an object directly.
- *Inheritance* is the process of reusing code by declaring a class as a particular type (or child) of another class. If a user calls a function inside the child class and the child class can't find it, it will look for it in the parent class, hence *inheriting* it.
- *Polymorphism* is the process of making a single piece of code (whether a function, object, or class) behave in more than one way.

The next section goes into great detail on these concepts. Right now, let's concentrate on the programming concept of abstraction. The OO philosophy (if it can be called as such) is centered around abstraction.

Abstraction

Abstraction is a slippery term to define and understand. *Abstraction* is a point of focus. When you are looking at things at a high abstraction level, you are looking at them without concern for the details (i.e., if you talk about the Internet, for example, saying something like "the Internet is growing rapidly"). This is a high level of abstraction, because you are not looking at details such as routers, computers, IP addresses, and so forth. You could also make a strong case that this is a "glittering" generality because it doesn't say much about anything.

The concept of abstraction has a very important role in the manufacture and design of complex systems. Consider an everyday object such as the CPU of your computer:

1. The transistors are at the lowest level.
2. The combinations of transistors form logic gates (AND and OR gates, for example).
3. These logic gates are, in turn, combined into circuits called *adders,* which actually do the computations.
4. The adders are combined into circuit groups called *units,* as in the Floating Point Unit, Arithmetic Logic Unit, etc.
5. These units are finally combined into the CPU of your computer.

This is an *abstraction* scale. At each point in the abstraction scale the point of focus gets higher, as if we were pulling a camera away from the CPU so we could see things only at a certain level of detail. Furthermore, each element can be *composed* of elements in the lower levels of the abstraction.

This abstraction scale is essential in order to make and use the CPU. It would be ridiculous if an engineering VP had to focus on making custom-designed transistors or logic gates for every CPU to be shipped—nothing would ever get done. If each transistor was hand-designed, then each chip would have hundreds of flaws. Likewise, we, as consumers of this chip, would have to custom-design our programs for each and every individual CPU.

As programmers, we are totally dependent on a large number of components working correctly: CPU, operating system, compiler, etc.

How does OO programming fit into all of this? Well, you can make an abstraction chain out of a programming language as well. With Perl, one starts with statements, then goes to functions, and then to programs. As stated, the next two steps in this abstraction chain are the elements that allow Perl to be OO-capable: modules and objects.

A *module* is a bundled set of subroutines, all of which have a common purpose. An *object* is a set of data that has subroutines associated with it that perform operations on that data. A *subsystem* is a coherent set of modules/objects that are related to each other.

These structures are explained in detail later. Modules, objects, and subsystems are introduced here to demonstrate the abstraction chain for Perl.

Here is an abstraction chain for Perl:

1. At the lowest level are data structures that the computer understands directly such as ints, floats, characters, and so on, as well as low-level operations on those data structures. Perl handles all this internally.
2. Combinations of these simple data structures compose the data structures we are familiar with (hashes, arrays, and scalars).
3. Combinations of these simple data structures with functions and operators make expressions. For example:

```
push(@array, 5);
```

4. Combinations of expressions make subroutines. For example:

```
sub swap
{
    my ($pos1, $pos2, $arrayref) = @_;
    @{$arrayref}[$pos1,$pos2] = @{$arrayref}[$pos2,$pos1];
}
```

5a. Combinations of subroutines make modules. The following:

```
package Array;
    sub swap {}        # code as above.
    sub reverse { my($arrayref)  =@_; @a = reverse(@a);   }
```

is a module, with the following usage:

```
Array::swap(1,2,\@array);
Array::reverse(\@array);
```

Array happens to be a module that Perl provides by default in its syntax.

5b. Combinations of data structures with subroutines to manipulate those data structures make objects:

```
package Array;
    sub new
    {
        my ($type, $args) = @_;
        my $self = {};
        $self->{data} = [@$args];
        bless $self, $type;
    }
    sub swap
    {
        my ($self, $pos1, $pos2) = @_;
        my $arrayref = $self->{data};
        @{$arrayref}[$pos1, $pos2] = @{$arrayref}[$pos2, $pos1];
    }
```

6. Combinations of modules/objects make a subsystem. For example, if you had a Perl script that needed to run on both Sybase and Access databases, you might create a database subsystem, as in the following:

```
package DatabaseAccess
```

which is composed of

```
Database::Sybase
```

and

```
Database::Access
```

7. Combinations of subsystems make a system. This, too, is a simplification, but a useful one.

The process of truly learning a computer language is, in effect, learning each level in this abstraction chain. You learn the data elements (level 2). You then learn how to manipulate them via expressions (level 3). You then learn how to put them into subroutines (level 4). Unfortunately, this is where many programmers stop in the learning curve.

Note

Now, it isn't *always* bad to stop at the subroutine level. Sometimes you simply need to get something working and get it working fast, and don't want to think about reuse of code. Furthermore, if you are learning the language for the first time, you probably want to concentrate on the building blocks of the language: hashes, arrays, and subroutines. It is also a virtue of Perl that you can do extremely rapid prototypes by ignoring issues such as code reuse.

Remember, however, if you stick to the lower levels of the abstraction scale, you are condemning yourself to small projects and maintenance nightmares for a long time to come. We will see this shortly.

You don't buy nuts and bolts at the hardware store and put them together inside an automobile engine, do you? Unfortunately, that is what many programmers do when they concentrate on using the power of Perl's syntax to make subroutines (abstraction levels 3 and 4). A formal definition of procedural programming is as a programming technique that concentrates on the series of steps that the computer performs in order to get something done. If the programmer stops here, he or she is not using the object-oriented capabilities of Perl.

Object-oriented programming, on the other hand, is the process of programming by concentrating on the object (abstraction levels 5b, 6, and 7). Instead of concentrating on the procedure (the subroutines and data structures), the programmer concentrates on building bundles of data and subroutines called *objects,* which can be used and reused in programs. In other words, object-oriented programming is a programming technique that concentrates on the object and how objects fit together. These objects then perform the tasks that make the application run.

This requires the programmer and project designer to shift focus and concentrate on the big picture. Instead of thinking about each task in isolation and then writing a bunch of statements to perform the task, as in:

```
open(FD, ">>log");
print FD "first log message\n";
close(FD);
```

think about the possibility of making a *log* object first, and then using the log as in:

```
my $log = new Log("log");
$log->write("first log message");
```

See the difference? Both are a series of statements, and both get something done. However, in the second piece of code, we forget about the details of a log, and concentrate instead on the higher-level operations of that log. These higher-level operations are *creating it* (rather than operating on a low-level filehandle) and *writing to it,* rather than printing to a low-level filehandle.

This may not look like much, but consider when we want to change our log policy (the example we will give in the section "Object Examples" will be adding a timestamp to all our logs). What if there were 100 scripts that write to 100 logs? In the procedural example, we would have to change all these examples to look like:

```
open(FD, ">>log");
print FD localtime() . "\n";
print FD "first log message\n";
close(FD);
```

whereas in the second example, we would only need to change the method `write`.

> **Note**
>
> This is a bit of a simplification, because you could make a `logwrite` subroutine that is not an object, and still be better off than with this stuff.

It is a much-abused phrase, but what we are talking about is *code reuse*. Paying attention to code reuse will help you be much more productive.

A Short Discourse on the Difficulty of Learning Object-Oriented Programming (Especially for Procedural Programmers)

Although object-oriented programming looks deceptively simple, it is quite a paradigm shift from procedural programming. There are many reasons why, but one of the main technical reasons is that it adds a level of indirection in what you are doing when compared to procedural programming. Indirection goes side by side with abstraction. Once something is abstracted, then it can't be directly seen, so you need to trust that the abstraction was correct.

It is easy to concentrate on the task at hand with a procedural program written without subroutines. You take a series of steps, without worrying about the consequences of those steps. Programs are assembled in the same way you would bake a cake, by following a recipe.

The use of subroutines adds the first level of indirection in procedural programming. This adds power, but it also adds complexity, because you do not directly see what you are doing. If something goes wrong, you must track down what went wrong, often through several layers.

Object-oriented programming is, of course, another level of indirection. This adds more power (considerably more), but it also adds more complexity. Not only do you not see what you are doing, but you also must think about how to put the objects together, and how different subroutines work together. Thinking in both the macro and the micro levels is not particularly easy.

But, more than that, learning OO is a matter of psychology. It is often hard to learn because people are comfortable with the procedural paradigm. Procedural programming works for them: it is relatively simple; it has its warts, but, generally, it is pretty powerful (especially Perl procedural programming). Remember the saying, "If all you know how to use is a hammer, everything looks like a nail!" Object-oriented programming puts a few extra tools in your programmer's tool belt.

The First Step of Learning OO

What is the best road to take to overcome the barriers that hinder learning object-oriented programming? The first step is to recognize the limitations of procedural programming. What follows is a short exercise in looking at the gymnastics required by procedural programming to get certain tasks done.

Suppose you wanted to make a program that takes input interactively, and then puts this input into a file based on a switch in the command line. One possible bit of code would look something like what is shown in Listing 13.1:

Listing 13.1
Sync.pm

```
1   #!/usr/local/bin/perl
2
3   open (FD, "> input_log");          # opens up the input log for
```

```
4                                    # the input to follow.
5   if (grep (/-input/, @ARGV))      # looks for the input switch in the
6   {                                # arguments on the command line.
7
8       do
9       {
10          my ($answer, $amount) = ('',0.00);
11
12          print "What do you want for christmas?\n";
13          chop($answer = <STDIN>);
14          push(@output, $answer);
15
16          print "How much will it cost?\n";
17          chop($amount = <STDIN>);
18          if ($amount > 100.00)
19          {
20              print "That's way too expensive\n";
21          }
22      } while ($amount > 100.00);
23  }
24
25  print FD "@output\n";
26  close(FD);
```

This is extremely easy to program, which is great if you want to get a program out the door quickly. This program hovers around abstraction levels 2 and 3 in that there is:

1. Direct, raw access to filehandles:

    ```
    open(FD, "> input_log");
    ```

2. Direct access to standard input:

    ```
    chop($line = <STDIN>);
    ```

Finally, we are repeating what looks like similar loops of logic inside the code, as in asking how much the gift will cost, what we want, etc. Moreover, the results of this program are not put into a data structure.

The upshot of all this is that this sort of programming has long-term cost:

1. If we want to add to this program (in any way) we are going to have to type quite a bit. For example, to add an extra question with an extra condition, we have to type four lines: the print statement, the prompt, the `if` condition, and the action if the condition is faulty.
2. Suppose we want to add an extra flag, say, a `-gift` flag that fills in the answer to "What do you want for Christmas?" at the command line. There is no way to do this without rearranging the entire program.
3. Suppose we want to make a series of programs, all of which do basically the same thing (i.e., a "gift" series of programs) various values from the command line. How do we ensure that the look and feel of the program remains the same?

These are all important questions as programs seldom stay constant. They fluctuate and respond to the demands people put on them. People demand features of programs, and if your programs are not designed to be malleable, you will ultimately get overwhelmed. The way I see it, if you are programming like this consistently, it is like custom-designing each brick in making a house; it is labor-intensive, and ultimately costly to maintain.

Realizing the long-term cost of not abstracting code is the first step.

The Second Step of Learning OO

The second step of learning object-oriented programming is to recognize the terror of cut and paste.

On the face of it, one solution to the problem of adding new code is cut and paste: reusing existing code by copying it. Now everybody knows that this is a bad idea (whether from gut feeling or from analysis), yet everybody does it (including myself). But I have managed to limit myself from doing it by reiterating to myself why this is so bad.

With cut and paste, you can save a little time in the short run; in the long run, you can render your programs completely unmanageable. Suppose you cut and paste 1,000 lines of code into another program. And then, lo and behold, a user of your program asks you for a certain change.

Now you are going to do one of a number of things:

1. You will remember to change the code in both places and get the change correct.
2. You will remember to change the code in both places, and get the changes correct, but make it "right" in two different ways.
3. You will remember to change the code in both places and get one correct, and make a mistake and create a bug in the other.
4. You will remember to change the code in both places and get two different bugs, one in each place.
5. You will only remember to change the code in one place, and forget the other one.

Only two of these changes are acceptable from the point of view of your users: the ones in which you changed both places and got both changes right. And only one should be acceptable to *you*, namely the one where you made the same change in both places. Code tends to take on a life of its own. Once the two sets of copied code diverge, you will find it very difficult to merge them again.

In other words, if you cut and paste (in any language), you are multiplying the amount of code you need to maintain unnecessarily. As I'm sure you are aware, this is *not* a good thing! Your day will be split into fixing the same types of bugs over and over again.

Once you feel that you have a handle on things, someone will ask for additions or changes, and you will go through the same cycle of needless bug fixes. With Perl this is an extra danger, because the free form of the language tempts and/or almost invites the cutting and pasting mentality, which, as I said, works well in the short run, but not so well in the long run.

To summarize: if you notice in your own code that you seem to be solving the same problem over and over again; you keep on hitting the cut and paste function to manage changes; you change code in one place, and then users report the same bug, but in a different script; or your code has hundreds of control blocks spread throughout it then you are probably *not* abstracting your code correctly.

A Guide for the Uninitiated and Unaware to Learning Object-Oriented Programming

Step #1: Learn the Syntax for, and Use Modular Programming

One of the simplest ways to get used to object-oriented programming is by walking before you start to run. Remember, modular programming is the process of taking related subroutines, and putting them into modules for reuse.

Perl provides a very convenient syntax for modular programming, which, if you are trying to learn OO, provides a good bridge for getting to OO. By using modular programming, you get into the habit of categorizing your thoughts, and splitting your design into reusable chunks. We have devoted an entire chapter to the technique and use of modular programming.

Step #2: Learn the Syntax for Making and Using Objects

Actually making Perl objects takes some getting used to, as the syntax is a bit difficult to grasp. Therefore, you should learn it well.

Perl also has some major differences from C++ in the way it does object-oriented programming. Hence, you should realize exactly what the policy is for Perl on OO issues such as memory management, privacy, and how Perl stores its objects.

Step #3: See Examples of Objects In Action

One of the biggest objections people have to object-oriented programming is that they can't get a good, real-life example of objects to work. On the accompanying CD (and available on the Internet) we have put all the source code that we use in this book, plus more. Please take advantage of this opportunity, and take the time to copy this source code (along with your installation of Perl) onto your home computer.

Chapter 17, "The Common Object," goes through the mindset, the steps, and some common problems Perl OO programmers face. It covers such issues as consciously thinking about reuse, steps in construction of objects, maintainability, looking toward new designs, and toward the future.

If you understand the process well enough to create a Perl object, then you will naturally gravitate toward Perl's OO and procedural programming will not seem very clean.

Step #4: Use the Examples for Objects in Your Own Code

I designed these examples specifically so that people could use them. They deal with very generic, low-level problems that everybody faces (log output, document code, and options processing), so you should be able to transfer them into your codebase fairly easily. Furthermore, they are not very difficult so you should be able to follow the flow pretty easily.

Step #5: Create Your Own Objects

Now that you see the examples in action and have traced how they work, go ahead and design and implement a couple of your own objects. They could be enhancements to the ones we have done in detail, or new objects. CPAN will give you some good ideas for objects, as well as helping you become more productive.

Step #6: Learn the More Advanced Perl OO Concepts

Advanced Perl object-oriented concepts such as typing, inheritance, polymorphism, containers, and iterators are very useful to know. Notice that I put this step after you have used OO and grouped a lot of stuff into it. This is because you really don't need to know these for some time. You can be productive in object-oriented Perl without knowing these features. We have dedicated much material to these concepts because they are useful. But they are not essential to the beginning Perl programmer. Following are some capsule definitions and where they will be covered in the text.

Inheritance

Inheritance is the ability of a class to "borrow" methods from another class if they have not defined them themselves.

See Chapter 19, "Inheritance and Perl," for the use of inheritance, how to learn it, and how to apply it to your code. You should understand this fully before you apply it to your code.

Polymorphism

Polymorphism is a technique for making different functions or classes "transparent" from the point of view of people who would use that function. For example, if you define an add function used like add(1,2), you might want to have this function take any number of arguments instead of defining a function like add3(1,2,3). The section "Polymorphism and Perl" goes into this in more detail.

Make no mistake, we will mention these different techniques as they arise in the chapters that lie ahead. But we will not dwell on them. Far too many programmers concentrate on learning everything at once, instead of trying to build their knowledge on top of simple foundations.

Step #7: Look at Some Actual Object-Oriented Perl Projects

Finally, the last few chapters of the book will cover some useful Perl projects. Look over these examples, and feel free to incorporate some of the code into your own projects.

Objects are the building blocks in Perl. Projects are the ways those blocks are put together. By seeing the culmination of thinking and programming in an OO way, you will be more likely to think this way yourself.

Summary

Object-oriented programming is a method for building up large structures out of simpler objects, and building on foundations. When you learn OO, you go through the same process, learning step by step: If you worry about understanding objects and understanding object design concepts at the same time, chances are you will become frustrated and quit. Hence, learn at a steady pace. Don't rush through the next few chapters. Take your time to learn, understand, and apply the principles that are given.

The next few chapters should give you a solid footing in learning Perl's OO, even if you are unfamiliar with object-oriented programming. If they don't, we are not doing our job.

Perl is one of the easiest programming languages to teach object-oriented programming, and in part, the next few chapters are designed for that very purpose. But be forewarned: for many people, OO programming does not come easy. You are best off reading the next few chapters in tandem with the programs we provide on the accompanying CD-ROM. Everything will go smoother if you can document, trace, look, tinker, and feel your way around the objects we provide.

So let's get going. Object-oriented programming is an extremely cool thing to know, especially in Perl! OO can be frustrating at first, but once you get into it, you will see all sorts of wonderful ways to improve your designs. Perl helps a lot, as it is so easy to do OO in Perl. After studying the next few chapters, you should have a pretty good idea of how to actually program the OO way.

14

The Syntax of Libraries and Modules

The purpose of this chapter is to add some substance to the theoretical material on object-oriented programming we outlined in Chapter 13. This chapter gives you the syntax behind the larger building blocks of Perl: libraries and modules.

This chapter is a good reference, but most of these elements will be covered in detail in later chapters. If you have simply used Perl as a one-liner language, you might want to read this chapter in its entirety; otherwise skim ahead, and refer back when you have questions about syntax.

Although the syntax for libraries, objects, and modules is simple, it requires frame of mind when actually using it. Always remember that while it is one of the biggest temptations to cut and paste code, it is also the most harmful type of code reuse. Use code modularity instead.

For more information, there are the **perlmod** (Perl modules) and the **perltoot** (object bag of tricks) man pages that come with the documentation and elaborate on the subjects in this chapter quite well.

Chapter Overview

In this chapter, we will introduce some of the major concepts you will need to know before getting into modular programming, and into object-oriented programming.

The main concepts are as follows:

- *Namespaces* are places to segregate code so that one piece of code does not conflict with another.
- *Libraries* are similar to modules, but are included in the application while the program is running, rather than at compile time.
- *Modules* are defined code that can be included into scripts (via `use module`).
- `@INC` and `%INC` are variables in Perl that define which library or module will be loaded into the code with `use module` or `require library`.

Namespaces

Before we talk about libraries and modules, we really should bring up a basic concept that will help you scale up your programs quite well: the namespace.

Namespaces are tags that let you segregate variables and functions into different compartments. A *tag* is a way to find something that has been put in a file. Tags define or point to where a variable or function may be found.

How do namespaces work? Every function and all global variables have a given namespace with which they are associated. For example:

```
A::function();
```

calls the namespace A's version of `function()`, and:

```
B::function();
```

calls the namespace B's version of `function()`.

Principles of Namespaces

The namespace mechanism in Perl is an elegant one. In fact, it is one taken directly from C, C++, filesystem design, and several other sources. In Perl, namespaces are stored in a *hierarchical* way. A filesystem's power comes from storing files in a directory tree. This makes it possible to access thousands and thousands of files by going only a couple of steps down in the tree. For example, a standard Windows hierarchy might look something like this:

```
C:\MSOFFICE
C:\MSOFFICE\EXCEL
C:\MSOFFICE\WINWORD
```

Although only three directories are listed, hundreds of files could be safely stored in each, lending order to chaos.

Perl stores functions and variables inside a similar hierarchy. The Windows hierarchy example above might be represented in Perl as:

```
MSOFFICE
MSOFFICE::EXCEL
MSOFFICE::WINWORD
```

in which each of the namespaces are homes for functions and variables. Here, the `::` is the separator, just as `\` is the separator in Win32, and `/` is the separator in Unix.

In this case, `MSOFFICE::EXCEL` might refer to functions and variables that implement the Excel program, `MSOFFICE::WINWORD` might refer to the functions and variables that implement WINWORD, and `MSOFFICE` might refer to the functions and variables that tie the functionality of the whole package together.

And the important point is that the variables/functions in `MSOFFICE::EXCEL` are different than the variables in `MSOFFICE::WINWORD`. You can use the scalar `$MSOFFICE::EXCEL::A`, and the variable `$MSOFFICE::WINWORD::A` without fear of stepping all over yourself.

All of this is quite hypothetical. Figure 14.1 shows the actual hierarchy that comes with the centralized distribution of Perl. Each node in this figure is a module that has its own namespace, functions, variables, and that may be an object. (For more details on the central distribution, the documentation that comes with Perl has over 200 pages of information.)

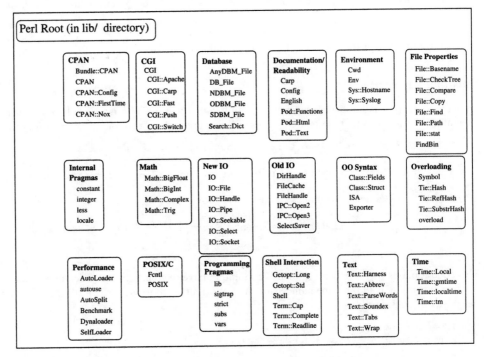

Figure 14.1
Central
Distribution of
Perl Object Tree

You can look at this hierarchy as a functionality map. Each entry has its own niche of functionality which it covers. There is no need for you to program for this functionality on your own. Instead, you should be reusing the modules listed earlier by looking in the documentation to see what is available to you.

In creating your own projects, you should be thinking about creating your *own* functionality map, creating your *own* hierarchy, and generally thinking "Have I implemented this before?" before starting to code. This mindset is essential to scaling up your projects to begin looking at the world in an object-oriented way.

Now, let's get a little more pragmatic, and look at the means Perl provides for accessing, and working with, namespaces.

Accessing a Namespace

There are two basic ways to work with a namespace: you can access it directly, or you can use the package keyword to access it.

Direct Access

One way of getting to variables and functions inside a namespace is to simply append the namespace to the beginning, plus : :. For example:

```
S::execute();
```

refers to namespace S's version of the `execute` function, and:

```
$Mail::hello;
```

refers to namespace `Mail`'s version of the `hello` scalar. Namespaces are hierarchical, so something like:

```
print keys(%level1::level2::hashName);
```

prints out the keys of `level1::level2`'s variable `hashName`.

package keyword

Directly accessing a namespace as we just did can be quite painful. This is especially true when there are several variables and functions that are related. Suppose you were writing a simple sort function as follows:

```
1 for ($sort::xx = 0; $sort::xx < @sort::elements; $sort::xx++)
2 {
3     for ($sort::yy = $sort::xx+1; $sort::yy < @sort::elements; $sort::yy++ )
4     {
5         @sort::elements[$sort::xx, $sort::yy] =
                 @sort::elements[$sort::yy, $sort::xx]
                 if ($sort::elements[$sort::yy] < $sort::elements[$sort::xx]);
6     }
7 }
```

This code contains way too many colons! We shouldn't have to go into the gory details about where each variable is when everything is in the same namespace. As a shortcut, Perl provides the `package` keyword, which simplifies this code considerably:

```
1 package sort;
2 for ($xx = 0; $xx < @elements; $xx++)
3 {
4     for ($yy = 0; $yy < @elements; $yy++)
5     {
6         @elements[$xx,$yy] = @elements[$yy, $xx];
7     }
8 }
```

This does exactly the same thing as the first piece of code: $xx, $yy, and @elements are aliased to $sort::xx, $sort::yy, @sort::elements. package therefore acts as a default namespace, and cuts down on the amount of syntax traffic (or code noise, take your pick) in the code.

Package Declaration Rules

To make all the variables and functions that follow part of a given namespace, say something like the following code snippet. The package declaration has the syntax:

```
package Packagename;
```

This simply tags whatever follows as part of the package `Packagename`.

You need to remember the following three rules of package declaration.

Rule 1: Packages supercede each other. Any package declarations are superseded by any other package declarations. In this code fragment:

```
package One;

package Two;
execute();
```

_execute() refers to Two::execute() rather than to One::execute() because package Two was the last package to be mentioned.

Rule 2: Packages have scope. If you declare a package statement, the package declaration is only good up to the end of the scope that it is included in. (See "Scoping Rules" in Chapter 5 for more details on scope.) The following statement:

```
package Two;
{ package One; }
print $b;
```

prints out $Two::b, because even though package One is the last one declared and mentioned, it was put inside brackets and, therefore, has gone out of scope. However, if you had said:

```
package Two;
package One;
print $b;
```

then print $b refers to print $One::b instead.

Rule 3: Although packages have scope and you can use curly brackets to delimit them, *package variables and lexical variables are totally separate concepts.* In other words, you cannot declare a my variable and have it associated with a package *and*. This may not bite you often, but when it does, it can cause problems. Take the following code:

```
$a::variable = 3;
package a;
my $variable = 1;
package b;
my $variable = 2;
print $a::variable;
```

What does Perl print when it sees this code? Well, the prudent answer would be 1, since my $variable = 1; was put under the package a; banner. However, the correct answer is 3.

In my opinion, this result is counter-intuitive and should be changed, but it vividly shows how Perl has been programmed. What is going on here?

Again, namespaces and lexical variables have absolutely nothing in common with each other. $a::variable = 3 sets a global variable inside the namespace, while package a; my $variable = 1; sets a variable without a namespace. It sets what is called a lexical variable, which is associated with the scope it is in: In this case, the file scope. Since there can be multiple namespaces in a given scope, the following code:

```
package a;
my $variable = 1;
package b;
my $variable = 2;
```

actually sets the same variable twice: first to 1, and then to 2, even though it looks like it is setting $a::variable and $b::variable.

Perl, thankfully, warns you about this type of error, but I still think it is a design flaw of the language that should be fixed. Unfortunately, that is easier said than done (since it would cause a lot of code already out there to change as well).

Practical Namespace and Package Tips

As we shall see, namespaces are the mechanism by which you will create modules, libraries, objects, classes, and other fun stuff. If you are getting into OO, you will be seeing a lot of them. In fact, namespaces will probably be the center around which you program.

Since namespaces will be the center in which you program, here are three quick tips that can save you much time and hassle when working with them.

Tip 1: One Namespace per File and One File per Namespace

As a general rule, there should be one namespace per file, and one file per namespace. If you follow this rule, you will overcome any "weirdness" with the difference between scoping and namespaces as described earlier, and will be able to instantly track down a given subroutine in your code. If you say something like:

```
Module::function();
```

when calling your functions, then you will instantly think "Aha, I need to go to **Module.pm** to find that." (I think of this in terms of "where the code lives.")

The keyword use provides a convenient way to follow this rule.

Tip 2: Use the Special Variable (%{namespace}::) to Track Down Problems

You can use the variable %<namespace>:: to get a list of all the global symbols in a given namespace. For example:

```
foreach $key (keys %Time::)
{
    print "\$$key => $Time::{$key}\n"
    print "\@$key => @$Time::{$key}\n";
    print "\%$key => @{[%$Time::{$key}\n"]}\n";
}
```

prints out all of the variable names and their values that have been globally declared in the namespace Time. This trick does not work for my variables as they are totally different. Again, this is a major stumbling block for people when dealing with Perl.

Tip 3: Develop Your Own Code Hierarchy

The central task of any project should be to develop a code hierarchy of your own. The Perl libraries that come with the standard distribution give a good example of how to make a large Perl project, essentially giving you 30,000 lines of code for free. Building your project as a hierarchy is one of the basic tasks of object-oriented programming.

Summary of Namespaces

Namespaces are where functions and variables "live." The simple way of accessing any variables or functions in a namespace is to say Namespace::function() or @Namespace::variable to directly access it, or to say package Namespace; in front of any code you want interpreted as having its own namespace.

Namespaces are used so you do not have to worry about name collision, which occurs when two variables have the same name. Namespaces allow:

```
$my::variable = 1;
```

and

```
$your::variable = 2;
```

in the same program without having the second variable overwrite the first.

Libraries and Keyword require

Before Perl 4, the only way to make a large-scale Perl project, or scale up your code, was to make functions and segregate variables into scopes. You could get pretty far with just these, but it limited Perl to "one shot" scripts–scripts that were useful, but didn't have reusable components.

Perl 4 came along, and added libraries or collections of functions that were related, which we shall address here. To make a library, you `require` it, just as you used modules.

Usage of require

The model for creating and using libraries in Perl is fairly simple:

1. To make a library, create a Perl program that you are going to reuse in several places. Usually, this file has the suffix **.pl** (for Perl library).
2. To use that library, say `require 'library.pl'` in the program in which you wish to use it.

This is shown in Figure 14.2. For example, say that you have created the following library, which performs certain translations to words. It is stored in the file **wordtrans.pl:**

Figure 14.2
Perl's Model for
Requiring
Libraries

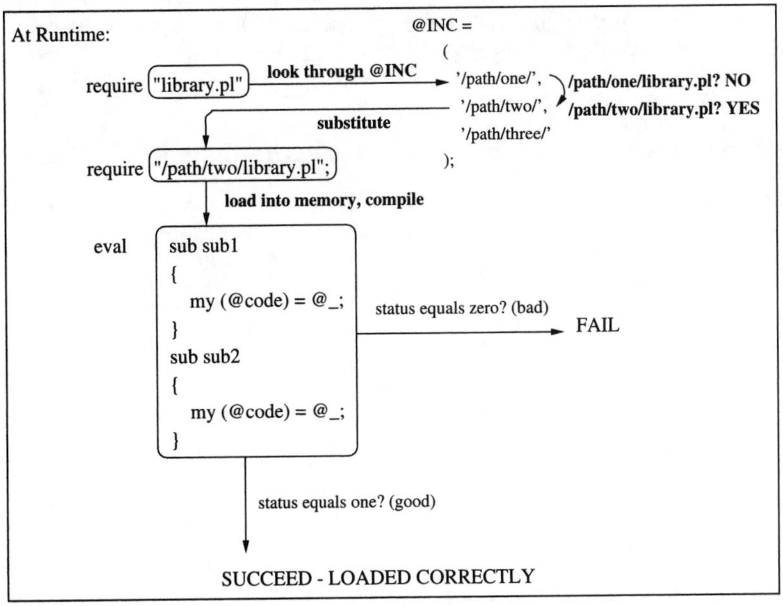

```
1   sub anagram { return(reverse($_[0])); }
2
3   sub rot13
4   {
5       my ($word) = @_;
```

```
6      $word =~ tr"A-Za-z"N-ZA-Mn-za-m";
7      return($word);
8  }
9  sub piglatin
10 {
11     my($word) = @_;
12     my (@letters) = split('', $word);
13     my ($first, $rest) = ($letters[0], join('', @letters[1..$#letters]));
14     return($rest . $first . "ay");
15 }
```

To use this library, put the following:

```
require "wordtrans.pl";
```

at the beginning of any script that wants to call piglatin, rot13, or anagram. The following code:

```
1 require "wordtrans.pl";
2 my $word = rot13('theseus');
3 print $word;
```

will do a simple encryption of theseus by shifting each letter 13 places to the right (A becomes M, B becomes N, etc.). Hence, this will print gurfrhf.

Principles

This may sound simple, but there is one issue we haven't discussed: exactly how this mechanism works. Of course, I should point out some of the small "gotchas" that can trouble new Perl programmers.

So, what happens when you say "require **perlprog.pl**"? There are two things to remember here, which I describe next.

Principle 1: When You require a Library, You Execute the Code Inside that Library

The main principle to remember is that when you write a library, and include it in a program, Perl simply executes the code in **library.pl** at the point when you say "require **library.pl**." For example, if you put the following statement inside the file **library.pl**:

```
1 print "Testing of require!n";
```

and then inside a program:

```
1 require "library.pl";
2 print "Done with require!\n";
```

starting execution at line 1, Perl opens, parses, and then executes the code inside **library.pl**. This prints the following:

```
Testing of require!
Done with require!
```

Principle 2: require Is a Run Time Statement

The library code is not inserted into the main code until run time. When you say "require **program.pl**," Perl executes that statement in exactly the place where it is called. Hence, the following:

```
1 use Config;
2 if ($Config{'osname'} =~ m"nix"i)
```

```
3 {
4     require "UnixLibrary.pl";
5 }
6 else
7 {
8     require "NTLibrary.pl";
9 }
```

does exactly what you might expect, namely, checking the operating system, and seeing if it is a variant of Unix. If so, it requires the library **UnixLibrary.pl**. Otherwise, it assumes you are using NT (we could make an explicit test here, too: **Config** would return `MSWin32`).

This principle *can* be abused to make very illegible code. (In fact, the preceding example could be considered an abuse if used irresponsibly.) For example, you could say something like:

```
1 $library = "mylib";
2 require $library;
```

Since `require` is run time, `require $library` becomes `require mylib`. Hence, we dynamically decide, based on a variable, which library to include.

If you do this often, it will become almost impossible to sort through how you structured your program. The less said about this the better, since the poor soul who has to maintain your code will be cursing your name as he searches through the layers of logic.

Principle 3: require Can Be Used to Open Up a File Directly

Finally, unlike the keyword `use`, `require` has two different usages. If you say something like:

```
1 require library;
```

or

```
1 require "library.pl";
```

then Perl uses the `@INC` variable to search for the module `library`. In the first case, "require library" looks by default for `library.pm`. In the second case, "require `library.pl`", Perl explicitly looks for `library.pl` in `@INC` and then opens it. However, you can override this behavior by saying:

```
1 require "/path/to/library.pl";
```

This opens the file directly, bypassing the magic search. This is helpful for applications such as versioning. Suppose that you want to be able to include differing versions of the same library inside a script. You can say:

```
1 use Getopt::Long;
2 GetOptions(\%varb, "version:s");
3 require "/path/to/perl/libraries/$varb->{version}/library.pl" ||
4   die "Couldn't open version $varb->{version}!";
```

where line 3 assumes that there are multiple versions of `library.pl` stored in different directories, and line 2 gets (and runs) the version of the library that the user wants to run.

require Caveats

`require` is the older way to include code in Perl; therefore, there are some caveats of which you should be aware. (`use` overcomes these caveats, so you are advised to learn it.) These caveats are listed next.

Caveat 1: Beware of Namespace Collision

Since `require` does not enforce any type of convention for functions, there is always the chance that the names of functions will collide, or overlap, each other, for example:

```
lib1.pl:
1 sub get { print "lib1's version of get\n"; }
2 sub put { print "lib1's version of put\n"; }
lib2.pl:
1 sub get { print "lib2's version of get\n"; }
2 sub put { print "lib2's version of put\n"; }
```

Now what happens when you say something like the following?

```
1 require "lib1.pl";
2 require "lib2.pl";
3 get();
```

Well, the first thing Perl does is open `lib1.pl`, and include the functions `get` and `put`. But then Perl goes on to open `lib2.pl` and include `lib2`'s versions of the same functions. This means that when you say `get()` in line 3, Perl prints:

```
lib2's version of get
```

This is a name collision, which has caused Perl to ignore `lib1` and run `lib2`'s version instead. This error can waste time, and the amount of wasted time increases exponentially as the size of the project grows.

The best way to avoid name collisions is by using namespaces (as we will see later), so that your functions aren't in "one big happy family" (i.e., the main namespace), but many smaller families. The flag -w will also show when namespaces collide.

However, even then, in large projects you will get some name collision. You are best off using modules and the keyword `use` instead.

Caveat 2: Beware of require's Run Time Nature

This is a simple one, but you'd be surprised how many times it can catch you. Look at the following code:

```
1 if ($var1 !=1 ) { require "lib2.pl"; } else { require "lib1.pl"; }
```

in which `lib1.pl` and `lib2.pl` look like:

```
lib1.pl:
1 print "This has a Syntax Error!\n
lib2.pl:
1 print "This doesn't have a syntax error!\n";
```

Now, if $var1 is not equal to 1, then the program will:

1. Hit the statement `require "lib2.pl"`.
2. Parse the code in `lib2.pl`.
3. Run correctly (and print `This doesn't have a syntax error`).

In other words, it will do exactly what you expect, because `lib2.pl` contains valid Perl code.

However, if $var1 equals 1, then you will trigger the other part of the `if` clause, and things aren't so simple. What happens? Perl will:

1. Hit the statement `require "lib1.pl"`.
2. Parse the code in `require "lib1.pl"`.
3. Die with a syntax error (since `lib1.pl` has a syntax error in it.)

This can be rather nasty, because the process that you run could have gone for hours before, and then and only then tell you that there is a problem in your code.

What to do about this? Well, the best thing to do is *minimize* your use of this form of require. In fact, I would go as far as to say that you should use require this way only when doing portable coding, or when you want to run a particular version of a module:

```perl
if ($UNIX) { require "UNIXLibrary.pl"; } else { require "NTLibrary.pl"; }
```

I would also take the further precaution of wrapping this in a use statement, since use statements include code before any of the code is actually run, that is, in the compile step. We will talk about this a bit later on, when we get to use.

Summary of require

In short, require lets you include code just as if the code was typed on the spot: require program.pl opens the Perl file **program.pl**, inserts it into the spot where require was called, checks it for syntax, and then runs it. Hence, it can be useful in cases where you are not sure which library to call. However, in general, use is, well, more useful, as we shall see next.

Modules with use

Libraries are a good start for Perl, but, in many ways, they are *too* flexible. In particular, since they are run time, this means that their syntax is checked during the middle of a run. This means, as we saw earlier, your script could be merrily going along, and then hit a require statement in the middle, along with a syntax error inside that library, and stop dead in its tracks. Also, it is too easy to get into poor programming practices with libraries, for reasons given earlier.

Hence, Perl 5 introduced the use statement, and the concept of modules to Perl. Modules are bits of related code that sit together in a specialized compartment, and follow a semi-strict naming convention which helps the programmer organize his or her code.

This has many advantages over require. In fact, you should be programming with use about 90 percent of the time (there will be a couple of places where you will have to resort to require, which we shall mention).

Usage of use

The model for creating modules with use is almost as simple as the one for require. There are a couple of layers thrown on top, as follows:

1. To make a module, write a Perl program that has the suffix **.pm**, as in **Module.pm**.
2. To use that module, say use Module in the program in which you want to include it.

So far, so good. In fact, this is exactly the same thing as in the case with libraries up above. However, as said, there are the following quirks which may seem like a pain starting off, but will make your life really easy when you get used to them:

1. The actual program, **Module.pm**, must have the header package Module; in front of any code that exists in the module.
2. You may include a special function, import, in the module, which will be executed at the point of the module's inclusion in a program.

The general form of programming and using modules is shown in Figure 14.3. There are several equivalencies here. The filename of the module (without the **.pm**) is equal to the package name of the module, which is equal to the namespace of the module, which is equivalent to the prefix put in front of every function in the module. If you don't have these relationships in your code, it will fail (with an empty package error). One of the simplest modules in Perl is:

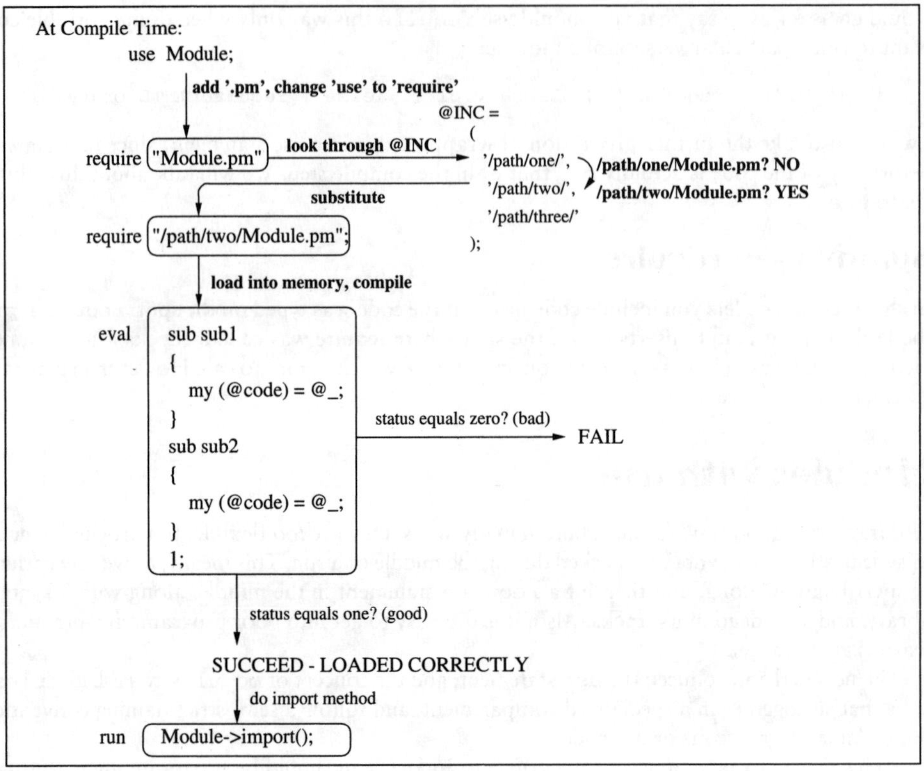

Figure 14.3
Module Form
in Perl

```
module Simple.pm:
1 package Simple;
2 sub True { return (1); }
3 sub False { return (0); }
client (client.p):
1 use Simple;
2 print Simple::True();    # (prints 1);
```

Or, as in the more complicated example:

```
module SubClass/Class1.pm:

1 package SubClass::Class1;
2 sub True { return(1); }
3 sub False { return(0); }
client (client.p):

1 use SubClass::Class1;
2 print SubClass::Class1::True();
```

Aside from accessing True() from the namespace Simple (or SubClass::Class1), this is very much like programming a Perl library. And to the casual user, it behaves much the same as require.

However, there are a few things that set use apart from require, which we discuss next.

Principles of use

As said, require can bite you because of the fact that it is done too late, *after* Perl has compiled the script. (This was the motivation for a separate compile phase in which you could alter the way the script was run. There used to be no way to do this in Perl 4.) use makes things much cleaner by following two principles, which are detailed next.

Principle 1: use Is Done at Compile Time

Each instance of use is run at compile time. This means a very helpful syntax check of all modules that are included in scripts is performed, before they are actually executed. However, this means one very misleading thing. Consider the following code:

```
1 if ($time eq 'now')
2 {
3     use Module1;
4 }
5 else
6 {
7     use Module2;
8 }
```

This does not mean "include Module1 if time equals 'now', otherwise include Module2." Instead, at compile time, Perl rips out each use statement, and parses the code on the fly, leading to something that executes like the following:

```
1 use Module1;
2 use Module2;
3
4 if ($time eq 'now')
5 {
6 }
7 else
8 {
9 }
```

This can mislead the new Perl programmer who is constantly thinking in terms of require. They are effectively using use as if it were require. Both keywords have their place, but this isn't one of them for use. Programmers are strongly encouraged to encapsulate all their require statements *inside* a use. We will show how to do this a little later. It makes the interface for client programs of the module much easier.

Principle 2: use Lets You Modify the Code By Making an Import Function Inside Modules Made By use

There is another twist here: the import function. import lets you pass parameters to the use statement, exactly as if use were a function.

import is Perl's mechanism for making what are called directives. A *directive* is a line of code that modifies the environment Perl is working in, so that programs that look at the directive are modified to run in a certain way at compile time.

Remember use strict? Well, this uses import internally. When you say use strict, Perl calls the function strict::import() at compile time, which then modifies the way that the Perl interpreter parses code. Remember use Config? This also uses import internally to gather information about what environment Perl has been compiled in, and store it in the hash %Config. Both are directives you use to your benefit.

As a simpler example, let's implement addition in a kind of an offshoot way, as a directive. Again, the client is the one with the use statement, and the module is the one that implements the package:

```
client:
1 use Add 2,2;
Module (in Add.pm):
1 package Add;
2 sub import
3 {
4     my ($type, @parameters) = @_;
5     my ($param, $answer) = (0, 0);
6     foreach $param (@parameters) { $answer += $param; }
7     return($answer);
8 }
9 1
```

Again, this is a rather strange way of doing addition, but a good example of import. When Perl sees use Add 2,2, it does two things:

1. Parses Add.pm (checks it for syntax errors, imports functions into the current code space, etc.).
2. Calls the function Add::import('Add',2,2), which passes the parameters that the use statement called. (Note that the first function parameter is the name of the package being used.)

When you consider that you can put anything into import, you get a very powerful mechanism. Indeed, different import functions, such as the one in the optional module filter, have been used to modify the syntax of Perl itself on the fly! (We used **filter** at my workplace to make the syntax of Perl look more like C++, for example.)

Common use Directives

Let's now look at actual use samples. You can get more information about these from the documentation itself, but they are so common that you will be constantly using them in the programs you write.

use strict

We just mention it here, but we have been using it throughout the book, and no summary of directives would be complete without it. See Chapter 22, "Perl Debugging Tips" for more information on *use strict*.

use Config

Again, we have used this before. It populates a hash named %Config, which is really a synonym for this file called **config.sh**, which is created when you compile and install Perl. By dumping the keys and values in this hash, you can get a complete list of the elements of which Config is aware.

Here's a sample program that prints some of the more common attributes:

```
1 use Config;
2 print $Config{'osname'};    # prints your operating system name.
3 print $Config{'cc'}         # prints the compiler which compiled Perl
4 print $Config{'ccflags'}    # prints the options which were used to compile Perl
```

As said, these are the most common values. There are about 447 others you can print! See the on-line documentation for more details.

use Env

use Env is a simple workaround that allows you to pretend that the environment is actually variables inside your program. It takes the elements of the hash %ENV, and makes a scalar for each element it finds. For example, if you say something like:

```
use Env;
print $PATH;
```

then Perl will print the current path for you, rather than having you say:

```
print $ENV{'PATH'};
```

use vars

use vars is used when you want to have a global variable and also want to have the strict directive in force in the program. For example, say you had the following code:

```
use strict;
$file = 1;
```

This will fail because $file is a global, and strict doesn't allow globals that are undeclared (don't have an occurrence without the package in front of them, like $main::file). However, if you say:

```
1 use strict;
2 use vars qw($file);
3 $file = 1;
```

then line 2 predeclares $file for you; this can work. It tells Perl "Yes, I know that a variable named $file exists; it is not just a typo."

use Exporter

This is the big kahuna, so to speak, of directives; people use it quite a bit (too much, actually). It lets you export functions and variables into an environment.

What does this mean? Remember the code we programmed before (the **Simple** module)?

```
module Simple.pm:
1 package Simple;
2 sub True { return (1); }
3 sub False { return (0); }
client (client.p):
1 use Simple;
2 print Simple::True();    # (prints 1);
```

In line 2 of the client, we said print Simple::True(). We had to fully qualify the namespace to the function that we were using. If you exported this function instead, you could say:

```
1 use Simple;
2 print True();
```

without knowing that True() was inside Simple.

How to do this? Well, Perl provides `Exporter` to do this very thing. You say:

```
module Simple.pm
1 package Simple;
2 use Exporter;
3 @ISA = qw(Exporter);
4 @EXPORT = qw(True);
```

Don't worry about the mechanics of how this works for now. All lines 2–4 are saying is "Export the function `True` into any place that says `"use Simple"`." This is called *exporting by default*. When you say:

```
use Simple;
```

in your script, Perl loads `Simple`, and then copies the `True` function into the namespace where `use Simple` is called. Don't worry, we will get to this when we talk about inheritance.

Exporting by default is not necessarily the best thing to do. The two things that follow are pretty nasty:

1. You can forget where your functions are coming from. There is something supremely satisfying about seeing `Simple::True()` instead of `True()`, because you know exactly where to look in case of problems.
2. Since there is a lot of stuff going on here (inheritance, globbing, using the import function, and so on), you are best off knowing about how it works, before actually using it. We treat `Exporter` as a good example of inheritance in that chapter, so you might want to read this before using it.

The documentation has more in the way of examples on `use Exporter`. You don't necessarily need to export by default; you can export by choice, give a list of patterns to export (or not export) variables, and so on. See the documentation for more information.

More Examples of use

OK, now let's supplement the `use` examples from the distribution with some of our own. Let's look at three more simple examples applying this to writing modules and using them in code.

Example of Functions In a Module: Converting the "WordTrans" Library (require to use)

First, let's take the 'word translation' library we wrote earlier, and convert it to a module. We call this file WordTrans.pm:

```perl
1   package WordTrans;
2
3   sub anagram { return(reverse($_[0])); }
4
5   sub rot13
6   {
7       my ($word) = @_;
8       $word =~ tr"A-Za-z"N-ZA-Mn-za-m";
9       return($word);
10  }
11  sub piglatin
12  {
13      my($word) = @_;
14      my (@letters) = split('', $word);
15      my ($first, $rest) = ($letters[0], join('', @letters[1..$#letters]));
```

```
16      return($rest . $first . "ay");
17 }
18 1;
```

Note two things here. One, the code is exactly the same. We have simply taken our three subroutines (anagram, rot13, and piglatin) and cut and pasted them into **WordTrans.pm**, our module file. Second, note the **package WordTrans**; and 1; statements at the beginning and end of the file. These statements enforce the convention that what you are doing is separating your functions off into a namespace.

When we get around to including our module into a program, we will call these functions differently. The client, or program that uses the module, will need to put WordTrans on the front of any functions it uses:

```
1 use WordTrans;
2 my $word = WordTrans::rot13('theseus');
3 print $word;
```

Instead of require "WordTrans.pl", we have use WordTrans. We are assuming that the module is called **WordTrans.pm** and that the functions we include are all in the WordTrans namespace.

Example of Using the import Function: A Simple "Version Checker" for Programs

Second, let's take a look at an example of import: the function that runs code inside a module when it is first imported, or compiled, into the program. Here, we will implement a simple version checker in Perl. You will probably be familiar with the main problem here if you have ever worked on a software project bigger than two people.

The problem is keeping things *in sync*. If you are using a module that has function A, that is no guarantee that previous versions of that module have function A.

In fact, if a script of yours is using version 1.005 of the module, and it happens to ooze its way into a place that only has version 1.004 (which doesn't have function A), then users of this module will get the following rather rude message:

```
Undefined subroutine A at line ...
```

The users of your module will have to go through your code to see what is going on (all the while thinking unpleasant thoughts about you). Not good. We will substitute this message with:

```
Version 1.005 required! You only have version 1.004! Please get the latest version
from (....) (source name)
```

How to do this? Well, with the import function it is straightforward. Assume our module is called Widget. We want to block any code older than version 1.005, so we say so inside our client:

```
client.p
use Widget 1.005;
```

Now, the 1.005 is passed to the import function as an argument. This will be executed when the Widget module is first applied. To get the behavior that we want, we program Widget as follows:

```
1 package Widget;
2 my $_actualVersion = 1.004;
3 sub import
4 {
5      my ($type, $neededVersion) = @_;
6      die "the module $type requires a version!\n" if (!defined $version);
7      if ($neededVersion > $_actualVersion)
```

```
8        {
9                print "Version $neededVersion required! You only have version
$actualVersion! Please get the latest version from (....) (source name)";
10       }
11 }
```

This mechanism can be added to any package to get this useful behavior. It is pretty much a universally applicable function. In fact, when we get to the `Exporter`, we will see a standard way of handling revisioning.

Example 3: Using use to Make Portable Code

This is a very generic example (in fact, we will cover it in more detail when we get to polymorphism), but it is a good example of how you can get the bulletproof nature of use, and still maintain the flexibility of `require`.
Consider the simple example that we had before with `require`:

```
1 use Config;
2 if ($Config{'osname'} =~ m"nix")  { require "UNIXMailLib.pl"; }
3     else { require "NTMailLib.pl"; }
```

Supposedly, `UnixLib.pl` and `NTLib.pl` are pieces of code that do the same thing on different platforms, and the above is a workaround to get a piece of code to run on both.
However, there are some drawbacks to that code. First, it does not shield the user from the details of how the code is working. We see the "gunk," the internal glue, which makes the code work.
Second, it suffers from the drawbacks of `require` that we discussed before: namespace pollution, and the fact that it is executed at run time. The second drawback is particularly irksome, because we may not be warned of any errors in our programs until the code is actually hit.
Hence, it would be natural for us to want to stuff all this messy code into a module. We would say:

```
use Mail;
```

and get the behavior we want. With use, and the `import` function in use, this is easy, as shown in the following code:

```
1 package Mail;
2 use Config;
3 sub import
4 {
5
6 if ($Config{'osname'} =~ m"nix")  { require "UNIXMailLib.pl"; }
7     else { require "NTMailLib.pl"; }
8 }
9 1;
```

In fact, we may want to make this error checking more stringent. Suppose that, in the same example, our script depends on a couple of executables being installed. Since we are working with pseudocode that implements a **Mail** module, let's use this as an example. We can take the preceding code and augment it with a couple of checks for code that we need:

```
1 package Mail;
2 use Config;               # module to get config details.
3 use Carp;                 # module to get debugging output.
4 sub import
5 {
6     if ($config{'osname'} =~ m"nix")
7     {
```

```
8              if (`which elm` =~ m"not found") { confess "Couldn't find elm\n"; }
9              require "UNIXMailLib.pl";
10    }
11    else
12    {
13             require "NTMailLib.pl";
14    }
15 }
```

Here, lines 8 and 13 check to see if the appropriate executables that we use (`elm, MSmail`) are installed, and `confess` (the process spilling its guts telling exactly when and where it died) if the executables are not there.

Summary of use

As you can see from the examples, `use` can be extremely powerful, providing a lot of extra functionality that `require` does not even approach. However, many former Perl programmers don't take the time to become familiar with `use`, out of habit or stubbornness. Whatever the reason, there is one simple way to remember how `use` is different from `require`: they are almost the exact opposites.

`require` is executed at run time, and `use` is executed at compile time. This makes it so that code forms such as if (`$a`) { use A; } else { use B; } don't work.

`require` has no naming conventions to follow to make it work. `use` needs the module name in use <ModuleName> to be equal to the filename (plus `.pm`), which is equal to the package name.

`require` simply imports the code with no questions asked. `use` allows you to write an import function which lets you do anything Perl allows to interrogate the code in order to learn about the environment it is running in before actually importing the function.

In other words, `use` makes you go through more hoops to get things done, but in doing so, it makes your job a lot easier, and makes your code more scalable. Hence, you should be using `require` only in specialized circumstances.

Loading Modules and Libraries From Disk

The preceding concepts (`require`, `use`, and namespaces) are the logical elements that make Perl able to process libraries and modules. You write a module, and then `require` it into your program, or use it. By doing so, you populate the variables and functions that make your program go.

However, there is a flip side of the coin: Your modules and libraries must come from somewhere. They are stored on disk, then must be loaded into memory and parsed before they can be used by the Perl interpreter.

All of these are physical concerns, and they account for much of the overhead in actual projects.

Where you actually get the code to be loaded into memory can make all the difference in the world: Was it a test version you loaded, or a preproduction version? Has the code gone through quality assurance, and so on? I have spent the better part of some days tracing down an elusive bug in Perl code, only to find that I was using the wrong version of the module, running from the wrong machine, or even using the wrong version of Perl.

These errors can trip you up time and time again, and Perl provides several facilities to stop this from happening. The following section goes over some of those facilities. Read these carefully, and we believe you will come to less grief as time goes on.

The Library and Module Road Map: @INC and %INC

The best way to avoid problems with loading the wrong libraries or modules is to understand how Perl finds the libraries it loads into memory. We cover this in detail next.

@INC

The central variable here is called @INC (short for *include*); if you remember anything from this section, remember this.

@INC is an array provided by Perl that tells Perl (and you) which directories to search to find libraries and modules. Ninety percent of your problems with version mismanagement can be solved by putting this simple statement at the beginning of your program:

```
print "@INC\n";
```

This gives you a list of places Perl is looking in to find your libraries. The central rule about @INC you should remember is that Perl goes through each of the directories *in order* looking for the module or library you are including. If it cannot find it in one directory, it goes to the next.

Printing out @INC shows exactly the order Perl is taking to get the libraries.

This seems to be confusing for some, so let's go further into an example of the way Perl does this lookup, and a session in troubleshooting.

Suppose you had a simple client that looks something like:

```
client1.p
use Devel::Peek;
```

and you find that, for some reason, Perl is saying something like the following:

```
Can't locate Devel::Peek in @INC at line
```

The first thing to do is comment out the offending line (use **Devel::Peek**) to get a working program, and print the "@INC\n" variable as the script sees it, to get something like:

```
/usr/local/lib/perl5 /usr/local/lib/perl5/sun4-solaris . /home/ed/WORK/Devel
```

Good enough. The second thing to do is print what is in each of those directories, as follows:

```
/usr/local/lib/perl5:              <Bunch of files, no Devel directory>
/usr/local/lib/perl5/sun4-solaris: <Bunch of files, no Devel directory>
.:                                 <Bunch of files, no Devel directory>
/home/ed/WORK/Devel:               Peek.pm, SelfStubber.pm
```

In tracing this down, we follow in Perl's footsteps. Perl goes through the following machinations:

1. Perl looks in /usr/local/lib/perl5, and tries to find /usr/local/lib/perl5/Devel/Peek.pm.
2. It fails, so it goes to the next directory (/usr/local/lib/perl5/sun4-solaris) and tries to find /usr/local/lib/perl5/sun4-solaris/Devel/Peek.pm.
3. It fails here, too, so it goes to the next directory (., or the current working directory) and tries to find ./Devel/Peek.pm.
4. This fails, so it finally goes to /home/ed/WORK/Devel to find /home/ed/WORK/Devel/Devel/Peek.pm.
5. It finally gives up and registers an error.

Note one important thing here: Perl does not find Peek.pm inside /home/ed/WORK/Devel because the directory /home/ed/WORK/Devel is the root directory that Perl tries to match. It sticks Devel/Peek.pm on the end of the root, to get:

```
/home/ed/WORK/Devel/Devel/Peek.pm
```

So, in solving the problem, we notice that there is an extra **Devel** on the end of our @INC which is causing mischief. The simple solution therefore is to change @INC to include /home/ed/WORK instead of /home/ed/WORK/Devel.

For those of you who like logic diagrams, Figure 14.4 shows the process in pictorial form. This is fairly straightforward if you understand "Perl-think." Learning include paths like Perl's will pay off tenfold (in other compilers, tools, etc.). It is a common design tactic in computer science.

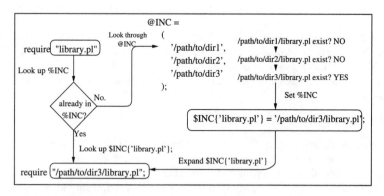

Figure 14.4
Perl's Process of Including Libraries

%INC

@INC is fairly well-known by people who program Perl regularly, but %INC is not. This is unfortunate, because %INC can be used to track down problems that would take much longer to track down with @INC.

If @INC contains a list of *directories* Perl searches for modules, then %INC contains a list of actual *modules* Perl has loaded from the environment. For example, the following code:

```
use Benchmark;
foreach $key (sort keys(%INC))
{
    print "$key => $INC{$key}\n";
}
```

will print:

```
Benchmark => '/usr/local/lib/perl5/Benchmark.pm'
```

assuming that **/usr/local/lib/perl5** is the first library that Perl stumbles across.

As you can see, this can be extremely helpful. For one thing, it can save you the trouble of searching through the include path (@INC) to find a library out of sync, but, more importantly, it is exactly what Perl sees, so there is no chance of human error in tracking down these problems.

It also has one more benefit, one that you will get without any effort on your part, but for which you will be grateful. Take the following code:

```
for ($xx = 0; $xx < 10; $xx++)
{
    require "lib1.pl";
}
```

On the surface this code would cause the library **lib1.pl** to be included several times. In most languages, this would cause severe problems. C++, for instance, has "compile guards," which are put around all header files, something like this:

```
#ifndef HEADERA
#define HEADERA 1
#include "headera.h"
#endif
```

This is essentially a hack to prevent a header from being included several times (and getting "xxx redefined" errors).

Perl does not need this. Instead, each time a Perl library is included into your script, Perl records the fact inside %INC. The next time that library is encountered in require or use, Perl recognizes that fact, and stops right there! Hence, no problems, and a vast savings of time and resources.

Let's use %INC to solve another resource problem. Suppose that you have written a script, and get several weird errors, such as:

```
Undefined subroutine File::Path::seek() line ...
```

Now, File::Path is a module that you have written to do basic things like open a bunch of files (say in a "tree" format), and when you open up the file **File/Path.pm**, and whatever else, you *see* the subroutine seek. Furthermore, the module **File/Path.pm** is in your @INC variable when you start Perl.

After a couple of minutes of double-checking yourself, your first reaction should be that this is a path problem, that somehow, you are including the wrong module into your program (Perl doesn't lie, after all).

Therefore, you should insert the following line into your program:

```
foreach $key (sort keys(%INC)) { print "$key => $INC{$key}\n"; }
```

This is exactly as we did before, except now when we run the program, we see (in the midst of the output):

```
File::Path => /usr/local/lib/perl5/File/Path.pm
```

So, at a glance, you see that somehow, **/usr/local/lib/perl5** has a module **File/Path.pm** instead of the expected **/home/ed/WORK** having **File/Path.pm**. What happened? You have gotten unlucky, and accidentally called your module the *same name* as one included in the central distribution! The solution? Rename your module **File/MyPath.pm** (and change the package definition inside) and everything compiles successfully.

In short, learning to use %INC (and @INC) can mean saving hours of effort. Problems like the one just described can be fairly common, especially in large projects, and tracking them down can be trivial, or difficult, depending on your knowledge.

Setting @INC

The variable @INC is such an important beastie to Perl that there are several different ways of setting its value. Each way has advantages and disadvantages; you should be aware of them all (especially when debugging projects.)

The Default Value of @INC

Unlike most variables in Perl, the default value of @INC is not blank. Instead, it is a value that is set at the moment which Perl has been compiled. If you look inside the **config.sh** file that comes with your Perl distribution, you will see this value. (Or, probably easier, the one-line script **perl -e 'print "@INC\n"'** will do the same.)

This path points to the place where the Perl installation has put all the libraries that came with the standard distribution (see the namespace diagram earlier).

The Environmental Variable PERL5LIB

The first way you should know about setting @INC is via the environmental variable PERL5LIB. This is a good way to set the environment for the purposes of a cron job, or to set the environment temporarily so you can test new code.

If you say something like:

```
prompt> set PERL5LIB = "my_path";
```

on Win32, or:

```
prompt> export PERL5LIB="my_path";
```

on ksh, then you prepend my_path to the @INC variable. Hence, if @INC was:

```
"/usr/local/lib/perl5", "/usr/local/lib/perl5/sun-solaris"
```

it becomes:

```
"my_path", "/usr/local/lib/perl5", "/usr/local/lib/perl5/sun-solaris"
```

with my_path being the first place Perl will search for libraries.

Setting PERL5LIB does have some drawbacks. Because you are setting the environment rather than putting your instructions into the code itself, you must be very careful when moving between environments. Forgetting to set PERL5LIB is an easy thing to do—caution is advised.

use lib 'my_path'

use lib 'my_path' is the second way to set @INC, and probably the best, most stable way of doing it. It has the following benefits:

1. It is done inside code, so you see exactly what is going on.
2. It works well with some Perl internals (in particular, MakeMaker, which you can read about in the Perl on-line documentation).
3. It uses a module, so your code will automatically get benefits of any further enhancements to the @INC mechanism.

When you say:

```
use lib 'my_path';   (ex: use lib '/home/epeschko/lib';)
```

at the beginning of any code, Perl does exactly the same thing as with PERL5LIB. Namely, it takes my_path and prepends it to @INC.

Setting @INC Directly

Finally, we mention the fact that you can set @INC directly, for closure. But to tell the truth, it is not such a hot idea. You can say:

```
BEGIN { unshift(@INC, "my_path"); }
```

which does the same thing as both PERL5LIB, and:

```
use lib 'my_path'
```

but it is unclear, ugly, and nonencapsulated (i.e., it shows the guts of the logic, rather than hiding the details).

Do yourself a favor and stick to the two other methods.

Summary of the Library and Module Road Map

@INC is the one major variable used to actually piece the script together out of the several modules and libraries that are require'd and use'd by your program.

Perl looks at @INC one directory at a time, trying to find modules. When it finds them, it notes the fact that it has found them in the hash %INC.

As @INC is so important, there are several methods for setting it:

1. By default: Perl looks at how you have configured Perl to find the libraries it needs.
2. By PERL5LIB: an environmental variable. This prepends a list of directories to @INC.
3. By saying use lib "path", which changes @INC at compile time.
4. By directly manipulating the variable @INC.

Setting Up a Development Environment

Now is the time to look at how you might set up an environment in which you can have different stages of Perl code development. There are some issues here that are outside the scope of this book (source control being the big one), but right now we are interested in the issues that have to do with code–how we can program for scalability.

Architecture

We have four such areas at our work right now:

1. *Development* is where the majority of the brainstorming, new ideas, blunders, and other associated mishaps happen with new code development.
2. *Test* is where the first swag of testing comes in, where the ideas that were first expounded in development get their trial by fire.
3. *Preprod* is where the code is released to a larger audience, and gets a chance to "cool down" with a large-scale (and usually lengthy) test, a staging area before the next environment (*production*). This stage is also sometimes called the *integrated test area*.
4. Production is where a final, clamped-down version of code is created which is supposed to be bullet-proof.

The general plan of attack we will have in this example is to set up a different directory tree for each environment we are working in. Figure 14.5 shows how it will all look. Each directory tree represents a complete picture, in which scripts can run using the modules that are associated with the tree. In this simplistic model we have four different directories:

1. **modules/.** This will be where all of the in-house modules will reside, the ones we will program. This is where we will set up our code tree.
2. **perl_extensions/.** This will be where the Perl extensions that come from the Net will reside.
3. **scripts/.** This is where the scripts we will program will reside, the ones that use the Perl extensions and modules.
4. **perl_source_code/.** This is where the Perl source code (the actual source for Perl) will reside.

It is a good idea to keep track of modules and scripts with these four directories. However, you may want to have a system administrator keep track of the **Perl_extensions** and **Perl_source_code.**

However, if you keep track of your Perl extensions and Perl source code, you can have complete confidence and control that your scripts will always work. (Well, OK, not complete confidence; the operating system or any supporting tools you use might change.)

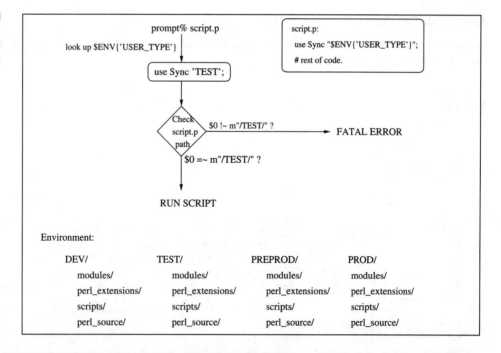

Figure 14.5
Module Form
in Perl

Note

Anyway, if you choose to keep track of your Perl source code, you can install your own Perl binary inside the tree by choosing the correct installation command for Perl. (We don't have room to talk about it here, but the install script on the CD gives a rather large example of a portable installation script. By using different values, you can install any combination of modules (from the CD, the Internet, or a website). If you have questions on it, drop me a line or an email.

The point of this is that you want to minimize the number of variables that can impact the scripts, and you definitely don't want these types of variables to affect you when people are counting on your scripts in a production environment, and your scripts fail.

Issues

Setting up different environments is not free, however. There are three issues when we set up something like this:

1. Change control and populating the different environments is the source code control issue I was talking about. You want to have a way to test your development code, before releasing it to test, and having a way to release it into preprod, etc. There are several good source control tools out there (such as CVS or PerForce). You can also write a Perl wrapper to handle your source control.
2. Code changes to make the environments work–The scripts you write must have some way to find the modules they are going to use. For example, if you say use MyModule; you have to make sure that MyModule is in a directory that is in @INC.
3. Synchronization issues–Making sure that production scripts don't use test or development modules. This can be a horror, as alluded to before. If a production script uses a development module, it may not be compatible with the production world, and things will break all over the place.

As said, issue 1 is outside the scope of this book. But issues 2 and 3 are different. In fact, there are very helpful directives in Perl that can ensure stability in scripts and minimize these two types of problems.

Implementation

Recognizing the preceding problems, here is a possible solution. Let's call the module we write **Sync**, (synchronization), and list it next (Listing14.1):

Listing 14.1
Sync.pm

```
1   package Sync;
2   use Carp;
3
4   sub import
5   {
6       my ($type, $place) = @_;
7       BEGIN
8       {
9           $ROOT = ($place eq 'TEST')?           "/code/tree/TEST":
10                  ($place eq 'DEVELOPMENT')? "/code/tree/DEVELOPMENT" :
11                  ($place eq 'PRODUCTION')?  "/code/tree/PRODUCTION" :
12                  ($place eq 'PREPROD')?     "/code/tree/PREPROD" :
13          -        ($place eq '')?                    confess "You need to provide a type of
     environment!\n" :
14                                            confess "Unknown place $place!\n";
15          my $script = $0;
16          if ($script !~ m"$ROOT")
17          {
18              - confess "The script $script is needs to be running under the tree
     $ROOT since it is a $place type of script!\n";
19          }
20      }
21      use lib "$ROOT/modules";
22  }
23  1;
```

Pretty simple logic, but following a strategy like this can help you out a great deal. Lines 4–22 are the `import` function, which will be called at compile time before any of your script is run. In lines 9–14, we figure out, based on what was passed to this module, which library tree we are to use: TEST, DEVELOPMENT, PRODUCTION, or PREPROD. If `import` is passed TEST, then the place that becomes the `$ROOT` to where we locate our modules becomes:

    /code/tree/TEST

Continuing, line 15 gets the full path to the script (i.e., the name of the script that actually includes this module) and lines 16–19 check to make sure that the name of the script is under the same tree as the modules that it includes. In other words, if the script you are running is:

    /code/tree/PRODUCTION/scripts/my_script.p

and because `$ROOT` has become:

    /code/tree/TEST

the test:

    '/code/tree/PRODUCTION/scripts/my_script.p' !~ m"/code/tree/TEST"

succeeds, and flags the problem as a mismatch (because the script as run is not inside the directory **/code/tree/TEST**), and the script dies (confesses) because of it.

Therefore, the code consists of two parts: one that figures out what the root will be, and one that flags potential problems with the code that one might encounter. And the usage? Well, each script that you put into this system should have something like the following lines:

```
use Sync "$ENV{USER_TYPE}";
# .... code comes here
```

In this case, we tell from the environment what type of module we use. This comes from the simple observation that most of the time, people are developers, testers, or users of the code you write. Hence, when people log on, you could set up the environmental variable $USER_TYPE to tell what type of user they are, and have **Sync import** the right modules automatically.

Why go to this trouble? Well, figure the alternative. If you say something like:

```
use Sync 'TEST';
# .... code comes here
```

then you pretty much condemn your code to be in TEST 'heck' for eternity. On the other hand, you could edit the code each time you move it from TEST to PREPROD, and PREPROD to PROD (or even have a Perl script to do it), automatically but you really want to avoid this type of magic. Making changing code is (most likely) a maintenance nightmare.

If you don't like the environmental idea, there are others you could try. People in testing usually work from a certain type of machine, or are in a certain group. You could "auto-magically" figure out what type of code out from these sources, or perhaps others.

In fact, some people take something like this a step further. Just food for thought, but we have seen something (done in Perl) like what is shown in Figure 14.6. Yes, that's right, there are many arrows, and it can usually be done only in a Unix environment (last time I checked, NT didn't have links). The trick is that each person has his or her own personal environment, which has links to the centralized environments. That way, when they check out something, everybody sees that something is checked out. And when someone puts something back, everybody sees it put back, so they are instantly affected.

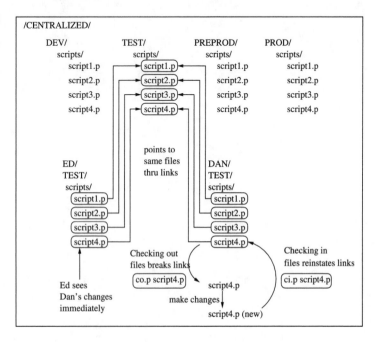

Figure 14.6
Personalized Environments

This scheme has, I admit, some maintenance involved, but if you get it working, it can do wonders. Each person has his or her own "playspace" in which he or she can do anything without affecting any other people. And if you do it right, the speed of code change gets faster and goes smoother.

Summary

We have covered a lot of territory here. Your basic weapons in the fight for scaling up code are the namespace (and the keyword `package` to implement namespaces), the library (with `require`), and the module (with `use`). `use` should be preferred over `require`, since `use` gives you some freebies in debugging your code, and is generally more scalable. There are times when you will need `require` (such as for portability issues), but these should be rare.

In Chapter 15, we will go through a lot more examples of modules and directives, and in a lot of detail. Perl has many simple, useful modules you can write to manage projects among other things, and we will go through how to spot and program them.

15

Abstraction and Modular Programming in Perl

Chapter 14 discussed the syntax of modules and libraries, along with examples on how to create a Perl project. In this chapter, we expand on those concepts and give more examples of the thought patterns behind making modules in Perl.

Making modules in Perl is the first step to scaling up code. The best way to think about modules is as collections of functions, whereas objects are collections of functions and associated data.

This means modules are easier to make than objects are, because there is no need to worry about as many technical details going on at the same time. To put it another way, programming with modules is like juggling three balls simultaneously. Programming with objects is like juggling with four or five, perhaps six balls at the same time. It is the purpose of this chapter to flesh out these concepts with examples.

If you aren't a Perl programmer, or are used to programming "quick" scripts in Perl, you will want to read this chapter.

We hate to beat it into the ground, but if you are going to do any of the following:

- Build anything larger in Perl than programs approximately 1,000 lines long
- Build a set of related programs
- Maintain your code
- Not rely on job security through code obscurity
- Build a foundation for object-oriented programming in Perl

You should have an intimate understanding of modular programming and how to use it effectively in Perl. Even if you aren't going to be a large-scale

OO programmer, learning modular programming will go a long way toward making you feel more comfortable with the language, as well as make you more efficient in it.

Modular Programming Concepts

Modular programming is based on a rather simple concept, that, if followed regularly, gives you incredible power over your programs. There are challenges in becoming a good modular programmer, and they are not all technical.

In fact, the technical side of modular programming is rather simple. The simple concept involves creating subroutines and pigeon-holing them into a common place, the *package*. Instead of having functions sitting at the bottom of scripts, they are abstracted out by putting them in a place where they can be found again. That's about it!

You can think about this in terms of a client/server relationship. We will use these terms a lot, and since they are bantered around quite a bit, it is a good idea to know what they mean in an object-oriented context.

- A *client* is a program that uses bits and pieces of other programs.
- A *server* is not a program in itself, but bits of functionality that a client would find useful.

The client gets its requests filled from the server whether those requests are to format a date, obtain a file, etc. You can get more complicated than this, too; clients can be servers of other clients. Something like *client => server/client => server*; is a three-tiered client/server system. The first client forks its requests off to the first server, which then fills other requests from the second server.

The trick of programming in a modular way is to recognize which functions are reusable, or what can and cannot be abstracted. That is what the bulk of this chapter is about. But we would be remiss if we didn't bring up the costs of programming in a modular way before we got started.

The Costs of Modular Programming

As introduced in Chapter 13—the introduction to object oriented programming—an unfortunate number of programmers cling to the lower ends of the abstraction scale. In other words, they never get above the point where they are putting subroutines in their individual scripts. This is good for throwaway scripts, but horrid when you're trying to do something really big in Perl.

However, there are some reasons for clinging to the lower level of abstraction, and never attempting to make anything larger than a subroutine. Some of these reasons are valid, and some are misplaced. Let's look at some of them now.

1. *Larger up-front time commitment.* Modular programming is synonymous with design. To make a set of modules in which you can pigeon-hole effective functions, there must be a design, and with design comes the time to design.
2. *Modular programming involves a level of "indirection."* Indirection is best defined by example—it is simply a matter of "I'm calling this function here, but the function actually lives in a module, over there!" In a way, this is harder to debug, and you have to think more on how to debug it.
3. *There is a psychological cost to modular programming.* Face it: People generally like to make simple scripts in which everything is there, in front of them, and they don't need to look anywhere else to debug. There are many reasons for this: habit, wanting to get something working fast, the sheer joy of hacking, and so on. But realize that when you are getting something done quickly by using shortcuts, you are not actually getting stuff done quickly; there is a hidden cost to what you do.
4. *Modular programming can limit flexibility.* This is a difficult concept for nonprogrammers (especially nontechnical managers) to understand. When making modules, you are making, in essence, building blocks. Building blocks are great for creating things quickly, but if the particular block does not fit exactly, it can be difficult to make it fit. What often looks like a difficult problem may actually be very trivial, and what looks like an easy problem can be just the opposite. Good modules limit the amount of problems that fall in the second category.

5. *There are many outside pressures that can prevent you from programming correctly.* Because modular programming takes more time up-front, let's not forget the outside pressures that can come from programming for profit, before programming for fun.

Each of these points affects people differently. For example, I didn't get snagged up by points 1, 2, and 3, but point 5 was a real kicker, because I primarily program for profit.

In fact, we have a name for this last point at my workplace. It is affectionately known as the "Scotty syndrome," named after the "Star Trek" character of the same name. This is the situation in which a Kirk-like manager comes in and says to the unfortunate Perl programmer, "Please, if you don't get this done in the next hour, WE'RE ALL GONNA DIE!" Because Perl sometimes lets you do very complicated things in a short space of time, Perl programmers are in demand in the workplace but they can be pigeon-holed into doing production fixes and only production fixes.

I digress. The main point is that if you aren't used to modular programming, and want to learn it, it will take resolve, determination, and drive, as well as working smarter rather than harder. Believe me, if you aren't thinking in a modular state right now, it is well worth it to do so when you start doing ten times the work in half the time.

Note

Do yourself a favor and don't get stuck in a rut where you are always making quick fixes to a problem. Consider the Scotty syndrome if you are in position where you are constantly on the critical path. If you always give way to the desire/orders to do that quick fix, then as sure as rain is wet, there will come a day when there will be a true problem where serious fallout will occur. Then, you won't be able to get it done, because it will not warrant a quick fix, but an overhaul to the entire process.

If you are in a situation like this, do not hesitate to tell the manager something such as: "Yes. I can do this (insert quick fix here). But this quick fix will probably cost us more time in the future than if I (modularized/objectified/designed) the problem correctly now." In other words, be up front with the manager's demands, and above all, learn how to fix the problems correctly.

I wish I had a dollar for every time quick fixes remained in production for years. And, by definition, quick fixes are usually devoid of comments, so everyone is afraid to get rid of, or fix, the program. Repeat after me: Nothing is an emergency unless there is blood on the floor!

Converting a Procedural Script to a Modular Script

I do code reviews at my work, with a red pen, an empty conference room, and lots of caffeine to tide me over until the code review is done. Code reviews are held for different purposes, but let's assume that we are taking a bit of code someone has written from scratch. We want to fit it into an already existing project by abstracting out what we can and putting it into modules. (We only consider modules here; we will see later that some of these modules are better off as objects.)

By an amazing coincidence, the script we will consider is one we discussed earlier in Chapter 13, the one that started this whole discussion on code reuse (shown in Listing 15.1).

Listing 15.1
procedual_code.p

```
1   #!/usr/local/bin/perl -w
2
3   use strict;                    # makes it so we adhere to strict rules
4   open (FD, "> input_log");      # opens up the input log for
5                                  # the input to follow.
6   if (grep (/-input/, @ARGV))    # looks for the input switch in the
7   {                              # arguments on the command line.
8       my ($answer, $amount, @output);
9       do
```

```
10    {
11        undef (@output);
12        print "What do you want for Christmas?\n";
13        chop($answer = <STDIN>);
14        push(@output, $answer);
15
16        print "How much will it cost?\n";
17        chop($amount = <STDIN>);
18        if ($amount > 100.00)
19        {
20            print "That's way too expensive\n";
21        }
22        push(@output, $amount);
23
24    } while ($amount > 100.00);
25 }
26
27 print FD "@output\n";
28 close(FD);
```

What can we make of this?

Well, any good program design consists of two steps. First, figure out what makes sense to abstract. Second, figure out how to implement the abstractions. If I had my red pen, I'd mark up this script to resemble something like Figure 15.1.

Figure 15.1
Marked Up
Procedural Code

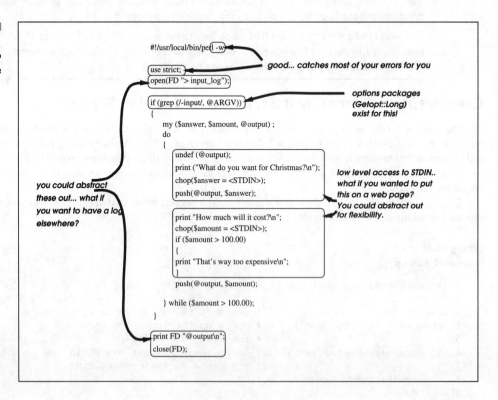

Three things come to mind from Figure 15.1:

1. Log files can be accessed directly.
2. Standard input can be accessed directly.
3. Options from the command line can be accessed directly.

Each of these represents classes of items that Perl programmers consistently do not abstract, which, as we said earlier, is a good and bad thing depending on your intentions. Hence, we will look at them in isolation and in detail. Let's take the first step, and consider how we wish to abstract each of these items.

Point 1: Abstracting the Log File into a Module

There were two lines in the code that dealt with logging:

```
4  open (FD, "> input_log");    # opens up the input log for
27 print FD "@output\n";
```

Now, this might not be a problem in itself—the script might be a one-liner—but we have a problem if this was part of a bunch of Perl scripts.

This is a problem if we want to do something more sophisticated than simply print the input as we do in line 27. Say we want to print a timestamp, or to log which program is using the log file, or to keep a running tally of gifts:

```
Oct 24 1996 13:45:02 Stretch Armstrong 14.95
Nov 14 1996 14:05:02 Hunchback of Notre Dame 15.95
```

Or perhaps we want to load this data into a database and make the elements in it pipe-delimited:

```
Oct 24 1996 13:45:02|Stretch Armstrong|14.95
Nov 14 1996 14:05:02|Hunchback of Notre Dame|15.95
```

In each case, if we don't abstract it and have more than one program that does similar logging, we will have to change every single occurrence in every single program that uses this logging. Therefore, it does make sense to abstract it out.

As we shall see in Chapter 17, this is a good candidate for an object (see that chapter for the rationale). But for now, let's make this a module. Modules, after all, are easier to do, both technically and conceptually. Finally, (this is important!) making it a module does not preclude making it an object later. Later, we will convert this module into an object to show how easy (if tedious) it is to do.

Let's start abstracting the above code by making three subroutines at the beginning of the program. We'll call them logOpen, logClose, and logWrite. Let's also make the usage for our log functions as simple as possible. In other words, the filehandle and the name of the file are now associated with the functions that are accessing them. This way, the call to our logOpen(), logClose(), and logWrite() functions will take only one argument. The code will look something like Listing 15.2.

Listing 15.2
procedural_code_mod.p

```
1  #!/usr/local/bin/perl
2
3  my $fh;
4  sub logOpen
5  {
6      my ($log) = @_;
7      $fh = new FileHandle("$log");
8  }
```

```
 9  sub logClose
10  {
11       close($fh);
12  }
13  sub logWrite
14  {
15       my (@output) = @_;
16       print $fh "@output";
17  }
18
19  logOpen('log_file');        # open(FD, ... )
20                              # the input to follow.
21  if (grep (/-input/, @ARGV))    # looks for the input switch in the
22  {                              # arguments on the command line.
23      my ($answer, $amount, @output);
24      do
25      {
26          undef @output;       # clear any mistakes.
27          print "What do you want for Christmas?\n";
28          chop($answer = <STDIN>);
29          push(@output, $answer);
30
31          print "How much will it cost?\n";
32          chop($amount = <STDIN>);
33          if ($amount > 100.00)
34          {
35              print "That's way too expensive\n";
36          }
37      } while ($amount > 100.00);
38  }
39
40  logWrite(@output);
41  logClose();
```

This program is the equivalent of the previous program. The code in boldface we are going to move to a package, but it makes sense to keep it here for ease of testing.

After we are done testing, we then abstract the three functions into their own package. As before, we do this in the same file for ease of testing (Listing 15.3).

Listing 15.3
procedural_code_mod2.p

```
 1  #!/usr/local/bin/perl
 2  package Log;
 3  my $fh;
 4  sub open
 5  {
 6      my ($log) = @_;
 7      $fh = new FileHandle( "$log");
 8  }
 9  sub close
10  {
11       close($fh);
12  }
```

```
13 sub write
14 {
15      my (@output) = @_;
16      print $fh "@output";
17 }
18 1;
19 package main;

20 Log::open("log_file");
# ..... all the other stuff.
# .....
40 Log::write(@output);
41 Log::close();
```

So, logOpen becomes Log::open; logClose becomes Log::close, and logWrite becomes Log::write. The Log:: tag shows that they are related in the same module.

In this case, our client is the program that actually does the asking about Christmas gifts. The server is our log module, which will be used by the Christmas gift program.

Cut the package out of the client; that is, remove everything between package Log; and 1. Put this code in its own place, say, a directory denoted by an environmental variable MYLIB. (We saw how to create MYLIB in the last chapter.) The client becomes what is shown in Listing 15.4.

Listing 15.4
procedural_code_mod3.p

```
1 #!/usr/local/bin/perl
2 use lib "$ENV{MYLIB}";
3 use Log;
4
5 Log::open("log_file");
6 # ..... all the other stuff.
7 # .....
8 Log::write(@output);
9 Log::close();
```

Then make a file named **Log.pm** (Listing 15.5).

Listing 15.5
Log.pm

```
1   package Log;
2   my $fh;
3   sub open
4   {
5       my ($log) = @_;
6       $fh = new FileHandle(">> $log");
7   }
8   sub close
9   {
10      close($fh);
11  }
12  sub write
13  {
14      my (@output) = @_;
```

```
15      print $fh "@output";
16 }
17 1;
```

Of course, there are several ways to stick **Log.pm** in its own central place. Using the following directive:

```
use lib "/directory/path"
```

is the easiest. It simply says to Perl "OK, the first place you are going to look for a module is inside "**/directory/path,**" before you look in any of the centralized places."

Summary of Abstracting Out Input Into a Log

This is a simple example of "modularizing" a program. We recognized that a few of the functions, `open(FD,..)`, `print FD`, and `close(FD)`, were doing work that was too low-level for the problems at hand. If we wanted to change our interface, for example, we would have had problems. We may also wish to reuse the concept of a log file, and would hate to throw away all that good code.

We also realized that it would probably be better if this log file was in fact an object rather than a module, and in the future, we would probably be better off converting it to an object.

We took five steps to modularize the routines:

1. Realization of the problem, and that the three functions were better off in a module/object.
2. Design of the new subroutines.
3. Prototyping, making each of the functions into a subroutine that abstracted out the low-level data (filehandles, etc.).
4. Making the subroutines into a package, which existed in the same program where the packages were used.
5. Making a module in a centralized place (`$ENV{MYLIB}`) that will contain all of the modules that we are going to use. We then pointed the client to use that module via `use lib`.

Now that we have this flexible code that can be reused in other programs, we might add to this with ideas for the future: thinking of how to expand our log module by adding features like the timestamp we talked about.

This is one of the fun things about programming in modules and objects. One almost never comes up with a perfect module or object. There are always ways to improve/add to your design, and since you are putting things in a centralized place, you are (in essence) solving 1,000 scenarios at once.

Point 2: Abstracting out Calls to Standard Input

Let's use this same line of thinking for the second problem on our list, the problem about standard input. Again, we have two questions that are being asked from the command line in the loop:

```
1  do
2  {
3      undef @output;      # clear any mistakes.
4      print "What do you want for Christmas?\n";
5      chop($answer = <STDIN>);
6      push(@output, $answer);
7
8      print "How much will it cost?\n";
9      chop($amount = <STDIN>);
10     if ($amount > 100.00)
11     {
12         print "That's way too expensive\n";
```

```
13      }
14 } while ($amount > 100.00);
```

How can this code be abstracted out of the main code?

Any given interaction between the user and the program consists of three things:

1. A question being asked.
2. A response being given for that question.
3. A validation for that question that tells the computer whether or not the answer is appropriate.

Therefore, this looks like the perfect case for a "killer" subroutine (i.e., one that kills 1,000 different problems at once), or a couple of killer subroutines that abstract out all of the input problems up above. Let's call this package **InputHandle**.

Now, unlike our first log module, I believe that the **InputHandle** package should ultimately be a module, not an object. In this case, we are doing a straightforward action: getting input from the user. Because modules consist of functions *only*, it makes sense not to introduce the extra complexity an object offers.

This is also the perfect example to create a low-level subroutine, one useful in a wide variety of situations, i.e., the "killer."

Let's call our low-level subroutine get and place it inside the module **InputHandler** so there is no name conflict with Perl. There will be only one subroutine in this module. In accordance with the requirements of the program, the subroutine will have two arguments:

1. The question that is going to be asked.
2. An optional function pointer that will be used to validate whether or not the function returned an appropriate value.

The usage of the get function looks something like this:

```
1 push (@output, InputHandler::getInput('What do you want for Christmas?'));
```

which will do the equivalent of:

```
1    print "What do you want for Christmas?\n";
2    chop($answer = <STDIN>);
3    push(@output, $answer);
and
1 $answer = getInput('How much does it cost?', \&validation);
```

which will do the same thing as:

```
1    chop($amount = <STDIN>);
2    if ($amount > 100.00)
3    {
4        print "That's way too expensive\n";
5    }
```

except that the cost validation is abstracted out into a subroutine called validation that the user controls. Listing 15.6 is the subroutine in its entirety.

Listing 15.6
InputHandler.pm

```
1    package InputHandler;
2    sub getInput
3    {
```

```
4      my ($question, $validFunction) = @_;
5
6      die "improper usage!\n" if (ref($validFunction) ne "CODE");
7                                   # simple type checking.
8      my $answer;
9
10     print "$question\n";        # print out the question
11     chop($answer = <STDIN>);    # get the answer via
12                                 # standard input.
13
14     $answer = &$validFunction($answer);  # try to validate the input
15                                          # assign the result to the
16                                          # return value. Example of
17                                          # a function pointer.
18     return($answer);            # return the validated input.
19 }
```

We then abstract and put it in its own module, and our client becomes what is shown in Listing 15.7.

Listing 15.7
procedural_code_mod4.p

```
1  #!/usr/local/bin/perl5
2  use lib $ENV{MYLIB};
3  use Getopt::Long;
4  use InputHandler;
5  use Log;
6
7  my $options = {};
8  GetOptions($options, '-input');
9
10 Log::open('log_file');     # open(FD, ... )
11                            # the input to follow.
12 if ($options->{input})     # looks for the input switch in the
13 {                          # arguments on the command line.
14     do
15     {
16         my ($answer, $amount) =
17             (
18                 InputHandler::getInput("What do you want for Christmas?\n"),
19                 InputHandler::getInput("How much will it cost\n",\&tooMuch);
20             );
21    } while ($amount eq 'NO_GOOD');
22 }
23
24 Log::write($answer, $amount);
25 Log::close();
26
27 sub tooMuch
28 {
29     my ($amount) = @_;
30     if ($amount > 100.00)
31     {
32         print "That's way too expensive\n";
33         return("NO_GOOD");
```

```
34      }
35      return($amount);
36 }
```

See how this is working? We are molding the internal loop, and abstracting it so that it contains only the main points of the action. Before the abstraction, we had bare filehandles and access to the standard input.

 We have also gotten ahead of ourselves and added command line processing, GetOptions. The reason we did this is that this is a trivial usage of GetOptions. If you want more information on option processing, see the next section.

Note

Notice that you need not abstract everything out of a given operation for a module to be useful. Take the case of the function pointer as used by getInput. From the point of view of **InputHandler::getInput**, this function is a black box. **InputHandler::getInput** calls it, not caring what this function is, and uses the results of that call to filter the input the user gave at the keyboard.

This function pointer is also called a *callback*. Callbacks are used to supply a missing piece of functionality to the module, a piece of information that the module cannot possibly know. (For more information on callbacks, see Chapter 11.)

For example, the **InputHandler** module cannot know whether a value passed to it is good or bad. **InputHandler::getInput** doesn't know whether the string that we pass it is asking about Christmas gifts, or steel girders. **InputHandler::getInput** shouldn't know (or care) what function we use to validate the data. These details should also be abstracted from the point of the module.

We simply say that the user (not the module itself) is going to define a function, a function that **InputHandler::getInput** simply calls without knowing what it is. Let's look at that code again (Listing 15.8).

Listing 15.8
InputHandler.pm

```
1   package InputHandler;
2   sub getInput
3   {
4       my ($question, $validFunction) = @_;
5
6       die "improper usage!\n" if (ref($validFunction) ne "CODE");
7                                   # simple type checking.
8       my $answer;
9
10      print "$question\n";        # print out the question
11      chop($answer = <STDIN>);    # get the answer via
12                                  # standard input.
13
14      $answer = &$validFunction($answer);  # try to validate the input
15                                           # assign the result to the
16                                           # return value. Example of
17                                           # a function pointer.
18      return($answer);                     # return the validated input.
```

The line:

```
14 $answer = &$validFunction($answer);
```

calls the function pointed to by $validFunction, passing the value $answer, which we get from the command line:

```
chop($answer = <STDIN>);
```

Here are some examples of how it is useful in this context:

```
$integer = InputHandler::getInput('give me a float..', \&roundUp);
sub roundUp { my ($float) = @_; $float += .999999999; return(int($float)); }
```

This gets a float from the command line, and rounds it up to the nearest integer. And:

```
do
{
} while (
    $number = InputHandler::getInput
            (
            'give me a number from 1 thru 10..',
            \&rejectdigit
            )
    );

sub rejectdigit
{
  my ($input) = @_;
  return('') if (($input > 0) && ($input<11));
  return($input);
}
```

keeps trying to get a number from the command line, while the user refuses to type a number, and types a string instead. \&rejectdigit is called, and the user input is validated, returning '' (false) if the input is not between 1 and 10. Otherwise, it returns the value the user typed.

This is enough about callbacks for now. Perceptive readers may recall that we first covered them in Chapter 11, and we will see them again. Just be aware that they are there, and remember that they are used in different ways.

Now let's think to the future on how we could expand **InputHandler::getInput**. One of the most obvious ways is that we could add an option for "shadowing" (i.e., not displaying the text to screen) when the user was to enter a password. Another might be to make it so getInput could automatically be mirrored into a log file, to record what the user had typed into a file.

Summary of Abstracting Out Standard Input

The process of creating this module was very similar to the previous one. We recognized the problem and figured out what we were going to abstract. We then abstracted the standard input problem, this time into a common module called **InputHandler**.

This time, however, we added a wrinkle: modularizing a client, but modularizing it while still relying on the script to do some of the processing. In this example, we did this by the use of a function pointer, a callback.

Callbacks are functions that let you abstract a problem out, but not completely. In this case, we used callbacks to make a powerful getInput routine, which could be used to get any standard input we want.

Abstracting Out Argument Processing: An Example of Getopts in Detail

There is one more point we must address in this example: argument processing. The array to manipulate is @ARGV, the standard options library. *Argument processing* is the teething ring upon which every Perl programmer learns Perl libraries. There are hundreds of option processing libraries.

There is a very good option processing library passed out with the standard distribution. It is called Getopt, and has two flavors:

```
Getopt::Long;
Getopt::Std;
```

You can therefore consider this example to be one of successful reuse. As we shall see, this is probably one wheel that you don't want to reinvent.

Getopt::Long Example

Consider a common situation in which there is a function that takes five different command line directives:

1. **-name** takes a nonoptional string argument.
2. **-age** takes a nonoptional integer argument.
3. **-occupation** takes an optional string argument.
4. **-married** is a switch (i.e., it is either there or not).
5. **-police_record** takes an array of strings as an argument.

The following example uses Getopt to stuff all the options from the command line into the hash reference called $options, and takes them out of the @ARGV array in the process:

```
use Getopt::Long;

my $options = {};

GetOptions($options, "-name=s", "-age=i", "-occupation:s",
          "-married", '-police_record:s@');
```

$options is an example of passing a reference to a subroutine to be filled. Using this code with the following input:

```
prompt% script.p -name 'Ed Peschko' -age '28' -occupation 'Data Migrant' -
police_record 'jaywalking' -police_record 'snorkeling without a license' other_arg1
other_arg2
```

results in a hash reference, $options, which contains:

```
{ name => 'Ed Peschko',
   age => 28,
   occupation => 'Data Migrant'
   police_record => ['jaywalking', 'snorkeling without a license']
}
```

And @ARGV becomes:

```
( 'other_arg1', 'other_arg2')
```

because these arguments cannot be processed by Getopts::Long. Hence, they are left in the surrounding array. Or you could say:

```
prompt% script.p -name 'Ed Peschko' -occupation -age '28'
```

and get:

```
{ name => 'Ed Peschko',  occupation => '', age => 28 }
```

Getopt Advantages

The Getopt module is pretty complicated, but very useful. Be sure to read the documentation that comes with it to get a taste of its complexity. I primarily use the option for stuffing everything into a hash reference because:

1. All the command processing is on one line.
2. All the options go into one hash reference, which can be passed to subroutines.

In addition, there are hundreds of command line options modules out there for your use. Getopt::Long is the best of them. Getopt::Long has three, inherent advantages, as follows:

1. *It has lots of functionality, and is very resilient.* There is a consistent interface with Getopt::Long, and one that is very user-resistant. Switching the order of the options has no effect on the actual use of those operations.
2. *It is distributed with Perl itself.* Hence, you are guaranteed that other people will be able to use your module.
3. *It is the standard that has been tested for years.* Most every program out there uses Getopt::Long.

Keep in mind that nothing is perfect, and Getopt::Long is no exception. We discuss its warts next.

Getopt::Long Defaults, Good and Bad

To use Getopt::Long effectively, it is necessary to make you aware that there are two package variables that must be set in order to make things work correctly. These package variables are already set in the package, but I dislike the defaults. Here is one:

```
$Getopt::Long::ignorecase
```

ignorecase is a package variable that controls the case-sensitivity of the command line options. Do yourself a favor and set this to 0. By default it is 1, which means that -U and -u are the same thing, which, to many programmers, is just plain wrong.

Here is the other package variable that needs to be changed:

```
$Getopt::Long::passthrough
```

This package variable controls whether options are passed through or ignored if they cannot be understood by Getopt::Long. "Passed through" means that they will remain in @ARGV to be processed later. Without the passthrough option, they will be "eaten" by Getopt::Long.

This passthrough is a new option, and it is essential to make a class of Perl programs called *wrappers* around other functions, which we talk about next.

Getopt::Long and Perl Wrappers

The statement $Getopt::Long::passthrough = 1 facilitates the creation of wrappers around already existing commands. Wrappers inherit the functionality of a given command without having to rewrite that functionality. If you set passthrough to true, and call the function **script.p** as so:

```
prompt% script.p -option_not_defined 'a' -defined_option 'b'
```

in which the command line is passed to

```
use Getopt::Long;
GetOptions($options, '-defined_option:s');
```

then this will leave the undefined option alone. @ARGV will become (-option_not_defined, a) and $options will contain { 'defined_option' => 'b' }.

Example of Passthrough: Database Interface

Here is an example of why passthrough is so useful. All major databases come with a command line interface, for example, in which you can directly type commands to the underlying Sybase engine. For example, if you have used Sybase before, then you are familiar with the infamous isql command, which is Sybase's command line interface with its database.

In Sybase, you can say something like:

```
isql -U user -P password -S server -i SQL_file
```

This will take the SQL in `SQL_file` and apply it (`-I`) to the server given by `-S`.

However, this is usually no good from the command line, since we want to apply our SQL file to a particular database, not a server. Hence, we could add a `-D` argument which would take the `SQL_file` and directly apply it to a database. Therefore, we could do something like what is shown in Listing 15.9.

Listing 15.9
Command Wrapper Example isql.p

```
 1  #!/usr/bin/perl
 2  use Getopt::Long;
 3  use FileHandle;
 4  $Getopt::Long::passthrough = 1;
 5  $Getopt::Long::ignorecase = 0;
 6  my $options = {};
 7  GetOptions($options, '—D:s', '—i:s');
 8  my $file;
 9  if ($options->{D})
10  {
11      _$tempfile = _addDB($options);
12  }
13  system("isql @ARGV -i $tempfile");     # we pass through the arguments.
14  unlink($tempfile);
```

The meat of the statement occurs in line 13.

If a user says:

```
isql -U user -P password -S server -D database -i SQL_file.
```

then the arguments `-D database` and `-i SQL_file` are picked up by `Getopt::Long`. `-P password` and `-S server` pass through (i.e., they stay in the argument list). Hence

```
system("isql @ARGV -i $tempfile");
```

becomes

```
system("isql -U user -P password -S server -i <temp_file>,
```

This is a vanilla, every-day **isql** command, with a difference. What's the trick? Well, we shall make `temp_file` a direct copy of the input file given on the command line, only we shall add a header telling where the SQL is going to be executed. If our SQL looked something like:

```
select * from account
```

```
go
```

then, inside `temp_file`, code will look something like:

```
use <database_name>
```

```
go
select * from account
go
```

Usually this editing would be done by hand (i.e., we would insert use <database_name> go into the file before processing). In this case, the editing is done by Perl.

This is especially helpful if you have a large, sprawling database model with tables inside different servers, and different databases.

Here is the implementation. Again, note the technique of undefining $/ and slurping an entire file into a string via $line = <$fd>; (Listing 15.10).

Listing 15.10
isql.p (continued)

```
1   sub _addDB
2   {
3       my ($options) = @_;
4       my ($database, $sqlfile) = @_;
5       local($/) = undef;   # lets us suck all the data down in one fell swoop;
6       my $fh = new FileHandle("$sqlfile") ||
7                       die "Couldn't open file $sqlfile\n";
8       my $fh2 = new FileHandle("> $$.SQL");
9       my $line = <$fh>;           # sucks in the whole file;
10      print $fh2 "use database $database\n";
11      print $fh2 "$line;
12  }
```

Note how easy this translates into Perl code. We have a program, **isql**, that does not exactly fit our needs. We want **isql** to take a database parameter, and it doesn't. Hence, we add that functionality on top, as it were.

Your cup of tea may not be database administration, but you can use this technique quite successfully no matter what you do. For example, suppose you want to log any **del** commands you type (Listing 15.11):

Listing 15.11
dellog.p

```
1 #!/usr/local/bin/perl5
2 use Log;
3 Log::open("del_log");
4 my $path = getcwd();
5 Log::write("$path; del @ARGV");
6 system("del @ARGV");
```

Now, if you convert this into a batch file (**dellog.bat**) using **pl2bat.bat** (see Chapter 3), and you put it in your path, each time you type

```
C:\> dellog
```

you will store all of the del commands that you type. (Not much use in Windows, one might argue, since they wrap up everything into the Explorer file. But for larger projects, such a trail of breadcrumbs is essential to figure out. You must weigh the convenience that the Recycle Bin gives you against the lack of traceability.)

Advanced Argument Processing

You can do a lot with simple wrappers, but there are some cases in which you are going to want to get more fancy than GetOptions permits. Suppose you have a bunch of scripts that all use the same options:

```
prompt% record.p -name 'Ed Peschko' -age '28' -occupation 'Data Migrant' -
police_record 'jaywalking' -police_record 'snorkeling without a license' other_arg1
other_arg2

prompt% get.p -name 'Ed Peschko' -age '28' -occupation 'Data Migrant' -police_record
'jaywalking' -police_record 'snorkeling without a license' other_arg1 other_arg2
```

record.p may record the information given at the command line into a file or database. **get.p** may simply get the information out of that file or database.

In this case, it makes sense to reuse the functionality of the command line in both scripts. Say we want to have a common usage for both scripts. If you want to do this, then simply reuse that functionality by placing it in a module. Define a module, **CommonOptions**, which uses a specific set of behaviors from the **Getopt** module. Do something like what is shown in Listing 15.12.

Listing 15.12
CommonOptions.pm

```
1 package CommonOptions;      # in file CommonOptions.pm
2 use Getopt::Long;           # using the module Getopt::Long;
3 use strict;                 # we want to have built in tracing.
4
5 my ($options) = {};
6
7 sub myopts
8 {
9     my (@extraOptions) = @_;
10
11    GetOptions($options, "-name=s", "-age=i", "-occupation:s",
12        "-married", "-police_record:s@", @extraOptions);
13
14
15    return($options);
16 }
17
18 # package CommonOptions.pm
```

This puts the information in a centralized place. It says that we will have -name, -age, -occupation, -married, and -police_record as standard options.

Any time we want a client to get these standard options, all we have to say is what is shown in Listing 15.13.

Listing 15.13
comm_opt_client.p

```
1 #!/usr/local/bin/perl
2
3 use lib $ENV{MYLIB};
4 use CommonOptions;
5
6 my $options = CommonOptions::myopts();
7 # ......
8 # rest of script comm_opt_client.p
```

Line 6 populates the hash reference $options with our standard options (-age, -name, etc.) such that if we said

```
prompt% comm_opt_client.p -age 15 -name Ed
```

$options will become

```
$options = { 'age' => 15, 'name' =M> 'Ed' };
```

and

```
print $options->{'name'};
```

would print Ed.

Now suppose that we want to have all the standard options for our script, plus an extra option that could take an array of elements. All we do is pass the CommonOptions ::myopts() function a parameter (extraComments:s@) as shown in Listing 15.14.

Listing 15.14
comm_opt_client2.p

```
#!/usr/local/bin/perl
use lib $ENV{MYLIB};
use CommonOptions;

my $options = CommonOptions::myopts('—extraComments:s@');
# ......
# client record.p
```

Both these commands will inherit, by default, the name, age, occupation, married, and police record options. In the second case, we added -extraComments:s@, which will let us turn the command line:

```
prompt% comm_opt_client2.p -name Paul -age 31
          -extraComments comment1 -extraComments comment2
```

into the data structure:

```
$options = { 'name' => 'Paul', 'age' => 31,
              'extraComments' => ['comment1','comment2']
```

This second script is a simple example of delegation. Here is a small definition:

Delegation is a programming technique in which a module or an object gets an argument or function, and if it cannot handle this argument/function, it passes it to a module that can.

The module **CommonOptions::myopts** cannot handle the argument **@extraOptions**, so it is passed to a module that can handle it, namely **Getopt::Long**. This merges both the common options (-name, -age, -occupation, married, -police_record) and noncommon options (-extraComments) together.

Now, having made a **Common Options** module, we can do lots of cool things with it. If we say:

```
use CommonOptions;
my $options = CommonOptions::myopts();
```

at the beginning of every script we write, then we have a way to make each script do a common action. In Listing 15.15 we overload it to keep a log of what commands have been typed, and at what time.

Listing 15.15
comm_opt_client2.p

```
1   package CommonOptions;
2   use Config;
3   use Getopt::Long;
4   use Log;
5   use strict;
6
7   my $logDir = "$ENV{LOG_DIRECTORY}";   # we make one log directory where
8                  # we will keep all of our logs. Could
9                  # actually be put in the Log module.
```

```
10
11 my $command = ($Config{'osname'} =~ m"in32")?
12                                    substr($0, rindex($0,"\")+1):
13                                    substr($0, rindex($0,"/")+1);
14                             # another hack that really should be
15                             # abstracted into a module, if
16                             # not only to ensure portability. It
17                             # simply gets the name of the script
18                             # run ('/export/home/epeschko/a.p')
19                             # becomes 'a.p'.
20 sub myopts
21 {
22     my (@extraOpts) = @_;
23     my $options;
24
25     _logOptions();       # 'private' function, written below
26
27     GetOptions($options, @extraOpts);
28 }
29
30 sub _logOptions
31 {
32     Log::open("$logDir/$command.log");
33
34     my $time = localtime();    # gets 'localtime': ie,the current time
35     Log::write("$time: $0 @ARGV");
36             # writes all of the options out to the
37             # log file, prefaced by the time. This could be made a default
38             # behavior of the 'Logger.'
39     Log::close();
40 }
```

If you get in the habit of saying

```
use CommonOptions;
```

at the beginning of each script, you will not only get the common options (that you don't have to retype) but you will also get a log, per command, of every single time someone typed that command, which version of the command they typed, and which arguments they used for the commands. The center of the log here is line 41, where we write to the **$command.log** file.

You also get this interface project-wide, which means you can do wondrous things with your interfaces. Following are a few examples of what you can do by using the concept of a common environment.

Q: Do you need all your scripts to have a common GUI interface through CGI scripting?
A: Simply overload the myopts function to recognize that it is being called through CGI, and then construct a GUI screen to handle this.
Q: Do you need all your scripts to have a mode where they can read from a configuration file, rather than from the command line?
A: Simply overload the myopts function to take a special argument, **config**, which then recognizes that all of the arguments are going to be coming from a **config** file instead of from the command line.
Q: Do you need all your scripts to have a default set of options? (Say we want to assume everybody has an age of 30 instead of being told otherwise.)
A: Simply overload the myopts function to default to the age of 30, and then use that default, unless given the option on the command line.

All of this is really cool, and comes from the paradigm shift of looking at changes to programs as if they occurred in bins. Once you get accustomed to looking at things in a modular and/or object-oriented way, changes to your programs will become easy to manage. Change will become a process of deciding which bin you are going to throw the changes into. In this example, it so happens that a very convenient bin to throw stuff into is the configuration bin, because that's the point at which every single program will inherit the stuff you gave to it.

Summary of Abstracting Command Line Processing

In this section, we introduced the reuse of code. There are hundreds of command line interfaces that Perl programmers have created. We choose the standard, Getopt, to discuss.

The module **Getopt::Long** does a wonderful job of abstracting out command line interfaces. It consists of a generic interface that is extremely flexible. We went through a simple example of its use, and also considered some caveats.

Finally, we thought about how we could further abstract out the command module in order to put our scripts into HTML, and do common setup routines, along with many other wide-reaching things.

Example Conclusion

This has been a rather long and arduous example, but let's see where it has taken us. Here is the script again, after our code review (Listing 15.16).

Listing 15.16
procedural_code_mod4.p

```
 1  #!/usr/local/bin/perl5
 2  use lib $ENV{MYLIB};
 3  use CommonOptions;
 4  use InputHandler;
 5  use Log;
 6
 7  my $options = {};
 8  my ($options) = CommonOptions::myopts('-input');
 9
10  Log::open('log_file');      # open(FD, ... )
11                              # the input to follow.
12  if ($options->{input})      # looks for the input switch in the
13  {                           # arguments on the command line.
14      do
15      {
16          my ($answer, $amount) =
17              (
18                  InputHandler::getInput("What do you want for Christmas?\n"),
19                  InputHandler::getInput("How much will it cost?\n",\&tooMuch);
20              );
21      } while ($amount eq 'NO_GOOD');
22  }
23
24  Log::write($answer, $amount);
25  Log::close();
26
27  sub tooMuch
28  {
```

```
29        my ($amount) = @_;
30        if ($amount > 100.00)
31        {
32            print "That's way too expensive\n";
33            return("NO_GOOD");
34        }
35        return($amount);
36 }
```

What have we gotten out of this?

Well, the first thing you will notice is that the code actually increased in length. Before our modifications there were 28 lines of code, afterwards 36. Abstraction usually results in a code reduction (but not always).

However, if we gained in size, we also gained in stability and flexibility. Here are some of the things we won by abstracting stuff out, by line number:

Line 8 (CommonOptions::myopts()) ensures that this script works well with other scripts of its type.

Lines 10, 24, and 25 (Log::open(), write(), close()) ensure that the log this script opens will have a consistent interface.

Lines 18 and 19 ensure our input from the user will be of the same format—everywhere—thereby ensuring a consistent look and feel of our code.

In addition, we now have the power to change our interface, the look and feel of our scripts by changing code in one place.

If we used the old, procedural method (where subroutines were at the bottom of each script), making a consistent interface is a question of "herding cats." Your code will take the path of diverging, rather than converging, on a central goal.

Other Things to Abstract

Following are some quick ideas on other things to put into modules. They have counterparts on CPAN (and the accompanying CD) so you might want to take a look there as well.

Dates and Times

Instead of preferring to rely on localtime, try making a generic module to handle dates and times. You might consider having a Date module in which you can say:

```
use Date;                               # includes the module 'Date'.
$daysApart = Date::dateDiff
        (
            '1996-12-12',
            'Mon Dec 15 02:52:13 1996',
            'day'
        );
```

and have the module return the number of days that two dates are apart. Another idea is:

```
$goodDate =Date::isReal ( 'Mon Dec 15 02:52:13 1996' );
```

which returns true if the given date is a real date, or false if it is a false date. To this end, check out the modules **Date::Parse** and **Date::DateCalc**. These two modules are available via CPAN.

Command Wrapping (for portability's sake)

Another useful abstraction into modules is system calls to other programs. A system call to a program such as **ls**, **dir**, or more exotic calls such as source control (**sccs**) or database control (**isql, bcp**), can be easily abstracted into modules. Saying something like:

```
system("ls");
```

is just begging your program to become unportable, since **ls** does not exist on NT. Instead, say:

```
use Commands;
Commands::dir();
```

This is much safer. Here, the particular command ls is abstracted into the generic `Commands::dir()`.

If you need to make it portable, you just hide the details inside the module **Commands**, and you need not worry about it in the interface. A lot of this has been done in the central distribution.

Variable Wrapping (for portability's sake)

A third opportunity for abstraction into modules is paths and variables. This really corresponds to two types of abuse. If you say:

```
$line = "/export/home/epeschko/a.p";
$line2 = "/export/home/epeschko/b.p";
```

then you are not abstracting your variables properly. It is better written as:

```
$path = "/export/home/epeschko";
$line = "$path/a.p";
$line2 = "$path/b.p";
```

In commonly used paths, this is also better off as:

```
use CommonPaths;
$line = CommonPaths::get('homepath') . "a.p";
$line = CommonPaths::get('homepath'} . "b.p";
```

because `homepath` tells you the *function* of what you are getting, and not the particular instance.

People also have the habit of saying:

```
my $command = substr($0, rindex($0,"/")+1);
             # gets the command name
             # as above:
             # /export/home/epeschko/a.p
             # becomes 'a.p'.
```

which is probably better off as:

```
use Path;
my $command = Path::getName($0);
```

because the details of the path, namely the delimiter, are abstracted out. Also, moving between Unix and NT will not be nearly as difficult when using this syntax.

Debugging and Data Structures

A fourth area which lends itself to abstraction is debugging and saving data structures.

Perl programmers waste a lot of time printing and storing data structures. This time could be saved by using the **Data::Dumper** module as it exists on CPAN. If you find yourself doing something like:

```
my $a = [{'complex', 'data','reference'}];

foreach $element (@$a)
{
    foreach $key (keys (%$element))
    {
      print "$element->{$key}\n";
    }
}
```

throw it all away! Instead, do:

```
use Data::Dumper;
print Dumper($a);
```

which will make much better printout.

Installation and Configuration Management

Installing newer versions of Perl modules is yet another area ripe for abstraction. Perl is the master of configuration management, and there are modules that handle this quite well.

We don't have a chance to talk about it here, but you can look on the accompanying CD. We have made an **install.p** script that helps keep you up to date on the most current modules.

Common Subroutines

Finally, by all means, don't be a purist when it comes to modularizing your programs! It is perfectly OK to have a module like **CommonSubs**, in which the only thing in common for the functions in **CommonSubs** is that they are all common! Building the module **CommonSubs** simply consists of:

1. Recognizing that a subroutine is common.
2. Changing that subroutine to the preface **CommonSubs::<sub_name>**, where *sub_name* is the name of the program.
3. Dumping that subroutine into the **CommonSubs** bucket.

For example, suppose you find that you are often using the subroutine `typeOf`. Remember `ref`? It was a function that let you determine whether something is a reference or not. Well, `typeOf` could be considered an extension of `ref`, because it doesn't care whether what you pass to it is a reference or not. So

```
$scalar = "scalar variable";
typeOf($scalar);
```

will return SCALAR, and

```
typeOf(@array);
```

returns ARRAY, and

```
$ref = ['1','2','3'];
```

returns ARRAYREF.

One way to code this is shown in Listing 15.17.

Listing 15.17
typeOf.p

```
 1 sub typeOf
 2 {
 3     my (@variable) = @_;
 4     my $reference;
 5     if (@variable > 1) { return("ARRAY"); }
 6
 7     if ($reference = ref($variable[0]))
 8     {
 9          return($reference."REF");
10     }
11     else
12     {
13          return("SCALAR");
14     }
15 }
```

Take these 15 lines out of your code, and dump them into **CommonSubs**. Now, you can do this:

```
$type = CommonSubs::typeOf(@reference);
```

This is an easy way to reuse code. We find a helpful subroutine, and instead of keeping it in the bottom of some script, we pull it out and stick it in a bin with a bunch of other subroutines. Then, when this bin becomes full, we simply look at it, and then decide how to better sort these functions.

Summary of Common Things to Abstract

You can think of the previous examples as templates to get started on the thought process to start modularizing your code. Of course, there are thousands of different functions you can possibly extract. Picking the best places to cut up code and put it into bundles is a bit like cutting a diamond; it takes a little practice, and some precision is involved.

Hence, lots of practice here could be considered a good thing. Here are the six things that you might consider abstracting/modularizing in your own Perl code:

1. Dates and times.
2. Command wrapping (for portability's sake).
3. Date and time wrapping (for portability's sake).
4. Debugging and data structures.
5. Installation and configuration management.
6. Common subroutines.

Looking at the Perl distribution is also good for showing the technique of modularizing your code. Finally, CPAN also gives you some good examples.

Examples of Modular Programming

Let's take this further and actually implement some more modules. You will ultimately want to start digging into the Perl distribution and/or CPAN to get prebuilt functionality (and there is a lot out there).

However, seeing how modules are implemented by example should ease the learning curve quite a bit, especially if you are unfamiliar with Perl syntax and/or modular programming. They aren't that complicated (well some of them aren't complicated), but they perform some pretty cool tasks that could help you out quite a bit, especially when you get to throwing scripts onto the Web. Let's start with a crucial issue that everybody seems to be concerned about these days: portability.

Example 1: Unix/NT Portability via CommonVarbs

If you have used both Unix and NT, then you know that they have similar concepts, yet do things just a little bit differently. The most common example of this is that NT makes its paths look like \TEMP; with backslashes, whereas Unix has a path separator of /tmp with forward slashes.

The backslash example is just one of many examples that are very annoying, especially for cross-platform programmers.

 This is just a "straw-man's" argument. Perl handles the /,\ issue internally (for the most part). Nonetheless, it is a good example of a common type of problem.

Note

One way of dealing with these low-level differences is to put them into a module. If we say something like:

```
use CommonVarbs qw($DSEP);
${DSEP}tmp${DSEP}tmp2;
```

and let Perl get the path separator for us, then our portability goes up, even if our readability goes down. Or, even more readable:

```
pathify("/tmp/tmp2");
```

which would then turn "/tmp/tmp2" into a format that Perl can handle internally. If you are wondering how to do this, a subroutine like:

```
sub pathify { my ($return) = @_; $return =~ s"[/\\]"$DSEP"g; $return }
```

should do it.

There are many of these little quibbles between the operating systems, and it makes sense to put them into a centralized CommonVariables subroutine. Something like Listing 15.18 is a good first try.

Listing 15.18
_CommonVarbs.pm

```
1    package CommonVarbs;
2
3    use strict;
4    use Exporter;
5    use Config;
6    use Cwd;
7    use Sys::Hostname;
8
9    BEGIN
10   {
11       use vars qw (@varlist);
12       @varlist =
13               qw(
14                   $HaveSend $HaveUtil $DEFAULT_EDITOR $USERNAME $DOMAIN
15                   $MAILING_ADDRESS $TEMPDIR $PATHSEP @PATHDIRS @PAGERS $DSEP
16                   $BINMODE $CWD $IGNORECASE $FORCE_WRITEABLE $ABS_PATH $HOSTNAME
17                   $CONSOLE $RM $RMDIR @ISA @EXPORT_OK
18                   );
19   }
20
```

```
21   use vars (@varlist);
22   @ISA = qw(Exporter);
23   @EXPORT_OK = (@varlist);
```

Here, we simply define all the variables before they are used. This is a quick, cheap way of getting the benefits of use strict without having to say something like $CommonVarbs::DEFAULT_EDITOR the first time we use this variable.

Finally, it creates a good way of self-documenting what this module is supposed to do. This module will determine the environment in which the script is running, and what are the values of the following:

Variable	Description
$DEFAULT_EDITOR	the default editor on the platform
$USERNAME	the username of the person executing the code
$DOMAIN	where the person is running the code (*netscape.com*)
$MAILING_ADDRESS	the person who is using this script's e-mail address
$TEMPDIR	where this platform keeps temporary files
$PATHSEP	a : or a ;—how the platform separates its paths
$PAGERS	commands to output a file to the screen
$DSEP	directory separator (/, \)
$BINMODE	whether or not there is binary and ASCII mode
$CWD	function pointer to get the current working directory
$IGNORECASE	whether the OS is case-insensitive or not
$ABS_PATH	a pointer to the function that gets the absolute path of a file
$HOSTNAME	the name of the machine
$CONSOLE	the name of the place where you get data from the keyboard
$RM	the name of the remove command
$RMDIR	the name of the remove directory command

Each of these varies between Unix and NT, and this module will define them all so you need not worry about doing a check each time you run into a platform dependency.

Line 23 is a simple way of exporting the variables back to whatever script uses the module. This is what lets us say:

```
use CommonVarbs qw($DEFAULT_EDITOR);
```

to get the $DEFAULT_EDITOR as seen by the module. But I digress. The module continues in Listing 15.19.

Listing 15.19
CommonVarbs.pm (continued)

```
24   BEGIN
25   {
26       eval "use Mail::Send;";      # stuff to determine domain more efficiently
27       $HaveSend = ($@ eq "");
28       eval "use Mail::Util;";
```

```
29          $HaveUtil = ($@ eq "");
30  }

31  sub import
32  {
33      my ($type) = @_;
34      if ($Config{osname} eq 'MSWin32')
35      {
36          _getWin32();
37      }
38      else
39      {
40          _getUnix();
41      }
42  }
```

Here, we define how we are going to split up the module. The module first looks at the operating system it is running on (use Config). If, as time goes on, we want to add more operating systems (OS2, VMS, and MacOS come to mind), we can simply tack on an extra subroutine.

For now, all we have to do is fill in the two pieces we have defined. Listing 15.20 shows the defaults for Win32.

Listing 15.20
CommonVarbs::_getWin32()

```
43  sub _getWin32
44  {
45      $DEFAULT_EDITOR = "notepad";
46      $USERNAME = $ENV{'USERNAME'};
47
48      if ($HaveUtil)  { $DOMAIN = Mail::Util::maildomain(); }
49      else            { $DOMAIN = $ENV{'USERDOMAIN'}; }
50
51      $MAILING_ADDRESS = "$USERNAME\@$DOMAIN";
52      $TEMPDIR = (defined ($ENV{'TEMP'}))? $ENV{'TEMP'} : '/tmp/';
53
54      $DISPLAYER = 'pod2text';
55      $PATHSEP = $Config{'path_sep'};
56      @PATHDIRS = grep( -d, split(m"$PATHSEP", $ENV{'PATH'}));
57
58      @PAGERS = qw (more< less notepad);
59      unshift (@PAGERS, $ENV{PAGER}) if (defined ($ENV{PAGER}));
60
61      $DSEP = "\\";
62      $BINMODE = 1;
63      $CWD = \&cwd;
64      $IGNORECASE = 1;
65      $FORCE_WRITEABLE = 1;
66      $ABS_PATH = \&abs_path;
67      $HOSTNAME = hostname();
68      $CONSOLE = "con";
69      $RM = "del";
70      $RMDIR = "deltree";
71  }
```

After we are done with NT and Windows 95, we fill in the Unix portion (Listing 15.21).

Listing 15.21
CommonVarbs::_getUnix()

```
 72   sub _getUnix
 73   {
 74
 75       $DEFAULT_EDITOR = "vi";
 76       $USERNAME = getpwuid($<);
 77
 78       if ($HaveUtil)  { $DOMAIN = Mail::Util::maildomain() }
 79       else            { $DOMAIN = `hostname` . "." . `domainname`; }
 80       $MAILING_ADDRESS = "$USERNAME\@$DOMAIN";
 81       $TEMPDIR = '/tmp/';
 82
 83       $DISPLAYER = 'pod2man';
 84       $PATHSEP = $Config{'path_sep'};
 85       @PATHDIRS = grep ( -d, split(m"$PATHSEP", $ENV{'PATH'}));
 86
 87       @PAGERS = qw (more less pg view cat );
 88       unshift (@PAGERS, $ENV{PAGER}) if (defined ($ENV{PAGER}));
 89
 90       $DSEP = "/";
 91
 92       $BINMODE = 0;
 93       $CWD = \&cwd;
 94       $IGNORECASE = 0;
 95       $FORCE_WRITEABLE = 0;
 96
 97       $ABS_PATH = \&abs_path;
 98       $HOSTNAME = hostname();
 99       $CONSOLE = "/dev/tty";
100   }
101   1;
```

Whew! I guess the point of this module is that about 90 percent of the portability issues you will face will be related to the small issues, such as those in the preceding code. You want to get a list of directories where you can find executables? Well, you can either say:

```
if ($Config{'os name'} eq 'MSWin32')
{
    @PATHDIRS = grep (-d, split(m"$Config{'path_sep'}, $ENV{'PATH'});
}
```

each time you want to get this particular item, or you can say:

```
use CommonVarbs qw(@PATHDIRS);
print "@PATHDIRS\n";
```

to let tested code do the work for you, and not worry about the internal details.

One more point: You might wonder how I went about writing this particular module. Well, part of it was memory, but you must remember that the code in the Perl distribution has ten years of experience dealing with these sorts of portability issues. So, yes, I looked to those thousands of lines of experienced, world-weary Perl code in order to glean parts of the example.

Example 2: Using Switches Inside a Script, Rather Than at the Command Line

Example 2 will come in pretty handy for those of you working on Windows 95 or NT, or even VMS or OS2. As we have seen, there are certain flags (**-w, -d, -c**) that you can set at the command line that let you tell Perl what to do, "above and beyond the call of duty." The following checks the syntax of **script.p**:

```
prompt% perl -c script.p
```

Now, what happens if you are running in a place where you don't want to use the command line, but still use the command switches? For example, Windows 95 and NT aren't set up very well for this whole switch thing, and it is a drag to have to open up a command shell each time you run a Perl script.

The following module lets you do stuff like the following:

```
use Switch qw(-c);
# my script here...
```

Now, when you run your script, with something like:

```
C:\> perl script.p
```

Perl will do a syntax check on your script for you (instead of running it) as in Listing 15.22.

Listing 15.22
Switch.pm:

```
 1  package Switch;
 2
 3  sub import
 4  {
 5      my ($type, @switches) = @_;
 6
 7      my $perl = "$^X";          # perl interpreter name.
 8      my $script = $0;           # perl script name
 9
10      my @run = ($^X, @switches, $script, @ARGV);
11      $script =~ s"\W""g;
12      $script = substr($script,0,6);
13
14      if (!$ENV{"SCRIPT_$script"})
15      {
16          $ENV{"SCRIPT_$script"} = 1;
17          exec(@run);
18      }
19  }
20  1;
```

Here, line 5 takes whatever switches the user passes in, and lines 7 and 8 proceed to get the name of the Perl executable (line 7) and the name of the script that was run (line 8). Line 10 puts all this information together into a run statement, such that if you said:

```
use Switch qw(-w);
#####
```

in the script calling **Switch.pm**, and then you said:

```
C:\> perl script.p 1 2 3
```

the variable $run would become:

```
perl -w script.p 1 2 3
```

as shown in Figure 15.2.

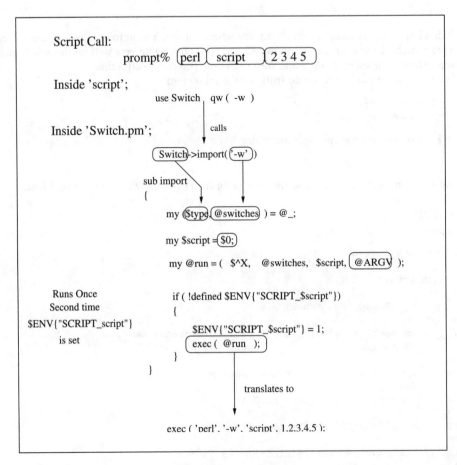

Figure 15.2
Command Line
Maker

Script Call:
        prompt% perl script 2 3 4 5

Inside 'script';
                        use Switch qw (-w)

Inside 'Switch.pm';   calls

                Switch->import('-w')

        sub import
        {
                my ($type, @switches) = @_;

                my $script = $0;

                my @run = ($^X, @switches, $script, @ARGV);

Runs Once   if (!defined $ENV{"SCRIPT_$script"})
Second time   {
$ENV{"SCRIPT_script"} $ENV{"SCRIPT_$script"} = 1;
  is set   exec (@run);
                   }
        }
                                        translates to

                exec ('perl'. '-w'. 'script'. 1.2.3.4.5);

Now, in lines 14–18, we proceed to "exec"ute this code. We set an environment variable, $ENV{'SCRIPT_scriptp'}, to leave a bread crumb for the script that follows, and to prevent an infinite loop from the script executing itself over and over again. Then, in line 17, we:

```
exec ('perl', '-w', 'script.p', 1, 2, 3);
```

which immediately takes the place of the original process. We've seen this before (in Chapter 11).

The upshot is that we have a portable way of doing command line switches which does not take too much time (this exec trick is fairly efficient) and is portable between operating systems. This particular trick will work pretty much anywhere, not just Unix and NT.

Note, again, always use the exec form of

```
exec (@run);
```

rather than

```
exec("@run");
```

To see why, if you say something like:

```
prompt% a.p \"1 2 3
```

where you have embedded quotes, if you use `@run`, Perl will munge your quote for you when you `exec (@run)`. Your argument list will become:

```
@ARGV = (1,2,3);
```

and the quote goes silently away! This is a very subtle bug, and although it doesn't bite often, when it does bite, it can cause you hours of pain. Remember this, especially when dealing with and writing programs for the shell (whether it be a Unix shell, NT shell, or other type of shell).

Let's show another example of this type of module in action. This time, we shall consider scripts that are run noninteractively (via cron or a browser).

Example 3: Getting the By-Product of Shell Scripts Inside of Perl

Both NT and Unix share the convenience, and the exasperation, of having startup scripts that set up a person's environment. On Unix, they are kshrc, bashrc, and .tcshrc, named resource files, and on NT the main one is **autoexec.bat.**

Usually, when you run scripts on the command line, they inherit the variables you have set up. But with a cron job, or a script run by a CGI server, they don't get inherited, which can cause developers a lot of pain.

Here is a module to take what we learned in Chapter 11 to its logical conclusion. We already talked a little bit on how to set such variables as `LD_LIBRARY_PATH, PERL5LIB` and other hard-to-set variables by the `exec` trick. This module will take the environment as produced by a shell script and import it inside your Perl script. Hence, if you say:

```
use ShellScript "ksh -c '. shellfile.ksh'";
# my script
print "$ENV{'PERL5LIB'}\n";
```

and **shellfile.ksh** sets `PERL5LIB`, then you will inherit and be able to use `PERL5LIB` inside your script.

Again, it is important to realize why the following will not work:

```
system("ksh -c shellfile.ksh");
```

Many people get tripped up on this one. The environment for the system call is copied from the parent's environment, and lives as long as the system call is in process. And it dies when the system call is done, and doesn't effect the parent. Hence, `PERL5LIB` will never change inside the script which calls `system`. Listing 15.23 is the workaround for this, again, using the exec trick.

Listing 15.23
ShellScript.pm

```
1  package ShellScript;
2
3  use strict;
4  use FileHandle;
5  use CommonVarbs qw($TEMPDIR $DSEP $RM);
6
```

Here we set up which modules we are going to use. Notice that we are already using `CommonVarbs` to help with our portability! We use the variable `$TEMPDIR` to tell us where we are going to put our temporary files, and

$DSEP to tell us what type of delimiter to use for directories (/ or \). Now, we need to define an import function that actually implements the statement use ShellScript 'ksh -c shellfile.ksh' (Listing 15.24).

Listing 15.24
ShellScript.pm (continued)

```
7   sub import
8   {
9       my ($type, $statement) = @_;
10
11      my $script = $0; my $perl = $^X;
12      @run = ($perl, $script, @ARGV);
13      $script = s"\W""g;
14      $script = substr($script, 0, 6);
15
16      if (!$ENV{'SHELL_$script'})
17      {
18          $ENV{'SHELL_$script'} = 1;
19
20          my $envfile = "$TEMPDIR${DSEP}env.$$.p";
21          my $fh = new FileHandle("> $envfile")
22                          || die "Couldn't open environment file!\n";
23
24 print $fh <<"END_OF_CODE";
25          foreach \$key (keys \%ENV)
26          {
27              print "\$ENV{'$key'}='\$ENV{\$key}';\\\n";
28          }
29 END_OF_CODE
30          close($fh);
31
```

A note on what's going on here: Again, we are using that old environment trick ($ENV{'SHELL_$script'}) to avoid an infinite loop where exec calls exec, which calls exec. However, we have thrown in the additional trick of using a code generator. Lines 25–28 generate a small Perl script, one that prints out the environment for us. Remember this later as we shall use this script that we generate to great effect. The code continues in Listing 15.25.

Listing 15.25
ShellScript.pm (continued)

```
32          my ($code, $perl, $file);
33
34          foreach $file (@files)
35          {
36              $perl = $^X;
37              my $code =
38                  `$statement;$perl $envfile; $RM $envfile`;
39              eval $code;
40          }
41      exec(@run);
42      }
43 }
```

Now this code may look a little "noisy" and, well, it is! But if you understand how this logic works, you will be able to program many cool things.

What is going on here? Well, remember that file we created in lines 25–28? In line 38, we use it. This line is the heart of the program. When translated, it looks something like this:

```
`ksh -c '. shellfile.ksh';/usr/local/bin/perl5 /tmp/env.1333;rm -f /tmp/env.1333`
```

In other words, we execute the shell statement, thus getting a modified environment. We then run our created Perl script (**/tmp/env.1333**), get some output, and then remove the traces of the file we created (**rm -f /tmp/env.1333**).

What we are left with, then, is a string with the environment we would have gotten had we done ksh -c '. shellfile.ksh' on the command line alone.

There is another twist here. The output of our generated script is in the form:

```
$ENV{'VARIABLE'}='value';
$ENV{'VARIABLE2'}='value2';
```

In other words, the output is a legal Perl script. When we get to line 39:

```
eval $code;
```

we then use the eval statement to run this code, producing the environment we want (the one from the shell script). Line 41 cements this environment into our original Perl script, by calling exec(@run) to fork off a child with the correct environment.

In other words, we used a Perl script to generate Perl code, which is in turn used to generate Perl code. This code is then evaluated to get the right environment. That environment is sent to an exec() which then re-executes the code to pass the effects to the original script, which then continues. This module's one mercy is that it is brief and therefore somewhat maintainable.

I admit I had fun programming it, and it does have a helpful effect, but one more level of indirection and any sane programmer would go mad! Use the techniques in this example with discretion, and wear your safety helmet.

Example 4: Diff Module

Let's look at one more example. This one is more straightforward. As said, one of the big advantages of Perl is that you can represent any data structure in terms of arrays, hashes, and scalars. The module **Data::Dumper** shows that strength by dumping out any data structure to the screen.

However, say you have some huge data structures you needed to compare, or you just made a change to a data structure that caused a bug in your code. It would be helpful if you could go through the data structure, and only look at the points that changed.

In other words, given the data structures:

```
$arrayRef1 = [1,2,3,4,5];
$arrayRef2 = [1,2,3,4,6];
```

we somehow want to point our attention to the fact that the only elements that differ are the last two (5 and 6). This way, we can trace what caused our error much easier. It also helps with changing your software. If we make several small, incremental changes, and test them carefully in this way, we are less likely to introduce new bugs.

So how do we do this? Well, note that if we compare each of the elements:

```
$arrayRef1->[0] eq $arrayRef2->[0];
$arrayRef1->[1] eq $arrayRef2->[1];
```

we could basically cancel out all the elements that are equal. If we do so, we are left with:

```
$diffRef = [undef, undef, undef, undef, XXXXX];
```

where XXXXX equals a difference in our data structure. The question is then what do we fill in for XXXXX?

Well, it makes sense to fill it in with something meaningful to our searching for bugs. Hence, we would probably want to stick in the two values that differ here. Unfortunately, as it stands we only have one position to put two elements (5 and 6), so what do we do? We use Perl's malleability in data structures to cheat, and put *both* elements here.

We define a **diff** as the following: If the elements in a position of the data structure are the same, then we register an **undef**. If the elements are different, we put in an array consisting of the elements that differ. For our array this turns into:

```
$diffRef = [undef, undef, undef, undef, [5,6]];
```

That way, we can see differences at a glance, and not lose any information. We also don't reinvent any of the functionality that is already in Data::Dumper. We reuse Data::Dumper by letting it be the function which prints this diff structure. It would be wasteful to make an elaborate print function, when **Data::Diff** does it for you.

Now, what functions make sense to be in our module? Well, three come to mind:

```
Diff::checkData($ref1,$ref2);
Diff::checkEq($ref1,$ref2);
Diff::patch($ref1, $ref2);
```

Diff::checkData($ref1, $ref2) will create this diff data structure we are talking about. Diff::checkEq($ref1, $ref2) will simply check if $ref1 is equal to $ref2. After all, sometimes we only want that minimum amount of information. Diff::patch($ref1, $ref2) will return a list of Perl commands to change $ref1 to $ref2.

We will implement the first two functions. Recursion will obviously play a part, since an arbitrary data structure in Perl is recursive. Also, notice that we have to worry about hash references, array references, and scalars. Once we hit a scalar, we hit the edge of the data structure, and we don't have to recurse any more. Hence, the pseudocode will look something like:

```
sub checkData
{
    if arg1 is scalar { compare arg1 to arg2; return difference }
    if arg1 is array { go through each element in arg1 and arg2 recursively }
    if arg1 is hash { go through each key in arg1 and arg2 recursively }
}
```

Each time we recurse, we keep going until we hit bedrock when we hit the scalars. Of course, it becomes more complicated than this. We must deal with cases in which the elements are not of the same type, and associated details. The code starts in Listing 15.26.

Listing 15.26
Diff.pm

```
1   package Diff;
2
3   use strict;
4   use Carp;
5   use Data::Dumper;
6
7   ##########################################################################
8   # Gives a data structure that shows the differences between two data structures
9   #
10  # $data = _checkData([1,2,3], [1,2,4]);  # $data = [undef, undef,[3,4];
11  #
12  ##########################################################################
13
14  sub checkData
```

```
15 {
16     my ($dst1, $dst2) = @_;
17     confess "You need to pass two arguments/data structures\n" if (@_ != 2);
18     my $return = _checkData($dst1, $dst2);
19 }
```

To be clear, we define the function checkData() in terms of an internal function _checkData(), which is called a *private* function. It isn't meant to be called by any external scripts that use *Diff.pm*. (You can, Perl won't prevent you from doing it, but it still is a good idea not to do so.) We will see more private functions later. The leading _ is a clue that whatever you are looking at is private.

We now define the _checkData() function (Listing 15.27), which will be heavily recursive. The recursive calls are in boldface.

Listing 15.27
Diff.pm (continued)

```
20 sub _checkData
21 {
22     my ( $dst1, $dst2 ) = @_;
23     my $return;
24
25     if ((!ref($dst1)) || (ref($dst1) ne ref($dst2)))
26     {
27         $return = _scalarEqData($dst1, $dst2);
28     }
29     elsif (ref($dst1) eq 'ARRAY')
30     {
31         my $xx;
32         for ($xx =0; $xx < @$dst1; $xx++)
33         {
34           $return->[$xx] = _checkData ( $dst1->[$xx], $dst2->[$xx] );
35         }
36         for ($xx = @$dst1; $xx < @$dst2; $xx++)
37         {
38             $return->[$xx] = _scalarEqData ( undef, $dst2->[$xx] );
39         }
40     }
41     elsif (ref($dst1) eq 'HASH')
42     {
43         my $key;
44         foreach $key (keys(%$dst1))
45         {
46           $return->{$key} = _checkData( $dst1->{$key}, $dst2->{$key} );
47         }
48         foreach $key (keys(%$dst2))
49         {
50             next if ($dst1->{$key});
51             $return = _scalarEqData ( undef, $dst2->{$key} );
52         }
53     }
54     return($return);
55 }
56 sub _scalarEqData
```

```
57 {
58     my ( $dst1, $dst2 ) = @_;
59     ($dst1 ne $dst2)?  [ $dst1, $dst2 ] : undef;
60 }
```

There are three things to notice about this code. First, the $return data structure mimics the structure that it finds inside $dst1. If $dst1 and $dst2 happen to be array references, line 34 ($return->[$xx]) creates an array element for each array element it finds in @$dst1. If $dst1 and $dst2 happen to be hash references, line 46 $return->{$key} creates a hash element for each hash element it finds in %$dst1.

Second, notice that it isn't quite as simple as the pseudocode we gave earlier. We need to compare each element together, true, but there is also the case where $dst1 and $dst2 have a different number of elements. The data structures:

```
$arrayRef = [1,2,3]; $arrayRef2 = [1,2,3,4];
```

are different, too. We would want our final data structure to look like $diffRef = [undef, undef, undef, [undef, 4]]. It is the job of lines 36–39 and 48–52 to deal with unequal numbers of array elements and hash elements.

Finally, notice we hit bedrock if $dst1 is a scalar and $dst1 is not the same data type as $dst2.

In these cases, _scalarEq() is called, which is a simple subroutine that compares the two elements. If they are equal, the subroutine returns undef. If not equal, _scalarEq() returns an array reference containing the two differing elements.

Once we get this structure created, the subroutine to check if the two data structures are equal is a lot easier.

To program this, we simply reuse the checkData() function that we already coded. This internal code reuse can help you out quite a bit. We need not go through all the work that we did in order to make the data structure in the first place. This means that our code is a bit shorter:

Listing 15.28
Diff.pm (continued)

```
61 sub checkEq
62 {
63     my ($dst1, $dst2) = @_;
64     confess "You need to pass two data structures\n" if (@_ != 2);
65     my $diff = checkData($dst1, $dst2);
66
67     my $status = 1;
68     _diffData($diff, \$status);
69     return($status);
70 }
71
72 sub _diffData
73 {
74     my ($return, $status) = @_;
75
76     return(0) if ($$status = 0);
77
78     if (!ref($return))
79     {
80         $$status = 0 if (defined($return));
81     }
82     if (ref($return) eq 'ARRAY')
83     {
```

```
84              foreach (@$return) { _diffData($_, $status ); }
85      }
86      elsif (ref($return eq 'HASH'))
87      {
88         foreach (keys (%$return))  { _diffData($return->{$_}, $status);}
89      }
90 }
```

Again, we outline the recursive calls. _diffData() is pretty simple. All it does is go through the data structure we have created via checkData($dat1, $dat2) and look for defined elements (in line 80). If we find any, our status is set to zero, meaning we have found a difference, and that short-circuits the subroutine in line 76 (any other recursive calls immediately return 0).

Note one more thing: $status is an example of a way to share variables between recursive subroutine calls. Because we are passing a reference to a scalar, other recursive calls will immediately see what $status actually is. If we had passed a scalar rather than a scalar reference, we would have been passing multiple copies around.

We could modify this to handle code references and object references, but we are running out of space.

Summary

Code abstraction into modules is the first step in a thought process that leads to object-oriented programming. The goal is code reusability across programs and platforms. This process allows you to develop code once, test it for validity, and then use it endlessly in other programs.

The best way to prove this assertion is through examples. As Perl syntax is so expressive, the scope and breadth of possible Perl modules is incredible. And to get the most out of Perl, you should use your imagination in coming up with the broadest, simplest modules you can think of! In the preceding code, we have:

1. Manipulated the way you can call Perl (switches).
2. Received effects from the execution of another language and used these effects in a Perl script (**ShellScript.pm**).
3. Made an all-purpose module to do data structure testing (**Diff**).
4. Centralized the interface of all of our Perl scripts (**CommonOptions**).

In most other languages, these goals are the exclusive territory of language design committees! In other words, you would need to redefine the language itself to get the required effects that we accomplished in 400 or so lines of code.

Anyway, in Chapter 16 we take the next big step in the quest to scale up our code: we talk about the syntax of the object. The rest of the book will be about object-oriented programming and examples, so make sure you understand much of what has been covered here.

The Syntax of Objects

If there were an alternative theme to this book, aside from the obvious one of teaching Perl programming, it would be that the process of truly learning a computer language is learning how to scale up that computer language and to do larger, more complicated projects.

In fact, the same thing could be said about all of computer history. One of the main motivations in computer science is to scale up projects: to make larger and larger projects for less and less money. Currently, all the research in software engineering points to the object as the best way to make the largest projects and to make them cheaply.

Therefore, the rest of this book will be devoted to how to make effective objects in Perl: object syntax, object-oriented techniques, useful object code, and finally, a few examples of object-oriented applications. This chapter will be a starting point: we will concern ourselves with the syntax of objects. For now, don't worry about the theory behind objects, or object-oriented techniques. We will cover plenty of that later!

If you are familiar with Perl object-oriented programming, you might want to skim this chapter. Others will want to read it at least once, and then come back to it again and again as they become familiar with objects.

After you become accustomed to the concepts and syntax presented in this chapter, you are strongly advised to check out the **perltoot, perlobj,** and **perlmod** documentation provided in the Perl distribution. perltie also helps, if you want to do what is called tie-ing (a certain type of object we discuss later in the chapter).

Chapter Overview

This chapter serves the same purpose as Chapter 14 did for modules: to provide a thorough grounding in the syntax of objects, and then take that basis and implement some simple examples. We will cover a lot of territory here. First, we cover object principles, giving an idea of the viewpoint object-oriented programming imposes on programming.

Second, we take these object principles and consider how they look implemented in Perl-ish syntax. We look at each piece of the object, and see how the pieces are implemented.

Third, we take a look at the difference between the class and the object, and discuss how this difference will affect how you program.

Fourth, we consider inheritance, the much misunderstood programming practice that lets you reuse code by getting it from another, related parent module. We will also see the syntax for implementing it.

Last, we consider overloading, which lets you treat symbols (+, -, and so on) differently with the different objects that you implement. We will see the syntax for doing overloading, plus some examples. Along with this, we will look at `tie`-ing, a Perl-specific form of overloading that allows you to make hashes, arrays, or scalars "objects in disguise;" objects that look like a Perl data structure, but actually do programmable things.

So, let's look first at a more rigorous view of what makes up an object. We have been hinting at this for long enough; let's flesh it out a little more.

Basic Object Principles

Those of you who are new to object-oriented programming should remember that it is not rocket science. It is simply a viewpoint that takes a bit of getting used to. Currently, you may look at code as being composed of several objects which have their own data and functions, rather than composed of several statements and subroutines you explicitly write inside your scripts. To get a task done, you call an object's functions, and they do the job for you.

This is rather abstract, so let's consider a simple example: a clock. A clock is an object in the common sense of the word, but it also makes a good example of a computer object. A clock has three elements:

1. Data: A clock contains the current time, sometimes the current date, and so on.
2. Methods or functions to get at and manipulate that data: A clock has a dial for reading the time, buttons for setting the time, and maybe a dial for winding it.
3. Elements that make the clock work: A clock has dials, gears, the verge and foliot, and various interactions of these components. These might be called the *algorithms* of the clock.

Objects in the computer sense are very much the same. In Perl, objects are implemented in special modules called *classes*, which create objects; the objects they create have three very similar elements in them:

1. Object data: This is data the object holds. It is what distinguishes one object from another object of the same type.
2. Object methods: These are functions that manipulate the data the object has, or return data from the module, or any one of a number of things. They are the constant for objects of the same type.
3. Object algorithms: These are the algorithms used to implement the object's methods.

In addition, objects have the following special functions:

1. A constructor or constructors: Constructors are used to make the object and to set the data the object will later use.
2. A destructor: Destructors are functions that destroy your objects when they are done with them. They are implicitly called when the object goes out of scope, or the program ends.

A Simple Example

We will take a look at each of these elements in detail later. But first, let's take this a bit further. Let's implement a *clock* class in Perl (again, classes are the modules that implement objects). It will not do very much, but it will illustrate the concepts, especially if you are a beginning Perl-object programmer:

```
1   package Clock;
2
3   sub new
4   {
5       my ($type) = @_;
6       my $self = {};
8       $self->{time} = time();
9       bless $self, $type;
10  }
11  sub get
12  {
13      my ($self) = @_;
14      return($self->{time});
15  }
16  sub set
17  {
18      my ($self, $secs) = @_;
20      $self->{time} = $secs || time();
21      return(1);
22  }
```

As I said, this does not do very much, but it illustrates a great deal about how Perl objects work. Our object is called $self in the class, and it has one data member in it: time. It has two methods: get, which gets the time, and set, which sets the time. It has no destructor. This clock is frozen at the point of creation, and shows its time in seconds since January 1, 1970.

But it is an object, and 75 percent of your objects will be advanced versions of this simple model. Let's see how you might use this object in a script of yours:

```
1 use Clock;
2 my $clock1 = new Clock();
3 bigNastyHairySubroutine();
4 my $clock2 = new Clock();
5
6 print "Big Nasty Hairy Subroutine started at ", $clock1->get(), "\n";
7 print "Big Nasty Hairy Subroutine ended at ", $clock2->get(), "\n";
8 print "Big Nasty Hairy Subroutine took ", $clock2->get() - $clock1->get(), "seconds";
```

All of the pertinent object calls are in boldface. Line 2 creates a Clock (called $clock1) before the bigNastyHairySubroutine. This calls the subroutine new inside the class Clock: This is our *constructor*. It also happens to freeze the time at which it was called into the element: $clock1->{time}.

Line 3 calls the bigNastyHairySubroutine, and line 4 makes another Clock object, this time called $clock2. Lines 5, 6, and 7 use the method get of the Clock object to retrieve the times associated with those clocks and print out how long the subroutine took.

Simple, but there are many mechanics behind how this is actually working. Let's take a closer look at how Perl allows you to make objects in this fashion. Perl's mechanism to do this is quite elegant. Knowing how it works will contribute quite a bit to your understanding of the language. As said, there were five parts to a simple class and its associated object: the constructor, the object methods, the object data, the object algorithms, and the destructor. Let's take each element in turn.

The Constructor

The constructor is the first required part of an object. The constructor is used to make an object when needed. To make a constructor, simply put a function in your class that returns a blessed reference to the main routine. A *blessed reference* is designated by the keyword **bless**. Its purpose is to set the type of the reference based on the type of the object called.

In the following:

```
my $self = bless {}, 'Object';
```

$self is a blessed reference of type Object.

Figure 16.1 shows the clock example again, this time with a bit of a play-by-play description and some added features to make the example more universal.

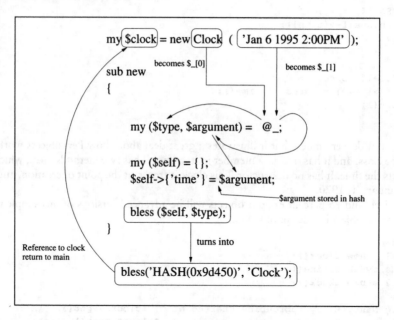

Figure 16.1
The Clock
Constructor

What's going on here? There are three major points we should cover.

Point 1: The Arguments In a Constructor Aren't a Straightforward Match with the Constructor Call

First of all, notice that we have done a little bit of a switcheroo on the arguments here. The statement:

```
my $clock1 = new Clock('argument1');
```

becomes the subroutine call:

```
Clock::new('Clock', 'argument1');
```

In other words, the first argument is the name of the Class!

Note

The answer has to do with *inheritance* and in particular *multiple inheritance*, the over-hyped, much-feared object-oriented technique we will cover later.

You will never want to use the `Clock::new('Clock', 'argument1')` form, ever. This is because of the inheritance principle (which we talk about later). For now, simply store this principle in the back of your brain, do the mental gymnastics to turn new `Clock('argument1')` into `Clock::new('Clock', 'argument1')`, and you will be fine. And if you want more detail on why, check out inheritance later.

You will get weird runtime errors if you forget to put the type as the first argument in your constructor and do something like this:

```
1 package Clock;
2 sub new
3 {
4 my (@arguments) = @_;          # $arguments[0] is the TYPE of class
5 my $self = {};                 # we are dealing with. NOT the bolded element
6                                 # $clock = new Clock('a')
7 return(bless $self, 'Clock');   # VERY BAD!!!! You have hard-wired what type $self
8                                 # is. What happens when you want to use inheritance?
9 }
```

This is a major "gotcha." This code looks valid and creates a Clock, but it will bite you later when you get to inheritance, in which you can have different types of clocks, all of which inherit off of a central Clock object. It takes a long time to get used to the extra argument, but if you do so, it will pay off many times over.

Point 2: The Object Starts Off as a Simple Reference

The statement my `$self = {}` shows the fundamental starting point of the object, and of all objects. All objects in Perl, complicated or simple, are composed of a simple reference. They continue to be simple references as long as they are alive.

What does this mean? When you say:

```
my $clock2 = new Clock('');
```

instead of saying:

```
$clock2->get();
```

to return the time associated with that clock, you could instead say (although ill-advised):

```
$clock->{time};
```

You can reach directly into the object itself and get the data associated with it, without going through the method to get it. This is called *breaking encapsulation*, and it is a bad practice indeed. Objects are meant to be inviolate and untouchable; you are supposed to be going through an interface and you are reaching in to grab the data directly! But it does show the nature of Perl's objects quite well to see their "bare nature" as references.

Objects can be made any type of data reference: hash references, array references, and scalar references. Hash references are the most common because you can have many named data elements in them, but sometimes it is helpful to have scalars instead.

Point 3: The Keyword bless Is Used to Make and Return the Object to the Function That Called It

Note the line:

```
bless $self, $type;
```

This is the last line in the constructor, and the value that comes out of it will be returned to the subroutine. So what is this doing? This call translates into:

```
bless $self, 'Clock';
```

When you then print out $self, you get something that looks like:

```
Clock=HASH(0x9d450)
```

This indicates that $self is both a hash reference and a Clock reference. bless is therefore identifying (tagging) $self as a clock. $self is returned to the main program in:

```
my $clock = new Clock();
```

then, $clock is printed out. It will also say `Clock=HASH(0x9d450)`. The "Clockness" is carried by the reference; it is therefore persistent, and will be transferred to any copy of the reference you make.

All these points will bear heavily on what we discuss next: object methods and how they work.

Object Methods

Just as the object's constructor has two parts, so do the object's methods: define and call the method.

Figure 16.2 shows these two parts in tandem and how they work together. Again, the clock example is extended to be more universal. There are three points to consider here.

Figure 16.2
An Object
Method, and How
It Works

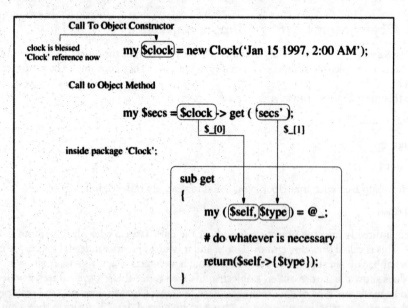

Point 1: The Method Call Has the Object Itself as the First Argument

The first thing to notice here is that there is the same basic mismatch between the arguments. There is one argument to get when we call the method, but two arguments when we actually write the method.

As stated, the first argument is the object itself. In other words, when you say:

```
$clock->get('argument1');
```

you are in effect saying:

```
Clock::get($clock, 'argument1');
```

assuming, of course, that $clock is a Clock object. Why? Well, the method somehow needs access to the data inside the object. And, since an object in Perl is simply a blessed reference, the way Perl does this is by passing the object reference around every time it sees something of the form $self->method();.

Note

This argument chicanery, passing the object itself as the first argument, was done for two reasons (instead of having some "magic" that hides the object argument). First, it makes things much more flexible and explicit when you write your methods. You can chose extremely unorthodox object models when you get fancy with Perl object orientation.

Second, it provides a much more consistent interface for functions. Instead of having one type of function for methods, and another for regular functions, Perl uses the same mechanism for both.

Point 2: Perl Finds Which Method to Call by Looking at the Reference Type

Remember blessing? Well, when you say something like:

```
bless $clock, 'Clock';
```

then Perl has tagged $self as being of type Clock. What does this mean? Well, this has everything to do with how Perl actually *finds* the methods when you say something like:

```
$clock->get();
```

This logic is more thoroughly spelled out in Figure 16.3.

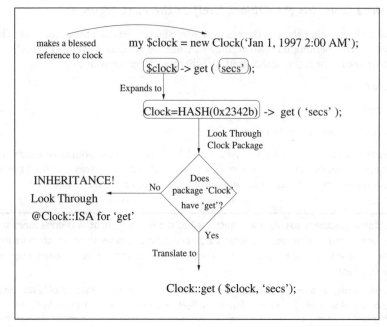

Figure 16.3
A Reference
Finding an Object
Method

Let's take this step by step. When you say:

```
bless $clock, 'Clock';
print $clock;
```

this will print the reference `$clock`.

```
'Clock=HASH(0x9d450)'
```

Hence, when you say something like:

```
$clock->get();
```

you are actually saying:

```
(Clock=Hash(0x9d450))->get();
```

Perl then knows the type of reference that it is, and therefore, opens the correct function to go along with it. Again, it passes the object as the first argument:

```
Clock::get($clock);
```

and then the function is actually called.

These two points summarize how Perl actually finds the correct method to call, and then what functions it uses to actually call it. Of course, it is not necessary to memorize this logic to actually program classes and objects. But it sure doesn't hurt. I don't know how many times I have forgotten to put `$self` at the beginning of a method, only to be bitten by it later, or how many times I have paused to act since I wasn't sure what mechanism Perl used to perform its magic.

Well, now you know. And it will pay dividends when we get to how Perl does inheritance.

Object Data

Object data is fairly simple in Perl. As objects are a simple reference (hash, array, or otherwise), there is no reason to declare object data in Perl as is necessary in most other OO languages (such as C++).

Consider, again, our Clock:

```
1 my $clock = new Clock();
2 print $clock->{time};
3 print $clock->get();
```

Here, lines 2 and 3 do exactly the same thing. The call to `$clock->get()` is really a wrapper around a hash call which returns `$self->time()`:

```
1 package Clock;
2
3 sub get
4 {
5     my ($self) = @_;
6     return($self->{time});
7 }
```

On the face of it, it seems that the form `$clock->get()` does not gain anything compared to `$clock->{time}`. It is slower and longer to write.

However, it does have one benefit over `$clock->{time}`: It is more flexible. If you change how the Clock object itself tells time, then you can make the method get much more complicated, whereas `$clock->{time}` cannot be enhanced in this way.

Again, here is an example of how encapsulation is your friend and why we devote Chapter 17 to making a sample object. Encapsulation allows you to scale up your projects by "divorcing the usage from the implementation." We will have a lot to say about this in Chapter 17.

Object Algorithms

The way you implement Classes has a large bearing on how useful their objects will be. The one golden rule about how you design your Classes is:

You can change the *implementation* of your objects, but, by all means, keep the *interface* the same.

The point is that if you change the way a method is written, but leave the interface alone, you will only have to change one piece of code: the method itself. If you change the way programs call that method (or how results are returned), then you have to change code everywhere that method is used.

Let's look at our clock again. Suppose we have thousands of programs using clocks with the statement:

```
my $clock = new Clock();
my $time = $clock->get();
```

Now, one day, we decide that we want our clock to have the ability to return seconds, hours, days, or years since 1970. Currently, our algorithm is:

```
sub get
{
    my($self) = @_;
    return($self->{time});
}
```

If we enhance this by adding a parameter, as in:

```
1   my $conversion = {
2                       'seconds' => 1, 'minutes' => 60,
3                       'hours' => 3600,'days' => 86400,
4                       'years' => 31557600
5                   };
6   sub get
7   {
8       my ($self, $type) = @_;
9       (print ("Unknown type $type!\n"), return(undef))
10                          if (!defined $conversion->{$type});
11      return(int($self->{time}/$conversion->{$type}));
12  }
```

then consider what happens to all of the programs that use get:

```
1 my $clock = new Clock();
2 my $time = $clock->get();
```

Line 2, which used to get the number of seconds since 1970, will now return Unknown type $type!. By making this one change, you have broken thousands of programs.

The solution? All you must do is ensure backward compatibility by adding a workaround. We could either:

1. Make a new function, and call it newget() (that way, we need not worry about backward compatibility).
2. Alter the old function to have a *default*. (The default happens to be the old data.)

Sometimes the first course is the right way to go, and sometimes the second course is correct. It depends on the situation. In this case, let's alter the function to be backward-compatible:

```
1   my $conversion = {
2                       'seconds' => 1, 'minutes' => 60,
3                       'hours' => 3600,'days' => 86400,
4                       'years' => 31557600
5                   };
6   sub get
7   {
8       my ($self, $type) = @_;
9       $type ||= 'seconds';
10      (print ("Unknown type $type!\n"), return(undef))
11                          if (!defined $conversion->{$type});
12      return(int($self->{time}/$conversion->{$type}));
13  }
```

Note the new line 9. Here, our workaround is simply to make the default type that we get from our clock the number of seconds. That way, any existing programs will still get the number of seconds when they pass no arguments to get.

The old interface has therefore been preserved. However, new programs that use the Clock object are able to say $clock->get('hours') with no strings attached.

Of course, this isn't a rule set in stone, but it is useful when your projects become more stable, and you get a large body of code. Perhaps it should be called "only change your interface when necessary." Sometimes, the cost of keeping the interface constant outweighs the cost of changing it.

But in general, the larger the project, or the more clients your program has, the more dangerous changing your interface is. This is an important point, and will shadow much of the design we do later.

The Destructor

Destructors are methods that occur when objects are destroyed. This occurs either by garbage collection (going out of scope) or when the program exits. Perl typically calls these for you, so you don't see them in the program.

You can make destructors in Perl, although they are not nearly as important in Perl as they are in languages like C++ and SmallTalk. This is because the traditional role of the destructor is to free up memory when the object is no longer needed, and Perl handles memory management for you.

As it stands now, we need no destructor in our Clock object to clean up after us. Nonetheless, let's make the Clock an "alarm clock" which goes off when it is being destroyed:

```
package Clock;
sub DESTROY
{
    my ($self) = @_;
    print "Destroying the clock now!\n";
}
```

Now, when we use the clock in a program, by saying:

```
destroy1.p:
1 use Clock;
2 my $clock = new Clock();
```

or

```
destroy2.p:
1 use Clock;
2 use strict;
3 my $xx;
4 for ($xx = 0; $xx < 10; $xx++) { my $clock = new Clock(); }
```

we implicitly are calling the destructor, which prints out `Destroying the clock now!` one time in **destroy1.p** and ten times in **destroy2.p**.

Typically, in Perl, you will need a destructor only when a nondata element is in your object. This nondata element could be a file, a database connection, a Web connection, etc. Since most of your objects will be data objects, you won't need a Destroy function too often.

Basic Object Principles Summary

As you can see, there is a lot going on behind even the simplest object in Perl, and you are well-advised to practice writing small classes of your own—and knowing how they work—before diving into more complicated stuff. At the very minimum learn the following:

1. Object Constructor: Know that my `$clock = new Clock('argument')` turns into
   `Clock::new('Clock', 'argument')` to construct objects.
2. Object Methods: Know that `$self->get('argument')` turns into `Clock::get($self, 'argument')`. If possible, know the mechanism.
3. Object Data: Know that an object in Perl is also a reference, and hence, all the data is held as members inside that reference.
4. Object Algorithms: Know that it is important to write your object's algorithms so that the *interface* to the outside world stays relatively the same.
5. Object Destructor: Know that the special function `sub DESTROY` is called when the object gets garbage collected.

Also realize that when you are doing object-oriented programming, you have two things to worry about: the object itself, and the programs that use the object. The object itself has to be clean, and not violate encapsulation. But, it also needs to be easily *usable*.

Intermediate/Advanced Object Principles

Don't forget that you can do a lot with even the so-called "basic" object principles. However, if you want to get more complicated, Perl has support in its syntax for the following two types of objects:

1. A specific syntax for inheritance.
2. A specific syntax for different types of overloading.

However, most complicated object designs in Perl come from the flexibility of its syntax. You can do marvelous things with the simple syntax Perl gives you. In fact, a large part of the rest of the book is devoted to proving this.

Let's look at how Perl does its inheritance, what exactly is meant by tie-ing, and one issue that we kind of ignored above: the relationship between class and object.

Class versus Object

In object-oriented programming, there are two concepts that are widely misunderstood: the object and the class. In fact, it is easy to get the two mixed up with one another, and the tendency is to use them interchangeably.

The first thing to realize is that they are *not* the same. The class can be seen as the *container* for the object. Let's take another look at the clock example:

```
1   package Clock;
2
3   sub new
4   {
5       my ($type) = @_;
6       my $self = {};
8       $self->{time} = time();
9       bless $self, $type;
10  }
11  sub get
12  {
13      my ($self) = @_;
14      return($self->{time});
15  }
16  sub set
17  {
18      my ($self, $secs) = @_;
20      $self->{time} = $secs || time();
21  }
```

This class contains the functions/methods new, get, and set. These functions *never change*. However, the object in this picture ($self) changes from instance to instance, even though it *uses* the class's functions new, get, and set. Hence, the relationship between the Clock object and the Clock class is something like what is shown in Figure 16.4.

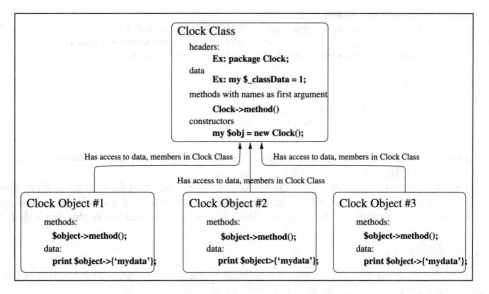

Figure 16.4
Relationship
between Object
and Class

This relationship is a one-to-many relationship: one class, many objects. The class consists of items that are automatically shared between objects, and the object consists of items that are unique.

This means we can use this relationship to our advantage. If we want functions that do something in common for all objects, we make a *class method*. If we want data that is shared between objects, we make *class data*.

Class Data

Perhaps an example will make this distinction clearer. Remember our proposal to enable the Clock class to give back not only seconds, but minutes, hours, and so on? The code looked like:

```
1   package Clock;
2
3 my $conversion = {
4                   'seconds' => 1, 'minutes' => 60,
5                   'hours' => 3600,'days' => 86400,
6                   'years' => 31557600
7               };
8
9   sub new
10  {
11     my ($type) = @_;
12     my $self = {};
13     $self->{time} = time();
14     bless $self, $type;
15  }
16   sub get
17   {
18       my ($self, $type) = @_;
```

```
19      $type ||= 'seconds';
20      (print ("Unknown type $type!\n"), return(undef))
21                            if (!defined $conversion->{$type}));
22      return(int($self->{time}/$conversion->{$type}));
23 }
24 sub set
25 {
26      my ($self, $secs) = @_;
27      $self->{time} = $secs || time();
28 }
```

The boldface code is added; the hash reference $conversion is what we are concerned with here. It is the perfect example of class data.

Since $conversion is defined at the top, outside of a function, it does not go with any given object (member of the class) but is instead used as a *translator* that converts the $type which is passed to get seconds, minutes, hours, etc., into the number of seconds. This translator can be used in any object; it is shared between them.

Class Methods

The other type of shared class resource is a function that affects all objects. For this, let's consider a clock function we can use to resynchronize all of the clocks to the current time.

How would we do this? Well, let's alter the constructor of our clock so that it makes a copy of the object onto a central stack:

```
1 my @objectStore;
2 sub new
3 {
4      my ($type) = @_;
5      my ($self) = {};
6      push (@objectStore, $self);
7      $self->{time} = time();
8      bless $self, $type;
9 }
```

In line 6, @objectStore keeps a record of all the clocks we have made. It is class data, again, and this means it is common to all objects.

Our resync function will then use this "universal" information to synchronize each object in an orderly fashion:

```
1 sub resync
2 {
3      my ($time) = @_;
4      my $clock;
5      foreach $clock (@objectStore) { $clock->set($time); }
6 }
```

Here, line 5 actually reaches into each clock we have "registered" in the constructor, and sets it for us. Hence, if we said in a client:

```
1 use Clock;
2 my $clock1 = new Clock();
3 sleep(60);
4 my $clock2 = new Clock();
```

```
5 Clock::resync(time());
6 print $clock1->get() - $clock2->get();
```

then line 5 is the class method call. It sets all the clocks to exactly the same time. The current time is evaluated and passed to `Clock::resync()`. Line 6, then, will always print out zero, rather than the expected '60'.

There are some cool things you can do with Class methods and Class data by understanding the difference between Class and Object. We will see more examples of this as we proceed. One primary use of this is to construct Configuration hashes that tell what the default behavior is for an object.

Class Methods, Part Two

You don't need to use the format `Class::method()`. You can instead use the format:

```
Class->method();
```

Why would you want to do this? Well, when we get to inheritance, we will find that the class `Class` can *inherit* subroutines from other classes, so `subroutine()` may or may not come from the class `Class`. We will get to how inheritance works later in this chapter.

These forms, therefore, are not exact synonyms. I don't use inheritance much, but if you are going to do so, use the `Class->method()` form instead. `Class::method()` ties you down to only using methods that are found in `Class`.

Summary of Class versus Object

Class and object are two concepts that are routinely mixed up by people just beginning to learn OO programming. Classes can be thought to contain objects, the one class containing the many objects. To make objects that share data, or a function that acts on one of the objects inside that class, make a class method or class data to do so.

This is done by making functions or data which aren't connected with any particular object. (Figure 16.5 provides a short template.)

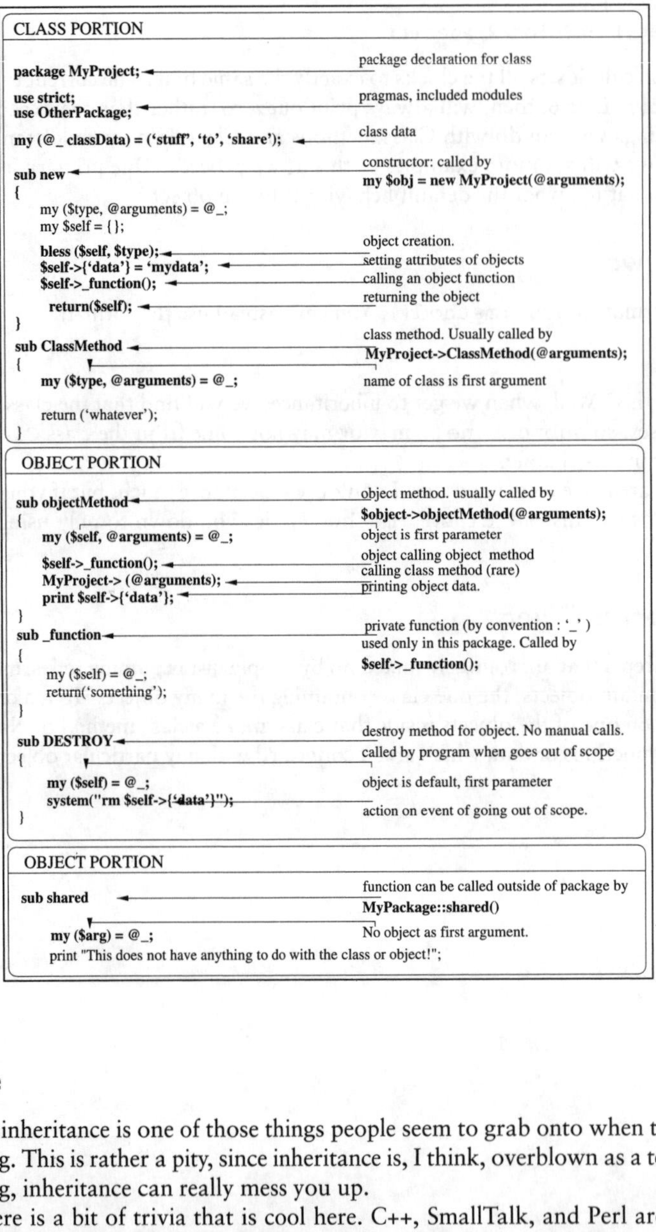

Figure 16.5
A Typical Class
with Class
Methods and Data

```
CLASS PORTION

package MyProject;                              package declaration for class

use strict;                                     pragmas, included modules
use OtherPackage;
my (@_ classData) = ('stuff', 'to', 'share');   class data

sub new                                         constructor: called by
{                                               my $obj = new MyProject(@arguments);
    my ($type, @arguments) = @_;
    my $self = { };
                                                object creation.
    bless ($self, $type);                       setting attributes of objects
    $self->{'data'} = 'mydata';                 calling an object function
    $self->_function();                         returning the object
    return($self);
}
                                                class method. Usually called by
sub ClassMethod                                 MyProject->ClassMethod(@arguments);
{
    my ($type, @arguments) = @_;                name of class is first argument

    return ('whatever');
}
```

```
OBJECT PORTION
                                                object method. usually called by
sub objectMethod                                $object->objectMethod(@arguments);
{
    my ($self, @arguments) = @_;                object is first parameter
                                                object calling object method
    $self->_function();                         calling class method (rare)
    MyProject-> (@arguments);                   printing object data.
    print $self->{'data'};
}                                               private function (by convention : '_' )
sub _function                                   used only in this package. Called by
{                                               $self->_function();
    my ($self) = @_;
    return('something');
}
                                                destroy method for object. No manual calls.
sub DESTROY                                      called by program when goes out of scope.
{
    my ($self) = @_;                            object is default, first parameter
    system("rm $self->{'data'}");
}                                               action on event of going out of scope.
```

```
OBJECT PORTION
                                                function can be called outside of package by
sub shared                                      MyPackage::shared()
{
    my ($arg) = @_;                             No object as first argument.
    print "This does not have anything to do with the class or object!";
}
```

Inheritance

As we said earlier, inheritance is one of those things people seem to grab onto when they first get into object-oriented programming. This is rather a pity, since inheritance is, I think, overblown as a technique. If you don't know what you are doing, inheritance can really mess you up.

That said, there is a bit of trivia that is cool here. C++, SmallTalk, and Perl are said to be object-oriented because they support inheritance. There are, however, true object languages (Ada is one of them) and they get along perfectly fine without inheritance. So take the following with a grain of salt.

We will also cover inheritance in more detail later (we devote Chapter 19 to inheritance), but for now, let's look at the syntax of how it works in Perl.

Inheritance is the practice of reusing code by defining a particular specific type of class in terms of a more generic one. An *inherited class* (or *subclass*) then places the code that has been abstracted out, into a *base* class. Figure 16.6 shows the basic relationship.

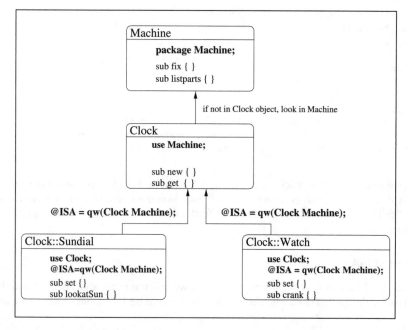

Figure 16.6
The Inheritance
Relationship

Suppose we want to make two different types of clocks: one that gets the time by looking at the sun (**Clock::SunDial**), and one that gets the time by the standard means of asking the operating system what the time is (**Clock::System**).

We could set it up so that we have one base class, which contains all the functions in common, and subclasses, which contain what is unique between the two types of clocks.

The Base Class

As said, we want to make it so both of them have the same interface (getting the number of seconds since 1970). The two different types of clocks have something in common, so we shouldn't have to duplicate code for each one.

What do they have in common? We can include the function get, because we have mandated that both types of clocks return the same value (the number of seconds since 1970) in the same way. We can also include the constructor new because we can define the construction of the clock in terms of setting the clock.

What we find in common, we put in **Clock.pm**. This is the base class:

```
1   package Clock;
2
3   my $conversion = {
4                       'seconds' => 1, 'minutes' => 60,
5                       'hours' => 3600,'days' => 86400,
6                       'years' => 31557600
7                   };
8
9   sub new
10  {
11      my ($type) = @_;
12      my $self = {};
```

```
13       bless $self, $type;
14       $self->set();
15       $self;
16  }
17  sub get
18  {
19       my ($self, $type) = @_;
20       $type ||= 'seconds';
21       (print ("Unknown type $type!\n"), return(undef))
22                            if (!defined $conversion->{$type});
23     return(int($self->{time}/$conversion->{$type}));
24  }
```

Note that we have done something tricky here: in line 14 we have defined our constructor new with the object method set. We don't know at this point what set will look like; it will differ with each subclass. We then say in the constructor "call the set function, whatever it is." With inheritance, "magic" will happen, and the correct set function will be called.

Subclasses and @ISA

Now that we have the base class, we must determine what we will put in the subclasses. The only function left is set, which differs for the System clock and the SunDial. Implement both versions of set, and store them in their own files:

Clock/System.pm

```
1 package Clock::System;
2 use Clock;
3 @ISA = qw(Clock);
4 sub set
5 {
6      my ($self, $secs) = @_;
7      $self->{time} = $secs || time();
8 }
```

Clock/SunDial.pm
```
1   package Clock::SunDial;
2   use Clock;
3   @ISA = qw(Clock);
4   sub set
5   {
6        my ($self, $secs) = @_;
7        $self->{time} = $secs || lookAtSun();
8   }
9   sub lookAtSun
10  {
11       print "Looking at the Sun for the time!\n";
12       return(time());
13  }
```

Two things here: one, note the special phrase '@ISA = qw(Clock)'. This is a key variable used for inheritance. It indicates that Clock::SunDial *is* also a Clock, and if a method/constructor/destructor is not found inside

`Clock::Sundial`, Perl then looks inside `Clock` to find it. If Perl can't find it there, Perl looks through the next member of `@ISA`, and so on. (If Perl runs out of `@ISA` entries to look in, it makes a last ditch attempt, and looks through a special class called UNIVERSAL.)

Figure 16.7 shows the path which is taken, in this case, `my $sundial = new Clock::Sundial()`.

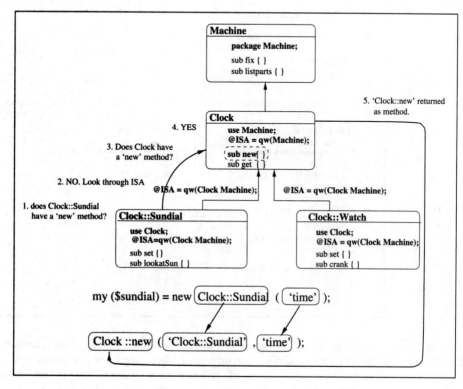

Figure 16.7
Perl Using
Inheritance to
Determine the
Constructor

Let's take this step by step. First, Perl looks for the constructor `new` inside `Clock::Sundial`. It can't find it, it then looks in `@ISA` and notes that a `Clock::Sundial` *is* also a `Clock`.

Second, Perl looks for the constructor `new` inside `Clock`. It finds it there, so the statement:

```
my $sundial = new Clock::Sundial();
```

is translated into

```
my $sundial = Clock::new('Clock::Sundial');
```

Remember the oddity about having the type be the first argument to the constructor? Here is where it is used most heavily. The `Clock::Sundial` may use the `Clock`'s constructor, but since the type of clock is passed to the `Clock` constructor, `Clock::new()` will create a `Clock::Sundial` instead of a `Clock`.

This is important to understanding how Perl actually calls the correct method. (Figure 16.8 shows how.)

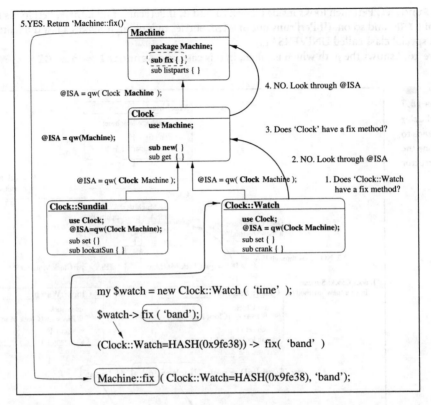

Figure 16.8
Perl Using
Inheritance to
Determine a
Method

Again, `$watch->fix('band')` translates into a form like `(Clock::watch=Hash(0x1f476))->fix('band')`. From this construct, we know that `$self` is a `Clock::watch`, and by `@ISA`, that is also a `'Clock'`, and a `'Machine'`. Since `Clock::watch` doesn't have a `'fix'` method, Perl then looks in its parent class `'Clock'`, and failing to find `'fix'` there, into its next parent class, `'Machine'`.

Hence:

```
$watch->fix('band')
```

translates into

```
machine::fix($watch, 'band');
```

If we had said `$watch->set()` on the other hand, this would translate into

```
Clock::watch::set($watch)
```

because `Clock::watch` has a `set` method.

No need to worry about speed with all these lookups: Perl caches the result of the lookup in a lookup table so it doesn't do the same work each time. Likewise, you need not worry about defining two versions of `set` (one for the base class, and one for the subclass) and then have them conflict with each other. Perl always picks the first method it finds.

The base method acts as a sort of default. If you decide that you need a specialized method for a given subclass, then Perl will always use that, and never use the base method again.

Inheritance Minutia

There are some minor concepts to know when dealing with inheritance. They are covered next, and when you get really fancy, you might consider using them in your own class.

UNIVERSAL

Remember when we said that if an object runs, and can't find a method in `@ISA`, it fails? Well, there is an exception to this.

There is a special class called *UNIVERSAL*, which all objects inherit from. It has the following methods, which are helpful when dealing with versioning and whatnot:

- `isa`—tells whether or not a reference is a certain type. `$self->isa('class')` returns 1 if `$self` is a class, and 0 if it is not. It does a search through the `@ISA` variable for you.
- `can`—tells whether or not a reference can do a given method. `$clock->can('get')` would say if `$clock` had a get method. If so, it returns a reference to the correct subroutine.
- `VERSION`—`Clock->VERSION('1.00')` will go into the Clock package and see if it is at least version 1.00 or better.

This is a quick summary of what the on-line documentation says in much more detail. Look at **UNIVERSAL.pm** in your favorite editor, or look at the Perl modules documentation. Both have much more to say about this.

SUPER::

If you have two methods that have the same name in an inheritance relationship, then the one in the subclass will be executed first. In code terms, the object call:

```
my $self = new SubSubClass();
$self->get();
```

with `SubSubClass` defined as:

```
package SubSubClass;
use BaseClass;
use SubClass;
@ISA = qw(SubClass BaseClass);
```

will first try to translate `$self->get()` to:

```
SubSubClass::get($self);
```

then

```
SubClass::get($self);
```

then

```
BaseClass::get($self);
```

then

```
UNIVERSAL::get($self);
```

and then finally die if it cannot find the method get in any of these places. Now what happens if you have a SubSubClass::get() defined, but still want to call SubClass::get()?

This is what SUPER:: is for. If you say:

```
package SubSubClass;
@ISA = qw(SubClass, Base);
sub get
{
$self->SUPER::get()
}
```

Perl will ignore SubSubClass::get(), and then look up the @ISA chain to find the next get() method (starting at SubClass::get()).

Note

Note that

```
$self->SUPER::get()
```

must be in the package SubSubClass. If you say:

```
my $self = new SubSubClass();
$self->SUPER::get();
```

it won't do what you want. Perl tries to look for the next get() function from the point of view of the package that you are in. See the on-line documentation for more detail on why this is.

SUPER:: is termed a *pseudoclass*. It allows you to call methods that are not directly inherited, but are still there. SUPER:: is seldom used, but when you do use it, it is invaluable.

Sometimes you may want to define a subclass method in terms of a base method. For example, suppose you wanted to log each time your clock was used (each time you set it). You call the subclass Clock::System::Log, and set it up as such:

```
Clock/System/Log.pm
1   package Clock::System::Log;
2   use Clock::System;
3   use Clock;
4   use FileHandle;
5   @ISA = qw (Clock::System clock);
6   sub set
7   {
8       my ($self, $secs) = @_;
9       $self->SUPER::set($secs);
10      my $fd = new FileHandle(">> clocklog");
11      print $fd "Clock set at ", $self->get(), "Seconds";
12  }
```

In line 9, then, we set up the set method defined in terms of Clock::System::set(). We simply append the extra stuff that we are going to do with this particular version of clock (such as open a log and append onto it the time with which it was set).

When we say:

```
my $clock = new Clock::System::Log();
```

```
$clock->set();
```

Perl goes through a flurry of activity to find which set method you mean. The main point here is that by saying SUPER:: you don't need to explicitly state which method you want, and you don't have to know that the set method is in Clock::System. The SUPER::construct finds it for you.

Inheritance Summary

Inheritance is a relatively complicated technique you should attempt only if you really know what you are doing. Perl supports inheritance, but there is quite a bit of logic you must know before you'll understand exactly what is happening when you program. You should understand:

- The inheritance relationship—the fact that a subclass inherits methods from the base class, and that the subclass goes through a bit of syntactical gymnastics to find which method to execute.
- @ISA—the @ISA variable is the main way you do inheritance. @ISA = ('Base', 'Super'); means that the class that you are working in is both a Base and a Super class.

Understanding the syntactical gymnastics with inheritance helps too. Perl does it for you, but if you understand exactly what Perl is doing for you (or *to* you!), it will make it much easier to handle any problems you might have.

Overloading

We are getting into rather esoteric territory with this subject. You probably don't even want to approach overloading until you've gotten a good handle on the basic types of objects. In fact, overloading is sort of a side road in the object network, and you can get along without it quite well.

Overloading refers to taking a function that is represented by a symbol (+, -, %, /, etc.) and giving it a function that is meaningful to a class.

What does this mean? The classic example is a class that implements complex numbers. If $a = '1+2i' and $b = '2+3i', then you obviously want $a+$b to equal '3+5i'. This means overloading the plus operator (+) so that it behaves differently when dealing with a complex number object.

There are two types of overloading in Perl: overloading of symbols and overloading of data structures. The first form is done with the help of a special use directive called use overload. The second form of overloading is called tie-ing.

Using Overload

Let's take the complex number example a bit further and define the plus and minus operations, as well as the quotes operations, for a complex number object.

First we need to write the complex object:

```
package Complex;
sub new
{
    my ($type, $real, $imaginary) = @_;
    my $self = {};
    $self->{real} = $real || 0;
    $self->{imaginary} = $imaginary || 0;
    bless $self, $type;
}
```

Here, we simply make a constructor, and stop. This class will have no direct methods. We want to make an interface that looks something like this:

```
my $complex1 = new Complex(5,4);
my $complex2 = new Complex(2,3);
my $complex3 = $complex1 + $complex2;
print "$complex3\n";
```

If we define our interface correctly, the last line shows print '7 t7I'.

We can do this with overloading. In some cases, especially mathematical ones, it vastly simplifies the interface. You could say:

```
my $complex3 = new Complex();
$complex3->add($complex1);
$complex3->add($complex2);
```

But why say that when:

```
$complex3 = $complex2 + $complex1;
```

does exactly the same thing, albeit much clearer?

Now let's implement this package. We start by declaring what symbols we are going to overload:

```
1   package Complex;
2
3   use overload "+" => \&plus,
4                "-" => \&minus,
5                "=" => \&equals,
6                '""' => \&print;
```

Here, each line indicates a callback that we will use to substitute for that given symbol. *Callbacks*, again, are functions that are supplied to provide extra information that a module or object doesn't know about, or needs to know on the fly.

In this case, every time the Perl engine sees $a + $b, where $a and $b are objects of type Complex, it executes a &Complex::plus($a, $b) instead. When Perl sees a $a - $b it executes &Complex::minus($a, $b) instead. print "$a" triggers &Complex::print($a), and so forth.

So all we need to do here is fill in the blanks, and write some functions that perform these various actions. plus will return the sum of the real parts and the imaginary parts, and create a new Complex as well. (Complex->new() is just a synonym, again, for 'new Complex().)

```
7   sub plus
8   {
9       my ($complex1, $complex2) = @_;
10      return (
11              Complex->new
12                  (
13                      $complex1->{real}+$complex2->{real},
14                      $complex1->{imaginary}+$complex2->{imaginary}
15                  )
16          );
17  }
```

minus does the exact opposite:

```
18
19  sub minus
20  {
21      my ($complex1, $complex2) = @_;
22
```

```
23          return (
24              Complex->new
25                  (
26                      $complex1->{real}-$complex2->{real},
27                      $complex1->{imaginary}-$complex2->{imaginary}
28                  )
29              );
30 }
31
```

`equals` creates a new complex (`$complex1`) and then assigns it the values from the complex on the right-hand side of the equation.

```
32 sub equals
33 {
34      my ($complex1, $complex2) = @_;
35      $complex1 = new Complex($complex2->{real}, $complex2->{imaginary});
36 }
```

Finally, `print` handles situations of the form `print "$complex"`.

```
37 sub print
38 {
39      my ($complex1) = @_;
40      if ($complex1->{imaginary} < 0)
41      {
42          return "$complex1->{real} $complex1->{imaginary}i\n";
43      }
44      else
45      {
46          return "$complex1->{real} + $complex1->{imaginary}i\n";
47      }
48 }
```

Instead of `print "$complex"` doing the regular thing (turning `$complex` into a string) it executes the print command instead, substituting the text:

```
"$complex1->{real} $complex1->{imaginary}i\n";
```

for any complex reference that Perl goes to print. Figure 16.9 shows the relationship between the usage of overloading and its output.

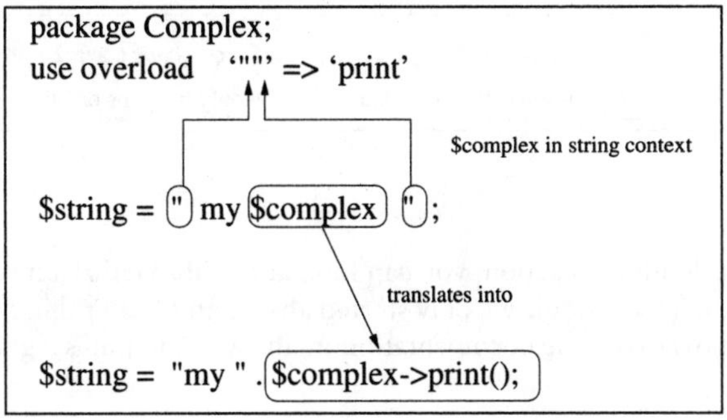

Figure 16.9
Overloading—
Relationship
Between Usage
and Arguments

```
package Complex;
use overload     '""' => 'print'
```
$complex in string context

$string = " my $complex ";

translates into

$string = "my " . $complex->print();

All this said, exactly what can you overload? Well, the documentation will give you a complete picture of what you can do, but Figure 16.10 gives you a handy summary for what can get overloaded, and where the arguments transfer when you use them.

Figure 16.10
Overloading—A
Summary of
Usage

Operation				Syntax for Operation	Overloaded Equivalent (need overload directive)
Math and String Operations					
+	+=	-	-=	$var + $var2	$var-> *plus*($var2);
*	*=	/	/=	$var x= $var2	$var-> *stringmult* ($var2);
%	%=	**	**=	$var ** $var2	$var-> *exponent* ($var2);
<<	<<=	>>	>>=	$var<<=$var2	$var-> *shiftbiteq* ($var2);
x	x=	.	.=	$var . $var2	$var-> *concatenate* ($var2);
Numeric Comparison					
<	<=	>	>=	($var > $var2)	$var-> *greaterthan* ($var2);
==	!=	<=>		($var <=> $var2)	$var-> *numcompare*($var2);
String Comparison					
lt	le	gt	ge	($var cmp $var2)	$var-> *stringcompare* ($var2);
eq	ne	cmp		($var eq $var2)	$var-> *isequal* ($var2);
Bit Operation					
&	^	|	neg	- $var	$var-> *negate*( );
!	~			! $var	$var-> *not* ( );
Increment, Decrement					
++	--			++$var, $var++	$var-> *increment* ( );
Conversion operators					
bool	""	0+		if ($var); # bool	$var-> *boolean* ( );
				print $var; # ""	$var-> *sprintf* ( );
				int($var); # 0+	$var-> *numconvert* ( );
Trigonometric operators					
atan2				atan ($var, $var2);	$var-> *atan2* ($var2);
cos	sin	exp	abs	cos($var);	$var-> *cos* ( );
log	sqrt			sqrt($var);	$var-> *sqrt* ( )
Copy Constructor					
=				$var=$var2;	$var-> *copy* ($var2);
				# some change to var	# only happens on change

If you want a real tour de force of overloading in action, you can look at the **lib/Math/Complex.pm** page in the standard distribution. It fully implements the module we only started above, and I can't think of a better real-life example to look at. For what you can overload, the documentation in **lib/overload.pm** is a good in-depth report too.

Tie-ing

Since use overload provides you with the ability to overload *symbols* like +, –, etc., you can overload *data structures* by the use of the special function tie.

Many objects act sort of like a glorified hash. We have already seen this in our Clock object. In fact, the get function in our Clock was equivalent to a hash access:

```
print $clock->get();
```

and

```
print $clock->{time};
```

were exactly the same.

Tie-ing takes this to its logical extreme. When you tie an object, you use the syntax of a hash, an array, or a scalar, but each time you use the syntax, a *method* call is called which actually does the work. This is accomplished by the **tie** command. You say:

```
tie(%hashname, 'ClassName',@argumentsToClassConstructor);
```

This makes an object by calling the constructor ClassName->TIEHASH(@argumentsToClass Constructor). (You can also make tied arrays, tied scalars, and tied handles—see the documentation **perltie** for more information on this.)

This object is then accessible by the **tied** command. If you say:

```
my $object = tied(%hashname);
```

it retrieves the object created by the constructor ClassName->TIEHASH() and puts it into the object. When you are done with the tied hashes, you can untie them:

```
untie(%hashname);
```

which then destroys the object behind the hash in the process.

Example: Smart Hashes

Let's give a simple example. Suppose you want a "smart hash" that keeps track of how many times a given key is accessed, stored, and deleted. This is the perfect application for tie. We shall make a package, **SmartHash.pm**, that we use in the following way:

```
1 use SmartHash;
2 tie (%hash, 'SmartHash');
3 my $hashObject = tied(%hash);
4 $hash{'a'} = 1;
5 $hash{'a'} = 2;
6 $hash{'b'} = 1;
7 print $hash{'a'};
7 delete $hash{'a'};
8
9 print $hashObject->get('deleted','a');
```

Line 2 actually takes the %hash object and *ties* it to the object SmartHash. What this then does is make an object associated with %hash that "shadows" its every move. We get this hash in line 3 and call it $hashObject.

Now, when we set a key in the hash $hash{'a'} it calls the method $hashObject->STORE(). When we access an element in %hash (print $hash{'a'}) it calls the method $hashObject->FETCH() for us.

When we delete an element it calls `$hashObject->DELETE()`, and so on. Figure 16.11 shows all of the methods provided for hash tie-ing, what they do, and when they are triggered.

Figure 16.11
Tie-ing Methods
Provided for
Hashes

Tied Hashes

TIEHASH	my $tiedhash = tie(%hash, 'MyHash', 'argument');	MyHash->TIEHASH('argument');
FETCH	print $hash{'value'};	print $tiedhash->FETCH('value');
STORE	$hash{'value'} = 1;	$tiedhash->STORE('value', '1');
DELETE	delete $hash{'value'};	$tiedhash->DELETE('value');
CLEAR	undef (%hash)	$tiedhash->CLEAR();
EXISTS	if (defined ($hash{'value'})) { }	$tiedhash->EXISTS('value');
FIRSTKEY	while (($key, $value) = each(%hash))	my $key = $tiedhash->FIRSTKEY();
NEXTKEY		my $value = $tiedhash->FETCH($key); # first time through

```
while ($key = $tiedhash->NEXTKEY())
{
    my $value = $tiedhash->FETCH($key);
    return($key, $value);
}
```

Tied Arrays

TIEARRAY	my $tiedarray = tie(%array, 'MyArray', 'argument');	$tiedarray = MyArray->TIEARRAY('argument');
FETCH	print $array[1];	print $tiedarray->FETCH('1');
STORE	@array = (1,2,3);	$tiedarray->STORE(0,1); $tiedarray->STORE(1,2); $tiedarray->STORE(2,3);
DESTROY	untie @array;	$tiedarray->DESTROY();

Tied Scalars

TIESCALAR	my $tiedscalar = tie($scalar, 'MyScalar', 'argument');	$tiedscalar= MyScalar->TIESCALAR( )
FETCH	print $scalar	print $tiedscalar->FETCH();
STORE	$scalar = 4;	$tiedscalar->STORE();
DESTROY	undef$scalar;	$tiedscalar->DESTROY();

Now, all we have to do is program each individual method in such a way so that the hash "remembers" what has happened to it during its lifetime. Let's go into a little more detail about the method of the most commonly used type of `tie` ing; *hash* `tie` ing.

The TIEHASH Method

Let's start with `TIEHASH`:

```
1   SmartHash.pm
2   package SmartHash;
3   sub TIEHASH
4   {
5       my ($type) = @_;
6       my $self = {hashval => {}};
```

```
 7       $self->{'accessed'} = {};
 8       $self->{'stored'} = {};
 9       $self->{'deleted'} = {};
10       bless $self, $type;
11 }
```

TIEHASH is the constructor for the SmartHash object. It is called when we first execute the **tie** command.

tie(%hash, 'SmartHash'); tells Perl to make a new object, SmartHash, and tie it to the variable %hash, so when we access, change, delete, or do anything to %hash we immediately call a method inside this class. %hash is merely the front end to the object created by this constructor.

As for our strategy in making a SmartHash, notice that we make three entries inside the object: one for each time an element is accessed, stored, and deleted. We also make a place for actually storing the hash that we are to build: inside $self->{hashval}.

The FETCH Method

Here is our FETCH method, the one called when we say something like print "$hash{orange}\n":

```
12 sub FETCH
13 {
14     my ($self, $key) = @_;
15     my $accessed =  $self->{'accessed'};
16     my $hash =  $self->{'hashval'};
17     $accessed->{$key}++;
18     return($hash->{$key});
19 }
```

In this case, orange becomes $key in my ($self, $key) = @_, and the method stores the fact that it accessed orange (line 17). It then retrieves the value of orange from the hash and returns it (line 18).

The STORE Method

STORE is the method called when we actually store a new value to the hash ($hash{'orange'} = 2, for example). Here's our STORE method:

```
20 sub STORE
21 {
22     my ($self, $key, $value) = @_;
23     my $stored =  $self->{'stored'};
24     my $hash =  $self->{'hashval'};
25     $stored->{$key}++;
26     $hash->{$key} = $value;
27 }
```

Here, we keep track that we have in fact stored the key orange (line 25), before we actually store the value into the hash itself (line 26).

The DELETE Method

DELETE is the method called when we say delete $hash{"key"}:

```
28 sub DELETE
29 {
```

```
30      my ($self, $key) = @_;
31      my $deleted =  $self->{'deleted'};
32      my $hash =  $self->{'hashval'};
33      $deleted->{$key}++;
34      delete $hash->{$key};
35 }
```

Again, this is exactly like a regular delete (line 34) but we keep track that we have deleted the key in the first place, storing the fact in $self->{'deleted'}(line 33).

The CLEAR Method

CLEAR is the method called when we are clearing out the hash (something like undef %hash):

```
36 sub CLEAR
37 {
38      my ($self) = @_;
39      my $key;
40
41      my $hash = $self->{'hashval'};
42      foreach $key ( keys %$hash ) { $self->DELETE($key); }
43 }
```

Again, because we are keeping a log of what has happened in the hash, we must wrap up our delete calls in a way that records this activity. The easiest way to do this is to call the DELETE method ourselves (line 42). This ensures that we mark each delete when it occurs.

If we had said delete $hash->{$key}, then no such marking would have occurred.

The EXISTS Method

```
44 sub EXISTS
45 {
46      my ($self, $key) = @_;
47      my $hash = $self->{'hashval'};
48      return (1) if (exists $hash->{key});
49      return (0);
50 }
```

EXISTS is called when we say something like if (exists $hash{'key'});. It is questionable whether or not calling EXISTS is an access of that variable. Here we assume it is not, and don't track it.

The FIRSTKEY and NEXTKEY Methods

FIRSTKEY and NEXTKEY are used for looping through each element in a hash, as in keys(%hash) and each(%hash). Here they are:

```
51 sub FIRSTKEY
52 {
53      my ($self) = @_;
54      my ($key, $value) = each(%{$self->{'hashval'}});
55    return($key);
56 }
```

```
57
58 sub NEXTKEY
59 {
60     my ($self, $lastkey) = @_;
61     $self->FIRSTKEY();
62 }
```

In other words, they provide a means to iterate through our tied hash, and get all the information out of it.

User-Provided Methods

Whew! Now we have come to the end of the methods that we need to program in order for the tie-ing to work. In the process of stuffing the hash in the first place, we have ensured that we have a log of activity about what actually has occurred with the hash. Now, we only have to figure out how to retrieve this log. We do it via get:

```
63 sub get
64 {
65     my ($self, $type, $key) = @_;
66     print "Undefined type!\n" if (!defined $self->{$type});
67     return($self->{$type}->{$key} || 0 );
68 }
```

Here, $type is one of three things: accessed, deleted, or stored. A call to $self->get('accessed', 'phaedrus') will get the number of times that the key phaedrus has been accessed.

This is the only user method we have to define. It satisfies our purpose for retrieving log information we have stored. There are eight methods that are necessary to define how the tie-ing will work, and one method that is user-defined.

There is a lot of excess typing you must do to make tie-ing work. But when it is done, you have a pretty slick interface.

Usage

Enough typing. Let's use the interface we have developed. We can say:

```
1 use SmartHash;
2 tie(%myHash, 'SmartHash');
3 $myHash{'element1'} = 2;
4 $myHash{'element2'} = 4;
5 $myHash{'element3'} = $myHash{'element2'};
6 # ....
7 my $object = tied(%myHash);
8 print $object->get('accessed', 'element2');
```

This will print out 1. We have accessed element2 one time since we tied the hash to an object.

The SmartHash has a lot of potential applications that we only touch on here. Suppose you made a hash element for each link that you had on a CGI Web page. You could use the SmartHash to automatically figure out which links are the most popular.

Or suppose you have to figure out how often a customer is accessed in a database. Again, the SmartHash can tell you at a glance which keys were accessed most often.

tie-ing has all sorts of uses. Next, we will briefly point out one tied hash which is very popular: the ability to make hashes permanent—stored on disk.

Example: DBM Files

No discussion of tie-ing would be complete without mentioning DBM files. DBM files allow you to manipulate a file on disk, as if it were a hash. (You guessed it, they are implemented by tie-ing.)

There are several types of DBM files (described in length in the on-line documentation). Each has its plusses and minuses. The one that we will look at is the **SDBM_file** since it is portable, and the source actually comes with Perl. However, it is slow so you might want to use **NDBM_file** instead (the interface is exactly the same) or the **GDBM_file**.

DBM usage

To tie to a DBM file, simply make a statement like:

```
use SDBM_file;
tie(%hash, 'SDBM_file', 'FileName', 1, 0);
```

Any writes or accesses to %hash will actually cause the file FileName to be written to and/or accessed. The hash is stored in this file for later retrieval. Hence:

```
$hash{'key'} = 'store';
```

will write to FileName the key, store pair. When you want to access it, you can say:

```
print $hash{'key'};
```

This is an easy way to share information between processes, and some implementations of DBM are very fast. The best, most supported, version of DBM is the Berkeley DBM which is included on the accompanying CD.

DBM Issues

However, don't get overzealous. One of the issues DBMs have, especially when sharing information between processes, is that you must be scrupulous about *locking* your DBM files while other files read it.

The other thing to mention is that DBM files can become really big, which is part of their usefulness. When they become really big, you are probably going to want to traverse through them with the function each:

```
while (($key, $value) = each(%hash))
{
     #
}
```

If you used the function keys with a large DBM file, you can end up eating a lot of memory, so be careful.

Summary of Overloading

This is just a fraction of what there is to know about overloading (both overloading operators and overloading data structures), and you would do well to go back to the documentation for more detail.

However, the information discussed in this section is really the central knowledge that you need to know to use overloading:

1. Overloading is simply the process of making an object use an expression like $c = $a+$b$, instead of $c = $a->add($b)$.
2. use overload "=" =>\= is an example of a statement that makes a class use overloading.

3. `tie`-ing is the process of making a data structure (hash, array, scalar, or handle) implemented in terms of an object to make it more flexible.

4. Tie objects to data structures with `tie(%hash, 'Object', @args)`, and get the object they are tied to with `my $object = tied(%hash)`. You can untie objects with `untie(%hash)`.

5. You need to define eight methods that go along with `tie`-ing a hash: `TIEHASH`, `FETCH`, `STORE`, `DELETE`, `CLEAR`, `FIRSTKEY`, `NEXTKEY`, and `DESTROY`.

Overloading is a cool thing to do, but it is not that widely used (I personally don't like to type that much). You can stick with basic object programming, ignore inheritance and overloading, and do just fine.

Note

To be fair, there is a lot of typing in overloading, but fortunately Perl provides two packages, **Tie::Hash** and **Tie::StdHash**, that let you inherit some of these methods by default. Go to **Tie::Hash** and **Tie::StdHash** in the standard distribution for more detail. We will also consider this more in the chapter on inheritance, when we see exactly how much typing you can avoid.

17

The Common Object

Chapter 16 introduced quite a bit of object syntax. This included the definition of Perl object variables and methods, the syntax of inheritance and overloading, building objects out of ordinary references, and the difference between a class and an object.

Just having the syntax isn't enough when dealing with object-oriented programming. You need to be patient and experiment. You also need to look at many examples, and when possible, get your feet wet in programming your own. It is quite easy to get frustrated, so be prepared. However, there is a bright side: There are many similarities you will run across when you program objects. Certain functions and variables are used over and over and they do the same basic thing in every single object.

We have dubbed this the *common object*. The purpose of this chapter is to give a good feel of how objects might look when you get into the full swing of things, without actually worrying about making anything useful.

Chapter Overview

The focus of this chapter is the creation of a "mock class," one complicated enough to show how an actual class might work, but not where we have to worry about real issues. The example we have chosen to illustrate objects is a board game.

First, we will give an overview of important class terms, as well as review some of the important terms from Chapter 16. Then, we will consider one of the foundation classes that will be the start of this game, the Piece, which we will implement as if we were actually seriously considering making the full game.

We will then look at the following five types of elements in the class Piece:

1. Common class data
2. Common object data
3. Common object methods (ones in pretty much every class)
4. Usually common object methods (ones in most classes)
5. Common private object methods

Finally, we will provide some code snippets on how to use these methods to manipulate the Piece object, and some ways of combining the low-level methods that you will find in pretty much any object into higher-level ones. But first, an overview of what we will cover.

The Common Object

As stated in the last chapter, any object you see will consist of the following five items:

1. A constructor or constructors—one or more functions that construct an object, give it form, and return a reference to that object.
2. A destructor—the function called for the destruction of the module. Since memory management is done by Perl itself, you need only destroy things that are used by the object (such as temporary files). This is optional.
3. Object data—the data that the object holds. Usually in a hashkey, as in `$self->{data}`.
4. Object methods—the functions associated with the object.
5. Object algorithms—the algorithms associated with the object; how the object is implemented.

When we talk about the common object, we are talking about methods and data. These methods and data are so common that they come up over and over again in the course of writing an object. Once you start writing lots of objects, these common methods are so ingrained in your psyche that you will say to yourself: "Oh—that needs a get method" or "Oh—that needs a store method." You will then add the appropriate method to your object in order to solve that particular problem.

Let's start with a fairly abstract problem. Let's consider making a board game, and consider the first object that we would have to make in that game, a Piece.

But first, let's go over definitions we are going to use in the following examples.

Common Class and Object Definitions

These definitions will figure prominently in the next examples. We have gone over some of them briefly in Chapter 16, but consider this a review.

- *Class methods* are methods shared between objects. For example, there might be a class method named `reset` that goes through all the objects that have been initialized by it and resets them back to an initial state.
- *Class data* is data shared between objects. Each object inside the class has access to that data. This is used to make common configurations to share between all objects.
- *Accessor methods* are a special type of method which is used to access the class or object's data.
- *Mutator methods* are used to set a class or object's data.
- *Private methods* are supposed to be internal to the object or class and are not meant to be called from the outside.
- *Private data* is data meant for consumption of the object only.

Perl's policy toward class data and class methods is pretty much consistent through all of the object-oriented world. However, Perl has a very unique way of handling private object methods and data: there *is* no syntax for private object methods or data.

In other words, methods and data are private, not by enforcement, but by convention. In C++ you could say:

```
class A
{
    private:
            int xx;
            int yy;
             A();
            int myfunction();
    public:
            int method();
}
```

in which `myfunction()` can only be called by objects in class A, and nowhere else. But the equivalent class header in Perl would be defined as follows:

```
package A;
sub new
{
    my ($type) = @_;
    # rest of object
}
sub method { }
sub _myfunction { }
```

Notice the _ in front of `_myfunction()`. This indicates that `_myfunction()` should not be called from the outside world. However, Perl isn't going to give you a compile time error if you do in fact call `_myfunction()`.

It is an unwritten contract between the person who writes the clients and the person who writes the modules to not tread on each other's toes. The unwritten contract we have on my current project is that _ means "Private! Hands off."

Why this flexibility? Well, the flexibility lets you break good programming rules (like respecting other people's wishes for a variable to be private) on a temporary basis to get an instant productivity gain. It is usually a bad idea to break these rules, because by doing so, you create silent traps in the code and it will break as soon as the private interface changes; it can be worthwhile, if you know what you are doing.

With that review let's do some real design. We start with the example overview, and then do a partial implementation of it.

Example Overview: Board Game Strategem

For our example, we will consider a mock game called *Strategem*. It is almost exactly like the Milton Bradley game *Stratego*, except that we will be using the flexibility the computer provides us to make the rules more complicated, have the pieces change in the middle of the game, and so on.

Furthermore, Strategem is used in this example because it is based on a relatively simple game. It has a square board, and pieces can be defined by generic attributes (such as *attacking_rank*, *movement*, *defending_rank*, and *position*). For the sake of this example, we can create the Strategem pieces in the abstract, showing how to use the methods that we create, and how we might use them in the game program itself.

A Little Bit About the Game

Stratego is a Milton Bradley board game that pits two players against each other in an attempt to capture the opponent's flag. Each player maneuvers pieces around the board either moving or attacking on alternating turns. The board itself consists of a 10x10 grid similar to a chess board. Game pieces each have a rank, and when an attack occurs, the piece with the highest rank wins. During play each player alternates either moving or attacking using one of the 40 game pieces each player starts with. The pieces consist of Admiral, General, Colonels, Majors, Captains, Lieutenants, Sergeants, Miners, Scouts, Spy, Bombs, and a Flag.

When pieces of equal rank attack, both lose. A losing piece (or pieces) is permanently removed from the board. Players may either move or attack on their turn, but not both. Any piece, except bombs or the flag, can move. A move can be made to any adjoining empty square, forward, backward, or sideways, but not diagonally. All pieces, except miners, can move only one square. Miners can move any number of empty squares in a single direction. An attack can happen (but is not required) between any two adjoining opposing pieces. The spy is the lowest ranked piece, but will win when attacking a marshal. Bombs destroy any piece that attack it except miners. Miners that attack bombs cause the bombs to be removed from the board.

The pieces are constructed so that only the piece's owner can see the name and rank of each piece when placed on the board. Each player initially places all his or her pieces on his or her own side of the board (again, similar to chess). However, the players can place any of their pieces in any location (unlike the constraints put on chess pieces). Pieces can move one (and only one) square either forward, backward, or sideways, but cannot move diagonally. The only exceptions are scouts, bombs, and the flag. Scouts can move any number of open squares in a single direction. Bombs and the flag cannot move at all once positioned at the beginning of the game.

These are the rules for the pieces of *Stratego*. Notice that there are a few constraints here:

1. Pieces that are captured are removed from the board permanently.
2. Pieces remain constant throughout the game.

In our Strategem game, we will design our piece object in such a way that these constraints are removed. Pieces will be able to be promoted (go up a rank) if they capture so many enemy pieces, or demoted if they retreat from battle. Recruits are another possibility, in which a side that is losing can gain more pieces and build more.

Keep these rules in mind while we are making the design. Understanding these rules of play is necessary in designing the object Piece.

Design of the Object Piece

What is the best way to go about implementing objects for the game? Remember, there are three major parts to designing an object:

1. Visualizing the data behind the object.
2. Visualizing the methods behind the object.
3. Visualizing the interface behind the method.

Let's look at each in turn.

Designing the Piece Object's Data

I like to start a design by thinking about the object's data. It tends to be a simple part of the design (although not the simplest) and it also tends to help me picture the object in my mind.

I start thinking of the attributes for the piece, and how they might be stored. I can think of several off the top of my head:

*   The type of piece it is.
*   How much the piece moves.

- The piece side (blue or red).
- The rank of the piece.
- The coordinates of the piece.

Furthermore, we have some wrinkles in the "problem domain," as computer programmers like to call it. You may have noticed in the design specifications that there were a few special rules on how pieces attacked:

1. Bombs, when attacked, always kill their opponent unless it is a miner.
2. Spies always lose when they are attacked. Spies who attack always lose unless their opponent is an admiral.

What is the best way to handle these exceptions? In a way, it would be really nice if we could say something like:

```
$piece = { 'type' => 'bomb',
           'movement' => 1,
           'side' => 'blue',
           'rank' => -1,
           'xcoord' => 3,
           'ycoord' => 5 }
```

in which each element in the hash corresponds to the list we made earlier. Attacking would then become a function of comparing the ranks between two pieces. If they are on opposing sides, the one with the lowest rank wins. Unfortunately, a bomb is *always* of rank -1, *always* invincible. So we need to somehow make the rank conditional on the piece that is attacking.

In other words, the piece's rank depends on something it has no idea about: another piece's rank—the rank of the piece attacking it, or the rank of the piece defending it. Object-oriented programming has a specific technique for solving this, one we have seen before. To get that other piece's rank, we rely on a *callback*. We do something like this:

```
$piece = { 'type' => 'bomb',
           'movement' => 1,
           'side' => 'blue',
           'rank' => sub {
                           $rank= -1 unless $_[0]->type() eq 'miner';
                           $rank = 99999 if  $_[0]->type() eq 'miner';
                           return($rank);
                       },
           'xcoord' => 3,
           'ycoord' => 5
         }
```

Now, the bomb's rank isn't a value per se, but depends on the boldfaced subroutine. This way, we separate what we cannot know from the object itself. If we then said something like:

```
my $callback = $piece->{'rank'};
&$callback($someotherpiece);
```

in which $someotherpiece was a piece of opposing rank, this translates into:

```
$rank = -1 unless $someotherpiece->type() eq 'miner';
$rank = 99999 if $someotherpiece->type() eq 'miner';
return($rank);
```

which is exactly what we need. This is a way of representing data based on a condition we don't know. After all, one time we call this, the rank may be –1, other times it may be 99999. We only know this information at the time when the two pieces attack each other.

So let's think of another case in our design, and see if the callback will handle it: Will this handle the condition that spies always lose when they are attacked, unless their opponent is an admiral?

The way it stands, we could accommodate this. The key point is that spies have a different rank depending on whether they are attacking or defending. Instead of trying to stuff this second point into the same callback and make it more complicated, split up the rank into two types of ranks, a *defending* rank and an *attacking* rank:

```
$spy_piece =
          {
              'type' => 'spy',
              'movement' => 1,
              'side' => 'blue',
              'attacking_rank' =>
                  sub {
                         my $attacking_rank;
                         $attacking_rank = 99999 unless($_[1]->type() eq 'admiral');
                         $attacking_rank = -1 if ($_[1]->type() eq 'admiral');
                       },
              'xcoord' => 3,
              'ycoord' => 5
          }
```

When the spy attacks anything but the admiral, its rank resolves to:

```
$attacking_rank = 99999 unless($_[1]->type() eq 'admiral');
```

meaning, of course that the spy's rank is the lowest of the low unless the piece it is attacking is an admiral. If the piece is an admiral, then the row:

```
$attacking_rank = -1 if ($_[1]->type() eq 'admiral');
```

gets evaluated instead and the spy is then all powerful and the admiral is captured.

Summary of Piece's Data Design

The main point to get out of this is to start simple with the data, and then think of worst-case scenarios to flesh out the details. We started with a simple hash as the object, and then looked at two special cases in our problem domain to see whether they would be problems. They were, which forced us to split the rank into two pieces, which we then supplemented with callbacks to provide the functionality we needed.

Special cases, or exceptions to the rule, will always be problematic. That is the reason behind the old 80/20 rule. Eighty percent of the work will take 20 percent of the time. These are the easy cases. On the other hand, 20 percent of the work will take 80 percent of the time. Following are the special cases.

Method Design for Piece Object

Now that we have the data designed, we must deal with the methods that manipulate that data. The secret to successful method design is to think of simple methods first, and then combine these methods to make more complicated things happen.

For example, we have probably isolated three methods: attack(), move(), and promote(). But we shouldn't have to directly implement these methods. Just as bronze is made of copper and tin, our move function is going to be composed of set() and get().

attack() and move() are composite methods. set() and get() are our mutator and accessor methods. They are *simple*.

Let's think of the methods we can have. The bulk of this chapter will be implementing the simple methods, and we will consider implementing the complex ones at the end.

- **new()**—the function that actually creates the object.
- **configure()**—the function that sets low-level data in the subroutine.
- **set()**—the function that sets high-level data and data that is commonly changing in the subroutine.
- **get()**—the function that gets data out of the hash.

These are the low-level functions. We then can define some more functions, such as common things to do with our pieces:

- **store()**—stores pieces to disk.
- **retrieve()**—retrieves pieces from disk.
- **debug()**—prints a helpful trail to debug.
- **copy()**—copies a given piece to another piece.
- **sprintf()**—'pretty prints' our piece, perhaps in something like a piece report.
- **grep()**—looks for an attribute for a given piece.

These are the actions to take in an application. We thus make a small code skeleton and put them all in so we can see how much work we have cut out for ourselves:

```
package Piece;
sub new { }
sub configure { }
sub set { }
sub get { }
sub store { }
sub retrieve { }
sub debug { }
sub copy { }
sub sprintf { }
sub grep { }
```

We are now ready to consider the basic interface issues we are going to face and then start coding.

Summary of Methods

The best design for methods is to keep things simple at first. Try not to rush and think of the actual things that you are going to do at the end, but instead think of the building blocks you will use to get there. You may want to consider only the simple, necessary basics at first. As we shall see, new, `configure`, `set`, and `get` will take us a long way.

Interface Issues

Now that we have our code skeleton, it is time to think of how to fill it. To do that, we think of exactly how we want to use this module. What is the easiest way of doing this?

First, consider the constructor, the function that will create our object. We somehow have to make a viable piece in one function statement, yet it would be a real drag to have to say:

```
my $piece = new Piece(
                        { 'type' => 'bomb', 'attacking_rank' => 'NA',
                          'movement' => '0', 'piece_side' => 'blue'
                          'defending_rank' =>
```

```
                                sub {
                                $defending_rank= -1 unless $_[0]->type()eq 'miner';
                                $defending_rank = 99999 if  $_[0]->type() eq 'miner';
                                return($defending_rank);
                                'xcoord' => 3,
                                'ycoord' => 5
                        }
                );
```

in which we define the whole object then and there on the command line! After all, bombs are always (at least starting out) going to have a movement of zero, a type of bomb, and a special attacking and defending rank.

These details should be handled by the object not the constructor call. Therefore, we simplify the constructor to only including the things that always change, that make sense to be variable.

```
    my $piece = new Piece('bomb', 'blue', 3,5);
```

defines a bomb that is *blue* on the square 3,5. Thus, the constructor is simplified so the client need not worry about it. As far as implementing this constructor, we don't worry how to do it, for now. We simply decide what we would like to use, and then evaluate whether it is easy or not to program.

For configure and set, the easiest way to implement is with something like this:

```
    $piece->configure({'attribute1' => 'this', 'attribute2' => 'that'});
    $piece->set({'attribute1' => 'this', 'attribute2' => 'that'});
```

configure and set, again, will be used to change the object with something like a 'key' => 'value' pair relationship. The preceding code would set attribute1 to this, and attribute2 to that.

By putting all the usage into one hash, rather than saying something like:

```
    $piece->configure('attribute1' => 'this', 'attribute2' => 'that');
```

we free up the other arguments for other uses later.

Remember, we think of usage right now, and then think of how to program it! Most of the time, you can program any interface you want with Perl; sometimes the interfaces are easy, and sometimes they are difficult.

Summary of Interfaces

You need to have an idea of how the interface to your class will look; after that you can start implementing. Usually, I implement top down. I think of how a given object will work from an abstract level, and then work down to actually implement it. In this case, the main goal we have in the interface is to hide all the details of the Piece object from the client, or user of the module. Once we have that down, the interface of the rest of the module should fall into place.

Let's implement each of the public functions given earlier, going in the order in which they appear in the module. We will start with something that is not actually in the class, but is necessary to make the simple interface that we want: class data.

Common Class Data: $_config

The first thing in the object will be a $_config variable. It is a hash reference that contains sensible defaults for the user that can be used to take some of the drudgery out of typing a lot of information. Remember, we want to avoid the horror where the user has to type the following in order to make a 'piece':

```
    my $piece = new Piece(3,5,
                            { 'type' => 'bomb', 'attacking_rank' => 'NA',
```

```
                             'movement' => '0', 'piece_side' => 'blue'
                       'defending_rank' =>
                          sub {
                          $defending_rank= -1 unless $_[0]->type()eq 'miner';
                          $defending_rank = 99999 if  $_[0]->type() eq 'miner';
                          return($defending_rank);
                                }
                  );
```

which creates a piece on the coordinates 3 x 5 of type bomb, with a strength of special and a movement of zero. The special abilities are a code reference (callback) which bombs the ultimate rank (–1, lower being better) unless the attacking piece is a miner (in which case the rank is 99999, and can be disarmed).

What a waste of typing! It is error-prone and way too tiresome. We will probably be defining more than one bomb, so if we force the clients of our module to type all this, we will end up with many bugs.

In this example, we are only going to have one type of bomb. "Bomb-like" behavior is internalized into the class itself. We can say what is shown in Listing 17.1.

Listing 17.1
Piece.pm   (Header and Default config)

```
1      package Piece;
2
3      use strict;
4      use Carp;
5      use Data::Dumper;
6      use FileHandle;
7
8      my $_config =
9              {
10                  'bomb' =>      {      # bomb defaults
11                                       'attacking_rank' => 'NA',
12                                       'movement' => 0,
13                                       'defending_rank' =>
14                                            sub {
15                                   my $defending_rank;
16                              $defending_rank=-1 unless ($_[0]->type() eq 'miner');
17                              $defending_rank =99999 if ($_[0]->type() eq 'miner');
18                                  return($defending_rank);
19                                            }
20
21                                 },
22              'admiral' => {      # admiral defaults
23                                 'attacking_rank' => 1,
24                                    'movement' => 1,
25                                    'defending_rank' => 1
26                                 },
27
28              'scout' =>      {      # scout defaults
29                                 'attacking_rank' => 9,
30                                 'movement' => 100,
31                                 'defending_rank' => 9
32                                 },
```

```
33              'spy'   =>   {    # spy defaults
34                                 'attacking_rank' =>
35                                     sub {
36                   my $attacking_rank;
37                   $attacking_rank = 99999 unless($_[1]->type() eq 'admiral');
38                   $attacking_rank = -1 if ($_[1]->type() eq 'admiral');
39                                          }
40                                 }
41              };
42              my $_pieceNo = 1;      # internal tracking info
43
```

This makes the class more complex, but as a result we get the interface that we want. We can say:

```
my $piece = new Piece('bomb', 'red',3,5);
```

to define a bomb. By adding a configure hash at the end to our original design, we can customize our pieces at the command line. In the unlikely event that we need another type of bomb, as in a bomb that could move, the code could be modified so that a call could be:

```
my $piece = new Piece('bomb','red' ,3,5, { movement => 1 });
```

in which the hash at the end of the constructor supplements the default at top.

Note that we are doing something a bit tricky here. We are defining some of our attributes, defending_rank and attacking_rank, as a code reference, or callback (for the spy and the bomb, lines 14–19, lines 35–39). This is because we can't put a regular value here. The value in some cases depends on the type of the piece that is attacking. This is why we need to make the value dependent. When anything attacks a bomb—except a miner—the bomb is invincible, killing anything (–1 rank). When a miner attacks a bomb he disarms it (the bomb gets a defending rank of 999999).

We thus leave the rank to be figured out at the time when it attacks a piece or defends against attack. This will become important when we write an attack function.

We use the $_config attribute to fill in the object data, detailed next.

Common Object Data: $self->{config}

The $_config defined in the class header is usually used to set object data in the objects themselves. In the object there is usually a statement like the following:

```
$self->{config} = $_config;
```

which copies $_config (or a portion of it) into the object itself. This is usually then modified by the caller of the object, such as:

```
%{$self->{config}} = (%{self->{config}}, $config);
```

in which $config is a variable that comes from the user of the module. This will be seen more clearly when we talk about the new() constructor and the private functions used to validate the configuration data (_validate(), _fill()) discussed next.

Common Object Methods

All we must do now is fill out the meat of the object, namely the methods associated with it. Let's start with the function that will build our object in the first place, the constructor new, and continue downward.

The Constructor: new( )

Based on the data above, the constructor becomes what you see in Listing 17.2.

Listing 17.2
Piece.pm (constructor)

```
44  sub new
45  {
46      my ($type, $piece_type, $piece_side, $xcoord, $ycoord, $config) = @_;
47
48
49      (print(STDERR "Incorrect Args!\n", Carp::longmess()), return(undef))
50                                  if (@_ != 5 && @_ != 6);
51      $config = $config || {};
52      %$config = (%$config,
53
54
55                      );
56      my $self = bless {}, $type;
57      $self->_fill
58              ( piece_side => $piece_side,
59                  { piece_no = $_pieceNo,
60                      'type' => $piece_type,
61                      'xcoord' => $xcoord,
62                      'ycoord' => $ycoord,
63                  },
64                  $config
65              );
66
67      $self->_validate();
68      $self->_recordDebug('after') if ($self->{'debug'} eq 'on');
69                      # retrofitted for function debug() see debug method below.
70      return($self);
71  }
72
```

The idea behind this subroutine is validation. First, the constructor checks that the user has given the correct arguments (lines 49 and 50) and we make a blank $config hash in the case that the user has not defined it. Then, $config is standardized so that it has a default value if the user has not defined it and we add information about what side the piece is on, and its identifier number (line 51).

The object then calls a couple of private functions that will be exceedingly important: _fill() and _validate(). These functions are important enough that they deserve a big side note.

The constructor we listed is short, mainly because of the two functions we defined: _fill() and _validate().Why make such a big fuss over these functions? Because they will make our life much easier.

Many of the bugs in object-oriented programs are because of:

1. Creating an incomplete object
2. Creating an object with incorrect data

Take, for example, an object that accepts a dollar amount as a piece of data, and the code said something like:

```
my $total = $self->{dollar_amount} + _interest($self->{dollar_amount});
```

or suppose there was code that used a filehandle:

```
my $fh = $self->{fh};
```

and you forgot to make the filehandle, or the dollar amount, or the filehandle did not open correctly—the code would blow up.

The _fill() and _validate() functions: make sure the object has all of the information it needs; validate that the user of the object opened everything up correctly, and didn't define the wrong attribute. If, for example, there was no x coordinate or y coordinate, the code would surely blow up somewhere.

This is a conscious design choice. Some programmers do without functions to watch their backs, and instead sprinkle validation into the code itself. I prefer to do validation through functions because it makes the rest of the code clean, and as you will see, we will reuse _fill() and _validate().

For now, we hazily define these as the functions that will actually assign the object's values for us, and then validate that we have a good object. And, in the case of _fill(), we define how the function is going to be called:

1. Argument 1 will consist of all the rapidly changing attributes, such as the piece's coordinates, or attributes that affect other attributes, like the type of the piece, which determines how it moves, attacks, etc. We will use this argument for our set() function.
2. Argument 2 will consist of all the fixed, or slowly changing attributes, like the color of the piece and how the piece attacks. These will be filled in by the $_config hash reference we defined earlier. We will use this argument for our configure() method.

However, we will actually implement them last, because _fill() and _validate() become complicated, and we don't want to have to reimplement them because we overlooked something that they needed to do.

configure()

Once we have created the object, we may want to change it. The first step is to define a configure method, whose job is to change the configuration hash inside the object to be something different. In this case, if we wanted to make a red spy, we could say:

```
my $spy = new Piece('spy','red', 3, 5);
```

which would create a spy on square 3, 5. But if we decided that we wanted this spy to assassinate miners instead of admirals, we could say, afterward:

```
$spy->configure( { 'attacking_rank' =>
                sub {
                      $attacking_rank = 999999 unless($_->type() eq 'miner');
                      $attacking_rank = -1 if ($_->type() eq 'miner');
                      $attacking_rank;
                }
              )
            );
```

which changes the attacking rank of the spy to take out miners instead of admirals. If we wanted to make the spy invincible in attacking everybody, we could:

```
$spy->configure( { 'attacking_rank' => -10 } );
```

which would make the spy able to assassinate even bombs! The configure function is shown in Listing 17.3.

Listing 17.3
configure

```
73
74
75  sub configure
76  {
77      my ($self, $config) = @_;
78
79      $self->_recordDebug('before') if ($self->{'debug'} eq 'on');
80                        # retrofitted for function debug() see debug method below.
81
82      $self->_fill( {}, $config);
83      $self->_validate();
84
85      $self->_recordDebug('after') if ($self->{'debug'} eq 'on');
86  }
```

Now, in this example, the configure method won't be used very frequently, since usually pieces have set attributes that fall into 'types' like bombs or lieutenants. We just include it for completeness. The next function, set(), will be used more.

set()

set() is like configure(), in that it is a mutator method, and used to change an object's data. However, set() is used to change the more common attributes, or to change the higher attributes (like what type of piece it is). For example, the following code:

```
my $obj = new Piece('admiral', 2,1);
$obj->set({xcoord => ($obj->get('xcoord') - 1)} );
```

is an awkward way of making and moving an admiral one step to the left, and:

```
my $obj = new Piece('admiral', 2, 1);
$obj->set( {'type' => 'spy'} );
```

turns a newly created admiral into a spy, giving the admiral all of the spy's attributes. The set() method is shown in Listing 17.4.

Listing 17.4
set()

```
87  sub set
88  {
89      my ($self, $config) = @_;
90
91      $self->_recordDebug('before') if ($self->{'debug'} eq 'on');
```

```
92                        # retrofitted for function debug() see debug method below.
93
94        $self->_fill( $config, {});
95        $self->_validate();
96
97        $self->_recordDebug('after') if ($self->{'debug'} eq 'on');
98                        # retrofitted for function debug() see debug method below.
99   }
```

Again, set is merely a wrapper around _fill() and _validate(). What the user passes in ($config) is directly passed to _fill() and then the results are validated.

Note

Some people dislike having two mutator methods that alter different parts of the object; I like it because you could inadvertently configure the wrong type of attribute. For example, if there were a set method that could do anything, you could inadvertently say:

```
$obj->set({'attack_rank' => 99999 });
```

and not know that attack_rank is something you are not supposed to set very often. Other people like to have a different mutator method for each attribute, something like:

```
$obj->setType('spy');
$obj->setAttackRank(999999);
```

but that seems to be the opposite extreme.

These two mutator methods will be the only ones our object has. We must now define the opposite, the accessor methods, which actually retrieve data for us. We will have one named get().

get()

Accessor methods are extremely important for the object that you are going to write. Since objects in Perl are simply references, the tendency is to say something like:

```
my $obj = new Piece('spy',1,2);
print $obj->{'type'};
```

to directly print out the type of the object. Don't do this! If you want to stay sane, always say:

```
my $obj = new Piece('spy',1,2);
print $obj->get('type');
```

This "extra level of indirection" (given by $obj->get('type')) separates the object from the use of that object, so that the object's programmer is free to change how the object works internally.

The main accessor method for our object will be get(). Unlike the design of mutator functions, I like to have one main accessor method that can get everything, and several, small accessor methods that are specialized to get important things. We have already seen one: $obj->type() gets the type of object $obj. We used it in making a configuration file.

So get() is, as one might expect, the opposite of set(). But it is more generic than set, being able to access everything. The get() method is shown in Listing 17.5.

Listing 17.5
get ( )

```
100  sub get
101  {
102      my ($self, $element) = @_;
103      my $config = $self->{config};
104      if (defined ($self->{$element}))
105      {
106          return($self->{$element});
107      }
108      elsif (defined ($config->{$element}))
109      {
110          return($config->{$element});
111      }
112  }
113
```

Now, even if our object changes and we add more elements either to config or to the hash itself, this function will still work. It is resistant to change. If you can program in general terms like this, avoiding making references to specific elements inside the object, by all means do so. The best bugs are the ones you prevent through careful programming.

Summary of Common Object Methods and Data

These are the four most common methods you will see in objects:

- new ( )—The constructor that actually creates the object.
- configure ( )—A function to configure the more hidden attributes of the object (ones that are usually left alone).
- set ( )—A function to configure the more changeable parts of the object (ones that often change).
- get ( )—A function to get any attribute that the object has (the ones you want the client to see).

These four methods also made great use of two different pieces of data:

- $_config—A piece of class data that sits at the top of the module, defining the most common way that pieces could be set up.
- $self->{config}—A piece of object data used to hold the base attributes of the object, ones that usually weren't for outside consumption.

Now, if that was all there were to programming objects, life would get boring pretty fast. There are an infinite number of methods out there—it's your task to find them—but let's take it to the next level and look at some other common methods.

Somewhat Common Methods

You will find the previous four methods in most any object; they follow the basic principle of most, if not all, object design: *think simple*.

In other words, you can accomplish a lot given only the simplest methods: set ( ), get ( ), configure ( ), and new ( ). Even though these methods represent simple concepts, they are extremely adaptable to many diverse situations. The simpler the method, the more likely you will find it in many objects.

On that note, here are six more common—but not *as* common—methods you will find in many objects; they can make your life extremely easy in the quest for a good interface.

They are: copy(), store(), retrieve(), debug(), sprintf(), and grep(). Once you feel comfortable with the simple methods, try adding them to your classes.

The copy() Method

copy() is used to make an actual, physical copy of an object. We have already seen something like this when we overloaded the equals operator (Chapter 16), saying:

```
use overload '=' => \&copy;
```

This code aliased = to the function copy(), so if you said:

```
my $obj = new Vector();
my $obj2 = new Vector();
$obj2 = $obj;
```

this would copy $obj2 into $obj.

Now, if you are going to copy objects, you will want to create a copy() method. Why? Remember that Perl always makes a reference to an object, and keeps the actual object in memory only to be accessed via that reference. If you say something such as:

```
my $obj = new Vector();
my $obj2 = $obj;
```

where you haven't overloaded =, then you've made a copy of the *reference*, not the data structure itself. And if you say:

```
$obj2->set(1,2,3);
```

to set $obj2 to the coordinate 1,2,3, then you've set $obj as well!

Listing 17.6 is a quick copy method that works on almost 95 percent of all objects. In fact, it will work on any class that is made simply out of data, and also code references. If you are doing fancy things like manipulating things that are not Perl data structures; you can't do this, but if you are dealing with simple data, like we are with our Piece class, this works just fine.

Listing 17.6
copy()

```
114
115 sub copy
116 {
117     my ($self) = @_;
118     my $text = Dumper($self);
119     my $VAR1;
120     eval ("$text");
121     $VAR1->_fill();
122     $VAR1->_validate();
123     return($VAR1);
124 }
```

Think a moment about what this is doing. When you say my $text = Dumper($self); in line 118, you make a string that looks something like:

```
$VAR1 = bless ( {
                ycoord => 1,
```

```
            piece_no => 1
            # ....
       }, 'Piece' );
```

and store it into the variable $text. Then, in line 120, you **eval** it. This creates a valid object of type Piece. Because you are doing a direct assignment, $VAR1 is an exact duplicate of $self. (Well, almost exact.) Since _fill() is purely vaporware anyway, we sweep another couple of issues into our _fill() function, which is probably by now becoming a little complicated. This was as anticipated, so this is OK (I guess).

The store() Method

Another common thing you are going to want to do in Perl object-oriented programming is store objects to memory. This is called making the object *persistent*, which means that the object stays around after the program itself is gone.

In our case, we can get the same 95 percent solution by, again, using the **Data::Dumper** module, and then sweeping the issues about restoring the module under _fill() and _validate(). Listing 17.7 shows our store() method.

Listing 17.7
store()

```
125
126 sub store
127 {
128     my ($self, $filename) = @_;
129
130     my $fh = new FileHandle("> $filename")
131         || (print(STDERR "Couldn't open $filename for writing!\n"), return());
132
133     print $fh Dumper($self);
134     close($fh);
135 }
136
```

This works by using the **Data::Dumper** trick, but this time we store everything to a provided file. When we retrieve the object, it won't be perfect, and some holes will be there. To use this method, say something like:

```
my $obj = new Piece('spy',1,2);
$obj->store('filename');
```

There are some other object storing packages on CPAN you can use as well. **FreezeThaw** is one, and **ObjectStore** is another. (If you are lucky enough to have **ObjectStore**, the object-oriented database management system, you cannot only store and restore your objects in Perl, but restore them in C++ and Java as well. **ObjectStore** will also allow you to store C++ and Java objects, and retrieve them in Perl.)

The retrieve() Method

We now have to make a complementary function to store(), a retrieve() method, which works to retrieve the stored function from disk.

Because retrieve actually creates an object out of a file, we implement it as another constructor. Instead of saying:

```
my $piece = new Piece(.....);
```

we say

```
my $piece = retrieve Piece("mypiece");
```

where mypiece is the name of a file that has been created under store(), and $piece becomes a blessed, piece reference.

_fill() and _validate() are again used to fill in some holes in the object (which I will talk about soon). Listing 17.8 shows our retrieval function.

Listing 17.8
retrieve()

```
137 sub retrieve
138 {
139     my ($type, $filename) = @_;
140
141     my $self = {};
142     my $fh = new FileHandle("$filename")
143             || (print("Couldn't open $filename for writing!\n"), return());
144
145
146     local($/) = undef;
147     my $text = <$fh>;
148     my $VAR1;
149     close($fh);
150     eval("$text");
151
152     $self = $VAR1;
153     $self->_fill({},{});
154
155     $self->_recordDebug('after') if ($self->{'debug'} eq 'on');
156     $self->_validate();
157     $self;
158 }
```

We could therefore say:

```
my $obj = new Piece ('bomb', 'white', 0,0)
$obj->store('file');
my $obj2 = retrieve Piece('file');
```

to do a roundabout copy of $obj into $obj2.

The debug() Method

debug() isn't strictly a method, but more of a practice. You can easily debug by putting in a bunch of printf statements. You can also implement debug as a flag, saying something such as:

```
my $obj = new Piece('miner','red', 0,0, { 'debug' => 1 });
```

However, sometimes you want something more permanent than this. The idea behind debug is to leave a trace of important information so that you can find out what is going on if there is an error later.

If you implement debug as a flag, it usually prints out everything: function entry, exit, etc. This is one way to implement a trace. You can also say something such as:

```
my $obj = new Piece('miner', 0,0);
$obj->debug('on');
## do stuff ###
$obj->debug('off');
```

with the idea that, when you are doing stuff like this, you are saving everything you have done to a "debug" member of the object. For instance (Listing 17.9):

Listing 17.9
debug()

```
159
160 sub debug
161 {
162     my ($self, $type) = @_;
163
164     if ($type eq 'off') { $self->{'debug'} = 'off'; }
165     elsif ($type eq 'on')  { $self->{'debug'} = 'on';  }
166     else { print "IMPROPER DEBUG CALL $type\n"; }
167 }
```

To make this work, we must retrofit every one of our methods already developed, putting in a function call at the beginnings and endings. However, if you look at the methods that we already implemented, notice that we were being real sneaky again and already did this with a function called _recordDebug().

For example, we retrofitted set as shown in Listing 17.10.

Listing 17.10
set() retrofitted

```
167 sub set
168 {
169     my ($self, $config) = @_;
170
171     $self->_recordDebug('before') if ($self->{'debug'} eq 'on');
172
173     $self->_fill( $config, {});
174     $self->_validate( $config, {});
175
176     $self->_recordDebug('after') if ($self->{'debug'} eq 'on');
177 }
```

_recordDebug() is a private method used to save what the object looked like when the method was entered, and when the method was left. It also saves which method called which method. It looks like what is shown in Listing 17.11.

Listing 17.11
recordDebug()

```
168 sub _recordDebug
169 {
170     my ($self, $flag) = @_;
171
172     my $debugstuff = $self->{'debug'};
173     my $no = @$debugstuff;
```

```
174
175     if ($flag eq 'before')
176     {
177         $debugstuff->[$no][0] = "Before: \n" . Carp::longmess();
178         $debugstuff->[$no][1] = Dumper($self);
179     }
180     elsif ($flag eq 'after')
181     {
182         $debugstuff->[$no-1][2] = "After: \n" . Carp::longmess();
183         $debugstuff->[$no-1][3] = Dumper($self);
184     }
185 }
```

Now, all we have to do is print out the debug as follows:

```
my $obj = new Piece('miner', 0,0);
$obj->debug('on');
## do stuff ###
$obj->debug('off');
my $debugstuff = $obj->get('debug');
print Dumper($debugstuff);
```

and we can get a direct trace of exactly what is going on in our Piece object, albeit in gory detail. In fact, it might be too detailed. We may want to replace our _recordDebug() function with what is shown in Listing 17.12.

Listing 17.12
recordDebug()

```
sub _recordDebug
{
    my ($self, $flag) = @_;

    my $debugstuff = $self->{'debugstuff'};
    my $no = @$debugstuff;

    if ($flag eq 'before')
    {
        $debugstuff->[$no][0] = "Called By:\n" . Carp::longmess();
        $oldself = $self->copy();
    }
    elsif ($flag eq 'after')
    {
        $oldself->{'debugstuff'} = undef;
        my $newself = $self->copy();
        $newself->{'debugstuff'} = undef;
        $debugstuff->[$no-1][1] = "After: ". Diff::checkData($self, $oldself);
    }
}
```

Note that we are reusing both the copy method we developed earlier, and the Diff::checkData function that we developed in Chapter 15. This lets us see exactly which elements of the Piece object changed, which may speed up our bug tracking time quite a bit.

The *sprintf()* Method

sprintf() performs exactly like its Perl-ish equivalent. It prints out to a formatted string some or all of the information contained in an object. Unlike debug(), it "prettifies" its output for the purpose of being printed out, or being used in the program itself. We may, for example, want to make a summary of all the pieces on the map. It may look something like:

```
Piece #1: Admiral      Coordinates # X = 4   Y = 5
Piece #2: Spy           Coordinates # X = 1   Y = 2
```

and so forth. sprintf() is often quite easy to implement, since it usually is a simple wrapper around a bunch of native Perl sprintf() calls.

Listing 17.13 is sprintf for our Piece class.

Listing 17.13
sprintf()

```
186
187 sub sprintf
188 {
189
190     my ($self) = @_;
191     return(sprintf("Piece #%.3d: %.15s      Coordinates # X = %.3d   Y = %.3d\n"));
192 }
193
```

Now we say:

```
my $piece = new Piece('miner', 2,4);
my $text = $piece->sprintf();
```

$text will contain the required text, looking something like:

```
Piece #1: miner         Coordinates # X = 2   Y = 4
```

You can then use this text in any reporting function you like.

The *grep()* Method

One more example of a somewhat common method is grep(). grep() is a very successful function inside Perl. Why not make it work for objects?

Suppose you want to make a list of bombs. Well, you could define a function:

```
$obj->isBomb();
```

and in an array of Pieces you could say something like:

```
foreach $piece (@pieces)
{
    push (@stack, $piece) if $piece->isBomb();
}
```

but this seems kludgey, because you often want your criteria to be more complicated than simple things like this.

This is the perfect place for grep. You could rewrite the preceding foreach loop like:

```
foreach $piece (@pieces)
{
    push(@stack, $piece) if ($piece->grep(sub { $_[0]->type() eq 'bomb' }));
}
```

Here, grep takes another callback in the first position, and then executes it on the object $piece to return back whether or not $piece is of type bomb. In this case, it is not that much of an improvement, and you could get the same results by saying:

```
foreach $piece (@pieces)
{
    push (@stack, $piece) if ($piece->type() eq 'bomb');
}
```

but to tell you the truth, we can't make an effective demonstration of grep simply because the Piece example is too small. But we will put it to good use later, because grep can take any subroutine that Perl can muster, whereas an if clause cannot.

Listing 17.14 is Piece's version of grep().

Listing 17.14
grep()

```
194 sub grep
195 {
196     my ($self, $callback) = @_;
197
198     return (&$callback($self));
199 }
200
```

You can take this code and adapt it for your particular situation.

Summary of Somewhat Common Methods

The following six functions complement the most common methods quite well.

- copy()—Copies an object because Perl uses references to store objects.
- store()—Stores an object to disk. Relevant modules for this are **Data::Dumper**, **FreezeThaw**, and **ObjectStore** (which is not included on the accompanying CD because it is platform-specific). **Data::Dumper's** usage was shown before.
- retrieve()—Does the opposite of store() and gets modules back from disk.
- debug()—Stores debug information in the object so we can retrieve it later.
- sprintf()—Prints the object into a scalar so we can use it later in some sort of method.
- grep()—Returns whether or not a given object has a certain characteristic; used with code references.

As a last point, any one of these methods can have a class equivalent. Hence, we can say

```
my @bomblist = Piece::grep( sub { $_[0]->type() eq 'bomb } );
```

with the understanding that Piece has (registered) a list of pieces that have been constructed.

Common Private Methods

There are two common private methods that come up again and again. They are listed last because you usually write them last since they support pretty much all of the methods above, and each one of the methods above have a "common assumption" that these two methods are going to work.

Because they support most all the methods in the class, they tend to get complicated. They do much of the verifying that what the user entered is correct, and shuffle bits of data around inside the object. These methods are _fill() and _validate(). Although we used them up in other code, we implement them now. To understand _fill() and _validate(), we need to take a moment and describe *persistence*.

Perl and Persistence: The "Data Structure Copy" Example

We alluded to holes in the code several times in the preceding sections. In the copy() and retrieve() functions we used $self->_fill() and $self->_validate(). One might think that because **Data::Dumper** dumps out any Perl data structure, that our copy() function would be as simple as:

```
my $text = Dumper($self);
my $VAL1;
eval("$text");
return($VAL1);
```

where eval creates the object $VAL1 which is a direct copy of $self, and return() returns it to the main routine.

Alas, the copy() and retrieve() functions are not this simple. Unfortunately for us, at this point, Perl does not "keep around" the text of the code that it keeps in code references. Test this yourself. If you say:

```
my $a = { 'a' => sub { print "HERE!\n" } };
```

and then say:

```
print Dumper($a);
```

you will get text that looks like:

```
$VAR1 = {
           a => sub { "DUMMY" }
        };
```

What happened is that the text of the code went away, becoming an internal thing to Perl that looks like:

```
CODE(0xafe5c)
```

which you may recognize as a reference to code.

Thus, there are two elements that lose their value when your code exits:

1. Code references and the like.
2. Elements outside of Perl's domain, such as database handles.

These two things are the challenges that persistent programming offers us. Note that if we didn't use code references, our copy(), store(), and retrieve() functions would be much simpler.

In this case, we use the _fill() function to fill in the gap, which we talk about next.

_fill()

fill's job is to make an object that is reasonable from the rest of the class's point of view. We saw fill in many places: the constructors new() and restore(), and inside the copy() and set() functions.

Here it is, implemented to work with all of these methods.

The fact that it is so complicated is a good and bad thing: bad because complexity is generally unmaintainable, but good because all the complexity is in 'one place'. In practice, methods like this are constructed via iteration; you start out simple, and then add things as you go. Anyway, the result is shown in Listing 17.15.

Listing 17.15
Piece.pm (_fill())

```
201 sub _fill
202 {
203     my ($self, $elemhash, $config) =@_;
204     $self->{'debugstuff'} = $self->{'debugstuff'} || [];
205     $elemhash = $elemhash || {};
206     $config   = $config   || {};
207     my $status = 0;
208     $status += _returnIfWrongTypeandDefined($elemhash, 'argument 1', 'HASH');
209     $status += _returnIfWrongTypeandDefined($config,   'argument 2', 'HASH');
210
211     return(undef) if ($status > 0);
212
213     %$self = (%$self, %$elemhash);
214
215     my $piece_type = $elemhash->{'type'} || $self->{'type'} ||
216             print(STDERR "Couldn't get a piece type!\n", Carp::longmess());
217
218     my $default_config = $_config->{$piece_type} || {};
219     if (!defined ($self->{'config'}) || defined ($elemhash->{'type'}))
220     {
221         %{$self->{'config'}} = %{$default_config};
222     }
223     else
224     {
225         my $key;
226         foreach $key (keys(%$default_config))
227         {
228             if (!defined $self->{'config'}->{$key}
229                         || $self->{'config'}->{$key} =~ m"CODE")
230             {
231                 $self->{'config'}->{$key} = $default_config->{$key};
232             }
233         }
234     }
235
236     if (ref($config) eq 'HASH')
237     {
238         %{$self->{'config'}} = (%{$self->{'config'}}, %$config);
239     }
240
241
242
243 }
```

Now let's take this very slow. There are three major areas to this function:

1. Type checking and default setting: Lines 204–206 set arguments that the user hasn't entered. The effect of line 206:

    ```
    $config = $config || {};
    ```

    is to ensure that `$config` gets at least an empty hash reference. The fancifully named private function `_returnIfWrongTypeandDefined()` in lines 208 and 209 is responsible for finding out if the user has entered in the right types to the `_fill()` function. If the user entered something other than a hash reference, this returns a 1. However, it also lets the user enter in something like:

    ```
    $self->_fill();
    ```

    without any arguments for convenience's sake. If the user enters *something*, but that something is not a hash reference, then

    ```
    return(undef) if ($status > 0);
    ```

    will short-circuit the function before continuing.

2. Filling commonly accessed object elements: Now remember, in our design, there were two possible hashes that you could pass to `_fill()`. Lines 213–222 deal with the assignment of the elements which are the most common. Line 213:

    ```
    %$self = (%$self, %$elemhash);
    ```

    is a common pattern you will see. It says, basically, "set all of `%$self`'s elements that are in `%$elemhash`, overriding the values that are already there." If you started with a hash that looked like:

    ```
    $self == { 1 => 2, 2 => 3};
    ```

    and then said

    ```
    %$self = (%$self, {1 => 4, 3 => 2});
    ```

    you would end up with a hash that looked like:

    ```
    $self == { 1 => 4, 2 => 3, 3 => 2 };
    ```

    in which the `3 => 2` was appended and `1 => 4` replaced `1 => 2`. This statement handles most of the common cases. However, there is one special case we need to take care of. Suppose we say:

    ```
    $self->_fill({'type' => 'spy' }, {});
    ```

    If we make a piece a different type, then that piece has to copy all the attributes that the new piece type has. We do this in lines 218–223 . If `$elemhash->{'type'}` is defined, we override `$self->{'config'}` to be:

    ```
    %{$self->{'config'}} = %{$_config->{$elemhash->{'type'}}};
    ```

    and this gives the piece the proper elements.

3. Filling in the configuration hash: The rest of the hash is dedicated to the second form of _fill() in which you say:

    ```
    $self->_fill({}, $configure);
    ```

    where `configure`, as you may remember, is infrequently set attributes like movement and xcoord. In this case, we have the problem of holes in the data set. If you say:

```
        my $piece2 = $piece->copy();
```

and `$piece` has any code references in it at all, then they will get dropped on the floor. The code snippet:

```
226             foreach $key (keys(%$default_config))
227             {
228                 if (!defined $self->{'config'}->{$key}
229                         || $self->{'config'}->{$key} =~ m"CODE")
230                 {
231                     $self->{'config'}->{$key} = $default_config->{$key};
232                 }
233             }
```

prevents this from occurring. It looks for code references (`$self->{'config'}->{$key} =~ m"CODE"`) and assumes they are bad, replacing them with a good code reference in line 231.

Whew! This might be a good place for inheritance to take some of the complexity out of our function. Maybe. We shall consider using inheritance to simplify the interface here when we get to inheritance (Chapter 20).

All that's left now is having to write our supporting private routine `_returnIfWrongTypeandDefined`:

```
244
245 sub _returnIfWrongTypeandDefined
246 {
247     my ($element, $stuff, $type) = @_;
248
249     if (ref($element) eq $type || !defined($element))
250     {
251         return(0);
252     }
253     else
254     {
255         print(STDERR "$stuff has to be of type $type\n", Carp::longmess());
256         return(1);
257     }
258 }
259 1;
```

which is fairly straightforward, if awkwardly named. It would be a good idea.

Because these "behind the curtain" methods can get so complicated, you may, at first, postpone implementing a `_fill()` method, and instead let the object grow naturally by spreading bits and pieces of `_fill()` throughout the code. Then, when you are ready, take all these pieces and consolidate them into one function. This is twice as much work as being up front about it, but it is a good learning exercise.

_validate()

validate's job is to make sure that `fill` has done its job: to take the object that has been created and make sure that no unknown pieces of information enter into it. Validation methods are often ignored, but you will save a lot of time in the useful life of your class if you are up front about implementing them.

Like _fill(), _validate() tends to become complicated quickly, with a little bit of fancy footwork to implement. Listing 17.16 shows the _validate() method for our Piece class.

The Common Object

Listing 17.16
Piece.pm (_validate())

```
260 sub _validate
261 {
262     my ($self) = @_;
263
264
265     my $type = $self->{'type'};
266     my $config = $self->{'config'};
267     my @errors;
268
269     push (@errors, "Bad piece type :$type:!\n")
270         if (!defined ($_config->{$type}));
271
272     my ($key) = '';
273     my $typeconfig = $_config->{$type} || {};
274
275     foreach $key (keys %$config)
276     {
277         push (@errors, "invalid key :$key:!\n")
278             if (!defined ($typeconfig->{$key}));
279     }
280     print (STDERR @errors, Carp::longmess()) if (@errors);
281 }
282
```

There is an error stack here that keeps track of all the inconsistencies found in $self->{'config'}. Since $_config contains what should be in a correct object, all we have to do is make sure that each element in $self->{'config'} is also in $_config. We do this in lines 275–279:

```
foreach $key (keys %$config)
{
    push (@errors,... if (!defined ($typeconfig->{$key}));
}
```

keeping this error stack handy in case our object has more than one problem. In line 280 we then print out all of the accumulated errors along with a stack trace (Carp::longmess()).

Again, this is becoming a bit complicated, and you may want to spread your validations throughout the code instead, and consolidate them into a _validate() function later.

Summary of Common Private Methods

In general, all the stuff that you are doing internal to the module and that is done in more than one place should be consolidated into a private method for your objects to call. In general, put a _ in front of every private method you have (saying "hands off") and proceed to call them as you would normal methods.

The _fill() and _validate() methods are particularly common in modules, but there are a whole slough of private methods. In fact, in many modules, there are more private methods than ones available to the outside world.

Private methods tend to use less generic names than public methods. Some are named _execCode() and _isaFlag(), and you can usually recognize them because they do less generic operations than do public methods.

If you find that you are calling these private methods over and over again, make them public. After all, Perl isn't imposing the private boundaries for you: You are.

Using the Object and Composite Methods

OK, a couple more notes. It would not be fair if we didn't give an idea of how this module would be used. Since we haven't defined the OO structure of the game itself, it is hard to get too detailed, but we can give you an idea of some tests, and some code which we would use the Piece class. And here are a couple of 'composite' methods which we might define.

Here's a couple of snippets.

Pseudocode for Testing Pieces

The following code:

```perl
my @pieces = ();
while (chop($line = <STDIN>))
{
      my ($type, $xcoord, $ycoord) = split(/:/, $line);
      push (@pieces, new Piece($type, $xcoord, $ycoord);
}
```

tests the constructor, giving a list of pieces in @pieces given by typing on the command line.

```perl
And:
foreach $piece (@pieces)
{
      print $piece->sprintf($piece);
}
```

prints out all the configuration information for the pieces that have been created.

We really should go ahead and define a couple of the Piece-specific functions, such as move() and attack(). Let's do that for the sake of showing how it is done. We have defined some basic methods, and attack() and move() should merely be composites of the simple methods.

The move() Method

Just like blue and yellow form green, get() and set() form move. Listing 17.17 shows our move() method.

Listing 17.17
Piece.pm (move())

```perl
283 sub move
284 {
285     my ($self, $newxcoord, $newycoord) = @_;
286
287     my $xcoord = $self->get('xcoord');
288     my $ycoord = $self->get('ycoord');
289     my $movement = $self->get('movement');
290
291     my $xval = abs($newxcoord - $xcoord);
292     my $yval = abs($newycoord - $ycoord);
293
```

```
294      (print(STDERR "Cannot move to $newxcoord $newycoord\n"), return(undef))
295                              if ($yval > 0 && $xval > 0);
296
297      if (($xval <= $movement) && ($yval <= $movement))
298      {
299          $self->set( { 'xcoord' => $newxcoord });
300          $self->set( { 'ycoord' => $newycoord });
301      }
302      else
303      {
304      print(STDERR "Cannot move to $newxcoord $newycoord!Too far!\n");
305      return(undef);
305      }
306 }
```

Here, we assume that the x coordinate and y coordinate will be entered in the function call, and then we go through some calculations (lines 287–295) to figure out if where we are moving is at a right angle.

If it is, then we check whether the movement attribute is greater than how far we are to move (line 297). If we can legally move, then go ahead and set the new attributes. Otherwise, return an error.

The attack() Function

Finally, here is the attack function. It uses those code references that complicated the design so much:

```
307 sub attack
308 {
309      my ($self, $enemy) = @_;
310
311      my $attack_rank  = $self->get('attacking_rank');
312      my $defend_rank  = $enemy->get('defending_rank');
313
314      if (ref($attack_rank) eq 'CODE')
315      {
316          $attack_rank = &$attack_rank($self, $enemy);
317      }
318      if (ref($defend_rank) eq 'CODE')
319      {
320          $defend_rank = &$defend_rank($self, $enemy);
321      }
322      return("CAPTURED!") if ($defend_rank < $attack_rank);
323      return("VICTORIOUS!") if ($attack_rank < $defend_rank);
324      return("STALEMATE!") if ($attack_rank == $defend_rank);
325 }
```

In other words, both $self and $enemy are Piece references; we call get() on both to get their attacking defending rank, respectively. Here comes the tricky part.

If the attacking or defending rank is a code reference, this indicates that we are going to use the code reference to find out what the rank is. Hence line 314 to line 318. The call:

```
$defend_rank = &$defend_rank($self, $enemy);
```

is one that you probably couldn't do in any other language (at least that I know of). It calls the code reference that is $defend_rank, using the Piece references $self and $enemy as arguments. As soon as it gets a result, the $defend_rank ceases to be a code reference, and becomes a number instead.

We then compare the numbers to get a result, which we return (either `CAPTURED!`, `VICTORIOUS!`, or `STALEMATE!`).

Summary

If we were to really implement this object, of course, this code would need more modifications. First, there is no provision for two pieces not occupying the same square. A board object might be in order to be a traffic handler.

Second, we would probably want move() and attack() to be linked in some way, so that when the pieces move into a square, they automatically attack any pieces that may be there. Again, a board object might be in order here.

Anyway, for now, this is it for the sample object. In Chapter 18, we'll take this object a step further, and consider both of the first design decisions we are going to have to face: whether to make what we program a module or an object, and good ways of turning procedural code into objects.

18

Turning Old Code into Object Code

This chapter takes the next big step in the process of learning object-oriented programming. First, we went over the syntax of how Perl objects work (Chapter 16). Then we went over a mock class, in which we implemented a fundamental class (the Piece class) for the game Strategem, and saw some of the common methods that are in objects.

Now it's time to look at your own code to see how much of it should become modules and objects, and how much should be left alone. If you are just starting to learn Perl, this chapter will help you dig into somebody else's code that you may need to maintain.

Chapter Overview

This chapter is divided into two sections. We will consider some simple decisions you will have to make. The primary design decision that anybody faces when doing object-oriented programming is:

To decide whether or not the overhead of making an object is worth the flexibility it gives you.

We will talk about this overhead, consider three different cases, go through the pros and cons for object versus module, and then implement what we decide is the best choice.

We will also consider making a scavenger hunt through old code, to search for objects. We will consider the **ftp.p** and **expect.p** scripts we have written, and dig through these to unearth any objects we can find. Then, we will rewrite **expect.p** in an object-oriented way to see what it buys us.

The emphasis here will be on examples. There is much work to do here so let's get going! The first step is to look at the module versus object design decision that all object-oriented programmers must make.

Design Decision: Modules versus Objects

Modules versus objects is the first decision to make when you are planning your code. The syntax for objects and for modules is a bit different. The mindset for modular programming and object-oriented programming is different too: modular programming seems to be easier for most people to grasp.

So we need to recognize the benefits and drawbacks of each approach. Since modular programming is the easier one, we start with it.

Modular Programming Features

Modular programming is the process of taking subroutines out of code and centralizing them into a separate place, the package.

In Perl, these packages are named **.pm** files; the function to include them is called use; and they are included via the @INC variable, which searches the disk to include them. But these principles are much the same for any computer language; here, they just come under different guises.

The concept of gathering subroutines together into packages is very powerful, but notice that it does not deal with any issues associated with data. There is a distinction between:

1. The functions in the module themselves
2. The data the functions take as arguments

For example, suppose that you were writing a **Vector** module, and defined the functions shown in Listing 18.1.

Listing 18.1
VectorModule.pm

```
1   package VectorModule;
2   sub add
3   {
4       my ($firstvec, $secondvec) = @_;
5       my $returnvec = [];
6       my $element;
7       die "You cannot add vectors of differing lengths!\n"
8                                   if (@$firstvec != @$secondvec);
9       for ($element = 0; $element <= @$firstvec; $element++)
10      {
11          $returnvec->[$element]
12                  = $firstvec->[$element] + $secondvec->[$element];
13      }
14      $returnvec;
15  }
16
17  sub subtract
18  {
19      my ($firstvec, $secondvec) = @_;
```

```
20   my $returnvec = [];
21   my $element;
22   die "You cannot subtract vectors of differing lengths!\n"
23                                      if (@$firstvec != @$secondvec);
24   for ($element = 0; $element <= @$firstvec; $element++)
25   {
26       $returnvec->[$element]
27                = $firstvec->[$element] - $secondvec->[$element];
28   }
29   $returnvec;
30 }
```

Note that the data ($firstvec, $secondvec, $returnvec) is separate from the functions (add, sub-tract). To use this module, you would say something like what is shown in Listing 18.2.

Listing 18.2
use_vecmodule.p

```
1  use VectorModule;
2  my $vec1 = [0,0,0];
3  my $vec2 = [0,1,2];
4  my $vec3 = VectorModule::add($vec1, $vec2);
```

$vec1 and $vec2 are defined by the client, and $vec3 is returned by the module. This separation between data and functions is the limiting factor in scaling up modular code. This is because if you change the module to use a different representation for vectors, then the underlying code you use in the clients will break.

The clients that use the module will still be representing the vector in an "old way," and will not work with the new representation inside the module. This means that you will need to change the module and all clients that use it. This is the flaw that object-oriented programming overcomes.

Object-Oriented Programming and Encapsulation

The great advance in object-oriented programming is that it eliminates the separation between data and functions. A capsule definition of object-oriented programming could be as follows:

Object-oriented programming is the process of taking modules, and the data these modules use in their inter-face, and stuffing that data inside the module so that multiple copies of that module can exist.

Another term for this is *encapsulation*. The definition is as follows:

Encapsulation is the process of taking functions and associated data, and "packing" them in objects so that the internal structure of the object can change without needing to change all of the clients that use it.

The main difference between objects and modules is that:

- *Modules* are packs of functions, whose functionality can be reused effectively.
- *Objects* are packs of functions combined with their own private bits of data.

To illustrate this point, let's rewrite the **VectorModule** function as an object (Listing 18.3).

Listing 18.3
VectorObject.pm

```
1  package VectorObject;
2
3  use overload '+' => \&add, '-' => \&subtract;
4  sub new
5  {
```

```
 6        my ($type, @elements) = @_;
 7        my $self = {};
 8        $self->{elements} = \@elements;
 9        bless $self, $type;
10  }
11
12  sub length
13  {
14        my ($self) = @_;
15        my $elements = $self->{elements};
16        my $length = @$elements;
17        return($length);
18  }
19
20  sub add
21  {
22      my ($self, $other) = @_;
23
24      my ($element, $returnelem) = ('', []);
25
26      my ($elements1, $elements2) =
27                          ( $self->{elements}, $other->{elements});
28
29      die "You cannot add vectors of differing lengths!\n"
30                                  if ($other->length() != $self->length())
31
32      for ($element = 0; $element <= $self->length(); $element++)
33      {
34            $returnelem->[$element] =
35                        $elements1->[$element] + $elements2->[$element]
36      }
37      return (new VectorObject(@$returnelem));
38  }
39  sub subtract
40  {
41      my ($self, $other) = @_;
42
43      my $element;
44      my ($elements1, $elements2) =
45                          ( $self->{elements}, $other->{elements});
46
47      die "You cannot subtract vectors of differing lengths!\n"
48                                  if ($other->length() != $self->length())
49
50      for ($element = 0; $element <= $self->length(); $element++)
51      {
52            $returnelem->[$element] =
53                        $elements1->[$element] - $elements2->[$element]
54      }
55      return(new VectorObject(@$returnelem));
56  }
```

Now, forget about the code for a second, and concentrate on the *interface*, how people will use the code. With the module, if you wanted to add two vectors together, you would say something like what is shown in Listing 18.4.

Listing 18.4
use_vecmodule.p

```
1 use VectorModule;
2 my $vec1 = [0,0,0];
3 my $vec2 = [0,1,2];
4 my $vec3 = VectorModule::add($vec1, $vec2);
```

and, after this addition, you would get the new vector (an array reference) inside $vec3.

With the object, however, if you wanted to add two vectors together, you would say something like what is shown in Listing 18.5.

Listing 18.5
use_vecobject.p

```
1 use VectorObject;
2 my $vec = new VectorObject(0,0,0);
3 my $vec2 = new VectorObject(0,1,2);
4 my $vec3 = $vec->add($vec2);
```

Or if you wanted to use the overloading we provided, you would do something like what is shown in Listing 18.6.

Listing 18.6
use_vecobject2.p

```
1 use VectorObject;
2 my $vec  = new VectorObject(0,0,0);
3 my $vec2 = new VectorObject(0,1,2);
4 my $vec3 = $vec + $vec2;
```

This is a lot of coding for such a small change in syntax! What exactly have we gained from the additional expense of 26 extra lines of code, and two extra functions?

The main thing we have gained is the encapsulation of the data (the addition of the data to the package). In particular, notice that:

```
my $vec = [0,0,0];
```

directly sets what the vector is, and what the data is inside the vector. Whereas:

```
my $vec = new VectorObject(0,0,0);
```

has a function call surrounding the creation of the vector. This function call removes the responsibility of knowing what actually makes a vector. In the first case, we can see that it is an array reference. In the second, we don't need to know.

Because only the creator of the module needs to know how the object is implemented, he or she can change it at will, provided the interface preserves "backward compatibility." For example, if we wanted to add an element that shows the distance of that element from the origin (0,0,0...), we could change the new function like so:

```
1  sub new
2  {
3       my ($type, @elements) = @_;
4       my $self = {};
5       foreach (@elements) { $self->{distance} += $_ ** 2; }
5       $self->{elements} = \@elements;
6       bless $self, $type;
7  }
```

In the module version, there would be no clean way to add this to the data structure. We could change it so that our functions add and subtract take the following data structures:

```
use VectorModule;
my ($vec) =
    {
        distance => VectorModule::getDistance([0,1,2]),
        elements => [0,1,2]
    }
my ($vec2) =
    {
        distance => VectorModule::getDistance([0,0,0]),
        elements => [0,0,0]
    }
my $vec3 = VectorModule::add($vec, $vec2);
```

in which the boldface hash references are the data structures that we pass to `VectorModule::add()`. Now, this does exactly the same thing, only not as clearly.

But more importantly, it does it in the client, and this is exactly the point. It is more difficult to change the code that uses the module (the client) than it is to change the module itself (the server).

After all, you actually use your module/class in clients many times, but you code the module/class once. Think of object-oriented programming and modular programming as basically putting all your eggs in one basket: coding the functionality you need one time, and then guarding that functionality with care so that existing clients that use that code don't have to change.

The difference between the two is that sometimes it makes sense to make your baskets contain only functions (in the case of modules) and sometimes contain functions with their own data (in the case of objects).

Choosing Between Object and Module

So, how do you choose between a module and an object? This is the first design decision you make when tackling a problem. Let's consider three separate examples to illustrate the choices between object and module:

1.   **Diff**—getting the difference between two data structures.
2.   **PathNames**—turning path names from absolute to relative, and vice versa.
3.   **LogFile**—creating a log file with a certain format.

One very prudent approach is to always prefer objects over modules, because objects are more flexible and extendable than modules (a module is simply an object with no data in it). However, you may want to consider other approaches.

One reason is that objects, although more flexible and extendable than modules, are also more complicated. Just look at our **Vector** example. The physical differences between the two:

1.   The `VectorObject` had 26 more lines of code than the `VectorModule`.
2.   The `VectorObject` had 2 more functions than the `VectorModule`.
3.   The `VectorObject` had 3 more variables than the `VectorModule`.

This is a cost associated with the use of objects in maintenance, programming, and complexity. Objects also have a cost in ease of usage and performance.

However, if you find that you in fact need a class when you have a module instead, you may not find it that easy to backtrack. This is especially true the more complicated your modules get. If you someday decide that you need two or more of the same module working concurrently, you will be able to hack your way through (Perl is great at that!) but it will not be much fun to do this hacking. Therefore, the decision isn't an easy one to make.

Let's look at the three different problems in which you might be called on to make such a decision.

Example 1: `Diff` Revisited

One of the most common tasks of a Perl programmer is finding differences. It might be finding differences in arrays and hashes, in anonymous data structures, or in tables, indexes, directory structures, and so forth.

In fact, we have already started such a "Diff" code repository. In Chapter 15 we made a **Diff** module. The two functions defined were:

- checkEq();
- checkData();

These functions were designed to look at two arbitrary data structures, check to see if they were equal, and return a structure with the difference between the two.

You may have a situation in which you would want to extend this functionality. Let's consider a function that returns the difference between two arrays (Listing 18.7).

Listing 18.7
Diff.pm

```
1   package Diff;
2
3   # Other subs checkData, checkEq, etc.
4
5   sub array
6   {
7       my ($ref1, $ref2) = @_;
8       my (%MARK1, %MARK2,%MARKTOTAL);
9       my $returnRef = [];
10      die "Need to pass two array references!\n"
11              if ((ref($ref1) ne 'ARRAY') || (ref($ref2) ne 'ARRAY'));
12      foreach (@$ref1) { $MARK1{$_} = 1; }
13      foreach (@$ref2) { $MARK2{$_} = 1; }
14      %MARKTOTAL = (%MARK1, %MARK2);
15      foreach (sort keys(%MARKTOTAL))
16      {
17          if (!defined($MARK1{$_}) || !defined ($MARK2{$_}))
18          {
19              push (@$returnRef, $_);
20          }
21      }
22  return($returnRef);
23  }
```

Given this type of code, you then could call this function via:

```
use Diff;
my ($ref1, $ref2) = ([1,2,3,4,6], [4,3,2,1,5]);
my $ref3 = Diff::array($ref1, $ref2);
```

which would make $ref3 equal to [5,6] because 5 and 6 are the only differences between the two array references.

Now, the question is whether this should be a module or an object. Let's look at the same client code, only coded as an object:

```
use Array;
my ($ref1, $ref2) = (new Array(1,2,3,4,6), new Array(4,3,2,1,5));
my  $ref3 = $ref1->diff($ref2);
```

Here, we make `Array` a "first class object," meaning that we would go through the `Array` object methods to manipulate the `Array`. As such, `diff` is a simple property of the object `Array`.

The design decision comes down to this: is `diff` something that you do (and hence be in its own module), or should `diff` be a property of the datastructure that calls it (and be part of an object)? In other words, is `diff` being used as a verb or as a noun? If `diff` is being used as a verb, then the decision should be to make this a module. If `diff` is being used as a noun then it should be made an object.

There are arguments to both sides here. The first type of code, where `diff` is made a module:

```
Diff::array($array1, $array2);
```

is more standard. "Traditional" Perl programmers will recognize it, and be able to acclimate to it more quickly.

The second type of code, where `diff` is a property of an Array object:

```
my $a = new Array(1,2,3);
my $b = new Array(1,2,4);
my $c = $a->diff($b);
```

seems cleaner. We could add other functionality to the array that does not have to do with `diff`-ing; merge strikes me as another function we could attach to an `Array` object. This function would merge all the elements of an array, take out the duplicates, and stuff them into its own array. So, what to do?

In this case, I would vote for the module. The kicker? In order to use the `diff` function when attached to an `Array` object, you need to use the `Array` object most everywhere.

What happens if you have a regular array reference, and then try to use the `diff` function by mistake, as in:

```
my $array = [1,2,3,4,5];
my $secarray = [1,2,3,4,5,6];
my $thirdarray = $secarray->diff($array);
```

In this case you would get:

```
Can't call method "diff" on unblessed reference at script.p line 7.
```

This is a fatal error because Perl cannot find the method `diff` for a regular array reference. The code would then die.

Since there is no way of guaranteeing that all array references you will encounter will be `Array` objects, you are limiting yourself if you attach `diff` to a specialized `Array` object instead of making it global. Put it into a module, and wait for the days when Perl data structures (hash references, array references, scalar references) are objects in their own right.

Example 2: `PathNames`

The whole problem of path names is a nagging one. Suppose that you want people to be able to enter in, as usage for a script:

```
script.p ..\..\..\scripts\path_to_file
```

in which `path_to_file` is a "relative" path—the `..\..\..` goes up three directories, down into the `scripts` directory, and points to `path_to_file` which happens to be there. In this situation, you might want to check to see if `..\..\..\scripts` is in a legal place for **script.p** to work on it (such as in the **\windows32** subdirectory).

What is required is a path converter, something that takes `..\..\..\scripts\path_to_file` and turns it into `\windows32\scripts\path_to_file`—a routine that does the job for you. Again, let's look at the potential solutions, from the point of view of the clients who use them:

- Object:
  ```
  my $path = new Path('..\..\..\scripts\path_to_file');
  print $path->abs();    # prints absolute path
  print $path->rel();    # prints relative path, to current working directory
  ```

- Module:

```
my $abs = Path::rel2abs('..\..\..\scripts\path_to_file');
my $rel = Path::abs2rel('\windows32\scripts\path_to_file');
```

Again, this is a difficult choice. Does the advantage of having things encapsulated, as in the object, outweigh the disadvantage of having the code more complicated? After all, a path to a file is a string, and it is not going to become much more complicated than that. This means that issues such as independence of representation and changeability are relatively minor.

On the flip side, there is not much of a cost in making it an object.

In cases like this, it is best to play it safe and go with the object, even though it may take a little extra time. Since objects are more flexible, you gain a bit of insurance, just in case you think of something really cool that you wanted to do to Path as an object.

You may be able to do this "cool thing" to an object and not a module. Always keep this in mind: If arguments weigh evenly between a module and an object, pick the object. Because if you miscalculate the complexity of what you are designing, you have more room to maneuver if you do so.

Listing 18.8 shows the Path functions we talked about as an object.

Listing 18.8
Path.pm

```
1   package Path;
2   use strict;
3   use Carp;
4   use CommonVarbs qw ($CMD $DSEP);       # developed in Chapter 15.
5                                          # gives common variables for OSes
6   use File::Basename;                    # gives basenames, filenames.
7
8   sub new
9   {
10      my ($type, $path) = @_;
11      my $self = \$path;                          # reference to a scalar
12
13      bless $self, $type;
14  }
15
```

One note about this code: notice in line 9 that I did not choose to make this object a hash reference. Why? I thought that a scalar would have been more flexible in order to work with other code. Since $path is a scalar reference as well as a Path object, you can say:

```
my $path = new Path('..\..\..');
if (-d $$path) { print "$$path is a directory!!!\n"; }
```

where you can simply test whether or not $path is a directory by dereferencing it.

The cost of this design choice is that you do not have nearly as much room to maneuver in your object. If you decide that you need to have a hash-based object (instead of a scalar) you are stuck. You will either have to change all of your clients to reflect this change or create a totally new object without this limitation.

The code (-d $$path) is a subtle way of breaking encapsulation. We are reaching into the object and stealing its data.

However, instinctively, I feel that giving the object Path all the power of Perl's file operators compensates for this loss of flexibility. You can treat a $path object as if it were a path to a file, just by dereferencing it. The code continues in Listing 18.9.

Listing 18.9
abs() in Path.pm

```
16 sub abs
17 {
18      my ($self) = @_;
19      my ($dir, $file);
20      my $path = $$self;
21      my $cwd = &$CWD();                    # could say 'use Cwd';  cwd();
22      if (-d $path)
23      {
24          $dir = "$path");
25          $file = '';
26      }
27      else
28      {
29          $dir  = dirname ($path);       # gotten from File::Basename.
30          $file = basename($path);       # gets directory name, filename
31      }
32
33      chdir($dir);
34      my $return = &$CWD();
35      chdir($cwd) || warn ("couldn't change directory");
36      $return .= $DSEP . $file if ($file);
37      return($return);
38 }
```

Here, we are a bit sneaky. If you think about it, a relative path is a parsing nightmare. The . means current directory, .. means the directory above the current one, .\ is a relative path to the current working directory, .\.\.\. which is really (redundantly) the same thing, etc., etc., etc. Therefore, it is easier to chicken out. We let the shell do the hard work. If $path is a directory, or does not exist (lines 19–23), then note that $path is the path we are looking for.

If not, we split the file into its directory and file parts (lines 26 and 27). Processing then proceeds to lines 30–34 where we change to the directory given by the ., .., .\, etc., calls, and then figure out the path by the shell itself in line 31. The shell knows better than us what the path is, and although creating a parser like this is possible, it sure is tedious and it doesn't have the knowledge the shell does about what exists in the environment.

On the downside, using the shell to get information about the path creates a dependency. We are now dependent on having access to the directory that we want to change, in order to use the Path object.

The function rel() is useful for places which you need to move things around. If you have relative path names in HTML documents, then you can move them from place to place, rather than "nailing them down" to a certain area.

An example relative path is '..'. We won't implement rel here, but leave it as an exercise.

A hint regarding the exercise: If you make the path "absolute" first (no matter what), then you can use the same algorithm to compute relativeness. If your current path is:

```
c:\winnt\system32\tmp\tmp2\tmp3
```

and you want to go to:

```
c:\winnt\system32\tmp\tmp1
```

then you can cancel out winnt\system32\tmp, and manipulate the rest to get ..\..\tmp1.

Example 3: Making Logs with LogFile

In Chapter 15, we went through the process of taking some procedural code and modularizing it by extracting the common functions and putting them into their own API. As part of this API, we came up with a Log module, whose interface looked like:

```
5 Log::open("log_file");
6 # ..... all the other stuff.
7 # .....
8 Log::write(@output);
9 Log::close();
```

Now, should we be happy with this interface? Should Log stay a module or should we make it an object?

We should definitely make it an object. We tested the waters of implementing a simple Log module, and came up with what is shown in Listing 18.10.

Listing 18.10
Log module

```
1  package Log;
2  my $fh;
3  sub open
4  {
5      my ($log) = @_;
6      $fh = new FileHandle("> $log");
7  }
8  sub close
9  {
10     close($fh);
11 }
12 sub write
13 {
14     my (@output) = @_;
15     print $fh "@output";
16 }
17 1;
```

There are a couple of things that you should immediately notice in this code that should tip you off to the design decision to make. First, there is data that is separate from the functions themselves.

We define the filehandle $fh in line 2, which is shared with the whole module. If we try to say something like:

```
Log::open("log_file");
Log::open("log_file2");
```

then we will have problems. The first call to open will work, but the second one will overwrite the first one because it is using the same file descriptor internally. This can be changed by adding a parameter to the write function:

```
my $fd = new FileHandle("> log_file");
Log::write($fd, @output);
# etc...
```

but this hardly does the job. The log isn't self-contained, and the code isn't any cleaner than:

```
print $fd "@output\n";
```

which basically does the same thing without the overhead of a module call.

Second, we have made some design decisions about what the output should look like (line 15). The following code:

```
print $fh "@output\n";
```

specifies that our log will simply consist of space-separated input.

Now, what happens if we want to have more than one type of format, i.e., one log will have a timestamp, another will be pipe-delimited, another has the associated script name attached to it, another notifies users when problems occur? In this case, the one write function will not suffice.

By making Log a module we are splitting the data from the functions, and limiting our flexibility. Let's see how the interface of an object would change this:

```
1 my $log  = new LogObject( "log_file",
2                             { type => 'regular', action =>'append' });
3 my $log2 = new LogObject("log_file2",
4                             { type => 'stamped',action => 'overwrite'});
5 $log2->open();
6 $log2->write("@data\n");
```

Lines 1–4 now associate 1) the name of the file, 2) the type of log we are going to be using, and 3) the action that it will be taking (either appending or overwriting the file).

When we get to line 5, we can pick and choose which log to open and which log to write. $log2->write("@data\n") then writes to the file "log_file2", with the addition of a timestamp. We implement it as shown in Listing 18.11.

Listing 18.11
LogObject.pm - headers, **new()**

```
1  package LogObject;
2  use strict;
3  use Carp;
4  use FileHandle;
5  use Diff;
6  use Data::Dumper;
7
8  my $_defaultConfig = { 'type' => 'regular', 'action' => 'append' };
9  my $_legal = { 'action' => { 'append' => '> ','overwrite' =>'> ' },
10               'type' =>    { 'regular' => 1, 'stamped' => 1 }
11             };
12
13 sub new
14 {
15     my ($type, $filename, $config) = @_;
16     my $self = {};
17     my %fullconfig;
18
19     confess "Config has to be a hash!\n" if($config && ref($config) ne 'HASH');
20     $config = $config || {};
21
22     $self->{filename} = $filename;
23     $self->{type} = $type;
24
25     %fullconfig = (%$_defaultConfig, %$config);
26     print Dumper(\%fullconfig);
27     bless $self, $type;
28     $self->{config} = \%fullconfig;
29     $self->_validate();
30     $self;
31 }
32
```

The constructor, new, is pretty straightforward, but with an added twist we haven't seen before. The third parameter to new is a config hash: It contains information that is pretty much essential for telling the LogObject to work. In line 6 we are being nice; `$_defaultConfig` gives a default configuration so users do not have to type as much. If they say:

```
my $log = new LogObject("filename");
```

then `filename` will be interpreted as a regular, appending sort of `Log`. Lines 8–11 are more niceties, telling us which configurations are legal. Lines 19 and 20 are still more niceties. The routine validates that users have typed the correct information before continuing.

These niceties are almost always a necessary evil when writing real modules. The less strict users need to be, and the more free they are to put anything into a method and have the computer understand what they are saying, the more accepted your modules and objects will become.

Believe me, you will be glad you took the time to code the extra functionality here and that Perl gives you the flexibility to do your own checking easily.

Once the new routine has completed, there is a legal `LogObject` available for our use. Since the checks have been done up front, we need not worry about checking for legality in arguments anywhere else. Processing then proceeds to `open` and `write` (Listing 18.12):

Listing 18.12
LogObject.pm (open, write)

```
33 sub open
34 {
35      my ($self) = @_;
36      my ($config) = $self->{config};
37      my $legalacts = $_legal->{'action'};
38      my ($action, $filename) =
39                      ( $legalacts->{$config->{action}}, $self->{filename} );
40      my $fh = new FileHandle("$action $filename");
41      $self->{filehandle} = $fh;
42 }
43
44 sub write
45 {
46      my ($self, @text) = @_;
47      my $config = $self->{config};
48      my ($type, $fh) = ($config->{type}, $self->{filehandle});
49      if    ($type eq 'regular') { $self->_writeRegular(@text); }
50      elsif ($type eq 'stamped') { $self->_writeStamped(@text); }
51 }
52
53 sub close { close($_[0]->{filehandle}); }
54
55 sub _writeRegular
56 {
57      my ($self, @text) = @_;
58      my $fh = $self->{filehandle};
59      print $fh "@text\n";
60 }
61
62 sub _writeStamped
63 {
64      my ($self, @text) = @_;
65      my $fh = $self->{filehandle};
```

```
66      my $script = $0;
67      my $time = localtime();
68      print $fh "$script:$time: @text\n";
69 }
```

There are more shenanigans here. Line 40 opens a filehandle and we store it for further use in line 41.

To determine how to open the filehandle, the method open() looks at $config->{action}. If the user gives an action of append, it opens with >, and if the user gives an action of overwrite it opens it with >.

Lines 49 and 50 determine exactly how the write will occur. If the type of log is regular, then the private function _writeRegular() is called; otherwise, _writeStamped() is called—each write to the log files in different ways. We then stuff the actual details of how the writing is being done out of sight.

All this code is relatively clean because we have placed all of the validation logic into one bucket (Listing 18.13), but it isn't a very pretty sight.

Listing 18.13
LogObject.pm (_validate)

```
70 sub _validate
71 {
72      my ($self) = @_;
73      my (@errors);
74      my ($hash, $filename) = ($self->{config}, $self->{filename});
75
76      my ($_actions, $_types ) =
77                      ($_legal->{'action'}, $_legal->{'type'});
78
79      push (@errors, "Incorrect action $hash->{'action'}! Needs
80 to be one of :@{[ keys %$_actions ]}:\n")
81                          if (!defined $_actions->{$hash->{'action'}});
82
83      push (@errors, "Incorrect type $hash->{'type'}! Needs to be one of
84 :@{[keys %$_types]}:\n")
85                          if (!defined $_types->{$hash->{'type'}});
86
87      my @keys = keys (%$hash); my @legal = keys (%$_legal);
88      my $diff = Diff::array(\@keys, \@legal);
89      push(@errors, "Incorrect keys :@$diff: passed to LogObject!\n")
90                                                  if (@$diff);
91      push(@errors, "Unwriteable log file! $filename\n")
92                          if (!(new FileHandle("> $filename")));
93      confess ("@errors") if (@errors);
94 }
95 1;
```

This code is devoted to making the user behave, to make them type the correct responses. Lines 79–92 make a stack of errors, things that _validate() has found wrong with the input parameters. If it has found any, it confesses them, and dies in line 93.

So if the user types:

```
my $log = new LogObject("file", { 'type' => 'reglur' }
```

Perl will catch the spelling error for you and die. If the user types:

```
my $log = new LogObject("file");
```

and the "file" happens to be unwritable, then Perl will die. Since all of the errors are written to a stack, Perl keeps track of each error for us:

```
my $log = new LogObject("file", 'type' => 'reglur');
                                # both illegal type and unreadable.
```

Note

For example, on the CD, we use a logging to keep track of good installs, and bad installs. This way, if a problem does occur, you can simply mail it off to someone.

Now when you run this script it will say something like:

```
Incorrect type rglr! Needs to be one of :regular stamped:
 Unwriteable log file! filea
        LogObject::_validate called at LogObject.pm line 29
        LogObject::new called at script.p line 5
```

Good log files are pretty much essential to get file jobs done. They are windows into what the computer is doing, and can save your skin 1,000 times over. If something goes wrong, it better be logged somewhere, because a problem that is untraceable is one that is unfixable, and unfixable problems make people very nervous.

We are finished with this example for now, but not for good. In Chapter 19 we will see how it can be improved by inheritance; we will throw on a couple of more features just for good measure. The key to improving it is to think about all the validation code, and to get rid of it so the maintenance of the module is easier.

Summary of Modules versus Objects

The three examples in this section demonstrate design decisions between making routines modules or objects. In each case we had a different criteria in choosing.

In the first case, Diff—functionality to get the difference between two simple data structures—we decided that the routine was better off as a module by itself. To make it an effective object, it would have to be tied with an array object (or hash object or scalar object), and that would mean that to use Diff, you would have to use the array object exclusively (rather than the built-in data structure).

In the second case, we decided that PathNames—functions to convert a path from absolute to relative and vice versa—should be an object, even though the deck was stacked about 50/50 in either case. The tipping factor was that even though we did not think that PathNames could get much more complicated, we weren't sure. Since we weren't sure, it was better to play it safe and make it an object.

In the third case—the LogFile—we definitely decided to make it an object because we want LogFile to be mainly bulletproof, yet customizable. We will need all the power of the object to do this.

So what can we say about this whole decision process? The following are two good basic, nonbulletproof rules to follow:

1. If what you want to program has to do with a verb, then make it (prototype it) as a module. A verb implies action, and action implies a function (by itself). Here, we had diff as the function we wanted to program. If you prototype it, and use the module, it will take less effort if you decide to convert it to an object.
2. If what you want to program is a noun, then make it an object. A noun implies that there is data associated with whatever it is you are modeling, hence Pathname and LogFile.

Finally, realize that you always want to favor your decision-making process toward the object if you are uncertain. Sometimes, all it takes is a 90 percent shift in viewpoint to think of verbs in terms of nouns. In the diff case, all we did is think about what we were acting on (namely an array) to see a plausible object implementation. The only reason we hesitated is because this would force you to have all of your arrays to be objects. (You would need to say my $array() = new array all the time, in order to get $arrays diff().)

Turning Procedural Code into Objects

Suppose for an instant that you land a new job, or that you have a large body of code that is procedural (scripts with functions sitting at the bottom of them). Now, you are going to try to reuse much of that code if feasible, as the code is basically a "gift-for-free." If a script works to automate a given problem, then no matter how spaghetti-like that script is, it has value. (The problem comes when people try to cling to that spaghetti-like code, causing much lost time in the process.)

Whenever you get a chance, recycle that code! Following are two examples of code that we will recycle into objects. We originally saw the scripts behind them in Chapter 12; they did some very useful things for us (automating ftp, and telnet, and reading a configuration file into memory). By turning them into objects, we can make them even better because they don't have to be tied to a specific command.

Example 1: ftp and telnet Expect Objects

The first step in recycling any procedural code and turning it into objects is to make a functional diagram for that code, to figure out its structure. Fortunately, we have already done this for the **telnet.p** script that we wrote in Chapter 12. We reproduce it in Figure 18.1. And just for kicks, let's make the equivalent calling tree for **ftp**, shown in Figure 18.2.

Figure 18.1
telnet Functional
Diagram

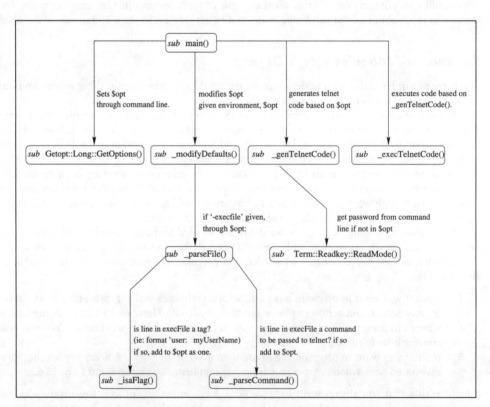

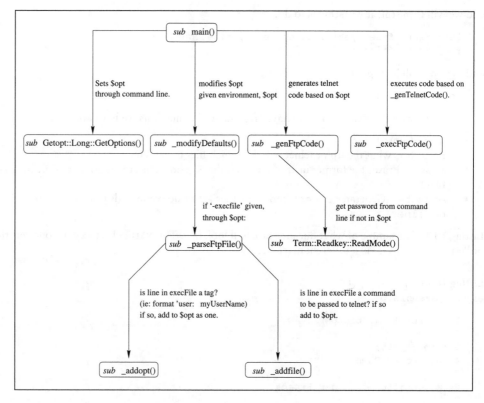

Figure 18.2
ftp Functional
Diagram

Look somewhat similar, don't they? We are basically doing two things:

1. Generating Expect code.
2. Executing Expect code.

> There are also about 150 lines of filler that deal with interfaces. These interfaces include getting arguments from the command line and getting arguments from a file. Both of these are dealt with in other sections of this book; the arguments to the command line we dealt with in Chapter 15, and in **Getopt::Long** getting command from a file we will deal with in this chapter.

Note

In addition, we have one global variable, `$opt`, which is filled either by the command line or a configuration file. Finally, the four functions `_genTelnetCode()`, `_genFtpCode()`, `_execFtpCode()`, and `_execTelnetCode()` are almost ready to order, doing some very basic functionality for us.

In fact, `_execFtpCode()` and `_execTelnetCode()` are exactly the same! It looks like we could gain some savings in code lines if we combined the two into an object.

We now have to come up with what will be the name of the object, and what the interface into the object will be. Since what the module automates is Don Libes' **Expect**program, let's choose that as a name.

From this flows our interface. We shall make a new `Expect` object:

```
my $obj = new Expect ( { 'configuration' => 'of', 'expect' => 'application' } );
```

and we will then stuff it with things to do:

```
$obj->set('filetoget1','filetoget2','filetoget3');
$obj->set('filetoget4');
```

and then we will let it perform those operations:

```
$obj->execute();
```

which will execute the Expect code we have created. So the functions we have are:

- new—Constructor.
- set—Sets what the **ftp** or **telnet** will do (which files to get, etc.).
- reset—Erases the former instructions that the Expect object was going to do, and sets them to blank.
- execute—Generates Expect code, to either get or do commands (whether or not it is of type ftp or telnet).

Listing 18.14 is a sample of what our interface will look like. This particular piece of code gets the latest version of Perl, and installs it via a different machine.

Listing 18.14
expect_example.p

```
1   #!/usr/local/bin/perl5 -w
2
3   use Expect;
4   use Data::Dumper;
5
6   my $objftp     = new Expect
7                    (
8                            {
9                                    'type' => 'bin' , 'site' => 'ftp.cs.colorado.edu' ,
10                                   'objtype' => 'ftp'
11                           }
12                   );
13
14  my $objtelnet = new Expect
15                   (
16                          {
17                                  'objtype'  => 'telnet' , 'site' => 'rock_lobster',
18                                  'userprompt' => 'ogin:','passwordprompt'=>'Password:',
19                                  'user' => 'epeschko'
20                          }
21                   );
22
23  chdir ("/net/mount");
24  $objftp->set('/pub/perl/CPAN/src/5.0/latest.tar.gz');
25  $objftp->execute();
26
27  $objtelnet->set
28           (
29                  ['epeschko', 'cd /net/mount'],
30                  ['epeschko', 'unzip latest.tar.gz'],
31                  ['epeschko', 'tar xvf latest.tar'],
```

```
32                ['epeschko', 'cd perl5.005'],
33                ['epeschko','sh configure -prefix="/home/perl/install"],
34                ['epeschko', 'make'],
35                ['epeschko', 'make test'],
36                ['epeschko', 'make install'],
37                ['epeschko', 'exit']
37            );
38 $objtelnet->execute();
```

We simply set up our `Expect` object exactly like we set up the **telnet.p** and **ftp.p** scripts, namely we configure them via a hash. Here the hash was provided by the user, and in the script examples, the hash was provided from the command line.

Then we let the script chug along by running `execute()`.

The only difference between this and the scripts **ftp.p** and **expect.p** is that this object is much more easily reused than the script's code. Of course you could use the **telnet.p** and **ftp.p** scripts of Chapter 12 in your code by saying:

```
system("telnet.p -file telnetfile");
system("ftp.p -site my.site");
```

where your code reuse is dependent on many system calls to scripts that you have already written. This can be good if your project stays small.

However, as soon as you try to scale this up, you will hit a major brick wall. I know, because I have tried to scale up code dependent on system calls, before Perl 5 and before Perl's version of the object, and yes, I hit a brick wall.

Note

I guess the reason why this doesn't work so well has to do with communication. When you depend on system calls like this, you can't get anything back from the call except for a status, which tells you whether or not the code has succeeded. In an operating system, this status code is a simple number, something like 0, and usually stored in $?. Of course you could say:

```
$text = `ftp.p -file ftpfile`
```

and then get back the text that this system call generates, but even then you are on slippery ground. You are dependent on the structure of the file that **ftp.p** reads, which itself is dependent on how **ftp.p** has implemented this. All these dependencies tend to make your code like a house of cards: A simple puff of wind from any direction can bring this house of cards down.

In Listing 18.15 we deal with the constructor and headers.

While you are going through the following, note the boldface code; this is code we have directly stolen from the **ftp.p** and **expect.p** modules introduced in Chapter 12.

Listing 18.15
Expect.pm header and constructor

```
1    package Expect;
2
3    use Carp;
4    use Term::ReadKey;
5    use strict;
6    use Data::Dumper;
```

```
7
8      my $_legalTypes =
9                       {
10                  telnet =>
11                      { 'site' => 1, 'expect' => 1, 'pass' => 1,
12                        'telnet' => 1,'debug' => 1, 'objtype' => 1,
13                        'user' => 1,'pass' =>1,'passwordprompt'=>1,
14                        'userprompt' => 1,'commands'=>1,'RESET'=> 1
15                        'ignore' => 1
16                      },
17                  ftp =>
18                      { 'site' => 1, 'expect'=> 1, 'ftp' => 1,
19                        'user' => 1, 'pass' => 1, 'type' => 1,
20                        'debug' => 1, 'objtype' => 1, 'RESET' => 1.
21                        'ignore' => 1
22                      }
23                  };
24
25  sub new
26  {
27      my ($type, $config) = @_;
28      my $self = {};
29      bless $self, $type;
30      $self->{config} = $config || {};
31      $self->_validate();
32      $self->_fill();
33      $self;
34  }
```

Two things here: 1) the hash reference $_legalTypes was directly copied from the **ftp.p** and the **telnet.p** examples from Chapter 12, with a few modifications (we removed the stuff that didn't have anything to do with Expect at all, such as (getting options from a file); and 2)we added an `ignore` flag, which tells the Expect module to ignore legal checks.

We do this for the sake of backward compatibility. We want to slide this module in, as easily as possible, to the existing code. At this point, this hash contains all of the information about the options an Expect object can do.

We then come to the constructor, new, which takes a configuration hash from any client that wants to make a new Expect object. Line 29 takes this $config hash and makes a copy of it for the object itself. $config tells us what the object actually looks like. When you say:

```
my $objtelnet = new Expect
                    (
                        {
                            'objtype'  => 'telnet' , 'site' => 'rock_lobster',
                            'userprompt' => 'ogin:','passwordprompt'=>'Password:',
                            'user' => 'edward'
                        }
                    );
```

we are making the telnet object of type telnet, connect to rock_lobster, and so on.

In line 30, we check to make sure that the configuration hash the user passed us is legal, with $self->_validate(). And line 31 helps the user with $self->_fill(), which fills in some common defaults so the user doesn't have to fill in each detail.

These two functions are private so we put them at the end of our module. In fact, we need not write them until the rest of the module is written; we simply assume that they are there so we can assume that we have a legal Expect configuration we can deal with.

As a further convenience, we also provide a `configure` function, as shown in Listing 18.16.

Listing 18.16
`configure()`

```
35  sub configure
36  {
37      my ($self, $configure) = @_;
38      if (defined ($configure->{'RESET'}))
39      {
40          $self->{config} = ($configure)
41      }
42      else
43      {
44          %{$self->{config}} = (%{$self->{config}}, %$configure);
45      }
46      $self->_validate();
47  }
48
```

This function allows us to reuse an existing Expect object. Say we defined the Expect object as shown:

```
my $objftp      = new Expect
                    (
                        {
                            'type' => 'bin' , 'site' => 'ftp.cs.colorado.edu' ,
                            'objtype' => 'ftp'
                        }
                    );
```

Now it would be a pain to have to type all of this again, when all we wanted to do is change the type from binary to ASCII, for example. So instead, we could say:

```
$objftp->configure( { 'type' => 'ascii' });
```

which would override the type of file transfer in the constructor call, but leave everything else intact, as in the site, password, etc.

With this convenience out of the way, all we must do is write the three major functions, namely `set`, `reset`, and `execute` (Listing 18.17). Then, of course, we must fill in the private functions.

Listing 18.17
`set()`, `reset()`, `execute()`

```
49  sub set
50  {
51      my ($self, @options) = @_;
52
53      my $opt = $self->{'config'};
54      if ($opt->{'objtype'} eq 'telnet')
55      {
56          $self->_telnetset(\@options);
```

```
57          }
58      else
59      {
60          $self->_ftpset(\@options);
61      }
62  }
63
64  sub reset
65  {
66      my ($self, @options) = @_;
67      if ($self->{'objtype'} eq 'telnet')
68      {
69          $self->_telnetset(\@options, 'RESET');
70      }
71      else
72      {
73          $self->_ftpset(\@options, 'RESET');
74      }
75  }
76
77  sub execute
78  {
79      my ($self) = @_;
80      my $opt = $self->{'config'};
81      if ($opt->{'objtype'} eq 'telnet')
82      {
83          $self->_genTelnetCode();
84      }
85      else
86      {
87          $self->_genFtpCode();
88      }
89      $self->_execCode();
90  }
```

set and reset are simply more ways of setting the attributes of the object. If the object is of type telnet, then we call the private function _telnetset(); if the type is ftp, we call _ftpset().

execute is the one function that actually does anything useful! Again, if the object type is telnet, we call _genTelnetCode(), and if the object type is ftp, we call _genFtpCode(), which generates the code we are to run. And line 89, _execCode(), actually executes this code.

Hence, out of the 90 lines of code we have made so far, only one line (line 89) even alludes to doing anything. We haven't yet reused the bulk of the code!

This is what we are talking about when we talk about the overhead of programming objects. Although objects themselves are powerful, in programming them, one tends to go through a lot of this interface stuff. Interface, although it doesn't do anything directly, will become really important when you come to actually using your objects.

Notice another thing. We are doing quite a bit of programming like:

```
sub XXXXX
{
    my ($self) = @_;
    if ($type eq 'ftp') { _doFTP(); }  else { _doTelnet();  }
}
```

If you see this pattern in your code (if something is of type `ftp`, then do this, otherwise do something else), this is a good clue that you should be using inheritance to split out the code into more manageable chunks.

Why? Because, when you add more and more pieces to this code (say you added a mail module, which automatically read your mail for you through `Expect`), then you are not going to want to be constrained by saying `set` and `execute`, since these functions don't really fit with `mail()`. We might therefore want to make Expect::Telnet, Expect::Ftp, and Expect::Mail modules, and have them all inherit Expect.

Anyway, we will go through all of this in Chapter 19, when we actually split this via inheritance. For now, all we have to do is fill in the blanks for this particular module. First, the `set` private functions (Listing 18.18):

Listing 18.18
telnetset(), _ftpset()

```
 91
 92  sub _telnetset
 93  {
 94       my ($self, $options, $flag) = @_;
 95       my $opt = $self->{'config'};
 96       if (defined($flag))
 97       {
 98           $opt->{'commands'} = [];
 99       }
100       else
101       {
102           push (@{$opt->{'commands'}}, @$options);
103       }
104  }
105
106  sub _ftpset
107  {
108       my ($self, $options, $flag) = @_;
109       my $opt = $self->{'config'};
110       if (defined($flag))
111       {
112           $opt->{'files'} = [];
113       }
114       else
115       {
116           push (@{$opt->{'files'}}, @$options);
117       }
118  }
119
```

These actually set the internal attributes for us: `telnet` has a list of commands set in line 102, and `ftp` has a list of files set in line 116.

Now, we turn to the `validate` function (Listing 18.19), which we used in the constructor:

Listing 18.19
validate()

```
120  sub _validate
121  {
122       my ($self) = @_;
123       my $config = $self->{config};
```

```
124     my $type    = $config->{objtype};
125     my $legals = $_legalTypes->{$type};
126
127     my (@errors);
128
129     if (!defined ($_legalTypes->{$type}))
130     {
131         push (@errors, "A Type of :$type: isn't legal!\n");
132     }
133     else
134     {
135         my $key;
136         foreach $key (keys(%$config))
137         {
138             if ((!defined ($legals->{$key})) && (!$config->{'ignore'}))
139             {
140                 push (@errors, "The key :$key: isn't legal!\n");
141             }
142         }
143     }
144     confess "@errors" if (@errors);
145 }
146
```

We have seen this type of function before in LogObject; we simply go through each of the keys that we know are legal, push the errors we find onto a stack, and then confess them if we find any (confess is covered in Chapter 22, "Debugging Perl" Tips"), so the user can fix the code (line 144). As a sop to backward compatibility, we make it so that we can pass a special config flag, ignore, to override these legality checks.

The _fill() function comes directly out of **ftp.p** and **telnet.p**. Remember, we had a bunch of defaults in the **ftp** and **telnet** scripts. We don't want these defaults to go to waste, so we cut and paste them into _fill() (Listing 18.20):

Listing 18.20
fill()

```
147 sub _fill
148 {
149     my ($self) = @_;
150     my $opt = $self->{'config'};
151
152     if ($opt->{'objtype'} eq 'ftp')
153     {
154         $opt->{'expect'}= $opt->{'expect'} || $ENV{'EXPECT_EXEC'} ||
155                                               "expect -i";
156
157         $opt->{'user'}  = $opt->{'user'}|| $ENV{'EXPECT_USER'}||
158                                               "anonymous";
159         $opt->{'pass'}  = $opt->{'pass'}||$ENV{'EXPECT_PASS'}||"me@";
160         $opt->{'ftp'}   = $opt->{'ftp'} ||$ENV{'FTP'}        ||"ftp";
161         $opt->{'type'}  = $opt->{'type'}||$ENV{'EXPECT_TYPE'}||"bin";
162         $opt->{'site'}  = $opt->{'site'}||$ENV{'EXPECT_FTP_SITE'} ||
163                     confess "You need to define a site to go to!\n";
164         $opt->{'files'} = $opt->{'files'} || [];
```

```
165        }
166        elsif ($opt->{'objtype'} eq 'telnet')
167        {
168
169            $opt->{'site'}    =
170        (defined($opt->{'site'}))? $opt->{'site'} :
171        (defined $ENV{'EXPECT_TELNET_SITE'})?$ENV{'EXPECT_TELNET_SITE'}:
172                    confess "You need to define a site to go to!\n";
173
174        $opt->{'telnet'} = $opt->{'telnet'}||$ENV{'TELNET'}||  "telnet";
175        $opt->{'expect'} = $opt->{'expect'}|| $ENV{'EXPECT_EXEC'}
176                                                ||"expect -i";
177
178        $opt->{'user'}    = $opt->{'user'} || $ENV{'TELNET_USER'} ||
179                        $ENV{'USERNAME'} || getpwuid($<) ||
180                        confess "Couldn't get a user!\n";
181
182        $opt->{'passwordprompt'} = $opt->{'passwordprompt'} ||
183                    confess "You need to define a password prompt!\n";
184
185        $opt->{'userprompt'} = $opt->{'userprompt'} ||
186                    confess "You need to define a userprompt!\n";
187        $opt->{'commands'}  = $opt->{'commands'}  || [];
188         $opt->{'pass'} = $opt->{'pass'} || 'INTERACT_PASSWORD';
189        }
190 }
```

With the exception of line 188 (which we will put to good use later), this is exactly the same code as is in **ftp.p** and **telnet.p**, only munged a little bit to fit. (We are taking time to rethink our password policy. Previously, setting the password had to be done before filling in defaults occurred.) We set up an if clause:

```
if ($opt->{'objtype'} eq 'ftp')
{
    # set up ftp options from ftp.p
}
else
{
    # set up telnet options from telnet.p
}
```

and then dump all the options, defaults, and so forth we had from **ftp.p** and **telnet.p** into the if clause. Again, we are thinking of splitting the code apart.

Finally, we have the _genFtpCode(), _genTelnetCode(), and _execCode() functions. These are directly lifted, in their entirety, from the **ftp.p** and **telnet.p** scripts. With minor changes, we make them work with the module, as shown in Listing 18.21.

Listing 18.21
genFtpCode()

```
191 sub _genFtpCode
192 {
193     my ($self) = @_;
194     my $opt = $self->{'config'};
195
```

```
196     my $line = '';
197        my $key;
#  ...........
# lines 191 through 284 directly taken from ftp.p-See chapter 12,
# or the CD that comes with this book for
# more detail; Makes ftp code and stuffs it in $line.
#  ...........
283     $self->{'code'} = $line;
284 }
```

We cut out the lines in question, merely to emphasize the changes we need to make the _genFtpCode function work with the Expect class. (If you want to see the _genFtpCode() function, turn to Chapter 12 or see the accompanying CD.)

The main thing to notice here is that the hash $opt, which we used in the actual **ftp.p** code and came from the command line (and **ftp** file) is now $self->{'config'}, which is set by the constructor.

To make things easy, we simply rename $self->{'config'} to $opt to use the code without modification. (If you can do this, you will save a lot of testing time because you are sure the code will work.) We now proceed to do the same thing with **telnet** (Listing 18.22):

Listing 18.22
genFtpCode()

```
285
286 sub _genTelnetCode
287 {
288     my ($self) = @_;
289     my $opt = $self->{'config'};
290
#  ...........
# lines 286 through 355 directly taken from telnet.p - Again,
# see chapter 12 page XXXXXXXX, or the CD that comes with
# this book for more detail;
#  ...........

353 ;
354     $self->{'code'} = $line;
355 }
```

Again, we make the code out of the $opt hash, stuff the code into $line, and then into the object variable $self->{'code'}. Since this string is legal code for Expect, when someone says $obj->execute(), we execute it via _execCode(), as shown in Listing 18.23.

Listing 18.23
execCode()

```
356
357 sub _execCode
358 {
359     my ($self) = @_;
360
361     my $opt = $self->{'config'};
362     my $exec = ($opt->{'expect'});
363
```

```
364        if ($opt->{'pass'} eq 'INTERACT_PASSWORD')
365        {
366            print "Enter password for $opt->{'user'}\n";
367            ReadMode 2; $opt->{'pass'} = <STDIN>; ReadMode 0;
368            $opt->{'code'} =~ s"INTERACT_PASSWORD"$opt->{'pass'}"sg;
369        }
370
371        if ($opt->{'debug'})
372        {
373            print "Generated code:\n$self->{'code'}\n";
374        }
375        else
376        {
377            open (EXPECT, "| $exec");
378            print EXPECT $self->{'code'};
379            close(EXPECT);
380        }
381        $self->{'code'} = '';
382 }
```

Again, we are being a little sly here. Instead of directly copying over the function from either ftp.p or telnet.p, we take the chance to better handle passwords.

We give the user the chance to have an interactive password, via setting the variable $opt->{'pass'} to INTERACT_PASSWORD. When Perl sees this, it knows that the user must give the class a password. Then it hands over control to the keyboard in lines 364–369, getting the user to enter a password. (Read Line is a function that does this from the package Term::Readkey.)

There is one problem: By this time, we have generated the Expect code, and the code has (as a password inside it) a line that looks like:

```
expect {
#......
    "Password:", send "INTERACTIVE_PASSWORD\r".
#......
}
```

If we simply executed this code as is, it would fail since the password is incorrect. So what to do? Well, there are certain advantages of linking the getting of the password with the actual time the code is executed. This ensures that we have the password inside the code for the smallest amount of time possible, and makes the code more secure, for instance. (After all, we set the code back to ' ' after completion.)

We again take advantage of Perl's flexibility. In line 368, we simply substitute the string INTERACT_PASS-WORD with the string we have received from the user. This turns the code into something that looks like:

```
expect {
#......
    "Password:", send "my_password \r".
#......
}
```

where my_password is what the user has typed on the keyboard.

This ends the first part of our code replacement exercise. Out of 368 lines, we have reused 203: over half of our old code. On the other hand, 165 are new lines of code, the price of making it a class. We will incur a bigger cost in terms of code lines for making it use inheritance.

For now, until you get used to Perl's object syntax, try to keep things as simple as possible, and don't go into inheritance too deeply. Although this code is in some ways more difficult to maintain, it is also a simpler design than splitting up your modules via inheritance, and you should always feel comfortable with the syntax of something before moving on to the next level.

Example 2: Configuration Files

Let's continue with the **expect.p** and **ftp.p** scripts, and see what other pieces of information we can abstract out. Remember, in **ftp.p** and **expect.p** we had the option execfile specified in GetOptions:

```
GetOptions
        (
                $opt, "-site:s", "-execfile:s", "-expect:s", "-pass:s",
                "-telnet:s", "-debug"
        );
```

The execFile option lets us take our input from a file, which seems like a good thing to do. Not only that, it seems like a common thing to do, something we would like to do again.

Therefore, we decide that it would be an especially good idea to make an object that is reusable and lets us take options from a file. Let's look at what we have so far. In line 34 of **telnet.p** we have:

```
34        $fileopt = (defined ($opt->{'execfile'}))? _parseFile($opt) : {};
```

which defines $fileopt either as blank, or from the output of _parseFile(). The file we want to parse looks like:

```
    site:               rock_lobster

    ogin:,              peschko
    assword:,           INTERACTIVE_PASSWORD
    epeschko*,          tcsh
    epeschko*,          ls
    epeschko*,          exit
    epeschko*,          exit
```

where we have two categories of entries. First, we have <flag>:   <value> and second is a series of comma-separated values, which are by themselves on a line.

Our strategy will be to reuse the code in _parseFile(), writing a new class to substitute for it. Let's call this object Config::CSV indicating that it is a **Config** file class of subtype **CSV**. We will define two functions that are accessible to the outside world:

*   get()
*   new()

new() will parse our configuration file for us, returning legal values. get() will be our interface to actually get those values out of the hash.

First we define the headers and the constructor (Listing 18.24):

Listing 18.24
execCode()

```
1    package Config::CSV;
2
```

```
3    use FileHandle;
4    use strict;
5    use Text::ParseWords;
6    use Carp;
7    use String::Edit;
8
9    my $_legalTypes =
10                  {
11                          'special' => 1, 'firstline' => 1,
12                          'secondline' => 1,  'thirdline' => 1,
13                          'elementsperline' => 1
14                  };
15
16   my $_config = { 'special' => 'specialelem' };
17
18   sub new
19   {
20       my ($type, $file, $config) = @_;
21       my $fh = new FileHandle("$file") || confess "Couldn't open $file!\n";
22
23       my $self = bless {}, $type;
24
25       $self->{fh} = $fh;
26       $self->{config} = $_config;
27       %{$self->{config}} = (%$_config, %$config) if (defined ($config));
28
29       $self->_parse();
30       $self;
31   }
32
```

A couple of notes here. Just for fun (and for the sake of speed) we define a default configuration hash $_config, rather than defining _validate() and _fill() functions as we did in the Expect object.

This was partly to have variety but it also *lets you not commit yourself until you have used the object for a while*. It is simpler to be flexible with a couple of statements rather than writing a complex validation routine and having to rewrite it later.

Second, line 30 (_parse()) does the actual parsing, and we return back the object to the main routine.

Now, let's look at what our usage is going to be, given the parameters. If we say something like:

```
my ($config) = new Config::CSV("configfile",
                            {
                                'special' => 'commands',
                                'firstline' => ['userprompt','user']
                                'secondline'=> ['passwordprompt','password']
                            }
                        );
```

this is saying "OK, let's open the file named "configfile," and then take all the flags (lines like "site: my.site.edu") and then process them." Hence our target transformation looks something like Figure 18.3. The subroutine that will do this for us is called _parse(). For now, we don't worry how to implement it; we just go on to do our other, nonprivate function, get() (Listing 18.25).

Figure 18.3
Target
Transformation

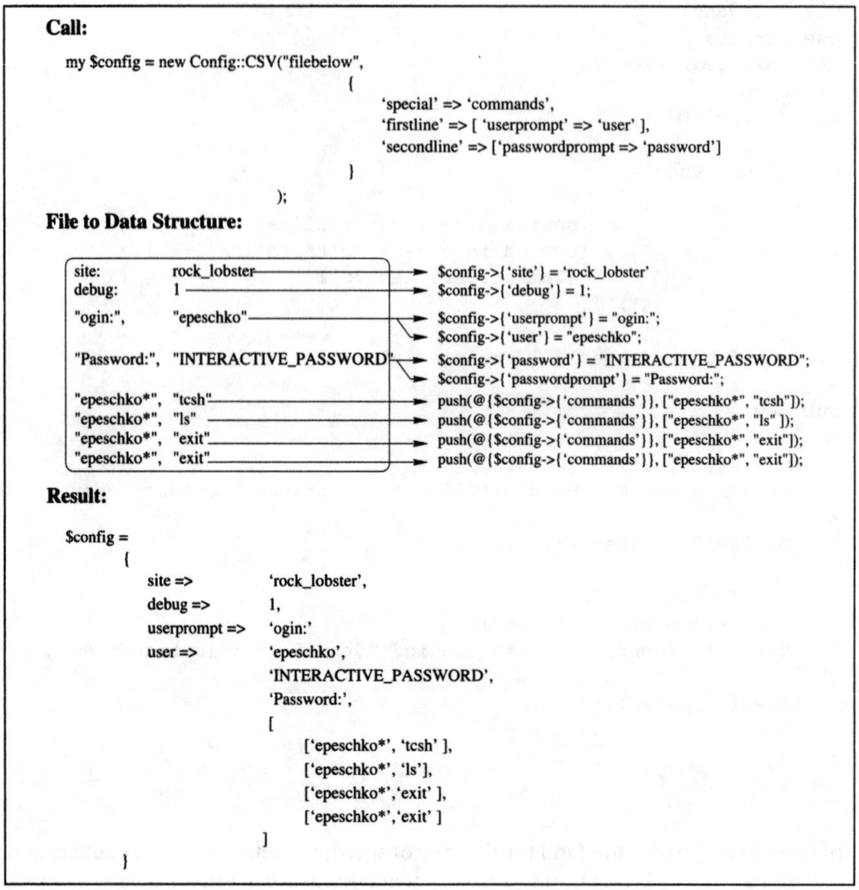

Call:

```
my $config = new Config::CSV("filebelow",
                            {
                              'special' => 'commands',
                              'firstline' => [ 'userprompt' => 'user' ],
                              'secondline' => ['passwordprompt => 'password']
                            }
                           );
```

File to Data Structure:

site:	rock_lobster	→ $config->{'site'} = 'rock_lobster'
debug:	1	→ $config->{'debug'} = 1;
"ogin:",	"epeschko"	→ $config->{'userprompt'} = "ogin:";
		↘ $config->{'user'} = "epeschko";
"Password:",	"INTERACTIVE_PASSWORD"	→ $config->{'password'} = "INTERACTIVE_PASSWORD";
		↘ $config->{'passwordprompt'} = "Password:";
"epeschko*",	"tcsh"	→ push(@{$config->{'commands'}}, ["epeschko*", "tcsh"]);
"epeschko*",	"ls"	→ push(@{$config->{'commands'}}, ["epeschko*", "ls"]);
"epeschko*",	"exit"	→ push(@{$config->{'commands'}}, ["epeschko*", "exit"]);
"epeschko*",	"exit"	→ push(@{$config->{'commands'}}, ["epeschko*", "exit"]);

Result:

```
$config =
        {
                site =>         'rock_lobster',
                debug =>        1,
                userprompt =>   'ogin:'
                user =>         'epeschko',
                                'INTERACTIVE_PASSWORD',
                                'Password:',
                                [
                                        ['epeschko*', 'tcsh' ],
                                        ['epeschko*', 'ls'],
                                        ['epeschko*','exit' ],
                                        ['epeschko*','exit' ]
                                ]
        }
```

Listing 18.25
get()

```
33
34   sub get
35   {
36       my ($self, $elementName) = @_;
37       my $values = $self->{values};
38       if (defined ($elementName))
39       {
40           if (!defined ($values->{$elementName}))
41           {
42               print "Warning!!! :$elementName: not defined!\n";
43           }
44           else
45           {
46               return($values->{$elementName});
```

```
47                 }
48          }
49          else
50          {
51                 return($values);
52          }
53   }
54
55
```

Again, this is pretty simple. All we do is assume that we have already parsed the file, and stored the values in $self->{values}. To make it even easier (and compatible with how **telnet.p** and **ftp.p** worked before) we give the special option to get(), which returns *all* the configuration values if no parameter was given. Hence:

```
my $user = $config->get('user');
```

would return the user name that was in a **Config** file whose attached object was $config, and

```
my $vals = $config->get();
```

would return the whole thing. The difficult bit, the parsing, is left until last (Listing 18.26):

Listing 18.26
parse()

```
56   sub _parse
57   {
58       my ($self) = @_;
59       my $return = {};
60       $self->{values} = $return;
61
62       my $fh = $self->{fh};
63       my $opt = $self->{config};
64       my @lines = <$fh>;
65
66
67       my ($line, $xx, $keep) = ('', 0, '');
68
69       foreach $line (@lines)
70       {
71          chop($line);
72          next if (!$line);    # ignore blanks
73
74          my @array;
75          if (@array = _isaFlag($line))
76          {
77                 $return->{$array[0]} = $array[1];
78          }
79          else
80          {
81              if (defined ($opt->{firstline}) && ($xx == 0))
82              {
83                  my (@elements) = $self->_parseCommand($line);
84                  my $keys = $opt->{firstline};
85                  $self->_set($keys, \@elements);
```

```
 86                  }
 87                  elsif (defined ($opt->{secondline}) && ($xx == 1))
 88                  {
 89                      my (@elements) = $self->_parseCommand($line);
 90                      my $keys = $opt->{secondline};
 91                      $self->_set($keys, \@elements);
 92                  }
 93                  elsif (defined ($opt->{thirdline}) && ($xx == 2))
 94                  {
 95                      my (@elements) = $self->_parseCommand($line);
 96                      my $keys = $opt->{thirdline};
 97                      $self->_set($keys, \@elements);
 98                  }
 99                  else
100                   {
101                      my (@elements) = $self->_parseCommand($line);
102                      my $key = $opt->{'special'};
103                      push (@{$return->{$key}}, \@elements);
104                   }
105                  $xx++;
106              }
107          }
108      return($return);
109 }
```

Not pretty. But neither is our problem, so that is OK. The boldface lines are either wholly or partially borrowed from **telnet.p** so it's not as bad as it looks. Basically, @lines contains all the lines in the configuration file,
and we go through each of them, one by one, in the foreach loop, just like before.

However, whereas before we hardcoded the values, like:

```
my ($passwordprompt, $password ) = _parseCommand($line);
                $opt->{'passwordprompt'} = $passwordprompt;
```

in our original script, we generalize this to fill our hash based on the config hash given in $self->{'config'}.
If the line was:

```
"epeschko*",        ls
```

and $opt->{'special'} was equal to commands, then:

```
my $key = $opt->{'special'};
```

makes $key equal to commands, and:

```
push (@{$return->{$key}}, \@elements);
```

is equal to:

```
push (@{$return->{'commands'}}, [ "epeschko*", "ls" ]);
```

In other words, our new code returns the same results as it did when stuffed at the bottom of **telnet.p**! It is simply
more general than the code before. It has to be; we are making a general module here, and we can't have hard-
coded elements.

All that is left to do is the actual parsing (Listing 18.27); the data structure we have made is in place, and we
have to fill in the blanks. Boldface code, again, is code that we have reused:

Listing 18.27
parse()

```
110
111 sub _set
112 {
113     my ($self, $keys, $values) = @_;
114     my $return = $self->{values};
115     my $xx = 0;
116     for ($xx = 0; $xx < @$values; $xx++)
117     {
118         $return->{$keys->[$xx]} = $values->[$xx];
119     }
120 }
121
122 sub _parseCommand
123 {
124     my ($self,$line) = @_;
125     my $keep = 0;
126
127     my (@args) = quotewords("\s*,\s*", $keep, $line);
128     if (defined ($self->{elementsperline}) &&
129                         @args != $self->{elementsperline})
130     {
131         print "Warning!!!! Number of arguments in line :$line: is not correct!
132 Should be $self->{elementsperline}\n";
133     }
134     @args = trim(@args);
135     return(@args);
136 }
137
138 sub _isaFlag
139 {
140     my ($line) = @_;
141     my $keep = 0;
142     my (@array) = quotewords("\s*:\s*", $keep, $line);
143     @array = trim(@array);
144     if (@array == 2)
145     {
146         return (@array);
147     }
148     else
149     {
150         return(());
151     }
152 }
153 1;
```

Rewriting telnet.p

With these two objects in place, we are now in a position to rewrite the **telnet.p** from Chapter 12. Considering that our original **telnet.p** was 216 lines long, let's see exactly how much we can improve on it. There are three steps to writing this code:

1. Using the correct modules
2. Getting configuration data
3. Running the expect portion

Our first step, therefore, is to go through our old code, seeing where it makes sense to replace the hard coded values with our objects we created (Expect, Config::CSU) Figure 18.4 does this.

We continue to do this for the whole code, marking up where it makes sense to put stuff in the objects that we have written (as in Figure 18.4).

Figure 18.4
Marked UP Code:
Where Things Go

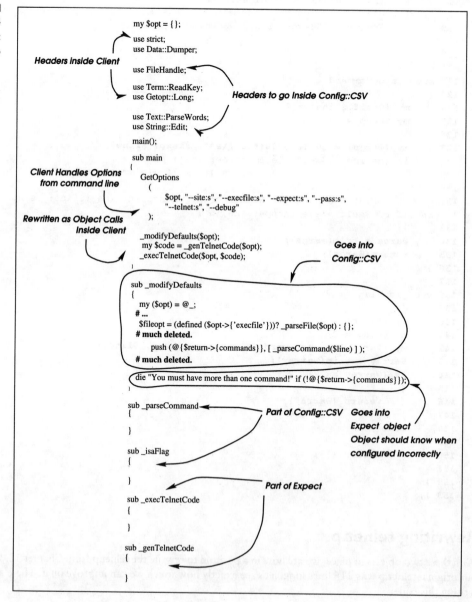

```
use strict;
use FileHandle;            # inside Config::CSV
use Term::ReadKey;         # inside Expect
use Getopt::Long;
use Text::ParseWords;      # inside Config::CSV
use String::Edit;          # inside Config::CSV
```

We still need `strict` and `Getopt::Long`, but now `FileHandle`, `Term::ReadKey`, `Text::ParseWords`, and `String::Edit` are no longer being directly used, instead being inside either `Config::CSV` or `Expect`.

Now our headers look like Listing 18.28. Having had a preliminary look at the code, we are ready to draw up the new code. First, we make a stub file, one that shows all the new modules we will be using (Listing 18.28):

Listing 18.28
telnet

```
use strict;
use Getopt::Long;
use Config::CSV;
use Expect;
```

Now, having done this, we fix each of the parts of the code, retrofitting them with objects. We first take the headers and change them, Before, they were:
we then proceed to test this stub with a `'perl -c'`

```
prompt% perl -c telnetobject.p
```

and it compiles (assuming that all of these modules are in your @INC directory).

Second, we look at what we need to change and then add them piece by piece. The first thing **telnet.p** does is take the arguments from a file (given the flag `--execfile`), and then gives the user the chance to override these arguments from the command line.

Well, since we made `Config::CSV`, the "arguments taken from a file" turns from a subroutine to a method call (Listing 18.29):

Listing 18.29
telnetobj.p (continued)

```
 7
 8
 9  main();
10
11 sub main
12 {
13      my $opt = {};
14      GetOptions
15          (
16                  $opt, "-site:s", "-execfile:s", "-expect:s", "-pass:s",
17                  "-telnet:s", "-debug"
18          );
19
20      if ($opt->{'execfile'})
21      {
22          my $filecfg = new Config::CSV
23                      (
24                              $opt->{'execfile'},
```

```
25                                    {
26                                        'firstline' =>['userprompt', 'user'],
27                                        'secondline'=>['passwordprompt','pass'],
28                                        'special' => 'commands'
29                                    }
30                            );
31            my $fileopt = $filecfg->get();
32            %$opt = (%$fileopt, %$opt);
33      }
```

The key lines here are in boldface; our objective is to get the `$fileopt` hash to look right, which contains the parsing of our configuration file in lines 22–31. Now we make a simple test file:

```
site:              rocky_horror
ogin:,             epeschko
Password:,         INTERACT_PASSWORD
epeschko*,         tcsh
epeschko*,         ls
epeschko*,         exit
epeschko*,         exit
```

and then add the line:

```
print Dumper($fileopt);
```

to our script. When we say:

```
%prompt telnetobj.p -execfile telnetfile
```

we hope to have a data structure that looks like

```
$VAR1 = { site => 'rocky horror',
          userprompt => 'ogin:'
          user =>  'epeschko'
          passwordprompt => 'Password:',
          pass => 'INTERACT_PASSWORD',
          commands => [ 'epeschko*' => 'tcsh',
                        'epeschko*' => 'ls',
                        'epeschko*' => 'exit',
                        'epeschko*' => 'exit'
                      ]
        };
```

We then cycle through, debugging as we go, until we get this output.

Finally, we add the merge of the command line and the file that our old file had, as well as the call to Expect (Listing 18.30).

Listing 18.30
telnetobj.p

```
33 %$opt = (%$opt, %$fileopt);
34 }
35
36      my $expectobj =new Expect({ 'objtype' => 'telnet','ignore' => 1, %$opt });
37      $expectobj->execute;();
38 }
```

That is it. Now I admit, it is difficult to believe that this 38-line program (which could probably be condensed even more) is the same 216-line behemoth we wrote before! Yet I hope it hasn't been too much of a surprise.

The key here is in line 33. Line 33 merges the options from the command line, and the options in the file that we provide on the command line. But (being sneaky as always) we have designed it so that the %opt file hash that we create from the program is plug-'n-play compatible with our Expect module.

Think about this for a second: each of the lines that comes out of the hash shown in Figure 18. has a use in Expect, the module. It should be. We were the ones who programmed Expect.pm! We therefore designed Expect.pm to take the original interface, and then collapsed all the configuration difficulties into Getopt::long and Config::CSV.

In a sense then, there is a usage relationship here between Config::CSV and Expect. Config::CSV has the job of sifting the input (which can be quite complicated), and then Expect knows that this input has been validated. Now, it can do its job, which is to actually run the **telnet** job!

This did not come totally seamlessly. I had to do testing, yes, and the module Data::Dumper came as an invaluable asset to knowing exactly what was going on.

Summary

Sometimes object-oriented programming is most fun and worthwhile when you are searching your old code (or somebody else's code) for objects. Much of the time, it cannot be done as quickly as the preceding examples, but there are times that you can glean diamonds out of your own code, and then ease them into existing code in a very seamless way.

The last example above may be a bit extreme, going from a 216-line client to 38-line one, but it is not by any means the only time that this has happened to me, and to programmers I know. The trick to doing this is:

1. A heavy analysis phase—understanding what you have and documenting down in detail how your code works (via a calling tree).
2. Actually ripping your code apart for scraps, and pigeon-holing what you see into several categories.
3. Designing your new interface with the old one in mind.
4. Coding the new interface, and slipping it in and testing it a step at a time.

You will get a lot out of doing this recycling job: You will learn more about your thinking processes if you do this stripmining of your code, and build it back in a better way. I am constantly doing it; if a module becomes unwieldly, I always sell it for parts. Often this is the only way to learn, and I recommend it highly.

In this chapter, we have 1) gone through some of the common methods, 2) learned about some of the ways to decide modules versus objects, and 3) learned to stripmine the objects for code.

In Chapter 19, let's build a real object from scratch. We will consider everything: problem recognition, available resources, design, and implementation—everything.

Inheritance and Perl

So far, we have considered objects by themselves, or as being used by scripts. However, on any large project, the objects you create will not only be used inside scripts, but will also be used, or intermingled, with other objects. To this end, *object hierarchies* are formed in a large project, which allow useful, high-level objects to be built out of low-level objects. These hierarchies may be several levels deep on large projects. Managing the complexity of large projects is a major goal of object-oriented programming.

For example, an application object (such as a spreadsheet or drawing program) might be built from several screen objects and user-input objects. Of course, actual object hierarchies are more complicated than this.

The two primary techniques at your disposal in building these object hierarchies are:

1. Inheritance
2. Layering

We shall save the second technique—layering—for the next chapter. The purpose of this chapter is to discuss inheritance. Inheritance is not a very well-understood technique and it takes quite a bit of finesse to use it well. I suggest that you understand not only what inheritance is, but when it is appropriate to use it (and when you should use layering instead) in your code.

Chapter Overview

Inheritance is, above all, a design choice. Inheritance should be used to compose projects that are bigger than just making an object and using it in a script (as we have done in previous chapters). As inheritance is a design technique, this chapter will be heavy on examples. The term *inheritance* is fairly straightforward, but the application of inheritance can be more complicated.

First, we will look at the second major tool—the first being functional diagrams—which is helpful in understanding how inheritance works, the *object diagram*—the blueprint of the computer science world. Building object diagrams for your projects is essential in understanding how to put things together cleanly.

From there, we will briefly review inheritance, go into its definition, its plusses and minuses, and some circumstances in which you would want to use inheritance. Finally, we will look at examples where we are asked to scale up some code. We will ask ourselves whether inheritance is the correct way to accomplish a given design. If so, we will see how we should implement it.

More Tools of the Trade: Object Diagrams

Readers who are already familiar with object-oriented programming techniques are probably familiar with object diagrams. Once you get into programming complicated projects, you will bump your head against logical diagrams that explain how you are going to do what you intend to do. We have already seen a class of diagrams that can be helpful to the software engineer. This was the functional diagram, which was covered in Chapter 17. These were used to outline how functions call each other.

Object diagrams take that logic a step further. *Object diagrams* describe how two or more objects are related to, and dependent on, each other. In other words, object diagrams do the same thing as functional diagrams, only at a higher level of abstraction. They take functions and hide how they relate to each other, only showing where objects are dependent on other objects. There are several forms of object diagrams. I use a deviant of a Booch diagram that tends to give more detail than the classic Booch diagram.

If you aren't already familiar with it, Booch's methodology is a formal "C++-ish" way of picturing object hierarchies. Booch has several books on the subject of OO design.

Note

To understand object diagrams, you must understand the concepts of ISA and HASA. We talk about these in conjunction with object diagrams next.

ISA

ISA denotes the type of relationship between two objects. It is used in close conjunction with inheritance. If something has an ISA relationship with something else, it probably is modeled using inheritance.

The best way of getting a grip on the definition of ISA is to think in colloquial terms. An object *ISA* (*is a*) child of another object if it is a specific type of that object. Hence, a sundial *ISA* clock, a dog *ISA* mammal, and a lake *ISA* body of water. Say we were making a program that models the phylogeny, the "tree of life," and we were looking at how to model crustaceans (crabs, whelks, etc.). The resulting object hierarchy might look something like Figure 19.1. Here, a whelk *ISA* crustacean *ISA* arthropod, and a spider *ISA* arachnid *ISA* arthropod.

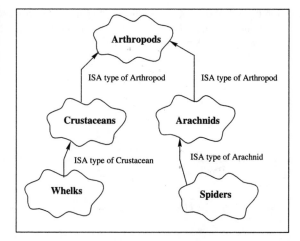

Figure 19.1
Object Diagram
Showing
Crustaceans

Thinking about things this way, although not 100 percent effective, gives you a good idea of when to use inheritance. Inheritance by and large has to do with cutting up and designing things along the lines of variants. If something is a variant of another thing, then it probably can be modeled in an ISA relationship, or an inheritance relationship.

HASA

HASA (has a) is also a term that denotes the relationship between two or more objects. While ISA is closely associated with inheritance, HASA is closely associated with layering.

Again, if you want to understand HASA, you should think colloquially. For example, we can model a person by looking at his or her component parts and how they relate, as shown in Figure 19.2. Here, a person *HASA* skeletal system, a nervous system, and a cardiovascular system. In turn, a skeletal system has bones, joints, and ligaments. We can do the same thing with the nervous and cardiovascular systems.

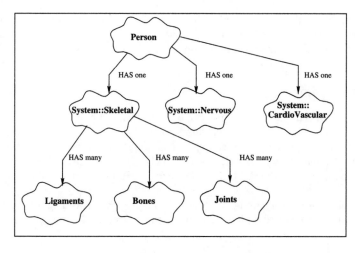

Figure 19.2
Object Diagram
Showing
Reduction of
Person

This technique is called *reducing* a system to its working parts, and is by far the most common way to make an object hierarchy. Although we have not pointed it out earlier, it has been common for use to have a HASA or layering relationship in the objects we have used so far. When we say something like:

```
package MyPackage;
use FileHandle;

sub new
{
    my ($type, $filename) = @_;
    my $self = bless {}, $type;
    $self->{fd} = new FileHandle("$filename") || die "Couldn't open $filename!\n";
    return($self);
}
```

we are in fact making a HASA relationship. `MyPackage` *HASA* `FileHandle`, and we store it inside the object itself.

Summary of Diagrams

We have pointed out the second major type of diagram to scale up projects. This is the object diagram and it shows how objects themselves relate to each other.

Furthermore, object diagrams have two major types of relationships: ISA and HASA. ISA relationships have to do with inheritance. ISA points out a "family relationship" between objects: if something *ISA* variant of something else (as quartz *ISA* rock), chances are an inheritance relationship is appropriate.

HASA relationships have to do with layering, with analyzing something and breaking it into smaller parts. This is illustrated by a person *HASA* skeletal system, a car *HASA* motor, and a computer *HASA* CPU. If you see something like this, your first instinct should be to model your problem in terms of layering.

Now, let's go into the details of inheritance. If you are interested in layering, check out Chapter 20.

Inheritance Overview

We have already talked a bit about the syntax of inheritance (see Chapter 16 for more detail), but we have not gone into detail about when or why you would want to use inheritance. This chapter discusses appropriate usage of inheritance. But first, let's have a short review of inheritance and how it works.

Short Review of Inheritance

Let's go over how inheritance works in the abstract. You can find the details of how it works technically in Chapter 16. Remember, *inheritance* is the process of making a class a particular version of another class, with the intention of having the parent class act as a default that supplies functionality if the child does not have it.

The example we gave in Chapter 16 was a clock. The parent class, **Clock**, kept all the information about how to actually get the time from the system. The child classes (**System** and **Sundial**) contained information on how to set the time.

The result is a simple relationship, something that looks like Figure 19.3. This diagram is an object diagram. We have, however, gone a bit further and added a couple of things that make it easier to go from this diagram to code.

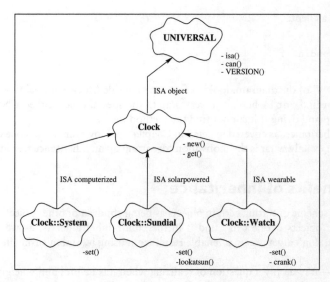

Figure 19.3
Inheritance
Relationship for
Clock Object

Each object has two labels: the name of the object and the filename that corresponds to the object. We have also, for clarity's sake, included each method that each object defines. Finally, the arrow points to the parent in the child-parent relationship that is shown here.

The key word in this diagram is *ISA*. The Clock::Sundial *ISA* Clock, which in turn *ISA* UNIVERSAL object. You can translate this into the skeleton code (which is never explicity defined) shown in Figure 19.4.

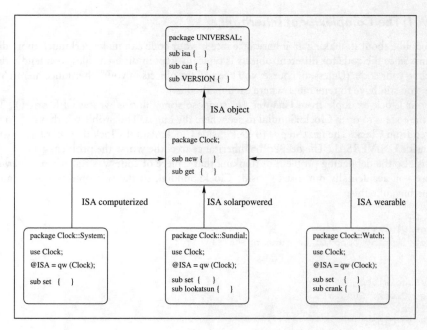

Figure 19.4
Skeleton Code for
Clock Object

When this code is called inside a client:

```
use Clock::Sundial;
my $sd = new Clock::Sundial();
print $sd->get();
```

Perl will then "follow the arrows" of the diagram, looking for `get()` inside **Clock::Sundial** first, then traversing up to **Clock** next. If Perl cannot find `get()` here, it traverses up to the special object called **UNIVERSAL** looking for `get()`, finally giving up and dying if it cannot find the method there.

This is the bare bones of inheritance, as covered in detail in Chapter 16. However, there is one question that we failed to answer in that chapter: exactly what is the motivation for setting up an inheritance tree in this manner?

Drawbacks and Benefits of Inheritance

Why go through this elaborate scheme of setting certain objects as being children of other objects, and then looking for functionality in parent objects if one can't find it in the child? Inheritance is, as we shall see, not a "win/win" type of concept; you don't always gain a tenable result from using it, and misusing inheritance can be quite harmful.

However, people do use it—it is simply a question of realizing when it is helpful and when it is harmful, the benefits and drawbacks. There are three of each we will talk about here. We start with the drawbacks.

Inheritance Drawbacks

There are three major drawbacks to inheritance. These are the *complexity* inheritance entails, the *overhead* it involves, and the *dependencies* inheritance can create between parent and children.

Drawback 1: The Complexity of Inheritance

There is no doubt about it: making an inheritance tree in your code can make Perl much more difficult to debug and program. Since the code for different objects is typically kept in different files, you tend to bounce from file to file to debug your code. (Unless, of course, you keep all the objects in your inheritance hierarchy open yourself. In this case, you still have to remember where each method is.)

Using our Clock example from Chapter 16, suppose something is wrong with `set()`. The first step in debugging the code is to open **Clock::Sundial** to see where the bug is. The problem is that `set()` is not there, but was inherited from **Clock**. The next step is to look inside **Clock**. And if **Clock** does not have `set()`, you would next look inside **UNIVERSAL**. The deeper the inheritance tree, the worse the problem gets.

There is also the debugging problem of thinking that a piece of code was run when *something else actually ran*. Suppose you accidentally put `set()` inside **Clock::Sundial**, so the two objects **Clock** and **Clock::Sundial** looked something like this:

```
Clock.pm
package Clock;
sub set { print "Should be running this!\n"; }


Clock/Sundial.pm
package Clock::Sundial;
use Clock;
@ISA = qw(Clock);
# ... other code
sub set { print "Mistake"; }
```

Now, when you run a program that looks like:

```
use Clock::Sundial;
my $a = new Clock::Sundial();
$a->set('Jul 15 1997');
```

Perl will run the call:

```
Clock::Sundial::set($a, 'Jul 15 1997');
```

and print out Mistake. Why? Because Perl takes the following path to execute 'set':

1. It tries to run **Clock::Sundial:set()**.
2. If it can't find **Clock::Sundial::set()**, only then does it run **Clock::set()**.

In this example, when Perl runs across a **Clock::Sundial::set()**, Perl executes this version. However, if you are not careful, you may be looking in **Clock.pm** instead, and keep changing **Clock.pm**'s version of set(), and wondering why your stupid computer is not responding to your code changes. Do not snigger; I have done this several times and it is a royal pain to track down!

Drawback 2: Inheritance Has Programming Overhead

Just as object-oriented programming has overhead compared to modular programming, programming with inheritance has overhead over object-oriented programming. Inheritance requires you to keep track of inheritance trees, create multiple files to hold child objects, worry about putting use statements in each of the children, sync everything up, and, of course, test.

The fact that all this is going on at the same time makes it more difficult to concentrate on what you are doing when setting up an inheritance tree.

The best way to show this overhead is by looking at the before and after effects in a diagram. Figure 19.5 shows how our code will change when we introduce inheritance to the picture. Not only are there more files to

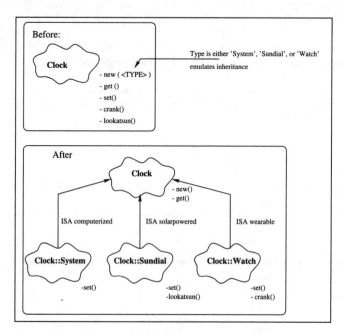

Figure 19.5
Before and After
Inheritance
Diagram

write, we also have to create a directory (to put in System.pm, Sundial.pm, and Watch.pm), and make sure the three files work as a team to get the desired effect.

Drawback 3: Inheritance Decreases Flexibility

Most of the time, there is also a third, more subtle drawback for inheritance. This is the lack of flexibility that inheritance can cause for your code; when you make an inheritance relationship between objects, you are implying a dependency of one on the other.

Notice that if you set up **Clock::Sundial** as a child of **Clock** so they can share functionality, it makes **Clock::Sundial** dependent on **Clock**.

Suppose **Clock** has an element, time, which it uses when you call set():

```
Clock.pm:
package Clock;
sub set
{
    my ($self, $time) = @_;
    $self->{'time'} = $time;
}
```

Programming set() in this way commits to having an element inside the object called time. Any child object of **Clock** must know about the object element time if it wants to use the results of the set function.

For example, say we wanted to make a get function inside **Clock::System:**

```
package Clock::System;
@ISA = qw (Clock);
sub get
{
    my ($self) = @_;
    return($self->{'time'});
}
```

In this case, the **Clock::System** object needs to know about the time element as set in **Clock**. Without it, there would be no way of returning the time element as made by the **Clock::set()** method call!

Note

Notice, however, that this lack of flexibility is from the point of view of the *programmer* and not the *user.* If you want, you can do something like:

```
my $type = 'Clock::Sundial';
my $clock = new $type('Dec 15 1995');
```

This is dynamic-type binding and it is much more difficult to do in C++ than in Perl! This facility in Perl makes inheritance much more practicable.

Of course, we could program our own set() function inside **Clock::System,** something like:

```
package Clock::System;
@ISA = qw(Clock);
sub set
```

```
{
    my ($self) = @_:
    $self->{'mytime'} = time;
}
sub get
{
    my ($self) = @_;
    return($self->{'mytime'});
}
```

Because there is a separate set() function, we break the dependency that **Clock::System** has on the element time. We call the relevant element mytime instead. However, we also are not using inheritance often. In fact, we are avoiding inheritance for the sake of flexibility.

If one of your objects inherits from the other, but you are rewriting your code in this way quite a bit, you should probably be splitting these objects into two separate, unrelated objects. Inflexibility in design can be a real killer, especially at the early stages of object design.

Inheritance Benefits

You might be wondering why people would even use inheritance in the first place. Some people do find the above drawbacks too much of a liability and never use inheritance. However, there are three positive benefits of inheritance that can outweigh the negatives.

Inheritance Enforces Programming Consistency

You might think of this rule as the direct corollary of the "loss of flexibility" rule given earlier. Every ounce of flexibility you lose by using inheritance, you gain in programming consistency.

Consider what we did to the **Clock::System** object, for example. We were forced to keep a certain structure for the objects we created. Since **Clock::set()** used the element $self->{'time'}, **Clock::System::get()** also had to use the element $self->{'time'}.

Thus, we can use inheritance to tie two different implementations together so that they don't diverge from one another. Of course, if you then change the parent object so that it uses $self->{'mytime'} itself, you then have to change all your child objects to use $self->{'mytime'} as well.

Inheritance Models Subtypes Well

This is the reason why most people use inheritance, and it is quite true. (It is difficult to discuss this except by example, and we will get to these later on.) The important thing to remember is that inheritance can model the subtype relationship well, but it doesn't necessarily have to. Following is a small example (a caveat) of a time when you perhaps would not want to model a subtype relationship in this way.

Caveat in Inheritance Modeling Subtypes

Consider if you were to make an object that represented "money." You might have subtypes, such as bonds, stocks, currency, and gold, and your design might look something like Figure 19.6.

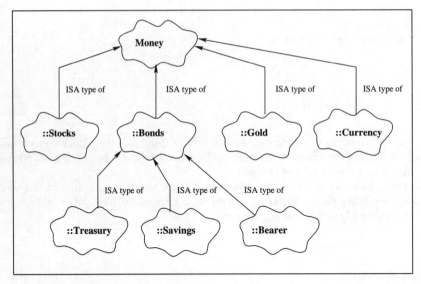

Figure 19.6
Inheritance
Relationship for
Money Objects

The next step is to make a money parent object, and then several inherited objects with attributes of their own. We could then define an object as:

```
my $a = new Money::Bonds::Savings('100.00');
```

to make $100 worth of savings bonds. However, this is a short-sighted design. What happens if we want to change our bonds into currency? We are then stuck with the ignoble task of taking our object, destroying it as it currently stands, and then recreating it as currency!

This would require an additional converter object that knows how to convert between different types of currency. We therefore have added a bunch of complexity that we do not need.

What went wrong here is that modeling money is a fluid problem, whereas inheritance imposes a certain rigidity on the problem domain. Here, the disadvantage of "lack of flexibility" overwhelms the advantage of how inheritance can model subtypes. We will see a lot of this give and take when we get to the examples.

Inheritance Lets You Split Up Monolithic Code

One common practice of beginning object-oriented programmers is to have one, big object, which is infinitely configurable. In fact, we have already seen some objects like this in previous chapters: the **LogObject** object in Chapter 18, the **Piece** object in Chapter 17, and also the **Expect** example in Chapter 18.

All these objects had one thing in common. They had a `type` attribute, which was really doing the inheritance work. When we defined the **LogObject**, we had the following private data at the top of the object:

```
8   my $_defaultConfig = { 'type' => 'regular', 'action' => 'append' };
9   my $_legal = { 'action' => { 'append' => '> ','overwrite' =>'> ' },
10              'type' =>    { 'regular' => 1, 'stamped' => 1 }
11          };
```

The only purpose of the `type` information in this code is to get information from the user for the object. Hence, we had the `write()` function, which looked something like:

```
44 sub write
45 {
```

```
46      my ($self, @text) = @_;
47      my $config = $self->{config};
48      my ($type, $fh) = ($config->{type}, $self->{filehandle});
49      if     ($type eq 'regular') { $self->_writeRegular(@text); }
50      elsif ($type eq 'stamped') { $self->_writeStamped(@text); }
51  }
52
```

In other words, this is a big if-then statement. It makes a call to a different private function (in bold) based on the type passed to the object from the user.

This design isn't necessarily a bad thing. For example, it puts all your functionality in one place. Some folks would vehemently disagree with this statement, they would say the design becomes inflexible because of this. I disagree. Because all the functionality is in one place, it is quite easy to trace, and can be easy to debug. If you used inheritance, it would be more difficult to debug because the code is spread into several objects.

Realize, though, that this practice is not scalable. If you do a lot of this, your code can become tangled up in itself, and the code can be long. I have seen modules 5,000 lines long!

Negative Effects of Monolithic Code

There are two major ways monolithic code can cause problems. The first is that modification of the code becomes difficult. If your code becomes monolithic, it starts to control you, rather than you controlling it.

Consider source control problems. If you have a 5,000-line module and two different people need to make changes in it simultaneously, there will be a bit of a tug-of-war. You will need to simultaneously check the code, make changes, and then merge the changes. If you have ever done any merges, you know they are not fun. If two people change the same piece of code at the same time, then it's going to be a puzzle to figure out which was the right change.

The second problem that can be caused by monolithic code is that your code can become entangled. Once your code becomes a certain length, it will be almost impossible to pull apart. Suppose for example that _writeStamped() calls _writeRegular(), something like:

```
sub _writeStamped
{
    my ($self, @text) = @_;
    my $fh = $self->{filehandle};
    my $script = $0; my $time = localtime();
    print $fh "$script:$time ";
    $self->_writeRegular();
}
```

This works because _writeStamped() simply writes the script name, the time the entry was made, and the output of _writeRegular() afterward. However, the two lines of code this action saves you also create a dependency of _writeStamped() on _writeRegular().

When you try to move _writeStamped() to its own file, you will find that it depends on _writeRegular() and the function will not work. Also, when you try to change _writeRegular(), you also change _writeStamped() by default! This is almost worse, since it is a silent error, and will make your program die without telling you.

When objects become large, in the 1,000–5,000 line range, these interdependencies can choke your objects like lilies choke a stagnant pond. Figure 19.7 shows a dependency diagram that shows how functions call each other in our simple example (before and after). Note how this change has turned the dependency diagram from a strict hierarchy (in the first part of the diagram) into a triangle, a loop. This is what causes things to become much more immobile. The objects become like a house of cards; if one card moves or is displaced, the whole structure collapses.

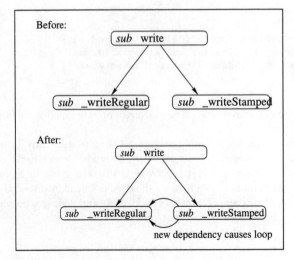

Figure 19.7
Dependency
Diagrams for
LogObject>

Of course, you can simply avoid these interdependencies by not using inheritance to help you. However, inheritance can be used as a blockade. With an inherited structure, `_writeRegular()` would be moved to its own file, so you can never call it like this.

Think of inheritance as a tool for cleaving monolithic code into pieces that would otherwise stick together, and be difficult to break apart. By enforcing a strict hierarchy, inheritance makes it easier for you to better design. As always is the case with OO principles, take this advice with a bit of caution!

Summary of Inheritance Benefits and Drawbacks

Inheritance is by no means a panacea—to think you should always use it is a mistake. In fact, you should weigh quite carefully whether or not you should be using inheritance every single time your project reaches a growth point and you must make a decision on how to scale up code. Remember: Inheritance is not your only choice; layering is a reasonable alternative that we discuss in Chapter 20.

In brief, here are the drawbacks and benefits of inheritance that we discussed earlier. The drawbacks are:

1. Using inheritance makes a solution more complicated than if it were a one-object solution.
2. Inheritance has a larger overhead than a one-object solution.
3. Inheritance lessens flexibility in structuring objects.

The benefits are:

1. Inheritance enforces consistency on objects; it forces them to work with each other.
2. Inheritance can model relationships where one object is a variation of another (hydrogen *ISA* atom).
3. Inheritance can split up monolithic code.

Now, the process of actually using inheritance is a question of seeing whether the advantages of inheritance fit more closely with your problem than the disadvantages. Next, we consider three different examples and how inheritance could be used in them.

Examples of When or When Not to Use Inheritance

You should think things through well before you decide to scale up code by using inheritance. I generally go through a four-step process in designing and/or implementing an inheritance solution. The steps are:

1. Define the problem. Defining the problem gives you a lot of information about what will and will not work, as well as giving ideas on how to implement. If the design looks like it might be a potential candidate for inheritance, I go to step 2.
2. Write the object diagram (i.e., code skeleton) as if it were one object, and the equivalent object diagram as if it were inherited. This solidifies how you are going to implement the solution, and gives you an idea about whether or not the object is a good candidate for inheritance. In an inherited solution, how much overlap will there be? Too much? Too little?
3. List the pros and cons of inheritance for the problem. Here, be brutally honest, cataloging what are the benefits and the negatives of inheritance in this situation. The important part of this step is honesty; it does not pay to design and implement inheritance and find out that it was a bad idea (although everybody does it sometimes).
4. Make a decision. After doing all this preparatory work, make a decision on what to do. If the answer is a clear "yes," implement inheritance. If it is a "maybe," look at other solutions. I usually wait a while for the answer to become clear. If it is a "no," we should look at layering.

So let's look at three examples and go step-by-step through the process of deciding whether or not something is fit for inheritance. Let's start with the **Piece** example we developed in Chapter 17.

Example 1: The `Piece` Class: Inheritance or Not?

We developed the **Piece** class with the idea that it was going to be the foundation class for our game *Strategem*. Hence, it has the potential to become pretty complicated. Should inheritance be used to scale up this particular class?

The Problem

The way we wrote **Piece.pm** had some difficult points. We had several different types of pieces stuffed into a single class. We could define an *admiral* by saying:

```
my $admiral = new Piece('admiral','red',3,5);
```

to define an *admiral* on the red side on the square 3,5, and we could say:

```
my $scout = new Piece('scout', 'black',3,2);
```

to define a *scout* on the black side on the square 3,2. However, this flexibility had a cost. The _validate() function, which we wrote to do some checking, was getting pretty complicated, as was _fill(). Can we get rid of some of this complexity by using inheritance by saying:

```
my $admiral = new Piece::Admiral('red',3,5);
```

instead, and letting inheritance take some of the job of validating the pieces (seeing if they are correct)?

Write Object Diagrams, Inheritance versus Noninheritance Solutions

To determine the answer to this question, lay the object diagrams down side by side and compare them. Which functions do we put in the parent? Which in the child? Which ones don't we know about? The best diagram I could come up with is shown in Figure 19.8. What is fairly apparent here is that there is not much to inherit. The only function we have included in our child objects is new(). Furthermore, we have to rename new() to _new() in the parent object, since some of the work will still be done by the parent in constructing its children; there is some stuff in all places that is in common.

Figure 19.8
Object Diagram
for **Piece** Class

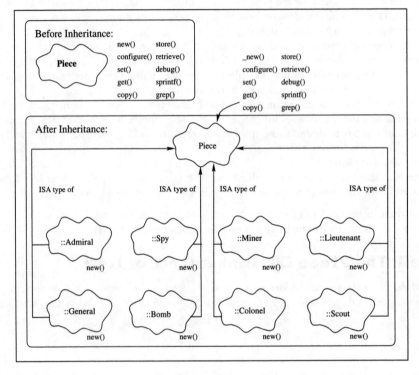

Let's go back to the implementation of the **Piece** example. Notice that everything in the **Piece** object was dependent on one hash, the config hash.

For example, the get object was programmed as follows:

```
100  sub get
101  {
102      my ($self, $element) = @_;
103      my $config = $self->{config};
104      if (defined ($self->{$element}))
105      {
106          return($self->{$element});
107      }
108      elsif (defined ($config->{$element}))
109      {
110          return($config->{$element});
111      }
112  }
113
```

which then went into the config hash to get a particular element. As it stands, there is a default config hash that looks like:

```
8    my $_config =
9            {
22              'admiral' => {
23                              'attacking_rank' => 1,
24                                  'movement' => 1,
25                                  'defending_rank' => 1
26                          },
27
28              'scout' =>    {
29                              'attacking_rank' => 9,
30                              'movement' => 100,
31                              'defending_rank' => 9
32                          },
33              # REST OF HASH.
34          }
```

This has quite an impact on how we would implement inheritance. The only way to implement an inheritance tree (without having to rewrite everything) is to split the packages along data lines, and not along functional lines. If we do not do this, then we will have to change the entire strategy on how we write get, set, store, etc. Each child class would have a header that looks like Listing 19.1.

Listing 19.1
Piece::Admiral header

```
Piece/Admiral.pm
1   package Piece::Admiral;
2
3   use Piece;
4   @ISA = qw (Piece);
5   use strict;
6
7   my $_config =                {
8                                   'attacking_rank' => 1,
9                                   'movement' => 1,
10                                  'defending_rank' => 1
11                               };
```

We have taken the config hash from the parent, and turned it into a one-dimensional hash that contains only the attributes for *admirals*. Again, @ISA is used to show that **Piece::Admiral** inherits from the class **Piece**. We have to include that functionality by saying use Piece at the beginning of the package.

When we are done with this, we must have a way to actually convey that information to the main **Piece** class, so it can store the information inside $self->{config}.

Note

An alternative is to write our own _fill() and _validate() functions inside each of the nine objects, for a total of 18 functions. Because pieces only differ by data and not by functionality, these _fill() and _validate() functions will look exactly the same!

We must write our own constructor for each class to pass $_config to the main parent class. This constructor might look something like Listing 19.2.

Listing 19.2
Piece::Admiral new() constructor

```
12  sub new
13  {
14      my ($type, $color, $xcoord, $ycoord, $config) = @_;
15      my $self = bless {}, $type;
16      $self->_new($color, $xcoord, $ycoord, $config, $_config);
17      $self;
18  }
```

The key line is line 16. Here, we put $_config into a call of the old constructor, the one defined inside **Piece.pm**. This is why we need to rename new inside **Piece::Admiral**. Since we already have a new function there, if we do not rename it, it won't be called. Anyway, it makes sense to rename it to be private since **Piece::_new()** is now private: it should never be called directly by any client that uses the **Piece::** hierarchy.

Since we are now calling **Piece::_new()** in the clients, we must reflect that change inside the parent object itself. We therefore change our constructor to look something like Listing 19.3.

Listing 19.3
Piece::Admiral constructor after inheritance

```
44  sub _new
45  {
46      my ($self, $piece_side, $xcoord, $ycoord, $config, $_config) = @_;
47
48
49      (print(STDERR "Incorrect Args!\n", Carp::longmess()), return(undef))
50                              if (@_ != 6);
51      $config = $config || {};
52      %$config = (%$config,
53                      piece_side => $piece_side,
54                      piece_no = $_pieceNo
55                  );
56  #  my $self = bless {}, $type;  take out.
57      $self->_fill
58          (
59              {
60                  'type' => $piece_type,
61                  'xcoord' => $xcoord,
62                  'ycoord' => $ycoord,
63              },
64              $config, $_config
65          );
66
67      $self->_validate($_config);
68      $self->_recordDebug('after') if ($self->{'debug'} eq 'on');
69                      # retrofitted for function debug() see debug method below.
70      return($self);
71  }
72
```

The boldface arguments are new; the rest of the constructor can stay the same. Note that we have to change new() into a function that takes a class name as an argument into one that takes an object. This is because the children are now calling the constructor as an object method and not a class method. We would have to go through and change _fill() and _validate() as well, because they have some dependencies on $_config. Since we have gone this far, we might as well show the new versions:

```
201 sub _fill
202 {
203     my ($self, $elemhash, $config $_config) =@_;
204     $self->{'debugstuff'} = $self->{'debugstuff'} || [];
205     $elemhash = $elemhash || {};
206     $config   = $config   || {};
207     my $status = 0;
208     $status += _returnIfWrongTypeandDefined($elemhash, 'argument 1', 'HASH');
209     $status += _returnIfWrongTypeandDefined($config,   'argument 2', 'HASH');
209     $status += _returnIfWrongTypeandDefined($_config,  'argument 3', 'HASH');
210
211     return(undef) if ($status > 0);
212
213     %$self = (%$self, %$elemhash);
214
215     # my $piece_type = $elemhash->{'type'} || $self->{'type'} ||
216     #        print(STDERR "Couldn't get a piece type!\n", Carp::longmess());
217
218     #  my $default_config = $_config->{$piece_type} || {};
219     if (!defined ($self->{'config'}))    # removed piece stuff.
220     {
221         %{$self->{'config'}} = %{$_config};  # used to be default config
222     }
223     else
224     {
225         my $key;
226         foreach $key (keys(%$_config))           # used to be default config.
227         {
228             if (!defined $self->{'config'}->{$key}
229                     || $self->{'config'}->{$key} =~ m"CODE")
230             {
231                 $self->{'config'}->{$key} = $default_config->{$key};
232             }
233         }
234     }
235
236     if (ref($config) eq 'HASH')
237     {
238         %{$self->{'config'}} = (%{$self->{'config'}}, %$config);
239     }
240 }
```

All we did is take out the code concerned with typing (lines 215–218), and substitute the variable $default_config for what we got from the child ($_config). $default_config is going away because the work it does (getting the different types for pieces) is going to be taken over by our inheritance tree. We do the same substitution of $default_config for $_config in the function _validate():

```
260 sub _validate
261 {
262     my ($self, $_config) = @_;
263
264
265     my $type = $self->{'type'};
266     my $config = $self->{'config'};
267     my @errors;
268
269     # push (@errors, "Bad piece type :$type:!\n")
270     #     if (!defined ($_config->{$type}));
271
272     my ($key) = '';
273     # my $typeconfig = $_config->{$type} || {};
274
275     foreach $key (keys %$_config)
276     {
277         push (@errors, "invalid key :$key:!\n")
278             if (!defined ($_config->{$key}));
279     }
280     print (STDERR @errors, Carp::longmess()) if (@errors);
281 }
282
```

The boldface lines are taken out; these lines have to do with the old way of doing things by looking up the correct values inside the old, global hash reference $_config.

List Pros and Cons of Inheritance for the Example

What can be said about this solution so far? After we would be done with our inheritance implementation, there are the following drawbacks:

- Nine extra files
- Nine extra new() constructors inside the nine new files
- Nine extra class variables (one $_config per class)
- One extra directory (**Piece/**)
- A more complicated path to trace when debugging and coding
- Changing three functions inside the central parent **Piece** class

As for the plusses, we would have:

- A slightly simpler _validate() and _fill()

So, based on this thought experiment (which we actually implemented to show what goes into making something use an inheritance hierarchy) we have come up with six negatives, and one shaky positive. It is pretty easy to determine the best decision.

Make a Decision on Inheritance

The decision is that we don't want to make this problem use inheritance. Not only have we made things more complicated by using inheritance (with nine files and nine extra functions to boot), but also we must ask ourselves how the loss of flexibility we get by putting things into an inherited format will affect the solution of our problem.

We were, in fact, being a bit naive. In this case, inheritance actually makes finding a solution more difficult. To see why, I quote part of the domain example:

> In our mock Strategio game we will remove these constraints [rigidity of pieces, etc]. Pieces should have the ability to be promoted, to go up a rank if they capture so many enemy pieces, demoted if they retreat from battle. Recruits are another possibility, in which a side that is losing can gain more pieces and build more.

What does "promoted" or "demoted" mean in the context of this example? It means that if we have constructed an object as follows:

```
my $object = new Piece::General('red',3,1);
```

we somehow must be able to turn this piece into an *admiral* (promote it) or turn it into a *colonel* (demote it). Before, when we had everything in one object, we could say something like:

```
$object->set({'type' => 'admiral' });
```

to actually "flip the switch" and make the object an *admiral*. However, the way it stands now, we have no way to perform this promotion. We would have to dump the data structure out into a hash, and then "re-bless" the **Piece::General** to be a **Piece::Admiral**.

Not only does inheritance make the project more complicated here, it actually doesn't fit the problem domain as well as a simple, one-object solution did.

Summary

There are many things to be said about this example. We went through the process of making a before and after diagram, and then thought about the pros and cons of making the **Piece** object an inheritance hierarchy.

Just for kicks, then, in thinking about these pros and cons, we implemented the object as it would look using inheritance. Finally, we decided that it was not the best idea to have the **Piece** class use inheritance after all.

However, there are some more abstract points to be made. I really expected the **Piece** object to be suitable for inheritance; in fact, I designed the example with inheritance in mind! When it came time to actually implement it, though, I thought carefully and in much detail as to what inheritance would require, including the benefits and drawbacks. All the information pointed to inheritance being the wrong tool for the job, so I switched my outlook 180° and decided not to force the issue.

I'm all for experimentation, but I advise that you be 100 percent honest with your own code, realizing that no code is perfect, and that mistakes will always be plentiful. I hope I'm not preaching the obvious, but I have fallen in this trap many times. Try to save yourself by being impartial with your code.

Example 2: The `LogObject` Object: Inheritance or Not?

Now let's look at a more practical example borrowed from Chapter 18. As you may remember, the **LogObject** was an object that spit out log files, which, as we left it, were of two types:

1. **regular**—simply spit out the text as the user passed it to the **LogObject** function.
2. **stamped**—was a time-stamped type of log for the **LogObject** function. It not only tells when a log entry was made, but also shows which script made the entry.

As of now, we have the **LogObject** in one centralized class. Does it make sense to split it into several smaller classes?

The Problem

When we implemented the **LogObject** in Chapter 18, we noted a couple of things. First, an average call to create a **LogObject** looked something like this:

```
my $object = new LogObject
                (
                    'filename',
                    { 'type' => 'regular', 'action' => 'append'}
                );
```

Even when we wrote this down, we remarked that it was complicated. When we gave it an explicit type like this (type => 'regular'), the main code that was affected was the write function, which looked something like this:

```
44 sub write
45 {
46     my ($self, @text) = @_;
47     my $config = $self->{config};
48     my ($type, $fh) = ($config->{type}, $self->{filehandle});
49     if    ($type eq 'regular') { $self->_writeRegular(@text); }
50     elsif ($type eq 'stamped') { $self->_writeStamped(@text); }
51 }
52
```

Lines 49 and 50 show what we might want to do: split up our object so that our constructor call looks something like:

```
my $object = new LogObject::Regular('filename', { 'action' => 'append' });
```

Should we use inheritance to make this change, and if so, how?

Object Diagrams: Before and After

As we did in the last example, let's look at the object diagrams generated from a before and after snapshot view of what inheritance will do. Figure 19.9 shows the results. As a part of looking toward the future, we have put in

Figure 19.9
Before and After
Shots of
LogObject

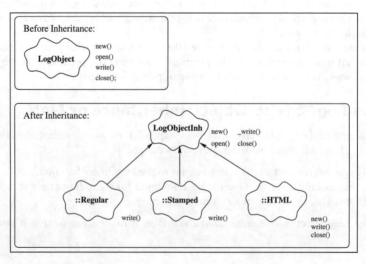

an extra object here: **LogObjectInh::HTML**. We name it **LogObjectInh** to differentiate from **LogObject** on the accompanying CD.

Now, by looking at this diagram, we can come up with a few observations about inheritance and how we would apply it to this problem. Note that this example falls almost squarely into the "inheritance hierarchy" concept. The child objects create one of their own functions, primarily across the board, and this one function is then modified for each object, to model how the child differs from the parent.

Now, the question is: how does this work? After all, we need to justify that the design is sound; we must be able to turn these pictures into code. Our main design point revolves around what `write` does.

Right now, our code for `write` looks like:

```
44 sub write
45 {
46     my ($self, @text) = @_;
47     my $config = $self->{config};
48     my ($type, $fh) = ($config->{type}, $self->{filehandle});
49     if    ($type eq 'regular') { $self->_writeRegular(@text); }
50     elsif ($type eq 'stamped') { $self->_writeStamped(@text); }
51 }
52
```

with `_writeStamped()` and `_writeRegular()` both doing the job of writing stuff to a file. Now, suppose we want to make it so we can write the text out to a database as well. We would have to write code that looks something like:

```
sub write
{
    my ($self, @text) = @_;
    my $config = $self->{'config'};
    my ($type, $fh) = ($config->{type}, $config->{dbase}, $self->{filehandle});
    if ($type eq 'regular' && $place eq 'file')
    {
        $self->_writeRegular('file', @text);
    }
    elsif ($type eq 'regular' && $place eq 'dbase')
    {
        $self->_writeRegular('dbase', @text);
    }
    elsif ($type eq 'stamped' && $place eq 'file')
    {
        $self->_writeStamped('file', @text);
    }
    elsif ($type eq 'stamped' && $place eq 'dbase')
    {
        $self->_writeStamped('file', @text);
    }
}
```

This is a parody: Don't write like this at home! It also gets worse when we add the ability to print out HTML. This is written to make a point: the preceding code is not doing a very good job of segregating out its tasks. The job of actually producing the text (`_writeStamped()`, `_writeRegular()`) is also in charge of deciding where the text is being printed (database or file).

We would like to make it so each `write()` function is in charge of producing the type of text it wants to print out, and **LogObjectInh::_write()**—the central source—is in charge of where to print our text. In other words, if we say:

```
my $object = new LogObjectInh::Regular('filename', { 'action' => 'append' } );
$object->write("my god! Its full of stars!");
```

this translates into:

```
LogObjectInh::Regular::write($object, "my god! It's full of stars!");
```

which should then call:

```
LogObjectInh::_write($object, "my god! It's full of stars!");
```

This function directs exactly where to print the text. Much more reuse! In fact, we can show this reuse by looking at another before and after diagram. Figure 19.10 is a functional diagram. In short, in the after diagram, `_write()` is used as a juncture point. All the child subroutines we will write go through it, so if we want to switch and write everything to e-mail or to a database, we can do so.

Figure 19.10
Functional
Diagrams
Showing Impact
of Inheritance

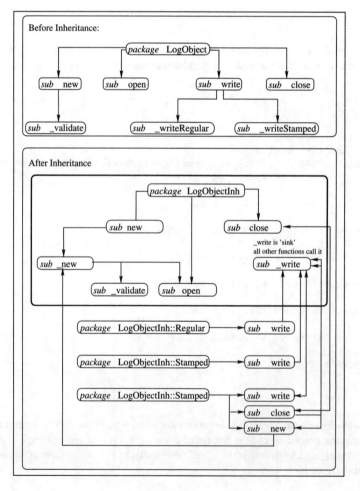

List Pros and Cons of Inheritance for this Example

We have gone through quite enough speculation. Now it's time to take what we have and turn it into a concrete list, something we can base a decision on.

Looking at this, we get the following cons:

- Multiple files: changing one file into four.
- Increased complexity of debugging inheritance.

The pros of using inheritance are:

- Cleaner design: We segregate the functionality well, so inheritance is doing the job of organizing our code for us.
- More scalable: We have already experimented with how (conceptually) we could add HTML support, and database support.

Furthermore, listing the pros and cons gives us a chance to go ahead and rethink our design. Right now, we have something that looks like this for an interface:

```
my $object = new LogObject('filename',{'type' => 'regular','action' => 'append'});
$object->open();
$object->write("my god! It's full of stars!");
```

which, to me is just a tad on the non-user-friendly side. Let's think of making it more along these lines:

```
my $object = new LogObject::Regular('> filename');
$object->write("my god! It's full of stars!");
```

This is one step shorter, has no `config` hash in the constructor (so we can save that for really important things, such as where to output the data), and generally looks much easier to use.

Make a Decision

Now let's implement **LogObject** using inheritance. Looking at the list, it looks like the advantages outweigh the disadvantages, and it gives us a good chance to rethink our design. Plus, even if it turns out not to be as helpful as we hoped, we still learn about objects and inheritance in the process. Whatever lessons we get from trying this out, we will probably get in the first few weeks of usage. We can then take this experience and apply it to an even better solution later. The only thing we have to think about is how to implement this; this is what we turn to next.

Implementation

Actually implementing inheritance is an iterative process. Each person has his or her own method for implementation, but I generally take the following four steps in making an inheritance hierarchy:

1. Lay out inheritance diagrams and, at the same time, look carefully at existing code (if there is any).
2. Implement one (and only one) of the children. Because this child will be using functions inside the parent that have not been written yet, there is no way to test the code at this stage.
3. Change the parent, or make a new parent to use that child and test that change. For the sake of being able to back out, I usually name the parent code something different than it was before (**LogObjectInh** instead of **LogObject**).
4. Implement the rest of the children. One at a time, I test the children with the parent to make sure each of them is working correctly.

This way, I have a nice incremental process to work with. If I do not like the results, I back up and start looking for other solutions. Let's go do this, and see where it gets us.

Implementing `LogObjectInh::Regular`

The first child we should implement is **LogObjectInh::Regular** because it is the simplest. It will give you a good starting point from which to work. In Listing 19.4, the module is pretty easy:

Listing 19.4
LogObjectInh::Regular

```
LogObjectInh/Regular.pm

1   package LogObjectInh::Regular;
2
3   use LogObjectInh;
4   @ISA = qw (LogObjectInh);
5
6   sub write
7   {
8       my ($self, @text) = @_;
9       $self->_write("@text\n");
10  }
11  1;
```

Here, as we said earlier, the write function's job is merely to determine what to write. In this case, it is an easy job. It is merely the concatenation of all the text supplied by the user. The actual job is done by the central function `LogObjectInh::_write()`, not locally. Other than that, be careful to put the `@ISA` relationship in, and be sure to `use LogObjectInh;`. These two steps are necessary to make the inheritance work transparently.

Implementing `LogObjectInh::Stamped`

Because that was so easy, let's implement the second child module **LogObjectInh::Stamped**. I would usually integrate the child into the parent at this stage, but the two are so similar that it is probably a good idea to compare both of them one after another.

LogObjectInh::Stamped primarily comes from the same mold as our first child class; the only difference between it and **LogObjectInh::Regular** is that **LogObjectInh::Stamped** "pretty prints" its log text. It looks like Listing 19.5.

Listing 19.5
LogObjectInh::Stamped

```
LogObjectInh/Stamped.pm

1   package LogObjectInh::Stamped;
2
3   use LogObjectInh;
4   @ISA = qw (LogObjectInh);
5
6   sub write
7   {
8       my ($self, @text) = @_;
9       my $script = $0;
10      my $time = localtime();
11      $self->_write("$script:$time:@text\n");
12  }
13  1;
```

This is exactly the same as our other child class, except that we get the script name in line 9 and the time in line 10 and then write it out, along with the text passed from the user, in line 11. We again use the central _write() function, gotten through inheritance, to do the actual printing. From the point of view of the child, we have no clue where the output is going.

Integrating the Children into the Parent

Our job now is to make sure that the children work with the parent. The obvious function that must change is write(), for the reasons just stated. However, there are other things that must change. The headers and the new() function must change, because, as of now, they have "typing" information whose job is being taken over by our inheritance hierarchy.

Note

We are also going to cheat and split the **new()** constructor into two parts. This is to support a change necessary for **LogObject::HTML**. Usually, this would be an iterative change, happening over the course of using it, but our space is limited.

Start with the headers, and the new function. They have changed quite a bit, as shown in Listing 19.6.

Listing 19.6
LogObjectInh headers and new()

```
LogObjectInh.pm
1   package LogObjectInh;
2
3   use strict;
4   use Carp;
5   use FileHandle;
6   use Diff;
7   use Data::Dumper;
8
9   # my $_defaultConfig = { 'type' => 'regular', 'action' => 'append' };
10  # my $_legal = { 'action' => { 'append' => '> ','overwrite' =>'> ' },
11  #                'type' =>    { 'regular' => 1, 'stamped' => 1 }
12  #            };
13  #
14
15  my $_defaultConfig= {'action' => '> ' };
16
17  sub new
18  {
19      my ($type, $filename, $config) = @_;
20      my $self = bless {}, $type;
21      $self->_new($filename, $config);
22  }
```

The first thing to notice is that we have vastly simplified the class data ($_defaultConfig and $_legal). Instead of four lines being devoted to configuration information, we now have one. This makes the module cleaner and easier to understand.

Second, the new() constructor is now a simple wrapper around _new(). Why do this? The idea is that the _new() function will consist of all the "common code"—the code that every child class will use. new() will simply be a wrapper that calls _new()—it is provided as a default constructor for the object.

Then, if we come across a child class with different requirements for being constructed, we can have that class do something like the following:

```
1   package LogObjectInh::ObjectWithDifferentNew;
2   use LogObjectInh;
3   @ISA = qw (LogObjectInh);
4
5   sub new
6   {
7       my ($type, @args) = @_;
8       # do other things with the arguments
9       my $self = bless {}, $type;
10      # do even more...
11      $self->_new(@args);
12      # do even more....
13  }
```

The important line is line 11. We do other things inside the child's version of the constructor, and then call the parent's constructor, so we get a consistent interface.

The next thing is the _new() function that actually does all the work (Listing 19.7).

Listing 19.7
LogObjectInh::_new() private function

```
14  sub _new
15  {
16      my ($self, $filename, $config) = @_;
17      my (%fullconfig, $action);
18
19      confess "Config has to be a hash!\n" if
20                      ($config && ref($config) ne 'HASH');
21
22      $config = $config || {};
23      if ($filename =~ m"(>*)") { $action = $1; }
24      $filename =~ s"[> ]""g;
25
26      $config = { %$_defaultConfig,
27                  'action'=>$action,%$config } if ($action);
28      $config = { %$_defaultConfig, %$config } if (!$action);
29
30      $config = { 'action' => $action, %$config };
31      $self->{filename} = $filename;
32
33      %fullconfig = (%$config);
34      $self->{config} = \%fullconfig;
35      $self->_validate();
36      $self->open();
37      $self;
38  }
```

We are doing a couple of things here. First, we turn the function from one that takes a class name ($type) into an object method (using $self) in line 16. We do this to support variations of constructors in the children, as outlined.

Second, we take the opportunity to change the interface: lines 22–30 support the syntax:

```
my $file = new LogObjectInh::Regular('> filename');
```

Instead of looking at a hash attribute {'action' => 'append'}, simply look for > signs in our first argument. If we find any, then those are what we use to figure out whether or not we are going to append.

In fact, this uses exactly the same syntax as open(FD, "> filename"); and my $fh = new FileHandle("> filename");, so we get the added benefit of a consistent interface with the rest of the file code. Note also the $self->open() in line 36. This makes it so we, the users, don't have to type this. (After all, what is the use of a closed **LogFile**?)

Now, all we have to do is write the functions that do the work (write, close, and open), as shown in Listing 19.8.

Listing 19.8
LogObjectInh: close(), open(), write()

```
39 sub open
40 {
41     my ($self) = @_;
42     $self->{'closed'} = 0;
43     my ($config) = $self->{'config'};
44     my ($action, $filename) = ($config->{'action'}, $self->{'filename'});
45     my $fh=new FileHandle("$action $filename") || die "Couldn't open$filename";
46
47     $self->{filehandle} = $fh;
48 }
49
50 sub _write
51 {
52     my ($self, @text) = @_;
53     my $config = $self->{config};
54     my $fh = $self->{filehandle};
55
56 #     if    ($type eq 'regular') { $self->_writeRegular(@text); }
57 #     elsif ($type eq 'stamped') { $self->_writeStamped(@text); }
58
59     print $fh "@text";
60 }
61
62 sub close
63 {
64     return(1) if ($self->{'closed'});
65     close($_[0]->{filehandle});
66     $self->{'closed'} = 1;
67 }
```

These three functions are almost exactly like they were before. open() is identical, as is close() except for one change: we have added a toggle switch that prevents us from closing a file twice, which is more an enhancement than anything else. It is only _write() that is an oddball. Lines 55 and 56 (where we decided what write function to call based on the type) is history, and has been replaced by the simple statement in line 58.

Again, the idea is to make it so that _write (and open() and close()) is the focus of attention rather than having the functionality spread over different subroutines. All we have to do is make sure that the object is correct. We do this with our _validate() function (Listing 19.9), which essentially remains unchanged.

Listing 19.9
LogObjectInh::_validate() private function

```
sub _validate
{
    my ($self) = @_;
    my (@errors);
    my ($config, $filename) = ($self->{config}, $self->{filename});

    my @keys = keys (%$config); my @legal = keys (%$_defaultConfig);
    my $diff = Diff::array(\@keys, \@legal);
    push(errors, "Incorrect keys :@$diff: passed to LogObject!\n")
                                            if (@$diff);
    push(errors, "Unwriteable log file! $filename\n")
                          if (!(new FileHandle("> $filename")));
    confess ("@errors") if (@errors);
}
```

With these changes, we are ready to implement the last of the children we will consider, **LogObject::HTML**. This will be the true test of how well our inheritance scales up, since the process for making an HTML file is more difficult than simply writing text to a filehandle.

Implementing `LogObjectInh::HTML`

So what should we do to actually implement a **LogObjectInh::HTML** class? Notice that writing out an HTML file requires two things that are not a necessary part of simply writing out a log file.

First, an HTML file requires a suffix to be attached to its name in order to be interpreted as HTML. This suffix is either *.htm or *.html. Hence, any object that outputs HTML files will have to either check to see if the user has input the correct type of file, or actually enforce this standard for the user.

Second, in order for HTML to be interpreted as HTML, it requires tags at the beginning of the file, such as <HTML><BODY>. It also requires tags at the end of the file to match the ones at the beginning, such as </BODY></HTML>.

Finally, let's assume we want to restrict people to only appending to a file; we want to keep a complete record of what transpires in any HTML file. (If we allow overwrites, then any HTML log we made in the past would vanish. This isn't a necessity; it's just kind of cool to see how it's done.)

Doing all this will be more difficult with the **LogObjectInh::HTML** than the other two. Figure 19.11 is the object diagram that shows the new relationship that we are striving for. Therefore, we need to implement three different functions. We will implement a new(), because we will need to add the "beginning tags" to the HTML file. Then come write() and close() functions. A different close() function is necessary because we need to add the "ending tags" to the HTML file.

Finally, there must be a DESTROY() function. Why? Well, when a user says:

```
my $html = new LogObjectInh::HTML('> filename');
$html->write('here!!!!');
```

and forgets to say $html->close(), we must add the ending tags to the HTML file to make it a complete HTML file. The DESTROY() function does this quite well, executing the close() function for us if we forget.

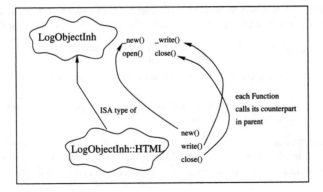

**Figure 19.11
LogObject
Inh::HTML**
Object Diagram

Let's implement this. First are the headers and the new() function:

```
LogObjectInh/HTML.pm
1   package LogObjectInh::HTML;
2
3   use LogObjectInh;
4   @ISA = qw (LogObjectInh);
5
6   use strict;
7
8   my $_defaultConfig = { 'action' => '>' };
9   sub new
10  {
11      my ($type, $filename, $config) = @_;
12      my $self = bless {}, $type;
13
14      if ($filename !~ m"\.htm(1)?$") { $filename = "$filename.html"; }
15
16      $config = $config || {};
17      $config = { %$_defaultConfig, %$config };
18
19
20      $self->_new($filename, $config);
21      ($self->{config}->{'action'} eq '>')
22                      || die "Need to use append!\n";
23      $self->open();
24      my $time = localtime();
25      $self->_write
26                      (
27  <<"EOL"
28  <HTML>
29  <HEAD>
30  <TITLE>log: $filename. Created by $0 at $time.</TITLE>
31  </HEAD>
32  <BODY>\n
33  EOL
34                      );
35      $self;
36  }
```

Compared to the previous children, this is much more elaborate. Needless to say, the other children didn't even have new() functions! We are doing five basic things here to satisfy the requirements of our problem domain:

1. Overriding the default configuration so that (by default) we append (line 8).
2. Making sure that the log has the suffix ***.htm** or ***.html** attached (line 14).
3. Making the configuration hash based on what the user has passed to us and the default for the package (lines 16 and 17).
4. Calling the function `$self->_new()`, which is translated into `LogObjectInh::_new()` (line 20).
5. Writing the headers to the HTML file (lines 26–34).

The way we are handling the configuration files is beginning to irritate me; it is just a bit unclean, since it directly accesses the configuration hash, two levels deep (lines 21 and 22). However, it is fine to make a solution like this, see how it works, and then tidy it up later. So make a mental note that we will return to the "scene of the crime" when we tidy this up later.

All we need to do now is write the last four functions (Listing 19.10):

Listing 19.10
LogObjectInh::HTML write() close() DESTROY()

```
37 sub write
38 {
39    my ($self, @text) = @_;
40    $self->_write("@text\n");
41 }
42
43 sub close
44 {
45    my ($self) = @_;
46    return(1) if ($self->{'closed'};
47    $self->_write(
48 <<"EOL2"
49 </BODY>
50 </HTML>
51 EOL2
52                    );
53    $self->SUPER::close();
54 }
55
56 sub DESTROY { my ($self) = @_; $self->close(); }
57 1;
```

Here, `close()` is the really interesting function. It is actually doing double duty. First, we must make sure that the file isn't closed (line 46), returning if it is, and then we must write out the information necessary to make the HTML file complete.

Summary of Example

As you can see from this discussion, inheritance requires a lot of thought, design, discussion, and give-and-take. It is, one might say, 90 percent thought and 10 percent action. And even after all of this thought and action, I'm still not satisfied with the result. For example, what happens if we want to print out a time-stamped entry into a HTML file? Do we say something like:

```
print LogObjectInh::HTML::Stamped;
```

making another layer of inherited objects? I am more inclined to perhaps extend the objects we have, maybe getting rid of **LogObjectInh::Stamped**, and concentrate on different types of items (like a "Regular" item, or a "Stamped" item). This is termed "layering" and will be covered in Chapter 20. Next, however, let's consider an example where we know that we are going to use inheritance, and simply do it.

Example 3: Using the Standard Distribution to Inherit: Tie::WatchHash

The standard distribution contains quite a few modules that are designed to do inheritance. **Autoloader, Exporter, DynaLoader**, and all the Tie modules (**Tie::Hash, Tie::Scalar**) are specifically for the purpose of inheritance. Here, we will be using an example of a common way to use one of these modules to lessen the pain of tie-ing a hash.

The Problem

Everybody has gone through a very common pain before. For some reason, the program does not work, they don't know why it doesn't work, and they spend a lot of time figuring out why it doesn't work. After hours of searching, they look at line 257, and find out that when they said:

```
257 if ($a{'value'} = 1)
258 {
259    doThis();
260 }
```

they have only put *one* equal sign when it should have been two.

Note

Although, if we were using -w in the first place, this mistake would never have happened.

What would be helpful here (and in other places) would be a way of putting a trace on a variable. When we say the following statement:

```
$a{'value'} = 2;
```

we would want to have our program print out:

```
%a - changed the key value to 2 at script.p line 257
```

to show that **script.p** has in fact changed the value of the key value to 2.

The easiest way to do this is via tie-ing. tie-ing lets you redefine what happens when a subroutine is stored, fetched, and so forth. However, you may recall from Chapter 16 (when we implemented a tied hash to count accesses to the hash) that tie-ing can be a lot of work. When we tie something, we need to define nine different subroutines:

```
TIEHASH
STORE
FETCH
FIRSTKEY
NEXTKEY
EXISTS
```

```
DELETE
CLEAR
DESTROY
```

Consider which of these subroutines are actually necessary for us to implement the WatchHash. Do we need a constructor to implement the functionality? No. STORE function? Yes. We need to print something every time we store something. FETCH? No. FIRSTKEY? No. NEXTKEY? No. EXISTS? No. DELETE? Yes. We need to print a message to the effect that something was destroyed. CLEAR? No. If we program it right, CLEAR can be defined in terms of DELETE, and in terms of FIRSTKEY and NEXTKEY, because all it is now is a bunch of deletes in a row. DESTROY? DESTROY could be defined in terms of CLEAR, so the answer is no.

This limits the functions we must define to STORE and DELETE. And although we won't actually need a constructor, we will define one anyway; as you will see, it will make the package more user-friendly. Hence, we come up with a preliminary object diagram, something that looks like Figure 19.12.

Figure 19.12
Preliminary
Inheritance
Diagram

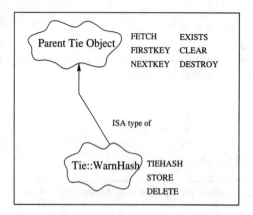

All we need to do is come up with something to inherit from. We look in the standard distribution (or go to CPAN), and come up with **Tie::Hash**. Opening it up, we find:

```
1   package Tie::StdHash::Encap;
2
3   @ISA = qw(Tie::Hash);
4   # The Tie::StdHash:Encap package implements standard Perl hash behavior, just
5   # like Tie::StdHash, but with a difference. All the data for the hash is put
6   # inside a '_tied' attribute. This makes it so you don't have key collisions
7   # inside your hash.
8
9
10  sub TIEHASH  { bless {}, $_[0] }
11  sub STORE    { $_[0]->{'_tied'}{$_[1]} = $_[2] }
12  sub FETCH    { $_[0]->{'_tied'}{$_[1]} }
13  sub FIRSTKEY {my $a=scalar keys %{$_[0]->{'_tied'}}; each %{$_[0]->{'_tied'}} }
14  sub NEXTKEY  { each %{$_[0]->{'_tied'}} }
15  sub EXISTS   { exists $_[0]->{'_tied'}{$_[1]} }
15  sub DELETE   { delete $_[0]->{'_tied'}{$_[1]} }
```

This is exactly what we need. It fills in almost all the holes. It ties the hash so that if you say:

```
my $obj = tie (%a, 'Tie::StdHash::Encap');
```

then `$obj` will return the object that is `tied` (i.e., connected to) `%a`, and such that:

```
$a{'array'} = 1;
```

actually calls:

```
$obj->STORE('array','1');
```

which in turn is translated into:

```
$obj->{'_tied'}{'array'} = 1;
```

All of the hash is designed this way so you get default hash behavior, yet can override certain methods through inheritance. The only methods left that aren't defined here are CLEAR and DESTROY. To get these, see that **Tie::StdHash::Encap** actually inherits off of **Tie::Hash**. When we look at that part of the file, we see:

```
1   sub CLEAR {
2       my $self = shift;
3       my $key = $self->FIRSTKEY(@_);
4       my @keys;
5
6       while (defined $key) {
7           push @keys, $key;
8           $key = $self->NEXTKEY(@_, $key);
9       }
10      foreach $key (@keys) {
11          $self->DELETE(@_, $key);
12      }
13  }
```

Aha! We find a CLEAR function, but not a DESTROY function. So our expanded inheritance hierarchy looks something like Figure 19.13. We therefore just need to define TIEHASH, STORE, and DESTROY. This follows next.

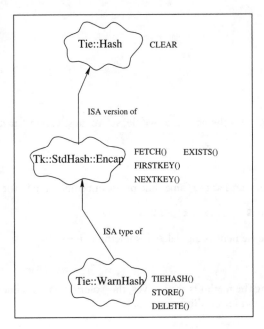

Figure 19.13
Improved
Inheritance
Diagram

Implementing *Tie::WarnHash*

```
1   package Tie::WarnHash;
2
3   use Tie::Hash;
4   use Carp;
5
6   @ISA = qw (Tie::StdHash::Encap);
7   use strict;
8
9   sub TIEHASH
10  {
11      my ($type, $name) = @_;
12      bless { 'name' => $name, '_tied' => {} }, $type;
13
14  }
15
16  sub STORE
17  {
18      $_[0]->{'_tied'}->{$_[1]} = $_[2];
19      print "\%$_[0]->{'name'} - element '$_[1]' changed to "
20                      ,"$_[2]",Carp::longmess();
21  }
22
23  sub DELETE
24  {
25      delete $_[0]->{'_tied'}->{$_[1]};
26      print "\%$_[0]->{'name'} - element '$_[1]' deleted ",Carp::longmess();
27  }
28
29  sub DESTROY
30  {
31      $_[0]->CLEAR();
32  }
33  1;
```

That's about it. TIEHASH associates a name with the hash that we tie, so we must create our hash elements by saying:

```
tie(%a, 'Tie::WarnHash', 'a');
```

STORE then does all assignments of hash keys, and at the same time prints out something in the format:

```
%a - element 'length' changed to 2 at script.p line 257
```

Finally, DELETE and DESTROY print out the element being deleted, something like:

```
%a - element 'length' deleted
```

By using inheritance instead of implementing the methods themselves, this solution has less lines of code associated with it, fewer subroutines to maintain, and fewer idiosyncrasies.

Implementing *Tie::WarnHashNew*

In fact, since that was so easy, let's make an additional hash that does just a bit more than the previous one. After this example is done, you will want to check out the public domain package **Tie::Watch**, which does this monitoring not only for hashes, but also for arrays and scalars.

We have done all the hard work in the example by thinking about how to do the inheritance, so now it is just a question of plug-and-play if we want projects that are similar. First, we think of how we can improve the preceding example. One way becomes clear pretty soon. Sometimes we don't want to monitor all of the hash. Say we wanted to monitor only the hash keys that start with *h*. Then, we would want to be able to say:

```
tie (  %hash, 'Tie::WarnHashNew', 'hash',
                sub {
                        my ($key, $value) = @_;
                        return(1) if ($key =~ m"^h");
                        return(0);
                }
       );
```

Here, we have added a callback to the end of **Tie::WarnHash**. This (optional) callback filters out which keys we want to monitor, and which keys we do not. In this case, we say we want to monitor it if $key =~ m"^h" (starts with an *h*) and we return a 1. If it doesn't start with an *h*, we fall through and return 0.

These return values are used by **Tie::WarnHashNew** to do this selective filtering. In general, the logic will look like:

```
my $cb = $self->{cb};
if (&$cb($key, $value)) { print "key changed!\n"; }
```

where $cb is the callback that we entered into the tie function, and $key and $value are the items we are putting into the hash. The actual code gets rougher. It's listed next:

```
1   package Tie::WarnHashNew;
2
3   use Tie::Hash;
4   use Carp;
5
6   @ISA = qw (Tie::StdHash::Encap);
7   use strict;
8
9   sub TIEHASH
10  {
11      my ($type, $name, $cb) = @_;
12      confess "$cb needs to be a code reference\n"
13                              if (defined($cb) && !ref($cb) eq 'CODE');
14
15      bless { 'name' => $name, 'cb' => $cb }, $type;
16  }
```

First, do the constructor. $cb holds the callback we discussed previously. We pass that as the last argument, and it in turn gets put into the object (in line 15) for storage.

```
17 sub STORE
18 {
19     $_[0]->{'_tied'}->{$_[1]} = $_[2];
20     if (($_[0]->{'cb'}) && (&{$_[0]->{'cb'}}($_[1], $_[2])))
```

```
21    {
22         print "\%$_[0]->{'name'} - element $_[1] changed to".
23                                " $_[2]", Carp::longmess();
24    }
25 }
26
27 sub DELETE
28 {
29    delete $_[0]->{'_tied'}->{$_[1]};
30    if (($_[0]->{'cb'}) && (&{$_[0]->{'cb'}}($_[1],'')))
31    {
32         print "\%$_[0]->{'name'} - element $_[1] deleted ",Carp::longmess();
33    }
34 }
35
36 sub DESTROY
37 {
38    $_[0]->CLEAR();
39 }
40 1;
```

In turn, STORE and DELETE take the callback to see if it is defined. If it is defined, we try it (lines 20 and 30). If the true value is returned from the callback, we print out that the element has changed, as we did before. If it is one of those hash keys we can ignore (and 0 or ' ' or undef) is returned, then we don't print it out.

Summary of Inheriting from Standard Distribution

Perl has quite a few built-in packages you can inherit from and you will probably want to check them out in the standard distribution. Packages such as **Autoloader** can make your Perl scripts faster by splitting them into chunks. **Dynaloader** is almost essential for linking C and C++ into Perl. **Exporter** we have already seen; it lets you move functions between packages so that you don't need to fully qualify them.

The main benefit of using these modules is that the work has already been done for you; by interfacing with them, you can learn better inheritance practices yourself.

Summary

As you can probably see, inheritance is not a technique to be taken lightly. It involves splitting code into multiple files, which always adds complexity, and sometimes leads to inflexibility.

Hence, inheritance is a tricky thing to do well; even after you are done with it, it is a hard thing to do in such a way that you aren't tweaking your code for a long time to come. You should always look at an inheritance plan very closely, and judge the solution you come up with against the other major alternative—layering, which we cover in Chapter 20.

20

Layering and Perl

This chapter deals with layering, the second major technique for scaling up projects (the first being inheritance). Layering is one of the great, unsung-hero techniques of object-oriented programming. When C++ came out, people went ga-ga over inheritance, thinking it was the great blessing that would cure all their programming woes. This is an exaggeration of what the literature said, but only a slight one.

What tended to be forgotten in all the excitement was that perfectly reasonable object languages existed before C++. The "oriented" part of "object-oriented" is because of inheritance; languages such as Ada and Modula were programming in an object paradigm and doing just fine for quite some time.

The technique these languages used for making objects work with each other was *layering*. I predict that layering will be used 90 percent of the time that you are creating object-oriented projects.

Chapter Overview

We have not yet formally discussed the layering technique. However, we have used it; it is difficult to perform organized object programming without using layering. This chapter will be one of formal recognition of layering, and expansion on the concept.

The first thing we need to do is understand what layering is by giving a formal definition, and see how we applied layering to programs in previous chapters. The second thing we need to do is to go into detailed examples about the concepts of which layering is composed. There are quite a few. We will cover:

- HASA, modifies, and uses
- Polymorphism
- Delegation

In addition, there are classes of design patterns that determine how you piece your objects together. We will cover:

- Singletons
- Containers
- Iterators

We will also go through examples of their use.

Finally, we will give real examples of how to use layering, which draw on earlier examples, and extend and enhance them. We will also consider a small but very viable (and useful) object-oriented project in PerlTk, which will set the stage for the chapters to come.

Layering Overview

Because you are doing 90 percent of your project building via layering, it is probably a good idea for you to understand what layering is. *Layering* (or *composition-* or *component-based programming*) is a technique of object-oriented programming in which an object is built from several different subobjects, each with its own role and functionality.

Some terms associated with layering are: *HASA*, *modifies*, and *uses*.

We briefly covered HASA in the last chapter. HASA sums up the layering relationship quite well. A cat *ISA* mammal, but a cat *HASA* tongue, claws, and a tail. A watch *ISA* clock, but a watch *HASA* dial, face, buttons, etc.

Modifies is a relationship between two objects such that one does not contain another, but instead one object changes another. A cat *HASA* tongue, and a cat *HASA* head of hair, but the tongue does not *HASA* head of hair. Instead, the tongue *modifies* the hair (i.e., it could clean it).

Likewise, *uses* is a less intrusive version of modifies; instead of changing another object's state, it gets information from that object. A piece of paper *uses* a paperclip (i.e., it takes from it the property to be able to bind paper). But it does not modify the properties of the paperclip itself.

Polymorphism and delegation are the relevant process terms of how layering is accomplished. *Polymorphism* is the ability to be able to call an object's method without knowing the object's type when you call it. Since Perl could care less about the type of the object and does all of its method checking at run time, Perl is known as *polymorphously perverse*. This means that it probably has more polymorphism than you would ever care to use!

Delegation is the process of passing functionality from one class to another, sort of like a manager handing out work to his or her employees. The manager may not know how to get the work done, but knows which employee is best for the job. Delegation is often used in conjunction with polymorphism.

In addition, there are design patterns you will use to construct your object-oriented projects. There are quite a few of these, so we will talk about a couple of major ones and let you discover the others on your own.

Singleton, container, and iterator are three of these design patterns. These design patterns are by no means exhaustive, of course. In fact, you could spend a long time learning all the possible design patterns.

Note

If you are interested in exactly what design patterns are available, the best resource is *Design Patterns: Elements of Reusable Object-Oriented Software*. If you want to learn object terms showing the structure of how they are used with many object diagrams, this is the text for you.

However, you can get by with just these three, and we give capsule definitions below:

- *Singleton:* A class that ensures that there is one and only one instance of itself (i.e., one and only one object created). Usually, this one instance is then available via a global pointer.

- *Container:* An object whose primary purposes are twofold: 1) to hold other objects or data, and 2) to provide a user interface to manipulate these objects or user data without exposing their underlying representations.
- *Iterator:* A class whose main task is to provide a user interface to access a list of contained objects, and which keeps track of its position inside that object list so the user of that class can cycle through them.

All these terms could earn their own chapter, but I will instead give some simple expansions of these capsule definitions, and then rely on examples to flesh them out.

Note

Since these patterns are so important, some might object to this treatment, saying that the best way to learn is by learning the theory first, and only then going to examples. I disagree. One of Perl's best strengths is that you can learn by doing. I have found that writing programs in OO Perl gives people a "reverse understanding" of OO design principles. I don't know how many times I have discovered a concept through Perl's rich language, and its rubberband syntax, without knowing it. Then, one day I rummaged through my favorite object-oriented textbook, only to say, "Hey, I did that!"

Of course, there are many things you can do in Perl that don't have technical names in the literature, generally because they can't be done in any other object-oriented language. But then again, they get the job done.

Recognizing Layering When You See It

Of course, the first thing you must know about layering is how to identify the layering relationship when you see it. To that end, there are three dead giveaways that something is in a layering relationship. The following cases go from the strongest type of layering relationship to the weakest. (In this case, strong means the type of relationship that binds the two objects close together, whereas weak means a looser relationship that can be pulled apart easier.)

Case 1: Object Storage

When you have an object that is stored inside another object, you are making a very strong tie between the two. Our **LogObjectInh** object in the last chapter had this type of relationship as shown when we said (in **LogObjectInh::open()**):

```
49 sub open
50 {
######
54     my $fh = new FileHandle("$action $filename")
                              ||die "Couldn't open $filename";
######
56     $self->{filehandle} = $fh;
57 }
```

Line 56 is the point at which the object was layered. **LogObjectInh** now contains the filehandle $fh.

Case 2: Using Objects in Callbacks and Functions

When you use callbacks and functions of another module or object inside an object, you are tying those two objects together in a very strong way, too.

Suppose you have an object that happens to use another object inside a callback, as in this example taken from the mail-filter program in Chapter 12:

```
38 my $field = $textwindow->Scrolled
39                          (    'Text',
40                               '-scrollbars' => 'e',
41                               '-wrap' => 'word',
42                               'relief' => 'sunken',
43                               'borderwidth' => 2,
44                               'setgrid' => '1'
45                          );

###### CODE #####

50 my $save = $textwindow->Button
51                          (
52                               'text' => 'Save',
53                               'command' =>
54                          [ \&savetext, $field, $file  ]
55                          )
```

Line 54 is a callback internal to the **Button** object $save, which uses the **$field** object created by **$textwindow->Scrolled()** in line 38. **$save** uses the **$field** object, implying a dependency of the **Button** object on the Scrolled object.

Case 3: Using Objects or Modules Inside Objects

We do not have to store objects inside other objects in order to have a layering relationship. The simple use of one object or module inside another is sufficient. In our **Expect.pm** object, there was the following call:

```
356 sub _execCode
357 {
    ######
365         print "Enter password for $opt->{'user'}\n";
366         ReadMode 2; $opt->{'pass'} = <STDIN>; ReadMode 0;
    ######
382 }
```

Here, line 366 made use of the **ReadLine** module (available via **CPAN** and on the accompanying CD) in order to make the input invisible so that we could enter a password. The **Expect** module is therefore the **ReadLine** module; it is in a layering relationship.

Summary of Recognizing Layering

As you can see, the layering relationship comes in many forms such as:

1. Storing objects in other objects.
2. Having objects used in functions or callbacks within an object.
3. Making an instance of a module or object inside another object.

Each of these forms is a use of layering, because having or using one object inside another implies a dependency of one on the other. And if there is a dependency, such as object A being dependent on object B, *any* change to the interface of object B could cause object A to break.

Therefore, the question is, what do we do now that we recognize what layering looks like? Well, we understand the concepts behind the forms, and because we are computer engineers, we make drawings of the concepts we see.

Layering Concepts in Detail

Let's put some substance in the concepts that we listed in the previous section. Here are some detailed explanations, as well as simple examples of how these concepts play out when you see them in code.

HASA, Modifies, and Uses

As we stated in the last chapter, HASA is not really a programming technique, but a relationship between two objects. One contains another, much in the same way that sentences contain words, or books contain pages; hence the meaning of the phrase "component-based programming." One object has other objects as components.

Likewise, modifies is not really a programming technique. Instead, *modifies* indicates when one object changes another's state through its methods. *Uses* is where one object gets another's data, without modifying it.

The best way to understand the HASA relationship is to be able to take code and turn it into an object diagram, or vice versa. Remember our script running example of Chapter 12? We wrote it in Tk, which is an interesting combination of inheritance and layering. It consisted of several method calls that packed windows with things such as buttons, frames, etc.

If we distill the code into these function calls, getting rid of the arguments that have nothing to do with the layering relationship, the result looks something like this:

```
12   my $window = new MainWindow();

20   foreach $text (@labels)
21   {
22       my $frame = $window->Frame( )-> pack( );
23
24       my $entry = $frame->Entry( ) -> pack( );

32       my $label = $frame->Label( ) -> pack( );

37       $entries{$text} = $entry;
40   }

42   my $frame = $window->Frame( )->pack( );
43
45   $text = $window->Scrolled( );
46
47   my $runbutton = $frame->Button ('command'=>[ \&run, \%entries, $text ] )
48   $runbutton->pack( );

55   my $savetextbutton = $frame->Button('command'=>[ \&saveas, \%entries, $text])
56   $savetextbutton->pack( );

62   my $scbutton =        $frame->Button('command'=>[\&scommand, \%entries,$text] )
63   $scbutton->pack( );

70   my $lcbutton = $frame->Button('command'=>[\&loadcommand,\%entries, $text ] )
71   $lcbutton->pack( );
```

```
78   my $clearbutton = $frame->Button ( 'command' => [\&clear => $text ] )
79   $clearbutton->pack( );

85   my $quitbutton = $frame->Button( 'command' => [$window => 'destroy'] )
86   $quitbutton->pack( );
```

Now, the special thing about this skeleton code—from the point of view of layering—is that each time the code says ->pack(), it actually affects the object which created it.

In other words, when you say:

```
my $button = $frame->Button();
```

the frame $frame doesn't actually have the button yet. It has just created a button that is sort of floating in space. The frame can't use it because it doesn't know what properties it has yet. When you say:

```
$button->pack();
```

this actually puts the button in the frame, with the desired look and feel.

What does this have to do with HASA, modifies, and uses? Well, it is a good example of all three. $button->pack() creates the HASA relationship here, where the frame *HASA* button. It also shows *modifies* in action. The button *modifies* the frame by more or less inserting itself into the frame. The resulting Booch-like diagram looks something like Figure 20.1.

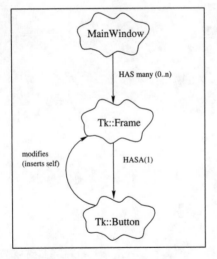

Figure 20.1
Diagram Showing
HASA-Modifies
Relationship

This is an unusual object-oriented relationship (in any other language beside Perl, that is). It was built this way so we could do the following:

```
my $frame = $window->Frame()->pack();
```

which basically does the same thing as:

```
my $frame = $window->Frame();
$frame->pack();
```

In other words, it lets you do two things in one. Instead of having to split the statement in two, we chain the statements together, in a very Perl-ish way.

Note

This is not the only way that this design could have been done. Nick Ing-Simmons, the developer of PerlTk, could have done something more conventional like:

```
my $frame = new Frame('attribute1', 'attribute2');
$window->pack($frame, 'frame', 'attributes');
```

in which the window is passed the frame that would be then configured by the window's pack function. Or even:

```
$window->pack(Frame->new('attribute1','attribute2'), 'frame', 'attributes');
```

which is the equivalent one-line statement that would create a frame. However, doing the packing this way puts a lot of burden on the `Window::pack()` subroutine. If we add a widget, say, `widget1`, the `pack()` function will need to know how to pack it.

Nonetheless, there are difficulties with the current design, too. It all comes down to a design choice. GUI development, especially the very flexible GUI development that PerlTk provides, is very difficult to do and PerlTk does it admirably.

Looking at the pseudocode we could make the object diagram shown in Figure 20.2. Hence, a window *HASA* frame, a frame *HASA* button, and a button *HASA* TopLevel. (We have stripped all the ->pack() *modifies* relationships for clarity.)

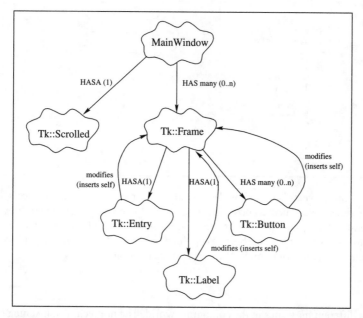

Figure 20.2
Fuller Diagram showing HASA-Modifies Diagram

Now, what can we say about the quality of this design? Just like when we were dealing with @ISA and inheritance, we want to have nice hierarchical designs, with few loops and few places where an object reaches out horizontally to modify its neighbor objects directly.

Unfortunately, when dealing with most any GUI program, this type of diagram does not give nearly enough detail about the quality of the program. The problem is that this diagram is at a class level. And since individual objects in a GUI are windows, frames, buttons, etc., there is an incentive to make an object-level diagram, something like Figure 20.3. Figure 20.3 gives an idea of how the actual program works. You can almost see how the GUI functions at this level of detail: when each button is pressed, what things it does, which windows it generates, and so forth. For example, when we push the **Save** button, we generate a **FileDialog** box which is connected with its parent entry window.

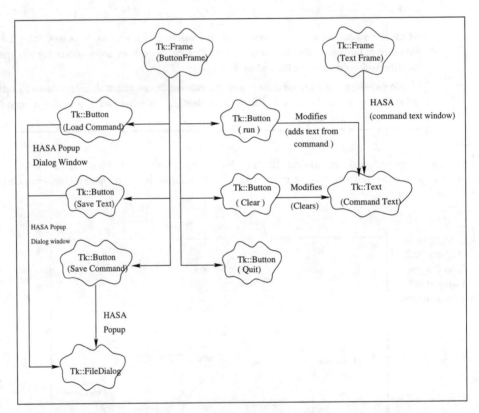

Figure 20.3
Object-Level
HASA Diagram

The level of detail in your projects is up to you. When I am working with non-GUI projects, I settle for a class diagram, and try to make it as hierarchical as possible. When I am doing GUI development, however, it is almost necessary to make a class-level diagram and lay out the relationships between buttons, windows, entries, frames, and other associated widgets. Again, it is desirable to keep things hierarchical. When you get loops—very difficult to avoid in GUI development—you should make them as tight as possible.

Polymorphism

Polymorphism has three different meanings in the computing world. The nontechnical meaning of polymorphism is one entity that has many different forms. Which, ironically, means that polymorphism is a polymorphic term in itself!

The three types of polymorphism in the computing world are:

- *Argument polymorphism* is making many different types of an argument mean the same thing to a function.
- *Functional polymorphism* is using some criteria (argument list, environment) to determine what that function will do.
- *Object/class polymorphism* is being able to call a different object method or class method based on the type of the object or class.

Most of this chapter will deal with object/class polymorphism, but it would not be fair to ignore the other types. We have actually used them before in this book (it is difficult to program Perl without them), and it is now time to give these techniques their due.

Argument Polymorphism

Argument polymorphism is the process of making a function user-friendly by letting multiple versions of a given argument be translated for a given function so the function knows what to do. One of the chief techniques of making programs more user-friendly is to incorporate some good, clean argument polymorphism into the function. The classic example is the `Date` function, which translates a user-supplied date into seconds:

```
use Date::Format;
my $secs = str2time('Jun 27, 1997');
```

How much more user-friendly this function is with argument polymorphism! Since the first argument of `str2time` can contain most any date format under the sun, you can blithely use any date that you want (absolute dates, that is) and Perl will understand it! This is an actual module, available via **CPAN**, and it is a life-saver (thank Graham Barr for this little gem). Likewise, when we say:

```
my $fh = new FileHandle("   >   file");
```

how much easier it would be if `FileHandle` stripped out the spaces for us, so that we need not be concerned about them. (It doesn't do this right now—a hint to Perl developers out there!)

All these statements use argument polymorphism, "normalizing" an argument of a function into a form that the function can handle. As the function is doing the job of recognizing that spaces, format, or whatever else is unimportant, it makes it so the user of the function needs to know less of the details.

Functional Polymorphism

Functional polymorphism is mostly akin to argument polymorphism, only much more ingrained into the language. *Functional polymorphism* allows a function to have multiple meanings based on what is passed to it, or have the return value contain multiple meanings based on the context in which it was called. For example, the built-in function:

```
$arg1++;
```

lets you have either integers, floats, or strings passed to it. If `$arg1` is an integer, Perl knows that it should increment that argument, that is, set `$arg1` to be one greater than it is right now. However, if `$arg1` is a string, then the natural action is to increment aa to ab.

Perl's internals are primarily built around functional polymorphism. Another example, which we covered in detail in the first section of this book, is contexts. When we said something like:

```
my $length = @array;
```

we were showing off the functional polymorphism in Perl. Since `@array` is in scalar context, `$length` becomes the length of the array. If you say:

```
my $scalar = $otherscalar;
```

then Perl does a regular assignment.

Of course, you probably recognize much of this now from the earlier part of the book. Indeed, built-in functions show the same duality, doing different (but related) acts based on what you pass to them: reverse(), < >, and chop() all use functional polymorphism.

Most user-built functional polymorphism is based on the two following operators: defined() and ref(). defined() is used to create functions that have optional arguments. If you say:

```
sub myFunc
{
    my ($arg1, $arg2) = @_;
    if (defined ($arg2)) { doSomething($arg1, $arg2); }
    else { doSomethingElse($arg1); }
}
```

then you are defining myFunc as having two different usages: myFunc($arg1); and myFunc($arg1, $arg2);. Both usages are legitimate, they just do different things based on the number of arguments. Likewise, if you say:

```
sub myFunc
{
    my ($arg1) = @_;
    if (ref($arg1) eq 'ARRAY')        { doSomethingArrayRef($arg1)); }
    elsif (ref($arg1) eq 'HASH')      { doSomethingHashRef($arg1)); }
    elsif (ref($arg1) eq 'SCALAR')    { doSomethingScalarRef($arg1));}
    elsif (!ref($arg1))               { doSomethingScalar($arg1); }
}
```

you are actually making myFunc do the job of four functions. More accurately, you are making myFunc a wrapper that hides the complexity of four separate functions from the user. Again, this benefits user-friendliness dramatically, since programmers do not need to remember four functions, only the one.

Example of Functional Polymorphism: A Dual Delete Method

You can use functional polymorphism to create methods that have a dual purpose. They may be both object and class functions depending on how they are called. In the process of creating these dual purpose methods, we will deal with a couple of issues that can arise when you implement them.

For example, suppose we wanted to create a delete method that had this dual purpose. We would want it to be able to be called as an object method. The syntax:

```
my $obj = new Object();
$obj->delete();
```

would delete the object referenced to by $obj.

We also want it to be able to be called as a class method. The syntax:

```
Object->delete();
```

would delete all the objects known by the class Object.

To do this, Perl checks the first argument of the delete function:

```
1   package Object;

##### constructor code deleted.. see below

14  sub delete
15  {
```

```
16        my ($classOrObject) = @_;
17        if (ref($classOrObject))
18        {
19            splice(@$_objects, $self->{'position'}, 1);
20            delete ($classOrObject);
21        }
22        else
23        {
24            my $obj;
25            foreach $obj (@$_objects) { $obj->delete(); }
26            undef (@$_objects);
27        }
28 }
```

When making an object method call, the first argument will be a reference, and lines 18–21 will be called, deleting the one object. If the first argument is not a reference, lines 11–15 will be called, and all the objects that the package knows about will be deleted.

Now, in this particular instance, there are a couple of side effects we need to keep track of. First, we now have to keep track of all the objects we create in the constructor. The list of objects deleted in line 24 must come from somewhere.

Second, we must manage the list of objects each time we delete one. Each time an object goes away, we need to modify @$_objects, as in line 20. The object must know about its position in the list @$_objects.

In this case, the easiest way to keep track of these two lists is in the constructor:

```
1    package Object;
2    my $_objects = [];
3
4    sub new
5    {
6        my($type) = @_;
7        my $self = bless {}, $type;
8        $self->{'position'} = @$_objects;
9        push(@$_objects, $self);
10       # code....
11       $self;
12 }
```

Line 9 keeps a list of all the objects we have created, and line 8 keeps track of the position where our object is in our grand list of objects (@$_objects).

Class/Object Polymorphism

Although the two techniques just described are invaluable, they should be old hat to you by now. The type of polymorphism we will use here is called *class* or *object polymorphism*. Another common name for it is *true polymorphism*, as it is the most commonly discussed of the three techniques.

Class or object polymorphism is a technique that makes classes more streamlined by letting the object reference discern which method it needs to call, rather than having the user figure it out. Let me explain: Suppose you made a **Polygon** class with the idea of having different shapes drawn. You could make an interface like:

```
package Polygon;
sub create_circle   { }
sub create_square   { }
sub create_triangle { }
```

```
sub draw_circle     { }
sub draw_square     { }
sub draw_triangle   { }
1;
```

where `create_*****` are constructor functions, and `draw_****` are functions that actually draw the shape to the screen. You could then write something like:

```
my $shape1 = create_circle Polygon();
my $shape2 = create_square Polygon();
my $shape3 = create_triangle Polygon();
$shape1->draw_circle();
$shape2->draw_square();
$shape3->draw_triangle();
```

This is not good! Just because you can do something does not mean that it should be done. In fact this interface sins in three major ways:

1. It has nongeneric functions: `create_*` and `draw_*` are difficult to remember, which means it will be difficult to use.
2. It is monolithic: We will find this code hard to split apart. If we add other shapes, we will have to add more functions to our one class.
3. It is complicated and error prone: The user must remember which draw function goes with which reference. It is perfectly legal to create a circle and then try to draw it as a square!

Polymorphism can help here in a major way. We take the monolithic interface and change it into three separate objects:

```
Polygon/Circle.pm
package Polygon::Circle;
sub new  { }
sub draw { }


Polygon/Square.pm
package Polygon::Square;
sub new  { }
sub draw { }


Polygon/Triangle.pm
package Polygon::Triangle;
sub new  { }
sub draw { }
```

Notice the simple names for the methods—simple names, simple usage. By splitting up the code in this way, we have, for the most part, taken care of the other two drawbacks as well. Our usage becomes:

```
1 my ( @shapes ) = (
2                       new Polygon::Circle(),
3                       new Polygon::Square(),
4                       new Polygon::Triangle()
5                   );
6
7 foreach $shape (@shapes) { $shape->draw(); }
```

which, as you can see, is much cleaner; the user doesn't need to keep track of which variable is which type. The program does it. Line 7 is where object polymorphism comes in. Perl does not care what object is calling the `draw()` method. It just cares that the method is attached to the given object. Hence, `$shape` could be any type of object with the `draw()` method. The user is spared the mental effort in having to coordinate the method name with the type of object.

This, by the way, is the reason that we want simple methods for objects. If we have simple methods, then our user interface is consistent. The more consistent the user interface is, the more usable it becomes. The usability will directly determine how popular your code is.

Summary of Polymorphism

Polymorphism is a term that, ironically, has many definitions in computer science. The primary types of polymorphism we discussed were:

Argument polymorphism, which is used to make functions easier to use by taking many forms of arguments, which are basically the same to the human eye, and being able to process them in the same function.

Functional polymorphism, which is used to make one function the gateway of many other functions based on the type of arguments passed to that function.

Object/class polymorphism, the most commonly used definition of polymorphism, which is used to make many different objects' methods (with the same name) be called transparently, depending on the objects' type.

We shall see next that polymorphism is used in many different ways, especially with GUI code such as Tk.

Delegation

Delegation and object polymorphism go hand in hand. In fact, delegation is a way for a programmer to use object polymorphism.

Consider the scenario we used in our small definition of delegation. A manager has several employees: an accountant, a programmer, a driver, and a masseuse. The job of the programmer is different from the driver's job, which is different from the accountant's, and so forth. However, we want to have the manager be the focal point that forwards requests to the employees. The relationship might look something like Figure 20.4. This is fairly straightforward: the Manager *HASA* group of employees, each with his or her own set of skills. The diagram turns into the pseudocode shown in Listing 20.1.

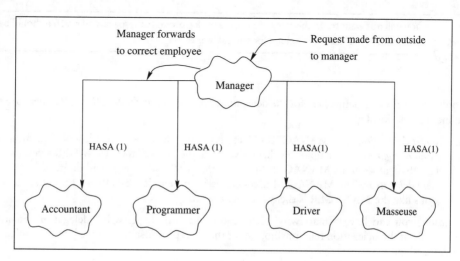

Figure 20.4
HASA Diagram
for Delegation

Listing 20.1
Employee Packages (Accountant, Programmer, Driver, Masseuse)

```
1  package Employee;           # Dummy package for Employees.
2  1;
3
4  package Accountant;
5  sub new       { bless {}, $_[0]; }
6  sub add       { print "Adding!\n"; }
7  sub subtract { print "Subtracting!\n"; }
8  sub fudge     { print "Fudging!\n"; };
9  1;
10
11 package Programmer;
12 sub new         { bless {}, $_[0]; }
13 sub program     { print "Programming!\n"; }
14 sub debug       { print "Debugging!\n";    }
15 sub surfInternet { print "Surfing Internet!\n"; }
16 1;
17
18 package Driver;
19 sub new         { bless {}; $_[0]; }
20 sub driveHome   { print "Driving Home!\n"; }
21 sub driveWork   { print "Driving to Work\n"; }
22 1;
23
24 package Masseuse;
25
26 sub new         { bless {}, $_[0]; }
27 sub therapy     { print "Doing therapy!\n"; }
28 1;
```

We have filled in each of the methods for the sake of making things complete. We have also made it easier to see what is going on by putting all the employees into one file.

Note

You will not want to do this very often. One package, one namespace, and one file should be the general rule you hold. In this case, it is helpful for the sake of testing.

The only file we need to define here for the delegation relationship is the **MANAGER**. There are three basic ways to define this relationship:

1. *Smart delegation:* The **MANAGER** object knows which is the correct job of each employee.
2. *Blind delegation:* The employees themselves take the jobs off the **MANAGER**'s desk, so to speak. They basically tell the **MANAGER** "I can do this job" and then go and do it.
3. *Wily delegation:* The **MANAGER** takes credit for his employees' efforts. From the outside world, it looks like the **MANAGER** is the one doing the jobs.

In addition, you can have "smart wily" delegation and "blind, yet wily" delegation. So item 3 is really a characteristic of the delegation relationship, rather than a type in itself. Let's see how to implement each delegation relationship.

Smart Delegation

In smart delegation, the **Manager** object has some built-in information in which he or she knows which task the **Employee** objects can perform. In this case, make this information a hash, as in Listing 20.2.

Listing 20.2
Manager::Smart

```
Manager/Smart.pm:

1   package Manager::Smart;
2   use Employee;
3
4   my $_delegateInfo =
5       {
6           'add'           => 'Accountant',
7           'subtract'      => 'Accountant',
8           'fudge'         => 'Accountant',
9           'program'       => 'Programmer',
10          'debug'         => 'Programmer',
11          'surfInternet'  => 'Programmer',
12          'driveHome'     => 'Driver',
13          'driveWork'     => 'Driver',
14          'therapy'       => 'Masseuse'
15      };
16
17  sub new
18  {
19      my ($type) = @_;
20      my $self = bless {}, $type;
21      $self->{'Accountant'} = new Accountant();
22      $self->{'Programmer'} = new Programmer();
23      $self->{'Driver'}     = new Driver();
24      $self->{'Masseuse'}   = new Masseuse();
25      $self;
26  }
27
28  sub delegate
29  {
30      my ($self, $function, @arguments) = @_;
31      my $employee = $_delegateInfo->{$function};
32      print "Sorry... can't do $function! No employee I know can do it!\n"
33                                          if (!defined($employee));
34      return ($employee->$function(@arguments));
35  }
```

Here, lines 4–15 define the hash for us. It is merely a dictionary of what functions are available and who performs them. This is the "smart" part of smart delegation. When we get to the constructor (lines 17–26), we form the layering relationship. The **Manager::Smart** constructs an accountant, programmer, driver, and masseuse and stores them inside itself in the fields 'Accountant', 'Programmer', 'Driver', and 'Masseuse'.

When we then get to delegation (lines 28–35), we simply take the function that was passed in and look up the employee that performs this task (line 30). Line 31 then calls the function passed in with the associated arguments. Notice that in line 32 we do not need to know the name of the function *a priori* in order to call the correct function.

In the client, we would say something like this:

```
1 my $manager = new Manager::Smart();
2 foreach $task ('program', 'add', 'subtract', 'surfInternet')
3 {
4     my $status = $manager->delegate($task);
5 }
```

Line 4 takes each task we require to be done, and then passes it to **Manager::Smart**, which then goes ahead and passes it to one of the **Employees**.

Blind Delegation

Once you understand smart delegation, it is not a far leap to understand the concept of blind delegation. In smart delegation, there was a hash of who could do what. Blind delegation does away with this necessity, instead letting each component class (i.e., the employees) figure out what to do. The **Manager::Blind** can't see what his employees do for him. Listing 20.3 shows the **Manager::Blind** model in practice.

Listing 20.3
Manager::Blind

Manager/Blind.pm:

```
1  package Manager::Blind;
2  use Employee;
3
4  sub new
5  {
6      my ($type) = @_;
7      my $self = bless {}, $type;
8      $self->{'Accountant'} = new Accountant();
9      $self->{'Programmer'} = new Programmer();
10     $self->{'Driver'}     = new Driver();
11     $self->{'Masseuse'}   = new Masseuse();
12     $self->{'employees'}=
13              [ 'Accountant', 'Programmer' , 'Driver' , 'Masseuse'];
14     $self;
15 }
16
17 sub delegate
18 {
19     my ($self, $function, @arguments) = @_;
20     my $employees = $self->{'employees'};
21     my $employee;
22     foreach $employee (@$employees)
23     {
24         if ($employee->can($function))
25         {
26             return($employee->$function(@arguments));
27         }
28     }
29     return ($employee->$function(@arguments));
30 }
```

Notice that the constructor is exactly the same here as it is in smart delegation, except for the fact that it explicitly lists the employee types in lines 12 and 13.

We then use this list in the actual delegation. In lines 22–28, we cycle through all the employees that the package knows about and query them if they know how to do the given function. The **UNIVERSAL** function can comes in very handy here. It simply returns whether or not the given employee can do the passed function.

The first employee that we find who knows how to do the function is then asked to do the job in line 26.

Advantages/Disadvantages of Blind Delegation

What can be said about this type of delegation compared to smart delegation? This form has three advantages. First, we can control which component classes are tried first, and which are tried last. This is, in OO design terms, a *chain of responsibility*. The accountant component is tried first, the programmer second, and so forth. If one isn't responsible for a certain task, we check the next.

Second, this form is more flexible than smart delegation. We could have just as easily told all the employees who knew how to do something to just go and do it.

Third, this form is easier to maintain than smart delegation. The manager class does not even know what types of employees it has, and it can still process requests!

Likewise, there are disadvantages. First, this form of delegation is slower than smart delegation. Since the manager is cycling through employees to find out if they can do certain requests, each cycle takes time. And second, some folks consider this type of delegation way too flexible for its own good.

In short, if you can learn not to abuse the power that blind delegation gives you, it can be a useful technique.

Dynamic Layering with Blind Delegation

In practice, it is the third advantage that makes blind delegation smarter than smart delegation. Let's add a secretary type that looks something like:

```perl
package Secretary;

sub new { bless {}, $type; }
sub scheduling { print "Scheduling!\n"; }
1;
```

What we want to do is to add the secretary to **Manager::Blind**'s list of employees, but we do not want to make **Manager::Blind** responsible for the employees that are added. We therefore add an assign function to **Manager::Blind**, that looks something like what is shown in Listing 20.4.

Listing 20.4
Manager::Blind (continued)

```perl
32 sub assign
33 {
34     my ($self, $employee) = @_;
35     my ($employees) = $self->{'employees'};
36     if ( grep (ref($employee) eq $_, @$employees))
37     {
38         print "Already have an employee of type $employee!!!\n";
39     }
40     else
41     {
42         $self->{ref($employee)} = $employee;
```

```
43          push (@$employees, $employee);
44      }
45 }
```

This adds the employee to the manager's object (line 42) and then adds the fact that the employee has been registered with the manager to the list (line 43).

The important thing here is that nothing else in the object has to change. Since each employee figures out what he or she going to do, when we say the following in a client:

```
1  my $manager = new DumbManager();
2  my $secretary = new Secretary();
3
4  $manager->assign($secretary);
5  $manager->delegate('scheduling');
```

then inside the delegate function we run into logic that looks like:

```
22      foreach $employee (@$employees)
23      {
24          if ($employee->can($function))
25          {
26              return($employee->$function(@arguments));
27          }
28      }
```

Since we have assigned the secretary to the manager, line 22 now has a secretary at the end of the array. When line 24 comes up and the $employee is a secretary, the routine finds that the secretary can now do scheduling. This is all automatic.

Wily Delegation

Let's briefly consider wily delegation (my own term) in which the **manager** class takes most all the credit for what its **employees** (component) classes do. In other words, we will have no delegate function. Instead, when we say:

```
my $wilyManager = new WilyManager();
my $status = $wilyManager->add(1,1);
```

magic will happen. Even though it looks like the manager is doing the adding, he or she is actually calling on the accountant to do it. Listing 20.5 is a wily manager in print.

Listing 20.5
Manager::Wily

```
Manager/Wily.pm:
```

```
1  package Manager::Wily;
2  use Employee;
3
4  sub AUTOLOAD
5  {
6      my ($self, @arguments) = @_;
7      my $function = $AUTOLOAD;
8      $function =~ s"(.*)::""g;
9      return if ($function =~ m"^DESTROY$");    # we don't want to delegate
10                                                # any DESTROY functions.
```

```
11          foreach $employee (@{$self->{'employees'}})
12          {
13              if ($employee->can($function))
14              {
15                  return($employee->$function(@arguments));
16              }
17          }
18          print "Couldn't do the function $function!\n";
19 }
```

This is where all the delegation happens in the wily manager package. The $AUTOLOAD variable holds the method name that was called:

```
$wilyManager->add(1,1);
```

However, $AUTOLOAD does not simply contain the string add. Instead, the $AUTOLOAD variable contains a fully qualified version of add, something like WilyManager::add, which shows from where Perl thinks the method is supposed to be applied. So in line 8 we take the name of the package from $AUTOLOAD, storing it in the more generic variable $function.

Line 9 takes away the DESTROY functions (we don't want to propagate these). If we wanted to, we could add functions that we do not want to propagate, something like:

```
(print ("Sorry I don't fudge books!\n"), return())
                              if ($function =~ m"fudge");
```

and this would act as a gateway to prevent dangerous functions. Lines 11–15 then do the delegation by dynamically figuring out the function to call in line 13.

The rest of the listing is exactly the same, looking like Listing 20.6.

Listing 20.6
Manager::Wily (continued)

```
20 sub new
21 {
22     my ($type) = @_;
23     my $self = bless {}, $type;
24     $self->{'Accountant'} = new Accountant();
25     $self->{'Programmer'} = new Programmer();
26     $self->{'Driver'}     = new Driver();
27     $self->{'Masseuse'}   = new Masseuse();
28     $self->{'employees'}=
29                 [ 'Accountant', 'Programmer' , 'Driver' , 'Masseuse'];
30     $self;
31 }
32
33 sub assign
34 {
35     my ($self, $employee) = @_;
36     my ($employees) = $self->{'employees'};
37     if ( grep (ref($employee) eq $_, @$employees))
38     {
39          print "Already have an employee of type $employee!!!\n";
40     }
41     else
42     {
```

```
43          $self->{ref($employee)} = $employee;
44          push (@$employees, $employee);
45      }
46 }
```

What can we say about wily delegation? Well, in a way it is nothing but syntactic sugar. Instead of:

```
my $mgr = new Manager::Blind();
$mgr->delegate('driveHome', 'address');
```

there is:

```
my $mgr = new Manager::Wily();
$mgr->driveHome('address');
```

which at least looks cleaner. Whether or not I use the first form, which is explicit about the delegation it performs, or the second, in which the delegation is implicit, depends on what problem I am trying to solve; it is a *stylistic* choice.

Summary of Layering Concepts

These concepts go a long way in building up the larger structures in a project. Objects can:

1. Own other objects through a *HASA* relationship.
2. Change the properties of another object through a *modifies* relationship.
3. Get attributes from another object through a *uses* relationship.

From there, we can diagram the structure of our project in the large by making class diagrams, and labeling each place where classes interact with each other.

Making these relationships effective is the job of the other two techniques we talked about: polymorphism and delegation. Polymorphism's job is to make an interface more user-friendly by allowing users of the class to not have to:

1. Worry about details such as what format an argument takes (argument polymorphism).
2. Memorize several different function-call names, and instead compact them into one simpler function call with multiple uses (function polymorphism).
3. Know which particular class is doing a job when he or she calls a method (class polymorphism).

Class polymorphism is used quite heavily in delegation. In delegation, if one object does not know how to do something, it delegates the job to another object. We gave three forms of this delegation (smart, blind, and wily).

In summary, these are the major syntactic techniques we will use in putting together patterns in software development.

Basic Design Patterns

Design patterns are the stock and trade of the object-oriented industry. *Design patterns* are recurring forms of logic and code. It is through design patterns that the object-oriented programming world turns ideas into applications, making such staple products as spreadsheets, word processors, and Web browsers.

There are two points you need to know about using design patterns in Perl. These points are polar in thought and use. First, the fact that Perl is so syntactically flexible means that you can make simple designs that translate into complicated projects that work. If we rewrote the delegation examples in C++, for example, we would have much more complicated syntax on our hands than we did with Perl.

Second, and conversely, the syntactic flexibility of Perl means that you can have much more complicated designs in Perl than in a language such as C++! Supposedly then, these complicated designs would lead to very complicated projects.

But all this is beyond the scope of this book. Let's concentrate instead on simple patterns. The three we are going to consider are the singleton, the container, and the iterator.

The Singleton Pattern

A *singleton class* is a class that enforces the fact that there is only one instance in a given program. Usually, a singleton object (an instance of a singleton) is kept in a global variable, so everybody can access it.

Singletons are useful in instances when:

1. You want to restrict the access to a resource within the process to only one copy of the object (or one copy of the underlying resource).
2. You are not sure whether something should be a module or an object, but you don't want to limit yourself to the module approach.

Point two is fairly uninteresting. Writing the **Diff** module so it looks like:

```
my $Global::diff = new Diff();
my $diffs = $Global::diff->array($a, $b);
```

pretty much sums it up. We expect **Diff** to have only one instance; in fact, we program it with the expectation that it will. However, just to be safe, we wrap it in an object, which does not make much sense in Perl because it is so easy to translate modules into objects.

Hence, we will concentrate on the first point, which shows some interesting things about implementing singletons.

Example: Restricting Resource Access: FileHandle::Single

Suppose you wanted to make sure that you do not have two filehandles pointing to the same file at the same time. In fact, suppose you wanted to make it a fatal error to say something like:

```
my $fh = new FileHandle("> write");
print $fh "Hello\n";
my $fh2 = new FileHandle("> write");
print $fh2 "Hello2\n";
```

which makes sense because the second write (print $fh2) will overwrite the first.

The simple singleton class approach is to ensure that there is only one **FileHandle** object at the same time. Let's call this **FileHandle::Single** (Listing 20.7).

Listing 20.7
FileHandle::Single

```
1   package FileHandle::Single;
2   use FileHandle;
3   use vars qw($AUTOLOAD)
4   use strict;
5
6   my $_count = 0;
7   sub AUTOLOAD
```

```
 8  {
 9      my ($self, @arguments) = @_;
10      my $fh = $self->{fh};
11      my $function = $AUTOLOAD;
12      $function =~ s"(.*)::""g;
13      return() if ($function =~ m"^DESTROY$");
14      $fh->$function(@arguments);
15  }
16
17  sub new
18  {
19      my ($type, @arguments) = @_;
20      (print("Can't create more than one filehandle!\n"), return())
21                                                if ($_count == 1);
22      $_count = 1;
23      my $self = bless {} , $type;
24      $self->{fh} = new FileHandle(@arguments);
25      return($self);
26  }
```

This is not only a good example of the singleton concept, but it also shows delegation quite well. We do not want to have to write all the filehandle methods, as a filehandle knows how to do its job quite well. Instead, we use the AUTOLOAD mechanism to intercept the function that is being called and redirect it to the filehandle stored in memory.

So, when a user types:

```
my $fh = new FileHandle("a");
my $fh2 = new FileHandle("bb");
```

the second call will cause the message:

```
Can't create more than one filehandle!
```

and then return the undef value into $fh2.

This is a simple type of singleton, but it is not very usable in this instance. Sometimes we need more than one filehandle, so we could look at having ten filehandles as the limit. In other words, we should have the $_count variable give an error when it reaches ten rather than on the first instance.

Example: Restricting Resource Access FileHandle::Cached

A much more flexible solution would be something that keeps track of filehandle pollution. Everybody does this at one time or another. It is easy to be careless with filehandles, and we sometimes step on ourselves in the process. If you did something such as:

```
my $fh = new FileHandle("> file");
my $fh2 = new FileHandle("> file");
```

you are asking for a catastrophe. This is because writes to the second filehandle will overwrite the first. Much better would be something like:

```
my $fh = new FileHandle::Cached("> file");
my $fh = new FileHandle::Cached("> file");                    # error
```

which would make sure that when one file was opened, subsequent calls to open the same file would ensure that there is only one filehandle per given file. We economize on filehandles, and we ensure that simple problems like this do not occur.

What is the best way to do this? Well, Perl provides the ideal method: through the hash. Listing 20.8 shows more detail:

Listing 20.8
FileHandle::Cached (AUTOLOAD)

```
1    package FileHandle::Cached;
2    use Path;
3    use FileHandle;
4    use vars qw($AUTOLOAD);
5    use strict;
6
7    my %_fhCache = ();
8    my %_fhType  = ();
9
10   sub AUTOLOAD
11   {
12       my ($self, @arguments) = @_;
13
14       my $fh = $self->{fh};
15       my $function = $AUTOLOAD;
16       $function =~ s"(.*)::""g;
17       return() if ($function =~ m"^DESTROY$");
18       $fh->$function(@arguments);
19   }
```

The first part is the same: delegation as usual. However, notice that there are hashes in lines 7 and 8. The %_fhCache is going to contain the filehandles that we want; the %_fhType is going to contain the type of file-handles (append, read, overwrite).

We must keep track of the types in this way because it would be disastrous if we opened an overwrite file-handle on top of a read filehandle, because we would trash whatever data was there!

These hashes are then used in the constructor, where we fill up the cache based on whether or not we have seen the file before, as shown in Listing 20.9.

Listing 20.9
FileHandle::Cached (new())

```
20
21   sub new
22   {
23       my ($type, @arguments) = @_;
24
25       my ($file) = $arguments[0];
26
27       my $writetype = ($file =~ m">\s*>")? 'append' :
28                       ($file =~ m">")?      'overwrite' :
29                                             'read';
30
31       my $self = bless {}, $type;
```

```
32      $self->{'fh'} = _getFH( $file, $writetype, \@arguments);
33      return($self);
34 }
35
```

Here, lines 27–29 determine what type of filehandle the code is opening. By looking at the file, we see if the file has two >, meaning append, or one >, meaning `overwrite` otherwise, we assume it is a `read`. Note that this means that this class only supports usages that look like:

```
my $fh = new FileHandle::Cached("> file");
```

and it will not work (as is) on things that look like:

```
my $fh = new FileHandle::Cached("file", "r");
```

although we could make it work that way. Line 32 stuffs **Cached** with filehandles in a private function called _getFH. It looks like Listing 20.10.

Listing 20.10
FileHandle::Cached (_getFH())

```
36 sub _getFH
37 {
38     my ($file, $type, $arguments) = @_;
39
40     $file =~ s"[>\s]*""g;
41     $file = Path::abs($file)              # defined in CH.28 gives absolute path
42     if (defined($_fhCache{$file}) && ($_fhType{$file} eq $type))
43     {
44          return($_fhCache{$file});
45     }
46     elsif (defined($_fhCache{$file}))
47     {
48          print "You already have a filehandle of type $_fhType{$file} open!
49 You requested a file of type $type which is incompatible.\n";
50     }
51     else
52     {
53          $_fhCache{$file} = new FileHandle(@$arguments);
54          $_fhType{$file} = $type;
55          return($_fhCache{$file});
56     }
57 }
58 1;
```

This function's sole purpose is to make sure we do not step on ourselves by opening the same file two different ways (lines 46–50). It also makes sure that we reuse all the filehandles we possibly can (lines 43–45).

Lines 53–55 are the ones that actually keep the cache. If we have not seen the file before, line 53 makes a new filehandle. We then store the type of file we created in line 54, and return the new filehandle, with the result being that a copy of the reference is stored in the object itself.

That's it! By going this route, we guarantee a minimum amount of filehandle usage, but there are some drawbacks of which you should be aware. By keeping this cache, we have minimized the number of filehandles we create, but we also keep the filehandles we have for the duration of the program. Why? Again, with Perl's garbage collection, keeping a filehandle in line 54 makes sure that the reference count never goes down to zero.

The usage (as written) is limited. You need to say:

```
my $fh = new FileHandle::Cached("> file");
$fh->print("HERE!\n");
```

instead of:

```
my $fh = new FileHandle::Cached("> file");
print $fh "HERE!!!\n";
```

because print expects a glob reference. It is an internal function, and is hard-wired to expect globs in the first parameter.

To sum up, this approach works quite well to limit resources (filehandles, directory handles, memory, etc.) because the codes are hard-wired into it.

The Container Pattern

The second type of pattern we will consider is the *container* pattern. A *container object* is an object whose main job is to hold other items so that the access to those items is easier, more structured, or more streamlined. There are two basic types of *container* objects:

1. Containers used to hold a group of other objects and simplify their access.
2. Containers used to hold and simplify access to physical items such as files and databases.

We have come across quite a few containers of each type in this book, but have only named them *containers* here.

For the type in which objects are used to simplify access to a certain physical object, there was the **LogObject** class, which managed a log file. Likewise, the **Expect** object was (in a way) a container class, because it managed the connection to other machines via the **Expect** program.

 Some people would say **Expect** is not a container, and think of a container class as something that simplifies access to data. I disagree; in fact, one of the coolest things you can do is make it so that you don't care whether the place you are sending your data is a file, or a pipe, over the network or whatever. The **IO::** modules of the central distribution do this quite well.

A good example of the type of container that holds a group of other objects was the **Manager** object. Also good examples were the smart filehandles that controlled access to filehandle objects.

In any case, the effect of using a container object is to simplify the interface. Instead of saying:

```
my $accountant = new Accountant();
my $driver = new Driver();
$driver->driveHome('2001 park avenue');
$accountant->add(1,1);
```

where we know what each object does, we say:

```
my $manager = new Manager::Wily();
```

```
$manager->driveHome('2001 park avenue');
$manager->add(1,1);
```

to do the equivalent. This is much cleaner; when the number of objects you need to keep track of becomes great enough, it is often worth it to pack information into a centralized place. Following are more examples of container objects.

Example 1: Password Screen (Tk::Password)

The first example to consider is one that shows a container that simplifies access to several subobjects. The example is the password entry screen so common to applications that need to vet (in other words, validate) access into a system.

Problem Domain

If you have used any browser, or had an account on a Unix or NT machine, you are probably familiar with a password screen. The screen looks something like Figure 20.5. As you enter the password, your characters are shadowed; they do not show up on the screen as is, but instead show up as asterisks (or blanks, or whatever). Furthermore, when you hit the **clear** button, the text in the user and password fields is emptied.

Figure 20.5
Password
Protection Screen

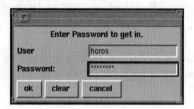

This looks simple enough. Now notice that this screen consists of at least five types of widgets or objects. They are listed next, with their Tk names:

- **Window**—The whole conglomeration is a window, with links into the windowing system (try resizing the window once and see what happens).
- **Frame**—The screen is partitioned into sections or frames. Each section is nailed down to a certain region of the window, which make up the object.
- **Label**—The Enter Password, User, and Password text is packed onto a label, which is then packed onto a frame.
- **Entry**—The place where the user enters text is in an entry window, which is in turn on a frame, which is in a window.
- **Buttons**—The OK, clear, and cancel buttons are all nailed to a frame, which is in turn nailed to a window.

As you can see, this apparent simplicity is quite misleading. There is much complexity in this application and it does not stop here. Because the clear button affects the user and password entries, there must be a link between the clear button and the entry button. When the smoke clears, there is a Booch diagram that looks something like Figure 20.6.

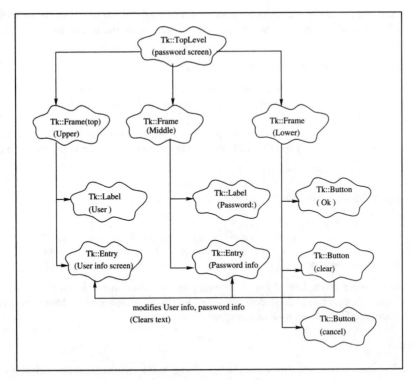

Figure 20.6
Password Entry
Screen Object
Diagram

The point of this is that it would be very difficult to recreate this window every single time we needed to have a password screen! If we look at this complexity (if we wanted to have a screen like this in our program), all we have to care about is:

- The user and password fields that the person entered in the application.
- Whether or not the user hit the cancel button.

In addition, we may want to do a little customization of the screen by having a different title, different caption on top, or link callbacks to each of the buttons. These are trivial issues compared with having to rewrite the password screen from scratch.

Hence, this is the perfect place for a container object that packs the windows, frames, buttons, and so forth in a very reusable fashion. First, we will consider the interface.

Interface Issues

How do we want to structure this object? First, notice that the **Password** object must be associated with a Tk widget (that is just a basic fact about how Tk works). This means the constructor call will look something like:

```
my $passwordWindow = new Tk::Password($window);
```

This associates the password window with a widget that we pass in ($window). This call will make a vanilla password window object.

Next, we must display the password window. This should be simple:

```
$passwordWindow->show();
```

However, we are missing a good opportunity for making this very simple to use. Because we care only about the return values (user, password, whether user pressed cancel), we can tie the return value to the fact that we are showing the window. This code:

```perl
my $enteredValues = $passwordWindow->show();
```

says "show the window, wait for the user to enter in some values, and then, and only then, return the value setting it inside $enteredValues." We therefore want to have the code wait for an OK or cancel event before continuing with the rest of the code.

Following is a complete program that creates a password window, waits for the user to enter in some value, and performs a simple validation of what the user typed. It continues only if the user enters the correct values:

```perl
1 my $window = new MainWindow();
2 my $passwordWindow = new Tk::Password($window);
3 my $values = $passwordWindow->show();
4
5 (print ("Got it right"), exit())
6                         if (($values->{'user'} eq 'hephaestus') &&
7                             ($values->{'password'} eq 'godoffire'));
8 print "Got it Wrong!\n";
```

The key to this short program is in lines 2 and 3. By encapsulating the complexity of the password window, and sticking it into the variable $passwordWindow, we allow for simple programming. More importantly, this action allows for a common interface between all our programs.

Implementation

Let's implement this code. It will be helpful to have two things handy while going through this exercise:

1. Tk documentation on-line. You can use a browser to view this (go to
    /perl/html/lib/site/Tk/UserGuide.html on NT or *<TkDistribution>/doc/Tk-UserGuide.htm* on Unix).
2. The sample Tk applications. If you say widget at the command line, you should get a menu of the different widgets available.

Let's use sample Tk applications to find some code to use as a template. After all, the password screen exercise is not the most complicated problem, and one of these prebuilt applications just might fit the bill to be modified to create the password screen.

Look at the widget demo called **Simple RolodexÆ Demo**. The screen looks like Figure 20.7. Click the button **See Code**, which spills the contents of what makes this particular demo tick. In this case, the code looks like Listing 20.11.

Figure 20.7

Simple Rolodex
Demo

Listing 20.11
(`form.pl` from demonstration Tk widgets)

```perl
 1  sub form {
 2  # form.pl
 3
 4  use vars qw/$TOP/;
 5
 6  sub form {
 7
 8      # Create a top-level window that displays a bunch of entries with
 9      # tabs set up to move between them.
10
11      my($demo) = @ARG;
12      my $demo_widget = $MW->WidgetDemo(
13          -name    => $demo,
14          -text    => 'This window contains a simple form where you can type in the
15  various entries and use tabs to move circularly between the entries.',
16          -title   => 'Form Demonstration',
17          -iconname => 'form',
18      );
19      $TOP = $demo_widget->Top;   # get geometry master
20
21      foreach ('Name:', 'Address:', '', '', 'Phone:') {
22          my $f = $TOP->Frame(qw/-borderwidth 2/);
23          my $e = $f->Entry(qw/-relief sunken -width 40/);
24          my $l = $f->Label(-text => $ARG);
25          $f->pack(qw/-side top -fill x/);
26          $e->pack(qw/-side right/);
27          $l->pack(qw/-side left/);
28          $e->focus if $ARG eq 'Name:';
29      }
30      $TOP->bind('<Return>' => [$TOP => 'destroy']);
31
32  } # end form
```

Even if we know nothing about Tk, this gives a wealth of information about how to program in it. We simply compare the code in Listing 20.11 with the **Rolodex** form that we have in Figure 20.7 and we can see that:

1. To make a place to enter text, make a frame, make an entry, and finally make a label (lines 22–24).
2. To Pack the objects, give them a location on the screen (line 25–27). Starting at line 21, each loop packs a frame at the top, and stacks the frames on the window from top to bottom.
3. If we want to bind a key to something, use the term bind (line 30).
4. To place the cursor in a certain place, focus it (line 28).

This is the first line of attack. The difficult part of making a working Tk object has been done for us. All we have to do is modify something that already works. Only if we must do something outside the scope of the sample application do we default to the documentation.

The implementation follows pretty closely to the template that we just created. We need deal only with the following issues:

1. *Configuration.* Since the demo application is not an object, we have to come up with a good interface that is not overly complicated, yet provides enough power to do the job.
2. *Object storage.* Again, we need to store object in an easy-to-access form.

These two issues will play themselves out when we actually create the object. So let's start coding, and see how we solve these issues as we proceed. First, we make the constructor and headers (Listing 20.12).

Listing 20.12
Tk::Password constructor and headers

```
Tk/Password.pm
1    package Tk::Password;
2    use strict;
3    use Carp;
4
5
6    sub new
7    {
8        my ($type, $widget, $desc, $title) = @_;
9
10        my $self = bless {}, $type;
11       $self->{'callbacks'} = {};
12
13       $self->{'title'} = $title || 'Password Screen';
14       $self->{'desc'} = $desc   || 'Enter Password to get in.';
15
16       $self->{'widget'} = $widget;
17       my $window = $self->{'window'} = $widget->TopLevel();
18       $window->title($title);
19       $self;
20   }
```

This is fairly straightforward. We take the name of a widget to tie the newly created window and we take the title and description with which we will tag the window.

In the bare-bones usage of this module, we need only the widget. However, I can see why people might want to have a different title to their password screen, depending on their application.

The description and title are optional and configurable in lines 13 and 14. The window's title is set in line 18.

Next, we must draw the object with the show() function, as in Listing 20.13.

Listing 20.13
(Tk::Password show())

```
21
22   sub show
23   {
24       my ($self) = @_;
25
26       my $window =    $self->{'window'};
27       my $attrib =    $self->{'attrib'};
28       $self->_packCallbacks();
29       $self->_pack();
30
31       $window->waitVariable(\$self->{'pass'});
32
33       return
```

```
34                  (
35                     {
36                         'user' => $self->{'user'},
37                         'pass' => $self->{'pass'},
38                         'cancel' => $self->{'cancel'}
39                     }
40                  );
41  }
42
```

This is mostly wrapper code. Wrapper code is called for because we are not exactly sure how we are going to implement the _pack() and _packCallbacks() functions. Two things to realize here are that the calls in line 28 and 29 are doing all the work (stuffing the details into private functions), and that line 31 does a really cool thing.

What is that cool thing? Well, if you think about how GUI code works, it usually follows this pattern: *set up everything and wait for the user to input events.*

The screen is set up by saying:

```
1 my $screen = new MainWindow();
2 my $button = $screen->Button('text' =>'ok','command' => [\&doSomething, @args]);
```

and:

```
3 MainLoop();
```

is an infinite loop to process any user events. When the button with the text OK is pressed, then (and only then) is the doSomething function executed.

Now, this is usually a good thing. However, it does mean that 100 percent of the time, the code is looping in line 3, waiting for events to happen. Code objects are redrawn and redisplayed in this time, out of the programmer's control except through callbacks as in line 2. This means that getting a return value from a window will not work as is. If the main loop is always being executed in order to display GUI objects, it means that each call to create a GUI object must be transparent: It must be registered with the MainLoop and the code must go on.

This statement:

```
31          $window->waitVariable(\$self->{'pass'});
```

commandeers the event loop. It tells Perl: "Wait here for the $self->{'user'} variable to change. When it does change, you can go on, but not before then." The basic idea is to draw the password screen, wait until one of the callbacks inside the password screen changes the value of $self->{'user'}, and then return the values after this event has occurred.

Where did we get this idea? Again, we looked at the code that came with Tk, in this case inside the **FileDialog.pm** box. This is another reason to keep your eyes open and dig through other people's code; you learn a lot! Let's implement the configure function (Listing 20.14).

Listing 20.14
Configure function

```
43  sub configure
44  {
45      my ($self, @config ) = @_;
46      my $xx;
47      my $callbacks = $self->{'callbacks'};
48
49      for ($xx = 0; $xx < @config; $xx++)
```

```
50        {
51            my $type =        $config[$xx];
52            my $cb    =        $config[$xx+1];
53            push(@{$callbacks->{$type}}, $cb);
54        }
55   }
56
57   sub _packCallbacks
58   {
59       my ($self) = @_;
60
61       my $callbacks = $self->{'callbacks'};
62       push(@{$callbacks->{'ok'}}, [ \&_setpass, $self, 'ok' ]);
63       push(@{$callbacks->{'ok'}}, [ $self->{'window'}, 'withdraw' ]);
64
65       push(@{$callbacks->{'clear'}}, [ \&_setpass, $self, 'clear' ] );
66
67       push(@{$callbacks->{'cancel'}}, [ \&_setpass, $self, 'cancel' ]);
68       push(@{$callbacks->{'cancel'}},[ $self->{'window'}, 'withdraw']);
69   }
70
```

The idea is that we can configure our object by adding callbacks that will do extra things after someone hits a button, whether the button is **OK, clear,** or **cancel.**

This functionality should not be needed very often: 99 percent of the time, all you have to do is check the return hash that comes out of the show function, and then do something from there. This functionality is added as insurance for unusual circumstances. All we have to do is draw the object and set up how this drawing interacts. Again, the code in Listing 20.15 comes almost straight from the **form** object.

Listing 20.15
_pack function

```
71   sub _pack
72   {
73       my ($self) = @_;
74
75       my $window = $self->{'window'};
76       my $attribs = $self->{'attribs'} = {};
77
78       my $labelFrame= $window->Frame( 'borderwidth' => 2 )->pack('side' => 'top');
79       my $userFrame = $window->Frame( 'borderwidth' => 2 )->pack('side' => 'top');
80       my $passFrame = $window->Frame( 'borderwidth' => 2 )->pack('side' => 'top');
81                                               # pack the frames from top to
bottom
82       my $topLabel = $labelFrame->Label('text' => $self->{'desc'} )
83                                               ->pack( 'side'=>'left' );
84
85       my $userLabel =
86               $userFrame->Label('text' => "User\t\t")->pack('side' => 'left');
87
88       my $passLabel =
89               $passFrame->Label( 'text' => "Password:\t")
90                                               ->pack('side' => 'left');
91       my $userEntry = $userFrame->Entry( 'relief' => 'sunken', 'width' => 20 )
92                                               ->pack('side' => 'left');
```

```
93
94      my $passEntry = $passFrame->Entry(
95                                          'relief'=> 'sunken',
96                                          'width' =>20,
97                                          '-show' => '*')
98                                                  ->pack('side' => 'left');
99      my $buttonFrame =
100            $window->Frame('borderwidth' => 2 )->pack('side' => 'left');
101
102     my $okButton = $buttonFrame->Button
103                                          (
104                                          'text' => 'ok',
105                                          'command' =>[$self, 'packedSubs','ok']
106                                          )
107                                          ->pack('side' => 'left');
108
109     my $clearButton = $buttonFrame->Button
110                                          (
111                                              'text' => 'clear',
112                                              'command' =>
113                                                  [$self, 'packedSubs', 'clear']
114                                          )
115                                          ->pack('side' => 'left');
116
117     my $cancelButton = $buttonFrame->Button
118                                          (
119                                              'text' => 'cancel',
120                                              'command' =>
121                                                  [ $self, 'packedSubs', 'cancel']
122                                          )
123                                          ->pack('side' => 'left');
124
125     $self->{'attrib'} = {
126                              'labelFrame'   => $labelFrame,
127                              'userFrame'    => $userFrame,
128                              'passFrame'    => $passFrame,
129                              'topLabel'     => $topLabel,
130                              'userLabel'    => $userLabel,
131                              'passLabel'    => $passLabel,
132                              'userEntry'    => $userEntry,
133                              'passEntry'    => $passEntry,
134                              'buttonFrame'  => $buttonFrame,
135                              'okButton'     => $okButton,
136                              'cancelButton' => $cancelButton
137                          };
138 }
```

The first thing to realize about this code is that it closely resembles building the window via Lego blocks. Again, each frame is positioned relative to another. When we say something like:

```
my $frame1 = $window->Frame() -> pack ('-side' => 'top');
my $frame1 = $window->Frame() -> pack ('-side' => 'top');
my $frame1 = $window->Frame() -> pack ('-side' => 'top');
```

we are making a structure that looks something like Figure 20.8.

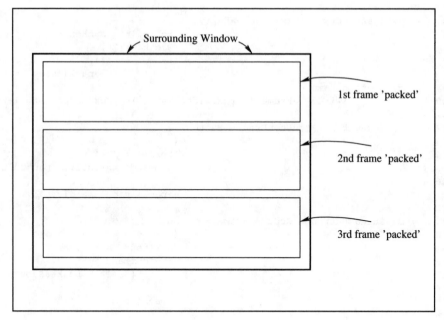

The second thing to realize is the code that glues the object together, the bulk of the work, is done by callbacks that look like:

```
117     my $cancelButton = $buttonFrame->Button
118                                         (
119                                             'text' => 'cancel',
120                             'command' =>
121                             [$self,'packedSubs','cancel']
122                             );
```

This says if the `cancel` button is hit, the command `packedSubs` is executed with the arguments `$self` and `cancel`. The rest of the module is devoted to writing these callbacks (Listing 20.16).

Listing 20.16
callbacks (_packedSubs())

```
139
140 sub packedSubs
141 {
142     my ($self, $type) = @_;
143
144     my $callbacks = $self->{'callbacks'};
145     my $buttoncallbacks = $callbacks->{$type};
146
147     my $call;
148     foreach $call (@$buttoncallbacks) { my ($cb, @args) =@$call; &$cb(@args);}
149 }
150
```

The subroutine _packedSubs() is actually a subroutine dispatcher. Since this object has configurable callbacks associated with each button, _packedSubs figures out which subroutines to call, and then calls them. When we say:

```
$self->_packedSubs('cancel');
```

it looks inside the callbacks that are configured for that particular button, as in the following:

```
144     my $callbacks = $self->{'callbacks'};
my $buttoncallbacks = $callbacks->{$type};
```

It then executes them without even knowing what they are:

```
148     foreach $call (@$buttoncallbacks) { my ($cb, @args) =@$call; &$cb(@args);}
```

In other words, the result is a meta-callback: a callback that calls callbacks! And one of the callbacks that _packedSubs() calls is essential to how the module works: _setpass(), as shown in Listing 20.17.

Listing 20.17
callbacks (_setpass())

```
151 sub _setpass
152 {
153     my ($self, $type) = @_;
154
155     my $userEntry = $self->{'attrib'}->{'userEntry'};
156     my $passEntry = $self->{'attrib'}->{'passEntry'};
157
158     if ($type eq 'ok')
159     {
160         $self->{'cancel'} = '';
161         $self->{'user'} = $userEntry->get();
162         $self->{'pass'} = $passEntry->get();
163     }
164     if ($type eq 'clear')
165     {
166         $userEntry->delete('0', 'end');
167         $passEntry->delete('0', 'end');
168     }
169     if ($type eq 'cancel')
170     {
171         $self->{'cancel'} = 1;
172         $self->{'user'} = '';
173         $self->{'pass'} = '';
174     }
175 }
176 1;
```

This is the main function of our module, the one that makes the whole thing come together. How does it work? Well, when we created the windows with the statement:

```
my $password = $passWindow->show();
```

the code froze at the statement:

```
31      $window->waitVariable(\$self->{'pass'});
```

with the intent to wait for the variable $self->{'pass'} to change (it is now undefined). When somebody hits the OK button, the code:

```
102     my $okButton = $buttonFrame->Button
103                                       (
104                                       'text' => 'ok',
105                                       'command' =>[$self, 'packedSubs','ok']
106                                       )
```

is executed. It translates into $self->packedSubs('ok'). Since we "packed the subs" in _packCall-backs(), this turns into the following two subroutine calls:

```
62      push(@{$callbacks->{'ok'}}, [ \&_setpass, $self, 'ok' ]);
        push(@{$callbacks->{'ok'}}, [ $self->{'window'}, 'withdraw' ]);
```

which in turn execute the following code in _setpass():

```
155     my $userEntry = $self->{'attrib'}->{'userEntry'};
156     my $passEntry = $self->{'attrib'}->{'passEntry'};
157
158     if ($type eq 'ok')
159     {
160         $self->{'cancel'} = '';
161         $self->{'user'} = $userEntry->get();
162         $self->{'pass'} = $passEntry->get();
163     }
```

which then sets the user and pass variables to whatever the user has set them. Finally, since the pass variable has changed, the statement:

```
31      $window->waitVariable(\$self->{'pass'});
```

senses this, and lets the code continue. This triggers:

```
33      return
34          (
35              {
36                  'user' => $self->{'user'},
37                  'pass' => $self->{'pass'},
38                  'cancel' => $self->{'cancel'}
39              }
40          );
```

which returns the values to the main subroutine.

Whew! Writing GUIs requires you to disassociate the GUI part of the code from the non-GUI part. The GUI part simply consists of a big loop that keeps spinning, looking for the user to do something. When the user does something, the callbacks associated with that code fire, and do the actual work, but they return the control to the main loop, which then looks for more user input.

Example 2: Unix Mail Messages

The second container example we will look at is making an OO interface into a physical resource, in this case, a piece of Unix mail. [Note that you will probably be better off using **MailTools** and **MailFilter** (which are on the accompanying CD) because they work transparently between NT and Unix, but this sure does make a good example.]

We saw this filtering example in Chapter 12, but we did not really touch on how the filter worked. This example is intended to fill in that gap a bit, as well as show how you might build physical containers of your own.

Problem Domain

This problem is one that many people are familiar with: they want processes to be able to read and sort mail, and even get rid of certain mail. Perl's `text` processing abilities will come in handy to do this. We want to make our interface as flexible as possible, considering the amount of things for which people use mail. We will also need to use some old Perl tricks to make the interface easier.

Interface Issues

To make a good interface, we must consider how the source data looks. The average Unix mail message looks something like:

```
From prince_of_darkness@satco.com Wed May 15 14:03 MDT 1996
Date: Wed, 15 May 1996 14:02:58 -0600
From: prince_of_darkness@satco.com
To: who_it_may_concern@above.com
Subject: Late on payment
Content-Length: 1219
X-Lines: 39
Status: O

This is the second notice in a series of three. You are again late on your contractual
payments, and if you persist in this manner, dire consequences will occur.

Yours,

B.B.
```

Note that this message consists of three parts. First is the `From` header, which tells the subject of the message. Second, there is a series of lines that look like:

```
Date:
From:
To:
```

In other words, these are tags that have values. You might also think of them as keys that have values, which immediately suggests storing them in a hash. The lines are separated by `:`.

Third is the actual message. What does this imply for our interface? First, the constructor should be fairly simple. We will say something like:

```
my $message = new UnixMail::Letter($text);
```

which converts the Unix mail `$text` into a message object we can manipulate. When we manipulate it, we will say:

```
my $subject = $message->get('subject');
```

and this retrieves the `Subject` header from the given message.

The essence of the physical container object is to take a piece of physical data and turn it into an internal format that can be manipulated—It can spit out the data that we want. If we were truly going to make this a read-and-write container, we would be able to say:

```
$message->set('Subject', 'forgery');
$message->write();
```

which would then set the internal format, and write it out to either a text representation of the mail message, or write it out to disk. However, for now, we will make it a read-only object. If you want to play around with a read-and-write container, you can take a look at **MailTools** on the accompanying CD.

Implementation

We are now ready to implement the **UnixMail::Letter** object. There will be two major functions, new and get. new will make the internal representation of the mail message a hash, and get will retrieve pieces of that object for us to look at. First, let's make the constructor and the headers (Listing 20.18).

Listing 20.18
UnixMail::Letter (new() constructor)

```
1    package UnixMail::Letter;
2
3    use Date::Parse qw (str2time);
4
5
6    sub new
7    {
8        my ($type, $text) = @_;
9        my $self = {};
10       my $header;
11
12       if ($text =~ m{
13                         (
14                             (?:^|\n)                    # beginning
15                             From (\S+) (.+?)            # From header, actual text
16                         )(?=\n)                          # up to next '\n'
17               }sgx)
18       {
19           $self->{'from'} = $2;
20           $self->{'date'} = $3;
21           $header = $1;
22       }
23       while
24           ($text =~ m{
25                         (
26                             \n([A-Za-z\-]+?): \s*(.*?)     # from tag.
27                         )
28                         (?=\n[^\n]+:|\n\n)                # up to next tag.
29                 }sgx
30           )
31       {
32           my $tag = $2;
33           my $value = $3;
34           $tag =~ tr"A-Z"a-z";
35           $self->{$tag} = $value;
36           $header .= $1;
37       }
38
39       $text =~ m"(.*?\n\n)"sg;
40
41       $header .= $1;
42       $self->{'header'} = $header;
43       if ($text =~ m"(.*)"sg) { $self->{'text'} = $1; }
44
```

```
45        if (!$self->{'from'})
46        {
47             return(undef);
48        }
49        if (!$self->{'subject'})
50        {
51             $self->{'subject'} = "*BLANK*";
52        }
53        bless $self, $type;
54   }
55
```

This code is performing quite a bit of work, but most of it pertains to the actual translation of the text into a hash. The constructor is split into three parts.

Lines 12–22 actually find out what the subject is going to be, along with the date. This allows sorting the mail by the date if we so desire. The g modifier to the regular expression keeps track of where we are, and stores what we have found about the header inside the variable $header.

Lines 23–37 go to the next step, taking all the tags we were talking about (From: Ed, Subject: hmm, etc.) and turns them into actual hash values. Line 34 turns the tags into lowercases, so it is easier to remember which tag is which.

Lines 38–55 do the cleanup, taking the rest of the text—the body—and turning it into another hash element. The whole header is then saved, and a check for a from element is performed. If there is no "From" element, chances are that it isn't a legal mail message. If there is no subject associated with the mail message, one is given.

All this is done to standardize the mail message into a hash. Notice that we have taken great pains to create code so that embedded mail messages are allowed. If there is junk in front of a mail message, we eliminate it by virtue of the regular expression in lines 12–17, which starts the parsing at the first "From" it meets.

If there are other mail messages at the end of the message, line 39 gets rid of them, since mail messages are always delimited by two newlines and then a From.

After we put the mail into this format, the get function (Listing 20.19) is trivial.

Listing 20.19
UnixMail::Letter (get ( ))

```
56   sub get
57   {
58        my ($self, $criteria) = @_;
59
60        if (!$self->{$criteria})
61        {
62             warn "The only criteria that are available are ",
63                  "@{[keys(%$self)]}\n";
64        }
65        return($self->{$criteria});
66   }
67
```

Not only is this a generic function (we don't care about the type of tags that a mail message has), it is self-documenting. The number of attributes a mail message can have is not fixed: there are no set tags (other than subject and from) that can be fixed.

Lines 62 and 63 output the possible tags for the given mail message rather than giving a fixed message.

The only other function that we have is a seconds function:

```
68
69   sub seconds
70   {
71       my ($self) = @_;
72       my $date = $self->{date};
73
74       return(str2time($date));
75   }
76
77   1;
```

This gives the number of seconds (since 1970) since a given message was written. This will come in handy when we get to iterator objects.

Summary of Container Objects

Container objects are handy for simplifying an interface. As we saw in the two examples, we could:

- Take a complicated mesh of objects, logic, and functionality, (the **Tk::Password** screen) and make it look like one, simple object from the point of view of the client.
- Take a file format, and make it look like a simple hash (**UnixMail::Letter**).

In both cases, the key to the container's success was *simplicity of interface*. A client should not care how the internal workings of the container operate.

In a sense, the container is the pattern in OO where the "buck stops." Any project that used the **Tk::Password** object could really simplify the object diagram that it had from what is shown in Figure 20.9.

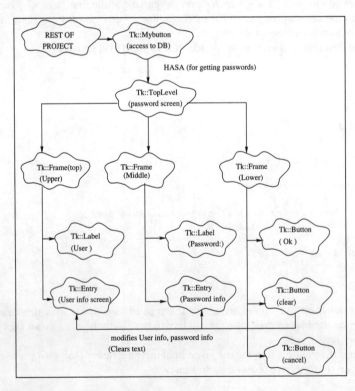

Figure 20.9
Project with
Password Entry
Screen Object
Diagram

to something that looks like what is shown in Figure 20.10.

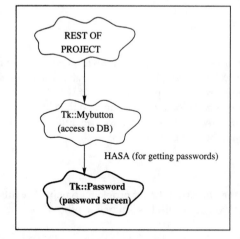

Figure 20.10
Simplified
Password Object
Diagram

After all, we know that the **Tk::Password** has buttons, objects, and the like, but what do we care? Putting all the detail in the object diagram just muddles the overall design of the program.

The Iterator Pattern

The last type of pattern we consider is the iterator pattern. The *iterator* is a common, specialized container that simplifies access to a list of simpler objects. It also manages issues such as boundary conditions [e.g., what happens when the last object is gone through (in the iterator) or what happens when the number of objects stored in the iterator goes to zero?].

The object diagram for the iterator looks something like Figure 20.11. It is common to see methods in the iterator pattern such as `next` and `previous`. The methods keep track of an internal counter that tells the iterator where it is in the list of objects it controls. Similarly there is usually a `reset` function.

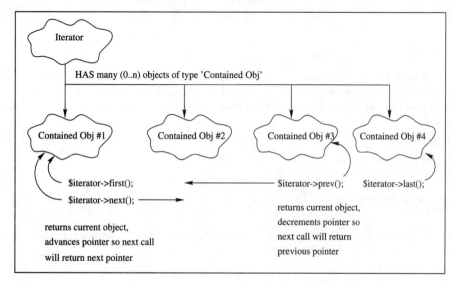

Figure 20.11
Simplified
Password Object
Diagram

The best way to look at the iterator is by example. So let's continue along the same lines as the **UnixMail::Letter** object.

Example: UnixMail::LetterIter

The **UnixMail::Letter** object is not all that useful, unless you have it in context. Usually, letters reside in a mailbox, with each mailbox containing several letters. What we would like to do is have a structured way of accessing, sorting, and otherwise manipulating those letters so we can pick them out at will.

This points to the need for an iterator which takes a mailbox, opens it up, and then looks at its contents. Once we have these letters in the form of an array of lower-level objects, we can look through them using the **UnixMail::Letters** accessor functions, and we should be doing OK.

Problem Domain

This problem domain is pretty much the same as the **UnixMail::Letter** problem domain. The difference this time is that we are dealing with it from a higher level, through the mechanism of a mailbox.

Interface Issues

What interface do we want for the letter iterator? It would be nice to create a simple version of the constructor:

```
my $mailiter = new UnixMail::LetterIter('mbox');
```

which then creates the **$mailiter** object for us, tying it to the file **mbox**. However, we may want to have complicated usage, something that looks like:

```
my $mailiter = new UnixMail::LetterIter
                (
                    'mbox',
                    { 'CRITERIA' =>
                        sub {
                            my ($message) = @_;
                            return(1) if ($message->get('subject') !~ m"junk");
                            return(0);
                        }
                    }
                );
```

This should probably be in its own subroutine (rather than an anonymous sub), but you get the idea. The CRITERIA determines which messages will be included in the **$mailiter** based on each message's attributes. This is incredibly powerful; by having this simple filter mechanism, you can use any piece of Perl syntax to sort through your mailbox.

Finally, we have the 'next' function. To actually go through the **LetterIter** object, say something like:

```
my $mbox = new UnixMail::LetterIter('mbox');
while ($message = $mbox->next())
{
    # do something with each message.
}
```

which gives internal access to each and every **UnixMail::Letter LetterIter** knows about. We then can manipulate these messages through the **UnixMail::Letter** methods.

Implementation

This implementation is pretty easy because most of the details about mail messages are being handled by **UnixMail::Letter**. All we have to do is be able to take a Unix mailbox, chop it into messages, and then feed these messages to **UnixMail::Letter**. Again, there are only two functions: new() and next(). new handles parsing, and next returns the next **UnixMail::Letter** object in the chain. First let's look at the constructor (Listing 20.20):

Listing 20.20
UnixMail::LetterIter (constructor)

```
1    package UnixMail::LetterIter;
2
3
4    use strict;
5    use UnixMail::Letter;
6    use Carp;
7
8    sub new
9    {
10       my ($type, $mbox, $config) = @_;
11       my $self = {};
12       my (@messages, $message);
13
14       bless $self, $type;
15
16       $self->{filename} = $mbox;
17       my $fh = new FileHandle($mbox) || die "couldn't open $mbox\n";
18       local($/) = undef;
19
20       my $msgtext = <$fh>;
21       close($fh);
22
23       while ($msgtext =~ m{
24                           (.*?)                        # actual message text
25                           (?=\nFrom [^\n]*\d\d\d\d\n\S+:|$) # next header.
26                     }sgx
27          )
28       {
29           my $message = new UnixMail::Letter($1);
30           if ($config->{CRITERIA})
31           {
32               my $callback = $config->{CRITERIA};
33               if (&$callback($message))
34               {
35                   push (@messages, $message);
36               }
37           }
38           else
39           {
40               push(@messages, $message);
41           }
42       }
43
```

```
44
45         @messages = sort { $b->secs() <=> $a->secs() } @messages;
46
47         $self->{'messages'} = [@messages];
48         $self->{'messageno'} = 0;
49         bless $self, $type;
50    }
```

The major piece of logic that splits a mailbox into its component messages is lines 23–41. We read the whole mailbox into one scalar (line 20), and then look for everything up to and including From [^\n]*\d\d\d\d\n\S+:. More informally, this is looking for the lines of the form:

```
From prince_of_darkness@satco.com Wed May 15 14:03 MDT 1996
```

where the four digits and then a newline are a dead giveaway that this is an actual mail header. The text we get from the `while` loop goes into the constructor in line 29, and gets filtered through the callback mechanism in line 33.

We finally sort the messages by their respective dates (`str2time` comes in so useful) and set the internal iterator that we are going to use in `next` to 0 (Listing 20.21).

Listing 20.21
UnixMail::Letter (next)

```
51
52    sub next
53    {
54         my ($self, $config) = @_;
55
56         my @messages = @{$self->{messages}};
57         my $messageno = $self->{'messageno'};
58
59         my $return = $messages[$self->{'messageno'}];
60
61         if (defined($return)
62         {
63              $self->{'messageno'} = 0;
64         }
65         else
66         {
67              $self->{'messageno'}++;
68         }
69         return($return);
70    }
71    1;
```

What we have here is your basic ring structure. We keep track of where we are in the ring by the internal `messageno` pointer, and increment it in line 67. If we run out of mail messages, this is sensed in line 61. The message number is reset to zero. We do, however, return `undef`; this short-circuits any loop that is calling the `next` function.

Summary of the Iterator Pattern

The iterator pattern is a simple, but widely used pattern in object-oriented programming. Whenever you have something that is directly composed of a bunch of similar subcomponents, it should be a clue that you might want to make an iterator on top of it.

In this case it was pretty obvious. Mailboxes are composed of messages; therefore, it makes sense to split modeling into two objects and make one the handler of the other. Other places where iterators are helpful are:

- Database accesses, in which each row can be thought of as part of an overall query.
- Graphical objects, which can be thought to compose a graphical canvas.
- Various file formats (of which Mailboxes can be an example).

In all these cases, the iterator is the natural method of modeling patterns.

Final Layering Example

Let's look at how we could use the concepts of layering to make a true-to-life application, rather than just components of applications as we have done heretofore. Going from the "write object" stage to thinking about writing object-oriented projects seems like it would be a big jump to make, but it is not a big deal.

We have been creating applications, almost the whole time. The automation of **telnet** and **ftp** in Chapter 17 is a sample of a nontrivial application through the use of an object. However, this is not how most people think of applications. When people think of applications, they usually think of the GUI environment. (This is a pity because there is much overhead in the GUI approach, and you can often do more for less with a text-based approach.)

Ah well. There's no way to change minds about the type of applications users would like to use, so you might as well put GUIs on things. This is what we will do here.

Problem Domain

The problem domain we consider here is the personal data assistant (PDA). The particular personal data assistant we are interested in here is the calendar application. Users enter plans they have for a certain day and the computer remembers the plans.

Interface and Design Issues

Because this is a GUI application, the interface and design issues for it go pretty much hand in hand. Our calendar application should be:

- Simple
- Robust
- Flexible

Simple means that there should only be a couple of buttons on the calendar at most and not too many options in menu bars. The calendar will not do everything under the sun. It will just be a reliable way of putting calendar notes in a safe place.

Robust means that there is no way of fooling the calendar into losing information, and there are few, if any, holes that lead to weird behavior.

Flexible means the application can adapt to an individual's needs. Some people can have many different activities going at the same time, or might need several scheduled days visible concurrently. Flexibility requires that the interface does not get in the way of using the calendar. Granted, these are touchy/feely terms; however, it is the job of the programmer to turn these terms into a concrete design and that is what we are going to do.

Again, to find role models for the application we are going to write, type:

```
C:\> widget
```

which brings up that awesome list of sample applications from which we can safely steal data. The one that we look at this time is called "A 15-puzzle made up of buttons," which has an interface looking something like Figure 20.12.

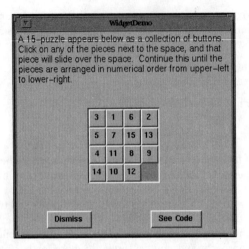

Again, a perfect fit! You can see the calendar forming already. The "trough" for the tiles becomes the calendar border, as well as the colors for the calendar. The buttons at the bottom become scrolling elements, and so forth and so on. Hit **See Code** and the following pops up (in part):

```
my($i, $num, $frame_num);
for ($i=0; $i<15; $i++) {
    $num = $order[$i];
    $xpos{$num} = ($i%4) * 0.25;
    $ypos{$num} = (int($i/4)) * 0.25;
    $frame_num = $frame->Button(
        -relief             => 'raised',
        -text               => $num,
        -highlightthickness => 0,
    );
    $frame_num->configure(
        -command => [\&puzzle_switch, $frame_num, $num, \%xpos, \%ypos],
    );
    $frame_num->place(
        -relx      => $xpos{$num},
        -rely      => $ypos{$num},
        -relwidth  => 0.25,
        -relheight => 0.25,
    );
}
```

This shows us how to put the buttons in the format we want. We use the **place** command, and then have four elements to define:

1. `-relx` is the relative *x* position in the frame from 0 to 1.
2. `-rely` is the relative *y* position in the frame from 0 to 1.
3. `-relwidth` is the relative width compared to the frame that the button is in from 0 to 1.
4. `-relheight` is the relative height compared to the frame that the button is in from 0 to 1.

Again, the metaphor is the same. We blatantly mimic the code that we get for free in the standard distribution, and adapt it to our needs. There are several possible designs, but the one in Figure 20.13 pops to mind first. This is straightforward and extremely linear. A calendar object *HASA* bunch of month objects, which in turn *HASA* bunch of date objects.

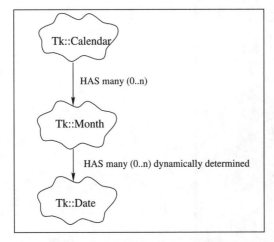

Figure 20.13
Object Diagram
for Calendar
Application

By making it this way, we should have few of the surprise behaviors we mentioned in our discussion on robustness. With a simple design, we facilitate a simple application. As for flexibility, this is where PerlTk comes in. It is difficult not to design a flexible application in PerlTk. Because each object can have almost any other object in the Tk library combined with the flexibility of Perl's syntax, you can easily create programs that look like they took about 20 to 100 times the equivalent C-code.

Let's look at how the preceding object diagram translates into graphics. First we have the calendar object (Figure 20.14).

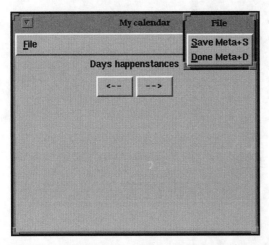

Figure 20.14
Calendar Objects

This contains all the menus, buttons, and so forth of the final product. Right now, there are only two buttons—**forward** and **back**—and one menu that consists of Save and Done. Nice and simple.

Each calendar consists of several month objects (Figure 20.15).

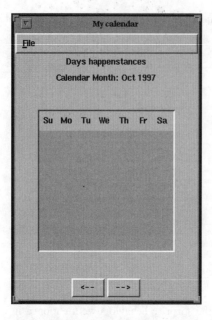

These objects consist of the trough where the month is defined, the headers (Su, Mo, Tu, We, etc.), and the position of the first days of the month as well as the last days. Finally, the month object has a bunch of day objects, which look something like what you see in Figure 20.16.

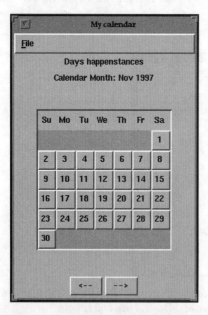

These objects have a button. The button knows when it has been pressed by the user, whether or not anything is scheduled on that day, and whether or not that day is the current day (in which case there are different color codes).

All of this translates into the final interface (Figure 20.17). Figure 20.17 shows a calendar at work with the shaded squares being days that have text associated with them and an opened day, which shows how people make appointments.

Figure 20.17
Final Calendar
Object

It is important to consider how the calendar object will be used in code. The usage should be as flexible as possible. Unlike such entities as the **Password** screen that we implemented earlier, we want the calendar object to be able to stand on its own, or be a subobject of another window. Therefore, we will want one usage that looks like:

```
my ($window) = new MainWindow();
my $calendar = new Tk::Calendar($window);
$calendar->draw();
MainLoop();
```

which ties the **$calendar** object to a certain window. The other usage we want to have is something that looks like:

```
my $calendar = new Tk::Calendar();
$calendar->draw();
MainLoop();
```

in which the calendar stands by itself. While this looks easy enough, the question is whether the implementation is as easy as it looks.

Implementation

We cannot possibly go into as much detail as we have previously about the following code as it is just too long. We can, however, point out certain stumbling blocks we came across in implementing it, as well as point out tricky places in the code that we came across. We point out where the different design patterns we have discussed made a difference while we were implementing the code.

We have three separate files: **Tk::Calendar.pm, Tk::Month.pm,** and **Tk::Date.pm.** I implemented them in this order so it would be easier to have a framework (**Tk::Calendar.pm**) in which I could place months and dates. We will start with **Tk::Calendar.pm** and work downward.

Tk::Calendar

Tk::Calendar.pm is responsible for the high-level interface issues in the calendar. It handles, for example, the way the next button will move to the next month, and how save will save and exit the application.

In rough terms, then, **Tk::Calendar** is a container for **Tk:Months**, although it does more than that. Figure 20.18 shows the object diagram generated by **Tk::Calendar**.

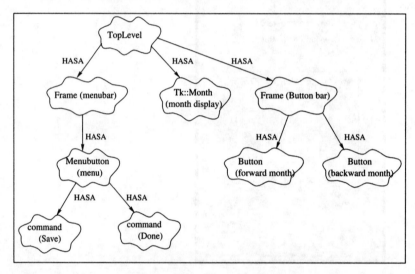

Figure 20.18
Tk::Calendar
Hierarchy

The only thing that was difficult about this design was the switching of the months. When a user had windows open, and pressed the **forward** key, the previous month's windows would close without saving. Therefore, I needed to implement a function called `_closeScreens()` that called the function:

```
my $dates = Tk::Date::getopen();
```

which is a class function in **Tk::Date**. It gets a list of open dates which then get closed (and saved) before proceeding to the next month, via a FileDialog box.

Here is the code:

```
1    package Tk::Calendar;
2
3    use Tk::Month;
4    use strict;
5
6    sub new
7    {
8        my ($type, $widget, $title, $descript, $date) = @_;
9        my $self = bless {}, $type;
10
11       $title ||= 'My calendar'; # title for calendar
12       $descript ||= 'Appointment listings';    # name for display
13       $date ||= localtime();
14
15       if ($widget)
16       {
```

```
17              $self->{'widget'} = $widget;
18              $self->{'window'} = $widget->TopLevel();
19          }
20      else
21          {
22              $self->{'widget'} = 'me';
23              $self->{'window'} = new MainWindow();
24          }
25      $self->{'window'}->title($title);
26      $self->{'description'} = $descript;
27      $self->{'date'} = $date;
28      $self;
29  }
30
```

Note the dual constructor in lines 15–24. If we are given a widget, tie the calendar to the widget. Otherwise, make a new main window. Following is the "guts" of GUI code:

```
31  sub draw
32  {
33      my ($self) = @_;
34      $self->_pack();
35  }
36
37  sub _pack
38  {
39      my ($self) = @_;
40
41      my $window = $self->{'window'};
42      my $attribs = $self->{'attribs'} = {};
43      my $date = $self->{'date'};
44
45      ##############################################################################
46
47      my $menuBar = $window->Frame('-borderwidth' => 2, -relief => 'raised' )
48      # menu buttons for the different      ->pack( '-side' => 'top', '-fill' => 'x'
);
49      # calendar options
50      my $menu = $menuBar->Menubutton
51                      (
52                          '-text' => 'File',
53                          '-underline'   => 0,
54                          '-borderwidth' => 2,
55                      ) -> pack (
56                              '-side' => 'left',
57                              '-padx' => 2
58                          );
59
60      $menu->command
61                  (
62                      '-label' => 'Save',
63                      '-accelerator' => 'Meta+S',
64                      '-underline' => 0,
```

```
65                             '-command' => [ $self, '_savecheck' ]
66                  );
67
68        $menu->command
69                  (
70                     '-label' => 'Done',
71                     '-accelerator' => 'Meta+D',
72                     '-underline' => 0,
73                     '-command' => [ $self, '_donecheck' ]
74                  );
75
76    #############################################################################
77
78        my $labelFrame= $window->Frame( 'borderwidth' => 2 )->pack('-side' =>'top');
79
80        my $topLabel = $labelFrame->Label('text' => $self->{'description'} )
81                                ->pack( '-side'=>'left' );
82
83        $self->{'currentmonth'} = new Tk::Month($window, $date);# create the month
84        $self->{'currentmonth'}->draw();
85
86        my $buttonFrame= $window->Frame( 'borderwidth'=> 2 )
87                                        ->pack    ( 'side' => 'top' );
88
89        my $backButton = $buttonFrame->Button    # button to go back a month
90                                  (
91                                     'text' => '<-',
92                                     'command' => [ $self, 'backamonth']
93                                  ) -> pack ( 'side' => 'left' );
94
95        my $forwardButton = $buttonFrame->Button # button to go forward
96                                  (
97                                     'text' => '->',
98                                     'command' => [ $self, 'forwardamonth']
99                                  ) -> pack ('side' => 'right' );
100
101        $self->{'attrib'} = {
102                           'labelFrame'    => $labelFrame,
103                           'topLabel'      => $topLabel,    # we save everything
in
104                           'month'   =>    {      # ourself, for later
105                                               "$self->{'currentmonth'}" =>
106                                               $self->{'currentmonth'}
107                                           },
108                           'menubar'       => $menuBar,
109                           'menu'       => $menu,
110                           'backButton'       => $backButton,
111                           'forwardButton' => $forwardButton
112                      };
113 }
```

The menu is associated with two callbacks (shown below) that exit the application. The **forward** and **back** buttons are associated with moving the calendar backward and forward a month, given the time.

```
114
115 sub backamonth
116 {
117     my ($self) = @_;
118
119     my $month = $self->{'currentmonth'};
120     my $window = $self->{'window'};
121
122     my $ok = _closeScreens($window, 'peaceful');
123     return() if (!$ok);
124
125     $month->undraw(); # we need to get rid of the
126     my $time = $month->last();      # old month, and get
127     my $newmonth = new Tk::Month( $window, $time ); # a new one
128     $newmonth->draw();
129
130     $self->{'currentmonth'} = $newmonth;
131
132     $self->{'attribs'}{'month'}{"$newmonth"} = $newmonth;    # save ourselves again
133 }
134
135 sub forwardamonth      # same as back a month
136 {        # except going forward
137     my ($self) = @_;
138
139     my $month = $self->{'currentmonth'};
140
141     my $window = $self->{'window'};
142
143     my $ok = _closeScreens($window, 'peaceful');
144     return() if (!$ok);
145
146     $month->undraw();
147
148     my $time = $month->next();
149     my $newmonth = new Tk::Month( $window, $time );
150     $newmonth->draw();
151
152     $self->{'currentmonth'} = $newmonth;      # set our current month.
153
154     $self->{'attribs'}{'month'}{"$newmonth"} = $newmonth;
155
156 }
```

Note the heavy use of **Month** methods to figure out what the next month is, to actually draw the new month being displayed and to undraw the old month. Months know their time and place, and have methods to return this information. Following is the code associated with **forward** and **back** buttons.

```
157 sub _donecheck
158 {
159     my ($self) = @_;
160
161     my $window = $self->{'window'};
162     my $ok = _closeScreens($window, 'destructive'); # function to close all
```

```
163        $window->destroy() if ($ok);      # date windows. Destroy self
164 }
165
166 sub _savecheck
167 {
168        my ($self) = @_;
169
170        my $window = $self->{'window'};
171        my $ok = _closeScreens($window, 'peaceful');    # peaceful means be nice
172        $window->destroy() if ($ok);       # and save things
173 }
174
```

Lines 162 and 171 have the @_closeScreens() function, which reaches directly into the dates of the months to figure out what to close. (This function could probably be moved to the month itself, but I was lazy.) Finally, following is the _closeScreens() function that gets the data for each date that is open (i.e., has an open screen) and closes them all.

```
175 sub _closeScreens        #
176 {
177        my ($window, $type) = @_;
178
179        my $dates = Tk::Date::getopen();     # -again, class method getting
180        my $kill;   # all registered dates
181        if ($type eq 'destructive') { $kill = "Text will be lost in them."; }
182        else { $kill = ''; }
183
184        if ($dates)
185        {
186            my @titles = map ($_->get('dbmstring'), @$dates);    # each $ dates is a date
187            # object
188            my $dialog = $window->DialogBox #
189                                (
190                                    '-title' => 'Open Screens',
191                                    '-buttons' => [ 'OK', 'Cancel' ],
192                                    '-default_button' => 'Cancel'
193                                );
194            my $text = $dialog->add ( 'Text' ) -> pack('side' => 'top');
195
196            $text->insert( '0.0',    # show all titles
197                "The following windows are still open: @titles. $kill Close them?"
198            );
199
200            my $grab = $dialog->Show();
201
202            return(0) if ($grab eq 'Cancel');
203
204            my ($date);
205            if ($type eq 'destructive')
206            {
207                foreach $date(@$dates) { $date->cancel(); }
208            }
209            else
```

```
210             {
211                     foreach $date (@$dates) { $date->savetext(); }
212             }
213     }
214     return(1);
215 }
216 1;
```

Tk::Calendar relied quite heavily on the **Tk::Month** methods to fill in the gaps of functionality that **Tk::Calendar** did not know (such as which month is last, and such). This is where we turn next.

Tk::Month

Tk::Month goes to the next level of detail. It provides the GUI and informational support about what a month is supposed to look like inside the calendar widget. If you think about it, months are tricky items to program. They are nonstandard (some months have 28 days, 29 days, etc.). There is no standard about which day of the week is the first day of the month. Just when you get this figured out, there are also several exceptions to rules—anything from leap years to the "add a day every four hundred years" rule.

What do we do about this? We let the operating system handle this, through Perl. Perl has a function called `localtime()` that returns a string for a given time, expressed in seconds since 1970. This function works cross-platform and is very easy to program.

We know that there are 86,400 seconds in a day, and that fact never varies. Therefore, when we are given the constructor for a new month:

```
my $month = new Month($widget, 'Jun 15, 1998');
```

we take that date, turn it into seconds, and then, in the function `_getStartDate()`, subtract days from this date until we reach the starting day of the month. From there, we can tell where to draw the first day of the month. The `Date::Parse` and `Date::Format` modules provided by **CPAN** are instrumental in making this a user-friendly operation. By using `str2time()`, we can take almost any form of date and turn it into seconds. By using `time2str()` we can take the seconds and extract any type of information out of the date we want (the year, name of the day in the week, etc.).

The second problem I came across while programming this was that some of the items (such as the background of the calendar and the days of the week for the calendar) did not merit having multiple copies of themselves, one per month. After all, they were drawn only once, and drawing them again would be a waste.

To that end, I made a few class variables (`%_cachedMonths`, `$_cachedFrame`, `$_cachedBody`, `$_cachedLabel`, `$_cachedWeekLabels`) that prevented excess copying. I needed to cache the months because I really did not want two copies of the same month floating around; that would mean that there could be two entries for the same date, which is not what I wanted. Listing 20.22 shows **Tk::Month**.

Listing 20.22
Tk::Month

```
TK/Month.pm

1    package Tk::Month;
2
3    use Date::Parse;
4    use Date::Format;
5    use Tk::Date;
6
7    use strict;
8
```

```
 9   my $_cachedMonths = {};          # class data
10   my $_cachedFrame = undef;        #
11   my $_cachedLabel = undef;
12   my $_cachedBody = undef;
13   my $_cachedWeekLabels = [];
14
15   sub new
16   {
17       my ($type, $widget, $date) = @_;
18       my $self = {};
19
20       if (ref($widget) eq 'Tk::TopLevel')
21       {
22
23
24           my ( $startingday, $secs, $monthstring ) = _getStartDate($date);        # -
             stuff to get dates
25               if ( defined($_cachedMonths->{ $monthstring }) )     # we return an already
26               {       # -created month if it has
27                   return ($_cachedMonths->{$monthstring}); # been opened before
28               }
29               else
30               {
31                   ( $self->{'startingday'}, $self->{'secs'}, $self->{'monthstring'})
32                       = ( $startingday, $secs, $monthstring );
33
34                   $self->{'xcoord'} =  .1428571428571428; # -we are splicing it up into
35                   $self->{'ycoord'} =  .1428571428571428; # -seven rows
36
37                   $self->{'widget'} = $widget;       # -we record the widget object
38               }        # -inside the object
39       }
40       else
41       {
42           print "You need to have a Frame widget to fill!\n";
43           return();
44       }
45
46       bless $self, $type;
47   }
48
```

Again, new caches the months that it has already seen (lines 25–28) and calculates a lot of information about the month that has been passed via the constructor by calling _getStartDate();.

```
49   sub next
50   {
51       my ($self) = @_;
52
53       my $secs = $self->{'secs'};
54       do { $secs += 86400 } while (!_diffMonth($secs, '+'));  # -simple function to
         calculate
```

```
55        $secs+=86400;        # if the month needs to change
56
57        return(scalar(localtime($secs)));
58  }
59
60  sub last        # simple function to calculate
61  {
62        my ($self) = @_;    # if the month needs to
63        my $secs = $self->{'secs'};         # change coding backwards
64        while (!_diffMonth($secs, '-')) { $secs -= 86400; }
65        $secs -=86400;
66
67        return(scalar(localtime($secs)));
68  }
69
```

These functions will be used by **Tk::Calendar.pm** to increment and decrement the month. Following is where we actually draw and undraw the month:

```
70
71  sub draw
72  {
73        my ($self) = @_;
74        $self->_packLabel();        # function to make label
75        $self->_drawButtons();      # and to call the month's 'date'
76  }          # object
77
78  sub undraw
79  {
80        my ($self) = @_;
81        $self->_undrawButtons();   # we need to get rid of buttons
82  }          # but not frames
83
84  sub _packLabel
85  {
86        my ($self) = @_;
87
88        my ($widget, $monthstring, $xcoord, $ycoord ) =
89                (
90                      $self->{'widget'}, $self->{'monthstring'},
91                      $self->{'xcoord'}, $self->{'ycoord'}
92                );
93
94
95        my $header = _getTopFrame($widget);
96        my $topLabel = _getTopLabel($header, $monthstring);
97        my $body = _getBody ($widget);
98
99        my $weekLabels = _getWeekLabels($body, $xcoord, $ycoord);
100
101       $self->{'attribs'}{'weeklabels'} = $weekLabels;
102       $self->{'attribs'}{'body'} = $body;
```

```
103        $self->{'attribs'}{'header'} = $header;
104        $self->{'attribs'}{'topLabel'} = $topLabel;
105 }
106
```

Lines 95–97 are actually calls to functions which determine whether or not a month has been drawn before. If so, then the header, body, etc., are not drawn again. Following is where the buttons are drawn:

```
107 sub _drawButtons
108 {
109     my ($self) = @_;
110
111     my ($secs, $startingday, $monthstring, $xcoord, $ycoord, $body) =
112             (
113                     $self->{'secs'}, $self->{'startingday'},
114                     $self->{'monthstring'},
115                     $self->{'xcoord'}, $self->{'ycoord'},
116                      $self->{'attribs'}{'body'}
117             );
118
119     my $newsecs = $secs;
120     my $day = $startingday;
121     my $oldday = $startingday - 1;
122     my $date = 1;
123     my (@buttons);
124     my $row = 1;
125
126     for (   # funky for loop to
127             $day = $startingday;; # determine dates
128             ( $secs+=86400, $day++, $day = $day%7, $date++ )
129         )
130     {
131         $row++ if ($day != ($oldday + 1));          # next week
132         push (       # keep an array of buttons
133                 @buttons, new Tk::Date
134                         (
135                                 $body, $monthstring, $day,
136                                 $date, $row, $xcoord, $ycoord
137                         )
138             );
139
140         $oldday = $day;
141         last if (_diffMonth($secs, '+'));
142     }
143
144     $self->{'attrib'}{'buttons'} = \@buttons;
145     grep($_->draw(), @buttons);
146 }
147
```

This is closely related to the place function we mentioned earlier, but the details are held inside **Tk::Date**. Note that we start with $startingday and then have logic for figuring out which row and day each button holds.

Following is where we do the reverse, and undraw the month information, plus *getStartDated*, which figures out the first day of the month:

```
148 sub _undrawButtons
149 {
150     my ($self) = @_;
151     my $buttons = $self->{'attrib'}{'buttons'};
152
153     my $button;
154     foreach $button (@$buttons) { $button->undraw(); }
155 }
156
157 sub _getStartDate
158 {
159
160     my ($date) = @_;
161
162     my $secs= str2time($date);
163
164     my $year = time2str("%Y", $secs);
165     my $month = time2str("%b", $secs);
166
167     while (!_diffMonth($secs, '-')) { $secs -= 86400; } # go back a day at a time
168     # until in a different month
169     my $startingday = time2str("%w", $secs);      # display time information
170
171     my $monthstring = "Calendar Month: $month $year";
172     return( $startingday, $secs, $monthstring );
173 }
174
175 sub _diffMonth     # -code to figure out different month
176 {
177     my ($secs, $type) = @_;
178     my $month= time2str("%b", $secs);     # get just month.
179     $secs = ($type eq '+')? $secs + 86400 : $secs - 86400;
180     my $newmonth= time2str("%b", $secs);
181
182     return(1) if ($month ne $newmonth);
183 }
184
185 sub _getTopFrame   # we cache everything so
186 {   # when we create a new month
187     my ($widget) = @_;     # we can reuse components.
188
189     if (defined($_cachedFrame))
190     {
191         return($_cachedFrame);
192     }
193     else    # -only create if not done so already.
194     {
195         my $frame = $widget->Frame( 'borderwidth' => 2)
196                                         ->pack('side' => 'top');
```

```
197            $_cachedFrame = $frame;
198            return($frame);
199        }
200 }
201 sub _getTopLabel
202 {       # again we cache top Labels
203     my ($widget, $monthstring) = @_;
204
205     if (defined($_cachedLabel))        # For reuse single on.
206        {
207            $_cachedLabel->configure( '-text' => $monthstring );
208            return($_cachedLabel);
209        }
210     else
211        {
212            my $label = $widget->Label( 'text' => $monthstring );
213
214            $label->Label('text' =>$monthstring );
215            $label->grid ( '-row' => 0, '-column' => 0);
216
217            $_cachedLabel = $label;
218            return($_cachedLabel);
219        }
220 }
221
222 sub _getBody   # we get 'through' for the month
223 {
224     my ($widget,$scroll) = @_;
225
226
227     if (defined ($_cachedBody))
228        {
229            return($_cachedBody);
230        }
231     else
232        {
233        my $scroll = $widget->Scrollbar();    #
234        my $body = $widget->Frame       # This allows us to make
235                            (    # an indentation.
236                                    '-width' => 210,
237                                    '-height' => 210,
238                                    '-borderwidth' => 2,
239                                    '-relief' => 'sunken',
240                                    '-background' => $scroll->cget('-troughcolor')
241                            ) ->pack
242                                    (
243                                            '-side' => 'top', '-padx' => '1c',
244                                            '-pady' => '1c'
245                                    );
246
247
248        $scroll->destroy();
249
```

```
250              $_cachedBody = $body;
251
252              return($_cachedBody);
253      }
254 }
255
256 sub _getWeekLabels      # we name each of
257 {            # the days on the calendar.
258      my ($widget, $xcoord, $ycoord) = @_;
259
260      my @dayarray = ('Su', 'Mo ', 'Tu ', 'We ', 'Th ', 'Fr ', 'Sa ' );
261
262      my ($xx, @weekLabels);
263
264      if (@$_cachedWeekLabels)
265      {
266          return($_cachedWeekLabels);
267      }
268      else
269      {
270          my ($xx);
271
272          for ($xx = 0; $xx < 7; $xx++)
273          {
274              push (@weekLabels, $widget->Label ( 'text' => $dayarray[$xx] ));
275              $weekLabels[-1]->place
276              (
277                  '-relx' => ($xx%7) * $xcoord , '-rely' => 0,
278                  '-relwidth' => $xcoord, '-relheight' => $ycoord
279              );
280          }
281          $_cachedWeekLabels = \@weekLabels;
282      }
283 }
284 1;
```

_getWeekLabels draws the Mo, Tu, We, Th, etc. top header, and _getBody draws the frame where the calendar is kept.

Tk::Date

Tk::Date contains the lowest level of detail. I had to concern myself with several things here. We want to have each button an entity unto itself, such that when the user presses the button, it pops up a screen that looks something like Figure 20.19. The question is: How do we store all of that data, in a way that is easy to use, portable, and moreover doesn't have much overhead to manipulate? We could have multiple files, but that seems to fall into the "lots of overhead" category. I chose to make the storage mechanism a single DBM hash ($_dbm) stored in a single DBM file ($_dbmfile). Because it is a single DBM file, there is no overhead on storing it. Moreover, DBM files can update, delete, and insert entries without any difficulty. Since DBM files are stored on disk, they are persistent. They are also portable, and do not require any specialty software like SQL databases to implement.

Figure 20.19

Opening Up a
Button for a
Certain Date

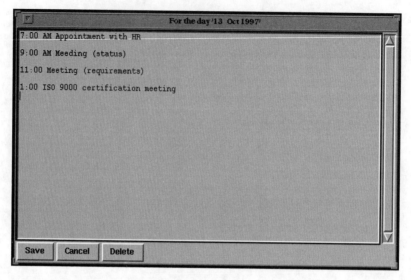

Another issue I encountered was how to distinguish between dates that had no information associated with them and dates that did. I chose to color the buttons differently:

- **firebrickred1** if the date is equal to the current date and there are appointments on it.
- **chartreuse4** (green) if the date is greater than the current date and there are appointments on it.
- **gray90** elsewhere.

In addition, I added the touch that the button flashed, once a second, if you happened to have an appointment on the current date.

These colors came out of the widget demonstration package again through:

```
C:\> widget
```

when Perl is installed.

There was also the issue of open entries, and maintaining the color scheme that showed which dates had appointments. If a date had no appointment, when the user clicked the button associated with that date and then closed that date, the color had to be updated as well.

Finally, there was the issue of open windows when the month switched or when either the **save** or **cancel** button was hit. In this case, I ended up maintaining an open list of all the dates that had open windows associated with them.

That was about it for the design challenges. **Date** was the most difficult object of the three to program, and I've found that it usually is that way: the highest level is easiest, and it gets more difficult on the way down. The code follows in Listing 20.23.

Listing 20.23
Tk::Date

Tk/Date.pm

```
1    package Tk::Date;
```

```
2
3    use AnyDBM_File;
4    use Fcntl;
5    use Tk::Dialog;
6    use strict;
7    use Date::Parse;
8
9    my $_dbm;
10   my $_dbmfile = $ENV{'CALENDAR_DBM'} || "$ENV{'HOME'}/.calendar";
11   my %_open;
12
13   sub new
14   {
15       my ($type, $widget, $monthstring, $day, $date, $row, $xcoord,
16            $ycoord) = @_;
17       my $self = bless {}, $type;
18
19       if (!defined ($_dbm))  # hash to hold date
20       {          # appointment info
21           $_dbm = {};
22           tie(%$_dbm, 'AnyDBM_File', $_dbmfile, O_RDWR|O_CREAT, 0640);     # Again, cached
23       }
24
25       (
26           $self->{'monthstring'}, $self->{'day'},
27           $self->{'date'}, $self->{'row'},
28           $self->{'xcoord'}, $self->{'ycoord'}, $self->{'widget'}
29
30       )     = ($monthstring, $day, $date, $row, $xcoord, $ycoord,$widget);
31
32       my $string = $self->{'monthstring'};
33       $string =~ s"Calendar Month:""g;
34       $string = $self->{'date'} . " $string";
35
36       $self->{'secs'} = _getSecs($string);
37       $self->{'dbmstring'} = $string;
38
39       return ($self);
40   }
```

Again, here is where we set up the access mechanism. Lines 19–23 are a portable way of setting up a DBM (database file). We use **AnyDBM_File**, which means "Hey—I don't care what type of DBM file we use, just use one!" Since SDBM comes with the standard distribution, we are guaranteed that this will work.

```
41
42   sub getopen
43   {
44       my $key;
45       my $return = undef;
46
47       foreach $key (sort keys %_open)
48       {
49           push(@$return, $_open{$key});
```

```
50          }
51
52          return($return);
53      }
54
```

getopen() is the class method we mentioned earlier. %_open maintains which dates have open screens. We simply cycle through all of them and return the associated %_open record.

```
55  sub get
56  {
57      my ($self, $attrib) = @_;
58      print "'$attrib' is not an element!\n" if (!defined($self->{$attrib}));
59      return($self->{$attrib});
60  }
61
```

'get' is the generic accessor function through which we get the data from our Date Object. The function draw:

```
62
63  sub draw
64  {
65
66      my ($self) = @_;
67
68      my ($monthstring,$day, $date, $row, $xcoord, $ycoord, $dbmstring,$widget ) =
69              (
70                  $self->{'monthstring'}, $self->{'day'}, $self->{'date'},
71                  $self->{'row'}, $self->{'xcoord'}, $self->{'ycoord'},
72                  $self->{'dbmstring'}, $self->{'widget'}
73              );
74
75      my $xpos = ($day%7) *              $xcoord;
76      my $ypos = $row        *          $ycoord;
77
78      my $button = $self->{'button'} = $widget->Button
79                                          (
80                                              '-relief' => 'raised',
81                                              '-text' => $date,
82                                              '-highlightthickness' => 0,
83                                              '-command' =>[ $self, 'press']
84                                          );
85
86          $button->place     (
87                                  '-relx' => $xpos, '-rely' => $ypos,
88                                  '-relwidth' => $xcoord,
89                                  '-relheight' => $ycoord
90                              );
91
92          $self->_makeCurrent();
93  }
94
```

is where the bulk of the drawing is done. Lines 75 and 76 figure out what the relative position of the button will be; line 86 then actually places the button in the correct spot. Line 92 then calls _makeCurrent(), which is a method for doing the shading (if the button corresponds to a date with information and is above the current calendar day).

```
95  sub undraw
96  {
97       my ($self) = @_;
98       $self->{'button'}->destroy();
99  }
```

This is a simple function to get rid of buttons so the next month can come in.

```
100
101 sub press
102 {
103      my ($self) = @_;
104      my $button = $self->{'button'};
105
106      my $string = $self->{'dbmstring'};
107
108      my $error;
109
110      if ($self->{'ispressed'}) # Are we pressed?
111      {   # should probably be $self->{'ispressed'}
112          my $dialog = $button->Dialog
113                          (
114                                      '-title' => 'Error',
115                                      '-text'  =>
116          "Button '$string $self->{'date'}' is already pressed" ,
117                                      '-bitmap'=> 'error'
118                              ) ->Show();
119          return();
120      }
121      $self->{'ispressed'} = 1;
122      $_open{$string} = $self;
123
124      $self->_makeScreen($string);
125 }
126
```

This is main callback, which happens if a **Date** button is pressed. We issue an error if the button is already pressed, in the form of a `Dialog` widget.

```
127 sub lightup     # make button a different color
128 {
129      my ($self, $color) = @_;
130      my $button = $self->{'button'};
131
132      $button->configure('-background' => $color);
133 }
134
135 sub lightoff    # turn it back the way it was
136 {
137      my ($self) = @_;
138      my $button = $self->{'button'};
139      $button->configure('-background' => '#d9d9d9');
```

```
140 }
141
```

These are two major functions that do lighting of the methods. lightup is called if the day is after the present day, and has scheduling information. This then changes the color of the background of the date button.

```
142 sub _makeScreen
143 {
144     my ($self,$string) = @_;  # make the screen associated
145     my $button = $self->{'button'};   # with the button
146
147     my $screen = $self->{'screen'} = $button->TopLevel();
148
149     $screen->title("For the day '$string'");
150
151     my $field =  $self->{'field'} = $screen->Scrolled # make a scrolled window
152                           (       'Text',
153                                   '-scrollbars' => 'e',
154                                   '-wrap' => 'word',
155                                   '-relief' => 'sunken',
156                                   '-borderwidth' => 2,
157                                   '-setgrid' => '1'
158                           ) -> pack ('-expand' => 'yes', '-fill' => 'both');
159
160     $field->insert('0.0', $_dbm->{$string});
161     my ($save) = $screen->Button      # save, cancel delete
162                             (        # are from left to right
163                             'text' => 'Save',
164                             'command' => [$self, 'savetext'],
165                             ) -> pack ( 'side' => 'left' );
166
167     my ($cancel) = $screen->Button
168                             (
169                             'text' => 'Cancel',
170                             'command' => [ $self, 'cancel'],
171                             ) -> pack ( 'side' => 'left' );
172
173     my ($delete) = $screen->Button
174                             (
175                             'text' => 'Delete',
176                             'command' => [ $self, 'deletetext'],
177                             ) -> pack ( 'side' => 'left' );
178 }
179
```

This is the main code that makes a screen if the button is pressed. We tie the three buttons to callbacks which save, delete, or cancel the changes made in the window.

```
180 sub savetext    # save date text to file:
181 {       # uses NDBM
182     my ($self)  = @_;
183
184     my $field = $self->{'field'};
185     my $screen = $self->{'screen'};
```

```
186      my $string = $self->{'dbmstring'};
187
188      $_dbm->{$string} = $field->get('0.0', 'end' );   # get the text assoc.
189         # with the button
190      delete $_open{$string};
191
192      $self->{'ispressed'} = 0;
193      $screen->destroy();
194
195      $self->_makeCurrent();      # we need to do same
196  }        # cleanup..date
197          # (or not)? have text
198  sub cancel
199  {
200      my ($self) = @_;
201
202      $self->{'ispressed'} = 0;
203
204      my $string = $self->{'dbmstring'};
205      my $screen = $self->{'screen'};
206
207      delete $_open{$string};
208
209      $screen->destroy();         # get rid of screen.
210
211      $self->_makeCurrent();
212  }
213
214  sub deletetext
215  {
216      my ($self) = @_;
217      my $field = $self->{'field'};
218
219      $field->delete('0.0', 'end');
220  }
221
```

These are the main functions which manipulate the text inside the windows. This is because we are maintaining a list of screens that are open we need to modify the %_open hash (lines 190 and 207).

```
228  sub _makeCurrent       # function to determine
229  {        # whether or not a date is current
230      my ($self) = @_;
231      my $dbmstring = $self->{'dbmstring'};
232      return() if (!defined($_dbm->{$dbmstring}));
233
234      $self->unflash();
235      if (($_dbm->{$dbmstring} =~ m"\S" ) && $self->_sameday())
236      {
237          $self->lightup('firebrick1');
238          $self->flash();
239      }
240      elsif (($_dbm->{$dbmstring} =~ m"\S") && !$self->_pastdate())
241      {
```

```
242          $self->lightup('chartreuse4');
243     }
244     else
245     {
246          $self->lightoff();
247     }
248 }
```

This is the function to make a button light up if it is ahead of the present and has data in it. Notice also the hooks into flash (line 238) and unflash (line 234). We assume the button is flashing and turn the flashing property off, and then determine whether it should be flashing. This simplifies the logic. Following are the functions we call, flash() and unflash():

```
249 # code to flash the button
250 sub flash
251 {
252     my ($self) = @_;
253     my $button = $self->{'button'};
254     $self->{'flashid'} = $button->repeat(1000, [$button, 'flash']);
255 }
256 sub unflash     # code to set buttons
257 {          # to normal
258     my ($self) = @_;
259     my $flashid = $self->{'flashid'};
260     if ($flashid)
261     {
262          my ($button = $self->{'button'};
263          $button->afterCancel($flashid);
264     }
265 }
```

The key to these two functions is in line 254, which solves the problem of animation in a very clean way. Remember how Tk works with the event loop, which essentially puts the computer on standby, waiting for events to occur? Well, line 254 takes advantage of this, registering the button to flash every 1,000 milliseconds, with a function called repeat().

When it registers this code, it also saves an ID inside $self->{'flashid'}. When we want the button to stop flashing, line 263 cancels this effect, with the function called afterCancel(). More than one piece of code can be happening at a time, and afterCancel() uses the ID made by repeat() to determine which piece of code to cancel.

This trick can be used to do quite a few things, not just control animation. If we wanted to warn the user every five minutes that he or she had an appointment on the same day, we could say:

```
$self->{'flashid'} = $button->repeat(300000, [$button, 'warn']);
```

where warn does this updating. We could also use this code to solve a subtle bug this program has. Right now, as it is, there is no way of telling the program that "Hey—a day has passed. September 27 is no longer the current date; you have to move forward!" We could put a function in the constructor that looks like this:

```
$self->{'flashid2'} = $button->repeat(3600000, [$button, '_makeCurrent']);
```

Now, without any intervention at all, our program will update the buttons' flashing status. Every hour, Tk will check for us whether or not our buttons have the current date. If so, buttons that weren't flashing the day before will suddenly flash when the correct day rolls around.

The code continues.

```
266 sub _getSecs
267 {
268
269     my ($string) = @_;
270     return(str2time($string));
271 }
272
273 sub _pastdate
274 {
275     my ($self) = @_;
276     my $secs = $self->{'secs'};
277     my $button = $self->{'button'};
278     my $today = time;
279     if (($secs - $today) < -86400) { return(1); }
280     return(0);
281 }
282
283
284 sub _sameday
285 {
286     my ($self) = @_;
287     my $secs = $self->{'secs'};
288     my $button = $self->{'button'};
289     my $today = time;
290     if (abs($secs - $today) < 86400) { return(1) }
291     return(0);
292 }
293
294 1;
```

These are generic functions that deal with time issues such as whether or not a button is on the same day as the current system time, or past the current date.

Using the New Application

That is it! Overall, the server piece of the code takes 777 lines. However, from the client side of the code, all we have to do is add the following six lines of code to a file:

```
use Tk;
use strict;
my $date = localtime();
my $calendar = new Tk::Calendar($date);
$calendar->draw();
MainLoop();
```

which draw the calendar. We can now go ahead and try out our application. We save these six lines inside **calendar.p** and say something like:

```
C:\> perl calendar.p
```

which displays our application, looking something like Figure 20.20.

Figure 20.20
Calendar Startup

We've seen this before, however, so we start clicking on various buttons. First, we click the **next** button, and we get the next month in the calendar, as shown in Figure 20.21.

Figure 20.21
Next Calendar
Month

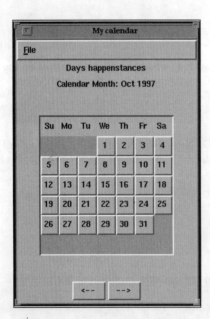

Then, we proceed to open some windows, and type some text into them, as in Figure 20.22.

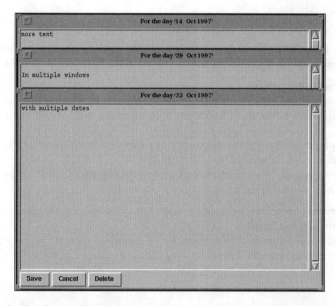

Saving the calendar dates makes the colors of the dates change, notifying us that we have a calendar appointment on that particular day (Figure 20.23).

This is just too cool! We have spent about one tenth of the effort we would have taken if we were to do the application in C, and about one hundredth of the effort of doing it in X-windows. In fact, the difficulty level is comparable to Visual Basic, and probably easier because of the tricky date issues. Moreover, the application is completely portable to Mac, OS/2, Unix, NT, and Windows 95. With the compiler, we can make a binary for each of these systems, which saves on startup times, and lessens the dependencies on the Tk GUI libraries.

Summary

This has been a long chapter but with good reason. This is probably the most important chapter in this OO section. You will want to learn the following concepts before you go to the next section of the book:

- **HASA**—A basic layering relationship.
- **Modifies**—The relationship between objects where one object modifies another without owning it.
- **Uses**—The relationship between objects in which one object uses the parts of another object without owning it.
- **Polymorphism**—The process of having one piece of syntax stand for many different things, or many different pieces of syntax stand for one thing.
- **Delegation**—The process of passing methods that a certain object doesn't know how to handle to objects that do know how to handle them.

In addition, there were three types of objects we discussed: singleton, container, and iterator, as well as a bunch of examples of their application. Quite a handful.

This is the last of the theoretical chapters. The next section concentrates on real Perl projects and the tools and programming methods for making your Perl programming the most effective possible.

21

Perl Development Environment

Perl does not leave you blind when it comes to tracking down bugs, distributing your programs, and figuring out performance bottlenecks in your code. Far from it. Perl goes quite overboard with its developer's support. There are debuggers, performance profilers, coverage testers, and other testing tools, all of which are essential to a rapid software development cycle.

There is also a compiler, which is just as important. By compiling your Perl code into a stand-alone executable you can:

- Lessen your dependency on external libraries
- Deliver an easily "packaged" product
- Lessen startup times of your code
- Improve the performance of your code ()

Note

Some folks also like the computer because it hides code from the users of that code—the "hide so you can sell" concept. I hardly ever do this sort of thing; it robs me a lot of free testing. Instead, I sell both the code and services—users pay for licenses and training.

Also note that the compiler, as of this writing, is rather experimental. It should be solid by the time you need this, and if you install from CPAN or my web site (see installing on the CD for more information), you should be OK.

Chapter Overview

This goal of this chapter is to go over some of the tools that can help you with your programming. Make no mistake about it, there are "cookie cutter" tools that provide functionality in your day-to-day programming chores. The way Perl implements these tools is a fascinating study in modular design itself. There will be four parts to this chapter.

First, we will provide an overview of how Perl is structured to handle programming tools. The programming tools in Perl are self-referential; in other words, they are themselves programmed in Perl! This means that if you don't like the default Perl debuggers, you can easily create your own.

Second, we will go over the default debugger that comes with the Perl executable itself. The debugger is full, option-rich, and, of course, has a Perl-ish syntax, which makes it familiar and easy to use.

Third, we will go over some of the alternative debuggers written for Perl, such as the speed profiler **DProf**, the small speed profiler **SmallProf**, and the coverage tester. All three of these modules are on the accompanying CD.

Finally, we will consider the compiler module. We will look at its usage, and see how its judicious use can save you many headaches in managing your code base.

Development Programs: The Perl-ish Model

Perl has an elegant way to handle programs such as debuggers, profilers, etc. These programs help the programming process itself. There are two basic types of extensions Perl defines:

1. Extensions for debugging: profilers (for performance testing), debuggers, and coverage checkers.
2. Extensions to manipulate the internals of Perl code: **Lint** and the compiler.

Instead of making one built-in program to do the work of a profiler and another to do the work of a debugger, Perl provides hooks that allow programmers to look inside the code as it is running or look at how it is compiled. Let's look at each extension in turn.

Debugging Extensions

Perl supports programmable debugging extensions, as well as a built-in debugger. For example, if you say:

```
C:> perl -d program.p
```

this tells Perl to turn on a special debugging flag internally. This flag tells Perl to tuck aside additional bits of information about what is happening inside the process, storing them for later use. It then fires up the default debugger, which is a Perl file that we shall describe later.

Programming Your Own Debugger

It sounds simple enough, but if you say:

```
C:\> perl -d:MyDebugger program.p
```

then instead of the default debugger, the debugger stored in **Devel::MyDebugger** runs. As we will see, creating your own debugger is not that difficult. How would you actually program **Devel::MyDebugger**? The on-line documentation (**perldebug**) has more detail, but when you say -d, Perl provides the hooks for a debugger programmer made through the package called **DB**.

Each time a new expression in a program with the -d flag is called, the function DB::DB is called behind the scenes. The following is a debugger that simply counts the number of statements you run in any given program:

```
Devel/MyDebugger.pm

1   package Devel::MyDebugger.pm
```

```
2   my $_noOfStatements = 0;
3   sub DB::DB { $_noOfStatements++; }
4   END { print "This program had $_noOfStatements statements.\n"; }
5   1;
```

Line 3 keeps a running tally. Each time a statement is called, the counter is incremented. At the end of the program, the **END** block is called, and if you run this script on the following example:

```
C:\> perl -d:MyDebugger -e 'for ($xx = 0; $xx < 5; $xx++) { 'print "HERE!\n"; }'
```

you get the following output:

```
This program had 8 statements
```

Figure 21.1 shows this relationship. Each time a statement is run and then the DB namespace is dumped into so you can take a look at its comments and manipulate them. One such manipulation is DB::DB being run after each statement. Another is the array @{$main::{'<_' . $filename}} being set to the lines in the file.

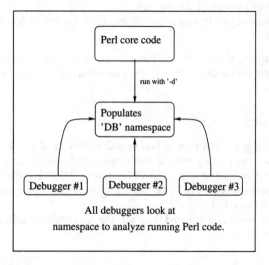

Figure 21.1
Relationship between Debuggers and Perl Core

Perl core code

run with '-d'

Populates 'DB' namespace

Debugger #1   Debugger #2   Debugger #3

All debuggers look at
namespace to analyze running Perl code.

By using caller() inside DB, you can get the package, filename, and line number from code you call. From there, you can get the text of the line being executed. For example, if you say:

```
Devel/MyDebugger2.pm
```

```
1  sub DB::DB
2  {
3      my ($pkg,$filename,$line) = (caller(0))[0..2];
4      print "$pkg: $filename: $main::{'_<' . $filename}[$line]\n";
5  }
```

then when you say:

```
perl -d:MyDebugger2.pm -e 'for ($xx = 0; $xx < 5; $xx++) { print HERE\n"; }'
```

you will get the following echoed back:

```
main:     -e:      for ($xx = 0; $xx < 5; $xx++) { print "HERE\n"; }
HERE
main:     -e:      for ($xx = 0; $xx < 5; $xx++) { print "HERE\n"; }
HERE
```

```
main:    -e:      for ($xx = 0; $xx < 5; $xx++) { print "HERE\n"; }
HERE
main:    -e:      for ($xx = 0; $xx < 5; $xx++) { print "HERE\n"; }
HERE
main:    -e:      for ($xx = 0; $xx < 5; $xx++) { print "HERE\n"; }
HERE
main:    -e:      for ($xx = 0; $xx < 5; $xx++) { print "HERE\n"; }
```

Perl rotates here between executing the debugger function DB::DB, and executing the actual code, which prints HERE to the screen. We have basically implemented the trace function, which we describe later.

For more information on this topic the best place to go is inside the standard distribution, in: lib/perl5db.pl. This is the standard debugger, the one that is called automatically when you say perl -d on the command line. It is heavily documented, so you can see what is going on fairly easily.

You can also look at:

- **Devel::SmallProf**—The small profile item we will address later.
- **Devel::Coverage**—A good example of a coverage testing tool.
- **Devel::DProf**—The standard profiler everybody uses although its help is limited to novices because it is written in C and linked into Perl.

We will cover each of these items later (including the standard debugger, of course). If you want to see the magic behind the scenes, start digging into the source code that comes with the **perldebug** page which comes with the central distribution.

Compilers and Bug Checkers

Some people are surprised that the Perl debugger is not part of Perl or a C add-on, and that it is written in Perl itself. But because Perl's forte is manipulating and parsing text, all Perl writers need to do is hang on the hooks we talked about before, and *voilá*: 50,000-line debugger (if written in C) becomes a 2,000-line Perl debugger. More powerful, too, because we can use all the powers of Perl to "talk" to the applications we debug. You might not be surprised that the Perl compiler itself is written in Perl.

Again, the logic of the compiler is much more complicated than was the case with the debugger, but what is going on is something that looks like Figure 21.2.

Figure 21.2
Relationship between Compiler and Perl Core

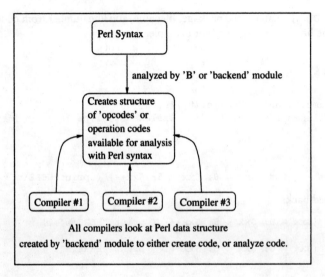

Perl Syntax

analyzed by 'B' or 'backend' module

Creates structure of 'opcodes' or operation codes available for analysis with Perl syntax

Compiler #1   Compiler #2   Compiler #3

All compilers look at Perl data structure created by 'backend' module to either create code, or analyze code.

Here, instead of Perl populating a run-time data structure, the compiler reuses parts of the interpreter. This lets Perl do the difficult part of actually figuring out the meaning of a particular symbol. For example:

```
${"main::$variable"};
```

is a scalar, but I'd like to see the regular expression that can parse this correctly, along with the other thousand or so ways to express scalars! The compiler piggybacks on the shoulders of the interpreter to turn this into the correct address for the compiler to generate C code or byte code.

Note that this is a high-level description of what is occurring to make the **Compile** and **Lint** modules work. It is not nearly as easy to program your own warnings as it is to program your own debuggers. To do so, you must know the outline of how a Perl program actually splits up into "op" codes, or operation codes. This is not an easy task.

For a good start on this subject, I suggest *Advanced Perl Programming* by Sriram Srinivasan, or the on-line documentation called **perlguts**. But this is a formidable task, and it probably will take time to get to the point where you can do this successfully.

Development Programs: The Perl-ish Model

Perl differentiates itself from almost every other language by making it easy to program debugging tools and fiddle around with the language itself with Perl's dynamic, adaptable syntax. We distinguished two types of auxiliary tools: *debuggers*, which use a special package called DB (that Perl itself provides via the -d flag), and *compilers*, which use the Perl interpreter itself to figure out how to parse, compile, and otherwise gauge your code.

The Perl Development Tools

Now it is time to look at examples of these principles in action. Some of you might be thinking that I am going backward with this. After all, we showed you how to program a debugger, albeit a simple one, and only now am I actually getting into the default Perl debugger. Surely the second one is the easier topic!

I think this sequence is correct. You will be a much more powerful Perl programmer when you realize exactly how malleable, bendable, and otherwise shapeable Perl syntax can be. Perl's debugger is only one of a multitude that could possibly exist, because, as you have seen, seldom is anything hard-coded into the Perl core. Perl is in many ways the duct tape of languages. Larry Wall calls it a "glue language" and, well, Perl itself is used to glue different parts of Perl together!

The Default Perl Debugger

The program most people think of when they consider tools to help them out in a Perl development environment is the Perl debugger. As we noticed earlier, when you say something like:

```
prompt% perl -d program.p
```

Perl magically comes back with a prompt, looking something like:

```
Stack dump during die enabled outside of evals.

Loading DB routines from perl5db.pl patch level 0.94
Emacs support available.

Enter h or `h h' for help.

A::(a.p:16):    1;
DB<1>
```

The prompt (DB<1>) indicates that you are interacting with the Perl debugger. What is going on behind the scenes is that you have silently loaded the following file:

lib/per15db.pl

which loads a debugger programmed in Perl into memory. You interact with the debugger with a series of one-word commands, which do such tasks as setting breakpoints, tracing, etc.

However, because the debugger is itself in Perl, you have the power to actually interact with the program you are tracing. Suppose you were writing a program that had an extremely large `for` loop in it, with the relevant code looking something like:

```
script.p
#
#
55 for ($xx = 0; $xx < 10000; $xx++)
56 {
57     print "HERE!\n";
58     # do something interminably long based on $xx
59 }
```

To test this, you obviously have to cut short the `for` loop. You could do this either by changing the code itself (not a very good idea), or by causing the loop to end prematurely. If we opt for the second, the debugger is the perfect way to handle it. All we need to do is load the debugger into memory on the script:

```
prompt% perl -d script.p
Stack dump during die enabled outside of evals.

Loading DB routines from per15db.pl patch level 0.94
Emacs support available.

Enter h or `h h' for help.

A::(a.p:16):    1;
DB<1>
```

Now set a simple breakpoint in the script:

```
DB<2> b 57
```

This will stop the script as soon as it hits the line 57. Then we proceed to run it:

```
DB<3> r
main::(script.p:57): print "HERE!!!\n";
```

We have now broken the script at line 57. The printing of the line indicates that the line is about to be executed. It has *not* been executed already.

Because we are now inside the loop itself, we can modify it to our heart's content. We can execute any legal Perl command here. If we say:

```
DB<4> $xx = 9998;
DB<5> D
Deleting All Breakpoints.
```

we set the iterator to 9998 so there are only two more rolls of the loop to be executed. The D then deletes all the breakpoints we have assigned, so that we will not be stopped the next time we hit 57. Hence, when we say:

```
DB<6> c
```

to continue, the script only iterates twice through the loop rather than the full complement of 10,000 iterations.

This seems pretty simple. The fact that the Perl debugger is so simple and so powerful has made it very popular. To get the full picture of the debugger, the best source is the on-line documentation (**perldebug**) as well as looking at the source code itself. Next, we give a quick overview of the most popular commands.

Common Debugger Functionality

There are 32 separate flags in the Perl debugger. Following are the 12 most common flags used, along with some examples of their usage.

On-line Help with h

There are two forms of on-line help you should be aware of. Type:

```
prompt% perl -d script.p
Stack dump during die enabled outside of evals.

Loading DB routines from perl5db.pl patch level 0.94
Emacs support available.

Enter h or `h h' for help.

DB<1> h
```

to get a list of all the commands in gory detail. Type:

```
DB<1> h h
```

to get a nice, handy cheat-sheet of all the operations listed next, plus many others. This cheat sheet is so handy, I reproduce it in Figure 21.3.

Figure 21.3
Cheat Sheet
for Debugger

List/search source lines:		Control script execution:	
l [ln|sub]	List source code	**T**	Stack trace
- or .	List previous/current line	**s [expr]**	Single step [in expr]
w [line]	List around line	**n [expr]**	Next, steps over subs
f filename	View source in file	**<CR>**	Repeat last n or s
/pattern/	Search forward	**r**	Return from subroutine
?pattern?	Search backward	**c [line]**	Continue until line
Debugger controls:		**L**	List break pts & actions
O [...]	Set debugger options	**t [expr]**	Toggle trace [trace expr]
< command	Command for before prompt	**b [ln] [c]**	Set breakpoint
> command	Command for after prompt	**b sub [c]**	Set breakpoint for sub
! [N|pat]	Redo a previous command	**d [line]**	Delete a breakpoint
H [-num]	Display last num commands	**D**	Delete all breakpoints
= [a val]	Define/list an alias	**a [ln] cmd**	Do cmd before line
h [db_cmd]	Get help on command	**A**	Delete all actions
|[|]dbcmd	Send output to pager	**![!] syscmd**	Run cmd in a subprocess
q or ^D	Quit	**R**	Attempt a restart
Data Examination:			
expr	Execute Perl code, also see: s,n,t expr.		
S [[!]pat]	List subroutine names [not] matching pattern.		
V [Pk [Vars]]	List Variables in Package. Vars can be ~pattern or !pattern.		
X [Vars]	Same as "V current_package [Vars]".		
x expr	Evals expression in array context, dumps the result.		
p expr	Print expression (uses script's current package).		

If you want more information on each of these commands, you can say:

```
DB<1> h =
= [alias value] Define a command alias, or list current aliases.
```

to get a more detailed version of the command's text.

Interacting with the Debugged Program: Running Perl Expressions, and *x* for Expand Data Structure

As we said earlier, the Perl debugger is a Perl debugger in more than one sense of the word. It debugs your programs, but it is also written in Perl so you can modify your program's attributes when you debug it. The following debugging session uses the **LWP::UserAgent** module introduced in Chapter 12. It is used to give a command line browser. In other words, you can interact with the Net without the GUI attached, and even without writing Perl programs. First, load a dummy program:

```
c:\> perl -d a.p
Loading DB routines from perl5db.pl version 1
Emacs support available.

Enter h or `h h' for help.
```

and then load functionality into it:

```
DB<1> use LWP::UserAgent;
```

Assuming that you have the user-agent module of Perl installed, this gives you all the power necessary to get files off target servers and put them into memory:

```
DB<2> $ua = new LWP::UserAgent();
DB<3> $request = new HTTP::Request('GET', "ftp://ftp.cs.colorado.edu/ls-lR.gz");
DB<4> $result = $ua->request($request, "target_file.gz");
DB<5> system("gunzip target_file.gz");
DB<6> open(FD, "target_file");
DB<7> @lines = <FD>;
DB<8> @lines = grep(m"perl"i, @lines);
DB<9> print @lines;
# output deleted...
```

Note that all of these commands are being done in the debugger. Perl is essentially acting as a shell here, performing each of your commands one by one, and immediately executing them. This (interactive) process gets the file ls-lR.gz from *ftp.cs.colorado.edu*, unzips the file, and reads the file's lines into memory. Perl then looks for the string Perl in these lines and then prints them out. The debugger acts as a mixture of shell and Perl combined.

Note, however, that we are not using my because Perl uses eval internally. If we used my variables, they would go out of scope immediately.

Printing Data Structures with *x*

Remember **Data::Dumper**, that handy module for printing out data structures? Well, the debugger has its own form of **Data::Dumper**, which you can access via x. In the following debugger session, you could print the contents of @array1 by saying:

```
prompt%perl -d script.p;
```

```
Loading DB routines from perl5db.pl patch level 0.94.
Emacs support available.

Enter h of 'h h' for help;
  DB<1> @array1 = ( 0, \
  cont:                [1,2,3,4], \
  cont:                 [5, [6,7,8,9], \
  cont:                  5,6, 7], \
  cont:            1
  cont:            );
  DB<2> x @array1
0  0
1  ARRAY(0x23234ab)
   0  1
   1  2
   2  3
   3  4
2  ARRAY(0x23424ac)
   0  5
   1  ARRAY(0x23242ab)
      0  6
      1  7
      2  8
      3  9
   2  5
   3  6
   4  7
3  1
```

As you can see, this output is designed more with visual debugging in mind than is **Data::Dumper**. At a glance, you can see which array elements go with which subscripts, although this clarity comes at a cost. The output is not nearly as good for making Perl tests, because **Data::Dumper** outputs legal Perl syntax. But if you want to use this output in your own programs, look in the standard distribution for *dumper.pl*.

Also notice that we used a \ on the end of the line to make a multiline Perl script in the debugger. This is just one trick that makes complicated debugging easier here.

Flow Control Under the Debugger: r for Run, t for Trace, c for Continue; n, s, and <CR> for Step

When you start up the Perl 5 debugger, Perl waits for you to start running the program you loaded. Now, as always, there are quite a few ways to do this, which are detailed next.

Running Programs with r

The first way to run programs is with r. When you get a debugger prompt, simply type r:

```
DB<2> r
```

Your program will run until it finishes executing your code (and returns to the debugger prompt), or until the program catches a fatal error. In the case of a fatal error, the debugger dumps the sequence of calling routines (i.e., the *stack trace*) of where the program died.

Tracing with t

The next most common flag you will use in conjunction with the debugger is t. The t command is used for showing verbose detail about the expressions being executed by Perl at any given time. When you say something like:

```
DB<1> t
Trace=on
```

then you are putting Perl in *trace mode*, which tells the Perl debugger to print out all the statements that pass through. In fact, the combination of t and r, as in:

```
DB<1>   t
Trace=on
DB<2>   r
```

will often be all you need to trace through code errors. Suppose your program looks something like Listing 21.1.

Listing 21.1
Insertion-Sort

```
1   #!/usr/local/bin/perl5
2
3   my @array = (1, 66,2);
4   insertion(\@array);
5
6   sub insertion                                    # insertion
7   {
8       my ($array) = @_;
9       for ($xx = 0; $xx < @$array; $xx++)
10      {
11          for ($yy = $xx+1; $yy < @$array; $yy++)
12          {
13              swap($array-> [$xx], $array-> [$yy])
14                      if ($array-> [$xx] >  $array-> [$yy]);
15          }
16      }
17 }
18
19 sub swap                                          # could be @_[0,1] = @_[1,0]
20 {
21      my ($tmp) = $_[0];
22      $_[0] = $_[1];
23      $_[1] = $tmp;
24 }
```

This is a simple insertion-sort. Let's look at the algorithm in action in Listing 21.2.

Listing 21.2
Recursive Headers

```
1       DB<2>   r
2   context return from : undef
3   main::(as.p:5): for ($xx = 0; $xx < @array; $xx++)
4   main::(as.p:6): {
```

```
 5  main::(as.p:11):          }
 6  main::(as.p:7):           for ($yy = $xx+1; $yy < @array; $yy++)
 7  main::(as.p:8):           {
 8  main::(as.p:10):          }
 9  main::(as.p:9):                       swap($array[$xx], $array[$yy])
10                                                if ($array[$xx] > $array[$yy]);
11  main::(as.p:9):                       swap($array[$xx], $array[$yy])
12                                                if ($array[$xx] > $array[$yy]);
13  main::(as.p:7):           for ($yy = $xx+1; $yy < @array; $yy++)
14  main::(as.p:8):           {
15  main::(as.p:10):          }
16  main::(as.p:9):                       swap($array[$xx], $array[$yy])
17                                                if ($array[$xx] > $array[$yy]);
18  main::swap(as.p:17):      my ($tmp) = $_[0];
19  main::swap(as.p:18):      $_[0] = $_[1];
20  main::swap(as.p:19):      $_[1] = $tmp;
21  main::(as.p:7):           for ($yy = $xx+1; $yy < @array; $yy++)
22  main::(as.p:8):           {
23  main::(as.p:10):                        }
24  main::(as.p:13):          print "@array\n";
```

Although this output takes time to get used to—the parenthesis positions in the for loops are counterintuitive—it is fairly easy to see what is going on. The test array is (1,66,2). We try to swap in lines 9–12, but without success, because $array[0] is already the lowest and does not need to be swapped.

In line 16, we swap $array[1] and $array[2], as indicated by the fact that we actually go into the subroutine swap (main::swap in lines 18–20).

Continuing with c

The flags r and t are what you might call "bludgeons" for finding bugs. Half of my debugging sessions consist of:

```
DB<1>  t
Trace=on
DB<2>  r
```

and then being lazy, watching all the debugging text fly by as we have just seen. Sometimes I save the output to files for later perusal (by using script on Unix—I'm not sure of the equivalent syntax on NT).

Sometimes you need a more delicate approach. Suppose, for example, there was a lot of overhead in starting your code and you were testing only a small part of it, such as a new merge-sort algorithm to replace the insertion-sort one.

This is a job for c. Instead of typing r, which runs through the whole program (or dies or hits a breakpoint), c can stop at any particular place. Say your code looked like Listing 21.3.

Listing 21.3
Merge-Sort (algorithm code listed only)

```
# other stuff at beginning.
150 my @array;
151 @array = (11112,12,442,1231);
152
153 mergesort (\@array);
```

```
154    print "@array\n";
155
156    sub mergesort
157    {
158        my ($array) = @_;
159        mergesort($array, 0, scalar(@$array) - 1)
160    }
161
162    sub _mergesort #
163    {
164        my ($array, $low, $high) = @_;
165
166        my $middle;
167
168        if ($low < $high )
169        {
170            $middle = int(($low + $high)/2);
171            _mergesort($array, $low, $middle);    # use recursion
172            _mergesort($array, $middle+1, $high);        # spilt problem into sub probs
173            _merge($array, $low, $middle, $high);
174        }
175    }
176
177    sub _merge
178    {
179        my ($array, $low, $middle, $high) = @_;
180
181        my $sorted_array = [];
182
183        my ($lowcounter, $highcounter) =  ($low, $middle+1);
184
185
186        while (($lowcounter != $middle + 1) || ($highcounter != $high + 1))
187        {
188            if ($lowcounter == $middle +1)
189            {
190                push(@$sorted_array, $array-> [$highcounter]);
191                $highcounter++;
192                next;
193            }
194            elsif ($highcounter == $high + 1)
195            {
196                push(@$sorted_array, $array-> [$lowcounter]);
197                $lowcounter++;
198                next;
199            }
200            elsif ($array-> [$lowcounter] < $array-> [$highcounter])
201            {
202                push(@$sorted_array, $array-> [$lowcounter]);
203                $lowcounter++;
204            }
205            else
206            {
```

```
207                push (@$sorted_array, $array-> [$highcounter]);
208                $highcounter++;
209            }
210        }
211    splice(@$array, $low, scalar(@$sorted_array), @$sorted_array);
212 }
```

We probably do not want to have to wade through the first 150 (or so) lines of Perl we have written. We certainly do not want to do this if we have thousands of lines of Perl that we included from other modules and objects, such as **Data::Dumper**. (Yes, the Perl debugger will go through its own code as well.) Instead, let's tell the interpreter to run up to a certain point and then stop.

```
DB<1>  c _merge
```

This does us the favor of running all the code we are not interested in silently. We stop right at line 179 where we can now either trace the rest of the code or step through it.

Stepping Through Code with s and <CR>

Suppose we were having difficulty with the _merge portion of the merge-sort algorithm. The process of merge-sort is a divide and conquer strategy: It splits up an array to be sorted into subarrays, which are then split up until they are reunited in a process that looks something like Figure 21.4.

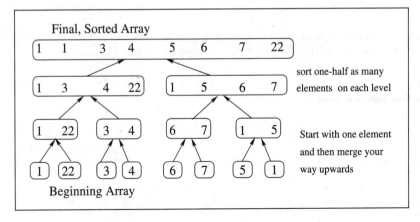

Figure 21.4
Merge-Sort
Algorithm

The _merge algorithm is a key component of merge-sort. The two separately sorted arrays:

```
Array #1:  1 2 5 6     Array #2: 1 3 4 6
```

must be sorted into:

```
Array #1:  1 1 2 3 4 5 6 6
```

This array can now be passed back to its parents to be merged into a larger array. However, there is a catch: for merge-sort to work correctly, we cannot be sloppy in our sorting. We must go through Array #1 and Array #2 only once.

So we come up with a plan. We will directly compare the leftmost elements inside Array #1 and Array #2, take the smallest of these elements, and stuff it into a temporary array. We will repeat this process until there are no elements left in either of the children arrays (#1 and #2).

The best way to see how this works is by looking at it in action. Fire up the debugger and type:

```
    DB<1>  c _merge
main::_merge(merge.p:180):              my ($array, $low, $middle, $high) = @_;
```

which brings us up to the point where the merge happens. We proceed to step through the code, first with *s*:

```
    DB<2> s
main::_merge(merge.p:182):              my $sorted_array = [];
```

and then <CR> for return.

```
    DB<3>
main::_merge(merge.p:38):               my ($lowcounter, $highcounter) =
                                                    ($low, $middle+1);
```

If we are eager to look at any of these values, say:

```
    DB<3>  x @_
0   ARRAY(0x173e78)
    0   11112
    1   12
    2   442
    3   1231
1   0
2   0
3   1
```

which gives us what has been passed to the subroutine. $low is zero, $middle is zero, and $high is one, so it looks like we are at the tail end of Figure 21.4. We continue stepping in Listing 21.4.

Listing 21.4
The _merge Function in Action

```
 1   DB<4>
 2   main::_merge(merge.p:186):           while (($lowcounter != $middle + 1) ||
 3                                                 ($highcounter != $high + 1))
 4   main::_merge(merge.p:187):           {
 5   DB<4>
 6   main::_merge(merge.p:188):               if ($lowcounter == $middle +1)
 7   main::_merge(merge.p:189):               {
 8   DB<4>
 9   main::_merge(merge.p:194):                   elsif ($highcounter == $high+1 )
10   main::_merge(merge.p:195):                   {
11   DB<4>
12   main::_merge(merge.p:200):               elsif ($array-> [$lowcounter]
13                                                   < $array-> [$highcounter])
14   main::_merge(merge.p:201):               {
15   DB<4>
16   main::_merge(merge.p:207):                 push (@$sorted_array,
17                                                     $array-> [$highcounter]);
18   DB<4>
19   main::_merge(merge.p:208):                 $highcounter++;
20   DB<4>
21   main::_merge(merge.p:188):               if ($lowcounter == $middle +1)
22   main::_merge(merge.p:189):               {
23   DB<4>
```

```
24 main::_merge(merge.p:194):            elsif ($highcounter == $high + 1)
25 main::_merge(merge.p:195):              {
26   DB<4>
27 main::_merge(merge.p:196):              push(@$sorted_array,
28                                                  $array-> [$lowcounter]);
29   DB<4>
30 main::_merge(merge.p:197):                  $lowcounter++;
31   DB<4>
32 main::_merge(merge.p:198):                  next;
33   DB<4>
34 main::_merge(merge.p:211):     splice(@$array, $low,
35                                    scalar(@$sorted_array), @$sorted_array);
```

At each step in this process, we can stop, peek, investigate, and generally see what is going on in any Perl expression that we like. Line 34 shows the major step here. We have built up @$sorted_array to hold the part of the array that has been sorted by _merge(). We then replace the nonsorted part of our array with a sorted one. Because our sample array looks like:

```
@array = (11112,12,442,1231);
```

and the underlined members of the array are what is being tested here, this array should end up as:

```
@array = (12, 11112, 442, 1231);
```

In other words, an operation like what is shown in Figure 21.5 should have occurred.

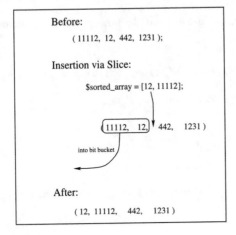

Figure 21.5
Operation to do
Merge-Sort

Before:
(11112, 12, 442, 1231);

Insertion via Slice:

$sorted_array = [12, 11112];

(11112, 12, 442,   1231)

into bit bucket

After:
(12, 11112, 442,   1231)

We can indeed test this by checking what x has to say:

```
DB<5>  x $sorted_array
0   ARRAY(0x2e8630)
    0   12
    1   11112

DB<6>  x $array                # Before
0   ARRAY(0x1985ec)
    0   11112
    1   12
    2   442
    3   1231
```

```
DB<7>  x $array                    # After
0   ARRAY(0x1985ec)
    0    12
    1    11112
    2    442
    3    1231
```

As you can see, the sorted array has inserted itself into the total, sorted array we are collecting.

n for Stepping Through Code (Over Subroutines)

For a high-level version of what is occurring within the processing, we can use n instead of s. Suppose we wanted to get a higher-level view of what is happening in merge-sort. We want to go through only one level of recursion, instead of hitting rock bottom (as we did with _merge() only having one element).

We can step over the subroutines and say something like:

```
prompt% perl -d merge.p
Stack dump during die enabled outside of evals.

Loading DB routines from perl5db.pl patch level 0.94
Emacs support available.

Enter h or `h h' for help.

main::(merge.p:150):      my @array;
  DB<1>  c _mergesort
```

We now step as we did before, but this time, we use n, and do not show the recursion when we hit _mergesort():

```
  DB<2>  c _mergesort
main::_mergesort(merge.p:164):      my ($array, $low, $high) = @_;
  DB<3>  n
main::_mergesort(merge.p:166):      my $middle;
  DB<3>
main::_mergesort(merge.p:168):      if ($low < $high )
main::_mergesort(merge.p:169):      {
  DB<3>
main::_mergesort(merge.p:170):          $middle = int(($low + $high)/2);
  DB<3>
main::_mergesort(merge.p:171):          _mergesort($array, $low, $middle);
  DB<4>  x @{$array}[$low..$middle]
0   11112
1   12
2   442
3   1231
  DB<5>  x @{$array}[$middle+1..$high]
0   3232
1   23421
2   5453
3   222
```

Just doing a sanity check here: The arrays should be unsorted before we call _mergesort() recursively. But after we step again:

```
  DB<6>
main::_mergesort(merge.p:172):          _mergesort($array, $middle+1, $high);
```

```
DB<7>  !4    # does 4th command - DB<4>
x @{$array}[$low..$middle]
0  12
1  442
2  1231
3  11112
```

we miss the internals of the merge-sort completely. Notice that the subarray is completely sorted. Continuing with the following:

```
DB<7>
main::_mergesort(merge.p:173):           _merge($array, $low, $middle, $high);
DB<8> !5    # does 5th command - DB<5>
x @{$array}[$middle+1..$high]
0  222
1  3232
2  5453
3  23421
DB<9>
main::(merge.p:154):    print "@array\n";
DB<1 0>
12 222 442 1231 3232 5453 11112 23421
```

we have conclusive proof that _mergesort() is working, at least at a higher level. After all, both subarrays are sorted, and in line 154, we show that they are combined to become a sorted array. Of course, there is more than one way to do this tracing. Two other ways are through breakpoints and action points, which we discuss next.

Breakpoints and Action Points with b, d, D, L, a, and A

The c function (continue) gives you a certain amount of control over where your programs are executed. The next step in control is breakpoints. Breakpoints are where you can set a place where code execution stops, so you can take a look at what is going on. The four main ways of setting breakpoints are described next.

Setting the Breakpoints with b

The key b sets a breakpoint. When you then hit *r* (for run), the code continues until the next breakpoint you have set. You are then at a command prompt next to the statement on which you set the breakpoint. There are several ways you can set breakpoints in your code. For a complete bestiary, go to the on-line documentation in **perldebug**. Following are the most important features.

Setting breakpoints on line numbers is the least exciting way to set breakpoints. All you have to do is say:

```
DB<3>  b 30
```

and your program will dutifully break every single time line 30 comes around. Generally, this is slow and inefficient because people think of code more in terms of subroutines than line numbers. But when you are setting breakpoints on subroutines, you say:

```
DB<3>  b sync
```

and Perl looks for the function sync, and sets the breakpoint after the function was called. For example, in the following listing, the breakpoint will be set right here:

```
sync('variable1','variable2');
sub sync
{
```

```
#### breaks right here.
my ($name, $args) = @_;
}
```

You are, therefore, inside the subroutine; if you want to examine the arguments passed to that subroutine, you can say:

```
DB<4>   x @_;
```

x is the printout function (we are getting a bit out of order here), but this is a perfect example of nonintrusive debugging techniques. An internal variable (@_) holds all the information about what has been passed to the subroutine. Since the debugger is written in Perl, we can access @_ and print it out. The x @_ statement results in:

```
DB<4>   x @_;
0 'variable1'
1 'variable2'
```

where variable1 is the zero-th element of the array and variable2 is the first.

When setting breakpoints with conditionals, you should remember that there is one more way to set breakpoints for a given program. That is, not to run the breakpoints automatically, but instead run them with a condition attached. In other words, you can say something like:

```
DB<5>   b 20 ($variable > 5);
```

which will break if and only if $variable is greater than 5. Notice the lack of an if here. The reason for this is, again, Perl's crowded syntax. If we put an if here, the line would have been treated as a Perl expression, and would have been wrongly executed. This is one of the drawbacks of having a program that tries to tie in its own language and still uses Perl's functionality. Perl has such a large syntactical footprint (i.e., almost all syntax, good or bad, is legal in Perl) that there is almost nothing left for the designer.

Setting conditional breakpoints is my favorite way to handle breakpoints. In fact, you can do things with conditional breakpoints that you could not possibly do any other way as far as debugging goes.

Consider our **MergeSort** code. We wanted to trace the functionality of _merge(), and we partially did so. However, since the recursion "broke up" @$array into one-element chunks for handling by _merge(), we didn't get to test all the conditions that could possibly arrive. We tested the part of the _merge() algorithm that merged single elements together into pairs, as shown in Figure 21.6.

Figure 21.6
Merge-Sort
Algorithm
(Tested Cases)

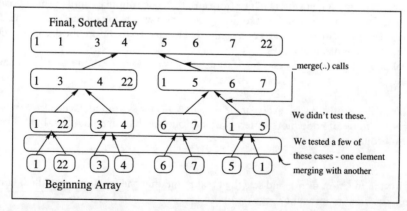

We now need to test the cases of _merge() in which there are more than two elements in each subarray being merged. With conditional breakpoints this is easy:

```
   DB<2>  c _merge              # gets us up to _merge function.
main::_merge(merge.p:179):          my ($array, $low, $middle, $high) = @_;

   DB<3>  b _merge $_[3] - $_[1] >  3;
   DB<4>  c
main::_merge(merge.p:179):          my ($array, $low, $middle, $high) = @_;
   DB<5>  s
```

The command DB<3> b _merge ($_[3] - $_[1] >   3) puts a breakpoint at the place where the $high element is three elements greater than the $low element. In other words, the command puts a breakpoint where more than two elements in each subarray are being merged.

One might ask, why is the direct access of the @_ variable necessary? Well, when you say b _merge, this tells the debugger to stop before any values are actually read in. Then, if we tried to print out $low or $high, we would get undef.

After DB<5>, we are ready to step through our algorithm. (See the section on s for more details.)

Breaking a Conditional with d

The keystroke d does almost the exact opposite of b: It gets rid of one breakpoint instead of making one breakpoint. It is, however, of limited use. You can only say something like:

```
   DB<6>  d 20
```

where the argument to d is a line number. The format d <subroutine_name> doesn't work; neither does setting a conditional deletion d 20 ($varb >   5);.

Listing All Conditionals with L

The L command simply lists the conditionals you have already set inside your program. If, for example, you have set three conditionals at three different spots in your program as follows:

```
   DB<7>  b qsort
   DB<8>  b qsort
   DB<9>  b partition $pivot >  5
```

the following command will then print all the conditional points:

```
   DB<1 0>  L
   12:              my ($array) = @_;
       break if (1)
   18:              my ($array, $pivot, $right) = @_;
       break if (1)
   31:              my ($array, $pivot, $right) = @_;
       break if ($pivot >  5)
```

If you so desire, you can go through and selectively delete them with d.

Deleting All Breakpoints with D

The D command goes through and deletes all breakpoints set in your program. This is quite handy when you have set 15 different breakpoints in ten different module files, and just want to start over from scratch.

Action Points with **a**

Action points allow you to insert temporary code into your script so that it is executed each time the statement is hit. For example, if you wanted to count how many times a certain loop was performed in the following code:

```
1 my $xx;
2 for ($xx = 0; $xx < int(rand(600)); $xx++)
3 {
4     if (_isPrime())
5     {
6         calc_code();
7     }
8 }
9 1;
```

we could insert a temporary variable that does this counting, but that requires a change to the code, and sometimes you don't or can't change the code (as in debugging production systems). Hence, instead you can use the debugger:

```
C:\> perl -d randscript.p
Loading DB routines from perl5db.pl version 1
Emacs support available

Enter h or 'h h' for help.

Main::(randscript.p):1 for ($xx = 0; $xx < int(rand(600)); $xx++)
  DB<1> a 6 $count++;

  DB<2> a 9 print "$count\n";

  DB<3>  r

142
```

This gives a count of how many times the subroutine is run. Note that again we make $count a global since the debugger is working via an eval statement.

Deleting Action Points with **A**

A does the opposite task of a; it deletes all the action points. Unfortunately, there is no easy way to delete just one, but a request report has been filed to do so.

Debugger Shell Commands

Perl's default debugger is quite flexible; in fact, one could say that it is almost like a shell. It is possible to alias commands, interact with a command history, and cycle back and forth through your commands like doskey or most Unix shells. The debugger is also hooked into the code that you are executing, so you can search through the code for patterns, and list out pertinent sections.

Cycling Through Commands with the Up Arrow and Down Arrow

Each time you type a command in the debugger interface, Perl internally stores that command in a buffer that you can traverse by hitting the up arrow and down arrow. You need **Term::ReadKey** to get this magic to work. You can get this code on either **CPAN** or on the accompanying CD. Suppose you typed the following commands:

```
DB<1>   t
Trace=on
DB<2> b mysub
DB<3>   s
DB<4>   x @my_value
```

The idea behind this is that you want to manually track what @my_value is, and stop when that value changes. So now, instead of having to type x @my_value every time, you can type:

```
DB<4>   <CR>
```

to step, and then:

```
DB<4> <up arrow>   <CR>
```

to get back the text x @my_value. Do this several times and you get something like:

```
DB<4> x @my_value
# print out
DB<5>
# print next line
DB<5>   x @my_value
# print out value
DB<6>
```

In other words, you get an extremely rapid turnaround, seeing each line of code, and then immediately seeing how that line of code affected your variable, all by typing three characters in sync (<CR>, <up arrow>, <CR>).

History of Commands with H

There is another way of accessing this buffer in addition to the step-by-step method we listed earlier. If, instead, you want to get a list of all the commands you typed, you can say:

```
DB<6>   H
```

which will output everything you have typed so far this session, prefixed by a number telling you what you had done. You can get a partial history by saying:

```
DB<6>   H -5
```

which shows the last five commands. In the example of fetching a file via **LWP::UserAgent,** the output to this command would look something like:

```
10: H -5
9: print @lines;
8: @lines = grep(m"perl"i, @lines);
7: @lines = <FD> ;
6: open(FD, "target_file");
```

You can now redo these commands with our next command: !.

Redoing Commands with !

Suppose you want to redo the seventh command in the previous stack of commands. By saying:

```
DB<11>   !7
```

Perl accesses the internal stack, and redoes the seventh command in its memory. If you say:

```
DB<11>   !!
```

then Perl will redo the tenth command, the last one typed (H–5—therefore, you will get a history). And if you say:

```
DB<11>   !@
```

then Perl will reach back and get the last pattern that starts with @. In this case, it will read all the lines back into memory with @lines = <FD>;.

Aliases with =

When you find something that you want to do over and over again, you can save it. You simply say:

```
DB<1> = <alias_name>   <command_name>
```

Hence, if you said:

```
DB<1> = x1 'x @variable1'
```

then any time you type x1 you will get a listing and history of the variable x1. If you want to save your aliases, you will have to put them into a file that Perl evaluates before it starts the debugger, called $ENV{'HOME'}/.perldb. The preceding alias would become an entry in that file:

```
$DB::alias{'x1'} = 's"^x1(.*)"x $1"';
```

For more information about the $ENV{'HOME'}/.perldb file, see the on-line documentation **perldebug**.

Looking Through Code with V and S

Let's look at some more ways of searching through code. Perl has many commands we won't consider here, such as /pattern/ to search forward, ?pattern? to search backward, l to print out lines, and w to get a screen's worth of code. However, V and S are the best of these commands, because they let you do things that a straight editor, such as vi or emacs, couldn't.

Looking at Variables with V

Perl has a way of doing a total variable dump: with a capital V. Simply say something like:

```
DB<1>   V main
```

and you will get a couple of screenfuls of your environment, variables included via use and require, any arguments passed to the script, and whatnot. All the global variables are available. If you said:

```
DB<1>   V main ~ENV
```

it would show you the environment as seen by main.

Since my variables do not show up in the symbol table, they are not included in this list.

Looking at Subroutines with S

The V command has limited uses because of Perl's policy with variables (lexical variables don't show up in the symbol tables). However, the S command to list subroutines is quite cool since it shows you exactly the API that you can use in modules.

For example, suppose you wanted to see the internals of the **CPAN** module. You could say something like:

```
C:\>  /home/ed/perl5.004_50/install/bin/perl -d -MCPAN -e shell
which goes into the debugger:
Loading DB routines from perl5db.pl version 1
```

```
Emacs support available.

Enter h or `h h' for help.

main::(-e:1):    shell
  DB<1>
```

We then ask what subroutines the debugger knows about:

```
DB<1>  S
AutoLoader::AUTOLOAD
AutoLoader::BEGIN
AutoLoader::import
CPAN::AUTOLOAD
CPAN::Author::as_glimpse
CPAN::Author::email
CPAN::Author::fullname
CPAN::BEGIN
CPAN::Bundle::as_string
CPAN::Bundle::clean
CPAN::Bundle::contains
CPAN::Bundle::find_bundle_file
CPAN::Bundle::force
CPAN::Bundle::get
CPAN::Bundle::inst_file
CPAN::Bundle::install
CPAN::Bundle::make
CPAN::Bundle::readme
CPAN::Bundle::rematein
CPAN::Bundle::test
CPAN::Bundle::xs_file
CPAN::CacheMgr::BEGIN
CPAN::CacheMgr::as_string
CPAN::Distribution::MD5_check_file
CPAN::Distribution::called_for
CPAN::Distribution::clean
CPAN::Distribution::dir
CPAN::Distribution::eq_MD5
CPAN::Distribution::force
CPAN::Distribution::get
CPAN::Distribution::install
CPAN::Distribution::look
CPAN::Distribution::make
CPAN::Distribution::new
CPAN::Distribution::perl
CPAN::Distribution::pm2dir_me
CPAN::Distribution::readme
CPAN::Distribution::test
CPAN::Distribution::untar_me
CPAN::Distribution::unzip_me
CPAN::Distribution::verifyMD5
CPAN::END
###### MUCH DELETED ######
readline::rl_getc
readline::savestate
readline::substr_with_props
```

```
strict::bits
strict::import
strict::unimport
subs::import
vars::BEGIN
vars::import
```

All in all, when you give S to the command line, you get 394 subroutines back, just from the command `perl -MCPAN -e shell`! Although this might seem intimidating, it isolates the problem. You can now see any subroutine that happens to run when you are doing different commands through CPAN in action. For example, we now set a breakpoint on `CPAN::Distribution::perl`:

```
DB<2> b CPAN::Distribution::perl
```

Then we run the program:

```
DB<3>  r
cpan shell — CPAN exploration and modules installation (v1.30)
ReadLine support available (try ``install Bundle::CPAN'')


cpan>  i Bundle::CPAN
## MUCH DELETED #####

Trying with /usr/local/bin/ncftp to get
     ftp://ftp.digital.com/pub/plan/perl/CPAN/authors/id/HAYASHI/CHECKSUMS
Issuing "/usr/bin/ftp -n"
Local directory now /home/ed/.cpan/sources/authors/id/HAYASHI
GOT /home/ed/.cpan/sources/authors/id/HAYASHI/CHECKSUMS
Checksum for /home/ed/.cpan/sources/authors/id/HAYASHI/Term-ReadLine-Gnu-0
.09.tar.gz ok
x Term-ReadLine-Gnu-0.09, 0 bytes, 0 tape blocks
x Term-ReadLine-Gnu-0.09/typemap, 166 bytes, 1 tape blocks
x Term-ReadLine-Gnu-0.09/eg, 0 bytes, 0 tape blocks
x Term-ReadLine-Gnu-0.09/eg/ptksh+, 2649 bytes, 6 tape blocks

CPAN::Distribution::perl(/home/ed/perl5.004_50/install/lib/CPAN.pm:2652):
2652:        my($self) = @_;
  DB<2>
```

The debugger puts you exactly where you would want to be in order to trace that given function. You can then simply step through to see how **CPAN** figures out where your Perl executable is located, in order to install it correctly:

```
CPAN::Distribution::perl(/home/ed/perl5.004_50/install/lib/CPAN.pm:2653):
2653:        my($perl) = MM-> file_name_is_absolute($^X) ? $^X : "";
  DB<2>
CPAN::Distribution::perl(/home/ed/perl5.004_50/install/lib/CPAN.pm:2654):
2654:        my $getcwd = $CPAN::Config-> {'getcwd'} || 'cwd';
DB<2>  x $perl
0  '/home/ed/perl5.004_50/install/bin/perl'

  DB<3>
```

We could go into much more detail, but for now, we will limit ourselves to this. It looks like this subroutine determines what "Perl" you are looking at by seeing if $^X (the variable that holds the Perl executable name) is absolute or relative.

Summary of Debugger Commands

This section has shown only a subset of the debugger commands available for your use in a debugging session. You can also:

- Fork off commands to the shell.
- Set "actions" with *a* so that a certain Perl command is executed before a piece of code is executed.
- Print sessions and save them in a file.

In addition, we have not even scratched the surface of customization. Do an h O to see what commands can be customized (how many array elements are printed with x, what history limit can be set, etc.).

If you are a fan of the editor emacs, the debugger can run inside emacs by installing **cperl-mode.el** inside emacs and typing:

```
M-x perldb <CR>
script <CR>
```

cperl-mode.el does many other things for you. Its thrust is syntax highlighting: highlighting variables, keywords, and subroutines so you do not make as many syntax mistakes. You can find it under the **emacs/** directory in the standard distribution.

The commands covered are in Table 21.1.

Table 21.1
Common Perl debugger Expressions

Key	Meaning
N/A	Running Perl expressions through the debugger
h	Getting on-line help
x	Printing data structures
A	Deleting all actions
b	Setting a breakpoint
d	Deleting a breakpoint
D	Deleting all breakpoints
L	Listing all breakpoints
<up arrow>	Cycling up through commands in the stack
<down arrow>	Cycling down through commands in the stack
H	History of all commands
!	Redoing commands
=	Making aliases
r	Running programs
t	Setting tracing on/off
c	Continuing a run
s or <CR>	Stepping through a program line by line (<CR> works after you press s once)
r	Running a program under the debugger
a	Setting an action
V	Printing global variables
S	Printing subroutines

These commands should do more than get you started. They should be about 95 percent of what you need from the debugger. Anything else you should be able to get with a combination of C:\> perldoc perldebug, DB<1> h h, and DB<1> h <key>. Next, we will try to fill in some of the gaps of the keys we did not cover.

An Example of Debugger Usage

Let's go through some more cases where we would use the debugger. In my experience, I have noticed that the best use for the debugger is on the small- to medium-sized projects. In other words, you will want to use the Perl debugger with local, precise problems. For bigger issues and specialized debugging, see Chapter 22.

In short, the best time to use the debugger is when you have algorithm bugs, and want to step through, in detail, where the algorithm is going wrong. Since we have primarily stuck with a sorting algorithm motif in this chapter, we might as well continue.

Example: Finding a Logic Bug in Heap Sort

Heap sort is another sorting technique developed to sort "in place," so you need not copy elements around. It is almost exactly like merge-sort, as it runs in about the same amount (i.e., same order of magnitude) of time. However, heap sort does not use heavy recursion. There is never a tree of the same subroutine running at the same time, and it is more predictable than merge_sort. It is, however, a bit more complicated. It rests on the idea that an array has parent elements and child elements (i.e., an array element i has children 2i + 1 and 2i + 2). Each child can have children of its own. The heap property states that every child has lower values than its parent. Figure 21.7 shows a heap in action.

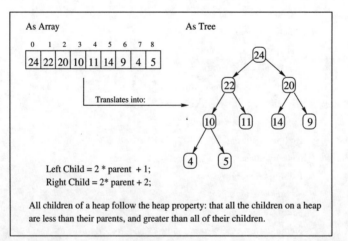

Figure 21.7
A Heap in Action

As Array

As Tree

```
 0  1  2  3  4  5  6  7  8
24 22 20 10 11 14  9  4  5
```

Translates into:

Left Child = 2 * parent + 1;
Right Child = 2* parent + 2;

All children of a heap follow the heap property: that all the children on a heap are less than their parents, and greater than all of their children.

The trick here is that after you have made something a heap, you know that the parent of everybody (on the left-hand side) is the largest element. If we made the array into a heap, saved the element at the end, and then continued to make a heap out of the remaining elements in the array, we could, ultimately, sort the whole array one element at a time. Figure 21.8 shows this process.

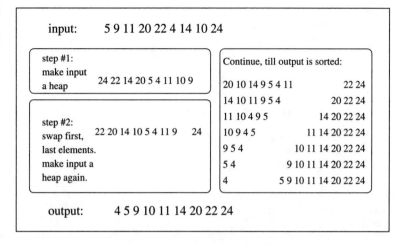

Figure 21.8
Heap Sort
in Action

Given the code for heap sort, there would be two steps in our algorithm. To debug it, we could:

- Make heapify, a subroutine that turns an array into a heap.
- Call heapify several times to sort the numbers in the array.

Listing 21.5 shows the actual heap sort code in Perl, that is, the actual heap sort code in Perl before a couple of bugs were removed by debugging it.

Listing 21.5
heapsort.p

```perl
1   use strict;
2
3   my (@array) = (4,2,5,1,6,6,33,1,2);
4   heapsort(\@array);
5   print "@array\n";
6
7
8   sub heapsort
9   {
10      my ($array) = @_;
11
12      my $heapsize;
13      build_heap($array, \$heapsize);    # we build our heap
14
15      my $xx;
16
17      for ($xx = $heapsize; $xx > = 0; $xx-)     # we swap our heap elements
18      {    # after beautifying
19          swap($array-> [0], $array-> [$xx]);
20          $heapsize-;
21          heapify($array, 0, \$heapsize);
22      }
23  }
24
25  sub build_heap
```

```
26 {
27     my ($array, $heapsize) = @_;
28
29     my $xx;
30     $$heapsize = @$array;
31
32     for ($xx = int($$heapsize/2); $xx > = 0; $xx−)
33     {
34         heapify($array, $xx, $heapsize);
35     }
36 }
37
38 sub heapify
39 {
40     my ($array, $index, $heapsize) = @_;
41     my $left = leftify($index);
42     my $right = rightify($index);
43
44     my $largest = $index;
45     $largest = $left if (($left <= $$heapsize)
46                             && ($array-> [$left] > $array-> [$index]));
47
48     $largest = $right if (($right <= $$heapsize) &&
49                             ($array-> [$right] > $array-> [$largest]));
50
51     if ($largest != $index)    # swap if lower
52     {
53         swap( $array-> [$largest], $array-> [$index] );
54         heapify($array, $largest, $heapsize);
55     }
56 }
57
58 sub leftify  { return (2 * $_[0] + 1); }     # get children
59 sub rightify { return (2 * $_[0] + 2); }
60
61 sub swap { my $tmp; $tmp = $_[0]; $_[0] = $_[1]; $_[1] = $tmp; }
```

The trick is to find the bugs in the fewest steps possible. To do this, we must know what is going on in the code.

We first build a heap in line 13, passing a reference around. Then, we continue to make heaps in the loop from lines 17–22. Each time through, though, we save an element, so the next heap we make is one element shorter than the first.

This may be where we want to start debugging. At each stage of the algorithm, we should see the sorted array growing on the right, and see heaps on the left. Let's start the debugger:

```
prompt% perl -d wrongheap.p
Stack dump during die enabled outside of evals.

Loading DB routines from perl5db.pl patch level 0.94
Emacs support available.

Enter h or `h h' for help.

main::(wrongheap.p:3):  my (@array) = (4,2,5,1,6,6,33,1,2);
  DB<1>
```

This seems to be the job for a. We will set a line of code to be executed that prints our array each time the call to heapify to make an array out of a heap in our main loop is done. As we can see, this is in line 20, but if we were not sure where it was in the code, we could use the debugger to find out:

```
    DB<1>  /heapify/
20:             heapify($array, 0, \$heapsize);
```

This looks for the first occurrence of the string heapify inside the code. After we have found it, we can list the context around line 20:

```
      DB<2>  l 15+10

16:             for ($xx = $heapsize; $xx > = 0; $xx-)
17:             {
18:                 swap($array-> [0], $array-> [$xx]);
19:                 $heapsize-;
20:                 heapify($array, 0, \$heapsize);
21:             }
22:         }
23:
24:         sub build_heap
25:         {
```

which says "list 10 lines around line 15."

Note I do not usually use the debugger to look at the code. Instead, I usually have a power editor (vim or emacs) open on the side and then reference the code directly that way. The exception to this is the **S** function. I usually look through the project I'm working on with **S** just to see an overarching view of the code. This can really help your understanding.

We can now insert our action into the for loop, and watch heap sort in action:

```
    DB<3>
    DB<4>  a 21 print "@{$array}[0..$xx]        > @{$array}[$xx+1..$#array]<\n";
    DB<5>  r

33 6 6 2 2 4 5 1 1
 6 6 2 2 4 5 1 1 33     > <
1 2 6 1 2 4 5  6      > 33<
 2 5 1 2 4 1 6       > 6 33<
1 2 4 1 2  5      > 6 6 33<
 2 1 1 2 4      > 5 6 6 33<
 2 1 1 2      > 4 5 6 6 33<
 1 1 2       > 2 4 5 6 6 33<
1  1      > 2 2 4 5 6 6 33<
 1      > 1 2 2 4 5 6 6 33<
      > 1 1 2 2 4 5 6 6 33<
 1 1 2 2 4 5 6 6 33
```

As you can see, something weird is going on here. In the second line, a ghost element seems to have arisen. The text is sorting correctly, but there is a >< element, which is a dead giveaway that a blank element has arisen.

We can see this more plainly by doing our own test call to heap sort, and then printing the results (unfortunately, the my variables go out of scope):

```
DB::fake::(/usr/local/lib/perl5/perl5db.pl:2043):
2043:        "Debugged program terminated.  Use `q' to quit or `R' to restart.";
  DB<6>   @array = (1,2,3,4,0);

  DB<7>   main::heapsort(\@array);
4 2 3 1 0
 2 3 1 0 4     > <
0 2  1 3       > <
0 1  2      > <
 0 1      > <
0        > <
0        > <
  DB<8>  x @array
empty array
  DB<9>
```

This is even worse. Here, it looks like our bug is actually eating the elements up. So how do we track it down?

We track it down by noticing that sometime between the action at 16 and the action at 21, the array size changed. Let's try to rerun the script through the debugger. For length's sake, I've eliminated our old actions:

```
  DB<1>   c 16
main::heapsort(wrongheap.p:16):          for ($xx = $heapsize; $xx > = 0; $xx—)
main::heapsort(wrongheap.p:17):          {
  DB<2>   x $array
0 ARRAY(0x1cacec)
  0   33
  1   6
  2   6
  3   2
  4   2
  5   4
  6   5
  7   1
  8   1

  DB<3>   n
main::heapsort(wrongheap.p:18):          swap($array-> [0], $array-> [$xx]);
  DB<3>   n
main::heapsort(wrongheap.p:19):          $heapsize—;
  DB<3>   x $array
0   ARRAY(0x1cacec)
  0   undef
  1   6
  2   6
  3   2
  4   2
  5   4
  6   5
  7   1
  8   1
  9
```

Aha! When we swap elements in line 18, we bring in an unwanted element. Remember how Perl automatically creates elements for you when you access an element outside array boundaries? This is what is happening here. $xx is too big by one, so $heapsize is too big by one. We look up to where $heapsize is being set, and we see:

```
12 build_heap($array, \$heapsize);
```

This looks suspicious to me, as heapsize is being passed in as a reference to build_heap so build_heap can change its value. We can trace this by hand:

```
29 $$heapsize = @$array;
```

$$heapsize is set to @$array or the length of the array. But since Perl has a zero subscript (instead of one), $array-> [$$heapsize] translates into an *empty element*, one past the bounds of the array.

Let's go into our editor, and change the offending line to:

```
29 $$heapsize = @$array - 1;
```

(I wish there were a way to modify it temporarily in the debugger, but there isn't, because of very deep-seated reasons of the way eval works.) Run it again. This time, when we run it, it looks like this:

```
33 6 6 2 2 4 5 1 1
1 2 6 1 2 4 5 6        > 33<
1 2 5 1 2 4 6        > 6 33<
1 2 4 1 2 5      > 6 6 33<
2 2 1 1 4      > 5 6 6 33<
1 2 1 2      > 4 5 6 6 33<
1 1 2      > 2 4 5 6 6 33<
1 1      > 2 2 4 5 6 6 33<
1      > 1 2 2 4 5 6 6 33<
1 1 2 2 4 5 6 6 33
```

This is much better. Each time the loop occurs, the sorted part of the string grows by one, until finally the whole array is sorted.

Summary of Debugger Example

That was a pretty easy bug in retrospect and pretty easily caught by -**w**. But believe me, Perl's ability to blur the line between programming and debugging will help you create bug-free programs fast. At low-level coding, the debugger represents your eyes into how the program works, whether that debugger is the one just listed, or by putting simple print statements in the code to figure out what is going on.

However, this is not the only way we can trace down logical bugs. The other major way of tracing down bugs is by performing *coverage testing*, where you know which parts of your code have been executed and which ones have not.

Coverage Testing with Devel::Coverage

Coverage testing is concerned with if or how often a piece of code has been executed. To that end, there is a **CPAN** module named **Devel::Coverage**, which is now in alpha state and should be out in beta before this book hits the shelves. (However, I have not had any problems using it so far.)

Why the need for coverage testing? If you have any conditional statements in your code at all, then you may have holes in your testing logic. Say you had the following code in **script.p**:

```
1 if (_$ARGV[0] >  $ARGV[1])  { _doSomethingNice(); }
2 if (_$ARGV[0] <  $ARGV[1])  { _dieAHorribleDeathAndTakeDownTheOSWithMe();  }
```

If you just tested this code with the following:

```
prompt% perl script.p 22 11;
```

Perl would execute _doSomethingNice(). Believing that this code was ready for production, you could release it with the bug in line 2.

Note

The _dieAHorribleDeathAndTakeDownTheOSWithMe() bug actually might happen if you are doing something particularly dangerous, and are running the script with a user that has special authority. In these cases, coverage testing is a necessity, and you will get bitten quite hard if you don't do it assiduously. Needless to say, you are going to want to do a lot of testing for scripts that run as "root" or "superuser," and therefore could potentially execute line 2 if you underestimate what you are doing.

This shows the need for coverage testing, in which you would have exercised the code in line 2 (preferably with a user with less authority that cannot do the things that the bug entails). **Devel::Coverage** deals with this issue by keeping track of the lines of code you have tested, and saving the file's lines plus the number of times they were executed, into a **.cvp** file. Then, use a tool called **coverperl** (which is installed into the Perl binary directory and should be in your path) to read the contents of this file, and display them to the screen.

For example, let's see how well our heap sort code fares under the coverage test. We would say:

```
prompt% perl -d:Coverage rightheap.p
prompt% coverperl rightheap.cvp
Total of 1 instrumentation runs.

/home/ed/rightheap.p
     1    main::build_heap
          1    line 26
          1    line 28
          1    line 29
          1    line 31
          5    line 33
    27    main::heapify
         27    line 39
         27    line 40
         27    line 41
         27    line 43
         27    line 44
         27    line 47
         27    line 50
         13    line 52
         13    line 53
     1    main::heapsort
          1    line 9
          1    line 11
          1    line 12
##.... stuff deleted
    22    main::swap
         88    line 60
     3    line 1
     1    line 3
     1    line 4
     1    line 5
```

The lines like `1  main::heapsort` show how many times a subroutine has been executed. They are also indented. Lines inside subroutines are indented relative to their parent subroutine, and lines that are from the main loop are not indented. This is pretty straightforward. The only slight complication comes with lines such as:

```
22 main::swap
    88    line 60
```

This is saying that **main::swap** was called 22 times, but line 60 (part of the subroutine swap) has been executed 88 times! What's going on here?

Well, if we look at line 60, we see:

```
60 sub swap { my $tmp; $tmp = $_[0]; $_[0] = $_[1]; $_[1] = $tmp; }
```

which has four different statements in it. Therefore, the coverage tool is sensitive to each expression in a line, not the line itself. Unfortunately, they are currently jumbled so we cannot see which expression has been run and which ones have been ignored (did I mention this was alpha software?), but that problem could be addressed by the time this book is released.

A couple of more things about the coverage tool: First, it resets itself each time you modify your script in any way. If you change things, the coverage tool has no way of knowing whether the change you made was serious or not. Therefore, if you add a space to the end of a line, your previous coverage tests are gone. It makes sense to save them often if you want a history of what you have tested. Either that, or save the coverage testing for last.

Second, the coverage tool will avoid the `import()` directives, and everything else at compile time. This is a simple fact about how the debugger works. It needs compiled bytecode before it can start.

It is very important to realize that just because the coverage tester says there has been more than one execution of a line, does not mean that the code is bug-free. It is obvious that if a line says:

```
0    main::mysub
```

that this is a hole, a bug, because the code has never been tested before. However, it is not obvious that the following:

```
1    main::mysub
```

is bug-free. Many people get a false sense of security from coverage tools. They say, "Oh, I've already covered that branch; it must be OK." Here is a simple example that shows otherwise.

If you wanted to match the integer part of any number, you might try this code:

```
$data = '234222';
my ($number) = ($data =~ m"(\d+)\.");
```

If we run this under the coverage testing tool, we will get the comforting statement:

```
Total number of instrumentations: 1
1    line 1
1    line 2
```

However, there is a bug in this code. The fact that a . is essential in the regular expression causes the match to fail, and $number to remain undefined. We must go on to other methods that we will talk about in the debugging chapter, Chapter 23 (-w, use strict) to supplement our debugging arsenal.

Debugging for Speed: Profilers

To this point, we have covered logical bugs, in which the bugs were dependent on outright coding mistakes. However, as far as anyone can attest, there are other bugs that can occur. For example, you know there is something wrong if you get a transfer rate of four characters per second while downloading a Web page, even though the functionality is correct.

For this purpose, Perl has two profilers which concentrate on two different scopes of measuring performance. First, there is **Devel::DProf**, the most popular debugger. It is designed with the large-scale application in mind. Second, there is the more recently introduced **Devel::SmallProf**, which is just as helpful in dealing with algorithm speed debugging. We will go over an example of each. But first, we will look at a very helpful module Perl has in the standard distribution called Benchmark, which will immensely help your debugging for speed problems.

Benchmark Module

Benchmark.pm is a gem of a module that comes with the standard distribution. It is invaluable for doing speed comparisons of code, especially on those small pieces of code that add up and make a large impact on your system, but that there is no way to benchmark without being run thousands of times.

Suppose, you wanted to find out how much the copy in the following:

```
sub add { my ($a, $b) = @_; $a + $b }
```

slows down the add function, as compared to:

```
sub add { $_[0] + $_[1]; }
```

which does no such copy because you are directly accessing the elements here. Well, **Benchmark** gives you a quick way of testing this:

```
addtest.p
use Benchmark;

sub addcopy { my ($a, $b) = @_; $a + $b }
sub add { $_[0] + $_[1]; }
timethese(1_000_000, { 'addcopy' =>  'addcopy(543,111);',
                          'add' =>  'add(543,111);' } );
```

`timethese()` is a quick and dirty test suite runner. Its job is to run (in this instance) one million `addcopy()` and `add()` subroutines, and display the elapsed time of each piece of code. In this case:

```
prompt% perl addtest.p
Benchmark: timing 1000000 iterations of add, addcopy . . .
       add: 13 secs (12.333 usr  0.00 sys = 12.33 cpu)
   addcopy: 18 secs (18.33 usr 00 sys = 18.33 cpu)
```

Each copy of an integer (at least one less than 32 bits) took approx six seconds /1,000,000 trials / two integers per trial = three millionths of a second. If we wanted to test the effect of larger integers on how long addition takes, we could say:

```
sub addcopy { my ($a, $b) = @_; $a + $b }
sub add { $_[0] + $_[1]; }
timethese(1_000_000, { 'addsmall' =>  'add(543,111);',
                          'addlarge' =>  'add(543234234234232422,111);' } );
```

and get the following:

```
Benchmark: timing 1000000 iterations of addlarge, addsmall . . .
    addlarge: 14 secs (13.56 usr  0.00 sys = 13.56 cpu )
    addsmall: 14 secs (13.50 usr  0.00 sys = 13.50 cpu )
```

which shows that there is no appreciable difference between the two.

Benchmark is infinitely useful. If you are just beginning with Perl, you can use it to get a feel for how fast or slow Perl is at certain things. Later, you can use it to test possible performance replacements for subroutines, to make sure they actually make a performance improvement. This second use is what we will exploit next with the profilers **Devel::DProf** and **Devel::SmallProf**.

Devel::DProf

Devel::DProf is the older of the two profilers. It is written in C, with the purpose of interjecting as little overhead as possible in timing Perl code. It is not in the standard distribution, so you must pick it up from **CPAN** or from the accompanying CD.

The use of **Devel::DProf** is analgous to **Devel::Coverage**. In fact, all the debuggers outside the default borrowed their usage from **Devel::DProf**:

```
C:\>  perl -d:DProf insertion.p
```

This runs our insertion sort under the profiler (with 100 numbers being sorted), saving the information inside **tmon.out**. You then can extract this information by saying:

```
C:\>  dprofpp -F
```

The -F is necessary because the underlying C code is persnickety about the way Perl handles exiting subroutines. This produces output looking something like:

```
Total Elapsed Time =    2.33 Seconds
User+System Time =    2.18 Seconds
Exclusive Times
%Time Seconds       #Calls sec/call Name
 52.2   1.140            1   1.1400 main::insertion
 46.7   1.020         5050   0.0002 main::swap
```

which, of course, is not that meaningful to us. We know that insertion-sort spends most of its time in swap mode. We also know that **main::swap** is called by **main::insertion**. Hence, the second number is indicative of the first. If we did not know the calling order, we could find out with:

```
C:\>  dprofpp -T -F
```

This is not very good in this case because insertion sort is calling swap *5050* times in a row, leading to an output that looks something like:

```
main::insertion
    main::sort
    ### repeated 4999 times.
)
```

DProf is not as good at the small projects as it is at finding the bottlenecks in larger projects, especially larger text applications. Unfortunately, we do not really have something to show off **DProf**'s talents in this book. The best thing we have is the calendar project from Chapter 20.

Let's use **DProf** to see bottlenecks in the calendar. From there, we can tell whether or not we want to improve any subroutines.

Example: Profiling the Calendar Application

Start by firing up the profiler, along with a client that uses the **Tk::Calendar** object:

```
C:\>  perl -d:DProf calendar.p
```

where **calendar.p** looks like

```
use Tk;
use Tk::Calendar;
use Data::Dumper;

my $screen = new Tk::Calendar();
$screen-> draw();

MainLoop();
```

Simple enough: make a calendar as the main window, draw it, and then go into the event loop. We need to exercise this code as much as we possibly can in order to get an idea of which functions are the bottlenecks. Cycle through the different operations that the calendar allows, such as:

- Going to the next and previous months.
- Entering text into the associated calendar screens.
- Having different types of notified boxes (flashing and stable).

If we were doing this formally, we would want to either:

1. Split the non-GUI components from the GUI components, and set up a scheme to test the non-GUI components with a file.
2. Use WinPerl++ (*aka* Guide) to make a regression test for the PerlTk script. Unfortunately, right now Guide is only available on Win32 platforms, but that may change in the future.

For now, we will just play around. Start up the calendar with:

```
prompt% perl -d:DProf calendar.p,
```

and wait for the screen to load. When I was doing this particular test, I did the following:

- Hit the **forward month** button four times.
- Clicked on four different dates in the same month.
- Entered **Coding Perl** as the plan for each of these days.
- Closed one of these windows.
- Tried to go back a month, opening up the file dialog box.
- Said **yes** to the save question, closing all three dates.
- Went back three more months, opened the current day.
- Entered **book done** as the plan.
- Closed this window.
- Opened another date.
- Hit **Done** in menu, bringing up the Open Screens window.
- Hit **OK** to exit program.

You get the idea. Tests like this in real life can be much more complicated than this, but they don't necessarily have to be. If you can pull off this sort of test on your code with a significant amount of interaction, you will get approximately 90 percent of the data about the performance of your code.

Here are the results of the performance analysis. The profiler shows only the top 15 subroutines by default. Let's go with this default for now. Type:

```
prompt% dprofpp -F
```

The -F is almost a necessity, but there are other interesting options we could have used here:

- -o 1000 to show all the subroutines profiled.
- -v to sort by the amount of time each subroutine takes rather than the total time involved.

Here is a sample of the output, with the subroutines we can control in boldface:

```
Faking 118 exit timestamp(s).
   Total Elapsed Time =    69.39 Seconds
     User+System Time =     5.24 Seconds
   Exclusive Times
   %Time Seconds      #Calls sec/call Name
    7.63   0.400        1125  0.0004 Date::Format::Generic::time2str
    6.30   0.330         369  0.0009 Tk::Widget::new
    3.24   0.170           1  0.1700 Tk::MainLoop
    3.05   0.160         299  0.0005 Tk::button
    2.86   0.150         284  0.0005 Time::Local::timelocal
    2.67   0.140        1125  0.0001 Date::Format::Generic::_subs
    2.48   0.130         672  0.0002 Tk::configure
    2.48   0.130         253  0.0005 Tk::destroy
    2.10   0.110         275  0.0004 Tk::Date::new
    2.10   0.110           1  0.1100 main::CODE(0xb1588)
    2.10   0.110        1107  0.0001 Date::Format::Generic::format_b
    2.10   0.110         284  0.0004 Date::Parse::CODE(0x30257c)
    2.10   0.110         127  0.0009 Tk::Derived::configure
    1.91   0.100         549  0.0002 Tk::Month::_diffMonth
    1.91   0.100         235  0.0004 Tk::Derived::Subconfigure
```

Even though we have actually interacted with the calendar program for 70 seconds, we have exercised the system for only 5 seconds or less.

What can we make out of the subroutines that take the most time? Well, `time2str` is used in more than one place, which can be confirmed either by looking at the code (the easiest way) or, if you are desperate, analyzing the output of:

```
%prompt dprofpp -T
```

which will give you the calling tree with reams of output. Since this subroutine occurs in many places, if we optimized it, we would get the most "bang for our buck." However, this particular subroutine is not a good candidate for optimization because we do not own it. Either that or we optimize it, and tell the author Graham Barr about it so that he can fix it inside the release that he gives to the world.

In fact, out of all these 15 subroutines, we can only optimize two that we have directly programmed: **Tk::Date::new()** and **Tk::Month::diffMonth()**. Let's look at the code of **Tk::Date::new()**:

```
13 sub new
14 {
15     my ($type, $widget, $monthstring, $day, $date, $row, $xcoord
16         $ycoord) = @_;
17     my $self = bless {}, $type;
18
19     if (!defined ($_dbm))
20     {
21         $_dbm = {};
22         tie(%$_dbm, 'AnyDBM_File', $_dbmfile, O_RDWR|O_CREAT, 0640);
23     }
24
25     (
26         $self-> {'monthstring'}, $self-> {'day'},
27         $self-> {'date'}, $self-> {'row'},
28         $self-> {'xcoord'}, $self-> {'ycoord'}, $self-> {'widget'}
29
30     )     = ($monthstring, $day, $date, $row, $xcoord, $ycoord,$widget);
```

```
31
32      my $string = $self-> {'monthstring'};
33      $string =~ s"Calendar Month:""g;
34      $string = $self-> {'date'} . " $string";
35
36      $self-> {'secs'} = _getSecs($string);
37      $self-> {'dbmstring'} = $string;
38
39      return ($self);
40 }
```

There does not seem to be much we can optimize here. The only call that is moderately labor-intensive is the tie to the DBM file, and we have already optimized it by caching it! The only reason **Tk::Date::new**() takes up so much total time is because each button is a date, and each time we go to a next or previous month, we must recreate and draw 30 or so buttons.

By making the **Tk::Month** a canvas, and putting dates directly on that canvas, we may make a performance improvement. But because this particular item takes up only 2.1 percent of the time, the redesign is probably not worth it. We might want to verify that **Tk::Date::new**() is efficient by looking at **Devel::SmallProf**, but otherwise I think that the extra work would not be worth it.

The second call that we can optimize is **_diffMonth**(). **_diffMonth**() was used to calculate whether a month was different or not, and looks like this:

```
sub _diffMonth
{
    my ($secs, $type) = @_;
    my $month = time2str("%b", $secs);
    $secs = ($type eq '+')? $secs + 86400 : $secs - 86400;
    my $newmonth = time2str("%b", $secs);

    return(1) if ($month ne $newmonth);
}
```

Now, considering that time2str had the highest profile listed above (taking 7.63 percent of the time), we might want to consider substituting the subroutine for a call to localtime, which can do the same task.

This subroutine follows:

```
sub _diffMonth
{
    my ($secs, $type) = @_;

    my $month = (localtime($secs))[3];
    $secs = ($type eq '+')? $secs + 86400: $secs - 86400;
    my $new_month = (localtime($secs))[3];

    return(1) if ($month eq $newmonth);
}
```

How can we be sure that the new _diffMonth does what it says it does and increases the performance of a given application? Well, we could place this code in a second version of our calendar program, and then use **DProf** to see the results. If I had an automated test suite, that might be just what we would do. After all, the best way to test something is to see how it performs in real life.

However, in this case, the **Benchmark** module will do very nicely. Define a **Benchmark** test case (Listing 21.6):

Listing 21.6
`diffmonthtest.p`

```
 1  #!/usr/local/bin/perl5
 2
 3  use Benchmark;
 4  use Date::Format;
 5
 6  my $t = timeit( 10000, '_diffMonth1(100000)');
 7  my $v = timeit( 10000, '_diffMonth2(100000)');
 8
 9  print timestr($t), "\n";
10  print timestr($v), "\n";
11
12  sub _diffMonth1
13  {
14      my ($secs, $type) = @_;
15
16      my $month = time2str($secs, "%b");
17      $secs = ($type eq '+')? $secs + 86400: $secs - 86400;
18      my $new_month = time2str($secs,"%b");
19
20      return(1) if ($month eq $newmonth);
21  }
22
23  sub _diffMonth2
24  {
25      my ($secs, $type) = @_;
26
27      my $month = (localtime($secs))[3];
28      $secs = ($type eq '+')? $secs + 86400: $secs - 86400;
29      my $new_month = (localtime($secs))[3];
30
31      return(1) if ($month eq $newmonth);
32  }
```

which uses the explicit version of the **Benchmark** modules `timeit()` and `timestr()` to provide a method of carrying around results of a benchmarking run. `timeit()` is used to actually make the benchmark, and `timestr()` turns that result into a string. The results are:

```
time2str:  8 secs (7.87 usr 0.00 sys = 7.87 cpu)
localtime: 1 secs (1.77 usr 0.00 sys = 1.77 cpu)
```

The results are quite a bit different. If we replaced all of our `time2str()` calls with `localtime()` calls, we could save:

```
.400 - .400 * 1.77/7.87 = .309 secs
```

A whopping .309 seconds! Not much, perhaps, but it does take the subroutines we can control out of the top 15 CPU hogs. To make a long story short, here is the profile as it exists after we make the change:

```
prompt% dprofpp -F
Faking 104 exit timestamp(s).
Total Elapsed Time =    70.21 Seconds
  User+System Time =     4.89 Seconds
```

```
Exclusive Times
%Time  Seconds      #Calls sec/call Name
 6.95   0.340          379  0.0009  Tk::Widget::new
 4.09   0.200            1  0.2000  Tk::MainLoop
 3.48   0.170          284  0.0006  Time::Local::timelocal
 3.07   0.150            1  0.1500  main::CODE(0xb1588)
 3.07   0.150          302  0.0005  Tk::button
 3.07   0.150            1  0.1500  Tk::Text::CODE(0xccd3c)
 2.86   0.140          254  0.0006  Tk::destroy
 2.66   0.130          284  0.0005  Date::Parse::CODE(0x30257c)
 2.66   0.130          284  0.0005  Date::Parse::str2time
 2.66   0.130          142  0.0009  Tk::Derived::configure
 2.45   0.120          720  0.0002  Tk::configure
 2.25   0.110          386  0.0003  Tk::Widget::CreateArgs
 1.84   0.090          282  0.0003  Tk::Widget::place
 1.84   0.090          369  0.0002  Tk::Widget::SetBindtags
```

We got rid of the two items we could control that even showed up on the scanner of **DProf**. We could also do the same for str2time, but my hunch is that it is probably worthwhile to keep str2time around for flexibility's sake.

The question now is does all of this tinkering make the calendar object a better object? In this case, I would say yes. Even though .309 seconds doesn't sound like a great deal, when you are actually maneuvering around in the calendar application, response time is very critical.

Many people's perception of the Internet is that one-half second between clicks of the mouse can be intolerable, let alone 20 to 30 seconds between mouse-click time. Indeed, I did notice the speed difference in our example. Multiply this by the speed difference you will get by doing things like this in real life, and you've made your applications twice as usable.

Summary of DProf

DProf is a good tool to do debugging "in the large." To profile something, simply say:

```
C:\>  perl -d:DProf file.p
```

resulting in a **tmon.out** file, and then say:

```
C:\>  dprofpp -F
```

to get a printout of the functions that take the most time. There is much functionality that we have not listed. In their own way, **dprofpp** and **DProf** are just as complicated as the debugger. The flags you can pass to **dprofpp** are listed in Table 21.2.

Table 21.2
dprofpp Flags

Flag	Meaning
-O	Maximum number of subroutines to display
-a	Sort subroutines in alphabetical order
-l	Sort by number of calls to subroutines (for inlining)
-v	Sort by average amount of time spent in subroutines
-T	Show the call tree (shown earlier)
-t	Show the compressed call tree (not very compressed though!)

Table 21.2
dprofpp Flags
(continued)

Flag	Meaning
-q	Don't print headers
-u	Use user time rather than user plus system
-s	Use system time rather than user plus system
-r	Use real elapsed time rather than user plus system
-U	Do not sort subroutines
-E	Subtimes are reported exclusive of child times
-I	Subtimes are reported inclusive of child times
-V	Print **dprofpp**'s version
-p script	Profile script script, and generate a report
-Q	Used with -p to profile the script and then quit before generating report

This is straight from the script **dprofpp** (stored in the central distribution when you install it). **dprofpp** has a great deal of elaboration on these explanations, which is stored in the script itself as a **pod** file, so you may want to check it out.

Devel::SmallDProf

The second profiler we will look at is called **Devel::SmallDProf**. It is a relatively new (beta) piece of software which allows you to trace the performance of Perl code line by line. For example, you could see exactly how much time each line in the code in Listing 21.7 took.

Listing 21.7
multvsadd.p

```
multvsadd.p
1 $DB::print_lines = 1;
2 my $yy = 1;
3 my $zz = 1;
4 for ($xx = 0; $xx < 100000; $xx++)
5 {
6     $yy = ($yy * 2)    % 100001;
7     $zz = ($zz + $zz) % 100001;
8 }
```

Two things here: First, use $DB::print_lines = 1, because that gives verbose output with the actual text of the lines (rather than just their numbers). Second, add the module 1000001 to multiplication just so the numbers don't get unreasonably big. We then use **SmallDProf**, and say:

```
prompt% perl -d:SmallDProf multvsadd.p
```

and see the file **smallprof.out**. It looks like:

```
==================================================
 Profile of multvsadd.p
```

```
=====================================================
     0  0.00000000  #!/usr/local/bin/perl5
     0  0.00000000
     0  0.00000000
     1  0.00003397  $DB::print_lines = 1;
     1  0.00003409  my $yy = 1;
     1  0.00003493  my $zz = 1;
     1  0.00004101  for ($xx = 0; $xx < 100000; $xx++)
     0  0.00000000  {
     0  0.00000000
100000  3.98235953         $yy = ($yy*2) % 100001;
100000  4.77289319         $zz = ($zz + $zz) % 100001;
     0  0.00000000  }
=====================================================
```

Hence, we can see that multiplying by two is faster than adding a number to itself.

Selective Profiling

By default, **SmallProf** profiles everything that is Perl. It does not profile C code linked into Perl, because those lines of code are outside the range of the -d flag. If you are dealing with a large program that includes lots of modules, you will not want to profile everything. In cases like these, you are going to want to skip certain modules in order to pinpoint performance bugs. **SmallProf** has two ways of doing this, which are listed next.

$DB::smallprof_on

Devel::SmallProf has two ways of skipping modules. First, there is the flag **$DB::smallprof_on**, which can be used to start and stop the profiling of data. For example, if you said something like:

```
$DB::smallprof_on = 0;

# do lots of other stuff

DB::smallprof_on = 1;
for ($xx = 0; $xx < 10; $xx++)
{
    print "Profiling!\n";
}

$DB::smallprof_on = 0;
```

then **SmallProf** would profile only the for loop and leave the rest of your code alone. Note that the default for **DB::smallprof_on** is 1, so unless you want the beginning of your program profiled, you must switch it off manually.

@DB::packageprof_on

Of course, it would be a real pain to have to turn off profiling each time you enter into a different package, or call a method based on that package. Therefore, **SmallProf** provides a simple way of turning off tracing for all but a subset of packages. If you say something like:

```
use Data::Dumper;
@DB::packageprof_on = ('Data::Dumper', 'main');
use Date::Format;
```

```
my $time = time();
time2str("%b", $time );
```

it will trace only the times of the calls in main. Hence, you will find out how much time time2str takes, and how long the time() call takes.

That's about it. As this is beta software at the moment, there isn't too much functionality in it. Now let's take a look at an example of **Devel::SmallProf**, to compare three different sorting algorithms (that basically do the same thing) in a statistically sensible manner.

Example: Comparing Three Sorting Algorithms

We have outlined three different types of sorting algorithms: insertion-sort, merge-sort, and heap sort. There are two more search algorithms that are just as popular: quick sort and radix sort.

In addition, Perl sports its own internal version of quick sort, which we discussed earlier. Just for kicks then, let's compare:

- A radix sort coded in Perl.
- A quick sort coded in Perl.
- The built-in quick sort.

This will probably be embarrassing. Perl does so much better on math-like tasks with built-in functions and C extensions to Perl than it does with native, Perl functionality. But doing such a comparison really helps you understand what is quick in Perl and what is not so quick.

Plan of Attack

The first step to perform this comparison is to code radix sort and quick sort. Second, we must make a *test harness*. We notice that one simple test will not be adequate, because a sorting algorithm might work one way with a small set of input, and another way with a totally different set of input. Third, we need to combine the two together, run **SmallProf**, and analyze the results.

Coding Radix Sort and Quick Sort

I'm not going to dwell too much on how radix sort or quick sort work. Following is a small, very high-level explanation.

Note

For more details, see the book *Introduction to Algorithms*, by Thomas H. Cormen, Charles E. Leiserson, and Ronald L. Rivest. This is the seminal book on tons of algorithms including quick sort and heap sort.

Radix sort works on the principle of collating input: looking at the least significant digit, then looking at the next significant digit, and so on, up to the top digit. You sort that output in the digit order that you see, sort of like Figure 21.9. By the time you get to the last digit, the output is sorted.

Quick sort is like merge-sort in that it is a recursive divide-and-conquer algorithm. Instead of dividing in half as does merge-sort, quick sort divides according to an algorithm called *partition*, which sorts an array in place. Partition works like Figure 21.10. The key here is that the partition algorithm does a partial sort so that one side of the array is guaranteed to always be smaller than the other side (although nothing can be said about the ordering in either of the two sides). Also, partition returns the location of where this split between small-half and large-half occurs, so that quick sort knows how to divvy up the array next. By the time quick sort gets to the bottom of the array (has divied-up the array into segments of one), the whole array is sorted.

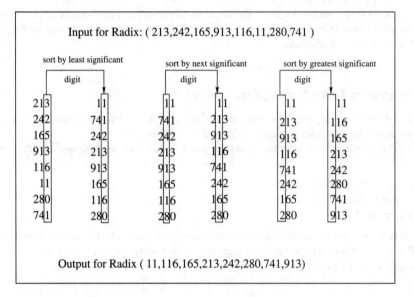

Figure 21.9
Radix Sort
in Action

Figure 21.10
Partition
Algorithm in
Quick Sort

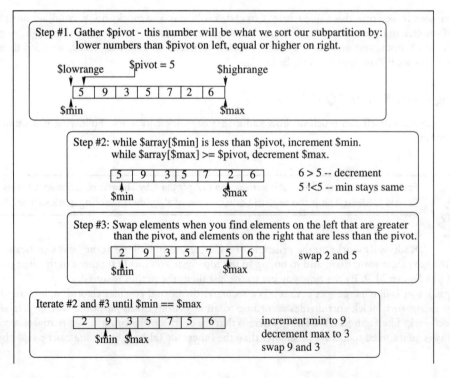

Figure 21.10 (continued)

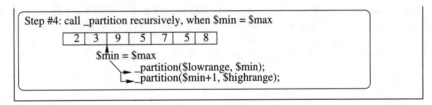

Step #4: call _partition recursively, when $min = $max

$min = $max
_partition($lowrange, $min);
_partition($min+1, $highrange);

Again, these are only high-level explanations of how the two processes work, and in any case I just lifted the pseudocode from *Introduction to Algorithms* and fleshed out the details. Listing 21.8 shows the working versions of the code.

Implementation of Radix Sort

Let's implement radix sort first.

Listing 21.8
radix.p

```perl
1  use strict;

2  sub radix
3  {
4      my ($array) = @_;
5      my ($elem, $max, $xx);
6      my (@arrayelem);

7
8      foreach (@$array) { $max = (length($_) >  $max)? length($_) : $max; }

9
10     for ($xx = 0; $xx <= $max; $xx++) # go number at a time
11     {
12         @arrayelem = ();
13         foreach $elem (@$array)
14         {
15             my ($key) = substr($elem, $xx, 1);
16             push(@{$arrayelem[$key]}, $elem);        # push onto a temporary stack
17         }
18         straighten(\@arrayelem, $array);
19     }
20 }
21
22 sub straighten  # take the Array of Array's
23 {          # and flatten it
24     my ($arrayelem, $return) = @_;
25     my ($array, $elem, $xx) = ('','',0);
26
27     foreach $array (@$arrayelem)
28     {
29         next if (!defined $array);
30         foreach $elem (@$array)
31         {
32             $return-> [$xx++] = $elem;
33         }
34     }
35 }
```

Lines 15 and 16 are the key. First, we get one character in each substring and sort it by putting it inside a bucket. This means that if we saw a zero, we'd put the element associated with it in bucket 0; if we saw a one, bucket 1; and so forth. In line 18, then, we rearrange the array by the subroutine straighten, taking the contents of these buckets and stringing them together (line 31). By the time we arrange the last elements, the sort is done.

Quick Sort Implementation

Let us now implement quick sort. Again, the key algorithm is the partition subroutine, which tells quick sort how to split up the problem, and does the sorting in place (Listing 21.9).

Listing 21.9
qsort.p

```
1   #!/usr/local/bin/perl
2
3   use strict;
4
5   sub qsort
6   {
7       my ($array) = @_;
8       _qsort($array, 0, scalar(@$array) - 1);
9   }
10
11  sub _qsort
12  {
13      my ($array, $pivot, $right) = @_;
14      my $new_pivot;
15
16      if ($pivot < $right)
17      {
18          $new_pivot = _partition($array, $pivot, $right);    # partition is key
19
20          _qsort($array, $pivot, $new_pivot);
21          _qsort($array, $new_pivot+1, $right);
22      }
23  }
24
25  sub _partition # -partition: compare left object with right object
26  {
27      my ($array, $low, $high) = @_;
28
29      my $element = $array-> [$low];
30      my $left = $low;
31      my $right = $high;
32      my $action_taken = 0;
33
34      while ($left != $right)
35      {
36          $action_taken = 0;
37          if ($array-> [$left] < $element)  { $left++; $action_taken = 1; }
38          if ($array-> [$right] > $element) { $right-; $action_taken = 1; }
39
40          if ($array-> [$left] >  $element)
41          {
```

```
42                swap ($array-> [$right], $array-> [$left]); $action_taken = 1;
43            }
44            if ($array-> [$right] < $element)
45            {
46                swap ($array-> [$right], $array-> [$left]); $action_taken = 1;
47            }
48
49            if (($array-> [$right] == $element)&&($action_taken == 0)) { $right--; }
50        }
51        return($left);
52 }
53
54 sub swap { my ($tmp) = $_[0]; $_[0] = $_[1]; $_[1] = $tmp; }
55 1;
```

As said, _partition is the important algorithm here. The loop in lines 35–50 looks at the elements at the left of the array, and only swaps them with the right-side elements if they are smaller than the central "pivot" element (line 42). _partition also looks at the elements to the right of the array, and swaps them with the left elements only if they are smaller than the central pivot element (line 46).

In addition, we skip elements that are in the "right" place: Lines 37 and 38 keep track of where we have searched in the array, constantly moving toward each other as the algorithm proceeds. When they merge together ($left == $right), we return the place where they merge as the new place for quick sort to partition.

That's about it for our contenders. The **qsort** that comes with Perl is easy to code; all we have to do is say:

```
@elements = sort (@elements);
```

and this will do the job.

Performance Testing Code

Now that we are done coding the contending algorithms, we need a series of arrays to sort. In this case, the **Benchmark** module isn't very useful, because we want to test the properties of sorting on differing arrays, not the same array a thousand times.

We must come up with a test harness, something that generates tests and actually executes them. Fortunately, Perl is very good at that. The natural structure for this problem is an array of arrays, actually three arrays of arrays, one for each sorting algorithm we are going to test.

The test harness is in Listing 21.10.

Listing 21.10
testharness.p **Test Harness for Sorting Comparison**

```
 1 use Data::Dumper;
 2 use strict;
 3
 4  require "qsort.p";
 5  require "radix.p";
 6
 7  my $xx;
 8  my ($radix_sort, $perl_qsort, $internal_qsort) = ([],[],[]);
 9
10  for ($xx = 0; $xx < 100; $xx++)
11  {
12      my ($no_of_elements) = int(rand()*100) + 2;
13      my $sort_array = _makeRand($no_of_elements);
```

```
14
15      $radix_sort->[$xx] = [@$sort_array];
16      $perl_qsort->[$xx] = [@$sort_array];
17      $internal_qsort-> [$xx] = [@$sort_array];
18 }
19
20 for ($xx = 0; $xx < 100; $xx ++)
21 {
22      qsort($perl_qsort-> [$xx]);
23      radix($radix_sort-> [$xx]);
24      @{$internal_qsort-> [$xx]} = sort (@{$internal_qsort-> [$xx]});
25 }
26
27 sub _makeRand
28 {
29      my ($no_elements) = @_;
30      my $return = [];
31      my $xx;
32      my $range = int(rand() * 100) + 2;
33
34      for ($xx = 0; $xx < $no_elements; $xx++)
35      {
36          $return-> [$xx] = int(rand()*$range);
37      }
38      return($return);
39 }
```

This is what you might call the "scattershot" approach to testing. First, we require the **qsort.p** and **radis.p** programs even though we know we coded them for stand-alone applications (this is a quick way to test functionality without having to cut and paste code). We then create a bunch of arrays with random length, random order, and random element. Then, we copy them three times and stuff them into a double dimension array. This ensures the following:

1. An even distribution of array sizes.
2. Good variability in their order.
3. Some atypical arrays; **qsort** may work well on totally random arrays, for example, but how does it work on sorting (1 2 1 3 1 2 3) where the elements are not too far apart?

In real life, we would want to do a lot more of this variability testing. We might want to test already sorted arrays (1 2 3 4 5) or arrays with patterns in them (1 2 3 1 2 3 1 2 3) to see how it affects the time.

For a good example of real-life testing, look at the **t/** directory (for tests) inside the Perl standard distribution. This gives an idea of how much variability a test suite can comprise, although Perl itself might be a worst-case scenario.

Testing with SmallProf

We now have our test harness and our code. All we have to do is fire up **SmallProf,** and see what happens:

```
C:\>  perl -d:SmallProf testharness.p
```

and print the output: (in *smallprof.out*).

```
=======================================================
 Profile of qsort.p
=======================================================

    0 0.00000000     #!/usr/local/bin/perl
```

```
  0 0.00000000
  3 0.00011611      use strict;
  0 0.00000000
  0 0.00000000      sub qsort
  0 0.00000000      {
100 0.00416720          my ($array) = @_;
100 0.00485253          _qsort($array, 0, scalar(@$array) - 1);
  0 0.00000000      }
  0 0.00000000
  0 0.00000000      sub _qsort
  0 0.00000000      {
112114 4.70423114       my ($array, $pivot, $right) = @_;
112114 3.67239106       my $new_pivot;
  0 0.00000000
112114 4.88533628       if ($pivot < $right)
  0 0.00000000          {
56007 1.99951482            $new_pivot = _partition($array, $pivot, $right);
  0 0.00000000
56007 2.12438154            _qsort($array, $pivot, $new_pivot);
56007 2.35733151            _qsort($array, $new_pivot+1, $right);
  0 0.00000000          }
  0 0.00000000      }
  0 0.00000000
  0 0.00000000      sub _partition
  0 0.00000000      {
56007 2.34353590        my ($array, $low, $high) = @_;
  0 0.00000000
56007 2.31031060        my $element = $array-> [$low];
56007 1.96292341        my $left = $low;
56007 1.96854722        my $right = $high;
56007 1.94039702        my $action_taken = 0;
  0 0.00000000
56007 1.87235343        while ($left != $right)
  0 0.00000000          {
696038 24.10507333          $action_taken = 0;
1193510 43.92413342         if ($array-> [$left] < $element)
                                { $left++; $action_taken = 1; }
1330440 49.74650681         if ($array-> [$right] >  $element)
                                { $right--; $action_taken = 1; }

  0 0.00000000
842032 32.56550169          if ($array-> [$left] >  $element)
                            {
                                swap ($array-> [$right], $array-> [$left]);
                                $action_taken = 1;
                            }
888644 34.93133080          if ($array-> [$right] < $element)
                            {
                                swap ($array-> [$right], $array-> [$left]);
                                $action_taken = 1;
                            }

  0 0.00000000
814161 35.19384336          if (($array-> [$right] == $element )
                                    && ($action_taken == 0)) { $right--; }

  0 0.00000000          }
56007 2.81549573        return($left);
```

```
    0  0.00000000        }
    0  0.00000000
507900 18.91453564        sub swap { my ($tmp) = $_[0]; $_[0] = $_[1]; $_[1] = $tmp; }
    0  0.00000000        1;
=================================================


=================================================
Profile of radix.p
=================================================


    0  0.00000000        #!/home/epeschko/perl5.004_50/install/bin/perl
    0  0.00000000
    3  0.00011599        use strict;
    0  0.00000000
    0  0.00000000        sub radix
    0  0.00000000        {
  100  0.00426257            my ($array) = @_;
  100  0.00358534            my ($elem, $max, $xx);
  100  0.00347233            my (@arrayelem);
    0  0.00000000
56173  3.00032341            foreach (@$array) { $max = (length($_) >  $max)?
                                length($_) : $max; }

    0  0.00000000
  100  0.00402462            for ($xx = 0; $xx <= $max; $xx++)
    0  0.00000000            {
  391  0.18335211                @arrayelem = ();
  391  0.01458871                foreach $elem (@$array)
    0  0.00000000                {
218686  8.74936187                  my ($key) = substr($elem, $xx, 1);
437372 19.37564433                  push(@{$arrayelem[ord($key)]}, $elem);
    0  0.00000000                }
  391  0.01633441                straighten(\@arrayelem, $array);
    0  0.00000000            }
    0  0.00000000        }
    0  0.00000000
    0  0.00000000        sub straighten
    0  0.00000000        {
  391  0.01596546            my ($arrayelem, $return) = @_;
  391  0.01618814            my ($array, $elem, $xx) = ('','',0);
    0  0.00000000
  391  0.01507688            foreach $array (@$arrayelem)
    0  0.00000000            {
16963  0.69085145                next if (!defined $array);
 3136  0.11467004                foreach $elem (@$array)
    0  0.00000000                {
218686 10.01768053                  $return-> [$xx++] = $elem;
    0  0.00000000                }
    0  0.00000000            }
    0  0.00000000        }
    0  0.00000000        1;
=================================================


=================================================
Profile of testharness.p
```

```
=====================================================
    1 0.00003302      $DB::print_lines = 1;

    1 0.00004196      for ($xx = 0; $xx < 100; $xx ++)
    0 0.00000000      {
  100 0.00549781          qsort($perl_qsort-> [$xx]);
  100 0.00527000          radix($radix_sort-> [$xx]);
  100 4.26977360          @{$internal_qsort-> [$xx]} =
                              sort (@{$internal_qsort-> [$xx]});
    0 0.00000000      }
```

I've cut out all but the most essential elements, but I hope you get the idea. The internal sort took a total of approximately four seconds, radix took about 25, and **qsort** programmed in Perl took about 140. More important, we can see exactly how the two algorithms work, and which statements take the most time. The qsort's partition function looks horrendously inefficient. For example, out of approximately 140 seconds in quick sort, 120 are being used to shuffle pointers to elements, and only 18 are being used to do the swapping! I must confess I perpetrated this particular crime of an algorithm: *Introduction to Algorithms* has a typo somewhere in their version of partition, and I didn't want to track it down.

Anyway, through this sort of analysis, you can see—down to the statement—where your bottlenecks are. With a little effort, we could probably bring quick sort's time down to about 25 seconds, which is still eight times the built-in speed. If we really wanted to make an algorithm different than the built-in, we would probably have to resort to making a C-extension anyway, discussed at length in the **perlXS** on-line manual.

Summary of SmallProf

SmallProf is pretty new software, but it has already changed the way I view my debugging for speed. By using **SmallProf** often, you get an intuitive feel for what Perl does fast, and what Perl does slow. There is a really cool chapter in the book *Programming Perl* by Larry Wall, the author of Perl, Tom Christiansen, and Randal Schwartz. (It's the one with the camel on the cover.) It covers different efficiencies you can make. I suggest looking there for more detail.

The chapter gives many efficiency tips. Here are some summarized from that section (there are many more there):

- Array access is faster than hash access.
- Hash access is faster than searching through an array (linear search).
- Short-circuit alternation is faster than regular expressions (most of the time), /a/ || /b/ is faster than /a|b/.

You can see all of these things in action by using **SmallProf**. We have just seen that things that might look fairly innocuous (compares, array accesses) can make a big difference if you lazily throw them around (as I did) in a loop that is called often.

The Perl Compiler

Now, about the Perl compiler. On the face of it, compilers are not the most exciting of programs. They don't actually let you do more. Compilers are concerned with how scripts are packaged, rather than any new functions or features in the language.

However, if you think about it, having a compiler and using it well can give you a lot of associated benefits. With a compiler you can:

1. Eliminate parsing time. Since Perl does not need to parse through all the lines of code after you hit return, scripts longer than 1,000 lines are suddenly much faster to parse than they would have been otherwise.

2. Speed up execution time over interpreted code. This is not much of a deal in the Perl world, because code is already pretty optimized with the current byte code interpreter. However, for some things such as object access, it is a major improvement.

3. Eliminate dependencies. The compiler can create a stand-alone executable for you. It is stand-alone in the sense that you need not have the setup of libraries in the correct place like you usually would with the interpreter.

4. Hide code that can still be executed, although this is a curse as well as a blessing, as I said in the Introduction to this book.

Hence, when Perl got its own compiler (circa **perl5.004**) it was a real plus to the language. The way that the compiler was programmed—as an extension to the language—was also a big boon. Malcolm made it so that you could see how Perl parses its source code, into an operation code tree (or *opcode* tree) which has led to the development of tools that can see "good style" or "bad style" code without actually executing the code itself.

Also, the way that the compiler is programmed allows for many different types of compilation, such as:

1. Compilation as a stand-alone executable. This is the main type of compilation in which a script is turned into a binary executable, which can be run without the need for supporting libraries.

2. Compilation of modules into linkable binary shared objects. Lots of available extensions include **.xs** code, which is really C code that is compiled into an **.so** (shared object) file. And when you say:

```
use Object;
```

the binary libraries are loaded into your Perl script in no time flat. The compiler supports making these **.so** libraries, which cuts down on the loading time of the object you have compiled.

3. Compilation of modules and scripts into byte code. The interface for this is still being worked out, but eventually the Perl compiler will allow you to compile objects into machine-independent byte code. This is much like Java's, except this byte code should be portable anywhere as it doesn't have to worry about competing and incompatible virtual machines. Although the interface for this is not nailed down (we won't cover it here), this is something to watch. Byte code gives you most of the advantages of compiled code (the start-up time is minimal), yet it is just as portable as regular Perl. Again, stay tuned. In fact, I would consider the Perl compiler beta as of the time of this writing.

Usage of the Compiler: The perlcc Front-end

Since Perl supports such a wide variety of platforms (each of which has its own rules about C code and how to compile it), the Perl distribution provides a front-end to the complicated rules that are necessary to perform compilation. This front-end is named **perlcc** (after the Unix c compiler) and it is quite easy to use. @T:First, if you want to get all of the options for **perlcc**, you can say:

```
prompt% perlcc -h
```

or:

```
prompt% perlcc
```

which lists all the options available in compiling programs. Not that this is any big deal; suppose we wanted to compile the calendar program we developed in Chapter 20. We would say:

```
prompt% perlcc calendar.p
```

Then, Perl will go into your **calendar.p** program, parse how the calendar needs to be laid out to perform the compilation, and actually compile **calendar.p** into the program **calendar**. Note that you need a stand-alone C compiler to do this. That way, you can run:

```
prompt% calendar
```

from anywhere the calendar program is installed, without having to worry about having PerlTk installed. This means, of course, that you can distribute the binary by itself, without needing Perl attached.

The second way of compiling using **perlcc** is turn libraries into shared objects. This has the benefit that you can still see what is going on with your application code (your central scripts that use the compiled libraries stay the same) but the resulting shared objects can still have dependencies on other shared objects depending on how it was compiled.

If we wanted to compile the **Tk::Calendar Perl** source code into a shared object, we could have said:

```
prompt perlcc -mod Tk/Calendar.pm
```

Again, this makes an **.so** file, but does not lessen the dependencies of **Tk::Calendar** on the objects it uses, **Tk::Month** and **Tk::Date**. (Note that the shared object type of compilation is not available on Win 32 as of this writing.)

Perl Compiler Caveats

There are two things you should be aware of when using Perl's compiler. First, it does not support all the nuances of Perl syntax. You can do things in Perl such that the code happens at run time, which means that the compiler can't possibly know about it. For example, the following code:

```
my $xx = 2;
LABEL1: print "HERE2!\n";
LABEL2: print "HERE3!\n";
goto "LABEL". $xx;
```

figures out the place where the code will jump at the time it actually does the jumping. This means that Perl does not know where to jump until the exact moment of jump. Perl will warn you about such problems, so you have a chance to change your syntax. In 99.9 percent of the cases, if you are fooling the Perl compiler, your code should probably be changed to something more simple.

Second, note that the compiler is a new piece of software, and hence is somewhat experimental on some systems. The compiler front-end, **perlcc**, will warn you if you try to do something that the compiler does not support on your given platform. It is also a little buggy, which means I have not used it (as much as I could).

Summary of the Compiler

The compiler will be your primary way of enabling your scripts to be passed from machine to machine. Working with an interpreter inevitably leads to dealing with many dependencies, as in when a module is stored in a certain place, which leads to you supporting a directory structure, which leads to your scripts being tied down to a certain location. The compiler frees those dependencies to a large extent. Type `perlcc -oscript script.p`, and see your scripts run by themselves via `script`.

Summary

We covered quite a bit in this chapter:

1. Making your own debuggers.
2. The Perl internal debugger.
3. Coverage testing scripts.
4. Perl profilers that allowed you to do performance testing.
5. The Perl compiler that turns your scripts into executables.

As time goes by, the amount of these tools will expand quite a bit. Perl's success at developing tools to manipulate Perl programs is due to the fact that its debugging/profiling/coverage testing/compiling ability is programmable. All these tools were programmed in Perl itself. This means that each one of the tools listed is extremely versatile, because Perl itself is extremely versatile.

In Chapter 22, we will continue in this vein: talking about how to debug and manipulate your Perl programs. All of the tools in this chapter were fairly generic (you could find them in other languages). There are quite a few techniques that are Perl-specific, though, and which help you debug in ways quite alien to other languages. We will cover these tools next.

Perl Debugging Tips

Perl is a free-form language compared to other languages, and the programming process in Perl tends to be free-form as well. When a Perl script is running, it is also being compiled.

Similarly, when you are designing your application you are inevitably doing some of its programming at the same time. The usual software development life cycle (SDLC) stages tend to blur and/or become compressed with Perl, and you usually do more than one part of the cycle at once. Iterations of the "gather requirements, plan, design, program, test, implement, and mantain" stages tend to come more closely together than in most other languages.

The same is true for debugging Perl programs. We covered the more ordinary tools in the Perl programmer's toolbox in the last chapter: debugger, profiler, coverage tester, compiler. But even here, the "ordinary" tools weren't ordinary at all, because they were built out of Perl itself.

This chapter goes one step further and covers some very Perl-specific debugging techniques that will make your programming life much easier. The purpose of this chapter is to go over these techniques in detail so you can get the most out of your programming time.

You will definitely want to read this chapter if you are unfamiliar with large-scale Perl projects. This chapter covers the gamut of debugging tricks that are not in the on-line documentation, along with examples of their use in real life.

Chapter Overview

Each programming language has its own tips and tricks to obtain maximum efficiency in debugging the language, and Perl is no exception. Perl is just unique in that many of the tips and tricks are integrated into the language itself. Because Perl makes it possible to program your own warnings and errors in modules and objects, the line between programming and debugging gets even thinner.

Hence, this chapter will be a bit of a grab bag. We discuss lots of the hooks and tricks that have surfaced, some of which are very powerful. The chapter consists of the following sections:

1. Tips for error-free programming—includes information such as how to interpret Perl error messages, learning to program Perl with style, and so on.
2. Perl safety guards-includes `use strict`, `use diagnostics`, `-w`, and the new **Lint** module (that comes with the compiler).
3. Stack tracing code-includes `use Carp` and all of its associated functions.
4. Debugging on the fly-includes exception handling, and how it is covered in Perl.
5. Data debugging-covers using **Data::Dumper** and **Tie::Watch** effectively to find data problems.
6. The `-D` option to Perl—what `-D` covers, how to use `-D`, and using the `-D` option to debug regular expressions.
7. Programming your own debugging modules—making a module to capture and retain warnings and fatal errors, and how to catch programming errors via a module that makes a class more strict.

As you can see, this is a scattershot group of topics. So let's take time to orient yourself on how to actually fit all this information together.

Orienting Yourself to Debug-Programming in Perl

Debugging in Perl is really a craft. With a little effort, you can get more useful results than you can with languages such as C or C++, and hence, can make more powerful programs faster than usual.

I have found when programming that the more information that is available about the environment you are working in, the quicker you can track down problems. In many ways, this is a self-evident principle.

Anyone who has programmed in assembly languages knows that it is a major pain when your program says something like `Stack Fault in 0x1233fd`. This is a bare-bones error that reveals absolutely nothing about the surrounding conditions. Did you misalign the stack? Or perhaps there was an overflow in one of the variables?

This error could signal different problems, and you have nothing but your own knowledge to figure out which of these possible causes it could have been. The same thing goes with the mysterious `General Protection Fault` error that every Windows user has experienced. What exactly does `General Protection Fault` mean? One of a trillion different things could be wrong with:

*   Windows (the OS itself).
*   The application layer.
*   Memory leaks in the program itself.

Furthermore, since you probably don't have the source code to Windows, there is no way of telling where the error occurred. Good luck figuring this out!

The key to effective debugging then, is information. When something goes wrong, you want to have information about:

*   The exact place in the program that has the error.
*   The surrounding conditions that may have caused the error.
*   The state of the data when the program had an error.

Since Perl's specialty is manipulating text, you can get tons of information about any error that might occur. It is a simple question of organizing the information you receive.

Now, of course, the first thing you have to do is make your program parse in Perl. This is the point we turn to next.

Tips for Error-Free Programming

Let's assume that you have written a program and need to make it run. What points should you be aware of to make this job easier?

Perl's Error Messages

Point 1: Perl Is Generally Correct When It Tells You Where Your Programs Have Errors, but Not Always

The accuracy of Perl in pinpointing your errors is incredible, given how complicated the language is. Nonetheless, Perl does make mistakes. Take the following program:

```
print FD "Statement1
print FD "Statement #2"
```

Here, Perl correctly diagnoses the problem of not having a parentheses and prints:

```
Bare word found where operator expected at a.p line 4, near "print FD "Statement2"
    (Might be a runaway multi-line "" string starting on line 3)
        (Do you need to predeclare print?)
syntax error at a.p line 4, near "print FD "Statement2"
Can't find string terminator '"' anywhere before EOF at a.p line 4.
```

However, in the following, admittedly contrived, program:

```
1 #!/usr/local/bin/perl5
2 $line = s' ';
3 $print = 1;
4 $summation = 2;
5 $line = ';1';
```

we get the error:

```
String found where operator expected at a.p line 6, at end of line
        (Missing operator before ';
?)
Can't find string terminator "'" anywhere before EOF at a.p line 6.
```

even though the error is actually in line 2. Perl has been fooled by thinking you intended the following, boldface text to be a statement:

```
1 #!/usr/local/bin/perl5
2 $line = s' ';
3 $print = 1;
4 $summation = 2;
5 $line = ';1';
```

To Perl, it looks like there must be another single quote at the end of the whole thing. Likewise, when there are missing brackets:

```
1 #!/usr/local/bin/perl5
2 sub a
3 {
4     print "Subroutine missing bracket!\n";
5
6 sub b
7 {
8 }
```

Perl gives the same type of error, diagnosing that you need a closing bracket at the end of line 8, even though the error really starts at line 3.

There are two ways/tricks of finding exactly where these errors are:

1. If you have an editor such as emacs or vi, and are getting an unmatched parentheses/bracket error, you can use the editor to "bounce" the parentheses against each other. (In vi, this function is **Shift-5**, emacs has an 'auto bounce' mode. Start at the top, and bounce each bracket with each other, looking for mismatches.)

2. You can stick __END__ in the appropriate places, until the error disappears. Take the problem with the mismatched brackets:

```
1 #!/usr/local/bin/perl5
2 sub a
3 {
4     print "Subroutine missing bracket!\n";
5
6 sub b
7 {
8 }
```

Now, to figure out where the error is, we can insert __END__ at specific points:

```
1 #!/usr/local/bin/perl5
2 sub a
3 {
4     print "Subroutine missing bracket!\n";
5
6 __END__
7 sub b
8 {
9 }
```

When we compile this changed program, it says the error is at line 6, instead of line 9. This means that the error must be above line 6. When we move the __END__ up to the next bracket that could possibly mismatch (line 1), we get:

```
1 #!/usr/local/bin/perl5
2 __END__
3 sub a
4 {
5     print "Subroutine missing bracket!\n";
6
7 sub b
8 {
9 }
```

Voilá: the error disappears! Hence, the missing bracket must be between lines 1 and 6. We can use this information to narrow our search area.

Point 2: If You Are getting a Weird Error, the First Thing You Should Do Is Go to perldiag

Let me give you a little advice, although nobody ever really follows it until they get burned. Perl has a wonderfully useful man page called **perldiag**. It gives all the errors you would ever hope to come across with the Perl interpreter. It even includes errors that occur when you run a Perl script but are not the fault of Perl itself.

    perldiag is a treasure trove of debugging tips you should consult often. To show how useful it has been to me, following is an example in which I had a problem that could have been easily solved with **perldiag**.

    Someone asked me why a certain Perl script, wrapped in a shell script, wasn't working. It was giving the following error message when execScript was typed on the command line (execScript was the shell script wrapper):

```
Can't execute perlscript.p
```

The first thing I did was check to see whether execScript was executable. It was. The second thing I did was to check that the right version of Perl was running, by saying:

```
perl -v
```

which gave me 5.003 with EMBED. No problem there. The third thing that I did was to check that **perlscript.p** was in the correct place. It was.

    So, after scratching my head for a bit, I opened up the shell script to see how it was actually executing the Perl script. It said:

```
exec perl5 -S perlscript.p $0 $1
```

Hmm... People who read the chapters on running Perl and Perl Syntax (1 and 2) might recognize this statement as a version of the universal Perl header, the one that can be used to port Perl scripts to almost anywhere without changing the path to Perl in a #! statement. So what was unusual about this?

    It turned out to be the -S. Remove the -S, and the script ran fine. Why? Well, it turned out that the error message:

```
Can't execute perlscript.p
```

was because **perlscript.p**, *$self*, and not the wrapper, had the wrong permissions.

    Usually, when you say perl perlscript.p, Perl ignores what permissions **perlscript.p** has. perl -S perlscript.p overrides that fact.

    Yuck. This was a very subtle bug, and a total waste of debugging time. If I had just swallowed my pride, and went to the error list in **perldiag**, I would have seen the following message:

```
Can't execute %s:
    (F) You used the -S switch but the script to execute could not be found in the
PATH, or at least not with the correct permissions.
```

This message told me exactly what I needed to know, without my having to go through two hours of debugging.

    Hence, **perldiag** is your friend. Every time you have a bug you don't know, your knee-jerk reaction should be to go to this man page.

Point 3: Get to Instinctively Know the Perl Parser

After you get to know the syntax, and above all the foibles behind Perl's syntax, creating and executing a Perl program will be much easier. To this end, Perl comes with a "syntax highlighter" for emacs called **cperl-mode.el**. When you load a Perl file into **cperl-mode.el**, it automatically highlights for you, in different colors or fonts, the functions, matched parentheses, matched brackets, and what not, and makes it infinitely easier for you to learn Perl syntax by heart. Refer to the distribution for more detail; **cperl-mode.el** comes with embedded documentation. The documentation contains many common errors people make, as well as a complete description of what the errors mean. The **perldiag** man page is the key document here.

Because Perl inherited its functionality from almost every computer language on the planet (except COBOL), the **perltrap** man page contains common problems people have coming from certain backgrounds. (For example, If you are a "Cerebral C" programmer, you should be aware that the `else if` C construct is `elsif` in Perl.)

Style Tips

Understanding the previous section can help you compile programs, but does not make up for the time you can waste if you don't follow conventions. This section looks at coding conventions that should save you a lot of pain.

Point 4: Program with Style: perlstyle

Look at, nay memorize, the **perlstyle** documentation page. It gives some very good guidelines for coding, each of which will make your programs less buggy and easier to debug when you have problems.

I personally do not agree with some of the conventions there, but it always pays to have some sort of method to your madness. For example, I like to spread out my code a bit more than **perlstyle** prefers:

```
sub aaa
{
}
```

But I have a reason: I like to see which brackets belong with each other at a glance, and I like to see lots of white space for logic's sake. However, on some occasions I do the opposite:

```
sub aaa {    }
```

especially when there is only one line to a given function. This way, I see all the logic that goes with that subroutine on the *same line*.

The point is that you have conventions and that they seem reasonable to you; and that Perl style gives you plenty of advice about this.

Perl Safety Guards

Having assiduously studied the **perlstyle** man page, you have resolved to code in style, and avoid the spaghetti-like code that comes from not thinking issues through properly. Furthermore, you have gotten lots of practice in writing Perl code efficiently. There are, in general, three types of scripts you will program:

1. Throwaway scripts—meant to be used once, and then discarded.
2. Transition scripts—meant to fulfill a role for a limited amount of time, and then be discarded.
3. Keepers—meant to fulfill a role, and are programmed correctly.

Part of the process in figuring out how much attention you want to pay to style, and how much protection you want for your code, is to figure out the type of script you are dealing with.

If the script is a throwaway, you really don't care about its style. If it is a transition script, you should take a little more care. If your script is a keeper, you avoid bad styles like the plague.

Perl has a few tools to keep you in good style. I call them *safety guards*, and we go over them here. As we said earlier, you will want to use these safety guards in differing amounts depending on whether your script is throwaway, transition, or a keeper.

use strict

`use strict` is a biggie among safety guards, and we have pretty much peppered this book with `use strict` for good reason. Simply put, `use strict` should be in about 90 percent of your code, if not more. Why? Well, it protects you from yourself.

The only place you shouldn't have `use strict` is where you dynamically export variables. Code such as `use Exporter` can't be programmed without soft references. See Chapter 11 for more details on globbing and dynamic exporting of variables.

Because Perl compiles and executes on the fly without checking the correct use of variables, without the aid of `use strict` you are vulnerable to many simple errors. Consider the following pieces of code:

```
Probable Error #1;
$variable = 2;
print $varbiable**2

Probable Error #2;
if ($condition) { my @array = (1,2,3); }
    else { my @array = (1,2,3,4); }
print "@array\n";

Probable Error #3;
my $arrayRef = 'scalar';
print @$arrayRef;

Probable Error #4;
my $scalarRef = 'scalar';
print $$scalarRef;

Probable error #5;
$value = function; # (function meant to be a
                   # function returning a value, but not defined)

Probable error #6;
sub function { &do_stuff; }
$value = function;
```

Each of these probable errors represents a possible run-time, "tear my hair out to the roots" scenario you may go through and probably will, if you don't use `use strict`. Let's look at them more closely.

strict Variables

Consider the first two errors:

```
Probable Error #1;
$variable = 2;
print $varbiable**2

Probable Error #2;
if ($condition) { my $scalar = 1; }
    else { my $scalar = 2; }
print "$scalar";
```

Error #1 illustrates the common mistake of mispelling a variable ($varbiable) and, therefore, making the `print` statement print zero. Error #2 shows a scoping problem. The $scalar variable is created within the `if { }`, and, therefore, the $scalar variable outside the scope is blank.

Both errors are because of the nonstrictness of the variables. `use strict` prevents these errors by forcing the following convention: You must either fully declare a regular variable, namespace included, or declare it as a `my` variable that is correctly scoped. Consider how this prevents the two errors described before. If we say:

```
my $variable = 2;
print $varbiable ** 2;
```

then Perl registers the variable $variable as being a my variable, but then it comes to $varbiable and sees no such reference. Hence, it prints out:

```
Global symbol "varbiable" requires explicit package name at as.p line 5.
```

In other words, you would have to say $package::varbiable instead of $varbiable in order to make this mistake, which isn't likely.

As for the scope error, if we say:

```
if ($condition) { my $scalar = 1; }
    else { my $scalar = 2; }
    print "$scalar\n";
```

then Perl recognizes the fact that the variable $scalar inside the brackets is not the same as the $scalar inside the print. When you try to compile this, Perl again says:

```
Global symbol "condition" requires explicit package name at a.p line 4.
Global symbol "scalar" requires explicit package name at a.p line 6.
```

Perl with use strict warns us of a potential error that we didn't even notice, the fact that condition hasn't been declared with a my, which could bite us later.

strict References

Now let's talk about errors #3 and #4:

```
Probable Error #3;
my $arrayRef = 'scalar';
print @$arrayRef;

Probable Error #4;
my $scalarRef = 'scalar';
print $$scalarRef;
```

Both of these errors are perfectly legal statements in Perl, without use strict. Even though you obviously meant to make $arrayRef an array reference, it ended up a scalar. This is the same with $scalarRef.

Since Perl has the ominous soft references, which are extremely useful 10 percent of the time, this must be legal. But 90 percent of the time, you don't want to use soft references.

Strict references will help you here. They tag the code with the errors:

```
Can't use string ("scalar") as an ARRAY ref while "strict refs" is in use at a.p, line
5.
```

and:

```
Can't use string ("scalar") as a SCALAR ref while "strict refs in use at a.p, line 5
```

This helps a lot, even though this check is made while the program is running, rather than being the compile-time error that strict vars provided. It sends you straight to the source of the error, rather than having the error occur, and you not noticing till two subroutines later, when you find that the certain variable you are tracking is empty.

strict subs

The third type of strict that Perl provides is strict subs. This is demonstrated in the probable errors #5 and #6:

```
Probable error #5;
my $value = function_name;  # (function meant to be a
                            # function returning a value, but not defined)
Probable error #6;
my $value = function_name;
sub function { &do_stuff; }
```

These examples are poor programming style in themselves, but with strict subs they become syntax errors. The first one, $value = function;, is particularly bad, because it could mean two things to Perl:

```
$value = 'function_name';
```

or:

```
$value = function_name();
```

depending on whether or not the function function is defined before or after the statement $value = function;. This has to do with the way Perl parses the program in the first place, and it is a long story why. ("Just say it is because of forward references," one person from the Net says. In a nutshell, Perl doesn't know that function is in fact a function until it sees the sub function { } statement. Enough said.)

This is why $value = function; is a no-no. There is no clarity of intent; this statement says two things at once, and that is a bad thing. Likewise, function could become a future keyword, so you are setting yourself up for errors in the future. Compounding this, you can do it accidentally. Hence, use strict blocks this:

```
Bareword "function" not allowed while "strict subs" in use at a.p line 4.
```

This allows you to clarify, and say what you actually mean, before you do it.

Partial Use of strict

As I said, sometimes you want to have nonstrict variables, nonstrict references, or (although I never have had the need) nonstrict functions. You'll know the time when you come to it. In fact, some of our examples in the object-oriented part of this book needed to turn off strict for the time being.

Should that need ever arise, this is how you do it. If you say:

```
use strict "vars";
```

this directive will make only the variables strict. This means that you must fully declare variables or say my $varbname. Likewise:

```
use strict "refs";
use strict "subs";
```

will only do strict references and strict functions, respectively. You can use the prefix no to turn off strictness, and can do so at the level of the block. For example:

```
1 use strict "vars";
2 my $a = 1;
3 if (defined $a)
4 {
5     no strict "vars";
6     $b = $a;
7 }
```

compiles, even though in line 6, we have not declared $b. no strict "vars" turns off strictness within the brackets, from lines 4–7. If we said in line 8:

```
8 $b = 1;
```

then the code wouldn't have compiled.

use strict *Caveat*

There is only one caveat that you should be aware of when you use use strict, and that is the caveat that goes along with many of the directives.

```
use strict is lexically scoped, not globally scoped.
```

In other words if you say, in the file **a.pm** (containing the class *a*):

```
a.pm
package a;
use strict;
# package a's code.
```

the use strict only covers package a. Likewise, if you then say in the file **b.pm** (containing the class *b*):

```
b.pm
package b;
# package b's code.
```

neglecting to say use strict in package b's code, then class *a*'s use strict will not affect class *b*. Hence, you should make it a rule that your first statement after every package statement or beginning Perl line say:

```
#!/usr/local/bin/perl5
use strict;
```

or:

```
package a;
use strict;
```

And if you are foolish enough to say:

```
{
    use strict;
}
```

well, you should expect trouble. After all, because use strict is lexically scoped, the strictness goes out of scope after the closing bracket.

use strict *Summary*

use strict is your first line of defense against the constant assault of typos and logical mistakes that every programmer makes. Everybody makes these types of mistakes, but the mark of a good Perl programmer over a struggling one is in the way they handle finding these types of errors, and how quick they fix them.

Give yourself a good Perl programming habit and use use strict almost all the time. Only in exceptional circumstances should you neglect it.

The -w Flag and use diagnostics

The first line of defense you have is use strict, but a close second is -w. -w is the warning flag: It warns you against code that may be wrong, but of which you cannot be sure. You will quickly develop a love/hate relationship with -w until you learn instinctively how to write code that avoids -w errors.

Why? Well, many beginning Perl programmers write code and get really discouraged when they either say:

```
perl -w filename;
```

or:

```
#!/usr/local/bin/perl -w
```

for the first time, and their code outputs thousands of warnings to the screen. That is what happened to me the first time I used –w. These warnings are notoriously difficult to get rid of. If you are the verbose type, then you might prefer

```
use diagnostics;
```

instead, because use diagnostics will do the same thing as –w except it is more verbose. For example, –w will give you a warning that looks like:

```
print (...) interpreted as function in line 4.
```

whereas use diagnostics will provide:

```
print (...) interpreted as function in line 4.
    (W) You've run afoul of the rule that says that any list
    operator followed by parenthesis turns into a function,
    with all the list operators arguments found the parentheses.
    See perlop/Terms and List Operators (Leftward)
```

Some people like the longer warnings, and some people think they are redundant. I prefer the longer warnings when working with people new to Perl—after all, look at exactly how much information this is telling you about Perl! It gives you a long explanation of what is going on and a place to find more information on the reasoning about why Perl is put together in a certain way.

On the other hand, if you are running a program that generates 50,000 error messages, you will probably get sick of this rule.

Functionality Provided by –w

What code problems does –w catch? Following, are some of them:

1. Writes and reads on closed and undefined filehandles:

   ```
   print STDERRR "Aha!\n";        # mean STDERR?
   $line = <STDNI>;               # mean STDIN?
   open (FD, "non_existant_file");# open fails, and you neglect to check status
   $line = <FD>;
   ```

2. Writes and reads on closed and undefined sockets:

   ```
   accept(NOTHING, NOBODY);
   connect(NOTHING, $inetadr);
   ```

3. Ambiguous usages and their resolution:

   ```
   print ${map};                  # is this print ${map()} or print $map?
   ```

4. Variables that are used just once:

   ```
   print $sefl;                   # sure its not '$self?'
   ```

5. Undefined variables, and array/hash elements:

```
$scalar = undef; print $scalar
$condition = undef; if ($condition) { do_something();}
$hash{'val'} = 1; print $hash{'vall'};
```

6. System and execute calls that fail because of permission problems and/or nonexistent executables:

```
system("dirr");
system("wrong_permission_file");
```

7. Places where you try to write to a read-only filehandle, or read from a writable filehandle:

```
open(FD, "> writeFile");       # writing to a file
$line = <FD>;                  # reading from that file
```

8. Probable syntax errors, but ones Perl can't be sure about:

```
open FD, "filename" || die;    # should be open(FD, "filename") || die;
                               # or open FD, "filename" or die;
@array['aaa'];                 # Can't use string as array element!
@key = (1,2,3); $hash{@key};   # meant $hash{$key}?
@array[1];                     # not an error, but $array[1] is cleaner
%hash{$key}                    # meant $hash{$key}?
my $a, $b = @_;                # means my ($a), ($b = @_);
if ($a = $b) { do_something;}  # do you mean ==? I *wish* this warning was in C!
$array[0,0,0];                 # should be $array[0][0][0]
```

9. "Void" contexts (where a variable is dropped into nothingness):

```
if ((1,2,3) < (4,5,6))         # means 1 < 4
$aa = ('this','drops','words'); # sets $aa == 'this'
```

10. Redefined subroutines:

```
sub subname { print "HERE!\n"; }
sub subname { print "HERE2!\n"; }
subname();
```

11. Conflicts between strings and numbers:

```
if ('a' < 'b') { }
$a = 'aaa'; $b = 'bbb'; $a <=> $b;
```

12. User-defined warnings:

```
use Carp;
warn "oh dear. it happened again.\n";
```

These are just some of the warnings −w gives you, albeit the main ones. As you can see, they are quite a treasure trove, especially to the new Perl programmer! In fact, I would go so far as to say that, if you are programming correctly, you have debugged about 90 percent of your program if the program runs successfully without warnings.

Overcoming the Not Use −w (or use diagnostics) Barrier

This is a fair warning. If you are not used to it, the −w flag will be a wet blanket at first by always slowing you down, and making your programming go twice as slow as it did before.

Here is the pattern I went through in my encounter with the warning flag.

1. Being unaware of −w: First, I was unaware of −w flag, and I bloodied my nose by making many of the same mistakes that −w could catch over and over again.

2. Trying and rejecting -w: I then heard of -w, and testing the waters, put it in my script. I immediately got disgusted with exactly how many potential errors there were in my script.
3. Acceptance of -w: After a long, hard struggle with my habits, I finally steeled myself to use -w in my programs.

This is the "ignorance, denial, and acceptance" cycle, and I doubt that I'm the only person who has gone through it. The simplest thing to do is skip stages 1 and 2 and go directly to 3. I daresay you will be a much stronger programmer if you learn to program under the constraints that use strict and -w provide.

However, this is easier said than done, because it can be a big discomfort when you are starting out to get rid of warning messages, especially if you think the code is already correct. Next, however, we give some quick ways to get rid of some of the more impertinent warning messages.

Common Warnings and How to Avoid Them

Following are some warnings you will encounter in your Perl programs, and some advice on how to avoid them. But if you get a persistent -w error that you can't get rid of, the best way to get rid of the error is to understand the logic of how Perl is parsing the annoying expression use of unitialized value.

Use of *uninitialized value*

This is an extremely common error, and it occurs when the code:

- Accidentally passes a null value to a subroutine.
- Accidentally accesses a null hash element.
- Otherwise tries to read a null value.

Most of the time, you will be plagued by these errors when you have a subroutine, or method call, and you hand it to other users. In calling your subroutine, they will try your code in ways that you didn't think possible, and report to you exactly the errors they get. It is up to you to use things like -w to debug the errors they bring up.

In all cases, the fix for the use of unitialized value error is the same. Suppose you have a subroutine, that is being passed the variable $variable. The solution is to either put guards, using the keyword defined, that prevent null values from being passed to a subroutine:

```
die if "variable needs to be defined!\n" (!defined $variable);
```

or, put the guard by the variable access itself:

```
$variable =~ m"string" if (defined $variable);
```

or, more kindly, provide a default in case a null value is passed in:

```
$value = (defined $value)? $value : 0;
```

In each case, the trick is to make the guard as unobtrusive as possible. If you need more than one line to make a default, or do a check, chances are you will want to put the guard in a subroutine:

```
$value = (defined $value)? $value : make_default('my_sub', 'value',0);
sub make_default
{
    print
    "
    The subroutine $_[0] took the parameter $_[1]
    in which you passed a null value. Assigning a default of $_[2]!
    ";
    $_[2];
}
```

If you do stuff like this, you not only prevent warnings in your code, you also warn that the other programmers should pass in a value for a given subroutine.

"Ambiguous use of ..." Error

This is a bit of a nasty error, because sometimes you can't get rid of it cleanly, without making use strict complain! For example, suppose you have the following code:

```
print "${map}_show_me_map\n";
```

The reason Perl is complaining is that it doesn't know whether or not ${map} means ${map()} (i.e., that you are taking the function map and turning the value into a variable, or ${map} means $map).

It assumes that you meant ${map} to mean $map (99 percent likely), but it is ugly to have it report this.

However, saying ${"map"} to avoid the error doesn't work! Because now, you are making ${"map"} a symbolic reference, and use strict complains! And if you say:

```
print "$map_show_me_map\n";
```

then you are saying something the opposite of what you originally intended, printing the variable $map_show_me_map. The only answer to this problem is to rename the variable:

```
print "${mapp}_show_me_map\n";
```

Ugly ("sigh"), but you can't have everything.

"%s (...) interpreted as function" Error

This is another weird error that comes up from time to time. It usually happens when you say:

```
(print ("HERE!!!\n"), exit());
```

You have used the (statement1, statement2); form to print stuff and then exit, but Perl is getting confused because of the extra space here. Say:

```
print("HERE!!!\n"), exit();
```

instead.

Other Warnings

The other warnings that Perl's -w provides (useless use of variable in void context, strings interpreted as numbers, etc.) are fairly straightforward. Getting them usually stems from carelessness or from a misunderstanding of Perl-ish logic. For example:

```
if ('x' < 'y') { print "HERE!!\n"; }
```

will generate the error:

```
Argument "x" isn't numeric in lt at ... line ...
```

Here, the -w flag points out to you that < is supposed to work on numbers and numbers alone. The correct statement should be:

```
if ('x' lt 'y') { print "HERE!!\n"; }
```

If you pay attention to these types of warnings, and correct them constantly, you will learn Perl's logical rules a lot faster than going it alone.

Warnings –w Does Not Cover

Once a Perl programmer finds and starts using –w, there is a tendency to overcompensate, especially if that user was reluctant to start using –w in the first place. In other words, the tendency is to think that a combination of use strict and –w will solve all the ills of Perl-kind. However, there are a few errors –w does not cover, and you should be aware of them:

1. Mismatching numbers of arguments— –w does not warn you of errors that look like:

    ```
    $scalar = (1,2);

    subroutine($a,$b,$c);
    sub subroutine { my ($a, $b) = @_; }
    ```

    where the number of arguments are different. In this case, the boldface elements (1, $c) will be dropped.
2. Undefined variables inside an if clause— –w does not warn you that:

    ```
    $self->{'key'} = 1;
    if ($self->{'ky'}) { print "HERE!\n"; }
    ```

    has a blank element, ($self->{'ky'}). This is a real problem with objects, and we will address it later.
3. Misusing hashes as arrays, and arrays as hashes— –w does not point out that:

    ```
    %hash = (1,2,3,4);
    function(%hash);
    sub function { my (@array) = @_; print "@array\n"; }
    ```

    will scramble the elements in %hash, and have an indeterminate order.

Finally, –w does not point out several logical errors when the programmer gets really fancy! As we said, you can have your code approach the level of "code noise" (with more special characters than there are letters). If this happens, all bets are off. Don't do this unless you feel really fancy.

Finding the Source of Warnings

Finally, I might note that it is sometimes more difficult to find the source of the warning than it is to fix it. This is especially true of warnings found in subroutines, because it is usually the case that the bug is found inside the calling code rather than inside the subroutine itself.

We saw this earlier. When you say:

```
1 $a = undef;
2 subroutine($a);
3 sub subroutine { my ($a) = @_; print "$a\n"; }
```

and use –w, this will point the error out in line 3 (i.e., in the subroutine) rather than the true source of the error, which is line 2 (the code that called the subroutine).

To get a more descriptive error that points to line 2, you will have to redefine the __WARN__ signal handler. We talk about this later in the chapter, after we cover stack traces. Read stack traces first, and then see the section "Debugging on the Fly" for more details.

The Lint Module

Let's go over the **Lint** module, which has the potential to make some serious advances in the process of actually finding errors before they bite you in Perl. It is relatively new, and has already spawned some extremely useful features.

What does **Lint** actually mean? Lint is named after the Unix C program of the same name, which in turn is named after the pieces of fluff that embed themselves inside clothing. (According to the on-line computer dictionary at *http://wagner.princeton.edu/foldoc*, that is. Kind of boring, in comparison to some of the etymologies you can find there.)

The job of the **Lint** module is to "vacuum" the bugs that dwell inside your Perl code. These bugs form two cases:

1. Items that are not obviously bugs: bugs that can't be caught with `use strict` because they might have genuine uses.
2. Items that you want to catch at compile time rather than run time: This excludes using -w, because -w is a run-time check.

To fill in this gap—warnings that aren't necessarily errors but need to be found at compile-time—Malcolm Beattie developed the **Lint** module in combination with the compiler. It is basically a programmable module with an interface on the way the Perl interpreter works. (This is done through a module called **B.pm**: B stands for *back-end*. To understand **B.pm**, you must understand how the components of Perl are built. See **perlguts**, and the book *Advanced Perl Programming* for more detail.)

Usage of the Lint Module

To use the **Lint** module, you run it much like you ran the debugger in the last chapter. You simply say the following:

```
perl -MO=Lint perl_script.p
```

to check for **Lint** warnings in your program. Perl will then list the warnings it finds, and then return you to the prompt. Usually, **Lint** checks your main program only for warnings. To turn on debug checks for all modules included in your program, you can say:

```
perl -MO=Lint,-u perl_script.p          # VAPORWARE?
```

This is my preferred method of checking my scripts, because it is a compile-time check, and it doesn't hurt to see all the warnings that are generated in modules. If you want to be more selective, you can say something like:

```
perl -MO=Lint,-uMyModule,MyModule2 perl_script.p
```

to selectively cover the script **Prl_script.p**, and the modules **MyModule** and **MyModule2**.

Lint provides quite a few warnings. If you want to selectively turn them on and off, you can say:

```
perl -MO=Lint,coverage perl_script.p
```

to only turn the `coverage` test on, and ignore the rest of the subroutines.

The only thing left then, is to know what options the **Lint** module has available. This is a rapidly growing topic, but the current ones are listed next.

Lint Debugging Checks

Lint has existed only for a couple of months as of this writing, but the following tests have already been incorporated into its interface. I list them next, each with a small explanation of how it can be so helpful in real life.

The undefined-subs Test

This is perhaps the most useful of the **Lint** checks, and it fills in a great hole that existed prior to the **Lint** module. This hole can be demonstrated quite vividly. Suppose you had the code shown in Listing 22.1.

Listing 22.1
`scaletest.p`

```
1   scale1();
2   scale22();
3
4   sub scale1
5   {
6        print "do re mi fa sol la ti..";
7        sleep(36000);
8   }
9   sub scale2
10  {
11    print "do\n";
12  }
```

When you run this code, you will get a run that looks like:

```
prompt% perl scaletest.p
do re mi fa sol la ti..
Undefined subroutine &main::_scale22 called at scaletest.p line 3;
```

Because you hit line 7, you waited 10 hours just to see that your program bombed before completing its task-all because there was an extra digit on the end of _scale2! This was one of my biggest pet peeves with Perl, because it meant that you needed to be very careful not to make a syntax error in a method name (before **Lint**, that is). Now, when you say:

```
prompt% perl -MO=Lint,undefined-subs a.p
```

or:

```
prompt% perl -MO=Lint a.p
```

you get a warning:

```
Warning: Undefined subroutine &main::_scale22 to be called at scaletest.p line 3!
```

immediately, before you actually start the script! Much better (and 10 hours saved).

You might also notice that you can have similar problems occur with methods (either class methods or object methods). If you say:

```
Class->method();
```

and `method` doesn't exist either in `Class` or in `Class`' parents through `@ISA`, you have problems. However, this option finds these errors quite nicely. When Perl gets strong typing (which may be true by the time this book is released), you will be able to say:

```
1 my Dog $spot = new Dog('chihuahua');
2 $spot->wooff();
```

and have line 2 flagged as an error as well, since you probably meant "woof." (Line 1 designates that `$spot` is always going to be a dog, so you can make certain assumptions about him.)

The context Test

The 'context' test simply flags down warnings that look something like:

```
$length = length(@array);
$length = @bar;
```

in which you are converting to a scalar from an array, say, to find the length of it. I'm not too fond of this test, because I am always saying statements like:

```
if (@a > @b) {   }
```

but it is helpful for new Perl folks who constantly run into the following trap:

```
sub
my_sub { my $arg = @_; }
```

(which makes $arg equal to the length of @_, not the first element in @_) when programming subroutines. If you want to get rid of the warning, you can say:

```
my $length = scalar(@array);
```

implicit-read, implicit-write

Again, these two tests get rid of common, new Perl programmer mistakes: dealing with $_ unintentionally. For example:

```
my $value = m"value";
```

does not look for the pattern value inside the variable $value. Instead, it looks inside $_ and sets $value equal to '' or 1, depending on whether this match found anything. This is much to the dismay of new Perl programmers. Likewise:

```
$value = s"value"other_value"g;
```

does a substitution of value for other value on $_ rather than value, and again trashes the value of $value (setting it to the number of times the string value was substituted for other_value inside $_). Saying the following:

```
prompt% perl -MO=Lint script.p
```

prevents these errors.

Dollar-Underscore

The dollar-underscore option looks for places where $_ is said explicitly, such as:

```
$_ = 1;
```

or implicitly inside print, like:

```
print, "Hi there!\n";
```

private-names

Finally, there is one more variable we cover: private-names. private-names gives you a gentle reminder of when you are using method names outside the scope in which they were intended.

For example, if you define a package as:

```
package A;
sub _function1 {}
sub _function2 {}
1;
```

and then someone making a script goes ahead and uses the private functions in a script, as in:

```
script.p
use A;

my $object = new A();
$object->_function1();
```

then that person is breaking your implicit rule that the function was in fact private. To warn of such potentially dangerous behavior, you can use the `private-names` routine. When you say:

```
prompt% perl5 -MO=Lint.pm,private-names script.p
```

then Perl will emit a warning, like:

```
Warning! The function _function1() is a private function, used in a non-private
context!
```

This especially helps on large projects, where you need to insure internal privacy rules.

Future Directions for Lint

Those are the only options currently available for **Lint**, because of how young it is. However, the situation may be vastly different by the time you read this sentence, so **Lint.pm** is a module to watch.

Because Lint is programmable—much like the debugger facilities in Perl (see Chapter 21)—one may soon be able to enforce a coding standard much stricter than one can do today, simply by programming a **Lint**-like module to warn about certain types of syntax. Here are some directions I would like to see **Lint** take in future versions:

1. Simple usage. The **Lint** module could use a simplified front-end, much like when you say:

   ```
   prompt% perl -d script.p
   ```

   you run the debugger. Perhaps an `-L` flag could be created, one that links the **Lint** module in, so you could say:

   ```
   prompt% perl -L script.p
   ```

   to get the desired, **Lint**-ing effect.
2. Customizability. The Perl debugger has a **.perldb** file that lets you set debugger commands. I'd like to see a **.perllint** file that lets you pick and choose which **Lint** warnings you want suppressed, as well as modules that you either always want to check, or always don't want to check.
3. Ease of programmability. Right now, to program your own **Lint** module, you need to specify it to the compiler back-end, something like:

   ```
   prompt% perl -MO=MyLint
   ```

   and know quite a bit about the internal workings of the compiler. I'd like to see the same usage for the **Lint** module as for the debugger, where you would say something like:

   ```
   prompt% perl -L:MyLint file.p
   ```

   which would then run the **Lint::MyLint** module on file **file.p**.
4. Adding an `ignore` flag. No matter how much one tries, one is not going to get rid of all the warnings that **Lint** generates (nor does one want to). Therefore, I would like to see an option for putting a `# IGNORE` comment around items that I know are warnings. This would save time tracing down false warnings.

5.   Auxilliary programming tools. Because **Lint**, and other "back-ends," are directly accessing how Perl is putting together your source code into a compilable program, it now becomes possible to build any number of tools that parse Perl programs themselves. Tools that make visual representations of your scripts are no longer out of the question. You could make a Perl program to automatically generate a functional diagram of your code, for instance. Other tools, such as Perl-aware editors and Perl project builders are not out of the question, and a visual Perl has become.

In short, **Lint** is new software and can be expanded quite a bit.

Summary of `use strict`, `-w`, `use diagnostics`, and `Lint`

The safety nets `-w`, `use strict`, `use diagnostics`, and the **Lint** module are essential tools that should be in the toolbox of every Perl programmer. These tools point out simple potential problems with code, such as:

1. Mistyped variables.
2. Undefined variables.
3. Code logic errors.
4. Assorted other errors.

All serious Perl programs should be warning-proof and `use strict`. In addition, you should run all serious Perl programs through:

```
prompt% perl -MO=Lint,-u
```

to point out dangling subroutine references, misused contexts, and so on. These four tools provide as much support as you can reasonably expect to get from automatic tools. The next level of error checking comes from items you add to the body of your code, such as stack tracing (next) or exception handling.

Pinpointing Errors: Stack Traces with *use Carp*

Suppose you have some complicated code, one with a fairly deep calling tree that looks something like Figure 22.1.

Figure 22.1
Usage Tree for
Complicated
Perl Code

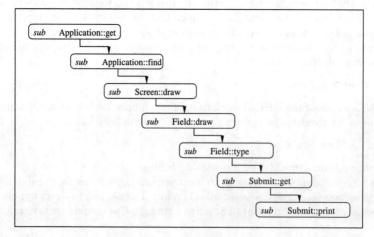

In other words, module **Application** uses module **Screen**, which uses module **Field**, which uses the module **Submit**. Now suppose a bug occurs in **Application**, but the source of the bug is in **Submit**. Let's say that the code responsible looks something like:

```
Submit.pm
1 sub print
2 {
3 ### code skipped.
4     if ($wrong_argument)
5     {
6          die "You can't pass the SEND parameter to the function 'print'!";
7     }
8 }
```

Now what happens when line 6 gets hit? Well, Perl dutifully exits the code, saying something like:

```
You can't pass the SEND parameter to the function 'get'! at line 6
```

but the source of the error is not in **Submit.pm**, it is in **Application.pm**! Hence, this code is next to useless. It points out, that yes, there was an error, but you will spend the next five hours traipsing through the code, trying to find where the real error is located.

What to do about this? Well, because the true error lies somewhere up the call chain, we need to somehow see the path Perl used to actually get to the module **Submit.pm**. In other words, we need what is called a *stack trace*.

How to get this stack trace? Well, remember the function caller(); caller's purpose was to give varying types of stack traces, and we can use that here.

Perl has four very helpful wrappers around caller() that you may want to use instead of directly calling caller(). They are carp(), cluck(), confess(), and croak(). All these routines are included in source code by saying:

```
use Carp;
```

at the beginning of any module or script that uses them. Let's look at each of them and see what they will do for you.

carp()

carp() is the least intrusive function of them all. It prints out the stack trace from the tip of the trace (where the carp call actually resides) to the point at which Perl enters the package itself. For example, suppose the stack trace of the complicated code given earlier looked something like:

```
Application::get() calls:
    Application::find() calls:
        Screen::draw() calls:
            Field::draw() calls:
                Field::type() calls:
                    Submit::get() calls
                        Submit::print()
```

in which each function calls the function on the following line. If Submit::print() had in it:

```
1     if ($wrong_argument)
2     {
3         die "You can't pass the SEND parameter to the function 'print'!";

4     }
```

and the user indeed had a "`$wrong argument`" so that the code was executed, then `carp` would display something like:

```
Submit::print called at Submit.pm line 54
Submit::get called at Submit.pm line 30
```

In other words, `carp` stops the trace at the point where the module **Submit.pm** is entered, printing the trace from the bottom up so to speak. The code continues executing, exactly as if you did a `print`.

Carp thus acts as a "signpoint function"—not supplying an overwhelming amount of information, just printing it out to the screen as a warning.

cluck()

`cluck()` is exactly like `carp()`, except that `cluck` goes through the entire stack trace. Given the same calling tree:

```
Application::get() calls:
    Application::find() calls:
        Screen::draw() calls:
            Field::draw() calls:
                Field::type() calls:
                    Submit::get() calls
                        Submit::print()
```

cluck() prints out:

```
Submit::print called at Submit.pm line 54
Submit::get called at Submit.pm line 30
Field::type called at Field.pm line 65
Field::draw called at Field.pm line 144
Screen::draw called at Screen.pm line 11
Application::find called at Application.pm line 65
Application::get called at Application.pm line 42
```

Hence, it prints the entire stack up to the root, and then continues with the program. This is useful for tracing the logic behind convoluted programs: simply insert a `cluck()` every once in a while to keep the program honest, and so that you don't lose track of the logic.

Note

One more thing; You don't get *cluck* by default when you say use **Carp**. You must export *cluck* manually. You need to say:

```
use Carp qw(cluck);
```

because of concerns in the Perl development community of exporting extra functions (cluck is a newcomer).

---

croak()

`croak()` is the fatal version of `carp()`. In other words, given the calling tree:

```
Application::get() calls:
    Application::find() calls:
```

```
        Screen::draw() calls:
            Field::draw() calls:
                Field::type() calls:
                    Submit::get() calls
                    Submit::print()
```

`croak ()` prints out:

```
    Submit::print called at Submit.pm line 54
    Submit::get called at Submit.pm line 30
```

and it dies. This is good for places where you are debugging an object or module, and are sure that any errors you get will fall inside the module itself.

confess()

Finally, we come to my favorite, `confess()`, which acts as a catch-all procedure, and will save you hours, especially when you pass the code to other people to use.

```
    confess() is the fatal version of cluck(). Given the calling tree:
     Application::get() calls:
        Application::find() calls:
            Screen::draw() calls:
                Field::draw() calls:
                    Field::type() calls:
                        Submit::get() calls
                        Submit::print()
```

`confess()` prints out the entire tree down to the point at which `confess` is hit:

```
    Submit::print called at Submit.pm line 54
    Submit::get called at Submit.pm line 30
    Field::type called at Field.pm line 65
    Field::draw called at Field.pm line 144
    Screen::draw called at Screen.pm line 11
    Application::find called at Application.pm line 65
    Application::get called at Application.pm line 42
```

and then it kills the program.

I cannot stress how much `confess()` contributes to making Perl a scalable language. Without confess(), making a program with more than one level of depth is treacherous, and the level of maintenance you will expend in order to maintain your applications will mushroom.

In fact, I would go so far as to say that you always want to use `confess` in your modules (instead of `die` or `croak`). You cannot have too much information in debugging a module, and it is better to have more than less.

Summary of use Carp

Perl has given you (as a gift with the standard distribution) a great tool for scaling up your programs, and finding where elusive bugs lie. This is the module `Carp`, and it provides the following four functions:

- `carp()`—which acts like `print()` but prints out a mini-stack trace.
- `cluck()`—which acts like `print()` but prints out a full stack trace.
- `croak()`—which acts like `die()` but prints out a mini-stack trace.
- `confess()`—which acts like `die()` but prints out a full stack trace.

Of these, `cluck()` and `confess()` are most useful, because they give you the most information. They will save you a great deal of time. If you are a Perl programmer who hasn't heard of or used them, then you will wonder how you ever coded without them once you do.

Debugging on the Fly: Finding Problems Dynamically

You will want to read this section if you are involved in large Perl projects. In any large project, 10 percent of the errors you encounter come from out of the blue. An error hits because of an unforeseen test case, a logic error, or a physical error.

If you do not catch these errors while they occur, they will never be corrected, which is totally unacceptable. The designers and programmers of Perl should be congratulated that they found a solution; it was elegant, and it saved a lot of time.

We talked about functions that provide a stack trace, and warning messages that come out of -w. Wouldn't it be great if these two concepts were combined? After all, since most warnings come out of functions, and the culprit is actually found in the code that calls these functions, there seems to be good reason for making something that can catch a stack trace for unplanned errors.

So it was done. Perl lets you redefine the logic that happens when a fatal error occurs or a warning occurs. In doing so, Perl provides a simple way to track down a bevy of problems. We go over how to do this next.

%SIG, $SIG{'__WARN__'} and $SIG{'__DIE__'}

We have seen %SIG before. %SIG is Perl's special hash used to trap signals from the operating system. The classic example is:

```
$SIG{INT} = sub { "Ouch!!!!\n"; die };
```

which means if Perl gets a break signal (someone hits **Control-C**), then Perl will die with the message Ouch!, instead of the regular, more jerky method of simply returning a prompt.

Usually, signals are reserved for places where the operating system sends you a message. In Perl, there is an additional twist: *You can have signals that come from the program itself—either warnings or errors.*

These special signals are $SIG{'__WARN__'} and $SIG{'__DIE__'}.

$SIG{'__DIE__'}

Let's look at how we might handle trapping errors that are fatal, but unplanned. Consider the following code:

```
use Carp;
$SIG{'__DIE__'} = sub { confess "@_"; };
```

and see how this can help you in your fight against bugs that come up in run time. A good example of a run time bug is when you accidentally use a hash reference as an array reference. The following code, for example, will die unexpectedly:

```
1 $hashref = {};
2 print @$hashref;
3 print "Will never get Here!!\n";
```

This will never get to line 3. Instead, at line 2, you will unceremoniously get the error:

```
Not an ARRAY reference at a.p line 4.
```

What happens in line 2 is called an *exception*, and it will make your life interesting. An exception is one of those errors I mentioned earlier that come out of the blue. Either the user pressed **Control-C**, or, as before, we came across a piece of data that should have been an array reference, but turned out to be a hash reference.

Consider, again, what happens if this is buried deep inside your code:

```
Application::get() calls:
    Application::find() calls:
        Screen::draw() calls:
            Field::draw() calls:
                Field::type() calls:
                    Submit::get() calls
                        Submit::print()
```

Suppose the offending code that causes the error is in **Application::get()**, and the actual error code is in **Submit::print()**. Then this error won't be most helpful. What we need is a way to catch the error, and print out something other than:

```
Not an ARRAY reference at Submit.pm line 54.
```

In languages such as C++, this is a rather complicated affair. You define a `try { } catch { }` function per class that knows how to handle the errors it "catches."

Again, in Perl, something like:

```
use Carp;
$SIG{'__DIE__'} = sub { confess "@_"; };
```

will suffice. Now, instead of calling the default signal handler, as soon as you hit the statements:

```
Submit.pm
53 $hashref = {};
54 print @$hashref;
55 print "Will never get Here!!\n";
```

you will get the statements:

```
Submit::print called at Submit.pm line 54
Submit::get called at Submit.pm line 30
Field::type called at Field.pm line 65
Field::draw called at Field.pm line 144
Screen::draw called at Screen.pm line 11
Application::find called at Application.pm line 65
Application::get called at Application.pm line 42
```

This process is called *exception handling*. Try it in your own applications! This type of information is invaluable in tracing down exactly where errors lie in your program. Ninety-nine percent of the time, you won't need something more complicated than:

```
use Carp;
$SIG{'__DIE__'} = sub { confess "@_"; };
```

If you do need something more complicated (a `try, catch` mechanism, for example), trust me—it will soon be there.

$SIG{'__WARN__'}

So far, so good. $SIG{'__DIE__'} was used to catch fatal errors. Now, lets use $SIG{'__WARN__'} to catch pesky warnings.

Sick of having thousands of warnings thrown out to the screen, where they whiz past, doing absolutely no good? Well, simply add the following signal handler to your scripts:

```
1  use Carp
2  use FileHandle;
3  $SIG{'__WARN__'} = \&warnHandler;
4
5  sub warnHandler
6  {
7      my $fd = new FileHandle("> $0.log") || die "Couldn't open $0.log!\n";
8      my $text = Carp::longmess(@_);
9    print $fd $text;
10     close($fd);
11 }
```

What does this do? Well, it assigns the __WARN__ handler to be the function &warnHandler. Hence, when you get the warning:

```
Use of unitialized value at Submit.pm line 60
```

Perl calls the warnHandler function, sets @_ to be the warning message's value (Use of..), opens a file (the name of your process plus the appendage log), and then prints (in gory detail) the whole stack trace of the warning:

```
Submit::print called at Submit.pm line 59
Submit::get called at Submit.pm line 30
Field::type called at Field.pm line 65
Field::draw called at Field.pm line 144
Screen::draw called at Screen.pm line 11
Application::find called at Application.pm line 65
Application::get called at Application.pm line 42
```

This means you have a trail of breadcrumbs you can mull over to find the source of your problems.

You may want to go farther than this. You may want to sort the errors, and make a log for each package you encounter. You may want to e-mail the trace to yourself so you need not be dependent on the people who use your code to tell you of the problems.

There are hundreds of things you can do to insure that your final product is solid, reliable, and capable of being more sophisticated. The better the foundation for your code, and the more hooks you have, the more cool things you can do.

Successful Data Debugging: `Data::Dumper()` and `Tie::Watch()`

As said above, the more data you have about a bug, the quicker you can kill it. To that end, there is an essential Perl module, included on the accompanying CD, called **Data::Dumper()**, which will make your Perl programming life much easier.

Data::Dumper()'s purpose in life is printing out data structures. No matter how complicated your data structures are, no matter how dense, how intertwined, what type they are, whatever: If they are legal in Perl, you can print them out by saying:

```
use Data::Dumper;
print Dumper($varb);
```

use Data::Dumper gives you the function Dumper() by exporting it into your current namespace. Here, $varb is any legal Perl variable. If you said something like:

```
$a = {1 => [1,2,3,4], 2 => $a->{1}};
print Dumper($a);
```

Perl will dutifully print out your data structure for you:

```
$VAR1 = {
          1 => [
                 1,
                 2,
                 3,
                 4
               ],
          2 => $VAR1->{1}
        };
```

Note two things about this example. First, the output that comes out of Dumper() is perfectly legal Perl code. Hence, if you printed this into a file and then ran that file, it would recreate $a as it was when it was "Dumped."

Hence, Dumper() is a boon for regression testing, where you are trying to come up with tests that decide whether or not your code is behaving correctly. If you say:

```
if (Dumper($var1) ne Dumper($var2)) { print "Test failed!\n"; }
```

then this compares the data structure $a with the data structure $b point for point. If they are any different, the strings from Dumper() will be different, and the test will fail.

Second, note that Dumper() successfully recreates when a data structure references itself. If you said

```
$a = {1 => [1,2,3,4]};
$a->{2} = $a->{1};
```

then this is subtly different than:

```
$a = {1 => [1,2,3,4], 2=> [1,2,3,4]};
```

In the first case, if you change $a->{1}, you also change $a->{2}, whereas in the second example, $a->{1} is separate from $a->{2}.

Dumper() and Debugging Objects

Dumper() is also very astute at debugging objects. Since objects are simple references in Perl, you can say something like:

```
my $object = new ComplicatedObject('arguments');
print Dumper($object);
```

and Dumper() will slice through the object like hot butter, displaying all the internal members of that object! For example, remember our first object, the clock? Well, if you said:

```
my $object = new Clock();
print Dumper($object);
```

it would print out:

```
$VAR1 = bless( {
                 time => 868147042
               }, 'Clock' );
```

showing you not only the data in the class, but also the fact that it is a clock.

C++ programmers may be cringing at this thought, as it "breaks encapsulation" of the object, but think about it for a minute:

1. When you say Dumper($object) to get data like this, you are not affecting the object in any way.

2. You need not write a bunch of routines for debugging. `Dumper()` will do most all you need.

3. This approach goes hand in hand with rapid development.

It is perfectly reasonable to use `Dumper` this way, to reach in and see the guts of objects. If anything, it makes the debugging and improvement of these objects easier.

Tie::Watch

Finally (for this section), we will consider the module **Tie::Watch,** which also makes tracking down data problems very easy. We already created an object called **WarnHash** in the chapter on inheritance. This module warned us when a hash changed one of its values. **Tie::Watch** takes this logic to its natural conclusion, letting you watch the way that any of your data changes.

In other words, let Perl do the hard work, and sit back; when things change, you then decide on whether the change is a bug. For example, in Chapter 22 we used the debugger to track down a problem in our heap sort algorithm. We could have used **Tie::Watch** instead. We could have programmed a test harness as in Listing 22.2.

Listing 22.2
tietestharness1.p

```
1  use Tie::Watch;
2
3  require "wrongheap.p";
4  my @array = (14, 12, 144, 55, 1, 910);
5  my $watch = new Tie::Watch(-variable => \@array, -store => \&store);
6
7  print "@array\n";
8
9  sub store
10 {
11     my ($tie, $key, $value) = @_;
12     $tie->Store($key, $value);  # does the store for us…
13     print "Storing value :$value: into index :$key:\n";
14 }
```

In line 5, you set a subroutine to "watch" when a given array value is stored. The callback subroutine `store` is called each time somebody does something such as:

```
@store = (1);
$store[1] = 2;
```

then the subroutine in line 9 is called. Because `heapsort` does so much in the way of switching elements around, we should see a lot of activity when we run this. Following is the output I got when running it:

```
Storing value :14: into key :0:
Storing value :12: into key :1:
Storing value :144: into key :2:
Storing value :55: into key :3:
Storing value :1: into key :4:
Storing value :910: into key :5:
Storing value :144: into key :5:
Storing value :910: into key :2:
Storing value :12: into key :3:
Storing value :55: into key :1:
Storing value :14: into key :2:
Storing value :910: into key :0:
```

```
Storing value :14: into key :5:
Storing value :144: into key :2:
Storing value :: into key :0:
Storing value :910: into key :6:
```

The second to the last line is where something is going wrong. Also notice that we are storing a 910 into element 6, whereas there are only five elements in the array that we are sorting. So we must track this down, where the first "fetch" of element 6 happens. So we add a `fetch` function to our test harness, as in Listing 22.3.

Listing 22.3
tietestharness2.p

```
1  use Tie::Watch;
2
3  require "wrongheap.p";
4  my @array = (14, 12, 144, 55, 1, 910);
5  my $watch = new Tie::Watch(-variable => \@array,
6                             -store => \&store, -fetch => \&fetch);
7
8 print "@array\n";
9
10  sub store
11 {
12     my ($tie, $key, $value) = @_;
13     $tie->Store($key, $value);  # does the store for us…
14     (print ("Storing value :$value: into index :$key:\n"), cluck(@_))
15                                             if ($value eq '');
16 }
17 sub fetch
18 {
19     my ($tie, $key) = @_;
20     my $value = $tie->Fetch($key);
21     ( print ("————————————————\n",
22       "Fetching the value :$value: out of index:$key:\n"), cluck(@_))
23                                             if ($value eq '');
24     return ($value);
25 }
```

The `fetch` function now prints out the values fetched from the array if the value of the element so happens to be `''` (an error). We have also added a `trace` (so we see exactly what has called what), and restricted `store` to outputting in case of an error.

If we run this now, we get something like:

```
Fetching the value :: out of index:6:

Tie::Watch::Array=ARRAY(0xb991c) 6
at /home/ed/perl5.005/install/lib/site_perl/Tie/Watch.pm line 329

    Tie::Watch::callback('Tie::Watch::Array=ARRAY(0xb991c)', '-fetch', 6) called at
/home/ed/perl5.005/install/lib/site_perl/Tie/Watch.pm line 505

    Tie::Watch::Array::FETCH('Tie::Watch::Array=ARRAY(0xb991c)', 6) called at
wrongheap.p line 48

    main::heapify('ARRAY(0x103fbc)',2,'SCALAR(0xb1df4)') called at
wrongheap.p line 33
```

```
    main::build_heap('ARRAY(0x103fbc)', 'SCALAR(0xb1df4)') called at
wrongheap.p line 12

main::heapsort('ARRAY(0x103fbc)') called at tietestharness2.p
```

This is the first time we have fetched the value '' out of the index key 6, so this list of lines should contain our error. We just need to track backward. Is the error in Tie::Watch (329 or 505);? No. Is the error in the FETCH? Well, the corresponding line is:

```
$largest = $right if (($right <= $$heapsize) &&
                      ($array->{$right} > $array->{$largest}));
```

So in this case, either $right or $largest is 6, because these are the two accesses that are made. Look back, and see that **main::heapify** was called with the arguments:

```
    main::heapify('ARRAY(0x103fbc)',2,'SCALAR(0xb1df4)') called at
wrongheap.p line 33
```

so it must be one of these arguments that is causing problems.

At this time, we have pinpointed our problem to one statement. It shouldn't be that hard to track down now. Using **Tie::Watch** alone seldom finds problems. Instead, it gives you a ballpark in which to look for bugs. You need not search through all your code; given the context, and the area where the bugs are happening, you can narrow your search and then concentrate your efforts using the debugger.

TIEDARRAY Support is relatively new, so in order to make **Tie::Watch** work corrects with arrays, I suggest installing the website, or **CPAN** version of Perl, and NOT the one on the CD.

Note

Summary of Successful Data Debugging

We covered two of the most useful tools for tracking down data problems: **Tie::Watch** and **Data::Dumper**. Perl programmers are infinitely innovative when it comes to making new modules to track down problems, so you might want to check **CPAN** for new developments, or talk on *comp.lang.perl.misc* to discuss new ideas for data debugging.

The Debugging Flag (-D)

The debugging flag is a bit of an odd duck, but it really is helpful if you get stuck on debugging unusual problems. This is especially true of difficult problems that sometimes are not your fault. -D is a flag you can supply to a Perl script, which assumes you have debugging turned on in your script.

As we said in Chapter 1, to get -D, you must make a "debug" version of the Perl executable. If you have not done so already, go to that chapter, and do this. You don't want to have the debug version of Perl as a default. It makes too much of a demand on computer resources.

We give a short overview of how -D is used next.

Values for -D

Once you have the debugging executable, realize what it gives you. If you have compiled the debugging executable correctly, you get what is shown in Table 22.1.

Table 22.1

Number	Letter	What the Option Does
1	p	Shows exactly how your Perl program is parsed (good if you are a fan of lex and yacc)
2	s	Shows exactly what is on the 'stack' at a given time
4	l	Same as *s*, but labeled clearly
8	t	Low-level trace of execution
16	o	Shows how your object methods are traced (good for debugging inheritance)
32	c	Shows conversions from strings to numbers (not that useful, use -w instead)
64	P	Shows preprocessor command. Anachronism. (Nobody uses #ifdef, #endif, #define, etc. anymore in Perl)
128	m	Memory trace. Shows memory usage in gory detail (good as a last refuge if you have a memory leak)
256	f	Shows how formats are processed. Good if you have a format that just doesn't quite work
512	r	Regular expression parse (this section)
1024	x	Syntax tree generator (shows the results of the parse in option -Dp)
2048	u	Shows tainting checks (tainting is an option that occurs in Unix when you are running with setuid or setgid bits set on. See **perlsec** for more detail
4096	L	Used to show memory leaks. Compile with make pureperl or make quantperl, or make purecovperl instead
8192	H	Shows exactly how your hashes are stored. For Perl debuggers only

**Table 22.1
(continued)**

Number	Letter	What the Option Does
16384	X	Shows a summary of memory allocation (the "scratchpad"). Much like -Dm but in summary detail
32768	D	"Cleaning up," shows what steps Perl takes between the end of executing your script, and when it returns to the prompt

If you want to get into actually changing the Perl source code itself, these flags, are invaluable, because they give (in great, gory detail) everything that the Perl binary is doing.

You can also use these flags to debug your programs. To actually use these flags, you have two choices: you can call your program with the flag -D plus the options you want:

```
prompt%  perl -DrX script.p
```

or, equivalently:

```
prompt% perl -D16896 script.p      # (16384(X) + 512(r) = 16896)
```

which then would run **script.p** for you, with the regular expression checker turned on, and the memory allocation checker turned on for the whole script. This is the first, less useful way. The other way is to set the $^D (dollar Control-D) variable (which does the same thing) yourself.

This is to prevent the torrent of output that comes with the flag -D. Remember: the debugging flag was made for debugging the Perl executable first, not your Perl script. Hence, it makes sense to look only at areas you are interested in. Next we use $^D to debug some regular expressions.

Debugging Regular Expressions

The thing I do the most, with Perl's debugging option, is debug my regular expressions. As with most debugging flags, -Dr gives a torrent of output, so I tend to turn it on and off as needed.

To get a feel of what is going on, let's look at debugging the following expression:

```
$expr = 'abacabac';
$expr =~ m"a(.*)c(.*)b";
```

Now, this expression is a good example because it is simple and nontrivial (it will go through some backtracking), so we can get a feel for the output. The first thing to do is put the correct $^D values before and after our example:

```
open (STDERR, "> log");
$^D = 512;     # Turn on regular expression debugging
$expr = 'abacabac';
$expr =~ m"a(.*)c(.*)b";
$^D = 0;       # Turns off debugging.
```

Now, we have bounded our problem. (open(STDERR, "> log"); redirects STDERR to a file named **log**. I usually run my script by saying something like:

```
%prompt: perl script.p
```

and then I open the file log to see what it has captured. In this case:

```
1      1:BRANCH   <abacabac>
2      5:EXACT     <abacabac>
3     11:OPEN1     <bacabac>
```

```
4       17:BRANCH       <bacabac>
5       21:STAR         <bacabac>
6          29:CLOSE1        <>
7          35:EXACT         <>
8          29:CLOSE1        <c>
9          35:EXACT         <c>
10         41:OPEN2      <>
11         47:BRANCH     <>
12         51:STAR       <>
13            59:CLOSE2       <>
14            65:EXACT        <>
15         29:CLOSE1        <ac>
16         35:EXACT         <ac>
17         29:CLOSE1        <bac>
18         35:EXACT         <bac>
19         29:CLOSE1        <abac>
20         35:EXACT         <abac>
21         29:CLOSE1        <cabac>
22         35:EXACT         <cabac>
23         41:OPEN2      <abac>
24         47:BRANCH     <abac>
25         51:STAR       <abac>
26            59:CLOSE2       <>
27            65:EXACT        <>
28            59:CLOSE2       <c>
29            65:EXACT        <c>
30            59:CLOSE2       <ac>
31            65:EXACT        <ac>
32            59:CLOSE2       <bac>
33            65:EXACT        <bac>
34            71:END          <ac>
```

Now, what to make of this? It isn't the easiest thing to read, but it contains some useful information about what is going on. The main points to realize about this output are that:

1. The text between < and > is the text left in the pattern that is being matched. Hence, at the end, <ac> is all that remains of the expression.
2. Each in indentation indicates an extra place where the regular expression can backtrack; each out indentation indicates where the backtrack failed. Hence, in line 14, there is a backtrack, since a(.*)c tried to match abacabac, but was too greedy and failed.
3. You can see greediness in action. At line 15, a(.*)c tries to match abacabac, then abacabac, and then finally abacabac and then branches in line 26.

Now, do your own matches! For example, you can learn quite a bit by saying:

```
$a = "'a\\''";
$a =~ m/'((?:[^'\\]|\\.)*)'/;
```

and watch Perl go through its twists and turns to see how it matches your regular expression. This, if you remember, is the regular expression that matches any single-quoted string, as seen in the book *Mastering Regular Expressions*, by Jeffery Friedl, and it contains quite a bit of logic that you can exploit.

Summary of -D and Debugging Regular Expressions

In the debugging version of Perl, -D is your brute force, last resort if you have a bug you cannot find (well, that and reporting bugs via **perlbug**). By use of different flags, you can see various ways Perl is actually running your program.

The debugging version of Perl is also the road to successfully fiddling around with the Perl internal code, if you so desire, as well as a refresher on linking C code with Perl code, and a whole bunch of other exotic things. If you are so inclined . . .

Programming Auxiliary Tools for Debugging

As you can see, debugging Perl code isn't nearly like debugging something like C or C++. The debugging process and the coding process are so intertwined that you sometimes feel as if you are coding to debug your program, and debugging to code your program!

The two are, therefore, almost indistinguishable from each other, and it is a tribute to how indistinguishable that we can write an entire chapter on debugging without talking about the Perl debugger itself!

This chapter finishes with two examples of how you can make packages which help extend debugging—extra layers of protection against the stray errors you might encounter.

Example 1: Warning Directive or Pragma

First, we will get rid of the necessity to redefine the $SIG{'__WARN__'} and $SIG{'__DIE__'} handlers every time you write a script. We will write a directive, or pragma, that will do it for us.

The code in question is the code to redefine $SIG{'__DIE__'}:

```
use Carp;
$SIG{'__DIE__'} = sub { confess "@_"; };
and $SIG{'__WARN__'}:
 use Carp
2 use FileHandle;
3 $SIG{'__WARN__'} = \&warnHandler;
4
5 sub warnHandler
6 {
7      my $fd = new FileHandle("> $0.log") || die "Couldn't open $0.log!\n";
8      my $text = Carp::longmess(@_);
9      print $fd $text;
10     close($fd);
11 }
```

There are two problems with this code. First, it must be put in front of every script. Second, it hard-codes the log we create as **$0.log**, which we may want to change, or not overwrite. Hence, this is the perfect place for a pragma, or directive. We want to say:

```
use FullWarn "file";
```

and have the signal handlers defined for us, and all the output from warnings and errors stuffed into the file **"file"**.

Hence, we will make a package (**"FullWarn.pm"**) and stuff the code into it. We will make it a wrapper much in the same way we have transformed scripts into modules:

```
FullWarn.pm:
1   package FullWarn;
2
3   use Carp;
4   use FileHandle;
5   sub import
6   {
```

```
7        $FullWarn::log = $_[1];      # use second argument as log name.
8        $SIG{'__DIE__'} =  \&dieHandler;
9        $SIG{'__WARN__'} = \&warnHandler;
10 }
11 sub warnHandler
12 {
13       my $fd = new FileHandle("> $log") || die "Couldn't open $log!\n";
14       my $text = Carp::longmess(@_);
15       print $fd $text;
16       close($fd);
18 }
19 sub dieHandler
20 {
21       my $fd = new FileHandle("> $log") || die "Couldn't open $log!\n";
22       my $text = Carp::longmess(@_);
23       print $fd $text;
24       close($fd);
25       confess(@_);
26 }
27 1;
```

Note two things here. First, because we are in a directive, we can be more explicit than we were before, defining both the warnHandler and dieHandler to display output.

Second, the signal handler requires a global variable $FullWarn::log, because $SIG{'__WARN__'} and $SIG{__DIE__} cannot take arguments.

You could make this method more fancy, separating errors into different packages or even dumping these errors to a centralized log. You may even want to make it so that you have a rigorous, "warnings check" before you hand off your code to anybody else (or put it into source control).

Example 2: Using `tie` to Make a Safe Object

Let's get a bit more fancy, and look at how to make a 'safe' object—one that has stronger type checking than Perl supplies internally.

Note

Actually, this sample code is a simpler version of a module already in the standard distribution called **Class::Fields**. Use that one for real, and take a look at this only as an example.

In C++, you have the convention where you can say:

```
class ClassName
{
    private:
        int a;
        int b;
    public:
        int c;
        int d;
};
```

In other words, you can declare your variables as int a, etc.

Let's implement a small "tied" class that does the same thing for Perl. We will inherit this class, so you can say:

```
1 use MyClass;
2 @ISA = qw(SmartObject);
3 sub new
4 {
5     my ($type, @args) = @_:
6     my $self = bless {}, $type;
7     $self->declare('a','b','c','d');
8     $self;
9 }
```

In other words, line 7 will make it so anyone trying to access:

```
$self->{'e'};
```

will provoke the message:

```
Element 'e' is not a 'blessed' data part of the object MyClass!
```

So how do we go about doing this? Well, we will make $self a *tied* class, so that any time we access an element of $self, we get a run-time check that this element is OK. As we did before, let's split this into all the functions we are to program.

The Inherited Functions: *declare* and *TIEHASH*

Here is the code for our declaration function:

```
SmartObject.pm
1   package SmartObject;
2   sub declare
3   {
4       my ($self, @elements) = @_;
5       tie (%$self, 'SmartObject', ref($self), @elements);
    }
```

Here, we declare that our object ($self) is also a SmartObject and hence, will go through the following functions when its elements are accessed, changed, etc. Line 5 calls the following constructor:

```
7   sub TIEHASH
4   {
5       my ($type, $beginType, @elements) = @_;
6       my $self = {hashval => {});
7       $self->{'element_list'} = {};
8       $self->{'type'} = $beginType;
9       my $list = $self->{'element_list'};
10      foreach (@elements) { $list->{$_} = 1; }
11      bless $self, $type;
12  }
```

In line 10 then, we register all the elements the user passed in (a, b, c, d). We will remember this declaration later, when we decide whether an element is appropriate or not. We now make a small shorthand function that checks to see if a data member is registered:

```
13  sub isRegistered
14  {
```

```
15      my ($self, $key) = @_;
16      my $list = $self->{'element_list'}1
17      if (!defined $list->{$key})
18      {
19          print "Element '$key' is not a 'blessed' data part of the object ",
20          $self->{type}, "!\n"; return(undef);
21      }
22 }
```

Now, we are ready to make our "tied" methods.

The *FETCH* method

When someone tries to access $self->{'e'}, the FETCH method is called:

```
23 sub FETCH
24 {
25      my ($self, $key) = @_;
26      if ($self->isRegisted($key)) { return($self->{hashval}->{$key}); }
27      return(undef);
28 }
```

Line 26 acts as a filter. Here is where we check on whether or not we have registered the element $key. If not, we are given a warning, and return an undefined key in line 27.

The *STORE* Method

STORE is the opposite of FETCH. Here is where we check to make sure that our class is not storing an element which we do not want:

```
30 sub STORE
31 {
32      my ($self, $key,$value) = @_;
33      if ($self->isRegisted($key)) { $self->{'hashval'}->{$key} = $value }
34      return(undef);
35 }
```

When we say $self->{'e'} = 1, line 33 stops us. The key is not registered, and undef is returned.

Other *tie* Methods in *SmartObject*

The other methods are simple consequences of the preceding methods. DELETE, CLEAR, EXISTS, FIRSTKEY, and NEXTKEY all are either regular hash calls, or have the filter:

```
36 sub DELETE
37 {
38      my ($self, $key) = @_;
39      if ($self->isRegisted($key)) { delete $self->{'hashval'}->{$key}; }
40      return(undef);
41 }
42 sub CLEAR
43 {
44      my ($self) = @_;
45      my $key;
```

```
46
47      my $hash = $self->{'hashval'};
48      foreach $key ( keys %$hash ) { $self->DELETE($key); }
49 }
50 sub EXISTS
51 {
52      my ($self, $key) = @_;
53      if ($self->isRegistered($key))
54      {
55          return(1) if (exists $self->{'hashval'}->{$key});
56      }
57      return (0);
58 }
59 sub FIRSTKEY
60 {
61      my ($self) = @_;
62      my ($key, $value) = each(%{$self->{'hashval'}});
63    return($key);
64 }
65
66 sub NEXTKEY
67 {
68      my ($self, $lastkey) = @_;
69      $self->FIRSTKEY();
70 }
```

Through the magic of inheritance then (see the section on inheritance for more detail), the method

```
$self->declare('a','b','c','d');
```

calls the method:

```
SmartObject::declare($self, 'a','b','c','d')
```

which then constructs a "guard" through tie-ing a SmartObject "around" the hash reference.

There are two points to this example:

1. You can probably see why it is necessary to keep close track of your warnings and errors in complicated code. We have three levels of depth here:

    ```
    $self->declare() (in package MyClass) references
        SmartObject::declare() which calls
            SmartObject::TieHash();
    ```

    In addition, if there are any bugs, they will happen in **MyClass**, or the application that calls **MyClass**. Hence, carp(), confess(), and crew, plus redefining the signal handlers, are essential to keep our sanity and to debug our classes.
2. You can see exactly how malleable Perl is! Any feature of other object-oriented languages (privacy, etc.) can be implemented in Perl, albeit at run time. It is up to you to decide exactly how strict you want the language.

This is the last of the chapters that emphasize concepts in programming. Next, we turn to Perl projects, where we are concerned about making an application, rather than individual objects.

23

Creating CGI Scripts from Existing Tools

The code and text in this chapter were contributed by Randy Ray.

One of the problems that faces companies of all sizes as they migrate operations to the World Wide Web is what to do with their existing pool of applications that are either GUI- or screen-based. While the Web makes great inroads to creating and promoting a consistent appearance and interface, the nature of the HTTP protocol yields an environment devoid of state and persistence. This is not news. Hundreds of papers and publications mention this and address it, but there has not been much said about ways to work with it when faced with a great deal of legacy code from pre-WWW days.

Moving a tool to the Web means resolving conflicts in several areas. These areas include (but are certainly not limited to) input parameters (command-line arguments versus HTML form elements), persistence of information from one page to the next, security of information, and handling of error conditions. Any of these are viable chapters in a book devoted to Web and/or CGI, but in this chapter, they will be examined from the viewpoint of trying to adapt older code to the Web API.

Make no mistake: There is no Perl library or wrapper that will automatically (or auto-magically) make screen-based or batch-execution scripts suddenly work as CGI scripts with comparable interfaces. In fact, this would not be a very good thing if it did exist, because as a totally different API, the Web has more to offer than just a generic graphical tool to browse information. Perl scripts running via CGI have limitations, but they also have access to a well-documented, widely accepted graphical user interface.

Rather than try to run old tools blindly under CGI, or completely reengineer tools for CGI at the expense of screen interfaces, this chapter will try to examine means to move scripts to a point in between, where they are useful on both fronts.

From the Start: Command-Line Options

The first and most noticeable difference between traditional scripts and CGI scripts is the handling of input. CGI scripts do not have @ARGV populated as traditional scripts do. The STDIN file descriptor will not be a viable source of input, either. A CGI script must retrieve its startup data from a combination of environment variables and STDIN, depending on the method used (GET or POST). Existing means of retrieving run-time options are all beholden to the @ARGV array. To start with, let's abstract the fetching and manipulation of run-time options.

An Abstracted Options Reader

We'll start with a simple module to read options in a more abstracted way. For this example, we'll use an object-oriented model, **Options.pm**, as shown in Listing 23.1.

Listing 23.1
Options.pm

```
1    package Options;
2
3    use strict;
4    use Carp;
5    use Getopt::Long;
6
7    1;
8
9    sub import
10   {
11       my $class = shift;
12
13       @Options::Argv = @ARGV;
14       @Options::Argv = () if ($#Options::Argv == -1);
15
16       if (defined $_[0] and $_[0] =~ /^-?pass/oi)
17       {
18           Getopt::Long::config('pass_through');
19       }
20
21       1;
22   }
23
24   sub unimport
25   {
26       my $class = shift;
```

```
27       $class = ref($class) || $class;
28
29       carp "Command `no $class;' not implemented";
30
31    1;
32  }
33
34  sub new
35  {
36      my $class = shift;
37      my @opts = @_;
38
39      $class = ref($class) || $class;
40
41      my $self = bless {}, $class;
42
43      $self->{RAW_ARGV} = [@Options::Argv];
44      $self->{RAW_OPTS} = [@opts];
45
46      my %opts;
47      local @ARGV = @Options::Argv;
48
49      if (! GetOptions(\%opts, @opts))
50      {
51          croak "Invalid option(s). Exiting";
52      }
53
54      $self->{opts} = \%opts;
55
56      $self;
57  }
58
59  sub option
60  {
61      my $self = shift;
62      my $arg  = shift;
63
64      my $type;
65
66      return undef unless (defined $self->{opts}->{$arg});
67
68      if ($type = ref($self->{opts}->{$arg}))
69      {
70          if (! wantarray)
71          {
72              return ($type eq 'ARRAY') ? scalar(@{$self->{opts}->{$arg}}) :
73                  scalar(keys %{$self->{opts}->{$arg}});
74          }
75          else
76          {
77              return ($type eq 'ARRAY') ? (@{$self->{opts}->{$arg}}) :
78                  (%{$self->{opts}->{$arg}});
79          }
80      }
```

```
81        else
82        {
83            return $self->{opts}->{$arg};
84        }
85   }
86
87   sub option_names
88   {
89        my $self = shift;
90
91        my @list = sort keys %{$self->{opts}};
92   }
```

This is a simple class that provides a few simple methods. The `import` method, starting at line 9, is designed to preserve a copy of @ARGV at initialization. This allows the rest of the module to operate without destroying @ARGV.

It then looks for the only currently supported option to the package itself, a string starting with -pass. This will tell **Options** to set the value in the core **Getopt::Long** module that allows options other than those specifically requested. This is useful for tools that in turn, call other tools, and thus receive options intended for the other tool.

When this is done, `import` returns. There is an `unimport` method provided for completeness, so that should someone code a line that reads no `Options`, they are informed that this is not a valid invocation.

The `new` method is the heart of any given class. This method is responsible for creating the new object and returning it. Lines 36–37 read in the arguments to the method (remember that the object calling convention automatically puts `$class` as the first argument). Line 39 is a little sleight of hand to allow the constructor to be called as either a static or dynamic constructor; one can create an object as `$obj = new Options ...` or one can create from an existing object of the class via `$obj2 = $obj->new(...)`.

Each object keeps a copy of the raw command line (line 43) and requested options list (line 44) for debugging purposes. In lines 46–47, a new hash table is created, and the special variable @ARGV becomes localized to the current scope, in preparation for the call to **Getoptions**. Line 49 does the call, using `croak` to report any errors and exit if need be. Assuming success, the hash is stored on an internal key and the reference is returned to the caller. But how are the options actually accessed?

The methods `option_names` and `option` are the access methods for the class. When the caller gets an object of class **Options**, they do not get any indication of which options were present, only that no illegal options were. The method `option_names` returns a list of the options that were successfully read (sorted).

Given the names, calls can be made to the `option` method to retrieve an actual value. The caller is responsible for knowing if said method invocation should return something other than a scalar. Lines 61 and 62 get the object reference and desired option from the call. Line 66 returns the special value `undef` if the requested option is not in the table. Other null values such as zero (0) could actually be valid option values, so `undef` is used.

On line 68, the value associated with `$arg` is checked to see if it is a reference. Jumping to the second half of the condition, lines 81–84, if it isn't a reference it is treated and returned as a scalar. If it is a reference, then a test is done to see if the caller is calling in a scalar or list context. In a scalar context (lines 72 and 73, when `wantarray` returns 0), the number of elements is the return value: the size of the array, or the number of keys in the hash table. If the context is an array context (lines 77 and 78), then the reference is simply dereferenced and the caller receives either the array or hash table, as appropriate.

Our **Options** class is best illustrated by Listing 23.2:

Listing 23.2
opttest.p

```
1    #!/usr/bin/perl -w
2
```

```
3    use Options;
4
5    my $opts = new Options qw(-list=s@ -int=i -any=s);
6
7    print "No options specified.\n" unless ($opts->option_names());
8
9    for $name ($opts->option_names())
10   {
11       printf "Option %-10s: %s\n", $name, join(" ", $opts->option($name));
12   }
13
14   exit;
```

This test script will accept –int followed by an integer, any number of –list specifications followed by general strings, and –any followed by a general string. Line 5 gets a new object of class **Options** with these specifications. Line 7 informs the user that there were no options, if none were found. Assuming that there was at least one, line 9 loops over the names returned by options_names. For each iteration of the loop, line 11 displays the name and value of the option. Note that the call to the option method on line 11 is forced into a list context by being called within join(). Thus, if the value of option $name is a list or hash table, all parts will be returned and joined into one string using a single space as the separator. If the script is run as:

```
test_opt -int 5 -list a -list b -any thing
```

the output will be:

```
Option any       : thing
Option int       : 5
Option list      : a b
```

but this:

```
test_opt -int bad
```

yields:

```
Value "bad" invalid for option int (number expected)
Invalid option(s). Exiting at test_opt line 6
```

A good start. But it clearly still uses @ARGV and standard argument parsing approaches. Where does CGI come in?

Subclassing the Basic Options

With a basic framework of a class in place, it is easy to subclass it to handle more complex features. Specifically, it is desirable to detect at compile time if the program is running under CGI or not, and act accordingly. What follows in Listing 23.3 is a subclass of **Options** called **Options::Common**.

Listing 23.3
Options::Common

```
Options/Common.pm
```

```
1    package Options::Common;
2
3    use strict;
```

```
4    use vars qw($running_under_cgi);
5    use Carp;
6    use Options;
7    use Detect;
8
9    @Options::Common::ISA = qw(Options);
10
11   1;
12
13   sub import
14   {
15       my $class = shift;
16       $class = ref($class) || $class;
17
18       if ($Detect::cgi && $#_ != -1) # ANYTHING in use line triggers this
19       {
20           print STDOUT "Content-type: text/plain\n\n";
21       }
22
23       $class->SUPER::import(@_);
24
25       1;
26   }
27
28   sub new
29   {
30       my $class = shift;
31       $class = ref($class) || $class;
32       my $self = bless {}, $class;
33
34       if (! $Detect::cgi)
35       {
36           return $self->SUPER::new(@_);
37       }
38       require CGI;
39
40       my @opts = @_;
41       my %opts;
42       my $cgi_obj = new CGI;
43       my ($item, $name, $type);
44
45       $self->{RAW_OPTS} = [@opts];
46       $self->{RAW_ARGV} = [@Options::Argv];
47       $cgi_obj->import_names('ARG');
48
49       no strict 'refs';
50
51       for $item (@opts)
52       {
53           $item =~ s/^-//o;
54           ($name, $type) = split(/=/, $item, 2);
55           if ($type =~ /\@$/o)
56           {
57               my @list;
```

```
58              if (defined @{"ARG::$name"} or defined $ {"ARG::$name"})
59              {
60                  @list = @{"ARG::$name"};
61                  @list = ($ {"ARG::$name"}) unless (@list);
62              }
63              if ($type =~ /^i/oi)
64              {
65                  croak "All arguments for $name must be integers"
66                      if (grep(! /^-?\d+$/o, @list));
67              }
68              $opts{$name} = [@list] if (@list);
69          }
70          elsif ($type eq 'i')
71          {
72              if (defined $ {"ARG::$name"})
73              {
74                  $opts{$name} = $ {"ARG::$name"};
75                  croak "Arg $name requires an integer (got $opts{$name})"
76                      unless ($opts{$name} =~ /^-?\d+$/o);
77              }
78          }
79          elsif ($type eq 's' || $type == '')
80          {
81              if (defined $ {"ARG::$name"})
82              {
83                  $opts{$name} = $ {"ARG::$name"};
84              }
85          }
86          else
87          {
88              croak "Unrecognized option type specifier: $type";
89          }
90      }
91
92      $self->{opts} = \%opts;
93
94      $self;
95  }
```

In subclassing **Options**, **Options::Common** starts by declaring **Options** as the parent class (line 9) and then redefines the methods import and new. Looking first at import, variable $Detect::cgi is examined. This is set by the **Detect** module referenced on line 7 and explained later. If the running program is in a CGI environment, this value will be true. If it is, and if anything was put after the use Options::Common akin to importing, then the string text/plain is output. This will simplify converting batch-style scripts to CGI in the short term.

Whether this is done or not, the parent class import method is then called using the special namespace identifier SUPER. None of the functionality of **Options::import** was replaced, only a little extra added at the start.

The real changes come in the new method. Lines 30–32 are basically the same as the old, but the resemblance stops there. In line 34, CGI context is checked again. If this is not a CGI process, then the superclass new method is called instead, with its return value directly passed back to the caller.

If this tool is a CGI script, things are now handled much more differently. Line 38 makes sure that the CGI library is loaded. Lines 40–47 declare variables and make local copies of options and @ARGV just as the parent new does. Line 47 itself uses the import_names method of the CGI class to copy all of the input values into variables in the ARG:: namespace. Fortunately, the CGI library abstracts POST and GET input methods, so the programmer need not worry at that level; all values are reachable via the same access method (a design very similar to what we are doing right now with command-line arguments).

Line 49 disables the strict checking of references. Normally, symbolic references are disallowed by the strict pragma, but the rest of new needs them. In lines 51–90, the requested options are examined one by one. The leading hyphen is removed (line 53) and the value split into name and type (line 54). If the type specifier starts with a @ character, then a list is requested. CGI doesn't have a data specification means that translates into a hash, so this loop can ignore hashes.

All the values under that name (tested both as a list or a scalar) are stored in a temporary list which is in turn stored on the **opts** key under $name. If there are no values, then no storage takes place.

Before leaving this branch of the conditional, the type specifier is checked to see if they requested a list of integers. Lines 65 and 66 check the list, in this case. If the type requested was not a list, then it must be a scalar value. The block in lines 70–78 checks to see if they specifically want an integer and tests the value, if there is one, for this. The default falls through to lines 79–89, where a specifier of s or no specifier at all results in a scalar value with no type tests, and if the identifier was something other than @, i, or s, an error is reported.

In a more detailed implementation, one would want to use the **CGI::Carp** package in a CGI context, so that the error messages were directed to the error logs and possibly the browser. As a simpler example, this communicates the point. At line 92, the %opts table is assigned to the object, and the object reference is returned. The caller now has an object of class **Options::Common**, but the retrieval of option names and values is exactly the same as it was for the command line version.

Detect

For the purposes of compile-time detection of a CGI context, it was necessary to throw together a small module to check the appropriate environment variables. We code a **Detect** module, which understands which environment, CGI or shell, a given script is running in. The code for this is shown in Listing 23.4.

Listing 23.4
Detect

Detect.pm

```
1   package Detect;
2
3   use strict;
4   use Carp;
5   use vars qw($cgi $webserver $server_version);
6
7   1;
8
9   sub import
10  {
11      my $class  = shift;
12      my $params = shift || {};
13
14      $cgi = $webserver = $server_version = '';
15
16      if (defined $params->{cgi} and ref($params->{cgi}) eq 'CODE')
17      {
18          $cgi = &{$params->{cgi}};
19      }
20      else
```

```
21      {
22          $cgi = (defined $ENV{GATEWAY_INTERFACE}) ? 1 : 0;
23      }
24
25      return 1 unless ($cgi);
26
27      if (defined $params->{webserver} and
28          ref($params->{webserver}) eq 'CODE')
29      {
30          ($webserver, $server_version) = &{$params->{webserver}};
31      }
32      else
33      {
34          my $srv_string = $ENV{SERVER_SOFTWARE} || '1/0';
35          ($webserver, $server_version) = split('/', $srv_string);
36      }
37
38      1;
39  }
40
41  sub unimport
42  {
43      my $class = shift;
44      $class = ref($class) || $class;
45
46      carp "Command `no $class;' not implemented";
47
48      1;
49  }
```

This module only needs import. The unimport function is provided as protection against no Detect. The import method takes and ignores the class passed in as the first argument, but takes note of the second argument, which is expected to be a hash reference. An empty hash reference is used if none was given.

The first test is on lines 16–23. The default (basic) test for CGI context is the presence of the environment variable named GATEWAY_INTERFACE. This is also the case when Perl is running under Windows 95 or NT. However, if the user wants more done, or more specific checking (such as specific gateway protocol revision), they can pass in a reference to an existent subroutine as the value to a key called cgi in the input hash. If this key exists and points to a code reference, that routine is called instead.

Note that since this is all running at compile time, the routine will have to be declared either within a BEGIN block prior to using this module, or passed as a closure. The return value of the routine should be 0 or 1. The default is sufficient to identify a CGI context. On line 25, we return if there is no CGI context, because there is nothing else worth checking. But if this is a CGI environment, then lines 27–36 check the name and version of the Web server software. As with the CGI detection, the user can specify a routine to use, or the default just takes the SERVER_SOFTWARE environment variable. In case this is not set (such as debugging a CGI program from a command line), the string defaults to 1/0, so that testing the variable $Detect::webserver still returns true.

A sample usage of this module might look like what is shown in Listing 23.5. Note that the $Detect::cgi variable determines whether or not to output HTML tags.

Listing 23.5
testdetect.p

```
1   #!/usr/bin/perl
```

```
2
3    use Detect;
4
5    if ($Detect::cgi)
6    {
7        # ... output HTML start-up tags and headers
8    }
9
10   # ... normal script processing, with output format also based on the CGI
11   # ... test, maybe even testing $Detect::webserver for some features
12
13   if ($Detect::cgi)
14   {
15       # ... output HTML closing tags
16   }
17
18   exit;
```

Nothing too new, but the ready availability of the value $Detect::cgi allows easy in-line selection of output styles.

Error Reporting and Management

Earlier it was noted that the simplified implementation of **Options::Common** suffered from the fact that it did not take into account the CGI context when reporting errors (or warnings).

This is another major area where the transition from traditional scripts to CGI is significant. Errors and warnings generally go to STDOUT, which in a CGI context goes to the server's error logs. The CGI library provides an additional module **CGI::Carp** that redefines **die, warn, carp,** and **croak** to send their output to the logs in a format consistent with HTTP error reporting. It is also possible to have errors echoed to the browser. Of course, you don't want your script to load either of CGI or **CGI::Carp** unless it is actually running in a CGI context. This makes for a more challenging issue.

To maintain maximum transparency, using the test on $Detect::cgi to choose either croak or CGI::Carp::croak is undesirable. Better to use **eval** after the CGI context has been identified:

```
eval { use CGI::Carp; }
            if ($Detect::cgi);

        die "Something bad has happened!";
```

Putting this in **Detect.pm**'s import function would require using Perl's caller function and calling **CGI::Carp**'s import directly. Putting it in the script itself makes it more verbose, but leaves a clearer distinction (remember, there will be no "auto-magic" conversion).

This package can be made to also send fatal errors to the browser by importing a special function called fatalsToBrowser:

```
eval { use CGI::Carp qw(fatalsToBrowser); }
            if ($Detect::cgi);

        die "Something else bad has happened!";
```

Yet another means of fine-tuning the control over errors and warnings comes from a routine called carpout. It is not a very good performer, and is mostly recommended for handling warnings in such a way as to echo them to the browser (the fatalsToBrowser predicate only affects errors). The carpout routine is not exported by default, and must be requested:

```
eval { use CGI::Carp qw(carpout); carpout(STDOUT); }
        if ($Detect::cgi);

    warn "Something non-fatal just happened";
```

It is called with an open, writeable filehandle. An important subtlety here is that in order to catch compiler errors this way, the **eval/if** would need to be in a `BEGIN` block, likely requiring that the call to **Options::Common** (or maybe just directly to Detect) occurs there as well. Not worrying about compile-time errors for now, the earlier test script can be enhanced as follows:

```
1   #!/usr/bin/perl -wT
2
3   use Options::Common;
4
5   eval { use CGI::Carp qw(fatalsToBrowser); } if ($Detect::cgi);
6
7   my $opts = new Options::Common qw(-list=s@ -int=i -any=s);
8   die "No options specified" unless ($opts->option_names);
9
10  print "Content-type: text/plain\n\n" if ($Detect::cgi);
11  for $name ($opts->option_names)
12  {
13      printf "Option %-10s: %s\n", $name, join(" ", $opts->option($name));
14  }
15
16  exit;
```

There is no need to show specific outputs, as the core of the script has not changed at all; compare lines 7 and 11–14 with lines 5 and 9–12 in the first version of this test. The only difference is the use of **Options::Common** instead of **Options**. Here, there is the **eval/if** combo, and an additional test on the `$Detect::cgi` value, to spit out a simple text/plain header. Any errors trapped by **CGI::Carp** will have sent their own headers.

A successful run under a browser results in input that looks exactly like the sample input earlier. But if an error occurs in the argument parsing or in the case of no arguments, then the error message on the browser references the line in which the error occurred and clearly notes that this is an error. This is an improvement over the more typical behavior of getting an empty document with no explanation.

Of course, if the legacy code handles its errors and warnings with print's to `STDERR` and the occasional exit, then that is a different matter. But if all the diagnostics are managed via `warn/die`, or the `confess/croak/carp` set, then switching between terminal and Web browser contexts should not be too much hassle.

On the Inside: Input, Output, and Persistent Data

HTTP, as a protocol, is stateless. CGI, reliant upon HTTP, is therefore also stateless. If you've read any other sources on either HTTP or CGI, you have heard this before.

Much of the reason for the repetition (including the repetition here) is that matters of information persistence between sessions rank high on the list of things that developers new to CGI must overcome. Most programs with any degree of user interaction, particularly legacy code, follow a design of forward processing. They proceed from start to finish, polling data as needed. When a CGI application runs, it goes straight through.

The only user input is that which is gleaned from the query. Many CGI scripts are self-referencing, running anywhere from a few to a few dozen times for one session of one end user. Web designers have taken a number of approaches to implementing data persistence across sessions while also structuring the programs themselves to run in different states based on the combination of input data. This section will start by looking at some of these approaches.

Squeezing the Most out of POST

The most obvious way to carry data from one session to the next is as part of the URL in a GET method, or in the data of a POST method. Using GET methods results in very cryptic URL strings which are limited to an arbitrary length (which can vary based on the server or browser). On the other hand, such a URL can be checkpointed and jumped to directly at a later time.

With POST methods, there are fewer limitations on the size of the data passed from session to session, but it isn't possible to checkpoint any one page and return to it later. As such, if this is the preferred method of data persistence, the choice boils down to whether the end user should be able to bookmark the process at some internal point or not. For on-line ordering systems, this is probably not a requirement. For other systems, it may well be.

This is also one of the easiest means by which to move your data from session to session. It requires no external packages (not even the CGI library, though this chapter assumes that it is being used) or juggling of the data. When browsing a site via one of the commercial search engines such as *Yahoo!* or *Altavista*, take note of the URL displayed in the browser's location window. Cryptic as it may appear, it contains all the information relevant to the ongoing search session taking place, including browsing through page after page of results.

Using a Database Index Key for Sessions

If you use a database system with your CGI project (whether a simple system like DBM or a commercial SQL-based system), then the data can be held on the server, and the browser need only remember the unique key from page to page. If the database sessions are meant only for the short term, the key can be in a hidden form element and the progression from page to page done by POST (useful if there are other forms to be filled out along the way). If the key is indexing data that may persist over a longer period, the key could be part of the URL for a GET method, and thus bookmarked for later use (also see the next section on browser cookies).

By using this approach, the quantity, persistence, and freshness of data are at the leisure of the CGI developer. This approach is further enhanced by the fact that Perl itself includes multiple DBM-style interfaces in the core of the language: GNU GDM, Berkeley DB, standard Unix DBM and NDBM, as well as a local implementation called SDBM that runs on the ports of Perl to Windows platforms. While the best choice may be to install an extra package such as Berkeley DB, an application can be quickly prototyped with the Perl extension called **AnyDBM_File**, which picks the first DBM implementation it can find that is implemented on the system. The data can be moved to a specific database format for the production code.

Browser-Specific Features: Cookies

Some browsers support the concept of data tokens stored locally on the user's machine. They are transmitted to a particular host or domain whenever the browser requests a page from that host or domain.

Cookies can be given a lifespan, set to be sent only for a certain area of the target host, and carry flags that indicate the cookie should be sent only if communicating on a secure channel. Cookies don't generally transmit a large chunk of data. However, they are a good way to sustain a database key across sessions, or store data that is by definition smaller (such as end user preferences for the Web site, whether to use frames, text-only, etc.). The pitfall of this approach is the browser-specific nature of cookies, limiting their usefulness to visitors who do not use a compatible browser.

Back to the Issue at Hand: Data

Those tools that are the most interactive in their execution and gathering of data will be the most difficult to bring to a CGI environment. If the pool of scripts awaiting conversion is mostly made up of single-purse, short administrative scripts, the task will be much easier. Take as an example the following, very basic rolodex utility (shown in Listing 23.6).

Listing 23.6

rolodex.p

```
1    #!/usr/bin/perl -w
2
3    BEGIN { @AnyDBM_File::ISA = qw(DB_File SDBM_File NDBM_File) }
4    use AnyDBM_File;
5    use Options;
6    use Carp;
7
8    $opts = new Options qw(-name=s -add -delete=s);
9
10   $name = $opts->option('name')    || '';
11   $add  = $opts->option('add')     || 0;
12   $del  = $opts->option('delete')  || '';
13
14   croak "Only one of -add or -delete may be specified, stopped"
15       if ($add and $del);
16
17   tie %rolo_hash, 'AnyDBM_File', '/u/rjray/locarolo.dex';
18
19   if ($name)
20   {
21       if (exists $rolo_hash{$name})
22       {
23           @data = split("\n", $rolo_hash{$name});
24           %data = map { split(/=/, $_, 2) } @data;
25           for (qw(NAME PHONE EMAIL))
26           {
27               printf "%-10s: %s\n", ucfirst lc $_, $data{$_};
28           }
29           for (grep(/^ADD/, sort keys %data))
30           {
31               printf "%-10s: %s\n", ucfirst lc $_, $data{$_};
32           }
33       }
34       else
35       {
36           carp "No record for ``$name'' in the rolodex.\n";
37       }
38   }
39   elsif ($add)
40   {
41       $line = '';
42       @addr = ();
43
44       print "Creating new record:\n\nNew Name:\n";
45       $new_name = <STDIN>;  chomp $new_name;
46       croak "NAME is a required field, stopped" unless ($new_name);
47       croak "NAME $new_name already exists, stopped"
48           if (exists $rolo_hash{$new_name});
49
50       print "New phone:\n";
51       $new_phone = <STDIN>; chomp $new_phone;
```

```
52      print "E-Mail address:\n";
53      $new_email = <STDIN>; chomp $new_email;
54
55      print "Enter address information. Enter '.' to end input:\n";
56      do
57      {
58          $line = <STDIN>; chomp $line;
59          push(@addr, $line) unless ($line eq '.');
60      } while ($line ne '.');
61
62      $data = "NAME=$new_name\nPHONE=$new_phone\nEMAIL=$new_email\n";
63      $count = 1;
64      $data .= join("\n",
65                      map { sprintf("ADDR%d=%s", $count++, $_) } (@addr));
66
67      $rolo_hash{$new_name} = $data;
68   }
69   elsif ($del)
70   {
71      croak "DELETE: Name ``$del'' is not in the rolodex, stopped"
72          unless (exists $rolo_hash{$del});
73
74      delete $rolo_hash{$del};
75   }
76   else
77   {
78      for (sort keys %rolo_hash)
79      {
80          print "$_\n";
81      }
82   }
83
84   untie %rolo_hash;
85
86   exit;
```

When this is described as basic, understand that the word is not used lightly. A real system would offer more in terms of data validation, flexible searching, and a host of other options. But for the sake of illustration, this is sufficient.

Picking the tool apart in sections, lines 3–6 control the use of outside libraries. The use of the BEGIN block on line 3 forces the order of preference in the module **AnyDBM_File**. Doing this, the Berkeley DB library gets preference, falling through to **SDBM_File** if **DB_File** is not present. In case neither are, the last choice is **NDBM_File**. Line 4 pulls in the **AnyDBM_File** superclass, and line 5 pulls in the now-familiar **Options** library. The **Carp** library is referenced on line 6 as a matter of preference for the flexibility in error message routing it offers (this will be a boon later).

Lines 8–12 create the **Options** class instance and assign some local names for the requested options. This also allows for defaulting these variables to empty strings or zeros as appropriate (a step that prevents warnings of the variety "Use of uninitialized value"). Line 17 connects to the database.

Lines 17–38 are the first of three cases that demand specific action. The if clause looks for a requested name to have been passed in via the -name command-line option. If a name was passed, it is checked to see that it actu- ally exists in the database (DB). If this test succeeds, the information is retrieved from the DB, unpacked accord- ing to the simple format used, and then displayed in a neatly formatted manner. If the requested name is not found, an error message is displayed using the croak function.

The second operative case is the addition of a new record, tested for and handled in lines 39–68. Rather than have the -add option provide some subset of the data, this block handles all the new data input to reduce the potential for confusion. After the name is read on line 45, it is checked against the current rolodex to ensure that said key is not already in use.

Lines 50–60 read the remaining data, with the simple loop being used to allow an arbitrary number of lines for the surface-mail address. Lines 62–65 pack the data for storage, and line 67 handles the assignment to the rolodex database.

For deletion requests, the blocks in lines 69–75 take the name from the -delete command-line option, check for existence in the database (lines 71 and 72 with a croak if it is not found), and perform the delete. Nothing fancy, though it could probably benefit from a confirmation.

The last block is executed only when none of the other options were requested. It simply displays the names in the rolodex in alphabetical order, using a simple for loop and the built-in sort function. Lastly within the script, line 84 forces a release of the database handles (often a redundant operation, but in some cases an explicit untie can be very necessary) and line 86 exits gracefully.

The First Steps Toward CGI Coexistence

For this first stage of transformation, the focus will be on simply making the existing **rolodex** script run under a Web browser, without adding any new or fanciful features. Listing 23.7 is the text of **rolodex2**.

Listing 23.7
rolodex2.p

```
1    #!/usr/bin/perl -w
2
3    BEGIN { @AnyDBM_File::ISA = qw(DB_File SDBM_File NDBM_File) }
4    use AnyDBM_File;
5    use Options::Common;
6    use Detect;
7    use Carp;
8
9    $opts = new Options::Common qw(-name=s -add -delete=s
10                                  -new_name=s -new_phone=s -new_email=s
11                                  -new_addr=s@);
12
13   $name = $opts->option('name')   || '';
14   $add  = $opts->option('add')    || 0;
15   $del  = $opts->option('delete') || '';
16
17   if ($Detect::cgi)
18   {
19       eval "use CGI; use CGI::Carp";
20
21       croak "Error bringing in CGI support: $@, stopped" if ($@);
22   }
23
24   croak "Only one of -add or -delete may be specified, stopped"
25       if ($add and $del);
26
27   tie %rolo_hash, 'AnyDBM_File', '/u/rjray/locarolo.dex';
28
29   if ($name)
```

```perl
30  {
31      if (exists $rolo_hash{$name})
32      {
33          print "Content-Type: text/html\n\n" if ($Detect::cgi);
34          @data = split("\n", $rolo_hash{$name});
35          %data = map { split(/=/, $_, 2) } @data;
36          for (qw(NAME PHONE EMAIL))
37          {
38              printf "%-10s: %s\n", ucfirst lc $_, $data{$_};
39              print "<br>" if ($Detect::cgi);
40          }
41          for (grep(/^ADD/, sort keys %data))
42          {
43              printf "%-10s: %s\n", ucfirst lc $_, $data{$_};
44              print "<br>" if ($Detect::cgi);
45          }
46      }
47      else
48      {
49          carp "No record for ``$name'' in the rolodex.\n";
50      }
51  }
52  elsif ($add)
53  {
54      if ($Detect::cgi)
55      {
56          my $Q = new CGI;
57
58          if ($new_name = $opts->option('new_name'))
59          {
60              $new_phone = $opts->option('new_phone') || '';
61              $new_email = $opts->option('new_email') || '';
62              @addr      = $opts->option('new_addr')  || ();
63
64              chomp ($new_phone, $new_email, $new_name, @addr);
65
66              $data = "NAME=$new_name\nPHONE=$new_phone\nEMAIL=$new_email\n";
67              $count = 1;
68              $data .= join("\n",
69                          map { sprintf("ADDR%d=%s",
70                                          $count++, $_) } (@addr));
71
72              $rolo_hash{$new_name} = $data;
73              print $Q->header, $Q->start_html(-title => 'Entry Added');
74              print $Q->p("The new data for: $new_name");
75              print $Q->p("has been added to the rolodex.");
76              print $Q->end_html;
77          }
78          else
79          {
80              print $Q->header;
81              print $Q->start_html(-title => 'Add new rolodex entry');
82              print $Q->center($Q->h1('Add new rolodex entry'));
83              print $Q->p();
```

```
84                  print $Q->startform('POST', $Q->script_name);
85                  print "New Name: ";
86                  print $Q->textfield(-name => 'new_name', -maxlength => 30),
87                      $Q->br;
88                  print "New phone: ";
89                  print $Q->textfield(-name => 'new_phone', -maxlength => 12),
90                      $Q->br;
91                  print "E-Mail: ";
92                  print $Q->textfield(-name => 'new_email', -maxlength => 30),
93                      $Q->br;
94                  print "Address:", $Q->br;
95                  print $Q->textarea(-name => 'new_addr', -rows => 5,
96                                     -columns => 40);
97                  print $Q->br;
98                  print $Q->submit(-name => 'add'), " this data", $Q->br;
99                  print $Q->reset, " the form";
100                 print $Q->endform;
101                 print $Q->end_html;
102             }
103         }
104     else
105         {
106         $line = '';
107         @addr = ();
108
109         print "Creating new record:\n\nNew Name:\n";
110         $new_name = <STDIN>;  chomp $new_name;
111         croak "NAME is a required field, stopped" unless ($new_name);
112         croak "NAME $new_name already exists, stopped"
113             if (exists $rolo_hash{$new_name});
114
115         print "New phone:\n";
116         $new_phone = <STDIN>; chomp $new_phone;
117         print "E-Mail address:\n";
118         $new_email = <STDIN>; chomp $new_email;
119
120         print "Enter address information. Enter '.' to end input:\n";
121         do
122             {
123             $line = <STDIN>; chomp $line;
124             push(@addr, $line) unless ($line eq '.');
125             } while ($line ne '.');
126
127         $data = "NAME=$new_name\nPHONE=$new_phone\nEMAIL=$new_email\n";
128         $count = 1;
129         $data .= join("\n",
130                       map { sprintf("ADDR%d=%s", $count++, $_) } (@addr));
131
132         $rolo_hash{$new_name} = $data;
133         }
134 }
135 elsif ($del)
136 {
137     croak "DELETE: Name ``$del'' is not in the rolodex, stopped"
```

```
138            unless (exists $rolo_hash{$del});
139
140     delete $rolo_hash{$del};
141     print "Content-Type: text/html\n\n" if ($Detect::cgi);
142     print "Record ``$del'' has been deleted.\n";
143 }
144 else
145 {
146     my $Q = new CGI
147         if ($Detect::cgi);
148
149     print $Q->header, $Q->start_html(-title => 'rolodex') if ($Detect::cgi);
150     for (sort keys %rolo_hash)
151     {
152         if ($Detect::cgi)
153         {
154             ($name = $_) =~ s/ /+/go;
155             print $Q->a({ -HREF => $Q->script_name . "?name=$name" },
156                         $_);
157             print $Q->br;
158         }
159         else
160         {
161             print "$_\n";
162         }
163     }
164
165     print $Q->end_html;
166 }
167
168 untie %rolo_hash;
169
170 exit;
```

In this example, you will see that much of the code is the same as the previous version. The first noteworthy addition is on lines 9–11, where **Options::Common** is used instead of plain **Options** (as was specified on the use statement on line 5). new is given four more potential parameters to watch for. These will be checked later.

The **Detect** module is also directly referenced here, though mostly for the sake of clarity. Nothing is exported by it, and the rest of the code will be checking the value of the variable $Detect::cgi directly, with full package qualification.

The block from lines 17–22 replaces the previous usage of the **Carp** library. Now, if the script is running in a CGI context, the CGI library and the **CGI::Carp** library are both used. Otherwise, the **Carp** library is left in place and used, as was the case previously. As a result, for the remainder of the script, any use of carp or croak will be properly handled for both CGI and command-line contexts.

Line 29 is where the core of the script starts, in the series of if statements that decide what course of action to follow. On line 33, within the block that will output the data "card" for a requested name, the value of $Detect::cgi is tested. If the script is in a CGI context, a simple header (Content-Type) is output, identifying what follows as HTML. None of the actual data output is altered. HTML tags that cause line breaks are output after each line to keep it from running together in the browser, but again these are done conditionally based on the value of $Detect::cgi.

This is the extent of change to the block that handles the –name command-line functionality. Any errors were reported with croak, which will act accordingly based on the context. There is no need to examine the various print statements to see which are error messages to be specially handled. The alternation of **Carp** and **CGI::Carp** takes care of this.

Skipping over the block that handles adds (we'll return to it last) to line 135, there is even less change to the block that handles deletions. Only the output of the `Content-Type` header, to satisfy the browser. As with the name-display block, errors are routed correctly through `croak`.

From lines 144–166, the default action of displaying the names alphabetically is handled, but with a twist this time, due to the CGI support. Rather than try to emit a great deal of HTML manually, this block creates an object of the CGI class if `$Detect::cgi` indicates such a need. This object is used to reference the HTML shortcuts that the library provides.

In this block, the desire is not just to list the names to the browser, but to actually make them links to this same script, but with a specific name specified for display. Now that the CGI object and its attendant methods are available, line 149 uses those methods to emit the relevant HTTP headers (the `$Q->header` method) and start the HTML code with proper initialization and directives (the `$Q->start_html` method, which also provides a document title).

The loop that actually lists the names now has an `if` clause, allowing it to simply print the names in a command-line context, or do much more in the CGI context. In the latter, the name is first slightly altered so that spaces are marked by the +. This is for the sake of the CGI protocol for passing arguments in a `GET` method. Without this, the name data would not be transmitted correctly.

Then the method `$Q->a` is used to effect an anchor, the familiar HTML A tag. All the shortcuts that follow a basic pattern have the same interface: if the first argument is a hash reference, it is treated as a list of attributes for the HTML tag. In this case, the only attribute being passed is the well-known `HREF` for specifying the link. Its value is created by using another CGI method, `script_name`, that returns the URL of the current script for the sake of self-referencing CGI applications such as this one.

Following the hash reference (if it is present at all) is the text that should be enclosed within this tag and the tag's closing specifier. For this example, that text is the unchanged name. The doctored name was used in specifying the URL for the `HREF` attribute. As with the earlier block that also displayed multiple lines, the `BR` tag is emitted to force line breaks. Only in this case, it is called as a method on the CGI object instead of emitted directly.

This takes us to the `add` block, the block from lines 52–134. Unlike the logical blocks that only produced output, the `add` functionality of **rolodex** required several pieces of input from the user. As a result, the block looks drastically different now that CGI support is required. Note lines 104–133 are unchanged from the original script, just moved to a block where they serve as a clause to the testing of `$Detect::cgi`. Line 56 starts the CGI-specific block with the creation of a CGI class object.

The test on line 58 is the first reference to the four new options specified on lines 9–11, in the new method call to **Options::Common**. If this parameter has a value, then it can mean only one thing: the script has already been through once. This is because the second part of this `if` evaluation, the case in which new_name has no value, is the only other reference to the parameter.

Looking at this second block first, lines 80–101 use a variety of HTML shortcut methods provided by the CGI object to emit HTTP headers, start the HTML page, create a form, and end the page. Look closely at the names of the shortcuts; they are designed to be very similar, or outright identical to the resulting HTML. (Rather than explain each one here, the reader is referred to the manual page for the **CGI.pm** library.) Line 84 is noteworthy as it starts the form declaring that it will be sent as a `POST` method, and that the action to be taken is to call this same script again. (Note the lack of trailing information on the URL, since this method is `POST` rather than `GET`.)

The sequence from lines 85–87 is essentially repeated for the other parts of data. The sequence prints a simple textual label followed by an entry box. The specification of the box gives a name to the form field produced, and also specifies size. When the form is posted (when the **Submit** button is pressed), the data in these fields will be passed along using the specified names. This is how the test for new_name can tell that the script is on its second cycle, and thus avoids redisplaying the form.

Returning to the processing of the form data, lines 60–76, the variable $new_name was set as a side effect of the test, and the other values are set by querying the **Options::Common** object. Line 64 is a safety measure to ensure that no trailing white space or newline characters are left in. Then the block from lines 66–72 performs the same processing of the data that the old version of the script did (and still does in lines 127–132). A short message is output to the browser using the CGI shortcuts, indicating a successful addition of data.

What does this illustrate? Those blocks that were not dependent on user-interactive input showed very little change. But the block that did require input from the user was drastically altered. This repeats the point made earlier, that there is no one-pass, off-the-shelf solution to this process.

The goal here is to simplify, not automate. All the same, this second-generation script still has many shortcomings. It simply is not easy to use in a WWW environment, and that, after all, is the goal.

One More Iteration Through

Now that the impact of the differences in input handling have been illustrated, one more pass at the **rolodex** script should be made. This will better its appearance and make it more user-friendly, in the WWW sense of the term. For this example, the CGI class will be subclassed in order to add a little twist to the IMG tag: automatic size information. A few icons and small graphics can add a better sense of life to the generated page. However, CGI scripts are not static things. The various tools available to stream-edit HTML code and add height and width attributes to images cannot be used on CGI scripts. For this next example to run, the **Image::Size** library from CPAN will be needed. The library is pure Perl code, requiring no compilation, and should install very easily.

First, the code for the subclassed CGI approach, called simply **NewCGI** (Listing 23.8).

Listing 23.8
NewCgi

```
1    package NewCGI;
2
3    use CGI;
4    use Image::Size qw(attr_imgsize);
5    use vars qw(@ISA);
6
7    my $img_path = '/u/rjray/html';
8
9    @ISA = qw(CGI);
10
11   sub img
12   {
13       my $self = shift;
14       my $args = (ref($_[0]) eq 'HASH') ? shift : {};
15
16       my ($key) = grep(/^-?src$/oi, keys %{$args});
17
18       if ($key)
19       {
20           my $url = $args->{$key};
21           my $path;
22           ($path = $url) =~ s|^/~rjray|$img_path|;
23           if (-e "$path")
24           {
25               %{$args} = (%{$args}, attr_imgsize($path));
26           }
```

```
27
28              return CGI->img($args, @_);
29          }
30      else
31          {
32              return CGI->img(@_);
33          }
34  }
```

There is little remarkable here. The goal of this is to allow a local version of the img() method to be used. To do this, all that must be done is to refer to CGI as the parent class (line 9) and define our own img() method (lines 11–34). The new version of img is done very simply here, for the sake of illustration. Only those image URLs that start with the string /~rjray are handled. The URL is translated into a viable path, and then that path is passed to the subroutine attr_imgsize to get height and width.

The attr_imgsize routine takes an image file, finds the size, and then returns a four-element list that is tailored to the style of attributes used in the CGI library. This makes it easier to "in-line" these values directly into the existing attributes. Because the **CGI.pm** library is designed well from an OO standpoint, all other methods (including new) are automatically available through an object of class **NewCGI**.

Now, on to the last example of a rolodex (Listing 23.9).

Listing 23.9
rolodex3.p

```
1   #!/usr/bin/perl -w
2
3   BEGIN { @AnyDBM_File::ISA = qw(DB_File SDBM_File NDBM_File) }
4   use AnyDBM_File;
5   use Options::Common;
6   use Detect;
7   use Carp;
8   use NewCGI;
9
10  $opts = new Options::Common qw(-name=s -add -delete=s
11                                 -new_name=s -new_phone=s -new_email=s
12                                 -new_addr=s -del_name=s);
13
14  $name = $opts->option('name')   || '';
15  $add  = $opts->option('add')    || 0;
16  $del  = $opts->option('delete') || '';
17
18  if ($add and $del)
19  {
20      if ($Detect::cgi)
21      {
22          print $Q->header, $Q->start_html(-title => 'ERROR');
23          print $Q->p("Only one of `add' or `delete' may be specified, ",
24                      "stopped at line " . __LINE__);
25          print $Q->p();
26          print $Q->p($Q->img({ -SRC => '/~rjray/g/bluediam.gif',
27                                -ALIGN => 'BOTTOM' }), " ",
28                      $Q->a({ -HREF => $Q->script_name },
29                          "Return to the list of entries")));
30          print $Q->end_html;
31          exit -1;
```

```
32       }
33     else
34     {
35         croak "Only one of `add' or `delete' may be specified, stopped";
36     }
37 }
38
39 tie %rolo_hash, 'AnyDBM_File', '/u/rjray/locarolo.dex';
40
41 if ($name)
42 {
43     if (! exists $rolo_hash{$name})
44     {
45         if ($Detect::cgi)
46         {
47             print $Q->header, $Q->start_html(-title => 'ERROR');
48             print $Q->p("No record for ``$name'' in the rolodex, ",
49                         "stopped at line " . __LINE__);
50             print $Q->p();
51             print $Q->p($Q->img({ -SRC => '/~rjray/g/bluediam.gif',
52                                   -ALIGN => 'BOTTOM' }), " ",
53                         $Q->a({ -HREF => $Q->script_name },
54                               "Return to the list of entries"));
55             print $Q->end_html;
56             exit -1;
57         }
58         else
59         {
60             croak "No record for ``$name'' in the rolodex, stopped";
61         }
62     }
63     else
64     {
65         @data = split("\n", $rolo_hash{$name});
66         %data = map { split(/=/, $_, 2) } @data;
67         if ($Detect::cgi)
68         {
69             my $Q = new NewCGI;
70
71             print $Q->header;
72             print $Q->start_html(-title => "Rolodex entry for: $name");
73             print $Q->p($Q->img({ -SRC => '/~rjray/g/bigblueball.gif',
74                                   -ALIGN => 'BOTTOM' }),
75                         $Q->font({ -SIZE => '+3' },
76                                  $Q->b($Q->i(" Rolodex Entry for: $name"))));
77             print $Q->p();
78             print $Q->table({ -BORDER => 0, -CELLPADDING => 3 },
79                             (map {
80                                  $Q->TR($Q->td({ -ALIGN => 'RIGHT' },
81                                                ucfirst lc $_ . ':'),
82                                         $Q->td(),
83                                         $Q->td($data{$_}))
84                             } (qw(NAME PHONE EMAIL),
85                               (grep(/^ADD/, sort keys %data)))));
```

```
86                  print $Q->p();
87                  print $Q->p($Q->img({ -SRC => '/~rjray/g/bluediam.gif',
88                                        -ALIGN => 'BOTTOM' }), " ",
89                          $Q->a({ -HREF => $Q->script_name },
90                                  "Return to the list of entries"));
91                  print $Q->end_html;
92              }
93          else
94          {
95              for (qw(NAME PHONE EMAIL))
96              {
97                  printf "%-10s: %s\n", ucfirst lc $_, $data{$_};
98              }
99              for (grep(/^ADD/, sort keys %data))
100             {
101                 printf "%-10s: %s\n", ucfirst lc $_, $data{$_};
102             }
103         }
104     }
105 }
106 elsif ($add)
107 {
108     if ($Detect::cgi)
109     {
110         my $Q = new NewCGI;
111
112         if ($new_name = $opts->option('new_name'))
113         {
114             if (defined $rolo_hash{$new_name})
115             {
116                 print $Q->header, $Q->start_html(-title => 'ERROR');
117                 print $Q->p("NAME $new_name already exists in database. ",
118                             "Stopped at $0, line " . __LINE__);
119                 print $Q->p();
120                 print $Q->p($Q->img({ -SRC => '/~rjray/g/bluediam.gif',
121                                       -ALIGN => 'BOTTOM' }), " ",
122                         $Q->a({ -HREF => $Q->script_name },
123                                 "Return to the list of entries"));
124                 print $Q->end_html;
125                 exit -1;
126             }
127             $new_phone = $opts->option('new_phone') || '';
128             $new_email = $opts->option('new_email') || '';
129             my $addr   = $opts->option('new_addr');
130             @addr = split("\n", $addr);
131
132             chomp ($new_phone, $new_email, $new_name, @addr);
133
134             $data = "NAME=$new_name\nPHONE=$new_phone\nEMAIL=$new_email\n";
135             $count = 1;
136             $data .= join("\n",
137                             map { sprintf("ADDR%d=%s",
138                                           $count++, $_) } (@addr));
139
```

```
140              $rolo_hash{$new_name} = $data;
141              print $Q->header,
142                  $Q->start_html(-title => "Entry $new_name Added");
143              print $Q->p($Q->img({ -SRC => '/~rjray/g/bigblueball.gif',
144                                     -ALIGN => 'BOTTOM' }),
145                       $Q->font({ -SIZE => '+3' },
146                               $Q->b($Q->i(" New Entry for: $new_name"))));
147              print $Q->p("The new data for: $new_name", $Q->br,
148                          "has been added to the rolodex.");
149              print $Q->p($Q->img({ -SRC => '/~rjray/g/bluediam.gif',
150                                    -ALIGN => 'BOTTOM' }), " ",
151                       $Q->a({ -HREF => $Q->script_name },
152                             "Return to the list of entries"));
153              print $Q->end_html;
154          }
155      else
156          {
157          print $Q->header;
158          print $Q->start_html(-title => 'Add new rolodex entry');
159          print $Q->p($Q->img({ -SRC => '/~rjray/g/bigblueball.gif',
160                                -ALIGN => 'BOTTOM' }),
161                   $Q->font({ -SIZE => '+3' },
162                           $Q->b($Q->i(" Add a new rolodex entry"))));
163          print $Q->p();
164          print $Q->startform('POST', $Q->script_name);
165          print $Q->table({ -BORDER => 0, -CELLPADDING => 3 },
166                   $Q->TR(
167                       $Q->td({ -ALIGN => 'RIGHT' },
168                               "New Name:"),
169                       $Q->td($Q->textfield(-name => 'new_name',
170                                           -maxlength => 30))
171                         ),
172                   $Q->TR(
173                       $Q->td({ -ALIGN => 'RIGHT' },
174                               "New phone:"),
175                       $Q->td($Q->textfield(-name => 'new_phone',
176                                             -maxlength => 12))
177                         ),
178                   $Q->TR(
179                       $Q->td({ -ALIGN => 'RIGHT' },
180                               "E-Mail:"),
181                       $Q->td($Q->textfield(-name => 'new_email',
182                                             -maxlength => 30))
183                         ),
184                   $Q->TR({ -VALIGN => 'TOP' },
185                       $Q->td({ -ALIGN => 'RIGHT' },
186                               "Address:"),
187                       $Q->td($Q->textarea(-name => 'new_addr',
188                                           -rows => 5,
189                                           -columns => 40))
190                         ));
191          print $Q->br;
192          print $Q->submit(-name => 'add'), " this data", $Q->br;
193          print $Q->b("or"), $Q->br;
```

```
194                    print $Q->reset, " the form";
195                    print $Q->endform;
196                    print $Q->p($Q->img({ -SRC => '/~rjray/g/bluediam.gif',
197                                          -ALIGN => 'BOTTOM' }), " ",
198                             $Q->a({ -HREF => $Q->script_name },
199                                   "Go back to the list of entries"));
200                    print $Q->end_html;
201            }
202        }
203    else
204        {
205            $line = '';
206            @addr = ();
207
208            print "Creating new record:\n\nNew Name:\n";
209            $new_name = <STDIN>;  chomp $new_name;
210            croak "NAME is a required field, stopped" unless ($new_name);
211            croak "NAME $new_name already exists, stopped"
212                if (exists $rolo_hash{$new_name});
213
214            print "New phone:\n";
215            $new_phone = <STDIN>; chomp $new_phone;
216            print "E-Mail address:\n";
217            $new_email = <STDIN>; chomp $new_email;
218
219            print "Enter address information. Enter '.' to end input:\n";
220            do
221            {
222                $line = <STDIN>; chomp $line;
223                push(@addr, $line) unless ($line eq '.');
224            } while ($line ne '.');
225
226            $data = "NAME=$new_name\nPHONE=$new_phone\nEMAIL=$new_email\n";
227            $count = 1;
228            $data .= join("\n",
229                          map { sprintf("ADDR%d=%s", $count++, $_) } (@addr));
230
231            $rolo_hash{$new_name} = $data;
232        }
233 }
234 elsif ($del)
235 {
236    if ($Detect::cgi)
237        {
238            my $del_name;
239            my $Q = new NewCGI;
240
241            if ($del_name = $opts->option('del_name'))
242            {
243                unless (exists $rolo_hash{$del_name})
244                {
245                    print $Q->header, $Q->start_html(-title => 'ERROR');
246                    print $Q->p("DELETE: Name ``$del_name'' not in the rolodex, ",
247                                "stopped at line " . __LINE__);
```

```
248                    print $Q->p();
249                    print $Q->p($Q->img({ -SRC => '/~rjray/g/bluediam.gif',
250                                          -ALIGN => 'BOTTOM' }), " ",
251                              $Q->a({ -HREF => $Q->script_name },
252                                    "Return to the list of entries"));
253                print $Q->end_html;
254                exit -1;
255            }
256
257        delete $rolo_hash{$del_name};
258
259        print $Q->header;
260        print $Q->start_html(-title => "Rolodex - $del_name deleted");
261        print $Q->p($Q->img({ -SRC => '/~rjray/g/bigblueball.gif',
262                              -ALIGN => 'BOTTOM' }),
263                    $Q->font({ -SIZE => '+3' },
264                             $Q->b($Q->i(" Entry $del_name Deleted"))));
265        print $Q->p();
266        print $Q->p("The rolodex entry ``$del_name'' has been deleted.");
267        print $Q->p($Q->img({ -SRC => '/~rjray/g/bluediam.gif',
268                              -ALIGN => 'BOTTOM' }), " ",
269                    $Q->a({ -HREF => $Q->script_name },
270                          "Go back to the list of entries"));
271        print $Q->end_html;
272    }
273    else
274    {
275        print $Q->header;
276        print $Q->start_html(-title => "Rolodex - Select Name to Delete");
277        print $Q->p($Q->img({ -SRC => '/~rjray/g/bigblueball.gif',
278                              -ALIGN => 'BOTTOM' }),
279                    $Q->font({ -SIZE => '+3' },
280                             $Q->b($Q->i(" Select a name to delete:"))));
281        print $Q->p();
282        print $Q->startform('POST', $Q->script_name);
283        my @boxes = $Q->radio_group(-name => 'del_name',
284                                    -values => [sort keys %rolo_hash],
285                                    -default => '-',
286                                    -nolabels => 1);
287        print $Q->table({ -BORDER => 0, -CELLPADDING => 3 },
288                        (map {
289                            $Q->TR($Q->td(shift(@boxes)),
290                                   $Q->td($_))
291                        } (sort keys %rolo_hash)));
292        print $Q->br;
293        print $Q->submit(-name => 'delete', -value => 'Delete');
294        print " the selected entry";
295        print $Q->p($Q->img({ -SRC => '/~rjray/g/bluediam.gif',
296                              -ALIGN => 'BOTTOM' }), " ",
297                    $Q->a({ -HREF => $Q->script_name },
298                          "Go back to the list of entries"));
299        print $Q->end_html;
300    }
301 }
```

```
302      else
303      {
304          croak "DELETE: Name ``$del'' is not in the rolodex, stopped"
305              unless (exists $rolo_hash{$del});
306
307          delete $rolo_hash{$del};
308          print "Record ``$del'' has been deleted.\n";
309      }
310 }
311 else
312 {
313      if ($Detect::cgi)
314      {
315          my $Q = new NewCGI;
316
317          print $Q->header;
318          print $Q->start_html(-title => 'Rolodex');
319          print $Q->p($Q->img({ -SRC => '/~rjray/g/bigblueball.gif',
320                                -ALIGN => 'BOTTOM' }),
321                      $Q->font({ -SIZE => '+3' },
322                              $Q->b($Q->i(" Welcome to WWW-Rolodex"))));
323          print $Q->p();
324          for (sort keys %rolo_hash)
325          {
326              ($name = $_) =~ s/ /+/go;
327              print $Q->img({ -SRC => '/~rjray/g/bluediam.gif',
328                            -ALIGN => 'BOTTOM' }), " ";
329              print $Q->a({ -HREF => $Q->script_name . "?name=$name" },
330                          $_);
331              print $Q->br;
332          }
333
334          print $Q->startform('POST', $Q->script_name);
335          print $Q->submit(-name => 'add', -value => 'Add a new entry');
336          print "   ";
337          print $Q->submit(-name => 'delete', -value => 'Delete an entry');
338          print $Q->endform;
339          print $Q->end_html;
340      }
341      else
342      {
343          for (sort keys %rolo_hash)
344          {
345              print "$_\n";
346          }
347      }
348 }
349
350 untie %rolo_hash;
351
352 exit;
```

Clearly, a more serious script! For starters, there is no longer the pretext of only reading in the CGI support if so needed. The **CGI** (and **NewCGI**) modules are very lightweight until used. No great amount of code is compiled initially, so there is very little added to the start-up time. Also, testing this showed that referring to the **CGI::Carp** library within an **eval** interfered with some of the "sanity checks" it performs. Instead, errors are handled natively, which also allows for the addition of a link to allow the user return to the full list.

Rather than slowly going over each changed line (as there are so many), the explanation will address blocks. The reader is encouraged to examine the blocks more closely, to help in understanding.

The block that displays a record is now redesigned to make the output somewhat nicer. The technique used here will be repeated in later blocks. A table with no border is used to manage the spacing of lines and elements. By doing this, it is possible to create effects such as having the field labels all right-justified, while having the field values left-justified. Whatever the width of the browser window or length of the data, these will persist. A few graphics are dropped in to add a splash of color. However, these will not slow the display of text, because the **NewCGI** version of the img method provides height and width information. This allows a browser to render the text before it finishes loading the image.

The adding of a new record is still handled in two steps, a self-referencing process. Again, a few graphics are thrown in for color. As before, a "transparent" table is used to force the alignment of the screen elements.

In this case, all the form entry elements are aligned with each other. If so desired, the **submit** and reset buttons could be better aligned using a second table. A common approach is to put the left-most button in a cell that is left-aligned, and the right-most in a right-aligned cell. The visual effect is that the buttons are on opposite edges, regardless of broswer width (see Figure 23.1).

Figure 23.1
Rolodex Version 1

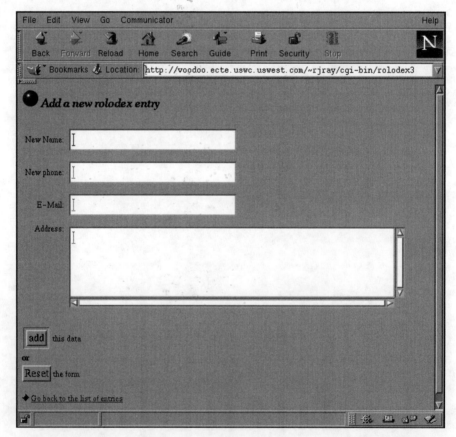

The delete block has now undergone a major revision from the previous incarnation. Because it was previously assumed that the name to be removed would already be in the parameter list, little was changed over the non-Web version. In this newer case, the user is offered a nicer interface.

In the absence of the name to delete (denoted as `del_name`), a form is presented with all the current rolodex names in alphabetical order. Each has a radiobutton beside the name. The user can select which name to delete and press the **Delete** button. This submit button is named *delete*, which means that the next iteration of the script will still detect a value for the parameter `delete` in the form data. The selected name will be in the parameter `del_name`. Note that a table is once again used. If the call to the CGI method `radio_group` (line 283) provided the labels, there would be no visible space between the button and the name. By saving the returned list from `radio_group` and using those elements in a table, the more professional layout is achieved (see Figure 23.2).

Figure 23.2
Form with
Rolodex Names

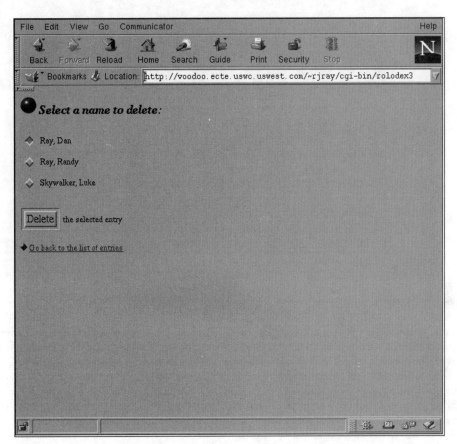

Lastly, the main loop displays the names in the rolodex, allowing the user to select one to display. As Figure 23.3 shows, this page is not changed much; the layout of names-as-links is the same as it was. But graphical "dots" (or diamonds, in this case) are added for effect, and at the bottom are two submit-style buttons, one to add a new record and the other to delete a record. These are given names **add** and **delete**, and if either is pressed, the tests for non-null values in either of these parameters will succeed, taking the correct action. Where the command-line version relied on `-add` and `-delete`, this is the best approach for the CGI context.

Figure 23.3
Display of
Rolodex Names

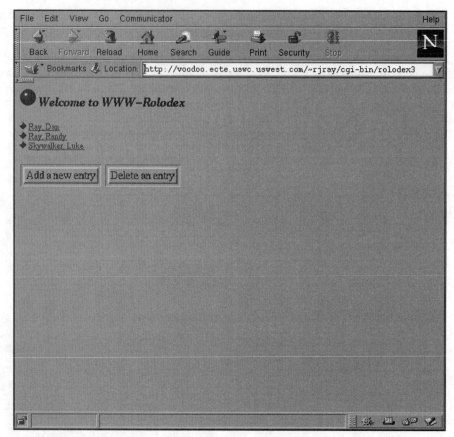

Summary

Migrating command-line scripts to CGI is not impossible, and does not have to be difficult. Although the concepts of application design are beyond the scope of this chapter, designing your scripts with the intent to operate in both arenas can help a great deal. The problem is, many people are faced with legacy code that was designed and developed before there was a World Wide Web. There may be cases where it is more cost-efficient to simply rewrite the application than to try to convert it.

When designing for both arenas, try to isolate the input-driven sections so that the different techniques do not get in each other's way. Output is not as strictly segregated, but taking the effort to use the full capacity of HTML on the Web side of the application may be worth the time.

In these examples, some things were glossed over in order to keep the code readable to newer Perl programmers. There are many things that could be added to this application to make it into a truly useful interoffice (or personal) tool: options to edit existing records, better handling of graphics by the NewCGI class, and better handling of non-command-line contexts in Options::Common, just to name a few. Hopefully, the basic code can provide a starting point for experimentation and exploration.

Syntax Patterns

Below are (about 300) Syntax Patterns that you might find useful. They range from the simple to the not-so-simple. As Perl programmers get more skillful, their basic tendency is to take patterns like this and connect them into larger 'sentences' and 'paragraphs'.

I have divided them by the chapters in which they first appear. (Not all chapters have a representative syntax sample because they primarily deal with examples or techniques). Of course, if you need elaboration on any of the syntax you find, please refer to the chapter listed.

Chapter 1: Setting Up the Perl 5 Environment

Two basic sections here: One, to compile the OS and the other, to compile extensions.

Compiling On Unix

To compile the standard distribution of Perl onto unix, first get Perl (as a quick reference, you can pick it up at *ftp://www.perl.com/pub/perl/CPAN/src/latest.tar.g*. Use the CPAN nearest you). Then say:

```
prompt% sh Configure
                # sh configure --help for info on installing automatically)
prompt% make
prompt% make test
prompt% make install
```

Compiling On NT/Win 95

To compile with VC++ onto Windows 95:

1. get Perl (*ftp://www.perl.com/pub/perl/CPAN/src/latest.tar.gz*)
2. use winzip to unzip files

edit Makefile—customize which drive (INST_DRV) and which directory (INST_TOP) you want Perl to go. Then type:

```
C:\path\to\C++> VCVARS32.BAT  # batch file for VC++; sets environment
C:\path\to\perl\download> nmake
C:\path\to\perl\download> nmake test
C:\path\to\perl\download> nmake install
```

Installing on Macintosh

To install on Macintosh:

Open a browser, go to *ftp://ftp.cs.colorado.edu/pub/perl/CPAN/ports/mac/* (or any other CPAN site under /ports/mac)

get a file that look likes Mac_Perl*appl.bin (*ftp://ftp.cs.colorado.edu/pub/perl/CPAN/Mac_Perl_520r4_bigappl.bin* is most current, and comes with the most 'stuff')

Unexpand with stuffit expaneder. (*http://www.aladdinsys.com/expander/expander_mac.html*)

Installing on OS/2

First, get EMX (as a prereq *ftp://ftp.cdrom.com/pub/os2/emx09c/emxrt.zip*)
    Now, get the OS/2 port of Perl (*ftp://ftp.cs.colorado.edu/mirrors/CPAN/authors/id/ILYAZ/os2/*) You are going to need get all the files there. Then, unzip plinst10.zip (unzip source: *ftp://ftp.cdrom.com/pub/infozip/OS2/*) Type (in installed directory):

```
[h:] install.exe
```

Installing on VMS

You are going to need gunzip, tar, a C compiler, and MMS or MMK.

gunzip can be found at: *ftp://ftp.digital.com/pub/VMS/*

tar can be found at: *ftp://ftp.digital.com/pub/VMS/*

gcc (freeware compiler) can be found at: *ftp://ftp.cco.caltech.edu/pub/rankin/*

MMK (freeware VMS make) can be found at: *ftp://ftp.wku.edu/madgoat/*

Install all these packages, then get Perl.

Perl can be found at: *ftp://ftp.cs.colorado.edu/pub/perl/CPAN/src/latest.tar.gz*

If you are using Netscape (or some other smart client) it will rename it for you. (VMS doesn't accept names with two dots in them.)

Then:

```
$ gunzip latest.tar-gz
$ tar -xvf latest.tar
$ set default [ .perl ] # to change directories
```

Edit config.vms (parameters for VMS in compilation) And, as an example, Perl installation:

```
$ mms/descrip=[.vms] /macro=("decc=1", "__AXP__=1")
$ mms/descrip=[.vms] /macro=("decc=1", "__AXP__=1") test
$ define/translation=concealed perl_root disk$dka200: [perl5_004_01.]
$ mms/descrip=[.vms] /macro=("decc=1", "__AXP__=1") install
```

(You will need to modify this command for your particular installation. Look at config.vms for details.)

Installing on MSDOS (via binary)

You will need djgpp, and unzip in order to make the binary installation work. For unzip go to *ftp://www.winsite.com/info/pc/win3/util/pk260w16.exe*. For DJGPP go to http://www.delorie.com.

For a WAY COOL (I mean WAY COOL) way of jumpstarting your use with DJGPP, go to *http://www.delorie.com/djgpp/zip-picker.html*. This will tell you exactly what you need, along with giving you commands for installation.

For a binary version of the Perl executable (in dos) go to (*ftp://ftp.cs.colorado.edu/pub/perl/CPAN/ports/msdos/LMOLNAR/perl542b.zip*).

If you want to install in C:\perl, type:

```
C:\perl> pkunzip -d perl542b.zip C:\perl> bin/perl -i~ -pe
"s'C:/djgpp'C:/perl'i" lib\perl\Config.pm
```

Installing Extensions

To use CPAN to install an extension, say:

```
prompt% perl -MCPAN -e shell;
cpan> i /Net/             # gets information about modules named 'Net'
cpan> install Net::Ident  # installs the module Net::Ident
```

To install Extensions without CPAN on unix and NT, type:

```
# Unix;
prompt% PATH=$PATH:/usr/local/bin; # or where you installed Perl.
prompt% ftp ftp.cs.colorado.edu    # connect as anonymous login.
                                   # go to any CPAN site

ftp> cd /pub/perl/CPAN/modules      # or path to CPAN

ftp> cd by-category                 # if you want to look by subject
```

or:

```
ftp> cd by-module          # if you want to look for individual mods

ftp> get                   # to get the module

prompt% gunzip             # WinZip on NT, or gnu's gunzip
prompt% tar xvf            # WinZip handles this too on NT.
prompt% perl Makefile.PL
prompt% make
prompt% make test
prompt% make install
#NT
C:\>   PATH="%PATH%; C:\perl\bin"; # (where you installed perl)
C:\>
C:\>   cd
C:\>   perl Makefile.PL
C:\>   nmake
C:\>   nmake test
C:\>   nmake install
```

Chapter 2: Perl at 30,000 Feet: An Overview of Perl

In this chapter, there is both an overview of how to run Perl, and an overview of variables. Since we covered variables in the following chapter, we shall concentrate on how to run Perl.

Running Perl

There are quite a few ways to run a Perl executable, differing on Unix and NT. We list them below.
You can run Perl anywhere by saying:

```
C:\> perl scriptname.p
```

You can run Perl from the command-line on a unix platform, without 'perl' at the front of the command-line:

```
# Inside script 'program.p'
# Add #!/path/to/perl to beginning of script

prompt% chmod 755 program.p
prompt% program.p (runs program)
```

You can run Perl from the command-line with NT/95, without 'perl' in front. Assuming your script is named 'program', you can type:

```
C:\> cd \lib
C:\> copy runperl.bat program.bat
C:\> program
```

'program' then runs the script named 'program'. This assumes that 'program.bat' is in your PATH. Type:

```
C:\> PATH="%PATH%; C:\path\to\batfiles";
```

to set it up so program.bat is inside your path (batfiles is the place where program.bat is located).

Chapter 3: Variables in Perl

There were four types of variables: Scalars, Arrays, Hashes, and Handles, and we covered all of them in this chapter, as well as the common functions behind them. Here is a summary:

Simple Scalar Assignment

To assign to a scalar, in a simple way:

```
$scalar1 = 1.111;        # setting a scalar to a number

$scalar2 = "George";     # setting a scalar to a string
$scalar3 = "Romero";

$scalar4 = "$scalar2 $scalar3";    # sets $scalar4 to 'George Romero'
```

More Complicated Scalar Assignment

```
Perl has quite a few special characters (backslashed characters) that let you assign
complex types of data. Examples of this are listed below:

$scalar1 = "hello all!\n";

$scalar2 = "\LREALLY LOWER CASE";    # makes $scalar2 'really lower case'
                                     # \L forces to lower case

$scalar3 = "\ued Peschko";           # makes $scalar3 'Ed Peschko' \u
                                     # forces 'e' to upper case

$scalar4 = "\Q$@$%^$#@!#"            # makes string
                                     # '\$\@\$\%\^\$\#\@\!\#' - ie
                                     # backslashes everything. Good for
                                     # regular expressions (see below)

$scalar5 = " A bunch of special Characters:\n\r\f\t\b\cM\021\x4f ";
                                     # a newline '\n', return, '\r',
                                     # form feed '\f', tab '\t',
                                     # backspace '\b', control-M '\cM',
                                     # octal character '\021'
```

```
                                        # 'hex character '\x4f'

$scalar6 = '$scalar4';                  # Note single quotes;
                                        # $scalar5 equals string $scalar4';

$scalar7 = "\$scalar4";                 # same deal. Note '\$' makes Perl
                                        # interpret dollarsign as a literal
                                        # dollarsign, not evaluated.

$scalar8 = 'This is a \' single quote'; # lets a single quote co-exist
                                        # in a single quoted string

$scalar9 = "This is a \" double quote"; # same thing for double quotes.
```

Scalar Operations

Here are the main functions that you will use to manipulate scalars:

```
$length = length($scalar);                   # gets length of scalar
                                             # (how many characters)

$reverse = reverse("This is how to do it"); # reverses string makes
                                             # 'ti od ot who si sihT'

$concat = 'concatenate '.'two strings'       # dot concatenate operator.
                         # $concat = 'concatenate two strings'

print "Goodbye world..\n";                   # prints standard output.

print substr('fullstring', 0, 2);            # prints letters 'fu'.

$scalar = 'Substitute';
substr($scalar, length($scalar) -2, length($scalar)) = substr($scalar, 0, 2);
                                             # swaps last two characters
                                             # with first two;
                                             # equals 'tebstituSu'

$scalar2 = 'te' x 5;                         # Scalar concat operator.
                                             # 'multiplies' 'te' by 5 to
                                             # make $scalar2 =
                                             # 'tetetetete'
```

Simple Array Assignment

Arrays are ordered sets of scalars, or simply lists of scalars, so all of the above scalar syntax applies to each element inside the array. Here are some array assignments:

```
@array = (1,2,'Dog', 4);              # each element is a scalar

$array[2] = 'te' x 5;                 # s/'Dog'/'tetetetete'/;

$array[-1] = 'dog2';                  # replaces last element
                                      # with 'dog2'.
```

More Complicated Array Assignment

But like always, since Perl is about flexibility, there are quite a few ways to deal with arrays:

```
$array[10000] = '';                      # Makes 10001th element in
                                         # array equal to blank (and
                                         # creates the other 10000
                                         # elements in the process.


@array = (3,4,5);
@array[1,2] = @array[2,1];               # Makes @array (3,5,4);
                                         # swaps elements 1 and 2.


@array[0..4] = @array[reverse(0..4)];    # reverses array section
                                         # ( 1st through 4th
                                         # elements in array).
                                         # Subscripted 0 through 4.
```

Array Operations

There are quite a few functions to deal with arrays, too:

```
@array = (1,2,3);
push (@array, 4);                   # makes array equal to (1,2,3,4);


@array = (1,2,3);
shift(@array, 0);                   # makes array equal to (0,1,2,3);


@array = (1,2,3);
$first_element = unshift(@array);   # makes '$first_element' equal to 1,
                                    # '@array' equal to (2,3)


@array = (1,2,3);
$last_element = pop (@array);       # makes '$last_element' equal to 3,
                                    # '@array' equal to (1,2)

@array = (1,2,3,4);
@splice_out = splice(@array, 1,2);      # makes '@array' equal to (1,4).
                                        # 'splice out the two elements,
                                        # at element position #1, and
                                        # continue for 2 elements.
                                        # makes @splice_out == (2,3)
                                        # (bold chars spliced out.)


@array = (1,2,3,4);
@splice_out = splice(@array, 1,2,(4,5,6));
                                        # makes @array == (1,4,5,6,5)
                                        # and @splice_out == (2,3). Read
                                        # as 'take two elements starting
                                        # at element #1, replace with
                                        # the elements (4,5,6).


@chars = split('', "SCALAR");           # makes array @chars equal to
                                        # ('S','C','A','L','A','R');
@words =split(' ',"SCALAR TO ARRAY");   # makes array @words equal to
                                        # ('SCALAR', 'TO','ARRAY');
```

```
@words = reverse(@words);           # makes array (@words) equal to
                                    # ('ARRAY','TO','SCALAR');

chop(@words);                       # makes array (@words) equal to
                                    # ('ARRA','T','SCALA');

$scalar = join(' ', @words);        # makes scalar $scalar equal to
                                    # 'ARRA T SCALA'
@words = ('ARRAY','TO','SCALAR');
$length = scalar(@words);           # gets length of array. Notice
                                    # NOT $length = length(@words).
                                    # That gives you the length of the
                                    # string resulting from the *number*
                                    # of elements in the string

                                    # Hence, length(@words) gives you the
                                    # string '3' if @words is 101
                                    # elements long.
print $#words;                      # prints out last subscripted
                                    # element in in array 'words'

print "@words";                     # prints out 'ARRAY TO SCALAR'
print "@words[0..1]\n";             # prints out 'ARRAY TO'.
```

Hash Assignment

Hashes are like dictionaries, or 'arrays that have any element' (not just numbers) as a key. Since they don't have a subscript to put them in place, they don't have order. Below are some assignments to hashes.

```
$hash{1} = 2;                       # makes hash key '1' equal to '2'.
$scalar = $hash{1};                 # makes $scalar equal to '2'.
%hash = (1,2,3,4);                  # sets entire hash
%hash = (1 => 2, 3 => 4);           # sets entire hash, same as above except
                                    # a little bit clearer 1 and 3 are keys,
                                    # 2 and 4 are values.
@hash{'dog','boy'} = @hash{'boy','dog'};
                                    # swap the values of the hash key 'dog'
                                    # and the hash key 'boy'
```

Hash Operations

Below are some functions to get information out of hashes.

```
%hash = (1 => 2, 3 => 4);
print keys(%hash);                  # prints out all the keys in no particular
                                    # order (1,3) or (3,1)
print values (%hash);               # prints out all the values inside a hash
                                    # in no particular order
delete $hash{1};                    # deletes the element 1 inside '%hash'.
undef %hash;                        # clears hash of all values

while (($key, $value) = each(%hash)) # prints out all key value pairs, one
```

```
{                                       # at a time.
    print "$key => $value\n";
}

%hash = reverse(%hash);           # switches the keys in a hash for its values,
                                  # %hash =(1=> 2,3=> 4) becomes (2=> 1,4 =>3);
```

FileHandle Operations

FileHandles are special in Perl. They are the main way for Perl to interact with the operating system (files, directories, pipes of information, etc.) I mostly use the '*FileHandle*' package; below shows the built-in FileHandle operators instead.

```
open (FD, "file");                # open FD for reading from the file 'file'
$fd = new FileHandle("file");     # same thing, except you can pass $fd around
                                  # to functions more easily.
$line = <FD>;                     # read one line from a file.
@lines = <FD>;                    # read all lines from a file ('\n' delimited)
chomp(@lines = <FD>);             # read all lines from file, chomp off the
                                  # '\n';
open(FD, "> file");               # open FD for writing.
print FD "HERE!!!\n";             # prints 'HERE!!!' to the file file
close(FD);                        # closes the file handle FD.
open(FD, "ls -1 |);               # gets output from a command pipe.
                                  # (Works on Win95, WinNT)
@lines = <FD>;                    # gets all the lines from that command
print "@lines\n";                 # print them out.
open(FD, "| grep hello");         # puts output into a command pipe.
$lines = "this\nis\na\nbunch\nof\nlines\nOne\nof\nthem\nsays\nhello\n";
print FD $lines;
close(FD);                        # sends text to grep to look for hello
                                  # see the 'grep' command below for better
                                  # ways of doing this.
```

Chapter 4: Perl Control Structures and Operators

There are quite a few control structures; this is one of the main things that gives Perl its expressability. Just remember that Perl's control structures are the same as C's:

Looping Constructs

Looping constructs allow you to execute the same statement, over and over under conditions. Here are while, foreach, for, and until.

while

```
while (defined ($line = )) # prints out all lines in data pointed to
{                                   # by filehandle FD
    print "$line\n";
```

```
}
while ($xx++ < 10)                    # prints out 1 2 3 4 5 6 7 8 9 10
{
    print "$xx\n";
}

$xx =0;
do                                    # prints out 0 1 2 3 4 5 6 7 8 9 10
{
    print "$xx\n";
} while ($xx++ < 10);
```

foreach

```
@array = (0..10);
foreach $xx (@array)                  # prints out 0 1 2 3 4 5 6 7 8 9 10
{
    print "$xx\n";
}

foreach $xx (@array)                  # makes '@array' =
{                                     # (0,2,4,6,8,10,12,14,16,18,20);
    $xx *= 2;                         # (ie: modifies array);
}
```

for

```
@array = (0..10);
for ($xx = 0; $xx < @array; $xx++)   # prints out 0 1 2 3 4 5 6 7 8 9 10
{
    print "$array[$xx]\n";
}
for ($line = ; defined($line); $line = )
{
    print $line;                      # does same thing as
}                                     # 'while (defined($line = ))'
```

until

```
until ($xx++ > 10)                    # prints out 1 2 3 4 5 6 7 8 9 10
{                                     # Exactly opposite of 'while'
    print "$xx\n";
}
```

Loop Control: last, next, redo—and labels

Loops in Perl are much more controllable than they are in a low level language like C. Below are ways of breaking out of loops (last), skipping to the next iteration (next) and redoing a loop (redo).

next

```
for ($xx = 0; $xx < 4; $xx++)          # prints 0 0 - 0 1 - 0 2 - 0 3
{                                      #             1 0 - 1 1 - 1 2 - 1 3
    for ($yy = 0; $yy < 4; $yy++)      #             2 0 - 2 1 - 2 2 - 2 3
    {                                  #             3 0 - 3 1 - 3 2 - 3 3
        print "$xx $yy - ";
        next if ($yy > 1);             #     GOES to statement in bold
    }
}

LABEL: for ($xx = 0; $xx < 4; $xx++)   # prints      0 0 - 0 1 - 0 2
       {                               #             1 0 - 1 1 - 1 2
           for ($yy = 0; $yy < 4; $yy ++) #          2 0 - 2 1 - 2 2
           {                           #             3 0 - 3 1 - 3 2
               print "$xx $yy - ";
             next LABEL if ($yy > 1);  # GOES TO bold $xx loop w/LABEL
           }
       }
```

last

```
for ($xx = 0; $xx < 4; $xx++)          # prints    0 0 - 0 1 - 0 2
{                                      #           1 0 - 1 1 - 1 2
    for ($yy = 0; $yy < 4; $yy ++)     #           2 0 - 2 1 - 2 2
    {                                  #           3 0 - 3 1 - 3 2
        print "$xx $yy - ";
        last if ($yy > 1);             # SHORT CIRCUITS bold $yy loop
    }
}

LABEL: for ($xx = 0; $xx < 4; $xx++)   # prints 0 0 - 0 1 - 0 2
       {
           for ($yy = 0; $yy < 4; $yy ++)
           {
               print "$xx $yy - ";
             last LABEL if ($yy > 2); # SHORT CIRCUITS BOLD $xx loop
           }
       }

foreach $line (@codelines)             # assumes @codelines
{                                      # contains lines of code.
    next if ($line =~ m"^#");          # skip comments (start with #)
    last if ($line eq '__END__');
    print $line;
}
```

redo

```
for ($xx = 0; $xx < 4; $xx ++)         # prints  0 0 - 0 1 - 0 2
{                                      #          0 2 - 0 2 - 0 2
```

```perl
    for ($yy = 0; $yy < 4; $yy++)          # INFINITE LOOP
    {
        print "$xx $yy - ";
        redo if ($yy > 1);                 # REDOES $yy loop
    }
}

LOOP:                                      # forces user to enter
{                                          # number between 3 and 18
    print "Enter Charisma:";
    $chr = ;
    redo LOOP if ($chr < 3 || $chr > 18);
}
```

Conditionals—if, unless

'if' works exactly like it does in C, except that it has multiple forms. (as shown below). 'unless' is the opposite of 'if'.

```perl
if ($xx < 10)  { print $xx; }         # simple form with statements last
print $xx if ($xx < 10);              # form with statement first
(print ("PRINTING $xx"), next) if ($xx < 10);
                                      # multiple statements prior to if

unless ($xx < 10) { print $xx; }      # exactly the opposite statements
print $xx unless ($xx < 10);          # to the 'if' ones above.
(print ("PRINTING $xx"), next) unless ($xx < 10);
```

Truth

Perl also has a very unique notion of truth in that it has to deal with the fact that numbers and strings are both represented by the same datatype, the scalar.

```perl
if (0){}            # FALSE. zero evaluates as false
if ("0"){}          # FALSE. string zero hence false
if (""){}           # FALSE. empty string, hence false
if (0.0){}          # FALSE. 0.0 evaluates to 0, becomes false
if ('0.0'){}        # TRUE. Besides '0', non-zero length strings ('0.0')
                    # are always true
if (undef){}        # FALSE. undef value is always false.
if ((undef, undef)){} # FALSE. (undef, undef) resolves undef, becomes false.

$a = undef
if ($a){}           # FALSE. $a resolves to undef, becomes false.
@a = (undef);
if (@a){}           # TRUE. @a has one element in it, becomes 'if (1){}'
@a = ();
if (@a){}           # FALSE. @a has no elements in it,becomes 'if (0){}'
```

Operators

There are tons of operators in Perl (see Chapter 3 for a summary). However, we concentrate below on the main ones for flow control, like short-circuiting.

```perl
$number || = 10;                        # sets $number to 10 if not set

my $fh = new FileHandle("f") || die;   # dies if cannot open $fh.
$number = $a || $b || $c || die "Couldn't set number!\n";
                                        # examples of short-circuiting.
                                        # if $a is false, tries to set to $b.
                                        # if $b is false, tries to set to $c.
                                        # if $c is false, dies.


$fullday = ($day eq 'mon')?  'monday' : # multiple clauses.  Tries setting
           ($day eq 'tue')? 'tuesday' : # $day to 'monday', then 'tuesday'
           'otherday';                  # gives up if $day ne 'mon', 'tue'
                                        # sets to 'otherday'.
```

Chapter 5: Functions and Scope

Scope and functions are intertwined. There are two types of scope: Lexical and dynamic, and they are used to make sure that you can have the same named variables without having them trample on each other. Functions are used to segregate bits of functionality, to compartmentalize certain complex operations that are used over and over.

Function Calls

Perl has only one stack which it passes functions through, the variable '@_'. You pass formal parameters through parens, and then assign to arguments inside the function.

Regular Function Call

```perl
function('aa','bb');                    # sets $aa equal to 'aa'
sub function                            # $bb equal to 'bb'
{
    my ($aa, $bb) = @_;
}
```

Function Call Mistake: Dropping Arguments

```perl
function ('aa','bb','cc');              # DROPS 'cc' OFF THE FACE OF THE
sub function                            # EARTH!  YOU are responsible
{                                       # for balancing arguments
    my ($aa, $bb) = @_;

}
```

Function Call Dropping Rest of Arguments into a 'Default' Argument Bucket

```perl
function('aa','bb','cc');
sub function
{
    my ($first, @rest) = @_;            # $first = 'aa',
}                                       # @rest = ('bb','cc');
```

Recursive Functions

```perl
sub recursive                          # recursive function
{
    my ($low, $high) = @_;             # need lexical (my) scope
    print $low if ($low == $high);     # in order to work.
    recursive ($low, int ($high/2));
    recursive (int ($high/2), $high);
}
```

Lexical Scoping

Lexical scoping (keyword 'my') is by far the most widely-used scoping in Perl today (as opposed to dynamic.) It allows for truly private variables which are distinct from each other and use brackets as the form of distinguishing what 'territory' they cover.

Brackets Making New Scope

```perl
my $scalar = 2;
{
    my $scalar = 1;
}

print $scalar;                         # prints out 2 - inner
                                       # scope is gone
```

File Scoped Variables

```perl
my $scalar = 1;                        # file-scoped variable.. not
{                                      # internal to any brackets.
}

sub function
{
    print $scalar;                     # prints 1; since the first
}                                      # scalar is outside the scope
                                       # of the brackets
```

Dynamic Scoping

Dynamic scoping (local) is much looser than lexical scoping. Instead of being confined to a certain area, dynamic variables 'replace' global variables (push them aside) until they go out of scope. This means that inside functions, a dynamically scoped variable will still be seen.

```
$scalar = 0;                         # global
{
    local($scalar) = 2;              # 'hides' global by turning
    function();                      # it into 2, pushes '0' back.
}
sub function
{
    print $scalar;                   # prints 2.
}
```

Local versus my

```
my ($scalar, @array);                # RIGHT way to declare 'my' variables
my $scalar, @array;                  # WRONG way to declare 'my' variables,
                                     # equal to my ($scalar), @array;

local($") = undef;                   # Use local only for special variables
                                     # like this.
```

Chapter 6: Contexts in Perl 5

Contexts are tricky, but powerful, and a proper understanding of contexts will make your life easy. There are two main types of context: scalar and list. Examples are listed below.

Scalar Contexts

```
$scalar = $scalar2;           # simple array assignment
$scalar = @array;             # $scalar equals number of elements array
$scalar = length(@array);     # 'length' evaluates @array as scalar,
                              # @array = (0,2,3,1);
length(@array);               # becomes length('4'), becomes 1.  Hence
                              # $scalar equals '1'. Not usually what you
                              # would want.

if (@array1 > @array2) {  }   # compares number of elements in @array1
                              # with those in @array2

if (keys(%hash1) > keys(%hash2)) {   }
                              # compares number of elements in hash1 with
                              # those in hash2.

@array = (0,1,5,4);  @array2 = (1,1);
@elementlist = (scalar(@array), scalar(@array2);
                              # the function 'scalar' always forces
                              # scalar context. @elementlist = (4,2);
$xx = [ @array ];             # makes $xx a reference to a copy of
                              # @array.
$line = ;                     # getting one line from a file
if ( =~ m"Y"i) { }            # Checking a users input for a 'Y'.
```

List and Void Contexts

```
($key1, $key2, $key3) = ($key2, $key3, $key1);
                              # swap all values

($key2, $key1) = ($key1, $key3, $key2);
                              # $key2 gets dropped because
                              # not enough elements on lhs
$key1 = ($key2, $key3, $key1);  # simplifies to $key1 = $key1. Not
                              # enough elements on lhs.

($key1) =($key2, $key3, $key1);  # makes $key1 = $key2. Confusing, eh?
                              # use -w to point out errors

(@array, $xx) = ($xx, @array);  # makes $xx = $array[$#array]
                              # and $array[0] = $xx;

($xx, @array) = (1,2,3,4,5,6);  # makes $xx = 1, @array=(2,3,4,5,6)

(@array1, @array2) = (@array2, @array1);
                              # does NOT swap @array1 and @array2!
                              # instead, makes @array1 both arrays,
                              # and @array2 = ('');
```

More List Contexts (with the 'List' Being an Array)

```
@array = (1,2,3,4);
@array = $scalar;                # @array contains one element in it:
                                 # $scalar
@array[1,2,3] = (4,4,4);         # assigning to part of an array

@linearray = (, );
                                 # making @linearray equal to the lines
                                 # in both  and

@hash{('key1','key2','key3')} = @hash{('key2','key1','key3')};
                                 # swapping hash elements
```

Chapter 7: References

References are Perl's way of building complicated data structures— if you create a reference, you are creating a symbol which points to a particular piece of data rather than the data itself. And, as such, you can make two-dimensional or three-dimensional arrays (Arrays of Arrays, and Arrays of Arrays of Arrays), as well as linked lists or what have you.

Scalar References

Scalar references simply are references which point to a scalar, symbolized by putting a '\' in front of a scalar.

```
$scalar = 1.22231;
my $reference = \$scalar;         # setting a reference to another variable
```

```
    print $$reference;                    # prints 1.22231;

    my $string = 'seventeen letters';
    print "${\( length($string) )}\n";     # prints out 17.
    my $scalarref = \'Scalar Reference';   # setting a reference to a string. Makes
                                           # a 'read only' reference.
    print $$scalarref;                     # $ plus reference dereferences.
                                           # prints 'Scalar Reference'.
```

Array References

Array references are symbolized either by putting a '\' in front of an array or by putting square brackets around a list [1, 2, 3].

```
    my @array = (1,6,7,1.1,5);
    my $arrayref = \@array;               # array reference to '@array' set by '\'

    my $arrayref2 = [ @array ];           # another way of making a reference
                                          # ($arrayref2) point to the same values
                                          # as @array - does a copy instead.

    my $arrayref3 = [1,2,3,4,5];          # 'anonymous' array reference (the
                                          # data itself has no name attached, you
                                          # only 'point' to it.

    print @$arrayRef;                     # prints out entire array
    print @{$arrayref2}[0..2];            # printing a slice of array, prints 1,2,3
    print $arrayref2->[0];                # printing an individual array.  prints 1

    @{$arrayref}[1,2] = @{$arrayref}[2,1];
                                          # swapping two elements of $arrayref

    my $arrayref3 = [1,2,3, sqrt(2)];
                                          # functions can be called inside references

    my %hash = (  'onekey' => 'oneval', 'twokey' => 'twoval'};
    print "@{[sort keys (%hash)]}\n";
                                          # interpolation trick to evaluate function
                                          # inside of parens prints 'onekey twokey'

    $group2 = ref($group) eq 'ARRAY')? [@$group] :
              (ref($group) eq 'HASH')? [%$group] :
              (!ref($group))? [$group];
                                          # universal data copy statement.
                                          # makes group2 equal to an array
                                          # reference that contains the data
                                          # in 'group';
```

Hash References

Hash references are symbolized by either putting a '\' in front of a '%', or by putting brackets around an even valued list {1 => 2, 3 => 4 }.

```
$hashref->{'array'} = 1;          # sets a hash reference key directly.
                                  # creates hash if $hashref is null, gives
                                  # error if $hashref is not a hash reference

my $hashref = { 'element' => '1', 'element2' => '2' };
                                  # makes an 'anonymous' hash reference.
my $hashref2 = { %$hashref };     # copies the anonymous hash reference just
                                  # created into another 'anonymous' hash
                                  # reference.

my %hash = ( 'onekey' => 'oneval', 'twokey' => 'twoval' );
my $hashref3 = \%hash;            # creates reference to hash 'hash'.

print $hashref3->{'onekey'};      # prints out 'oneval'

print @{$hashref}{'onekey', 'twokey'};
                                  # prints out 'oneval','twoval'.

print { key => 'value', key2 => 'value2'}->{'key'};
                                  # prints 'value'. Dereferencing on fly.
```

Complex References

Complex references are made by nesting hash references inside array references, or array references inside hash references, and so on. You can make references arbitrarily complicated, as below (which is an Array of Hashes of Arrays):

```
$triplearrayref = [              # each level of [, { indicates
                    [            # another array or hash level.
                     [   1,2,3,4   ],
                     [   5,6,7,8   ]
                    ],
                    [
                     [   9,10,11,12 ]
                    ]
                   ];

print $triplearrayref->[0][0][2]; # prints 3
```

Manipulation of References

So far, we have just created references. To manipulate them, '->' is used to point 'into' the reference. Of course, you can use the syntax of references to assign to any part of the data structure.

```
$aa = [0,1,2];
$bb = $aa;
$aa->[0] = 4;
print $bb->[0];                  # prints 4. Since $bb references the
                                 # same data as $aa, assignment of $aa->[0]
                                 # changes $bb->[0]

$aa = [0,1,2];
```

```
$bb = [ @$aa ];                    # makes copy of data in $aa
@$bb = (4,5,6);
print $aa->[2];                    # prints 2. Since [@$aa] copied contents to
                                   # $bb, modifying contents of $bb doesn't
                                   # change $aa.


$aa = \'3.1415927';                # makes reference to scalar;
$$aa = 1;                          # causes syntax error because $aa is a 'read
                                   # only value.


my $bb;
{
    my $aa = [1,2,3,4];
    $bb = $aa;
}
print "@$bb\n";                    # prints '1 2 3 4' even though $aa has gone
                                   # out of scope.


my $bb = [1,2,3,4];
                                   # bad idea ... $bb never gets freed. because
{                                  # the refcount never gets to zero
    $bb = \$bb;
}
```

Chapter 8: More on Perl 5 References and Common Data Structures

We went over four different common data structures. Array of Arrays, Array of Hashes, Hash of Arrays, and Hash of Hashes. Of course, you can take the archetype further, and get quite complicated...

(reference to) Array of Arrays

Array of arrays is a good structure when dealing with files that have more than one field, where each field stands for something and you need to preserve order. Below are some examples of manipulating them.

```
my $AoA = [                        # creating a two dimensional array
            [1,2,3,4],
            [5,6,7,8]
          ];

print $AoA->[0][1];                #  prints '2';
                                   # referencing the second element
                                   # of that array
print "@{$AoA->[0]}\n";            #  prints '1 2 3 4';
                                   # printing out the entire first
                                   # 'sub-array'


my $array = $AoA->[1];             # making the reference to the second
print $array->[2];                 #  prints '7';
                                   # part of the array.
```

```
    my @elements = map($_->[1], @$AoA);      # getting the first 'slice' of the
    print "@elements\n";                     #  prints "2 6";

    foreach $array (@$AoA)                    # printing out all of the elements
    {                                         # of the array '@$AoA'
        foreach $element (@$array)            # prints '1 2 3 4'
        {                                     #         '5 6 7 8'
            print "$element ";
        }
        print "\n";
    }
```

(reference to) Array of Hashes

An Array of Hashes is good for cases when you need to name your data; it may be more intuitive if you can refer to a row's employee_id by $row->{emp_id} rather than $row->[1]. Below is a sample Array of Hashes.

```
    my $AoH =
        [                                           # creating an Array of Hashes
            { 'tin' => 'mine', 'feel' => 'good' } # anonymously
            { 'sam' => 'hill', 'what' => 'ever' }
        ];

    print $AoH->[0]{'tin'}; #  prints 'mine';
                                                # getting one of the AoH
                                                # elements.

    print "@{ [ keys (%{$AoH->[1]}) ] }\n";     # prints 'sam what';
                                                # getting all of the keys
                                                # in one slice of the array
                                                # reference.

    print "@{ [ values (%{$AoH->[0]} ] }\n";    # prints 'mine good';
                                                # getting all of the values
                                                # out of one of the hashes

    my $hash = $AoH->[1];
    @array = %$hash;                            # prints 'sam hill what ever'
                                                #  OR 'what ever sam hill';

    print "@array\n";                           #  prints entire hash in one of the
                                                #  array keys and values in
                                                #  non-determinant order

    print "@{ [ keys (%$hash); ] }\n";          # prints 'sam what'
```

(reference to) Hash of Arrays

Hash of Arrays are good when you have a file where each row has a different amount of data, and you want to distinguish between the rows by a 'key'; ie., $HoA->{'key1'} has data [1,2,3], and $HoA->{'key2'} has data [4,5,6].

```
my $HoA =
        {                                   # creates an anonymous hash of array
            'key1' => [1,2,3,4],
            'key2' => [5,6,7,8]
        };

print $HoA->{'key1'}[2];                #  prints '3'
                                        # prints one element in the array
                                        # pointed to the hash key 'key1'
print $HoA->{'key2'}[2];                # prints '6'
                                        # same, except under 'key2'

print "@{[ keys (%$HoA) ]}\n";          # prints 'key1 key2' OR 'key2 key1';
                                        # prints all of the keys for the
                                        # hash of arrays in random order.

print "@{[$HoA->{'key1'}]}\n";          # prints '1 2 3 4';
                                        # prints the array inside 'key1'.

my $array = $HoA->{'key2'};             # makes a place holder so we can get
                                        # the array inside 'key2' later.
print $array->[0];                      # prints '1';

print "@{   [map ($_->[2], values(%$HoA))   ]}\n";

                                        # 'prints '3 7' or '7 3'
                                        # prints a 'horizontal slice' of the
                                        # HoA (elements going down)

my $HoH =                               # An Anonymous Hash of Hashes.
        {
            'key'  => { 'subkey' => 'subvalue', 'subkey2' => 'subvalue2' }
            'key2' => { 'subkey3' =>'subvalue3','subkey4' => 'subvalue4' }
        };

print $HoH->{'key2'}{'subkey4'};        # prints subvalue4;
                                        # prints one of the keys inside the
                                        # hash of hashes

print "@{[  keys(%$HoH) ]}\n";          # prints 'key key2' or 'key2 key'
                                        # prints all of the keys at the
                                        # 'first level' of the HoH
                                        # (horizontally, going down)

print "@{[ keys(%{$HoH->{'key'}}) ]}"; # prints 'subkey subkey2' or
                                        # 'subkey2 subkey'
                                        # reaches in to the keys inside one
                                        # of the sub-hashes... and prints
                                        # them out in an array.

print "@{[ values(%{$HoH->{'key2'}}) ]}\n";
                                        # prints 'subvalue3 subvalue4'
                                        # or 'subvalue4 subvalue3'
                                        # reaches in and gets the values
```

```
                                        # for the hash signified by
                                        # $HoH->{'key2'};
```

Chapter 9: Regular Expressions

Regular expressions are really a language inside of a language; you will find them infinitely fascinating (hopefully), and for a small while at least, infinitely frustrating. It's my job to try to minimize this second period of time. But persevere, because they will make your job a heck of a lot easier.

Translating

Translating involves substituting one group of characters for another group of characters (like turning uppercase to lower).

```
$value = 'abcdefghijklmnopqrstuvwxyz';

$value =~ tr[a-z][A-Z]                   # makes $value into
                                         # ABCDEFGHIJKLMNOPQRSTUVWXYZ

$value =~ tr[A-Z][N-ZA-M];               # rot13 encryption - shifts all
                                         # the letters 13 positions into
                                         # NOPQRSTUVWXYZABCDEFGHIJKLM

$cnt = ($value =~ tr[A][A]);             # counts number of A's in $value
$value2 = 'lots of         spaces';
$value2 =~ tr[ ][]s;                     # makes $value2 'lots of spaces' -
                                         # turns multiple spaces into one.

$value3 = 'abcdefghijklmnopqrstuvwxyz';
$value3 =~ tr[aeiou][ ]cs;               # c = complement; ie: take all of
                                         # the non vowels and turns them into
                                         # spaces. s squishes the multiple
                                         # resulting spaces into one;
                                         # turns string into 'a e i o u'
```

Simple Expressions

Here are some simple expressions. Note that you can use a literal string ("city mouse") on the left-hand side of a regular expression; this is good for testing.

```
"city mouse" =~ /mouse/;                # matches because mouse is
                                        # substring of city mouse


my $string = "city mouse";
$string =~ s/mouse/rat/;                # makes 'city mouse' 'city rat'

"city mouse" =~ m/mouse/;               # same thing. m is optional with //

'/usr/local/bin/perl' =~ /bin\/perl/;  # matches bin/perl (note backslash of /)
'/usr/local/bin/perl' =~ m"bin/perl";  # alternate character for delimiter:
                                        # matches bin/perl.No backslash needed

"city mouse" =~ m'mouse';               # any character (' for instance) can
```

```
                                           # be used instead of //
         "city mouse" =~ m{mouse};         # can also use brackets;
```

Simple Wildcards, Backreferences

Wildcards are special characters in regular expressions which say 'match more than one character': \w matches any word character (A-Za-z0-9), for instance. Backreferences save pieces of text from a match, so you can manipulate them later.

```
         "city mouse" =~ m"mo...";         # matches because . is wildcard that

                                           # matches any character
         "city mouse" =~ m"\.\.";          # DOES NOT MATCH. \. makes it a literal
                                           # dot ('.')

         "city mouse" =~ m"(mo)use";       # matches, saves 'mo' in $1;

         my ($first,$second) = ("city mouse" =~ m"(mo)(use)");

                                           # matches, saves 'mo'
                                           # in $first, 'use' in $second

         if ('city mouse' =~ m"(mo)(use)") # common way of doing the same thing.
         {                                 # better because you can check error
             ($first,$second) = ($1,$2);   # statuses.
         }

         $pattern = 'aabb';
         my $pattern =~ s"(aa)(bb)"$2$1";   # makes pattern
                                           # 'aabb' => 'bbaa';

         'bbbbaaaa' =~ m"(bb)(\1)";        # \1 is internal modifier.
                                           # \1 equals 'bb' - matches 'bbbb'

         my ($first, $second) = ("city mouse" =~ m"(country)(rat)");
                                           # doesn't match, makes $first and
                                           # $second blank

         'city mouse' =~ m"(\w+)"          # word matcher (\w+). Matches 'city' in
                                           # 'city mouse'. Always matches first
```

Alternation

Alternation means 'match more than one pattern in any given spot(al(or)b)'. Always put the most specific pattern in the first position.

```
         'this always matches a not aa' =~ m"(a|aa)";
                                           # if the first part of an alternation
                                           # is a subset of the second, it will
                                           # always be matched first.

         'this always matches a not ab' =~ m"(ab|a)";
                                           # likewise, the first appearance of an
```

```
                                            # alternation gets matched before the
                                            # second.

'this matches "double quoted \"string\""' =~ m/"((?:[^\\"]|\\\\")*)"/s;
                                            # alternation with quantifiers
                                            # matches 'd','o','u'..., ' ' with
                                            # first alternation, then '\"' with
                                            # second, then 's','t','r','i','n','g'
                                            # with first then '\"' with second,
                                            # followed by '"' to finish.
```

Character classes, complicated back references, minimal matching: Here are more in the way of character classes. Note minimal matching (.*?), which works to match the least amount of characters.

```
'city mouse' =~ m"((\w+\s*)*)";        # Nested ) matches 'city mouse' -
                                       # $2 first matches city, then mouse
                                       # $1 becomes 'city mouse'


"/* C Comment */  /* another C commment */" =~ m"/*(.*?)*/";
                                       # matches, saves ' C comment '
                                       # in $1. Does NOT match
                                       # 'C Comment */  /* another C comment */'
                                       #  Shows minimal matching


'<a href = "http://a.b.c"> a.com
 <a href = "http://d.e.f"> b.com ' =~ m"()";
                                       # matches href tag
                                       # '<a href = "http://a.b.c"> a.com '
                                       # into $1.


"aeiou_except_maybe_not_y" =~ m"([aeiou]*)";
                                       # character class. matches 'aeiou'.
                                       # stops at
                                       # '_' because it wasn't
                                       # in the character class


"ababacmafga" =~ m"([a-ei-m]*)";       # character class example.
                                       # Matches 'ababacma', stops at
                                       # 'fga' since not in character class


"fgfghmasd" =~ m"([^a-ei-m]*)";        # negated character class (note '^' at
                                       # beginning). Matches fgfgh - stops
                                       # at 'm' since that is part of negated
                                       # character class


$dgt = '[0-9\-\.]+';                   # regular expressions can be stored in
                                       # vars


'this contains the float 9.5 embedded in it' =~ m"($dgt)";
                                       # matches - stores 9.5 in $1.


'this contains, at the end, the float 9.5'   =~ m"($dgt)$";
                                       # matches - 9.5
                                       # - '$'  indicates end of line:
```

```
"my number is 1,233,444" =~ m"(\d{1,3}(,\d{3,3})*)"
                                    # Note embedding of ).
                                    # matches, saves 1,233,444 in $1,
                                    # 233,444 in $2

"my number is 444"        =~ m"(\d{1,3}(,\d{3,3})*)"
                                    # also matches, saves  444 in $1,
                                    # '' in $2. The '*' indicates zero/many

'fee fie foe fum' =~ m"((f.. )*)";  # matches 'fee file foe fum' in $1
                                    # 'fum' in $2.

'fee fie foe fum foo' =~ m"((f..)((f..){1,3}))"
                                    # matches 'fee fie foe fum' in $1,
                                    # 'fee' in $2, 'fie foe fum' in $3
                                    # and 'fum' in $4

'fee fie foe fum' =~ m"((f..)((f..){1,3}?))"
                                    # matches 'fee fie' in $1, 'fee' in $2,
                                    # 'fie' in $3 and 'fie' in $4.  Minimal
                                    # matching changes the meaning of the
                                    # regexp, so 1 match of 'f..' is
                                    # preferred over 3.
```

More Character Classes, Zero-Width Assertions

Here, we have even more characters that have special meanings. These are good for matching binary data, since you can match any given character.

```
$variable =~ m{
    \e              # matches escape character ('esc')
    \r              # matches carriage return (control-M)
    \s              # matches a space
    \S              # matches a non-space
    \w              # matches [a-zA-Z0-9]
    \W              # matches a non-space
    \t              # matches tab character
    \n              # matches return
    \cM             # matches (control-M)
    \x5d            # matches hexadecimal 5d
    \0              # matches a null (could have been \x00)
    \043            # matches octal '43
}x;                 # again, extended format. Readable expressions

"this matches word boundaries" =~ m"\bboundries\b"; # matches the word
                                                    # 'boundaries'.
                                                    # \b is zero width
                                                    # assertion.

"this matches word boundaries" =~ m"\Sboundries\S"; # doesn't match the
                                                    # word boundaries.
                                                    # Non-zero-width
                                                    # assertion (\S) has to
```

```
                                        # match a space on the
                                        # end, and there is none

$line = 'a1111e1111f1111i11111';

while ($line =~ m"\G([aeiou]1111)"sg)   # matches 'a1111' first
{                                       # then 'e1111' then
    print "$1\n";                       # stops, since \G only
}                                       # allows matches at beginning
                                        # where last 'g' left off.


'this does not match' =~ m"^does";      # does not match since
                                        # ^ 'nails' match to the
                                        # beginning


'this doesn't match 87 in $1, it matches 89 in $1' =~ m"(\d+)in \$1$";
                                        # mathces '89' since '$'
                                        # nails pattern to the end.
```

Special Functionality With '?' Construct

Perl's regular expressions are extendible; by means of a question mark plus a special symbol (?:, for instance), Perl allows different behaviors which are useful. (?# is a comment in a regex, for example).

```
'fee fie foe fum' =~ m"((?:f.. )*)";   # matches 'fee fie foe fum' in $1.
                                        # No match into $2. (?:) does not
                                        # save back references)

'catches everything ' =~ m"(.*?(?=pattern)|.*)";
                                        # $1 becomes 'catches everything -
                                        # uses second alternative.

'catches till here, but not second here' =~ m"(.*?(?=pattern)|.*)";
                                        # $1 becomes 'catches till ' since
                                        # the pattern 'here' is hit, and
                                        # not included. Next time, the string
                                        # 'here, but not second 'would
                                        # be matched.

'this does not match, followed by orange' =~ m"by (?!orange)";
                                        # since 'by' is followed by the string
                                        # orange, does not match. (?!)
```

Modifiers to Regular Expressions, and Regular Expression Patterns

By putting a letter on the end of a regular expression, you can modify its behavior, too. m" "s forces the regex to be a single line, so '.' matches everything, for instance. In addition, Perl provides a (?) syntax which lets you make a regular expression case insensitive (?i), one line (?s), or whatever, based on the data.

```
"ThIs Is NoT VeRy ConSiStent" =~ m"consistent"i;
                                # matches - 'i' makes items
                                # case insensitive

"ThIs Is NoT VeRy ConSiStent Too" =~ m"(?i)consistent";
```

```
                                      # matches - '(?i)' makes items
                                      # case insensitive inside the
                                      # expression

    my $pattern = '(?i)consistent';
    "ThIs Is NoT VeRy ConSiStent Too" =~ m"$pattern";
                                      # (?i) can be put inside a scalar
                                      # then interpreted.


    $expression = m{
            This            #EMBEDDED COMMENT
            is a really     #EMBEDDED COMMENT2
            long
            expression
         }sx;                         # using 'x' modifier to make a long, long
                                      # regular expression with comments.


    undef $/;

    my ($FD1, $FD2) = (new FileHandle("file1"), new FileHandle ("file2"));
    grep($MARK{$_}++, (<$FD1> =~ m"\b(\w+)\b"));

    @diffWords = grep(!$MARK{$_}, (<$FD2> =~ m"\b(\w+)\b"));
                                          # Gives words that are
                                          # in file2 but not in file1.


    if ($pattern =~ m"(\S+)\s*=\s*(\S+)")
    {
        my ($variable, $value) = ($1,$2);
        $variable{$1} = $2;
    }
                                            # makes hash record out of
                                            # first row that looks like
                                            # PATH=/usr/bin:/usr/local/bin;
                                            # in input string pattern


    while ($pattern =~ m"(\S+)\s*=\s*(\S+)"sg)
    {
        my ($variable, $value) = ($1,$2);
        $variable{$1} = $2;
    }                                       # does the same thing, except
                                            # via 'g', iterates through
                                            # the entire input string
                                            # $pattern. 'A=B; C=D;'
                                            # makes %variable =
                                            # ( A => B, C => D );


    undef $/;
    open(FD,"file");
    %values = (=~ m"(\S+)\s*=\s*(\S+)"g);   # same effect as above, except
                                            # reads the values from a
                                            # file, and does it in one
                                            # step.


    @cutUpLines = ($pattern =~ m".{1,79}\b"sg);   # cuts up lines along word
```

```
                                          # boundaries, up to 80
                                          # characters long.
```

Chapter 10: Perl Built-In Functions and Variables

Perl has tons of built-in functions—here are some common expressions constructed out of them.

HERE documents

Here documents are good for generating code, and making long strings. Some examples are listed below:

```
@variables = (1,2,3);
$scalar =<<"END";
Interpolation of "@variables"
END
                              # makes $scalar 'Interpolation of "1 2 3"'.
                              # note that double quotes do NOT have to be quoted


$scalar =<<'END';
multi-line,
single quoted
$scalar
END
                              # makes $scalar
                              # 'multi-linesingle quoted$scalar'
                              # note that $scalar is not interpolated.


$executefrom=<<`END`;
ls
cd ..
ls -l
END
                              # executes three commands (note back-ticks.)
                              # helpful for embedding a shell script
                              # inside your script. Unix only.
```

Directing Output

The print operator, and open are extremely flexible. Below are some examples of redirecting output based on filehandle.

```
my $fd = new FileHandle("> file");
print $fd "text";                              # prints out to file handle
                                               # fd

print { $stout ? *STDOUT : *STDERR; } "TEXT";  # can be a function returning
                                               # a file handle.
print { $filehandle? $filehandle: *STDERR; }  "TEXT";
                                               # same for mixing and matching
                                               # filehandles and user defined
                                               # filehandles
```

```
open(STDERR, ">STDOUT");              # redirects all stderr
                                      # statements to STDOUT;
                                      # doesn't work on win95 yet.
```

Directing Input

Perl also has extreme flexibility in reading data in, too. You can read in a line at a time, treat a script as data, read the whole thing in (slurp mode), or read in via buffers.

```
while (defined ($line = <FD> ))       # script and data as one.
{                                     # everything after the
    print $line;                      # 'defined' tag is considered
}                                     # a line of data.
__DATA__
1
2
3

my $fh = new FileHandle("ls |"); # ;   # piping the results of an
$line = <$fh>;                        # expression to a filehandle

local($") = '|';                      # printing out something pipe
print "@array\n";                     # delimited.

local($/) = undef;                    # slurp mode.
my $fh = new FileHandle ("huzzah");

$lines = <$fh>;                       # snarfing all the text from a
                                      # filehandle into '$lines'

open (FH, "file");
while (read(FH, $line 65536))          # processing of text. Gets text
{                                     # in 64K blocks and 'processes'
    process($line);                   # it
}
```

grep, map, and sort

The three functions you really should learn are grep, map, and sort—with them, you can manipulate data to a great extent—getting the differences between arrays, or getting error lines out of a file, or what have you.

```
my @largeInts = grep { $_ > 999999; } @integers; # looks for large integers
                                                  # inside group of integers

open(FD, "filename");
@errorLines = grep(m"ERROR", );       # looking for error lines
                                      # inside a filehandle.

open(FD, "filename");
$numberofErrors = grep (m"ERROR", );  # counts number of errors
                                      # in open file handle FD
```

```
  grep($MARK{$_}++, @array1);
  my @differences = grep(!$MARK{$_}, @array2); # getting differences between
                                               # array 1 and array 2
  my @same        = grep($MARK{$_},  @array2); # getting elements in common
                                               # between array1 and array2

  @chars = ('a'..'z');
  @integers = map(ord($_) - ord('a')), @chars);  # makes @integer =('0..25').
  foreach (@chars) { push(@integers, ord($_)); } # does the same thing.

  @chars = ('a'..'z');
  %char2int = map(($_, ord($_) - ord('a')), @chars);
                                      # creats the hash
                                      # (a => 0, b => 1, .. z => 25 )

  @index = (0..$#array);
  @array = @array[ sort { $array[$a] <=> $array[$b] } @index ];
                                      # sorting an array via index rather
                                      # than via the array elements
                                      # themselves
```

Anonymous, Useful Things

Here's a grab-bag of useful tricks that I've learned. Of course, they aren't exhaustive; you will find thousands of them yourself...

```
  local($") = "','";
  @array = ('this','is','array');
  print CODE "\@eval = ('@array');\n";      # code generation. prints to file
                                            # handle CODE - @eval =
                                            # ('this','is','array').Note use of
                                            # $" to 'fill in' gaps inbetween
                                            # this is, and array

  local($") = " ";
  print CODE "\@eval = qw (@array);\n";     # produces @eval=qw(this is array);
                                            # lets Perl do the hard part quoting
                                            # wise. Note \ of @eval.

  my $time = sprintf ("%02d:%02d:%02d", $hours, $minutes, $seconds);
                                            # way of getting standard time
                                            # format

  $VERSION = do {my @r = (q$Revision$ =~ /\d+/g); sprintf "%d." .
            "%02d"x$#r, @r};
                                            # working with RCS to get a
                                            # version number out of an
                                            # RCS tag.

  my ($secs, $mins, $hours, $monthdays, $months, $year, $weekdays,

  $yearday, $daylightsavings) = localtime($secs);
```

```
                              # common way of parsing time.
                              # $sec = 0-59 $min = 0-59
                              # $hours = 0-23 $monthdays = 1-31
                              # $year = 69-137 (+1900)
                              # $weekdays = 0-6
                              # $yearday = 1-365
                              # $isdst = 0 (not) 1 (is daylight)
```

Chapter 11: Perl 5 Odds and Ends

Perl Odds and Ends are things that simply don't fit into the categories we have discussed so far (code references for example, are references but they aren't really references to data). Below are the six 'odds and ends' we've talked about.

Formats

Formats allow you a quick, dirty way of making ascii reports (STDOUT_TOP is the top of the sheet, STDOUT is the body). Just don't use 'my' with formats; they aren't compatible.

```
format STDOUT_TOP =
@<<<<<<<<<<<<<   @>>>>>>>>>>>>>         @|||||||||||||
$field1,         function($field2),    $field3
.
                                 # simple header... on top of each page makes
                                 # $field1 left justified, function($field2)
                                 # right justified and $field3 centered.


format STDOUT =
@<<<<<<<<<<<<<   @>>>>>>>>>>>>>         @|||||||||||||
$field4 ,          $field5,            $field6
.

^<<<<<<<<<<<<<<<<<<<<<<<<<<<<<<<<<<<<<<<<<<<<<<
$longtext


^<<<<<<<<<<<<<<<<<<<<<<<<<<<<<<<<<<<<<<<<<<<<<
$longtext
.
                                 # per each call to 'write'

local($field1, $field2, $field3) = ('top', 'of', 'field');
foreach $array (@$AoA)
{
     ($field4, $field5, $field6, $longtext) = @$array;
     write(STDOUT);
}
                                 # prints out to format. Notice no my statement.
                                 # my and format are not compatible (this is
                                 # probably a bug )
```

Code References

Code references are used really often, especially in conjunction with perltk, and with objects. Closures are the most powerful form of code reference—for they allow the creation of subroutines 'on the fly'.

```perl
$a = sub {   print "this is an anonymous sub\n"; }
&$a;                            # calling an anonymous sub without arguments
                                # $a is callback or code reference

sub subroutine
{
    my (@args) = @_;
    print "@args\n";
}
$coderef = \&subroutine;
&$coderef(1,2,3);               # calling an anonymous sub with arguments
                                # prints '1 2 3'
                                # $coderef is another code reference

sub a
{
    my ($b, $c) = @_;
    return ( sub { $b * $c; } } ) # callback
}
my $b = a(4,3);                 # $b is a code reference
my $c = a(2,3);                 # $c is a code reference
print &$b;                      # prints 12.
print &$c;                      # prints 6.
```

Globbing

Globbing allows you to make constants, and to alias variables together (so when one changes, the other changes). It is indicated by a '*' in front of a variable; this says that you are looking at a variable as a reference rather than data.

```perl
*PI = \3.1415926535;        # makes a scalar, read only constant
print $PI;                  # prints this scalar out.
sub PI($)  { return(3.1415926535); }
print PI;                   # does same thing through prototypes.
                            # (only good use for prototypes I've found
                            # so far - but then again they are in transition.

$scalar1 = 11;
*scalar2 = \$scalar1;       # aliases $scalar2 for $scalar1
$scalar1 = 13;              # changes $scalar2 as well as $scalar1
print $scalar2;             # prints 13.
open(FH, "filehandle");
process(*FH);               # passing a filehandle to a subroutine
sub file                    # use FileHandle instead?.
{
    my ($fh) = @_;
    $line = <$fh>;
    print $line;
}
```

BEGIN/END

BEGIN and END allow flow control, so you can have statements which are executed at the beginning of a program (before the actual program starts, at compile time) and when the program is about to exit.

```
BEGIN                                   # executing a script over, defining a
{                                       # certain environmental variable first.
    if (!$ENV{'LD_LIBRARY_PATH'})       # useful for places where you are linking
    {                                   # with C-libraries
        exec($0, @ARGV);
        $ENV{'LD_LIBRARY_PATH'} = 'blah';
    }
}

BEGIN { print "1 "; }
BEGIN { print "2 "; }
BEGIN { print "3 "; }

print "4";

END { print "7 ";    }
END { print "6 ";    }
END { print "5 ";    }               # prints '1 2 3 4 5 6 7' - BEGINS are executed
                                     # first-in-first-out, ENDS are executed
                                     # last-in-first-out

BEGIN { while (-e 'lock') { sleep(60); } }
BEGIN { system("touch lock"); }
                                     # cheap way of making a MUTEX.
# .... program                       # touches the lock a lock file
END { system("unlink lock"); } # and holds all other similar processes
                                     # at bay whilst processing.
```

eval

eval lets you run a string as if it was a 'mini-Perl program'. This has lots of benefits, including efficiency, and being able to check the syntax of code so otherwise 'fatal' errors are not fatal.

```
$code = 'print "HERE!!!!\n";';
eval( "sub { $code }");         # checking code for syntax errors without
                                # actually executing it.

eval<<"END_OF_CODE";            # uses a here document to evaluate a piece
# ... CODE ...                  # of code inside a script?
END_OF_CODE;

eval("use NT_module;") || eval("use UnixModule;") || die;
                                # tries to use the NT version of a module
                                # first, and if that fails, tries the Unix
                                # version. If not, dies.
```

Chapter 14: The Syntax of Modules and Libraries

Libraries are represented by 'require' in Perl, and modules are a special form of library inside a namespace, and is usually included at compile-time with a 'use Module'.

Libraries

Below is a simple example of a library in Perl. The first file is the actual library, the second is how to include that library in a script, and call the functionality inside.

```
# in file library.pl          # standard library syntax - just
sub mysub                      # normal Perl code, with a 1; tagged on
{                              # the end.
    print "In mysub\n";
}
1;

# in file script.p            # requiring the library imports the code
require "library.pl";
mysub();                       # mysub() then prints out the values.
```

Modules

Same thing applies for a Module. Note that the 'import' function is called at compile time, as soon as the Perl interpreter sees it.

```
# in file Module.pm           # standard module syntax, same as
package Module;                # libraries except 'import' function
                               # is called first.
sub import
{
    my ($modulename, @arguments) = @_;
    print "Calling $modulename with @arguments\n";
}

sub mysub
{
    print "In mysub\n";
}
1;
# in file script.p
use Module 1,2,3;              # prints out 'Calling Module 1 2 3' at
Module::mysub();              # CompileTime function call, packed
                              # inside namespace Module.
```

Auxiliary Variables to Handle Libraries

There are quite a few ways of physical control over where libraries and modules are accessed from (ie., how they get from the filesystem into your script). Below are some examples of how to control which version of libraries you use.

```
use lib "/my/libraries";        # adds to front of @INC, so libraries can
                                # come from a different place

use lib "$ENV{'CODEROOT'}";     # can be an environmental variable,
                                # have production, development code run
                                # transparently

C:> PERL5LIB='C:\my\libraries';
                                # sets @INC in the environment on NT;

print "@INC\n";                 # prints out all directories where libraries
                                # could come from.

use Data::Dumper;               # need to install Data::Dumper for this to work
print Dumper(\%INC);            # prints out the names of libraries, modules
                                #  that are included, along with which actual
                                # file is being looked at:
                                # ('Config.pm' => '/usr/local/lib/Config.pm')
```

Chapter 16: The Syntax of Objects

The following is a complex object (actually an object hierarchy) to be used as a template for your code. It shows inheritance, autoloading (ie., catching unknown subroutines), constructors, destructors, class data, class methods, and actual methods, plus how they can be used in your scripts.

```
# -------------------------------------------------------------------------
# one complete object hierarchy showing all the syntax you would need for
# an object (and probably more than you would need)
# -------------------------------------------------------------------------

# inside 'MoreBaseClass.pm'; - file

package MoreBaseClass;          # We set up a Base class for inheritance.

sub foo                         # methods
{
    print "Running Basic Foo!!!!!\n";
}
1;

sub bar
{
    print "Running Bar!!!!!\n";
}
1;

# inside 'BaseClass.pm'

package BaseClass;              # We set up a derived class off of the
                               # 'MoreBaseClass'. This in turn will be used
                               # as a base clase
```

```perl
use MoreBaseClass;              # we require functionality of base class.
@ISA = qw(MoreBaseClass);       # this says that a BaseClass inherits off of
                                # MoreBaseClass.

sub foo
{
    print "Running Foo!!!!\n";
}
sub basefoo                     # By using 'SUPER::', we can call
{                               # 'MoreBaseClass'es foo(). prints
    my ($self) = @_;            # Running Basic Foo!!!!! when done.
    $self->SUPER::foo();
}
1;
# -------------------------------------------------------------------------
# inside 'Class.pm';
# -------------------------------------------------------------------------

my @_config;                    # Class data (shared between objects)

package Class;                  # Here is our derived class, uses both
use BaseClass;                  # BaseClass and MoreBaseClass
use MoreBaseClass;

@ISA = qw (BaseClass);          # gets methods from 'BaseClass'; inheritance
                                # then from 'MoreBaseClass' (if not found in
                                # BaseClass\n";
use OtherClass;                 # module gets functionality from 'OtherClass'.
                                # (Layering)

sub import                      # called when package is imported (right after
{                               # parsing)
    my ($type, @args) = @_;
    @_config = @args;           # sets the class data based on 'use' statement.
}

sub AUTOLOAD                    # AUTOLOAD catches any unknown method
{
    my ($self) = @_;
    print "CAUGHT AN UNKNOWN FUNCTION $AUTOLOAD!!!\n";
}

sub classmethod                 # Class method, not dependant on individual
{                               # objects. prints out the class configuration
    print @$_config;
}

sub new                         # Constructor. First argument is the type of
{                               # class to construct as called inside client.
    my ($type, @args) = @_;
    my $self = { args => [@args] };
    bless $self, $type;
}
```

```perl
sub print                          # sample method. First argument is object
{                                  # itself
    my ($self, $arg) = @_;
    my $args = $self->{args};
    print $args->[$arg];
}

sub DESTROY                        # destructor. Called when object goes out of
{                                  # memory.
    my ($self) = @_;
     print "RUNNING DESTROY for $self! WHEN GOING OUT OF MEMORY!\n";
}


# ------------------------------------------------------------------------
# The corresponding client script
# ------------------------------------------------------------------------

# inside client script.p;

use Class 1, 2, 3, 4;              # calls import method with args 1 2 3 4
                                   # sets @_config to be (1,2,3,4);
Class::classmethod();             # prints out '1 2 3 4';

my $object = new Class('args','to','class');
                                   # object $object is created
print ref($object);               # prints out 'Class';

$object->print;                    # prints out 'to', calls Class::print($object, 1);
$object->foo();                    # looks in 'Class' for method foo, can't find it.
                                   # looks in 'BaseClass' for method foo, calls
                                   # BaseClass::foo($object).
                                   # prints "Running Foo!!!!\n";
$object->basefoo();                # looks in 'Class' for method basefoo,
                                   # then in 'BaseClass'. Finds it, calls
                                   # $self->SUPER::foo(), which turns into
                                   # MoreBaseClass::foo($self).
                                   # prints 'Running Base Foo'.

$object->bar();                    # prints 'Running Bar!'. Looks inside 'Class'
                                   # for 'bar()' method, then 'BaseClass', and
                                   # then 'More Base Class'.

$object->unfoundmethod();         # prints CAUGHT AN UNKNOWN FUNCTION
                                   # Class::unfoundmethod!!! Uses import as filter
                                   # for unfound functions\n";

# After script ends, prints RUNNING DESTROY FOR Class=HASH(0x432ad) WHEN
# GOING OUT OF MEMORY!
```

Chapter 21: Perl Development Environment

Perl is special in that you can program Perl development tools in Perl itself. There are debuggers, compilers, profilers, coverage testers, and more—below are examples of existing environments.

```
prompt% perl -d script.p          # starting the debugger.

Stack dump during die enabled outside of evals.
Loading DB routines from perl5db.pl patch level 0.94
Emacs support available.

Enter h of `h h' for help.
Main::(aa.p:3): $line = 'a';

  DB<1> h h                       # gets help for debugger.
  DB<2> exit                      # exits debugger.

prompt% perl -d:DProf script.p
                                  # runs profiler on script.p (not
                                  # installed by default). Creates
                                  # file called 'tmon.out' with
                                  # information about your program

prompt% dprofpp -F                # analyzes output

prompt% perl -d:Coverage script.p
                                  # shows coverage testing for script.
                                  # creates a 'cvp' file
                                  # (not installed by default; get
                                  # from disk or CPAN

prompt% coverperl script.cvp      # analyzes output for coverage test

prompt% perl -d:SmallProf script.p
                                  # creates a file... 'smallprof.out'
                                  # for analysis. Shows line by line
                                  # how long each statement took..

prompt% perlcc script.p           # compiles script into executable (called
                                  # a.out by default

prompt% perlcc -oscript script.p
                                  # compiles script into executable called
                                  # 'script'.

prompt% perlcc -h                 # shows help for compiler
```

Chapter 22: Perl Debugging Tips

Perl also blurs the line between programming and debugging. There are several flags, libraries, pragmas, and modules (including Lint, strict, -w, diagnostics), all which are designed to help you track down problems. Below are some examples.

```perl
#!/usr/local/bin/perl5 -w        # warning flag... catches quite a bit

prompt% perl -w script.p         # equivalent of warning flag on command-line.

use strict;                      # strict module... prevents

use strict vars;                 # only use the 'vars' part of strict.

use strict subs;                 # only use the 'subs' part of strict.

use strict refs;                 # only use the 'refs' part of strict

use vars qw(varb1 varb2);        # way of making globals possible.

use Carp qw(cluck);
$SIG{__WARN__} = sub { cluck(@_); }    # prints out stack trace w/warnings.
$SIG{__DIE__}  = sub { confess(@_); }  # prints out stack trace on error.
$SIG{INT}      = sub { print "Ouch!!! Hit control-C!!\n"; }
                                       # prints when control-C is hit.

confess("Died here!!!\n");             # gives stack trace showing how
                                       # program reached this sorry fate.
                                       # dies afterwards.

croak("Died Here!!!\n");               # gives 'one-level' stack trace (less
                                       # verbose than confess, at least).
                                       # dies afterwards.

carp::cluck("Warning!!!\n");           # gives full stack trace (verbose)
                                       # showing where output
                                       # is used.

carp("warning!!!!\n");                 # gives one-level stack trace
prompt% perl -MCarp=verbose script.p   # makes 'carp' equal to 'cluck'
                                       # and 'croak' equal to 'confess'
                                       # to show more detailed output.

prompt% perl -MO=Lint -u script.p      # checks for 'bad style' type of
                                       # errors in script.p

prompt% perl -Dr script.p              # debugs Perl regular expression
                                       # (-Dr) Need to compile debug version
                                       # of Perl executable.
```

Summary

Well, that's about it. If there are any cool patterns that are not in the listing above, and you would like me to include, let me know (through the apxtech address—*perlhelp@apxtech.com*). If you program, and come up with your own list—it works wonders on your programming style.

Index

About the Authors

Ed Peschko has been a Perl veteran since Perl 3 and has used Perl in applications ranging from system administration to database administration, from CGI programming to data warehousing. He is also the chief technical officer in Apex Technical Consulting, a firm devoted to writing specialized enterprise applications and comprehensive technical support for Java, C++, and Perl.

Michele DeWolfe is a project manager, university instructor, and owner of an Internet retail firm, *www.eTeapot.com*. She has co-authored three books including *Peter Norton's Guide to Java* and *Perl 5 Complete*.

ABOUT THE CD

Installation Instructions

To install the CD:

1. go into the directory at the head of the CD
2. type 'install.sh' (unix) and 'install' (WinNT, Win95) to get started
3. type in the answers (as the questions are asked).

This should install the entire contents of the CD. (If you decide to, you can be selective as to what you install. Simply answer the questions appropriately.)

NOTE: Unlike some books out there, this CD is an integral part of the book. All of the syntax, examples, techniques, and so forth that we have discussed in this book are pointless—if you have nowhere to go with them. The CD is therefore meant as this book's 'second half', and is meant for you to:

1. experiment with the code supplied in the book itself
2. try out new Perl modules, and see what functionality they provide
3. perhaps even try posting a module yourself.

For more detailed information on the contents of the CD, read Appendix B on the CD-ROM.